FRASER & STEWART

COMPANY LAW OF CANADA

Sixth Edition, 1993

BY

HARRY SUTHERLAND, Q.C.

together with

DAVID B. HORSLEY, Q.C.
GRAHAM TURNER
CHRISTOPHER D. WOODBURY
SHONA BRADLEY

all of Fraser & Beatty

CARSWELL
Thomson Professional Publishing

Canadian Cataloguing in Publication Data

Main entry under title:

Company law of Canada

6th ed.

At head of title: Fraser & Stewart.

First ed. published in 1901 under title: Canadian company law.

Includes index.

ISBN 0-459-56778-0 (bound) ISBN 0-459-55771-8 (pbk.)

1. Corporation law - Canada. I. Sutherland, Harry, 1930- . II. Horsley, David B.

KE1369.C65 1993 346.71′066 C93-094668-5
KF1384.C65 1993

1st edition 1901
2nd edition 1920
3rd edition 1929
4th edition 1941
5th edition 1962
6th edition 1993

Typeset by: Video Text Inc., Barrie, Ontario

CARSWELL
Thomson Professional Publishing

One Corporate Plaza, 2075 Kennedy Road, Scarborough, Ontario M1T 3V4

Customer Service:

Toronto 1-416-609-3800

Elsewhere in Canada/U.S. 1-800-387-5164

Fax 1-416-298-5094

PREFACE

The last edition of this work appeared in 1962 and this edition reflects the new legislation which has been enacted and the many decisions which have been handed down since 1961, which was the date as of which the last edition was written. The present edition is largely based on the 5th edition and its predecessors dating back to 1901 and the great indebtedness of the present team to the distinguished lawyers who were their predecessors is cheerfully recorded. Our appreciation for the assistance received from our colleagues at Fraser & Beatty is gratefully acknowledged. They have assisted in many ways and the comments and suggestions made by each of them have been most constructive and helpful.

In this edition the law is dealt with as at January 1, 1993.

Toronto, June 1, 1993 H.S.

TABLE OF CONTENTS

PART I

CANADA BUSINESS CORPORATIONS ACT

PART II
THE WINDING-UP ACT

TABLE OF CASES

PART I

CANADA BUSINESS CORPORATIONS ACT

Chapter 1

INTRODUCTION

Cross-references: Ontario Act, ss. 1, 2.

Introductory

In its legal sense the word "company" is used to describe the relationship of those associated for business purposes. This relationship can take the form of a partnership or similar type of association, or a corporation. There are of course a number of different types of corporations. These include municipal corporations, which are basically regulated by provincial statute; religious corporations; non-business corporations, which cater to various educational, charitable, scientific, vocational and leisure interests; and business corporations. Under the constitutional division of powers in Canada, both the federal and provincial legislatures are given power to incorporate companies.

Some of the earliest companies were formed for trading purposes, with one example dating back to 1800 B.C., when the King of Assyria sanctioned the organization of a trading association among certain merchants. In some companies formed for overseas trade, a group of merchants, each of whom had their own stock, would band together to use a common ship. Other companies had joint stock which was owned in common by all the members and could be subscribed for in varying shares by the members. This joint stock and the profits made from it were divided among the members after each voyage. Thus, after one particular voyage a dividend of 311 per cent was declared. There are a number of companies still in existence that were incorporated many years ago, notably the Hudson's Bay Company of Canada, originally incorporated by Royal Charter in 1670, and the Storra Kopparbergs of Sweden, originally incorporated about 1288.

The word "company" can be used in other senses, for example, to describe a group of mercenaries fighting for profit. Indeed, one of the authors well remembers attending a lecture on business principles in which reference was made to the *The Art of War* by Sun Tzu, who was a Chinese general during the 4th century B.C.

The word "corporation" is ordinarily used throughout this work to describe a business corporation (or company), except where the word "company" appears in a quotation.

History and application of Act

We are concerned in this work with business corporations with particular reference to the *Canada Business Corporations Act*, now c. C-44 of the Revised Statutes of Canada, 1985. This Act was proclaimed in force in 1975 and replaced the *Canada Corporations Act* of 1964-65, which had extensively revised the former *Companies Act*, 1934, which in turn was a revision of the 1902 Act, whose predecessors were the *Canada Joint Stock Companies Act* of 1877 and the *Canada Joint Stock Companies Letters Patent Act* of 1869. Pre-confederation legislation of a general nature was passed in 1850, 1860 and 1864.

The present Ontario Act is the *Business Corporations Act*, c. B.16 of the Revised Statutes of Ontario, 1990, which, after the 1982 amendments, generally parallels the federal Act. It was originally enacted in 1970 to replace *The Corporations Act*, 1953, which replaced the Companies Acts of 1907 and 1912, which in turn replaced the *Ontario Companies Act* of 1897 and the *Ontario Joint Stock Companies Letters Patent Act* of 1874. Prior to Confederation, over 200 business corporations had been incorporated in Ontario. A useful account of these early corporations is given in an article by Professor Risk, "The Nineteenth Century Foundations of the Business Corporation in Ontario" (1973), 23 University of Toronto Law Journal 270. The first two business corporations to be formed by the legislature in Upper Canada were both banks, the Bank of Kingston and the Bank of Upper Canada, in the year 1819. It will be noted that the provisions of *The Corporations Act*, R.S.O. 1990, c. C.38 are still in force so far as non-profit companies under Part III of that Act are concerned.

Federal corporations may be incorporated by one of the following methods: (1) certificate of incorporation pursuant to the *Canada Business Corporations Act*; (2) pursuant to the provisions of another federal Act, such as the *Trust and Loan Companies Act*; (3) by special act of incorporation, which in recent years has not been used for business corporations, although, of course, Parliament still has power to do this (this method is more usually utilized for non-profit bodies, such as the Girl Guides of Canada); (4) non-profit companies can be incorporated by letters patent under the provisions of Part II of the *Canada Corporations Act*, which is still in force so far as such corporations are concerned; (5) by a charter or letters patent pursuant to the Royal Prerogative (which, while still possible in theory, has not ocurred in practice in Canada in recent years). This list is also applicable to most provincial jurisdictions including Ontario.

It will be noted that the provisions of the *Winding-up Act*, R.S.C. 1985, c.W-11, are not applicable to corporations incorporated under the *Canada Business Corporations Act*, see s. 3(3) of that Act. The *Winding-up Act* is, however, still applicable to a number of types of corporations, including banks, insurance companies, provincial companies and foreign companies which are sought to be wound up on the ground of insolvency.

Interpretation

It is important to note that in addition to the definitions set out in s. 2, there are other definitions which are applicable only to a particular part, thus the word "insider" is defined in s. 126 and is applicable to Part XI and the word "solicit" is defined in s. 147, applicable to Part XIII only. In certain cases a definition is applicable to a certain section, for example, the word "shareholder" is defined in s. 226 to include the heirs and legal representatives of a shareholder so far as that section is concerned.

A discussion of the definitions will be found under the various headings of this work. It should be noted here, however, that a corporation is a body incorporated or continued under the *Canada Business Corporations Act*, whereas a body corporate includes a company or other body corporate wherever or however incorporated. It will also be noted that the terms "affiliated corporation", "control", "holding body corporate" and "subsidiary body corporate" all have a common thread; that is, the requirement of ownership of more than 50 per cent of the securities carrying the right to elect a majority of the directors (other than by way of security for a loan). The test is legal—not working—control. As to the meaning of the word "control" see *Purdom v. Doherty*, [1929] 3 D.L.R. 719 (S.C.C.), at 721 (possession of more than half the voting power of the company) and *M.N.R. v. Wrights' Canadian Ropes Ltd.*, [1947] 1 D.L.R. 721 at 727 (P.C.) (holding of less than 50 per cent conclusive against existence of control). As to the meaning of the term "controlling interest" see *British American Tobacco Co. Ltd. v. I.R.C.*, [1943] A.C. 335 (H.L.); *Vancouver Towing Co. v. M.N.R.*, [1946] Ex. C.R. 623 (Ex. Ct.); *Army & Navy Department Store Ltd. v. M.N.R.* [1954] 1 D.L.R. 177 (S.C.C.); M.N.R. v. Sheldons Engineering Ltd., [1954] Ex. C.R. 507 (Ex. Ct.); *Barclays Bank Ltd. v. I.R.C.*, [1959] 1 Ch. 341, (Ch.D.) and cases reviewed therein. In *International Mercantile Factors Ltd. v. R.* (1990), 90 D.T.C. 6390 (F.C. T.D.), the court considered whether a corporation was controlled "directly or indirectly, in any manner whatsoever" by one or more public corporations. In that case two public corporations each owned 25 per cent of the voting rights and a private corporation held the other 50 per cent. The board of directors consisted of five in number. Under a shareholders agreement between the three shareholders, two were nominated by each of the public corporations and one by the private corporation. The court held that neither of the public corporations on the one hand or the private corporation on the other hand had control of the corporation in question but since neither side could effectively alter the composition of the board of directors during the currency of the shareholders agreement the public corporations had legal and effective control of the corporation concerned. An appeal was dismissed without reasons on December 15, 1992.

While ordinarily the word "individual" relates to a natural person rather than an artificial person, it may include a corporation. See *R. v. Sommers (No. 4)* (1958), 26 W.W.R. 246 (S.C.), where Wilson J. held that the word "individual" in s. 158(e) of the Criminal Code, R.S.C. 1927, c. 36 included a corporation. He said at p. 248: "A corporation is, in the purest sense of the word, an individual. It is *persona juridica*; it is recognized as a juridical entity in the eyes of the law and it is as much an individual in respect of its acts." It will be noted that s. 33(1) of the *Interpretation Act* (Canada) provides that words importing male persons includes females and corporations and that the definition of the word "person" in s. 35 of the same Act includes a corporation.

In accordance with the ordinary rules of statutory interpretation, neither headings nor marginal notes can control the plain meaning of the words of the enactment, though they may, in some cases, be looked at if there is any ambiguity in the meaning of the sections on which they can throw light: *R. v. Hare*, [1934] 1 K.B. 354 (C.C.A.). See also s. 14 of the *Interpretation Act* (Canada) so far as marginal notes and references to former enactments are concerned.

The *Interpretation Act* (Canada) provides in s. 21 that words establishing a corporation are to be construed: (a) to vest in the corporation power to sue and be sued, to contract and be contracted with by its corporate name, to have a common seal and to alter or change the same, to have perpetual succession, to acquire and hold personal property for the purposes for which the corporation is established and to dispose of the same; (b) where a corporation has a name consisting of an English and a French form or a combined English and French form to vest in the corporation power to use either or both forms of its name and to show on its seal both forms or to have two seals, one showing the English and the other showing the French form of its name; (c) to vest in a majority of its members the power to bind the others by their acts; and (d) to exempt from personal liability for its debts, obligations or acts, such individual members of the corporation who do not contravene the provisions of the enactment establishing the corporation. Where the corporation is a body consisting of three or more members, s. 21(2) of the same Act provides that at least one half of the number of members provided for by the enactment, if a fixed number, or at least one half of the number of members in office, if there is a range having a maximum and a minimum and the number in question is within the range, constitutes a quorum and an act or thing done by a majority of the members of the body present at a meeting, if the members present constitute a quorum, is deemed to have been done by the body and a vacancy in the membership of the body does not impair the right of members in office to act or invalidate the constitution of the body if the number of members in office is not less than a quorum.

Purposes of Act

Section 4 of the *Canada Business Corporations Act* provides that the purposes of the Act are to revise and reform the law applicable to business corporations incorporated to carry on business throughout Canada, to advance the uniformity of law applicable to business corporations in Canada, and to provide a means of permitting an orderly transference of certain federal companies incorporated under various federal acts to the *Canada Business Corporations Act.* The purpose of uniformity of law with respect to business corporations is gradually being fulfilled since provincial legislation similar to the format of the *Canada Business Corporations Act* has been passed in the provinces of Alberta, Manitoba, New Brunswick, Newfoundland, Ontario and Saskatchewan. A similar but optional procedure is available for incorporation under Part IA of the Quebec Act. Incorporation by registration of a memorandum of association is the method of incorporation in the provinces of British Columbia and Nova Scotia. The provinces having provision for incorporation by letters patent are Prince Edward Island and Quebec.

Traditionally, the distinction between the two types of incorporation was that a corporation incorporated by letters patent was regarded as having the powers of a natural person so that the doctrine of *ultra vires* was not applicable to it in the absence of any restriction in the governing statute or in the letters patent incorporating it. A corporation incorporated by memorandum of association, however, was ordinarily confined to the powers set out in the memorandum itself and accordingly the doctrine of *ultra vires* would be applicable. However, the British Columbia Act confers upon a memorandum of association company incorporated under it the power and capacity of a natural person subject to the Act. For a further discussion of powers of corporations, see Chapter 3. As to the circumstances under which a certificate of incorporation can be attacked, see Chapter 2.

Chapter 2

FORMATION OF NEW CORPORATIONS

Cross references: Federal Act, ss. 264, 265
Ontario Act, ss. 3, 4, 5, 6, 7, 8, 10, 11, 12, 21, 273, 275

General

Prior to the present federal Act coming into force, corporations were incorporated by either letters patent or by memorandum of association, apart from those few cases where incorporation by special act was applied for. In all such cases great care and particularity was used in drafting the objects clauses; that is, what the corporation could do. Each Act contained ancillary powers and in addition, it was normal to have a number of ancillary powers forming part of the objects. Under the current practice, a federal corporation is incorporated by articles of incorporation which require any restriction on the corporation's business to be set out in the articles of incorporation. The usual practice is to say that there are no restrictions and with this change in practice much of the earlier law has become solely of academic interest.

However, it should be noted that the federal Act does not apply to a bank, insurance company, trust company or loan company and no corporation incorporated under the federal Act is to carry on such a business.

It should also be noted that the Ontario Act contains a similar provision that does not apply (unless otherwise provided) to a corporation within the meaning of the *Loan and Trust Corporations Act* (Ontario). In addition, the Ontario Act will not apply to a corporation (a) where the objects are in whole or in part of a social nature, (b) to which the *Co-operative Corporations Act* (Ontario) applies, (c) that is an insurer within the meaning of s. 141(1) of the Corporations Act (Ontario), or (d) to which the *Credit Unions and Caisses*

Populaires Act (Ontario) applies. Section 3(1) of the Ontario Act also contains restrictions on the practice of a profession by a corporation.

Accordingly, it is only in a very limited sense that questions of jurisdiction with respect to corporations are now of consequence so far as an ordinary manufacturing or trading corporation is concerned. However, the discussion is preserved since a provincial corporation has no power to carry on certain businesses, for example, banking, as this head is reserved exclusively to corporations under the federal legislation.

Federal and provincial jurisdiction with respect to corporations

The power to incorporate corporations is derived both by federal and provincial authorities from the *Constitution Act, 1867* (hereinafter referred to as the "B.N.A. Act"). These two levels of government between them possess complete power to incorporate all corporations; however, complicated questions arise respecting the distribution of that power between them.

From the realm of power to incorporate is first carved the exclusive power of the provinces to incorporate corporations with provincial objects conferred by head 11 of s. 92 of the *B.N.A. Act.* The residue of the power to incorporate is federal.

Ever since the enactment of the *B.N.A. Act* in 1867 the courts have defined the respective powers of the federal and provincial legislatures with respect to corporations and as a result certain principles may now be regarded as reasonably settled. Some of these may be stated as follows:

1. A corporation is endowed with such powers only as the state or province creating it has power to bestow upon it and if the state or province assumes to confer upon the corporation greater power than it is able to bestow, the act of the state or province is itself *ultra vires* and the corporation will not possess the powers which its charter assumes to confer: *Weyburn Townsite Co. v. Honsberger* (1918), 43 O.L.R. 451 at 460 (Ont. H.C.); *Bank of Augusta v. Earle* (1839), 13 Peters 589 (P.E.I.); *Canadian Pacific Railway v. Western Union Telegraph Co.* (1889), 17 S.C.R. 151 at 163; *John Deere Plow Co. v. Wharton*, [1915] A.C. 330 (P.C.); *Linde Canadian Refrigerator Co. v. Saskatchewan Creamery Co.* (1915), 51 S.C.R. 400 at 403; *Great West Saddlery Co. v. The King*, [1921] 2 A.C. 91 (P.C.). For example, if a federal charter were to be granted for a local cemetery corporation or for a rural telephone corporation, such as is described in *Canadian Bank of Commerce v. Cudworth Rural Telephone Co.*, [1923] S.C.R. 618, it would probably be held that this was a corporation with provincial objects only and that the power to incorporate it belonged exclusively to the province. So, on the other hand, an attempt by a provincial authority to confer on a corporation actual and direct powers to carry on its operations beyond the geographical boundaries of the province would be invalid, but see also 8 below.

2. The power of legislating with reference to the incorporation of corporations with other than provincial objects belongs exclusively to the federal Parliament as being a matter which does not fall within the classes of subjects assigned exclusively to provincial jurisdiction under s. 92 of the *B.N.A. Act* but

which does fall within the meaning of the initial words of s. 91 as being a matter affecting Canada generally and covered by the expression "the peace, order, and good government of Canada."

Citizens Insurance Co. v. Parsons (1881), 7 App. Cas. 96; *Colonial Building & Investment Assn. v. A.G. Que.* (1883), 9 App. Cas. 157 (P.C.); *John Deere Plow Co. v. Wharton*, [1915] A.C. 330 (P.C.); *A.G. Can. v. A.G. Alta. (The Insurance Case)*, [1916] 1 A.C. 588 (P.C.); *Lukey v. Ruthenian Farmers' Elevator Co.*, [1924] S.C.R. 56 at 70. The federal jurisdiction over corporations under s. 91 extends to the local works and undertakings which are excepted from provincial jurisdiction under clauses (a), (b) and (c) of head 10 of s. 92; see principle 11 below.

3. The fact that a corporation incorporated under an Act of the federal Parliament with power to carry on its business throughout Canada confines the exercise of its powers to one province cannot of itself affect its status or capacity as a corporation.

Colonial Building & Investment Assn. v. A.G. Que. (1883), 9 App. Cas. 157 (P.C.); *Traverse de Lévis v. Lemieux* (1940), 79 Qué. S.C. 52.

4. Federal corporations have a status which enables them to exercise their powers in all the provinces. They cannot be interfered with by any provincial law in such a way as to derogate from their status and their consequent capacities or, as a result of such restriction, be prevented from exercising such powers as have been validly conferred on them by federal authority or suing in the courts.

Dobie v. Temporalities Board (1881), 7 App. Cas. 136; *Toronto (City) v. Bell Telephone Co.*, [1905] A.C. 52 (P.C.); *John Deere Plow Co. v. Wharton*, [1915] A.C. 330 at 343 (P.C.); *Great West Saddlery Co. v. The King*, [1921] 2 A.C. 91 at 100 (P.C.); *La Compagnie Hydraulique de St. Francois v. Continental Heat & Light Co.*, [1909] A.C. 194; *A.G. Man. v. A.G. Can.*, [1929] A.C. 260 at 267; *Charlottetown (City) v. Foundation Maritime Ltd.*, [1932] 1 D.L.R. 453 (P.E.I. C.A.); affd on other grounds [1932] S.C.R. 589; *Montreal-Canada Fire Insurance Co. v. National Trust Co.* (1917), 35 D.L.R. 445 (Que. S.C.) (insurance company incorporated under federal statute); such legislation is not saved by the fact that there is no special discrimination against federal corporations: *A.G. Man. v. A.G. Can., supra.*

A provincial legislature cannot delegate to the executive or to an official an unfettered discretion with respect to the exercise by a federal corporation of its powers: *Re Royalite Oil Co.*, [1931] 2 D.L.R. 418 (Alta. C.A.).

5. The power to regulate trade and commerce conferred by the second head of s. 91 upon federal Parliament enables it to prescribe to what extent the powers of trading corporations whose objects extend to all of Canada should be exercisable and what limitations should be placed on such powers.

John Deere Plow Co. v. Wharton, [1915] A.C. 330 at 339-41 (P.C.); *In re Board of Commerce Act*, [1922] 1 A.C. 191 (P.C.); *Lukey v. Ruthenian Farmers' Elevator Co.*, [1924] S.C.R. 56 at 70.

6. Such legislation in so far as it interferes with "civil rights" (head 13

of s. 92) will be valid only if it is necessarily incidental to the effective constitution and operation of the corporation so incorporated.

Toronto Electric Commissioners v. Snider, [1925] A.C. 396 at 409-10 (P.C.); *Re Insurance Contracts* (1926), 58 O.L.R. 404 at 417-19 (C.A.); *Montel v. Groupe de Consultants P.G.L. Inc.* (1982), 142 D.L.R. (3d) 659 (Que. C.A.).

In the reference *Re Section 110 of the Dominion Companies Act*, [1934] S.C.R. 653, it was held by the Supreme Court of Canada that the section fell within the federal power to incorporate corporations with objects not provincial and that the liability thereby imposed on directors was part of the definition of the constitution of the corporation. A different view had previously been expressed by the Ontario Court of Appeal in *Meyer Malt & Grain Corp. v. Coombs*, [1933] O.R. 259 (C.A.).

7. It is within the power of the federal Parliament, by properly framed legislation, under heads (2) and (25) of s. 91 of the *B.N.A. Act*, to require a foreign corporation to take out a federal licence, even where the corporation desires to carry on its business only within the limits of a single province: *A.G. Can. v. A.G. Alta. (The Insurance Case)*, [1916] 1 A.C. 588 at 597 (P.C.), followed in *Farmers Mutual Hail Insurance Assn. v. Whittaker* (1917), 37 D.L.R. 705 (Alta. C.A.); *Matthew v. Guardian Assurance Co.* (1918), 58 S.C.R. 47.

8. Provided it does not interfere with the constitution or status of a federal corporation, it is submitted that a provincial authority may confer on a corporation incorporated elsewhere the right to exercise within the province powers additional to those embraced in its original incorporation if such powers are not inconsistent with its original constating instruments: *Sun Life Assurance Co. v. Sisters Adorers of Precious Blood*, [1942] O.R. 708 (C.A.).

9. A federal corporation is subject to provincial laws of general application, in relation to provincial subject matter such as laws imposing taxes, relating to mortmain, requiring licences for certain purposes, as to forms of contracts, prescribing the way in which any business shall be carried on in the province, as to offering its shares unless it does so through a registered person or is itself registered, and as to making returns.

Citizens Insurance Co. v. Parsons (1881), 7 App. Cas. 96 (P.C.); *Colonial Building & Investment Assn. v. A.G. Que.* (1883), 9 App. Cas. 157 (P.C.); *Bank of Toronto v. Lambe* (1887), 12 App. Cas. 575; *John Deere Plow Co. v. Wharton*, [1915] A.C. 300 at 340-1 (P.C.); *R. v. Regina Wine & Spirit Ltd.*, [1922] 1 W.W.R. 195 (Sask. C.A.) (*The Saskatchewan Temperance Act*, R.S.S. 1920, c. 194, requiring returns); *R. v. Gebhardt (No. 2)*, [1926] 2 D.L.R. 950 (Sask. C.A.); *Reference Insurance Act (Canada)*, [1932] A.C. 41 at 45 (P.C.); *Lymburn v. Mayland*, [1932] A.C. 318 (P.C.) (*Alberta Security Frauds Prevention Act*, 1930); *R. v. Arcadia Coal Co.*, [1932] 2 D.L.R. 475 (Alta. C.A.) (*Alberta Coal Miners' Wages Security Act*, 1928, c. 46); *Motor Car Supply Co. of Canada v. A.G. Alta.*, [1939] 3 D.L.R. 660 (Alta. T.D.) (*Licensing of Trades and Businesses Act*, 1937); *International Harvester Co. of Canada v. Provincial Tax Commission*, [1949] A.C. 36 at 52, 54 (P.C.); [1948] C.T.C. 307 at 323 (*The Income Tax Act*, 1932, c. 9 and *The Income Tax Act*, 1936, c. 15 of Saskatchewan); *A.G. Que. v. Imperial Oil Ltd.*, [1945] C.T.C. 233 (Que.) (*The Corporation Tax Act*, R.S.Q. 1941, c. 77); *Manitoba*

(Provincial Treasurer) v. Wm. Wrigley Jr. Co., [1950] A.C. 1 (P.C.) (The Income Tax Act, R.S.M. 1940, c. 209); *R. v. New Westminster (City)* (1965), 54 W.W.R. 238 (*sub nom. Ex parte Canada Wirevision Ltd.*) (B.C. C.A.); affg 53 W.W.R. 373 (B.C.) (municipal act a provincial law of general application); *C.T.C.U.Q. Canada (Comm des champs de bataille nationaux)*, [1990] 2 S.C.R. 838, 74 D.L.R. (4th) 23; *Reference re Sections 91 & 92 of Constitution Act, 1867, Corporations Act and Business Names Registration Act*, [1991] 4 W.W.R. 193 (Man. C.A.)—legislation which required registration of a business name applies to all companies wherever incorporated.

Provincial laws which do not impair or destroy the essential status and capacities of federal corporations are *intra vires* the province. Where a federally incorporated corporation's assets were expropriated by the province, the corporate being was unaffected as the corporation retained its structure and ability to raise new capital and issue shares. See *Churchill Falls (Labrador) Corp. v. Newfoundland (A.G.)* (1984), 1 S.C.R. 297, 8 D.L.R. (4th) 1 (S.C.C.), which overruled *B.C. Power Corp. v. British Columbia (A.G.)* (1963), 44 W.W.R. 65 47 D.L.R. (2d) 633 (B.C. S.C.) where it was held that legislation purporting to expropriate the shares of a provincial corporation which was a wholly owned subsidiary of a federal corporation was *ultra vires*, since the legislation was not of "general application" and its effect was to put an end to the federal corporation's status as controlling shareholder.

10. The sanctions by which such provincial laws are supported cannot "validly be so directed . . . as indirectly to sterilize . . . if the local laws are not obeyed . . . the capacities and powers which the Dominion had validly conferred": *Great West Saddlery Co. v. The King*, [1921] 2 A.C. 91, at 100.

Where provincial laws substantially duplicate federal provisions but do not conflict with the federal provisions, the provincial laws are not rendered inoperative in respect of federally incorporated corporations. Provincial insider trading provisions of the *Securities Act* are therefore applicable to federal corporations and both laws apply by virtue of the double aspect doctrine. See *Multiple Access Ltd. v. McCutcheon*, [1982] 2 S.C.R. 161, 138 D.L.R. (3d) 1 (S.C.C.).

11. If the business of the corporation is such that power to incorporate and make laws in relation to it belongs exclusively to Parliament (e.g., federal railways, federal telephone corporations, sea coast and inland fisheries, navigation and shipping, etc.), the exclusive power to legislate in relation to such subjects not only enables Parliament to prescribe the powers exercisable by such corporations and what limitations should be placed on such powers, but also to a certain extent enables it to affect proprietary rights within the several provinces, and where the legislative power cannot be effectually exercised without affecting the proprietary rights of individuals or of the provincial legislature the power so to affect those rights is necessarily involved in the legislative power.

A.G. Can. v. A.G. Ont., Que. & N.S., [1898] A.C. 700, 713 (P.C.); *Canadian Pacific Railway v. Bonsecours (Parish)*, [1899] A.C. 367 (P.C.); *Toronto (City) v. Bell Telephone Co. of Canada*, [1905] A.C. 52 (P.C.); *A.G. B.C. v. Canadian*

Pacific Railway, [1906] A.C. 204, 210 (P.C.); *A.G. Que. v. Nipissing Central Railway*, [1926] A.C. 715 (P.C.); *United Manufacturing Co. v. St. Maurice Power Co.*, [1926] A.C. 708 (P.C.).

The exclusive federal jurisdiction covers those local works and undertakings specified in clauses (a), (b) and (c) of head 10 of s. 92 as if such local works and undertakings were inserted in one of the classes of subjects assigned to Canada under s. 91: *Montreal (City) v. Montreal Street*, [1912] A.C. 333 at 342 (P.C.); *A.G. Ont. v. Winner*, [1954] A.C. 541 at 568 (P.C.). The words "works and undertakings" in s. 92(10)(a) " . . . works and undertakings connecting the province with any other or others of the provinces, or extending beyond the limits of the province . . ." are to be read disjunctively, so that if either "works" or "undertakings" connect the province with others or extend beyond its limits Parliament is alone empowered to deal with them: *A.G. Ont. v. Winner*, [1954] A.C. 541 at 572 (P.C.). In that case it was held that it was not within the legislative jurisdiction of New Brunswick to prohibit an operator of public motor buses from carrying passengers from points outside the province to points within the province and vice versa and from taking up and setting down passengers within the province. In *Campbell-Bennett Ltd. v. Comstock Mid-Western Ltd.*, [1953] 3 D.L.R. 594 (B.C. C.A.) the British Columbia Court of Appeal held that proceedings to enforce a lien under the *Mechanics' Lien Act* of that province could not be taken against a corporation incorporated by special Act of Canada in its operation of an oil pipeline between Alberta and British Columbia.

By legislation passed pursuant to s. 92(10)(c), Canada may assume jurisdiction over such works and undertakings as are declared by Parliament to be for the general advantage of Canada or for the advantage of two or more provinces. An express declaration is necessary in every case: *St. John & Quebec v. Jones* (1921), 62 S.C.R. 92. Such legislation declares the undertaking of the corporation specified to be a work for the general advantage of Canada and the corporation to be a body politic and corporate within the legislative authority of the Parliament of Canada. Where the usual procedure has been followed in respect of a street railway corporation, the corporation is not subject to the jurisdiction of a public service commission created by the province: *Quebec Light & Power Co. v. Montcalm Land Co.*, [1927] S.C.R. 545; and a municipal by-law imposing an assessment on a telephone corporation, the works of which have been declared to be for the general advantage of Canada, in default of an alteration (even temporary) in the physical structure of its lines and equipment is beyond any power which a provincial legislature can delegate to a municipality: *Bell Telephone Co. v. Harwich (Township)*, [1945] O.R. 852 (C.A.) (affd on other grounds *loc. cit.*). As to what will be comprised in the term "undertaking" in such a statute, see *Beauport v. Quebec Railway Light & Power Co.*, [1945] S.C.R. 16.

But see *Northern Manufacturing Co. v. St. Lawrence Power Co.*, [1926] 3 D.L.R. 209 (S.C.C.).

12. Subject to the above principle the *B.N.A. Act* does not enable Parliament to confer upon others proprietary rights where it possesses none itself.

A.G. Can. v. Atts. G. Ont., Que. & N.S., [1898] A.C. 700, 713 (P.C.); *A.G. Can. v. A.G. Que.*, [1921] 1 A.C. 413, at 420 (P.C.); *Montreal (City) v. Montreal Harbour Commissioners*, [1926] A.C. 299, at 312, 313 (P.C.).

13. The power of the provinces to incorporate corporations is derived from s. 92 head 11 whereby "In each Province the Legislature may exclusively make laws in relation to the Incorporation of Companies with Provincial objects."

The meaning of the phrase "with Provincial objects" was, after much discussion in the courts of Canada, considered, explained and determined by the Privy Council in the cases of *Bonanza Creek Gold Mining Co. v. The King*, [1916] 1 A.C. 566 (P.C.); *A.G. Can. v. A.G. Alta.*, [1916] 1 A.C. 588, at 597 (P.C.), and by the Supreme Court of Canada in *Honsberger v. Weyburn Townsite Co.* (1919), 59 S.C.R. 281.

The result of these cases appears to be that, while the actual powers and rights which the provincial authority can bestow are limited to powers and rights exercisable within the province, the provincial authority is not precluded by the *B.N.A. Act* from conferring on the corporation created by it capacity to accept extraprovincial powers and rights. Accordingly, a provincially incorporated fire insurance corporation is not inherently incapable of entering, outside the province of incorporation, into a valid contract of insurance relating to property situate in a foreign country: *Canadian Pacific Railway v. Ottawa Fire Insurance Co.* (1908), 39 S.C.R. 405; and a corporation incorporated under the laws of a province for the purpose of carrying on the business of insurance has power to do business and effect policies outside the province of incorporation: *Kittles v. Colonial Assurance Co.* (1917), 35 D.L.R. 588 (Man. C.A.) (corporation incorporated by special Act); *Re Anglo-American Fire Insurance Co. (No. 2)* (1919), 16 O.W.N. 150 (Ont. H.C.) (corporation incorporated by letters patent and holding federal and provincial licences). See further the notes, *infra*, with reference to provincial legislation conferring on provincially incorporated corporations the general capacity which the common law ordinarily attaches to corporations created by charter.

In *Honsberger v. Weyburn Townsite Co., supra,* the Supreme Court of Canada negatived the view expressed by Masten J. in (1918), 43 O.L.R. 451, at 461, viz., that the implied permission to carry on its business outside the boundaries of the province of incorporation which, in recognition of the doctrine of comity, would be ascribed to a corporation incorporated by plenary sovereign authority, is not enjoyed by a corporation incorporated under a provincial statute.

Provincial legislation, dismissing the directors of a provincially incorporated railway and providing for the appointment of others in their place, is *intra vires: St. John & Quebec Ryailway v. Jones* (1921), 62 S.C.R. 92; affg (1921), 57 D.L.R. 477 (N.B. C.A.).

14. Provincial corporations if insolvent are subject to the federal *Winding-up Act* and the *Bankruptcy Act.* Federal powers to legislate in relation to bankruptcy and insolvency enable Parliament to determine by legislation the relative priorities of creditors under a bankruptcy or authorized assignment: *Royal Bank v. Larue,* [1928] A.C. 187 (P.C.); and legislative provisions as to compositions, by which bankruptcy is avoided but which assume insolvency,

are within the sphere of bankruptcy legislation: *A.G. B.C. v. A.G. Can.*, [1937] A.C. 391 (P.C.). Provincial legislation is *ultra vires* if it substantially invades the exclusive legislative powers of Canada in relation to bankruptcy and insolvency and obstructs actual federal legislation on this subject: *A.G. Alta. v. A.G. Can.*, [1943] A.C. 356, at 375 (P.C.) (Reference re *The Debt Adjustment Act*, 1937, of Alberta).

Provincial corporations must observe the requirements of federal law as to navigation and shipping: *Queddy River Driving Boom Co. v. Davidson* (1883), 10 S.C.R. 222.

But a railway which is constituted by Act of a provincial legislature, is wholly situate within one province and has not been declared by the federal Parliament to be a work for the general advantage of Canada is not bound by federal legislation relative to through traffic carried over its lines: *Montreal (City) v. Montreal Street Ry.* [1912] A.C. 333.

Corporation a distinct legal entity

A corporation is regarded at law as a persona or entity distinct from the shareholders who compose it. It is not like a partnership, a mere collection or aggregation of individual units. This distinction between the corporation as a body corporate and its shareholders is fundamental.

At common law it had been held that in order for a corporation to be created there must be first a group or series of natural persons to constitute the corporation: *Hague v. Cancer Relief & Research Institute*, [1939] 4 D.L.R. 191, at 194 (Man. K.B.). Under the present Act it is clear that one or more bodies corporate may incorporate a corporation (see s. 5(2)). The Ontario Act provides that any individual or corporation or any combination may incorporate a corporation by signing articles of incorporation (see s. 4(1)).

Rules arising from separate legal personality of corporations

Particularly in the case of what have been called "one man companies" it is essential that there should be no confusion between the respective rights, powers, assets and transactions of the corporation and its corporators, or in regard to their respective liabilities in cases where it is sought to impose personal liability on shareholders or directors in lieu of or in addition to the liability of the corporation.

A consideration of the cases appears to establish the following rules:

1. In questions of property and capacity, of acts done and rights acquired or liabilities assumed, the corporation is always an entity distinct from its corporators. It is not an alias or a sham, the general principle of the *Salomon* case, *infra*, stands unimpaired. It is only in the most exceptional of circumstances that the corporate veil should be lifted.

Salomon v. Salomon & Co., [1897] A.C. 22 at 42, 51 (H.L.); *Rielle v. Reid* (1899), 26 O.A.R. 54; *Kodak, Ltd. v. Clark*, [1902] 2 K.B. 450, [1903] 1 K.B. 505 (C.A.); *Janson v. Driefontein Consolidated Mines Ltd.*, [1902] A.C. 484 at 497, 498, 501 (H.L.); *Rainham Chemical Works Ltd. v. Belevedere Fish Guano Co.*, [1921] 2 A.C. 465 at 475, 476, 501 (H.L.); *Meadow Farm Ltd. v. Imperial*

Bank of Canada (1922), 66 D.L.R. 743 (Alta. C.A.); *British Thomson-Houston Co. v. Sterling Accessories Ltd.*, [1924] 2 Ch. 33; *Associated Growers of B.C. Ltd. v. Edmunds*, [1926] 1 W.W.R. 535 (B.C. C.A.) (leave to appeal to P.C. refused); *Waldron v. Hogan*, [1934] 3 D.L.R. 800 (B.C. Co. Ct.); *Export Brewing & Malting Co. v. Dominion Bank*, [1937] 3 D.L.R. 513 (P.C.); *R. v. Meilicke*, [1938] 3 D.L.R. 33 (Sask. C.A.); *Re Hydro-Electric Power Commission of Ontario and Thorold and Pelham (Townships)* (1924), 55 O.L.R. 431 at 435 (C.A.); *Carter v. Fournier* (1937), 75 Que. S.C. 530 (C.S. Qué); *Dion v. Banque Provinciale du Canada* (1939), 66 Que. K.B. 344 (C.A.); *Beckow v. Panich & Toronto Jobbing Co.* (1940), 69 Que. K.B. 398 (C.A.); *White v. Bank of Toronto*, [1953] O.R. 479 (C.A.); *Bank Voor Handel en Scheepvaart N.V. v. Slatford*, [1953] 1 Q.B. 248 at 269; *Lee v. Lee's Air Farming Ltd.*, [1961] A.C. 12, 3 W.L.R. 758 (P.C.) (director, as agent of the corporation, may enter into an employment contract with himself); *Clarkson Co. v. Zhelka*, [1967] 2 O.R. 565, 64 D.L.R. (2d) 457 (Ont, H.C.); *Fidelity Developments Inc. v. Chief of Resources*, [1979] W.W.R. 151 (N.W.T.) and *Ian J. Ward & Co. v. Gilbert* (unreported) November 9, 1990 (B.C. C.A.).

Thus, for example, in the case of *Macaura v. Northern Assurance Co.*, [1925] A.C. 619 (P.C.) it was held that a shareholder had no insurable interest in the property of a corporation in which he was sole shareholder. The Supreme Court of Canada followed the *Macaura* case in *Guarantee Co. of North America v. Aqua-Land Exploration Ltd.*, [1966] S.C.R. 133 [1965] I.L.R. 1-153 (S.C.C.) in refusing to lift the corporate veil in order to find that one of three shareholders in a corporation had an insurable interest in its assets. *Macaura* was also followed by the Supreme Court in *Wandlyn Motels Ltd. v. Commerce General Insurance Co.*, [1970] S.C.R. 992, 3 N.B.R. (2d) 6 (S.C.C.) in which the court did not regard the motel owned by a man who held all but two shares of Wandlyn Motels Ltd. as the property of the corporation. However, in *Kosmopoulos v. Constitution Insurance Co.*, [1987] S.C.R. [1987] I.L.R. 1-2147 the Supreme Court refused to follow the *Macaura* case. The court did leave the corporate veil intact, deciding the case on the basis of insurance principles. Wilson J., writing for the majority, noted at p. 10:

> As a general rule a corporation is a legal entity distinct from its shareholders: *Salomon v. Salomon & Co.*, [1897] A.C. 22 (H.L.). The law on when a court may disregard this principle by "lifting the corporate veil" and regarding the company as a mere "agent" or "puppet" of its controlling shareholder or parent corporation follows no consistent principle. The best that can be said is that the "separate entities" principle is not enforced when it would yield a result "too flagrantly opposed to justice, convenience or the interest of the Revenue" L.C.B. Gower, *Modern Company Law*, 4th ed. (1979), p. 112.

Wilson J. concluded that while it was theoretically possible to lift the veil in the case before the court, to do so would result in an arbitrary distinction between corporations with more than one shareholder and corporations with only one shareholder. The majority of the court was of the view that the corporate veil could not be lifted. However, the court reconsidered the insurance principle that a person can have an insurable interest only in legally enforceable rights as established in the *Macaura* and *Aqua-Land* cases holding that it was a rule that should no longer be followed. As Mr. Kosmopoulos had a "sufficient interest" in the property, the court held he had an insurable interest in it.

2. For the purpose of determining the conditions on which the capacity to act is enjoyed and acts are done by the corporation, the personalities of the natural persons who are its corporators and the predominant character of its shareholders and corporators are open for consideration.

Daimler Co. v. Continental Tyre & Rubber Co., [1916] 2 A.C. 307 (H.L.); *Trahan v. Painchaud* (1918), 53 Que. S.C. 445 (C.A.) (sale to corporation fictitious or fraudulent).

3. If a corporation is formed for the express purpose of doing a wrongful act or if, when formed, those in control expressly direct a wrongful thing to be done, the individuals as well as the corporation are responsible. The mere machinery to do an illegal act will not purge its illegality.

Dominion Royalty Corp. v. Goffatt, [1935] S.C.R. 565; *Patton v. Yukon Consolidated Gold Corp.*, [1934] O.W.N. 321 (C.A.); *Daimler Co. v. Continental Tyre & Rubber Co., supra*, at 316; *Rainham Chemical Works Ltd. v. Belvedere Fish Guano Co., supra*, at 476; *R. v. Sommers (No. 7)* (1958), 26 W.W.R. 254 (B.C. S.C.); *Jones v. Lipman*, [1962] 1 All E.R. 442 (Ch. D.); *Wawanesa Mutual Insurance Co. v. J.A. (Fred) Chalmers & Co.* (1969), 69 W.W.R. 612, [1969] I.L.R. 1-301 (Sask. Q.B.); *Fern Brand Waxes Ltd. v. Pearl*, [1972] 3 O.R. 829, 29 D.L.R. (3d) 662 (Ont. C.A.); *Pacific Rim Installations Ltd. v. Tilt-Up Construction Ltd.* (1978), 5 B.C.L.R. 231 (B.C. Co. Ct.); *Saskatchewan Economic Development Corp. v. Patterson-Boyd Manufacturing Corp.*, [1981] 6 Sask.R. 325, 2 W.W.R. 40 (Sask. C.A.); *Lockharts Ltd. v. Excalibur Holdings Ltd.* (1987), 47 R.P.R. 8, 83 N.S.R. (2d) 281 (N.S. T.D.); *B.G. Preeco I (Pacific Coast) Ltd. v. Bon Street Holdings Ltd.* (1989), 43 B.L.R. 67, 60 D.L.R. (4th) 30 (B.C. C.A.); *Austin v. Habitat Development Ltd.* (1991), 105 N.S.R. (2d) 91, 284 A.P.R. 91 (N.S. T.D.)

4. Whether an individual has constituted the corporation his agent is a question of fact, but the fact that the controlling corporator holds a majority or even the whole of the shares and is the managing director will not alone suffice to establish the relationship of principal and agent between himself and his corporation.

Gramophone & Typewriter Ltd. v. Stanley, [1908] 2 K.B. 89 at 96 (C.A.); *I.R.C. v. Sansom*, [1921] 2 K.B. 492 (C.A.); *Rainham Chemical Works Ltd. v. Belvedere Fish Guano Co., supra*, at 475 and 488; *British Thomson-Houston Co. v. Sterling Accessories Ltd.*, [1924] 2 Ch. 33 at 38; *Performing Right Society Ltd. v. Ciryl Theatrical Syndicate Ltd.*, [1924] 1 K.B. 1 at 14; *Patton v. Yukon Consolidated Gold Corp. Ltd., supra*; *Allen General Supplies Ltd. v. Ritchie*, [1934] O.W.N. 273 (H.C.); *Dominion Royalty Corp. v. Goffat*, supra; *Royal Bank v. Port Royal Pulp & Paper Co.*, [1937] 4 D.L.R. 254 (N.B. C.A.); *Discount & Loan Corp. v. Superintendent of Insurance*, [1938] 4 D.L.R. 225 (Ex. Ct.); *Clarkson Co. v. Zhelka, supra*; *Frankel Structural Steel Ltd. v. Goden Holdings Ltd.*, [1971] S.C.R. 250.

Similarly, whether a subsidiary corporation acts as agent for its parent corporation is a question of fact. In the absence of an express agency, an implied agency may be found where the parent corporation so dominates the function of the subsidiary that the subsidiary has no separate existence. *A.G. Can. v. Coleman Products Co.*, [1929] 1 D.L.R. 658 (Ont. H.C.) (relationship between closely interlocked corporations that of principal and selling agent); *Assiniboia v. Suburban Rapid Transit Co.*, [1931] 2 D.L.R. 862 (Man. C.A.) (parent corporation not liable under a franchise of the subsidiary); *Palmolive Manufacturing Co. (Ontario) v. R.*, [1933] S.C.R. 131 (one subsidiary acting as agent for the other); *Electric Chain Co. v. Art Metal Works Inc.*, [1933] S.C.R. 581 (subsidiary had no cause of action for infringement of patent owned by its parent corporation and should not have been joined as plaintiff); *The King v. Leon L. Plotkins*, [1939] Ex. C.R. 1 (partnership and limited corporation held to be independent trading units); *The King v. B.C. Brick & Tile Co.*, [1936] 3 D.L.R. 23 (Ex. Ct.) (degree of control not present and the corporations constituted independent trading units); *Smith Stone & Knight Ltd. v. Birmingham Corporation*, [1939] 4 All E.R. 116 (K.B.); *Aluminum Co. v. Toronto (City)*, [1944] S.C.R. 267 (agency rejected); *Lunney v. Welland Securities Ltd.*, [1942] O.W.N. 262 (H.C.) (agency not established): *Ebbw Vale Urban District Council v. South Wales Traffic Licensing Authority*, [1951] 2 K.B. 366 (C.A.) (agency not established); *The Queen v. Waverly Construction Co.* (1972), 4 N.S.R. (2d) 232, 30 D.L.R. (3d) 224 (N.S. C.A.) (subsidiary did not act as agent for parent corporation and parent therefore not liable for the negligent acts of the subsidiary's employee); *Canada Life Assurance Co. v. Canadian Imperial Bank of Commerce* (1974), 3 O.R. (2d) 70, 44 D.L.R. (3d) 486 (Ont. C.A.) (no agency where sufficient degree of dependence not established); *Aluminum Co. of Canada v. Regional Assessment Commissioner, Region No. 5* (1984), 46 O.R. (2d) 614, 26 M.P.L.R.I. (H.C.); affd (1986), 54 O.R. (2d) 249, 26 D.L.R. (4th) 475 (Div. Ct.) (subsidiary carrying on independent business and not a mere "puppet" of the parent corporation); See also *Sun Sudan Oil Co. v. Methanex Corp.* (1992), 5 Alta. L.R. (3d) 292 (Q.B.); *Seagrams Distillers (Ont.) Ltd. v. Regional Assessment Commissioner, Regions 9 and 10* (1986), 54 O.R. (2d) 289, 12 O.A.C. 313 (Div. Ct.) (subsidiary assessable at the tax rate of the parent corporation as the subsidiary was a puppet of the parent corporation); *Bank of Montreal v. Canadian Westgrowth Ltd.* (1990), 72 Alta. L.R. (2d) 319 102 A.R. 391; affd April 15, 1992 Alta. C.A. unreported (Q.B.) (agency not established even though officers and directors identical, subsidiary funded by parent and assets purchased with interest-free loans from parent). Where the controlling shareholder so controls the functions of two affiliated corporations that it appears the one corporation has acted as the "puppet" of the other, the corporate veils of both corporations may be pierced; *Kristian Equipment Ltd. v. Campbell West Ltd.*, [1992] 2 W.W.R. 69 (Sask. Q.B.).

5. Where the evidence brings the case within rule 3 or where it establishes that the corporation is a mere agent of the controlling shareholder (rule 4) it may be appropriate to characterize the corporation as a paper sham, a simulacrum, cloak, alias or alter ego; but otherwise the indiscriminate use of these or similar terms is liable to lead to confusion of thought and possible injustice.

Salomon v. Salomon & Co., *supra*, at 42; *Rainham Chemical Works Ltd. v. Belvedere Fish Guano Co.*, *supra*, at 488; *I.R.C. v. Sanson*, *supra*; *Clark v. Gaytree Studios Inc.*, [1930] 4 D.L.R. 1038 (Sask. K.B.); [1931] 1 D.L.R. 346 (Sask. C.A.); *Dominion Royalty Corp. v. Goffatt*, *supra*; *Export Brewing & Malting Co. v. Dominion Bank*, *supra*, at 523; *White v. Bank of Toronto*, *supra*.

6. A transaction, even though within the powers of the corporation, will be treated as unenforceable if the corporation acting through the directors, without the authorization of the shareholders in general meeting, has purported thereby to apply its property for the benefit of the directors; *Export Brewing & Malting Co. v. Dominion Bank*, *supra*.

Parent and subsidiary corporations

The distinction between a corporation and its shareholders is equally applicable to parent and subsidiary corporations and to related corporations owned by a common shareholder.

A corporation and its wholly owned subsidiary are separate and distinct legal entities: see *Aluminum Co. v. City of Toronto*, *supra*, at 271; *Barnes v. Saskatchewan Co-Operative Wheat Producers Ltd.*, [1946] 1 W.W.R. 97 at 113 (Sask. C.A.), appeal dismissed [1947] S.C.R. 241; *Aluminum Co. of Canada v. Regional Assessment Commission Region No. 5*, *supra*; *Re Seagrams Distillers (Ont.) Ltd. v. Regional Assessment Commission, Regions 9 and 10*, *supra*.

As stated in *Ebbw Vale Urban District Council v. South Wales Traffic Licensing Authority*, *supra*, at p. 370:

> Under the ordinary rules of law, a parent company and a subsidiary company, even a 100 per cent, subsidiary company, are distinct legal entities, and in the absence of an agency contract between the two companies one cannot be said to be the agent of the other.

Where there is no express or implied agency, fraud, conspiracy, or evidence that the two corporations are alter egos of the corporate principals, the corporate veil will not be lifted.

The distinction between corporation and shareholder also applies where a person owns and controls two separate corporations. Where there is no evidence of fraud, conspiracy, agency, or that the corporations are alter egos of the owner, there is no reason to pierce the corporate veil to make one corporation liable for the obligations of the other. See *Northern Electric Co. v. Frank Warkentin Electric Ltd.* (1972), 27 D.L.R. (3d) 519 (Man. C.A.) and *B.G. Preeco I (Pacific Coast) Ltd. v. Bon Street Holdings Ltd.*, *supra* (corporate veil not lifted).

Exceptions

While certain exceptions to the *Solomon* principle have been articulated where the courts seek to discover the true relationship between a corporation and the individuals who control it, between a subsidiary corporation and its parent corporation or between related corporations, as pointed out by Wilson J. in the *Kosmopolous* case, the case law is difficult to reconcile. Such exceptions include: where one corporation in fact acts as agent of another; where there is fraud or a lack of a legitimate corporate purpose; where the lifting of the veil makes enforcement of a taxing statute reasonable; and where, although the corporations are in law separate entities, the two corporations in fact constitute one enterprise.

Corporation as an agent or alias of controlling shareholder

In some cases, the principal of the corporation has been perceived as the true vendor or purchaser of property. These are not truly "corporate veil" cases but merely examples of individuals contracting in a personal capacity. For example, in *Patton v. Yukon Consolidated Gold Corp.*, *supra*, a person was treated as vendor where he owned substantially all the shares of a corporation which he used as a vehicle or instrument for effecting a sale of assets to another corporation of which he was a director. See also *Provincial Electric (1969) Ltd. v. Registered Holdings Ltd.* (1977), 34 N.S.R. (2d) 100, 59 A.P.R. 100 (N.S. Co.Ct.).

In *Allen General Supplies Ltd. v. Ritchie*, *supra*, the president and controlling shareholder of a corporation was held liable as an undisclosed principal where the corporation on his direction ordered goods intended for him personally.

Where an individual has carried on a business and has a personal account with a supplier and after incorporation continues to purchase goods from the supplier presumably on behalf of the incorporated corporation, the onus is on him (debtor) to prove that the supplier (creditor) knew of the incorporation and has agreed to accept the corporation in place of the individual: *Royal Stores Ltd. v. Brown* (1956), 5 D.L.R. (2d) 146.

In a case where the officers of a new corporation did not advise suppliers that the new corporation was responsible for goods sold and delivered, it was held that they were personally liable for the debt. It was an obligation on a party who intended to rely on the fact of incorporation to claim limited liability protection to give ample notice to suppliers of a change in status, particularly where the new business was carried on in the same premises and the former name was used. See *Trail Tire Service Ltd. v. Scobie*, [1976] 5 W.W.R. 409 (Alta. Dist. Ct.).

However, in a case where a corporation had been struck off the register and a director was not aware of this fact, he was not held personally liable for payment for goods supplied to the corporation which had been struck off. It was pointed out that the situation would have been different where a director knew a winding-up procedure and dissolution had taken place and incurred a liability on behalf of the corporation as in such a case the director would be personally liable. See *Olympia & York Developers Ltd. v. Price*, [1976] 5 W.W.R. 347 (B.C. Co. Ct.) but see *Royal Bank v. Starr* (1985), 31 B.L.R. 124 (Ont. Dist. Ct.) where a corporation gave a note to the plaintiff but at the time had been dissolved, the sole shareholder and director were liable, not on the note itself, but on the basis of breach of warranty of authority, negligent misrepresentation, and unjust enrichment.

Where a jeweller's claim ticket gave no indication that the customer dealt with a limited corporation and all dealings were on a personal basis, the jeweller was found personally liable for negligence in the loss of the customer's watch.

See *Chaing v. Heppner* (1978), 6 B.C.L.R. 76, 85 D.L.R. (3d) 487 (B.C. Co. Ct.).

Where the plaintiff entered into contracts with the defendant on behalf of a named corporation and made the payments personally, the plaintiff was successful in an action to recover moneys due. There were broad failures to comply with the formal requirements of the former Alberta *Companies Act* which made limited liability unavailable. See *Tato Enterprises Ltd. v. Rode* (1979), 17 A.R. 432 (Alta. Dist. Ct.). See also *Frankel Structural Steel Ltd. v. Goden Holdings ltd.*, [1971] S.C.R. 250, 16 D.L.R. (3d) 736 (S.C.C.).

Where a one-man holding corporation purchased a shopping centre and it was disclosed at the time of the purchase that the corporation was a mere shell for other investors, the court refused to lift the corporate veil to hold the sole shareholder liable as actual purchaser. See *390346 Ontario Ltd. v. Malidav Holdings Ltd.* (1980), 31 N.B.R. (2d) 72, 75 A.P.R. 72 (N.B. Q.B.). See also *Chenier v. Johnson* (1964), 48 D.L.R. (2d) 380 (B.C. S.C.).

Where the defendant owners of a corporation purchased goods from the plaintiff and had incorporated a new corporation but failed to make it clear to the plaintiff that he dealt with a limited corporation, the plaintiff succeeded in an action for the price of goods as against the defendant owners personally. The defendant's invoices had been marked with the new corporation's name but there was no indication that the business was to be a limited corporation. See *Interlake Packers Ltd. v. Vogt* (1987), 47 Man. R. (2d) 268 (Man. Q.B.). See also *Re Pahmer (St. George Lumber Company Limited)* (1969), 12 C.B.R. (N.S.) 261 (Ont. S.C.); *Data Business Forms Ltd. v. MacIntosh* (1986), 76 N.S.R. (2d) 418, 189 A.P.R. 418 (T.D.); *Morse Electro Products (Canada) Corp. v. Central Discount House Ltd.* (1978), 5 B.C.L.R. 340 (B.C. Co.Ct.); *Victor (Canada) Ltd. v. Farbetter Addressing & Mailing Ltd.* (1978), 3 B.L.R. 312 (Ont. H.C.); *Corkum v. Lohnes* (1981), 43 N.S.R. (2d) 477, 81 A.P.R. 477 (N.S. C.A.); *W.R. Benjamin Products Ltd. v. Saulnier* (1982), 40 N.B.R. (2d) 537, 105 A.P.R. 537 (N.B. Q.B.); *Jenkins v. Cox* (1983), 56 N.S.R. (2d) 301, 117 A.P.R. 301 (N.S. T.D.); *Spilsbury Communications Ltd. v. Fentronics-NSI Ltd.* (1986), 73 N.S.R. (2d) 86, 176 A.P.R. 86 (T.D.).

For cases in which the corporation was held to be liable as there was sufficient notice see *William A. Flemming Ltd. v. Fisher* (1978), 29 N.S.R. (2d) 338, 45 A.P.R. 338; *Vanier v. Learmonth* (1976), 23 N.S.R. (2d) 37; *Hellekson v. Canadian Pacific Ltd.* (1976), 1 B.C.L.R 321, [1977] 2 W.W.R. 216 (B.C. S.C.).

In other cases, the corporation has been considered the agent of the controlling corporate principals. The key factor which persuades a court that a corporation acts as agent is the degree of control which the shareholder exercises. Where, for example, a subsidiary corporation has no existence of its own and is subservient to and dependent upon the parent, the parent will be unable to shelter behind the corporate veil. For cases where the court has gone behind the legal organization to determine whether a corporation is an agent or alias for the individuals who control it, see the cases referred to under rules 3, 4 and 5 above.

In most cases, there will be no formal agency agreement between the shareholder and the corporation or between related corporations. Whether or not an implied agency arises depends on the facts. Certain factors would appear to influence a court in determining whether an agency exists. In *Smith, Stone & Knight v. Birmingham Corp., supra*, at 121, Atkinson J. set out the following six factors for determining whether a company acts as agent for another company:

1. Were the profits treated as the profits of the company?
2. Were the persons conducting the business appointed by the parent company?
3. Was the company the head and brain of the trading venture?
4. Did the company govern the adventure, decide what should be done and what capital should be embarked on the venture?
5. Did the company make the profits by its skill and direction?
6. Was the company in effectual and constant control?

These six factors were not considered determinative of the issue by the Nova Scotia Court of Appeal in *The Queen v. Waverly Construction Co. Ltd., supra*, The court held that the parent corporation was not vicariously liable for the negligent act of an employee of its subsidiary. While the two corporations shared office premises and had common management, there was insufficient proof that the subsidiary acted as agent for Waverly. See also *Sun Sudan Oil Co. v. Methanex Corp.* (1992), 5 Alta. L.R. (3d) 292 (Q.B.).

The Ontario Court of Appeal has also enunciated several factors which may be helpful in determining the agency question: see *Canada Life Assurance Co. v. Canadian Imperial Bank of Commerce, supra*, wherein it was held that an affiliated Canadian bank did not carry on the business as agent of an American bank for the purposes of service under the Ontario Rules of Civil Procedure. The following criteria were considered by Gale C.J.O., at p. 84:

1. the capitalization of the subsidiary;
2. the degree of observance of corporate formalities;
3. the extent of the relationship between the business of parent and subsidiary;
4. the nature and extent of the business dealings between parent and subsidiary;
5. the corporate histories of both parent and subsidiary;
6. the relationship between the boards of directors and upper management personnel of parent and subsidiary, and
7. the extent of the ownership interest of the parent in the subsidiary.

While in the above cases certain factors were specifically laid down as indicative of agency, it would appear that similar criteria were considered in the following cases even though not formally articulated as such.

In *Palmolive Manufacturing Co. (Ontario) Ltd. v. The King, supra*, the court concluded that Palmolive, which sold goods to Colgate-Palmolive-Peet Co., a related corporation, acted as the agent of Colgate because of the degree of control exercised by Colgate over Palmolive's production. The court noted that while the two corporations were separate legal entities, in fact and in practical terms, Palmolive was part of Colgate because it was subject to the direction and control of Colgate. See also *A.G. Can. v. Coleman Products Co., supra.*

In *The King v. B.C. Brick and Tile Co., supra*, the court concluded that such degree of control was not present. Each corporation financed and conducted its own business, kept separate business records and had no arrangement to divide shared profits and losses. In the court's view, it would be dangerous to conclude an agency was established on the mere basis that the corporate shareholders and officers were the same and the two corporations had "business relations". See also *The King v. Leon L. Plotkins, supra.* Nor will the fact that all the shares of a subsidiary (except qualification shares) are owned by the parent corporation, and that all the officers are officers of the parent corporation make the parent corporation liable under a franchise of the subsidiary: see *Assiniboia v. Suburban Rapid Transit Co., supra.*

In *Aluminum Co. v. City of Toronto, supra,* the court considered whether the provisions of the *Assessment Act of Ontario* would apply to the income of wholly owned subsidiary corporations because the subsidiaries acted as agents for the parent corporation. The agency argument was rejected by the court. Kerwin J. simply found that the subsidiaries did business with other unrelated people or corporations. Rand J., in a concurring judgment, stated at p. 271 that the business of the first corporation can in some circumstances embrace the nominal business of another corporation where the second corporation is in fact a "puppet" of the first corporation. The question, apart from any formal agency, was whether the first corporation so dominates the second, that the second has no independent functioning. See also *Aluminum Co. v. Regional Assessment Commissioner, Region No. 5, supra,* and *Seagrams Distillers (Ont.) Ltd. v. Regional Assessment Commissioner, Regions 9 & 10, supra,* which followed Rand J.'s comments in *Aluminum Co. v. City of Toronto, supra.*

In *Bank of Montreal v. Canadian Westgrowth Ltd., supra,* Brennan J. was unwilling to find either an express or implied agency contract on the facts. The Bank had taken an assignment of a customer's interest under a guaranteed rental agreement executed by Westgrowth Petroleums Inc., a wholly owned American subsidiary of a Canadian corporation, Westgrowth Petroleums Ltd. The Bank claimed the rental shortfall against both the subsidiary and parent corporations, alleging that the subsidiary was the agent of the parent and that the parent was the de facto contracting party as the alter ego of the subsidiary. Despite the fact that the officers and directors of both corporations were identical, that the subsidiary was funded by the parent, and that the assets were purchased with interest-free monies loaned by the parent, Brennan J. refused to lift the corporate veil between the corporations. The Court of Appeal affirmed the trial judgment. Coté J.A., writing for the majority, could find no evidence that the contracting parties intended that the parent corporation be a party to the agreement.

In *Kristian Equipment Ltd. v. Campbell West Ltd., supra,* the controlling shareholder of the defendant corporation also controlled another corporation, Urano Rentals Ltd. Urano had purchased goods for resale to the plaintiff. When Urano was unable to complete the purchase, the defendant corporation bought the goods. It then resold the goods to Urano, financing the purchase by way of an unsecured loan. When the loan was not repaid, the defendant registered a security interest and purported to retain the goods in satisfaction, the plaintiff's action for damages against the defendant was successful. Batten J. upon examining the structure of the two companies and the nature of the transaction, concluded that Urano has acted as a mere puppet in the transaction.

Such factors have been considered in the labour relations context in determining if a union is entitled to picket at the premises of a related corporation. In *Nedco Ltd. v. Clark and Communications Workers of Canada, Local No. 4*, [1973] 6 W.W.R. 425, 43 D.L.R. (3d) 714 (Sask. C.A.) it was held that no injunction was available against the respondent union to prohibit picketing outside the business premises of Nedco, a wholly owned subsidiary, because Nedco was directed, controlled and so dominated by its parent that it constituted an integral part of the parent's business. See also *Nedco Ltd. v. Nichols*, [1973] 3 O.R. 944, 38 D.L.R. (3d) 664 (Ont. H.C.) and *Canada Safeway Ltd. v. Canadian Food and Allied Workers, Local 212 and Local 373*, [1974] 4 W.W.R. 453, 46 D.L.R. (3d) 113 (B.C.S.C.) (no injunction granted). But see *Imperial Oil Ltd. v. Oil, Chemical and Atomic Workers International Union, Local 9-601* (1969), 69 W.W.R. 401; affd 69 W.W.R. 702 (B.C. C.A.) (injunction granted where there was no suggestion that the parent corporation had transferred one phase of its operation to a wholly owned subsidiary to avoid labour problems or for any other improper motive); *Security Building Supplies Ltd. v. Massey and International Woodworkers of America, Local 1-184*, [1978] 6 W.W.R. 755, 92 D.L.R. (3d) 146 (Sask. Q.B.) where it was held that two substantial shareholders had no connection with the struck corporation and would be adversely affected should picketing be allowed at the plaintiff's premises.

Where the plaintiff was employed by a subsidiary corporation which was owned by two corporations in turn owned by a parent corporation, he sued the parent and subsidiary corporations for wrongful dismissal. The parent corporation was held liable for damages for wrongful dismissal as the evidence indicated that the parent corporation was in complete control of every aspect of the plaintiff's employment and considered to be the true employer. The intermediary corporations were not held liable as the mere fact they were shareholders of the nominal employer without more meant that no liability would flow from that relationship. See *Bagby v. Gustavson International Drilling Co.* (1980), 24 A.R. 181 (Alta. C.A.); varg (1979), 20 A.R. 244. See also *PCM Construction Control Consultants Ltd. v. Heeger* (1989) 67 Alta. L.R. (2d) 302, [1989] 5 W.W.R. 598 (Alta. Q.B.).

Fraud or improper purpose

Where the defendant corporation had conveyed its interest as purchaser under an agreement of purchase and sale to a corporation owned and controlled by the same individual to avoid a judgment registered against its interest in the lands, the court held that the transfer constituted a fraudulent scheme. Davison J. concluded that the principle in the *Salomon* case remains unimpaired, but where the veil is used as a sham or for a fraudulent or improper purpose, a court is entitled to look behind the corporate structure. The judgment was held to be binding against both corporations. See *Lockharts Ltd. v. Excalibur Holdings Ltd., supra.*

Similarly, in *Jones v. Lipman*, *supra*, specific performance of an agreement of purchase and sale was ordered where the defendant had conveyed the property to a corporation controlled by him to avoid the transaction with the plaintiff. The court found the corporation was a sham or mask and specific performance could not be resisted by a vendor who, by his absolute ownership and control of a limited corporation in which title had vested, was in a position to cause the contract to be completed.

Where the holder of all the shares of a corporation but for qualification shares failed to remit to the plaintiff insurance premiums which by statute were constituted as trust funds, he was held personally liable. The conversion of trust funds was a wrongful act directed by the shareholder. See *Wawanesa Mutual Insurance Co. v. J.A. (Fred) Chalmers & Co.*, *supra*.

Where one of the directors of the plaintiff corporation diverted funds—by way of loan to other corporations controlled by him as shareholder—to apply them against the debt owed to the plaintiff on a share subscription account, the director/shareholder was held personally liable for the fraudulently diverted moneys. See *Fern Brand Waxes Ltd. v. Pearl*, *supra*.

In *Austin v. Habitat Development Ltd.*, *supra*, the vice-president of the defendant corporation surreptitiously took $90,000 and converted it to his own use. The president stood by and allowed the appropriation of funds. The court found that while the individual had purported to act under the corporate veil, with no minutes or resolutions, the veil became "transparent". Because the funds had been paid to a corporation of which the vice-president was the controlling shareholder, the corporate veils of both companies were lifted as they related to both the vice-president and president. The vice-president and his company were ordered to return the funds or be in default, the plaintiffs would obtain judgment for that sum. The president was held jointly and severally responsible. In *Pacific Rim Installations Ltd. v. Tilt-Up Construction Ltd.*, *supra*, a shareholder and officer of the two defendant corporations negotiated a subcontract with the plaintiff but it was not entirely clear which of the two corporations actually entered into the agreement. Judgment was given against both corporations on the basis that they were the alter ego of the shareholder who had manipulated them to avoid payment.

If the corporation has been used to effect a purpose or commit an act which the shareholder could not effect or commit, the corporate veil may be lifted. See *Saskatchewan Economic Development Corp. v. Patterson-Boyd Manufacturing Corp.*, *supra*, where a debenture provided that the defendant corporation would not borrow from shareholders without consent and money was advanced by the shareholders through a new corporation, it was held that the newly incorporated corporation was enabling the shareholders to do something which they were unable to do in their individual capacity and the corporate veil was lifted. See, however, *B.G. Preeco I (Pacific Coast) Ltd. v. Bon Street Holdings Ltd.* (1989), 43 B.L.R. 67, 60 D.L.R. (4th) 30 (B.C. C.A.) where although the principals of the corporation were found to be guilty of fraud, the corporation had not been used to commit an act which the shareholders could not commit.

Group enterprises

The "group enterprise theory" as discussed by Professor Gower in *Modern Company Law* (3rd. ed.) at pp. 213 to 216 suggests that in some circumstances related corporations may be treated as one enterprise. This theory has been adopted by the English courts. See *DHN Food Distributors Ltd. v. London Borough of Tower Hamlets*, [1976] 3 All E.R. 462, 1 W.L.R. 852 (C.A.) wherein the court allowed the parent corporation compensation when land owned by its wholly owned subsidiary was expropriated, but see *Woolfson v. Strathdyde Regional Council* (1978), S.C. 90 (H.L.) wherein the House of Lords distinguished the *D.H.N.* case on its facts and denied compensation to the sole shareholder, Woolfson, of the occupying corporation. That corporation had no control over the owners of the land, Woolfson, and a related corporation of which Woolfson held the majority of the shares.

The theory has been recognized in Canada. Where the defendant, employed by a subsidiary of the plaintiff corporation, set up a business which was in competition with the parent corporation the court was willing to lift the corporate veil between parent and subsidiary, treating the two corporations as one enterprise. See *Manley Inc. v. Fallis* (1977), 2 B.L.R. 277, 38 C.P.R. (2d) 74 (Ont. C.A.).

In *Merrill Lynch Royal Securities Ltd. v. Blum* (1983), 23 B.L.R. 260 (Ont. H.C.) judgment was given against the three defendant corporations jointly and not against each corporation individually for the actual amount owing on their commodity trading accounts when the defendants became under-margined.

In *Equipment House Ltd. v. Canada* (1983), 28 L.C.R. 26, 148 D.L.R. (3d) 546 (F.C.T.D.) corporations which were wholly owned subsidiaries of a common shareholder were all held to be entitled to compensation when property in which only one of the corporations had an interest as lessee was expropriated. The corporations were treated as one enterprise. See, however, *The King v. Quebec Gas Co.* (1919), 59 S.C.R. 677 where it was held that a holding corporation has no *locus standi* to prosecute a claim for damages suffered by its subsidiary on the expropriation of property of the subsidiary.

The theory was noted by the Alberta Court of Appeal in *Bagby v. Gustavson International Drilling Co.*, *supra*, however, the case was decided on other grounds.

In *B.G. Preeco I (Pacific Coast) Ltd. v. Bon Street Holdings Ltd.*, *supra*, the plaintiff sought to fix a corporation with contractual liability for the misrepresentations of another corporation controlled by the same shareholders. Subsequent to entering into an agreement of purchase and sale with Bon Street Developments Ltd., the directors of Bon Street exchanged its name with that of a numbered shell corporation. "New" Bon Street refused to complete the transaction and was found liable for breach of contract. The plaintiff appealed with respect to the issue of whether the corporate veil should be lifted in order to fix old "Bon Street" and the directors with liability for the breach of contract by "new" Bon Street.

The Court of Appeal held that the plaintiff was not entitled to succeed on this basis, but could recover damages for fraud against the individuals and the corporation which committed the fraud. The court refused to pierce the veil on equitable grounds alone. In the court's opinion, the only basis upon which to pierce the veil would be fraud or improper conduct or on the basis of the "group enterprise theory." As "new" Bon Street had not been used to effect a purpose which the shareholders could not otherwise have effected, neither "new" Bon Street nor the shareholders were held liable for contractual damages.

Enforcement of taxing statutes

It is a question of fact whether a partnership, all or substantially all the members of which are shareholders of a corporation, is carrying on business for the corporation so as not to constitute independent trading units for tax purposes: *Canada Rice Mills Ltd. v. The King*, [1939] 3 D.L.R. 577 (P.C.).

In *Rodwell Securities Ltd. v. Inland Revenue Commissioners*, [1968] 1 All E.R. 257 (Ch. Div.) the court refused to grant an exemption from stamp duty to a wholly owned subsidiary corporation. The parent corporation held all the shares in two subsidiary corporations. One of the subsidiaries transferred property to a wholly owned subsidiary of the other wholly owned subsidiary. The transferee corporation claimed an exemption from stamp duty on the basis that the parent corporation was the beneficial owner of the share of the transferee. The court held that although the parent corporation might have a "controlling" interest, it did not beneficially own the assets of the subsidiary. The court refused to look behind the corporate veil to give effect to the taxing statute.

In *Littlewoods Mail Order Stores Ltd. v. McGregor*, [1969] 3 All E.R. 855, 1 W.L.R. 1241 (C.A.) the court disallowed a deduction of rent in calculating profits for tax purposes, concluding that the rent was in reality a sum paid for the acquisition of a capital asset through a wholly owned subsidiary.

In assessing the nature of the profit realized by a corporation on the purchase and sale of land, the investment policies of related corporations were considered. The taxpayer corporation was considered to be the instrument of the group of related corporations and the profit realized on the sale treated as taxable income. See *De Salaberry Realties Ltd. v. The Queen* (1976), 70 D.L.R. (3d) 706 (Fed. C.A.); affg (1974), 46 D.L.R. (3d) 100.

In *Re Jodrey* (1980), 2 S.C.R. 744, 8 E.T.R. 69 (S.C.C.) a majority of the Supreme Court of Canada concluded that the parent corporation, the shares of which were held by the testator's grandchildren, was "beneficially entitled" to the residue to the testator's estate which had been bequeathed to a wholly owned subsidiary corporation for purposes of Nova Scotia succession duty legislation. The majority was of the opinion that as the parent had absolute control of the named beneficiary, the subsidiary, and legal capacity to compel the subsidiary to turn over its share of the estate, the parent corporation and its shareholders would be considered "successors" of the property of the deceased.

Where seven Indian Bands incorporated a corporation to operate a resort, the corporation was not allowed an exemption from taxes granted in respect of Indian lands owned by an Indian or a band. In the absence of fraud or improper conduct, the separate legal existence of the corporation should not be disregarded, nor should an inquiry be made as to the shareholders' identity to determine liability. See *Kinookimaw Beach Assn. v. The Queen*, [1979] 6 W.W.R. 84; revg (*sub nom. Kinookimaw Beach Assn. v. Board of Review Commissioners*), [1978] 6 W.W.R. 749; leave to appeal refused to S.C.C. (1979), 1 Sask. R. 179n (S.C.C.).

Where to incorporate

The traditional view has been that where a corporation's activities are to be confined to one province, incorporation in that province is advisable; but that where a corporation will be carrying on business in a number of provinces or in foreign countries, consideration should be given to incorporation under the federal Act. The relative jurisdictional authority of Canada and the provinces to incorporate corporations as a matter of constitutional law are dealt with under the heading "Federal and provincial jurisdiction with respect to corporations", above, where it is indicated among other things that if a corporation is to carry on business in one province only it should be incorporated in that province and that, while Canada has the sole jurisdiction to incorporate corporations with other than provincial objects, the provinces may incorporate corporations with capacity to accept extraprovincial powers and rights. Subject to this constitutional point and in order to assess the soundness of the traditional view mentioned, it will be desirable to consider some of the factors which may be material in determining in a particular case the jurisdiction in which to incorporate.

If operations are to be carried on or financing undertaken outside Canada, a federal corporation may be preferable to a provincial corporation as a federal charter may carry greater prestige and the federal Act may be better known abroad. For similar reasons where foreign interests forming Canadian subsidiaries, may prefer federal as opposed to provincial corporations. Where such considerations are not paramount, various other factors may be taken into account in determining the jurisdiction of incorporation.

The decision may turn to some extent on the relative merits of the actual provisions of the federal Act and a particular provincial Act for the purposes of the proposed corporation. Certain provisions of the federal Act may be regarded in certain circumstances as disadvantageous. Thus, under s. 160 of the federal Act it is necessary for federal corporations, whose sales or assets (including those of affiliates) exceed prescribed limits or if its securities were distributed to the public and are held by more than one person, to file copies of its financial statements with the Department administering the Act. These are open for public inspection. At the present time, there is no similar requirement under any of the provincial Acts.

Federal corporations and corporations incorporated in eight of the provinces are incorporated by articles of incorporation or by letters patent; corporations incorporated in the other two provinces are incorporated by the registration of a memorandum of association. See the notes under the heading "Incorporation and organization under provincial Corporations Acts" below. The law applicable to articles of incorporation or letters patent corporations differs in a number of respects from that applicable to corporations incorporated by registration. In certain of the memorandum of association jurisdictions solicitors may be generally more familiar with the law applicable to provincial corporations than with that applicable to federal corporations and may tend as a result to incorporate corporations provincially. In addition the provincial authorities may afford more expeditions and convenient handling of corporate matters.

In most of the provinces corporations incorporated in other provinces or by Canada must be registered or licensed as a condition of doing business in the province. However, it should be kept in mind that the right of a federal corporation to carry on business throughout Canada cannot be taken away by the provincial requirements previously mentioned. A provincial corporation is not in this position and may in theory be refused registration or a licence in another province, although in practice registration or a licence will ordinarily be obtained without difficulty.

Generally speaking, incorporation fees and provincial licensing or registration requirements and fees are unlikely to vary sufficiently to affect a decision as to the jurisdiction of incorporation. It should be noted, however, that certain provincial jurisdictions may require the issue of a licence in or for a corporation to hold land in the province.

Summing up, it would appear that under current practice—unless operations outside Canada are contemplated, in which event a federal corporation may be preferable—the question of whether a federal or a provincial corporation is formed is unlikely to be of great practical importance no matter whether operations are to be carried on in one or more provinces. The circumstances of the particular case should always be taken into account, however, in determining the jurisdiction of incorporation. This will include any requirements as to the make-up of the board of directors which while generally requiring the majority of the board to be "resident Canadians" may offer variations which can be material in any particular case. For example in section 118(3) of the Ontario Act if there are only two directors, only one need be a "resident Canadian".

Points to be determined at time of incorporation and organization

The following is a brief list of the more important points on which instruction should be obtained before proceeding with the incorporation of a corporation:

(1) name;
(2) objects—if any;
(3) place of head office;
(4) authorized share capital, provisions applicable to preferred shares, if any;
(5) number of directors (ordinarily a minimum and maximum number is set), provision for division of directors into classes, if desired (s. 106);
(6) public or private corporation: if private corporation, what restrictions on the transfer of shares are desired;
(7) property to be acquired;
(8) how capital is to be obtained;
(9) what special matters are to be dealt with in the articles (see the heading "Additional provisions" below).

See further in connection with these matters the material under the heading "The articles" commencing below.

The following is a list of the more important matters which should be dealt with for the purpose of the organization of a corporation once incorporated:

(1) agreement under which assets to be acquired;
(2) subscriptions for shares;
(3) share certificates;
(4) seal of corporation;
(5) determination of persons to be authorized to sign contracts and other documents including banking documents;
(6) selection of bankers;
(7) selection of auditors;
(8) selection of transfer agent and registrar, if any;
(9) compliance with registration or licensing requirements of provinces in which business to be carried on;
(10) compliance with provincial requirements as to holding of land (see Chapter 3 under the heading "Provincial legislation affecting holding of land by federal corporations.");
(11) where a public offering of securities is contemplated:
—arrangements with underwriters or brokers,
—compliance with applicable provincial Securities Act requirements;
(12) organization meetings, minutes therefor (alternatively minutes to be signed by all directors and shareholders);
(13) general by-laws;
(14) unanimous shareholders' agreement;
(15) handing corporation over to new board;
(16) preparation of records called for by s. 20 and of books of account;
(17) registration of conveyances, etc.

See further the material under the heading "Organization", below.

Procedure for incorporation

Incorporation under the Act is obtained by filing articles of incorporation signed by one or more individuals or corporations, whereupon the Director of the Companies Division is to issue a certificate of incorporation. The articles are to be filed in duplicate as set out in s. 262(2).

Who may apply for incorporation

The Act, (s. 5), requires that each applicant be of the full age of eighteen years, and there may be one or more applicants. Aliens are not excluded.

It is well established that it is not illegal to form a so-called "one man" corporation, so long as all the requirements of the Act under which incorporation is obtained are complied with: *Salomon v. Salomon & Co.*, [1897] A.C. 22 (H.L.); and see *Lagunas Nitrate Co. v. Langunas Syndicate*, [1899] 2 Ch. 392 (C.A.); and promoters of a corporation are not bound to provide it with an independent board of directors, if the real truth is disclosed to those who are induced to join the corporation, per Lindley M.R. at p. 426. See on the same point *Wood v. Reesor* (1895), 22 O.A.R. 57; *Rielle v. Reid* (1899), 26 O.A.R. 54.

The articles

This topic will be dealt with under the following subheadings: (1) Name; (2) Objects; (3) Registered office; (4) Shares of the corporation; (5) Private corporations; (6) Additional provisions; (7) Number of directors; (8) Other formalities in connection with the articles; (9) Fees; (10) Certificate of incorporation; (11) Effect of certificate.

(1) Name

The articles must contain the name of the corporation. The name is to include the word "Limited", "Limitée", "Incorporated", "Incorporée", "Corporation", "Société par actions de régime fédéral", or "Société commerciale canadienne" or its corresponding abbreviation, "Ltd.", "Ltée", "Inc.", "Corp." "S.A.R.F" or "S.C.C." but a corporation may use and may be legally designated by either the full or the abbreviated form; the name may be set out in an English form, a French form, an English form and a French form or in a combined English and French form and the corporation may be legally designated by any such form; the corporation may also, for use outside Canada, set out its name in any language form and it may be legally designated by any such form outside Canada (s. 10(1)-(4)).

A corporation is not to be incorporated with, have or carry on business under or identify itself by a name that is, as prescribed, prohibited or deceptively misdescriptive or that is reserved for another corporation under s. 11 (s. 12(1)).

It is necessary prior to filing the articles to obtain a computerized corporate search as to the availability of the name and to file the report with the articles. It will be noted that a numbered corporation can be obtained, e.g., 516842 Canada Limited (or in Ontario 612590 Ontario Limited). The numbered corporation itself can carry on business under another name by making the appropriate filings for registration of business names or styles.

The use of certain words may be prohibited by federal or provincial statute, e.g., the use of the word "bank" or the words "trust company".

See also the comment under the heading Name "*infra*".

(2) Objects

The articles must set out whether there are any restrictions on the business the corporation may carry on. Ordinarily, the form will be filled in with the wording "no restrictions". It will be noted that s. 15 of the federal Act provides that a corporation has the capacity, and subject to the provisions of the Act, the rights, powers and privileges of a natural person.

Historically, corporations were incorporated either by royal charter or pursuant to legislative authority. In some cases the statute provided that a corporation had the same power and capacity as if it had been incorporated by royal charter. The courts distinguished the two general types of incorporation by saying in effect that a corporation incorporated by royal charter, or pursuant to a statute giving the same consequences, had all the powers and capacities of an ordinary individual subject to any restriction imposed by statute or as withheld by the letters patent pursuant to which the corporation was incorporated. This was not the case as far as a corporation incorporated by statute alone was concerned. These corporations were incorporated by articles of association and the courts held that if a power was not expressly granted either in the articles of association or the governing statute, such power must be deemed to be withheld. From this fundamental difference, searching examinations could arise as to whether a proposed corporate action was or was not *ultra vires* of the corporation. As time went on the various statutes were modified to provide a list of ancillary powers and to make specific provision for the power and capacity of a corporation incorporated under the particular statute. Even so, great care was taken in drafting objects clauses. With the new approach taken to the whole subject by the federal Act, the former cases have become largely irrelevant, but reference is made to the discussion of *ultra vires* in Chapter 3 under the heading "Effect of *ultra vires* Acts".

(3) Registered office

The articles must state the place within Canada where the registered office is to be located. The articles need only state the name of the relevant municipality and county or the geographic township and district, if applicable, and the province. The place of location of the registered office may be changed only by articles of amendment pursuant to a special resolution (s. 173).

A notice of registered office (Form 3) is to be sent to the director together with the articles of incorporation or articles of amendment, as the case may be. The directors may change the address of the registered office and notice of any such change is to be given to the Director (s. 20).

(4) Shares of the corporation

Certain particulars as to the shares that the corporation is authorized to be issued are required to be set out in the articles (s. 6(1)(c)). See the comment in Chapter 5.

(5) Private corporations

There is no definition of the expression "private corporations" contained in the federal Act. However, the term is defined in the various Securities Acts either as a corporation having restrictions on transfer, a limitation on the number of shareholders and a prohibition against offering any securities of the corporation to the public, or as a corporation not offering its shares to the public. Any restrictions on transfer and on the number of shareholders must be inserted in the articles as must any prohibition against offering any securities of the corporation to the public.

(6) Additional provisions

It is common practice to set out provisions similar to those of a general borrowing by-law which would make reference to mortgaging, hypothecating or pledging any property, moveable or immoveable, present or future. The reference to future property will enable a valid charge to be created on future property in the province of Quebec by virtue of the *Special Corporate Powers Act* (Quebec).

(7) Number of directors

The articles must specify the number of directors to be elected or provide for a minimum and maximum number of directors. In the latter case the shareholders may fix the number of directors to be elected and it will be observed that a majority of the directors must be resident Canadians. The articles on filing must be accompanied by Form 6 setting out the initial directors of the corporation.

(8) Other formalities in connection with the articles

The names in full and the residence address of each of the incorporators must be set forth in the articles. Initials only will not suffice. The application must be signed by each of the incorporators. If it is impractical for any incorporator to sign in person, he may sign by an attorney but the original power of attorney (or a notarized copy) must be produced. The power of attorney should be specific for the particular purposes. The articles must be filed in duplicate and be accompanied by a Notice of Registered Office (Form 3) and a Notice of Directors (Form 6).

(9) Fees

The fee for filing the articles of association is set out in Schedule II to the regulations, and is currently $500.

(10) Certificate of incorporation

Upon receipt of articles of incorporation in duplicate, the director is to endorse each copy, file one and to attach to the other copy a certificate of incorporation which is then sent to the corporation or its representative.

(11) Effect of certificate

Section 9 of the Act provides that a corporation comes into existence on the date shown in the certificate of incorporation. It will be observed that s. 262(3) states that a certificate may be dated as of the day the director receives the articles pursuant to which the certificate is issued or as of any later day specified by the person who signed the articles. See, however *Letain v. Conwest Exploration Co.*, [1961] S.C.R. 98, 33 W.W.R. 635 (S.C.C.); in that case there was an agreement whereby if a new corporation was incorporated on or before October 1, 1958 certain mining claims were to be transferred to the new corporation. The letters patent incorporating the corporation bore a date prior to October 1, 1958 but evidence was sought to be introduced to show that the new corporation had in fact not been incorporated until after October 1, 1958. The Supreme Court of Canada referring to a provision in the governing act that the date of incorporation appearing in the letters patent was conclusive proof of the fact, held that the corporation had acquired status as such as of that date but the issue in question was whether the provisions of the agreement had been complied with and that to determine that question the date of incorporation of the new corporation could be questioned. It will be noted that any clerical error in the articles must be corrected by filing articles of amendment. See also s. 265.

In interpreting s. 28 of the former Alberta *Companies Act* the court, in *C.P.W. Valve & Instrument Ltd. v. Scott* (1978), 5 Alta. L.R. (2d) 271, 3 B.L.R. 204 (Alta. C.A.); revg 1 B.L.R. 32, was of the view that the certificate was conclusive evidence of the date on which the corporate status was created, but did not operate to validate a contractual step required to be taken by such date.

The provisions of the *Business Corporations Act* of Alberta may have a different result. A corporation had applied for a certificate of continuance, which was granted. Articles of continuance had been signed but there had been no shareholders' meeting. The court held that because the statute provided that, " . . . and for all other purposes," failure to comply with statutory formalities such as shareholder ratification did not affect the validity of the certificate, see *Prim Investments Ltd. v. Madison Development Corp.*, [1983] 1 W.W.R. 697 23 Alta. L.R. (2d) 165 (Alta. Q.B.).

As to the circumstances under which a director will not be permitted to deny the existence of a *de facto* corporation, see *Williams v. Rice*, [1926] 3 D.L.R. 225, at 246.

Name

Requirements (s. 10)

Unless exempted by the director, the word "Limited", its abbreviation or one of the other wordings provided for in s. 10(1), are to form part of the name of every corporation. A corporation may use and be legally designated by either the full or abbreviated form. If the name is not prohibited, as to which see below, a corporation may have its name in an English form, a French form, a combined form, or both English and French and it may use and be legally designated by any such form; similarly, a corporation, for use outside Canada, may set out its name in its articles in any language form and may use and be legally designated by any such form outside Canada.

A corporation may carry on business or identify itself by a name other than its corporate name by filing a declaration of carrying on business in the appropriate name in each jurisdiction in which it so carries on business. However, the actual name of the corporation is to be set out in legible characters in all contracts, invoices, negotiable instruments and orders for goods or services issued or made by or on behalf of the corporation.

A summons served on a corporation omitting the word "Limited" is not, for that reason, bad: *Springate v. Questier*, [1952] 2 All E.R. 21 (C.A.).

Reserving name (s. 11)

The director may on request reserve for 90 days a name for an intended corporation, or for a corporation about to change its name.

In each case where a name is requested, a NUANS name search must be obtained as to its availability and a copy filed with the Director. In certain cases consents will be required for the use of the name requested if it is similar to that of an existing corporation.

Prohibited names (ss. 12, 13)

The federal Act provides that a corporation is not to be incorporated with, have, carry on business under, or identify itself by a name that is prohibited or deceptively misdescriptive or that has been reserved for another corporation or intended corporation. Sections 16 to 23 of the Regulations passed pursuant to the federal Act provide prohibitions against certain corporate names. Thus, certain specific words or their initials are forbidden as is any connotation that the corporation carries on business under royal, vice-regal or governmental patronage, approval or authority unless so requested by the appropriate government department in writing. Regulations 24 to 28 set out certain names which are not prohibited. Thus, for example, the use of a surname of an individual who is living or who has died within 30 years preceding the date of the application is prohibited unless it is established that the name has, through use, acquired and continues to have a secondary meaning at the time of such application. See in this regard regulation 19.

It will be noted that mere consent is not sufficient in case of confusion but that the existing corporation, society, association or firm giving the consent must be in the course of being dissolved or changing its name.

Similar sections appear in the Acts of the various provinces. It has been held that where the provision contained no geographical limitation, it permitted consideration of names of corporations not incorporated in Canada: *Re Universal Asbestos Cement Ltd.* (1958), 26 W.W.R. 411 at 426 (Man. C.A.).

In *Aerators Ltd. v. Tollitt*, [1902] 2 Ch. 319 an injunction was sought restraining certain individuals from proceeding with an application for incorporation under a name so nearly resembling that of the plaintiff as to be calculated to deceive. The application was refused.

Quite independently of any statutory provision, such as s. 12, a person has a common law right to prevent others from using his name or a similar name in such a manner as to cause confusion. In addition, the *Trade Marks Act* contains provisions restricting the use of trade names which are confusing (in the sense in which the word is used in that Act) with the trade names or trade marks of others or which cause or are likely to cause confusion in Canada between the wares, services or businesses of two traders. See further in this connection the notes under the heading "Restriction of wrongful use of corporate name," below.

If a person consents to a corporation using his name, this permission is irrevocable so long as the corporation continues to exercise the powers given to it by its charter, but upon the corporation becoming bankrupt and abandoning its charter, the rights of the owner of the name immediately revive and he may carry on business in his own name: *Hector L. Déry & Co. v. Déry* (1941), 70 Que. K.B. 433 (C.A.).

In the absence of any prohibition or restriction in the charter it is not *ultra vires* of a federal corporation to carry on a business under an assumed name: *Heriteau v. W.D. Morris Realty Ltd.*, [1943] O.R. 724 at 733 (Ont. H.C.). See *Re Len Plumbing & Heating Co.*, [1969] 2 O.R. 698, 13 C.B.R. (N.S.) 22 (Ont. H.C.) and s. 10(6) of the federal Act and s. 11(2) of the Ontario Act. However, it would appear that the corporation must comply with s. 10(5) of the federal Act or s. 10(5) of the Ontario Act, c.f. the *Business Names Act* (Ontario) s. 2(6).

Certificate of amendment of name (s. 13)

If a corporation is incorporated with a name that is forbidden under s. 12.1, s. 12.2 provides that the Director may direct the corporation in question to change its name in accordance with s. 173. If this is not done within 60 days from the service of the directive from the Director, the Director may revoke the name of the corporation and assign to it a name which will become its name thereafter until changed in accordance with s. 173. A certificate of amendment is to be issued which is to be effective on the date shown thereon (s. 13). An exception is made in the case of a corporation continued under this Act when the same name may be used unless the name is identical with or confusingly similar to the name of an existing body corporate. It will be noted that pursuant to s. 246 of the Act an appeal from the decision of the Director changing a name lies to the provincial Supreme Court. Fresh evidence relating to matters ought not to be introduced on appeal, the proper procedure is for the appellant to seek a new hearing by the Director: see *Citibank Canada v. Citicapital Financial Corp.* (1988), 24 C.P.R. (3d) 221 (Ont. Div. Ct.). See also *Help-U-Sell Inc. v. Help-U-Sell Real Estate Ltd.* (1988), 69 Sask. R. 142, 22 C.P.R. (3d) 370 (Sask. Q.B.); affd (1988), 72 Sask. R. 76 (C.A.); and *Unitel International Inc. v. Unitel Communications Inc.*, [1992] 3 W.W.R. 548 (Sask. Q.B.).

Cases where name changed

Re F.P. Chapple Co., [1960] O.R. 531 (C.A.); *Re C. Cole & Co.*, [1965] 2 O.R. 243 (Ont. C.A.); *Italia (Azzurri) Soccer Club Inc. v. Manitoba (Director of Corporations Branch)* (1988), 55 Man. R. (2d) 273 (Q.B.); *Re Golden Hope Resources Inc.* (1987), 18 C.P.R. (3d) 453; *Ordre des comptables agréés du Québec v. Canada (Minister of Consumer & Corporate Affairs)* (1987), 37 B.L.R. 275, 78 N.R. 112 (Fed. C.A.); leave to appeal to S.C.C. refused (*sub nom. Assn. des comptables généraux agréés du Can. v. Institute Canadien des comptables agréés*) (1987), 86 N.R. 263 (S.C.C.); *Perfect Tan Inc. v. Saskatchewan (Director of Business Corporations)* (1986), 55 Sask. R. 79 (Sask. Q.B.); *Manufacture Decoratek (1979) Inc. v. D.J. Shiller Stores Ltée* (1985), 32 B.L.R. 9 (C.A. Qué.); *Ebsco Investments Ltd. v. Ebsco Subscription Services Ltd.* (1975), 11 O.R. (2d) 305, 66 D.L.R. (3d) 47 (Ont. C.A.); *Northwest Trading Co. v. Northwest Trading Co.*, [1920] 1 W.W.R. 353; affd [1920] 3 W.W.R. 729 (B.C. C.A.); *Semi-Ready Ltd. v. Semi-Ready Ltd.* (1910), 15 B.C.R. 301 (S.C.); *Re Cap-Co Inc.* (1987),

17 C.P.R. (3d) 498; *Continental Cladding (Sudbury) Ltd. v. Continental Insulation Sudbury Ltd.* (1987), 14 C.P.R. (3d) 509; *Royal Canadian Legion v. Hamilton War Veterans' Poppy Fund Inc.* (1987), 15 C.P.R. (3d) 472; *Consul-Pak Inc. v. Cheeseman* (1986), 12 C.P.R. (3d) 394; *Re Ontario Bicycle Moto Cross Assn.* (1986), 11 C.P.R. (3d) 335; *Toronto & Regional Crime Stoppers Inc. v. Crime Stoppers Security Systems Inc.* (1986), 13 C.P.R. (3d) 323; *Spirax Sarco Ltd. v. Sarco Canada Ltd.* (1985), 8 C.P.R. (3d) 465; *Re Toronto Bocciofila Club* (1985), 7 C.P.R. (3d) 328; *87118 Canada Ltd. v. Canada* (1981), 13 B.L.R. 272, 56 C.P.R. (2d) 209 (Fed. C.A.); *T'Ease Fashions Ltd. v. Flory* (1980), 6 Sask. R. 133 (Sask. Q.B.); *Bumper's, The Beef House (Banff) Ltd. v. Alberta (Registrar of Cos.)* (1977), 4 Alta. L.R. (2d) 68, A.R. 349 (Alta. T.D.); *Fordprint Ltd. v. Ontario (Minister of Consumer & Commercial Relations)* (1976), 11 O.R. (2d) 434 (Div. Ct.); *Prime Locations Ltd. v. Prime Real Estate Ltd.* (1976), 30 C.P.R. (2d) 38 (Ont. Div. Ct.); *New World Pictures v. New World Video Inc.* (1986), 53 O.R. (2d) 794, 25 D.L.R. (4th) 434 (H.C.); *Questel Telecommunications Inc. v. Télésystèmes Societe Anonyme* (1985), 5 C.P.R. (3d) 96 (Ont. H.C.); *Re Hypocorp & Commerce Inc.* (1982), 64 C.P.R. (2d) 287 (Ont. Div. Ct.); *Paladium St-Robert Inc. c. Sparling*, [1980] C.S. 984 (Qué. C.S.); *Safeco Insurance Co. of America v. British Columbia (Registrar of Companies)* (1980), 33 B.C.L.R. 168 (C.F.S. Comm.); *Yellow Freight System Inc. v. Yellow Freight System Canada Ltd.* (1986), 12 C.P.R. (3d) 502 [1986] R.D.J. 247 (C.A. Qué.); leave to appeal to S.C.C. refused (1986), 12 C.P.R. (3d) 502n, 74 N.R. 320 (note) (S.C.C.); *Films Presto Inc. c. Service de Foto Presto Inc.*, [1982] C.S. 435 (Qué. C.S.); *Inter-City Express Ltd. v. Inter-City Truck Mines (Can) Inc.* (1979), 16 B.C.L.R. 37; affd (1979), 16 B.C.L.R. 43 (B.C. C.A.); *Coin-A-Matic Inc. v. Coin Automat Washing Machine Corp.* (1966), 35 Fox Pat. C. 46 (Que. S.C.); *Oxweld Acetylene Co. v. Oxyweld Co. of Canada* (1923), 53 O.L.R. 455 (C.A.); *W.M. Houston Co. v. W.S. Houston Ltd.*, [1920] 1 W.W.R. 463 (Sask. K.B.); *Canadian National Investors Ltd. v. Canadian National Estates, Ltd.* (1911), 1 W.W.R. 87 (B.C.); *Tire Specialists (Manitoba) Ltd. v. Manitoba (Director of Corporations)* (1991), 74 Man. R. (2d) 240 (Q.B.); *Dex Resources Ltd. v. Alberta (Registrar of Corporations)* (1992), 1 Alta. L.R. (3d) 240 (Q.B.); *Connell Chrysler Ltd. v. Connell Motors Ltd.* (1991), 304 A.P.R. 181 (Dir.).

Cases where name not changed

See *Canada Campers Inc. v. British Columbia (Registrar of Companies)* (1989), 28 C.P.R. (3d) 137, 46 B.L.R. 97 (B.C. S.C.); *Bargain Tire Centre Ltd. v. Flory*, [1984] 3 W.W.R. 85, 32 Sask. R. 12 (Sask. Q.B.); *Bell Insurance Agencies Ltd. v. Bell & Cross Insurance Agency Ltd.*, [1983] 4 W.W.R. 38, 21 B.L.R. 306 (Man. Q.B.); *Chartac Small-Business Services Ltd. v. Chartacc Computer Services Inc.* (1983), 44 B.C.L.R. 259, (C.F.S. Comm.); *I. Browns Packaging Inc. v. Canada (Department of Consumer & Corporate Affairs)* (1982), 24 B.L.R. 44, 80 C.P.R. (2d) 122 (Que. S.C.); *Office Overload Co. v. Driver Overload Ltd.*, [1968] 1 O.R. 292, 54 C.P.R. 162 (Ont. H.C.); *Travellers Insurance Co. v. Travellers Life Assurance Co. of Canada* (1910), 20 Que. K.B. 437 (C.A.); *Auccio Gucci S.p.A. v. Gucci Investments Inc.* (1988), 29 O.A.C. 241 (Ont. Div. Ct.); *Adelco Express*

Ltd. v. Adelco Supply Co. (1987), 14 C.P.R. (3d) 497; *Re Agri-Service Laboratory Inc.* (1987), 16 C.P.R. (3d) 260; *Re Artlab Communications Inc.* (1987), 16 C.P.R. (3d) 356; *Re Ashrae Controls Inc.* (1987), 16 C.P.R. (3d) 273; *Re Beverly Hills Motor Car Co.* (1987), 18 C.P.R. (3d) 334; *Re Esprit Communications Inc.* (1987), 18 C.P.R. (3d) 345; *Re New Land Design Inc.* (1987), 18 C.P.R. (3d) 495 (Ministry of Consumer & Commercial Relations Cos. Branch); *Re Prime Locations Ltd. v. Prime Realty Inc.* (1987), 14 C.P.R. (3d) 457 (Ont. Ministry of Consumer & Commercial Relations, Cos. Branch); *Re Telecorp Canada Ltd.* (1987), 16 C.P.R. (3d) 124; *Brydon Marine Products Ltd. v. ITT Industries of Canada Ltd.* (1986), 10 C.P.R. (3d) 361; *IBL Industries Ltd. v. IBL Container Refurbishing Ltd.* (1986), 11 C.P.R. (3d) 298; *WoodGreen Red Door Family Shelter v. Ontario (Ministry of Consumer & Commercial Relations)* (1986), 13 C.P.R. (3d) 298; *Medicine Hat & District Big Brothers Assn. v. Alberta (Registrar of Companies)* (1981), 32 A.R. 601, 81 C.P.R. (2d) 112 (Alta. Q.B.); *Action Plumbing Ltd. v. Alberta (Registrar of Companies)* (1976), 1 A.R. 296, [1977] 1 W.W.R. 123 (Alta. C.A.); *Executone Ltd. v. Executive Communications Ltd.* (1977), 34 C.P.R. (2d) 287 (Ont. Div. Ct.); *Re CC Chemicals*, [1967] 2 O.R. 248, 63 D.L.R. (2d) 203 (Ont. C.A.); *Re Menzies-Gibson Ltd.*, [1955] O.W.N. 657 (H.C.); *Wabco-Standard Ltd. v. Amstan Distributors Ltd.*, [1986] R.L. 250 (Que. C.A.); *Bay Travel Centre Ltd. v. British Columbia (Registrar of Travel Services)* (1981), 126 D.L.R. (3d) 685, 60 C.P.R. (2d) 6 (B.C. Co. Ct.); *Re Cantrade Sales & Import Co.* (1977), 1 B.L.R. 179, 32 C.P.R. (2d) 76 (Ont. Div. Ct.); *C.A. Fitzsimmons & Co. v. A.H. Fitzsimmons & Co.* (1975), 20 C.P.R. (2d) 285 (Ont. Div. Ct.); *Foster's Garden Chapel Ltd. v. Cy Foster Funeral Service Ltd.* (1965), 47 C.P.R. 21, 52 W.W.R. 364 (Alta. T.D.); *Canada Permanent v. British Columbia Permanent* (1898), 6 B.C.R. 377 (S.C.); *F.W.T.A.O. v. Ontario (Minister of Consumer & Commercial Relations)* (1984), 46 O.R. (2d) 645, 4 O.A.C. 200 (Ont. Div. Ct.).

For a discussion of the difference between an action in passing-off and whether registration should be granted see *StarTruck Taxi Assn. Ltd. v. Alberta (Registrar of Companies)*, [1975] W.W.D. 91 (Alta.). That case involved the refusal of the Registrar of Companies to register an extraprovincial corporation with a name similar to that of an existing entity and likely to deceive. On appeal the registration was permitted and the test was stated to include the visual and auditory qualities of the names, the objects and proposed business activities of the two corporations and the type of persons who might deal with them; the probability of deception was also a factor but the test was not the same as in a passing-off action; the mere possibility of deception not being sufficient. See, also, *Re Cantrade Sales & Import Co.* (1977), 1 B.L.R. 179, 32 C.P.R. (2d) 76 (Ont. Div. Ct.) where under the circumstances of the case an order requiring the appellant to change its name was rescinded. It was pointed out that the two corporations were engaged in totally dissimilar businesses and there was no evidence of any actual deception of the public and little likelihood of any confusion to the public or any part of it.

It has been held that under the provision (s. 10(1)) of *The Companies Act* of Manitoba corresponding to s. 13, the Provincial Secretary is performing an administrative function involving the exercise of a discretion and that his exercise of that discretion is in no way subject to the control of the court; as a result prohibition does not lie to prevent the Provincial Secretary from exercising his discretion in a particular case: *Re Application of Universal Asbestos Cement Ltd. & Supercrete Ltd.* (1958), 26 W.W.R. 411.

Change of name on application of corporation

Section 173 provides that the articles of a corporation may, by special resolution, be amended to change its name. Articles of amendment in prescribed form are to be delivered to the Director as set out in s. 177 of the Act.

The court will not interfere to restrain the corporation from acting upon a by-law providing for the change of the corporation's name: *Dover v. Breay* (1924), 27 O.W.N. 33 (H.C.), where it was indicated that any objections to the application must be made to the appropriate government officer. The change of name will not become effective until the issuance of articles of amendment. See *Shackleford, Ford & Co. v. Dangerfield* (1868), L.R. 3 C.P. 407. No alteration of name under s. 173 affects the rights or obligations of the corporation; see s. 179(2).

Right of corporation to protection and use of corporate name

Where a corporation has been incorporated under the federal Act, a provincial corporation subsequently incorporated will be restrained by injunction from operating under the same name: *Semi-Ready Ltd. v. Semi-Ready Ltd.* (1910), 15 B.C.R. 301 (B.C. S.C.). The judgment proceeded on the ground that once a corporation had been incorporated under the federal Act with a particular name, the field was exclusively occupied as far as that name was concerned. Conversely, where a corporation had been incorporated by special Act of the federal Parliament with a name similar to that of an American corporation, in an action brought by the American corporation to restrain the Canadian corporation from using its name an injunction was refused: *Travellers Insurance Co. v. Travellers Life Assurance Co. of Canada* (1911), 20 Que. K.B. 437 (C.A.). The basis of the judgment in that case was that, as Parliament had conferred the name on the corporation, it was not open to the courts to interfere with the use of such name, as such interference would amount to a denial of the right of the federal corporation to existence and the exercise of the rights and powers conferred on it by Parliament. Lavergne J., delivering the judgment of the court, pointed out that the case was one of a corporation incorporated by Act of Parliament and not by letters patent. In *Oxweld Acetylene Co. v. Oxyweld Co. of Canada* (1923), 53 O.L.R. 455 (C.A.) it was held that the Supreme Court of Ontario had no jurisdiction to cancel letters patent of an Ontario corporation except at the instance of the Attorney-General suing on behalf of the Crown or upon the relation of an interested party. Cancellation of the letters patent of an Ontario corporation which had been incorporated under a name similar to that of a foreign corporation was refused in an action brought by the latter, but an injunction was granted restraining the corporation from using the words "Oxweld" and "Oxyweld" in connection with the sale of certain apparatus.

Under the provisions of the *British Columbia Companies Act* (1910) c. 7,

s. 18, which were somewhat different from those of s. 25, where the registrar had permitted the registration of a corporation with a name so similar to that of a corporation previously incorporated as to be calculated to deceive, the corporation subsequently incorporated was restrained from carrying on business under such name: *Canadian National Investors Ltd. v. Canadian National Estates Ltd.* (1911), 1 W.W.R. 87 (B.C. S.C.); and as to the circumstances under which a foreign corporation may be entitled to compel a corporation incorporated by registration to change its name, see *Northwest Trading Co. v. Northwest Trading Co. Ltd.*, [1920] 3 W.W.R. 729 (B.C. C.A.).

A corporation incorporated by letters patent has the right to use, for all lawful and legitimate purposes, its corporate name granted by the letters patent although the use of the name or part of it for certain purposes may be restrained at the instance of another corporation with a similar name: *Boston Rubber Shoe Co. v. Boston Rubber Co. of Montreal* (1902), 32 S.C.R. 315, 333; *John Palmer Co. v. Palmer-McLellan Shoe-Pack Co.* (1917), 37 D.L.R. 201 (N.B. C.A.) at 207; and see *Lajoie v. Lacombe Ltd.* (1934), 37 Que. P.R. 406 (interlocutory injunction to restrain use of name refused); *Anglo-Canadian Fire Agencies Ltd. v. Anglo-Canadian Underwriters Ltd.*, [1942] 1 D.L.R. 550 (N.B. S.C.) (corporation incorporated in one province entitled, in the same way as an individual, to commence business in its own name in another province, provided it does so without intent to deceive the public).

Whatever rights a federal corporation may have (under the principles laid down in the above decisions) to the use of a corporate name, as distinguished from a trade name, which conflicts with that of another corporation, not being a federal corporation, in the absence of action under s. 12, the use of a trade name contrary to the provisions of the *Trade Marks Act* or contrary to the principles established in cases decided under the common law, will, it is submitted, be restrained notwithstanding that such trade name may be the same as the name of the corporation. See *General Doors Inc. v. Saskatchewan (Registrar under the Business Names Registration Act)*, [1988] 4 W.W.R. 337, 18 C.I.P.R. 257 (Sask. Q.B.). On the other hand, where there is no similarity between the name of a federal corporation and the name of a foreign corporation, the federal corporation will not be enjoined from using its name in connection with the sale of its products on the ground that the use of such name amounts to a representation that the goods were those manufactured by the foreign corporation: *Anheuser-Busch Inc. v. Canada Bud Breweries Ltd.*, [1933] O.R. 75 (H.C.). In that case Wright J. said at p. 83 "In cases respecting the use of a corporate name, the Court acts or interferes on the principle that one person is not to be permitted to represent himself as carrying on the business which is carried on by another.".

In *Groceteria Ltd. v. T. Eaton Co.*, [1926] 1 D.L.R. 26 (Alta. C.A.) the principles of the decided cases with reference to trade names were applied and the contention was rejected that incorporation under provincial laws gave a corporation the exclusive right to use the corporate name as a business or trade name within the province. And in *Boston Rubber Shoe Co. v. Boston Rubber Co. of Montreal* (1902), 32 S.C.R. 315 it was held that a federal corporation was not entitled to use its name by stamping it on goods manufactured and offered for sale, if by so doing it caused the public to believe that the goods were those of the plaintiff corporation. In that case the name of the defendant corporation embraced the plaintiff corporation's trade mark.

In a case where the Department of Consumer and Corporate Affairs (federal) had advised that the name appeared to be available, but subject to and conditional upon the applicant's assuming full responsibility for any risk of confusion with existing business names and trade marks, and subsequently a new search had revealed the existence of a corporation with the same name, with a consequent change of name of the plaintiff, the plaintiff sued for negligence in failing to advise it of the existence of the similarly named corporation. On appeal it was held that the action should be dismissed and that no action would lie against the Director under the circumstances: *87118 Canada Ltd. v. Canada* (1981), 13 B.L.R. 272 (Fed. C.A.); see also *Lampolier Manufacturing Co. v. Manitoba* (1967), 60 W.W.R. 459 (Man.); *Odyssey Development Corporation Ltd. v. Alberta (Registrar of Companies)*, [1984] 31 Alta. L.R. (2d) 288, 4 W.W.R. 288 (Alta. C.A.).

Restriction of wrongful use of corporate name

The principle on which the courts will act to restrain the use of a name is the same as that which protects persons in the use of trade marks, namely that, one trader is not permitted to represent his undertaking or his goods to be the undertaking or goods of his competitor: *Boston Rubber Shoe Co. v. Boston Rubber Co. of Montreal* (1902), 32 S.C.R. 315; *Sovereen Mitt, Glove & Robe Co. v. Simcoe Mitt, Glove & Robe Co.* (1904), 3 O.W.R. 681. The question to be answered by the court in each case is the simple one laid down by Halsbury L.C. in *North Cheshire & Manchester Brewery Co. v. Manchester Brewery Co.*, [1899] A.C. 83 at 84 (H.L.), "Is this name so nearly resembling the name of another firm as to be likely to deceive?" See also *Re F. P. Chapple Co.; Ex parte Chapples Ltd.*, [1960] O.R. 531, 20 Fox Pat. C. 179 at 539 (Ont. C.A.). It is not necessary to show an intent to deceive, the words "likely" and "calculated" meaning only "morally certain": *Hendriks v. Montagu* (1881), 17 Ch. D. 638 (C.A.) at 645; nor is it necessary to show fraud: *North Cheshire & Manchester Brewery Co. v. Manchester Brewery Co. Ltd., supra.*

In determining whether or not a name is likely to deceive, the court will not restrict itself to the question of similarity of names but will look at other factors: *Dominion Motors Ltd. v. Gillman*, [1959] Ex. C.R. 423; *Re F. P. Chapple Co.; Ex parte Chapples Ltd.*, [1960] O.R. 531 at 540 (C.A.).

Similarity of business may be an important factor: *Merchant Banking Co. of London v. Merchants' Joint Stock Bank* (1878), 9 Ch. D. 560; *Anglo-Canadian Fire Agencies Ltd. v. Anglo-Canadian Underwriters Ltd.*, [1942] 1 D.L.R. 550 at 559 (N.B. S.C.); as well as likelihood of confusion: *Laing Packing & Provision Co. v. Laing* (1904), 25 Que. S.C. 344 (S.C.); *Lamontagne Ltd. v. Girard* (1911), 39 Que. S.C. 179 (C.S.); *Jay's Ltd. v. Jacobi*, [1933] 1 Ch. 411; *Fred W. Matthews Co. v. Matthews*, [1945] O.R. 182 (C.A.). Evidence of actual cases of confusion and damage may not be essential if the continuance of a wrongful use of a trade name will be an injury to the plaintiff and amount to dishonesty: *A. A. Allan & Co. v. Kates & Conson*, [1948] O.R. 472 (C.A.).

The actual manner in which a name is used is relevant: *Re F. P. Chapple Co.; Ex parte Chapples Ltd.*, [1960] O.R. 531 at 540 (C.A.). The fact that the two businesses were carried on in different areas does not affect the situation: *Panhard & Levassor v. Panhard Levassor Motor Co.*, [1901] 2 Ch. 513; *Ewing v. Buttercup Margarine Co.*, [1917] 2 Ch. 1 at 10 (C.A.); *Re F. P. Chapple Co.; Ex parte Chapples Ltd.*, *supra*, at 544.

An individual, in the absence of fraud or false representation, may carry on business in his own name in competition with a similar business previously established under the same name: *Fred W. Matthews Co. v. Matthews*, [1945] O.R. 182 at 187 (C.A.). However, a person may not cause a corporation to be incorporated in his own name, if his name is the same as that of an existing corporation and there is likelihood of deceiving the public, if he has no real interest nor goodwill in the business proposed to be incorporated: *Fine Cotton Spinners v. Harwood Cash & Co.*, [1907] 2 Ch. 184; *Kingston Miller & Co. v. Thomas Kingston & Co.*, [1912] 1 Ch. 575; *W. M. Houston Co. v. W. S. Houston Ltd.*, [1920] 1 W.W.R. 463 (Sask. K.B.); *Re F. P. Chapple Co. Ltd.; Ex parte Chapples Ltd.*, *supra*, at 543.

An individual cannot use his own name in the conduct of his business if he does so for a deceptive purpose: *Hunt's Ltd. v. Hunt* (1924), 56 O.L.R. 349 (C.A.); *E. Herman & Co. v. I. Herman*, [1937] O.W.N. 594 (H.C.) (a passing off case); nor, without the intent of passing off his goods as those of another person, so use his name and persist in such use that it will have that effect: *Hurlburt Co. v. Hurlburt Shoe Co.*, [1925] S.C.R. 141; *Groceteria Ltd. v. T. Eaton Co.*, [1926] 1 D.L.R. 26 (Alta. C.A.) (neither registration of a name as a trade mark nor incorporation under that name gives the exclusive right to its use or the right to restrain another from using it in the absence of intention to deceive).

In some cases the right to use an existing trade name may be acquired, as, for example, where the goodwill of an existing business is purchased: *Canada Paint v. William Johnson & Sons* (1893), 4 Que. S.C. 253 (S.C.); *Rose v. McLean Publishing Co.* (1897), 24 O.A.R. 240; *Montreal Lithographing Co. v. Sabiston*, [1899] A.C. 610 at 613 (P.C.); *Boston Rubber Shoe Co. v. Boston Rubber Co. of Montreal* (1902), 32 S.C.R. 315; *Re Elkington & Co.* (1908), 11 Ex. C.R. 293; *Standard Ideal Co. v. Standard Sanitary Manufacturing Co.*, [1911] A.C. 78 (P.C.); *Kingston Miller & Co. v. Thomas Kingston & Co.*, [1912] 1 Ch. 575 at 581; *Strains Ltd. v. Nott* (1919), 49 D.L.R. 699 (Man. K.B.).

In *Acme Vacuum Cleaner Co. Ltd. v. Acme Vacuum Cleaner Co.*, [1953] Que. Q.B. 188 (C.A.), the plaintiff corporation had failed for several years to file its annual returns and although the Secretary of State had sent the corporation a notice under s. 125 of the Act, no action had been taken to revoke the corporation's charter. Upon the application of the individual defendants, the Secretary of State issued a charter incorporating them as a corporation under the same name as the corporate plaintiff. The Quebec Court of Appeal held that until the Secretary of State took proper action to set aside the letters patent of the corporation, its corporate existence continued, and consequently, the court affirmed the granting of a permanent injunction restraining the defendant corporation from using the plaintiff corporation's trade name.

Organization

General procedure

After issue of the certificate of incorporation, the directors are to hold an organization meeting at which the directors may make by-laws, adopt forms of security certificates and corporate records, authorize the issue of securities, appoint officers, appoint an auditor to hold office until the first annual meeting of shareholders, make banking arrangements, and transact any other business (s. 104(1)). Such meeting may be called by an incorporator or a director by not less than five days' notice by mail to each director stating the time and place of the meeting (s. 104(3)). An organizational meeting is not required in respect of a body corporate to which a certificate of amalgamation or a certificate of continuation has been issued (s. 104(2)).

The corporation may be organized by way of meetings of directors and shareholders or without meetings by utilizing the provisions relating to directors' and shareholders' resolutions. A resolution in writing signed by all the directors entitled to vote on that resolution at a meeting is as valid as if passed by a meeting of the directors (s. 117). Similarly, a resolution in writing signed by all the shareholders entitled to vote on that resolution at a meeting of shareholders is as valid as if it had been passed at a meeting of the shareholders (s. 142).

If the corporation is being organized by meetings of the directors, the following procedure may be adopted:

1. A meeting of the directors is called. It will be noted that notice may be waived. The first directors are those listed in the notice of directors filed with the articles and will often be members of the staff of the corporation's solicitors. At this meeting reference is made to the issuance of articles of incorporation. One or more subscriptions should be received and accepted from proposed shareholders in order that shares may be allotted and issued so that there will be at least one shareholder in existence to effect the organization of the corporation. A general by-law and a general borrowing by-law (and any other by-laws which it is necessary or desirable to pass during the organization stage) are passed. While it may be the usual practice to pass a borrowing by-law or by-laws, it is not necessary to do so, as the governing Acts provide that the power to borrow is deemed to be included in the articles of every corporation. The Ontario Act provides that it is not necessary for a by-law to be passed in order to confer any particular power on the corporation or its directors (s. 17(1)). In addition to the general borrowing by-law, a by-law may be passed in the form suggested by the corporation's bankers, although this is not necessary. At this meeting provision is made for calling a shareholders' meeting and the meeting then terminates.

2. A meeting of shareholders is held at which the by-laws are confirmed. Since the directors named in the first notice of directors hold office from the issue of the certificate of incorporation until the first meeting of shareholders, the shareholders at this meeting will generally elect permanent directors to hold

office until the first annual meeting, although the initial directors will remain in office if they fail to do so. The shareholders at this meeting may also appoint an auditor or may leave such appointment to be made by the directors.

3. A meeting of the permanent directors is held at which the directors appoint an auditor to hold office until the first annual meeting of shareholders (if not already appointed by the shareholders), elect officers and pass resolutions respecting banking and signing officers, the adoption of a corporate seal (if desired) and the approval of forms of share certificates. At this or a subsequent meeting the directors, if they are temporary or office directors, resign in succession if favour of the persons who are to act as the continuing directors of the corporation. Each director as he resigns may transfer his share, if any, to his successor who takes his place on the board; however, there is no requirement that a director be a shareholder of the corporation. The new board appoints new officers and the meeting then adjourns.

Where extensive dealing in the corporation's shares is anticipated a transfer agent and registrar should be appointed.

It is generally advisable at the outset to have a set of books opened by a firm of accountants.

If the corporation is to be organized through the signature of resolutions and by-laws, the resolutions and by-laws to be signed are those referred to above in respect of organization meetings. The corporation may be organized in part through the holding of meetings and in part through the signature of by-laws and resolutions by the directors and/or shareholders.

In organizing a corporation, consideration should be given as to whether a unanimous shareholder agreement would be appropriate. Section 146(2) of the Act provides that an otherwise lawful agreement in writing among all the shareholders of a corporation or among all such shareholders and a person who is not a shareholder, restricting in whole or in part the powers of the directors to manage the business and affairs of a corporation, is valid. Similarly, a written declaration by a sole shareholder restricting in whole or in part the powers of the directors to manage the business and affairs of a corporation is deemed to be a unanimous shareholder agreement. A shareholder who is a party to a unanimous shareholder agreement has by virtue of s. 146(5) all the rights, powers and duties of a director of the corporation to which the agreement relates to the extent that the agreement restricts the powers of the directors to manage the business and affairs of the corporation and the directors are accordingly relieved of their duties and liabilities, including any liability under s. 119 (which provides for the liability of directors for wages of employees up to a certain amount) to the same extent. See the comment on s. 146 in Chapter 10. It will be observed that an agreement between all the shareholders as to the manner in which the corporation is to be operated is not necessarily a unanimous shareholder agreement.

Compliance with provincial licensing requirements

The corporation must comply with any applicable legislation of the provinces in which it proposes to carry on business which requires it to take out a licence or to register before or upon commencing business therein. Corporations incorporated under federal jurisdiction are also required to comply with provincial registration and licencing legislation. See *Reference re Corporations Act (Manitoba)*, [1991] 4 W.W.R. 193 (Man. C.A.).

Public financing

If the corporation proposes to offer its shares or securities to the public, the requirements of s. 193 in respect of prospectuses and offers to the public must be complied with. In addition the corporation and/or the underwriters must comply with the requirements of the legislation and regulations applicable in any province where the shares or securities are offered by the corporation or on its behalf or are offered by an underwriter who has taken up such shares or securities for the purpose of resale to the public.

Purchase of property

No matter what business the corporation proposes to carry on, the acquisition of certain assets immediately upon incorporation is often contemplated; for example, lands, plant and other assets in the case of a manufacturing corporation, or mines or mining claims in the case of a mining corporation.

The entering into of a contract for the acquisition of such assets should be authorized by resolution of the directors and where the contract is of major importance by resolution of the shareholders.

If any director is interested in the sale to the corporation he must make full disclosure of his interest and refrain from voting in compliance with s. 120. See further the notes to that section in Chapter 8.

Pre-incorporation contracts

At common law a contract made on behalf of a corporation prior to its incorporation was not binding on the corporation and could not be ratified by it after incorporation. Thus, for example, a lease signed by a person for the benefit of a corporation before its incorporation would not be binding on the corporation and the fact that the corporation occupied the premises after its incorporation did not change the position: *In re A. Leclerc & Co.* (1926), 7 C.B.R. 712 (C.S. Qué.). Similarly, a corporation could not by adoption or ratification claim the benefit of a contract made on its behalf prior to its incorporation; in order to bind the corporation, the corporation would have to enter into a new contract on the same terms as contained in the pre-incorporation contract. See *Howard v. Patent Ivory Manufacturing Co.* (1888), 38 Ch. D. 156; *Re Dale & Plant Ltd.* (1889), 43 Ch. D. 255.

However, the position has been radically changed by the provisions of s. 14(2) of the federal Act which provides that a corporation may, within a reasonable time after it comes into existence, by any action or conduct signifying its intention to be bound, thereby adopt a written contract made before it came into existence in its name or on its behalf, and on such adoption it will be bound by the contract and entitled to the benefits thereof as though it had been in existence at the date of the contract and had been a party thereto and the person who purported to act on behalf of the corporation will cease to be bound by or entitled to the benefits of the contract; however, he, or any other party, may apply to a court for an order fixing obligations under the contract as joint or joint and several or apportioning liability between the corporation and the person who purported to act for it and the court may make any order it thinks fit (s. 14(3)). For cases involving this or similar provincial provisions see *Bank of Nova Scotia v. Williams* (1976), 12 O.R. (2d) 709, 70 D.L.R. (3d) 108 (Ont. H.C.); *Okinczyc v. Tessier* (1979), 8 R.P.R. 249 (Ont. H.C.). If it is expressly so provided in the contract, a person who purported to act for the corporation before it came into existence will not be bound by the contract or entitled to the benefits thereof in any event (s. 14(4)).

It will be observed that the common law rules will still apply to oral pre-incorporation contracts. Note that the Ontario Act specifically includes oral contracts (s. 24(2)). It will also be observed that the heading of the provision refers to pre-amalgamation contracts as well as pre-incorporation contracts. The reference to pre-amalgamation contracts would seem to be unnecessary since an amalgamated corporation is liable to all the debts and obligations and may claim any right or benefit under a contract by either of the amalgamating corporations.

It will be observed that s. 14(1) of the federal Act provides that a pre-incorporation contract results in personal liability to the person entering into the contract in the name of or on behalf of a corporation before it comes into existence and that he is also entitled to all the benefits thereof, subject to the conditions stipulated in the section.

It will be noted that problems of interpretation still exist. Thus, where an agreement was purported to be entered into on behalf of a corporation both parties believing that the person contracting on behalf of the corporation was so authorized and where no corporation existed, it was held by the Divisional Court that the agent was not liable since there was no evidence that the parties intended that the agent should be liable personally. The Ontario equivalent to s. 14(1) of the federal Act was not applicable since there was no contract. See *Westcom Radio Group Ltd. v. MacIsaac* (1989), 70 O.R. (2d) 591, 45 B.L.R. 273 (Ont. Div. Ct.). See also *Black v. Smallwood* (1965-66), 117 C.L.R. 52 (H.C.A.) which distinguished the earlier authority *Kelner v. Baxter* (1866), L.R. 2 C.P. 174 on the ground that in that case both sides knew that the corporation had not yet been formed and the documents indicated an intention that the defendants should be bound. See *Heinhuis v. Blacksheep Charters Ltd.* (1987), 19 B.C.L.R. (2d) 239 [1988] 2 W.W.R. 444 (B.C. C.A.) where a new post-incorporation contract was implied where the parties by their conduct showed an intention to be bound by a new contract containing terms identical to those in the pre-incorporation contract; an intention to be bound was inferred where there was part performance of the contract; see also *Borg-Warner Acceptance Can. Ltd. v. Moto Chaleur Cycle Ltée* (1987), 84 N.B.R. (2d) 211, 214 A.P.R. 211 (N.B. Q.B.).

Incorporation and organization under provincial corporations Acts

Letters patent jurisdictions

The procedure for incorporation of corporations under the corporations Acts which provide for the incorporation of corporations by letters patent, is substantially similar to that followed under this Act. Pamphlet copies of the provincial Act and of any regulations made thereunder with forms and schedules of fees are obtainable from the Queen's Printer in the respective provincial capitals. As to the basic procedure, see the notes under the heading "Procedure for incorporation," above.

The procedure for organizing corporations incorporated by letters patent is essentially the same as that under the federal Act.

Memorandum of association jurisdictions

Under the Companies Acts in force in some provinces incorporation is effected by the registration of a memorandum of association and, if desired, articles of association, and the issuance of a certificate of registration stating certain particulars. Pamphlet copies of the provincial Act, containing schedules of incorporation fees, and blank forms of memorandum of association are obtainable from the Queen's Printer in the respective provincial capitals.

Under these Acts a company is practically organized upon incorporation, as it has in its registered articles of association, or in the articles contained in Table A if no special articles have been registered, a complete code of regulations. At the first meeting of directors it will be necessary to appoint officers, make regulations as to meetings of directors (unless these have been fully provided for in the articles) and approve the forms of share certificates and the corporate seal. A resolution of the board appointing the bankers will also have to be passed. In some jurisdictions a resolution of the directors authorizing the exercise of borrowing powers may be requisite.

Advantages of incorporation

Business undertakings in Canada are almost invariably carried on through the medium of corporations incorporated with share capital. Brief mention may be made of the inherent characteristics and the advantages for business purposes of this form of organization.

A corporation is a distinct legal entity, a legal personality separate from its shareholders or members. It has a capital, contributed in the first instance by its shareholders, which belongs to it and which it employs in its operations. Its assets are owned by it and not by its shareholders and its liabilities are its and not their responsibility. Once its operations are on a firm footing it may be able to attract further funds for its purposes through the sale of additional shares. Its existence is in theory perpetual and is not legally affected by changes in its shareholders or managers which may occur by death or otherwise.

The shareholder or member holds shares in the corporation which represent a fractional part of the capital of the corporation and confer certain rights to participate in dividends paid during the corporation's existence and in the distribution of its assets if that existence is terminated. The shareholder has risked the amount paid or agreed to be paid on his shares but no more; once his shares are fully paid he is under no liability for the debts of the corporation. Assuming that his shares are voting shares, he may participate at shareholders' meetings in the election of the directors who are responsible for the day to day management of the corporation. He is eligible himself for election as a director or for employment by the corporation and may therefore participate actively in the conduct of its affairs. He may on the other hand remain simply an investor who leaves the management of the corporation to the directors and officers subject to their legal liability to account to the shareholders as a whole. He may himself contract or enter into business relations with the corporation. He may at any time, if a market for them exists, dispose of his shares (subject to any applicable restrictions on transfer); and such disposition does not affect the operations of the corporation.

It will be seen, therefore, that a corporation of the type under consideration is a relatively stable form of organization in which the shareholder has a proprietary interest to which limited liability attaches and which is relatively freely transferable. The fundamental characteristics of the corporate form of organization are such that almost all businesses of substantial size in Canada are now incorporated. Whether a smaller business should be incorporated will depend on the facts of the individual case but there will in certain circumstances be advantages from the taxation point of view, apart from those indicated above, in carrying it on through a corporation.

Holding corporations and family corporations

Apart from the cases where a person engaged in business finds it advisable to carry on the business by means of a corporation, important advantages may be secured by use of a corporation to hold and administer investments and assets rather than having them continue under the personal ownership of the individual. Thus, the ownership and control of assets and family businesses can be continued in a family without interruption by death of the individual owner. The payment of foreign succession duties and inheritance taxes can usually be avoided, as there is no change in ownership of the underlying assets in the case of the death of an individual shareholder. The principal shareholder of a corporation formed to acquire his assets can limit his holdings in the corporation to obligations or preferred shares or dispose of a part of his holdings in the corporation to members of his family or others before his death without necessarily losing control of the corporation and, in doing so, may frequently effect a saving in taxes of various kinds.

Syndicates and other unincorporated organizations

Unincorporated associations of several individuals or corporations are frequently formed pursuant to agreement for various purposes. Thus when promoters acquire property with the intention of ultimately forming and floating a corporation to acquire and work the property, they may wish to postpone the formation of the corporation until their plans mature or the value or the marketability of the property is proved. In such cases, the parties may form a syndicate, pursuant to a syndicate agreement, whereunder the persons who advance money or turn over property to the syndicate are entitled to a proportionate interest in the assets of the syndicate. For this purpose the syndicate may be divided into a given number of shares, each member being entitled to a certificate for shares in accordance with his holdings. Such shares or proportional interests in a syndicate are often referred to as "units". Syndicate managers may be appointed and provisions adopted for the holding of meetings of the members, forbidding the manager to pledge the credit of the syndicate for its members beyond the amounts actually paid in, etc. Sometimes the syndicate is effected by letters, verbal arrangements or other informal agreement. A syndicate is not an entity like a corporation but partakes more of the nature of a partnership and the carrying on of business in the name of a syndicate may easily, and often does, result in personal liability on the part of its members for the debts of the syndicate. For this reason, wherever the incurring of financial responsibility or liability by the syndicate can be foreseen, it is usually preferable to create a limited partnership under the provincial statute in force relating to limited partnerships, or to incorporate a private corporation. In addition to a syndicate, a joint venture may be formed. The basic rules applicable to such an organization are similar to those pertaining to syndicates but a joint venture is ordinarily formed for a limited purpose which is to be completed within a limited time span, for example, a construction contract in which there are a number of participants.

Where there is a common fund in which all the members of the syndicate have a common interest, each subscriber becoming liable to all his fellow members as a body, one member of the syndicate can maintain a class action to enforce a syndicate subscription: *A. E. Osler & Co. v. Solman* (1926), 59 O.L.R. 368 (H.C.).

As to the circumstances under which a person will be held liable as a partner for the debts of a syndicate, see *Canadian Bank of Commerce v. Patricia Syndicate* (1921), 51 O.L.R. 42 (H.C.); affd (*sub nom. Ross v. Canadian Bank of Commerce*), [1923] 3 D.L.R. 339 (P.C.) ; *Re General Fibre Board Syndicate* (1923), (*sub nom. Trustee v. Nichol*) 25 O.W.N. 304 (S.C.) and cases cited; *Wearmouth v. MacPherson*, [1936] 1 W.W.R. 623 (B.C. S.C.).

Where the relationship of the syndicate members is that of partners, in an action for the price of goods sold and delivered to the syndicate the individual members should not be joined as defendants: *Wabi Iron Works Ltd. v. Patricia Syndicate* (1923), 54 O.L.R. 640 (C.A.).

Membership in a syndicate formed to purchase property will give rise to a fiduciary relationship between the members of the syndicate: *Radford v. Stannard* (1914), 7 W.W.R. 986 (Alta. C.A.).

A member of a syndicate, who holds property as trustee for the syndicate, cannot purchase the syndicate property under authority of a resolution passed at a meeting of the syndicate, if a member of the syndicate who was notified, but did not attend, objects: *Perkins v. Lundy* (1925), 28 O.W.N. 300 (C.A.).

Where a syndicate was formed to buy a specific piece of land at a specific price and K, a member of the syndicate, had before its formation obtained an option (on behalf of himself and others) to purchase the land at a lower price, which option was exercised by K, his wife paying the purchase price, and the land was conveyed to a trustee for the syndicate at the specific price agreed upon, in an action by dissatisfied members of the syndicate it was held that the syndicate was properly charged with the agreed price as that was the basis of the contract between K and the other members of the syndicate and that there was no duty cast upon K to exercise the option for the benefit of the syndicate or to try to have the price reduced: *Merriam v. Kenderdine Realty Co.* (1915), 34 O.L.R. 556 (C.A.). In this same case it was held that K, who was the manager of the syndicate, was not entitled to charge the syndicate with the benefit it derived from his services or the amount he might have had to pay to another for such services, the syndicate agreement not providing for a salary or allowance to the manager. Nor could a clause in the syndicate agreement providing for meetings be relied upon to justify such a meeting giving away the funds of the syndicate to one of its members. In a proper case the court will appoint a receiver and manager of a syndicate: *Merriam v. Kenderdine Realty* (1915), 34 O.L.R. 563 (C.A.).

A member of a syndicate will be personally liable as a contributory in respect of shares of a corporation standing in his name, notwithstanding the addition of the words "trustee for syndicate" after his name in the certificate: *Winnipeg Hedge & Wire Fence Co.* (1912), 1 D.L.R. 316 (Man. K.B.).

An organization which is not a corporation or a quasi-corporation or a partnership, cannot be sued by its adopted name or served with process in the ordinary way: *Metallic Roofing Co. of Canada v. Local Amalgamated Sheet Metal Workers International Assn.* (1905), 9 O.L.R. 171 at 178 (C.A.); *Local Union No. 1562 v. Williams* (1919), 59 S.C.R. 240, 246, 251; *Robinson v. Adams* (1924) 56 O.L.R. 217 (C.A.); *Society Brand Clothes Ltd. v. Amalgamated Clothing Workers of America*, [1931] S.C.R. 321 (in this case it was also held that the legal incapacity of a defendant to be sued can be raised at any stage of the proceedings); *Body v. Murdoch*, [1954] O.W.N. 658; *Orchard v. Tunney*, [1957] S.C.R. 436; *Tel-Ad Advisors (Ont.) Ltd. v. Tele-Direct (Publications) Inc.* (1986), 8 C.P.C. (2d) 217, 11 C.P.R. (3d) 397 (Ont. H.C.). See also *Yue Shan Society v. Chinese Workers' Protective Assn.*, [1944] 2 D.L.R. 287 (B.C. C.A.) (judgment set aside by Court of Appeal in exercise of its inherent jurisdiction); *International Brotherhood of Teamsters v. Therien*, [1960] S.C.R. 265 (S.C.C.) (a trade union as defined in the British Columbia Labour Relations Act is a legal entity which may be made liable for damages either for breach of a provision of that Act or under the common law).

As to trustees of an unincorporated union being made defendants, see *Hemmingsen v. Bergen*, [1938] 1 D.L.R. 786 (B.C. Co. Ct.) and *Smith Transport Ltd. v. Baird*, [1957] O.W.N. 405 (H.C.); as to individual members of a voluntary unincorporated body, not carried on for profit, being made defendants, see *Smith v. Falk*, [1940] O.W.N. 271 (Master). An unincorporated association can be sued in tort in a representative action: *Metallic Roofing Co. of Canada v. Local Amalgamated Sheet Metal Workers International Assn.* (1905), 9 O.L.R. 171 (C.A.).

At common law, political parties, like trade unions, have no legal existence and could not sue or be sued: *McKinney v. Liberal Party of Canada* (1987), 61 O.R. (2d) 680, 21 C.P.C. (2d) 118 (Ont. H.C.).

Where the action is for damages in tort and there is no allegation of the existence of a trust fund to which the plaintiff, if successful, could resort, an order appointing individuals to represent an unincorporated association and authorizing them to defend the action for the association should not be made: *Barrett v. Harris* (1921), 51 O.L.R. 484 (H.C.); *Robinson v. Adams, supra*; *Bistry v. Cloak & Suit Contractors Assn.*, [1936] O.W.N. 511 (H.C.).

An association which is not a partnership nor a corporation nor a legal entity cannot sue: *Ottawa Lumbermen's Credit Bureau v. Swan* (1922), 53 O.L.R. 135 (C.A.); *International Ladies Garment Workers Union v. Rothman*, [1941] S.C.R. 388. A union may however be prosecuted for breaches of the *Criminal Code* and may be held liable for the common law contempt. See: *United Nurses of Alberta v. Alberta (Attorney General)*, [1992] 3 W.W.R. 481 (S.C.C.).

A lease cannot be made to an unincorporated body by its name: *Henderson v. Toronto General Trusts Corp.* (1928), 62 O.L.R. 303 (C.A.); an unincorporated body is incapable of making a lease: *Canada Morning News Co. v. Thompson*, [1930] S.C.R. 338; *Yue Shan Society v. Chinese Workers' Protective Assn.*, [1944] 2 D.L.R. 287 (B.C. C.A.).

Under Ontario Rule 8.07 any person, including a corporation, carrying on business in a business name other than his own name, may sue or be sued in such business name. Formerly such sole proprietorships could be sued in the firm's name but could not sue using the firm's name: *Towne & Countrye Pet Village v. Silver* (1986), 58 O.R. (2d) 287, 14 C.P.C. (2d) 271 (Ont. Div. Ct.). Most jurisdictions now permit the business to sue in the business name. A partnership by reason of s. 9 of *The Partnerships Registration Act*, (Ontario). cannot maintain an action in respect of a contract made in connection with the business carried on by it, if it has failed to file the prescribed declaration: *Gibb Manufacturing Co. v. Murray-Jones & Co.*, [1947] O.W.N. 1036 (C.A.) (action stayed); and, in this case on subsequent proof by the plaintiff that the declaration had been filed, the stay was removed: *Gibb Manufacturing Co. v. Murray-Jones & Co.*, [1948] O.W.N. 421 (H.C.). The inability to sue does not, however, affect substantive rights so that an incorporated corporation to which a contract was assigned by a partnership was entitled to sue thereon although the partnership could not have done so by reason of defects in the partnership declaration filed: *Roblin Motors Ltd. v. Pringle*, [1956] O.W.N. 153 (P.E.I. Co. Ct.).

Chapter 3

GENERAL POWERS AND DUTIES OF CORPORATIONS; CONTRACTS

Section 15. Capacity of a corporation
Section 16. Powers of a corporation
Section 17. No constructive notice
Section 18. Authority of directors, officers and agents

Cross references: Ontario Act, ss. 15, 16, 17, 18, 19.

Powers of corporations

Under the federal Act s. 15 provides that a corporation has the capacity and, subject to the provisions of the Act, the rights, powers and privileges of a natural person. It may carry on business throughout Canada and conduct its affairs and exercise its powers in any jurisdiction outside of Canada to the extent that the laws of such jurisdiction permit. A similar provision is contained in s. 15 of the Ontario Act which provides that a corporation has the capacity and the rights, powers and privileges of a natural person. These provisions virtually eliminate vexing questions which arose under former Acts relating to the capacity and power of a corporation which could vary depending on the method of incorporation and the provisions of the charter. However, a brief resume of such restrictions and of the doctrine of *ultra vires* is not inappropriate as some of the distinctions may still be applicable to certain provincial corporations not incorporated under a Business Corporations Act modelled on the federal Act, and some of the law may be relevant where there are express restrictions either in the governing Act, or the articles or which are implied by law.

It will be noted that the general exclusion against carrying on business as a trust corporation does not preclude a corporation from entering into an agreement whereby it acts as a trustee: see *Bank of Montreal v. Abacus Cities Ltd.* (1982), 40 B.C.L.R. 39 (B.C. S.C.); affd (*sub nom. Thorne Riddell Inc. v. Rolfe*), [1983] 6 W.W.R. 97, 47 B.C.L.R. 196 (B.C. C.A.).

Interpretation Act

Every corporation incorporated under federal authority possesses by virtue of its incorporation the powers set forth in the first subsection of s. 21 of the *Interpretation Act*, R.S.C. 1985, c. I-21 which reads as follows:

> 21(1). Words establishing a corporation shall be construed
>
> (a) as vesting in the corporation power to sue and be sued, to contract and be contracted with by its corporate name, to have a common seal and to alter or change it at pleasure, to have perpetual succession, to acquire and hold personal property for the purposes for which the corporation is established and to alienate that property at pleasure;
>
> (b) in the case of a corporation having a name consisting of an English and a French form or a combined English and French form, as vesting in the corporation power to use either the English or the French form of its name or both forms and to show on its seal both the English and French forms of its name or have two seals, one showing the English and the other showing the French form of its name;
>
> (c) as vesting in a majority of the members of the corporation the power to bind the others by their acts; and
>
> (d) as exempting from personal liability for its debts, obligations or acts individual members of the corporation who do not contravene the provisions of the enactment establishing the corporation.

Section 27 of *The Interpretation Act*, R.S.O. 1990, c. I.11 is to the same effect.

The provision contained in the *Interpretation Act* is *intra vires* of the Parliament of Canada: *John Deere Plow Co. v. Wharton*, [1915] A.C. 330 at 340 (P.C.); *Lukey v. Ruthenian Farmers' Elevator Co.*, [1924] S.C.R. 56 at 71.

Suits against Crown

It is well established law that the Crown or an emanation of the Crown can be sued in contract, but until the enactment of the *Crown Liability Act* an action in tort could only be brought by a petition of right granted by the Crown. The Act, now c. C-50 R.S.C. 1985, provides for liability in tort of the Crown or an emanation of the Crown, but it will be noted that certain procedural requirements are set out which must be followed. There is also a general limitation provision. These can have the effect of limiting a recovery, for example, where a pension or compensation has been paid or is payable in respect of the death or loss in respect of which the claim is made. In every case where proceedings against an emanation of the Crown are contemplated, reference should be had to the statute governing the body in question, as there may well be special provisions relating to the requirement of notice or a limitation of action or other special provisions.

At common law, the provision that a body corporate may sue or be sued does not affect the immunities of the Crown in respect of tortious acts of its servants: *Peccin v. Lonegan*, [1934] O.R. 701 (C.A.); and a commission, though a body corporate, which is a servant or agent of the Crown, is, as such, immune from liability in tort: *Summers v. Niagara Parks Commission*, [1945] O.R. 326 (H.C.), [1945] O.W.N. 817 (C.A.) (appeal dismissed); and a corporation such as the Canadian Broadcasting Corporation which is an emanation of the Crown is entitled to the same immunity as the Crown in respect of municipal taxation: *Re City of Toronto & Canadian Broadcasting Corp.*, [1938] O.W.N. 507 (C.A.). While the Crown or an emanation of the Crown cannot be sued in tort except in very exceptional circumstances, it can be sued in contract: *Gooderham & Worts Ltd. v. Canadian Broadcasting Corp.*, [1940] O.R. 130 at 137 (C.A.) and cases cited, where it was held, reading a special section of the Act of incorporation together with the powers conferred on the corporation, that the corporation was in essence one of commercial character and could sue and be sued in the ordinary way. See also *Canadian Broadcasting Corp. v. Cyr*, [1939] 4 D.L.R. 233 (Que. C.A.); leave to appeal to S.C.C. refused, (1938) 64 Que. K.B. 191 (Canadian Broadcasting Corporation subject to the jurisdiction of the ordinary courts in actions arising out of its contracts). The above cases were followed in *Gagnon v. C.B.C.*, [1944] 4 D.L.R. 77 (Que. S.C.) (contractual claim) and in *North v. Madden*, [1944] 4 D.L.R. 161 (C.A.) (private corporation, even though wholly owned by the Crown, may be sued in the ordinary courts by ordinary process for breach of contract); and interest on damages for breach of contract was allowed against a Crown corporation where the statute establishing the corporation provided that it might be sued in respect of obligations incurred on behalf of the Crown as if they had been incurred on its own behalf and the circumstances were such that interest would be payable by a private corporation: *Langlois v. Canadian Commercial Corp.*, [1956] S.C.R. 954. See also the *Crown Liability Act*, R.S.C. 1985, c. C-50.

In *International Railway v. Niagara Parks Commission*, [1941] A.C. 328 (P.C.), Luxmoore L.J., in delivering the judgment of the Judicial Committee of the Privy Council, said at p. 343 that the word "emanation" was hardly applicable to a person or body having corporate capacity and added that "it would avoid obscurity in the future if the words agent or servant were used in preference to the inappropriate and undefined word 'emanation'." In that case it was held that an action would lie against the Niagara Parks Commission, a corporation created by the Ontario Legislature with the power to sue and be sued, in respect of a contract expressly entered into on its own behalf as well as on behalf and with the approval of the Crown.

It was held by a majority of the Manitoba Court of Appeal in *Oatway v. Canadian Wheat Board*, [1944] 4 D.L.R. 381, that the Canadian Wheat Board, having regard to the control over it vested by the *Canadian Wheat Board Act*, 1935 in the Governor in Council, is a servant of the Crown entitled to share the Crown's immunity from suit and may not be sued in the ordinary courts for an accounting.

Incidental powers under general law

As to powers "necessarily and inseparably incident to every corporation" such as the power to sue and be sued, see *Powell-Rees Ltd. v. Anglo-Canadian Mortgage Corp.* (1912), 26 O.L.R. 490 at 493 (Ont. H.C.); *Rattenbury v. Land Settlement Board*, [1929] S.C.R. 52; the power to acquire capital by selling its shares: *Lukey v. Ruthenian Farmers' Elevator Co.*, [1924] S.C.R. 56 at 72; the right to appoint agents: *Ferguson v. Wilson* (1866), L.R. 2 Ch. App. 77 at 89; the power to compromise *bona fide* disputes: *Bath's Case* (1878), 8 Ch. D. 334 (C.A.).

Ancillary powers

In addition to any ancillary rights and powers expressly provided for by the governing Act, specific rights or powers are often provided for. For example, s. 43 of the Act provides that a corporation may pay a dividend in fully paid shares and subject to the provisions of s. 42 may pay a dividend in money or property.

Prior to the introduction of the present federal Act, a long list of ancillary powers were listed in the prior Acts. These followed with some variation clauses commonly incorporated in the memorandum of association of corporations formed under the English Act. These were first enacted in 1924 and were amplified in 1930 and 1934.

Inherent powers of corporations

The inherent powers of Canadian corporations, federal and provincial, differ in certain respects in consequence of differing methods of incorporation. The methods of incorporation employed are four in number.

1. By the filing of a memorandum of association subscribed by the incorporators and the issuance of a certificate of registration. This method obtains under the *Companies Acts* of British Columbia and Nova Scotia. It is similar to the method of incorporation under the *English Act.*

2. By special Act of the Parliament of Canada or of a Provincial Legislature.

3. By letters patent issued pursuant to the provisions of a general Companies Act. This method obtains in the case of Prince Edward Island and Part I of the *Quebec Act.*

4. Under the federal Act, and the Acts of Alberta, Manitoba, New Brunswick, Newfoundland, Ontario, Saskatchewan and Quebec (Part IA), incorporation takes place by the delivery to the appropriate director of articles of incorporation and the issuance of a certificate of incorporation affixed to a duplicate of the articles.

Under the first two methods the corporation thereby created is customarily described as a statutory corporation and under the last two as a common law corporation.

Corporations incorporated with memorandum of association

The powers of corporations incorporated with a memorandum of association were defined in the leading case of *Ashbury Ry. Carriage & Iron Co. v. Riche* (1875), L.R. 7 H.L. 653 (H.L.), where Lord Selborne said at p. 693:

> I only repeat what Lord Cranworth in *Hawkes v. Eastern Counties Railway Co.* [5 H.L.C. 331] . . . stated to be settled law, when I say that a statutory corporation, created by Act of Parliament for a particular purpose, is limited, as to all its powers, by the purposes of its incorporation as defined in that Act. The present and all other corporations incorporated by virtue of the Companies Act of 1862 appear to me to be statutory corporations within this principle. The memorandum of association is under that Act their fundamental, and (except in certain specified particulars) their unalterable law; and they are incorporated only for the objects and purposes expressed in that memorandum.

The method to be adopted for ascertaining whether any given act is *intra vires* or not is stated in *A.G. v. Mersey Ry.*,[1907] 1 Ch. 81 at 99 (C.A.), to be as follows:

> . . . the main purpose must first be ascertained; then the special powers for effectuating that purpose must be looked for, and then, if the act is not within either the main purpose as described in or the special powers expressly given by the statute, the inquiry remains whether the act is incidental to or consequential upon the main purpose and is a thing reasonably to be done for effectuating it.

The case was reversed in [1907] A.C. 415, but the above statement by Buckley L.J. was not dissented from.

In *Baroness Wenlock v. River Dee Co.* (1885), 10 App. Cas. 354 (H.L.), Lord Watson said at p. 362:

> Whenever a corporation is created by Act of Parliament, with reference to the purposes of the Act, and solely with a view to carrying these purposes into execution, I am of opinion not only that the objects which the corporation may legitimately pursue must be ascertained from the Act itself, but that the powers which the corporation may lawfully use in furtherance of these objects must either be expressly conferred or derived by reasonable implication from its provisions.

In *A.G. v. Mersey Ry.*, [1907] A.C. 415 at 415 (H.L.), Lord Loreburn said:

> The rule of law has been laid down in this House to the effect . . . that it must be shewn that the business can be fairly regarded as incidental to or consequential upon the use of the statutory powers; and it is a question in each case whether it is so or whether it is not so.

The objects and powers must not include anything in contravention of the Acts or the general law.

The rule that any purpose or object not specifically authorized by the memorandum is *ultra vires* is to be applied reasonably. Anything fairly incidental to the corporation's objects as defined is not (unless expressly prohibited) to be held *ultra vires: A.G. v. Great Eastern Ry.* (1879), 11 Ch. D. 449 at 480 (C.A.); *New Zealand Gold Extraction Co. v. Peacock*, [1894] 1 Q.B. 622 at 632 (C.A.); *Deuchar v. Gas, Light & Coke Co.*, [1925] A.C. 691 (H.L.); *A.G. v. Racecourse*

Betting Control Board, [1935] 1 Ch. 34 (C.A.); *Grand Trunk Ry. v. James* (1916), 10 W.W.R. 1075 (Alta. T.D.) (right to carry baggage to and from its own stations incidental to the statutory powers of a railway corporation).

To the above rules of construction must be added the "primary object" rule which is that, where the objects of a corporation set forth a number of powers, the paragraphs containing the main or dominant objects must first be looked at and all other clauses are to be regarded as merely ancillary to the main object and not as conferring independent powers: *In re German Date Coffee Co.* (1882), 20 Ch. D. 169 (C.A.); but the memorandum must be read as a whole and the primary object rule, being only of *prima facie* application, may be expressly excluded by the terms of the memorandum: *Butler v. Northern Territories Mines of Australia* (1907), 96 L.T. 41; and effect will be given to a statement in the memorandum that each paragraph is to be read separately and not restricted by any other paragraph: *Cotman v. Brougham*, [1918] A.C. 514 (H.L.); and the memorandum "must be read fairly and its import derived from a reasonable interpretation of the language which it employs": *Egyptian Salt & Soda Co. v. Port Said Salt Assn.*, [1931] A.C. 677 at 682 (P.C.). Thus, in the case of a corporation incorporated under the Companies Act of Alberta, the Supreme Court of Canada held that it was *ultra vires* for a corporation to make assessments on its shareholders for the purpose of providing revenue: *Edmonton Country Club Ltd. v. Case* (1974), 44 D.L.R. (3d) 554 (S.C.C.). See also *H. & H. Logging Co. v. Random Services Corp.* (1967), 63 D.L.R. (2d) 6 (B.C. C.A.); *Thorne Riddell Inc. v. Rolfe*, [1983] 6 W.W.R. 97 (B.C. C.A.), affg (*sub nom. Bank of Montreal v. Abacus Cities Ltd.*) (1982), 40 B.C.L.R. 39 (S.C.); *Angus v. R. Angus Alberta Ltd.*, [1988] 3 W.W.R. 737 (Alta. C.A.).

A somewhat unusual application of the "primary object" rule is to be found in *Northern Ontario Power Co. v. Lake Shore Mines Ltd.*, [1943] 3 D.L.R. 616 at 621 (Ont. H.C.); affd [1944] 2 D.L.R. 20 at 31 (Ont. C.A.). In that case it was held that the mere fact that the power to manufacture, buy, sell and deal in goods, wares and merchandise was placed first in the letters patent when the remaining purposes and objects indicated that the supply of public utilities was the one most prominently in the minds of the incorporators, did not prevent the corporation from being described as one incorporated for the purpose of supplying a public utility within the meaning of s. 58 of the *Public Utilities Act,* 1913 (Ontario), c. 41.

The governing Act may limit the powers of the corporation and any act of the corporation which is not authorized by the statutory provision will be *ultra vires: Neily v. Brooklyn Fruit Co.*, [1937] 3 D.L.R. 198 (N.S. C.A.).

After the decision of the Privy Council in *Bonanza Creek Gold Mining Co. v. The King*, [1916] 1 A.C. 566 (P.C.), as to which see the heading "Corporations incorporated by letters patent" below, legislation enacted by the province of Saskatchewan, by way of amendment of the Companies Act, provided, *inter alia*, that as to every corporation created by or under any general or special Act of the legislature

> unless the contrary intention is expressed in a special Act or ordinance incorporating the corporation or in a memorandum of association thereof, such incorporation shall,

so far as the capacities of such corporations are concerned, have and be deemed to have had the same effect as if the company were or had been incorporated by letters patent under the Great Seal.

In *Canadian Bank of Commerce v. Cudworth Rural Telephone Co.*, [1923] S.C.R. 618, it was held that a corporation organized under the *Rural Telephone Act* as a non-trading corporation without power to issue promissory notes and, pursuant to the provisions of that Act, registered under the Saskatchewan Companies Act, did not, by reason of the above statutory provision, acquire power to make a promissory note. Duff J. at pp. 628-9 expressed the view that the effect of the statutory provision upon corporations to which it applied was "not to abrogate entirely the doctrine of *ultra vires* but to establish a rule of construction which in effect is that such companies are to be deemed to have the capacities of a common law corporation, subject to such restrictions as the legislature has evidenced an intention of imposing on it."

Apart from statutory enactments such as that referred to above and subject to the rules of construction mentioned above and to certain general restrictions and limitations hereinafter mentioned, the powers exercisable by a corporation incorporated by memorandum of association are those expressly conferred by its constating instruments when read together, that is by its memorandum of association, its articles, and the Companies Act under which it is incorporated.

Corporations incorporated by special Act

The powers of a corporation incorporated by special Act are *prima facie* those which are conferred by the Act itself. Such powers are, however, supplemented in most cases by the powers conferred by general provisions embodied either in a separate "Companies Clauses Act", in a separate subdivision of a general Companies Act or in general legislation applicable to corporations of a particular type, for example, banks. For an example of such supplemental powers, see ss. 151 and 152 of Part IV of the *Canada Corporations Act* applicable to those federal corporations incorporated by special Act to which that Part applies. For an example of the application of the doctrine of *ultra vires* to a corporation incorporated by special act see: *Vézina (Sam) Inc. v. Laurentian Pilotage Authority* (1991), 49 F.T.R. 184 (T.D.); *Canadian Pacific Ltd. v. Telestat Canada* (1981), 32 O.R. (2d) 197; affd (1982), 36 O.R. (2d) 229; leave to appeal to S.C.C. refused (1982), 133 D.L.R. (3d) 321. See also *Alta. Mortgage & Housing Corp. v. Ciereszko* (1985), 41 Alta. L.R. (2d) 242 (Q.B.); (1987), 50 Alta. L.R. (2d) 289 with additional reasons at 54 Alta. L.R. (2d) 191 (C.A.); leave to appeal to S.C.C. refused 51 Alta. L.R. (2d) x1i (note); *Army, Navy & Air Force Veterans in Canada, Saskatoon Unit 38 v. Morguard Trust Co.*, [1982] 1 W.W.R. 632 (Sask. C.A.), leave to appeal to S.C.C. refused (1982), 16 Sask. R. 179.

Following the decision in the *Bonanza Creek* case, as to which see the heading "Corporations incorporated by letters patent", below, some provinces passed legislation declaring that *all* corporations incorporated under the authority of the province and to which the provincial Act was made applicable should possess the powers of a common law corporation. Such legislation extends to and includes corporations incorporated by special Act, subject, however, to any limitations or restrictions contained in the special Act by which, as its supreme authority, the corporation is governed. Such legislation has been enacted in Saskatchewan, as mentioned above, in Manitoba and in Ontario. The effect of the Ontario legislation is discussed below under the heading "Corporations incorporated by letters patent". The Manitoba legislation was considered by the Manitoba Court of Appeal in *Re Northwestern Trust Co.; Ex parte Pure Oil Co.*, [1926] 1 D.L.R. 689. In that case it was held that the Act did not give a trust corporation, incorporated by private Act of the Manitoba legislature, power to give a guarantee not authorized by the specific powers of its governing Act. The judgments draw a distinction between "capacities" and "powers". In *Emco Ltd. v. Manitoba Health Service* (1960), 32 W.W.R. 19 at 26 a corporation incorporated by special Act of the Manitoba legislature did not have the specific power to purchase real property but the majority of the Manitoba Court of Appeal held that such a power was fairly incidental to and consequential upon its objects and was a power which the legislature, by giving the corporation power to make by-laws "for charging, hypothecating, mortgaging or pledging any or all of . . . [its] real . . .property," intended the corporation to possess.

No such Act has been passed by the federal Parliament and the powers of corporations incorporated by a federal Special Act are subject to the doctrine of *Ashbury v. Riche* and not to that of the *Bonanza Creek* case. Their powers are to be found in the governing Act: *Canada National Fire Insurance Co. v. Hutchings*, [1918] A.C. 451 at 456 (P.C.); and may be limited by the governing Act: *Neily v. Brooklyn Fruit Co.*, [1937] 3 D.L.R. 198 (N.S. C.A.). A corporation incorporated by special provincial Act may sue in the absence of clear and unambiguous words in the constituent Act restricting its right to do so. See *Fathers of Confederation Buildings Trust v. Pigott Construction Co.* (1973), 4 Nfld. & P.E.I.R. 482 (P.E.I. S.C.). Where the corporation was empowered by the governing Act to acquire real estate for the purposes of its business, the corporation acting *bona fide* must be the sole judge of what is required for the purposes of its business: *Montreal & St. Lawrence Light & Power Co. v. Robert*, [1906] A.C. 196 at 200 (P.C.). Where the plaintiff corporation had the power by its incorporating statute to hold land at a value not exceeding $10,000 in value and the plaintiff attempted to sell the land for an amount greater than $10,000, the land did not automatically escheat to the Crown. The corporation had the power to sell and convey property before escheat proceedings were commenced and if the land was so sold, the purchaser was held bound to complete the purchase and would take title free from subsequent proceedings to establish escheat. See *Resolutes Amateur Athletic Club of Halifax v. African Methodist Episcopal Church of Halifax* (1980), 44 N.S.R. (2d) 250 (T.D.). As to the application of the *ejusdem generis* rule, see *Ottawa Young Men's Christian Assn. v. City of Ottawa* (1913), 29 O.L.R. 574 (C.A.). In *Re Ditchburn Boats & Aircraft (1936) Ltd.*, [1938] 2 D.L.R. 518 (Ont. H.C.), Urquhart J. held that the powers of a trust corporation under s. 18 of *The Loan and Trust Corporations Act*, R.S.O. 1937, c. 257, to act as attorney or agent for the transaction of business, did not extend to acting as proxy for others. An appeal having been taken, a motion to quash was allowed ([1938] O.W.N. 241 (Ont. C.A.)), the judgment pointing out that the court was not to be taken as giving any approbation to the order below.

In *Communities Economic Development Fund v. Canadian Pickles Corp.*, [1992] 1 W.W.R. 193 (S.C.C.), it was held that the appellant, a lending institution, could not recover in its action against the guarantors of a loan where the loan had been made in contravention of specific provisions of the constituent statute, *The Communities Economic Fund Act.* The making of a loan was *ultra vires.* One section of that Act granted the lending institution the capacities and powers of a natural person. Iacobucci, J. held that while normally such a provision would abolish the doctrine of *ultra vires,* the specific provisions of the Act qualified the otherwise wide grant of powers. Iacobucci, J. distinguished the Act from other business corporations legislation on the basis that no remedial provisions were provided for in the special Act and the remedial provisions of the Manitoba *Corporations Act* were expressly made inapplicable to the lender. Thus, the provisions of the Manitoba *Corporations Act* did not abolish the *ultra vires* doctrine in respect of corporations created by special Act where the constituent statute has the effect of making the usual remedial provisions of the *Corporations Act* inapplicable. It is unlikely that the decision will apply to corporations governed solely by business corporations legislation given the general remedial provisions of that legislation.

Where, however, a debtor alleged that a credit union had acted *ultra vires* of its permitted powers thus relieving the debtor of her obligation to repay the loan, Noble J. distinguished the *Canadian Pickles* case commenting that *Canadian Pickles* stands for the proposition that a guarantor may challenge the capacity of a lender if the guarantee documents do not specifically make him liable. A borrower stands on a different footing because of the doctrine of money had and received. See: *Kindersley District Credit Union Ltd. v. Dahl,* [1992] 3 W.W.R. 209 (Sask. Q.B.).

Corporations incorporated by letters patent

The earlier view adopted by the Canadian courts was that the doctrine of *ultra vires* was applicable to corporations incorporated by letters patent. Thus, for example, in *Union Bank of Canada v. McKillop & Sons* (1915), 51 S.C.R. 518, a guarantee given by a corporation so incorporated was held to be *ultra vires.* But, in what became the leading case on the subject, it was determined that such corporations derive their existence from the act of the Sovereign by the grant of a charter from the Crown, which confers on the corporation "a status resembling that of a corporation at common law, subject to the restrictions which are imposed on its proceedings": *Bonanza Creek Gold Mining Co. v. The King,* [1916] 1 A.C. 566 at 582 (P.C.). The *Bonanza Creek* case at pp. 583-4 decided that the doctrine of *ultra vires* is not applicable to corporations "incorporated by charter in the absence of statutory restriction added to what is written in the charter. Such a company has the capacity of a natural person to acquire powers and rights. If by the terms of the charter it is prohibited from doing so, a violation of this prohibition is an act not beyond its capacity, and is therefore not *ultra vires,* although such a violation may well give ground for proceedings by way of *scire facias* for the forfeiture of the charter".

The specific question under consideration in the *Bonanza Creek* case was whether a corporation incorporated by letters patent under the Ontario Companies Act could acquire *ab extra* powers and rights outside the boundaries of the province. It was held that the corporation—which was given by its charter power, *inter alia,* to carry on the business of mining and acquire real and personal property, including mining claims, with incidental powers—had no authority as of right to exercise powers outside the province of its incorporation, but that it had a status which enabled it to accept from the federal authorities the right of free mining and to hold the leases in the Yukon which were in question in the action. However, Viscount Haldane explicitly states that the doctrine of *ultra vires* does not apply to corporations incorporated by charter in the absence of some restriction in their constating instruments, and the case has been treated as a decision on the powers of all corporations coming within this class.

The broad powers of a corporation created by royal charter as established in the *Sutton's Hospital* case, 10 Coke's Rep. 1(a), have been described in subsequent cases as extending to the "power to do with its property all such acts as an ordinary person can do and to bind itself to such contracts as an ordinary person can bind himself to" per Bowen L.J. in *Baroness Wenlock v. River Dee Co.* (1883), 36 Ch. D. 675n at 685n (Ch. D.); and see the observations of Blackburn J. in *Riche v. Ashbury Ry. Carriage & Iron Co.* (1874), L.R. 9 Ex. 224 at 262 (Ex. Ch.).

For an illuminating discussion of the distinction between "capacities" and "actual powers and rights" as those terms are used in the *Bonanza Creek* case see the judgment of Duff J. (as he then was) in *Canadian Bank of Commerce v. Cudworth Rural Telephone Co.*, [1923] S.C.R. 618 at 629, and 630 concluding with the following observation:

> But there is, of course, nothing in Lord Haldane's judgment throwing a doubt upon the propriety and aptitude of the phrase 'corporate capacity' sanctioned by the widest and most inveterate usage as applied to the power now in question.

It would seem that the "capacity" referred to by Lord Haldane in the *Bonanza Creek* case is equivalent to a power to apply for and, if granted, to accept from another province or state the right to exercise within the confines of such province or state any or all of the powers with which it was endowed by its original incorporation.

As stated above, an amendment of the Ontario Companies Act, 6 Geo. V. c. 35, s. 6 passed after the decision in the *Bonanza Creek* case, expressly confers on the corporations thereby affected "the general capacity which the common law ordinarily attaches to corporations created by charter". The judgment of the Ontario Supreme Court, Appellate Division, in *Edwards v. Blackmore* (1918), 42 O.L.R. 105, while decided in reference to a corporation governed by the above mentioned statutory provision, followed the *Bonanza Creek* case and is applicable to all corporations incorporated by letters patent. The following propositions were laid down by Ferguson J.A.:

> . . . a corporation created by charter had at common law almost unlimited capacity to contract, and . . . statements in the charter defining the objects of incorporation do not take away that unlimited capacity, and . . . even express restrictions in the charter do not take it away, but are simply treated as a declaration of the Crown's pleasure in reference to the purposes beyond which the capacity of the corporation is not to be exercised, a breach of which declaration gives to the Crown a right to annul the charter (at pp. 116 and 117).
>
> . . . the enumeration in the charter of the objects for which the company is incorporated cannot be considered as a declaration that the company shall not do things other than those particularly set out, but . . . it requires at least express words of restriction in the charter, or the statute, to confine operations of the company, or even to confer upon a person aggrieved the right to apply by *scire facias* proceedings to cancel the charter. (at p. 118).

See also *Kittles v. Colonial Assurance Co.* (1917), 35 D.L.R. 588 (Man. C.A.) where a similar statutory provision (Man. 7 Geo. V, c. 12) was applicable.

Edwards v. Blackmore was not applied in *Canadian Bank of Commerce v. Cudworth Rural Telephone Co.*, [1923] S.C.R. 618 and in that case Mignault J. at p. 641, observed that the Ontario statute was differently worded from the Saskatchewan legislation, that the corporation was of a different nature and that he expressed no opinion as to the decision in the Ontario court. In *Re Northwestern Trust Co.; Pure Oil Co., Ex parte*, [1926] 1 D.L.R. 689, which was a case involving a trust corporation incorporated by special Act, the Manitoba Court of Appeal did not apply *Edwards v. Blackmore,* although the Manitoba legislation was similar to the Ontario legislation considered in that case. In some of the judgments in these cases the distinction is drawn between "capacities" and "powers".

Ontario cases involving the powers of corporations decided since the amendment above mentioned which is now reflected in ss. 15-16 of the Ontario Act include the following:

Diebel v. Stratford Improvement Co. (1917), 38 O.L.R. 407 (C.A.) (guarantee for performance of a contract not *ultra vires*).

Town of Cobalt v. Temiskaming Telephone Co. (1919), 59 S.C.R. 62 (an agreement by a municipality to permit, by irrevocable licence, a telephone corporation to occupy the streets with poles and wires was *ultra vires*).

Waterous Engine Co. v. Town of Capreol (1922), 52 O.L.R. 247 (C.A.) (the section does not apply to municipal corporations).

R. v. Long Branch Racing Association (1924), 56 O.L.R. 303 (C.A.) (the section cannot enable a corporation to do an act which the Criminal Code forbids or makes illegal).

Re Jacques Furniture Co., Canadian Radio Corp. v. The Trustee, [1933] O.W.N. 170 (C.A.) (it was held that the Court of Appeal was bound by *Edwards v. Blackmore, supra;* contract for use of broadcasting station was not *ultra vires*).

Royal Bank of Canada v. Fleming, [1933] O.R. 601 (C.A.) (it was held in respect of two corporations incorporated under the Ontario Act that the doctrine of *ultra vires* had no application, following *Edwards v. Blackmore, supra*).

Re W. N. McEachren & Sons Ltd., [1933] O.R. 349 (C.A.) (an agreement to purchase interests in a real estate syndicate was not *ultra vires*).

Export Brewing & Malting Co. v. Dominion Bank, [1934] O.R. 560 (C.A.) (it was held that the power of a federal corporation to become surety for the debt of a third party was conferred by the Act and the letters patent, without deciding whether the principle of the *Bonanza Creek* case applied; the Judicial Committee of the Privy Council, [1937] 3 D.L.R. 513, allowed the appeal of the guarantor corporation on other grounds without expressing a view that such a transaction as was there in question was *intra vires*).

The King v. Williams, [1942] A.C. 541 at 554 (P.C.) (Ontario corporation held to have capacity to maintain transfer agency and register of shareholders outside of Ontario in absence of any express declaration to the contrary, in view of s. 217 of the *Ontario Act*).

Stanishewski v. Tkachuk, [1955] O.R. 667 (S.C.) (The objects of a corporation incorporated by letters patent without share capital were, "To promote culture, education and Canadian citizenship among the Ukrainian people . . ." (at 669). As a result of friction between the members of the corporation, certain assets were conveyed to a particular religious body to which the majority of members belonged. Spence J. held that the conveyance must be set aside as *ultra vires*, being of the opinion that the conveyance of its assets to a religious body was not in furtherance of its objects; secondly, that the conveyance did not fall within the incidental powers to dispose of their assets conferred on corporations by s. 22(1) of the Ontario Corporations Act; and thirdly, that the conveyance could not be justified under the powers provided in s. 286 of that Act because the Act conferred specific powers with regard to the disposition of corporation property and the transaction could not be effected within the specific powers and was therefore *ultra vires*).

Galbraith v. Madawaska Club Ltd. (1959), 18 D.L.R. (2d) 424 (Ont. H.C.) (Ontario corporation held to have the capacity to operate a club in the absence of any express declaration to the contrary, in view of s. 286 of the Ontario Corporations Act).

Cases involving the powers of corporations arising in jurisdictions other than Ontario include the following:

Jacques Cartier Water & Power Co. v. Quebec Ry., Light, & Power Co. (1902), 11 Que. K.B. 511 (C.A.) (powers of these two corporations discussed in detail).

National Land & Loan Co. v. Rat Portage Lumber Co. (1917), 36 D.L.R. 97 (Man. K.B.) (trading corporation having power to sell land has implied power to execute assignment of an agreement for sale of land with usual convenant of guarantee against default of purchaser).

United Manufacturing Co. v. St. Maurice Power Co., [1926] A.C. 708 (P.C.) (power to construct and maintain dams in a river, after having acquired from the riparian proprietors the properties necessary for this purpose, will not operate as a grant of actual proprietary rights).

Sass v. St. Nicholas Mutual Benefit Association, [1937] S.C.R. 415 (power of Manitoba corporation to amalgamate with another society).

Quebec Construction Co. v. Concrete Column Clamps Ltd., [1940] S.C.R. 522 (power of corporation to submit to arbitration).

City of Winnipeg v. Canadian Pacific Ry., [1953] 4 D.L.R. 1 (P.C.) (The charter of incorporation of the railway corporation conferred all franchises and powers necessary or useful to the corporation to enable it to maintain, work and run its railway. The corporation gave the city of Winnipeg a deed of covenant to build and continue forever certain railway works within the city and in return received an exemption from all municipal taxes. The city sought to tax the corporation on the ground that the deed of covenant was *ultra vires* the corporation and thus the city was not bound thereby. The Judicial Committee of the Privy Council held that as the deed of covenant was incidental and useful to the corporation it fell within the charter powers and the city was bound by the deed and must grant exemption from municipal taxes.

Where a corporation incorporated under the laws of the province of Quebec and the Ontario Hydro-Electric Power Commission, a statutory corporation, had each received from its incorporating province not only all necessary power to act within its own province but also capacity to receive powers outside the province and each had received from the neighbouring province full authority there to exercise all its powers, the corporation and the Commission were to be deemed to be in the same position as individuals in respect of a contract entered into between them: *Ottawa Valley Power Co. v. A.G. Ont.*, [1936] 4 D.L.R. 594 at 608, 611, 624 (Ont. C.A.).

Where there was no law in New Brunswick prohibiting a corporation which did not carry on business within the province from suing in that province, the New Brunswick Court of Appeal held that a corporation incorporated under *The Companies Act of Quebec* by letters patent issued under the Great Seal of that province had the same right as a natural person to maintain an action in New Brunswick: *Aetna Factors Corp. Ltd. v. Breau* (1959), 15 D.L.R. (2d) 326 (N.B. C.A.).

Section 7(1)(b) of the former Act provided that the purposes of the proposed corporation were to be set forth in the application for incorporation (Form 1) and were to be limited to the purposes and objects which it was intended that the corporation would pursue; and under s. 5(4) the carrying on of any business not within the scope of the purposes and objects set forth in the charter or the exercising or professing to exercise any powers not reasonably incidental to those purposes or objects or any powers expressly excluded by the charter would subject the corporation to the risk of an application by the Attorney-General of Canada for its winding-up and dissolution. This provision recognized such a corporation as possessing the character of a common law corporation, whose acts, if unwarranted by its charter, are, generally speaking, not *ultra vires* but subject the corporation to the risk of dissolution at the suit of the Attorney-General.

The provisions mentioned relate only to the provisions of the charter and have no bearing on the result of a violation of provisions and restrictions contained in the statute. Section 212 of the former Act limited the application of s. 5(4) and s. 7(1)(b) to corporations incorporated on or after September 5, 1935, so that they did not apply to corporations incorporated prior to that date.

In *Machray's Department Store Ltd. v. Zionist Labour Organization,* (1965), 53 W.W.R. 218 (Man. Q.B.) a non-share corporation was held to be without power to purchase real estate, the court pointing out that, while the corporation was created by letters patent, the Act restricted the powers of the corporation and the powers permitting the acquisition of real estate by such a corporation were not complied with. Accordingly, the corporation could not sue for damages for failure to carry out an agreement to purchase land.

If a corporation incorporated by royal charter intends to do acts which are not authorized by its charter a member is entitled to ask for an injunction restraining the commission of acts which are outside of the scope of the charter and which may result in the forfeiture of the charter: *Jenkin v. Pharmaceutical Society of Great Britain*, [1921] 1 Ch. 392.

Corporations incorporated by articles of incorporation

The Act provides in s. 15 that every corporation incorporated under the Act has the capacity and, subject to the provisions of the Act, the rights, powers and privileges of a natural person. Accordingly, the position of a corporation incorporated under this and similar acts is analogous to corporations incorporated by the issue of letters patent. The articles must contain any restrictions on the businesses that the corporation may carry on (s. 6(1)(f)). The usual practice is to provide that there are no restrictions with the result that questions of *ultra vires* are ordinarily of no consequence with the exception of any restriction contained in the governing Act or acts which are illegal or contrary to the general doctrines of corporation law.

The provision under the Ontario Act (s. 15) is even wider since there is no reference to the restrictions contained in the Act. It will also be noted that s. 16 of that Act provides that a corporation has the capacity to carry on its business, conduct its affairs and exercise its powers in any jurisdiction outside Ontario to the extent that the laws of such jurisdiction permit.

Restrictions on powers

Section 16(2) of the federal Act provides that a corporation is not to carry on any business or exercise any power that it is restricted by its articles from carrying on or exercising nor is it to exercise any of its powers in a manner contrary to its articles. However, s. 16(3) provides that no act of a corporation including any transfer of property to or by it is invalid by reason only that it is contrary to the articles or the federal Act.

The old federal Act contained no express words qualifying the royal prerogative to create a common law corporation by royal charter, but it is submitted that it did by necessary intendment provide that the exercise of the royal prerogative, which for the purposes of this Act was delegated to the Secretary of State, was limited by the express restrictions contained in the Act (see s. 13) or necessarily to be inferred from its provisions, and that the corporation when incorporated could possess no greater powers than the Secretary of State in the exercise of the limited prerogative power delegated to him had power to bestow.

The result is that, though the corporation incorporated by letters patent resembled a common law corporation, it was limited in its powers by the express restrictions contained in the Act. It is submitted that a similar result is applicable to corporations incorporated by articles of incorporation.

If this view is correct, proceedings by the corporation in violation of such statutory restrictions are beyond its corporate powers (in spite of s. 16(3)) and in that sense appear to be *ultra vires.* For example, if a corporation were to carry on the business of a trust corporation, contrary to a provision of the Act, its proceedings would, it is submitted, be *ultra vires.*

Our courts have, moreover, been astute to find limitations on the broad scope of the powers of a common law corporation either by implication arising from the circumstances attending its incorporation or from the words of the charter. See, for example, *Northwestern Trust Co., Re, Ex parte Pure Oil Co.*, [1926] 1 D.L.R. 689 (Man. C.A.); *Canadian Bank of Commerce v. Cudworth Rural Telephone Co.*, [1923] S.C.R. 618; *Mutual Investments Ltd., Re* (1924), 56 O.L.R. 29 (H.C.); and *Stanishewski v. Tkachuk*, [1955] O.R. 667 (S.C.). However, where an Ontario corporation had sold a portion of its land and had taken from the purchaser, for the unpaid balance of the purchase price, a transfer of an existing charge upon lands which were not the property of the corporation, it was held that the transaction was *intra vires* (ss. 24(1)(q) and 26 of *The Companies Act,* R.S.O. 1937, c. 251 referred to): *Re York Land Co.*, [1939] 2 D.L.R. 775 (Ont. S.C.). And where a corporation took a short-term mortgage in its own name and also agreed to hold the proceeds of the mortgage in trust for its co-investors, both transactions were held *intra vires* (s. 23(1)(o) and (p) of *The Companies Act* R.S.O. 1950, c. 59 referred to): *Coupland Acceptance Ltd. v. Walsh*, [1954] S.C.R. 90. Somewhat different in its effect is a statutory restriction on the duration of a contract which may be entered into by a corporation for a specified purpose. Thus, s. 22 of *The Public Utilities Act*, R.S.O. 1927, c. 249, authorizing a public utility corporation to enter into contracts for the supply of a public utility for a maximum period of years, will restrict the capacity of a public utility corporation so to contract to such period, but on the other hand a contract purporting to extend beyond such period may be valid during such period: *Northern Ontario Power Co. v. LaRoche Mines Ltd.*, [1938] 3 D.L.R. 657 at 662 (P.C.); *Northern Ontario Power Co. v. Lake Shore Mines Ltd.*, [1943] 3 D.L.R. 616 at 619 (Ont. H.C.); affd [1944] 2 D.L.R. 20 (Ont. C.A.).

In *H. & H. Logging Co. v. Random Services Corporation* (1966), 57 D.L.R. (2d) 747 (B.C. S.C.) the defendant corporation had bid for a licence and contract to cut ground timber. The only other bidder for this right applied for a declaration that the contract was *ultra vires.* It was held that logging could be included if the directors believed it could conveniently be carried on in connection with dealing in logs and thus was *intra vires.*

Whether any particular provision of the statute is a restriction on the powers of the corporation, conditional or absolute, or is merely directory, is a question of the construction of that particular provision, and the same is true as to powers conferred by the statute subject to a condition. See *Pacific Coast Coal Mines Ltd. v. Arbuthnot*, [1917] A.C. 607 at 616 (P.C.). In *Banking Service Corp. v. Toronto Finance Corp.*, [1928] A.C. 333 (P.C.) it was held that a transaction in contravention of the provision of the Ontario Act corresponding to s. 16(2) of the former federal Act was *ultra vires.* Thus, under the former Act a loan to a shareholder might well have been found to be *ultra vires.* See *Henderson v. Strang* (1920), 60 S.C.R. 201. However, s. 44(3) of the federal Act specifically provides that a contract made by a corporation in contravention of the provisions prohibiting certain financial assistance may be enforced by the corporation or by a lender for value in good faith without notice of the contravention.

Apart from express restrictions and prohibitions contained in the Act, there remain to be considered implied limitations and restrictions. Such implication arises either by reason of express provisions of the Act, such as those in relation to the share capital of corporations, or by reason of general doctrines of corporation law which are regarded as fundamental.

Express provisions of the Act affecting the capital structure, such as provisions in relation to alteration of share capital requiring the carrying out of the procedure prescribed and the issuance of articles of amendment as a condition of such alteration being effectively carried out, by implication prevent such alteration of the share capital without compliance with the statutory requirements.

Other express provisions of the Act indicate that the status as a common law corporation of a corporation incorporated by letters patent does not entitle it to limit by contract the liability of a shareholder still further and to provide that he shall not be liable for the amount unpaid on his shares. See *Ooregum Gold Mining Co. of India v. Roper*, [1892] A.C. 125 at 133 (H.L.) and s. 33 of the federal Act.

An example of a general doctrine of corporation law, to which corporations incorporated by letters patent are subject, is the rule that a corporation cannot lawfully give away its property: *Trustee of the Property of C. E. Plain Ltd. v. Kenley & Royal Trust Co.* (1930), 66 O.L.R. 179 at 191 (H.C.); affd [1931] O.R. 75 (C.A.).

With respect to restrictions and limitations contained in the charter but not contained in the statute or implied by reason of any fundamental rule of corporation law it is clear that, even if the charter by express words forbids any particular act, the corporation can nevertheless do the act and, if it does it, is bound thereby and the result is only that ground is given for a proceeding by *scire facias* in the name of the Crown to repeal the charter or articles. *Sutton's Hospital Case*, 10 Coke's Rep. 1(a); *Riche v. Ashbury Ry. Carriage & Iron Co.* (1874), L.R. 9 Exch. 224 at 262 (Ex. Ch.); *Baroness Wenlock v. River Dee Co.*

(1883), 36 Ch. D. 675n at 685n. (C.A.); *Bonanza Creek Gold Mining Co. v. The King*, [1916] 1 A.C. 566 (P.C.); *Re W. N. McEachren & Sons Ltd.*, [1933] O.R. 349 at 360 (C.A.); *Dion Ltd. v. Banque Provinciale du Canada* (1939), 66 Que. K.B. 344 (C.A.).

Illegal acts

Acts of a corporation quite apart from their being prohibited by the charter or by the Act may be illegal as being contrary to public policy or forbidden by law. A corporation could not, for example, purchase land for the purpose of a lottery scheme: *Prevost v. Bedard* (1915), 51 S.C.R. 149. The prohibition of a contract by statute renders the contract void and of no effect: *Montreal Trust Co. v. Canadian National Railway*, [1939] A.C. 613 (P.C.), applying and approving the principle laid down in *Macdonald v. Riordon* (1899), 8 Que. Q.B. 555 (C.A.); appeal dismissed (1899), 30 S.C.R. 619.

The distinction between an illegal transaction and one which is *ultra vires* is that no right enforceable in a court of justice can be maintained on an illegal transaction, but a party may come into court and set up the existence of and the incompetence of a party to bind himself by a transaction which is *ultra vires*: *In Re Birkbeck Permanent Benefit Building Society*, [1912] 2 Ch. 183 at 232 (C.A.). In the case of a guarantee, however, when the liability of the guarantor is dependent on the existence of a valid obligation on the part of a principal debtor the guarantee will be equally unenforceable, whether the principal debt is the result of an *ultra vires* contract or a contract which is illegal: *MacDonald-Crawford Ltd. v. Burns*, [1924] 2 D.L.R. 977 (Sask. C.A.); but see *Garrard v. James*, [1925] 1 Ch. 616 (Ch. D.) and cases cited. As to *ultra vires* acts, see the notes under the heading "Effect of *ultra vires* acts", below.

Where moneys of the corporation have been illegally applied and the recipient knows or must be assumed to have known the illegality of the transaction, the moneys are recoverable: *Rountree v. Sydney Land & Loan Co.* (1908), 39 S.C.R. 614; and where the person benefitted is involved in such misapplication, so as to be answerable for it, the corporation is entitled to recover from him assets acquired with such moneys: *Chandler & Massey Ltd. v. Irish* (1913), 29 O.L.R. 112 (C.A.).

Manner of exercise of powers

Where a corporation has permissive powers which are capable of being exercised without the creation of a nuisance and which are conferred without provision being made for compensating persons injured by their exercise, they must be used so as not to create a nuisance: *Hopkin v. Hamilton Electric Light & Cataract Power Co.* (1901), 2 O.L.R. 240 (H.C.); affd (1902), 1 O.W.R. 486 (C.A.). The general rule of law is that if the thing complained of, although an act which would otherwise be actionable, be authorized by statute, then no action will lie in respect of it, if it be the very thing the legislature has authorized. If it be not the very thing authorized or if in exercising the power conferred on it the corporation acts "arbitrarily, carelessly or oppressively" an action against it for the injury occasioned will lie: *Guelph Worsted Spinning Co. v. Guelph*

(1914), 30 O.L.R. 466 (H.C.); *Chadwick v. City of Toronto* (1914), 32 O.L.R. 111 (C.A.); *Fieldhouse v. City of Toronto* (1918), 43 O.L.R. 491 (C.A.); *Campbell v. Morris* (1925), 54 O.L.R. 358 (C.A.); *Stevens v. Canadian Pacific Ry.* (1913), 15 Can. Ry. Cas. 28 (Ont. C.A.); *Leighton v. B.C. Electric Co.* (1914), 18 D.L.R. 505 (B.C. C.A.).

Powers granted to a corporation by charter cannot be delegated or transmitted: *Sandwich Windsor & Amherstburg Ry. v. City of Windsor* (1917), 13 O.W.N. 336 (H.C.), and cases cited; *Lynch v. William Richards Co.* (1907), 38 N.B.R. 160 (C.A.); *South-West River Driving Co. v. Lynch* (1907), 38 N.B.R. 242 (C.A.).

Effect of *ultra vires* Acts

Persons dealing with a corporation must at their peril satisfy themselves as to the existence of the power the corporation seeks to exercise: *Eastern Securities Co. v. City of Sydney*, [1923] 4 D.L.R. 717 (N.S. T.D.); *Collins v. The Hydro-Electric Commission of Renfrew*, [1948] O.R. 29 (C.A.) (contract, entered into without approval required by statute, a nullity).

An *ultra vires* transaction is void; it cannot be ratified even by the unanimous resolution of all the shareholders and does not give rise to any indebtedness on the part of the corporation: *Ashbury Ry. Carriage & Iron Co. v. Riche* (1875), L.R. 7 H.L. 653; *Sinclair v. Brougham*, [1914] A.C. 398 at 440 (H.L.); *Gnaedinger & Sons v. Turtleford Grain Growers Co-Operative Assn. Ltd.* (1922), 63 D.L.R. 498 (Sask. C.A.); *In re Allan Grain Growers' Co-operative Association, Ex. parte Robinson, Little & Co.* (1922), 65 D.L.R. 347 (Sask. K.B.); *Toronto Finance Corp. & Cook v. Banking Service Corp.* (1926), 59 O.L.R. 278 at 283 affd (*sub nom. Banking Service Corp. v. Toronto Finance Corp.*), [1928] A.C. 333 (P.C.).

No judgment based upon an *ultra vires* contract, whether by consent, by way of settlement, or by default, can be sustained unless it embodies a decision of the court on the issue of *ultra vires* or a compromise of that issue: *Great North-West Central Ry. v. Charlebois*, [1899] A.C. 114 (P.C.); *In re Jon Beauforte (London) Ltd.*, [1953] 1 Ch. 131. See also *Re New Zealand Land Co., Jackson's Case* (1888), 6 N.Z.L.R. 549 (S.C.); *Hughes v. Northern Electric and Manufacturing Co.* (1915), 50 S.C.R. 626 (judgment in a foreclosure action was based on *ultra vires* mortgage); *Dominion Dry Goods Co. v. Klotz*, [1923] 4 D.L.R. 197 (Sask. C.A.) (default judgment on *ultra vires* purchase of goods set aside).

A corporation will not be estopped by deed or otherwise from showing that the act which it purports to have done, or the contract which it is alleged to have made, was beyond its corporate powers, and is, therefore, a nullity as regards the corporation: *Baroness Wenlock v. River Dee Co.* (1883), 36 Ch. D. 675n. (C.A.); affd (1885), 10 App. Cas. 354 (H.L.); *Ex parte Watson* (1888), 21 Q.B.D. 301 at 302 (C.A.). Persons who deal with the corporation cannot hold it liable for an attempted exercise of powers which it does not possess: *Balfour v. Ernest* (1859), 5 C.B.N.S. 601 (C.B.); *Mahony v. East Holyford Mining Co.* (1875), L.R. 7 H.L. 869. This principle does not apply, however, where the act in question is not outside of the powers of the corporation altogether, but is one which has been performed without the observance of some formality which is a mere matter of internal management: *County of Gloucester Bank v. Rudry Co.*, [1895] 1 Ch. 629 (C.A.); *Mahony v. East Holyford Mining Co.*, *supra*, and *Royal British Bank v. Turquand* (1855), 5 E. & B. 248, affd 6 E. & B. 327 (Ex. Ch.). In such a case it will be assumed that the necessary requirements have been observed: *Colonial Bank of Australasia v. Willan* (1874), L.R. 5 P.C. 417, and the cases just cited above, and it is not incumbent on the person dealing with the corporation to ascertain that all its proceedings have been regular: ibid. This rule was applied in a decision upholding a sale of mining lands by directors: *Herrmann v. Canadian Nickel Co.* (1929), 64 O.L.R. 190 (C.A.), and see the authorities there cited and discussed. A completed transfer of shares to a corporation will not be set aside as against strangers as a nullity, where the corporation has the power under its memorandum to acquire such shares and the provisions of the governing Act, which have not been complied with, do not make the transaction unlawful: *Pacific Berry Growers Ltd. v. Western Packing Corp.*, [1929] 1 D.L.R. 814 (B.C. S.C.).

A corporation is bound by a contract for the purchase of goods where such purchase is *intra vires* even though the seller may have notice that the goods have been purchased for a purpose which is *ultra vires* of the corporation: *Re Contract Corp.* (1869), L.R. 8 Eq. 14.

An *ultra vires* transaction may be set aside in an action brought by the corporation: *Toronto Finance Corp. Ltd. & Cook v. Banking Service Corp.*, [1928] A.C. 333 (P.C.) or by the trustee in bankruptcy: *Trustee of the Property of C. E. Plain Ltd. v. Kenley & Royal Trust Co.*, [1931] O.R. 75 (C.A.); and a shareholder suing on behalf of himself and others may maintain an action to restrain or set aside an *ultra vires* transaction (see the notes to Chapter 16); but an ordinary creditor at common law had no status to maintain such an action: *The Michigan Central Ry. v. Wealleans* (1895), 24 S.C.R. 309 at 319; *Mills v. Northern Ry. of Buenos Ayres* (1870), L.R. 5 Ch. App. 621 at 628; *Lawrence v. West Somerset Mineral Ry. Co.*, [1918] 2 Ch. 250 (holder of debenture stock not constituting a charge on the assets); *International Mercantile Marine Co. v. Oceanic Steam Navigation Co.* (1938), 78 Sol. Jo. 350 (unpaid vendors).

While the issue of *ultra vires* will rarely arise where the corporation is governed solely by business corporations legislation, it is worth noting that the remedial provisions of the federal Act may now allow creditors standing to maintain an action to restrain or set aside an *ultra vires* transaction. Section 239 permits a "complainant" to apply to a court for leave to bring an action in the name of and on behalf of the corporation. Section 238 defines complainant as including "proper persons". Thus, a court might, in its discretion, grant standing to creditors. For a detailed discussion of the standing question see Chapter 16.

A bona fide transaction impeachable only on the ground of being *ultra vires* will be set aside only on terms that both parties will be restored to their original rights: *Re Irish Provident Assurance Co.*, [1913] 1 I.R. 352.

Moneys received from a corporation on an *ultra vires* claim may be directed to be repaid with interest, but there is no fixed rule on this point; and where directors have been guilty of delay in seeking to recover such moneys and of continuing to act under what they must have known to be an invalid resolution, the court only required the recipients to pay back the moneys actually received without interest: *Pacific Coast Coal Mines Ltd. v. Arbuthnot* (1921), 56 D.L.R. 452 (P.C.). Where goods have been acquired by a corporation under an *ultra vires* contract, the property in the goods remains in the vendor and the corporation will be ordered to return them; if the corporation has sold some of the goods to purchasers the corporation must account to the vendor for the amount so received: *Gnaedinger & Sons v. Turtleford Grain Growers Co-Operative Assn Ltd.* (1922), 63 D.L.R. 498 at 504 (Sask. C.A.); and see *Dominion Dry Goods Co. v. Klotz*, [1923] 4 D.L.R. 197 (Sask. C.A.). But in *Trades Hall Co. v. Erie Tobacco Co.* (1916), 29 D.L.R. 779 where goods had got into the possession of a corporation under an *ultra vires* contract and had been sold by it to others, the Court of Appeal in Manitoba held that the corporation must return the goods or pay their value. Cameron J.A. was of opinion that the property in the goods passed to the purchaser. See further *Sinclair v. Brougham*, [1914] A.C. 398 at 440 (H.L.). Moneys paid by the insured to an insurance corporation on a policy which the corporation had no power to issue can be recovered in an action for money had and received: *Hooper Grain Co. v. Colonial Assurance Co.*, [1917] 1 W.W.R. 1226 (Man. K.B.) and cases cited. See also *Niagara Public School Board (Section 4) v. Queenston Branch Women's Institute* (1926), 59 O.L.R. 213 (H.C.); *County of Halton v. Township of Trafalgar* (1927), 61 O.L.R. 45 (H.C.); *Re General Finance Corp. (Yarmouth)*, [1941] 1 D.L.R. 746 (N.S. T.D.) (bona fide holders of profit-sharing certificates, issued in the course of carrying on a loan business expressly prohibited and *ultra vires*, held to be entitled to repayment of the moneys paid to corporation therefor, in priority to preference shareholders in the winding-up of the corporation).

A guarantor of the due performance by a corporation of a contract, entered into in good faith and in the belief that it was valid, will be liable under the guarantee when the contract is merely *ultra vires* and the transaction is not illegal or *malum in se*: *Garrard v. James*, [1925] 1 Ch. 616 (Ch. D.); but see *MacDonald-Crawford Ltd. v. Burns*, [1924] 2 D.L.R. 977 (Sask. C.A.).

Where the corporation had no authority to carry on the operation of a store and the manager, without objection from the corporation, carried on a store on the premises of the corporation in its interests, he was not accountable for the profits: *Weitzen Land & Agricultural Co. v. Winter* (1914), 17 D.L.R. 750 (Sask. T.D.).

In the case of an *ultra vires* borrowing by a corporation the lender has no right of action against the corporation in respect of the contract of loan itself. Nor can he enforce any securities given for such loan. However, he does have certain rights in respect of the money received by the corporation under the transaction. If the money has not been disposed of by the corporation or has been used to acquire an asset that can be identified he has a right to claim the money or the particular asset. Further, if the money advanced has been expended in paying the lawful enforceable debts of the corporation, he is entitled to stand in the shoes of the creditors so paid off, but he is not entitled to the benefit of such securities as the creditors may have held in respect of their debts:

Blackburn Building Society v. Cunliffe, Brooks & Co. (1882), 22 Ch. D. 61 (C.A.), affd (1884), 9 App. Cas. 857 (H.L.); *Sinclair v. Brougham*, [1914] A.C. 398 at 413-414 (P.C.); *Royal Bank v. B.C. Accident* (1917), 35 D.L.R. 650 (B.C. C.A.); *McKinnon v. Campbell River Lumber Co.* (1922), 67 D.L.R. 528 (B.C. C.A.); *Smith v. Elrose Rural Telephone Co.*, [1928] 3 D.L.R. 51 (Sask. K.B.); *Douglas v. Maritime United Farmers' Co-op. Ltd.*, [1928] 3 D.L.R. 166 (N.B. C.A.); *In re Airedale Co-operative Worsted Manufacturing Society Ltd.*, [1933] 1 Ch. 639 (lender entitled to rank as creditor in the winding-up of the borrower). It is immaterial whether the debts were or were not in existence at the time of the advance: *Baroness Wenlock v. River Dee* (1887), 19 Q.B.D. 155 (C.A.).

Particular powers conferred by the Act or implied by law

The notes under this heading are to be read bearing in mind the wide powers given by the federal Act or which under *Bonanza Creek Gold Mining Co. v. The King* and *Edwards v. Blackmore*, *supra*, are ascribed to corporations incorporated by letters patent.

To give guarantees

In *Williams Machinery Co. v. Crawford Tug Co.* (1908), 16 O.L.R. 245 (Div. Ct.), it was held that a tug corporation had no implied power to guarantee the price of a boiler to be purchased for a tug owned by one of its employees; see also *Carter v. Columbia Bitulithic Co.* (1914), 18 D.L.R. 520 (B.C. C.A.) but see *A. E. Thomas, Ltd. v. Standard Bank* (1910), 1 O.W.N. 379 (C.P.) and 548 (Ont. C.A.), where under the circumstances in question the power to guarantee was implied. So also in *National Land & Loan Co. v. Rat Portage Lumber Co.* (1917), 36 D.L.R. 97 (Man. K.B.) a lumber corporation having power to sell land was held to have an implied power to give a guarantee against default of the purchaser on an assignment of an agreement for the sale of land.

In *Union Bank of Canada v. McKillop & Sons Ltd.* (1914), 30 O.L.R. 87 (C.A.), affd (1915), 51 S.C.R. 518, the defendant was a corporation incorporated under *The Ontario Companies Act*, R.S.O. 1897, c. 191, with power to buy, sell and deal in timber and lumber, operate saw mills, etc. The giving of a guarantee for a debt of a corporation whose sole connection with the guarantor was that of a customer was held to be *ultra vires.*

See also *Bank of Ottawa v. Hamilton Stove & Heater Co.* (1918), 44 O.L.R. 93 (H.C.); *Abbotsford Lumber Co. v. Stevenson*, [1925] 2 D.L.R. 1114 (B.C. S.C.), affd [1925] 4 D.L.R. 560 (B.C. C.A.); *Royal Bank of Canada v. Fleming*, [1933] O.R. 601 (C.A.); and *Re Jacques Furniture Co., Canadian Radio Corp. v. The Trustee*, [1933] O.W.N. 170 (C.A.); *Ontario Marble Co. v. Creative Memorials Ltd.* (1963), 42 W.W.R. 315 (Sask. Q.B.), affd 48 W.W.R. 239 (Sask. C.A.).

In *Export Brewing & Malting Co. v. Dominion Bank*, [1934] O.R. 560 (C.A.); revd [1937] 3 D.L.R. 513 (P.C.) the transaction attacked was not in terms a guarantee but the transfer to a bank of certain bonds, owned by the plaintiff corporation, as additional security for the personal debt of three individuals to the bank. In the Court of Appeal, Latchford C.J., Masten and Fisher JJ.A. held that under the provisions of the federal Act of 1927, similar to but not identical with subparagraphs (d) and (q) of s. 14(1) of the former Act and a provision (corresponding to subparagraph (k)) which in the 1927 Act read "to lend money to customers and others having dealings with the corporation and to guarantee the performance of contracts by any such persons," and the express powers of the corporation's charter which repeated the statutory provisions, the company was empowered in proper circumstances to become surety for the debt of a third party. The decision of the Judicial Committee of the Privy Council, reversing the decision of the Court of Appeal and holding that the corporation was entitled to the return of the bonds, proceeded on the grounds that the transaction was not for the corporation's benefit, but was detrimental to its interests; that the corporation (acting through its directors) was purporting to apply its property for the benefit of those directors; that the bank was not in the position of having no notice of anything extraordinary being done and that, in the absence of confirmation by the shareholders in general meeting, the transaction could not stand. The Judicial Committee of the Privy Council expressly refrained from deciding or expressing any view as to whether the transaction was *intra vires.*

In view of the above decisions it would appear that, where a statutory provision or provision in the letters patent or memorandum is relied upon to support a contract of guarantee, the relationship between the guarantor corporation and the corporation or person whose debt is guaranteed may be of vital importance. While the requirement of a prior or contemporaneous agreement of the type prescribed by the statute or in the charter laid down by Macdonald C.J.A. in *Abbotsford Lumber Co. v. Stevenson*, [1925] 4 D.L.R. 560 (B.C. C.A.) has not been adopted in the Ontario decisions, it would no doubt be prudent to have such an agreement entered into wherever possible, at any rate where co-operation, union of interests or other like arrangements are not established by, or must necessarily be inferred from, previous dealings or the relationship between the guarantor and the person whose debt is guaranteed. It would also appear that, where a statutory provision or provision in the letters patent or memorandum such as that contained in subparagraph (q) of s. 14(1) of the former Act is relied on then, unless shares, debentures or other obligations of the corporation whose debt is guaranteed are held by the guarantor corporation, pre-existing business relations are requisite. See also the comment on s. 44 below in Chapter 5.

The foregoing is subject to the application of the principle, above discussed, laid down in *Bonanza Creek Gold Mining Co. v. The King*, [1916] 1 A.C. 566 (P.C.) and subsequent cases, particularly *Edwards v. Blackmore* (1918), 42 O.L.R. 105 (C.A.) in the case of corporations incorporated by letters patent. See also *In re International Piano Co.; Ex parte Liquidation of Manufacturers' Finance Corp.* (1928), 10 C.B.R. 518 (Ont. S.C.).

To purchase shares of other corporations

There is nothing at common law to prevent one trading corporation from taking or accepting shares in another trading corporation: *In re Barned's Banking Co.; Ex parte Contract Corp.* (1867), L.R. 3 Ch. App. 105 at 113; *Royal Bank of India's Case* (1869), L.R. 4 Ch. App. 252 at 257; *McCausland v. Hill* (1897), 23 O.A.R. 738 at 752 (C.A.).

With regard to semi-public corporations it is well settled that they cannot, without express statutory authority, purchase, take or deal in the shares of other corporations: *Great Eastern Ry. v. Turner* (1872), L.R. 8 Ch. App. 149; *Great Western Ry. v. Metropolitan Ry.* (1863), 32 L.J. Ch. 382.

As to whether a corporation may accept shares owned by a person indebted to it as a compromise for a debt if not taken with the intention of retaining them as an investment, see *Re Lands Allotment Co.*, [1894] 1 Ch. 616 (C.A.); *Canada Life Assurance Co. v. Peel General Manufacturing Co.* (1879), 26 Gr. 477 (Ont. Ch.).

If a corporation has no power to purchase shares in another corporation it will be liable to repay money obtained through a representation by its agent that it has such power: *Whaley v. O'Grady* (1912), 4 D.L.R. 485 (Man. C.A.).

An instructive case on the question of the power of a corporation to invest in the shares of other corporations is *Re Atlas Loan Co.; Elgin Loan Co.'s Claim* (1905), 9 O.L.R. 250 (Ont. C.P.). The facts of this case were as follows: The Elgin Loan Company had a large savings account with the Atlas Loan Company and in order to enable the Atlas Loan Company to purchase a number of shares of a coal corporation, it was arranged that the Elgin Loan Company should lend the Atlas Loan Company $55,000, the amount required to purchase such shares, on the security of a debenture of the Atlas Loan Company for that amount; the Atlas Loan Company had power to invest in shares but the Elgin Loan Company did not; under the arrangement the Elgin Loan Company was to be permitted to call in the loan whenever it saw fit and was also to hold the shares purchased as collateral security and was to be paid five per cent interest on the money advanced, or at its option take the dividends on the shares, and was to receive one-half the difference between the purchase price and the selling price when the shares were sold. It was held by Meredith C.J. that the transaction was a bona fide one—not merely a device to enable the Elgin Loan Company to invest in shares—and the Elgin Loan Company was entitled, on the winding-up of the Atlas Loan Company, to rank as a creditor.

The provisions of the governing statute may prohibit the use by a corporation of its funds in the purchase of shares of any other corporation unless certain formalities, such as the enactment of a by-law and its approval by the shareholders, are observed. Such a provision merely imposes a restriction on the exercise of the power in the case of corporations which possess it, that is, they may not use their funds in the purchase of shares of other corporations without complying with the statutory requirement. It would appear that if shares have been acquired without the use of the corporation's funds for that purpose, the holding of such shares would be legal: *Victoria Montreal Fire Insurance Co. v. Strome* (1905), 15 Man. R. 645 (C.A.) (per Dubuc C.J.).

If the corporation has power by its letters patent to acquire shares, it will be liable upon a subscription for shares in another corporation even though no by-law as required by the governing Act has been passed, when the other corporation had no knowledge of the non-existence of the by-law: *Foley v. Barber* (1909), 1 O.W.N. 40 (Ch.); affd at 1029 (C.A.).

In the following special circumstances the transaction was held not to fall within the purview of a statutory restriction of the nature above indicated. A corporation purchased lands, for which, in lieu of cash, it transferred to the vendor shares in another corporation. The corporation agreed to take the shares back and pay cash at a specified rate per share for so many shares as the vendor required the corporation to take back: *Grant v. Dominion Loose Leaf Co.* (1925), 56 O.L.R. 508 (C.A.).

To borrow money and to mortgage

The power to borrow money implies the power to mortgage. Directors of a corporation incorporated under the Act of 1852, c. 2 (R.S. N.S., (3d) 750) had power to mortgage the property of the corporation to discharge obligations for which the shareholders were liable and would continue personally liable if there was no mortgage: *In re Nash Brick & Pottery Mfg. Co.* (1873), 9 N.S.R. 254 (T.D.).

Where the terms upon which money is borrowed or a mortgage given by a corporation are not illegal it is within its powers to pay a bonus for the accommodation obtained: *Farrell v. Caribou Gold Mining Co.* (1897), 30 N.S.R. 199 (C.A.).

When one of the objects for which the corporation is incorporated is to acquire, sell and dispose of lands of a certain description the corporation has power to give a mortgage as security for purchase money and to give a covenant therein to pay such purchase money: *Sheppard v. Bonanza Nickel Mining Co. of Sudbury* (1895), 25 O.R. 305 (Ch.); *Kirkpatrick v. Cornwall Electric Street Ry.* (1901), 2 O.L.R. 113 (C.A.). Osler J.A. said at p. 117:

> ... there is nothing in the Act which expressly or by implication restricts the exercise of the power to its then existing property. In this respect it seems to me that the company is invested with as large powers to mortgage its ordinary after acquired property as belong to a natural person.

See also *Re Perth Flax & Cordage Co.* (1909), 13 O.W.R. 1140 (Ch.), where a mortgage of a corporation's after acquired choses in action was held *intra vires*.

In *Eisenberg v. Bank of Nova Scotia*, [1965] S.C.R. 681 assets of the corporation were pledged to secure a loan made by the bank to a third party. There was no meeting of the board of directors to authorize the transaction and the person signing as secretary was in fact not an officer of the corporation. On the insolvency of the corporation, in an action to recover the proceeds of the assets from the bank, it was held that the transactions had been approved by the sole beneficial owner of the shares of the corporation and where a matter was *intra vires* of the corporation, and there was no fraud, the corporation could not be heard to deny a transaction to which all the shareholders had given assent, even when the assent was given in an informal manner or by conduct as distinguished from a formal resolution at a duly convened meeting of the board.

See also *Central and Eastern Trust Co. v. Irving Oil Ltd.*, [1980] 2 S.C.R. 29; *Re Newfoundland Brokerage Ltd.* (1978), 53 A.P.R. 408 (Nfld. T.D.); and *Re Sparkes v. Sparkes* (1980), 119 D.L.R. (3d) 330 (Nfld. T.D.).

To pay interest

In an action for the interest on bonds issued by a corporation under 37 Vict. c. 57 (Que.), the defendants pleaded that the legislature could not enact a law authorizing the corporation to enter into any contract binding on it by which a rate of interest higher than six per cent was to be paid, and the coupon being at the rate of seven per cent the obligation was void, or at most good only for six per cent. It was held, however, that the corporation being authorized to borrow could legally agree to pay seven per cent or such other rate as might be specially agreed upon: *Macdougall v. Montreal Warehousing Co.* (1880), 3 L.N. 64.

To issue negotiable instruments

A power to issue negotiable instruments will be readily implied in the case of a trading corporation. See *Re Peruvian Railways* (1867), L.R. 2 Ch. App. 617; *Kerr v. University Press Ltd.*, [1923] 2 W.W.R. 187 (Sask. C.A.).

A non-trading corporation, unless its instrument of incorporation expressly or by clear implication confers the power, has no power to incur liability on a bill of exchange or promissory note: *Canadian Bank of Commerce v. Cudworth Rural Telephone Co.*, [1923] S.C.R. 618. However, corporations without share capital which are subject to Part II of the *Canada Corporations Act* have such power, s. 14(1)(l) being made applicable to such corporations by s. 147 of that Act.

To lend money

Where the governing statute does not contain an express provision, the power to loan is a common power to be inserted in the memorandum and its omission from the memorandum of a trading corporation is significant. Thus, where there was no express power to loan it was held that a corporation incorporated to carry on a general contracting business had no implied power to make a loan to another corporation, and that a chattel mortgage taken therefor was invalid: *Columbia Bitulithic Co. v. Vancouver Lumber Co.* (1915), 21 D.L.R. 91 (B.C. C.A.). But a trading corporation can take chattel mortgages to protect credits which it has extended and may give a note to the creditor of the mortgagor to protect its own security: *Vancouver Engineering Works v. Columbia Bitulithic Co.* (1914), 16 D.L.R. 841 (B.C. S.C.). In the case of a corporation incorporated by memorandum and articles, the memorandum did not expressly authorize the lending of money, but included among the objects the doing of such things as were incidental or conducive to the attainment of the other objects; having regard to the terms of the articles, it was held that a loan to a faithful servant of the corporation was not *ultra vires*: *Rainford v. James Keith & Blackman Co.*, [1905] 2 Ch. 147 at 162 (C.A.).

Corporations other than banks may validly lend at any stipulated rate of interest: *Royal Canadian Insurance Co. v. Montreal Warehousing Co.* (1880), 3 L.N. 155; *McHugh v. Union Bank of Canada*, [1913] A.C. 299 (P.C.).

To acquire, hold and dispose of land

Apart from statutory provisions, the following cases illustrate the law:

1. The purchase of undivided interests or shares in the lands of a syndicate is within the specific provisions of a power enabling the corporation to purchase lands or interests therein: *Re W. N. McEachren & Sons Ltd.*, [1933] O.R. 349 (C.A.).
2. A corporation empowered to hold land for a definite purpose only may take a conveyance of land for another purpose, the Crown alone can take advantage of the disability, and the corporation can convey its defeasible title: *Becher v. Woods* (1865), 16 U.C.C.P. 29; *McDiarmid v. Hughes* (1888), 16 O.R. 570 (Q.B.). So also if a corporation has power to hold land for a definite period only, without any provision as to reverter, and holds beyond that period, the Crown alone can take advantage of it: *McDiarmid v. Hughes, supra.*
3. An insurance corporation had power to hold real estate for the immediate accommodation of the corporation "or such as shall have been bona fide mortgaged to it by way of security, or conveyed to it in satisfaction of debts previously contracted in the course of its dealing." It also had power to invest its funds in mortgages of real estate. The corporation sold a vessel and took from its vendee mortgages on real estate for securing the purchase money. It was held that this transaction was *intra vires: The Western Assurance Co. v. Taylor* (1862), 9 Gr. 471 (U.C. Ch.).
4. Only the Crown can take advantage of the forfeiture which a corporation incurs by holding land when not empowered to do so: *McDiarmid v. Hughes, supra.*
5. A bona fide agreement to sell is sufficient to prevent a forfeiture: *London & Canadian Loan & Agency Co. v. Graham* (1888), 16 O.R. 329 (Ch.).
6. A corporation incorporated by private Act, having obtained an indefeasible title to real property under the *Land Registry Act* for purposes not authorized by the incorporating Act, may enter into an agreement for sale of the property and sue to recover arrears of payments due thereon: *Creelman v. Hudson Bay Insurance Co.* (1919), 48 D.L.R. 234 (P.C.).
7. A power to sell any lands (short of disposing of the whole undertaking) may be implied from a power to purchase: *Brown v. Moore* (1921), 62 S.C.R. 487; *In re Kingsbury Collieries Ltd. & Moore's Contract*, [1907] 2 Ch. 259. The power to dispose of lands carries with it the power to lease: *Dominion Cotton Mills Co. v. Amyot*, [1912] A.C. 546 (P.C.).
8. In the case of a semi-public corporation created by special Act of Parliament the power to dispose of its property is limited by the rule that, apart from authority expressly given or appearing by necessary implication from its incorporating Act, such a corporation may not dispose of its property if by such disposition it should disable itself from carrying out its objects (in

which the public have an interest) for which its special powers were conferred upon it: *Esquimalt Waterworks Co. v. City of Victoria* (1906), 12 B.C.R. 302 at 318 (C.A.). Where it is the duty of a corporation to hold lands on trusts declared by statute, it cannot get rid of such duty by reincorporating under s. 12 of The Companies Act (Ontario): *Smith v. Humbervale Cemetery Co.* (1915), 33 O.L.R. 452 (C.A.).

9. A corporation formed to manage works in which the public have an interest may not assign all its rights and powers absolutely: *A.G. v. The Niagara Falls International Bridge Co.* (1873), 20 Gr. 34 (Ont. Ch.); but a railway corporation may lease a portion of its road to another corporation and assign all its rights and privileges as to the portion so leased: *Michigan Central Ry. Co. v. Wealleans* (1894), 24 S.C.R. 309; but see *Hinckley v. Gildersleeve* (1872), 19 Gr. 212 (Ont. Ch.), and see also *Montreal Telegraph Co. v. Law* (1883), 27 L.C. Jurist 257 at 277.
10. If a corporation has the power to deal with real property, it may enter into any reasonable covenant usually found in an instrument appropriate to the transaction: *Real Estate Investment Co. v. The Metropolitan Building Society* (1883), 3 O.R. 476 at 492 (C.P.) (covenant that assigned mortgages were valid charges upon the land).

To sell assets and undertaking

A power by statute or charter purporting to authorize a corporation to sell its undertaking does not, without express words, give a power to sell for shares in another corporation: *Hill v. Starr Manufacturing Co.* (1913), 15 D.L.R. 146 (N.S. C.A.). See also *McGregor v. St. Croix Lumber Co.* (1913), 8 D.L.R. 876 at 880 (N.S. T.D.). Where such power exists it is not destroyed by liquidation; the effect of liquidation is to make the power subject to the approval of the court and the superior rights of the creditors: *Re Bailey Cobalt Mines Ltd.* (1920), 47 O.L.R. 13 (C.A.).

A corporation, under the power to sell and dispose of real and personal property, can dispose of the same as distinguished from its undertaking: *Ritchie v. Vermillion Mining Co.* (1901), 1 O.L.R. 654, affd (1902), 4 O.L.R. 588 (C.A.) (all the mines of a mining corporation); *Dominion Cotton Mills Ltd. v. Amyot*, [1912] A.C. 546 (P.C.) (all the mills of a manufacturing corporation); *Wilson v. Miers* (1861), 10 C.B.N.S. 348 (all the ships of a shipping corporation); but see *Stanishewski v. Tkachuk*, [1955] O.R. 667 (H.C.), where a corporation purported, without consideration, to transfer all of its assets to another corporation and this was held to be *ultra vires.*

As regards the manner in which the power to sell the assets and undertaking may be exercised and the statutory formalities required to be observed in certain jurisdictions, see the notes under the heading "Sale of assets and undertaking," *infra.*

To purchase the assets of another corporation

The power to buy the assets of another corporation is not taken away by a prohibition against leasing, amalgamating or selling out to any other corporation: *Corporation of the City of Toronto v. Toronto Electric Light Co.* (1905), 10 O.L.R. 621 (C.A.).

The power to purchase assets cannot be used to give away the corporation's own assets for the special benefit of the directors. Thus, where a partnership was indebted to its bankers and the members of the partnership procured a purchase of certain of the partnership assets to be made by a corporation, of which the members were the directors, by the action of nominees added to the board for that purpose, as part of a scheme to take the assets of the corporation out of its treasury and apply them to reduce the indebtedness of the partnership, without the sanction of the shareholders, the transaction was set aside. Although there was no suggestion of impropriety in the action of the bankers it was held that they had sufficient knowledge to put them on enquiry and that the moneys paid to them could be recovered by the corporation: *McGill Shipbuilding & Transportation Co. v. Canadian Bank of Commerce*, [1925] 2 D.L.R. 1183 (N.S. C.A.).

To act as agent

A trading corporation, as incidental to the express powers conferred by the charter, has power to take an assignment of a chose in action and collect it by suit for the benefit of an assignor: *Stobart v. Forbes* (1900), 13 Man. R. 184 (K.B.).

To maintain an action in another jurisdiction

Although a corporation incorporated under the Companies Act of Quebec by letters patent issued under the Great Seal of that province did not carry on business in New Brunswick, it had the same right as a natural person to maintain an action in that jurisdiction, there being no provincial law prohibiting such a corporation from suing in New Brunswick: *Aetna Factors Corp. v. Breau* (1959), 15 D.L.R. (2d) 326 (N.B. C.A.). If the corporate status of a party is placed in issue then its incorporation must be proved; ordinarily it would be assumed to be incorporated unless it is challenged: see *International Harvester Credit Corp. v. Knight* (1975), 19 N.B.R. (2d) 620 (Co. Ct.). See also *Browning-Ferris Industries Inc. v. Browning-Ferris Industries Inc.*, [1976] 3 W.W.R. 759 (B.C. S.C.).

It may be noted that under a number of the Provincial Acts, an extraprovincial corporation, unless registered in the Province, is declared to be unable to maintain an action in the courts as a contract made in the Province.

Right of provinces to pass legislation affecting federal corporations

It is established that provincial legislatures may to a certain extent enact laws for the regulation, taxation, and licensing of federal corporations. The question of the legality of the various provisions now in force in the different provinces is beyond the scope of this note in which some of the decisions only and the principles therein laid down are referred to. See also the notes under the heading "Federal and provincial jurisdiction with respect to corporations" in Chapter 2. Thus, a federal corporation is bound by provincial laws of general application, for example, the *Municipal Act*. See *Regina v. City of New Westminster* (1965), 55 D.L.R. (2d) 613 (B.C. C.A.); and see *Multiple Access Ltd. v. McCutcheon* (1982), 138 D.L.R. (3d) 1 (S.C.C.) where the insider trading provisions of the *Ontario Securities Act* were held to be valid so far as a federal incorporated corporation was concerned and see *Churchill Falls (Labrador) Corp. v. A.G. Nfld.* (1984), 8 D.L.R. (4th) 1 (S.C.C.) where the province of Newfoundland was held to be entitled to pass legislation expropriating a corporation's assets even if that corporation were federally incorporated. The Supreme Court of Canada held that, while it was clear that a province could not legislate to impair or destroy the essential status and capacities of a federal corporation, a federal corporation was subject to all laws within the province and the mere deprivation of the business conducted by the corporation did not affect the corporate being of the corporation itself. See also *Wood v. Canadian Soccer Association*, (1984) 5 C.H.R.R. D/2024 (Can. Human Rights Tribunal); and *C.T.C.U.Q. v. Canada*, [1988] R.L. 146 (Que. C.A.).

Legislation excluding federal corporations—because not registered or licensed (where registration or a licence may be refused)—from resorting to the provincial courts to enforce contracts made in pursuance of the powers granted by their charter is *ultra vires: John Deere Plow Co. v. Wharton*, [1915] A.C. 330 (P.C.); *Linde Canadian Refrigerator Co. v. Saskatchewan Creamery Co.* (1915), 51 S.C.R. 400 at 403; and see *Great West Saddlery v. The King*, [1921] 2 A.C. 91 (P.C.). A province cannot interfere with the status and corporate capacity of a federal corporation insofar as that status and capacity carries with it powers conferred by Parliament to carry on business in every part of Canada: *John Deere Plow Co. v. Wharton, supra*. See also *B.C. Power Corp. v. A.G. B.C.* (1963), 44 W.W.R. 65 (B.C. S.C.) which was overruled in *Churchill Falls (Labrador) Corp. v. A.G. Newfoundland, supra*. On the other hand, Viscount Haldane L.C. said at *John Deere Plow Company* pp. 342, 343:

> It is true that even when a company has been incorporated by the Dominion Government with powers to trade, it is not the less subject to provincial laws of general application enacted under the powers conferred by s. 92. Thus, notwithstanding that a Dominion company has capacity to hold land, it cannot refuse to obey the statutes of the province as to mortmain (*Colonial Building & Investment Association v. A.G. of Quebec*, 9 App. Cas. 157 at 164); or escape the payment of taxes, even though these may assume the form of requiring, as the method of raising a revenue, a license to trade which affects a Dominion company in common with other corporations (*Bank of Toronto v. Lambe*, 12 App. Cas. 575). Again, such a company is subject to the powers of the Province relating to property and civil rights under s. 92 for the regulation of contracts generally: *Citizens Insurance Co. v. Parsons* (1881), 7 App. Cas. 96.

Their Lordships refrained from stating any general principles beyond observing that it might be competent to a legislature "to pass laws applying to companies without distinction, and requiring those that were not incorporated within the Province to register for certain limited purposes, such as the furnishing of information"; also "to enact that any company which had not an office and assets within the Province should, under a statute of general application regulating procedure, give security for costs".

Great West Saddlery Co. v. The King.

The legislation of the provinces of Ontario, Manitoba and Saskatchewan relating to extraprovincial corporations was reviewed by the Judicial Committee of the Privy Council in *Great West Saddlery Co. v. The King*, [1921] 2 A.C. 91. The main question was whether the provinces of Ontario, Manitoba and Saskatchewan had power to impose on federal corporations the obligation to obtain a licence from the provincial government as a condition of the exercise in these provinces respectively of the powers conferred upon them by Parliament. Viscount Haldane, at p. 120, said:

> If the condition of taking out a license had been introduced, not so as to affect the status of the Dominion company, but simply for the purpose of obtaining payment of a direct tax for Provincial purposes, or of securing the observance of some restriction as to contracts to be observed by the public generally in the Province, or of causing the doing, by that public generally, of some act of a purely local character only under license, their Lordships would, for reasons already given, have been prepared to regard the condition as one which it was within the power of the Province to impose. Even then it would have been requisite to see, as was pointed out by Lord Herschell in delivering the judgment of the Judicial Committee in the *Brewers and Maltsters* case ([1897] A.C. 231 at 237 (P.C.)), that the Provincial Legislature was not, under the guise of imposing such direct taxation in the form of which he was speaking as being within their power, really doing something else, such as imposing indirect taxation. As to any enquiry in the future whether this or anything analogous has been in substance attempted, their Lordships hold themselves unfettered. If, for example, such a question were to arise hereafter, involving consideration of whether the real effect of the license required by a Provincial law has been to abrogate capacity which it was within the power of the Parliament of Canada to bestow, or whether for a breach of conditions a Provincial Legislature could impose, not an ordinary penalty but one extending to the destruction of the status of the company and its capacity in the Province, nothing that has been here said is intended to prejudice the decision of such a question, should it occur. It is sufficient to observe once more that in such matters what cannot be done directly can no more be effected by indirect methods.

Applying the test laid down in the *John Deere Plow Co.* case (that provincial legislation cannot validly destroy the status and powers conferred on a federal corporation by Act of the Parliament of Canada) to the Ontario *Extra-Provincial Corporations Act* (R.S.O. 1914, c. 179), their Lordships held that the provisions under review could not be regarded as confined only to such limited purpose as would be legitimate and that they were therefore *ultra vires.* Their Lordships took a similar view of the Manitoba and Saskatchewan legislation and held that the Acts of all three provinces, in so far as they purported to apply to the appellant federal corporations, were *ultra vires* and the corporations were not precluded, by reason of not having been licensed or registered, from carrying on business and exercising their powers and were not liable to the penalties prescribed for having done so.

Attorney-General for Manitoba v. Attorney-General for Canada.

The *John Deere Plow Co.* case and the *Great West Saddlery Co.* case were applied in *A.G. Man. v. A.G. Can.*, [1929] A.C. 260 (P.C.), in which it was held that the *Manitoba Sale of Shares Act, 1924* and the *Municipal and Public Utility Board Act, 1926*, were *ultra vires* insofar as they purported to apply to the sale of its own shares by a federal corporation. The legislation under review prohibited corporations, including federal corporations, from selling their shares within the province without the permission of a provincial commissioner or board. Viscount Sumner, delivering the judgment of their Lordships, after summarizing the effect of the legislation, said at p. 265:

> In the case of a company, incorporated for purposes not wholly Provincial and under the powers of legislation of the Dominion of Canada, their Lordships cannot doubt that the Provincial legislation above summarized interferes, directly and not merely incidentally, in material respects and to a substantial extent, with the capacity of the company to raise capital, as and when its directors may deem it necessary to do so in accordance with its articles and the provisions of the Dominion Companies Act, and so derogates from its status and consequent capacities as a Dominion company.

See also *Lukey v. Ruthenian Farmers' Elevator Co.*, [1924] S.C.R. 56; *R. v. Henderson, Ex. parte Queen* (1924), 51 N.B.R. 346 (C.A.).

Re Royalite Oil Co.

The above and earlier cases were reviewed in *Re Royalite Oil Co.*, [1931] 2 D.L.R. 418 (Alta. C.A.), where Harvey C.J.A. delivering the judgment of the court as to whether certain provisions of the Alberta Companies Act were applicable to a federal corporation, held that:

(1) provincial requirements for payment of fees and furnishing information by statements and returns are justified if reasonable and uniform;
(2) a requirement calling for the furnishing upon an application for registration of "such other information as the Registrar may require", involving the possibility of such information being required as the company may not be able or should not be asked to furnish, and registration being dependent upon the furnishing of all information demanded, cannot apply to a federal company;
(3) a requirement that the company is to display its name prominently at its place of business in the province is valid, but the further requirement that the name of the company should appear in notices, advertisements, official publications, bills of exchange and other documents is to be interpreted as being intended to apply only within the province; and
(4) a table of fees payable on registration that is not in itself objectionable will apply to federal corporations if fixed by statute, but not if it is to be fixed by order-in-council, because the fees might be so increased as to make it practically impossible for a federal company to carry on its business in the province.

It was also held that the requirements in respect of the filing of a prospectus inviting subscriptions in the province and the information to be given offended against the principle laid down in *A.G. Man. v. A.G. Can.*, [1929] A.C. 260 (P.C.), *supra*. On this point, however, see *Lymburn v. Mayland*, [1932] A.C. 318 (P.C.), *infra*.

Lymburn v. Mayland.

A.G. Man. v. A.G. Can. was distinguished in *Lymburn v. Mayland*, [1932] A.C. 318 (P.C.). In that case it was held by the Judicial Committee of the Privy Council that the *Security Frauds Prevention Act, 1930*, of Alberta was *intra vires* and applicable to federal corporations. The Act in effect prevented a corporation from selling its shares except through a registered broker or salesman or unless the corporation itself was registered. Lord Atkin said at pp. 324 and 325:

> There is no reason to doubt that the main object sought to be secured in this part of the Act is to secure that persons who carry on the business of dealing in securities shall be honest and of good repute, and in this way to protect the public from being defrauded. Incidentally the net has been drawn so wide as to cover the issue of shares by a public company, with the result that a company cannot issue its shares to the public unless for that purpose it employs a registered broker or salesman, or unless the company itself is registered. It is said that these provisions so far as they affect Dominion corporations are *ultra vires* according to the principles adopted by this Board in *John Deere Plow Co. v. Wharton*, ([1915] A.C. 330 (P.C.)); *Great West Saddlery Co. v. The King*, ([1921] 2 A.C. 91 (P.C.)); *A.G. Man. v. A.G. Can.*, ([1929] A.C. 260 (P.C.)). In those cases there was a general prohibition to corporations either to trade at all or to issue their capital unless the company was registered. The legislation was held *ultra vires* because the legislative powers of the Province are restricted so that 'the status and power of a Dominion company as such cannot be destroyed' (*John Deere Plow Co.* case (*supra*)) and legislation will be invalid if a Dominion company is 'sterilized in all its functions and activities' or 'its status and essential capacities are impaired in a substantial degree' (*Great West Saddlery Co.* case (*supra*)). It appears to their Lordships impossible to bring this legislation within such a principle. A Dominion company constituted with powers to carry on a particular business is subject to the competent legislation of the Province as to that business and may find its special activities completely paralyzed, as by legislation against drink traffic or by the laws as to holding land. If it is formed to trade in securities there appears no reason why it should not be subject to the competent laws of the Province as to the business of all persons who trade in securities. As to the issue of capital there is no complete prohibition, as in the *Manitoba* case ([1929] A.C. 260 (P.C.)) in 1929; and no reason to suppose that any honest company would have any difficulty in finding registered persons in the Province through whom it could lawfully issue its capital. There is no material upon which their Lordships could find that the functions and activities of a company were sterilized or its status and essential capacities impaired in a substantial degree.

Provincial requirements as to registration or the taking out of a licence

In every province of Canada legislation exists requiring all or certain classes of corporations incorporated in other jurisdictions to become licensed or registered if they carry on business in the province. Certain aspects of such legislation are dealt with in the subheadings which follow.

The constitutional limitations on such legislation, so far as the same is sought to be made applicable to federal corporations, have been discussed above. As applicable to foreign corporations such legislation is within the powers of provincial legislatures: *International Text-Book Co. v. Brown* (1907), 13 O.L.R. 644 (Div. Ct.).

In *International Home Purchasing Contract Co. v. Registrar of Joint Stock Companies* (1913), 9 D.L.R. 297 (Alta. T.D.) it was held that a mandamus would not be granted to compel the Registrar of joint stock companies to register under the Foreign Companies Ordinance (Alta. Ord. 1911, c. 63) a corporation having only a provincial incorporation in another province.

A foreign corporation's failure to procure an extraprovincial licence under the *Ontario Corporations Act, 1953* does not immunize it against suits brought against it in the province; and its corporate existence is not impaired by its failure to procure such a licence, subject to the disability (incapability of maintaining an action in an Ontario court in respect of any contract made in whole or in part in Ontario in the course of carrying on business without a licence) imposed on the corporation by that Act by reason of such failure: *Webpax Ltd. v. Weill*, [1960] O.W.N. 325 (C.A.).

The acts of a licensed extraprovincial corporation using a greater amount of capital than the amount authorized are not invalid unless the licence is suspended or revoked: *Re West & Mullen* (1926), 30 O.W.N. 78 (H.C.).

Where a federal trust corporation has applied for a licence and as a term of receiving it has given a bond, neither the corporation nor the surety can attack the validity of the bond on the ground that the corporation could have done business in the province without a licence: *A.G. Ont. v. Railway Passengers Assurance Co.* (1918), 43 O.L.R. 108 (C.A.).

Carrying on business

What constitutes carrying on business in such a manner as to subject an extraprovincial corporation to local licensing requirements will depend primarily on the specific provisions of the applicable provincial statute.

Sales by travellers may not constitute carrying on business when they act merely as sales agents, have no showroom and carry no stock for the corporation and shipment is made direct to the customer who pays the corporation direct: *Standard Ideal Co. v. Standard Sanitary Manufacturing Co.*, [1911] A.C. 78 at 84 (P.C.); *Heney & Co. v. Birmingham* (1909), 39 N.B.R. 336 (S.C.) (action on guarantee in respect of a sale made by a traveller); and keeping a stock of merchandise in a public warehouse in a municipality does not necessarily involve doing business in the municipality: *City of London v. Watt & Sons* (1893), 22 S.C.R. 300.

A corporation was held to be carrying on business in the province when it had a resident agent although he did not solicit orders but took only those which came to him at his place of business: *Bessemer Gas Engine Co. v. Mills* (1904), 8 O.L.R. 647 (Div. Ct.); and when it had an office in the province:

International Text-Book Co. v. Brown (1907), 13 O.L.R. 644 (Div. Ct.); and when its resident agent displayed samples and accepted orders: *Brewster, Leeds & Co. v. Waldman & Stone Ltd.*, [1953] 4 D.L.R. 732 (Man. C.A.).

Cases decided on the question of carrying on business in a province for the purposes of taxation are often relevant to a question of corporate law.

Merely trading with some person within the province does not constitute doing business therein where no act is done by the corporation within the province. Thus, in *John Deere Plow Co. v. Agnew* (1913), 48 S.C.R. 208, the corporation had made an agreement in Winnipeg with a British Columbia resident under which the latter was given the exclusive right to buy and sell the products of the corporation within a defined area in British Columbia. Under the agreement goods were ordered and delivered f.o.b. a point outside British Columbia and were thereafter to be at the risk of the purchaser; payment was to be made by promissory notes dated at Winnipeg and payable at a place in British Columbia where some of them were signed. It was held that the transaction did not constitute the carrying on of business in the Province of British Columbia within the meaning of the British Columbia Companies Act. At p. 232, Duff J. suggested that a corporation would be subject to the legislation in question only if it had a fixed place of business at which it carried on some part of its own business within the province. This view was adopted in *White v. Donkin* (1914), 16 D.L.R. 446 (B.C. S.C.). In *Firestone Tire & Rubber Co. of Canada v. Commissioner of Income Tax*, [1942] S.C.R. 476 the majority of the court, applying *John Deere Plow Co. v. Agnew, supra*, held that the "distributor's warehouse contract" under consideration was not one of agency but of sale; and that—since the contract called for no act to be done within British Columbia to complete the sale—the manufacturer was not subject to taxation in that province under the *Income Tax Act*, R.S.B.C., 1936, c. 280. See also *The King v. Montreal Telegraph Co.*, [1945] S.C.R. 669.

Place and manner of delivery is sometimes a factor in determining whether or not a corporation carries on business in a province. For examples, see *Empire Cream Separator Co. v. Maritime Dairy Co.* (1907), 38 N.B.R. 309 (C.A.) (delivery of goods and notes therefor in New Brunswick involved carrying on business in New Brunswick although order accepted in Toronto); *Culbert v. McCall Co.* (1911), 40 N.B.R. 385 (C.A.) (passing of title at Toronto of goods shipped to consignee in New Brunswick, who was to pay freight, although in fact the consignor sent the goods by express prepaying the charges for which he was afterwards reimbursed, held to be conclusive as to consignor not carrying on business in New Brunswick); *Standard Fashion v. McLeod* (1914), 17 D.L.R. 403 (Alta. C.A.), followed in *Butterick Publishing Co. v. White & Walker Co.* (1914), 18 D.L.R. 636 (Alta. C.A.) (sale to a representative in Alberta of goods delivered f.o.b. outside the province held not to be carrying on business in Alberta); *Pacific Fruit & Produce Co. v. Dingle & Stewart* (1922), 65 D.L.R. 64 (Man. C.A.) (isolated sale by corporation, having no resident agent or place of business in Manitoba, effected by correspondence through a broker in Winnipeg to a purchaser in Winnipeg, sale being f.o.b. a point outside Manitoba, held not carrying on business in Manitoba); *Brewster, Leeds & Co. v. Waldman & Stone Ltd.*, [1953] 4 D.L.R.

732 (Man. C.A.) (sale effected by a corporation in New York, through its representative in Winnipeg, to a purchaser in Winnipeg held to be carrying on business in Manitoba, even though orders accepted in and goods shipped from New York); *Hickman, Williams & Co. v. J. L. Kerr & Sons Ltd.*, [1955] 1 D.L.R. 735 (Man. Q.B.) (where delivery of goods made and promissory notes therefor signed in Manitoba, business was carried on in Manitoba although orders and notes accepted in Minnesota); *Lainière de Roubaix, S.A. v. Craftsmen Distributors Inc.* (1991), 55 B.C.L.R. (2d) 103 (B.C.C.A.) (where a French corporation shipped yarn from France to the defendant in British Columbia and the defendant had no offices or telephone number in the province, no officers or employees were resident there and the corporation was not registered as an extraprovincial corporation, the corporation was not "carrying on business" in British Columbia within the meaning of the British Columbia Act. The fact that the sale price was in Canadian dollars and payment made by cheques drawn on a British Columbia bank did not transform a business operation in France into one carried on in British Columbia).

In some cases the fact that the transaction was an isolated one has been considered to be important: *Halifax Hotel Co. v. Canadian Fire Engine Co.* (1906), 41 N.S.R. 97 (C.A.); *Pacific Fruit & Produce Co. v. Dingle & Stewart, supra*; *Linde Canadian Refrigerator Co. v. Saskatchewan Creamery Co.* (1915), 51 S.C.R. 400 at 407; *Euclid Avenue Trusts Co. v. Hohs* (1911), 24 O.L.R. 447 (C.A.); *Montreal Trust Co. v. Abitibi Power Co.*, [1937] O.R. 939 (H.C.).

The mere taking of promissory notes has been held not to be of itself carrying on business: *Securities Development Co. of New York v. Brethour* (1911), 3 O.W.N. 250 (Div. Ct.); *Consolidated Investments v. Caswell* (1915), 21 D.L.R. 525 (Man. C.A.); *Ontario Wind Engine & Pump Co. v. Eldred* (1912), 2 D.L.R. 270 (Sask. T.D.); but for the opposite view see *Canadian Bank of Commerce v. Rogers* (1911), 23 O.L.R. 109 at 115 (Div. Ct.).

It has been held in Manitoba that if a foreign corporation enters into contracts with a Manitoba corporation which has no representation outside Manitoba, the contracts must be made in whole or in part in Manitoba with the result that the foreign corporation cannot sue on the contracts in the province unless it is licensed and registered: *Brewster, Leeds & Co. v. Waldman & Stone Ltd.*, [1953] 4 D.L.R. 732 (Man. C.A.); *Hickman, Williams & Co. v. J. L. Kerr & Sons Ltd.*, [1955] 1 D.L.R. 735 (Man. Q.B.).

In Quebec it has been held that a foreign corporation was not doing business by reason of taking subscriptions for capital stock: *In re Adanac Coal Co.* (1926), 7 C.B.R. 731 (Que. C.S.) and for a Saskatchewan decision to a similar effect, see *Canadian Co-op. Co. v. Trauniczek* (1908), 1 Sask. L.R. 143 (T.D.). The contrary was held in Ontario in *Canadian Bank of Commerce v. Rogers* (1911), 23 O.L.R. 109 (Div. Ct.), where notes had been given in payment for shares disposed of by the officers of the corporation in Ontario and negotiated with a bank.

In *Linde Canadian Refrigerator Co. v. Saskatchewan Creamery Co.* (1915), 51 S.C.R. 400, Anglin J. considered that the installation of machinery, sold to a purchaser at a price which includes such work, constitutes carrying on a part of the business of the corporation in the province. In the same case Idington J. expressed the opposite opinion. In *Kominick System Sandstone Brick Machinery Co. v. B.C. Pressed Brick Co.* (1912), 8 D.L.R. 859, the British Columbia Court of Appeal took the view that the erection of machinery constituted carrying on business, the case being reversed (1918), 56 S.C.R. 539 on other grounds.

The taking of a mortgage of lands in Ontario as collateral security for an advance made outside of Ontario is not carrying on business in the province: *Euclid Avenue Trusts Co. v. Hohs* (1911), 24 O.L.R. 477 (C.A.).

The bringing of an action in the province does not constitute doing business: *Charles H. Lilly Co. v. Johnston Fisheries Co. & A. R. Johnston* (1909), 14 B.C.R. 174 (C.A.).

The court will have regard to the essence of the contract as distinguished from its form. Thus, in *De Laval Separator Co. v. Walworth* (1907), 13 B.C.R. 74 (S.C.); *City of Halifax v. McLaughlin Carriage Co.* (1908), 39 S.C.R. 174 and *Butterick Publishing Co. v. White & Walker Co.* (1914), 18 D.L.R. 636 (Alta. C.A.), contracts purporting to appoint an agent were held in fact to be agreements for the sale of goods. In applying this rule the court will give consideration not only to the terms of the agreement, but also to the methods adopted by the parties to carrying it out and the course of dealings between them: *Firestone Tire & Rubber Co. of Canada v. Commissioner of Income Tax*, [1942] S.C.R. 476 at 482.

Position of extraprovincial corporations in court proceedings

Provincial legislation providing for licensing of extraprovincial corporations frequently provides that such a corporation, if unlicensed, may not maintain any proceedings in the provincial courts in respect of contracts made in the province in the course of carrying on the business for which it should be licensed. Such provisions do not apply to federal corporations: see *I.A.C. Ltd. v. Donald E. Hirtle Transport Ltd.* (1978), 29 N.S.R. (2d) 482 (C.A.); affg (1977) 27 N.S.R. (2d) 416 and should the provincial provisions deprive an unlicensed federal corporation of the right to sue in the courts of the province, they would be *ultra vires: Linde Canadian Refrigerator Co. v. Saskatchewan Creamery Co.* (1915), 51 S.C.R. 400.

Once the defendant shows that the plaintiff's name is not on the register of domestic or foreign corporations and the nature of the action itself shows that the plaintiff was doing business in the province, the onus lies on the plaintiff to establish its status to do business: *La Salle Extension University v. Freeman*, [1926] 3 W.W.R. 474 (Man. Co. Ct.); *Alexander Hamilton Institute v. Chambers* (1922), 65 D.L.R. 226 (Sask. C.A.). However, if the disability to sue depends on whether the corporation has been carrying on business in the province and, on the facts, the corporation has not been carrying on business in the province, there is no disability against suing in the province to recover in respect of a transaction which does not constitute carrying on business in the province: *John Deere Plow Co. v. Agnew* (1913), 48 S.C.R. 208; *White v. Donkin* (1914), 16 D.L.R. 446. See further the cases under the heading "Carrying on business", *supra.* See also *Re Huber and Pocklington Financial Corp.* (1982), 134 D.L.R. (3d) 532 (N.S. T.D.).

The Ontario provision does not declare a contract made by an unlicensed corporation to be void; it merely deprives the offending corporation of the right of maintaining any action in respect of the contract while unlicensed; the granting of a licence during the progress of an action is sufficient to support the right of action and puts the corporation's right of resort to the Ontario courts in the same position as if the licence had been granted before the institution of the action: *Honsberger v. Weyburn Townsite Co.* (1919), 59 S.C.R. 281. See also the notes under the heading "Contracts of unlicensed or unregistered extraprovincial corporations", below.

While the absence of a licence if proved will, in Ontario, result in the dismissal of the action, the action may be dismissed without prejudice to the plaintiff's right to bring another action after a licence has been obtained: *Bessemer Gas Engine Co. v. Mills* (1904), 8 O.L.R. 647 at 649 (Div. Ct.). The difficulty as to the want of a licence is removed by its production after the action has been instituted: *Honsberger v. Weyburn Townsite Co.* (1919), 59 S.C.R. 281, *Canadian Stock Breeders Service Ltd. v. Reimer,* [1976] 3 W.W.R. 448 (B.C. S.C.), revd on other grounds, [1976] 5 W.W.R. 405 (B.C. C.A.), or in the course of the trial: *C. C. Robbins Inc. St. Thomas Packing Co.* (1919), 17 O.W.N. 449 (H.C.); affd (1920), 18 O.W.N. 287 (C.A.), or after the argument of an appeal: *Semi-Ready Ltd. v. Tew* (1909), 19 O.L.R. 227 at 235 (Div. Ct.). The more usual course would be to make an order staying the action for a limited period of time until proof of a licence is filed, see: *New York & Pennsylvania Co. v. Holgevac* (1915), 9 O.W.N. 123 (H.C.); *Ben Ginter Construction Co. v. Primary Construction Co.* (1969), 4 D.L.R. (3d) 54 (Y.T.) where the action was stayed until the foreign corporation became registered; *All-Steel Erectors Ltd. v. Armco Canada Ltd.* (1983), 26 Sask. R. 221 (Q.B.); *408464 Ontario Ltd. v. Gogals Furniture Ltd.* (1983), 55 Sask. R. 147 (Q.B.). In Manitoba, the courts have permitted the action to continue provided the corporation registers within a certain period of time. The *Manitoba Corporations Act, 1977* provides that registration is deemed to authorize all "previous acts". The commencement of the action is considered to be an "act" which can be retroactively validated by the subsequent registration. See *Associated Fidelity Investigators Ltd. v. Kodiak Parking Services Ltd.* (1980), 12 Man. R. (2d) 404 (Q.B.); *Bassett Furniture Industries Inc. v. Sargent Color T.V. & Furniture Ltd.* (1981), 12 Man. R. (2d) 409 (Co. Ct.) and *Amco Enrg. Co. v. Custom Steel Products Inc.* (1981), 10 Man. R. (2d) 378; affd (1981), 13 Man. R. (2d) 149 (C.A.). See also *Webb Pax Ltd. v. Weill* (1960), 24 D.L.R. (2d) 350 (Ont. C.A.); *Marathon Watch Co. v. Knelman* (1963), 43 W.W.R. 310 (Man. C.A.). In some jurisdictions the writ may be set aside on summary application: *North Wyoming v. Butler* (1915), 23 D.L.R. 274 (Man. K.B.); *Empire Cream Separator Co. v. Maritime Dairy Co.* (1907), 38 N.B.R. 309 (N.B. S.C.); *La Salle Extension University v. Freeman,* [1926] 3 W.W.R. 474 (Man. Co. Ct.). As to the effect of a statutory provision entitling a corporation after being licensed or registered to maintain anew an action dismissed by reason of the corporation not having been licensed or registered, see *Kominick System Sandstone Brick*

Machinery Co. v. B.C. Pressed Brick Co. (1918), 56 S.C.R. 539. An extraprovincial corporation cannot maintain actions in Prince Edward Island courts without obtaining a certificate of registration: *Woodcraft National Canada Ltée v. Complete Home Centre Ltd.* (1989), 81 Nfld. & P.E.I.R. 91 (P.E.I. T.D.). See also *J. P. Hammill & Son Ltd. v. Kappa Services Ltd.* (1984), 153 A.P.R. 49 (Nfld. T.D.); *Troy Metal Industries Ltd. v. Nolte* (1984), 113 B.C. Corps. L.G. 78,228; *Bridgedale AG v. Metro Weldtech Inc.* (1984), B.C. Corps. L.G. 78,270. Thus, in *Dome Construction Ltd. v. Solarsystems Industries Ltd.*, [1983] 5 W.W.R. 285 (Sask. Q.B.), the court held that to defend an action was the same as maintaining it and the statement of defence was to be struck out unless the corporation registered under the Act. See also *80890 Canada Ltd. v. Frank B. Hall & Co.*, [1986] R.D.J. 544 (Que. C.A.); *Counsel Trust Co. v. Locke* (1985), 70 N.S.R. (2d) 34 (T.D.).

A prohibition against maintaining an action does not in most cases prevent a foreign corporation from commencing an action while unregistered: *Slater Shoe Co. v. Burdette* (1914), 14 D.L.R. 519 (Alta. T.D.); and see *Western Canada Ranching Co. v. Begg & Wyndham*, [1919] 2 W.W.R. 861 (Alta. Dist. Ct.) (non-registration not a ground for setting aside a default judgment); *Webpax Ltd. v. Weill*, [1960] O.W.N. 325 (C.A.) (non-registration not a ground for depriving a defendant, the president of the corporation, of a defence dependent on the corporate existence of the corporation); *Myer Bald Ltd. v. Country Wholesale Ltd.* (1965), 53 W.W.R. 765 (Alta. Dist. Ct.) where default judgement was held to be effective but execution proceedings were held invalid for non-registration. See also *C.B.M. Contracting & Developing Ltd. v. Johnstone* (1980), 39 N.S.R. (2d) 156 (C.A.) where the plaintiff was granted judgment despite the fact that its registration had been revoked before the trial of the action. However, execution was stayed pending renewal of the registration. In *Western Earth Moving Ltd. v. Saskatchewan (Minister of Highways & Transportation)* (1990), 81 Sask. R. 311 (C.A.); leave to appeal to S.C.C. refused (1990), 85 Sask. R. 240 (note), a corporation struck off the register was held to be incapable of commencing or maintaining court proceedings. In *Anaco Equipment Sales Ltd. v. Morsky Construction Ltd.* (1987), 61 Sask. R. 83 (Q.B.), it was held that where an unregistered extraprovincial corporation issued a garnishee summons, it was to be set aside even if the corporation had subsequently become registered under the *Saskatchewan Act* prior to the hearing of the application since the garnishee remedy was an extraordinary remedy requiring strict compliance with the legislation and at the time of the issue of the summons the corporation was not capable of maintaining the action. See, however, *D-B Service (Western) Ltd. v. Madrid Services Ltd.* (1975), 60 D.L.R. (3d) 299 (B.C. S.C.) in which it was held that the prohibition in the British Columbia *Companies Act* S.B.C. 1973 c. 18 against "maintaining" an action was designed to prevent the commencement of litigation. Therefore, "maintain" was interpreted to include "commencing". See also *Smith v. Draper Dobie & Co.* (1978), 8 Alta. L.R. (2d) 84 (T.D.), wherein it was held that the Alberta Companies Act, unlike the legislation in other jurisdictions, prohibited both the commencement and maintaining of an action if unregistered. However, in Nova Scotia it has been held that the failure of a New York corporation to register constituted a complete bar to an action on a contract under the *Corporations Registration Act,* R.S.N.S. 1967, c. 59. See *Seaworld International Seafood Ltd. v. A.M. Farmer & Assoc. Ltd.* (1981), 25 C.P.C. 183 (N.S. T.D.). See also *Counsel Trust Co. v. Locke* (1985), 70 N.S.R. (2d) 34 (T.D.). As to the right of a defendant to have the status of the plaintiff decided at the trial, where there has been failure by the plaintiff to allege registration and failure by the defendant to plead lack of registration, see *Ontario Wind Engine & Pump Co. v. Eldred* (1912), 2 D.L.R. 270. In Ontario, the objection to the absence of a licence should be pleaded: *National Malleable Castings Co. v. Smiths' Falls Malleable Castings Co.* (1907), 14 O.L.R. 22 at 23 (C.A.), and in Saskatchewan the defence that a foreign corporation has not the status entitling it to sue must be pleaded: *J. R. Watkins Co. v. Thole*, [1924] 3 W.W.R. 847 (Sask. K.B.).

The holding of a licence or registration does not make the corporation a resident in the jurisdiction so as to absolve it from giving security for costs: *Ashland Co. v. Armstrong* (1906), 11 O.L.R. 414 (Ch.); *Canadian Ry. Accident Co. v. Kelly* (1907), 5 W.L.R. 412 (Man. K.B.); *Frost & Wood Co. v. Howes* (1912), 4 D.L.R. 527 (Alta. T.D.); *La Salle Extension University v. Linley*, [1933] 3 D.L.R. 643 (B.C. C.A.); *Christian Community of Universal Brotherhood Ltd. v. Trafimenkoff*, [1937] 2 W.W.R. 340 (Sask. C.A.); *R. M. Buchanan-Sumner Co. v. Scottish Co-operative Wholesale Society Ltd.*, [1936] 1 W.W.R. 491 (Sask. K.B.) (affidavit of *nulla bona* unnecessary).

Registration of an extraprovincial corporation within the province does not make the corporation a resident of that province so as to give the courts of the province jurisdiction over the corporation in respect of a cause of action arising wholly outside the province: *Pearlman v. Great West Life Assurance Co.* (1912), 4 D.L.R. 154 (B.C. C.A.).

The mere fact that an extraprovincial corporation has its registered office in a certain county does not necessarily mean that it dwells or carries on business in that county within the meaning of a statute requiring an action to be brought in the county in which the defendant dwells or carries on business: *McNeil v. Morrison-Knudsen Company of Canada* (1953), 10 W.W.R. 354 (B.C. C.A.).

There are certain exceptions to the rule that an unlicensed extraprovincial corporation may not take proceedings or sue.

Where a licence is required only if the corporation carries on business in the province and the corporation does not in fact do so, it may sue in respect of a transaction which does not constitute carrying on business: *John Deere Plow Co. v. Agnew* (1913), 48 S.C.R. 208; *White v. Donkin* (1914), 16 D.L.R. 446 (B.C. S.C.). Thus, where the plaintiff was not carrying on business in Ontario, no licence was required in order to maintain an action in Ontario on a franchise agreement governed by the laws of New York. See *Weight Watchers International Inc. v. Weight Watchers of Ontario Ltd.*, [1973] 1 O.R. 549 (Ont. H.C.). Where the contract specified New Brunswick law governed, but the agreement was carried out in Alberta, the Supreme Court of Canada upheld the conviction of the accused unregistered New Brunswick corporation. The corporation was subject to the provisions of the Alberta Act. See *R. v. Thomas Equipment Ltd.*

(1979), 26 N.R. 499 (S.C.C.). See also *Uni-Spec Inspection Services (Nova) Ltd. v. Leclair* (1985), 170 A.P.R. 4 (Nfld. Dist. Ct.). See also *Valley Construction Co. v. Eberle*, [1974] 5 W.W.R. 537 (Man. Co. Ct.) where it was pointed out that the filing of a mechanics lien is not an action or other proceeding in a court but is a proceeding taking place in a Land Titles Office. See also *Basic Distributors Inc. v. F.D.R. Sales Ltd.* (1978), 7 B.C.L.R. 354 (Co. Ct.) and *Associated Fidelity Investigators Ltd. v. Kodiak Parking Services Ltd.* (1980), 12 Man. R. (2d) 404 (Q.B.).

In *Re Society Shirt Co.*, [1932] O.R. 104 (C.A.), the Court of Appeal held that the Ontario *Extraprovincial Corporations Act* then in force did not affect the right of an unlicensed foreign corporation to institute proceedings under the *Bankruptcy Act*; but for the position in Saskatchewan, see *Re Nelson Ford Lumber Co.* (1908), 1 Sask. L.R. 108 (T.D.).

An unregistered foreign corporation, in the absence of any express statutory prohibition, can sue on a foreign judgment: *Charles H. Lilly Co. v. Johnston Fisheries Co.* (1909), 14 B.C.R. 174 (C.A.); or upon a contract made on a foreign country: *Bondholders Securities Corp. v. Manville*, [1933] 4 D.L.R. 699 (Sask. C.A.); or upon a contract not made in whole or in part within the province in the course of its business where the applicable provincial legislation merely prohibited the maintaining of action in respect of contracts made in the province: *Basic Distributors Inc. v. F.D.R. Sales Ltd.* (1978), 7 B.C.L.R. 354 (Co. Ct.); or on behalf of itself and other creditors to set aside as fraudulent conveyances of real estate in the province made by a debtor: *Minot Grocery Co. v. Durich* (1913), 10 D.L.R. 126 (Sask. T.D.); or in respect of a tort: *Mickelson v. Mickelson* (1916), 28 D.L.R. 307 (Man. C.A.); or to enforce its rights incidental to the ownership of book debts there being no contractual relationship between the plaintiff and defendant: *Robertson & Son Ltd. v. Canadian Bank of Commerce*, [1920] 2 W.W.R. 1003. A foreign corporation, not licensed in Ontario, is entitled to sue for possession on a mortgage of lands in the province taken as collateral security for an advance made outside of Ontario: *Euclid Avenue Trusts Co. v. Hohs* (1911), 24 O.L.R. 477 (C.A.); but a foreign corporation which had not obtained a licence as required by Part 4 of c. 35, R.S.M. 1913, was held to be not entitled to maintain an action for specific performance of a contract to exchange lands in the foreign jurisdiction for lands in Manitoba: *North Wyoming v. Butler* (1915), 23 D.L.R. 274. Section 149(1) of *The Companies Act*, R.S.A. 1929, c. 14 (Alta.), providing that any foreign corporation registered under the Act may sue and be sued, does not by implication prohibit any right of action by an unregistered foreign corporation: *Lampson, Fraser & Huth Inc. v. Simpson*, [1942] 3 W.W.R. 238 (no evidence to show whether the cause of action arose in respect of a contract made in the course of business carried on in Alberta).

An unlicensed foreign mining corporation can sue its agent for an accounting necessarily incidental to the right to carry on mining operations under a federal licence: *McDonald v. Klondyke Government Concession Ltd.* (1906), 4 W.L.R. 151.

An extraprovincial corporation, which has ceased doing business, is not bound to take out a licence to enforce its rights under an agreement and is not precluded from instituting proceedings by reason of not being licensed: *International Ry. Co. & Niagara Parks Comm.*, [1936] O.R. 220.

A foreign corporation registered and carrying on business in Nova Scotia, being within the jurisdiction of the courts, is subject to garnishment for wages owing by it to an employee of a branch office within the province: *Gaul v. Yorke*, [1938] 3 D.L.R. 715. See *Kroetsch v. H. W. Domnik Industries Ltd.* (1985), 60 A.R. 69 (Q.B.).

Appointment of attorney

The legislation of the various provinces relating to the licensing of extraprovincial corporations usually provides for the appointment by such corporations of an attorney in the province upon whom service of process, notices and other proceedings may be made. As to the effect of the appointment of an attorney as regards dispensing with the necessity of obtaining an order for service *ex juris*, see *Reinhorn v. The Knetchel Furniture Co.* (1912), 8 D.L.R. 1047.

A power of attorney of a foreign corporation will be held valid until the contrary is proved if signed in its name by the president and secretary before a notary and bearing the corporate seal: *The Great Northern Ry. v. Furness, Withy & Co.* (1904), 6 Que. P.R. 404. In that case it was also held that a foreign corporation may give a general power of attorney to its solicitors to act in all causes in which it may be concerned; that the power of attorney could be given after the institution of the action; and that it was not necessary to attach a resolution of the board authorizing the signature by the officers. As to the powers of particular officers, powers of attorney have been held valid when executed under the corporate seal by the president: *Standard Trust Co. v. South Shore Ry.* (1903), 5 Que. P.R. 257 (no express delegation by the board to the president to prosecute suits required); by the president and secretary: *The Great Northern Ry. v. Furness Withy & Co.*, *supra*; by the managing director and secretary: *In re James A. Brook Co. and The I. & J. Stewart Leitch Co.* (1905), 7 Que. P.R. 301; and by the vice-president and assistant-secretary: *Amherst Investment Corp. v. Prudential Insurance Co. of Canada* (1934), 56 Que. K.B 128 (C.A.). Powers of attorney have been rejected in Quebec where there is no proof of authorization by the board and the power of attorney has been signed without the corporate seal by the treasurer of the corporation alone: *Leyser Green Co. v. Chaleger Co.* (1912), 14 Que. P.R. 96; and by the secretary-treasurer alone: *Alexandria Paper Co. v. Compagnie de Pulpe de Chicoutimi* (1919), 21 Que. P.R. 246. Powers of attorney have been rejected even where the corporate seal was affixed when signed by, but without evidence of authority having been given to, the manager: *The Trusts and Guarantee Co. v. Belanger* (1905), 7 Que. P.R. 301; and by the secretary and an assistant secretary: *Automobile Insurance Co. of Hartford Connecticut v. Newfoundland Canada Steamships Ltd.* (1935), 38 Que. P.R. 344. In *Atlanta Corp. Ltd. v. Richmond*, [1957] Que. P.R. 176 the court stated that neither the Quebec Civil Code nor the Federal or Quebec Companies Act required the corporate seal to be affixed to a power of attorney.

Contracts of unlicensed or unregistered extraprovincial corporations

Whether a contract entered into by an unlicensed or unregistered extraprovincial corporation, in the course of carrying on business in the province in the face of an express prohibition or when penalties are imposed, is to be regarded as illegal and void, or whether the contract is only unenforceable, so that the remedy of the corporation is suspended until it becomes licensed or registered, will depend on the provisions of the governing statute and the view which the court takes of their object and effect. The decided cases which have arisen in connection with litigation based on such contracts are by no means uniform or easily reconcilable.

In *Northwestern Construction Co. v. Young* (1907), 13 B.C.R. 297 (C.A.) it was held, following *Brown v. Moore* (1902), 32 S.C.R. 93, that a contract entered into by an unlicensed extraprovincial corporation was void and unenforceable as the statute prohibited corporations doing business until they had obtained a licence. The same view was adopted in *Kominick System Sandstone Brick Machinery Co. v. B.C. Pressed Brick Co.* (1912), 8 D.L.R. 859 (B.C.C.A.) and in *Willett Martin Co. v. Full* (1915), 24 D.L.R. 672, where the statute requiring the filing of a sworn statement by the extraprovincial corporation prior to carrying on business was regarded as prohibitive and imposed a penalty. However, in Alberta it was held that the effect of the former Companies Act in prohibiting the commencing or maintaining of an action was not to impair the corporation's right to contract but merely to prevent it from enforcing the contract if unregistered. Upon registration contracts, including those made prior to registration, become enforceable. See *Smith v. Draper Dobie & Co.* (1978), 93 D.L.R. (3d) 69 (Alta. T.D.)

For the constitutional aspects of such legislation, see *Great West Saddlery Co. v. The King*, [1921] 2 A.C. 91 at 123.

In Ontario, s. 21 of the *Extra-Provincial Corporations Act*, c.E.27, R.S.O. 1990, provides that certain extraprovincial corporations so long as they are unlicensed or do not have an agent for service in the province shall not be capable of maintaining any action or other proceeding in any court in Ontario in respect of any contract but that upon the granting of the licence (and appointing an agent) such action may be prosecuted as if the default had been corrected before the institution of the action. This restriction is not applicable to a federal corporation. Under similar legislation it has been held that contracts made by an unlicensed extraprovincial corporation are not void; the right of the corporation to maintain the action on the contract is merely suspended: *Bessemer Gas Engine Co. v. Mills* (1904), 8 O.L.R. 647; *Semi-Ready Ltd. v. Tew* (1909), 19 O.L.R. 227 (production of licence after argument on appeal sufficient); *Canadian Bank of Commerce v. Rogers* (1911), 23 O.L.R. 109; *Smith v. Western Canada Flour Mills Co.* (1911), 3 Alta. L.R. 348; *Slater Shoe Co. v. Burdette* (1914), 14 D.L.R. 519; *Consolidated Investments v. Caswell* (1915), 21 D.L.R. 525 (Man. C.A.) (corporation licensed before action but after promissory note sued upon); *Mickelson v. Mickelson* (1916), 28 D.L.R. 307 (Man. C.A.); *Assiniboia Land Co. v. Acres* (1916), 10 O.W.N. 328; *Wiley & Co. v. Cheesman* (1917), 34 D.L.R. 357 (registration *pendente lite*); *Honsberger v. Weyburn Townsite Co.*

(1919), 59 S.C.R. 281 (licence obtained *pendente lite*); *C.C. Robbins Incorp. v. St. Thomas Packing Co.* (1920), 18 O.W.N. 287 (following *Honsberger* case).

Provincial legislation affecting holding of land by federal corporations

On this question in *Great West Saddlery Co. v. The King*, [1921] 2 A.C. 91 (P.C.), Viscount Haldane said at pp. 119 and 120:

> Their Lordships will dispose in the first place of a subsidiary matter, which is whether a Dominion company can be precluded from acquiring and holding land in a province by a Provincial law of the nature of a general Mortmain Act. It is clear, both on principle and from previous decisions, that it is within the competence of a Provincial Legislature to enact such legislation, and the question is therefore answered in the affirmative. If there be a provision to this effect, occurring even in a statute which in other respects is *ultra vires*, and that provision be severable, it is valid. In the Ontario case there is therefore no doubt that the broad result of the contention of the Province under this head is well founded; for there the Legislature has passed a Mortmain Act of general application, and in regard to this Act a Dominion company is in no better position than any other corporation which desires to hold land.
>
> In Manitoba there is no general Mortmain Act, but s. 112 of the *Manitoba Companies Act* enables a corporation receiving a licence under Part IV of the Act, relating to extra-provincial companies, to acquire and hold land as freely as could any company under Part I of the Act. Even if the provision as to the licensing of extra-provincial companies is held to be *ultra vires*, so as to prevent such a provision from being operative, as being inseverable, it is plain that the substance of a provision which is of the character of a mortmain law is within the power of the Province.
>
> In Saskatchewan there is no general Mortmain Act, but the *Companies Act* of 1915, by s. 19, enables a company incorporated under the law of the Province to hold land. By s. 25 a company not so incorporated (and this includes a Dominion company) may, if it has been licensed, carry on its business as if it had been incorporated under the law of the Province. This enables it to hold land unless the provisions as to the grant to it of a license are inoperative. Their Lordships do not think that s. 29 of the Companies Act of Canada, which purports to enable a Dominion company to acquire and hold real estate requisite for the carrying on of its undertaking, can prevail against any severable provision by a Provincial Legislature restricting the power of corporations generally to acquire or hold real estate in the Province.

In the result it was held that in the case of the province of Ontario none of the appellant corporations could acquire and hold lands in the province without a licence under the provincial Mortmain Act, and that it was within the power of the other provincial legislatures to impose the requirement of a licence directed to this purpose. See also *Chaudière Gold Mining Co. of Boston v. Desbarats* (1873), L.R. 5 P.C. 277; followed in *Cooper v.McIndoe* (1887), 15 R.L.O.S. 276.

The Mortmain legislation in Ontario was abolished in 1982 and the *Extra-Provincial Corporations Act* provides that every corporation has power to acquire, hold and convey any land or interest therein in Ontario necessary for its actual use and occupation or if carrying on its undertaking if it was incorporated or continued under the laws of any province or is a federal corporation or incorporated under an ordinance of the Yukon or Northwest Territories. In order to have this power, corporations incorporated or continued under the laws of a jurisdiction outside of Canada must be licensed under the Act or be a class of corporation which is exempt from the licensing requirement. Section 15 of the regulations passed pursuant to the Act exempts the following from the provisions of the Act, namely, corporations licensed or registered under the *Insurance Act,* the *Investment Contracts Act* or the *Loan and Trust Corporations Act,* corporations incorporated to operate a banking business or the business of a savings bank, a railway, a telegraph corporation, an express corporation (over a railway), or the business of leasing or hiring sleeping parlour or dining cars run on a railway. Also exempted are corporations engaged in the brewing, distilling or making of wine that are licensed under the *Liquor Licence Act* or corporations not having gain for any of their objects.

Examples of provincial legislation affecting federal corporations

Agents of federal corporations are subject to the provisions of provincial legislation requiring peddlers to take out a licence: *R. ex rel. Nalder v. Barlow,* [1923] 1 D.L.R. 262 (Alta. C.A.); notwithstanding that the corporation was authorized by its charter to sell its goods by means of salesmen and agents: *R. v. Gebhardt (No. 2),* [1926] 2 D.L.R. 950 (Sask. C.A.). See also as to agents: *R. ex rel. Kane v. Haworth,* [1920] 2 W.W.R. 1043 (Sask. C.A.); *R. ex rel. Kyte v. Aune,* [1925] 2 W.W.R. 539; *R. v. Gebhardt (No. 1),* [1926] 3 D.L.R. 203 (Sask. C.A.).

A tax on contractors (not residents of the province but doing business in the City of Charlottetown) imposed by a by-law of the city passed pursuant to a provincial statute, was held invalid where the contractor was a federal corporation with power to construct buildings throughout Canada on the ground that it was an interference with the status and powers of a federal corporation: *Charlottetown v. Foundations Maritime Ltd.*, [1932] 1 D.L.R. 453; affd [1932] S.C.R. 589.

A federal corporation is, in common with other corporations, firms and persons engaged in similar business, liable to pay a licence tax imposed by a municipality: *Re Major Hill Taxicab & Transfer Co. & City of Ottawa* (1915), 7 O.W.N. 747. A municipality may require federal corporations to take out transient traders' licences if the by-law is not discriminatory against such corporations and does not attempt to penalize or exclude them: *R. v. Continental Salvage Corp.*, [1930] 2 W.W.R. 562 (Man. C.A.).

A provision of the city charter of Halifax prohibiting a federal corporation, with power to do business throughout Canada, from conducting such business within the city without first paying a licence fee, is *ultra vires: City of Halifax v. Lyall & Sons Construction Co.* (1922), 65 D.L.R. 305 (N.S. C.A.).

In *Re Dominion Marble Co., In Liquidation* (1917), 35 D.L.R. 63, it was held that a federal corporation is subject to the limitation that in carrying out its objects it must comply with the law relating to property and civil rights in each of the provinces. As a result it was held that the corporation in liquidation had no authority to create in favour of a trustee for bondholders, a privilege upon its moveable property in view of the local law in force in the province of Quebec, making moveables insusceptible of hypothecation. (By the Quebec *Special Corporate Powers Act*, authority is now given for the pledging and mortgaging of moveable property to secure bonds, and authorizing such pledges or mortgages).

Practically all the provinces have enacted similar legislation applicable to federal corporations as well as other corporations which prohibit corporations from selling their shares or securities to the public except through a registered broker or salesman or unless the corporation is itself registered. The Alberta *Security Frauds Prevention Act, 1930*, was held *intra vires* and applicable to federal corporations: *Lymburn v. Mayland*, [1932] A.C. 318.

The Ontario *Security Frauds Prevention Act, 1930* which prohibited any person from trading in any security unless he was registered did not impair the status and powers of a federal corporation, and consequently was *intra vires: R. v. Hazzard*, [1932] O.R. 139. Section 38 of the Ontario *Securities Act* requiring the filing of a prospectus with the Commission when trading in the securities of a mining corporation was *intra vires* as it was aimed at regulating the manner in which the business of selling securities should be conducted: *Smith v. R.*, [1959] O.R. 365 (C.A.); affd [1960] S.C.R. 776.

See further the notes to s. 193 under the heading "Provincial legislation with respect to dealing in securities", in Chapter 13.

Power of corporation to contract

A corporation is as fully capable of binding itself by contract as an individual: *Bateman v. Ashton-under-Lyne* (1858), 3 H. & N. 323, per Martin B. at 335; *Ooregum Gold Mining Co. v. Roper*, [1892] A.C. 125.

The general question of the powers of corporations is dealt with in the notes to ss. 15-16, *supra*, and the brief comments on the power to contract which follow should be read in conjunction therewith.

A corporation incorporated under this Act has the capacity, and subject to the provisions of the Act, the rights and powers of a natural person under s. 15 of the Act and by virtue of s. 21 of the *Interpretation Act* power to contract and be contracted with in its corporate name and, under the rule laid down in *Edwards v. Blackmore* (1918), 42 O.L.R. 105 (C.A.), a corporation incorporated by charter has all the powers of a common law corporation to enter into contracts. The powers of the corporation to enter into contracts may be limited or restricted by the charter and certain transactions may be prohibited by the Act, general law or may be dependent on the following prescribed procedure.

The powers of corporations incorporated by memorandum and articles or by special Act are exercisable only subject to the doctrine of *ultra vires* which is fully applicable except as modified by statute to such corporations.

A limitation on the powers of a corporation incorporated under this Act may also be prescribed by the general by-laws of the corporation, but a stranger dealing with the corporation will not be affected by such limitation unless he has notice thereof.

In some cases corporations are by their constitutions required to observe certain formalities when making contracts. In these cases the requirements of the constitution must be strictly carried out: *Cope v. Thames Haven & Dock Ry. Co.* (1849), 3 Ex 841; *Eaton v. Basker* (1881), 7 Q.B.D. 529; *Stevens v. Hounslow Burial Board* (1889), 61 L.T. 839; *Quinlan & Robertson v. Town of St. John* (1918), 41 D.L.R. 365 (Que.); *MacKay v. City of Toronto*, [1920] A.C. 208 (P.C.); *Waterous Engine Co. v. Town of Capreol* (1922), 52 O.L.R. 247 (C.A.); *Shuler v. Smith* (1990), 112 A.R. 321 (Q.B.) where the sole beneficial shareholder signed an agreement to relinquish her interest in certain business projects and the articles of the corporation required the signature of her husband for the transfer of interests, it was held that the corporation was bound by the agreement notwithstanding that the articles had not been complied with. It will be noted that in a case of a corporation subject to the federal Act a corporation or guarantor of an obligation of the corporation may not assert against a person dealing with the corporation or with any person who has acquired rights from the corporation that the articles have not been complied with unless he had or ought to have had by virtue of his position with or relationship to the corporation, knowledge to the contrary. See s. 18(a).

As regards certain contracts, compliance with statutory prerequisites may be required, for example, the authority of a special resolution in the case of the sale of the undertaking of a corporation as an entirety or substantially as an entirety other than in the ordinary course of business under s. 189(3); and any contract will be subject to the provisions of any law of general application which may affect it, for example, a bulk sale to which the provisions of the relative provincial *Bulk Sales Act* applies.

Necessity of by-law

The formal acts of the directors of a corporation at meetings of the board are expressed in the form of resolutions or by-laws. It has been said that a resolution applies to one act whereas a by-law is a permanent and continuing rule which is applicable to all future occasions. However, the federal Act now provides in s. 16(1) that it is not necessary for a by-law to be passed in order to confer any particular power on the corporation or its directors. A similar provision is contained in s. 17(1) of the Ontario Act. This means, for example, that borrowing by-laws are no longer necessary whether for a bank or to authorize the issuance of corporate indebtedness generally.

Authorization of contracts

The general agents of the corporation are the directors, to whom the management of the corporation's affairs is entrusted; and the board acting as such will, as a general rule, have power to bind the corporation by any arrangement or contract. A single director, not specially authorized, has no power to bind the corporation: *Bent v. Arrowhead* (1909), 18 Man. R. 632 (C.A.); *Swayze v. Grobb* (1915), 8 O.W.N. 316 (agreement with a single director for the allotment of shares); *Houghton & Company v. Nothard, Lowe & Wills Ltd.*, [1928] A.C. 1 (P.C.) (agreement by single director for pledge of proceeds of corporation's produce as security for advances to another corporation); *Kortzman v. O'Brien et al.* (1932), 41 O.W.N. 344 (agreement by director without special authority for a long-term lease); [1933] O.W.N. 215 (appeal dismissed); *Rama Corp. Ltd. v. Proved Tin & General Investments Ltd.*, [1952] 2 Q.B. 147 (action to recover money paid pursuant to an agreement made with a director acting without authority). The corporation may, however, be bound by the act of a director whom the corporation has allowed to act as manager: *Keystone Shingles & Lumber Ltd. v. Moody Shingles Ltd.*, [1942] 2 D.L.R. 311 (B.C.C.A.).

In *Roman Hotels Ltd. v. Desrochers Hotels Ltd.* (1976), 69 D.L.R. (3d) 126 (Sask. C.A.), three persons were the sole directors, officers and beneficiaries of a corporation whose sole undertaking was the operation of a hotel. In a telephone conversation the three unanimously agreed to sell the hotel and then an agreement of purchase and sale was executed. In an action for specific performance it was held that the purchasers were entitled to damages. Notwithstanding the statutory requirement of filing a resolution with the province in such cases, a corporate decision had taken place despite the lack of formality. A formal meeting was simply the best evidence but not the only evidence of the decision. The Act did not provide that the sale was invalid unless sanctioned by resolution.

While the Act provides that the affairs of the corporation are to be managed by the directors (s. 102(1)), the Board may and commonly does delegate the performance of many acts, to officers and employees of the corporation, who, to the extent of the agency expressly or impliedly delegated, are the agents of the corporation and are entitled to bind it by their acts. The matter is well expressed by Burton C.J.O. in *Thompson v. Brantford Electric & Operating Co.* (1898), 25 O.A.R. 340 at 345 (C.A.):

> The directors of a company are not, however, necessarily its only agents. It is generally necessary for them to employ other persons to act for the company, and where this is the case those persons will also have power to bind the company within the limits of their agency, and as a rule their authority cannot be denied unless their employment was beyond the power of the directors or they had been employed irregularly and the person dealing with them had notice of the irregularity.

The authority of particular officers or agents may be implied and the corporation will be bound by contracts entered into by such officers or agents within the apparent scope of their authority. However, where the authority of the officer or agent is doubtful, or in transactions of any magnitude, it may be advisable to insist on the production of a properly certified copy of a resolution of the board of directors authorizing the specific contract or transaction proposed to be entered into on the corporation's behalf.

See also the discussion under the heading "Liability for acts of agents and officers", *infra*.

Formalities in execution of contracts

Use of corporation name

Care should be taken to state accurately the name of the corporation in any contracts entered into by it, but so far as the liability of the corporation itself is concerned on documents to which the corporation is a party, such liability is not avoided by the use of the abbreviation "Ltd." even where the statute requires the word to be written in full: *A. E. Thomas Ltd. v. Standard Bank of Canada*, (1910) 1 O.W.N. 379 at 382 (H.C.); appeal to Divisional Court dismissed at p. 548. The same is true where the word "Company" is abbreviated to "Co.": *Thompson v. Big Cities Realty & Agency Co.* (1910), 21 O.L.R. 394. See also *Canadian Imperial Bank of Commerce v. Dene Mat Construction Ltd.*, [1988] N.W.T.R. 174 (S.C.). A slight variation in the name of the corporation in a written contract, for example, "M. Beatty & Sons Co., Lim.", where the proper name was "M. Beatty & Sons, Limited", will not invalidate the contract: *Schmidt v. M. Beatty & Sons Ltd.* (1916), 10 O.W.N. 230. Similarly where, during proceedings to change the name, the corporation enters into an agreement in which it is described by its old name but which it executes under its new name, this will not affect the liability under the contract: *Alliance Securities Ltd. v. Posnekoff*, [1922] 3 W.W.R. 1201. Where in a deed to a corporation it is described by its original name, which has been changed, there being no doubt as to what corporation was intended, the description is sufficient to make the grant effectual: *Grand Junction Ry. v. Midland Ry.* (1883), 7 O.A.R. 681 at 686. A variation in or omission from the name of a grantor corporation is immaterial where the identity of the corporation is readily known either from the instrument or other proof: *McRae v. Corbett* (1890), 6 Man. R. 426 (C.A.). Where cheques and promissory notes were mistakenly endorsed with the stamp of an affiliated corporation, the holders of the bills of exchange were not considered to be holders in due course under the *Bills of Exchange Act*, R.S.C. 1970 and were unable to rely upon provisions of that statute which provide that the signature of an officer of a corporation constitutes sufficient endorsement and deems the bill of exchange to have been made on behalf of the corporation. See *Hoeller v. Roberts* (1980), 19 B.C.L.R. 333 (Co. Ct.). Where the principal of the corporation failed to comply with the formalities of the former Alberta Companies Act in that he was incorrect respecting the proper name of the corporation which was never used and was in fact a shell corporation, the defendant recovered from the principal personally. The court found the defendant principal had contracted personally and was unable to take advantage of limited liability because of the broad failure to comply with the formal requirements of the Act. See *Tato Enterprises Ltd. v. Rode* (1979), 17 A.R. 432 (Dist. Ct.).

In many cases corporations carry on business under a style or name other than their corporate name, particularly if the corporate name is a number. In this case consideration must be given to the appropriate provincial Act as to the requirements of the use of such name. In Ontario the *Business Names Act*, R.S.O. 1990, ch. B. 17 provides that no corporation is to carry on business or to identify itself to the public under a name other than its corporate name unless the name is registered by that corporation. It will be observed that s. 2(6) of that Act provides that such a corporation is to set out both the registered name and the corporation's actual name in all contracts, invoices, negotiable instruments and orders involving goods or services issued or made by the corporation concerned. If, however, there is a partnership or business association consisting of two or more corporations which identifies itself or carries on business under a registered business name, the corporate names of the partners may be omitted by specifically identifying the business name by the words "registered name" or "registered style" or a similar abbreviation or identification.

Necessity of writing

Under certain statutes, such as *The Statute of Frauds* (Ontario), no action can be brought upon certain contracts, for example, contracts of guarantee, contracts of sale of lands, and contracts not to be performed within a year, unless the agreement sued upon or some memorandum or note thereof is in writing and signed by the party to be charged therewith or some other person thereunto by him lawfully authorized. For a similar provision see *The Sale of Goods Act* (Ontario). Where the terms of a contract have been embodied by reference in the minutes of a corporation, and the minutes have been signed by the president or chairman, this will be considered a sufficient writing to satisfy s. 4 of the Statute of Frauds: *Jones v. Victoria Graving Dock Co.* (1877), 2 Q.B.D. 314. The equitable rule of part performance taking the case out of the Statute of Frauds, applies to a corporation: *Howard v. Patent Ivory Mfg. Co.* (1888), 38 Ch. D. 156.

Use of corporate seal

The federal Act provides in s. 23 that an instrument or an agreement executed on behalf of a corporation by a director, officer or agent is not invalid merely because a corporate seal is not affixed thereto. It will be noted that this provision is different from that contained in the Ontario Act in s. 13 where it is provided that a corporation may, but need not, have a corporate seal. Interesting questions arise where common law requires the use of a seal and it might be argued that the provision in the federal Act is unconstitutional as purporting to deal with a matter relating to property and civil rights in a province; on the other hand, the provision might be upheld as being merely ancillary to the *modus operandi* of a creature of federal law. For registration under the Land Titles and Registry Acts of Ontario a statement under the signature or signatures that "we have authority to bind the corporation" will by virtue of the statutory provision relieve any requirement for a corporate seal. In some cases it might be possible to argue that a "wafer" seal could be used by a corporation which did not have a corporate seal but in such instance it would be necessary to show that that form of seal was authorized for use on behalf of the corporation.

Generally speaking, in any contract of importance the practice is for the corporation to affix its corporate seal.

The common law rule was that a corporation was not bound by a contract unless it was under the corporate seal but there were and are certain exceptions to this rule, namely, contracts in respect of trivial matters of every day occurrence, contracts of trading corporations entered into for the purposes for which they were incorporated, and contracts which had been fully carried out by the other party or contracts on which the corporation had acted or contracts to which the equitable rule of part performance applied. In these cases the corporation could be made liable even if the contract was not executed under the corporate seal.

A contract which is not under seal will be binding on the corporation if it is in furtherance of the corporation's objects, for example, a contract for sale of land with a view to enable the corporation to purchase other lands for the carrying on of its business: *Vansickler v. McKnight Construction Co.* (1914), 31 O.L.R. 531 at 537 (C.A.); affd (1915), 51 S.C.R. 374 at 384, where Duff J. following and approving the judgment of Bovill C.J. in *South of Ireland Colliery Co. v. Waddle* (1868), L.R. 3 C.P. 463; affd (1869), L.R. 4 C.P. 617, said:

> I may add that the decision in *Waddle's Case* is over fifty years old and it is, of course, perfectly well known that the business of trading corporations has now for many years been conducted on the assumption (based upon the observations of the learned judges who decided that case) that such corporations may express their consent in a binding manner to contracts within the scope of their business in the same way as an individual may do, provided that no statutory provision or regulation affecting them is infringed or departed from.

See also *Canadian Market Place Ltd. v. Fallowfield* (1976), 13 O.R. (2d) 456 (H.C.); *R. ex rel. Cameron v. Hurlbut*, [1956] O.W.N. 226 at 227, per Judson J.; *London Board of Education v. East Middlesex District High School Board*, [1967] S.C.R. 49; affg [1965] 2 O.R. 51; revg [1965] 1 O.R. 129 (*sub nom. Last Middlesex District High School Board v. London (Board of Education)*) wherein it was held that s. 293 of the former Ontario Act, R.S.O. 1960 c. 71 created a statutory exception in addition to the common law exceptions. Hence, where a contract had been entered into between the respective boards (both statutory corporations), but the corporate seal not affixed thereto, the contract was enforceable.

A contract is not in furtherance of the corporation's objects if it is not made for the primary benefit of the corporation, but is made for the benefit of others: *Merkur Brothers v. W. J. McCart & Co.*, [1944] O.W.N. 671.

A corporation signing an application to a municipal corporation in support of an early closing by-law, does so within the scope of its business and accordingly it is not necessary for the corporation to affix its seal: *R. ex rel. Cameron v. Hurlbut (supra)*, where Judson J. did not follow *Smith v. Galloway & Galloway*, [1950] O.W.N. 576, where in the same circumstances the court held that it was necessary to affix the corporate seal.

For examples where the corporation has been made liable on an executed contract, see *Campbell v. Community General Hospital* (1910), 20 O.L.R. 467 at 475; *Gowans-Kent v. Assiniboia Club* (1916), 25 D.L.R. 695 at 697; *Hawkins v. Allied Truck Co. Ltd.* (1919), 16 O.W.N. 379 at 381.

The term "trading company" is synonymous with a commercial corporation having gain for its object: *Hunt v. Wimbledon Local Board* (1878), 3 C.P.D. 208 at 213. See *Richardson v. Urban Mutual Fire Ins. Co.* (1916), 28 D.L.R. 12 (Man. C.A.) (mutual benefit association not a trading corporation) and *Brandon Construction Co. v. Saskatoon School Board* (1912), 5 D.L.R. 754 (building corporation is a trading corporation).

The distinction between executed and executory contracts is still of importance in the case of a non-trading corporation. The general rule as to such corporations is that, in the absence of a provision in its constitution or governing Act dispensing with the necessity for a seal, the corporation will not be liable if the contract is executory, but will be liable if the contract is executed: *Campbell v. Community General Hospital* (1910), 20 O.L.R. 467; *Gowans-Kent v. Assiniboia Club* (1916), 25 D.L.R. 695.

Where the governing statute prescribes the affixing of the corporate seal, as in the case of a municipal corporation, such direction must be observed and no recovery can be had against the corporation in the absence of a seal even though the contract is executed: *MacKay v. City of Toronto* (1917), 39 O.L.R. 34; on appeal (1918) 43 O.L.R. 17, [1920] A.C. 208; *Waterous Engine Co. v. Town of Capreol*, (1922) 52 O.L.R. 247 (C.A.); *London Board of Education v. East Middlesex District High School Board, supra.* If an instrument required to be under seal, for example, an assignment of a lessor's reversion in land, fails for want of due execution, the court will not grant relief against the irregularity unless it can be ascertained from the facts that the intention of the party sought to be bound was to enter into the contract. So where there was no by-law, resolution or evidence of any other corporate action to express the intention of the corporation to enter into the transaction, the person seeking to bind the corporation will not be granted such relief: *Glasgow Lumber Co. Ltd. v. Fettes*, [1933] 1 D.L.R. 66 (Sask. C.A.); and where a lease by a corporation purporting to be a lease for 20 years was not under seal, it was held to be void under the Statute of Frauds because not under the corporate seal, and an action upon the covenant could not be maintained on the ground that the parties had never gone beyond the stage of negotiations, which was one of the grounds on which it was decided in the court below that the action failed: *Newport Industrial Development Co. v. Heughan* (1928), 62 O.L.R. 364; affd [1929] S.C.R. 491. A lease to a corporation granted by deed signed by the lessor, and which, being for more than three years, comes within ss. 1 and 2 of the Statute of Frauds, is not void although the corporate seal of the lessee corporation is not affixed: *Kingston Motor Car Co. Ltd. v. Wright et al.*, [1941] 3 D.L.R. 778 (contract made for a purpose directly connected with the objects of a trading corporation). Where a lease under seal exists, the consequences of overholding and paying rent are the same for a corporation tenant as for an individual: *Young v. Bank of Nova Scotia* (1915), 34 O.L.R. 176 (C.A.). In *West City Motors Ltd. v. Delta Acceptance Corp.*, [1963] 2 O.R. 683 (H.C.), the corporate seal was improperly affixed to a chattel mortgage by the mortgagee. This unauthorized application was held to invalidate the chattel mortgage.

Where the contract is executed under the corporate seal it is executed in the name of the corporation by the proper signing officers whose designations appear under their respective signatures. However, the mere affixing of the corporate seal is sufficient without the signature of the officers, if delivery takes place: *Town of Eastview v. Roman Catholic Episcopal Corp. of Ottawa* (1918), 44 O.L.R. 284 (C.A.) at 295 and 296. As to the sanctity of an agreement to which the common seal of the corporation is attached, see *Re W. N. McEachren & Sons Ltd.*, [1933] O.R. 349 (C.A.).

Where an instrument is produced under seal of the corporation, the seal must *prima facie* be taken to be properly affixed, but the presumption is rebuttable: *D'Arcy v. Tamar Kit Hill & Callington Ry. Co.* (1867), L.R. 2 Ex. 158. In *Inter City Baking Co. v. Rosenblood,* [1954] O.W.N. 531 (C.A.) this presumption was relied upon where corporate seals had been affixed to conveyances of land.

If no formalities are prescribed by the governing Act or by the memorandum and articles, if the seal of the corporation has been affixed by the direction of the persons who manage the affairs of the corporation it will be considered to have been affixed by due authority: *In re Barned's Banking Co.; Ex parte. The Contract Corp.* (1867), L.R. 3 Ch. App. 105 at 116.

If there is nothing in the governing Act, memorandum or articles prescribing the manner in which or the authority under which the seal of the corporation is to be affixed, the president and general manager appointed with authority to conduct the corporation's business will be entitled to use the corporation's seal where necessary: *Regina Plumbing & Heating Co. v. Bruce Robinson Electric Ltd.*, [1933] 3 W.W.R. 469 (Sask. C.A.) at 475.

A corporation incorporated by memorandum can only function through agents authorized to act and acting within the limits of the relevant statutes and its memorandum and articles: *In re Cleadon Trust Ltd.*, [1939] Ch. 286 (C.A.). In the case of a corporation incorporated by memorandum, if articles require instruments under the corporate seal to be signed in a particular manner, for example, by two directors and the secretary, the instrument must be so signed to make it effective: *Re The Land Registry Act, 1911* (1916), 10 W.W.R. 634. In that case it was held that the requirement involved signatures of three persons and that one of the directors signing as such could not also sign as secretary. It was pointed out that if the instrument was not so signed a person dealing with the corporation acquired no rights under it, as even an outsider was deemed to have notice of the contents of the articles (see now however s. 18) and such contructive notice excludes the operation of the rule in *Royal British Bank v. Turquand: Glasgow Lumber Co. Ltd. v. Fettes*, [1933] 1 D.L.R. 66 (Sask. C.A.). In that case it was further held that a lessee, whom it was sought to make liable in pursuance of a defectively executed assignment of the lease, was entitled to attack the validity of its execution. As to the rule in *Royal British Bank v. Turquand* see the heading "Application of rule in *Royal British Bank v. Turquand*" in this chapter.

The corporation will not be bound where the seal has been fraudulently affixed by the secretary and the signatures of the other signing officers are forgeries: *Ruben v. Great Fingall Consolidated Co.*, [1906] A.C. 439, applied in *Kreditbank Cassel G.m.b.H. v. Schenkers, Ltd.*, [1927] 1 K.B. 826 (C.A.) and *South London Greyhound Racecourses Ltd. v. Wake*, [1931] 1 Ch. 496, where bills of exchange and share certificates, respectively, were treated as forgeries because the officers who affixed the seals did so fraudulently without the authority of the corporation, although the signatures themselves were genuine.

There is no general requirement under the *British Columbia Act* that the seal be authenticated by signature. See *Cafco Products Ltd. v. Douglas Eyrl Association Ltd.* (1982), 41 B.C.L.R. 135 (S.C.). An authority to an agent to execute a deed under seal must likewise be under seal: *Berkeley v. Hardy* (1826),

5 B. & C. 355. In the absence of any statutory provision, where the by-laws provide that the seal of the corporation is to be in a designated form, it is within the powers of the directors to authorize the sealing of documents in such form, employing a stamp usually kept at the head office or a stamp kept at a branch office: *Baird v. District Registrar of Titles*, [1938] S.C.R. 25.

Where a corporation was obligated under a statute to sign certain forms and did so by affixing a rubber stamp containing the corporate name with no signature to verify it, the method of signature was criticized by Denning L.J. in *Lazarus Estates Ltd. v. Beasley*, [1956] 1 Q.B. 702 at 710.

In *Atlanta Corp. Ltd. v. Richmond*, [1957] Que. P.R. 176, the court dismissed a motion to reject a power of attorney which did not bear the corporate seal, on the ground that there was no provision in the Quebec Civil Code or the Federal or Quebec Companies Acts requiring that the seal of the corporation must be affixed to such a document.

Pre-incorporation contracts

What follows is the position at common law or if the contract in question is not in writing. See also the discussion of s. 14 under the heading "Pre-incorporation contracts" in Chapter 2, *supra*.

Section 14 of the federal Act now provides that a corporation may, within reasonable time after coming into existence, adopt a written contract made before it came into existence in its name or on its behalf by any action or conduct signifying its intention to be bound thereby. Upon such adoption the corporation is bound by the contract and is entitled to the benefits thereof, as though it had been in existence at the date of the contract and had been a party thereto, and the person who acted in the name of or on behalf of the corporation ceases to be bound by or entitled to the benefits of the contract. Provision is made for an application to the court to determine the rights of the various parties. See *Mission Hill Tire & Auto Centre Ltd. v. Killerney Group Ltd.* (1989), 38 C.P.C. (2d) 64 (Alta. Master) and *Coast Wholesale Applicances Ltd. v. Buffalo* (1990), 103 A.R. 307 (Alta. Master) where it was held on the facts that the liability was that of the individual rather than of the proposed corporation.

At common law, a contract made on behalf of a corporation before incorporation was not binding on the corporation and could not be ratified by it after incorporation: *Kelner v. Baxter* (1866), L.R. 2 C.P. 174; *Re Empress Engineering Co.* (1880), 16 Ch. D. 125 (C.A.); *Waddell v. Dominion City Brick Co.* (1888), 5 Man. R. 119; *Cass v. McCutcheon* (1903), 15 Man. R. 667; *Newborne v. Sensolid (Great Britain) Ltd.*, [1954] 1 Q.B. 45 (C.A.) where *Kelner v. Baxter*, *supra*, is discussed. Nor will a corporation be liable for a pre-incorporation debt even when the persons who created the debt are the same as those who obtain incorporation and form the corporation: *King v. The Modern System Sign Service, Ltd.* (1922), 28 Rev. Leg. 324. A lease signed by a person for the benefit of a corporation before its incorporation is not binding on the corporation and the fact that the corporation occupied the premises after its incorporation does not change the position: *In Re A. Leclerc & Co. Ltd.* (1926), 7 C.B.R. 712. For cases involving pre-incorporation contracts where the principal was held liable see *Hotel St. John's Ltd. v. Parsons* (1978), 50 A.P.R. 386 (Nfld. Dist. Ct.); *B. & N. Flooring Supplies Ltd. v. Williams* (1978), 22 N.B.R. (2d) 239 (Q.B.); *Landmark Inns of Canada Ltd. v. Horeak*, [1982] 2 W.W.R. 377 (Sask. Q.B.); *Federal Business Development Bank v. Eldridge* (1985), 67 N.B.R. (2d) 93, affd (1986), 76 N.B.R. (2d) 399 (C.A.); *Mission Hill Tire & Auto Centre Ltd. v. Killerney Group Ltd.* (1989), 38 C.P.C. (2d) 64 (Alta. Master).

In *Murray Elias Ltd. v. Walsam Investments Ltd.*, [1964] 2 O.R. 381 it was pointed out that a corporation not yet in existence cannot have an agent and that a corporation when incorporated cannot ratify any contract made for it by an alleged agent, yet a contract can be made prior to incorporation provided it is made as a provisional contract; that is, one which is not really a contract unless and until the corporation comes into existence and acts upon it. In such case, the agent would not be liable for damages for the omission of the new corporation to comply with contractual terms of such an agreement unless he had expressly agreed to act in a specified way. See also *Westcom Radio Group Ltd. v. MacIsaac* (1989), 70 O.R. (2d) 591 (Div. Ct.); *General Motors Acceptance Corporation v. Weisman* (1979), 23 O.R. (2d) 479 (Co. Ct.). However, an individual signing may be liable for a breach of implied or express warranty of authority, see: *Delta Construction Co. v. Lidstone* (1979), 96 D.L.R. (3d) 457 (Nlfd. T.D.).

The subsequent adoption and confirmation by the corporation of a pre-incorporation contract does not impose any obligation on the corporation or establish any contractual relation between it and the other party to the contract: *North Sydney Investment Co. v. Higgins*, [1899] A.C. 263. Nor will the corporation be bound in such cases although the parties afterwards carry out some of the terms of the contract and act on the supposition that it was binding on the corporation: *Coit v. Dowling* (1901), 4 Terr. L.R. 464; and see *Bagot Pneumatic Tyre Co. v. Clipper Pneumatic Tyre Co.*, [1902] 1 Ch. 146 (C.A.). A new contract is necessary: *Re J. R. Morgan, Ltd.*, [1927] 1 D.L.R. 882 at 885.

In England a provision in the articles of association that the corporation shall adopt and be bound by such a contract, or shall enter into a particular contract still leaves the corporation free of obligation until it binds itself by a new contract: *Re Northumberland Avenue Hotel Co.* (1886), 33 Ch. D. 16 (C.A.); *Browne v. La Trinidad* (1888), 37 Ch. D. 1 (C.A.); *Re Dale & Plant, Ltd.* (1889), 43 Ch. D. 255.

Conversely, a corporation cannot by adoption or ratification claim the benefit of a contract made on its behalf before incorporation: *Natal Land & Colonization Co. Ltd. v. Pauline Colliery & Development Syndicate Ltd.*, [1904] A.C. 120; *Repetti Ltd. v. Oliver-Lee Ltd.* (1922), 52 O.L.R. 315 (C.A.).

There is nothing, however, to prevent the corporation, after incorporation, from entering into a new contract on the terms of the pre-incorporation contract: *Howard v. Patent Ivory Mfg. Co.* (1888), 38 Ch. D. 156; *Re Dale & Plant Ltd.* (1889), 43 Ch. D. 255. And where a person executed a document which was handed to the organization committee of a proposed corporation as his agents to hold the same and hand it over when the proposed corporation became incorporated, which was done, and the proposed corporation having become incorporated then executed the document, which was acted upon, it was held that the corporation could sue on it: *Associated Growers of B.C., Ltd. v. B.C. Fruit Land, Ltd.*, [1925] 1 D.L.R. 871. See also *Hudson-Mattagami Exploration Mining Co. v. Wettlaufer Bros Ltd.* (1928), 62 O.L.R. 387 (C.A.) (tentative contract with corporation becoming effective upon incorporation and payment by the corporation of purchase consideration); *Re Red Deer Milling & Elevator Co. Ltd.* (1908), 1 Alta. L.R. 237 (corporation having accepted goods purporting to be sold by agreement made in name of corporation prior to its incorporation and having paid promissory notes for portion of price, estopped against seller from denying that agreement valid and binding on corporation as if formally executed under corporation's seal after incorporation). See also *Heinhuis v. Blacksheep Charters Ltd.* (1987), 46 D.L.R. (4th) 67 (B.C. C.A.) and *Brown Brothers Motor Lease Canada Ltd. v. Kirkpatrick* (1992), 67 B.C.L.R. (2d) 141 (B.C. C.A.).

If the corporation merely takes the benefit of a contract made before its incorporation it will not be bound: *Re Rotherham Alum & Chemical Co.* (1883), 25 Ch. D. 103 (C.A.); *In re English & Colonial Produce Co.*, [1906] 2 Ch. 435 (C.A.); *In re National Motor Mail-Coach Co. Ltd.*, [1908] 2 Ch. 515 (C.A.).

As to goods supplied to an inchoate corporation, see *Seiffert v. Irving* (1888), 15 O.R. 173; as to services, *O'Dell v. Boston & Nova Scotia Coal Co.* (1896), 29 N.S.R. 385.

Sale of assets and undertaking

Section 189(3) of the Act provides that a sale, lease or exchange of all or substantially all the property of a corporation other than in the ordinary course of business requires the approval of the shareholders as set out in the section. It must be approved by a special resolution, namely, a resolution carried by a majority of not less than two-thirds of the votes cast by the shareholders who voted in respect thereof or signed by all the shareholders entitled to vote on such resolution. It will be noted that a right of dissent is given to shareholders pursuant to the provisions of s. 190 of the Act which provides for a method of valuing shares of shareholders who follow a prescribed course of conduct in dissenting from certain proposals. A similar provision is contained in s. 184(3) of the Ontario Act. The right of dissent is given by s. 185 of that Act. The question can arise as to what is "all or substantially all" the property of the corporation. Thus, if a corporation has two factories of approximately equal size and proposes to sell one of them, this would not usually constitute a sale of all or substantially all the property of the corporation. It is not easy to envisage a case in which it is in the ordinary course of business of a corporation to sell all or substantially all of its property. One example might be a corporation formed to realize on certain assets. See Chapter 12 for a further discussion of these provisions.

In the case of corporations incorporated under other jurisdictions, a sale of the assets and undertaking can be effected in pursuance, either of a power in that behalf contained in the letters patent or memorandum of association, or in pursuance of an ancillary power conferred by the governing Act. Any special procedure prescribed by the governing Act must be followed: *McGregor v. St. Croix Lumber Co.* (1912), 8 D.L.R. 876.

Sales of the assets or undertaking of a corporation may also be effected under such provisions as ss. 191-192 of this Act with regard to reorganizations or arrangements or under the provisions of the *Companies' Creditors Arrangement Act,* the *Winding-up Act* or the *Bankruptcy and Insolvency Act.* See *In re Sovereign Life Assurance Co.* (1889), 42 Ch. D. 540 at 547 (no power under governing Act for an insurance corporation to transfer its business to another corporation). In *Doyle v. Miniota Mutual Fire Insurance Co.*, [1924] 2 D.L.R. 471, a majority of the Manitoba Court of Appeal held that an arrangement under which a mutual fire insurance corporation was to assign all policies, premium notes, assessments, mortgages and contracts with agents, to another corporation, which agreed to re-insure the risks, was valid under s. 30 of the *Mutual Fire Insurance Act*, R.S.M. 1913, c. 101, as an arrangement for re-insurance, notwithstanding that the assignor corporation would be denuded of most of its assets. Dennistoun J.A. considered that the directors were entitled to enter into the transaction for the purpose of protecting the members from loss, following *Hovey v. Whiting* (1888), 14 S.C.R. 515 at 520.

Whether a sale of all the corporation's assets and undertaking can effectively be authorized by the directors or not, it is usual and proper to have the sale approved by the shareholders beforehand. In *Trans Mountain Pipe Line Co. v. Dawn Holdings Ltd.* (1986), 7 B.C.L.R. (2d) 165 (B.C. S.C.), a special resolution for the sale of its undertaking was approved by the shareholders; the resolution was general in nature without a specific buyer. At some later date a purchaser was found and a sale agreement was entered into by the corporation. The majority shareholder who was interested in another purchaser brought an application for an order preventing the said completion of the sale on the grounds that the special resolution had been spent and the transaction was not that prescribed in the resolution. The application was dismissed since the special resolution was not stale and the transaction was sufficiently similar to that described in the resolution. It was pointed out the resolution was to be given commercial rather than legalistic construction. The substance of the two transactions was sufficiently identical.

The power to sell assets is not destroyed by liquidation. The effect of liquidation is to make the power subject to the approval of the court and the superior rights of the creditors: *Re Bailey Cobalt Mines Ltd.* (1920), 47 O.L.R. 13 (C.A.).

An agreement for sale of the corporation's assets and undertaking entered into by a selling committee appointed by the directors is not binding on the corporation in the absence of approval by the directors and shareholders: *Peterson & Canwood Co-Operative Association Ltd. v. Cook* (1923), 16 Sask. L.R. 281. A managing director has no implied authority to sell the entire assets of the corporation as a going concern: *Picard v. Revelstoke Saw Mill Co. et al.* (1913), 9 D.L.R. 580; (1913), 12 D.L.R. 685 (B.C.C.A.) (managing director personally liable for implied warranty of authority). On the other hand, where a vendor has agreed to sell a business including the freehold premises, which are vested in a corporation absolutely controlled by the vendor, an enforceable contract will result if the vendor is in a position to compel the corporation to execute the necessary conveyance: *Harold Elliott & H. Elliott (Builders), Ltd. v. Pierson*, [1948] Ch. 452. And similarly, an option to purchase the assets of a corporation signed by the president (the principal shareholder) with the knowledge and consent of the other directors (holders of all the remaining shares) is valid and binding on the corporation although no formal resolution of approval was ever adopted: *Hayes v. Miron*, [1957] Que. Q.B. 538 (C.A.).

The provisions attaching to preferred shares may require the assent of the preferred shareholders, given at a meeting, to a sale of the assets and undertaking. Under s. 189(7) it is provided that holders of a class of shares of the corporation are entitled to vote separately as a class only if such class is affected by the sale, lease or exchange in a manner different from the shares of another class. Ordinarily, whether or not the share carries the right to vote, each share has a vote with respect to such a sale, lease or exchange, s. 189(6).

A shareholder is not debarred from voting for the approval of the sale of the corporation's assets by the circumstance of his having an interest in the subject matter of the vote: *Dominion Cotton Mills v. Amyot*, [1912] A.C. 546; *Ritchie v. Vermillion Mining Co.* (1902), 4 O.L.R. 588 (C.A.) (approving majority were also shareholders in a rival corporation the interests of which they were furthering in carrying out the sale). If a proposed sale is being conducted at such a time and in such a manner that it could only be regarded as an improvident or improper proceeding or as designed to enable interested parties to secure the assets at an inadequate price it may be restrained by injunction at the suit of shareholders suing on behalf of themselves and other shareholders: *Ritchie v. Vermillion Mining Co., supra*.

Minority shareholders suing on behalf of themselves and all other shareholders, except the defendants, are entitled to restrain the majority from carrying out a sale for an inadequate consideration in a manner oppressive and fraudulent upon the minority: *Elliott v. Orr Gold Mines Ltd.* (1920), 17 O.W.N. 447 and cases cited; or a sale where the statutory requirements have not been complied with: *Pellatt v. Dominion Sewer Pipe & Clay Industries Ltd.* (1929), 36 O.W.N. 298. Where a purchaser of a business is entitled to rescission on the ground of fraudulent misrepresentation and *restitutio in integrum* is impossible, the court will direct appropriate accounts to be taken: *Carter v. Golland*, [1937] 4 D.L.R. 513 (Ont. C.A.).

A sale to a new corporation is sometimes resorted to for the purpose of reconstruction; the existing corporation sells its assets subject to liabilities to a new corporation with the desired capitalization; the new corporation issues its shares in payment and these are distributed by the vendor corporation or its liquidator among the shareholders *pro rata*.

The sale agreement should explicitly state that the goodwill is included, when the undertaking of the corporation is being sold. However, the use of the words "assets" or "property" may include the goodwill without its being specifically mentioned: *Jennings v. Jennings*, [1898] 1 Ch. 378; *In re Leas Hotel Co.*, [1902] 1 Ch. 332. So also where a business is sold the goodwill passes without being expressly mentioned: *Shipwright v. Clements* (1871), 19 W.R. 599. A sale of the enterprise and undertaking as a going concern will include contracts and claims thereunder: *Provincial Transport Co. v. Montreal Sight Seeing Tours Ltd.*, [1933] S.C.R. 109. The sale of an asset, for example, a newspaper, the publication of which is discontinued by the purchaser, may result in the destruction of the office of an employee, for example, the chief sub-editor of such newspaper, in which case such sale involves a breach of contract for which the vendor is liable in damages: *Collier v. Sunday Referee Publishing Co., Ltd.*, [1940] 2 K.B. 647.

As to the principles on which covenants of a director or shareholder of the vendor corporation restricting the carrying on of a similar business will be enforced, see *Connors Bros. Ltd. v. Connors*, [1941] 1 D.L.R. 81 at 93 (P.C.). A common provision is for the vendor to covenant that, within a specified period and area, he will not "either solely or jointly with or as agent, officer, manager, servant, director or shareholder of any other person or corporation directly or indirectly carry on or assist in carrying on or be engaged, concerned, interested or employed" in a specified business. Where the business specified was a quarry and one of the vendors provided a sum of money to enable others to purchase a quarry and for working capital and took part on their behalf in preliminary negotiations for the purchase of machinery and equipment for the quarry, such acts were held to constitute a breach of a covenant in the foregoing terms: *Batts Combe Quarry, Ltd. v. Ford*, [1943] Ch. 51 (C.A.).

It may be a term of the contract that the vendor corporation is to distribute the proceeds of the sale among its shareholders and is to be wound up or surrender its charter. If any part of the consideration to be received by the vendor corporation consists of shares or securities of the purchaser corporation and either there is to be a distribution among shareholders of the vendor corporation, or the vendor corporation proposes to cease carrying on the business or part of its business so sold, the transaction is an "arrangement" as defined by s. 192(1). It may be that in such a case the sale must be carried out as an arrangement under that section.

The sale agreement is frequently expressed to operate as an actual transfer of the assets, in which case it should contain a covenant by the vendor to execute such further assurances as may be required to vest full title and ownership. Sometimes as an additional precaution the agreement or the general bill of sale, if one is given, contains a power of attorney to the purchaser to execute such further assurances in the name of the vendor. The necessary deeds, bills of sale, and transfers appropriate to the specific assets sold should be executed and registered.

A general transfer of assets may be insufficient where the statute requires the recording of a transfer: *Engineer Mining Co. Ltd. v. Fraser*, [1923] A.C. 228. In certain cases where special statutory provisions apply as, for example, on the purchase by a bank of the assets of another bank, the assets of the vendor corporation will vest in the purchaser corporation without more: *Bank of Montreal v. Irvine & Feinstein*, [1924] 3 D.L.R. 752 (Sask. C.A.) (purchaser bank entitled to sue on a note given to vendor bank without endorsement by vendor bank).

Where a vendor corporation has sold its assets and undertaking and assigned the benefit of an assignable contract to a purchaser, and has subsequently been completely wound up, the purchaser can sue on the contract without joining the vendor corporation as plaintiff: *Tolhurst v. Associated Portland Cement Mfg. (1900) Ltd.*, [1903] A.C. 414 at 420, applied in *British American Timber Co. Ltd. v. Ray W. Jones*, [1944] 2 D.L.R. 481 (B.C.C.A.) at 501.

Bulk Sales Acts

In the provinces where Bulk Sales Acts are in force a sale of the corporation's assets may be a "sale in bulk" and therefore subject to the provisions of the Act. Thus in Ontario the sale of part of a manufacturing corporation's business, plant and machinery, not in the ordinary course of business, comes within the provisions of the Act: *Interlake Tissue Mills Co. Ltd. v. George Everall Co. Ltd.* (1921), 50 O.L.R. 165; *Re St. Thomas Cabinets, Ltd.* (1921), 50 O.L.R. 492; and the same applies in Saskatchewan: *Barthels Shewan & Co. v. Sloane* (1915), 19 D.L.R. 547 (Sask. C.A.).

The sale of an interest in a business, in order to constitute a bulk sale, must include a stock of goods, wares and merchandise and the sale of a business and goodwill which does not include a stock of goods is not a bulk sale within the meaning of the *Nova Scotia Bulk Sales Act*: *Norris v. McKenzie*, [1933] 3 D.L.R. 713.

The provisions of the Quebec Civil Code as to bulk sales do not apply to a sale of the vendor's plant as a going concern, including stock in trade and other specified assets and goodwill, to a corporation incorporated for the purpose of acquiring the same in consideration of the issuance of the purchaser's shares and an undertaking to pay the vendor's liabilities: *D'Amours v. Darveau*, [1933] S.C.R. 503.

Bankruptcy and liquidation

A sale of the assets and undertaking subject to liabilities assumed by the purchaser may be attacked and set aside if the vendor is subsequently adjudged bankrupt. In *Re Simms*, [1930] 2 Ch. 22, where the cases are collected, a trader transferred his business to a private corporation for shares, the corporation agreeing to assume the liabilities. It was held that the substitution, in place of a going business and substantial business assets, of shares in a private corporation together with a right of action by the debtor against the corporation on its covenant to discharge his liabilities must necessarily have the result of delaying the creditors. The agreement was accordingly held to be a fraudulent transfer within the meaning of the English *Bankruptcy Act, 1914*.

If it can be established that the transfer of the assets by the vendor corporation to the new corporation and the surrender of the vendor corporation's charter was part of a fraudulent scheme to defeat the claims of any possible creditors of the old corporation and the directors of the old corporation have benefited from the fraud, the directors of the old corporation can be made liable. See *McLaughlin v. Solloway & Mills*, [1936] S.C.R. 127; revd in part *sub nom. Solloway et al. v. McLaughlin*, [1938] A.C. 247.

A corporation cannot by going into voluntary liquidation absolve itself from contractual liability. Thus a voluntary winding-up does not operate to dismiss the servants of the corporation: *Midland Counties District Bank v. Attwood*, [1905] 1 Ch. 357. Where the liquidator terminates his employment, an employee pursuing a claim for damages for wrongful dismissal may either prove in the liquidation or commence a separate action, and the court ought not to interfere with his discretion unless it is satisfied that circumstances (e.g., saving of expense) exist which justify the taking away from the employee of his choice of a tribunal: *Cook v. "X" Chair Patents Co., Ltd.*, [1959] 3 All E.R. 906.

In *Northern Ontario Power Co. v. La Roche Mines Ltd.*, [1937] O.R. 824 (C.A.), [1938] 3 D.L.R. 657 (P.C.) a mining corporation had entered into a contract for the supply of electrical power by a power corporation during the mining life of the corporation's properties. Having sold its properties, the corporation denied further liability under the contract and went into voluntary liquidation. An action was brought by the power corporation against the mining corporation and its liquidator for damages for breach of contract and the Judicial Committee of the Privy Council upheld the dismissal of the action on the ground that on the construction of the particular contract it came to an end on the sale of the mining properties, but the reasons for judgment do not indicate that upon a different construction of the contract the liability to the power corporation for damages would not have been a provable claim.

Provision for liabilities of vendor corporation

The sale agreement will often provide that the purchaser is to assume the liabilities of the vendor and indemnify the vendor against all proceedings and claims in respect thereof. Such a covenant does not enable creditors of the vendor, who are not parties to the sale agreement, to sue the purchaser as there is no privity between the creditors and the purchaser; nor does it create a trust in favour of creditors of the vendor corporation: *Re Excelsior Dairy Machinery Ltd.* (1922), 52 O.L.R. 225. In *Trustee Company of Winnipeg v. Manitoba Bridge & Iron Works Ltd.*, [1922] 1 W.W.R. 178 (Man. C.A.) an amendment was permitted adding the successor corporation as a defendant, a direct liability of the successor corporation being alleged.

The right of indemnity is, however, assignable, and, where the creditor has taken from the vendor corporation an assignment of the purchaser's obligation of payment and indemnity, the creditor can sue on the covenant: *Stewart v. Stratford Hotel Co.* (1908), 12 O.W.R. 157 (C.A.); *In re Perkins, Poyser v. Beyfus*, [1892] 2 Ch. 182. See also the first mentioned case as to the proper parties to the action.

There may, of course, be novation, that is, the liability of the purchaser may be substituted for the liability of the vendor corporation; but in such a case the creditor, the original debtor (the vendor) and the new debtor (the purchaser) must be parties to the transaction: *In re Manchester & London Life Assurance & Loan Association* (1870), L.R. 9 Eq. 643 at 649; *La Banque d'Hochelaga v. Auger* (1925), 39 Que. K.B. 288 (C.A.). Novation may be inferred from the acts of the parties: *In re National Provincial Life Assurance Society* (1870),

L.R. 9 Eq. 306; *British American Timber Co. Ltd. v. Ray W. Jones*, [1944] 2 D.L.R. 481 (B.C.C.A.) at 486 at 489. As to the requirements to effect novation under the laws of the province of Quebec see *Walker v. Barclays Bank (Canada)*, [1941] S.C.R. 491.

Sometimes the sale agreement provides that the purchaser is to enter into a direct covenant with the creditors to pay off their claims, but—unless actual novation is contemplated and can be effected—it would appear to be better for the vendor corporation to rely on an express covenant of indemnity.

The purchaser corporation, by admitting a claim and promising to pay it, may make itself liable: *In re Star Flooring Co. Ltd.* (1924), 4 C.B.R. 679. However, an admission of responsibility by the purchaser corporation, which has assumed the liabilities of the vendor corporation, will not operate as a release of the latter: *Freshwater v. Bulmer Rayon Co. Ltd.*, [1933] 1 Ch. 162 (C.A.).

If the vendor is a trustee of moneys received from creditors and those moneys are traced to the purchaser, the creditors can recover such moneys from the purchaser but must join the trustee either as co-plaintiff or as a defendant: *Best v. Beatty* (1920), 47 O.L.R. 265 (C.A.). Possibly the contract may be so framed as to create a trust for creditors of the vendor which they can enforce directly if they join the vendor: *Thompson v. Donlands Properties Ltd.*, [1934] O.R. 541 (C.A.), although that was a case of a sale of assets by an administratrix to a corporation, indicates that where the purchaser corporation undertakes to pay the liabilities the action can be so framed as to enable the court to order the corporation to carry out its undertaking and pay the creditor.

Unless there is novation or until the liabilities of the vendor corporation have been paid off in due course of operations of the purchaser, as in the case of ordinary trade liabilities, the existence of undischarged liabilities of the vendor corporation will be an obstacle to the surrender of its charter.

Income tax

The income tax aspects of any sale of the assets of the corporation and any distribution of the proceeds of sale to its creditors must be carefully considered.

Appointment of agents and officers

Section 121 provides that, subject to the articles, by-laws and any unanimous shareholders' agreement, the directors may appoint officers of the corporation.

An agreement between two persons who were both shareholders and directors of a corporation that one of them would be employed as general manager of the corporation as long as he desired that position and would also be president of the corporation was held to be invalid as being contrary to s. 90(d) and s. 92 of the former Federal Act: *Motherwell v. Schoof*, [1949] 4 D.L.R. 812.

However, in *Ringuet v. Bergeron* (1960), 24 D.L.R. (2d) 449, a majority of the Supreme Court of Canada held that an agreement between majority shareholders of a corporation whereby they would elect and name one another as directors and officers of the corporation was not contrary to public policy, did not contravene any provision of the *Quebec Companies Act* and was valid.

Pending the first meeting of a newly-elected board of directors to appoint new officers, there is an implied authority from the new board to the existing officers to continue to act as such; but where the board of directors of a corporation were unable to agree, at the first meeting after their election, on the appointment of a president and secretary of the corporation, and the old officers continued to act, the Supreme Court of Canada held that the old officers had automatically forfeited their positions on the election of the new board of directors, there being no provision indicating otherwise in the letters patent or by-laws of the corporation and the *Quebec Companies Act*, R.S.Q. 1941, c. 276, s. 86, providing that the directors after their election should elect a president: *Ghimpelman v. Bercovici*, [1957] S.C.R. 128.

Where the by-laws of a corporation provided that the chairman of the board of directors was to be "elected" by the directors, and in so doing, the directors used the word "appointed" and added "for the ensuing year and until his successor is elected" and then removed the chairman before the year had passed, the court held that the words "elected" and "appointed" were synonymous in this connection, that the right to nominate a chairman carried with it the power of removal and that the words "for the ensuing year" did not confer any vested right to hold the office until the expiration of the term: *Van Alstyne v. Rankin & St. Lawrence Corp. Ltd.*, [1952] Que. S.C. 12.

The by-laws usually provide that certain officers, for example, the president, vice-president, secretary and treasurer, are to be appointed by the board of directors and that the board may appoint other officers and agents of the corporation.

The appointment of senior officers of a corporation is usually made by the directors and such of these officers as are full-time employees may enter into formal employment contracts which may be executed by the corporation under seal. The duty of engaging other officers, employees and agents is commonly delegated to one of the senior officers of the corporation and the written employment contracts, if any, of such persons are usually less formal and will probably not be executed by the corporation under seal.

If a contract to serve the corporation is not to be performed within a year an agreement in writing is required to satisfy the Statute of Frauds: *Eley v. Positive Assurance Co.* (1875), 1 Ex. Div. 20; *Britain v. Rossiter* (1879), 11 Q.B.D. 123 (C.A.). A minute of the board signed by the chairman embodying a resolution incorporating the terms of a draft agreement setting out the terms of appointment is a sufficient memorandum in writing: *Jones v. Victoria Graving Dock Co.* (1877), 2 Q.B.D. 314 (C.A.). The contract must show the date when the service is to begin and should also contain some definition of the nature of the service: *In re Alexander's Timber Co.* (1901), 70 L.J. Ch. 767.

Where a liaison manager had been appointed by the directors of a corporation by a resolution which stipulated no time for the duration of the contract and upon being dismissed brought an action against the corporation for wrongful dismissal without notice, the court held that the resolution was not only *prima facie* evidence of the terms of the contract of service but it was the best available evidence thereof and that the affixing of the corporate seal to the resolution was not essential to its validity as a contract in view of s. 98(1) of the Saskatchewan *Companies Act*, which, read in conjunction with s. 3 of the *Saskatchewan Masters and Servants Act,* did not require a contract of hiring to be under seal: *Havard v. Freeholders Oil Co. Ltd.* (1952), 6 W.W.R. (N.S.) 413.

Where a by-law appointing an officer for a term of years, provides that an agreement is to be entered into fixing the amount of remuneration and no agreement is entered into, no enforceable contract for the term results: *Warren v. Superior Engravers Ltd.*, [1941] 1 D.L.R. 323 at 328 (Ont. C.A.). In *Jubilee Theatre Ltd.* (1956), 3 D.L.R. (2d) 624 (N.S. C.A.), a secretary who had been appointed without any fixed term of office made a claim for unpaid salary, which had been stopped at the request of the majority shareholder, and the court held that the secretary was entitled to recover on the basis that such an officer appointed without any fixed term held office during the pleasure of the board of directors or until he resigned or until some event (the winding-up of the corporation) happened which involved a termination of his employment.

Where a secretary-treasurer had been employed by resolution of the board to act during the pleasure of the board at a weekly salary and his services were terminated at a board meeting it was held to be immaterial that such termination was not shown by the recorded minutes: *Fancy v. Dealers Security Ltd.* (1932), 41 O.W.N. 500 (C.A.).

Where a director is appointed managing director he is not necessarily entitled to hold the appointment as long as he remains in office as a director: *Foster v. Foster*, [1916] 1 Ch. 532.

Where an agreement has been entered into between a managing director and a corporation, the terms of which are inconsistent with the exercise of the corporation's power to terminate his employment conferred on it by the articles, an action lies for wrongful dismissal in the event of the corporation exercising that power: *Southern Foundries (1926), Ltd. v. Shirlaw*, [1940] A.C. 701 followed in *Shindler v. Northern Raincoat Co.*, [1960] 2 All E.R. 239 (C.A.). In the *Southern Foundries* case a director was appointed managing director by contract for ten years and the articles of the corporation provided that subject to the provisions of any contract the managing director should *ipso facto* cease to be managing director if he ceased to be a director and that the corporation might by extraordinary resolution remove any director before the expiration of his period of office. The view of the House of Lords was that there was an implied term in the contract that the corporation would not remove him from his position as a director, and so unseat him as managing director, during the term of his appointment. Subsequently the corporation adopted new articles providing that another corporation, a stranger to the contract of employment, might remove from office any director of the corporation. A majority of the House of Lords (Viscount Maugham and Lord Romer dissenting) held that the fact that the removal was done by a third party, who was given power to do so under the new article, did not prevent the dismissal from being wrongful.

Where there was no contract of employment between a managing director and a corporation, and the articles besides authorizing the directors to appoint a managing director provided that the appointment should be subject to termination *ipso facto* if the corporation in general meeting so determined, the Court of Appeal held that the articles governed the appointment and that the managing director was not entitled to receive notice of the termination of his employment: *Read v. Astoria Garage (Streatham) Ltd.*, [1952] 1 Ch. 637.

And where the articles of a corporation provided that the appointment of the managing director was subject to termination at the pleasure of the board of directors, the British Columbia Court of Appeal held that the managing director of the corporation was not entitled to damages for wrongful dismissal, there being no contract of employment and the articles providing for a right of immediate dismissal on the part of the corporation: *Allish v. Allied Engineering of B.C. Ltd.* (1957), 9 D.L.R. (2d) 688.

If a corporation has a manager whom it desires to dismiss, it may pay him a lump sum out of its capital in satisfaction of all his claims under his management agreement: *Investment Trust Corp. Ltd. v. Singapore Traction Co.*, [1935] Ch. 615 (C.A.) 635 at 642.

Where the articles of association of a corporation provided that a director might contract with a corporation but expressly forbade his voting in respect of a contract in which he was interested, and the director voted in favour of the resolution appointing him managing director at a remuneration, it was held that there was a contract between the director and the corporation within the meaning of the article, that the appointment was irregular, but that the irregularity could be cured by a vote of the corporation in general meeting: *Foster v. Foster*, [1916] 1 Ch. 532. But see the view expressed by Idington J. in *Wade v. Kendrick* (1906), 37 S.C.R. 32 at 53. See also *Re Owen Sound Lumber Co.* (1917), 38 O.L.R. 414 (C.A.).

In *Slone & Holt v. Margolian et al.* (1957), 8 D.L.R. (2d) 115, the court held that a director was not prevented from voting for a resolution appointing himself managing director where the articles of association of the corporation authorized the directors to make such an appointment and did not forbid a director from voting in respect of a contract in which he was interested except only if the voter was a member of another corporation which had contracted with the corporation. At page 121, MacDonald J. pointed out that the director's participation in the vote did not render the resolution void but only voidable at the option of the corporation and that it was capable of ratification at a shareholders' meeting.

Where a managing director was appointed to "perform the duties and exercise the powers in relation to the business of the appellant company and the businesses of its existing subsidiary companies . . . which might from time to time be assigned to or vested in him by the board of directors of the appellant company" it was held that the board of directors might properly require the managing director to confine his attention to the affairs not of the parent but of a particular subsidiary: *Harold Holdsworth & Co. (Wakefield) Ltd. v. Caddies*, [1955] 1 All E.R. 725 (H.L.).

A corporation is liable in damages to its general manager for breach of contract of employment if, by resolution of the directors, it materially lessens his authority under such contract and makes it impossible for him to discharge his duties thereunder: *Montreal Public Service Co. v. Champagne* (1917), 33 D.L.R. 49 (P.C.).

As to the remuneration of officers and agents, see the notes to s. 121 in Chapter 8.

A receiver and manager appointed by debenture holders is not a manager or officer of the corporation within the meaning of ss. 455(1) (definition of "officer") and 333(1) (misfeasance proceedings) of the English *Companies Act, 1948* because he has no duty of managing the affairs of the corporation for the corporation's benefit but is appointed by the debenture holders to facilitate the enforcement of their security: *Re B. Johnson & Co. (Builders) Ltd.*, [1955] 1 Ch. 634 (C.A.).

Liability for acts of agents and officers

Application of rule in Royal British Bank v. Turquand

What is within the apparent scope of the authority of an officer or agent appointed under any particular title, such as manager, general manager, secretary, etc., is a question of fact rather than of law: *Foley v. Commercial Cars Ltd.* (1922), 52 O.L.R. 174 (C.A.) 178.

A person dealing *bona fide* with the apparent agent of a corporation acting within the apparent scope of his authority is entitled to the benefit of the rule in *Royal British Bank v. Turquand* (1856), 6 E. & B. 327. Under that rule persons dealing with a corporation were fixed with notice of the public documents of the corporation and with knowledge that its agents cannot do anything inconsistent therewith; they were not bound to enquire further and to determine whether the internal proceedings which might have been taken to confer authority on an agent or officer acting within the apparent scope of his authority were in fact taken.

Every corporation has an implied power to act through its agents, since being an artificial person it "cannot act in its own person, for it has no person": *Ferguson v. Wilson* (1866), L.R. 2 Ch. App. 77 at 89. See further on this point the comment under the heading "Authorization of contracts" and see the comment on s. 18 under the heading "Authority of directors, officers and agents (s. 18)" in this chapter.

No constructive notice

At common law a person dealing with a corporation was deemed to have notice of the documents of the corporation on public file; that is, in the case of a corporation incorporated under the former federal Act, this would include the Act itself, the letters patent and any supplementary letters patent and in the case of a corporation incorporated by articles of association would include notice of the contents of such articles.

Under the present Act, in the absence of actual or imputed knowledge, a person is not affected and is not deemed to have notice or knowledge of the contents of any documents concerning the corporation by reason only that the document has been filed by the director or is available for inspection at an office of the corporation (s. 17). Thus, articles of incorporation and articles of amendment would no longer be deemed to be known to any person dealing with the corporation.

Authority of directors, officers and agents (s. 18)

At common law a person dealing with a corporation was not bound to enquire whether internal proceedings had in fact been taken to confer authority on an agent or officer acting within the apparent scope of his authority. Thus, a contract signed on behalf of a corporation by the president and the secretary would ordinarily be binding on the corporation without any further evidence of authority. The federal Act (s. 18) provides that a corporation or a guarantor of an obligation of the corporation may not assert against a person dealing with that corporation or any person who has acquired rights from that corporation that (1) there has been failure to comply with the articles, by-laws or any unanimous shareholders' agreement; (2) the persons named in the most recent notice sent to the director are not the directors of the corporation; (3) the place named in the most recent notice sent to the director is not the registered office of the corporation; (4) a person held out by the corporation as a director, officer or agent has not been duly appointed or has no authority to exercise the powers and perform the duties that are customary in the business of the corporation or usual for such director, officer or agent; (5) that any document issued by a director, officer or agent of a corporation with actual or usual authority to issue the document is not valid or genuine; or (6) financial assistance as referred to in s. 44 or a sale, lease or exchange of property referred to in s. 189(3) was not authorized; unless in each case such person has or ought to have had by reason of his position with or relationship to the corporation knowledge to the contrary.

The rule that an outsider is deemed to have notice of the contents of articles of association does not apply in the case of by-laws which are not public property and are not accessible to those dealing with the corporation: *Montreal & St. Lawrence Light & Power Co. v. Robert*, [1906] A.C. 196 at 202; *Box v. Bird's Hill Sand Co.* (1913), 12 D.L.R. 556 at 561 (Man. C.A.); *Re W.N. McEachren & Sons Ltd.*, [1933] O.R. 349 at 365 (C.A.).

It is as a result not necessary for a person contracting with a corporation to satisfy himself that the officer or agent purporting to act for it has been duly appointed: *In re County Life Ass. Co.* (1870), L.R. 5 Ch. App. 288; *Mahony v. East Holyford Mining Co.* (1875), L.R. 7 H.L. 869 at 894; *Biggerstaff v. Rowatt's Wharf Ltd.*, [1896] 2 Ch. 93 at 106 (C.A.); *Doctor v. People's Trust Co.* (1914), 16 D.L.R. 192 (B.C.C.A.); *General Supply Co. of Can. Ltd. v. O'Neill Morkin Machinery Co.*, [1923] 2 W.W.R. 928; *Imperial Bank of Canada v. Dennis* (1926), 59 O.L.R. 20 at 22 (C.A.).

Any irregularity in the exercise of a power to appoint an agent will not affect a person dealing with the agent bona fide and without notice of the irregularity: *Biggerstaff v. Rowatt's Wharf Ltd.*, *supra*, at 104. A corporation cannot escape liability upon an agreement executed under its common seal with an outsider on the ground that its directors have not been regularly elected: *Re W. N. McEachren & Sons Ltd.*, [1933] O.R. 349 at 361 (C.A.); *Gray v. Yellowknife Gold Mines Ltd. (No. 1)*, [1945] O.R. 688, [1947] O.R. 928 (C.A.).

In the case of a person acting as managing director, a person dealing with him must look at the governing Act and the charter, or the memorandum and articles in the case of a corporation incorporated by memorandum, and if the transaction is apparently regular and it appears that the board could have given him the power which he purported to exercise, that is sufficient if the person is dealing with him bona fide: *Biggerstaff v. Rowatt's Wharf Ltd.*, *supra*, at 102, 103. In such a case the person dealing with the officer is entitled to assume that he has been duly clothed with the real authority which he was ostensibly exercising in making the contract: *National Malleable Castings Co. v. Smiths' Falls Malleable Castings Co.* (1907), 14 O.L.R. 22 at 28 (C.A.). In *Freeman & Lockyer (A Firm) v. Buckhurst Park Properties (Mangal) Ltd. et al.*, [1964] 2 Q.B. (C.A.) the plaintiff was successful in its action in contract against the defendant corporation when the plaintiff contracted with Kapoor, one of the directors of the defendant corporation. Provision had been made in the articles of association for the appointment of a managing director, but no such director had been appointed. The Court held that, although Kapoor had no actual authority to contract with the plaintiff, he had ostensible authority and had assumed the role of managing director to the knowledge of the Board. See also: *Hely-Hutchinson v. Brayhead, Ltd. et al.*, [1967] 3 All E.R. 98 (C.A.); affg [1967] 2 All E.R. 14.

Other cases where it was held sufficient that the managing director was the apparent agent of the corporation to transact business of the kind in issue are: *Doctor v. People's Trust Co.* (1914), 16 D.L.R. 192 (B.C.C.A.) (contract for a building made by managing director); *Vancouver Engineering Works v. Columbia Bitulithic Co.* (1914), 16 D.L.R. 841 (under the corporation's articles the managing director might have had the power to give promissory notes); *Dey v. Pullinger Engineering Co.*, [1921] 1 K.B. 77 (managing director without authority drawing bills of exchange which he might have been authorized to draw under the articles of the corporation); *In re British Columbia Bond Corp. Ltd. & Lang* (1931), 12 C.B.R. 213 (managing director under the articles of the corporation might have had the power which he purported to exercise).

The same rule was applied in the case of the chairman of the board in *British Thomson-Houston Co. v. Federated European Bank Ltd.*, [1932] 2 K.B. 176 (C.A.) (chairman acting in a matter normally entrusted to directors) and in the case of managers in *McArthur v. Imperial Trust Co.* (1911), 17 W.L.R. 415 (where acts were within the scope of the corporation's corporate powers and the joint managers' duties; liability grounded on estoppel); *Cox v. Canadian Bank of Commerce* (1912), 46 S.C.R. 564 (no notice of limitation of ostensible authority of manager); *McDougall Segur Exploration Co. v. Solloway Mills & Co. Ltd.*, [1931] 2 W.W.R. 516 at 523 (local manager); *Keystone Shingles & Lumber Ltd. v. Moody Shingles Ltd.*, [1942] 2 D.L.R. 311 (officer *de facto* manager).

In the following cases the apparent agent of the corporation was the president and the same rule was applied: *Garrison v. Thomsen & Clarke Timber Co. Ltd.*,

[1926] 2 W.W.R. 81 (contract made by president); *Bank of United States v. Ross*, [1932] S.C.R. 150 (promissory notes given by president in accordance with authority under the by-laws, but no resolution giving him express authority); *W. C. Pitfield & Co. Ltd. v. Jomac Gold Syndicate Ltd. et al.*, [1938] O.R. 427 at 438, 452 (C.A.) (option executed by the president and the secretary-treasurer); *Sellars v. Andrews Labrador Fisheries Ltd.* (1951), 28 M.P.R. 189 (director agreeing as to price); *Dorval Equipment Co. v. Franki Compressed Pile Co.*, [1953] Que. Q.B. 787 (C.A.) (the president had entered into an agreement with the lessee of the corporation's property varying the rent payable under the lease); *Cobetto v. Belanger Bowling Alley & Restaurant Ltd. & Genser*, [1955] Que. S.C. 301 (the corporation had leased certain premises and the president sublet the premises to a third party); *Desalliers v. Franmount Development Co. Ltd.*, [1957] Que. S.C. 307 (where, by reason of a course of conduct followed in the past, a real estate agent had reason to believe that the president of a corporation was acting on its behalf in listing certain property for sale with the agent, the corporation was held liable for his commission notwithstanding that the corporation did not own the property).

The rule was also applied in the case of the secretary-treasurer where there was evidence that the secretary-treasurer was the apparent agent of the corporation for the transaction of the kind of business which he undertook to do: *McKnight Construction Co. v. Vansickler* (1915), 51 S.C.R. 374 at 382, 287. And see *Dorfman v. Toronto Mutual Co.* (1932), 41 O.W.N. 27 (alteration of date on corporation's cheque was made by payee after obtaining the secretary-treasurer's approval; in the absence of notice of the corporation's by-laws it might be presumed that the secretary-treasurer could authorize such an alteration); *W. C. Pitfield & Co. v. Jomac Gold Syndicate Ltd., supra.*

Under s. 18 of this Act, contracts made by agents, officers or servants of a corporation within the apparent scope of their authority as such are expressly made binding on the corporation, in the absence of express or implied knowledge to the contrary. A corporation will be bound by contracts made by officers or agents acting within their express authority or within the powers which they could have under the constitution of the corporation, even if they are influenced by improper motives or are acting for their own benefit: *Bryant Powis, & Bryant, Ltd. v. Quebec Bank*, [1893] A.C. 170; *Hambro v. Burnard*, [1904] 2 K.B. 10 (C.A.); *Re J. Stanley Wedlock, Ltd.*, [1924] 4 D.L.R. 1178 (P.E.I.C.A.) and at 1180 (leave to appeal to Supreme Court of Canada refused).

Where payments are made under a bona fide mistake of fact by an authorized agent of the corporation, the fact that some other agent of the corporation had full knowledge of all the facts does not disentitle the corporation from recovering the money so paid, provided that the agent with the full knowledge did not know that the payments were being made on an erroneous basis: *Anglo-Scottish Beet Sugar Corp. Ltd. v. Spalding Urban District Council*, [1937] 2 K.B. 607, followed in *Turvey v. Dentons (1923), Ltd.*, [1953] 1 Q.B. 218 (mistake of corporation officials as the term of a lease taken by the corporation).

See also *Re Van-Ern Plumbing & Heating Ltd.; Canadian Credit Men's*

Association v. Van Kruse (1967), 64 D.L.R. (2d) 254 (Man. Q.B.) where it was held that the third party had acted in good faith throughout the transaction in question and there was nothing to show that the directors did not have authority to authorize the set-off in question. It was held that the third party was not put on inquiry having acted in good faith as the arrangement was a matter of internal management. See also *Canadian Imperial Bank of Commerce v. Crawford's Ltd.* (1970), 10 D.L.R. (3d) 497 (Sask. C.A.); *Chugal Properties Ltd. v. Levine*, [1971] 2 O.R. 331 (H.C.), (revd on other grounds, [1972] 1 O.R. 158, affd 33 D.L.R. (3d) 512 (S.C.C.). See also *Morguard Trust Co. v. Army, Navy & Air Force Veterans in Canada, Saskatoon Unit No. 38*, [1980] 6 W.W.R. 651 (Sask. Q.B.) and *Re Cosco Supply (1979) Ltd.* (1982), 135 D.L.R. (3d) 557 (19 Alta L.R. (2d) 387 (*sub nom. Toronto-Dominion Bank v. Coopers & Lybrand Ltd.)* (Alta. Q.B.); *Whitehorse Lounge Ltd. v. Bennett* (1984), 150 A.P.R. 91 (Nfld. T.D.); *Re Agra-voice Productions Ltd. (Agraland Enterprises); Flewitt v. Kelleher* (1986), 61 C.B.R. (N.S.) 280 (Man. Q.B.); *Kuklica v. Morguard Trust Co.* (1987), 50 Man. R. (2d) 136 (Q.B.).

Exceptions to rule in Turquand's Case

The rule does not apply (apart from cases where the corporation has held out the officer or agent as possessing the powers in question) when the officer or agent purports to enter into a contract which is beyond what might reasonably be considered to be within the ordinary scope of his powers and duties or where the transaction is unusual. Cases falling within this category include: *Hedican v. Crow's Nest Pass Lumber Co.* (1914), 17 D.L.R. 164 (B.C. C.A.) (no implied authority of a logging superintendent to enter into a contract for cutting logs extending over more than one season); *Pitt River Lumber Co. v. Shaake* (1914), 17 D.L.R. 768 (no implied authority of accountant to give notice of cancellation of agreement of sale); *Foley v. Commerical Cars Ltd.* (1922), 52 O.L.R. 174 (C.A.) (contract made by the manager in Canada of an English corporation which required it to form a Canadian corporation which was to issue paid up shares for certain patents, not within the implied power of such officer); *Kortzman v. O'Brien et al.* (1932), 41 O.W.N. 344, [1933] O.W.N. 215 (C.A.) (director without special authority could not bind corporation in transaction involving lease of part of corporation's premises for ten years); *Fred T. Brooks Ltd. v. Claude Neon General Advertising Ltd.*, [1931] O.R. 92, [1932] O.R. 205 (C.A.) (agent not a director or officer and transaction involving one corporation purchasing the outstanding shares of another, sufficiently out of the ordinary to put other party on enquiry to ascertain whether agent had authority); *Royal Bank of Canada v. Mack*, [1932] S.C.R. 488 (a branch bank manager has no implied authority to invest a customer's money); *Rama Corp. Ltd. v. Proved Tin & General Investments Ltd.*, [1952] 2 Q.B. 147 (no express or implied authority for a director of a corporation to enter into an oral agreement with another corporation whereby both corporations would contribute to a fund to be used to finance the sale of a certain article).

Where there is actual knowledge of the limitation of authority or the particular requirements, the indoor management rule cannot be pleaded. See

Coopers & Lybrand v. Ford Credit Canada Ltd. (1983), 59 N.S.R. (2d) 235 (N.S. T.D.); *Murray v. C. W. Boon & Co.*, [1974] 2 W.W.R. 620 (Alta. Dist. Ct.).

The rule does not apply where there is notice of the lack of authority of the agent: *Union Bank v. Eureka Woollen Mfg. Co.* (1900), 33 N.S.R. 302 (C.A.); *Dickson Co. of Peterborough v. Graham* (1913), 9 D.L.R. 813; *John v. Dodwell & Co. Ltd.*, [1918] A.C. 563 at 568; *Peterson & Canwood Co-Operative Association v. Cook* (1923), 16 Sask. L.R. 281; *London Guarantee & Accident Co. Ltd. v. Abrams*, [1923] 2 W.W.R. 1006; or where no agency is made out and the agreement is not in the ordinary course of the corporation's business: *Bird v. Hussey-Ferrier* (1913), 5 O.W.N. 60; *Sinclair v. Toronto Brick Co. Ltd.* (1916), 10 O.W.N. 250; *Export Brewing & Malting Co. v. Dominion Bank*, [1937] 3 D.L.R. 513 at 529 (P.C.).

If the corporation is seeking to set aside a transaction on the ground that the other party had notice or knowledge of the defective execution of the agreement it must prove such notice or knowledge: *Re W. N. McEachren & Sons Ltd.*, [1933] O.R. 349 at 365 (C.A.); so also where it is alleged that directors acting within their ostensible powers were abusing such powers and giving directions which they had no right to give: *Ticonderoga Pulp & Paper Co. v. Cowans et al.*, [1925] 4 D.L.R. 1 (P.C.).

A corporation has notice of the lack of authority of the agents or officers of another corporation if its own officers know of such lack: *John v. Dodwell & Co. Ltd.*, [1918] A.C. 563 at 568; *Retailers' Trust Co. Ltd. v. Dominion Bank*, [1935] 3 W.W.R. 165.

Nor does the rule apply where there is a lack of good faith and collusion between the officer making the contract and the party in whose favour the contract is made: *Rundle v. Miramichi Lumber Co.* (1922), 70 D.L.R. 713 (N.B.C.A.).

In *John v. Dodwell & Co. Ltd.*, [1918] A.C. 563, the manager of the plaintiffs, who was authorized by them to draw cheques on the plaintiffs' account, employed the defendants as his brokers and delivered to them cheques drawn on the plaintiffs' account in payment for shares purchased by him for his personal account. The cheques were received by the brokers without fraud, but with knowledge that the manager, without apparent authority, was drawing for his own purposes on the plaintiffs' funds. The brokers were held liable to account to the plaintiffs for the proceeds of the cheques. The law applicable was stated by Lord Haldane at pp. 569 and 570 as follows:

> For when an agent is entrusted by his principal with property be applied for the purposes of the latter, and to be accounted for on that footing, he is . . . in a fiduciary position, and any third person taking from the agent a transfer of the property with knowledge of a breach of duty committed by him in making the transfer holds what has been transferred to him under a transmitted fiduciary obligation to account for it to the principal. That there is no privity of contract between him and the principal does not make any difference, for the title does not rest on contract.
>
> If the appellants received such money with notice of the trust affecting it, they would be bound to account for it to the respondents.

So also, where a bank accepted as collateral security for an advance made to an officer of the corporation, notes under the seal of the corporation and duly signed, which were issued directly to the bank's nominees and represented amounts in excess of the authorized issue, and were issued in pursuance of a fraudulent scheme of the officer, the bank, having extended credit not to the issuer but to its agent, was put on inquiry, and, having failed to make such inquiry, was not entitled to claim as a creditor in respect of the notes: *Re Stadacona Rouyn Mines Ltd.*, [1945] 1 D.L.R. 420 (Que. C.A.).

Knowledge (or imputed knowledge) on the part of the person to be made liable is essential. Thus, in one case cheques were fraudulently drawn on the plaintiff corporation's bank account by its director and secretary-treasurer who were authorized by the corporation's by-laws to draw cheques. Such cheques were drawn in favour of the director and deposited by him in his personal account in another bank. An action by the corporation against the latter bank for the recovery of the money so misapplied failed on the ground that the bank had no knowledge that the cheques were improperly drawn on the corporation's account and the form of the cheques on their face was not notice of the fact that the director was appropriating the corporation's moneys to his own use: *Corporation Agencies, Ltd. v. Home Bank of Canada*, [1927] A.C. 318.

The rule is excluded by negligence on the part of the person dealing with the corporation and also where the officer in the transaction is not purporting to act as agent of the corporation. Thus, where the sole director of a corporation, who held all the shares but one, paid cheques payable to the corporation, and endorsed by himself for the corporation, into his private accounts with the defendant banks for collection, it was found that the true inference was that the director was acting in fraud of the corporation and the defendant banks having made no enquiries were liable for conversion of the cheques: *Underwood Ltd. v. Bank of Liverpool & Martins*, [1924] 1 K.B. 775 (C.A.).

The rule does not apply to a forgery: *Ruben v. Great Fingall Consolidated Co.*, [1906] A.C. 439 followed in *Kreditbank Cassel G.m.b.H. v. Schenkers, Ltd.*, [1927] 1 K.B. 826 (C.A.). So when a corporation was sued as the maker of a note, to which the corporation's signature had been forged, the corporation was not estopped from denying the genuineness of the signature in the absence of proof that the corporation had knowledge of the forgery at the material time, or that with such knowledge it deliberately refrained from disclosing it, and of any prejudice to the holder as the result of any breach of duty to disclose: *Industrial Acceptance Corp. Ltd. v. Lunenberg Outfitting Co. Ltd.*, [1934] 2 D.L.R. 558 (N.S. C.A.).

Liability based on holding out or estoppel

If the corporation has neither appointed an agent at all, nor held out anyone as agent, it cannot be made liable: *Bent v. Arrowhead* (1909), 18 Man. R. 632 (Man. C.A.); *McLeod v. United Canners Ltd.*, [1925] 3 D.L.R. 767 (unauthorized officer could not bind corporation by contract with a non-shareholder so as to give the latter the privileges of a shareholder). Where the plaintiff corporation was the purchaser of platinum from the defendant corporation, and the plaintiff's clerk devised a fraudulent scheme whereby he ordered platinum and then resold it to the defendant, the plaintiff was successful in its action against the defendant for conversion. There was nothing to show the plaintiff as the principal had placed the clerk in a position to hold himself out as having authority to arrange the resale of the platinum. Any representations regarding ostensible authority had been made by the clerk himself and the plaintiff could not be said to be responsible for such representations. See: *Canadian Laboratory Supplies Ltd. v. Englehard Industries of Canada Ltd.* (1979), 6 B.L.R. 235 (S.C.C.).

If the corporation has permitted its agent to act in a certain capacity without objection and his acts of agency have been acquiesced in by the corporation, the latter may be liable on the principle of holding out: *Central Canada Ry. Co. v. Murray* (1882), 8 S.C.R. 313; *Hamilton & Port Dover Ry. Co. v. Gore Bank* (1873), 20 Gr. 190; *Wilson v. West Hartlepool Ry. Co.* (1865), 34 L.J. Ch. 241; *Sheppard v. Bonanza Nickel Mining Co. of Sudbury* (1895), 25 O.R. 305; *Imperial Bank v. Farmers' Trading Co.* (1901), 13 Man. R. 412; *Muldowan v. German Canadian Land Co.* (1909), 19 Man. R. 667 at 672; *Brandon Construction Co. v. Saskatoon School Board* (1912), 5 D.L.R. 754 (revd on other grounds (1913), 13 D.L.R. 379); *French Gas Saving Co. v. The Desbarats Advertising Agency Ltd.* (1912), 1 D.L.R. 136 at 145 (Que. C.A.); *Acton Tanning Co. v. Toronto Suburban Ry. Co.* (1918), 56 S.C.R. 196; *Palmer v. Canadian Fish Producers Ltd.*, [1949] 2 D.L.R. 39 (Man. C.A.). *Rockland Industries Inc. v. Amerada Minerals Corp. of Canada*, [1980] 2 S.C.R. 2. Where the only knowledge of the corporation is through individual directors who are parties to an arrangement which is a fraud on the corporation, there is no acquiescence: *Houghton v. Northard, Lowe & Wills Ltd.*, [1928] A.C. 1; *In re Hampshire Land Co.*, [1896] 2 Ch. 743 at 749.

In *Russo-Chinese Bank v. Li Yau Sam*, [1910] A.C. 174 at 184 (P.C.), Lord Atkinson said that:

> in order that the principle of 'holding out' should in any given case of agency apply, the act done by the agent, and relied on to bind the principal, must be an act of that particular class of acts which the agent is held out as having general authority on behalf of his principal to do; and, of course, the party prejudiced must have believed in the existence of that general authority and been thereby misled.

A person cannot set up an ostensible or apparent authority unless he relied on it in making the contract or supposed contract: *Rama Corp. Ltd. v. Proved Tin & General Investments Ltd.*, [1952] 2 Q.B. 147 where Slade J. said at p. 149:

> Ostensible or apparent authority which negatives the existence of actual authority is merely a form of estoppel, indeed, it has been termed agency by estoppel, and you cannot call in aid an estoppel unless you have three ingredients: (i) a representation, (ii) a reliance on the representation, and (iii) an alteration of your position resulting from such reliance.

In that case, Slade J. held that a person, who at the time of making a contract with a corporation had no knowledge of the corporation's articles of association, could not rely on the articles as conferring ostensible or apparent authority on the agent of the corporation with whom he dealt.

The doctrine of "holding out" had no application where in a case between a customer and a bank, the bank acting on the directions of the customer's accountant did not concern itself about either the identity or the authority of the person who attached the customer's name to the requisition for payment of the customer's moneys: *Dominion Gresham Guarantee & Casualty Ltd. v. Bank of Montreal*, [1929] S.C.R. 572 at 579.

A person dealing with a supposed agent of a corporation cannot rely upon the fact that other contracts had been negotiated by the agent if he is at the time entirely ignorant of that fact: *Fred T. Brooks Ltd. v. Claude Neon General Advertising Ltd.*, [1931] O.R. 92 at 108; affd [1932] O.R. 205 (C.A.).

A corporation may furthermore estop itself from denying the authority of an officer, for example, if it has obtained advances on the strength of a note made or endorsed by him: *Bridgewater Cheese Factory Co. v. Murphy* (1897), 23 O.A.R. 66; affd (1896), 26 S.C.R. 443; *Canadian Bank of Commerce v. Bellamy* (1916), 25 D.L.R. 133 (Sask. C.A.).; *Bondholders Securities Corp. v. Manville*, [1933] 4 D.L.R. 699 at 703 (Sask. C.A.); or goods on the strength of a draft accepted: *Bank of Hamilton v. Mutual Fruit Co. Ltd.* (1921), 29 B.C.R. 448; or if it has accepted the services of an employee engaged by an officer: *Bloomfield v. Monarch Overall Mfg. Co.*, [1927] 3 D.L.R. 146; affd [1927] 4 D.L.R. 1137 (Man. C.A.); or if it has received an advance and has paid interest thereon: *Nickle v. Kingston & Pembroke Ry. Co.* (1906), 12 O.L.R. 349 (C.A.); or where the corporation has so conducted itself as to lead a third party reasonably to suppose that its agent at a branch office had the requisite authority to purchase goods; *Farm Products Ltd. v. MacLeod Flouring Mills Ltd.* (1918), 43 D.L.R. 770 (Alta. C.A.) (transaction in ordinary course of corporation's business and not of unusual proportions); or where the directors have passed a resolution conferring general authority on the manager, a certified copy of which resolution has been exhibited to the other contracting party: *Jardine v. Northern Co-operative Timber & Mill Association*, [1945] 1 D.L.R. 732 (B.C. C.A.); or where goods have been ordered by a *de facto* manager in the ordinary course and the corporation has taken the benefit of the transaction: *Keystone Shingles & Lumber Ltd. v. Moody Shingles Ltd.*, [1942] 2 D.L.R. 311 (B.C. C.A.); or where two officers of the corporation executed a guarantee but no resolution had been passed by the corporation authorizing the officers to execute the guarantee, the mortgagee could rely on s. 18 as the corporation had held out the officers as persons with authority to bind the corporation: *Canada Mortgage & Housing Corp. v. Edinburgh House Apartments Ltd.* (1991), 112 A.R. 104 (Q.B.).

Unauthorized acts of agents may be ratified by the corporation, either expressly or impliedly. Thus where the agent of a mercantile corporation purchased property for the corporation and gave the corporation's note in payment and the corporation received notice that it had been given and took no steps to repudiate it and subsequently entered into possession of the land, it was held that it had ratified the act of its agent and was bound by the note: *Ryan v. Terminal City Co. Ltd.* (1893), 25 N.S.R. 131 (C.A.). Cases to the same effect are *Leask Cattle Co. Ltd. v. Drabble*, [1923] 1 W.W.R. 126 (Sask. C.A.) (corporation bound by acquiescence of all the shareholders); *Price v. Indiana-Alberta Oil Co.*, [1926] 3 D.L.R. 82 (ratification by shareholders).

The corporation will also be bound on the principle of estoppel where the agent is apparently exercising an authority which he in fact possesses: *Ward v. Montreal Cold Storage, & Freezing Co.* (1904), 26 Que. S.C. 310; *McDougall Segur Exploration Co. v. Solloway Mills & Co. Ltd.*, [1931] 2 W.W.R. 516; *W. C. Pitfield & Co. v. Jomac Gold Syndicate Ltd.*, [1938] O.R. 427 (C.A.).

In such cases the apparent authority is held to be the real authority: *Bryant, Powis, & Bryant, Ltd. v. La Banque du Peuple*, [1893] A.C. 170; *MacKenzie v. Monarch Life Assurance Co.* (1911), 45 S.C.R. 232, but see the same case in the Privy Council (1913), 15 D.L.R. 695; *Re James Robinson Co. Ltd., Canadian Credit Men's Trust Association, Ltd. v. Molsons Bank* (1925), 38 Que. K.B. 479 (C.A.).

Authority of particular officers

President

In the normal course, the directors will appoint a president, who usually will be the chief executive or operating officer of the corporation.

The following cases have been concerned with the authority and powers of a president: *Standard Trust Co. v. South Shore Ry. Co.* (1903), 5 Que. P.R. 257 (the president without express authorization by resolution of the board might institute and prosecute actions for the corporation and appoint an attorney *ad litem*); *Tanguay v. Royal Paper Mills* (1907), 31 Que. S.C. 397 (only administrative acts and not discretionary powers of the board of directors may be delegated to the president); *Beaucage v. Winnipeg Stone Co.* (1910), 14 W.L.R. 575 (president had power without express authorization of board to sign contract of hire); *A. E. Thomas Ltd. v. Standard Bank* (1910), 1 O.W.N. 548 (guarantee for loan given by president); *Canadian Bank of Commerce v. Smith* (1911), 17 W.L.R. 135 (where the directors have power to borrow money and mortgage, the president and managing director are by virtue of their offices *prima facie* the proper officers to execute mortgages; a mortgage so signed and sealed with the corporation's seal is properly executed); *Schmidt v. M. Beatty & Sons Ltd.* (1916), 10 O.W.N. 230 (president had no actual authority but had implied authority to make a contract because the corporation possessed the power); *Acton Tanning Co. v. Toronto Suburban Ry. Co.* (1918), 56 S.C.R. 196 (where president had ostensible authority to bind the corporation and there was no notice of any limitation thereof, a verbal contract made by him and acquiesced in by the corporation for a number of years was not set aside); *The Country Club of Montreal v. Bell Telephone Co. of Canada* (1920), 58 Que. S.C. 56 (president cannot give away corporation's property without a resolution of the board); *Rundle v. Miramichi Lumber Co.* (1922), 70 D.L.R. 713 (N.B.C.A.) (power of president "to sign all contracts" did not cover one entered into in bad faith); *Re Petrie Manufacturing Co. Ltd.*, [1924] 4 D.L.R. 1308 (Ont. C.A.) (president engaged solicitor without authority); *Re E. J. Lane Ltd., Ex. p. Milligan*, [1924] 1 D.L.R. 269 (president agreed to a compromise of a claim against the corporation); *Gallagher v. Waterloo Motors Ltd.*, [1931] 2 D.L.R. 310 (corporation could not set up lack of authority of the president once it had accepted the services which were to be performed under a written contract executed under the corporate seal by the president who took an active part in the management of the corporation); *Fess Oil Burners Ltd. v. Hutchings*, [1934] 1 D.L.R. 335 (Man. C.A.) (effect of common form of by-law conferring authority on president considered in relation to a trade contract); *W. C. Pitfield & Co. Ltd. v. Jomac Gold Syndicate Ltd. et al.*, [1938] O.R. 247 (C.A.) (a contract negotiated and executed along with the secretary by the president was incidental to the ordinary business of the corporation and bound the corporation); *Dorval Equipment Co. v. Franki Compressed Pile Co.*, [1953] Que. Q.B. 787 (C.A.) (president renting the property of the corporation); *Cobetto v. Belanger Bowling Alley & Restaurant Ltd. & Genser*, [1955] Que. S.C. 301 (president sub-leasing corporation premises). Thus, in *Marv-Eon Signs Ltd. v. Vogue Shoppe Ltd. (1977) Ltd. and McClaine* (1983), 24 Man. R. (2d) 125 (Co. Ct.), the president of a corporation had signed his name at the bottom of a letter addressed to the individual defendant confirming continuance of rental payments pursuant to a contract signed by the president for rent. It was held that the president was not personally liable as he was signing in his capacity as president but that the corporation itself was bound. See also *Norval Leaseholds Ltd. v. Altador Heights Dev. Ltd.* (1981), 31 A.R. 587 (Q.B.). If a person signs as president of a corporation but in fact does not hold that position the doctrine of ostensible authority will be inapplicable and the corporation will not be responsible for the agreement. See *First City Capital Ltd. v. 105383 B.C. Ltd.* (1985), 29 B.L.R. 274 (B.C.C.A.).

Vice-president

The by-laws will usually provide for one or more vice-presidents. They may specify the duties of the vice-president(s); thus they may provide that the vice-president or, if more than one, the vice-presidents in order of seniority shall be vested with the powers and perform the duties of the president if the latter is absent or under disability. The vice-president when acting within his powers can bind the corporation: *Whaley v. O'Grady* (1912), 22 Man. R. 379 (C.A.).

See also *Ward v. Montreal Cold Storage & Freezing Co.* (1904), 26 Que. S.C. 310 (corporation liable to third parties where by-laws authorized vice-president to sign storage receipts but he did so fraudulently); *Foley v. Barber* (1909-10), 1 O.W.N. 40 (Q.B.), affd (1910), 1 O.W.N. 1029 (C.A.) (vice-president and manager); *Rutherford v. Royal Bank of Canada*, [1932] S.C.R. 131 (vice-president and treasurer signing bank's form of release under resolution passed pursuant to by-law).

General manager and managing director

A corporation may appoint a general manager or managing director with powers which may be very broad over the management of the corporation's affairs. It is not *ultra vires* of a corporation to give the general manager power over "all the administration of the business of the corporation subject only to such direction and control as it is the duty of the directors to exercise": *Montreal Public Service Corp. v. Champagne* (1917), 33 D.L.R. 49 (P.C.).

The manager may or may not also be a director. In his capacity as a director he would have no power individually to bind the corporation since the directors' authority is vested in them as a body. A managing director who is the sole director of a corporation may, however, in that capacity on behalf of the corporation enter into a contract with himself to serve the corporation, in this case, as a pilot: *Lee v. Lee's Air Farming Ltd.*, [1960] 3 W.L.R. 758 (P.C.).

The extent of the manager's authority is governed primarily by the by-laws, but the corporation may become liable for his acts on one or more of the principles above discussed; and the corporation will not necessarily escape liability even though there are no by-laws conferring authority on its officers or agents: *National Malleable Castings Co. v. Smiths' Falls Malleable Casting Co.* (1907), 14 O.L.R. 22 (C.A.).

In an English case in which the three directors of a corporation individually acted as its managers, it was held that their intention as demonstrated by their conduct could be treated by the court as the intention of the corporation: *H.L. Bolton Co. v. T.J. Graham & Sons*, [1957] 1 Q.B. 159. Denning L.J. made the following statement at p. 172:

> A company may in many ways be likened to a human body. It has a brain and nerve centre which controls what it does. It also has hands which hold the tools and act in accordance with the directions from the centre. Some of the people in the company are mere servants and agents who are nothing more than hands to do the work and cannot be said to represent the mind or will. Others are directors and managers who represent the directing mind and will of the company, and control what it does. The state of mind of these managers is the state of mind of the company and is treated by the law as such. So you will find that in cases where the law requires personal fault as a condition of liability in tort, the fault of the manager will be the personal fault of the company. That is made clear in Lord Haldane's speech in *Lennard's Carrying Co. Ltd. v. Asiatic Petroleum Co. Ltd.*, [1915] A.C. 705 (P.C.). So also in the criminal law, in cases where the law requires a guilty mind as a condition of a criminal offence, the guilty mind of the directors or the managers will render the company itself guilty. That is shown by *Rex v. I.C.R. Haulage Ltd.*, [1944] K.B. 551, to which we were referred and in which the court said:
>
> > Whether in any particular case there is evidence to go to a jury that the criminal act of an agent, including his state of mind, intention, knowledge or belief is the act of the company . . . must depend on the nature of the charge, the relative position of the officer or agent, and the other relevant facts and circumstances of the case.

Whether or not any specific act is within the authority of a manager or managing director depends on the facts of the particular case. The nature of the act of the manager or managing director in issue in each of the following cases is indicated in brackets after the citation thereof: *Thompson v. Bank of Nova Scotia* (1893), 32 N.B.R. 335 (a branch manager of a bank not presumed to have general authority to prosecute on behalf of the bank so as to make it liable for malicious prosecution); *Thompson v. Brantford Electric & Operating Co.* (1898), 25 O.A.R. 340 (a corporation bound by manager's contract to purchase a machine even though purchase made on terms different from those authorized because such purchase was in the ordinary course of business); *Joshua Calloway v. Stobart* (1905), 35 S.C.R. 301 (general manager could not make a binding agreement for the sale of the corporation's real estate without special authority for that purpose); *Foley v. Barber* (1909), 1 O.W.N. 40 (H.C.), affd (1910), 1 O.W.N. 1029 (C.A.) (power of managing director to purchase stock); *Dickson Co. of Peterborough v. Graham* (1913), 9 D.L.R. 813 (all parties knew that agreement made by general manager and vice-president was subject to ratification); *Picard v. Revelstoke Sawmill Co.* (1913), 12 D.L.R. 685 (B.C. C.A.) (managing director had no authority to sell the entire assets of the corporation as a going concern); *Ledwell v. Charlottetown Light & Power Co.* (1913), 13 E.L.R. 225 (general manger had implied authority to engage a physician for an employee injured at work); *Hedican v. Crow's Nest Pass Lumber Co.* (1914), 17 D.L.R. 164 (B.C. C.A.) (subordinate officer not in same position as managing director with respect to implied authority to contract); *Standard Construction Co. v. Crabb* (1914), 7 W.W.R. 719 (managing director has no implied authority to bring an action in the name of the corporation); *Olympic Stone Construction Co. v. Momsen & Rose* (1915), 8 W.W.R. 79 (B.C. C.A.) (general manager exercising a power which under the corporation's constitution he could have possessed); *Sinclair v. Toronto Brick Co.* (1916), 10 O.W.N. 250 (letter written by manager undertaking to discharge mortgage not in the ordinary course of business); *McGee v. Rosetown Electric Co.* (1917), 11 Sask. L.R. 68 (contract to sink well within implied power of managing director); *Canadian General Securities Ltd. v. George* (1919), 59 S.C.R. 641 (general manager did not repudiate representations made by the corporation's sales agent); *Bank of Ottawa v. Hamilton Stove & Heater Co.* (1918), 44 O.L.R. 93 (guarantee executed by manager and secretary under seal of corporation binding without authorization by directors); *Kennedy v. Victory Land* (1922), 70 D.L.R. 868 (S.C.C.) (no authority to sell land); *Northern Creameries Ltd. v. Rossington Produce Co.* (1922), 66 D.L.R. 548 (Alta. C.A.) (managing director used money to purchase property without authority); *Re J. Stanley Wedlock Ltd.; Ex parte Royal Bank of Canada*, [1924] 4 D.L.R. 1178 at 1180 (managing director exercising for his own advantage power which under the constitution of the corporation he could possess); *Mid-West Collieries Ltd. v. McEwen*, [1925] S.C.R. 326 (power of managing director to mortgage property to secure pre-existing debt); *Imperial Bank of Canada v. Dennis* (1925), 57 O.L.R. 203 (power of managing director to sign promissory note as collateral for loan to the corporation); *Wrathall v. Ripstein*, [1932] 3 D.L.R. 64 (Man. C.A.) (president and managing director agreed to pay commission to person for securing a lease); *Royal Bank of Canada v. Mack*, [1932] S.C.R. 488 (branch manager of bank undertaking duty not within the scope of the business of a bank according to the provisions of the *Bank Act*); *Re Jacques Furniture Co. Ltd., Canadian Radio Corp. Ltd. v. The Trustee*, [1933] O.W.N. 170 (C.A.) (contract signed by president and managing director of an Ontario corporation for use of broadcasting station and services of artists of another corporation and completely performed by latter binding on corporation); *Re Crescent Silver Cobalt Mines Ltd. Ex p. Barber*, [1934] O.W.N. 558 (duties of managing director same as those of a general manager); *Nova Scotia Trust Co. v. Auto Parts Co.*, [1936] 2 D.L.R. 441 (unauthorized loans to employees); *Andrews, Andrews & McBride v. Two-in-One Gold Mines Ltd.*, [1937] O.R. 482 (C.A.) (president and managing director retaining solicitors in pursuance of general authority conferred by resolution of board); *W.C. Pitfield & Co. Ltd. v. Jomac Gold Syndicate Ltd. et al.*, [1938] O.R. 427 (C.A.) (contract incidental to the carrying out of the ordinary business of the corporation).

Secretary

It is normal practice for the directors to appoint a secretary.

The secretary as such has no authority to bind the corporation: *Smith & Goldberg Ltd. v. Moyer & Co.* (1929), 63 O.L.R. 388 (C.A.) and cases cited; *Bianco v. Mathers & Son Ltd.*, [1938] 2 D.L.R. 175 (N.S. C.A.). Thus, the corporation cannot be held liable to repay moneys advanced for its benefit at the request of the secretary: *In re Cleadon Trust, Ltd.*, [1939] Ch. 286 at 310, 319 (C.A.). His duties are of a limited character: *George Whitechurch, Ltd., v. Cavanagh*, [1902] A.C. 117, and there is an important distinction between his position and that of a director: *Cloutier v. Dion*, [1954] Que. Q.B. 595 (C.A.). In matters within the scope of his authority or in trifling details he may bind the corporation: *Smith & Goldberg Ltd. v. Moyer & Co.*, *supra*.

Where the secretary is acting as agent of the corporation within the scope of his employment the corporation will be liable whether he is acting for its benefit or not: *Lloyd v. Grace, Smith & Co.*, [1912] A.C. 716; *Hambro v. Burnand*, [1904] 2 K.B. 10 (C.A.); *Bryant, Powis, & Bryant, Ltd. v. La Banque du Peuple*, [1893] A.C. 170. Forgery by the secretary seems to depend on a different rule; see *Ruben v. Great Fingall Consolidated Co.*, [1906] A.C. 439, where a corporation was held not bound by a share certificate to which the seal of the corporation had been affixed, the secretary having forged the signatures of the directors. So also a corporation may repudiate a cheque on which the signatures of the directors have been forged by the secretary: *Kepitigalla Rubber Estates Ltd. v. National Bank of India*, [1909] 2 K.B. 1010. See also *South London Greyhound Racecourses Ltd. v. Wake*, [1931] 1 Ch. 496 (share certificate to which corporation's seal fraudulently affixed treated as a forgery although signature of secretary and other signing officer genuine).

The secretary has no power without authorization to call a meeting: *In re Haycraft Gold Reduction & Mining Co.*, [1900] 2 Ch. 230; nor to sign a guarantee in the name of the corporation: *In re Williams Machinery Co. v. Crawford Tug Co.* (1908), 16 O.L.R. 245 (C.A.); nor to pass transfers of shares not fully paid up: *Chida Mines, Ltd. v. Anderson* (1905), 22 T.L.R. 27; nor to promise payment in a particular currency where there is a dispute, in the absence of evidence that his authority is other or more extensive than that of any other secretary: *Myers v. Union Natural Gas Co.* (1922), 53 O.L.R. 88 at 92; nor to binding the corporation by an arrangement whereby its property is applied to satisfy the debt of another corporation: *Houghton & Co. v. Nothard, Lowe & Wills, Ltd.*, [1928] A.C. 1; nor to terminate a lease: *Lebeault v. Venant Lebeault Ltée et Valiquette*, [1944] Que. S.C. 275; nor to bind the corporation by a settlement: *Smith & Goldberg Ltd. v. Moyer & Co.*, *supra*; nor has he any authority, in virtue of his position, in respect of the management of the ships of a navigation corporation: *Robin Hood Mills v. Paterson SS. Ltd.*, [1936] 2 D.L.R. 130; and he cannot be presumed to have authority to enter into a binding transaction for the sale of its goods: *Smith & Goldberg Ltd. v. Moyer & Co., supra.*

In *Vansickler v. McKnight Construction Co.* (1914), 31 O.L.R. 531, (1915) 51 S.C.R. 374, the signature of the secretary-treasurer to a contract in which the president concurred, but being absent did not sign, was held binding on the corporation, it appearing further that the secretary-treasurer was authorized to enter into a contract of the kind in question by the general course of business adopted by the corporation.

On the authority of a secretary-treasurer, see also *Hamilton & Port Dover Ry. Co. v. Gore Bank* (1873), 20 Gr. 190 (secretary-treasurer advising bank of certain terms regarding the corporation's debts, such terms not being authorized by the board, held not to be in the ordinary course of business); *Barnett v. South London Tramways* (1887), 18 Q.B.D. 815 (C.A.) (representations by secretary-treasurer to corporation's contractor that he could retain certain moneys held not in the ordinary course of business); *Dorfman v. Toronto Mutual Co.* (1932), 41 O.W.N. 27 (in absence of notice of corporation's by-laws the power of the secretary-treasurer to authorize change of date in cheque may be presumed); *Re W. N. McEachren & Sons Ltd.*, [1933] O.R. 349 (C.A.) (contract executed under seal by secretary and assistant secretary, such officers being also directors *de facto* held binding).

Personal liability of agents

An agent acting for a principal in most circumstances will incur no personal liability. The act is the act of the principal who is entitled to any benefit and must meet any liability resulting from such act. Where something is done by an agent within the apparent scope of his authority as such, s. 18 in effect affords a protection. The agent will be personally liable if: (a) his authority is defective or non-existent; or (b) through failing to make it clear that he contracted as agent, he is held to have contracted as principal or the personal liability of the agent was contemplated by the parties.

Where an individual who was an officer of a corporation was sued in his personal capacity for an amount due for services rendered, but the evidence was that in the dealings giving rise to the claim and previous dealings he was acting simply as an officer and agent of the corporation, he was held not to be personally liable for the amount due: *Webpax Ltd. v. Weill*, [1960] O.W.N. 325 (C.A.). See also *R. & B. United Trades Ltd. v. Tummonds* (1976), 25 N.S.R. (2d) 412 (N.S. T.D.). See also *Vivien Agencies Ltd. v. Butler* (1978), 58 A.P.R. 256 (Nfld. Dist. Ct.); *Fraser v. Pedlar Industrial Inc.* (1981), 16 B.L.R. 49 (N.S. T.D.); *Maclean v. Portland Masonry Ltd.* (1982), 55 N.S.R. (2d) 666 (T.D.); *Entreprises Croussette Ltée v. St.-Onge* (1983), 50 N.B.R. (2d) 414 (Q.B.); *Thomas v. Equipment Rebuilders Ltd.* (1974), 10 N.S.R. (2d) 225 (C.A.). Thus, in a case where a contract was made by the principal shareholder of a corporation without using the corporation's name it was held that the corporation itself was liable since the other contracting party was aware of the agency relationship. The onus, however, is on the agent to establish that the other party to the contract was aware that he was dealing with a limited corporation. See *Pennelly Ltd.*

v. 449438 Ontario Ltd. (1986), 20 C.L.R. 145 (Ont. H.C.); *Timmerman's Enterprises Ltd. v. Painter* (1986), 42 Man. R. (2d) 17 (Q.B.), affd (1986), 42 Man. R. (2d) 16 (C.A.); *Ellehammer Industries Ltd. v. Hanson*, unreported, Feb 6. 1990 (B.C.C.A.); *West Fraser Builder Supplies v. Vander Horst*, unreported, January 22, 1990 (B.C.C.A).

For cases in which the agent was held personally liable on a contract see: *Sign-O-Lite Signs Ltd. v. Dekker Chevrolet Oldsmobile Ltd.*, unreported, March 11, 1988, (Alta. C.A.); *City Leaseway Ltd. v. Symes* (1984), 58 N.B.R. (2d) 59 (C.A.); *Gulf Canada v. Cameron* (1981), 32 Nfld. & P.E.I.R. 136 (P.E.I.S.C.); *Fidelity Realty Ltd. v. Rockingham Realty Ltd.* (1975), 13 N.S.R. (2d) 54 (T.D.), revd on other grounds (1976), 17 N.S.R. (2d) 527 (C.A.); *Frankel Structural Steel Ltd. v. Goden Holdings Ltd.*, [1971] S.C.R. 250.

Where agent's authority defective or non-existent

Where an agent contracts without authorization he is liable to a third person not aware of the defect of authority as on an implied warranty of authority: *Collen v. Wright* (1857), 8 E. & B. 647; *Coit v. Dowling* (1901), 4 Terr. L.R. 464; *Douglas v. The Eastern Car Co.* (1915), 25 D.L.R. 481 (N.S.C.A.) 487; *Fred T. Brooks Ltd. v. Claude Neon General Advertising Ltd.*, [1932] O.R. 205 (C.A.).

So if a person enters into a contract on behalf of a non-existing corporation, he will be personally liable on an implied warranty of authority: *Coit v. Dowling, supra*; *Crane v. Lavoie* (1912), 4 D.L.R. 175 (Man. C.A.); so also an officer of an unincorporated society: *Finlay v. Black* (1921), 60 D.L.R. 422 and cases cited.

Where, however, an individual entered into an agreement on behalf of a corporation to be incorporated and the agreement excluded liability of the individual thereunder, he was not personally liable: *Diary Supplies Limited v. Fuchs* (1959), 28 W.W.R. 1 (Sask. C.A.). When a person named as a provisional director of a corporation was negligent while allegedly acting on its behalf the day prior to its incorporation, he was held personally liable as the corporation had no legal existence when the negligence occurred: *Montreal v. Sanders*, [1958] Que. S.C. 262. A provisional director is not necessarily liable on a pre-incorporation contract entered into by a promoter: *Federated Press Ltd. v. Archambault* (1924), 30 Rev. Leg. 220. See also s. 14 and the comment thereon in Chapter 2.

In an action against an officer of the corporation for breach of warranty of authority to make the contract absence of authority must be alleged and proved: *Fess Oil Burners Ltd. v. Hutchings*, [1934] 1 D.L.R. 335 (Man. C.A.).

Where agent liable as principal

An agent may be personally liable if he fails to make it clear that he was contracting as such on behalf of the corporation.

In *Vulcan Iron Works v. Leary* (1905), 1 W.L.R. 453 a manager was held personally liable where he ordered goods at a store, at which he had dealt personally before the corporation was incorporated, without making it clear that he was now ordering on behalf of the corporation. See also *Car Leasing (Alberta) Ltd. v. Swinhoe* (1978), 15 A.R. 22 (Co. Ct.); *Thompson & Sutherland Ltd. v.*

Redden (1978), 34 N.S.R. (2d) 91 (Dist. Ct.); *G.W. Turner Ltd. v. Lauze* (1981), 25 Man. R. (2d) 35 (Co. Ct.); *Bridge City Electric (1981) Ltd. v. Robertson* (1986), 49 Sask. R. 58 (Q.B.); *Selby's Electric Ltd. v. Bruce* (1984), 3 C.L.R. 1314 (Nfld.); *Gerco Services Co. v. Aston* (1981), 48 N.S.R. (2d) 541; *Gulf Canada Ltd. v. Cameron* (1981), 91 A.P.R. 136 (P.E.I. S.C.); and *Irving Oil Ltd. v. Colbourne* (1983), 130 A.P.R. 136 (Nfld. Dist. Ct.); *McKee v. Owl Construction Ltd.* (1987), 190 A.P.R. 162 (Nfld. C.A.); *Maritime Carpet Distributors Ltd. v. Reinders* (1982), 110 A.P.R. 421 (N.B.Q.B.); *Storey v. Price* (1981), 36 N.B.R. (2d) 317, affd (1983), 118 A.P.R. 181 (N.B.C.A.); *W. Rodgerson's Insulators Ltd. v. Bezanson* (1979), 39 N.S.R. (2d) 81 (C.A.).

Where directors contracted in their individual names without disclosing that they were in truth acting for the corporation they were held personally liable: *Litchfield v. Saskatchewan & Battle River Land & Development Co.* (1908), 7 W.L.R. 475.

A mere description of the contracting officers as "the directors of the A.B. company" will not release them from personal liability because such description does not purport to bind the corporation: *Aggs v. Nicholson* (1856), 1 H. & N. 165; *McCollin v. Gilpin* (1880), 5 Q.B.D. 390.

An officer or agent may become personally liable on a contract if he has entered into it on his own behalf, even though the agreement is signed in the name of the corporation only. In *Wood v. Grand Valley R.W. Co.* (1912), 27 O.L.R. 556, (1915) 51 S.C.R. 283, the president of the corporation signed an agreement "on his own behalf" signing the name of the corporation over his own name followed by the word "Prest". It was held that the obligation stated to have been assumed by the officer could not be void because he did not sign a second time in his individual capacity. So also where the president of the corporation, who was described as a party to the agreement together with the corporation, signed his own name and also affixed the corporation's signature with a rubber stamp, he was held to be liable: *Freeman v. McBride* (1924), 26 O.W.N. 375. Where a secretary of a corporation signed a share certificate at the request of the president and without knowing of any irregularity regarding it, the Quebec Court of Appeal found that he was not personally liable for damages: *Cloutier v. Dion*, [1954] Que. Q.B. 595.

If the liability of the corporation was contemplated it will be the corporation and not the officer who will be liable: *Gadd v. Houghton* (1876), 1 Ex. D. 357; even though the signature may be somewhat ambiguous: *Johnson v. Hamilton* (1856), 13 U.C.Q.B. 211, where the defendant who was president of the Victoria Bridge Company signed the agreement in question describing himself as "Pres. V.B.".

It is a question of fact whether a person has contracted so as to make himself personally liable or has contracted on behalf of a corporation: *Simpson v. Carr* (1862), 5 U.C.Q.B. 326. In *Frankel Structural Steel Ltd. v. Goden Holdings Ltd.*, [1971] S.C.R. 250 a corporation had been directed to pay to the plaintiff all advances after delivery of goods contracted for and the solicitors for that corporation assured the plaintiff that it would be paid if the steel were supplied. The solicitors were in fact the only officers and shareholders of the corporation which was used as a means of making interim building loans on behalf of the clients of the law firm. The corporation had no separate bank account and kept no books or records. Money contributed by clients appeared in the trust account of the law firm. The goods in question were supplied but only partial payment was made. It was held that the corporation and the solicitors were liable for breach of contract. The solicitors could not excuse themselves on the basis that their undertaking was given on behalf of the corporation and that their refusal to honour it involved the corporation but not them. The court held that the solicitors were the corporation in that they were the only shareholders and officers and had management and control of a corporation having no independent volition.

Bills of exchange and promissory notes

The most frequent instances of personal liability arising from failure to make it clear that the agent was contracting as such, and any personal responsibility was intended to be excluded, are found in the case of promissory notes signed by an officer or agent of a corporation. Special care should be taken in the case of bills of exchange, promissory notes, cheques, and endorsements of such instruments not only to sign for or on behalf of the corporation, but also to state the corporation's name accurately.

Section 51 of the *Bills of Exchange Act*, R.S.C. 1985, c. B-4 reads in part as follows:

> 51. Where a person signs a bill as drawer, endorser or acceptor and adds words to his signature indicating that he has signed for or on behalf of a principal, or in a representative character, he is not personally liable thereon but the mere addition to his signature of words describing him as an agent, or as filling a representative character, does not exempt him from personal liability.

Under s. 5 of the *Bills of Exchange Act,* however, the corporate seal of a corporation is sufficient as a signature of the corporation.

Generally, an individual may be personally liable on a bill of exchange unless it is clear on the face of the instrument or through the examination of extrinsic evidence that the parties intended only that the corporation be bound. In some cases, the notation of such words as "agent" on the instrument has not exempted the individual from personal liability where there was no indication on the face of the instrument as to the identity of the principal. In some cases, the individual has escaped personal liability where his corporate position has been indicated on the face of the instrument, however, in other cases the mere notation of the individual's corporate position has been insufficient to discharge personal liability. In short, the caselaw lacks coherency as to what circumstances will give rise to personal liability. For a full discussion of this issue, see Crawford and Falconbridge, *Banking and Bills of Exchange* (8th ed.) p. 1406-11.

It is a question of construction whether a promissory note is that of the corporation or not. Crawford and Falconbridge suggest that parol evidence will be admitted in two circumstances: to show an ambiguity on the face of the document and to show the parties' true intentions. See Crawford and Falconbridge, *supra* at p. 1407. The intent must normally be gathered from the face of the document unless there is some ambiguity which requires extrinsic evidence for its elucidation: *Schaffer v. Tubby Smith & Co.*, [1924] 1 D.L.R. 468 at 470; *Medic v. Taylor*, [1975] 6 W.W.R. 725 (B.C.S.C.); *Storm v. Holmes* (1963), 46 W.W.R. 181 (Alta. Dist. Ct.); *Pacific Western Airlines Ltd. v. Gauthier* (1977), 2 Alta. L.R. (2d) 52 (C.A.); *Armand v. Checotel Finance Corp.* (1985), 31 B.L.R. 203 (Que. S.C.); but where there was no *prima facie* ambiguity, extrinsic evidence was not admitted. See: *Canadian Acceptance Corp v. Noye & Raynor Construction Ltd.* (1980), 93 A.P.R. 361 (P.E.I.S.C.); *Beaver Lumber Co. v. Denis and Denis Sawmills Ltd.* (1963), 41 W.W.R. 570 (B.C.S.C.)

In *J.D.F. Builders Ltd. v. Albert Pearl (Management) Ltd. et al.*, [1975] 2 S.C.R. 846, affg [1973] 1 O.R. 594 (C.A.), revg [1972] 1 O.R. 208 (H.C.), the court examined the evidence of the parties to determine their intention. The promissory note in issue bore the words "we promise to pay" and the corporation's name was stamped in ink on the promissory note together with the signature of the individual in control of the corporation. The plaintiff sought judgment against both the corporation and the individual. Notwithstanding that there was no notation on the instrument clearly indicating that the individual had not signed in any personal capacity, the court was of the view that the evidence indicated that parties had intended that only the corporation be bound.

It is not necessary to use the words "for" or "on behalf of" to exonerate the signer from personal liability. Thus, in *Chapman v. Smethurst*, [1909] 1 K.B. 927 (C.A.) the name of the corporation was impressed by a rubber stamp with the words "Managing Director" underneath, made by the same stamp. Above these words the defendant signed his name and it was held that he was not personally liable. But in *Traders Group Ltd. v. Carroll* (1970), 2 N.S.R. (2d) 321 (C.A.) the notation "by" was made upon a promissory note, followed by the defendant's signature. No principal was indicated on the note. Under this line was another line, below which were the words "additional endorser." The plaintiff sued the defendant as an endorser of the note, but the defendant argued that he had signed as president of the corporation. On appeal it was held that the president was personally liable as endorser even though he had signed his name on the line usually reserved for the corporate officer and not on the line reserved for additional endorsers. The word "by" in front of his signature did not raise an ambiguity and extrinsic evidence could not be admitted. The court drew the inference that the president had endorsed the note to give added protecton to the plaintiff.

Schaffer v. Tubby Smith & Co., *supra*, followed in *McKale v. Martin*, [1946] Que. K.B. 435, the note was impressed with a rubber stamp bearing the name of the corporation and two dotted lines underneath. It was held that the signatures on these lines of the defendants followed by the words "Pres." and "Secy." respectively, linked these signatures with the name of the corporation in such a way as to indicate an intention to complete the signature to the notes on behalf of the corporation. The defendants were held not to be personally liable. In *Loczka v. Ruthenian Farmers' Co-operative Co.* (1922), 68 D.L.R. 535 (Man. C.A.) it was stated that coupling the signatures by a bracket or rubber stamp would indicate that the signatures were in reality one and that the signers were mere scribes on behalf of the corporation.

Where parties "describe themselves as directors or by any similar form of description, but do not state on the face of the document that it is on account or on behalf of those whom they might otherwise be considered as representing, — if they merely describe themselves as directors, but do not state that they are acting on behalf of the company, — they are individually liable": *Dutton v. Marsh* (1871), L.R. 6 Q.B. 361, per Cockburn C.J. at 364. So also the words "President" or "Mgr." written after the names of the parties are descriptive only and do not exempt them from personal liability: *Loczka v. Ruthenian Farmers' Co-operative Co., supra.*

A bill of exchange drawn on a corporation had been accepted by it and was endorsed with the name of the corporation impressed by a rubber stamp and underneath the names of the two defendants bracketed together followed by the word "directors". The plaintiff not being satisfied with the liability of the corporation alone had required endorsation by the directors. It was held that there was nothing in the form of the signatures which was conclusive as a matter of law that the signatures were for and on behalf of the corporation. Having regard to s. 26(2) of the *Bills of Exchange Act, 1882* and adopting the construction most favourable to the validity of the instrument it was held that the signature was the signature of the directors personally, since otherwise the endorsement would be valueless, the corporation being already liable as an acceptor: *Elliott v. Bax-Ironside*, [1925] 2 K.B. 301 (C.A.).

So also, where the president of a corporation gave a letter of guarantee signing the corporation's name per himself, it was held the signature was sufficient to charge the defendant personally: *Miles v. Zuckerman*, [1931] O.R. 368 (C.A.) *sed quaere.*

Conversely, in *Fraser v. Pedlar Industrial Inc.* (1981), 16 B.L.R. 49 (N.S.A.D.) where printed cheques upon which the corporation's name and address were inscribed were delivered and dishonoured, the president was not personally liable on the cheques. The cheques had been signed by the president who had not indicated on the cheques that he was an officer of the corporation, nor that he was signing on its behalf. Upon examining the cheques and the extrinsic evidence, the court concluded that the cheques were those of the corporation, the president signed as an officer of the corporation intending to bind only the corporation and that the respondent had accepted them with the same intent.

The word "we" instead of "I", used in a promissory note signed by an officer in his individual capacity, does not necessarily imply that the note was that of the corporation: *Lindsay-Walker v. Hilson* (1916), 27 D.L.R. 233 (Man. C.A.). See also *J.D.F. Builders Ltd. v. Albert Pearl (Management) Ltd., supra.*

Extrinsic evidence is not admissible to show that a promissory note signed by a managing director in his individual capacity was intended to be that of the corporation: ibid. See also *Wilton v. Manitoba Independent Oil Co.* (1915), 25 D.L.R. 243 (Man. C.A.); *Crane v. Lavoie* (1912), 4. D.L.R. 175 (Man. C.A.); *Fairchild v. Ferguson & Nolan* (1892), 21 S.C.R. 484.

In an action on a promissory note signed by a corporation and several individuals the question at issue was whether the note was that of the corporation only, or whether the individual signers of it were also liable. The note was in form, "we promise to pay" and signed "The Alberta Brick Company, Ltd. — W. C. Harris, Dir. Wm. M. Cross Mgr., F. C. Everard". It was held that there was nothing upon the face of the note to indicate that the individual signers of it were not personally liable: *Union Bank of Canada v. Everard* (1912), 5 Alta. L.R. 489 (C.A.).

Where promissory notes were signed in the name of a corporation by means of a rubber stamp and followed by the signatures of the corporation's three directors but their position as such officers was not indicated, the Court of Appeal held that the directors were personally liable as there was nothing on the face of the notes to show that they signed in a representative capacity: *Daymond Motors Ltd. v. Thistletown Developments Ltd. et al.*, [1956] O.W.N. 867. See also: *Beaver Lumber Co. Ltd. v. Denis and Denis Sawmills Ltd.*, *supra*. But see: *J.D.F. Builders Ltd. v. Albert Pearl (Management) Ltd. et al.*, discussed *supra*; *H.B. Etlin Co. Ltd. v. Asselstyne*, [1962] O.R. 810 (C.A.) and *Allprint Co. Ltd. v. Erwin* (1982), 38 O.R. (2d) 13 (C.A.). In both the *Etlin* and *Allprint* cases, the individual had signed a corporate cheque but did not indicate on the cheque that they held offices with the corporation.

In the former case, the cheque on printed stationary of the corporation, the size of the cheque number, the name of the corporation's bank printed on the cheque, the perforated stamp of the type commonly used by corporations and the signature of the defendant on the line provided for corporate signing officers made the cheque *prima facie* that of the corporation.

In the latter case, Dubin J.A. concluded that, apart from extrinsic evidence, and based on the following factors, one could readily conclude the cheque was a corporate cheque only: there was only one signature; the cheque was drawn on the corporate bank account; the name of the corporation was in bold face type; the signature of the corporation was provided by the printed corporate name and a line drawn thereunder for the signature of the signing officer. Dubin, J.A. suggested that in those cases where an individual has been held liable, it was because it was not clear on the face of the instrument that there was a corporate signature.

In *Bank of Montreal v. DeLatre* (1848), 5 U.C.Q.B. 362, the president of the corporation accepted a bill thus, "P. C. DeLatre, President N. H. & D. Co." In an action by the payee against the acceptor personally he was held to be liable and the addition of his description did not aid him. Officers of corporations were also held personally liable as acceptors in *Armour v. Gates* (1859), 8 U.C.C.P. 548; *Laing v. Taylor* (1876), 26 U.C.C.P. 416; *City Bank v. Cheney* (1855), 15 U.C.Q.B. 400.

Liability of corporation for torts of its agents

A corporation is liable for the acts of its agents and for the natural consequences of those acts when done by them in the ordinary course of the corporation's business. The state of mind of directors and managers who represent the directing mind and will of a corporation and control what it does is the state of mind of the corporation and is treated by the law as such: *H. L. Bolton Co. v. T. J. Graham & Sons*, [1957] 1 Q.B. 159 (C.A.), per Denning L. J., at 172. Hence, as a result of its agent's wrong, a corporation may be held liable for

Negligence: *Parnaby v. Lancaster Canal* (1839), 11 A. & E. 223; *Mersey Docks Trustees v. Gibbs* (1865), L.R. 1 H. L. 93; *Lennard's Carrying Co. Ltd. v. Asiatic Petroleum Co. Ltd.*, [1915] A.C. 705; *Lockhart v. C.P.R.*, [1941] S.C.R. 278; *Lord Nelson Hotel Ltd. v. Cambrian Construction Ltd.* (1975), 13 N.S.R. (2d) 79 (T.D.), affd (1976), 17 N.S.R. (2d) 336 (C.A.); *James Street Hardware & Furniture Co. v. Spizziri* (1985), 33 C.C.L.T. 209 (H.C.), revd on other grounds (1987), 43 C.C.L.T. 9 (C.A.); *Crown Diamond Paint Co. v. R.*, [1980] 2 F.C. 794 (T.D.), revd on other grounds [1982] 1 F.C. 837 (Fed. C.A.); *Robitaille v. Vancouver Hockey Club Ltd.* (1979), 19 B.C.L.R. 158 (B.C.S.C.), affd [1981], 3 W.W.R. 481 (B.C.C.A.); *Strilchic v. Lalonde, Koons & Thompson Cabs Ltd.*, [1972] 3 W.W.R. 50 (Man. Q.B.), affd [1973] 1 W.W.R. 500 (Man. C.A.); *Imperial Oil Ltd. v. Nadeau*, [1965] S.C.R. 534.

Trespass: *Maund v. Monmouthshire Canal Co.* (1842), 4 M. & G. 452; *Magnus v. Wiebe et al.*, [1942] 1 D.L.R. 458.

Malicious prosecution: *Edwards v. Midland Ry. Co.* (1880), 6 Q.B.D. 287; *Abrath v. North Eastern Ry. Co.* (1886), 11 App. Cas. 247.

Libel: *Whitfield v. S.E. Ry. Co.* (1858), E.B. & E. 115; *Tench v. Great Western Ry. Co.* (1872), 32 U.C.Q.B. 452; *L'Institut Canadien v. Le Nouveau Monde* (1873), 17 L.C.J. 296; *Freeborn v. Singer Sewing Machine Co.* (1885), 2 Man. R. 253 (C.A.); *Carroll v. Penberthy Injector Co.* (1889), 16 O.A.R. 446.

Defamatory words published by an employee within the scope and in the course of his employment: *Harrison v. The Joy Oil Co. Ltd. et al.*, [1938] O.R. 679 (C.A.); *Munro v. Toronto Sun Publishing Corp.* (1982), 39 O.R. (2d) 100 (H.C.)

Assault and battery: *Butler v. Manchester, Sheffield and Lincolnshire Ry. Co.* (1888), 21 Q.B.D. 207 (C.A.); *Verbeek v. Stefura and St. Albert Motor Inn (1972) Ltd.* (1981), 26 A.R. 497 (Q.B.); *Brown v. Doe and Aster Hotel Ltd.* (1980), 23 B.C.L.R. 34 (S.C.); *Frizzell v. Breckenridge and Field & Stream Inc.* (1974), 5 Nfld. & P.E.I.R. 457 (P.E.I.S.C.); *Wenz v. Royal Trust Co.*, [1953] O.W.N. 798 (H.C.); *Ferguson v. Roblin* (1888), 17 O.R. 167 (C.A.); *Jennings v. Canadian National Railway Co.*, [1925] 1 W.W.R. 918 (B.C.C.A.) and *Griggs v. Southside Hotel Ltd. and German*, [1947] O.R. 674 (C.A.).

Nuisance: *Rapier v. London Tramways Co.* (1893), 69 L.T. 361.

Fraud: *Barwick v. English Joint Stock Bank* (1867), L.R. 2 Ex. 259; *Mackay v. Commercial Bank of New Brunswick* (1874), L.R. 5 P.C. 394; *Houldsworth v. City of Glasgow Bank* (1880), 5 App. Cas. 317; *Moore v. Ontario Investment Association* (1888), 16 O.R. 269; *S. Pearson & Son Ltd. v. Dublin Corp.*,

[1907] A.C. 351; *London County Freehold & Leasehold Properties Ltd. v. Berkeley Property & Investment Co. Ltd.*, [1936] 2 All. E.R. 1039 (C.A.); *Uxbridge Permanent Building Society v. Pickard*, [1939] 2 K.B. 248 (C.A.); *B.P.I. Resources Ltd. v. Merrill Lynch Canada Inc.* (1986), 72 A.R. 6 (Q.B.), affd (1989), 43 B.L.R. 1 (C.A.); *A.G. Nova Scotia v. Christian* (1974), 49 D.L.R. (3d) 742 (C.A.); *Seven Oaks Manufacturing & Sales (1968) Ltd. v. Vaughan* (1976), 62 D.L.R. (3d) 577 (Sask. Dist. Ct.), affd [1977] 4 W.W.R. 119 (Sask. C.A.).

Breach of trust committed for the benefit of the corporation: *McCrindle v. London Scottish Canadian Investment Syndicate* (1922), 70 D.L.R. 612 (Alta C.A.).

A corporation will not be held liable for negligence of an employee while not engaged on the corporation's business and not under its control: *Dallas v. Hinton & Home Oil Distributors Ltd.*, [1938] S.C.R. 244; *Hoar v. Wallace et al.*, [1938] O.R. 666 (C.A.); *Colling v. Naden Habour Timber Ltd.* (1985), 33 M.V.R. 138 (B.C.S.C.), affd (unreported, April 15, 1987, B.C.C.A.)

A corporation may be estopped by the acts of its agents: *Burkinshaw v. Nicolls* (1878), 3 App. Cas. 1004; *Bloomenthal v. Ford*, [1897] A.C. 156; but not where the estoppel would prevent the corporation carrying out a statutory duty: *Maritime Electric Co. Ltd. v. General Dairies, Ltd.*, [1937] A.C. 610. A corporation may be held guilty of laches and bound by acquiescence: *Erlanger v. New Sombrero Phosphate Co.* (1878), 3 App. Cas. 1218; *Nicol's Case* (1885), 29 Ch. D. 421 (C.A.). For although it may not have eyes and see what is going on, it has agents who can see: *Crook v. Corporation of Seaford* (1871), L.R. 6 Ch. App. 551; and it can form an "intention" within the meaning of a civil statute: *Betty's Cafés, Ltd. v. Phillips Furnishing Stores, Ltd.*, [1958] 1 All E.R. 607 (H.L.).

A corporation on the ordinary principles of the law of agency is answerable for the manner in which its agent has conducted himself in transacting the business which he was authorized to do, and, if a sales agent sells shares and represents that his principal has power to repurchase them and will repurchase them, which the principal, an incorporated corporation, has no power to do, the principal will be bound to refund the money paid: *Whaley v. O'Grady* (1912), 4 D.L.R. 485 (Man. C.A.).

In *Montreal v. Sanders*, [1958] Que. S.C. 262, the provisional directors of a corporation permitted the corporation to carry on business before the letters patent were granted and during this period the defendant, one of the directors, while driving a truck bought on behalf of the corporation was involved in an accident. The court held that if the corporation was treated as having a *de facto* existence, the directors, including defendant, were liable for permitting the corporation to commence operations but as the corporation had no legal existence defendant was liable as the truck was in his care.

Chapter 4

REGISTERED OFFICE AND RECORDS

Cross references: Ontario Act, ss. 14, 139-141, 143-145, 13.

Registered office

A corporation is at all times to have a registered office in the place within Canada specified in its articles (s. 19(1)). Any change in the place where the registered office is to be situated will require articles of amendment under s. 173(1)(b). The address of the registered office within the place specified in the articles may be fixed and changed from time to time by the directors. A notice in prescribed form (Form 3) of the address of the registered office and of any change thereto is to be sent to the Director together with any articles designating the place or changing the place of the registered office (s. 19(2)).

Notice of a change of address of its registered office is to be given by a corporation to the Director within 15 days of such change. Until the foregoing requirements have been complied with, the head office of the corporation is unchanged. See *Re Smith Transportation Co.* (1928), 62 O.L.R. 203 at 208 (H.C.). It is not necessary that any part of the ordinary business operations of the corporation be carried on at or from the head office: *Re Smith Transportation Co.* (1928), 62 O.L.R. 203 at 208 (H.C.).

Nationality of corporations

A corporation is capable of having a nationality. Its nationality is the place of its registration or incorporation: *Princess of Reuss v. Bos* (1871), L.R. 5 H.L. 176; *A.G. v. Jewish Colonization Association*, [1901] 1 K.B. 123 (C.A.); *Janson v. Driefontein Consolidated Mines Ltd.*, [1902] A.C. 484 (H.L.); *Gasque v. Inland Revenue Commissioners*, [1940] 2 K.B. 80 (K.B.); *Kuenigl v. Donnersmarck*, [1955] 1 Q.B. 515 (Q.B.). See also the article "The Nationality of Corporations" by R.E.L. Vaughan Williams and M. Chrussachi in (1933) 49 Law Quarterly Review, p. 334.

Domicile of corporations

A corporation is capable of having a domicile. Its domicile is the place of its registration or incorporation and that domicile clings to it throughout its existence: *Gasque v. Inland Revenue Commissioners*, [1940] 2 K.B. 80 (K.B.); *National Trust Co. v. Ebro Irrigation & Power Co.*, [1954] O.R. 463 (H.C.); *Kuenigl v. Donnersmarck*, [1955] 1 Q.B. 515 (Q.B.). If, however, a corporation is reincorporated under the laws of another jurisdiction, it will acquire a new domicile.

The laws of a corporation's domicile govern not only its creation and continuing existence but also all matters of internal management, the creation of share capital and related matters, and the persons who are entitled to act as directors and the manner of their selection: *National Trust Co. v. Ebro Irrigation & Power Co., supra.* In that case a Canadian corporation owned shares and bonds of two Canadian subsidiary corporations which owned assets and carried on business in a foreign country. The courts in the foreign country adjudged the corporation bankrupt and persons purporting to act under that judgment seized the assets of the two subsidiaries (which had not been declared bankrupt), purported to issue new shares and elect new boards of directors of the subsidiaries and then transferred all the assets of the subsidiaries to a new corporation incorporated in the foreign country. It was held that the trustee for the bondholders of the Canadian parent corporation was entitled to a declaratory judgment that all the proceedings in the foreign country were an absolute nullity because they had been conducted without any regard to and in violation of Canadian law which, being the law of the two subsidiaries' domicile, governed the matters in question.

A corporation's domicile does not change by reason of the fact that the corporation comes under enemy control: *Kuenigl v. Donnersmarck, supra.*

Residence of corporations

While a corporation can have only one nationality and one domicile at any one time it can have more than one residence. The question of residence generally arises in cases involving such matters as liability to taxation, liability to suit, service of documents, change of venue, security for costs and enemy character. Each case depends not only on its own facts but on the wording of the statute or rule in question, for example, whether the word "resides" stands alone or is amplified by some words such as "carries on business". The question of residence for tax purposes is discussed under a separate heading below; the question of what constitutes carrying on business is dealt with in the notes in Chapter 3; other cases on residence are noted in the material that follows.

The principle that a corporation may have more than one place of residence is illustrated in *Bank of Toronto v. Pickering* (1919), 46 O.L.R. 289 (Ch.) (where Middleton J. relied on *Bruell, Ex parte; In re Bowie* (1880), 16 Ch. D. 484 (C.A.) and *R. v. Lovitt*, [1912] A.C. 212 at 219 (P.C.); *Ehmka v. Border Cities Improvement Co.* (1922), 52 O.L.R. 193 (H.C.) (where Lennox J. reviewed the English authorities); *The King v. National Trust Co.*, [1933] S.C.R. 670 (Duff C.J. at p. 674); *Royal Bank v. McMahon*, [1934] 4 D.L.R. 801 (P.E.I. S.C.) (following *Bank of Toronto v. Pickering, supra*); *Swedish Central Railways Co. v. Thompson*, [1925] A.C. 495 (H.L.) (dual residence for taxation purposes); *Union Corp. Ltd. v. I.R.C.*, [1953] A.C. 482 (H.L.) (dual residence for taxation purposes); and see *Cody's Ltd. v. Chester Branch Canadian Legion* (1962), 47 M.P.R. 203 (N.S. C.A.).

A corporation resides, for the purposes of suit, in as many places as it carries on business: *New York Life Insurance Co. v. Public Trustee*, [1924] 2 Ch. 101 at 120 (C.A.). It is in each case a question of fact whether the corporation carries on its business in any given place: *Haggin v. Comptoir D'Escompte de Paris* (1889), 23 Q.B.D. 519 (C.A.).

A corporation, having its head office and chief place of business in Toronto but a branch or agency in Hamilton, did not "reside or carry on business" in Hamilton so as to confer jurisdiction on the Division Court in the latter place under s. 64 of the *Division Courts Act*, R.S.O. 1927, c. 95: *Re Miles Transport Co. & The Mail Printing Co.*, [1935] O.W.N. 541 (H.C.).

In *Davies v. British Geon Ltd.*, [1957] 1 Q.B. 1 the Court of Appeal held that for purposes of a rule of practice which provided that an appearance should be entered where the defendant "resides or carries on business", the defendant manufacturing corporation resided and carried on business in London where its head office was situated but that this did not preclude the corporation from also carrying on business elsewhere, in this case where its factory was located.

Under a rule of practice, which provides that where the plaintiff resides out of the province security for costs may be ordered, security may be required in the case of an extraprovincial corporation notwithstanding that it is duly registered in the province: *Ashland Co. v. Armstrong* (1906), 11 O.L.R. 414 (Ont. Ch.); *Canadian Ry. Accident v. Kelly* (1907), 5 W.L.R. 412 (Man. K.B.); *Frost & Wood Co. v. Howes* (1912), 4 D.L.R. 527 (Alta. T.D.); *Buckeye Incubator Co. v. Rice Construction Co. Ltd.*, [1963] 2 O.R. 195 (H.C.); *Factory Tire & Rubber Co. Ltd. v. Timac Tire Sales Ltd. et al.* (1979), 9 Alta. L.R. (2d) 193 (T.D.). In several cases it has been held that the existence of *Reciprocal Enforcement of Judgments Acts* does not affect the right of a court to grant security for costs against a corporation registered as an extraprovincial corporation. See *Park Avenue Furniture Corp. v. Gandhi*, [1990] 2 W.W.R. 174 (Q.B.); *Alpina Equi-*

pamentos Industriais Ltda. v. Bennett Environmental Consultants Ltd. et al. (1990), 45 C.P.C. (2d) 15 (B.C.S.C.); *Ruko of Canada Ltd. v. Canadian Imperial Bank of Commerce* (1991), 49 C.P.C. (2d) 105 (B.C.S.C.). In British Columbia, there is no specific rule of practice governing security for costs and such an order is a matter within the inherent jurisdiction of the court. It is unclear whether the court also has a statutory power to make such order pursuant to s. 129 of the British Columbia *Companies Act*. See *Ruko of Canada Ltd. v. Canadian Imperial Bank of Commerce, supra* (statutory authority flows from s. 129) but see *Alpina Equipamentos Industriais Ltda., supra* (no statutory authority). In *La Salle Extension University v. Linley*, [1933] 3 D.L.R. 643 (B.C. C.A.), it was held that it was not sufficient to show residence in the province, as the fact that the corporation also had another residence outside the province entitled the court to make the order to give security for costs. Where the corporation had a branch office in Ontario in which a substantial business had been carried on, the corporation did not reside outside of Ontario. See *McDougall & Christmas Ltd. v. Genser*, [1963] 2 O.R. 737 (H.C.). A foreign corporation which held shares in a company with assets within the jurisdiction had an insufficient presence to be considered "resident" and the court ordered security for costs. A shareholder has no property in the physical corporate assets. See *Greenacres Inc. v. J. & M. Mills Ltd.* (1967), 60 W.W.R. 447 (B.C.S.C.). Where the keeping of an office is merely for purposes of a mailing address, this is an insufficient presence to be considered a resident. See *Pet Milk Canada Ltd. and Numilk Co. Ltd. v. Olympia and York Developments et al.* (1974), 4 O.R. (2d) 640 (Master). Evidence that the head office is in another jurisdiction is not in and of itself sufficient to establish non-residency. See *Valleyfield Construction Ltd. v. Argo Construction Ltd. et al.* (1984), 44 C.P.C. 107 (Ont. Master). Where the Statement of Defence asserted that the head office was in Texas and there was no further material before the Court, the company was found to be ordinarily resident outside Ontario and *prima facie*, the motion for security for costs was entitled to succeed. See *Community Web Printing v. Cosmos Graphics Inc.* (1985), 3 C.P.C. (2d) 209 (Ont. Master). See also *Gesco Industries Inc. v. Welby's Fine Furniture*, [1986] 6 W.W.R. 573 (Man. Q.B.). Where the plaintiff corporation, which sued on a policy of insurance, had been doing business in the province when the policy was purchased, but subsequently moved to Quebec, the defendant insurer's application was denied. See *Flèche Verte Ltée v. Dominion Insurance Corp.* (1987), 201 A.P.R. 236 (N.B.Q.B.). Where a contract between the plaintiff Florida corporation and the defendant Alberta corporation provided that the agreement was to be interpreted according to the laws of Alberta and that the parties attorned to the jurisdiction of Alberta courts, security for costs was ordered because the plaintiff was not registered in Alberta, did not carry on business there and had no assets there. See *Vesta Technology Ltd. v. Chem-Security (Alberta) Ltd.* (1991), 50 C.P.C. (2d) 167 (Alta. Master). A non-resident shareholder applying for the liquidation and dissolution of a corporation is, however, not compellable to post security for costs. See *Hurler v. M.L.E. Industries Ltd.* (1991), 45 C.P.C. (2d) 11 (Alta. Q.B.).

Having a branch office and carrying on business may constitute residence for certain purposes. Thus, it was held in *John v. Dodwell & Co.*, [1918] A.C. 563 (P.C.) that a statute, providing that if a person entitled to sue was beyond the seas time should not run until such disability was removed, did not apply to a corporation having its registered office outside the jurisdiction if it had a branch office and carried on business within the jurisdiction.

The question of residence may also arise in determining whether or not a corporation is an enemy either under a statute or at common law. Under the Revised Regulations Respecting Trading with the Enemy (1943), (S.C. 1947, chap. 24, s.1(a)(d)), the word "person" included a corporation and the word "enemy" included, *inter alia*, "any person who resides within enemy territory or proscribed territory". At common law a natural person bears an enemy character if he voluntarily resides among Her Majesty's enemies. In determining the voluntary residence of a corporation for this purpose the court looks at the residence of the persons in control of the corporation's affairs: *Daimler Co. v. Continental Tyre & Rubber Co. (Great Britain)*, [1916] 2 A.C. 307 at 339 (H.L.). In that case the corporation was incorporated in the United Kingdom, all the shareholders, save one, and all the directors were Germans resident in Germany and the House of Lords held that it could not sue for a trade account in England. At page 344, Lord Parker summarized the law on the subject:

> (1.) A company incorporated in the United Kingdom is a legal entity, a creation of law with the status and capacity which the law confers. . . .
>
> (2.) Such a company can only act through agents properly authorized, and so long as it is carrying on business in this country through agents so authorized and residing in this or a friendly country it is *prima facie* to be regarded as a friend . . .
>
> (3.) Such a company may, however, assume an enemy character. This will be the case if its agents or the persons in *de facto* control of its affairs, whether authorized or not, are resident in an enemy country, or, wherever resident, are adhering to the enemy or taking instructions from or acting under the control of enemies. . . .
>
> (4.) The character of individual shareholders cannot of itself affect the character of the company. . . . The enemy character of individual shareholders and their conduct may, however, be very material on the question whether the company's agents, or the persons in *de facto* control of its affairs, are in fact adhering to, taking instructions from, or acting under the control of enemies. . . .

A corporation which has acquired enemy character continues to owe its existence to the law of the country under which it was incorporated and it remains subject to that law: *Kuenigl v. Donnersmarck*, [1955] 1 Q.B. 515 at 535 (Q.B.). In that case the directors of an English corporation were residing in enemy territory and purported to enter into a contract with the enemy. McNair J. held that the authority of the directors was automatically determined on the outbreak of war between England and the enemy and that, consequently, the contract made by them was not the contract of the corporation.

Residence for purposes of taxation

The *Income Tax Act* (Canada) by s. 250(4) provides that a corporation is deemed to be resident in Canada throughout the taxation year if it was incorporated in Canada after April 26, 1965; or if incorporated prior to April 9, 1959 and was a foreign business corporation (as defined) controlled by a corporation resident in Canada and throughout the ten year period ending on June 18, 1971 carried on business in any one particular country other than Canada and during such period paid dividends to its Canadian resident shareholders on which such shareholders paid tax to the foreign country where the corporation carried on business, was incorporated in Canada and at any time in any taxation year commencing after 1971 was resident in Canada or carried on business in Canada; and if incorporated before April 27, 1965 it was incorporated in Canada and at any time in a taxation year ending after April 26, 1965 it was resident in Canada or carried on business in Canada. It will be noted that pursuant to s. 250(5) of *The Income Tax Act* (Canada) a corporation (except as proscribed) is deemed not to be resident in Canada if by virtue of an agreement or a convention between the Government of Canada and the government of another country having the force of law in Canada, it would at the time in question, if it had income from a source outside Canada, not be subject to tax thereon under Part I of the Act.

Apart from the statutory provisions, for the purposes of taxation a corporation may be deemed to be resident in a jurisdiction other than that of the place where its head office is situated: *De Beers Consolidated Mines, Ltd. v. Howe*, [1906] A.C. 455 (H.L.). In that case Lord Loreburn adopted the test that a corporation "resides for purposes of income tax where its real business is carried on" and "the real business is carried on where the central management and control actually abides". This test has been applied repeatedly in judicial decisions, the leading ones being *Bradbury v. English Sewing Cotton Co.*, [1923] A.C. 744 (H.L.); *Egyptian Delta Land & Investment Co. v. Todd*, [1929] A.C. 1 (H.L.) and *Unit Construction Co. v. Bullock*, [1960] A.C. 351 (H.L.); *Zehnder and Company v. Minister of National Revenue*, 70 D.T.C. 6064 (Ex. Cr.); *Bedford Overseas Freighters Ltd. v. Minister of National Revenue*, 70 D.T.C. 6072 (Ex. Cr.). Where Canadian shipping corporations were managed by a non-resident management corporation, virtually all of the shares were owned directly or indirectly by a non-resident individual, and almost all of the major decisions were made by the non-resident owner, but the Canadian directors opened bank accounts, signed cheques and performed other activities such as negotiating and signing agreements on behalf of the corporation, it was held in the above two cases that the corporations were resident in Canada because management and control were exercised to a substantial degree in Canada. See also *Sifneos v. Minister of National Revenue*, 68 D.T.C. 522 (T.A.B.); *Birmount Holdings Ltd. v. The Queen*, 78 D.T.C. 6254 (Fed. C.A.).

Where the central management and control actually abides is a pure question of fact: *Unit Construction Co. v. Bullock, supra*, at p. 363; and it makes no difference in determining this fact that the acts of management may be irregular, unauthorized or unlawful: *Unit Construction Co. v. Bullock, supra*. In that case the parent corporation in England exercised complete control over its three wholly owned subsidiaries in Kenya, even though the memoranda and articles of association of the subsidiaries vested complete control in the directors in

Kenya. The House of Lords held that the actual place of management, whether regular or irregular, and not the constitutionally lawful place of management was the factor that must be regarded in determining the question of management and therefore of residence. At page 363, Viscount Simonds said:

> The business is not the less managed in London because it ought to be managed in Kenya. Its residence is determined by the solid facts, not by the terms of its constitution, however imperative. If, indeed, I must disregard the facts as they are, because they are irregular, I find a company without any central management at all. For, though I may disregard existing facts, I cannot invent facts which do not exist and say that the company's business is managed in Kenya. . . . I come, therefore, to the conclusion, though truly no precedent can be found for such a case, that it is the actual place of management, not that place in which it ought to be managed, which fixes the residence of a company.

It has been held that a corporation, for tax purposes, may have two or more residences: *Swedish Central Railways Co. v. Thompson*, [1925] A.C. 495 (H.L.). In such a case the central management and control must be divided or distributed among the countries so that some part of it rests in the country where it is sought to establish the corporation's residence: *Union Corp. Ltd. v. I.R.C.*, [1953] A.C. 482 (H.L.). In considering both these cases in *Unit Construction Co. v. Bullock, supra*, at 369 Lord Radcliffe said that the facts in these cases were genuinely such as not to admit of a finding that central management and control was exercised in or from any one country and they constitute only one category of exception from the principle of the *De Beers* case and not an undefined second class. See also: *Minister of National Revenue v. Crossley Carpets (Canada) Ltd.*, [1968] C.T.C. 570 (Ex. Ct.).

As to facts which will result in a foreign corporation being deemed to be resident in Canada for income tax purposes, see *British Columbia Electric Ry. v. R.*, [1946] A.C. 527 at 538 (P.C.). As to the facts which will result in an extraprovincial manufacturing corporation not being resident for income tax purposes in a province where it conducts no manufacturing operations but does carry on some selling operations, see *International Harvester Company of Canada Ltd. v. Provincial Tax Commission*, [1949] A.C. 36 (P.C.) and *Wm. Wrigley Jr. Co. Ltd. v. The Provincial Treasurer of Manitoba*, [1947] S.C.R. 431.

Corporate records

A corporation is required to prepare and maintain at its registered office (or in any other place in Canada designated by the directors) records containing the articles, by-laws and any amendments thereto and a copy of any unanimous shareholders' agreement; minutes of meetings and resolutions of shareholders; copies of the notices of directors required to be sent to the Director (Form 6) and copies of the notice with respect to any change therein; and a securities register recording the securities issued in registered form showing with respect to each class of securities the names alphabetically arranged and the latest known address of each person who is or has been a security holder, the number of securities held by him and the date and particulars of the issue and transfer of each security (ss. 20(1), 50(1)). A corporation may appoint an agent to maintain a central securities register and branch securities register (s. 50(2)). The central securities register is to be maintained in any place in Canada and the branch securities register may be kept at any place in or out of Canada designated by the directors (s. 50(3)). See Chapter 6 "Transfers of Securities" for a discussion of transfer agents and securities registers.

Where a corporation has a substantial number of shareholders it is usual to appoint a trust corporation to perform as agent of the corporation the duties of passing upon the regularity of, and recording, transfers of shares and of keeping the register of shareholders. If the shares of the corporation are listed on a stock exchange, the exchange will require the corporation to employ a transfer agent and registrar and sometimes separate trust corporations are appointed, one to act as transfer agent and the other to act as registrar. Such requirements are designed to ensure that all transfers are regularly made and that on the death of a shareholder no transfer will be recorded without proper evidence of probate or administration having been granted being furnished.

The appointment of a transfer agent and registrar (and branch registrars of transfers) is made by resolution of the board of directors. The resolution also authorizes the corporation to execute an agreement with the transfer agent and registrar evidencing the appointment and embodying the obligations and duties relating to the appointment.

Where a foreign corporation has appointed a transfer agent in Ontario it may impose conditions upon the completion of the transfer by such transfer agent, for example, the payment to the transfer agent of such sum as the foreign corporation is, by the laws governing it, required to pay as a tax: *Galbraith v. Montreal Trust Co.* (10 February 1932), Rose C.J. [unreported]. The transfer agent cannot be compelled to do something beyond its authority from its principal, for example, to record a transfer until the transfer has been entered in the book kept in the state where the principal is incorporated, where the laws of that state so require: *Re Hatch & Fanny Farmer Candy Shops Inc.*, [1944] O.R. 586 (C.A.). *Quaere*, as to what remedy, if any, may be available to a person who has accepted and acted upon a share certificate containing a statement that the shares comprised therein are interchangeably transferable in Toronto or elsewhere as well as in New York where such is not the case: *Re Hatch & Fanny Farmer Candy Shops Inc., supra*, at p. 597.

If a branch register has not been set up a transfer of registered shares as between the shareholder and the corporation is deemed to take place where the register of transfers is located: *Black-Clawson Co. v. Montreal Locomotive Works Ltd.*, [1960] Que. Q.B. 514 (C.A.).

The Acts of most of the provinces contain specific authorization for maintaining books for the transfer of shares elsewhere than at the head office. Section 143 of the Ontario Act authorizes corporations incorporated under that Act to maintain branch registers of transfers either within or outside of Ontario. The former Ontario Act contained no such provision but it was held that a corporation incorporated thereunder had capacity to maintain a transfer agency and register of shareholders outside the province: *The King v. Williams*, [1942] A.C. 541 at 554 (P.C.); see also *Treasurer of Ontario v. Aberdein*, [1941] O.R.

227 at 243 (C.A.), affd [1947] A.C. 24 at 32 (P.C.) (New York transfer office on a parity with the Ontario transfer office).

Whether or not a branch register of transfers has been duly established is a matter for the law of the corporate domicile: *National Trust Co. v. Ebro Irrigation & Power Co.*, [1954] O.R. 463 (H.C.).

A corporation is also required to prepare and maintain adequate accounting records and records containing minutes and resolutions of the directors and of any committee thereof (s. 20(2)). These last mentioned records are to be opened for inspection by the directors at all reasonable times (s. 20(4)). Where accounting records of a corporation are kept outside Canada, accounting records are to be kept at the registered office or other office in Canada which are adequate to enable the directors to ascertain the financial condition of the corporation with reasonable accuracy on a quarterly basis (s. 20(5)).

Section 20(6) provides that a corporation failing to comply with the requirements of s. 20 without reasonable cause is guilty of an offence and liable on summary conviction to a fine not exceeding $5,000.

Form of corporate records

Registers and records required to be prepared and maintained under the Act may be in a bound or loose-leaf form or in a photographic film form or may be entered or recorded by any system of mechanical, electronic data processing or other information storage device capable of reproducing any required information in intelligible written form within a reasonable period of time (s. 22(11)). A corporation and its agents are required to take reasonable precautions to prevent loss or destruction of, or falsification of entries in, and to facilitate detection and correction of errors in such registers (s. 22(2)).

A person who contravenes the requirement of s. 22 without reasonable cause is guilty of an offence and is liable on summary conviction to a fine not exceeding $5,000 or imprisonment for a term not exceeding six months or to both (s. 22(3)).

Inspection of corporate records

The records in s. 20(1) may be inspected by the shareholders and creditors of a corporation as well as their agents and legal representatives and the director, all of whom may take extracts therefrom without charge; where the corporation is a distributing corporation, that is, any of the securities which are or were part of a distribution to the public and are outstanding and are held by more than one person, any other person may take such extract on payment of a reasonable fee (s. 21(1)).

A shareholder of a corporation is entitled to a copy of the articles and by-laws and any unanimous shareholder agreement without charge (s. 21(2)).

Similarly a list of shareholders can be obtained. Such list can be supplemented and include the holders of options. The list is to be furnished within 10 days from receipt of the affidavit required under s. 21(7) and is available to any shareholder or creditor of a corporation, his agent or legal representative and the director or where the corporation is a distribution corporation, any other person. A reasonable fee may be charged (s. 21(3)).

The affidavit under s. 21(7) is to state the name and address of the applicant (the name and address for service, if the applicant is a corporation) and that the basic list and any supplemental list will not be used except for specific purposes. In the case of a corporation the affidavit is to be made by a director or officer of a corporation (s. 21(8)). The list of shareholders obtained pursuant to the provisions in the article is not to be used by any person except as follows: (1) in an effort to influence the voting of shareholders of the corporation, (2) an offer to acquire shares of the corporation, or (3) any other matter relating to the affairs of the corporation (s. 21(9)).

It is provided that any person contravening s. 21 without reasonable cause is guilty of an offence and liable on summary conviction to a fine not exceeding $5,000 or imprisonment for a term not exceeding six months or both.

It has been held at common law that the books and papers of a corporation are the property of its shareholders and they are entitled to inspect them, but it has been further held that there is a duty cast on the shareholders not to disclose information so acquired and they may be restrained from doing so: *Brinsley, Ex parte* (1866), 36 L.J. Ch. 150. This rule was held to apply in the case of a shareholder who was also the solicitor for adverse parties engaged in litigation with the corporation: *R. v. Wilts. & Berks. Canal Navigation Co.* (1874), 29 L.T. 922. However, the common law right of a shareholder to inspect the books of the corporation is only a qualified and limited right. In the absence of statutory provisions, inspection will only be permitted by the court where, and to the extent to which, it is necessary for the purpose of some specific dispute or question pending in which the applicant has a special interest: *The Bank of Bombay v. Suleman Somji* (1908), 24 T.L.R. 698; and see *R. v. Merchant Tailors' Co.* (1831), 2 B. & Ad. 115. In *Klianis v. Poole*, (unreported), June 5, 1992, Ont. Ct. Gen. Div., the directors were held entitled to inspect.

Where the right is unqualified and statutory the motives of the person seeking to enforce it are immaterial and the court has no jurisdiction to enquire into them: *Davies v. Gas, Light & Coke Co.*, [1909] 1 Ch. 708 (C.A.). The fact that a shareholder acquired his shares at the instance of a rival corporation will not affect his right of inspection: *Mutter v. Eastern & Midland Ry.* (1888), 38 Ch. D. 92 (C.A.). As to what will constitute an unwarranted refusal of the right of inspection see *Michaud v. Cote* (1933), 39 Rev. de Jur. 504 and *Cooper v. Premier Trust Co.*, [1945] O.R. 35 (C.A.).

The right of inspection may be enforced by injunction restraining interference with such right: *Holland v. Dickson* (1888), 37 Ch. D. 669; or by action: *Cooper v. Premier Trust Co., supra.* In *Merritt v. Copper Crown Co.* (1903), 36 N.S.R. 383 (C.A.) mandamus was granted to a non-resident shareholder of a foreign corporation having its principal place of business in Nova Scotia to compel the corporation to permit him to inspect the books of the corporation.

The governing statute may impose restrictions on the right of inspection or the right to make extracts. For the prohibitions and restrictions on making, procuring and using lists of shareholders of an Ontario corporation, see s. 146

of the Ontario Act. In *Re MacMillan Bloedel Ltd.*, [1976] 6 W.W.R. 475 (B.C. S.C.) it was held that the language of the section must be followed exactly and that the declaration must contain the words as found in the B.C. Act that the list "is required and will be used only for corporate purposes". In the case in question a solicitor applied on behalf of an undisclosed principal and gave an affidavit rather than a statutory declaration which did not contain the above wording. An order was not granted to compel the corporation to provide him with a list. See also *Brunet v. Prince County Hospital* (1983), 23 B.L.R. 168 (P.E.I. S.C.).

The right of inspection ceases when the corporation is in liquidation: *In re Kent Coalfields Syndicate*, [1898] 1 Q.B. 754 (C.A.).

A director by virtue of his office has the right at any time, and not at board meetings only, to see and take copies of documents belonging to the corporation: *Burn v. London & South Wales Coal Co.* (1890), 7 T.L.R. 118.

No provision is made entitling shareholders to copies of minutes of meetings of directors. The minutes of meetings of directors are not properly open to the inspection of the shareholders and a provision entitling shareholders to inspect the books wherein the proceedings of the corporation are recorded has been held not sufficient to entitle them to see the minutes of the proceedings of the directors: *R. v. Marquita* (1858), 1 E. & E. 289.

There is now no statutory provision that any such minutes, if purporting to be signed by the chairman of the meeting or the chairman of the next succeeding meeting, are to be evidence of the proceedings. Such might be the case even apart from the statutory provision: *In re Portuguese Consolidated Copper Mines Ltd.* (1890), 45 Ch. D. 16 at 29 (C.A.).

The *prima facie* proof afforded by signed minutes may be displaced by the evidence of persons present at the meeting: *Bartlett v. Bartlett Mines Ltd.* (1911), 24 O.L.R. 419 at 435 (D.C.).

The minutes are not exclusive evidence of what took place at a meeting: *In re Fireproof Doors Ltd.*, [1916] 1 Ch. 142 at 149; *Fullerton v. Crawford* (1919), 59 S.C.R. 314 at 349; *Wilson v. Woollatt* (1928), 62 O.L.R. 620 at 627 (C.A.). Where the charter provides that a declaration of the president that a resolution has been carried and entry to that effect in the minutes is to be sufficient evidence of the fact, such declaration and entry is not conclusive evidence: *Gold v. Maldaver* (1912), 6 D.L.R. 333 at 335 (Ont. H.C.).

In the case of corporations incorporated with memorandum and articles, if the articles provide that minutes are to be conclusive evidence of the facts therein stated, the words "conclusive evidence" mean evidence which is not to be displaced: *Kerr v. John Mottram Ltd.*, [1940] 1 Ch. 657.

In *Harvard v. Freeholders Oil Co.* (1952), 6 W.W.R. 413 (Q.B.), the corporation contended that the signatures appearing on the minutes of a meeting of the directors at which an officer was appointed had not been proved and that without such proof the resolution appointing the officer could not be accepted in evidence in an action brought by him for wrongful dismissal. As the minutes of the meeting purported to be signed by the chairman and secretary of the meeting at which they were passed, the court, under a section of the Saskatchewan

Companies Act similar to s. 110(2), rejected the corporation's contention and held that the minutes of the meeting containing the resolution were acceptable in evidence and bound the corporation.

Section 257(2) of the Act provides that a certified copy of minutes or an extract from minutes of a meeting of directors or a committee of directors is, in the absence of evidence to the contrary, proof of the facts so certified without proof of the signature or official character of the person appearing to have signed the certificate, when such certificate is introduced as evidence in any civil, criminal or administrative action or proceeding.

Section 257(3) provides that an entry in a securities register is, in the absence of evidence to the contrary, proof that the person in whose name the security is registered is the owner of the securities therein described.

A certificate issued on behalf of a corporation stating any fact set out in the minutes of the meetings of directors or a committee thereof may be signed by a director, officer or transfer agent (s. 257(1)).

A corporation will not be allowed to set up its own want of books or improper bookkeeping or neglect to comply with the statutory provisions: *Re Sprouted Food Co., Hudson's Case* (1905), 6 O.W.R. 514 (U.C. K.B.). A liquidator is at liberty to draw conclusions as to the liability of contributories from books which are defective or do not comply with the Act: *Re Jones & Moore Electric Co.* (1909), 18 Man. R. 549 (C.A.).

False entry in corporate records

A person who, with intent to defraud, destroys, mutilates, alters, falsifies, or makes a false entry in, or omits a material particular from, or alters a material particular in, a book, paper, writing, valuable security or document is guilty of an offence under s. 397 of the Criminal Code.

Corporate seal

Section 23 of the Act provides that an instrument or agreement executed on behalf of a corporation by a director, officer or agent is not invalid merely because a corporate seal is not affixed thereto. For a full discussion of the use and necessity of a corporate seal see under the heading "Formalities in Execution of Contracts," in Chapter 3, *supra*. It will be noted that the general practice is to use a corporate seal for any contract of importance, even although this is no longer required under the Act.

Chapter 5

SHARES, SHAREHOLDERS AND DIVIDENDS

Cross references: Ontario Act, ss. 22-45

Nature of shares

A share is an aliquot separate integral part of the authorized capital of a corporation. The fractional part of the capital which a share represents depends on the number and classes of shares issued. In *Bradbury v. English Sewing Cotton Co.*, [1923] A.C. 744 at 767 (H.L.), Lord Wrenbury described shares as follows:

> A share is, therefore, a fractional part of the capital. It confers upon the holder a certain right to a proportionate part of the assets of the corporation, whether by way of dividend or of distribution of assets in winding-up. It forms, however, a separate right of property. The capital is the property of the corporation. The share, although it is a fraction of the capital, is the property of the corporator. The aggregate of all the fractions if collected in two or three hands does not constitute the corporators the owners of the capital — that remains the property of the corporation. But, nevertheless, the share is a property in a fractional part of the capital.

For a definition of the term "share" see *Borland's Trustee v. Steel Bros. & Co.*, [1901] 1 Ch. 279 at 288, and for a discussion of the nature of the attributes of shares see *Williams v. The King*, [1940] O.R. 403 at 413 (C.A.). The creation and issuance of shares are governed by the law of the corporate domicile: *National Trust Co. v. Ebro Irrigation & Power Co.*, [1954] O.R. 463 (Ont. H.C.). Where a lease provided that the landlord could cancel the lease on 60 days' notice of change of control of the tenant by sale or other disposition, and the tenant issued additional treasury shares which changed its control. which in turn was alleged to be a change by sale or other disposition, the court held that an issue of shares was included in the word "sale" as the shares had been issued for consideration. See *J.M.P.M. Enterprises Ltd. v. Danforth Fabrics (Humbertown) Ltd.*, [1969] 1 O.R. 785 (H.C.).

It is important to keep in mind the distinction between the share and the share certificate. The share certificate is a piece of paper which constitutes evidence of the title to shares as opposed to the share itself.

Shares in a corporation are personal estate and transferable as such: see *Re Polson Iron Works Ltd.* (1912), 4 D.L.R. 193 (Ont. H.C.) and see s. 41 of the Ontario Act. There is no comparable provision in the federal Act.

Shares are not goods, wares or merchandise within s. 17 of the English Statute of Frauds: *Watson v. Spratley* (1854), 10 Exch. 222; *Colt v. Netterville* (1725), 2 P. Wms. 304. But see *Evans v. Davies*, [1893] 2 Ch. 216. They are rather in the nature of choses in action, *per* Sir Charles Fitzpatrick C.J. in *Roche v. Johnson* (1916), 53 S.C.R. 18 at 23; for statements to the same effect, see *Harrold v. Plenty*, [1901] 2 Ch. 314; *In re V.G.M. Holdings Ltd.*, [1942] Ch. 235 at 241 (C.A.); *MacDougall v. Johnson*, [1946] 4 D.L.R. 412 at 416 (B.C. S.C.). However, in *Re C. A. Macdonald & Co.* (1959), 18 D.L.R. (2d) 731, the Alberta Court of Appeal concluded that shares represented a type of property which only a very wide definition of the term "choses in action" would include and that the ordinary methods of transferring ownership in choses in action would be inappropriate to shares as the various Companies' Acts provided the method by which shares were to be transferred; it also concluded that because of their nature shares probably did not come within the *Sale of Goods Act* of Alberta.

A share certificate as distinguished from the share itself was held to constitute a chattel and properly the subject of a claim for recovery within the meaning of Rule 33 (g) of the former Ontario Rules of Practice: *Gray v. Gray*, [1944] O.W.N. 399 (Ont. H.C.).

It is usually provided by the Execution Acts of the various provinces of Canada that shares may be seized and sold under execution and the method of so doing is there prescribed.

As to the limited liability of shareholders see the heading "Limited Liability of Shareholders" in this chapter.

In the case of corporations without share capital, the property of the corporation remains its property until a resolution is passed for its distribution. Until that is done no interest vests in any individual member and the right of members is merely potential, not actual. Upon distribution, the member's right is to an aliquot share along with all other actual members: *Kerr v. Dominion Millers Association* (1930), 38 O.W.N. 290 (Ont. H.C.).

Share certificates themselves are discussed in Chapter 6.

Shares without par value

Under former Acts the usual practice was that shares had a nominal or par value and in such a case the corporation was regarded as having an authorized capital consisting of so many dollars divided into so many shares, for example, an authorized capital of $1 million divided into 100,000 shares with a par value of $10 each. In some cases, the authorized capital would consist of shares both with and without par value in which case the authorized capital would be the number of shares with par value and the number of shares without par value. The par value could be fixed at any amount.

Under the present Act, shares can only be created without nominal or par value: see s. 24(1); where a corporation is continued under the federal Act having shares with par value prior to its continuance such shares are deemed to be without par value.

The authorized capital in such a case is the number of shares which the corporation is authorized to issue, which can now be unlimited in number.

Rights attaching to shares

Where there is only one class of shares the rights of the holders are equal in all respects and include the rights to vote at any meetings of shareholders, to receive any dividend declared and on dissolution to receive the remaining property of the corporation (s. 24(3)). In *Muljo v. Sunwest Projects Ltd.* (1991), 2 B.L.R. (2d) 221 (B.C.C.A.) the Court held that, on a winding-up, every share without par value is equal to every other such share, subject to rights or restrictions which attach to those shares, and thus there is no two-stage process on winding-up which would permit repayment of capital to paid-up shareholders before a distribution of surplus capital.

The articles may provide for more than one class of shares and if they so provide the rights, privileges, restrictions and conditions attaching to the shares are to be set out therein and the rights in s. 24(3) are to be attached to at least one class of shares but all such rights are not required to be attached to one class. It will be noted that the rights, privileges, restrictions and conditions need not be set out in the certificate itself if there is a statement on the certificate that the class or series of shares in question has such and that a copy will be furnished to a shareholder on demand and without charge (see s. 49(13)(b)).

Where the articles of incorporation provided that special common shares would carry ten votes per share in the hands of the initial holder but only one vote per share in the hands of any subsequent holder and an application was filed challenging the validity of the change in votes as well as the number of votes per share, the Ontario Court of Appeal held that the provision reducing the number of votes in the hands of a subsequent holder was invalid as there was a great opportunity for fraud but it was severable and as the provision for ten votes per shares had been in force for almost thirty years unquestioned by shareholders, the shares continued to carry ten votes per share: *Bowater Canadian Ltd. v. R.L. Crain Inc.* (1987), 62 O.R. (2d) 752 (Ont. C.A.).

Issuance

Subject to the articles, by-laws, any unanimous shareholder agreement and to s. 28 (providing for pre-emptive rights), shares may be issued at such times and to such persons for such consideration as the directors may determine (s. 25(1)). Shares issued by a corporation are non-assessable and the holders are not liable to the corporation or its creditors in respect thereof (s. 25(2)); no shares are to be issued until the consideration for them is fully paid in money or in property or past services that are not less in value than the fair equivalent of the money that the corporation would have received if the shares had been issued for money (s. 25(3)). In making such a determination the directors may take into account reasonable charges and expenses of organization and reorganization and payments for property and past services reasonably expected to benefit the corporation (s. 25 (41)). The word "property" as used in s. 25 does not include a promissory note or promise to pay (s. 25(5)), which would be applicable to a third party promissory note. The Ontario Act is worded differently (see s. 23(b)).

It will be observed that s. 118(1) provides that directors of a corporation who vote for or consent to a resolution authorizing the issue of a share under s. 25 for a consideration other than money are jointly and severally liable to the corporation to make good any amount by which the consideration received is less than the fair equivalent of the money that the corporation would have received if the share had been issued for money on the date of the resolution. Assuming that shares of a corporation have in fact been issued for an inadequate consideration, the question may arise as to whether the holder of such shares is liable to the corporation for the amount that should have been paid, or if not the holder then the original person to whom such shares were issued. The older authorities seem to indicate where the consideration for shares issued is property conveyed to the corporation, the property given will not normally be inquired into unless the transaction itself can be impeached, in which case the issue of the shares is set aside not because of the inadequate consideration but because the transaction itself is fraudulent or illegal. However, in the case of *Javelin International Ltd. (Receiver of) v. Hillier* (1988), 40 B.L.R. 249 (Que. S.C.) an application was made to direct the transfer agent to register into the applicant's name certain shares registered in the name of a stockbroker but endorsed in blank. The shares were part of an issuance of shares made in exchange for securities of another corporation coming into the possession of the father of the applicant in suspicious circumstances. The court held that the shares in question should not be registered as requested and that the shares should be annulled as having been issued for an inadequate consideration. It is submitted that this case is probably incorrectly decided since it fails to take into account the liability imposed on the directors pursuant to s. 118(1). It is also submitted that the older authorities should still be considered. In *Oakley v. McDougall* (1987), 37 B.L.R. 31 (B.C. C.A.) it was held that the issue of shares without payment is not null and void. The shares were validly issued but a director who authorized their issuance might be liable to the corporation. See also *Davidson v. Davidson Manufacturing Co.* (1978), Vancouver Registry No. C776454.

Where fraud or secret profit is involved, a vendor-promoter may still be liable to the corporation or the liquidator notwithstanding that the profit is obtained by a resale of shares without par value issued to the vendor. See *Jubilee Cotton Mills Ltd. (Official Receiver) v. Lewis*, [1924] A.C. 958 and [1922] 1 Ch. 100.

Shares without par value may be issued for a nominal consideration but they cannot be issued without any consideration: *Stone v. Young* (1924), 210 App. Div. N.Y. 303, 206 N.Y. Supp. 95 and see s. 25(3) of the federal Act.

On general principles shares without par value, like shares with par value, cannot be issued as a bonus without payment: *Re Manitoulin Quartzite Ltd.*, [1933] 4 D.L.R. 132 (Ont. C.A.). It is submitted that a subscriber, unless he is put on notice, would not be bound to satisfy himself as to the board having taken the requisite action to fix the consideration for the issuance of the shares without par value taken by him in conformity with the subscription price which he has agreed to pay. The American decisions appear to indicate that a subscriber for shares without par value, in the absence of fraud, cannot be made liable for more than or anything different from the consideration which he has agreed to pay or deliver to the corporation: *Johnson v. Louisville Trust Co.* (1923), 293 Fed. 857; *Piggly Wiggly Delaware v. Bartlett* (1925), N.J. Ch. 129, Atl. 413; *Hodgman v. Atlantic Refining Co.* (1924), 300 Fed. 590 (fraud proved).

Pre-emptive rights

If so provided in the articles, no shares of a class are to be issued unless the shares are first offered to the shareholders holding shares of that class who have a pre-emptive right to acquire the offered shares in proportion to their holding of shares of that class at such price and terms as may be offered by the corporation; this pre-emptive right does not apply to shares to be issued for a consideration other than money, as a share dividend or pursuant to the exercise of conversion privileges, options or rights previously granted by the corporation (s. 28).

Options and rights

A corporation may issue certificates, warrants or other evidences of conversion privileges, options or rights to acquire securities of the corporation and is to set out the conditions thereof in the certificates, warrants or other evidences themselves or in certificates evidencing the securities to which the conversion privileges, options or rights are attached. Such privileges, options and rights may be made transferable or non-transferable and the options and rights may be made severable or not severable from the securities to which they are attached. A corporation which has granted privileges to convert any securities or which has issued or granted options or rights is to reserve and continue to reserve sufficient authorized shares to meet the exercise of such conversion privileges, options and rights if the articles limit the number of authorized shares (s. 29).

Corporation holding its own shares

Subject to certain exceptions a corporation is not to "hold shares" in itself or its parent and is not to permit any of its subsidiaries to acquire its shares. No definition of the words "holding shares in itself" is provided in the Act. The rule in *Trevor v. Whitworth* (1887), 12 App. Cas. 409 (H.L.) prevented a corporation from acquiring shares in itself, thus preventing both any reduction in capital and any trafficking in the corporation's own shares. With the enactment of business corporations legislation, that rule was in substance abrogated. In its place, the current federal Act now provides numerous defined exceptions to the general prohibition on holding shares. Where a corporation cannot fit within one of these exceptions, the general prohibition will continue to apply. In that sense only, the rule in *Trevor v. Whitworth* can be said to have limited application.

If a subsidiary does hold shares of its parent corporation (for example if control is acquired of a company which holds shares of its new parent), the parent corporation is to cause the subsidiary to sell or dispose of those shares within five years of the date that the subsidiary became a subsidiary of the corporation or the corporation was continued under the Act (s. 30). As to whether the prohibition extends to sub-subsidiaries, see the discussion *infra* in respect of s. 44.

There are a number of exceptions to the general prohibition, namely, where the corporation is a legal representative without beneficial interest in the shares in question or where the shares are held for the purposes of a transaction entered into by the corporation in the ordinary course of business that includes the lending of money (s. 31). As to the scope of the "lending of money" excepton in s. 31, see the discussion *infra* in respect of s. 44.

The Ontario Court of Appeal held in considering the somewhat similar provision in the previous Federal Act that the provision was within the powers of the federal Parliament: see *Schiowitz v. I.O.S. Ltd.*, [1972] 3 O.R. 262 (Ont. C.A.).

Constrained shares

A corporation, any of the issued shares of which are or were a part of a distribution to the public and remain outstanding and are held by more than one person, may by special resolution amend its articles to constrain the issue or transfer of its shares in accordance with the regulations to persons who are not resident Canadians or to enable the corporation or any of its affiliates to qualify under any law of Canada or province to obtain a licence to carry on any business, to become a publisher of a Canadian newspaper or periodical or to acquire shares of a financial intermediary as defined in the regulations; a corporation may likewise constrain the issue, transfer or ownership of shares of any class or series in order to assist the corporation or any of its affiliates or associates to qualify under any prescribed law of Canada or of a province to receive licences, permits, grants, payments or other benefits by reason of obtaining or maintaining a specified level of Canadian ownership or control; provided that a constraint on the transfer of shares of any class or series of which any shares are outstanding is not permitted unless, in the case of a constraint in respect of a class, the shares of the class, or, in the case of a constraint in respect of a series, the shares of the series, are already subject to a constraint permitted under the paragraph (s. 174(1), (2)). Any constraint imposed may be removed by special resolution amending the articles accordingly; if a special resolution affecting an amendment to impose a constraint so provides, the directors may revoke such restriction before it is acted upon without further approval of the shareholders (s. 174(4), (5)). Regulations have been made pursuant to s. 174(6) with respect to the matters listed therein pertaining to a corporation that constrains the issue or transfer of its shares. An issue or transfer of shares or an act of a corporation is valid notwithstanding any failure to comply with s. 174 or the regulations thereunder (s. 174 (7)). Section 32(1) provides that such a corporation may hold shares in itself that are not constrained for the purpose of assisting the corporation or any of its affiliates or associates to qualify under the provisions referred to above or are shares into which shares so held were converted by the corporation that are constrained for the purpose of assisting the corporation to so qualify and that were not previously held by the corporation. A corporation is not to transfer shares held under this provision to any person unless it is satisfied on reasonable grounds that the ownership of the shares as a result of the transfer would assist the corporation or any of its affiliates or associates to achieve the purposes set out above (s. 32(2)). Penalties may be imposed upon the corporation or directors who proceed in violation of the provision (s. 32(3), (4)). Where shares are so held and are transferred by a corporation the provisions of s. 25 apply with such modifications as circumstances require in respect of the transfer as if the transfer were an issue of shares (s. 32(5)).

Shares owned contrary to such constraints may, after such notice and under such conditions as may be prescribed, be sold by the corporation; certain safeguards are provided (s. 46). The proceeds of a sale of such shares by the corporation are to constitute a trust fund for the benefit of the person entitled under s. 47(1) to receive the proceeds of sale and, if not claimed for a period of ten years after the date of the sale, vest in the Crown. The *Escheats Act* applies in respect of a trust fund so vesting in Her Majesty in Right of Canada (s. 47). Regulations 51-57 have been passed which are applicable to constrained share corporations.

Stated capital account

Every corporation is to maintain a separate stated capital account for each class or series of shares issued by it and add to the appropriate stated capital account the full amount of any consideration received for any shares issued by it and may not add a greater amount than the consideration received to such capital account. This capital account may not be reduced except in the manner provided in the Act (s. 26(1), (2), (4) and (10)). Special provisions are made for certain non-arm's length transactions and for the treatment of corporations continued under the Act. In addition, special provisions are made for an open-end mutual fund.

Voting shares

A corporation holding shares in itself or in its parent is not to vote or permit those shares to be voted unless the corporation holds such shares as a legal representative and has complied with s. 153 of the Act, which prohibits a nominee shareholder from voting unless a copy of the proxy circular has been submitted to the beneficial owner and the nominee has requested in writing instructions as to how to vote such shares, or where the nominee is already in receipt of written voting instructions from the beneficial owner (s. 33).

Acquisition of its own shares by a corporation

Subject to its articles, a corporation may purchase or otherwise acquire shares issued by it unless there are reasonable grounds for believing that the corporation is or, would after the payment, be unable to pay its liabilities as they become due or the realizable value of its assets would after the payment be less than the aggregate of its liabilities and stated capital of all classes (s. 34). A corporation may also purchase or otherwise acquire shares issued by it to settle or compromise a debt or claim asserted by or against the corporation, or to eliminate fractional shares, or to fulfil the terms of a non-assignable agreement under which the corporation has an option or is obliged to purchase shares owned by a director, officer or employee of the corporation (s. 35(1)). In addition, the corporation may purchase or otherwise acquire shares issued by it to satisfy the claim of a shareholder who dissents under s. 190 or to comply with an order under s. 241. Both these sections provide that a corporation shall not make such a payment if there are reasonable grounds for believing that the corporation is or would, after the payment, be unable to pay its liabilities as they become due or if the realizable value of its assets would thereby be less than the aggregate of its liabilities. There is a similar limitation under s. 35(3) for a purchase under s. 35(1) if the corporation is or would, after the payment, be unable to pay its liabilities as they become due or a realizable value of the corporation's assets would, after the payment, be less than the aggregate of its liabilities and the amount required for payment on a redemption or on a liquidation of all shares, the holders of which have a right to be paid prior to the holders of the shares to be purchased or acquired.

Where a corporation had agreed to acquire its own shares and alleged that it could not do so because it would be in violation of the solvency provisions, the court held that the onus is on the corporation to establish that the acquisition would be improper. It was pointed out that the work in progress is an asset to be considered in determining solvency under the provisions of the Alberta Act: *Wallinder v. Target Tunnelling Ltd.* (1989), 62 Alta. L.R. (2d) 125 (Q.B.).

Redemption of shares

Section 36 of the federal Act provides that, subject to certain limitations and to its articles, a corporation may purchase or redeem any redeemable shares issued by it at prices not exceeding the redemption price thereof stated in the articles or calculated according to a formula stated in the articles, but is not to make any payment in connection therewith if there are reasonable grounds for believing that the corporation is or would after the payment be unable to pay its liabilities as they become due, or if the realizable value of the corporation's assets would after the payment be less than the aggregate of its liabilities and the amount required to pay the holders of shares, who have a right to be paid on a redemption or liquidation ratably with or prior to the holders of any shares to be purchased or redeemed. In *Clarke v. Technical Marketing Associates Ltd. Estate* (1992), 8 O.R. (3d) 734 (Ont. Ct. Gen. Div.) the Court discusses both the liquidity and the solvency test and indicated that, for the purposes of the liquidity test, the guarantee could be disregarded as there was no evidence to demonstrate that there were reasonable grounds at the time of giving the guarantee for believing that the guarantee would be called upon so as to constitute a liability affecting liquidity. So far as the solvency test was concerned, the traditional valuation, namely, the price payable by a willing and knowledgeable vendor by a like purchaser, neither acting under compulsion, should be incorporated into the concept of realizable value.

Contract for purchase of shares

A contract with a corporation providing for the purchase of shares of that corporation is specifically enforceable against the corporation except to the extent that the corporation cannot perform the contract without being in breach of s. 34 or s. 35 dealing with the acquisition of its shares. In such a case until the corporation has fully performed the contract the other party retains the status of a claimant entitled to be paid as soon as the corporation is lawfully able to do so or on a liquidation, to be ranked subordinate to the rights of creditors but in priority to the shareholders (s. 40).

Adjustment of stated capital account

On a purchase, redemption or other acquisition the corporation is to deduct from the stated capital account (maintained for the class or series of shares of which the shares purchased, redeemed or otherwise acquired form part) an amount equal to the average value of the shares of the class or series in question immediately before the purchase, redemption or other acquisition (s. 39(1)). Under s. 39(3) an adjustment is required to be made in accordance with the stated capital account or accounts in accordance with any special resolution referred to in s. 38(2). Where shares have been converted from one class to another the corporation is to deduct from the stated capital account of the former class the average value of the shares of that class and to add the same amount to the stated capital account for the new class or series of shares into which the shares in question have been converted or changed (s. 39(4)). Shares or fractions thereof issued by a corporation and purchased, redeemed or otherwise acquired by it are to be cancelled or if the articles limit the number of authorized shares may be restored to the status of authorized but unissued shares of the class (s. 39(6)). If a corporation holding shares in itself is permitted to do so by s. 31(1) or (2), that is, as a legal representative or in connection with the lending of money, then it is deemed not to have purchased, redeemed or otherwise acquired such shares (s. 39(7)); constrained shares are provided for in s. 39(8).

It will be observed that debt obligations are not deemed to be redeemed by reason only that the debt has been repaid subject to the provisions of the applicable trust indenture or other agreement (s. 39(11)).

Voting rights

Section 24(3) of the federal Act provides that where a corporation has only one class of shares the rights of the holders are equal in all respects and include the right, among others, to vote at any meeting of shareholders of the corporation; subs. (4) provides that the articles may provide for more than one class of shares and, if so, the rights set out in s. 24(3) are to be attached to at least one class of shares but all such rights are not required to be attached to one class.

The former Act provided that no public corporation (i.e., a corporation which was not a private corporation) could have shares of any class or subdivision carrying an exclusive right to control the management of the business or affairs of the corporation; however, preferred shares could be created carrying the right to elect all or a majority of the board in a stated event, for example, when dividends were in arrears to a specified extent. As a result of the present provisions of the federal Act it is now possible to have both multiple votes per share and a class of shares without any entitlement to vote of any kind. However, in the latter case, consideration must be given to the provisions of s. 176(5) which provides that in the case of a fundamental alteration a class vote may be required and in such a case the holders of such shares have a right to vote whether or not such shares otherwise carry the right to vote. A similar provision appears in s. 183(3) relating to amalgamations. It will be observed that pooling agreements are dealt with in s. 146(1).

The subject of cumulative voting—in other words, each share having the number of votes for the election of directors as the number of directors to be elected — is dealt with in s. 107. Attention is drawn to s. 140(1) which provides that (unless the articles otherwise provide) each share of the corporation entitles the holder thereof to one vote at a meeting of shareholders (s. 140(2), (3)). If the corporation is itself a shareholder of another corporation, any individual authorized by resolution to represent the first corporation at meetings of shareholders of the corporation in question is to be recognized and in addition one of the joint holders may vote the shares held by them unless two or more of such holders are present in person or by proxy in which case they are to vote as one on the shares jointly held (s. 140(4)).

It will also be observed that where a record date has been fixed for a determination of shareholders entitled to receive notice pursuant to s. 134(2), the person named in the list prepared for that purpose is entitled to vote the shares shown opposite his name at the meeting, subject to certain exceptions set out in s. 138(2). If in the case of redemption or purchase of shares by a corporation the redemption amount is larger than the paid-up capital as defined in the *Income Tax Act* (Canada) the excess may constitute a deemed dividend with substantial tax consequences to the recipient of the amount. See also under the heading "Voting shares" above for a restriction on voting shares held by a corporation in itself or in a parent.

Situs of shares

A share, as distinguished from the certificate representing the ownership of the share, is intangible property, for which, for certain purposes, a situs (which may be purely of a fictional nature) must be found. Such situs, for certain purposes, may be different from the situs for other purposes, and the considerations and tests applicable for determining the situs vary having regard to the purpose for which the situs is to be ascertained: *The King v. Williams*, [1942] A.C. 541 at 549 (P.C.); *Secretary of State of Canada v. Alien Property Custodian for The United States*, [1931] S.C.R. 170 at 195; *Braun v. The Custodian*, [1944] Ex. C.R. 30 at 40, [1944] S.C.R. 339.

The situs of shares for the purpose of determining a dispute as to their ownership is in the territory of incorporation of the corporation: *Braun v. The Custodian*, [1944] Ex. C.R. 30 at 47, [1944] S.C.R. 339 at 346; *Re Fenwick* (1915), 35 O.L.R. 29 at 32; *Secretary of State of Canada v. Alien Property Custodian for the United States*, [1931] S.C.R. 170; *Spitz v. Secretary of State*, [1939] Ex. C.R. 162; *Lovibond v. Grand Trunk Ry. Co. of Canada*, [1939] O.R. 305 (C.A.); *Kieffer v. Secretary of State*, [1953] 2 S.C.R. 198. See also *Brown v. Beleggings-Societeit N.V.*, [1961] O.R. 815 (H.C.).

For purposes of constitutional law, the shares of a provincially incorporated railway corporation are to be considered as being situate within the province, so that the provincial legislature has power to legislate in respect of the title to such shares: *St. John & Quebec Ry. v. Jones* (1921), 62 S.C.R. 92.

As to the situs of shares for the purposes of the Execution Acts, in the case of a provincially incorporated corporation which is required to keep its share register in the province, see *Oliver v. Granby Consolidated Mining & Smelting Power Co.*, [1923] 1 D.L.R. 1163 (B.C. S.C.). See *Hunt v. Regina*, [1968] S.C.R. 323 which held that the situs of shares for the purpose of judicial execution was determined by the corporation's domicile.

For income tax purposes the shares of a corporation may have a situs where the corporation is resident: *Bradbury v. English Sewing Cotton Co.*, [1923] A.C. 744 (H.L.).

In *Black-Clawson Co. v. Montreal Locomotive Works Ltd.*, [1960] Que. Q.B. 514 (C.A.) it was held that in determining whether a foreign corporation could be sued in Quebec it was material that the corporation held shares of a Canadian subsidiary which were situate in Quebec since the only register of transfers of the subsidiary was there.

How the relationship of a shareholder may be established

After the incorporation of the corporation, a person may become a shareholder by contract with the corporation. Usually such contract is constituted by an application to the corporation for shares (the subscription), the issue of the shares applied for and notice to the applicant of the acceptance of his application. Even though the usual formalities are not followed, the acts of the corporation and of the alleged shareholder may be such as to raise a necessary implication that he has become a shareholder, both the corporation and the alleged shareholder being estopped by their conduct from asserting any different position. Whether in such circumstances the acts established in evidence are such as to constitute the relationship of shareholder is a question of fact in each case. See the notes under the heading "Application" in this chapter.

A person may also become a shareholder by taking a transfer of shares, by a transmission under a will or on an intestacy or by becoming a personal representative of a deceased shareholder. A person may also become a shareholder by way of gift and upon such gift the recipient has the same rights as if the transaction had been for full consideration. See *Miller v. F. Mendel Holdings Ltd.*, [1984] 2 W.W.R. 683 (Sask. Q.B.).

Rights of shareholders

When he becomes a shareholder of a corporation, a person acquires an asset of the nature described under the heading "Nature of shares" above. The status of shareholder carries with it certain rights and obligations which arise under the governing Act, under the articles of the corporation and under the general law. These rights and obligations are dealt with in various portions of this work but it may be convenient to refer to some of them here and in so doing to indicate the sections of the Act under which they are discussed.

Shareholders are not, as such, responsible for any liability, act or default of the corporation; their liability as shareholders is limited to paying any amounts unpaid on their shares (s. 45).

Shareholders as such may participate in dividend and in the return of capital (s. 24(3)). A return of capital may be effected in various ways: payment by way of reduction of capital (s. 38); payment as a result of the redemption or purchase for cancellation of shares (s. 36); payment as a result of a reorganization or arrangement (ss. 191-192); distribution upon the dissolution (Part XVIII of the corporation).

As a body the shareholders have the right to elect the directors (s. 106(3)) and auditors (s. 162). In addition certain corporate acts or steps must be authorized or taken by by-law or special resolution. Thus, for example, fundamental changes require an amendment of articles to be authorized by special resolution (see s. 173). These include a change of name, a change of the place where the registered office is situate and change or removal of any restriction on the business or businesses that the corporation may carry on, a change of any maximum number of shares that the corporation is authorized to issue, the creation of new classes of shares and a reduction or increase in its stated capital, a change in the designation of all or any of its shares and the addition, change or removal of any rights, privileges, restrictions and conditions, including rights to accrued dividends in respect of all or any of its shares whether issued or unissued, the change of the shares of any class or securities whether issued or unissued into different number of shares of the same class or series whether issued or unissued a different number of shares of a different class or series, to divide any class of unissued shares into series and to fix the number of shares in each series and to increase or decrease the number of directors, to add, change or remove restrictions on the transfer or ownership of shares or to add, change or remove any other provision permitted by the Act to be set out in the articles. In addition a special resolution is also required to authorize the sale, lease or exchange of all or substantially all of the property of the corporation (s. 189(3)). A special resolution is also required for approval of an amalgamation (s. 183(5)); continuance of the corporation under the laws of another jurisdiction; (s. 188) and in the usual case of continuance under the federal Act by virtue of the laws of the country of incorporation (s. 187). See, for example, s. 180 of the Ontario Act. By-laws may be made, amended or repealed by the directors (s. 103(1)), but such by-law or the amendment or repeal thereof is to be submitted to the shareholders at the next meeting of shareholders and the shareholders may by ordinary resolution confirm, reject or amend the same (s. 103(2)).

The Act confers other rights on the shareholders. Thus, a shareholder may bring proceedings against the corporation in appropriate cases where the shareholder has been oppressed, unfairly prejudiced or if his interests have been unfairly disregarded (s. 241). Also, the shareholder may (1) apply for the rectification of the corporation's registers under s. 243, (2) apply to the court if there has been default in holding an annual meeting under s. 144, (3) requisition a meeting under s. 143 if he and his fellow requisitionists hold not less than five per cent of the issued shares, (4) apply to the court for the appointment of an investigator pursuant to s. 229 or for a receiver pursuant to s. 214 or (5) apply to the court for certain orders pursuant to Part XVII which deals with takeover bids.

As to the relative rights of majority and minority shareholders, see the notes in Chapter 16.

Subscription for shares before incorporation

Under the provisions of the former Act, a corporation was incorporated by a memorandum of agreement containing a subV scription for shares. By virtue of the then provisions of the Act, a subscriber to such memorandum of agreement became, forthwith upon the incorporation of the corporation, a shareholder *ipso facto* holding the number of shares for which he had subscribed even if the shares had not been allotted. However, there is no such requirement under the present Act and in theory at least it would appear that a corporation could exist without the issuance of any shares. Shares are now issued only by the directors pursuant to s. 25 of the Act, subject to the articles, the by-laws and any unanimous shareholder agreement. Section 14(2) provides that a corporation may, within a reasonable time after it comes into existence, adopt a written contract made before it came into existence in its name or on its behalf and on such adoption the corporation is bound by the contract and is entitled to the benefits thereof as if it had been in existence at the date of the contract and had been a party thereto. In the absence of such adoption by the corporation it would appear that an agreement between individuals, made prior to incorporation, to take shares in a corporation to be formed, might be enforced as between the parties to it if by the breach of some, others suffer damage: *Re Nipissing Planing Mills; Rankin's Case* (1909), 18 O.L.R. 80 at 84 (Ch.); *Patterson v. Turner* (1902), 3 O.L.R. 373 (H.C.); *Purse v. Gowganda Queen Mines Ltd.* (1910), 16 O.W.R. 596 (C.A.). The plaintiff should sue on behalf of himself and all the other signatories: *Patterson v. Turner, supra.* An agreement between individuals and a syndicate to become shareholders in a corporation to be incorporated does not, however, create liability to the corporation per se. It is an executory agreement which only becomes executed by an application to the corporation on the part of the subscribers for allotment of shares therein. Nor can the syndicate assign such subscriptions to the corporation after incorporation so as to make the subscribers liable: *Re Bluebird Corp.* (1926), 59 O.L.R. 486 (C.A.) per Masten J.A. at 505. The agreement in question in that case did not expressly or impliedly authorize the syndicate to act as agent or attorney of the subscriber in applying in his name to the corporation for the shares subscribed for.

An offer to take shares as soon as the corporation is incorporated must be accepted by allotment and notice to the applicant after incorporation to constitute a binding contract: *Morse Co-operative Supply Co. v. Coates* (1918), 38 D.L.R. 92 (Sask. C.A.).

It will be noted that under the former Act, the directors received a subscription or an application for shares and the directors proceeded to allot the shares and could then issue them as partly paid. Under the present Act shares cannot be issued until the consideration has been received in full therefor. See s. 25(3); the only time when partially paid shares can exist under the present federal Act is where partially paid shares have been issued by a corporation incorporated under the former Act which is continued under the new Act with its partially paid shares still in existence.

In the comment which follows, the word "allotment" is used interchangeably with "acceptance".

Many of the authorities which follow deal with the question of the status of the shareholder in the light of whether the shareholder or the person holding the shares was liable to a call on partially paid shares either at the instance of the corporation or of the liquidator. From this point of view many of the authorities are not applicable in modern practice, but they still may be useful from other points of view and therefore the more important of them have been retained.

Application

The usual method by which an agreement to take shares is constituted is by an application for shares (the subscription), the issue of the shares applied for and notice to the applicant of such issue.

An application to be binding must be made to the corporation, and no contractual relation between the applicant and the corporation is established where, for example, the application is addressed to a syndicate holding issued shares of the corporation: *Consumers Cordage Co. v. Molson* (1912), 2 D.L.R. 451 (Que. C.A.). Nor will the signing, after the incorporation of the corporation, of the memorandum of agreement, which was signed by the incorporators before incorporation, operate as an application: *Re Dominion Milling Co.; Dennis's Case* (1915), 8 O.W.N. 496 (H.C.). But where the application read "We, the undersigned, severally subscribe for and agree to purchase from Edward Slade & Co." the shares in question, in the absence of evidence that Slade had agreed to take up the issue of shares himself and sell them on his own behalf, it was held that the application was really made to the corporation which could enforce it: *Forget v. Cement Products Co.* (1916), 28 D.L.R. 717 (P.C.). The basis of the decision was that Edward Slade & Co. were the intermediaries through whom the transaction was carried out. In the same case at p. 722 of the report it was stated that if the offer had been to buy shares from Slade, a transfer of the offer by him to the corporation would not enable it to sue.

Transfer of issued shares in lieu of issuance of shares

A corporation cannot in answer to an application for shares, instead of issuing unissued shares to the subscriber, cause to be transferred to him shares already issued to another person: *Fitzherbert v. Dominion Bed Manufacturing Co.* (1915), 23 D.L.R. 125 (B.C. C.A.) 126; and see *International Casualty Co. v. Thomson* (1913), 48 S.C.R. 167. The last mentioned case was applied in *Clay v. Powell & Co.*, [1932] S.C.R. 210. There the plaintiff was given to understand that he was purchasing unissued or treasury shares of the corporation and, having repudiated the transaction on discovering that shares of an officer of the corporation had been transferred to him to satisfy the contract, he was held entitled to recover the money paid. A person who has led another to believe that he was acquiring unissued shares and was dealing with the corporation is liable on the same principle: *Witcomb v. Toronto General Trusts Corp.*, [1931] 2 W.W.R. 545 (B.C. S.C.).

Where applicants repudiate such shares promptly on learning that they have not been allotted the shares applied for but that issued shares have been transferred to them, they will not be liable as contributories and will be entitled to have their names removed from the list of contributories: *Western Union Fire Insurance Co. v. Alexander, Loggin & Holmes* (1918), 39 D.L.R. 632 (B.C. S.C.); *Brydges v. Dominion Trust Co.*, [1919] 2 W.W.R. 510 (B.C. S.C.); *American Seamless Tube Corp. v. Goward*, [1931] 1 D.L.R. 878 (B.C. C.A.), and, where the corporation is in liquidation, will be entitled to recover interest on the moneys paid calculated to the date of the liquidation: *Brydges v. Dominion Trust Co.*, [1919] 3 W.W.R. 345 (B.C. S.C.).

If, however, it is shown that the corporation had shares available for issue, a tender to the subscriber of shares which had been issued to the president of the corporation and purported to have been surrendered will not of itself invalidate the allotment: *Graham Island Collieries v. McLeod* (1914), 16 D.L.R. 281 (B.C. C.A.).

Corporation other than the one in which shares were applied for

Where a person applies for shares in a corporation believing it to be a totally different corporation, there is no contract and the subscriber is entitled to repudiate: *Baillie's Case*, [1898] 1 Ch. 110. As no contract has been entered into the subscriber will be entitled to have his name removed from the list of contributories even though he takes no steps in that direction prior to the winding-up. Where payments had been made under a mistake of fact, the subscribers thinking they were paying, as they had subscribed, to a different corporation, it was held that they were not bound: *In re Victor Wood Works Ltd.* (1909), 43 N.S.R. 368 (C.A.); but see *Re Port Arthur Wagon Co.; Smyth's Case* (1919), 57 S.C.R. 388 where the court held that a reduction of the capital stock and change in name of the corporation did not warrant a rescission of the contract.

Application by agent

The application may be made either in person or by an agent duly authorized, and where made through an agent the ordinary principles of the law of agency apply: *Davidson v. Grange* (1854), 4 Gr. 377; *Re Standard Fire Insurance Co.* (1885), 7 O.R. 448 (Ch.); *Ingersoll & Thamesford Gravel Road Co. v. McCarthy* (1858), 16 U.C.Q.B. 162 (Q.B.); *In re Olympic Fire & General Re-insurance Co.*, [1920] 2 Ch. 341 (C.A.) (application by underwriters on behalf of a sub-underwriter).

The implied authority of a partner to bind the others does not extend, in the case of an ordinary trading partnership, to applying for shares in a corporation and the partner who applies on behalf of the firm without authority will be personally liable: *Masecar v. McKenzie & Son*, [1924] 2 D.L.R. 1242 (Sask. C.A.).

A person, in contemplation of the incorporation of a corporation, may effectively constitute an agent to apply on his behalf for shares of the corporation when incorporated: *Ottawa Dairy Co. v. Sorley* (1904), 34 S.C.R. 508. In that case it was further held that the authority might be given by the signing of an application and a promissory note and their delivery to a promoter to be handed over on the incorporation of the corporation; but that mere possession of such instruments should not of itself be taken as giving authority to apply for the shares and deliver the note and that the corporation was bound to enquire into the authority.

In a Quebec case, where the amount of the subscription and the number of shares were left blank when the subscriber signed the subscription, and the agent for the corporation soliciting subscriptions later filled in the blank for a greater amount of shares than the subscriber intended to apply for, and on the evidence of the agent this was done by him as mandatory or agent of the subscriber, his unauthorized act did not bind the subscriber: *Coté v. Stadacona Insurance Co.* (1882), 6 S.C.R. 193 at 205.

A subscription for shares by a person in his own name but really as a trustee, is valid: *Davidson v. Grange* (1854), 4 Gr. 377.

Application may be verbal, in writing, in writing under seal

The application for shares may be oral, in writing or in writing under seal.

Where the governing Act defined the term "shareholder" as "every subscriber to stock in the company" it was argued that every application for shares must be in writing subscribed by the applicant. See the definition of subscriber by Osler J.A. in *Re London Speaker Printing Co.; Pearce's Case* (1889), 16 O.A.R. 508 at 516 (C.A.), as "a person who has put down his name to a contract by which he binds himself to contribute to the extent of the number of shares for which he puts down his name." See also the argument for the appellants in *Re Queen City Refining Co.* (1885), 10 O.R. 264 (Ch.). However, it has been held that a person may become a shareholder without signing any written agreement to take shares: *Caston's Case* (1885), 12 O.A.R. 486 (C.A.); *Union Fire Insurance Co. v. O'Gara* (1883), 4 O.R. 359. In *National Insurance Co. v. Egleson* (1881), 29 Gr. 406, a holder of shares was held estopped from setting up that he had not subscribed.

The doctrine of *Nelson Coke & Gas Co. v. Pellatt* (1902), 4 O.L.R. 481 (C.A.) in which it was held that a subscription under seal cannot be withdrawn, makes the distinction between ordinary applications in writing and those under seal important. The matter is discussed below under "Withdrawal of application". It is accordingly important to consider what constitutes an application under seal and the better opinion would appear to be that the instrument must have been intended by the parties to be under seal and actually have a seal affixed, and the mere printing of a form of seal on the paper opposite the signature, without reference to the seal, is insufficient: *Farmers Bank v. Sunstrum* (1909), 14 O.W.R. 288 (Ex.); *Connor-Ruddy Co. v. Robinson-Whyte Co.* (1909), 19 O.L.R. 133 (K.B.). In *Re Buff Pressed Brick Co.* (1924), 56 O.L.R. 33 (H.C.) the stock book had a number of seals to subscriptions, but none opposite the signature of the contributory. The body of the instrument said "witness our hands and seals." It was held that the fact of sealing should be presumed. The debt being thus a specialty debt was not barred under the *Limitations Act*.

As to what will and what will not constitute a document under seal see *Clement and Donaldson* (1853), 9 U.C.Q.B. 299 (C.A.); *Whittier v. McLennan* (1856), 13 U.C.Q.B. 638; *Re Bell and Black* (1882), 1 O.R. 125 (Ch.) and cases cited; *Marchant v. Morton, Down & Co.*, [1901] 2 K.B. 829 (K.B.); *Sawyer & Massey Ltd. v. Bouchard* (1910), 13 W.L.R. 394 (Alta. T.D.) and cases cited; *Re Imperial Canadian Trust Co. & McKeague*, [1929] 4 D.L.R. 381 (Man. C.A.).

Withdrawal of application

Unless the application is under seal it may be withdrawn at any time before it has been accepted: *Re Canadian Tin Plate Decorating Co.; Mortons' Case* (1906), 12 O.L.R. 594 (C.A.); *Hodgins v. O'Hara* (1901), 22 C.L.T. Occ. N. 29 & 133; *Re Nipissing Planing Mills; Rankin's Case* (1909), 18 O.L.R. 80 (Ch.); *Kruger v. Harwood* (1907), 16 Man. R. 433 (C.A.); *In re Metropolitan Fire Insurance Co.; Wallace's Case*, [1900] 2 Ch. 671. But where an application has been made by an underwriter on behalf of a sub-underwriter, in pursuance of a sub-underwriting letter conferring an authority to apply for the shares (such authority being coupled with an interest and expressed to be irrevocable), the sub-underwriter is not entitled to withdraw the application, and an attempted withdrawal before notice of allotment is ineffective: *In re Olympic Fire & General Re-insurance Co.*, [1920] 2 Ch. 341 (C.A.). To the same effect, see *Hannan's Empress Gold Mining & Development Co.; Carmichael's Case*, [1896] 2 Ch. 643 (C.A.). Even after shares have been allotted, repudiation is in time if made and communicated to the corporation before notice of allotment has been posted; otherwise it is too late: *Byrne v. Van Tienhoven* (1880), 5 C.P.D. 343; *Harris' Case* (1872), L.R. 7 Ch. App. 587; *Stevenson v. McLean* (1880), 5 Q.B.D. 346; *North West Battery v. Hargrave* (1914), 15 D.L.R. 193; but due posting of the letter must be proved and the position of a trustee in bankruptcy in this respect is no different from that of the corporation: *Re Dominion Finance Guaranty Corp.* (1929), 36 O.W.N. 305 (S.C.); *Re Jenny Lind Candy Shops Ltd.; Trustee v. Forsyth* (1935), 16 C.B.R. 290 (Ont. S.C.). Repudiation is effective from the time when it reaches the corporation: *Henthorn v. Fraser*, [1892] 2 Ch. 27 (C.A.).

Notice of withdrawal, if given to the general agent of the corporation who procured the subscription, will be sufficient notice to the corporation: *Kruger v. Harwood* (1907), 16 Man. R. 433 (C.A.); but not a notice to a mere canvasser for subscriptions: *Re Globe Fire Insurance Co.* (1909), 2 Sask. L.R. 234 (T.D.).

It has been held by the Court of Appeal in Ontario that a subscription for a definite amount of shares when issued and allotted, if made under seal, is not revocable as a mere offer would be and that the subscriber could not get rid of his obligation by mere notice of repudiation and withdrawal: *Nelson Coke & Gas Co. v. Pellatt* (1902), 4 O.L.R. 481 (C.A.), explaining and distinguishing *Nasmith v. Manning* (1880), 5 O.A.R. 126, 5 S.C.R. 417. As pointed out at p. 491 of the report, the subscriber "might demand the shares, offering to pay, and in the event of refusal by the company, he would be discharged, or he might be entitled to relief by action for rescission, after notice calling upon the company within a reasonable time to give him the shares". He could not, however, successfully repudiate his subscription unless he could prove a case for rescission of the contract by the court: *Modern Bedstead Co. v. Tobin* (1908), 12 O.W.R. 22 (Ch.), a decision of Boyd C. Here the subscriber had signed the memorandum of agreement and stock book. See also *Manes Tailoring Co. v. Willson* (1907), 14 O.L.R. 89 at 95 (Ch.) where the court held that a withdrawal before allotment was invalid as the application was under seal.

For cases in which it was held that the shareholder could not withdraw his offer even though it was not under seal, see *McDowell v. Macklem* (1904), 4 O.W.R. 482 (H.C.) (transaction treated as offer by corporation to sell the shares and acceptance by subscriber); *Acadia Loan Corp. v. Wentworth* (1904), 40 N.S.R. 525 (N.S. C.A.) (transaction treated as complete); *Port Hope Brewing and Malting Co. v. Cavanagh* (1906), 8 O.W.R. 985 (H.C.) & (1907), 10 O.W.R. 531 (H.C.); *Anglo-American Lumber Co. v. McLellan* (1908), 14 B.C.R. 93 (C.A.) (transaction treated as a present purchase of shares); *Monarch Life Assurance Co. v. Brophy* (1907), 14 O.L.R. 1 at 15 (C.A.).

The *Pellatt* case was followed in *Re Provincial Grocers Ltd., Calderwood's Case* (1905), 10 O.L.R. 705 (C.P.), although the decision really turned on another point. Here there was a subscription under seal for one share, the subscriber agreeing to pay $100 therefor as follows: 10 per cent on application, 25 per cent two months thereafter and the balance as the directors might deem advisable. Before any action had been taken by the corporation on the application, the subscriber wrote cancelling his subscription. The subscriber was drawn on for the 10 per cent payable on application, but refused to accept the draft, and beyond entering his name in the list of shareholders the corporation thereafter did not treat him as a shareholder. It was held on these facts that the offer could not be withdrawn by the subscriber before acceptance, but that the corporation never intended to accept the subscriber as a shareholder unless 10 per cent was paid on application. It was further stated that even if the corporation had accepted the application there was a duty to communicate the acceptance to the subscriber and that in the absence of this he could not be made liable as a shareholder.

In the province of Manitoba it has been held that the fact of an application for shares in a corporation being under seal does not dispense with the necessity of a corporation accepting the offer and communicating its acceptance to the applicant to make a complete contract: *North West Battery v. Hargrave* (1913), 15 D.L.R. 193 (Man. K.B.).

Notwithstanding attempted withdrawal of the subscription subsequent conduct may amount to acceptance of the shares: *Re Ontario Accident Insurance Co.* (1911), 3 O.W.N. 140 (Ch.).

Application subject to conditions

In *Re Nanwa Gold Mines Ltd.*, [1955] 3 All E.R. 219 (Ch.) certain persons subscribed for shares in the corporation in response to a circular letter which provided that the issuance of the shares was subject to specified conditions and that the application money was to be kept in a separate account and refunded on the failure of such conditions. The conditions were not fulfilled and, in proceedings brought by the creditors to determine whether the money belonged to the corporation and therefore could be claimed by them or whether it was the property of the persons who had subscribed for shares, the court held that the subscribers were entitled to the repayment of the amounts subscribed.

Allotment

Allotment is the formal act of appropriation by the corporation of certain of its shares theretofore unissued to a particular person. It is a popular rather than a technical term.

The meaning of the term "allotment" is discussed in *Nicol's Case* (1885), 29 Ch. D. 421 (C.A.), where Chitty J. at 426, said:

> There is no difference, as has often been pointed out, between a contract to take shares and any other contract. What is termed "allotment" is generally neither more nor less than the acceptance by the company of the offer to take shares. To take the common case, the offer is to take a certain number of shares, or such a less number of shares as may be allotted. That offer is accepted by the allotment either of the total number mentioned in the offer or a less number, to be taken by the person who made the offer. This constitutes a binding contract to take that number according to the offer and acceptance. To my mind there is no magic whatever in the term "allotment" as used in these circumstances. It is said that the allotment is an appropriation of a specific number of shares. It is an appropriation, not of specific shares, but of a certain number of shares. It does not, however, make the person who has thus agreed to take the shares a member from that moment; all that it does is simply this — it constitutes a binding contract under which the company is bound to make a complete allotment of the specified number of shares, and under which the person who has made the offer and is now bound by the acceptance is bound to take that particular number of shares. In most cases the act of placing the person who has agreed to become a member on the register is a mere matter of form, and may be described as a mere ministerial act; but it appears to me that in point of law all that is done by the process I have just indicated, and all that was done in this case, was to make a complete and binding contract.

In *Spitzel v. Chinese Corp.* (1899), 80 L.T. 347 at 351, Stirling J. said: "What is an allotment of shares? Broadly speaking, it is an appropriation by the directors or the managing body of the company of shares to a particular person."

In *Nelson Coke & Gas Co. v. Pellatt* (1902), 4 O.L.R. 481 at 489 (C.A.), Maclennan J.A. said: "As applied to a fixed quantity of anything, or a fixed number of shares, the word "allotment" can mean nothing more than to give, to assign, to set apart, to appropriate."

As to the necessity of giving notice of allotment to an applicant for shares see the notes under the heading "Notice" in this chapter.

The word "issue" was something distinct from "allotment" and could have different meanings according to the circumstances. In s. 25 of the English *Companies Act 1862*, requiring registration of a contract before the issue of shares to be paid up otherwise than in cash, the term imports the doing of some act subsequent to allotment whereby the title of the allottee becomes complete: *In re Ambrose Lake Tin & Copper Co.; Clarke's Case* (1878), 8 Ch. D. 635 at

640 (C.A.). In that case the shares were held not to have been issued where nothing was done following the allotment pending the filing of the contract.

The issuance by a new corporation of an allotment letter, with a form of renunciation on it, to shareholders of an old corporation is not an "issue" of shares within the provisions of a taxing statute exempting such an issue from stamp duty: *Oswald Tillotson Ltd. v. I.R.C.*, [1933] 1 K.B. 134 (C.A.).

In modern corporate practice shares are no longer allotted but rather the subscription or application for shares is accepted and the shares are issued. It will be noted that under the provisions of s. 25(3) of the Act shares are not to be issued until the consideration for the shares is fully paid in money or in property or past services that are not less in value than the fair equivalent of the money that the corporation would have received if the shares had been issued for money. It would appear to be perfectly permissible to accept a subscription which provided that the consideration was to be payable at a later date so long as the resolution stated that the shares were not to be issued until the consideration in question had been received.

Necessity for allotment or acceptance

Ordinarily allotment is a necessary element in the contract to take shares: *In re Zoological Society of Ontario; Cox's Case* (1889), 16 O.A.R. 543 (C.A.); *Re Bolt & Iron Co.; Hovenden's Case* (1884), 10 P.R. 434 (Ont. Master); *Re Dominion Milling Co.; Dennis's Case* (1915), 8 O.W.N. 496 (H.C.); *Re Canadian Tin Plate Decorating Co.; Mortons' Case* (1906), 12 O.L.R. 594 (C.A.); *Robertsonville v. Bilodeau* (1914), 46 Que. S.C. 5 (C. de Rev.); *Alberta Rolling Mills Co. v. Christie* (1919), 58 S.C.R. 208 at 217; *In re Canadian Bee Supply & Honey Co.; Ex parte McCutcheon* (1922), 3 C.B.R. 460 (Ont. S.C.).

An unaccepted subscription cannot be enforced: *Duclos v. Bilodeau* (1914), 47 Que. S.C. 205; every subscription for shares must be accepted, if at all, as it is given: *Halifax Carette Co. v. Moir* (1895), 28 N.S.R. 45 (N.S. C.A.).

See also on acceptance of application: *Re Port Arthur Wagon Co.; Price's Case* (1916), 9 O.W.N. 358 (C.A.); *Re Bishop Construction Co.* (1914), 15 D.L.R. 911 (Que. C.A.); *In re Dominion Finance Guaranty Corp.; Ex parte Fleet* (1929), 10 C.B.R. 557 at 576 (Ont. S.C.) (applications forwarded to corporation for safekeeping under arrangement with agent whereby he was to hold subscriptions pending collection of certain payments).

Where an application for shares in a corporation incorporated in Manitoba, is obtained and signed in Saskatchewan and mailed to the corporation's head office in Manitoba, and accepted by allotment there followed by notice of allotment, the laws of Manitoba apply to the contract: *In re Northwestern Trust Co.*, [1924] 3 W.W.R. 625 (Man. C.A.).

Authority to act

One of the essentials to a valid allotment is the capacity and authority of the executive agency which purports to make the allotment, whether that agency is the board of directors or an executive committee or a meeting of shareholders. The question is, who is authorized by the constating instruments (that is, by the governing Act, the articles or charter and the by-laws, or, in the case of corporations incorporated by registration, by the Act, the memorandum of association and the articles) to make the allotment? Further, is there power in the board of directors or in the shareholders to delegate their authority? It is apparent that with differing Companies Acts, differing charters and differing by-laws, a decision in one case may afford little assistance in determining another case arising under a different statute, different articles or charter and different by-laws.

It will be observed that under the federal Act the directors are given power to issue shares at such times and to such persons and for such consideration as they may determine but subject to the articles, by-laws, any unanimous shareholders' agreement and any pre-emptive rights provided for in s. 28 of the Act. It will be observed that s. 115(1) provides that directors of a corporation may appoint from their number a managing director who is a resident Canadian, or a committee of directors and delegate any of the powers of the directors to such managing director or committee of directors, but such managing director or committee has no authority to issue a security except in the manner and on the terms authorized by the directors.

In *Re Pakenham Pork Packing Co.; Galloway's Case* (1906), 12 O.L.R. 100 the Court of Appeal held that the directors of a corporation incorporated under the Ontario Act, as it then stood, could not delegate to a subordinate officer their power to allot. The Ontario Act then contained a provision to the effect that if the letters patent contained no other definite provision, shares should be allotted "when and as the directors by by-law or otherwise ordain". See also *Re Bolt & Iron Co.; Hovenden's Case* (1884), 10 P.R. 434 (Ont. Master); *Fischer v. Borland Carriage Co.* (1906), 8 O.W.R. 579 (Ex.); affd (1907), 9 O.W.R. 193 (C.P.), where under the special circumstances of the case the subscriber was held to be bound; *Twin City Oil Co. v. Christie* (1909), 18 O.L.R. 324 (C.P.); *Re Bishop Construction Co.* (1914), 15 D.L.R. 911 at 913 (Que. C.A.). Subsequent to the decision in *Re Pakenham Pork Packing Co.*, the Ontario Act was changed by omitting the provision above referred to and in *Imperial Bank of Canada v. Dennis* (1926), 59 O.L.R. 20 the Ontario Court of Appeal held that under the provisions of the Ontario Act corresponding to s. 92(a) of the former Act, the directors could delegate to the acting manager director and the secretary the duty of allotting shares.

In *Re Sun Ray Manufacturing Co.* (1924), 27 O.W.N. 176 (C.A.) it was said that s. 46 of the *Companies Act*, R.S.C. 1906, c. 79 as amended which was there applicable, made it the exclusive duty of the board of directors to allot shares. The observation appears, however, to have been *obiter.*

In cases where an improperly constituted board attempted to act, the allotment was held to be ineffectual: *Toronto Brewing & Malting Co. v. Blake* (1882), 2 O.R. 175 (Ch.); *Re Nutter Brewery Ltd.* (1909), 1 O.W.N. 400 (H.C.); *Twin City Oil Co. v. Christie* (1909), 18 O.L.R. 324 (C.P.); *Re Carpenter Ltd.; Hamilton's Case* (1916), 35 O.L.R. 626 (H.C.); so also where the allotment was made by a bare quorum of the board at a meeting irregularly called: *In re Homer District Consolidated Gold Mines; Ex parte Smith* (1888), 39 Ch. D. 546. As to allotment by a *de facto* board and the effect of provisions in the governing statute or the articles covering irregularities, see *Traders Trust Co. v. Goodman* (1917), 37 D.L.R. 31 (Man. C.A.) and the cases cited. The rule in *Royal British Bank v. Turquand* (1855), 6 E. & B. 327 (Ex. Ct.) does not apply to the allotment of shares to a director, where in the transaction he was himself purporting to act as a director: *Morris v. Kanssen*, [1946] A.C. 459 at 475 (H.L.).

Method

Allotment must be made in conformity with the provisions (1) of the statute, (2) of the articles and, (3) of any applicable by-law.

The by-laws usually provided that shares were to be allotted by resolution of the board. If the charter or by-laws in pursuance of applicable statutory provisions provide for allotment in some manner other than by resolution, such provisions must be observed: *Stephenson v. Vokes* (1896), 27 O.R. 691 (Q.B.).

It is not necessary unless the Act so provides to identify with denoting numbers the particular shares allotted: *National Insurance Co. v. Eagleson* (1881), 29 Gr. 406 (Ont. Ch.). See, for example, s. 26 of the *Newfoundland Companies Act*, R.S.N. 1952, c. 168, s. 26 as amended 1954, c. 43, s. 5 which provided that each share was to be distinguished by an appropriate number.

It may be important from the corporation's point of view that the application should authorize the allotment of a smaller number of shares than the number applied for; otherwise the allotment of a lesser number will entitle the applicant to repudiate: *Ex parte Roberts* (1852), 1 Drew. 204; *Re Barber* (1852), 15 Jur. 51.

Allotment and entry of the name of the allottee as a holder of shares on the books of the corporation, without any application or conduct on the part of the allottee amounting to an admission that he is a shareholder, will not make the allottee a shareholder: *Re Whistle Co.*, [1925] 1 D.L.R. 1110 (Ont. S.C.).

A resolution allotting "all shares of stock subscribed for and transferred to date" is too vague: *McCurdy v. Oak Tire & Rubber Co.* (1918), 44 O.L.R. 571 at 574 (H.C.).

As regards formal requisites, if the subscriber expressly waives statutory formalities in connection with allotment he may be bound by an irregular and informal allotment: *Fort William Commercial Chambers Ltd. v. Braden* (1914), 6 O.W.N. 24 (H.C.); affd (1915), 7 O.W.N. 679 (C.A.); and see *Smart v. Bowmanville Machine & Implement Co.* (1875), 25 U.C.C.P. 503 at 510 (Ont.). Likewise a shareholder may be estopped by his conduct from setting up the irregularity of an allotment: *Union Bank v. Gourley* (1916), 31 D.L.R. 565 (Man. K.B.); affd (1917), 37 D.L.R. 599 (Man. C.A.). Thus, where a subscriber has accepted the shares, paid for them in part, attended shareholders' meetings and accepted a dividend, he will be estopped, after the making of a winding-up order, by his conduct from raising the defence that he is not liable as a shareholder by reason of the directors who made the allotment not having been qualified: *In re Acme Products Ltd.; Hopp's Case*, [1932] 4 D.L.R. 330 (Man. C.A.). See also *York Tramways Co. v. Willows* (1882), 8 Q.B.D. 685 at 699 (director joining in allotment to himself).

An allotment which is invalid, because made at a meeting irregularly held, will be effective if confirmed by a duly constituted meeting: *In re Portuguese Consolidated Copper Mines Ltd.* (1890), 45 Ch. D. 16 (C.A.).

Proof

A specific allotment may be proved by production of the minute book of the board of directors containing the minutes of the meeting at which the allotment was made and by proving the posting of the letter containing the notice of allotment: *North West Battery v. Hargrave* (1913), 15 D.L.R. 193 (Man. K.B.).

Allotment can also be shown by conduct of the parties: *Pierson v. Egbert* (1916), 28 D.L.R. 759 at 761 (Alta. T.D.), affd (1916), 29 D.L.R. 569 (Alta. C.A.), affd (*sub nom. Pierson v. Crystal Ice Co.*) [1917] 2 W.W.R. 1175 (S.C.C.) 1253; *In re R. T. Scott Co.; Robertson's Case* (1925), 5 C.B.R. 506 (Ont. S.C.) (payments made under subscription but formal resolution of allotment not proved); *In re Essex Provision Co.* (1925), 5 C.B.R. 549 (Ont. S.C.) (note given and accepted by corporation and payments made on account). So also the issue and delivery of share certificates and the sending of notices of meetings followed by the giving of proxies may supply the evidence which entry of allotment in the minute book and the giving of formal notice would afford: *Alberta Rolling Mills Co. v. Christie* (1919), 58 S.C.R. 208 at 217, 218.

Where a corporation purchased certain mining claims which were to be paid for by the allotment and issue of a number of its shares to the vendors, the Ontario Court of Appeal held that the corporation was under a contractual obligation to allot and issue the shares upon the vendors transferring the title to the mining claims to the corporation, that the title to the claims having been transferred the vendors acquired the status of *de facto* shareholders and the omission of the officers of the corporation to enter the vendors' names on the corporation's books and to issue them certificates did not deprive the vendors of that status nor the rights (in this case the power to transfer the shares) arising from that status: *Cooper v. Cayzor Athabaska Mines Ltd.* (1960), 24 D.L.R. (2d) 544 (Ont. C.A.).

Duties of directors

Directors in allotting shares must act *bona fide* in the interests of the corporation: *Percival v. Wright*, [1902] 2 Ch. 421 at 425; *Punt v. Symons & Co.*, [1903] 2 Ch. 506 at 514; *C. E. Plain Ltd. (Trustee of) v. Kenley & Royal Trust Co.*, [1931] O.R. 75 at 81 (C.A.); *Hebb v. Mulock & Newmarket Era & Express Ltd.*, [1945] O.R. 727 at 737 (C.A.).

Directors may not use their powers of issuing shares merely for the purpose of maintaining control or defeating the wishes of the majority: *Piercy v. S. Mills & Co.*, [1920] 1 Ch. 77; *Swayze v. Grobb* (1915), 8 O.W.N. 316 (H.C.); or so as to effect a prejudicial encroachment on the voting power of a minority: *Martin v. Gibson* (1908), 15 O.L.R. 623 at 632 (Ch.); or in order to obtain voting control: *Smith v. Hanson Tire & Supply Co.*, [1927] 3 D.L.R. 786 (Sask. C.A.); or in order to deprive a shareholder of control, even though they may believe that it is not in the best interest of the corporation that he should control its affairs and in that sense they have acted in good faith and in what they believe to be the best interest of the corporation: *Bonisteel v. Collis Leather Co.* (1919), 45 O.L.R. 195 at 199 (H.C.). In that case Rose J. appears to have considered that a distinction should be drawn between the allotment of shares of an issue, where the capital has been increased or where no shares have been issued for some time, and the allotment from time to time of shares of an issue which has been determined upon as a means of providing working capital. In *Martin v. Gibson, supra,* at p. 631, and in *Bonisteel v. Collis Leather Co., supra,* at p. 200, a right of existing shareholders to claim a *pro rata* division of a new issue or to protect their proportionate holding by taking up further shares appears to be assumed. See, however, *Harris v. Sumner* (1909), 39 N.B.R. 204 (C.A.) where, under the circumstances, it was held that the directors were not bound to offer to the shareholders *pro rata* unissued shares of the originally authorized capital; and *Spooner v. Spooner Oils Ltd.* [1936] 2 D.L.R. 634 (Alta. C.A.) where Harvey C.J.A. expressed the view at p. 636 that an issue of shares for the sole purpose of giving someone control of the corporation could be upheld if the directors honestly believed on reasonable grounds that such course was in the interests of the corporation. So also, where the directors made an allotment which gave effect to the objective which underlay an agreement among the shareholders, the allotment, which effected an equality among the shareholders, was upheld, on the ground that the directors had acted *bona fide* and in the interests of the corporation: *Hebb v. Mulock & Newmarket Era & Express Ltd.*, [1945] O.R. 727 (C.A.).

Thus, in *Olson v. Phoenix Industrial Supply Ltd.*, [1984] 4 W.W.R. 498 (Man C.A.); leave to appeal to S.C.C. refused (1984), 31 Man. R. (2d) 8n (S.C.C.) the directors of a corporation issued sufficient shares to divest a former majority shareholder of control in order to satisfy customers and suppliers that control would be vested in a person in whom they had confidence. The former majority shareholder sued for a declaration that the issue of shares was invalid. It was held to be valid since in issuing the shares the directors exercised their powers *bona fide* in the best interests of the corporation. The test was whether in issuing the shares the directors honestly believed they were acting in the best interests of the corporation and whether there were reasonable grounds for that belief. The corporation was insolvent, its shares were worthless and its survival was dependent on the removal of control from its majority shareholder. See also *Teck Corp. v. Millar,* [1973] 2 W.W.R. 385 (B.C. S.C.); *Howard Smith Ltd. v. Ampol Petroleum Ltd.*, [1974] A.C. 821 (P.C.); *Exco Corp v. N.S. Savings & Loan Co.* (1987), 35 B.L.R. 149 (N.S. T.D.); *Munden Acres Ltd. v. Oakes*, [1970] 1 O.R. 513 (H.C.).

Directors are not bound to issue shares at a price above par because they are quoted at a premium: *Harris v. Sumner* (1909), 39 N.B.R. 204 (C.A.); *Hilder v. Dexter,* [1902] A.C. 474 at 480 (H.L.); and it is not illegal for the corporation to give to a subscriber, in consideration of his taking shares, an option to take up at a future date further shares at par: *Hilder v. Dexter, supra.* Directors cannot, however, allot shares as fully paid where there is no consideration: *Warren v. Superior Engravers Ltd.*, [1941] 1 D.L.R. 323 at 333 (Ont. C.A.).

It will be noted that where shares are issued in violation of s. 25(3) the directors may be liable to the corporation under s. 118(1) of the Act. For a discussion of this section see Chapter 8.

Issue illegal, ineffective or open to attack

If the entering into of the contract to issue the shares is prohibited by statute, either in the given circumstances or at all, the contract is an illegal contract and is wholly void and the act of the corporation in issuing the shares is inoperative: *McAskill v. Northwestern Trust Co.*, [1926] S.C.R. 412 at 418; *Home Assurance Co. of Canada, Re; Patterson v. Burton*, [1950] S.C.R. 578 at 581; and see *Canadian Bank of Commerce v. Cudworth Rural Telephone Co.*, [1923] S.C.R. 618 at 627-631; *Lasell v. Hannah* (1906), 37 S.C.R. 324 (agreement for issuance of shares illegal and a breach of trust by which other shareholders defrauded); *Bigley v. Haffey*, [1941] O.W.N. 261 (C.A.) (cancellation refused as against innocent third party who had taken shares issued as fully paid in satisfaction of an execution).

If a corporation has power to allot shares for a certain consideration, the validity of the allotment will not be affected by a representation in the prospectus that such power has not been or will not be exercised: *Re Canadian Diamond Co.; Broad's Case* (1913), 11 D.L.R. 251 at 253. Where a corporation agreed to hold the purchase price of shares in trust until certain construction commenced, the Alberta Court of Appeal held that the corporation had no right to allot or issue the shares until such time as the construction commenced (because it was only then that the moneys were released from the trust) and that an allotment prior to such time was invalid: *Johnson v. Canada Theatres Ltd.*, [1955] 2 D.L.R. 850.

Where a statutory prerequisite to the entering into of a valid contract of subscription has not been complied with, so that the contract is void, the subscriber may be relieved even after a winding-up order has been made: *In re Dauntless Manufacturing Co.* (1922), 63 D.L.R. 457; *McAskill v. Northwestern Trust Co., supra.* If the statutory conditions precedent to the valid creation of the shares, for example, preferred shares, have not been complied with, there being no shares of the kind specified to allot, an allotment will be a nullity: *Manes Tailoring Co. v. Willson* (1907), 14 O.L.R. 89 (Ch.), and see *Re Pakenham Port Packing Co.; Galloway's Case* (1906), 12 O.L.R. 100 (C.A.); similarly where all the available authorized shares have already been issued to others: *In re R. T. Scott Co.; Robertson's Case* (1925), 5 C.B.R. 506 (Ont. S.C.). So also as regards shares purporting to have been created on an increase of capital illegally effected: *In re Ontario Express & Transportation Co.* (1894), 21 O.A.R. 646; *Twigg v. Thunder Hill Mining Co.* (1893), 3 B.C.R. 101 (repudiation by allottee on ascertainment of facts). Where, however, an unauthorized issue of increased capital has been validated, a subscriber for such shares may be estopped by his acts from disputing his liability as a shareholder: *In re New Zealand Banking Corp.; Sewell's Case* (1868), L.R. 3 Ch. App. 131.

While a subscriber, where an *ultra vires* issue of shares is made, is entitled to get his money back, if he has sold the shares he is no longer entitled to assert that the shares have been unlawfully issued or that there has been a total failure of consideration: *Linz v. Electric Wire Co. of Palestine.*, [1948] A.C. 371.

Notice

An offer to take shares, like any other offer, is not binding until it is accepted; the acceptance must be consistent with the offer and take place by means of a legal allotment and a communication of the allotment to the applicant: *Re Canadian Mail Orders Ltd.* (1910), 2 O.W.N. 882; *Rural Electric Light Co. v. Cauchon* (1924), 36 Que. K.B. 532 (C.A.) (withdrawal of subscription before notice of allotment).

Notice of allotment may be given orally or in writing or by conduct: *North West Battery v. Hargrave* (1913), 15 D.L.R. 193 at 205 (Man. K.B.); *Gunn's Case* (1867), L.R. 3 Ch. App. 40 at 45; *Imperial Bank of Canada v. Dennis* (1926), 59 O.L.R. 20 at 26 (C.A.) (notice of discounting of notes given for shares equivalent to notice of allotment); *Robert v. Eastern Townships Bank* (1907), 17 Que. K.B. 157 (C.A.) (assignment by a corporation to a bank of a subscription for a definite number of shares and notification thereof to subscriber constitutes allotment and notice thereof); and it has been held that taking the subscriber's money on account of his shares is conduct from which acceptance must be inferred: *North West Battery v. Hargrave, supra*; *Re Winding-up Act & Canadian Tractor Co.* (1914), 7 W.W.R. 562. See also *Hill's Case* (1905), 10 O.L.R. 501 (subscriber placed on list of shareholders and paid draft for 10 per cent of his subscription); *Re Western Canadian Fire Insurance Co.; Craig's Case* (1914), 19 D.L.R. 170 (receipt and retention of share certificates establishing *prima facie* case of liability).

Ordinarily communication by post of the allotment will be deemed to have been authorized and in such cases the contract is complete where a letter has been posted accepting the offer: *Harris' Case* (1872), L.R. 7 Ch. App. 587. Where notice of allotment is duly posted, the applicant is bound even though the notice never reaches him: *Household Fire Insurance Co. v. Grant* (1879), 4 Ex. D. 216; *North West Battery v. Hargrave* (1913), 15 D.L.R. 193 at 205 (Man. K.B.); *Howson v. Crow*, [1925] 1 D.L.R. 495. The posting of a letter properly stamped is evidence of the fact of the receipt thereof by the addressee: *Canadian Druggists' Syndicate Ltd. v. Thompson* (1911), 24 O.L.R. 108 at 111.

Formal notice of allotment is not necessary to make the subscriber liable if it appears that he had actual notice that the corporation accepted his application: *In re Universal Banking Corp.; Gunn's Case* (1867), L.R. 3 Ch. App. 40; *Re Publishers' Syndicate; Hart's Case* (1902), 1 O.W.R. 508; *Re Winding-up Act & Canadian Tractor Co.* (1914), 7 W.W.R. 562; *Re Monarch Bank; Murphy's Case* (1919), 45 O.L.R. 412 (C.A.); affd (*sub nom. Murphy v. Clarkson*) (1920), 17 O.W.N. 295 (S.C.C.). And where a subscriber received requests for payment of his shares although no notice of allotment had been given, he was held liable, the evidence being held sufficient to prove that he had knowledge of the acceptance of his offer to buy shares: *Denison v. Lesslie* (1878), 3 O.A.R. 536 (see especially the remarks of Moss C.J.O. at 547); *Forget v. Cement Products*

Co. (1916), 28 D.L.R. 717 (P.C.); *Re Winding-up Act & Canadian Tractor Co.; W.B. Hooker's Case* (1914), 7 W.W.R. 562.

Notice of a shareholders' meeting may be sufficient notice of acceptance of the subscription: *Traders Trust v. Goodman* (1917), 37 D.L.R. 31 at 33 and 43 (Man. C.A.); *Alberta Rolling Mills Co. v. Christie* (1919), 58 S.C.R. 208 at 214; *Re Manchester Stores Ltd.; Cook's Case* (1922), 51 O.L.R. 637 at 639; *Re Buff Pressed Brick Co.* (1924), 56 O.L.R. 33 (receipt of shareholders' notices and demands for payment of calls). But see *Morse Co-operative Supply Co. v. Coates* (1918), 38 D.L.R. 92 (sending of notice of meeting and attendance, without allotment or notice of entry on the register, insufficient).

Allotment or notice thereof or both may be waived by acting as a shareholder and director: *Lake Superior Navigation Co. v. Morrison* (1872), 22 U.C.C.P. 217; or as a shareholder: *Re Manchester Stores Ltd.; Frasers' Case* (1922), 51 O.L.R. 637; *Howson v. Crow*, [1925] 1 D.L.R. 495 (waiver of notice); *Re Bishop Engraving & Printing Co.; Ex parte Howard* (1887), 4 Man. R. 429 (acting as director; payment of calls; request to see subscription list).

Though the applicant receives no notice of allotment he may be held to be estopped by his acts from setting up want of notice and actual notice may be imputed to him from circumstances such as where he acts as a director: *Levita's Case* (1867), L.R. 3 Ch. App. 36; *Fletcher's Case* (1868), 37 L.J. Ch. 49; *Bird's Case* (1864), 4 De G.J. & S. 200; or where he has executed a transfer of the shares: *Crawley's Case* (1869), L.R. 4 Ch. App. 322; or has paid one call on the shares: *Morden Woollen Mills v. Heckels* (1908), 17 Man. R. 557 (C.A.); *In re R. T. Scott Co.; Robertson's Case* (1925), 5 C.B.R. 506 (payment under subscription); and see *Re S. Medine & Co. (Trustee) v. Rasminsky* (1925), 7 C.B.R. 578.

Allowing one's name to remain on the register and acting as owner of shares is sufficient: *Morrisburgh & Ottawa Electric Ry. v. O'Connor* (1915), 34 O.L.R. 161 (C.A.); and in *Re Gramm Motor Truck Co. of Canada & Bennett* (1915), 35 O.L.R. 224 (C.A.) it was held that Bennett, by allowing his name to be put on the register to qualify as director and vice-president, and voting and taking an active part in the corporation's affairs before shares standing in his name could be legally issued as paid up, thereby elected to take the shares with the liability attaching to them. Neither formal subscription nor allotment was necessary. See also *Traders Trust v. Goodman* (1917), 37 D.L.R. 31 (Man. C.A.) where the subscriber attended meetings and gave proxies.

Relationship of shareholder arising by implied contract, acquiescence or estoppel

In its proper sense, the term "allotment" signifies a positive act by which shares authorized but unissued are allocated to an applicant by the duly authorized executive authority of the corporation. In its wider sense, however, the term is neither more nor less than the acceptance of the corporation of an offer to take shares: *Imperial Bank of Canada v. Dennis* (1926), 59 O.L.R. 20 at 23 (C.A.) and cases cited.

The acts of the parties may establish the relationship of shareholders by way of implied contract, acquiescence or estoppel. Certain acts, such as payment on account of shares, active participation in the affairs of the corporation, knowingly allowing one's name to appear as a director of the corporation, are important, but not conclusive elements in determining whether the position of shareholder has been established: *Bank of Hamilton v. Johnston* (1906), 7 O.W.R. 111 at 116 (C.A.).

Where the status of a shareholder is acquired and the obligations of a shareholder are incurred by force of an implied contract or by estoppel it would appear to be unnecessary to assume an allotment by inference as is suggested in *Pierson v. Crystal Ice Co.*, [1917] 2 W.W.R. 1175 and 1253 (S.C.C.) and in *Alberta Rolling Mills Co. v. Christie* (1919), 58 S.C.R. 208 at 217 and 218. It is submitted that, without any such assumption, where the evidence establishes acts by the corporation and by the alleged shareholder which are consistent only with his status as a shareholder, it must be recognized that the subscriber has become a shareholder.

The question whether a person has or has not acquired the status of a shareholder, with its incidental rights and obligations, may come before the court in a variety of different proceedings, and sometimes the relevant considerations differ according to the form of the proceedings. For example, the question may arise in an application by the alleged shareholder to rectify the register, or in an action by the shareholder for rescission of his subscription. The subsequent conduct of the alleged shareholder frequently brings into operation the doctrines of estoppel, waiver and acquiescence, and in determining the question whether he has that status regard must be had to the particular Act or the provisions of the articles or the by-laws applicable in the case in question.

In every case the question is one of fact and the cases (sometimes conflicting in their results) appear not to establish any definite rules, but only to illustrate the view taken by the particular court of the facts adduced in evidence.

In the following cases the conduct of the parties was held to be sufficient to constitute the relationship of shareholder without formal subscription and allotment: *Re Wiarton Beet Root Sugar Co.; Alexander McNeill's Case* (1905), 10 O.L.R. 219 (transferring shares and acting as director); *Re Winding-up Act & Canadian Tractor Co.* (1914), 7 W.W.R. 562 (payment of call; part payment and attendance at meeting); *Re Dominion Milling Co.; Dennis's Case* (1915), 8 O.W.N. 496 (payment for shares and receipt of certificates); *Re Gramm Motor Truck Co. of Canada & Bennett* (1915), 35 O.L.R. 224 at 231 (C.A.) (acting as owner of shares); *Boulet v. Hudon* (1917), 51 Que. S.C. 29 (part payment for shares and giving of promissory note for the balance); *Alberta Rolling Mills Co. v. Christie* (1919), 58 S.C.R. 208 (retention of certificates and giving proxies); *Cooper v. Cayzor Athabaska Mines Ltd.* (1960), 24 D.L.R. (2d) 544 (Ont. C.A.) (acceptance by the president of a corporation of a transfer of shares and failure on the part of the corporation for several years to deny that the shares stood in the name of the transferor on the corporation's books). Whether there has been such action on the part of the corporation as to constitute an allotment or on the part of the shareholder as to waive the necessity for formal allotment and notice is largely one of fact: *Re Manchester Stores Ltd.; Taylor's Case* (1922),

51 O.L.R. 637 at 639. See also *Sovereign Bank of Canada v. McIntyre* (1911), 44 S.C.R. 157, where the subscriber was held liable on a note given for shares which had not been formally allotted, the subscriber having received dividends on the shares; and *Re Globe Fire Assurance Co.; Robertson's Case* (1909), 11 W.L.R. 45; affd 11 W.L.R. 293, where the applicant, in addition to receiving notice of allotment, had received his share certificate after it had been returned by him for correction.

See further as to the effect of conduct in establishing liability as a shareholder: *In re Empire Assurance Corp.; Leeke's Case* (1871), L.R. 6 Ch. App. 469 (assenting to act as director; attending meeting as chairman; implied agreement to accept shares constituting qualification of a director); *In re Great Oceanic Telegraph Co.; Harvard's Case* (1817), L.R. 13 Eq. 30 (acting as director; implied agreement to take number of shares required as a qualification); *In re Portuguese Consolidated Copper Mines Ltd.; Ex parte Lord Inchiquin*, [1891] 3 Ch. 28 (C.A.) (estoppel by acting as director where qualification shares allotted without director's knowledge and without application); *Re Port Arthur Wagon Co.; Smyth's Case* (1919), 57 S.C.R. 388 (elected a director and gave power of attorney to sign his name to prospectus of the corporation); *Re Burnsland Ltd.; Barr's Case* (1920), 53 D.L.R. 439 (agreement to sell the shares in question); *Re Farmers Bank of Canada; Lindsay's Case* (1916), 35 O.L.R. 470 at 483 (retention of certificates, attendance at meetings, receipt of dividends).

In *Re Home Assurance Co. of Canada; Patterson v. Burton*, [1950] S.C.R. 578 although the contracts of sale of the shares were void due to non-compliance with the Alberta Sale of Shares Act, the Supreme Court of Canada held that the holders of the shares by their subsequent conduct (accepting and keeping certificates, payment of calls, accepting dividends and attending meetings) had agreed to become shareholders and were to be treated as contributories.

In the following cases, which include cases where it was not merely alleged that there was no allotment, the conduct of the parties was held not to be sufficient to constitute the relationship of a shareholder: *Coté v. Stadacona Insurance Co.* (1882), 6 S.C.R. 193 (usual implication arising from receipt of dividends negatived); *Page v. Austin* (1885), 10 S.C.R. 132 (shares not legally authorized); *In re Macdonald, Sons & Co.*, [1894] 1 Ch. 89 (C.A.) (receipt of certificates, but no application, allotment or registration as a shareholder); *In re Moore Brothers & Co.*, [1899] 1 Ch. 627 (C.A.) (statement in prospectus that directors would take up all ordinary shares not taken up by vendors, not sufficient proof of agreement binding on corporation to allot and on director to accept shares); *Bank of Hamilton v. Johnston* (1906), 7 O.W.R. 111 (C.A.) (attendance at meetings insufficient to establish an agreement different from actual subscription which involved issuance of shares at a discount); *Re Pakenham Pork Packing Co.* (1906), 12 O.L.R. 100 (C.A.) (payments and attendance at meetings in ignorance of absence of allotment and of the fact that there were no shares authorized of the class applied for); *Farrell v. Manchester* (1908), 40 S.C.R. 339 (attendance at meetings, *inter alia*, not a bar to an action for rescission); *Re Nagrella Manufacturing Co.* (1915), 8 O.W.N. 452 (where the promoter, without authority, purported to complete and issue certificates for fully paid shares); *Re Dominion*

Trusts Co. and Allen (1917), 37 D.L.R. 251 (B.C. C.A.) (in the absence of allotment receipt of dividends insufficient where the statutory prerequisite to becoming a shareholder not complied with); *Western Union Fire Insurance Co. v. Alexander; Loggin & Holmes* (1918), 39 D.L.R. 632 (registration on the books of the corporation and receipt of certificates, but no contract by reason of shares transferred from other shareholders having been delivered); *Shymka v. Smoky Lake United Farmers Co.* (1922), 66 D.L.R. 729 (no acceptance of application, if any, of person already a shareholder; payment on account); *Farmers Packing Co. v. Tully*, [1927] 2 D.L.R. 749 (no evidence of allotment or entry of subscriber's name on register; subscriber held entitled to defend action on note given in payment although he had attended several meetings of shareholders); *In re Steel Service Ltd.; Jolly v. Trustee & H. Lunenfeld & Sons Ltd.* (1935), 16 C.B.R. 231 (no written application; no record of allotment; payment shown on corporation's books as a loan); *Gutche v. Kostiuk & Prudential Trust Co.* (1951), 3 W.W.R. (N.S.) 328 (corporation not registered under the Securities Act at time shares were issued, cheque given by plaintiff indicating it was in payment for a royalty interest, no application for shares, no prospectus received and no notice of allotment); *Setter & Hurlburt v. Mander & Red-Man Oils Ltd.* (1952), 6 W.W.R. (N.S.) 577 (subscription warrant and stock certificate issued by non-registered broker in contravention of Securities Act and forwarded to plaintiff who did not open envelope and did not in any way act as a shareholder).

Repudiation after allotment

Even where an application has been made and accepted by the corporation and shares allotted, the applicant may be entitled to relief on various grounds. For example, he may contend that his subscription was obtained by misrepresentation; or that the corporation was not the corporation in which he intended to apply for shares; or that the issuance and allotment of the shares was illegal or void; or that, his liability under the subscription having been disputed, the subscription had been cancelled; or that the application was subject to a condition which has not been fulfilled; or on the ground of total failure of consideration; or on the ground that the applicant is under age. The last three grounds are considered below.

Conditional subscription

An offer to take shares, like any other offer, may be absolute or conditional; in the latter case the condition may be a condition precedent or subsequent, or there may be a collateral agreement annexed to the application. If there is a condition precedent something is required to be done or some prerequisite complied with before the contract becomes complete. In the case of a condition subsequent or of a collateral agreement, on the other hand, the intention is that the subscriber is to become a shareholder *in praesenti*.

Whether any arrangement entered into with regard to a subscription for shares is a condition precedent or a condition subsequent or a collateral agreement appears in every case to be a question of fact. If there is an undertaking that something is to be done in the future, there may be a presumption against a condition precedent being intended: *Elkington's Case* (1867), L.R. 2 Ch. App. 511 at 524.

Condition precedent

Examples of conditions precedent may be found in the following cases: *Bullivant v. Manning* (1877), 41 U.C.Q.B. 517 (condition that a contract was to be awarded to applicant); *Re Standard Fire Insurance Co.; Turner's Case* (1885), 7 O.R. 448 (applicant was to be appointed a director); *Mallory's Case* (1902), 3 O.L.R. 552 (applicant to pay for shares out of money he expected to receive but did not); *Monarch Life Assurance v. Brophy* (1907), 14 O.L.R. 1 (C.A.) (provisional directors were to advance out of corporation funds the money to pay for shares of intending subscribers); *Gillespie v. Clover Bar Coal Co.* (1911), 3 Alta. L.R. 238 (condition that subscriber should be appointed a director); *Edge v. Security Life Insurance Co.* (1912), 8 D.L.R. 492 (Que. C.A.) and *Canadian Ohio Motor Co. v. Cochrane* (1915), 8 O.W.N. 242 (C.A.) (requirement that a definite amount should be subscribed for before applicant became bound); *Black's Case* (1915), 25 D.L.R. 703 (applicant to be appointed medical referee); *Re Sun Ray Manufacturing Co.; Ex parte Birkett* (1924), 27 O.W.N. 176 ("subject to your appointing us your sole and exclusive agents"); *Humphrey & Denman Ltd. v. Kavanagh* (1925), 41 T.L.R. 378 (application entrusted to agent on terms which prevented it from becoming effective).

Where preference shares are subscribed for on terms that the subscriber shall receive in addition a certain number of common shares, the corporation, before taking action for the enforcement of the subscription, need not do more than declare itself ready to deliver the common shares on payment; it is not necessary that the corporation should actually offer bonus shares to the subscriber and deposit them in court: *Forget v. Cement Products Co.* (1916), 28 D.L.R. 717 (P.C.).

However, in *Auditorium Ltd. v. Lumsden* (1926), 59 O.L.R. 496 (C.A.) the subscription contained a provision that upon payment of the subscription price there should be transferred to the subscriber one fully paid common share for every three preference shares. There was no evidence that the corporation was ever ready or willing or able to transfer the common shares to the subscriber and the court considered that the proposed use of shares held in trust for the corporation by a promoting syndicate was a device to issue its shares at a discount and refused to enforce the subscription. Moreover, in order that specific performance of such an agreement may be decreed, it is necessary that the agreement should not involve the performance by either party of obligations which the court cannot practically enforce. The court could not compel the transfer of the fully paid common shares to the subscriber from any outside source.

In Quebec an action was successfully brought against a subscriber for preference shares who was entitled to receive a bonus of common shares which had been issued as fully paid to the manager for services and tendered by him to the subscriber: *Prudential Trust Co. v. Norman* (1922), 67 D.L.R. 310 (Que. C.A.).

In the following cases it was held that there was only a condition subsequent or a collateral agreement.

Elkington's Case (1867), L.R. 2 Ch. App. 511 (shares partly paid for in cash, remainder to be set off against goods to be ordered by the corporation); *Bridger's Case* (1870), L.R. 5 Ch. App. 305 (shares to be paid for out of commission for selling other shares); *Sherrington's Case* (1885), 31 Ch. D. 120 (C.A.) (arrangement that certain money held by corporation was to be credited on shares); *Caston's Case* (1886), 12 S.C.R. 644 (defendant subscribed for shares on the understanding that he was to be solicitor for the corporation, that he was to pay no cash for the shares but that his remuneration as solicitor was to be credited on them); *Hamilton v. Stewiacke & Co.* (1897), 30 N.S.R. 166 (N.S.C.A.) (arrangement that subscription money should be used for a special purpose); *Re Wiarton Beet Root Sugar Co.; Jarvis's Case* (1905), 5 O.W.R. 542 (arrangement that subscriber should pay for his shares in goods to be supplied to the corporation); *Barrett v. Bank of Vancouver* (1917) 36 D.L.R. 158 (B.C. C.A.) (subscription conditional on subscriber effecting a sale of certain real estate); *Alberta Rolling Mills Co. v. Christie* (1919), 58 S.C.R. 208 (arrangement that applicant's money was to be used by corporation until one of the undertakings was successful and then to be applied in payment of shares); *Murphy's Case* (1918), 45 O.L.R. 412 (C.A.), affd (*sub nom. Murphy v. Clarkson*) (1920), 17 O.W.N. 295 (S.C.C.) (agreement to appoint subscriber a director); *Re Manchester Stores Ltd.* (1922), 69 D.L.R. 669 (arrangement that corporation was to purchase certain goods from subscriber and employ him); *Princess Copper Mines Ltd. v. Trelle*, [1922] 3 W.W.R. 59 (arrangement that corporation was to place subscriber in charge of certain operations); *Re National Stadium Ltd.* (1924), 55 O.L.R. 199 (balance payable when building operations commenced); *Vizzard v. E. W. Lancaster Co.* (1925), 28 O.W.N. 433 (arrangement that money subscriber paid for shares was to be used to build a store and he should be manager thereof); *Re Manitoulin Quartzite Ltd.*, [1933] 4 D.L.R. 132 (agreement that provision should be made for conversion of preferred shares into common shares on a specified basis).

Notwithstanding a condition subsequent which is unfulfilled, a subscriber may become a *de facto* shareholder where he has retained the shares and given proxies to vote thereon: *Alberta Rolling Mills Co. v. Christie* (1919), 58 S.C.R. 208. And in *Re Manitoulin Quartzite Ltd.*, *supra*, Sedgewick J., whose decision was affirmed on appeal, at p. 136 said (with reference to subscribers who had set up as a defence to a claim by the trustee in bankruptcy a condition which was held to be a condition subsequent) that as soon as the certificates were issued and they were entered on the register of shareholders or at any rate within such time thereafter as would enable them to make the necessary enquiries, they became *de facto* shareholders.

Non-compliance with condition

The corporation is not entitled to allot shares in disregard of a condition imposed by the applicant: *Ottawa Dairy Co. v. Sorley* (1906), 34 S.C.R. 508. If a subscription is subject to a condition precedent the subscriber does not become a shareholder unless the condition is fulfilled: *Re Great Northern Assurance Co.; Black's Case* (1915), 25 D.L.R. 703 (applicant to be appointed medical referee). In the case of a condition subsequent, on the other hand, the subscriber may be entitled to a right of action for indemnity or damages against the corporation, but he cannot repudiate his liability as a shareholder: *Clarke v. Union Fire Insurance Co.; Caston's Case* (1884), 10 P.R. 339. If the corporation is still a going concern, so that questions as to the rights of creditors do not arise, a person who has subscribed for shares on an express condition, for example, that business would be commenced and the subscriber would receive a definite appointment, is entitled to rescission of the agreement and the return of his money, if the condition is not fulfilled: *International Casualty Co. v. Thomson* (1913), 48 S.C.R. 167; *Re Winding-up Act & Canadian Tractor Co.; W. B. Hooker's Case* (1914), 7 W.W.R. 562; *Pard v. Auto Piston Ring Co.* (1920), 59 Que. S.C. 151. The right to rescind is, however, lost if a winding-up has intervened: *Re Standard Fire Insurance Co.; Caston's Case* (1886), 12 S.C.R. 644; *Fisher's Case* (1885), 31 Ch. D. 120 at 128 (C.A.); *Brownlee v. Hyde* (1906), 15 Que. K.B. 221; *Barrett v. Bank of Vancouver* (1917), 36 D.L.R. 158 (B.C. C.A.). So also if bankruptcy of the corporation occurs before an action has been brought by the shareholder to get his name removed: *Trusts & Guarantee Co. v. Smith*, [1924] 2 D.L.R. 211 (Ont. C.A.); *Re National Stadium Ltd.* (1924), 55 O.L.R. 199 (*Re Western Canada Fire Insurance Co.* (1915), 22 D.L.R. 19 (Alta. C.A.) not followed).

If as a condition of the offer to purchase, the corporation agrees to hold the purchase price of the shares in trust until the happening of a certain event, the corporation has no right to allot or issue the shares until the event takes place and the money is released from the trust and an allotment prior to such event is invalid: *Johnson v. Canada Theatres Ltd.*, [1955] 2 D.L.R. 850 (Alta. C.A.).

A stipulation in a subscription that the amount unpaid is to be satisfied by the application of dividends will not avail against a liquidator: *Re Investors Ltd.; Ball's Case*, [1918] 3 W.W.R. 180; nor will a stipulation that the balance is only to be payable when building operations commence: *Re National Stadium Ltd, supra.* A condition subsequent or collateral agreement by which under certain circumstances a subscriber is entitled to surrender the shares and demand the return of his money may be *ultra vires* as involving an illegal reduction of the corporation's capital: *Alberta Rolling Mills Co. v. Christie* (1919), 58 S.C.R. 208. That case was one decided in relation to a corporation governed by the Alberta Companies Ordinance, which contained strict provisions as to the conditions on which and the methods by which the corporation's capital might be reduced.

Evidence of existence of condition or collateral agreement

A condition precedent need not appear in the application itself. In *Monarch Life Assurance Co. v. Brophy* (1907), 14 O.L.R. 1 (C.A.) where the defendant signed a printed form of application and it was admitted that this did not represent the whole agreement, the court went into the evidence which established a condition precedent. For other cases where the condition precedent was not set out in the application, see *Re Canadian McVicker Engine Co.* (1909), 13 O.W.R.

916; *In re Publishers' Syndicate; Mallory's Case* (1902), 3 O.L.R. 552; *Re Globe Fire Insurance Co.; Robertson's Case* (1909), 2 Sask. L.R. 234; *In re Victor Wood Words Ltd.* (1909), 43 N.S.R. 368 (C.A.); *Silliker Car Co. v. Evans* (1909), 7 E.L.R. 560; *Carter v. C.N.R.* (1911), 24 O.L.R. 370 (C.A.); *Ontario Ladies' College v. Kendry* (1906), 10 O.L.R. 324 (C.A); *Les Verreries Nationale Ltée v. Perron & Fils* (1924), 38 Que. K.B. 122 (C.A.) (special arrangement as to payment made after signature of subscription). In *Ontario Ladies' College v. Kendry, supra*, the corporation's agent who had obtained the subscription having died before the commencement of the action, the uncorroborated evidence of the subscriber that the written agreement was made subject to a contemporaneous oral agreement was accepted in the absence of facts indicating the contrary.

Where the written subscription stated that it was made unconditionally, oral testimony was not admitted to establish the contrary: *St. Roch Hotel Co. v. Barbeau* (1915), 48 Que. S.C. 94; and to a similar effect, see *Wilson v. Société de Construction de Soulanges* (1880), 3 L.N. 79; *Christopher v. Noxon* (1883), 4 O.R. 672. Evidence is admissible of an independent oral collateral agreement with a third party to repurchase the shares subscribed for: *Macdonald v. Soulis*, [1925] 2 D.L.R. 926 (N.S. C.A.).

The subscriber should prove that the condition sought to be annexed to the subscription has been brought to the notice of the corporation: *Harrison's Case* (1868), L.R. 3 Ch. App. 633 at 638; *In re Publishers' Syndicate; Mallory's Case* (1902), 3 O.L.R. 552.

A collateral agreement may be bad because made by a person--for example, a provisional director—who is not entitled to bind the corporation thereby: *Wilson v. Ginty* (1878), 3 O.A.R. 124 at 129.

Waiver of condition

If the subscriber does not repudiate his subscription after notice of allotment before the condition has been complied with, he will be liable as a shareholder: *Wheatcroft's Case* (1873), 29 L.T. 324.

A condition may be waived by conduct, for example, if the subscriber attends meetings, acts as director, executes transfers of his shares, makes payments thereon or does other acts which show that he has assumed the position of shareholder. Some examples are: *Kingston Street Railway v. Foster* (1886), 44 U.C.Q.B. 552 (payment made); *Wiarton Beet Root Sugar Manufacturing Co.; McNeill's Case* (1905), 10 O.L.R. 219 (paid for part of shares and acted as director); *Bank of Hamilton v. Johnston* (1906), 7 O.W.R. 111 (elected a director and attended one meeting); *In re Victor Wood Works Ltd.* (1909), 43 N.S.R. 368 (N.S. C.A.) (payment of the call did not waive the condition); *Re Lake Ontario Navigation Co.; Davis's Case* (1910), 20 O.L.R. 191 (C.A.) (paid for shares and gave proxy to vote them but stopped payment, thus repudiating subscription); *Barrett v. Bank of Vancouver* (1917), 36 D.L.R. 158 (B.C. C.A.) (delayed repudiation until after winding-up proceedings launched); *Re National Stadium Ltd.* (1924), 55 O.L.R. 199 (delayed repudiation until after winding-up proceedings launched); *Re Sun Ray Manufacturing Co.; Robson's Case*, [1925] 1 D.L.R.

175 (subscription not cancelled by parol agreement with an officer of the corporation).

There must be full knowledge to admit of waiver; there can be no waiver where the acts of the subscriber which are relied on are done in the belief that the condition has been fulfilled: *Canadian Ohio Motor Car Co. v. Cochrane* (1915), 7 O.W.N. 698; affd (1915), 8 O.W.N. 242.

Total failure of consideration

If shares have been subscribed for on the basis of an arrangement which subsequently becomes impracticable and is abandoned so that the whole consideration for the subscription is gone, the subscriber is entitled to be relieved and recover back anything he may have paid on the shares: *Bullion Mining Co. v. Cartwright* (1905), 10 O.L.R. 438; but not where the shareholder was one of the original incorporators: *Giguère v. Colas* (1915), 48 Que. S.C. 198. In such a case the onus of proof is on the person sought to be made liable: *Sovereign Bank of Canada v. McIntyre* (1911), 44 S.C.R. 157 at 162.

Infancy

The contract of an infant to take shares, like other voidable contracts of an infant, is valid until repudiation, which, in order to be effective, must take place within a reasonable time after the attainment of majority. It will be noted that section 51(5) of the Act provides that where an infant exercises any of of the rights of ownership in shares, he cannot, as against the corporation, subsequently repudiate or avoid the contract. This provision may be unconstitutional as an infringement of rights governed by provincial law, and the fact that the Ontario Act has a similar provision (s. 67(5)) would not seem to alter this result. Laches or acquiescence or an affirmation of the position of a shareholder after majority will leave the former infant liable as a contributory in a winding-up: *Re Sovereign Bank of Canada; Clark's Case* (1916), 35 O.L.R. 448 (C.A.); *Re Prudential Life Insurance Co.; Re Paterson*, [1918] 1 W.W.R. 105 (receipt of a dividend).

If an infant is a shareholder when winding-up commences or if he is not then precluded from repudiating his shares, he does not lose that right by mere delay: *Re Central Bank & Hogg* (1890), 19 O.R. 7.

Where shares have been transferred to an infant by way of gift and he effectually repudiates the shares, they re-vest in the donor: *Re Sovereign Bank of Canada; Barnes's Case* (1916), 11 O.W.N. 103.

Cancellation of shares or subscriptions for shares

After shares have been allotted, if no dispute exists as to the liability of the shareholder, there is no power to cancel a subscription, unless such power is created by express words and, apparently, it will not be raised by implication: *Richmond's Case* (1858), 4 K. & J. 305; *Wheeler & Wilson Manufacturing Co. v. Wilson* (1884), 6 O.R. 421; *Kinney v. Plunkett* (1894), 26 N.S.R. 158. It has been held that the Ontario Act, which provided a mode for the reduction of capital, impliedly excluded such power of cancellation: *Livingstone v. Temperance Colonization Society* (1890), 17 O.A.R. 379; and see *Re McGill Chair Co.; Munro's Case* (1912), 26 O.L.R. 254, where the authorities are collected.

The power to cancel will be construed strictly: *Stanhope's Case* (1850), 3 DeG. & S. 198; *In re Patent Paper Manufacturing Co.; Addison's Case* (1870), L.R. 5 Ch. App. 294.

If a shareholder disputes his liability and is in a position to repudiate his subscription for fraud or misrepresentation, the allotment of his shares to him may be cancelled. Thus, where the defendant subscribed for shares on the faith of a statement of affairs prepared by the secretary of the corporation and on finding that the statement was false procured cancellation of his shares at a shareholders' meeting, it was held in an action by a creditor of the corporation, who had become such before the cancellation, that there was power to cancel the stock, and that the power was duly exercised: *Wheeler & Wilson Manufacturing Co. v. Wilson* (1884), 6 O.R. 421. An officer has no right to consent to a cancellation of a subscription in the absence of express authority from the corporation empowering him to do so: *Re Sun Ray Manufacturing Co.; Ex parte Robson*, [1925] 1 D.L.R. 175. See *Sutherland v. Peat Moss Plant Foods Ltd.* (1983), 23 B.L.R. 215 (N.B. C.A.) where the plaintiff was induced by one of the defendants to invest moneys through the defendant corporation. There was misrepresentation calculated to influence the judgment of the plaintiff—even if there was no intent to deceive—and since there was an essential error of a material kind, the plaintiff was entitled to elect to terminate the contract for the subscription and issue of shares and rescind the contract and to obtain restoration of moneys paid with interest.

A trading corporation has power to compromise all claims against it, including claims for cancellation of shares for fraud or misrepresentation, but cannot compromise a claim for damages not connected in any way with the validity of shares by a cancellation of them: *Livingstone v. Temperance Colonization Society* (1890), 17 O.A.R. 379; *Re International Electric Co.; McMahan's Case* (1914), 31 O.L.R. 348 at 359; *Re Alberta Loan & Investment Co.; Dr. Lafferty's Case*, [1919] 1 W.W.R. 603.

As to power to compromise with shareholders, see also *Fuches v. Hamilton Tribune Printing Co.; Copp's Case* (1885), 10 O.R. 497.

If shares have been agreed to be illegally issued and the matter is still *in fieri*, the subscription agreement may be cancelled, but after the shares have actually been allotted and issued there can be no cancellation: *Re Matthew Guy Carriage & Automobile; Thomas's Case* (1912), 1 D.L.R. 642. In that case there had been a subscription for shares to be issued at a discount. Before the shares had been allotted or any notice of allotment given or corporate action taken with respect to the subscription, a resolution was passed that all applications relating to bonus stock should be cancelled and that any certificates issued in respect thereof should be recalled. Certificates for the shares had been issued, but Middleton J. held that the return of the subscriptions pursuant to the above resolution and the substitution of new subscriptions thereafter was *intra vires* and binding upon the liquidator, who sought to make the defendant a contributory in respect of amounts on these shares. In *Re McGill Chair Co.; Munro's Case* (1912), 26 O.L.R. 254 at 262, Meredith C.J. in referring to the foregoing case said that he found on enquiry from Middleton J. that the latter had decided *Re Matthew Guy* on the basis that the contract to take the shares was still executory at the time the resolution to cancel the bonus shares was passed. If the matter no longer remains *in fieri* and shares have been issued, for example, at a discount, and the shares have been allotted, the certificate issued, and the subscriber has acted as a shareholder, then, even though the shares were illegally issued at a discount, it is too late to cancel the certificate of share actually issued and the shareholder will be liable in a winding-up as a contributory in respect of the shares: *Re McGill Chair Co.; Munro's Case, supra.* In that case the shareholders passed a resolution that all stock certificates which had been regarded in the light of bonus stock should be recalled into the corporation. This had been done in response to pressure on the part of shareholders holding such stock, and the defendant had been present at the meeting of shareholders and had voted in favour of the resolution. In pursuance of the resolution a new certificate had been issued to the defendant for the amount of shares which he had paid up in full. Meredith C.J. in his judgment reviewed the English authorities and held that cancellation or surrender of shares under the Ontario Companies Act then in force could only take place where forfeiture would be permissible.

Donated shares

A corporation may accept from any shareholder a share of the corporation surrendered to it as a gift, but may not extinguish or reduce a liability in respect of an amount unpaid on any such share, except in accordance with s. 38. This section provides that a corporation may by special resolution reduce its stated capital for any purpose including that of (1) extinguishing or reducing a liability in respect of an amount unpaid on any share, (2) distributing to the holder of a share of any class or series of shares an amount not exceeding the stated capital of that class or series, and (3) declaring that the stated capital be reduced by an amount that is not represented by realizable assets.

The special resolution must specify the stated capital accounts from which the reduction of stated capital will be deducted, and it is not to reduce its capital for any purpose other than declaring the stated capital be reduced by an amount that is not represented by realizable assets if the corporation is or would after the reduction be unable to pay its liabilities as they become due, or if the realizable value of the corporation's assets would thereby be less than the aggregate of its liabilities (s. 38). Section 38(4) provides that a creditor of a corporation may apply to a court for an order compelling a shareholder or other recipient to repay to the corporation an amount equal to any liability of the shareholder that was extinguished or that is contrary to the provisions of s. 38, or to pay or deliver to the corporation any money or property paid or distributed to the shareholder or other recipient as a consequence of a reduction of capital made contrary to the provisions of s. 38. An action to enforce this liability must be commenced within two years after the date of the act complained of. The provisions of the section do not affect any director's liability arising under s. 118.

Where the real transaction is not a purchase of shares for valuable consideration moving from the corporation but a compromise with the shareholders whereby the corporation disposes of valueless and burdensome property and the shares are surrendered as incidental to such compromise, there is no reduction of capital and the surrender is free from objection and is substantially a surrender of shares by way of gift pursuant to the statutory authority conferred by the British Columbia Companies Act: *B.C. Red Cedar Shingle Co. v. Stoltze Manufacturing Co.*, [1932] 1 D.L.R. 762 (B.C. C.A.) following *In re Denver Hotel Co.*, [1893] 1 Ch. 495 (C.A.). Where a corporation was empowered by supplementary letters patent to redeem its preferred shares or purchase them in the open market, and bought from a shareholder 50 preferred shares and 50 common shares (the two classes being traded as a unit) and then cancelled the preferred shares and registered the common shares in the name of the president in trust for the corporation, the majority of the Manitoba Court of Appeal held that as the common shares were valueless the essence of the transaction was a voluntary surrender by the shareholder and accordingly he was not entitled to be restored to the register in respect of the shares: *Re Northern Canadian Mortgage Co.; Moore v. Northwood* (1960), 22 D.L.R. (2d) 698 (Man. C.A.).

The power to accept a surrender of shares may, of course, be expressly given by statute, as to which see *Harte v. Ontario Express & Transportation Co.; Kirk & Marling's Case* (1893), 24 O.R. 340; *In re Ontario Express & Transportation Co.* (1893), 24 O.R. 216, (1894), 21 O.A.R. 646, (1895), 24 S.C.R. 716; *B.C. Red Cedar Shingle Co. v. Stoltze Manufacturing Co.*, [1932] 1 D.L.R. 762 (B.C. C.A.) (surrender by way of gift). See s. 37 of the federal Act.

Also, when there is a bona fide dispute between the shareholder and the corporation as to whether the shares have been legally issued, shares may be taken back by way of compromise, but not where the shareholder on the register admits that he is a shareholder: *Mother Lode Consolidated Gold Mines v. Hill* (1903), 19 T.L.R. 341. Nor can the corporation take back some of the shares and leave the shareholder with the balance: ibid. But as to this, *quaere*, and see *Patterson v. Vulcan Iron Works Ltd.*, *infra.*

A shareholder whose shares have been invalidly surrendered can compel the corporation to reinstate him as a shareholder: *Brosseau v. Brosseau & Co.* (1919), 58 Que. S.C. 455; even after a long interval, the corporation not having in the meantime reissued or otherwise dealt with the shares: *Bellerby v. Rowland & Marwood's Steamship Co.*, [1902] 2 Ch. 14 (C.A.).

In *Patterson v. Vulcan Iron Works Ltd.*, [1929] 4 D.L.R. 508; affd [1930] 2 D.L.R. 961 (B.C. C.A.) where the plaintiff, who was a vendor to the corporation, had surrendered his shares on a complaint that the property was overvalued and twenty years later sought to set aside the surrender, it was held that after his acquiescence and long delay he could not succeed; the action being barred at common law by the Statute of Limitations, the statute by analogy met the case in equity. It was held that there had been in reality no reduction of capital. An appeal to the British Columbia Court of Appeal was dismissed, two judges giving no reasons. The judgments of Martin J.A. and Macdonald J.A. proceeded on the ground that there was no real reduction of capital, while Martin J.A. also considered that the plaintiff was precluded from bringing action by reason of the long delay.

There is no objection to one shareholder, whether he is a director or not, with his own money buying the shares of another and so getting rid of an objectionable shareholder, per Macnaghten L.J. in *Trevor v. Whitworth* (1888), 12 App. Cas. 409 at 436. In a transaction of such a character the corporation cannot give a mortgage of its assets to secure the purchase price of the shares: *Re Inrig Shoe Co.*, [1924] 4 D.L.R. 625.

Nature of preferred shares

A preferred share is basically a share of a class which confers upon the holder a preference or right over the holders of shares of another class whether preferred or common. As to the types of preferences which may attach to preferred shares, see below. Under the federal Act, such shares have no special designation. Under the Ontario Act, they are called "special shares", but the term "preferred shares" is used in common parlance for this type of share under either Act.

Section 27 of the federal Act provides that the articles may authorize the issue of any class of shares in one or more series and it may authorize the directors to fix the number of shares in each series and to determine the designation, rights, privileges, restrictions and conditions attaching to such shares, subject to the limitations set out in the articles; no shares of a series authorized under this section are to be issued prior to filing articles of amendment in prescribed form to designate the series of shares; if any cumulative dividends or amounts payable on return of capital in respect of a series of shares are not paid in full the shares of all series of the same class participate rateably in respect of accumulated dividends and return of capital and it is also provided that no rights, privileges, restrictions or conditions attached to a series of shares authorized under this provision is to confer on a series a priority in respect of dividends or return of capital over any other series of shares of the same class then outstanding.

The rights, privileges, restrictions or conditions attaching to preferred shares

If a preference of any character whatever is given to the holder of a share, the fact that he is deprived of some of the usual rights of a holder of common shares does not prevent his shares from being properly designated as preferred shares: *Rubas v. Parkinson* (1929), 64 O.L.R. 87 (C.A.). Apart from any statutory prohibition, preferred shares may be validly issued and properly designated as such although containing no voting rights whatsoever: *Rubas v. Parkinson, supra.*

It is submitted that the "rights" of preferred shareholders as such are rights as between the different classes of shareholders and nothing more. Thus, the "right to receive" a fixed preferential dividend is not an absolute right entitling the holders of preferred shares to demand payment from profits where the directors, in the bona fide exercise of the right conferred upon them by the by-laws to set aside a reserve fund, failed to declare such dividend: *De Vall v. Wainwright Gas Co.*, [1932] 2 D.L.R. 145 (Alta. C.A.).

The rights are preferential as against ordinary shares and not as against creditors. Such a priority is the privilege of a mortgagee or debenture holder, not of a shareholder as such. See *In re Touquoy Gold Mining Co.* (1906), 1 E.L.R. 142 (N.S. T.D.); *Re General Finance Corp. (Yarmouth)*, [1941] 1 D.L.R. 746 (N.S. T.D.).

Every infringement or attempted infringement of the rights of a preferred shareholder will be restrained by injunction and the fact that the owner of preferred shares may have for years acquiesced in the declaration of a dividend on the common shares while there were arrears of dividend due on the preferred shares, will not deprive him of his right in respect of subsequent arrears though it will preclude him from making any claim in respect of these particular arrears: *Matthews v. Great Northern Railway Co.* (1859), 28 L.J. Ch. 375, and see also *Leeling v. Insurance Co.* (1865), 45 Barb. 510. Conversely, holders of common shares in a class action are entitled to a declaration construing the provisions applicable to the preferred and common shares respectively; declaring that dividends declared on the preferred shares in excess of the rights attaching to such shares are invalid; directing that excess dividends so paid are to be taken into account by a corresponding reduction in the next dividend declared; and to an injunction restraining the corporation from paying any dividends to holders of preferred shares except in accordance with such declaration: *Steel Co. of Canada v. Ramsay*, [1931] A.C. 270 (P.C.). So also a holder of common shares may bring a class action to determine whether preferred shares have been properly issued: *Andrews v. Gas Meter Co.*, [1897] 1 Ch. 361 (C.A.) (defendant holder of preferred shares appointed by the court to represent all holders of preferred shares).

The special rights conferred on the holders of preferred shares may include: (1) preference as to dividends, and the right to participate in dividends after a specified dividend has been paid on common shares, (2) preference as to return of capital in a winding-up and distribution of surplus assets, (3) rights as to the control of or interference in the management of the corporation's affairs by means of the election of a stated number of directors, (4) the right to convert preferred shares into common shares of an equal par value or into common shares without par value on a certain basis.

These are the more ordinary incidents of preferred shares, and are dealt with in what follows, but they do not exhaust the preferences or priorities that may be granted. If preferred shares are to be non-voting, there should be a specific provision to that effect.

Preference as to dividends

A corporation cannot contract to pay interest or dividends on its shares regardless of whether or not it could otherwise pay a dividend.

The dividend on preferred shares may be cumulative so that, if it is not paid in the year, it is carried forward and together with subsequent dividends must be paid before any dividend is paid on shares ranking junior to the preferred shares. The preferred dividend may, however, be made non-cumulative in which event if it is not paid within the time prescribed, the right to payment is lost. A preferential dividend, in the absence of words limiting the preference, is *prima facie* cumulative and means a dividend having preference over the whole income of the corporation during the whole period of its existence or during as many years as may be necessary to satisfy the claim of dividend, per Lord McLaren in *Miln v. Arizona Copper Co.* (1899), 36 Sc. L.R. 741. If, on the other hand, the preferred shareholders are declared to be entitled to be paid their dividend out of the net profits of each year, the dividend is not cumulative: *Staples v. Eastman Photographic Materials Co.*, [1896] 2 Ch. 303 (C.A.).

As to the meaning to be ascribed to the expressions "dividends accruing due" and "dividend accrued due" in provisions attaching to preferred shares and a testamentary provision respectively, see *In re Ganong Estate v. Belyea*, [1941] S.C.R. 125; *Belyea v. McBride*, [1942] 3 D.L.R. 785 (P.C.).

Where cumulative preferential dividends have been passed for a number of years and a dividend is declared sufficient in amount to pay off all arrears to date, the dividend is not in respect of each year but is in respect of the current year, although the amount of the dividend is determined by the whole amount of dividends unpaid: *In re Wakley*, [1920] 2 Ch. 205 (C.A.). In the absence of provisions giving an express priority to one year over another, where shares have been issued from time to time over a number of years, so that some shareholders have a claim for a longer period than others for arrears of cumulative dividends, and there are profits available for payment of arrears after payment of the dividend for the current year but not enough to clear off all the arrears, the fund available must be distributed rateably among the shareholders in proportion to their several maximum claims: *First Garden City Ltd. v. Bonham-Carter*, [1928] Ch. 53. *Quaere*, whether the above cases would be applied where the preferred share provisions require the corporation to pay the dividends in quarterly instalments and to pay earlier instalments which may be in arrear before subsequently accruing instalments.

If it is desired to confer on preferred shareholders the right to participate by way of dividends in addition to the fixed preferential dividend, it must be distinctly so stated; otherwise the right is impliedly negatived: *Will v. United Lankat Plantations Co.*, [1914] A.C. 11 (H.L.); *Steel Co. of Canada v. Ramsay*, [1931] A.C. 270 at 274 (P.C.); *International Power Co. v. McMaster University*, [1946] S.C.R. 178, per Kerwin J., at 190 and Taschereau and Estey J.J., at 205. *Prima facie*, the rights to dividends provided for in the share provisions are exhaustive: *Re Isle of Thanet Electric Supply Co.*, [1950] 1 Ch. 161 at 171 per Wynn-Parry J.

Ordinarily speaking, where a preferred shareholder receives his preferred dividend he can ask for no more: *Steel Co. of Canada v. Ramsay*, [1931] A.C. 270 at 274 (P.C.), citing *Will v. United Lankat Plantations Co.*, *supra.*

In *Steel Co. of Canada v. Ramsay*, *supra*, the letters patent provided that the net profits of the corporation, which it might be determined from time to time to distribute, were to be applicable first to the payment of a fixed cumulative preferred dividend of 7 per cent on the preferred shares and that in any further distributions of net profits the preferred shareholders should participate rateably with the common shareholders after the common shareholders had received dividends "equal to those paid on the preferred shares"; the regular cumulative 7 per cent dividend on the preferred shares had been paid every year but in some years the common shareholders had received a dividend of less than 7 per cent; the directors declared a dividend of 8 per cent on both the preferred and common shares and it was held that the provisions of the letters patent prevented the payment of a dividend greater than 7 per cent on the preferred shares until such time as the total dividends paid on the common shares since the incorporation of the corporation should equal, as to the rate thereof, that theretofore paid on the preferred shares.

The interpretation placed on the share provisions in *Steel Co. of Canada v. Ramsay*, *supra*, was that the common shareholders had a cumulative right to particular dividends before the preferred shareholders became entitled to their participating dividends. For more usual share provisions in which preferred shareholders were given a participating dividend and the right of the common shareholders to dividends was treated as non-cumulative, see *Re Isle of Thanet Electric Supply Co.*, [1950] 1 Ch. 161.

Preference as to return of capital and rights on distribution of surplus assets

A preference as to dividend does not carry with it a similar preference as to return of capital or distribution of surplus assets in a winding-up: *In re London India Rubber Co.* (1868), L.R. 5 Eq. 519. The general rule, which requires an express provision to exclude it, is that both classes of shareholders rank *pro rata*: *Morrow v. Peterborough Water Co.* (1902), 4 O.L.R. 324 at 329 (C.P.).

Where it is desired to confer a priority as to return of capital or on the distribution of surplus assets, apt words must be inserted in the articles or by-law creating the issue. It is a common provision that, in the event of liquidation, dissolution or winding up of the corporation or other distribution for the purpose of winding up the business of the corporation, the holders of preferred shares are to receive the redemption price (which may include a premium over the stated capital) of their shares, and accumulated and unpaid dividends and no more. Sometimes the provisions are silent as to what is to be done with any surplus assets which may remain after all the capital is repaid. In such a case it will depend on the construction of the provisions whether the holders of preferred shares are entitled to participate further in the surplus assets.

Until the decision of the House of Lords in *Scottish Insurance Corp. v. Wilsons & Clyde Coal Co.* [1949] A.C. 462, there were conflicting decisions in England as to whether the attachment to preference shares of the right to a fixed cumulative dividend and the right in a winding up to repayment of capital in priority to all other shares, deprived the holders of the preference shares of any right to share in the distribution of surplus assets *pari passu* with the holders of ordinary shares.

In a number of cases including *In re Espuela Land & Cattle Co.*, [1909] 2 Ch. 187; *In re Fraser & Chalmers Ltd.*, [1919] 2 Ch. 114; *Anglo-French Music Co. Ltd. v. Nicoll*, [1921] 1 Ch. 386; *In re John Dry Steam Tugs Ltd.*, [1932]

1 Ch. 594; *In re William Metcalfe & Sons Ltd.*, [1933] Ch. 142 (C.A.); *Re W. Foster & Sons Ltd.*, [1942] 1 All E.R. 314 (Ch. Div.), and *Re Wood Skinner & Co.*, [1944] 1 Ch. 323, it was held that such provisions did not exclude the right of participation in surplus assets. On the other hand in *In re National Telephone Co.*, [1914] 1 Ch. 755, on the construction of provisions conferring on the preference shareholders a fixed preferential dividend and repayment of capital in priority to the other shares but no other participation in profits, it was held that the right of further participation in surplus on a winding-up was excluded. Likewise, in *Collaroy Co. v. Giffard*, [1928] Ch. 144 where the provisions conferred the right to a fixed dividend and the right on a winding-up to repayment of capital in priority to the ordinary shares, it was held that these provisions contained an exhaustive delimitation of the rights of the preference shareholders and that they were not entitled to participate in surplus assets.

In *Scottish Insurance Corp. v. Wilsons & Clyde Coal Co.*, *supra*, the House of Lords approved the principles established by *In re National Telephone Co.* and *Collaroy Co. v. Giffard* and overruled *In re William Metcalfe & Sons Ltd.* The *Scottish Insurance Corp.* case was followed in *Prudential Assurance Co. v. Chatterley-Whitfield Collieries Co.*, [1949] A.C. 512 (H.L.) and *Re Isle of Thanet Electric Supply Co.*, [1950] 1 Ch. 161 where at 171 Wynn-Parry J. sums up the present position as follows:

> . . . the effect of the authorities as now in force is to establish the two principles . . . first, that, in construing an article which deals with rights to share in profits, that is, dividend rights and rights to share in the company's property in a liquidation, the same principle is applicable; and, second, that that principle is that, where the article sets out the rights attached to a class of shares to participate in profits while the company is a going concern or to share in the property of the company in liquidation, *prima facie*, the rights so set out are in each case exhaustive.

The onus is on the holders of the preference stock to show that the specified provision is not exhaustive: *Re Isle of Thanet Electric Supply Co.*, *supra.*

Where the provisions conferred a fixed cumulative preferential dividend, but did not confer any priority as regards capital, it was held on the construction of the articles that the surplus assets were distributable among all the shareholders, preference and common, *pro rata* in proportion to the amount paid up on their shares: *In re Madam Tussaud & Sons Ltd.*, [1927] 1 Ch. 657.

In *International Power Co. v. McMaster University*, [1946] S.C.R. 178, under the by-law creating the preference shares, the holders of preference shares were entitled to cumulative preferential dividends at a stated rate and further entitled to priority on any division of assets to the extent of repayment in full at par together with any accrued and unpaid dividends; but the provisions were silent as to distribution of surplus assets. Among the reasons alleged in support of the contention that the right of participation was not excluded, were that the Act in force at the time when the by-law was enacted provided that holders of preference shares should in all respects possess the rights of shareholders. It was held that the by-law did not expressly or by implication limit the rights of the holders of the preference shares to participate share for share with the holders of common shares in surplus assets. The judgments proceed upon the principle of equality among shareholders except to the extent that such equality is displaced by the terms of the contract. The judgments of Taschereau and Estey JJ. and Rand J. treat the question as one of construction and review and apply the English decisions, and for that reason it is important to bear in mind that this case was decided before the decision of the House of Lords in *Scottish Insurance Corp. v. Wilsons & Clyde Coal Co.*, [1949] A.C. 462 and the decisions referred to above which followed the principles laid down in that case. It does not appear that any different result would have been reached in the absence of provisions such as those contained in the Act.

Where the articles were silent as to the disposition of surplus assets, but provided that (subject to the preference as to assets and cumulative dividends) the profits were to be divisible among the holders of ordinary shares, and the principal source of the surplus assets was the excess of the write-off for depreciation, it was held that the holders of preference shares were not entitled to participate in surplus assets beyond a return of capital and accrued dividend up to the date of distribution: *Re Casino Co.*, [1947] 4 D.L.R. 380 (N.S. S.C.).

Where the dividend is cumulative, and it is provided that the surplus assets in the event of a winding-up are to be applied, first in repaying the preference capital, and secondly, in paying off arrears (if any) of the preferential dividend to the commencement of the winding-up, the preferred shareholders are entitled to payment of arrears of dividend out of surplus assets, even though no dividends have been actually declared: *In re New Chinese Antimony Co.*, [1916] 2 Ch. 115. It is immaterial whether there were profits or not: *In re Springbok Agricultural Estates*, [1920] 1 Ch. 563. The principles established by these latter two cases have been approved and followed in *Re Dominion Tar & Chemical Co.*, [1929] 2 Ch. 387 and *Re Wharfedale Brewery Co.*, [1952] 1 Ch. 913, in which case Wynn-Parry J. disapproved of the earlier decision in *Re W. J. Hall & Co.*, [1909] 1 Ch. 521. But compare *In re Roberts & Cooper Ltd.*, [1929] 2 Ch. 383, where the provisions relating to the preference shares stated that the holders thereof should receive on a winding-up "any arrears of dividend due thereon" and it was held that no dividends having been declared for a period of four years prior to the winding-up, the preference shareholders were not entitled to receive anything for arrears of dividends for that period.

A provision that the preference shares, which were entitled to a fixed cumulative preferential dividend, should rank both as regards dividends and capital in priority to the ordinary shares, although there was no express provision for payment of arrears of preferential dividend in a winding-up, was held to entitle the preference shareholders, in priority to the ordinary shareholders, to payment of arrears of fixed cumulative preferential dividends and repayment of capital. The clause was regarded as one dealing with what was to happen in a winding-up and the word "dividends" was construed as meaning "arrears of fixed cumulative preferential dividends": *In re Walter Symons Ltd.*, [1934] Ch. 308, followed in *In re F. de Jong & Co.*, [1946] Ch. 211 (C.A.) and in *Re E. W. Savory Ltd.*, [1951] 2 All E.R. 1036. So also where the special resolution creating preference shares simply provided "such stock to be 6% cumulative preferred stock such stock to be preferred as to assets and dividends" it was held on the winding up of the corporation, that the holders of the preference shares were entitled out of surplus assets to be paid the preferential dividend to the time of payment : *Re Casino Co.*, [1947] 4 D.L.R. 380.

Where the provisions were similar to those in *In re Walter Symons Ltd.*, *supra*, but the preference shares were entitled simply to a fixed cumulative dividend rather than a fixed cumulative preferential dividend, it was held that the word "rank" must be intended to cover winding-up so far as capital was concerned but to apply when the corporation was a going concern as regards dividends and that the holders of preference shares were not entitled in liquidation to priority for arrears of dividends, there being no profits available for distribution: *In re Wood Skinner & Co.*, [1944] Ch. 323. In *Re E. W. Savory*, *supra*, at 1038, *In re Wood Skinner & Co.* was distinguished on the ground that there was no provision in the latter case for the cumulative dividend to be a preferential dividend and *In re Walter Symons Ltd.* and *In re F. de Jong & Co.*, *supra*, were followed.

Where the provision read that the holders of preference shares should be entitled to a fixed cumulative dividend at a specified rate and should on a dissolution or winding up of the corporation have priority over all other shares but should have no further right to participate in profits or assets, it was held that the preferential right on a winding-up was limited to a return of capital and that holders of the preference shares were not entitled to be paid arrears of dividends: *Re Kent Holding & Securities Ltd.*, [1943] O.W.N. 41 (H.C.). Roach J., in arriving at that conclusion, referred to and followed the opinion expressed by Maugham J. in *In re Walter Symons Ltd.*, *supra*, at p. 312 that, but for the words "and shall rank both as regards dividends and capital in priority to the ordinary shares", the holders of preference shares would not be entitled to claim in a winding-up arrears of fixed cumulative preferential dividend.

Where the provision was that the holders of preference shares should be entitled on liquidation, dissolution or winding up of the corporation or on the distribution of capital among shareholders, to repayment of the capital paid on such shares in preference to the right of the common shareholders but "shall not have a right to any further participation in the assets of the Company in any such event", Danis J., after reviewing the English and Canadian authorities held that such a provision could not be construed as entitling the preferred shareholders to arrears of dividends on winding-up: *Re Canada Tea Co.*, [1959] O.W.N. 378 (H.C.).

In the absence of any provision as to distribution of assets on a winding-up, if there is a surplus after discharging debts and liabilities it must be applied first in repaying to the holders of preferred and common shares the capital paid up on their shares, and any balance is to be divided among all the shareholders in proportion to the number of shares held by them respectively, where the shares are of the same par value, and not in proportion to the amounts paid up: *Birch v. Cropper* (1889), 14 App. Cas. 525 (H.L.). If the preferred and common shares are of different nominal amounts the surplus assets must be distributed rateably according to the nominal amount of the shares: *In re Espuela Land & Cattle*

Co., [1909] 2 Ch. 187 at 192. Presumably this would be in proportion to the paid up value where preferred and common shares are without par value.

Where the articles provided that in the event of the winding up of the corporation the surplus assets should be distributed among the holders of preference shares (which were entitled to a cumulative preferential dividend) and ordinary shares according to the amount paid up on them, it was held that the holders of preference shares were not entitled to have a sum remaining after repayment of the capital on the preference and ordinary shares applied in paying their dividends for the years in which they had received none: *In re Crichton's Oil Co.*, [1902] 2 Ch. 86 (C.A.). So also, where there was no provision as to distribution of surplus assets, the holders of preferred shares were held not entitled to have a balance to the credit of revenue account distributed in a winding-up as a dividend on the preference shares in the absence of a declaration: *In re Odessa Waterworks Co.*, [1901] 2 Ch. 190 (note).

The holders of preference shares may, under the provisions applicable thereto, be entitled to receive arrears of dividends down to the date of actual payment, but in the absence of an express provision to that effect they have a right to arrears only up to the date of the winding up of the corporation, when the whole position becomes crystallized: *Re E. W. Savory Ltd.*, [1951] 2 All E.R. 1036 at 1040 (Ch. Div.).

Under s. 25 of the *Coal Industry Nationalization Act of England, 1946*, the interests of all classes of shares in nationalized corporations were to be adjusted, giving effect to the substitution of compensation for the corporation's assets and the rights of priority conferred on such classes by the memorandum and articles of the corporation. In *Scottish Insurance Corp. v. Wilsons & Clyde Coal Co.*, [1949] A.C. 462 (H.L.) and *Prudential Assurance Co. v. Chatterley-Whitfield Collieries Co.*, [1949] A.C. 512 (H.L.), the House of Lords held that s. 25 did not give preference shareholders any right in addition to the right to participate in the assets of the corporation given in the articles of the corporation, and confirmed a valid reduction of capital which ignored s. 25. However, in *In re Old Silkstone Collieries Ltd.*, [1954] 1 Ch. 169, the preference capital had twice been reduced following statements to the preference shareholders that their right to claim adjustment of compensation under s. 25 would be unaffected by the reductions. The Court of Appeal held that this reservation conferred a special right on the preference shareholders and that, as a third reduction of capital which was proposed had not been approved at separate meetings of the two classes of preference shareholders as required by the articles of the corporation, such third reduction should not be approved.

Rights as to the control of or interference in the management of the corporation's affairs

The holders of preferred shares may have limited voting rights. Thus, the preferred share provisions may and frequently do deprive the preferred shareholders of the right to vote except where the preferential dividend is in arrears for a stated period, or where their interests are affected, for example, where it is proposed to wind-up the corporation, sell the assets, issue further preferred shares of equal or higher rank, modify the rights attaching to the preferred shares, or create a mortgage or a bond issue against the assets.

It is not unusual to provide that the holders of preferred shares are to be entitled to elect a stated proportion of the board of directors after the preferential dividend has gone in arrears for a certain period or to a specified amount. It strengthens such provisions materially from the point of view of the holders of preferred shares if in the events indicated they are given the right to elect a majority of the board.

It was held that a clause in the memorandum of association purporting to enable the holders of a specified block of shares to elect three out of five directors was null and void, the shares being held not to be preference shares within the meaning of the statute: *Colonist Printing & Publishing Co. v. Dunsmuir* (1902), 32 S.C.R. 679.

Conversion rights

Preferred shares are sometimes issued on the basis that the holders, at their option, may convert their preferred shares into common shares at a specified rate, for example, two common shares for each preferred share. The provisions in respect of conversion must be set out in the articles.

The provisions conferring the right of conversion should embody clauses to protect the privilege from dilution in the event of the corporation sub-dividing the common shares, declaring stock dividends payable in common shares or taking other steps with regard to the share capital which would reduce the value of the common shares and thereby make the conversion privilege less valuable.

Redemption or purchase of preferred shares for cancellation

Section 36 of the federal Act provides that subject to the articles and to what follows, a corporation may purchase or redeem any redeemable shares issued by it at prices not exceeding the redemption price as stated in the articles or calculated according to the formula stated in the articles; no payment is to be made to purchase or redeem any redeemable shares if there are reasonable grounds for believing that the corporation is or would after the payment be unable to pay its liabilities as they become due, or if the realizable value of the corporation's assets would after the payment be less than the aggregate of its liabilities and the amount that would be required to pay the holders of shares having the right to be paid on a redemption or on a liquidation rateably with or prior to the holders of the shares to be purchased or redeemed.

In addition to this provision it will be noted that s. 34 provides that a corporation may, subject to its articles, purchase or otherwise acquire shares issued by it but is not to make any payment to purchase or otherwise acquire such shares if there are reasonable grounds for believing that the corporation is or would after the payment be unable to pay its liabilities as they become due or if the realizable value of the corporation's assets would after the payment be less than the aggregate of its liabilities and stated capital of all classes.

It will be noted that the test under s. 34 is more severe than the test under s. 36. It would appear that the words "realizable value" would ordinarily be interpreted as referring to a corporation as an ongoing business rather than a corporation in liquidation. See the discussion in *Clarke v. Technical Marketing Associates Ltd. Estate* (1992), 8 O.R. (3d) 734 at p. 750. It should be noted that s. 39 provides for an adjustment to the stated capital account of any shares so purchased or redeemed; the corporation is to deduct from the stated capital account of the shares in question an amount equal to the result obtained by multiplying the stated capital of the shares of that class by the number of shares of that class so purchased, redeemed or otherwise acquired, divided by the number of issued shares of that class or series immediately before the redemption, purchase or other acquisition. It will be noted that when shares are redeemed for an amount in excess of the paid-up capital, the amount of the excess will result in a deemed dividend in the hands of the recipient for tax purposes. This in certain cases will also apply where shares are purchased.

Modification of the rights of preferred shareholders

Whether the rights of preferred shareholders may be modified depends on the terms of the issue, the wording of the provisions in which these rights are defined, and the provisions (if any) of the governing statute. Section 173 of the federal Act gives power to amend the articles by special resolution by changing any rights, privileges, restrictions and conditions attaching to any or all of its shares, including rights to accrued dividends. These also apply to the question whether the corporation is entitled to create further preferred shares, ranking in priority to, or *pari passu* with, existing preferred shares. As a general rule, the power to modify the rights of preferred shareholders is desirable from the point of view of the corporation and not objectionable from the point of view of the preferred shareholders, provided their interests are properly safeguarded.

If the modification involves a change of provisions in the articles the procedure prescribed by s. 173 must be followed.

A power to modify rights does not enable a majority to destroy such rights altogether. See on modification of rights: *Ashbury v. Watson* (1885), 30 Ch. D. 376 (C.A.).; *Underwood v. London Music Hall Ltd.*, [1901] 2 Ch. 309; *East v. Bennett Bros. Ltd.*, [1911] 1 Ch. 163.

In determining whether the rights of preferred shareholders are being modified or varied in such a way as to require their consent, it is necessary to distinguish between a modification of rights of shareholders in the strict legal sense and a modification of the position of shareholders from the commercial point of view. The former requires the consent of the shareholders, the latter does not. See the decisions in *Greenhalgh v. Arderne Cinemas Ltd. and Another*, [1946] 1 All. E.R. 512 (C.A.), *White & Bristol Aeroplane Co.*, [1953] 1 Ch. 65 and *In re John Smith's Tadcaster Brewery Co.*, [1953] 1 Ch. 308.

Where modification of the rights of preferred shareholders is not provided for in the provisions of the issue, it can be effected under the Act by appropriate proceedings pursuant to s. 173 or s. 192. The procedure under s. 192 may also be availed of, notwithstanding the existence of provisions for modification attaching to the preferred shares.

Sometimes a modification can be effected by a sale of the corporation's assets to a new corporation for preferred shares (with the required provisions) and common shares of the new corporation and the distribution of the shares of the new corporation among the shareholders of the existing corporation pursuant to an arrangement under s. 192.

Suggestions for drafting preferred share provisions

As has been indicated above, preferred shares may have varying characteristics. The rights and restrictions to be attached to an issue of preferred shares will depend in each case on the special circumstances and the object which the issuing corporation has in view in creating the issue.

In the case of small corporations, where the persons who agree to take preferred shares for the capital which they are willing to supply, will be in a position to exercise supervision and control over the operations of the corporation, very simple provisions will suffice. All that is essential is that the shares should carry a fixed preferential dividend (which may well be cumulative), priority as to return of capital, and the right to vote and possibly the right to elect a majority or a stated number of the board whenever dividends are in arrears for a stated period, for example, two years. A right to the corporation to redeem such shares at the redemption price or to purchase such shares at prices not exceeding the redemption price (as defined in the articles) is usually desirable.

Where the preferred shares are designed to attract investors upon an issue to the public, different considerations arise. The solicitor should confer with the brokers or underwriters or other persons who will assume the burden of making the issue a success and satisfy himself that he has adopted satisfactory provisions, having regard not only to the position and prospects of the corporation but also to the state of the market and to other recent successful issues of a similar character.

It will be apparent from the material under the heading "Preference as to dividends", *supra*, that the preferred provisions should deal in detail with the rights of the preferred shareholders to dividends (including participating dividends, if any) and on return of capital and distribution of surplus assets.

The preferred share provisions should also, where this is desired, contain provisions for the redemption of such shares, the purchase of such shares for cancellation and/or provisions for retraction. See further the notes under the heading "Redemption or purchase of preferred shares for cancellation", *supra*. Provision may be made for the setting aside of an annual amount, which may be a percentage of earnings or of the par value of the outstanding preferred shares, to be used as a sinking fund to be applied in the purchase for cancellation, if obtainable, or the redemption of the preferred shares.

The voting rights of the holders of the preferred shares should also be defined; see the notes under the heading "Rights as to the control of or interference in the management of the corporation's affairs" *supra*. The right to attend shareholders' meetings of the corporation may be withheld so long as there is no right to vote.

It will be noted that preferred shareholders are not entitled as of right to subscribe for any shares or obligations of the corporation, unless the articles so provide (s. 28).

Various restrictions may be inserted in the preferred share provisions for the protection of the holders of the preferred shares. Thus, the approval of the holders of such shares may be required for (1) the creation of shares ranking in priority to or *pari passu* with the preferred shares, (2) the issuance of preferred shares in excess of a particular number (there would often be an exception if at the time of issue of the new shares the assets and the earnings of the corporation met certain tests), (3) the creation or issuance of funded debt (with certain exceptions), (4) the payment off of any shares ranking junior to the preferred shares, (5) or the sale of the assets and undertaking of the corporation as an entirety or substantially as an entirety.

As preferred share provisions (which may be appropriate and satisfactory under the circumstances in existence at the time when the issue is made) may become unworkable, some provision for modifying them in case of need is desirable. See the material under the heading "Modification of the rights of preferred shareholders", *supra.*

It may also be desirable in certain circumstances to provide for the issuance of preferred shares in series, this being expressly provided for in s. 27.

Preferred shares as a mode of financing

When the circumstances or prospects of the corporation will permit, financing by means of preferred shares confers certain advantages over the issue of bonds or debentures. The corporation is freed from the burden of fixed interest charges and the risk of permitting default and consequent action by creditors to realize their security. By apt provisions, voting rights of preferred shareholders can be restricted, leaving the direction of the corporation's affairs largely in the hands of the common shareholders. Moreover, in the absence of any secured indebtedness or other restrictions, the corporation can, in case of need, finance further by an issue of bonds, debentures, notes or other obligations. By giving the preferred shareholders a right of participation in further dividends over and above the fixed cumulative dividend after the common shares have received a certain amount, or by giving the preferred shareholders a bonus in common shares, an option to purchase common shares at a favourable price, or a right of conversion into common shares, additional features are introduced which may afford greater attraction to such shares.

Bonds or debentures, on the other hand, as opposed to preferred shares, as a mode of financing, have the advantage that the corporation can deduct the interest thereon from its earnings for the purposes of income tax. Moreover, bonds or debentures, if sufficiently supported by assets and earnings, can usually be sold more easily and at a better price than preferred shares so that the corporation pays less for its financing, but at the price of encumbering its assets and obligating itself to meet fixed interest charges. In case the corporation gets into difficulties, it has been found on numerous occasions that the existence of a bond or debenture issue, properly secured by way of charge on the corporation's undertaking, enables a reorganization to be effected at the instance of the secured creditors by means of a receivership or other proceeding. In the absence of a bond or debenture issue, the corporation may find itself at the mercy of unsecured creditors who have no interest in making sacrifices to enable the corporation to continue in business. Frequently a combination of the two methods of financing can usefully be adopted. Thus, a bond or debenture issue may be placed to the extent of, for example, 50 per cent of the value of the fixed assets, followed by a preferred share issue based upon the established earnings of the corporation and upon the equity in the corporation's assets over and above the bonds or debentures. Apart from the relative advantages and disadvantages, from the point of view of the corporation, of preferred shares as a mode of financing, other questions, such as the position and prospects of the corporation, the nature and value of its assets, the title to its property (whether freehold or leasehold), the stability of its earnings, the nature of the industry, and the condition of the market all have to be taken into consideration in determining how to raise capital. In every case the financial structure of the corporation will depend upon the particular circumstances.

Limited liability of shareholders

At common law every member of an unincorporated partnership, whether it was an ordinary firm or a joint stock corporation with transferable shares, was personally liable for all debts contracted while he was a member. Numerous attempts were made to evade this rule but, owing to modern facilities for incorporation, they have ceased to be of practical interest. The fundamental rule of limited liability is that from the moment of incorporation the members of a body corporate are in no way liable for its debts, unless there is express statutory provision that the shareholders shall be liable: *Emerson v. Flint* (1858), 7 U.C.C.P. 161; and see *Salomon v. Salomon & Co.*, [1897] A.C. 22 (H.L.); *I.R.C. v. Sansom*, [1921] 2 K.B. 492 (C.A.).

In spite of the fact that shares may only be issued under the federal Act if the consideration is fully paid in money or in property or past services that are not less in value than the fair equivalent of the money that would have been received by the corporation had the shares been issued for money, and that shares issued by a corporation are non-assessable and the holders are not liable to the corporation or to the creditors in respect thereof (s. 25), in a case where partially paid shares were issued under the former Act, have remained outstanding as partly paid and the corporation has been continued under the federal Act, there will be liability both to the corporation and on a liquidation to the liquidator or the trustee in bankruptcy for the amount unpaid on its shares. The older cases on this subject may therefore be useful in these very limited circumstances apart from the questions of law for which they are still useful.

Section 45(1) of the Federal Act states that a shareholder of a corporation is not, as a shareholder, liable for any liability, act or default of the corporation except under certain specified sections: s. 38(4) where a shareholder is liable to repay within a two-year period of time certain improper payments in reduction of stated capital; s. 146(5) if the shareholder is party to a unanimous shareholders' agreement and has thereby assumed the rights, duties and liabilities of a director of the corporation concerned; or s. 226(5) where a representative action may be brought against shareholders of the corporation following its dissolution.

Section 45(2) states that the articles may provide that a corporation has a lien on a share registered in the name of a shareholder or his legal representative, for a debt of that shareholder to the corporation, including an amount unpaid in respect of a share issued by a body corporate on the date it was continued under the federal Act. Such lien is to be enforced by the corporation in accordance with its by-laws. It should be noted that there is no comparable provision in s. 45 to that contained in s. 40(2) of the Ontario Act which states that the provisions relating to a lien on the shares registered in the name of a shareholder or its legal representative for a debt of the shareholder to a corporation, does not apply to a corporation having shares listed on a stock exchange recognized by the Ontario Securities Commission.

When a British subject domiciled in Manitoba becomes the owner of shares of an American corporation, he becomes subject to the liabilities imposed on shareholders by the laws of the state where the corporation is incorporated and may be sued in Manitoba for the amount of his liability: *Allen v. Standard Trust Co.* (1919), 49 D.L.R. 399; affd (1921), 57 D.L.R. 105 (Man. C.A.).

But where an agreement to take shares in a California corporation had been made in British Columbia, it was held that the question whether there was a binding contract or not must be determined by British Columbia law; and that in the absence of a binding contract there was no liability in the absence of estoppel: *American Seamless Tube Corp. v. Goward*, [1931] 1 W.W.R. 509 (B.C. C.A.).

Mode of payment for shares

Shares may be paid for either in cash or in some other way. Thus, where an officer of the corporation had credited himself with disbursements properly made, it was held that his shares were paid up in this manner: *Re Ottawa Cement Block Co.; Macoun's Case* (1907), 14 O.L.R. 389 (Ch.). See also s. 25(4).

If the shares are not paid for in cash, they may be paid up as incidental to the acquisition of assets by the corporation from a vendor as part of the purchase price, and an appropriate provision made in the vendor's agreement. In such a case there should be authority from the vendor to the purchaser corporation to apply the requisite amount of the purchase money in paying up the incorporators' shares, failing such authority the vendor would be entitled to recover from the purchasing corporation the amount applied to pay up the incorporators' shares and the shares would have been treated as not paid up: *In re Benson-Johnston Ltd.* (1925), 5 C.B.R. 505 (Ont. S.C.).

In *C.B.C. Corset Co., Re* (1908), 12 O.W.R. 185 (C.P.) three persons agreed to sell the assets of a partnership to a corporation for 300 paid-up shares of the corporation. The three persons signed the stock book for two shares each for the purpose of incorporating the corporation; at that time it was agreed that on completion of the transaction with the corporation, there would be issued to them, as part of the sale consideration of 300 shares, two fully paid shares representing the two shares subscribed for by each. In holding that the liability on the shares was satisfied, Teetzel J. said at p. 186:

> None of the transactions are impeached as fraudulent, and it seems to me that it was competent for the company, with the assent of all parties concerned, to exchange *pro tanto* the obligation of the company to issue shares under the agreement of purchase for the obligations of the [three persons] to pay for the . . . shares subscribed for by them.

However, in *Re T. E. O'Reilly Ltd.* (1927), 60 O.L.R. 649 (H.C.) it was held that the incorporators were liable where the agreement was for the sale of assets to the corporation for a specified number of paid-up shares, the vendor directed one of such shares to be issued to each of the incorporators and a resolution was passed by the directors stating that the shares allotted to the incorporators should be in satisfaction of their subscriptions. The basis for the decision was that the corporation never received the money nor the money's worth for the incorporators' shares originally agreed to be taken.

Acceptance by a director of his qualifying shares from a promoter or vendor, while there are any questions open between the corporation and the promoter or vendor, constitutes a breach of trust on the part of the director: *Eden v. Ridsdales Ry. Lamp & Lighting Co.* (1889), 23 Q.B.D. 368 at 372 (C.A.). Thus, in the following cases it was held that schemes designed to relieve the incorporators from paying for their own shares were in effect gifts from the promoter or vendor, and the incorporators (directors) were liable to pay up their own shares: *In re Disderi & Co.* (1870), L.R. 11 Eq. 242; *In re Canadian Oil Works Corp.; Hay's Case* (1875), L.R. 10 Ch. App. 593; *In re London & South Western Canal Ltd.*, [1911] 1 Ch. 346.

Payment by promissory note

It will be noted that while it is proper to issue a share for property, the word "property" is defined by s. 25(5) as not including a promissory note or a promise to pay. Notwithstanding the authority of the former cases on this subject, shares may now not be issued in return for a promissory note or a promise to pay. In the Ontario Act, the same exception (s. 23(6)) is more widely worded, namely, "a document evidencing indebtedness of a person to whom shares are to be issued, or of any other person not dealing at arm's length with such person within the meaning of the term in the *Income Tax Act* (Canada), does not constitute property".

Payment in property or by services

Payment may be made in money's worth if the corporation has authorized such payment. As to the provisions of this Act with respect to the liability of directors where shares are improperly issued, see Chapter 8.

Apart from such special provisions, where a corporation chooses to take property, services or other consideration not possessing an obvious money value in payment of its shares, the value placed by the parties (the corporation and the shareholder) on such consideration will be accepted by the court and the court will not, whilst the contract stands (that is, is not impugned in an action to set it aside) examine into the adequacy of the consideration: *Pell's Case* (1870), L.R. 5 Ch. App. 11; *Jones v. Miller* (1893), 24 O.R. 268 (Q.B.); *Re Hess Manufacturing Co.* (1894), 23 S.C.R. 644; *Re Theatrical Trust*, [1895] 1 Ch. 771; *Re Wragg Ltd.*, [1897] 1 Ch. 796 (C.A.); *Re Co-operative Cycle & Motor Co.* (1902), 1 O.W.R. 778 (K.B.); *Re Innes & Co.*, [1903] 2 Ch. 254 (C.A.); *Hood v. Eden* (1905), 36 S.C.R. 476; *Re North Bay Supply Co.* (1905), 6 O.W.R. 85 (Ex.); *Re Modern House Manufacturing Co.; Goudy's Case* (1913), 29 O.L.R. 266 (C.A.); *National Trust Co. v. Frank*, [1917] 3 W.W.R. 43 (Sask. S.C.); *Compagnie d'Immeubles v. St. Amour* (1920), 59 Que. S.C. 391 (C.S.); *John E. Hayes & Sons v. Turner* (1924), 26 O.W.N. 456 (H.C.); *Toronto Finance Corp. & Cook v. Banking Service Corp.*, [1928] A.C. 333 (P.C.); *Re Dominion Combing Mills Ltd.* (1930), 65 O.L.R. 65 (C.A.); *Re R. P. Clark & Co. (Vancouver)l; Juke's Case*, [1938] 4 D.L.R. 806 (B.C. S.C.) (assignment of goodwill and negative covenant having real value).

If, however, it is plain on the face of a contract providing for the payment of shares that the consideration has no monetary value, then the court will examine into the adequacy of the consideration, even though no independent action impugning the contract has been taken: *In re White Star Line Ltd.*, [1938] Ch. 458 (C.A.).

Directors cannot allot fully paid shares for no real consideration and an action against a corporation to compel payment of a claim (which was found to be invalid) by the issuance of shares was accordingly dismissed: *Warren v. Superior Engravers Ltd.*, [1941] 1 D.L.R. 323 (Ont. C.A.).

If a contract providing for the issuance of shares is fraudulent or shows on its face that the consideration is illusory or is clearly not equivalent to the nominal value of the shares, the contract may be upset. It is difficult to formulate any exact rule as to when the consideration will be held to be colourable or illusory. Each case will depend upon its own facts: *Hood v. Caldwell* (1921), 50 O.L.R. 387 at 399 (C.A.); affd [1923] S.C.R. 488.

Where by contracts (approved by the shareholders) the corporation agreed to issue shares in consideration for services which all parties knew to be worth only a small part of the par value of the shares, it was held in an action by the corporation that the transaction was beyond the powers of the corporation, that all the shares for which no certificates had been issued were unissued, and that the register should be amended accordingly and the certificates held by the defendants delivered up for cancellation. In making the agreements, all parties assumed that the par value of the shares was not an element to be considered in fixing the consideration the corporation should receive for the shares, nor did they agree upon the money value for the services. The agreements therefore were not honestly entered into on the basis that the services or the agreement to perform them had or would have a value to the corporation equal to or greater than the par value of the shares. The agreements were therefore *ultra vires* and incapable of ratification: *Toronto Finance Corp. & Cook v. Banking Service Corp.* (1926), 59 O.L.R. 278; affd (*sub nom. Banking Service Corp. v. Toronto Finance*

Corp.) [1928] A.C. 333 (P.C.), and see *Signal Hill Oils Co. v. London Oil Securities*, [1927] 3 D.L.R. 984 (Alta. S.C.).

Where, however, in the case of the issuance of shares of a mining corporation, it was not proved that the parties were dealing on the basis that the interest in mining lands transferred to the corporation was worth less than the par value of the shares issued in exchange, it was held that the case was not within the doctrine of the *Toronto Finance Corporation* case: *Beaver Dam Mining Co. v. Larson* (1927), 32 O.W.N. 143 at 145 (H.C.); affd (1927), 33 O.W.N. 19 (C.A.). The leading cases were reviewed and the *Toronto Finance Corporation* case was followed in *Spooner v. Spooner Oils Ltd.*, [1936] 2 D.L.R. 634 (Alta. C.A.) where the issuance of shares was set aside as being in violation of the provisions of s. 16 of the former Act. The directors in allotting shares having a substantial par value for certain leasehold oil rights and cash did so with a view to raising money for the corporation and to giving the vendor control. No consideration was given to the actual value of the leasehold rights which it was known were worth only a fraction of the par value of the shares issued therefor.

Shares issued as fully paid, in consideration of an agreement to convey property which is specifically enforceable, may be fully paid although the shares are issued before the property is conveyed: *Re Modern House Manufacturing Co.; Goudy's Case* (1913), 29 O.L.R. 266 (C.A.).

A corporation cannot purchase property on terms that a proportion of future increases of capital shall from time to time be issued to the vendor and that all liability for calls shall be extinguished without payment. In such a case the obligation to allot is good, but the attempt to relieve the vendor from payment is bad: *Hong Kong & China Gas Co. v. Glen*, [1914] 1 Ch. 527.

Nor can a corporation convert a charge on future profits into a charge on capital and a present debt and issue fully paid shares in satisfaction of the debt created in that manner: *Famatina Development Corp. v. Bury*, [1910] A.C. 439 (H.L.).

The agreement to issue shares must be between the subscriber and the corporation, and if it is made between the subscriber and the person who solicited him to become a shareholder it will not bind the corporation: *Christin v. Union Navigation Co. (1882)*, Ramsay's Digest 391 (Q.B.). The same is true of an agreement made with a provisional director of a railway corporation on condition that the subscriber shall receive the contract for building the road: *Wilson v. Ginty* (1878), 3 O.A.R. 124 (C.A.), and see *Jones v. Montreal Cotton Co.* (1878), 24 L.C.J. 108, 1 L.N. 450.

A corporation may contract to pay in fully paid shares for completed services: *Inglis v. Wellington Hotel Co.* (1878), 29 U.C.C.P. 387 (C.A.).

The corporation cannot, however, enter into a contract for the issuance of shares which substitutes an action for breach of contract for the statutory liability to pay calls: *Pellatt's Case* (1867), L.R. 2 Ch. App. 527. Thus a condition that the applicant might pay up the balance on his shares by fees to be earned by his firm, which was to be appointed to a certain office, was *ultra vires*: *National House Property Investment Co. v. Watson*, [1908] S.C. 888 (Scot.). Nor can shares be paid up by a covenant (for example, to do something in the future), the remedy for the breach of which is limited to damages: *Toronto Finance Corp. & Cook v. Banking Service Corp., supra*; *Re Jones & Moore Electric Co.* (1909), 18 Man. R. 549 (C.A.) 571; *Winnipeg Hedge & Wire Fence Co.* (1912), 1 D.L.R. 316 (Man. K.B.). However, in the cases below the shares were treated as fully paid for the reasons indicated: *Re Theatrical Trust*, [1895] 1 Ch. 771 (contract to perform services but court not bound to inquire as to whether the consideration was reasonable); *Gardner v. Iredale*, [1912] 1 Ch. 700 (Parker J. considered that, if the contract could be read as one to perform the services in consideration of an immediate payment by the corporation, to be satisfied by the issue of fully paid shares, it would be valid); *Re Gibson, Pelican Lake Lbr. Co. v. Traders' Trust Co.*, [1929] 4 D.L.R. 1001 (Man. K.B.) (payment for shares by means of future services to be rendered to the corporation held valid as it was a bona fide transaction); *Waschysyn v. Kildonan Ice & Fuel Co.*, [1937] 2 D.L.R. 653 (Man. C.A.) (payment for shares by means of a contract for services was a matter of internal management and the court would not interfere); *Re R. P. Clark & Co. (Vancouver); Juke's Case*, [1938] 4 D.L.R. 806 (negative covenant with an assignment of goodwill was sufficient consideration for issuance of shares as fully paid because the transaction was not a sham but open and valid).

Payment for shares by means of services may be illegal as being in contravention of a statute: *Kenyon v. Darwen Cotton Manufacturing Co.*, [1936] 2 K.B. 193 (C.A.) (deductions from wages illegal under English Truck Acts applied on subscriptions for shares by employees); *Arnett v. Alouette Peat Products Ltd.*, [1942] 1 D.L.R. 175 (B.C. C.A.) (acceptance of shares in payment of services illegal under the *Truck Act*). See also the provisions of s. 23(3) of the *Ontario Act* referred to above restricting the consideration for which shares may be issued to cash or the equivalent in property or *past* services.

In the following cases the shareholder was held to have paid up his shares: *Inglis v. Wellington Hotel Co.* (1878), 29 U.C.C.P. 387 (Ont. C.A.), agreement for payment by performance of services; *Re Hess Manufacturing Co.* (1894), 23 S.C.R. 644, transfer of property; *Re Theatrical Trust*, [1895] 1 Ch. 771, agreement to render services; *In re Wragg Ltd.*, [1897] 1 Ch. 796 (C.A.), set-off of existing debt; *Hood v. Eden* (1905), 36 S.C.R. 476, transfer of property; *In re Ontario Fire Insurance Co.; Heighington's Case* (1916), 10 W.W.R. 911 (Alta. S.C.), set-off of existing debt; *Re Dorenwends Ltd.* (1924), 55 O.L.R. 413 (C.A.), stock dividend for past services.

In the following instances shares were held not to have been paid up: *Pellatt's Case* (1867), L.R. 2 Ch. App. 527, agreement to accept supply of goods in future; *Re London & Colonial Co.; Ex parte Clark* (1869), L.R. 7 Eq. 550, part of salary to be applied in payment of shares; *Scales v. Irwin* (1874), 34 U.C.Q.B. 545 (Q.B.), money owed by corporation was used to pay for shares in order to defeat creditors; *Re Almada & Tirito Co.* (1888), 38 Ch. D. 415 (C.A.), shares issued at a discount; *Re Collingwood Dry Dock; Weddell's Case* (1890), 20 O.R. 107 (Ch. Div.), services in connection with formation of the corporation: *Ooregum v. Roper*, [1892] A.C. 125 (H.L.), consideration illusory; *Re Eddystone Marine Insurance Co.*, [1893] 3 Ch. 9 (C.A.), agreement to issue shares in payment of past services; *In re Wragg Ltd.*, [1897] 1 Ch. 796 at 831 (C.A.), issue of paid up shares in satisfaction of a debt of less amount than their par value; *Union Bank v. Morris & Code* (1900), 27 O.A.R. 396; affd (1901), 31 S.C.R. 594, subscriber received back portion of amount paid in consideration for services rendered; *Moseley v. Koffyfontein Mines Ltd.*, [1904] 2 Ch. 108 (C.A.), option to debenture-holders to take fully paid shares in exchange for debentures; *Re Cornwall Furniture Co.* (1910), 20 O.L.R. 520 (C.A.), bonus stock; *Winnipeg Hedge & Wire Fence Co.* (1912), 1 D.L.R. 316, alleged consideration was the transfer of patent rights known to be of no real value to the corporation; *Colonial Assurance Co. v. Smith* (1913), 12 D.L.R. 113 (Man. K.B.), consideration unsubstantial and illusory; *Re Owen Sound Lumber Co.* (1917), 38 O.L.R. 414 (C.A.), shares allotted to promoters for profits in fact belonging to the corporation.

Calls

Under the former Act while shares could be issued without nominal or par value, it was often the case that shares with par value were issued. Historically, it was customary to issue shares with a par value of $100 although this in later years became a much smaller amount and often a par value of $1 per share was utilized. In cases where shares had a substantial par value it was often the practice to issue shares as partly paid and in such cases the shareholder was liable for the unpaid amount on his shares. This liability could be terminated by a transfer of the shares in question to a bona fide transferee. Obviously a transfer to someone without any funds to pay a potential call would not be recognized for the purpose of relieving the original shareholder of his liability. Under the present Act, no shares may be issued unless they are fully paid (s. 25) and it is specifically provided in that section that shares issued by a corporation are non-assessable and the holders are not liable to the corporation or its creditors in respect thereof. Accordingly, the case law which had developed under the former Act with respect to calls is no longer applicable except in a very limited case, namely, where a corporation was incorporated under the former Act, had issued shares which were partially paid and was continued under the present Act while such shares remained as unpaid. The liability to make payment in full for such shares continues under the present Act. A number of the more important cases are noted below.

Payments required to be made by a subscriber on allotment or upon application and allotment under the terms of subscription are not calls: *Croskey v. Bank of Wales* (1863), 4 Giff. 314 at 330, 66 E.R. 726; *Alexander v. Automatic Telephone Co.*, [1900] 2 Ch. 56 at 64 (C.A.); *Re Port Arthur Wagon Co.; Tudhope's Case; Shelden's Case* (1919), 45 O.L.R. 260, 47 O.L.R. 565 (C.A.).

The directors, in the absence of statutory restriction, can call up the whole amount unpaid at one time: *Lake Superior Navigation Co. v. Morrison* (1872), 22 U.C.C.P. 217; and the court will not interfere with the discretion of directors in making a call, for example, on the ground that the money is not wanted for the purposes of the corporation: *Odessa Tramways Co. v. Mendel* (1878), 8 Ch. D. 235 (C.A.).

It is the essence of a call that it should bear equally on all shares allotted; a resolution that "a call be made upon the directors" is not a valid call: *Re*

Port Arthur Wagon Co.; Tudhope's Case; Shelden's Case (1919), 45 O.L.R. 260 at 269; affd (1920), 47 O.L.R. 565. While the court will not interfere to determine whether a call is necessary or not if it is made upon all shareholders without discrimination or impartiality, if calls were made in such a way as to favour one set of shareholders the court might interfere to protect the others: *Christopher v. Noxon* (1884), 4 O.R. 672. Even where the articles of a corporation gave the power to make calls on some members and not on others it was held that this did not justify the making of a call on certain members only on the ground that they had been dilatory in paying former calls: *Galloway v. Hallé Concerts Society*, [1915] 2 Ch. 233. So, where directors in making a call excluded a large amount of shares held abroad, it was held, in an action for a call against a shareholder in Canada, that the assessment was not an equal assessment and was therefore bad. Although the directors were empowered in making an assessment to restrict it to one-half, it was held that this would not justify excluding part of the shares altogether, but at most allowed them to make an equal assessment on all the shares to that extent: *European & North American Ry. v. McLeod* (1875), 16 N.B.R. 3.

A corporation which is in difficulties may make a call to prevent the transfer of shares: *Gilbert's Case* (1870), L.R. 5 Ch. App. 559; and a call may be made to increase the saleable assets of a corporation by the amount thereof: *New Zealand Gold Extraction Co. v. Peacock*, [1894] 1 Q.B. 622 (C.A.).

Apart from any special agreement and prior to the corporation being wound up nothing is payable by a subscriber in respect of his shares until a call is made. Until a call is made and becomes payable the Statute of Limitations will not commence to run against the corporation: *In re Haggert Bros. Manufacturing Co.; Peaker & Runions' Case* (1892), 19 O.A.R. 582 at 589; *Re T. E. O'Reilly Ltd.* (1927), 60 O.L.R. 649.

An action upon a call being an action of debt on a statute is an action upon a specialty, for which the period of limitation is twenty years: *Cork & Bandon Ry. v. Goode* (1853), 22 L.J.C.P. 198. If, however, the corporation has been ordered to be wound up, the Statute of Limitations is not a defence to the statutory liability under the *Winding-up Act*: *Re Home Bank; Gillespie's Case* (1926), 59 O.L.R. 654 (C.A.); *Re Imperial Canadian Trust Co. & McKeague*, [1929] 4 D.L.R. 381 (Man. C.A.). In that case Trueman J.A. said at p. 388: "If by reason of lapse of time an action by the company on the call is barred, the defence prevails against the liquidator unless liability is imposed by statute, unaffected by the Statute of Limitations".

An agreement that a shareholder shall not be liable for calls is *ultra vires*: *Ex parte Clark* (1869), L.R. 7 Eq. 550; *Bunn's Case* (1860), 2 DeG. F. & J. 275, and see *Re Lake Ontario Navigation Co.; Davis's Case* (1910), 20 O.L.R. 191 (C.A.); *Re Port Hope Brewing & Malting Co.; Johnson's Case* (1912), 3 D.L.R. 426; and when a call has been made a shareholder cannot be released from his liability to pay it: *Mother Lode Consolidated Gold Mines v. Hill* (1903), 19 T.L.R. 341.

Where a call is made after the death of a shareholder his executors are liable to pay it out of his assets: *New Zealand Gold Extraction Co. v. Peacock*, [1894] 1 Q.B. 622 (C.A.).

If a person *sui juris* is beneficially entitled to shares and the registered holder has paid calls thereon, the beneficial owner is bound to indemnify him: *Hardoon v. Belilios*, [1901] A.C. 118.

Forfeiture for non-payment of calls

Section 43 of the former federal Act provided that if a shareholder, after the prescribed demand or notice had been given, failed to pay a call within the prescribed time, the directors could by resolution declare the shares to be forfeited in respect of which the call was not paid.

The directors were required to determine whether the forfeiture of shares or the enforcement of calls by action was in the interests of the corporation. The nature of the right to forfeit shares and the duty of the directors in exercising the right was explained by Lord Cranworth in *Spackman v. Evans* (1868), L.R. 3 H.L. 171 at 186, as follows:

> . . . the power to declare shares forfeited was intended only to give to the directors additional means of compelling payment of calls, or other money due from the shareholder to the company by virtue of the deed. The shares are, in substance, made a security to the company for the money from time to time becoming due from the shareholder. The duty of the directors, when a call is made, is to compel every shareholder to pay to the company the amount due from him in respect of that call; and they are guilty of a breach of their duty to the company if they do not take all reasonable means for enforcing that payment. In the present case it has never been even suggested that the Appellant was insolvent, that he was not perfectly able to pay the full 30*s*. per share, which was the amount of his call; and it was a plain breach of trust in the directors to take, in discharge of the money due from the Appellant, shares over which they had power as security only for the money due, but which shares they knew to be valueless. They were bound, as trustees for the body of the shareholders, to enforce payment of the whole 30*s*. per share, and for that purpose to take all proper legal proceedings, unless they *bona fide* believed that he was not in circumstances which would enable him to pay the sum for which he was sued . . . .

It was pointed out, however, by Duff C.J.C. in *Sun Trust Co. v. Bégin*, [1937] S.C.R. 305, that failure to pursue the personal remedy and proceeding by declaration of forfeiture might, where the shareholder is solvent, be evidence that the directors had acted in breach of their duty, or, if the shareholder were implicated, establish grounds for holding the forfeiture ineffectual. In *Sun Trust Co. v. Bégin* there were a large number of shareholders who failed to pay the call and the directors made no effort to ascertain the solvency of the shareholders whose shares they forfeited and there was no evidence as to their circumstances. On the evidence Duff C.J.C. said that it was impossible to say that the directors might not have thought that notice of forfeiture would, on the whole, be more productive than the recovery of judgment against defaulters.

Forfeiture had to be for the benefit of the corporation, not for the benefit of a shareholder: *Common v. McArthur* (1898), 29 S.C.R. 239; *Sun Trust Co.*

v. Bégin, [1937] S.C.R. 305 at 317; and though a forfeiture was presumed to be regular: *Webster's Case* (1863), 32 L.J. Ch. 135, yet if it were shown to be collusive or made for the benefit of the shareholder it was inoperative: *Richmond's Case* (1858), 4 K. & J. 305; *Re Agriculturist Cattle Insurance Co.; Spackman's Case* (1864), 34 L.J. Ch. 321 at 326. There were a number of grounds of defence to an action for payment of calls including a denial that the defendant ever became a shareholder or that there was a valid transfer of the shares before the call was made. Different considerations could arise when the action was brought by the corporation itself as opposed to by the liquidator of the corporation.

Commissions

At common law it had been held that a corporation could not enter into a valid contract for the underwriting of its shares but payment by way of brokerage could be upheld.

Section 41 of the federal Act provides that the directors may authorize the corporation to pay a reasonable commission to any person in consideration of his purchasing or agreeing to purchase shares of the corporation from the corporation or from any other person, or procuring or agreeing to procure purchasers for any such shares.

Dividends

Meaning of dividend

The word "dividend" is not a term of art to which a precise, definite or rigid meaning has been given in law. Rather, it is a general term to be given its normal and ordinary meaning. Fundamentally, a "dividend" is that which is to be divided. More particularly with reference to payments to shareholders, it has been described as the portion of the profit of a joint-stock corporation received by an individual holder as his share: *Re Carson*, [1963] 1 O.R. 373 (H.C.). A distribution by an operating corporation of retained income as opposed to capital constitutes a dividend: *Re Canadian Pacific Ltd.* (1990), 72 O.R. (2d) 545 (H.C.). The term "dividend" implies a payment related by way of entitlement to one's capital or share interest in the corporation and not to any other consideration: *Re Telsten Services Ltd.* (1981), 39 C.B.R. (N.S.) 68 (Ont. S.C.); *Re Waterloo Mechanical Contractors Ltd.* (1983), 49 C.B.R. (N.S.) 196 (Ont. S.C.). It appears, however, that some other considerations may be taken into account in some circumstances: *R. v. McClurg*, [1991] 2 W.W.R. 244 at 264 (S.C.C.). It is of the essence of a dividend that it apply rateably to all shareholders of the same class: *Re Telsten Services Ltd., supra, Priceville Fox Co. v. Jordon* (1929), 64 O.L.R. 172 (C.A.) and *Wunderlich Brothers v. Northwestern Mutual Fire Association*, [1936] 1 W.W.R. 297 (Sask. C.A.).

Declaration and payment of dividend

A corporation is authorized to pay dividends (s. 43). The Act does not, however, expressly identify the body within the corporation which has the authority to declare dividends (cf. s. 38(1) of the Ontario Act which specifically authorizes the directors to declare at least some kinds of dividends). Nevertheless, the necessary authority to declare dividends is given to the directors pursuant to their authority under s. 102 to manage the business and affairs of the corporation. The authority of directors to declare dividends under the Act is much the same as the power of directors in this regard at common law: *R. v. McClurg*, [1991] 2 W.W.R. 244 (S.C.C.). Because the managerial power of directors is a fiduciary one, directors must always act in good faith when declaring dividends and may only do so when it is in the best interests of the corporation: *R. v. McClurg, supra*. Directors may not delegate the authority to declare dividends to a managing director, to a committee of directors or to any officers of the corporation (ss. 115(3)(d) and 121(a)). In the exercise of their authority to declare dividends, directors are subject to the provisions of the corporation's articles and by-laws.

Although the declaration of dividends will *prima facie* be the responsibility of the directors, a unanimous shareholders' agreement may transfer the authority to declare dividends from the directors to the shareholders (s. 146). Apart from this, however, it would appear to be improper for the shareholders to attempt to declare a dividend as constituting an attempt to usurp the directors' powers of financial direction: see *Scott v. Scott*, [1943] 1 All E.R. 582.

Dividends are sufficiently declared by resolution of the directors and a by-law is not required: *James v. Beaver Consolidated Mines Ltd.* (1927), 60 O.L.R. 420 (H.C.). By-laws may be used, however, to impose restrictions on the discretion of the directors to declare dividends. A distribution which, in law, constitutes a dividend will be so considered even in the absence of a formal declaration: *Re Canadian Pacific Ltd., supra*, at 565.

The Act does not require that any notice be given of the declaration of a dividend but, if a record date (i.e., a date as of which the shareholders entitled to the dividend are determined) is fixed in respect of the payment of the dividend, unless notice of the record date is waived by every holder of shares affected, notice of the record date must be given not less than seven days before the record date by advertisement in a newspaper published or distributed in the place where the corporation has its registered office and in each place in Canada where it has a transfer agent or where a transfer of its shares may be recorded, and by written notice to each stock exchange in Canada on which the shares of the corporation are listed for trading (s. 134(4)). The record date may not be more than fifty days before the date on which the dividend becomes payable (s. 134(1)). In the case of a corporation whose shares are listed with a stock exchange, the notice requirements of that exchange must be complied with as well.

Unless otherwise provided by law, dividends must be paid in cash: *James v. Beaver Consolidated Mines Ltd., supra*, and *Priceville Fox Co. v. Jordan* (1929), 64 O.L.R. 172 (C.A.). Section 43(1) of the Act authorizes a corporation to pay a dividend in money, in property or by issuing fully paid shares of the corporation (i.e., a stock dividend).

It is not requisite that the dividend, otherwise proper, be declared and paid out of available cash and money may be borrowed to pay it: *Stringer's Case* (1869), L.R. 4 Ch. App. 475.

Dividends in money

The usual practice it to pay dividends by cheque sent by mail to the registered address of the shareholder. On other occasions the dividend may be deposited directly to the shareholder's bank account or be automatically used to purchase additional shares of the corporation in question. A by-law providing that dividends, unless otherwise directed by the registered shareholders concerned, were to be paid by cheque or warrant sent through the post, directed to the holder at his registered address, and that such cheque or warrant was to be sent at the risk of the shareholder, is binding and has the effect of a contract between each shareholder and the corporation: *Rands v. Hiram Walker, Gooderham & Worts Ltd.*, [1936] O.R. 488 (H.C.). To establish that the posting of a dividend cheque amounts to payment, the corporation must prove a request by the shareholder or an agreement between the shareholder and the corporation that payment should be so made. As to the circumstances from which such request may be implied, see *Thairlwall v. Great Northern Ry.*, [1910] 2 K.B. 509.

If the only obligation of the corporation is to post the dividend cheque, due posting of the cheque discharges the corporation and the corporation is not liable if the cheque is lost: *Thairlwall v. Great Northern Ry., supra*; or when the endorsement of the dividend cheque has been forged by an agent of the shareholder: *Rands v. Hiram Walker, Gooderham & Worts Ltd., supra.* It appears, however, that it is not universally the case that a corporation's by-laws limit its obligation to posting the dividend cheque.

It is common practice for the by-laws to provide that the mailing of dividend cheques to a shareholder satisfies and discharges all liability for the dividend unless the cheque be not paid on presentation. In the case of *Steen v. Gunnar Mining Ltd.*, [1963] 1 O.R. 329 (C.A.) a cheque was mailed to a shareholder and intercepted by a third party who forgedly endorsed it and cashed it. The funds had been recredited to the corporation by the bank. An action against the corporation for the dividend was dismissed on the grounds that the corporation had complied with the by-law. On appeal it was held that the trial judgment should be varied to provide that the cheque in question should be returned to the shareholder so that it could be presented for payment at the bank. In case of dishonour the plaintiff would have a valid cause of action against the corporation.

Dividends in property

There is no restriction on the type of property which may be distributed by a corporation to its shareholders as a dividend. In order to qualify as a dividend, however, the property must be distributed rateably among the shareholders of one or more classes of shares: see under the heading "Meaning of dividend," *supra*. For instance, a corporation might distribute to its shareholders by way of dividend the shares which it holds in another corporation.

Stock dividends

A corporation may prefer to issue its own shares in payment of a dividend, for instance, where the corporation does not have sufficient cash readily available to pay a dividend in cash. Such shares must be fully paid when issued and the declared amount of the dividend, in respect of which the shares are issued, stated as an amount of money, must be added to the stated capital account maintained or to be maintained by the corporation for the shares of the class or series issued in payment of the dividend (s. 43). As a result of a stock dividend, some shareholders may become entitled to a fraction of a share. Fractional shares may be issued by a corporation but the holder of a fractional share received by virtue of a stock dividend will not be entitled to exercise voting rights or to receive a dividend in respect of the fractional share (s. 49(15), (17)). For this reason, and to avoid the complications which would arise in keeping records of fractional shares, many corporations paying stock dividends offer cash to shareholders in lieu of fractional shares. This practice appears to be generally accepted although without specific statutory authority. A stock dividend is taxable under the *Income Tax Act* (Canada).

Right to sue for dividend

The court has no jurisdiction to control a decision of the directors, properly taken, as to the propriety of retaining profits undivided nor to require the distribution of profits among shareholders. Neither will the court interfere to say what is a fair or reasonable sum to retain undivided or what reserve fund may properly be required: *Burland v. Earle*, [1902] A.C. 83 (P.C.); *R. v. McClurg*, [1991] 2 W.W.R. 244 (S.C.C.); *Sparling v. Javelin International Ltd.* (1987), 37 B.L.R. 265 (Que. S.C.). The court can, however, review the decisions taken by directors to ensure that they have fulfilled their duty to act prudently and to consider all appropriate options. In any given situation and at any given time, that duty may permit the declaration and payment of a dividend, with a consequent reduction of retained earnings, or it may require the retention of surplus: *Westfair Foods Ltd. v. Watt*, [1991] 4 W.W.R. 695 (Alta. C.A.); leave to appeal to S.C.C. refused [1992] 1 W.W.R. lxv (note).

A dividend must be declared before suit can be brought for it, even where shares carry a fixed preferential dividend: *Burland v. Earle*, *supra*; *Bond v. Barrow Haematite Steel Co.*, [1902] 1 Ch. 353 followed in *De Vall v. Wainwright Gas Co.*, [1932] 2 D.L.R. 145 (Alta. C.A.); *Fairhall v. Butler*, [1928] S.C.R. 369.

A shareholder may, however, be entitled to sue for a declaration that, if such is the case, the corporation is bound by its articles (or other incorporating documents) to apply profits in payment of dividends, although no dividend has been declared. Such an action is one to determine the rights of shareholders *inter se* and although, when those rights have been ascertained, the result may be a payment by way of dividend to the plaintiff and others, the action is not strictly one to recover payment of a dividend. Thus, where the incorporating documents (memorandum of association) provided that the profits should be applied in payment of dividends and the accounts showed a balance sufficient to pay such dividends, but no dividends were paid, a shareholder was entitled to a declaration that the profits should be so applied and to an account on the footing of that declaration: *Evling v. Israel & Oppenheimer Ltd.*, [1918] 1 Ch. 101; see *Paterson v. Paterson & Sons* (1916), 53 Sc. L.R. 404 (2d Div.), 54 Sc. L.R. 19 (H.L.).

Further, in appropriate circumstances, a shareholder (or other "complainant") may bring an application to court under s. 241 (the "oppression remedy") for relief including, potentially, an order directing the declaration and payment of a dividend if the powers of the directors in not declaring and paying a dividend are being exercised in a manner that is oppressive or unfairly prejudicial to or that unfairly disregard the interests of the shareholder: *R. v. McClurg, supra*; but also see *Westfair Foods Ltd. v. Watt, supra.*

When a dividend is declared it is a debt and each shareholder is entitled to sue the corporation for his proportion: *The Custodian v. Blucher*, [1927] S.C.R. 420; *In re Severn and Wye & Severn Bridge Railway*, [1896] 1 Ch. 559; *Leclerc Ltd. v. Pouliot*, [1924] 1 D.L.R. 361 (Que. K.B.); *Re Sawtell; Ex parte Bank of Montreal*, [1933] O.R. 295 (C.A.); *Wunderlich Brothers v. Northwestern Mutual Fire Association*, [1936] 1 W.W.R. 297 (Sask. C.A.).

It has been suggested that once a dividend has been declared, it cannot be revoked or payment arbitrarily refused: *Leclerc Ltd. v. Pouliot, supra*; and see the statement of Wright J. in *James v. Beaver Consolidated Mines Ltd.* (1927), 60 O.L.R. 420 (H.C.), at 425:

> I have not discussed or considered the effect of the rescinding resolution of the 18th October, as, in view of my finding that the resolution [declaring the dividend] was invalid, it was not necessary to rescind it. If it were a valid resolution, then the dividend became a debt due from the company to the shareholder, and I do not see how the debt could be cancelled by another resolution, particularly in view of the fact that the plaintiff in the present case knew of the dividend being declared and purchased his stock upon the faith of it.

It would appear that the reasoning in support of this proposition proceeds on the basis that a debt has been created by a declaration of the dividend and it is therefore impossible for the directors to revoke the resolution dealing with the dividend and therefore unilaterally altering the debt. The American authorities which are referred to in 18 Corpus Juris Secundum at p. 619 (¶297) appear to indicate that dividends properly declared and payable in cash cannot be revoked by the subsequent action of the corporation. However, it is stated that this depends on the form of the resolution declaring the dividend and if it does not create an irrevocable debt against the corporation, or if it is not properly declared, the directors are free to rescind or alter the resolution. The position in England is governed by the provisions of the standard articles which provide that the shareholders of a corporation can declare a final dividend in a general meeting, but not in an amount higher than that recommended by the directors. In addition, the directors have power to declare interim dividends. The standard provision reads as follows: "Directors may pay such interim dividends as appear to the directors to be justified by the profits of the company." The final dividend as authorized by the shareholders cannot be altered by the directors once approved. However, so far as an interim dividend is concerned, see the case of *Potel v. Inland Revenue Commissioners*, [1971] 2 All E.R. 504 (Ch. D.) where it was held at p. 511 as follows: "In the case of an interim dividend which a board has resolved to pay, it is open to the board at any time before payment to review its decision and resolve not to pay the dividend." The authority for this proposition is given as *Lagunas Nitrate Co. v. Schroeder & Co.* (1901), 85 L.T. 22 (Ch. D.). In that case, an interim dividend had been declared and prior to the date of payment, the directors resolved that having regard to certain litigation pending, the payment of the proposed interim dividend would not be made, at least for the time being. This action was taken on advice of counsel as a result of litigation in which the corporation was involved. The corporation instructed its bankers to set aside to the credit of a special interim dividend account the amount of the dividend. As a result of the litigation, it was found it would not be proper to pay any interim dividend in respect of the period in question. The corporation requested payment of the amount at the credit of its special account and the bankers refused to pay the same, alleging that it was held for the benefit of the shareholders. It was indicated by the court that a final dividend was a debt due from the corporation to its shareholders, but the position with respect to an interim dividend was held to be different, Joyce J. stating at p. 512: "I do not see why the board of directors might not before an interim dividend is actually paid, acting *bona fide*, reconsider the question as to whether it ought to be paid at all." The banker was ordered to repay the money to the corporation.

A corporation incorporated under the federal Act could have arrangements for interim and final dividends and if such arrangements were in force, presumably the English rules would be applied. However, this is not the ordinary provision for dividends, and the standard form of by-law in use in Canada provides that the board of directors may from time to time declare, and the corporation may pay, dividends on the issued and outstanding shares in the capital of the corporation, except as may be provided in the articles of the corporation. If the courts were to treat such a power to declare dividends as equivalent to the English interim dividend, there would seem to be no reason why the English rule would not apply in Canada subject to possible questions of estoppel. However, there is no authority directly on point with the exception of *Leclerc Ltd. v. Pouliot, supra*. Thus, for example in *Denault v. Stewart, Denault & Co.* (1918), 54 Que. S.C. 209, a dividend had been declared by the board of directors and the question was whether such declaration could be revoked at a meeting of shareholders. The court held that the shareholders had no such power.

Where a dividend is declared payable in the future or in instalments, the declaration of the dividend creates a debt due to the shareholders but not payable until such future date(s) so that no steps can be taken to enforce the debt until the due date(s): *In re Kidner*, [1929] 2 Ch. 121; *Potel v. Inland Revenue Commissioners*, [1971] 2 All E.R. 504 (Ch. D.); *Inland Revenue Commissioners v. Greaves*, [1971] 3 All E.R. 1271 (Ch. D.).

Interest is recoverable by way of damages if payment of a dividend is wrongfully delayed: *The Custodian v. Blucher, supra.*

In the absence of any evidence of a trust relationship between a corporation and its shareholders respecting the payment of dividends, the legal relationship between them in respect of an unpaid dividend is that of debtor and creditor: *Re Northern Ontario Power Co.*, [1954] 1 D.L.R. (2d) 627 (Ont. H.C. Master); *Re Canada Tea Co.*, [1959] O.W.N. 378 (H.C.) and *In re Severn and Wye and Severn Bridge Railway, supra.* In the *Northern Ontario Power Co.* case, the fact that moneys originally set aside in a special account for the payment of dividends were transferred to the general account of the corporation upon the failure of shareholders to cash their dividend cheques, was said to negate completely any relationship of trustee and *cestui que trust.* An entry of the liability to pay a dividend in the corporation's books — at any rate when no special part of its assets is set aside as representing the dividend and no notice of the entry is given to the shareholder — does not establish the corporation as trustee: *In re Severn and Wye & Severn Bridge Railway, supra.*

Where there is nothing in the governing Act, the incorporating documents or the by-laws which constitutes the obligation in respect of dividends as a specialty debt, a claim for dividends relates to an ordinary contract debt and not a specialty (even though the share certificates are executed under seal, at any rate where the by-laws authorizing the payment of dividends are not under seal): *Re Northern Ontario Power Co., supra,* followed in *Re Canada Tea Co., supra,* and *Re Compania de Electricidad de Buenos Aires Ltd.*, [1978] 3 All E.R. 668 (Ch. D.).

Preference as to dividends

Where a corporation has only one class of shares, the rights of the holders thereof are equal in all respects, including the right to receive dividends (s. 24(3)). The articles of a corporation, however, may and often do provide for more than one class of shares in which case the rights and priorities of each class of shares as to dividends may vary (s. 24(4)). A discretionary dividend clause, giving to each class of shares the entitlement to be considered for a dividend at such times as is decided in the discretion of the directors, is valid and effective to create different rights as to dividends among different classes of shares: *R. v. McClurg*, [1991] 2 W.W.R. 244 (S.C.C.). A corporation's articles may also authorize the issuance of any class of shares in one or more series, but no priority in respect of dividends may be accorded to one series of shares over any other series of shares of the same class (s. 27(3)).

A prior right to a dividend is often known as a "preference" and the shares to which such a prior right is attached are often called "preferred shares" as distinct from "common shares". Previous corporate statutes used the terms "common" shares and "preferred" or "preference" shares to describe different classes of shares. The holders of common shares generally had the right to vote at meetings of shareholders, receive dividends and were entitled to a *pro rata* distribution of the property of the corporation on dissolution. Preferred shareholders typically had a preferred right of dividend, may have been able to vote at shareholders' meetings and usually were entitled only to a fixed return on dissolution. References to preferred and common shares are not strictly appropriate to a corporation subject to the Act as those terms are not found anywhere in the Act and there need not be any one class of shares which are designated as "common" (s. 24(4)). If there is more than one class of shares, there need only be different rights attached to different classes. In respect particularly of dividends, each class may have different rights with certain classes having rights in priority over other classes. Nevertheless, the term "preferred share" remains in common usage as, to a somewhat lesser extent, does the term "common share".

A "priority" in respect of dividends arises if a particular class of shares has attached to it the right to have a particular dividend declared, before a dividend on one or more other classes of shares is declared. Normally, preferred shares will have attached to them a fixed dividend rate, payable at specified times. Since no suit may be brought in respect of a dividend until it is declared, any entitlement to the stated dividend by the holder of such a preferred share is contingent upon the proper declaration of a dividend: *Bond v. Barrow Haematite Steel Co.*, [1902] 1 Ch. 353. See under the heading "Right to sue for dividend," in this chapter.

Two issues which frequently arise in connection with preferred shares are whether any right to a dividend is cumulative, that is, carried forward to a future period if, for any reason, the dividend is not declared in a given period and whether the preferred shares, in addition to the stated dividend, are entitled to share rateably with other shares in other dividends declared or whether they are limited to the stated preferred dividend. If the holders waive a dividend, careful consideration must be given to income tax legislation.

When dividend may be paid

The Act provides that a dividend (which includes a stock dividend) may not be declared or paid except when there are reasonable grounds for believing either that the corporation is, or would be after the payment, unable to pay its liabilities as they become due or that the realizable value of the corporation's assets would, after the payment, be less than the aggregate of its liabilities and stated capital of all classes of shares (s. 42). See *Clarke v. Technical Marketing Associates Ltd. Estate* (1992), 8 O.R. (3d) 734 for a discussion of the meaning of "liabilities" and "realizable value". Failure to satisfy either of these two tests requires that a dividend not be declared or paid. The stated capital of all classes of shares is the full amount of any consideration a corporation receives for any issue of shares (except in the case of non-arm's length transactions) (ss. 26(2), (3)).

While it is not entirely certain, it appears that these tests must be met not only with respect to dividends in money or in property but also with respect to stock dividends (s. 43(1)).

Prior to the enactment of the Act and similar provincial statutes, the law, largely created by the courts, dealing with when a corporation could and could not pay a dividend, focused on the distinction between the capital and profits of a corporation. The original reason for this distinction was that creditors were said to give credit to corporations on the basis of the implicit representation that they would not return their capital to shareholders: *Re Exchange Banking Co.* (1882), 21 Ch. D. 519 (C.A.). Accordingly, dividends were said to be payable only out of profits and not out of capital or, alternatively, that payment of a dividend could not "impair" a corporation's capital. While this proposition may be simply stated, it was far from easy to determine whether a specific dividend was being paid out of profits or capital: *Dovey v. Corey*, [1901] A.C. 477 at 487 (H.C.). There were also a number of qualifications to this general position. As well, there were statutory rules prohibiting the declaration of dividends when the corporation was or would as a result of payment of the dividend be "insolvent". However, no definition of what constituted insolvency was included. The result was a series of rules, referred to as a "confused mess" in *Proposals for a New Business Corporations Law for Canada* (1971) by R.W.V. Dickerson et al., vol. I, para. 140, which were often difficult to apply. An abbreviated discussion of the former law on this point follows.

A corporation's capital is generally considered to be the value paid to the corporation by shareholders in return for their shares: *Verner v. General & Commercial Investment Trust*, [1894] 2 Ch. 239 at 265 (C.A.). However, it was decided that a premium received by a corporation on the issuance of shares (i.e, an amount in excess of the par value thereof) was not part of the capital paid up on the shares but was a sum received by the corporation in excess of such paid-up capital: *Drown v. Gaumont-British Picture Corp.*, [1937] Ch. 402.

In addition, there were special rules developed regarding the payment of dividends by corporations with wasting assets, that is, assets subject to depletion, for example, a mine. In *Lee v. Neuchatel Asphalte Co.* (1889), 41 Ch. D. 1 (C.A.), it was said that under the general law there was no obligation to create a reserve fund out of revenue to meet depreciation in value of wasting property.

There were also rules directed at whether capital losses (both in prior years and in the current year) had to be made up before a dividend could be paid. The relevant cases drew a distinction between losses of fixed capital and losses of circulating capital. These terms appear to have corresponded to some extent to fixed assets and current assets.

In *Ammonia Soda Co. v. Chamberlain*, [1918] 1 Ch. 266 (C.A.), Swinfen Eady L.J. at pp. 286 and 287 defined fixed capital as:

> that which a company retains, in the shape of assets upon which the subscribed capital has been expended, and which assets either themselves produce income, independent of any further action by the company, or being retained by the company are made use of to produce income or gain profits.

and circulating capital as:

> . . . a portion of the subscribed capital of the company intended to be used by being temporarily parted with and circulated in business in the form of money, goods or other assets, and which, or the proceeds of which, are intended to return to the company with an increment, and are intended to be used again and again, and to always return with some accretion.

Fixed capital might have been lost either in prior years or the current year and the excess of current receipts over current expenditures could nonetheless be distributed by way of dividend: *Lee v. Neuchatel Asphalte Co.*, *supra*; *Verner v. General & Commercial Investment Trust*, *supra*; *In re National Bank of Wales*

Ltd., [1899] 2 Ch. 629 at 670 (C.A.); *Lawrence v. West Somerset Mineral Railway*, [1918] 2 Ch. 250.

It appears that losses of circulating capital in earlier years also need not have been made good before dividends could be paid out of current operating profits: see *In re National Bank of Wales, supra*, at 669, 670; *Bond v. Barrow Haematite Steel Co*, [1902] 1 Ch. 353.

On the other hand, the division by dividend of income arising from the consumption in the current year of circulating capital, without prior replacement of the capital consumed in producing the income, was considered to be a payment of dividend out of capital and forbidden: *Verner v. General & Commercial Investment Trust, supra*, at 266.

Further, the law was required to deal with whether dividends could be paid out of the increase in value of fixed assets. Any increase in value of fixed assets duly realized and turned into money, for example, through sale, could be treated as available for the purpose of dividends: *Lubbock v. British Bank of South America*, [1892] 2 Ch. 198; *Verner v. General & Commercial Investment Trust, supra*, at 265. There continued to be some doubt about whether unrealized capital appreciation could be distributed by way of dividend: *Bolton v. Natal Land and Colonization Co.*, [1892] 2 Ch. 124; *Dimbula Valley (Ceylon) Tea Co. v. Laurie*, [1961] Ch. 353; *R. and A.G. Sask. v. Meilicke*, [1938] 3 D.L.R. 33 at 45, 60 (Sask. C.A.).

All these former rules, however, appear now to have been either legislatively overruled or subsumed in the two tests established by s. 42 of the Act in respect of corporations subject to the Act or similar corporations legislation: *R. v. McClurg*, [1991] 2 W.W.R. 244 at 259, 260 (S.C.C.).

Because s. 42 of the Act avoids any reference to "capital", "profits" or "insolvency", there seems now to be no basis for continuing to apply the former rules or the old cases to the new test. The only questions relevant to an inquiry under s. 42 are whether, after payment of the dividend, there are reasonable grounds for believing that the corporation will be unable to pay its liabilities as they become due or that the realizable value of the corporation's assets will be less than the aggregate of its liabilities and stated capital of all classes. If it is reasonable to believe that either of these results would occur, the corporation should not declare or pay a dividend. The Act contains no special provision authorizing the payment of dividends when the test set out in s. 42 cannot be met by corporations with a large percentage of their assets being of a wasting character (s. 39 of the Ontario Act).

In deciding whether or not to declare and pay a dividend in money or in property, those responsible for that decision, normally the directors, must decide whether there are reasonable grounds for believing that either of the prohibited results would occur. The directors must, therefore, make sufficient inquiries before declaring or paying such a dividend to ensure that no such reasonable grounds exist. It will be a question of fact in each case whether this objective test has been met. A director is, however, entitled to rely in good faith on financial statements of the corporation, represented to him by an officer of the corporation, or in a written report of the auditor of the corporation, to fairly reflect the financial condition of the corporation (s. 123(4)). See also generally *Re Owen Sound Lumber Co.* (1917), 38 O.L.R. 414 (C.A.) and *Dovey v. Corey, supra.*

The Act indicates that a dividend should not be declared or paid in the circumstances referred to in s. 42: *633746 Ontario Inc. (Trustee of) v. Salvati* (1990), 73 O.R. (2d) 774 (S.C.). If circumstances change so that, although on the date the dividend was declared there were reasonable grounds for believing that the tests were met (and would be met following payment of the dividend), by the date of payment it is apparent that these tests are (or will, after payment) not be met, it is not clear what the directors should do and what rights shareholders may have. It is apparent, however, that the dividend should not be paid. Payment of the dividend in the circumstances referred to would be directly contrary to s. 42 of the Act and would expose the directors to liability: *633746 Ontario Inc. (Trustee of) v. Salvati, supra*, and see under "Liability of directors when dividends improperly paid," in this chapter. It is arguable that in such circumstances, the directors are authorized to and should retract or cancel the declaration of the dividend, or at the least, defer its payment. If that is the case, however, the result of the enactment of s. 42 has been to alter the long-standing position that a dividend once declared is a debt owed by the corporation to each of the shareholders entitled thereto which cannot be revoked. See "Right to sue for dividend," in this chapter. While that result is possible, there is no clear indication in s. 42 that that result was intended. Section 42 precludes payment of the dividend in these circumstances but does not expressly affect the declaration of the dividend or the consequences of its declaration.

It is suggested that, in these circumstances and assuming that the declaration cannot be revoked, the directors' best course of action is to suspend payment of the dividend until such time as it can be paid without contravening s. 42. This course of action recognizes that, upon declaration of the dividend, the corporation incurred a debt obligation to the shareholders from which it cannot unilaterally resile. It also recognizes that payment of a dividend contrary to s. 42 ought not to be permitted.

If the directors do suspend payment of the dividend until s. 42 can be complied with, it is doubtful that a shareholder could successfully bring an action for non-payment so long as the conditions set out in s. 42 were not satisfied. If a shareholder were to be successful in such an action, the result would be to require the corporation to pay a dividend in circumstances in which it is prohibited from doing so by s. 42. Such a result is unlikely. It follows that, if the corporation does pay the dividend as soon as s. 42 is complied with, a shareholder should not be entitled to interest from the original payment date. The result, in effect, is comparable to that in respect of a dividend declared payable in the future; no action to enforce payment can be taken until the dividend becomes payable. If the corporation becomes insolvent or bankrupt without ever again satisfying the conditions of s. 42, then the ability of a shareholder to make a claim against the corporation's estate in respect of the unpaid dividend would depend on the extent to which, under the applicable insolvency or bankruptcy legislation, debts payable upon the happening of a future event may be claimed for.

Liability of directors when dividends improperly paid

Directors of a corporation who vote for or consent to a resolution authorizing payment of a dividend contrary to s. 42 are jointly and severally liable to restore to the corporation any amounts so paid and not otherwise recovered by the corporation (s. 118(2)). Directors are deemed to have consented to all resolutions passed at meetings of directors, whether they were present or not, unless they take the appropriate steps to disassociate themselves from the resolution (s. 123).

A director who has satisfied a judgment rendered against him for voting for or consenting to a resolution authorizing payment of a dividend contrary to s. 42 is entitled to contribution from the other directors who voted for or consented to the act on which the judgment was founded (s. 118(3)). Those directors who relied in good faith on financial statements of the corporation represented to them by an officer of the corporation or in a written report of the auditor of the corporation fairly to reflect the financial condition of the corporation are apparently not subject to such obligation to contribute (s. 123(4)) but see, *contra*, Welling, *Corporate Law in Canada — The Governing Principles* (1984) at pp. 629-630.

Any director liable to restore to the corporation any amount improperly paid as a dividend contrary to s. 42 may apply to a court for an order compelling a shareholder to pay or deliver to the director any money or property that was improperly paid or distributed to the shareholder (s. 118(4)). The court may make any order it thinks fit, including an order requiring payment or delivery to the director of any money or property improperly paid to the shareholder. The court will only make any such order if it is satisfied that it is equitable to do so (s. 118(5)). Presumably, any order which might be made requiring payment to the director would be contingent on the director having first repaid such amount to the corporation.

Relative rights of tenant for life and remainderman to dividends

For corporate purposes, when deciding whether or not a dividend may be properly declared or paid, it is no longer necessary to determine whether the dividend is being paid out of profits or income or capital. See "When dividend may be paid," in this chapter. Nevertheless, when the shares in respect of which a dividend is declared and paid are held in trust for a tenant for life and for a remainderman, the distinction between income and capital may continue to have significance.

As between the tenant for life and the remainderman, the principle is that the tenant for life takes all dividends and bonuses declared in his lifetime: *Price v. Anderson* (1847), 15 Sim. 473, 60 E.R. 703; *In re Hopkins' Trust* (1874), L.R. 18 Eq. 696; *In re Armitage*, [1893] 3 Ch. 337 (C.A.); *In re Malam*, [1894] 3 Ch. 578.

For this purpose, any payment by a corporation, by means of which it parts with moneys to its shareholders, must be made by way of dividing profits, unless the corporation is in liquidation or the payment is incidental to a reduction of capital or dissolution. Subject to these exceptions and the different considerations which arise when undivided profits are capitalized in the form of additional shares which are issued to the shareholders *pro rata*, any payment or division of profits by a corporation to shareholders *prima facie* belongs to the person entitled to the income and no statement by the corporation that moneys paid to shareholders out of profits are, or are to be treated as, capital will affect the rights of beneficiaries: *Hill v. Permanent Trust Company of New South Wales*, [1930] A.C. 720 (P.C.); *Re Zacks* (1984), 17 E.T.R. 206 (Ont. H.C.).

The time when profits were earned by the corporation is immaterial as between the tenant for life and remainderman. Their rights have been made dependent on the legitimate acts of the corporation and are determined by the time, not at which the profits are earned by the corporation, but at which they are by the action of the corporation made divisible amongst its shareholders: *In re Bouch* (1885), 29 Ch. D. 635 (C.A.); and to the same effect in *Dale v. Hayes* (1871), 40 L.J. Ch. 244; *MacLaren v. Stainton* (1861), 3 De G.F. & J. 202, 45 E.R. 855; *In re Ogilvie* (1919), 88 L.J. Ch. 159; *In re Thomas*, [1916] 2 Ch. 331 (C.A.).

However, in certain cases another principle may be applied, viz., that when executors delay realizing corporate shares so as to nurse a doubtful asset, and this operates to deprive the life tenant of his income in the meantime, the whole loss cannot be thrown either upon capital or income, but must be distributed between capital and income: *Re Leys* (1911), 3 O.W.N. 464, and similarly see *Hibbert v. Cooke* (1824), 1 Sim. & Stu. 552, 57 E.R. 218; *In re Bird*, [1901] 1 Ch. 916; *In re Atkinson*, [1904] 2 Ch. 160 (C.A.); *In re Walkers Settlement Trusts*, [1936] 1 ch. 280 (assets insufficient to pay off debenture stock and arrears of interest apportioned between capital and income).

Where an extraordinary distribution of profits is made by way of dividend, the court may possess an equitable jurisdiction to apportion a dividend received by trustees as between income and capital but it may be that any such interference by the court could only be justified where the trustees had committed a breach of trust consisting of action or inaction: *Re Kleinwort's Settlement Trusts*, [1951] Ch. 860; *Re Rudd's Will Trusts*, [1952] 1 All E.R. 254, [1952] 1 T.L.R. 55 (Ch. D.); see also *Re Zacks, supra.*

Where a corporation, rather than distributing profits as such, capitalizes profits and makes a distribution of capital (e.g. a stock dividend), what is received by a trustee is capital and the remainderman rather than the life tenant is entitled thereto (unless the trust instrument otherwise provides). The exercise of the corporation's discretion in distributing profits as dividends or converting them into capital is binding on both the remainderman and the tenant for life: *Bouch v. Sproule* (1887), 12 App. Cas. 385; *In re Ogilvie, supra*; *In re Outen's Will Trusts*, [1963] 1 Ch. 291.

It was stated by Jenkins L.J. in *Re Duff's Settlements*, [1951] Ch. 923 (C.A.) at p. 929 that "the character, as a matter of company law, of any given distribution as it leaves a company determines its characters in the hands of the recipient." That statement was approved by the Supreme Court of Canada in *In re Waters*, [1956] S.C.R. 889.

If an option is given to the shareholders to take the dividend either in cash or shares, the dividend may be income: *In re Malam, supra*; *Inland Revenue*

Commissioners v. Coke, [1926] 2 K.B. 246; but not if it is apparent that the corporation intended to capitalize: *In re Taylor*, [1926] Ch. 923.

The mere fact of moneys being taken from undivided profits and carried to a reserve fund has been considered not equivalent to their capitalization: *In re Bridgewater Navigation Co.*, [1891] 2 Ch. 317 (C.A.); but see *Fisher v. Black & White Publishing Company*, [1901] 1 Ch. 174 (C.A.).

A provision in a trust instrument that bonus shares or stock dividends are to be treated as income or capital will bind the beneficiaries: *Re Mittam's Settlement Trusts* (1858), 4 Jur. (N.S.) 1077.

If the corporation is in liquidation, every payment by the liquidator to the shareholders, including any surplus of assets over and above the stated capital is capital and, when received by an executor, becomes part of the corpus of the estate. *In re Keating Estate*, [1934] S.C.R. 698; *Hill v. Permanent Trustee Company of New South Wales, supra*, followed in *Re McLarty*, [1943] 2 D.L.R. 425 (N.S. S.C.); and, as between tenant for life and remainderman, is capital and not income: *Re Anderson*, [1925] 4 D.L.R. 116 (Man. K.B.), following *In re Armitage, supra.*

Where a dividend is paid in respect of a period, which begins before the tenant for life's interest begins, or ends after such interest expires, such dividend may under provincial legislation be apportionable between the tenant for life and the other person interested during such period.

In Ontario, under the *Apportionment Act*, R.S.O. 1990, c. A.22, dividends as defined are deemed to have accrued by equal daily increments during and within the period for which the payment of the same is declared or expressed to be made. Only dividends which are declared in respect of a definite period fall within the Act: *Re Coulson*, [1960] O.R. 1 (C.A.).

The effect of the *Apportionment Act* with respect to dividends declared after the death of a tenant for life, but declared for a period entirely prior to the death of the tenant for life, is to make such dividends fall into the estate of the tenant for life: *In re Muirhead*, [1916] 2 Ch. 181.

Where a fixed cumulative preferential dividend has been allowed to go in arrears, by reason of lack of profits and failure to declare the dividend at the fixed rate, and a dividend is subsequently declared at a rate sufficient to absorb the arrears, that dividend is not declared and paid with respect to each year, but with respect to the current year, the amount being determined by the total amount of dividends unpaid: *In Re Wakley*, [1920] 2 Ch. 205 (C.A.); the same principle being applied in *In re Marjoribanks*, [1923] 2 Ch. 307. Similarly where dividends on preference shares were in arrears, and the holders of common shares pursuant to a scheme of arrangement surrendered part of their holdings to the preference shareholders in consideration of a waiver of their right to the arrears, it was held that the common shares so received should be treated as income and belonged to the tenant for life, the transaction being in effect a sale of the claim to arrears of dividends: *In re MacIver's Settlement*, [1936] Ch. 198; followed in *In re Smith's Will Trusts*, [1936] 2 All E.R. 1210 (Ch. D.).

If trustees, on the direction of the tenant for life, invest capital in the purchase of shares on which at the date of purchase dividends have been entirely earned and declared but not paid, the tenant for life is not entitled to such dividends; such dividends form part of the capital: *In re Sir Robert Peel's Settled Estates*, [1910] 1 Ch. 389. Under the rule in *Scholefield v. Redfern* (1863), 2 Dr. & Sm. 173, 62 E.R. 587, as explained in *Bulkeley v. Stephens*, [1896] 2 Ch. 241, the tenant for life is not entitled to be credited or charged with the proportionate part of accruing and undeclared dividends, on the sale or purchase by a trustee of shares sold or purchased *cum* dividend, in the absence of special circumstances justifying a departure from the rule; and to the same effect are the decisions in *In re Firth*, [1938] Ch. 517 and *In re Henderson*, [1940] 1 All E.R. 623 (Ch. D.). However, where the question had been raised by the life tenant and there was no difficulty in ascertaining the apportioned part of the dividend on shares sold *cum* dividend, it was held that, as between the remainderman and the life tenant who had died, it was proper for the trustees to account to the executors of the life tenant for the apportioned dividend: *In re Winterstoke's Will Trusts*, [1938] Ch. 158.

Guarantee of dividends

One corporation may guarantee the payment of dividends on the shares of another corporation, for example, a parent corporation may guarantee the dividends on preferred or common shares of a subsidiary corporation in order to make them more attractive to the public.

The guarantee should be by way of agreement between the guaranteeing corporation and a trust corporation and the share certificates may refer to the agreement and state that the original is on deposit with the trustee. It is obviously inconvenient to have the original guarantee endorsed on each certificate, since a new guarantee would have to be signed on each transfer of shares. The guarantee agreement should, *inter alia*, contain provisions whereby the trustee is required to enforce the guarantee on default on requisition of a stated proportion of the shareholders and under which no shareholder may sue the guarantor on default, as otherwise the guarantor would be exposed to as many actions as there are shareholders.

It will depend on the terms of the contract and the attending circumstances whether, on the liquidation of the corporation in respect of whose shares the guarantee was given, the amounts payable or set aside for payment under the guarantee belong to the corporation or to the shareholders individually. If the agreement is between a vendor and a purchaser and part of the purchase price is allocated and deposited with trustees to satisfy the guarantee, the fund belongs to the corporation and is divisible among its creditors: *In re Menell & Cie.*, [1915] 1 Ch. 759; *In re Stuart's Trusts* (1876) 4 Ch. D. 213. If, however, the vendor, having received the whole of the purchase money, enters into a mere personal obligation for the benefit of the shareholders to make up the profits to a certain amount, then, notwithstanding that payment is to be made to the corporation for distribution to the shareholders, the moneys payable under the guarantee will not form any part of the assets of the corporation: *In re South Llanharran*

Colliery Co. (1879), 12 Ch. D. 503 (C.A.); *Re Gelly Deg Colliery Co.* (1878), 38 L.T. 440 (payment to trustees).

Where there is a provision that the guarantor shall be entitled to be repaid by the corporation, the latter being made a party, the payment of any sum under the guarantee is *ultra vires* and void: *In re Walters' Deed of Guarantee, Walters' "Palm" Toffee, Ltd. v. Walters*, [1933] 1 Ch. 321. In that case, however, the declaration was made without prejudice to any claim of the guarantor to be subrogated to the rights of the preferred shareholders as to payments made in regard to dividends for the period covered by the guarantee or in regard to any rights of preferred shareholders in a winding-up. This was on the ground that preferred shareholders were not entitled to be paid twice over any part of the dividends which the guarantor had provided for distribution.

The right of subrogation, if any, which it is intended that the guarantor should have, should be clearly defined in the instrument of guarantee. If it is intended that there should be no such right, it should be expressly excluded.

When a vendor of shares undertook that he would "personally guarantee a 7 per cent. dividend on the preferred stock . . . which you hold", this was construed to be a promise for one dividend only: *Quance v. Brown* (1926), 58 O.L.R. 578 (C.A.). In the same case it was held that this was not a guarantee to which the Statute of Frauds applied; that is, it was not a special promise to answer for the debt, default or miscarriage of another and it was unnecessary for the consideration for the promise to appear in writing or by necessary inference from a written document. There was no undertaking in the share certificate to pay any dividend and, consequently, there was no debt of the corporation to be guaranteed. *Quaere*, whether, even if an undertaking to pay the dividend had appeared in the share certificate, the statute would have applied, for there could be no debt until a dividend had been declared.

Prohibited loans and guarantees

It is provided in s. 44(1) that subject to subs. (2), a corporation or any of its affiliates are not directly or indirectly to give financial assistance by means of a loan, guarantee or otherwise to any shareholder, director, officer or employee of the corporation or an affiliated corporation, or to an associate of any such person for any purpose or to any person for the purpose of or in connection with the purchase of a share issued or to be issued by the corporation or the affiliated corporation where there are reasonable grounds for believing that the corporation is or, after giving the financial assistance, would be unable to pay its liabilities as they become due or the realizable value of the corporation's assets, excluding the amount of any financial assistance in the form of a loan or which are pledged or encumbered to secure a guarantee, after giving the financial assistance would be less than the aggregate of the corporation liabilities and stated capital of all classes.

In *Mount View Charolais Ranch Ltd. v. Haverland*, [1974] 2 W.W.R. 289 (Alta. C.A.) the validity of a mortgage given by a corporation to secure the purchase of its own shares was in question. The mortgage was held to be valid as the exception in the Alberta Act was limited to public corporations. That provision stated that a public corporation should not give any financial assistance for the purpose of the purchase of any shares in the corporation. The Court also held that the principle in *Trevor E. Whitworth* (1887), 12 App. Cas. 409 was limited to the purchase by a corporation of its own shares. See also *Royal Bank v. Stewart* (1979), 15 B.C.L.R. 349 (S.C.); affd (1981), 31 B.C.L.R. 33 (C.A.); and *Murray v. C.W. Boon & Co.*, [1974] 2 W.W.R. 620 (Alta. Dist. Ct.), a case decided under a predecessor Act.

In *Clarke v. Technical Marketing Associates Ltd. Estate* (1992), 8 O.R. (3d) 734, a leveraged buy out was considered in which there was a guarantee of the obligation to pay for the shares secured by a general security agreement charging the assets of the purchased company. The purchasing company and the company giving the guarantee were then amalgamated and the amalgamated company subsequently went into bankruptcy. In a dispute as to the general security agreement the Court held that it was valid. The financial assistance was permitted pursuant to the provisions of s. 44(2)(c) of the Federal Act. As financial assistance to a holding body corporate by a wholly owned subsidiary such financial assistance did not have to meet the test laid down in ss. 44(1)(e) or 44(1)(d). The Court discusses both the liquidity test and the solvency test, holding that the guarantee could be disregarded as there was no evidence to demonstrate that there were reasonable grounds at the time of giving the guarantee for believing that the guarantee would be called upon so as to constitute a liablity affecting liquidity and so far as the solvency test was concerned the traditional valuation, namely, the price payable by a willing and knowledgeable vendor by a like purchaser, neither acting under compulsion, should be incorporated into the concept of realizable value. In *Nelson v. Rentown Enterprises Inc.* (1992), 5 Alta. L.R. (3d) 149 (Q.B.), it was held that the solvency test must be met both when the contract was made and when it was performed.

A contract made in violation of this provision may be enforced by the corporation or by a lender for value in good faith without notice of the contravention (s. 44(3)). See *Petro-Canada v. Cojef Ltd.* (1992), [1993] 3 W.W.R. 76 (Man. C.A.).

The protection afforded by the good faith exception was addressed in *Royal Bank of Canada v. Stewart et al.* (1979), 8 B.L.R. 77 (B.C.S.C.); affd (1981), 31 B.C.L.R. 33 (C.A.). In this case, the Bank was unsuccessful in its action for repayment of its loan. The Bank had been asked to lend sufficient funds for the purpose of buying the shares of one of the shareholders. The loan was secured by a corporate guarantee and collateral mortgage. When the loan was not repaid, the Bank sued on its security.

Proudfoot, J., in considering the British Columbia equivalent of s. 44, held that the loan had contravened the prohibition on granting financial assistance for the purchase of shares. In considering whether the Bank could rely on the lender exception, Proudfoot, J. found that the evidence indicated that the assistant manager of the Bank knew the purpose of the loan. The Bank's solicitors also were directly involved in the preparation of the security documents and thus the Bank had imputed notice through the solicitors. The conclusions of Proudfoot, J. were upheld on appeal.

The Alberta Law Reform Institute has suggested that the *Royal Bank* case puts into doubt the actual protection afforded to lenders under the "good faith" exception (see *Financial Assitance by a Corporation: Section 42, The Business Corporations Act (Alberta)* Report No. 54, August, 1989 at p. 11). In the Institute's opinion, few banks lend money without knowing the purpose of the loan.

It would appear that "notice" includes information sufficient to put the lender on inquiry. See *Petro-Canada v. Cojef Ltd., supra.*

The term "holding body corporate" is defined in s. 2(4) of the Act as being the parent of a subsidiary and the term "subsidiary" is defined in s. 2(5) as a body corporate controlled by another body corporate. Under s. 2(3) a body corporate is controlled by the holding of securities of the corporation in question to which are attached more than 50 per cent of the votes that may be cast to elect directors which are held (other than by way of security only) by or for the benefit of the parent. In addition, the votes attached to those securities must be sufficient if exercised to elect a majority of the directors of the corporation. Despite these definitions, it is unclear whether ss. 30(1) or 44(2) of the Federal Act are intended to apply to a sub-subsidiary of a corporation. On a literal reading of the Federal Act, one might conclude that this Act does not prevent a corporate grandchild from acquiring shares in its corporate grandparent pursuant to s. 30(1) nor would it prevent the giving of a guarantee where the guarantee is made by or in favour of the corporate grandchild pursuant to s. 44(2). In contrast, the definition in the Ontario Act in s. 1(2) provides that a body corporate is deemed to be a subsidiary of another if it is controlled by that other or that other and one or more bodies corporate, each of which is controlled by that other, or two or more bodies corporate, each of which is controlled by that other, or if it is a subsidiary of a body corporate that is that other's subsidiary. Accordingly, it seems clear that the comparable provision in the Ontario Act (s. 20(2)) has wider application than the federal Act. As a result, it is submitted that under the Ontario Act, a corporate sub-subsidiary will be considered a "subsidiary" of its corporate grandparent and ths cannot directly hold shares in the grandparent, but can guarantee the obligations of the corporate grandparent.

The concept of "control" is also relevant in any determination of how the Federal Act will be interpreted. The Act provides that a body corporate is a subsidiary if it is "controlled" by the other body corporate. The concept of "control" by definition includes shares held "for the benefit of a person." As a corporate grandparent does not hold shares in its corporate grandchild, it cannot be said to control the grandchild unless the shares which the intermediate corporation holds in the grandchild can be said to be held for the benefit of the grandparent. Applying the traditional rule that a shareholdern does not own or have any interest in the assets of the corporation in which such shareholder holds shares would lead to the conclusion that it would not be proper to regard the intermediate corporation as holding the shares of the grandchild for the benefit of the grandparent. It is submitted that unless the intermediate corporation was regarded as the nominee or trustee for the grandparent or circumstances exist which would permit the corporate veil to be pierced so that the grandparent and intermediate corporation would be regarded as one, the Federal Act, unlike its Ontario counterpart, does not prevent a corporate grandchild from acquiring the shares of its corporate grandparent.

However, it is noted that in both *Clarke v. Technical Marketing Associates Limited (Estate of)*, discussed above, and *Re Amoco Canada Petroleum and Dome Petroleum*, unreported July 14, 1988, Alta. Q.B., Forsyth, J., in interpreting the provisions of the Federal Act, both Farley, J. and Forsyth, J. held that a grandchild corporation should be considered a subsidiary under the Federal Act.

The question of whether the guaranteeing of the obligations of sister corporations is prohibited is more difficult. To put it simply, if corporations B and C are both wholly owned subsidiaries of A (and thus sister corporations of each other), can B guarantee C's obligations where the solvency test cannot be met? It is clear that the provision of financial assistance by B directly to C would contravene the Act. On the other hand, the giving of financial assistance by B to A and by A to C are, individually, steps that are permitted. However, it is unclear whether the upstream and downstream guarantees, if linked together, would be considered the "indirect" provision of financial assistance.

In *Amoco, supra*, Forsyth, J. considered whether back-to-back guarantees could be utilized to avoid the prohibition in s. 44 of the Federal Act. He concluded that this section does not specifically preclude the giving of linked guarantees and that the purpose of the secton is to allow financial assitance between interrelated companies.

For a further discussion of this issue, see: Levin, J.A., "Financial Assistance", 1985 Annual Institute on Continuing Legal Education CBAO; Levin, J.A., "Financial Assistance", Paper prepared for CBAO seminar, *Basics of a Secured Bank Financing*, April 1, 1989; Levin, J.A., "Financial Assistance", Paper prepared for CBAO seminar, . . . *And Enforceable in Accordance with its Terms — Enduring Problems in Legal Opinions*, February 9, 1990; Karvellas, J.D. and Daniel, G.J., "Limitations on the Power of an Alberta Corporation to Provide Guarantees and Other Financial Assistance: Section 42 of the (Alberta) Business Corporations Act (1985), 23 Alta. Law Rev. 479; Dietrich, N., "Financial Assistance", Paper prepared for L.S.U.C. seminar, *Working with the Ontario Business Corporations Act: The Practitioner's Experience*, April 8, 1992.

Section 44(2) provides that notwithstanding the foregoing provisions a corporation may give financial assistance by means of a loan, guarantee or otherwise in the following circumstances:

(1) to any person in the ordinary course of business if the lending of money is part of the ordinary business of the corporation;
(2) to any person on account of expenditures incurred or to be incurred on behalf of the corporation;
(3) to a holding body corporate if the corporation is a wholly owned subsidiary of the holding body corporate;
(4) to a subsidiary body corporate of the corporation; and
(5) to employees of the corporation or any of its affiliates

either to enable or assist them to purchase or erect living accommodation for their own occupation or in accordance with a plan for the purchase of shares of the corporation or any of its affiliates to be held by a trustee.

There are few cases in which any of these exceptions have been judicially interpreted. In interpreting the English equivalent of the "moneylending" exception, the House of Lords took a conservative approach. In *Steen v. Law*, [1964] A.C. 287 (H.L.) a corporation was to be turned into a wholly owned subsidiary corporation for tax purposes and to that end loaned money to the new parent corporation which in turn used the money to acquire the shares of the subsidiary. The loan was made without security and without interest. The court held that in order to come within the exception permitting financial assistance, the lending of money must be part of the "ordinary business of the company." This in effect means that there must be lending of money in the general sense of a registered moneylender or bank. The lending of money cannot be restricted to special uses or for particular purposes. In this particular case, the only lending of money by the subsidiary was the inter-corporate transfer of funds made without security or interest and was not considered a loan in the ordinary course.

Certain sections of the *Income Tax Act* also refer to the "business of lending money." The determination of whether or not a taxpayer carries on the business of lending money and whether or not the loan is made in the ordinary course of business is fact specific. However, the courts consider the following general principles: the level of loan making and pattern of lending money; whether or not a consistent system or procedure has been utilized in granting loans; and whether the purpose for making the loan is an "accommodation" and not made with a business purpose and in the expectation of profit. See, for example, *Charter Industries Ltd. v. MNR* (1975), 75 D.T.C. 270 (Tax Review Bd.) where a parent corporaton loaned money to a subsidiary, but did not lend to the general public or to disinterested third parties, the parent corporation was not in the business of lending money. In *Anderson & Miskin Ltd. v. MNR* (1969), 69 D.T.C. 536 (Tax Appeal Bd.) it was held that the placing of surplus funds from time to time in order to earn interest does not constitute "money-lending."

With respect to the permitted financial assistance to holding body corporates by wholly owned subsidiaries, the cases indicate that in determining whether this exception applies, the question of the requisite ownership of the subsidiary is not determined at the time the transaction is conceived. The relevant time to be considered is the time at which the financial commitment is given. See *Strait Line Contractors Ltd. et al. v. Rainbow Oilfield Maintenance Ltd.* (1991), 79 Alta. L.R. (2d) 169 (C.A.) and *Noren Investments Ltd. v. Brownie's Franchises Ltd.* (1987), 37 D.L.R. (4th) 1 (B.C.C.A.).

In the *Strait Line* case, the court concluded that the requisite ownership had not been established. The ownership was transitory and existed for only a short period of time, as dictated by the closing agenda for a share purchase agreement, and the shares of the corporations were subject to the lender's prior 35% equitable interest. In *Noren Investments* on the closing date of the transactions, the 100% ownership requirement was met, although it was lacking at the time the purchase scheme was devised. Such interest was considered sufficient.

It will be noted that s. 118(2) provides that directors who vote for or consent to a resolution authorizing financial assistance contrary to s. 44 are jointly and severally liable to restore to the corporation any amounts so paid and not otherwise recovered by the corporation. The action to enforce such liability must be commenced within two years from the date of the resolution authorizing the action complained of (s. 118(7)). It will be noted that under s. 118(4) a director who is liable under s. 118(2) may apply to the court for an order compelling the recipient to pay or deliver to the director any money or property paid contrary to s. 44. It would appear that this provision may be in conflict with the provisions of s. 44(3), but there is as yet no decided authority on the matter.

A contract made by a bank in contravention of the provisions of the *Banking Act*, 34 Vict., c. 5, s. 40, prohibiting the lending of money upon certain security, was held to be illegal and void: *Bank of Toronto v. Perkins* (1883), 8 S.C.R. 603; and where the governing statute prohibited a loan to a member in excess of a specified amount and made it an offence to do anything forbidden by the statute, subject to a penalty, it was held that a prohibited loan was an illegal and void transaction and the money advanced could not be recovered: *Lougher v. Molyneux*, [1916] 1 K.B. 718.

In *Batu Pahat Bank Ltd. v. Tan Keng Tin*, [1933] A.C. 691, a case decided by the Judicial Committee of the Privy Council, the statutory provision under consideration prohibited certain corporations from making loans on the security of their shares and specified consequences to ensue in the event of any loan being made in contravention of the statute; such consequences included a personal liability on directors and managers for a fine and "for the payment of any portion of the amount lent which remains unpaid after deducting the amount realized on the securities". The view was expressed that the provision recognized (1) the continuance of the security on which the loan was made, and (2) the discharge of the debt *pro tanto* by the proceeds of its realization. In that case the implication was held to be plain that the transaction was not void, for the words of the ordinance indicated that the corporation had power to enforce its security and would no doubt be obliged to do so before calling on a shareholder for any balance of the amount lent remaining unpaid.

The question arises as to whether financial assistance given in contravention of s. 44 is valid or void. In this regard s. 44(3) provides that a contract made by a corporation in contravention of the section may be enforced by the corporation or by a lender for value and good faith without notice of the contravention. This provision would appear to result in contracts which did not fit within the wording of subs. (3) being unenforceable or void. In *Central and Eastern Trust Co. v. Irivng Oil Ltd. et al.*, [1980] 2 S.C.R. 29, the purchasers of shares of a corporation arranged for the corporation to grant a mortgage on its assets to the plaintiff trust company as security for funds advanced by the trust company to the purchasers, which enabled them to pay the purchase price for the shares. When the trust company attempted to foreclose, it was argued that the mortgages were unenforceable as contrary to the provisions of the Nova Scotia Companies Act, which were in substance similar to the existng s. 44 of the Federal Act. The Supreme Court of Canada held that the moneys advanced had been used in contravention of the Act to assist in the purchase of shares. Accordingly, the Court was of the view that the mortgages were void and unenforceable.

However, inspite of this decision, in view of the penalty provided for in s. 118 on directors, it may be arguable whether this result should necessarily follow. Thus, under the former Act it was held that the section which provided for a liability on directors who authorized a loan in contravention of the section contained its own penalty and accordingly the liability under the loan would continue, see *Eanser v. Eanser et al* [1946] S.C.R. 54.

Under the English Act, where a contract, to which the corporation was a party, contained a provision under which a retiring director was to sell certain shares to another shareholder, the fact that the corporation provided the purchase moneys was held not to vitiate the agreement, since if the corporation had contravened s. 45 of the English Act of 1929 (now s. 151 of the 1985 Act), it had simply made itself liable to the penalty provided in the section: *Spink (Bournemouth) Ltd. v. Spink*, [1936] 1 Ch. 544. Under the corresponding subs. (1) of the English Act it has been held that the word "security" means "valid security" and that, where a debenture has been issued in contravention of the section, the penalty imposed on the borrowing corporation by the section is on the footing that the security is and remains valid: *Victor Battery Co. v. Curry's Ltd.*, [1946] Ch. 242. The decisions under the English Act may not however be applicable under s. 44 as that section, unlike the English provision, does not impose a penalty on the corporation for breach of its provisions. It will be noted, however, that s. 251 of the federal Act provides that it is an offence for any person, without reasonable cause, to contravene any provision of the Act for which no punishment is provided.

Chapter 6

TRANSFERS OF SECURITIES

Cross-references: Sections 6(1)(d), 32, 46-47, 174, 241(1), 241(3)(k), 243 and ss. 51-57 of the Regulations passed pursuant to the federal Act; Ontario Act ss. 29(4)-(7), s. 42(1), (2)-(4), ss. 53-91, 45, 248(1), (3)(k), 250.

Shares or securities

Section 48(3) of the Act provides that unless there is a restriction on transfer which is noted on the security in accordance with s. 49(8), a security is a negotiable instrument. The provisions of ss. 48-81 have been drafted to provide for a corporate securities transfer code, but there is some question as to whether the Act has attained its objectives because of the provisions for rectification of the register contained in s. 243, as to which see the discussion in Chapter 16. The term "securities" includes both shares and certain classes of corporate obligations. The definition in s. 48(2) includes a share participation or other interest in or obligation of a corporation. In what follows shares alone are dealt with unless the contrary appears. However, it will be noted that the same provisions relating to shares will also be applicable to obligations as well.

General

Shares in the capital stock of a corporation are personal estate and transferable as such by the shareholder: see *Re Polson Iron Works Ltd.* (1912), 4 D.L.R. 193.

The property represented by shares of a Canadian corporation is subject to Canadian law which can effectively prevent a transferee from acquiring a legal or equitable title to such shares: *Spitz v. Secretary of State of Canada*, [1939] Ex. C.R. 162 at 172; or can effectively divest the registered shareholder of the title to the share: *Lovibond v. G.T.R. & C.N.R.*, [1939] O.R. 305 (C.A.). The validity of a contract to transfer shares depends upon the laws of the country where the contract is made: *Colonial Bank v. Cady* (1890), 15 App. Cas. 267; *The King v. Cutting*, [1932] S.C.R. 410. The situs of shares of a corporation for the purpose of determining a dispute as to their ownership is the territory of incorporation of the corporation, which is the place where the shares can be effectively dealt with by the court: *Braun v. The Custodian*, [1944] Ex. C.R. 30 at 47; [1944] S.C.R. 339 at 346. See *Brown v. Beleggings-Societiet N.V.*, [1961] O.R. 815 (H.C.).

A corporation, as well as an individual, may become the owner of shares of another by transfer. As for the power of a corporation to acquire or deal in its own shares, however, see the notes to ss. 30-36, and as to the surrender of shares to a corporation, see the notes to s. 37 (both in Chapter 5).

After the commencement of a winding-up, no transfer of shares can be made without the sanction of the liquidator under the authority of the court; see the notes to s. 20 of the *Winding-up Act*, in Chapter 21.

After an assignment or receiving order under the *Bankruptcy and Insolvency Act* transfers of shares may be made and registered in the same manner as before: *Re Canadian Cereal & Flour Mills Co. Ltd.* (1922), 51 O.L.R. 316.

A share certificate "is a declaration by the company to all the world that the person is whose name the certificate is made out, and to whom it is given, is a shareholder in the company, and it is given by the company with the intention that it shall be so used by the person to whom it is given and acted upon in the sale and transfer of shares"; *In re Bahia & San Francisco Ry. Co.* (1868), L.R. 3 Q.B. 584, per Cockburn, C.J., at 595; and see *The Balkis Consolidated Co. Ltd. v. Tomkinson*, [1893] A.C. 396, 403, approving this statement.

Share certificates are not themselves contracts, nor are they specialities: *Treasurer of Ontario v. Blondé*, [1941] O.R. 227 at 247, and cases cited; *The King v. Williams*, [1942] A.C. 541 at 555. A share certificate is evidence of an obligation of the company to pay to the shareholder his proportionate share of dividends declard and of net assets upon a winding-up: *Williams v. The King*, [1940] O.R. 403 (C.A.) at 415.

A share certificate is not the title but the evidence of title to shares and statutory provisions providing that the certificate is *prima facie* evidence of the title of the shareholder to the shares mentioned therein, are merely declaratory of the law as established in the cases, for example, *Shropshire Union Railway & Canal Co. v. The Queen* (1875), L.R. 7 H.L. 496 at 513; *Union Bank v. Morris* (1900), 27 O.A.R. 396 at 409; *Longman v. Bath Electric Tramways Ltd.*, [1905] 1 Ch. 646 (C.A.) at 659; *Mackenzie v. Monarch Life Assurance Co.* (1912), 45 S.C.R. 232 at 258; *Lorsch & Co. v. Shamrock Consolidated Mines Ltd.* (1917), 39 O.L.R. 315 (C.A.) at 321; *Coplan v. Coplan*, [1958] O.R. 551 (C.A.).

The presumption of title in favour of the person in whose name the certificate stands may be rebutted: *Philipps v. Cameron Copper Mines Ltd.*, [1959] Que. S.C. 433. Where the company raises any question of ownership in a person other than the person in whose name the certificate stands, the burden of proof is on the company: *Re Champion & White Ltd.*, [1943] 1 D.L.R. 283 at 287.

Transfer provisions in Act

The federal Act in Part VII (ss. 46-81) sets forth what is intended to be a corporate securities transfer code. A number of different concepts are dealt with, including the concept of an adverse claim and the negotiability of securities in relation to the rights and liabilities between purchasers and sellers. Part VI contains definitions of terms and establishes certain presumptions; sets out the liabilities, rights and defences imposed upon or available to a corporation in respect of transfers of corporate securities; sets out the conditions, rights and liabilities as between the purchaser and seller; and establishes the duties of the issuer and its transfer agent in respect of those situations where liability may arise in regard to the registration of transfers. The following is a summary of some of the more significant provisions contained in the transfer code.

(1) Section 51 - subject to certain provisions, a corporation or a trustee under

a trust indenture may treat the registered owner of a security as the person exclusively entitled to vote, to receive notices, to receive any interest, dividend or other payment in respect of the security, and otherwise to exercise all the rights and powers of an owner of the security;

(2) Section 54 - except in certain circumstances and unless otherwise agreed, a person required to deliver securities may deliver any security of the specified issue in bearer form or registered in the name of the transferee or endorsed to him or in blank;

(3) Section 55 - a purchaser for value is deemed to have notice of the terms of a security including those stated on the security and those incorporated therein by reference to another instrument, statute, rule, regulation or order to the extent that the terms so referred to do not conflict with the stated terms, except that the purchaser is to be deemed not to have such notice of a defect going to the validity of the security even though the security expressly states that a person accepting it admits such notice;

(4) Section 56 - after an event that creates a right to immediate performance of the principal obligation evidenced by a security or that sets a date on or after which a security is to be presented or surrendered for redemption or exchange, a purchaser is charged with notice of any defect in its issue or any defence of the issuer (a) if the event is one requiring the payment of money or the delivery of securities or both on presentation or surrender of the security and such funds or securities are available on the date set for payment or exchange and he takes the security more than one year after that date; or (b) if he takes the security more than two years after the date set for surrender or presentation or the date on which such performance became due;

(5) Section 57 - an unauthorized signature on a security prior to or in the course of issue is ineffective except that the signature is effective in favour of a purchaser for value and without notice of the lack of authority if the signing has been done by (a) an authenticating trustee, registrar, transfer agent or other person entrusted by the issuer with the signing of the security or of similar securities or their immediate preparation for signing; or (b) an employee of the issuer or person referred to in (a) who in the ordinary course of business handles the security;

(6) Section 58 - where a security contains the signatures necessary to its issue or transfer but is incomplete in any other respect (a) any person may complete it by filling in the blanks as authorized; and (b) even though the blanks are incorrectly filled in, the security as completed is enforceable by a purchaser who took it for value and without notice of such incorrectness; and a completed security that has been improperly altered, even though fraudulently, remains enforceable but only according to its original terms;

(7) Section 60 - upon delivery of a security, the purchaser acquires the rights in the security that his transferor had or had actual authority to convey except in certain circumstances where a purchaser has been a party to any fraud or illegality affecting the security or as a prior owner had notice

of an adverse claim; moreover, a bona fide purchaser in addition to acquiring the rights of a purchaser also acquires the security free of any adverse claim.

(8) Sections 61-62 - a purchaser of a security, including a broker for the seller or purchaser, is charged with notice of an adverse claim if (a) the security, whether in bearer or registered form, has been endorsed "for collection" or "for surrender" or for some other purpose not involving transfer; or (b) the security is in bearer form and has on it a statement that it is the property of a person other than the transferor but the mere writing of a name on a security is not to be deemed such a statement; notice that a security is held for a third person or is registered in the name of or endorsed by a fiduciary does not give rise to a duty to inquire into the rightfulness of the transfer and is not notice of an adverse claim, except where the purchaser knows that the transaction is in breach of a fiduciary duty; an event that creates a right to immediate performance of the principal obligation evidenced by a security or that sets out a date on or after which a security is to be presented or surrendered for redemption or exchange does not of itself constitute notice of an adverse claim except in the case of a purchase (a) after one year from any date set for such presentment or surrender for redemption or exchange; or (b) after six months after any date set for payment of money against presentation or surrender of the security if funds are available for payment on that date;

(9) Section 64 - when a security in registered form has been delivered to a purchaser without a necessary endorsement, he may become a bona fide purchaser only as of the time the endorsement is supplied, but against the transferor the transfer is complete upon delivery and the purchaser has a specifically enforceable right to have any necessary endorsement supplied;

(10) Section 65 - an endorsement of a security in registered form is made when the appropriate person (as defined in s. 65) signs on it or on a separate document an assignment or transfer of the security or a power to assign or transfer it or when the signature of such person is written without more upon the back of the security; an endorsement of a security may be (a) in blank, including to bearer; or (b) a special endorsement specifying the person to whom the security is to be transferred or who has the power to transfer it and a holder may convert an endorsement in blank into a special endorsement;

(11) Section 66 - an endorsement of a security whether special or in blank does not constitute a transfer until delivery of the security on which it appears or, if the endorsement is on a separate document, until the delivery of both the document and the security;

(12) Section 67 - an endorsement of a security in bearer form may give notice of an adverse claim under s. 61 but otherwise does not affect any right to registration that the holder has;

(13) Section 69 - any person guaranteeing a signature of an endorser of a security warrants that at the time of signing (a) the signature was genuine; (b) the

signer was an appropriate person (as defined in s. 65) to endorse; and (c) the signer had legal capacity to sign, but the guarantor does not otherwise warrant the rightfulness of the particular transfer; a person by guaranteeing an endorsement of a security warrants not only the signature but also the rightfulness of the transfer in all respects but no issuer may require a guarantee of endorsement as a condition to registration of transfer;

(14) Section 70 - delivery to a purchaser occurs when he or a person designated by him acquires possession of a security or his broker acquires possession of a security specially endorsed to or issued in the name of the purchaser and in certain other specified circumstances as more particularly set out in s. 70;

(15) Section 73 - unless otherwise agreed, a transferor is required on demand to supply a purchaser with proof of his authority to transfer or with any other requisite that is necessary to obtain registration of the transfer of a security;

(16) Section 76 - where a security in registered form is presented for transfer, the issuer is under a duty to register the transfer as requested if (a) the security is endorsed by the appropriate person (as defined in s. 65); (b) reasonable assurance is given that the endorsement is genuine (as defined in s. 48) and effective; (c) the issuer has no duty to inquire into adverse claims or has discharged such duty; (d) any applicable law relating to the collection of taxes has been complied with; (e) the transfer is rightful or is to a bona fide purchaser; and (f) any applicable certificate fee has been paid; where an issuer is under a duty to register a transfer of a security, the issuer is liable to the person presenting it for registration for loss resulting from any unreasonable delay in registration or from failure or refusal to register the transfer;

(17) Section 77 - for the purpose of obtaining reasonable assurance that each necessary endorsement on a security is genuine and effective, the issuer may require a guarantee of the signature of the person endorsing and may also require (a) where the endorsement is by an agent, reasonable assurance of authority to sign; (b) where the endorsement is by a fiduciary, evidence of appointment or incumbency; (c) where there is more than one fiduciary, reasonable assurance that all who are required to sign have done so; and (d) in any other case, assurance that corresponds as closely as practicable to the foregoing;

(18) Section 78 - an issuer to whom a security is presented for registration has a duty to inquire into adverse claims if (a) written notice of an adverse claim is received at a time and in a manner that affords the issuer a reasonable opportunity to act on it before the issuance of a new, reissued or reregistered security and the notice discloses the name and address of the claimant, the registered owner and the issue of which the security is a part; or (b) the issuer is deemed to have notice of an adverse claim from a document that it obtained under s. 77(7), namely a copy of a will, trust or partnership agreement, by-law or similar document, in response to a demand for additional assurance; except in the foregoing circumstances

an issuer has no duty to inquire into adverse claims, and provided further that a written notice of an adverse claim received by an issuer is effective for only twelve months from the date when it was received unless the notice is renewed in writing; an issuer may discharge a duty of inquiry by any reasonable means, including notifying an adverse claimant by registered mail sent to the address furnished by him (or, in default, his resident or regular place of business) that the security has been presented for registration by a named person and that the transfer will be registered unless within thirty days from the date of mailing the notification either (a) the issuer is served with a restraining order or other order of a court; or (b) the issuer is provided with an indemnity bond sufficient in the issuer's judgment to protect the issuer and any registrar, transfer agent or other agent of the issuer from any loss which it or they may suffer by complying with the adverse claim;

(19) Section 80 - where a security has been lost, apparently destroyed or wrongfully taken and the owner fails to notify the issuer of that fact by written notice of adverse claim within a reasonable time after he knows of the loss, destruction or taking and if the issuer has registered a transfer of the security before receiving such notice, the owner is precluded from asserting against the issuer any claim to a new security; if the owner makes his request before the issuer has notice that the security has been acquired by a bona fide purchaser, furnishes the issuer with a sufficient indemnity bond and satisfies any other reasonable requirements imposed by the issuer, the issuer is required to replace the original security; if, after the issue of a new security, a bona fide purchaser of the original security presents it for registration of transfer, the issuer is required to register the transfer unless registration would result in an over-issue in which event the issuer's liability is governed by s. 52 and in addition to any rights on an indemnity bond, the issuer is entitled to recover the new security from the person to whom it was issued or any person taking under him except a bona fide purchaser;

(20) Section 81 - an authenticating trustee, registrar, transfer agent or other agent of an issuer has in respect of the issue, registration of transfer and cancellation of a security of the issuer a duty to the issuer to exercise good faith and reasonable diligence; and has the same obligations to the holder or owner of a security and the same rights, privileges and immunities as the issuer.

Subject to any applicable law relating to the collection of taxes, an executor, administrator, heir or legal representative of the heirs, of the estate of a deceased security holder is entitled to become, or to designate, a registered holder if he deposits with the corporation or its transfer agent the original or duly certified copy of probate or letters of administration (or an authenticated copy of a notarial will) together with an affidavit or declaration of transmission, the security certificate duly endorsed, if required, and any assurance under s. 77 required by the corporation (s. 51(7)).

Share certificates and registers

It is provided in the federal Act that every security holder is entitled at his option to a security certificate complying with the Act or a non-transferable written acknowledgement of his right to obtain the same in respect of the securities of that corporation; a fee of not more than $3 may be charged for the issuance of a security certificate (s. 49(1) and (2)). Each share certificate issued by a corporation is to state thereon the following: the name of the corporation, the words "Incorporated under the *Canada Business Corporations Act*", the name of the person to whom it is issued, and the number and class of shares and the designation of any series represented by the certificate. The failure to note a restriction on transfer or certain other matters on a share certificate renders the restriction ineffective against a transferee who took without actual knowledge. Apart from the restriction on transfer (except with respect to constrained share corporations), these are: liens in favour of the corporation, a unanimous shareholder agreement or an endorsement that a shareholder is a dissenting shareholder pursuant to the provisions of s. 190. If the corporation is continued under the Act and the words "private company" appear on the certificate the words are deemed to be notice of a restriction as above provided. The rights, privileges, restrictions and conditions attaching to each class and series are to be legibly stated thereon or a statement made that there are such rights, privileges, restrictions or conditions and that a copy thereof will be furnished on demand to a shareholder without charge. Except in the case of fractional shares or rights or script, each certificate must bear a manual signature of a director or officer of the corporation or of the registrar, transfer agent or branch transfer agent of the corporation. Any additional signatures may be printed or otherwise mechanically reproduced; the fact that the person whose signature is reproduced is no longer in office does not affect the validity of the certificate (s. 49).

Under the federal Act bearer share certificates are not possible (except in the case of script or fractional shares) since a share certificate by virtue of s. 49(7) is required to state the name of the person to whom it was issued. However, it would appear that there is nothing in the Act to prevent the issue of bearer share warrants entitling the holder thereof on presentation to the corporation to shares therein specified. Such a bearer share warrant could have coupons attached for the payment of dividends. It will be observed in this regard that s. 49(1) which entitles a security holder to a security certificate complying with the Act or a non-transferable written acknowledgement of his right to obtain such a security certificate is not phrased in terms which would prohibit the corporation from issuing bearer share warrants, which of course are transferable by delivery. See also s. 187(9).

A corporation is required to maintain a securities register in which it records the securities issued by it in registered form showing, with respect to each class or series of securities, the names alphabetically arranged and the last known address of each person who is or has been a security holder, the number of securities held by him and the date and particulars of the issue and transfer of each security; branch securities registers may be kept at any place in or outside of Canada designated by the directors and the central securities registers are to be maintained by the corporation at its registered office or at any other place in Canada designated by the directors; the corporation may appoint agents to maintain the central securities register and branch securities register. The central securities register is to contain particulars of the securities registered in a branch securities register (s. 50)).

Restrictions on transfer

The general rule is that if the right to transfer shares of a corporation is to be restricted, a statement to that effect and a statement as to the nature of such restrictions is to be contained in the articles (s. 6(1)(d)). Except where its transfer is restricted and noted on a security in accordance with s. 49(8), a security is a negotiable instrument (s. 48(3)). If a security certificate issued by a corporation, or by a body corporate before it was continued under the Act, is or becomes subject to a restriction on its transfer other than a constraint under s. 174, a lien in favour of the corporation, a unanimous shareholder agreement or an endorsement under s. 190(10), such restriction, lien, agreement or endorsement, is ineffective against a transferee of the security who has no actual knowledge of it unless it or a reference to it is noted conspicuously on the security certificate (s. 49(8)).

The legal position is dealt with below under the following headings: "General rules relating to shares of public corporations"; "Constrained share corporations"; "Shares of a shareholder who is indebted to the corporation"; "Shares in private corporations".

Under the provisions of the former Acts, there were provisions in effect prohibiting transfers of shares which were not fully paid without the consent of the directors.

The authorities with respect to these former provisions are no longer applicable since shares may now not be issued unless they are fully paid (see s. 25(3) and the comment thereon, *supra*). The old authorities provided that an express consent was not necessary but could be inferred by the way the shares were dealt with in the corporation's books. The principal grounds in exercising the discretion of the directors was whether a transferee was of less pecuniary responsibility than the transferor. If, however, the transferee was financially able to pay up the shares it was difficult to justify any refusal. It will be noted that the former provisions did impose liability on the directors if they consented to a transfer of partially paid shares to a person who was apparently not of sufficient means to pay up the shares fully.

General rules relating to shares of public corporations

Where a corporation has issued shares which are or were part of a distribution to the public and remain outstanding in the hands of more than one person, it cannot have a restriction on the issue, transfer or ownership of any of its shares except by way of a constrained share as provided by s. 174 (s. 49(9)).

If none of the issued shares of a corporation were part of a distribution to the public, then restrictions on transfer of the type indicated above may be made. However, there must be a conspicuous notation of the particular restriction on the share certificate itself if it is to be effective against a transferee without notice. Thus, a statement printed on a certificate that a corporation has a lien on a share registered in the name of a shareholder for debts of the shareholder to the corporation would be valid as against a transferee without any knowledge of whether there was a lien or the amount of it.

Such a restriction can be applicable to the shares of a public corporation provided the necessary requisites are met (and no issued shares were part of a distribution to the public) but it is more usual in the case of a private corporation.

In *Canada National Fire Insurance Co. v. Hutchings*, [1918] A.C. 451, a case decided with reference to a corporation incorporated under Part II of the Act then in force, in which it was held that a by-law giving the directors unrestricted power to disapprove transfers was *ultra vires*, Sir Walter Phillimore in discussing the sections of that Part said at p. 456:

> The latter section provides that stock shall be personal estate and transferable. No doubt the stock is transferable "in such manner only, and subject to such restrictions and conditions as are prescribed by this part "(of the Act)", or by the special Act or by the by-laws of the company" (s. 138). This provision, however, is not to be construed as empowering the company to make restrictive by-laws. The power to make by-laws is in s. 132, and it is confined in this matter to by-laws regulating " . . . the transfer of stock." Regulation does not mean restriction, still less subjection, to an arbitrary veto.

It was pointed out in the same case, at p. 458, that directors have a discretion in certain matters affecting transfers, including the right to take precautions against forged transfers; in the case of a deceased or bankrupt shareholder, the right to see that the title has duly devolved upon the transferor; the right to require a transfer in the prescribed form or satisfactory explanation and indemnity if the form is departed from; the right to refuse to register a transfer to an alien enemy; the right to exact a reasonable fee; and generally to see to matters of title and conveyance.

In *Ontario Jockey Club v. McBride*, [1927] A.C. 916 at 924, the Judicial Committee stated that it was unnecessary to consider whether the above decision extended beyond the question actually decided, that is, that the by-law in issue giving the directors an unrestricted power to disapprove transfers was *ultra vires*. See also *Emerson v. Provincial Secretary-Treasurer*, [1941] 2 D.L.R. 232 (N.B. C.A.) (New Brunswick close corporation).

Shareholders may, however, contract for value to submit to any reasonable restriction on the right to transfer shares which they choose to agree to; and while a restriction absolutely precluding the transferability of shares may be invalid, one which only gives a right of pre-emption is valid: *Ontario Jockey Club Ltd. v. McBride*, [1927] A.C. 916 at 923. Such a restriction, if notice thereof is given in the certificate, entitles the directors to refuse a transfer accompanied by the certificate bearing such notice. A copy of the agreement should be printed on the reverse side of the certificate and referred to on the face of the certificate. As a further precaution it is sometimes required that each transferee should become a party to the restrictive agreement by signing it or an agreement in like form on the reverse side of the certificate issued to him.

The importance of notice of the agreement is illustrated by *Re Belleville Driving & Athletic Association* (1914), 31 O.L.R. 79 (C.A.), where an agreement had been entered into by the incorporators before the issue of the letters patent to the effect that no shares should be transferred without the consent of the shareholders; a similar agreement it was alleged had been entered into between the shareholders and the corporation and by each shareholder with the others. It was held that there was no consideration for such an agreement on the part of the corporation, that agreements of such a nature between the shareholders did not attach to the shares the incident of non-transferability without the consent of all the shareholders so as to permit the corporation to refuse to register a transfer, and that the only remedy for a breach of such agreements was an action for damages, or, possibly, an injunction to restrain a threatened breach. The distinction between a restriction imposed by agreement and one appearing in the articles of association of the corporation, which has been held in English cases to be valid, is explained by Meredith C.J.O. at pp. 85 and 86 of the report, as follows:

> In the latter case the agreement forms part of the very constitution of the company, and every one who deals with the company or with respect to shares in it has an opportunity of examining it; while in the former it is a collateral agreement and is not embodied in its constitution, and such a person would have no means of knowing of its existence.

In *Barnard v. Duplessis Independent Shoe Machinery Co.* (1907), 31 Que. S.C. 362, an agreement signed by all the shareholders, engaging that before any sale of shares they should first be offered to certain individuals, was held to be binding only on the shareholders individually. The corporation being a stranger to the agreement could not enforce it.

A donee of shares agreed that she would not during a specified period dispose of any of the shares and executed in favour of nominees transfers of certain of the shares absolute in form. The transferees alleged that the transfers were made on condition that they should hold the shares as trustees for the transferor and transfer the shares to the transferor on demand. An interim injunction restraining the corporation from registering the transfers was continued to the trial, it being held that the question involved was not proper to be determined on a motion: *Simpson v. Gillespie* (1930), 38 O.W.N. 103 at 260.

Where under the governing Act or the articles of association the directors have a discretionary power to register transfers, the discretion must be exercised in a reasonable manner: *Poole v. Middleton* (1861), 29 Beav. 646; *Re London & Birmingham Banking Co.* (1865), 34 Beav. 332; and with reasonable promptitude: *In re Ceylon Land & Produce Co.; Ex parte Anderson* (1891), 7 T.L.R. 692.

A power of this kind is a fiduciary power to be exercised for the benefit of the corporation: *Re Coalport China Co.*, [1895] 2 Ch. 404 (C.A.); *Upton v. Hutchinson* (1899), 2 Que. P.R. 300; *Re Peterborough Cold Storage Co.* (1907), 14 O.L.R. 475.

Where the directors have a discretionary power to decline to register transfers, the secretary, in the absence of authority from them to register transfers at once, is not entitled to do so and the directors may refuse to pass a transfer so registered: *Chida Mines Ltd. v. Anderson* (1905), 22 T.L.R. 27.

Directors cannot refuse to register transfers of shares to nominees to increase the voting power of a shareholder unless there is express power to decline: *In re Stranton Iron & Steel Co.* (1873), L.R. 16 Eq. 559.

As to transfers on the eve of liquidation, see *Alexander Mitchell's Case* (1879), 4 App. Cas. 548; *Rutherfurd's Case,* ibid.; *Nelson Mitchell's Case,* ibid., 624.

For the position of a shareholder following dissolution of a corporation, see s. 226(4) and the comment thereon in Chapter 14; a shareholder receiving property on dissolution may be liable to a person claiming against the corporation as to the amount received by him; an action to enforce such liability must be brought within two years following the date of the dissolution of the corporation concerned.

Constrained share corporations

A corporation, any of the issued shares of which are or were part of a distribution to the public and remain outstanding and are held by more than one person, may by special resolution amend its articles to constrain the issue or transfer of its shares in accordance with the regulations to persons who are not resident Canadians or to enable the corporation or any of its affiliates to qualify under any prescribed law of Canada or a province to obtain a licence to carry on any business, to become a publisher of a Canadian newspaper or periodical, or to acquire shares of a financial intermediary as defined in the regulations. A corporation may likewise constrain the transfer of shares of any class or series (or limit the number or shares to be held by non-Canadians) in order to assist the corporation or any of its affiliates or associates to qualify under any prescribed law of Canada or a province to receive licences, permits, grants, payments or other benefits by reason of attaining or maintaining a specified level of Canadian ownership or control; provided that a constraint on the transfer of shares of any class or series of which any shares are outstanding is not permitted unless, in the case of a constraint in respect of a class, the shares of the class, or, in the case of a constraint in respect of a series, the shares of the series are already subject to a constraint permitted under that paragraph (s. 174(1)-(3)). Any constraint imposed may be changed or removed by special resolution amending the articles accordingly; if a special resolution affecting an amendment to impose a constraint so provides, the directors may revoke such resolution before it is acted upon without further approval of the shareholders (s. 174(4), (5)). Regulations have been made pursuant to s. 174(6) with respect to the matters listed pertaining to a corporation that constrains the issue or transfer of its shares. An issue or a transfer of a share or an act of a corporation is valid notwithstanding any failure to comply with s. 174 or regulations thereunder (s. 174(7)).

Sections 46 and 47 of the federal Act provide that where constrained shares are owned contrary to the constraints applicable thereto as determined by the directors, the corporation may sell such shares. The shares to be selected for sale are to be selected by the directors acting in good faith and in a manner not unfairly prejudicial to and not disregarding the interests of the holders of the shares in the constrained class taken as a whole. The proceeds of the sale constitute a trust fund in favour of the shareholder whose shares are sold.

Shares of a shareholder who is indebted to the corporation

It was held in *McMurrich v. Bond Head Harbour Co.* (1852), 9 U.C.Q.B. 333 that there was no common law lien for general indebtedness to the corporation.

When there was no express statutory provision entitling the directors to decline to permit the registration of any transfer of shares belonging to a shareholder who is indebted to the corporation, a power to enact such a by-law might be inferred from the general words of the governing Act authorizing the directors to regulate the transfer of shares: *Montgomery v. Mitchell* (1908), 18 Man. R. 37; *Box v. Bird's Hill Sand Co.* (1913), 12 D.L.R. 556 at 559 (Man. C.A.). In *Re McKain & Canadian Birkbeck Investment Co.* (1904), 7 O.L.R. 241 at 247 it was held that a by-law creating such a lien will not affect a purchaser in good faith who had no knowledge of the by-law, but some doubt was cast on this decision by Meredith C.J.O. in *Re Belleville Driving & Athletic Association* (1914), 31 O.L.R. 79 (C.A.). The purchaser's claim to have the transfer recorded may be defeated by reason of the by-law if he has notice of the lien before the execution of the transfer and the making of payment: *Box v. Bird's Hill Sand Co., supra.*

In *Montgomery v. Mitchell, supra*, it was held that the corporation can assert its lien against an execution creditor of the shareholder; so also the lien may be asserted against a person deriving title from an assignee for the benefit of creditors: *Box v. Bird's Hill Sand Co., supra.*

It would appear, where proceedings are necessary to enforce the lien, that the proper procedure is by way of action. See *New London & Brazilian Bank v. Brocklebank* (1882), 21 Ch. D. 302 (C.A.). A provision in the by-laws to the effect that the lien should be enforceable by forfeiture for debts due by the shareholder generally is invalid as involving an illegal reduction of capital and a clog on the equity of redemption: *Hopkinson v. Mortimer, Harley & Co.*, [1917] 1 Ch. 646. An injunction may be granted restraining the shareholder from selling or transferring the shares in respect of which the lien is claimed: *Walkerton Binder Twine Co. v. Higgins* (1902), 1 O.W.R. 403 (lien for amount owing on the shares).

As to when the corporation will be estopped from asserting its lien, see *Cook v. Royal Canadian Bank* (1873), 20 Gr. 1; *Lazard Bros. & Co. v. Union Bank of Canada* (1920), 47 O.L.R. 76 and 608 (C.A.) (failure by a bank which had a lien on some of its own shares to disclose this to a person the bank knew to be making advances to the shareholder on the security of the shares); *Bradford Banking Co. v. Briggs* (1886), 12 App. Cas. 29; *Rearden v. Provincial Bank of Ireland*, [1896] 1 Ir. 532. The lien of a bank on the shares in its own capital stock for any debt to the bank provided for in a former *Bank Act* does not lapse if the bank neglects to sell the shares within twelve months after the debt has accrued and become payable: *Re Bernier & Provincial Bank of Canada*, [1940] 4 D.L.R. 574.

An amendment of the letters patent, supplementary letters patent or by-laws conferring the power on the directors to decline to permit the registration of a transfer of fully paid shares belonging to a shareholder who is indebted to the corporation may be effective notwithstanding that the indebtedness was incurred prior to the amendment: *Allen v. Gold Reefs of West Africa Ltd.*, [1900] 1 Ch. 656 at 672 (C.A.); *Batu Pahat Bank Ltd. v. Tan Keng Tin (a Bankrupt)*, [1933] A.C. 691.

The indebtedness of the shareholder must exist at the time when the transfer is executed, and the fact that the shareholder has become indebted to the corporation before the application for registration by the transferee does not justify a refusal by the directors to register: *Re Polson Iron Works Ltd.* (1912), 4 D.L.R. 193. So where there was no evidence that the shareholder's liability to the corporation existed at the time of an assignment of the shares by way of security, the assignee was entitled under the assignment to a charge in priority to the rights of the corporation, which had seized the shares in execution of a judgment subsequently obtained against the shareholder: *Bank of N. T. Butterfield & Son Ltd. v. Golinsky*, [1926] A.C. 733. When the registered shareholder is a trustee, the corporation does not have a lien on the shares for the debt of the *cestui que trust*: *Re Perkins* (1890), 24 Q.B.D. 613 (C.A.). Even where the governing Act provides that no notice of any trust shall be entered on the register and the articles state that the corporation shall not be bound to recognize any equitable interest, the corporation, in the face of actual notice that the registered shareholder is not the beneficial owner, cannot make advances to the shareholder and assert a lien on the shares against the beneficiaries: *Mackereth v. Wigan Coal & Iron Co.*, [1916] 2 Ch. 293. The lien may be discharged by waiver, by agreement or by any arrangement between the corporation and the shareholder, the terms of which are incompatible with the continuance of the lien. Any such arrangement must indicate the intention of the parties that the lien is no longer to be enforced. An agreement by a corporation with a shareholder indebted to it that the corporation might sell certain of his shares without notice is not sufficient to warrant the inference that the corporation is abandoning its lien on his other shares: *Bank of Africa Ltd. v. Salisbury Gold Mining Co.*, [1892] A.C. 281.

A corporation may accept a deposit of its own shares by way of pledge as collateral security for indebtedness of a shareholder to it on the terms of an agreement under which the corporation cannot enforce the obligation by selling or otherwise dealing with the shares or suing on the obligation; such a transaction does not involve any trafficking by the corporation in its shares or any question of unauthorized reduction of capital: *British American Timber Co. v. Ray W. Jones*, [1944] 2 D.L.R. 481 (B.C. C.A.).

Shares in private corporations

A private corporation is a corporation where, pursuant to its articles of incorporation or articles of amendment, the right to transfer its shares is restricted and in addition the number of its shareholders exclusive of present or former employees can be no more than 50 and any invitation to the public to subscribe for securities of the corporation is prohibited. Various types of restrictions on transfer are discussed below.

Provisions restricting the transfer of shares must be so construed as not unreasonably to prevent shareholders from enjoying a fair and reasonable exercise of their powers as members of the corporation: *In re Hobson, Houghton & Co.*, [1929] 1 Ch. 300 at 304. Restrictions on the transfer of shares are not repugnant to the absolute ownership of the shares nor does the rule against perpetuities apply to such restrictions: *Borland's Trustee v. Steel Bros. & Co.*, [1901] 1 Ch. 279 at 288.

Restrictions on transfer may or may not apply to shares transmitted on the death of a holder to his personal representative, and if it is desired to control such a transmission it should be so stated in plain terms in the articles of the corporation: *Moodie v. Shepherd (Bookbinders) Ltd*, [1949] 2 All E.R. 1044 (H.L.).

Notwithstanding a complete failure to comply with the applicable restrictions on transfer, a purchaser of shares who had paid the full consideration therefor obtained an equitable right in the shares, which was held to prevail over the equitable right therein subsequently obtained by a judgment creditor of the selling shareholder under a charging order: *Hawks v. McArthur*, [1951] 1 All E.R. 22.

It is doubtful whether the corporation is bound to recognize any equitable or other interest claimed by a person other than the registered owner where restrictions on transfer exist: *Re Champion & White Ltd.*, [1943] 1 D.L.R. 283 at 287; but see the same case on appeal, [1943] 2 D.L.R. 145 (B.C. C.A.). In *Taylor v. Borger* (1964), 44 D.R.L. (2d) 605 (Alta. C.A.) the defendant shareholder agreed to purchase further shares in a private corporation. The price was to be paid in instalments, shares that had been fully paid for being released at the end of each year. Full voting rights from the date of the agreement were to be vested in the defendant. The directors refused to approve the purchase and the defendant purported to repudiate the agreement on the grounds of such refusal. The directors then approved the transfer and the plaintiffs commenced an action on the agreement. On appeal from a decision in favour of the plaintiffs the defendant argued that the voting rights could be exercised only if the shares were registered in his name. In dismissing the appeal the court held that it was not necessary for the shares to be registered in the defendant's name for him to be able to vote them since a proxy could be given to the defendant. It was therefore not necessary to imply that registration was either a term or a condition precedent of the agreement. Where the restrictions on transfer do not contemplate or permit the transfer of shares by way of security and the lender's nominees have been registered as the holders in contravention of such restrictions, the lender cannot make an effective sale of the shares or of the equitable interest therein: *Hunter v. Hunter*, [1936] A.C. 222.

Where the articles of a private corporation provided that the directors would purchase the shares of any member desirous of transferring his shares, it was held that the articles constituted an enforceable contract between the members of the corporation and thus, in an action to enforce the provision, the directors could be sued as members and there was no need to join the corporation as a party defendant: *Rayfield v. Hands*, [1958] 2 All E.R. 194.

An allotment made to nominees of a vendor pursuant to direction, where the contract entitles the vendor to require allotment to his nominees, is not a transfer of the shares so as to be subject to restrictions on a "sale or other disposition": *MacDougall v. Johnson*, [1946] 4 D.L.R. 412 (subsequent direction to allot to other nominees carried out by cancelling certificate in vendor's name and issuing others to nominees).

(1) Transfers requiring the consent of the board of directors

A common restrictive position is to the effect that shares shall not be transferred without the consent of the board of directors. Such a provision is valid: *Re Phillips and La Paloma Sweets Ltd.* (1921), 51 O.L.R. 125.

Where it was provided by the articles that shares should not be transferred without the consent of the directors, it was held that it was not necessary that the consent should be obtained before the execution of the transfer, but that it was sufficient if given prior to the completion of the transaction: *In re Copal Varnish Co.*, [1917] 2 Ch. 349. It was further held that the statement that a shareholder has a right to dispose of his shares, subject to any restrictions in the governing instruments, is as applicable to a private corporation as to a public corporation.

Where the charter of a private corporation provided that "the shares of the company shall not be transferred without the consent of the board of directors", the court, in the absence of evidence of *mala fides*, refused a mandatory order directing the directors of the corporation to record a transfer of shares seized by the sheriff under an execution and sold by the sheriff to a third party: *Re Phillips and La Paloma Sweets Ltd., supra.*

Where the restriction gives the directors an "absolute and uncontrolled discretion to refuse to register any transfer of shares", the court will not write into the provisions any limitation other than that a fiduciary power of this kind must be exercised *bona fide* in the interests of the corporation: *In re Smith & Fawcett Ltd.*, [1942] 1 Ch. 304 at 308 (C.A.). In *Robertson v. Daisy Dairy Ltd.*, [1948] 4 D.L.R. 483 at 491; affd [1949] 1 D.L.R. 44 (Ont. C.A.) it was held that the approval by the directors of a transfer which had the effect of shifting control was not open to objection on that ground, there being no evidence that the directors in approving the transfer were acting in other than the best interests of the corporation or that they were motivated by any ulterior motives prejudicial to the minority shareholders. The principle laid down in *Bonisteel v. Collis Leather Co.* (1919), 45 O.L.R. 195 (one-sided allotment with a view to affecting control) was held inapplicable to the approval of the transfer of shares. Where the letters patent of a private corporation provided that "no shares shall be transferred without the express sanction or approval of a majority of the directors", the Ontario Court of Appeal would not interfere with the action of the directors in refusing to approve a proposed transfer of shares, there being no evidence of bad faith: *Re Bondi Better Bananas Ltd.*, [1951] O.R. 845, approving and following *In Re Smith & Fawcett Ltd., supra.*

In the case of a trustee in bankruptcy, if the directors improperly refuse to register him as a shareholder, he should apply to the court for an order to compel them to do so. *Semble*, it should not be difficult for the trustee to show improper refusal in view of the shares having vested in him: *Re Fox Johnson & Co.*, [1942] 3 D.L.R. 784 at 788.

Where directors have power to refuse to register a transfer they are not bound to give their reasons for refusal if they act *bona fide* and have considered the question: *In re Gresham Life Assurance Society; Ex parte Penney* (1873), L.R. 8 Ch. App. 446; *In re Coalport China Co.*, [1895] 2 Ch. 404. If the provision gives the directors a complete discretion, the fact that the proposed transferee is already a shareholder will not enable him to question the directors' refusal to permit the registration, in the absence of evidence of *mala fides*: *In re Dublin North City Milling Co.*, [1909] 1 I.R. 179.

Where the resolution of the board refusing to permit the transfer specifies only one ground for such refusal, the corporation, on an application to rectify the register, is not restricted to such ground and other grounds are open to the corporation upon such application: *Re Champion & White Ltd.*, [1943] 1 D.L.R. 283 at 286; but see the same case on appeal, [1943] 2 D.L.R. 145 (B.C. C.A.).

The court will be opposed to drawing inferences from affidavit evidence as to the motives of directors in refusing to assent to a transfer: *In re Smith & Fawcett Ltd.*, [1942] 1 Ch. 304 at 308 (C.A.). A plaintiff is entitled to discovery of what one of several branches of the power to refuse the directors acted under, that is, the grounds which give rise to the exercise of the power as distinguished from the reasons which actuated them: *Sutherland (Duke) v. British Dominions Land Settlement Corp.*, [1926] 1 Ch. 746; but if the governing provision states that the directors are not to be bound to specify the grounds upon which the registration of the transfer is declined, discovery to ascertain the species of grounds on which they are acting will be refused: *Berry v. Tottenham Hotspur Football & Athletic Co.*, [1935] 1 Ch. 718.

Where the approval of the board is requisite and a transfer has been registered it may not be necessary to show a direct approval by the board, since such approval may be inferred from entries in the corporation's books: *In re Branksea Island Co.; Ex parte Bentinck* (1888), 1 Meg. 12.

Where the directors have the right to decline registration of a transfer, there must be an active exercise of the power by passing a resolution; and where under the circumstances this could not be done, it was held that the power had not been exercised and the register must be rectified by inserting the name of the transferee: *Re Hackney Pavilion Ltd.*, [1924] 1 Ch. 276; approved and followed by the House of Lords in *Moodie v. Shepherd (Bookbinders) Ltd.*, [1949] 2 All E.R. 1044. In the latter case, one of the two directors of a corporation was prepared to approve a transfer, but the other was not, and it was held that there could not in the circumstances be said to have been any refusal by the board to register the transfer and that it should accordingly be registered.

If the power is for directors to refuse to register transfers if in their opinion it is contrary to the interests of the corporation that the proposed transferee should be a shareholder, a refusal must be on grounds personal to the proposed transferee: *In re Bede Steam Shipping Co.*, [1917] 1 Ch. 123 (C.A.) (illustrations of unjustifiable refusal).

Directors who refused without giving any reason to register a transfer after entering into a contract with the transferee to do what might be reasonably required to cause the shares to be transferred were held to have acted *mala fide* and to have waived the benefit of the article of association giving them a discretion to refuse to register a transfer: *Re Shoal Harbour Marine Service Ltd.* (1956), 20 W.W.R. 312 and 448.

Where a corporation's by-law required the consent of the directors to transfer shares to non-shareholders, it was held that a transfer of preferred shares to a holder of common shares without the consent of the directors was permissible. The by-law could have referred to the class of shareholder but did not: *Nadeau v. Nadeau* (1972), 6 N.B.R. (2d) 512 (Q.B.).

(2) Transfers requiring the consent of the shareholders or of the directors or the shareholders.

In lieu of providing that transfers require the consent of the directors as in (1) above, the restrictions on transfer may require the consent of the shareholders, given in a prescribed manner, to any transfer.

A type of restriction on transfer slightly more elaborate and somewhat more flexible than either of these requires that no shares are to be transferred without either the sanction of the directors or the sanction of the shareholders, the sanction of the directors to be expressed either by a resolution or by an instrument or instruments in writing signed by a majority of the directors and the sanction of the shareholders to be expressed either by a resolution or by an instrument or instruments in writing signed by the holders of a majority of the shares outstanding.

(3) Transfers requiring preliminary offer of shares to existing shareholders

The restrictions may require a shareholder who wishes to dispose of his shares to give the remaining shareholders the right to purchase his shares at a price determined in a specified manner, as for example the fair value thereof determined in accordance with a set formula or by the auditors on a prescribed basis, or at the book value with or without an allowance for goodwill. Alternatively, the restrictions may provide that when a holder desires to sell or transfer any shares (to any person other than a registered shareholder) he must notify the corporation, specifying the number of shares desired to be sold and the price he wishes to obtain therefor, that the corporation is then to offer the shares to other shareholders who may take up the shares at that price *pro rata* to their holdings and that if the shares offered are not accepted by the other shareholders within a specified time, the holder may sell the shares or any of them to any one else at not less than the specified price; but that if such sale is not made within a limited time the shares again become subject to the requirements as to notice to the corporation and an offering to the other shareholders. It is important that such provisions should make it clear whether the other shareholders are to be entitled to take up all or any part of the shares offered or whether, if all the shares are not taken up by the other shareholders, the holder is to be entitled to sell to others the whole block offered or simply those not so taken up.

On the construction of particular articles providing for an offer to the shareholders of shares proposed to be transferred it was held that the offer must be considered as an offer of the whole block of shares specified and could not be accepted unless one or more shareholders agreed to take up the whole number offered. Accordingly, although the articles provided in part that "if the shares or any of them are not so accepted the holders may sell or transfer them or any of them at the same or any higher price . . . to third parties approved by the Board", the whole block offered not having been accepted by shareholders, the holder was entitled to sell all the shares to third parties: *Ocean Coal Co. v. Powell Duffryn Steam Coal Co.*, [1932] 1 Ch. 654. So where the notice of intended sale relates to the whole number of shares offered and not a part, it must be accepted, if at all, as to all the shares offered: *Re Champion & White Ltd.*, [1943] 1 D.L.R. 283 at 286; revd on other grounds [1943] 2 D.L.R. 145 (B.C. C.A.).

In the absence of a provision in the articles of a private corporation to the effect that no sale shall be made at a lower price than the price offered to the existing shareholders until there has been a new offer made at the reduced price, a shareholder, having made an offer which has not been accepted, may sell at any price: *Re Champion & White Ltd., supra.*

In view of the right of transfer inherent in the ownership of shares, a provision restricting the sale or transfer of shares should state clearly whether it is to apply to sales or transfers to both members and non-members: *Greenhalgh v. Mallard*, [1943] 2 All E.R. 234 (C.A.).

Where the restrictions on transfer provided that, before a sale was completed, notice should be given to existing shareholders stating the price and terms at which the shares were to be sold, the British Columbia Court of Appeal held that this provision meant the price and terms at which the shareholder had conditionally agreed to sell the shares to a person other than an existing shareholder: *Re Champion & White Ltd.*, [1943] 2 D.L.R. 145.

The words "first refusal" may mean either the opportunity of refusing a fair and reasonable offer by the owner to sell to the other party, or the opportunity of refusing the price offered by a third party, such price being acceptable to the owner: *Manchester Ship Canal v. Manchester Racecourse Co.*, [1901] 2 Ch. 37 at 48 (C.A.) (a case involving a first refusal to buy land).

Where the articles required a shareholder "desirous of transferring" his shares to notify the corporation so that other shareholders might have the opportunity to purchase the shares, it was held that if a holder had agreed to sell his shares to a person who was not a shareholder and received and retained the sale price, he must be deemed to be "desirous of transferring" and was bound to abide by the articles requiring notification; otherwise the purpose of the articles would be defeated: *Lyle & Scott Ltd. v. Scott's Trustees; Same v. British Investment Trust Ltd.*, [1959] 2 All E.R. 661 (H.L.).

Where the controlling shareholder of a private corporation, the articles of which provided that the shares should not be transferred to an outsider before the shareholders were given an opportunity to buy them, by his will left all his shares to an outsider, the court held that the proposal of the executors that they should use their majority voting power to eliminate the article restricting transfer so that they could give effect to the deceased's will, might legally be carried out provided this was done *bona fide* and in the best interests of the corporation: *Re Leigh; Royal Trust Co. v. Norrie* (1951), 3 W.W.R. (N.S.) 503 (B.C. C.A.).

In *Gaby v. Federal Packaging & Partition Co.*, [1966] S.C.R. 527 shareholders of a private corporation had by agreement the right to buy shares offered for sale in the proportion that their holdings bore to the total holdings of other parties. Pursuant to the agreement, the plaintiff purchased an additional number of shares and received a duly endorsed certificate, but did not then become registered. He held the shares in trust for a third party in part and in part for himself. Subsequently, a further offer of shares was made under the agreement and the plaintiff claimed to be entitled to those shares on the basis of his entire holding including the unregistered share certificate. It was held that the word "shareholder" in the agreement was not limited to registered shareholders. An equitable ownership was sufficient to entitle him to purchase the shares in question on the basis of his equitable rights.

In *Crocker v. Tornroos*, [1957] S.C.R. 151, the articles of association of a private corporation, the shares of which were owned equally by C., D. and T., provided that any shareholder who wished to sell or transfer his shares was required to give written notice to the directors who would thereupon give the other shareholders the first opportunity to purchase the shares. T. died, leaving a will appointing C. one of the executors and providing for investment of his estate in trustee investments only. D.'s shares came up for sale and C. purchased them on his own behalf. In an action brought by T.'s estate claiming that C. failed to exercise the right of pre-emption which enured to the benefit of T.'s estate, the Supreme Court of Canada held that C., in purchasing the shares as he did, was exercising nothing but a contractual right vested in him personally under the articles of association; the fact that the estate could not be a buyer because of the restrictive investment clause in T.'s will was not something for which C. was responsible.

When the shares of a retiring shareholder were to be transferred at the "fair value" which was to be a sum equal to the proportion of the assets of the corporation, exclusive of goodwill, appearing on the books of the corporation to which the shares should be entitled on winding-up, it was held that, in arriving at the fair value, the directors could write off a sum by way of depreciation: *Jacobsen v. Jamaica Times Ltd.* (1921), 90 L.J.P.C. 100.

As to amending the restrictive provisions by enabling the directors to purchase at a fair valuation the shares of any shareholder who is in business competition with the corporation, see *Sidebottom v. Kershaw, Leese & Co.*, [1920] 1 Ch. 154 (C.A.).

Articles of association of a corporation provided that shares might be transferred from one member to another but no shares were to be transferred to a non-shareholder if any shareholder was willing to purchase the shares. A shareholder bequeathed her shares in the corporation to a non-shareholder. The court held that the articles did not prohibit the bequest to the non-shareholder who could have them held in trust by the executors but so long as a shareholder was willing to purchase the shares the articles prohibited the entry of the shares in the non-shareholder's name in the share register: *Harvey v. Harvey*, [1979] 2 W.W.R. 661 (B.C. C.A.).

A requirement that shareholders offer their shares to other shareholders at book value was struck down as the power to regulate shares was held not to include the power to exclude alienation by means of a forced sale at less than market price: *Corporation de Placement Renaud Inc. c. Nor-Mix Ltée.*, [1980] C.S. 980 (Que.).

Voting trusts, pooling agreements and unanimous shareholder agreements

Section 146(1) provides that a written agreement between two or more shareholders may provide that in exercising voting rights the shares held by them shall be voted as therein provided. Section 146(2) provides that an otherwise lawful written agreement amongst all the shareholders of a corporation or among the shareholders and a person who is not a shareholder that restricts, in whole or in part, the powers of directors to manage the business affairs of the corporation is valid. A declaration by the person who is the beneficial owner of all the shares of the corporation which so restricts the powers of the directors is deemed to be a unanimous shareholder agreement under s. 146(3). A unanimous shareholder agreement will bind the transferee of shares unless the transferee has no actual knowledge or if there is no reference thereto on the certificate that was transferred to him (s. 146(4)).

A shareholder, who is a party to a unanimous shareholder agreement, has by virtue of s. 146(5) all the rights, powers and duties of a director of a corporation to which the agreement relates, to the extent that the agreement restricts the powers of directors to manage the business and affairs of the corporation and the directors are thereby relieved of their duties and liabilities including liabilities under s. 119 to the same extent.

Voting trusts

Freedom of transferability of shares of a public corporation may as indicated above be restricted by agreement among the shareholders. Such an agreement may involve a direct restriction on transfer or accomplish the desired result by providing for the transfer of the shares of the agreeing shareholders to a trustee who will hold them on specified trusts or to a holding corporation. Where what is desired is concentration of the voting power attaching to shares in particular hands without loss of the other rights arising from ownership of the shares, the shares may be deposited under a voting trust agreement. Under such an agreement the persons named as voting trustees are entitled to exercise the voting rights attaching to the deposited shares. The persons depositing their shares receive from the voting trustees, or from the depositary named in the voting trust agreement, voting trust certificates in respect of the shares deposited. These certificates evidence the right of the holders thereof to receive, upon the dissolution of the voting trust agreement, certificates for specified numbers of shares. In the meantime the holders of voting trust certificates are entitled to such rights as are given them by the voting trust agreement, under which the shares are deposited and which may include all the rights of shareholders in respect of the deposited shares except the right to vote and the right to transfer the shares as opposed to the voting trust certificates therefor. Voting trust agreements commonly provide that voting trust certificates may be transferred on the registration books of the depositary or the voting trustees. The voting trust agreement will generally provide for its termination on a specified date, or at a time to be determined in a particular manner, and will frequently provide for earlier termination by the voting trustees. It is submitted that the duration of a voting trust should not be such that it offends the rule against perpetuities.

The voting trust agreement may provide for restrictions on the transfer of voting trust certificates. It is submitted that in the case of a private corporation such restrictions should ordinarily be similar to the restrictions on the transfer of the shares of the corporation contained in the letters patent; and that the voting trust agreement should prevent the number of holders of voting trust certificates exceeding the maximum number of shareholders permitted under the statute.

Frequently, the agreement, under which the share certificates are transferred to one or more persons for voting purposes, is of a very informal character. An agreement under which shares were pooled for 18 months was upheld in *Christin v. Blondin* (1922), 60 Que. S.C. 446. See also *Re Sydney & Whitney Pier Bus Service Ltd.*, [1944] 3 D.L.R. 468 at 473 (voting trust agreement not illegal).

A breach of a pooling agreement by one of the parties will not entitle the others to treat the agreement at an end unless the breach is such that the other parties are entitled to conclude that the party committing the breach no longer intends to be bound by the provisions of the agreement: *Reed v. McVeigh*, [1931] 1 W.W.R. 257.

In *Waschysyn v. Kildonan Ice & Fuel Co.*, [1937] 2 D.L.R. 653 (Man. C.A.) an arrangement for adequate consideration under which certain shares were issued to the manager for voting purposes only and to prevent outsiders from obtaining control was supported as being in the nature of a voting trust and a matter of internal management.

In the absence of express authority conferred by the voting trust agreement, the voting trustees are not entitled to exercise their voting rights to terminate the corporation's business by sale: *Re Firstbrook Boxes Ltd.*, [1936] O.R. 15 (C.A.).

Where a voting trust agreement related to shares of two classes and one party to the agreement exchanged shares of one class for shares of the other held by a person who was not a party to the agreement, the shares so acquired by the party to the agreement were held to be subject to the trust to the extent necessary to ensure the voting control contemplated by the agreement: *Turvey v. Lauder* (1956), 4 D.L.R. (2d) 225 (S.C.C.).

Where a voting trust was applicable to both free and escrowed shares, and one of the shareholders transferred free shares for value to his wife in order to avoid the voting trust, the shareholder was held to be obliged to give a proxy for his escrowed shares but not for the shares which he had transferred. See *Milligan v. Bergman* (1978), 7 B.C.L.R. 103 (S.C.).

In *Field v. Bachynski* (1976), 1 A.R. 491 (C.A.) nine founding shareholders of a cable television corporation entered into an agreement constituting a voting trust so that the shareholders could vote as a block at shareholders' meetings. A question arose with respect to voting procedure under the agreement and the question was whether the voting was based on the shareholding of each party. The Court of Appeal held that the situation of the parties to the agreement was analogous to that of a partnership and therefore each party had one vote in accordance with the agreement.

In *Birks c. Birks* (1983), 15 E.T.R. 208 (C.A. Qué.) the question was raised as to whether a voting trust was contrary to the *Civil Code of Quebec*. At the trial court it was found that a voting trust was contrary to the Civil Code, but on appeal it was held that neither jurisprudence nor doctrine suggested that such an agreement would violate rights under the Civil Code and that a separation of voting rights and ownership was permitted by the Civil Code. The fact that the agreement was to last 74 years did not render the agreement void.

Pooling agreements and unanimous shareholder agreements

There have been a number of cases dealing with the question of voting and other rights pursuant to shareholder agreements.

In *Babic v. Milinkovic* (1972), 25 D.L.R. (3d) 752 (B.C. C.A.) an injunction application was brought to restrain wrongful voting pursuant to an alleged shareholder agreement. It was held that the application should be dismissed since doubt as to the duration of the agreement was sufficient on the grounds of convenience to allow the shareholders to vote their shares as they wished until such right could be determined at the trial of the matter. See also *Pizzo v. Crory* (1986), 71 N.S.R. (2d) 419 (T.D.), where damages for breach of a shareholder agreement were allowed.

In *Trimac Limited v. C.I.L. Inc.*, [1987] 6 W.W.R. 66 (Alta. C.A.) a shareholder agreement provided that when one of the shareholders served notice to buy the shares held by the other shareholder at a named price, the recipient of the notice had an option to sell at that price or to buy within a stated period of time the offeree's shares at that same price. Notice was given and the other shareholder responded by saying that it wished to buy the shares held by the shareholder giving the notice, either at the price named or at a price to be determined by the court. The original shareholder giving the notice claimed that the response was not unconditional and therefore was ineffective and that it was therefore entitled to buy the shares in question. The court held that the response was conditional and accordingly the original shareholder was entitled to buy the shares in question subject to other issues pending between the parties.

Thus, in *Ventures West Ltd. v. Bethlehem Copper Corp.* (1980), 23 A.R. 253 (C.A.) a shareholder agreement provided that it was to remain in force while each of the parties owned 30 per cent of the shares or more; one party acquired 50 per cent of the shares and attempted to increase the number of directors to seven, whereas the agreement provided the number of directors was to be limited to five. The agreement was held to be a binding contract for the constitution of the board and an injunction was granted to enforce the same.

In a subsequent decision involving *Trimac Ltd v. C.I.L. Inc.* (1989), 69 Alta. L.R. (2d) 113 (Q.B.), one shareholder had entered into an agreement with a third party for the sale of all shares of the corporation involved and offered to buy the shares of the other shareholder. That other shareholder submitted that the agreement with the third party was, in effect, a sale and furthermore that there was a breach of fiduciary duty by the first shareholder in its failure to disclose the arrangement. It was held that there was no fiduciary duty between the shareholders in the circumstances, and that even if there had been, there was no breach as both parties had acted fairly and honestly in their business negotiations. Furthermore, the agreement with the third party was conditional on the shareholder obtaining all the shares of the corporation in question and was therefore not a sale to a third party within the provisions of the shareholder agreement. See also *Solski v. Haymour* (1989), B.C. C.A. (unreported). The shareholder agreement in question contained a forced buy and sell arrangement. There was an offer made and accepted. The selling party repudiated the agreement and purported to forfeit the deposit on the basis of failure to perform certain conditions of the obligation to complete. The plaintiff sued successfully for his deposit and the appeal was dismissed. It was pointed out that at the time of cancellation the plaintiff was not in breach of his conditions since he had until the closing date to fulfil the same and the other condition was inconsequential and having regard thereto it was not likely that the parties had intended a breach to result in forfeiture of the deposit.

In *Kay v. Poirier & Lawson* (1990), 105 N.B.R. (2d) 395 (Q.B.) a shareholder died and his shares vested in his executor and sole heir. These shares were sold to one of the two surviving shareholders. The third shareholder sought an order preventing the sale of the shares on the grounds that he and the deceased had entered into a standstill agreement regarding the ownership of the shares in the corporation. The shares of the deceased were accordingly subject to a trust in favour of himself. The court dismissed the motion and in effect said that the trustee and legatee were not bound by any standstill agreement which in fact had not been agreed to.

In *Morton v. Asper* (1989), 62 Man. R. (2d) 1 (Q.B.) a shareholder agreement provided that the majority owner was to sell his shares to the other shareholders for the fair market value. The parties were controlling shareholders of various corporations affected by the agreement and were all officers and directors of the corporation being purchased. In negotiating a fair market value the plaintiffs did not disclose certain financial forecasts to the defendant which, if disclosed, might have resulted in a higher negotiated transfer price. The defendant repudiated the agreement and the plaintiffs sought an order for specific performance. The action was dismissed, the court saying that the relationship of the parties went beyond the normal relationship between majority and minority shareholders so as to constitute a fiduciary relationship, they were in fact *de facto* partners. This imposed a duty to make full and fair disclosure of all material facts known to them. The defendant was therefore entitled to expect such disclosure and because of the failure to do so was entitled to repudiate the agreement. See also *Klassen v. Klassen* (1989), 42 B.L.R. 261 (Man.Q.B.); *Canadian Western Natural Gas Co. v. Central Gas Utilities Ltd.*, [1966] S.C.R. 630.

In *Ringuet v. Bergeron*, [1960] S.C.R. 672 a majority of shareholders agreed to elect themselves as directors and vote unanimously, and had a right to call for a transfer of shares on a breach of the agreement. The agreement was held not to be contrary to public policy or to the *Quebec Companies Act*.

Sale of shares

Offer and acceptance

In a transaction for the sale and purchase of shares the ordinary law of contract applies and there must be an offer to purchase and an unqualified acceptance of that offer.

Where a person offers to sell shares and no time is mentioned within which the offer is to be accepted, the offer expires at the end of a reasonable time. The acceptance of the offer must be communicated within such reasonable time, and what constitutes a reasonable time depends largely on the nature of the particular offer and the circumstances of the case: *Nesbitt v. McCartney* (1922), 63 D.L.R. 93 (Alta. C.A.). A vendor, unless the contract fixes the time for the delivery of the shares, must deliver them within a reasonable time, and where unreasonable delay occurs the purchaser may refuse to accept the shares: *De Waal v. Adler* (1887), 12 App. Cas. 141. But if the price be payable by instalments the vendor need not transfer till payment is made in full: *Saunders v. Harvey* (1912), 43 Que. S.C. 54.

Because shares vary in price from day to day, a contract for the sale and purchase of shares is one in which time is of the essence: *Gamble v. Wright* (1927), 31 O.W.N. 482 at 483; affd (1927), 32 O.W.N. 193; but the circumstances may be such as to show that it was not the intention of the parties that time should be of the essence: *Hebb v. Mulock & Newmarket Era & Express Ltd.*, [1945] O.R. 727 (C.A.).

The mere quoting of a price and the giving of the information that the proposed vendor has the shares for sale will not evidence a contract for the sale and purchase of the shares in question. See *Harvey v. Facey*, [1893] A.C. 552; *Blackstock v. Williams* (1907), 6 W.L.R. 79 (C.A.); and *Gillespie v. Sheady*, [1931] S.C.R. 232.

Where employees purchased shares of a corporation on the condition that if they wished to sell the shares or left the corporation's employ, they would resell the shares to the corporation on certain terms, but there was no express covenant on the corporation's part to purchase the shares, the British Columbia Court of Appeal refused to imply an obligation on the corporation to purchase the shares: *Lyle v. Baynes Manning Ltd.* (1957), 21 W.W.R. 42.

For a case in which the plaintiff in an action for damages for non-delivery of shares failed because the corporation never became fully organized, see *Roche v. Johnson* (1916), 53 S.C.R. 18.

When an offer to sell shares is accepted by an agent professedly acting for an undisclosed principal the vendor is not entitled to be informed as to the identity of the principal as a condition of transferring the shares: *Duff v. Rudolph & Lunenburg Gas Co.*, [1929] 4 D.L.R. 813.

An offer to sell shares to the directors of a corporation, being made not to the directors personally but to the board, cannot be accepted by the surviving directors where some of the directors have died: *Reynolds v. Atherton* (1922), 127 L.T. 189.

As to when vendor and purchaser will be held to be *ad idem* where there is a dispute as to identity of the shares agreed to be bought, see *Lindsey v. Heron & Co.* (1922), 50 O.L.R. 1.

In the absence of special agreement, the vendor is not required to give the purchaser any particular shares nor shares standing in the vendor's name: *Maxted v. Paine* (1871), L.R. 6 Ex. 132 at 150, 151; but where the sale is not executory but is made by delivery against cash of a certificate with a transfer executed in blank by the holder named in the certificate, who is not the vendor, then the vendor must be taken to affirm that the *jus disponendi* of the shares is vested in him: *Castleman v. Waghorn, Gwynn & Co.* (1909), 41 S.C.R. 88 at 97. In that case the right to dispose of the shares was not vested in the vendor but in the executors of the deceased holder and the purchaser was entitled to recover the purchase price from the vendor.

If the contract is an entire one for the sale of a specific block of shares, viz., the vendor's own shares, and the vendor has delivered shares which he did not own in full or in part and as to some of which he had no title in order to make up the balance of the block, the purchaser is entitled to resist the vendor's demand for payment which is in effect a claim for specific performance, on the ground of lack of title in the vendor: *McTavish v. Langer*, [1933] 1 D.L.R. 151 (B.C. C.A.).

A representation that shares sold were "treasury shares", when in fact the shares sold were shares of the accused, is a false representation on which the accused may be convicted for false pretences: *Rex v. Jones & Manlove*, [1935] 2 D.L.R. 718 (B.C. C.A.).

Where the managing director of a corporation was authorized by the shareholders to sell the shares held by them to another and in the course of doing so made fraudulent misrepresentations, the selling shareholders, although they had no knowledge of the director's fraud, were held liable for damages to the purchaser of the shares: *Briess v. Woolley*, [1954] A.C. 333.

On a purchase of common shares, subject to a verified statement of assets and liabilities being produced, undeclared arrears of cumulative preferential dividends are a liability within the meaning of the contract: *Fairhall v. Butler*, [1928] S.C.R. 369.

A buyer of shares from a promoter may have an interest in compelling the promoter to carry out his obligations to the corporation. Thus, where a promoter sold a portion of his shares to the defendant and the latter maintained that he had stipulated that the purchase price should be applied by the promoter towards payment of certain liabilities of the corporation and in accordance with his promotion agreement, and the promoter sued the purchaser for payment of the purchase price, the Supreme Court of Alberta *en banc* stayed execution to enable the purchaser to enforce this term of the contract: *Lazier v. MacCullough* (1913), 14 D.L.R. 270 (Alta. C.A.).

After the par value of shares has been reduced and shareholders have been notified to turn in old certificates, in the absence of anything in the statute or the resolution of the shareholders effecting the reduction, a sale may be completed by delivery of the old certificate with transfer endorsed: *Duff v. Rudolph & Lunenberg Gas Co.*, [1929] 4 D.L.R. 813.

Where a government transfer tax is payable by the transferor, he must affix the revenue stamps or otherwise provide for payment of the tax.

Where shares are sold with a right reserved to the vendor to repurchase, a condition that failure to exercise the right within a stipulated time terminates the right must be strictly complied with: *McRae v. Law*, [1936] 2 W.W.R. 60.

Where, under an option to purchase shares, it is provided that the optionee is to take and pay for a specified number of shares on or before a certain date, the optionee must make actual payment or tender, unless the optionor repudiates or it is shown that tender would be useless; where the option states that it is given for value received, the onus of showing that there was no consideration is upon the optionor: *Bishop v. Gray*, [1944] O.W.N. 700 (Ont. C.A.).

Sale of controlling interest

It is a common transaction for one or more owners of a majority of the issued shares of a corporation to sell their shares to a purchaser who desires to obtain the controlling interest in the corporation. For a discussion of the duty of directors to disclose information or the possible liability of the purchaser to make an offer to purchase minority shareholdings, see Chapter 13.

As to the circumstances under which an agreement for sale of control may be dissolved on account of impossibility, see *Lieberman v. Roseland Theatres Ltd.*, [1946] 1 D.L.R. 342.

Vendors of shares should bear in mind that, after the purchaser of a controlling interest has secured the appointment of his nominees as directors, the corporation, at the instance of the new board, may bring an action against the former directors for any wrongful acts committed by them during their term of office: *Ammonia Soda Co. v. Chamberlain*, [1918] 1 Ch. 266 (C.A.) (payment of dividends attacked); *Regal (Hastings) Ltd. v. Gulliver*, [1942] 1 All E.R. 378 (H.L.) (directors required to account for profits on transactions).

As to the binding effect of a convenant not to engage in a similar business given on the sale of control, see *Connors Bros. Ltd. v. Connors*, [1941] 1 D.L.R. 81 at 94 (P.C.).

Registration of transfer after sale

The agreement for sale of shares does not impliedly bind the vendor to procure the registration of the transfer: *Castleman v. Waghorn, Gwynn & Co.* (1909), 41 S.C.R. 88 at 96; *Beaton v. Cooper*, [1938] 2 D.L.R. 191 (Sask. C.A.). His duty is performed when he hands over to the transferee the duly executed transfer together with the certificate or its equivalent: *Skinner v. City of London Marine Insurance Corp.* (1885), 14 Q.B.D. 882 (C.A.); *London Founders Assn. v. Clarke* (1888), 20 Q.B.D. 576 (C.A.); *Fortin v. Hardy* (1938), 44 Rev. Leg. 11; *Davidson v. Brooker* (1924), 27 O.W.N. 195. The transferor, however, is under an implied obligation not to prevent or delay registration of the transfer: *Hooper v. Herts*, [1906] 1 Ch. 549 (C.A.); *Boultbee v. Wills & Co.* (1911), 15 O.L.R. 227.

The seller, moreover, must do all in his power to enable the purchaser to put himself into legal ownership of the shares; if the seller is the transferor he must not object to registration; the seller's obligation is not lessened if he completes the contract by tendering a transfer by another of whom the purchaser knows nothing except that he is the owner of the number of shares contracted to be sold: *Hichens, Harrison, Woolston & Co. v. Jackson & Sons*, [1941] 2 K.B. 176 (C.A.).

In the case of a broker accepting an order from a customer to purchase shares in a private corporation (known by the customer to be such) which cannot be transferred without a resolution of the directors, if the broker accepts the money and agrees to supply the shares, the customer is not obligated to accept an unapproved transfer; the broker's obligation can only be fulfilled by making the customer the owner within a reasonable time and a tender of street certificates is insufficient: *Born v. Premier Investments (Victoria) Ltd.*, [1948] 1 D.L.R. 596 (B.C. C.A.).

The measure of damages for breach of obligation of the transferor not to prevent or delay registration was held in *Hooper v. Herts, supra*, to be the difference between the price at which the purchaser had contracted to resell and the price he afterwards obtained when registered as owner. When the number of shares in question is large, however, other considerations may enter in, as to which see *Hooper v. Herts, supra*, at p. 562.

If the corporation will not register the transfer, the vendor is a trustee for the purchaser and must pay over to him any dividends received on the shares: *Stevenson v. Wilson*, [1907] S.C. 445.

Entitlement to dividends

Where a contract for the sale of shares, not being a contract governed by the rules of a stock exchange as to sale *cum* dividend, is silent as to dividends, a dividend declared after the date of the contract belongs to the purchaser and is not apportionable, notwithstanding that the dividend is declared in respect of a period antecedent to the date of the sale: *Black v. Homersham* (1874), 4 Ex. D. 24; *In re Wimbush; Richards v. Wimbush*, [1940] 1 Ch. 92.

On a sale of shares with an option to re-purchase, the possibility of the payment of a dividend during the option period not having been contemplated or provided for, the court refused to imply a provision entitling the optionee to interim dividends which the optioner was entitled to as incidental to his ownership of the shares: *Herron v. Mayland*, [1928] S.C.R. 225. On the exercise of an option to purchase shares, instalments of dividends declared prior but payable subsequently to the date of the exercise of the option belong to the vendor: *In re Kidner; Kidner v. Kidner*, [1929] 2 Ch. 121.

Purchaser's liability to indemnify seller

Upon a sale of shares there is an implied contract on the part of the buyer to indemnify the seller against any calls or liabilities which may arise in respect of the shares subsequently to the transfer: *Kellock v. Enthoven* (1874), L.R. 9 Q.B. 241; *Levi v. Ayers* (1878), 3 App. Cas. 842. The liability to indemnify is not extinguished by the purchaser passing over the property to another. Thus, where B. agreed to sell to C. shares not paid-up and received a transfer in blank from A. (the registered holder), which he delivered to C., who delivered it to D., for whom the shares had been bought, and D. never became registered as the holder of the shares, but became bankrupt, and subsequently to the transfer to D., calls were made on A., who claimed indemnity from B., in an action by B. against C., B. was held entitled to indemnity: *Spencer v. Ashworth Partington & Co.*, [1925] 1 K.B. 589 (C.A.). The only way in which the purchaser can get rid of the liability to indemnify is by seeing that someone, himself or his nominee, gets registered as the holder of the shares. For, once the transfer is registered, except in the case of winding-up and the former registered holder being placed on the "B" list (in jurisdictions where such liability exists), the registration of the transfer frees the original vendor from liability for calls and leaves the registered holder liable.

Remedies for breach of contract for sale; damages and specific performance

Where a purchaser refuses to accept shares, the vendor can have damages or specific performance: *Helwig v. Siemon* (1916), 10 O.W.N. 296 (C.A.); *McGregor v. Currie* (1914), 31 O.L.R. 261; affd 25 D.L.R. 771 (P.C.); *David v. Dow* (1916), 27 D.L.R. 689 (Alta. C.A.).

The remedy of the buyer for breach of an agreement to transfer is damages, where other shares might have been purchased on the market. In such a case the transferee is not entitled to have the transferor declared a trustee of the shares for him: *Bureau v. Laurencelle* (1913), 11 D.L.R. 283. This case may seem inconsistent with *Stevenson v. Wilson*, [1907] S.C. 445, where it was held that the corporation having refused to register the transferee, while the latter retained the beneficial interest in the shares, the transferor must take the dividends as trustee for the transferee and pay them over to him. *Bureau v. Laurencelle*, however, was a case of shares which were being dealt with on the stock market and which had an assignable money value and therefore it was a case where the purchaser could be adequately compensated in damages.

In a contract for the sale of shares, the measure of damages for breach by reason of failure of the seller to deliver or failure of the buyer to take the shares is the difference between the contract price and the market price at the date of the breach: *Rodocanachi, Sons & Co. v. Milburn Bros.* (1886), 18 Q.B.D. 67 (C.A.); *Jamal v. Moolla Dawood, Sons & Co.*, [1916] 1 A.C. 175; *W.C. Pitfield & Co. v. Jomac Gold Syndicate Ltd.*, [1938] O.R. 427 at 457 (C.A.); and in *Kinkel v. Hyman*, [1939] S.C.R. 364 at 375, Davis J. said:

> Where there is a market in the shares, the proper measure of damages in general is the difference between the contract price and the market price of such shares at the time when the contract was broken, because if the purchaser has the money in his hands he may go into the market and buy.

The damages are not to be reduced on the supposition that the market price would drop if the shares were thrown on the market, the purchaser having the right, if delivery had been made, to market the shares as he sees fit: *W.C. Pitfield & Co. v. Jomac Gold Syndicate Ltd.*, *supra*, at 458; see, however, *Crown Reserve Consolidated Mines Ltd. v. MacKay*, [1941] 3 D.L.R. 461 (Ont. C.A.) where, in a case of judgment for the delivery up of shares, the market being inactive and the only sales at the relevant time being for relatively small amounts of shares, it was held that there was nothing to justify the price obtained on the sale of the small block being taken as a reasonable expectation on a sale of the large block of shares involved. Consideration will not be given to the fact that a purchase of the same number of shares on the market would enhance the price: *Mines Ltd. v. Woodworth*, [1940] 4 D.L.R. 676; revd on other grounds, [1941] 4 D.L.R. 101 (B.C. C.A.); and see as to damages the same case on appeal to the Supreme Court of Canada, [1942] 1 D.L.R. 135 at 141. See also *Bishop v. Gray*, [1944] O.W.N. 700 (C.A.) (proof of real loss or damage requisite).

As to the basis on which damages for non-delivery will be assessed where there is no evidence available of the corporation's shares having a market value, see *Johnson v. Roche* (1915), 24 D.L.R. 305 (N.S. C.A.); revd on other grounds (1916), 53 S.C.R. 18; *In re Bahia & San Francisco Railway* (1868), L.R. 3 Q.B. 584 at 595 (C.A.); *Goodall v. Clarke* (1910), 21 O.L.R. 614; affd (1911), 23 O.L.R. 57 (damages to be ascertained as well as possible on the whole evidence); *Nelles v. Hesseltine* (1911), 2 O.W.N. 643 (fair value determined by the court).

On default by the purchaser there is an obligation on the vendor to minimize the damages by obtaining the best price he can at the date of the breach. He is not bound, however, to reduce the damages by subsequent sales at better prices. If the vendor chooses to retain the shares after the breach, he is not liable to the purchaser for profits if the market rises, and he cannot make the purchaser account for subsequent losses if the market falls: *Jamal v. Moolla Dawood, Sons & Co.*, *supra*.

Where a vendor purported to sell a share as fully paid on which in fact there still remained a liability of 60 per cent, the buyer was held entitled to compel the vendor to pay the balance owing on the share: *Beauchemin v. Richelieu Foundry Co.* (1908), 34 Que. S.C. 261.

Specific performance of an agreement to sell shares may be granted: *W. C. Pitfield & Co. v. Jomac Gold Syndicate Ltd.*, [1938] O.R. 427 (C.A.) (transfer agent also joined); *McDougall Segur Exploration Co. v. Solloway Mills & Co.*, [1931] 2 W.W.R. 516; *Westman v. MacDonald*, [1941] 4 D.L.R. 793 (damages inadequate because shares involved assisted plaintiff in obtaining control). The corporation may be joined as a proper party: *Reardon v. Franklin* (1917), 35 D.L.R. 380; affd (1918), 55 S.C.R. 613. As to joinder of the legal owner in proceedings by a person claiming an equitable interest in shares through assignment, see *Dawson v. Leach*, [1936] 1 D.L.R. 31 (Alta. C.A.), and as to specific performance of an agreement to reassign and transfer shares, see *Lamoureaux v. Simpson* (1911), 20 O.W.R. 287. As to the circumstances under which specific performance of an oral contract to sell and deliver shares may be decreed, see *Eansor v. Eansor*, [1946] S.C.R. 54.

Where the buyer sued for specific performance and claimed damages in addition, and contracts made by the buyer for the resale of part of the shares had been adduced in evidence without objection, judgment was given for specific performance and damages were awarded on the foregoing basis for non-delivery of part of the shares: *W. C. Pitfield & Co. v. Jomac Gold Syndicate Ltd.*, [1938] O.R. 427 (C.A.).

When the vendor is resident out of the jurisdiction, the corporation should be joined: *Duff v. Rudolph & Lunenberg Gas Co.*, [1929] 4 D.L.R. 813. In the same case it was held that specific performance cannot be had where the vendor has sold the shares to a third party who had no notice of the prior agreement.

In *Mines Ltd. v. Woodworth*, [1941] 4 D.L.R. 101 (B.C. C.A.), where the plaintiff had elected to treat a contract for the sale of shares to him as subsisting and claimed specific performance, but was not entitled to specific performance by reason of his not being able, ready and willing to carry out the contract, O'Halloran J.A. held that damages could not be awarded in substitution for specific performance. On a further appeal to the Supreme Court of Canada ([1942] 1 D.L.R. 135) the point of election of remedies was not dealt with.

Specific performance of a contract for the purchase of shares will not be decreed where the directors, having the power to do so, refuse to assent to the transfer, so that the transferee named cannot be put on the register, unless it is a case in which the court can and will compel their assent: *Birmingham v. Sheridan* (1864), 33 Beav. 660.

Where the articles of association of a corporation required that before the sale of certain shares they should first be offered to the board of directors, an objection by an outside purchaser to complete the purchase by reason of non-compliance by the vendor with such article fails, if notice that the shares were for sale was given to the individual directors and the latter took no action towards exercising the right to purchase the shares: *Harvey v. Mitchell* (1914), 20 D.L.R. 134.

When a corporation had agreed to repurchase from the plaintiffs (at a fixed price, on or before a certain date) a block of shares of another corporation, or so many of them as should not have been previously sold or transferred by the plaintiffs, and the plaintiffs sold some and brought action for specific performance of the agreement to buy the balance, it was held that the plaintiffs were bound to make their election and give notice within a reasonable time after the specified date; but the corporation did not plead nor attempt to show that the notice was not given within a reasonable time, therefore it could not be found that the notice was too late: *Grant v. Dominion Loose Leaf Co.* (1925), 56 O.L.R. 508 (C.A.).

In an action for the price of shares, it has been held in Quebec that the plaintiff not having tendered the shares either before or with the action is not a ground for a dilatory exception asking for a stay of the action: *Abitibi Power & Paper Co. v. Smart* (1914), 20 D.L.R. 977. If the share certificates have actually been received and accepted by the purchaser, the vendor's action to recover the purchase price is a common law action to enforce a money demand under a contract to pay money, and the court in such an action is not invested with the discretionary powers which it exercises in actions of specific performance: *McTavish v. Langer*, [1933] 4 D.L.R. 609 (S.C.C.). If in such an action the purchaser sets up as a defence the existence of some legal or equitable ground on which the vendor was precluded from transferring the shares, the onus of proof is on the purchaser.

Criminal liability

Under s. 380(2) of the Criminal Code it is an indictable offence to conspire by deceit or falsehood or other fraudulent means, with intent to defraud, to affect the public market price of shares. In the absence of fraud or misrepresentation, transactions which involve making or maintaining a market may be legitimate, for example, where a pool is formed and those taking part in it agree with a broker to buy any surplus shares remaining after purchases made to maintain the market: *Sanderson & Levi v. British Westralian Mines & Share Corp.* (1898), Times, November 10; affd (*sub nom. Sanderson & Levi v. British Mercantile Mine & Share Co.*) (1899), Times, July 19.

Section 382 of the Criminal Code makes it an indictable offence, through the facility of any stock exchange, curb or other market, with the intent of creating a false or misleading appearance of active public trading in any security or with the intent of creating a false or misleading appearance with respect to the market price of any security, to (a) effect a transaction in such security which involves no change in the beneficial ownership thereof; or (b) enter an order for the purchase of such security with the knowledge that an order of substantially the same size at substantially the same time and at substantially the same price for the sale of any such security has been or will be entered by or for the same or different persons; or (c) enter an order for the sale of any such security with the knowledge that an order of substantially the same size at substantially the same time and at substantially the same price for the purchase of any such security has been or will be entered by or for the same or different persons. If the purpose of the trading is to stabilize the market price in the interest of the traders no offence has been committed: see *R. v. Jay*, [1965] 2 O.R. 471 (C.A.).

Importance of registration of transfer

In the absence of special provision in the governing Act or articles imposing conditions to the contrary, an assignment of shares duly executed by assignor and assignee, for good consideration, with proper notice to the corporation, is valid without further registration: *Crawford v. Provincial Insurance Co.* (1859), 8 U.C.C.P. 263 (C.A.).

Under the Act, registration of the transfer is required to complete it, so as to constitute the transferee a shareholder in the strict sense. Thus, s. 51(1) provides that a corporation may treat the registered holder of a security as the person exclusively entitled to vote and to receive dividends, notices and to exercise other rights and powers of an owner. It is the duty of the transferee to secure registration: *Smith & Osberg Ltd. v. Hollenbeck (No. 2)*, [1939] 4 D.L.R. 119 (B.C. C.A.).

Whether a share register or register of transfers of a corporation has been duly established, is to be determined by the law of the corporate domicile: *National Trust Co. v. Ebro Irrigation & Power Co.*, [1954] O.R. 463.

Even without registration, as between the parties, a transfer is valid: *Philipps v. Cameron Copper Mines Ltd.*, [1959] Que. S.C. 433.

Additional formalities, unless required by the articles or by-laws, are not necessary to make the transfer complete and effective; thus, where the transfer had been registered and the transferee had in fact accepted the shares, signature by the transferee of formal acceptance was held to be unnecessary, not being required by the incorporating Act, charter or by-laws: *Ross v. Machar* (1885), 8 O.R. 417; see also *Woodruff v. Harris* (1850), 11 U.C.Q.B. 490.

The significance of registration or non-registration of a transfer is dealt with further under the following headings: "Share certificates as negotiable instruments"; "Effect of transfer by endorsement in blank"; "Risks of holder of unregistered transfer"; "Estoppel"; and "Trustee in bankruptcy or liquidator claiming against rightful owner".

Share certificates as negotiable instruments

By virtue of s. 48(3) of the federal Act, a share certificate is a negotiable instrument. However, it should be noted that it is not a true negotiable instrument in that, if registered, it is not transferable by delivery. Section 64 provides that where a security in registered form is delivered to a purchaser without a necessary endorsement, the purchaser will become a bona fide purchaser only at the time of endorsement but as against his transferor the transfer is complete on delivery and the purchaser has a specifically enforceable right to have any necessary endorsement supplied. Section 71(2) provides that a transferor's duty to deliver a security under a contract of purchase is not fulfilled until the security is delivered in negotiable form to the purchaser or his designee, or the transferor causes an acknowledgement to be made to the purchaser that the security is held for him.

Under the prior law, it was clear that share certificates, although having some of the qualities of a negotiable instrument, were not negotiable instruments. Thus, see *Longman v. Bath Electric Tramways Ltd.*, [1905] 1 Ch. 646 at 665

(C.A.); and although they may pass by delivery this is subject to the equities: *Smith v. Walkerville Malleable Iron Co.* (1896), 23 O.A.R. 95. In this case the corporation had issued a certificate for shares (not numbered or identified) which stated that the shares were "transferable only on the books of the company in person or by attorney on the surrender of this certificate". This provision was not required either by the statute or the corporation's by-laws. The holder handed the certificate with assignment endorsed to the plaintiff, who gave valuable consideration therefor. The plaintiff failed to apply for registration or to notify the corporation for several months, and in the meantime his transferor transferred the shares for value to an innocent transferee, who got himself registered without production of the certificate. The Court of Appeal held that the plaintiff's equitable title was lost by virtue of the subsequent transfer and registration and that, although the corporation ought to have insisted on the production of the certificate, it was not compelled to so and was not estopped from denying the plaintiff's title.

Section 76 of the federal Act provides that where a security in registered form is presented for transfer, the following criteria must be met and the transfer is to be registered: (1) if it is properly endorsed; (2) reasonable assurance is given as to the genuineness and effectiveness of the endorsement; (3) there is no duty to enquire into adverse claims or any such duty has been discharged; (4) any applicable law relating to the collection of taxes has been complied with; (5) the transfer is rightful or is to a bona fide purchaser; and (6) any required fee has been paid. See *Javelin International Ltd. (Receiver of) v. Hillier* (1988), 40 B.L.R. 249 (Que. S.C.) where the alleged shareholder was not entitled to registration as the shares in question had been issued for inadequate consideration.

The delivery of a share certificate endorsed in blank is not equivalent to a transfer or alienation of the certificate: *Bonner v. Moray* (1914), 23 Que. K.B. 252 (C.A.).

Share certificates are to be distinguished from share warrants. The latter are negotiable instruments and are transferable by delivery: *Webb, Hale & Co. v. Alexandria Water Co.* (1905), 93 L.T. 339.

Effect of transfer by endorsement in blank

It is often inconvenient or impossible for the transferee, or each of successive transferees, to obtain registration as the holder of the shares dealt with. A transfer of shares may, accordingly, be regarded from two standpoints, first, from a commercial standpoint, and, secondly, from a strictly legal standpoint. In commercial practice, particularly on the stock exchange, delivery of shares which have been sold may be effected by delivery of the share certificates endorsed in blank with signature suitably guaranteed, the transfer not to be registered on the books of the corporation unless specially requested. The transfer confers on the holder of the certificate for the time being, authority to fill in the name of the transferee, and each successive holder passes on his authority when he delivers the certificate to his immediate transferee. In general, and subject to statutory provisions, the holder for the time being takes not the property in the shares but a title, legal and equitable, which will enable him to vest himself with the shares without risk of his right being defeated by any other person deriving title from the registered owner: *Colonial Bank v. Cady* (1890), 15 App. Cas. 267; *Smith v. Rogers* (1899), 30 O.R. 256 (C.A.); *Fuller v. Glyn, Mills, Currie & Co.*, [1914] 2 K.B. 168; *Macdonald v. Bank of Vancouver* (1916), 25 D.L.R. 567; *Stern v. The Queen*, [1896] 1 Q.B. 211; *Secretary of State of Canada & Custodian v. Alien Property Custodian for the United States*, [1931] S.C.R. 170 at 183; *Chartered Trust and Executor Co. v. Pagon*, [1950] O.R. 662; *Aitken v. Gardiner & Watson*, [1956] O.R. 589; *Melanson v. McCleave* (1958), 11 D.L.R. (2d) 579.

The existing practice of transfer by endorsement in blank and delivery of the certificate is expressly recognized by s. 71 of the Act; but the person so acquiring shares does not become a shareholder until he has the transfer registered, and a corporation cannot dispense with registration or issue shares expressed to be transferable by delivery: *Re General Company for Promotion of Land Credit* (1870), L.R. 5 Ch. App. 363. Furthermore, before registration, the transferee does not enjoy the right to receive notice of or to vote at meetings of shareholders. He also runs the risk of dividends being collected by the transferor, who, until the transfer is registered, is the only person known to the corporation and, therefore, the person to whom the dividend cheques will be sent.

Where the owner of a certificate endorses it in blank and delivers it to another person—understanding that such person is being given control of the certificate and is thereby enabled to dispose of it—a bona fide purchaser for value without notice who acquires the certificate becomes the owner of the shares represented by the certificate, free from any claim of the former owner; the transfer agent is bound to register the transfer on presentation unless prevented by injunction: *McLeod v. Brazilian Traction Light & Power Co.* (1927), 60 O.L.R. 253.

The rule is that the corporation, on presentation of a certificate in the name of the registered owner with a transfer executed by him, is bound to register the lawful holder and named transferee as owner, notwithstanding that the transfer may have been originally executed in blank. There must, however, be delivery of the certificate by or on behalf of the registered owner. Delivery by the agent or trustee of the registered owner in pursuance of a statute is sufficient: *Secretary of State of Canada & Custodian v. Alien Property Custodian for the United States*, [1931] S.C.R. 170 at 183.

Upon presenting a certificate endorsed in blank to the corporation for registration, the lawful holder of such a certificate need not explain the circumstances under which the certificate came into his possession. He is *prima facie* entitled to be registered on the books of the corporation as a shareholder and to have a new certificate issued to him (so long as he does not require the aid of an illegal transaction to establish that he is the lawful holder): *Coplan v. Coplan*, [1958] O.R. 551 (C.A.).

If there has been no delivery of the endorsed certificate by the owner, the certificate having been lost or stolen, and the certificate itself has not been purchased on the open market but through a clearing agent of the stock exchange and at the time of such acquisition the blank endorsement has been altered so as to put the purchaser on enquiry, the real owner is entitled to have the shares registered in his own name: *Whitehead v. Bridger, Hevenor & Co.*, [1936] 3 D.L.R. 408 (Ont. C.A.).

Where the transferee expects to hold the shares, it is, of course, advisable to have the transfer completed on the books of the corporation.

Risks of holder of unregistered transfer

The holder under an unregistered transfer takes the shares subject to any defect in the title of the person from whom he acquires them, for example, if they had been stolen he would get no title at all. Thus, where share certificates in "street" form were stolen from the owner and eventually delivered to and sold by a firm of stockbrokers, the person from whom they were stolen succeeded in an action of detinue against the brokers who were required to deliver to such person an equal number of shares or pay their value at the date of judgment: *Aitken v. Gardiner*, [1956] O.R. 589. See now, however, s. 72 of the federal Act and the provisions of s. 75 of the Act which provides that an agent or bailee, who in good faith, including the observance of reasonable commercial standards if he is in the business of dealing in securities, has received securities and sold, pledged or delivered them according to the instructions of his principal, is not liable for conversion even if the principal has no right to dispose of them. Section 68(1) provides that the owner of a security may assert the ineffectiveness of an endorsement against the issuer or any purchaser other than a purchaser for value without notice who has received a new security on registration of transfer unless the owner has either ratified the unauthorized endorsement or is otherwise precluded from alleging the ineffectiveness of an unauthorized endorsement. It will be noted that s. 53(b) provides that a signature is presumed to be genuine, but if its effectiveness is challenged, the burden of establishing it to be genuine is on the party claiming under it. See *Javelin International Ltd. (Receiver of) v. Hillier* (1988), 40 B.L.R. 249 (Que. S.C.) where the alleged shareholder was unsuccessful as the shares in question had been issued for inadequate consideration. The decision was based on what is now s. 76 of the Act.

A transferee, who fails to have his transfer registered, may lose his shares by a fraudulent transfer on the books of the corporation by the registered holder to a bona fide purchaser. In such case he has no action against the corporation for allowing the transfer: *Smith v. Walkerville Malleable Iron Co.* (1896), 23 O.A.R. 95; *Guy v. Waterlow Bros. & Layton Ltd.* (1909), 25 T.L.R. 515. See s. 72.

The right to registration does not depend on the possession of the certificate, and where the certificate states that it is transferable only "on surrender of this certificate", the corporation may waive such a provision: *Shropshire Union Railway & Canal Co. v. The Queen* (1875), L.R. 7 H.L. 496 at 509; *Smith v. Walkerville Malleable Iron Co., supra.* Such a note on the certificate is not a representation or contract, but a warning only: *Guy v. Waterlow Bros. & Layton Ltd.* (1909), 25 T.L.R. 515; *Rainford v. James Keith & Blackman Co.*, [1905] 1 Ch. 296; revd on other grounds [1905] 2 Ch. 147 (C.A.).

If a certificate has been lodged with the corporation for transfer, and the corporation by inadvertence returns the certificate to the transferor so as to enable him fraudulently to pledge it to a third person, the corporation is not liable to such third person on the ground that the corporation should have retained the certificate, for it owes no duty of safe custody to the public at large and the negligence is not the immediate cause of the loss: *Longman v. Bath Electric Tramways Ltd.*, [1905] 1 Ch. 646 (C.A.).

As between persons whose rights are equitable only, that is, where neither has perfected his title by registration or acquired an unconditional right to be registered, the title of the person whose equitable title is prior in time prevails: *Peat v. Clayton*, [1906] 1 Ch. 659.

Estoppel

Questions of estoppel arise where the person to whom a certificate for shares has been issued or a person claiming under him, relying on the represenation contained in the certificate as regards title to the shares has altered his position.

A share certificate is not a warranty of title on which an action can be brought against the company: *In re Ottos Kopje Diamond Mines Ltd.*, [1893] 1 Ch. 618 (C.A.); but under certain circumstances the certificate will operate by way of estoppel.

In order that the established principles of estoppel can apply against the company there must be a representation by it intended to be acted on by the party complaining and which has been acted upon by him to his prejudice without any knowledge that the statement is untrue: *Mackenzie v. Monarch Life Assurance Co.* (1911) 23 O.L.R. 342; (1912); 45 S.C.R. 232.

Where a company, acting upon a forged transfer from A. to B. issued a certificate to B., and C. relying on this certificate purchased the shares in good faith from B. and became the registered shareholder but the company on the forgery being discovered removed C. from the register, the company was held liable to C. for damages on the ground of estoppel: *In re Bahia & San Francisco Railway Co.* (1868), L.R. 3 Q.B. 584 (forged transfer); *In re Ottos Kopje Diamond Mines Ltd.*, [1893] 1 Ch. 618 (C.A.) (forged transfer), where Bowen, L.J., stated the true view of the *Bahia* case in these words:

> It was said that the case of *In re Bahia and San Francisco Railway Company* shews that there was a cause of action in the nature of an implied warranty upon the certificate, or breach of warranty arising out of the certificate. A certificate is not like a promissory note: it does not transfer a chose in action; it is only a representation. The case of *In re Bahia and San Francisco Railway Company* was, in truth, an attempt, which was successful, to make the company liable — although in the absence of fraud — through the estoppel created by the certificate. The way in which the Court made the company liable was this: they said that inasmuch as the certificate had been intended to be acted upon, it became a document the truth of which the company could not deny as against the transferee to whom it

was intended to be shewn; and, therefore, it precluded the company, as against such transferee, from denying the truth of what the certificate contained; they could not be in any better position than if the statement were true; but that only obliged the company to act as if the title, the goodness of which was certified, were in fact good. Until, therefore, the company did something which ought not to be done, or omitted to do something which ought to be done, as between them and the true owner of the shares, no cause of action would arise.

In both the above cases the measure of damages was held to be the value of the shares at the time of refusal to register.

In order for a person to whom a certificate for shares has been issued to recover against a company on the ground of estoppel, he must show that he relied on the certificate given by the company. Where a person received and submitted to the company a forged transfer and on the basis of it received a certificate from the company, he was not entitled to recover from the company because he had not relied on a statement by the company: *Simm v. Anglo-American Telegraph Co.* (1879), 5 Q.B.D. 188. However, if the person acts to his detriment on such a certificate, for example, by selling or mortgaging the shares or otherwise incurring liability in respect thereof, the situation is different. Thus where, upon receiving a certificate based on a fraudulent transfer, a person entered into a contract to sell the shares to a third party, he was entitled to recover from the company: *Balkis Consolidated Co. Ltd. v. Tomkinson*, [1893] A.C. 396. In that case the party, in order to fulfil his contract with the third party, bought other shares in the market and the amount so expended was held to be the measure of damages to which he was entitled. Moreover, mere inaction may lead to a claim; thus, where, upon receiving a certificate based on a fraudulent transfer, a person took no steps until all chance of recovery against the wrongdoer had gone (the wrongdoer had become bankrupt), he was entitled to recover: *Dixon v. Kennaway & Co.*, [1990] 1 Ch. 833.

There is no estoppel where the certificate as opposed to a transfer of the shares represented thereby is a forgery or where on the facts the certificate is to be treated as a forgery: *Ruben v. Great Fingall Consolidated Co.*, [1906] A.C. 439; *Fire Valley Orchards v. Sly* (1914), 17 D.L.R. 3; *South London Greyhound Racecourses Ltd. v. Wake*, [1931] 1 Ch. 496.

Like principles apply where the representation contained in the certificate is that the shares are fully paid. Thus a transferee of shares, not in fact paid up, relying in good faith on a certificte which shows that the shares are fully paid, is entitled to hold them as such: *Burkinshaw v. Nicolls* (1878), 3 App. Cas. 1004, 1026; even against the creditors of the company: *McCraken v. McIntyre* (1877), 1 S.C.R. 479. As a general rule in original allottee cannot rely on any estoppel created by the certificate but a lender of money to the company on the security of a certificate for shares purporting to be fully paid is entitled to rely oupn the representation contained in the certificate: *Bloomenthal v. Ford*, [1897] A.C. 156; *In re Charle H. Davies, Ltd., McNicol's Case* (1909), 18 O.L.R. 240; and if the shares have been allotted on the direction of a person who was entitled to have the shares issued to him as fully paid, the company may be estopped as against the original allottee: *Parbury's Case*, [1896] 1 Ch. 100. Even where the shares, if they remained in the hands of the person to whom they were originally issued, would be subject to cancellation the company will be estopped from questioning that such shares are fully paid if they come into the hands of *bona fide* purchasers for value: *Proprietary Mines Ltd. v. Mackay*, [1939] O.R. 461 (C.A.).

A defect in title of the immediate transferor will not in all cases prevent the transferee from getting himself registered; the registered owner of the shares may be estopped from denying the title of the holder, as was held under the following circumstances. The registered owner of shares in a corporation gave to her brokers, for the purpose of selling the shares, the certificate of ownership, upon the face of which the shares were said to be transferable on the books of the corporation in person, or by attorney upon surrender of the certificate, and upon which was endorsed a transfer and power of attorney signed by her, and having a blank left for the name of the transferee. The brokers improperly deposited the certificate as security for advances to them with a bank, who received it in the ordinary course of business without any notice of the owner's rights. There was evidence at the trial that, according to the usages of the stock exchanges of Ontario and Quebec, such a share certificate, so endorsed, passes from hand to hand and is recognized as entitling the holder to deal with the shares as owner, and to pass the property in them by delivery, or to fill in the blank with his own name, and have the shares so registered on the books of the corporation. The court held (1) that such a transfer passed the title to the bank; (2) that the original holder, having placed it in the power of her broker to transfer the shares, was estopped from questioning what had been done; (3) that, under the circumstances detailed, a transferee for value is not put on enquiry as to the rights of antecedent owners, nor as to the title of his immediate vendors: *Smith v. Rogers* (1899), 30 O.R. 256 (C.A.). It will be noted that s. 55(2) of the Act provides that a security is valid in the hands of a purchaser for value without notice of any defect going to its validity.

In the case of a delivery by executors of certificates standing in the name of the deceased, and endorsed in blank by an executor, his signature in his executorial capacity does not disclose whether he intended to dispose of the shares or to vest himself with them and such a blank transfer, being an ambiguous document, will not raise an estoppel against the executor from pleading that a broker to whom the certificates were delivered had no authority to pledge them: *Colonial Bank v. Cady* (1890), 15 App. Cas. 267 at 280.

A person taking certificates which have already been registered in the name of the executor under circumstances which place him on enquiry may, if he fails to make such enquiry, become liable to the estate and become bound to return the certificates. Thus, in *Cartwright v. Lyster*, [1934] O.R. 161 (C.A.), the bank took the certificate endorsed in blank by the executors, of whom the bank's customer was one, as security for the indebtedness of the executor with notice that it was the property of the estate and that the executor was applying it for the purpose of securing his own indebtedness. Under those circumstances the bank was put upon enquiry and, having failed to make such enquiry, became liable to the estate.

If the transferee either knows or has reason to believe that the interest of the person transferring the securities is limited, he is not a purchaser for value without notice and must inquire into the transferor's authority, whether the securities are negotiable or not: *Earl of Sheffield v. London Joint Stock Bank* (1888), 13 App. Cas. 333.

So also where shares are registered "in trust", a pledgee of the shares is under the duty to decline to take the transfer until he has ascertained that it was authorized by the nature of the trust: *Bank of Montreal v. Sweeny* (1887), 12 App. Cas. 617.

Persons who acquired, as bona fide purchasers for value without notice, certificates with transfers endorsed and executed in blank, the words of transfer including a power of attorney for registration, which certificates were delivered by the transferor to a third person so as to enable him to dispose of them, became the owners of the shares free from any claim on the part of the transferor: *McLeod v. Brazilian Traction Light & Power Co.* (1927), 60 O.L.R. 253 (shares listed on exchanges).

Where the owner has delivered shares endorsed in blank to a person with instructions to obtain a loan, he will be bound by the act of his agent, even though the latter exceeds his authority, for example, by depositing the shares as security for his own loan: *Fry v. Smellie*, [1912] 3 K.B. 282 (C.A.). And where the owner delivered shares endorsed in blank to her stockbroker with authority for him to use them as collateral security for his own loans, she was bound when he sold the shares to a bona fide purchaser for value, who had no notice of any limitation on his power to sell: *Melanson v. McCleave* (1958), 11 D.L.R. (2d) 579.

A lender, advancing money in good faith on shares deposited with him and endorsed in blank, is not bound to make enquiries as to whether the registered owner has any claim on the shares: *Macdonald v. Bank of Vancouver* (1916), 25 D.L.R. 567. In the last mentioned case, evidence of the usage of the monetary world that certificates endorsed in blank are regarded as bearer securities on which bankers make advances, if it was required at all, was supplied by the superintendent for British Columbia of a chartered bank. And in *Patrick v. Royal Bank*, [1932] 3 D.L.R. 532, similar evidence having been given at the trial as to mercantile usage, the British Columbia Court of Appeal held that share certificates endorsed in blank were negotiable instruments; and for an earlier decision to the same effect, see *Bank of Montreal v. Isbell*, [1925] 2 D.L.R. 30 (S.C.C.).

There will be no estoppel against the registered owner where the blank endorsement is followed by restrictive words. In *Mathers v. Royal Bank* (1913), 29 O.L.R. 141, the registered owner handed his broker a certificate for 46 shares instructing him to sell 25 shares and endorsed the certificate in blank, adding in writing the words "twenty-five" as indicating the number of shares to be dealt with. The certificate was deposited by the broker with a bank to secure advances, and the bank sold the shares in order to realize the security, the bank's agent striking out the words, "twenty-five", in the endorsement. It was held by Boyd C. that the manner of endorsement gave notice to all concerned that only 25 shares were to be used and the endorsement reading "hereby sell, assign and transfer unto . . ." was notice that the shares were to be used for selling, not pledging, and the bank was liable to account for the full value of the shares sold.

Nor will the person who has transferred shares in blank, where the transfer is not in order, be estopped if the person to whom the shares are handed, fraudulently deals with them. In *Colonial Bank v. Cady* (1890), 15 App. Cas. 267, executors not registered as shareholders in respect of shares of their testator had endorsed them in blank and the broker, to whom the shares had been handed, fraudulently deposited them with his bank to secure a personal debt. It was held that the fact of the certificates being signed by such executors put two possible interpretations on their leaving the certificates with the broker; either he was to sell them or procure registration in their names; the bank should have enquired which of the two reasons was the cause of the deposit, and the executors were not estopped.

Trustee in bankruptcy or liquidator claiming against rightful owner

Where the shareholder delivers his share certificate to a broker with instructions to sell part of the shares and the broker fraudulently has the balance of the shares transferred into his own name, his trustee in bankruptcy cannot hold the shares against the rightful owner: *Denman v. Tousaw, Hart & Anderson* (1922), 66 D.L.R. 572 (Que.). In such a case the client must identify the certificate which he asks to be returned as relating to his shares: *McKay v. Turgeon* (1922), 67 D.L.R. 607 (Que.).

Where a broker to secure his own indebtedness, wrongfully and fraudulently pledges a share certificate of a customer delivered to him as collateral security for the customer's marginal account, and the pledgee remains in possession of the share certificate after the customer's indebtedness to the broker has been paid and the broker's indebtedness to the pledgee has been paid, the customer is entitled as against the trustee in bankruptcy of the broker to have the share certificate delivered to him: *Haggart v. Trusts & Guarantee Co.* (1930), 65 O.L.R. 23.

A customer deposited with brokers certain bonds as collateral in lieu of cash margin on the purchase of shares through the brokers, the bonds by agreement to be pledged for no greater amount than one third of the purchase price. The brokers pledged the shares purchased and the bonds and, the brokers having made an authorized assignment, the trustee sold the shares for a price which left a credit balance in favour of the customer. It was held, following *Haggart v. Trusts & Guarantee Co., supra,* that the bonds being in the hands of the trustee must be delivered to the customer: *Re Wiggins Ltd.* (1930), 66 O.L.R. 391, [1931] O.R. 337 (C.A.).

Where shares are acquired by a stockbroker to fill the order of a customer who has purchased them on margin, the order having been placed with a branch office and forwarded to the head office which in turn purchases the shares from another firm, and the certificates, endorsed in blank and designated as being for the client's account, are delivered to the branch office, they become the property of the customer subject to payment of the balance due on them, and, funds for this purpose being in the hands of the stockbroker, the shares belong to the client and not to the liquidator of the stockbroker on his insolvency occurring before delivery of the certificates to the customer: *Re Stobie-Forlong-Matthews Ltd.; Re Kern Agencies Ltd.; Re Gillespie & Co.; Re Stewart; Re Leaney*, [1931] 3 D.L.R. 170 (Man. C.A.). A customer who has paid in full for shares purchased by a broker for his account but has not received the certificates is entitled to the shares against the liquidator on a winding-up if there are sufficient shares of the same kind to satisfy the demands of all purchasers, such shares being held by the broker to satisfy the demands of all purchasers of that particular stock. It is not necessary for the claimant to identify his particular shares: *Re Stobie-Forlong-Matthews Ltd.; Re Stewart, supra*; *Re J. T. Richards & Co.*, [1939] 1 D.L.R. 760.

If less of the shares of a particular stock are returned to the trustee in bankruptcy than there are claims, the claimants rank *pro rata*; if more are returned than claimed, the surplus remains in the hands of the trustee; if none of a claimant's shares are returned to the trustee, he cannot require that those whose shares have been returned should contribute: *Re J. T. Richards & Co., supra.*

On the other hand, when a customer purchases shares direct from a broker, not employed as the agent of the customer, no commission being charged on the transaction so that the relation between the broker and the customer is that of vendor and purchaser, then, though the customer has paid in full for the shares, if they have not been registered in his name or delivered to him or appropriated to his contract, no property in the shares passes to the customer and the liquidator is entitled to them: *Re Stobie-Forlong-Matthews Ltd.; Re Leaney, supra.* In *Re C. A. Macdonald & Co.* (1959), 18 D.L.R. (2d) 731, the Alberta Court of Appeal held that the law of seller and buyer and not that of broker and client applied where a broker sold his own shares to a client and that the fact that the purchaser had paid the price of a certain number of shares which were to come out of a larger number held by the broker did not, in the absence of a transfer and where there was no appropriation of the particular number of shares, give him any interest, equitable or other, in the broker's shares. Hence, when the broker's bankruptcy intervened before the purchase could be consummated, the title to the shares remained wholly with the bankrupt broker.

Section 64 of the Act provides that where a security in registered form is delivered to a purchaser without a necessary endorsement, the purchaser will become a bona fide purchaser only at the time that the endorsement is supplied; but as against the transferor, the transfer is complete on delivery and the purchaser has a specifically enforceable right to have any necessary endorsement supplied.

Section 51(2) of the federal Act provides that a private corporation must, and any other corporation may, treat a person as a registered security holder if the corporation is supplied with the stipulated evidence that the person in question is the executor, administrator, heir or legal representative of the heirs, of the estate of a deceased security holder; s. 51(7) provides that such a person, subject to any applicable law relating to the collection of taxes, is entitled to become a registered holder or to designate a registered holder if he deposits with the corporation, or its transfer agent, the original grant of probate or letters of administration or a copy certified to be a true copy by (a) the court granting probate or letters of administration, (b) a trust corporation or (c) a lawyer or notary acting on behalf of the executor, administrator, heir or legal representative of the heirs, together with an affidavit or declaration of transmission and a certificate for the security in question accompanied by any guarantee required by the corporation pursuant to s. 77.

A different situation arises when the claimant's shares have been realized upon and the proceeds form part of a fund made up of the proceeds of the sale of the securities of several claimants.

In *Re Wiggins Ltd.; Travers' and Spratt's Claims*, [1931] O.R. 573 (C.A.), Middleton J.A. said at p. 581:

> Where the insolvent hypothecates stock which is not his own and stock which is his own for his own purposes and without the authority of the client, the proceeds of the stock which he owns or has a right to discount must be applied first in the discharge of the debt, and those who have been wronged by the tortious act of the insolvent are entitled to claim that that which remains, after satisfying the claim against all the stock, must be in the first place regarded as the proceeds of the stock wrongfully converted. If the claims based upon wrongful conversion exceed the balance available, all such claims will rank *pro rata* upon the surplus available. The Court will not attempt to discriminate as between these preferred claimants and accord to one priority over the others. In order to invoke this principle, ownership of the stock sold must be satisfactorily proved by the claimants as well as the fact of its wrongful conversion.

In that case the claimants failed because they could not prove ownership. Accordingly, the fund was distributed as part of the bankrupt's assets in the bankruptcy proceedings, subject only to any equitable right which any claimant might succeed in proving. The principles enunciated by Middleton J.A. in this case were approved in *Re Heron & Co.; Ex parte Robertson*, [1933] O.R. 693.

Where shares of customers had been wrongfully pledged by a broker, and the latter's trustee in bankruptcy credited each of the customers with the value of the collaterals deposited by them, converting their debit balances into credit balances, and directed the pledgee to realize the securities held by it and remit the surplus, it was held that each customer was entitled to rank on the fund in proportion to the amount contributed by his security to the common fund. There was no suggestion that the securities ever came in specie to the trustee or that they were ever released in specie to the claimants and all the claimants desired to rank on the common fund: *Re Bryant Isard & Co.; Ex parte Turner* (1925) 29 O.W.N. 167, followed in *Re Nakashidze*, [1948] O.R. 254. As to the law in Quebec see *Grondin v. Lefaivre*, [1931] S.C.R. 102.

If a broker, being entitled to do so, has pledged as security for advances shares purchased for various customers, and the pledgees return to the trustee a surplus of cash and shares not required to satisfy the broker's indebtedness, the trustee will be directed to give notice to all customers to redeem or file a claim and then to sell all the shares and distribute to those who have filed claims their *pro rata* share of the proceeds and the cash already in his hands:

Re Carroll & Wright; Ex parte Bain, [1932] O.R. 474. It was further held that if the proceeds are insufficient to satisfy all claimants of the same class, the securities which survived the liquidation by the pledgee must contribute *pro rata* to those which did not survive the liquidation. This rule which is termed "sharing the burden of the loan" was adopted in *Re Clark Martin & Co.*, [1934] 1 D.L.R. 521 (Man. C.A.) where the pledge was wrongful and was held applicable to all classes of customers, irrespective of whether they had purchased the securities outright or were margin customers. The rule was also followed in *In re Miller, Court & Manley Ltd.*, [1940] 3 W.W.R. 184. However, where a broker pledges shares of customers, some with and some without authority from the customers, and the pledgee sells some but not all, those customers (whether their shares were pledged with or without authority) who are able to identify their shares among those unsold are entitled to have them returned, if fully paid for, or if not, on payment of the balance owing; and the rule of "sharing the burden of the loan" does not apply: *Re Nakashidze*, [1948] O.R. 254.

Where dividends were received by a trustee in bankruptcy of a stockbroker in respect of shares represented by street certificates, which were registered in the stockbroker's name but could not be located, the trustee in bankruptcy was in no different position than the stockbroker would have been in respect of the dividends, that is, he was a trustee for the persons who might subsequently establish entitlement thereto. He was directed to pay the amounts so received to the Receiver-General of Canada for the benefit of such persons as preliminary to his own discharge: *Re Stobie & Forlong; Re Stobie-Forlong Assets Ltd.*, [1950] O.W.N. 629.

The owner of shares in a corporation had purported to transfer them to his wife, the transfer of shares was noted in the share transfer register but no new share certificate was issued. The owner subsequently became bankrupt and the trustee attacked the validity of the transfer. The court held that the transfer was valid and pointed out that a share certificate is only *prima facie* evidence of title and there was nothing in the Act providing that a transfer was ineffective unless a share certificate was issued to the transferee: *Clarkson Co. v. Pace* (1983), 60 N.S.R. (2d) 182 (C.A.).

Transmission on death of shareholder

Section 51(8) of the federal Act provides that if the laws of the jurisdiction governing the transmission of a security of a deceased holder do not require a grant of probate or letters of administration, a legal representative of the deceased holder is entitled (subject to any applicable law relating to the collection of taxes) to become a registered holder or to designate a registered holder, if he deposits with the corporation the security certificate in question and reasonable proof of the governing laws relating to the deceased holder's interest in the security, and of the right of the legal representative or person he designates to become the registered holder.

Where a shareholder of a corporation dies, his shares, as personal estate, vest in his executors or administrators, and the estate is liable for any balance due on them: *Baird's Case* (1870), L.R. 5 Ch. App. 725; *Clarkson v. McLean*

(1918), 42 O.L.R. 1, but the executors or administrators do not *ipso facto* become members of the corporation at common law, nor is the corporation entitled without their consent to register them as members: *Buchan's Case* (1879), 4 App. Cas. 583 at 588.

An article of a private corporation, which provided that on the death of a member of the corporation his shares should be deemed to have passed to his widow, who should promptly be registered as the holder thereof, was held invalid as being contrary to a section of the English *Companies Act* prohibiting the registration of a transfer of shares unless a proper instrument of transfer was delivered; and it was ordered that the register should be rectified by registering the shares in the names of the personal representatives of the deceased: *Re Greene, Greene v. Greene*, [1949] 1 Ch. 333. See also *Kay v. Poirier* (1990), 105 N.B.R. (2d) 395 (Q.B.).

As to the procedure in Quebec where an heir desires transfer on the books of the corporation of shares inherited by him, see *Connolly v. Connolly Corp.* (1936), 40 Que. P.R. 36.

For a discussion of the distinction between a transfer and the transmission of shares see *Carter v. Roy M. Lawson Ltd.* (1981), 129 D.L.R. (3d) 214 (N.B. Q.B.). See also *H.A. Fawcett & Son Ltd. v. The Queen* (1980), 80 D.T.C. 6195 (Fed. C.A.) where a controlling shareholder of a corporation died and left a will appointing his son as sole executor and beneficiary. The court held that the son became the controlling shareholder of the corporation following his father's death, by operation of law and that it was irrelevant that the shares had not been registered in the son's name.

See further the notes under the heading "Transfer practice" in this chapter.

Lost or stolen certificates

Section 80 of the federal Act provides that where a security has been lost, apparently destroyed or wrongfully taken, and the owner fails to notify the issuer of that fact by written notice of his adverse claim within a reasonable time after becoming aware thereof, if the issuer has registered a transfer of the security before receiving such notice, the owner is precluded from asserting against the issuer any claim to a new security. However, it would appear open to the owner to argue that the register should be rectified if a forged endorsement of the owner's signature were involved. Where there is a claim that a security has been lost, destroyed or wrongfully taken, the issuer is to issue a new security if the owner so requests before the issuer has notice that the security has been acquired by a bona fide purchaser, the owner furnishes the issuer with a sufficient indemnity bond and satisfies any other reasonable requirements of the issuer. Section 80(3) provides that if, after the issue of such a new security, a bona fide purchaser of the original security presents it for registration of transfer, the issuer is to register the same unless the registration would result in an over-issue in which case the provisions of s. 52 of the Act apply.

While share certificates are negotiable, if a certificate is lost or stolen from the owner without fault on his part, his right to it is superior to that of any other person who may acquire it by purchase for value from any other holder, and he may maintain an action to establish his right to it against the corporation or the person who holds it: *Whitehead v. Bridger, Hevenor & Co.*, [1936] 3 D.L.R. 408 (Ont. C.A.). In that case the words "same name" had been filled in in the blank space for the name of the transferee and it having been assumed by the court that such words had been inserted when the certificate was delivered to the persons claiming as purchasers, that was sufficient to put them on enquiry. It will be observed that under the present Act, s. 60 provides that, on delivery to him, the purchaser acquires the rights in the security that his transferor had, unless he was party to any fraud or illegality affecting the security or had notice of an adverse claim. Section 60(2) provides that a bona fide purchaser, in addition to acquiring the rights of a purchaser, also acquires the security free from any adverse claim which would seem to include a forged endorsement but query whether this result would follow. Section 68(1) provides that an owner of a security may assert the ineffectiveness of an endorsement against the issuer or any purchaser until the security has been registered on transfer to the purchaser.

In *Aitken v. Gardiner*, [1956] O.R. 589 share certificates endorsed in blank were stolen from the owner and delivered to and later sold by a firm of stockbrokers. The court held that in an action of detinue against the brokers, the owner was entitled to recover an equal number of shares or their value at the date of judgment.

In *Chartered Trust and Executor Co. v. Pagon*, [1950] O.R. 662, P. lost the share certificate endorsed in blank by the registered owner, but immediately notified both the registered owner and the transfer agent who made a "stop transfer" notation in its books. P. applied for a new certificate and obtained one on giving a bond to indemnify the corporation and the transfer agent "against any and all loss, costs and expenses of whatsoever kind or nature by reason of the [transfer agent] issuing duplicate of the [certificate] . . .". Two years later the original certificate was presented to the transfer agent and by oversight the "stop transfer" was not discovered before the transfer had been recorded and new certificates issued. The transfer agent was compelled to buy shares in the market and deliver them to the corporation for cancellation and sought to recover the value of the shares under the bond. The court held that the transfer agent could not recover, its loss arising not as a result of issuing a duplicate certificate to P., but from the negligence of its officers and servants in accepting and acting upon the transfer of the original certificate against which its books recorded a stop-order.

Seizure and sale at instance of execution creditor

The Execution Acts of the various provinces contain special provisions regulating the procedure where it is desired to seize shares under an execution. Such procedure must be strictly followed: *Royal Bank v. Canadian National Fire Insurance Co.* (1920), 55 D.L.R. 272.

Where the transferor still retains an interest in the shares, for example, where the transfer is by way of pledge only and not an out and out transfer by way of sale, the Ontario *Execution Act*, R.S.O. 1990, c. E.24, s. 16, enables the equity of redemption to be sold by the sheriff.

Where an equitable interest in shares is not exigible under an execution, the appointment of a receiver by way of equitable execution may be granted: *Sayre v. Gilfoy*, [1925] 1 W.W.R. 992. See also *Miller-Morse Hardware Co. v. Smart*, [1917] 2 W.W.R. 439 (charging order); *Lehane v. Porteous*, [1917] 2 W.W.R. 560 (receiver appointed of dividends).

Section 14 of the *Execution Act*, R.S.O. 1990, E. 24, provides for the seizure of transferrable shares, or interests therein, by the sheriff; notice of the seizure is to be given by the sheriff to the corporation in question, the shares may be sold by the sheriff and the purchaser is to have the same rights as if he had purchased the shares for in the execution debtor at the time of service of the notice in the corporation.

Under the *Executions Act*, R.S.S. 1920, c. 52, s. 10, which provided for a charging order against any shares "standing in the name of any person in trust" for the judgment debtor, it was not necessary that there be some record or evidence of the trust on the books of the corporation: *Hudson's Bay Co. v. Hosie*, [1926] 4 D.L.R. 489 (Sask. C.A.). The governing statute provided that no notice of any trust should be entered on the register. Where by supplementary letters patent a class of shares is extinguished and replaced by a new class and it is provided that the rights of the holders of shares of the old class are to consist solely of the right to receive shares of the new class against surrender and/or cancellation of certificates representing shares of the old class, a purchaser of the shares of the new class at a sheriff's sale pursuant to execution is not entitled to compel the corporation to register him as holder of shares of the new class without surrender of the certificate for shares of the old class: *Sinclair v. Blue Top Brewing Co.*, [1947] 4 D.L.R. 561 (S.C.C.).

The provisions of the Ontario *Execution Act* providing for the seizure and sale of "transferable shares", at any rate before the enactment of the amendment to s. 15, did not extend to shares of a private corporation which can be transferred only with the consent of the directors: *Re Phillips & La Paloma Sweets Ltd.* (1921), 51 O.L.R. 125. In the same case it was held that in the absence of *mala fides* on the part of the directors of a private corporation in refusing to permit a transfer, a purchaser from the sheriff could not compel the corporation to register the transfer. The execution creditor of a shareholder was, however, not without a remedy in such a case. He could have a receiver appointed to receive all dividends payable.

Section 15 of the Ontario *Execution Act*, R.S.O. 1990, E. 24, now provides as follows:

> If a sheriff seizes the shares of an execution debtor in a private company, he shall first offer them for sale to the other shareholders or any of them in such private company, and if none of them will purchase the shares for a reasonable price, the sheriff may then offer the debtor's interest therein for sale to the public generally and sell and convey to the highest bidder.

It is now generally accepted that section 15 reverses the *Phillips* decision. (See the discussion by Dunlop, C.R.B., *Creditor-Debtor Law in Canada* at p. 166). In *Associates Finance Co. Ltd. v. Webber and Dixon*, [1972] 4 W.W.R. 131 (B.C.S.C.) Anderson, J. was of the view that *Phillips* did not apply even in the absence of any equivalent to s. 15 of the Ontario Act. In this case, the plaintiff sought a charging order against shares in two private companies. The articles of association contained restrictions on transfers without the consent of the other shareholders and granted an overriding power to the directors to refuse to register any transfer of which they did not approve. Anderson, J. held that notwithstanding the restrictions on transfer, the shares should be considered as "transferrable" and the plaintiff had a right to seize and sell the shares. Thus, the application for a charging order was dismissed. (See also: *Yorkshire Trust Co. v. Bennett*, [1987] 1 W.W.R. 238 (Alta. Q.B.) and *Bank of Montreal v. Melbay Development Inc.* (1984), 32 Sask. R. 143 (Q.B.)).

Where the corporation is a federal corporation having a place of business in Ontario but its head office in Quebec, *semble*, the remedy of an execution creditor in Ontario is to make a seizure of the shares under the *Execution Act*: *Herold v. Budding* (1916), 37 O.L.R. 605.

In *Goodbun v. Mitchell*, [1930] 1 D.L.R. 580 (Man. C.A.), it was held that shares in a federal corporation having its head office in Toronto and no place in Manitoba where service of process could be legally made were not subject to legal execution under the Manitoba *Executions Act*; and that since the shares were not subject to legal execution, they could not be subject to equitable execution and therefore the court would not grant an order appointing a receiver to sell the plaintiff's equity of redemption in the shares on the application of a judgment creditor.

Where a British Columbia corporation is bound to keep its share register in the province, the situs of the shares is in British Columbia so far as the provisions of the *Execution Act* are concerned: *Oliver v. Granby Consolidated Mining & Smelting Power Co.*, [1923] 1 D.L.R. 1163.

Rights of unregistered transferee against execution creditor

A creditor of the transferor, who causes an execution to be levied against the shares before they have been registered in the name of the transferee, does not, however, stand in a better position than the transferor as regards the shares. If the transfer is *bona fide* and for value, a sale under execution cannot defeat the title of the transferee as only the debtor's interest in the property seized can be sold: *Morton v. Cowan* (1894), 25 O.R. 529. In *Sinclair v. Blue Top Brewing Co.*, [1945] O.R. 359 (C.A.); affd [1947] 4 D.L.R. 561 (S.C.C.), Laidlaw J.A. said at pp. 372-373, "It is equally plain and well settled in law that a purchaser of shares at a sale under execution acquires only the debtor's interest in the property seized."

In *Morton v. Cowan* (1894), 25 O.R. 529, Boyd C. at p. 532 observed that the provision in the statute is not aimed at dealings between the holder and others pending which an execution intervenes. It does apply, of course, as between successive transferees: see *Moore v. North Western Bank*, [1891] 2 Ch. 599 and *Roots v. Williamson* (1888), 38 Ch. D. 485; and is intended to keep on foot the liability of the registered shareholder to the corporation and its creditors in respect of his shares (in the event of their not being fully paid-up) until the liability of a transferee whose title has become complete by registration is substituted; see *Denison v. Smith* (1878), 43 U.C.Q.B. 503.

As to the law in Quebec, see *Paquin v. Dunlop* (1933), 71 Que. S.C. 506; *Kennedy v. Williams* (1937), 75 Que. S.C. 65.

In *Hawks v. McArthur*, [1951] 1 All E.R. 22 it was held that a purchaser of shares who had paid the full consideration therefor but had not had the shares registered in his name obtained an equitable right in the shares which prevailed over the equitable right therein subsequently obtained by a judgment creditor of the selling shareholder under a charging order.

Informalities and irregularities

A transfer may be valid, if *bona fide*, even though made and registered without formally complying with the usual procedure: *Bush's Case* (1871), L.R. 6 Ch. App. 246; affd (*sub nom. Murray v. Bush*) (1874), L.R. 6 H.L. 37.

A transfer may be effected without physical delivery of a share certificate, for example, by directing an allotment to be made in the name of a nominee, followed by issuance of a certificate in the name of such nominee and communication to him of what has been done: *MacDougall v. Johnson*, [1946] 4 D.L.R. 412.

Where a shareholder, who was also a director, notified the corporation that he desired to withdraw and the provisional directors, there being at that stage of the corporation's organization no proper register of transfers and no by-laws governing the same, erased the shareholder's name from the corporation's books, noted the date on which the director retired, and purported to transfer the shares to a person who thereafter became president of the corporation, all of which was approved by the shareholders, the transaction was held to be in effect a transfer of the shares and a substantial compliance with the Act: *Re Sprouted Food Co.; Hudson's Case* (1905), 6 O.W.R. 514. But if there is no transfer in fact of shares and acceptance thereof by the transferee the case is different. In *Re Publishers' Syndicate; Paton's Case* (1903), 5 O.L.R. 392 (C.A.), the directors of a corporation, erroneously believing that there were no unallotted shares, procured powers of attorney from several persons authorizing an agent "to receive from the vendors a transfer" of a specified number of "shares in the company purchased by me from him" and "to sign in the books of the company my name and acceptance to the transfer" thereof. No transfer was actually made of the shares by any vendor and appointors who took shares from the corporation, some of them signing applications and some of them not, were held to be original allottees of the shares and liable as such. So also where the articles of a corporation required the transfer of shares to be in writing and to be accompanied by the certificate of the shares to be transferred and no certificate was issued and there was no transfer in writing, a purported minute of a meeting of the board, which was not in fact held, reciting a transfer did not entitle the transferee to compel the corporation to register him as a shareholder: *Davis v. Pallesen Dairy & Creamery Co.*, [1935] 4 D.L.R. 518 (Alta. C.A.).

A transfer which is irregular (e.g., because not executed by the transferee where so required) is not a nullity, and, after it has been acted upon and treated as valid for a long period, cannot be impeached: *In re Taurine Company* (1884), 25 Ch. D. 118 at 137 (C.A.). Where the transferee, who has not signed an acceptance of transfer as required by the governing Act, has paid calls, received dividends and appointed a proxy, he will be estopped from denying that he is a shareholder in an action for calls: *Bank of Liverpool v. Bigelow* (1878), 12 N.S.R. 236. See also *Boultbee v. Gzowski* (1898), 29 S.C.R. 54 where the transferee was estopped by his conduct even though the transfer had not been formally recorded on the transfer books.

Formalities in respect of transfers

A form of transfer and power of attorney is usually endorsed on the back of any share certificate.

Even though the by-laws contemplate some delay in the approval of transfers, for example, where the by-laws require all transfers to be submitted to and approved by the directors, the directors should not unduly delay transfers: *Gairdner, Clarke & Doherty v. Northern Life Assurance Co.* (1923), 25 O.W.N. 278.

Where a given form of transfer is made compulsory by the by-laws it must be followed and the directors should refuse to register a transfer not in proper form. Small deviations, however, will not justify the rejection of a transfer which substantially complies with the regulations. Thus it has been held that the absence of the denoting numbers of the shares (where the shares were required to be distinguished by number) and the absence of the address of the transferor, were immaterial where both were known to the directors and there was no doubt as to the identity of the shares intended to be transferred: *Re Letheby & Christopher Ltd.*, [1904] 1 Ch. 815. The same is true where the wrong numbers are inserted in the transfer: *Ind's Case* (1872), L.R. 7 Ch. App. 485, or where the numbers are inserted after execution: *Bishop's Case* (1869), L.R. 7 Ch. App. 296n, provided always that the identity of the shares transferred is clear.

If the transfer is executed in blank there is an implied authority to the transferee to complete it; the absence of a subscribing witness to the transfer is not fatal; if there is no by-law regulating the form, a transfer in the ordinary form endorsed on the certificate issued will be sufficient: *Goldfields Ltd. v. Harris Maxwell Co.* (1910), 2 O.W.N. 1373. See also s. 58(1).

Where the corporation had never delivered the certificate in respect of his shares to the shareholder, it was held by MacMahon J. in *Meyers v. Lucknow Elevator Co.* (1905), 6 O.W.R. 291, that an assignment of his shares by the shareholder was a transfer of his certificate in the hands of the corporation. It was not necessary for the shareholder to go through the formality of obtaining possession of the certificate and handing it to the purchaser.

Remedies for refusal to register transfer

A corporation owes a duty to a shareholder to permit the transfer of his shares in a proper case and in case of a wrongful refusal to permit a transfer is liable for the natural consequences of such breach: *Wolverton v. Black Diamond Oil Fields* (1915), 8 Alta. L.R. 283 (C.A.).

Mandamus

In Ontario and Quebec, mandamus will lie at the instance of a transferee of shares to compel the corporation to make the transfer on its books: *Crawford v. Provincial Insurance Co.* (1859), 8 U.C.C.P. 263; *Re Guillot and Sandwich & Windsor Gravel Road Co.* (1867), 26 U.C.Q.B. 246; *In re Macdonald & Mail Printing & Publishing Co.* (1876), 6 P.R. 309; *Cunningham v. Beaudet* (1878), 11 Q.L.R. 168; *Brady v. Stewart* (1887), 15 S.C.R. 82 (appeal from Quebec); *Upton v. Hutchinson* (1899), 2 Que. P.R. 300; *Rich v. Melancthon Board of Health* (1912), 26 O.L.R. 48.

The court cannot make an order in the nature of mandamus, directing the transfer agent to make, and the registrar to register, a transfer of shares of a foreign corporation, where the law under which the foreign corporation is incorporated requires, as a condition precedent to the validity of the transfer as against the corporation, entry in a book to be maintained at its office in the state of incorporation: *Re Hatch & Fanny Farmer Candy Shops Inc.*, [1944] O.R. 586 (C.A.).

A writ of mandamus must be addressed to the corporation, the principal: *The Queen v. Clements* (1891), 24 N.S.R. 64; *Re Hatch & Fanny Farmer Candy Shops Inc., supra*, per Laidlaw J.A. at p. 599.

Laches will disentitle a transferee from demanding this remedy: *Leadley v. Union Stock Yards* (1915), 8 O.W.N. 516.

A distinct refusal to register the transfer is necessary before mandamus will lie, but a refusal in effect, though not in direct terms, would be sufficient. No rule can be laid down for determining whether there has been a refusal or not: *Re Guillot and Sandwich & Windsor Gravel Road Co.* (1867), 26 U.C.Q.B. 246; *Goodwin v. Ottawa & Prescott Railway* (1863), 13 U.C.C.P. 254. Where directors were at fault in failing to hold a meeting to approve a transfer of a block of shares, failure to call upon the directors to proceed promptly disentitled the transferee to a mandamus to register the transfer: *Gairdner, Clarke & Doherty v. Northern Life Assurance Co.* (1923), 25 O.W.N. 278.

Executors applied to the transfer agents and registrars in Toronto to accept and register transfers of shares held by the deceased in Winnipeg Electric Railway Company, which had purported to establish a share registry and share transfer office in that city; the administrator of succession duties in Manitoba had warned the transfer agents and registrars that they would be held liable for payment of succession duty on the shares if the transfers were recorded and registered without requiring letters probate to be resealed in Manitoba, which had not been done. The transfer agents and registrars refused to accept or record the transfers. On a motion for an order of mandamus the application was refused on the ground that the law was still in such a state that the question arising should not be disposed of on a motion of that character when other interests than those of the parties to the application were involved: *Re Hobbs* (1931), 39 O.W.N. 383.

Where, however, there appeared to be little doubt that there could be no liability for succession duty to the province in which the corporation was incorporated, it was held that the transfer agent in Ontario—the certificates stating on their face that they were transferable in Montreal or Toronto and being endorsed in blank—was not entitled to make it a condition of transfer that the applicant furnish a clearance from the Quebec succession duty department: *Re Russell*, [1942] O.R. 466 (certificates endorsed in blank). This case was distinguished in *Re Hatch & Fanny Farmer Candy Shops Inc.*, [1944] O.R. 586 at 593 and 597 (C.A.), where, under the laws relating to a New York corporation, no transfer, valid as against the corporation, could be made without entry in a book kept in the State of New York. See also *Christie v. British American Oil Co.*, [1947] O.R. 455 and 842 (refusal to transfer in Ontario without an Ontario succession duty release shares held by residents of Manitoba and transferable in Toronto or Montreal upheld).

Suit

Where a corporation wrongfully refuses to register a transfer the transferee may sue in equity for a decree compelling the corporation to register the transfer, but such a decree is not to be made in the face of superior equities, or where there has been laches: *Smith v. Bank of Nova Scotia* (1882), 8 S.C.R. 558.

The transferee may also sue for damages for wrongful refusal to register his transfer: *McMurrich v. Bond Head Harbour Co.* (1852), 9 U.C.Q.B. 333; *Wolverton v. Black Diamond Oil Fields* (1915), 8 Alta. L.R. 283 (Alta. C.A.). Notwithstanding that a claim is made for damages against the corporation by one of the claimants, the corporation may interplead: *Re Underfeed Stoker Co.* (1901), 1 O.L.R. 42.

The writ must be directed against the corporation and not against the directors or an officer personally: *Cunningham v. Beaudet, supra*; *Upton v. Hutchinson, supra*; but see *Morton v. Cowan* (1894), 25 O.R. 529 where the writ was issued against both the president and the corporation.

The measure of damages for refusal to register a transfer may be the value of the shares at the time of the refusal. See *In re Ottos Kopje Diamond Mines*, [1893] 1 Ch. 618; *McMurrich v. Bond Head Harbour Co.* (1852), 9 U.C.Q.B. 333. Where the shareholder is suing, the corporation is liable for the natural consequences of the breach of duty to permit the transfer, which, in a case where a sale of shares is prevented, is the loss of the sale: *Wolverton v. Black Diamond Oil Fields* (1915), 8 Alta. L.R. 283 (C.A.) (refusal to register not *bona fide*). In *Grand Trunk Railway v. Webster* (1861), 6 L.C. Jur. 178, it was held that the measure of damages was the difference between the market price of the shares at the time of the first refusal to register and that at the time when the transfer was registered. Where the transferor is the plaintiff the corporation will not be liable for special damages arising out of an unusual contract of which the corporation had no notice: *Skinner v. City of London Marine Insurance Corp.* (1885), 14 Q.B.D. 882 (C.A.).

Application to rectify entries in books

Section 243 of the Act provides for an application for the rectification of entries in the records of a corporation, including the records pertaining to the registration and transfer of shares. See the notes to this section in Chapter 16 and see also s. 241(1) and 3(k). For examples of the application of circumstances in which the register will be rectified see *Re B.C. Aircraft Propeller & Engine Co.* (1968), 66 D.L.R. (2d) 628 (B.C. S.C.); *Mitchell v. Miller* (1983), 21 Sask. R. 407 (C.A.); *Mathers v. Mathers* (1989), 90 N.S.R. (2d) 354 (C.A.).

Other considerations

In certain cases where control of a Canadian business is being acquired by a non-Canadian either by the purchase of a majority of the voting shares of a corporation, or by the purchase of shares of a foreign entity which controls a Canadian business, the purchaser must comply with the provisions of the *Investment Canada Act.* In certain cases notice is required and in other cases prior approval is required. For an example of the circumstances in which an injunction may be granted if approval is required see *A. G. Canada v. Fallbridge Holdings Ltd.* (1979), 7 B.L.R. 275 (Fed. T.D.); affd (1985), 63 N.R. 17 (Fed. C.A.); leave to appeal to S.C.C. refused (1986), 69 N.R. 76 (note) (S.C.C.).

A purchase agreement for shares provided that a condition precedent to the purchaser's liability was the favourable opinion of solicitors for the purchaser to the due creation and issuance of the shares in question and certain other matters. The agreement further provided that the purchaser was entitled to rescind the agreement if the condition precedent was not fulfilled. Certain objections to title were made and the purchaser purported to rescind the agreement. The vendor alleged that he became entitled to forfeit the deposit. On a suit to recover the deposit, judgment was given in favour of the purchaser. The provisions of the agreement were plain and the opinion was genuinely and honestly entertained: see *Gordon Leaseholds Ltd. v. Metzger,* [1967] 1 O.R. 580 (H.C.).

Conflicting claims to shares before registration

If notice of an objection, on the part of the transferor to registration of the transferee, comes to the knowledge of the corporation, the directors are not bound to register the transfer forthwith, even though the transfer is in order: *Ireland v. Hart,* [1902] 1 Ch. 552. The directors are entitled to a reasonable time to make enquiries. What is a reasonable time is, of course, a question of fact. In *Nelles v. Windsor, Essex & Lake Shore Rapid Railway* (1908), 16 O.L.R. 359 (C.A.), Britton J. on an interlocutory application by the transferee thought that two or three days was a sufficient time and directed a mandamus to issue. The Divisional Court, however, set the order aside, holding that there was not sufficient urgency shown to call for summary action and that the question of unreasonable delay could be better disposed of on *viva voce* evidence at the trial. While mandamus may not be obtainable on an interlocutory motion, mandamus is the proper remedy where the directors refuse to register the transfer: *Re Polson Iron Works Ltd.* (1912), 3 O.W.N. 1269 at 1271. See also s. 78 of the Federal Act, which provides for a limited duty of enquiry. Ss. (2) provides that the duty may be discharged by any reasonable means including notice to the adverse claimant that the transfer will be registered unless within 30 days of mailing the notice either the issuer is served with a restraining order or other court order, or an indemnity bond is provided to the issuer as the result of complying with the adverse claim.

In the event of conflicting claims being set up to the shares by the transferor and transferee before registration and an action being brought, the corporation should interplead: *Re Underfeed Stoker Co.* (1901), 1 O.L.R. 42.

Shares held in trust

Questions may arise as to the right of a transferee of shares from a trustee to hold them against the *cestui que trust*. If the certificate shows on its face that the shares are held in trust the transferee is put on inquiry and is affected with notice that the transferor is not the owner of the shares: *Birkbeck Loan Co. v. Johnston* (1902), 3 O.L.R. 497, 6 O.L.R. 258 (C.A.); *London & Canadian Loan & Agency Co. v. Duggan*, [1893] A.C. 506 at 509. If, however, the trust is not clearly disclosed on the face of the certificate, the transferee is not, in the absence of actual knowledge, affected by the trust. Thus, in *London & Canadian Loan & Agency Co. v. Duggan, supra*, where the certificate was made out to the "manager in trust" of a bank, that indicated merely that he held the shares in trust for his employers, and did not indicate a trust in favour of some third person so as to affect a transferee with notice of such relationship.

See also sections 51, 62(1) and 78 of the Federal Act, which are discussed *supra*.

Loans on the security of shares

It is a common commercial practice to make loans upon the security of shares and the security may be taken in various ways.

If the shares are fully paid the lender should take a transfer to himself or a trustee, register the transfer and obtain a new certificate from the corporation prior to making the advance. This alone will give the lender absolute security. This method has one disadvantage in jurisdictions in which security transfer taxes are payable as such taxes will be payable on the transfer and retransfer. Another method is for the borrower to deposit with the lender the share certificates endorsed in blank, the lender retaining the certificates until the loan is repaid. As share certificates are not negotiable instruments and the title of the lender is not complete until registration, he runs the risk of having his security defeated by the prior registration of a subsequent transfer, see the notes under the heading "Risks of holder of unregistered transfer" in this chapter. The lender's security may also become impaired, if he has not had himself registered as a shareholder, by the fact of the borrowing shareholder being indebted to the corporation; the corporation may refuse to permit a transfer of the shares into the lender's name, or may retain dividends on the shares to meet liability for indebtedness. Furthermore, until registration of the transfer, the borrower will receive dividends and will be entitled to vote on the shares.

If the corporation registers in favour of the lender a transfer of fully paid shares, it loses its lien for any indebtedness of the prior shareholders.

The deposit of share certificates to secure a loan amounts to an agreement to transfer the shares by way of mortgage, an equitable mortgage, whether or not accompanied by a transfer in blank: *London & Midland Bank v. Mitchell*, [1899] 2 Ch. 161; *Harrold v. Plenty*, [1901] 2 Ch. 314; *Stubbs v. Slater*, [1910] 1 Ch. 632 (C.A.); *Ellis & Co.'s Trustee v. Dixon-Johnson*, [1924] 2 Ch. 451 (C.A.). The depositee being an equitable mortgagee and not a pledgee is entitled to a decree of foreclosure and is not restricted to a remedy by sale: *General Credit & Discount Co. v. Glegg* (1883), 22 Ch. D. 549; *Harrold v. Plenty, supra*.

A sale of shares, with an option to the vendor to re-purchase which has not been exercised in accordance with its terms, will not operate as a mortgage of the shares: *McRae v. Law*, [1936] 2 W.W.R. 60.

By taking an out and out transfer to himself or his nominee, followed by registration, the lender obtains absolute title to the shares to the extent of his advances. Where this was done and the lender acted in good faith, taking a transfer from brokers who were fraudulently pledging the shares of their client to secure their own account, the lender was entitled to hold the shares as against the brokers' client: *Fuller v. Glyn, Mills, Currie & Co.*, [1914] 2 K.B. 168. In that case it was also held that the lender was not put on enquiry by the mere fact of the brokers' depositing the shares to secure their own indebtedness, nor by the fact that the shares deposited were made out in the name of another party and by him endorsed in blank. If the endorsement is restricted or not "in order" and indicates that only a portion of the shares represented by the certificate are to be used and that the shares are to be sold and not pledged, the lender will be affected with notice and cannot retain the certificate: *Mathers v. Royal Bank of Canada* (1913), 29 O.L.R. 141. There is no custom or usage of banks or brokers or of the stock exchange justifying the deletion of such restrictive words.

Where a mortgagee of shares has agreed to vote the shares in accordance with the wishes of the mortgagor, the court will enforce such an agreement by mandatory injunction: *Puddephatt v. Leith*, [1916] 1 Ch. 200.

Lender's power of sale

Even in the absence of an express power of sale, a mortgagee of shares has an implied power to sell on default of payment at the appointed time or, if no time be fixed, on the expiration of a reasonable notice claiming payment on a certain date: *Deverges v. Sandeman, Clark & Co.*, [1902] 1 Ch. 579 (C.A.); *Young v. Croteau* (1925), 58 O.L.R. 76 and 303 (C.A.). A month's notice or less would probably be regarded as reasonable: *Deverges v. Sandeman, supra*, per Stirling and Cozens Hardy L.JJ. The manner in which the sale should take place depends on the law of each particular province. In *Toronto General Trusts Corp. v. Central Ontario Railway* (1905), 10 O.L.R. 347 (C.A.), the memorandum of hypothecation authorized the pledgee of bonds, on default, from time to time to sell the securities by giving 15 days' notice in a daily paper published in Ottawa, with power to buy in and re-sell without being liable for any loss. On the facts it was held that the sale was invalid, and at p. 353 of the report it was said that the sale should be by public auction. If the power of sale requires advertising a specified number of times with intervals of one week between each insertion, a full week excluding the day of publication must elapse between each publication: *Bartram v. Grice* (1912), 4 D.L.R. 682.

In a Quebec case it was held that a public sale duly advertised was necessary, and notice given by private circular to the shareholders was deemed insufficient: *Campbell v. Beyer* (1906), 30 Que. S.C. 86. See also *Young v. Croteau* (1925), 58 O.L.R. 76 and 303 (C.A.), where a private sale by the mortgagee was allowed to stand in part, although the point seems not to have been raised.

If there is a special agreement pledging the shares, the rights of the lender and borrower *inter se* will, of course, be governed thereby.

A mortgagee of shares with a power of sale is not a trustee of the power, which is rather a power given him for his own benefit, per Maclennan J.A. in *Daniels v. Noxon* (1889), 17 O.A.R. 206 at 211, citing *Warner v. Jacob* (1882), 20 Ch. D. 220. Consequently, there is no duty on him to sue a purchaser of the shares for completion of the sale, and he cannot be compelled by the mortgagor to do so except on the terms of the debt being paid. The court will not interfere, although the sale by the mortgagee is disadvantageous, if he exercises his power in good faith for the purpose of realizing the debt, without collusion with the purchaser, unless the price is so low as itself to be evidence of fraud: *Young v. Croteau* (1925), 58 O.L.R. 76 and 303 (C.A.).

A sale of shares or securities pledged should only be of a sufficient amount to pay off the debt: *Toronto General Trusts Corp. v. Central Ontario Railway* (1905), 10 O.L.R. 347 (C.A.), and if more are sold the mortgagee is liable to return the excess or pay damages: *Young v. Croteau, supra.*

The exercise of the implied power of sale by a mortgagee of shares will not be invalidated by reason of too much having been demanded in the notice requiring payment: *Stubbs v. Slater*, [1910] 1 Ch. 632 (C.A.). In the same case it was held that where the mortgagee held a single certificate and a blank transfer covering the number of shares specified in the certificate the mortgagee was entitled to sell the whole block of shares, the borrower being only entitled to an account of the proceeds.

It is the duty of the pledgee to take reasonable means to prevent a sacrifice and to act as a provident owner would have done: *Latch v. Furlong* (1866), 12 Gr. 303; *Bartram v. Grice, supra.*

The principle that a mortgagee is not entitled to sue for the mortgage debt, if he is unable to return the mortgaged security through having wrongfully parted with it, applies where the mortgaged property consists of shares as well as real property. However, if the shares are readily purchasable on the market, the court will not insist on a retransfer of the identical shares mortgaged but will substitute the value of the shares as of the date when they ought to have been returned to the mortgagor, namely, the date when the amount of the debt was ascertained and became payable: *Ellis & Co.'s Trustee v. Dixon-Johnson*, [1924] 1 Ch. 342, [1924] 2 Ch. 451 (C.A.).

The Statute of Limitations does not apply to proceedings for the redemption of personalty. Where shares had been deposited to secure a loan and no payments were made but, 21 years later, the dividends received by the mortgagee were sufficient to pay off the loan, the representatives of the borrower after the lapse of over 26 years from the making of the loan were held entitled to redeem, the mortgagee having taken no steps to sell or foreclose and the circumstances being such that no one had been prejudiced by the delay: *Weld v. Petre*, [1929] 1 Ch. 33 (C.A.).

Loan of shares

Where shares are lent among stockbrokers the borrower is not bound to return the specific shares borrowed, but may repay the loan with any shares of the same amount and kind. In such transactions the borrower has the right to return the shares at any time and demand the return to him by the lender of the security given for the loan of the shares. In the event of refusal by the lender to take back the shares the borrower need not make a formal tender thereof: *Wills v. Ford & Doucette* (1915), 35 O.L.R. 126 (C.A.).

If both parties admit the existence of a contract regarding shares, parol evidence is admissible to show that a transfer of the shares to the corporation, pursuant to the contract, is intended as a loan and not a gift: *Siscoe Gold Mines Ltd. v. Bijakowski*, [1935] S.C.R. 193.

It is becoming increasingly common for pension funds, insurance companies and other investment entities to engage in securities lending transactions which can have significant corporate and tax implications. It can be anticipated that jurisprudence and regulatory requirements will intervene to determine a number of the issues that arise from such transactions.

Transfer practice

This subject is discussed under various headings noted below. Reference is made to the provisions of s. 48 to s. 81 inclusive of the federal Act, which provide a code relating to certificates, registers and transfers. The sections dealing with transfers in particular are s. 76 to s. 81, the more important of which are commented on below. Section 78 of the Act provides that an issuer has a duty to enquiry into adverse claims, if written notice has been received which gives the issuer a reasonable opportunity to act on it, and the notice discloses certain required particulars. The duty of enquiry may be discharged by notifying an adverse claimant that a security has been presented for transfer and that the transfer will be registered, unless within 30 days from the date of mailing either a restraining or other order of the court is served on the issuer or the issuer is provided with an appropriate indemnity bond; written notice of an adverse claim is effective 12 months from the date on which it was received unless the notice is renewed in writing (s. 78(4)). Section 79 of the Act provides that there is no liability on the issuer to an owner as the result of a transfer of a security where the necessary endorsements were present and there was no duty to enquire into adverse claims or if such duty had been discharged.

Genuineness of signature

The corporation is bound not to take an existing shareholder off the register unless he has executed a transfer. The corporation may as a precaution advise the registered holder of a transfer, but the protection derived from this practice is apt to be illusory: *Sheffield Corporation v. Barclay*, [1905] A.C. 392 at 404. It is a more useful precaution to require the person presenting the transfer to procure the endorsement to be guaranteed by a bank or a trust corporation or by a member of a recognized stock exchange. While such procedure will afford the corporation a right of recourse against the guarantor, it does not release the corporation from responsibility to the registered owner if he has not in fact executed the transfer: *Racette v. The King*, [1942] S.C.R. 464.

A forged transfer is a nullity and the rightful owner is entitled to be registered as owner of the shares: *Barton v. North Staffordshire Railway* (1888), 38 Ch. D. 458; *Barton v. London & North Western Railway* (1889), 24 Q.B.D. 77 (C.A.). The Statute of Limitations commences to run from the time when the corporation refuses to treat the true owner as the shareholder: *Barton v. North Staffordshire Railway, supra.*

No estoppel exists as against the corporation in favour of the supposed transferee who has caused the corporation to issue to him a certificate on the faith of a forged transfer: *Simm v. Anglo-American Telegraph Co.* (1879), 5 Q.B.D. 188; and the corporation is entitled to be indemnified by the person at whose request a forged transfer is registered for any liability incurred to the real owner: *Bank of England v. Cutler*, [1908] 2 K.B. 208 (C.A.); *Sheffield Corporation v. Barclay, supra.* If, however, the corporation has issued a certificate to the person presenting a forged transfer, and a third person relying on such certificate purchases the shares, the corporation will be liable to such third person for damages for loss of the shares on the ground of estoppel: *In re Bahia & San Francisco Railway* (1868), L.R. 3 Q.B. 584.

The standard practice is to require the endorsement to be guaranteed by a bank, trust corporation or a member of a recognized stock exchange. This will ordinarily be a member of the stock exchange of the place where the certificate is presented for transfer. Section 77 of the Act provides that an issuer may require an assurance that each necessary endorsement on a security is genuine and effective by requiring a guarantee of the signature of the person making the endorsement and by requiring certain evidence of authority to sign where appropriate. The guarantee under ss. (2) must be signed by or on behalf of a person reasonably believed by the issuer to be responsible. Subsection (4) deals with the appropriate evidence of appointment of an agent or other representative.

Regularity of endorsement

The signature should correspond exactly with the name on the face of the certificate. Most forms of endorsement printed on the back of the certificate call for the witnessing of the signature of the transferor, but the absence of a subscribing witness is not fatal: *Goldfields Ltd. v. Harris Maxwell Co.* (1910), 2 O.W.N. 1373.

Where the transfer is executed not by the registered holder but by an attorney for him, the original power of attorney should be lodged with and retained by the corporation or its transfer agent, and should be carefully examined to see whether the transfer is within the power conferred. The corporation or its transfer agent should satisfy itself by enquiry that the power of attorney is still in full force and effect; that it has not been revoked by the grantor (unless it has effectively been made irrevocable); and that it has not been revoked by operation of law as by the death, insanity or bankruptcy of the grantor. By the *Powers of Attorney Act*, R.S.O. 1990, c. P.20, a limited protection is given in certain specified cases as regards acts done after the death or mental incompetency of the grantor. The risk to the corporation or a transfer agent in acting on a power of attorney is considerable as illustrated by *McLaughlin v. Daily Telegraph Newspaper Co. (No. 2)*, [1904] 1 C.L.R. 243 (*sub nom. Daily Telegraph Newspaper Co. v. McLaughlin*), [1904] A.C. 776, where a corporation was required to rectify the register on the ground that a power of attorney, in pursuance of which a transfer had been recorded, having been signed by the shareholder while he was insane to the knowledge of the attorney although not to the knowledge of the corporation, must be treated as a nullity. Transfers executed by persons other than the registered shareholder are discussed further in what follows.

Transfers to and by partnership firms

Under the former Act there was some question as to whether a partnership was entitled to become a shareholder because of the definition of the word "person". Under the present Act, s. 2(1) defines the word "person" as including a partnership. Accordingly there is no longer any doubt. In any event, the practice even prior to the present Act was to register transfers to partnership firms in the name of the firm and where this is done it is a proper precaution to obtain from the firm, for use when the shares are transferred by it, specimen signatures signed by each member of the firm authorized in the name of the partnership to transfer shares. The practice referred to is of particular importance as regards stock exchange firms. *Semble*, if shares are registered in the name of a partnership firm, the partners are joint holders: *In re Glory Paper Mills Co.; Dunster's Case*, [1894] 3 Ch. 473 at 482 (C.A.). Accordingly it can be argued that each partner should sign the form of transfer. However, ordinarily, a partnership agreement would deal with signature on behalf of the partnership for all matters including transfers and this would govern.

Transfers by corporations

A certified copy of the provisions of the by-laws with regard to execution of transfers of shares generally by the holders of particular offices, or a certified copy of a resolution of the directors authorizing the transfer by particular officers, should be produced, together in each case with evidence as to the persons holding the offices specified. The transfer must be signed by the proper officers, and the seal of the corporation should be affixed unless it is part of the usual business of the corporation to deal in shares, or the corporation is not required to, and does not, have a seal.

Change of name of shareholder

In the case of the marriage of a female shareholder and consequent change of name or in the case of any other change of name, a statutory declaration should be required setting out the facts and showing that the names on the face of the certificate and in the endorsement are those of the same person.

Joint holders

Section 51(6) of the federal Act provides that a corporation may treat as the owner of a security any survivors of persons to whom the security was issued as joint holders, if it receives proof satisfactory to it of the death of such joint holder.

Where shares stand in the names of two persons jointly, on the death of one the other is entitled to the shares by survivorship: *Garrick v. Taylor* (1861), 4 DeG. F. & J. 159; *Crossfield v. Such* (1853), 8 Ex. 825. However, where shares are registered in the names of two persons and one of them dies, the safer course is not to record a transfer upon the signature of the survivor only, unless there is furnished either (a) satisfactory evidence that the survivor is solely entitled by reason of the holding having in fact been a joint holding in the strict sense with resulting right of survivorship, or (b) the consent in writing of the personal representatives of the deceased holder and the letters probate or corresponding document or a duly authenticated copy. Such joint holding would be established if the shares are recorded in the names of two persons "as joint tenants, with right of survivorship and not as tenants in common", to which form of recording there does not appear to be any legal objection. In any event, consents of any appropriate succession duty or taxing authorities should be obtained. At common law it is impossible to create a joint tenancy between a corporation and an individual: *Law Guarantee & Trust Society Ltd. v. Governor & Company of Bank of England* (1890), 24 Q.B.D. 406.

Transfers by a married woman

As shares are personal estate and are governed by the law of the shareholder's domicile it may be necessary to obtain the concurrence of a spouse in the transfer of shares by a married shareholdern domiciled in a jurisdiction, for example, the Province of Quebec, where, unless it is established that the shareholder is separate as to property, such concurrence is necessary for a gift or gratuitous transfer of shares. When the domicile of such a shareholder is in doubt, it is advisable to obtain a declaration covering the matter. See *Re Parsons* (1926), 29 O.W.N. 430.

Transfers by or to an infant

Section 51(5) of the federal Act provides that where an infant exercises any rights of ownership in securities of a corporation no subsequent repudiation or avoidance is effective against the corporation. The cases which follow must be read with this provision in mind.

An infant may by contract become the holder of shares in a corporation. Such a contract is voidable by the infant and, like any other such contract, is valid until repudiated: *Re Sovereign Bank of Canada; Clark's Case* (1916), 35

O.L.R. 448 at 456 (C.A.); *Steinberg v. Scala (Leeds) Ltd.*, [1923] 2 Ch. 452 at 462 (C.A.).

A transfer of shares to an infant is good provided the corporation registers the transfer; but a corporation is not bound to register a transfer of shares to an infant: *In re Asiatic Banking Corp.; Symons' Case* (1870), L.R. 5 Ch. App. 298. The disadvantage to a corporation in registering a transfer of shares to an infant arises from the facts that the infant is entitled to repudiate the shares on attaining majority or within a reasonable time thereafter, and that in the meantime calls cannot be enforced against him: *Re Sovereign Bank of Canada; Clark's Case* (1916), 35 O.L.R. 448 (C.A.). In that case the infant after attaining majority withdrew from a bank money which represented accumulated dividends on the shares; the court held that this was a ratification of the infant's position as a shareholder and that she was liable as a contributory in respect of the shares in her name. Where an infant had effectually repudiated the shares, she was not liable as a contributory: *Re Sovereign Bank of Canada; Barnes's Case* (1916), 11 O.W.N. 103.

When the corporation has gone into liquidation, if it has acted innocently in recording the transfer, the transfer will be treated as a nullity: *In re Joint Discount Co.; Mann's Case* (1868), L.R. 3 Ch. App. 459n; *In re China Steamship & Labuan Coal Co.; Capper's Case* (1868), L.R. 3 Ch. App. 458. As pointed out in the latter case, questions of difficulty as to the effect of such a transfer might arise, if dividends had been received and the corporation was not in liquidation. If there has been laches on the part of the corporation in permitting the infant's name to remain on the register after discovery of the infant's age and liquidation has intervened, the liquidator will be disentitled to have the register amended by substituting the name of the adult transferor for that of the infant transferee: *In re European Central Railway; Parsons' Case* (1869), L.R. 8 Eq. 656.

It may be that a transfer of shares held by an infant can be effectively made only in pursuance of an order of the court having jurisdiction. In Ontario a guardian can apply to the court for advice under the *Trustee Act*, R.S.O. 1990, c. T.23, s. 60, and the court, on such an application, can give leave to sell or approve a sale: *Re Gurney* (1926), 31 O.W.N. 232. As to the transfer of shares belonging to a minor domiciled in Quebec, see *Raphael v. McFarlane* (1890), 18 S.C.R. 183.

As a transfer to an infant is not void but voidable, where shares were transferred to an infant, who transferred them to another infant, who in turn transferred them to an adult, all the transfers being registered, the intermediate transfers could not be avoided: *In re Contract Corp.; Gooch's Case* (1872), L.R. 8 Ch. App. 266.

If a foreign guardian applies for registration in his name of shares belonging to an infant domiciled abroad, the guardian must show that he is entitled to the shares by the law of the domicile of the infant or by an order of the court of the country where the infant is domiciled: *Kelly v. O'Brian* (1916), 37 O.L.R. 326, followed in *Re Burnett*, [1936] O.R. 506.

See also s. 51(2)(b) of the federal Act where a guardian is to be recognized under certain circumstances as acting for an infant.

Transfers by an incompetent or a committee of an incompetent

A transfer of shares by an incompetent will, it is submitted, be subject to the same rules as are applicable in the case of other contracts of an incompetent, as to which see *Wilson v. The King*, [1938] S.C.R. 317. A transfer made in pursuance of a power of attorney signed by an incompetent, so far as the corporation is concerned, at any rate where the fact of incompetency was known to the attorney, is wholly void: *McLaughlin v. Daily Telegraph Newspaper Co. (No. 2)*, [1904] 1 C.L.R. 243 (*sub nom. Daily Telegraph Newspaper Co. v. McLaughlin*), [1904] A.C. 776, and see *Wilson v. The King*, [1938] S.C.R. 317 at 335. The Ontario *Powers of Attorney Act* provides that power of attorney—expressly stating that it may be exercised during any subsequent legal incapacity of the donor—is valid, but not if a committee is appointed, or an order under s. 35 of the *Mental Incompetency Act* is made and a person appointed having the powers of a committee, or if the public trustee becomes committee of the estate of the donor. See also s. 51 of the federal Act where a private corporation is required to—and any other corporation may—treat a person as a registered security holder, entitled to exercise the rights of the security holder he represents, if certain documentation is filed and if he is the guardian or committee of the incompetent person.

When the committee of an incompetent requests the transfer of shares into his name, if the incompetent is domiciled in Ontario, the corporation should be furnished with evidence that the committee has given security as required by s. 10(d) of the *Mental Incompetency Act*, R.S.O. 1990, c. M.9, that the committee has been authorized by the court to have the shares transferred into his name or that a court order has been made vesting the shares in the committee. The courts are bound to recognize the rights conferred upon the committee of an incompetent by the laws of his domicile: *Re Hickson* (1927), 61 O.L.R. 180; see *Thiery v. Chalmers, Guthrie & Co.*, [1900] 1 Ch. 80.

Bankruptcy of the shareholder

A bankrupt's shares vest in the trustee who has power to transfer them: the *Bankruptcy and Insolvency Act*, ss. 15 and 30. The corporation should require evidence of permission having been granted by the inspectors to the trustee to transfer the shares. See also s. 51(2)(c) of the federal Act where a private corporation is required to—and other corporations may—treat a person as a registered security holder if that person furnishes the corporation with required evidence that he is a liquidator or trustee in bankruptcy for the security holder.

For the distinction between transfer and transmission to a trustee in bankruptcy see *In re Bentham Mills Spinning Co.* (1879), 11 Ch. D. 900 (C.A.); *In re W. Key & Sons Ltd.*, [1902] 1 Ch. 467 (trustee entitled to clean registration); but see *La Société Canadienne-Française de Construction de Montréal v. Daveluy* (1891), 20 S.C.R. 449. In the case of shares of a private corporation, where the right to transfer shares is prohibited without the sanction of the directors, it would appear that the trustee in bankruptcy does not acquire the full rights of a shareholder until he has himself recorded on the books of the corporation as such: *Re Fox Johnson & Co.*, [1942] 2 D.L.R. 784 at 788. Moreover, a trustee in bankruptcy may be bound by provisions in the charter of a private corporation requiring the sale of the shares to particular persons at a prescribed price not shown to be less than the fair price: *Borland's Trustee v. Steel Brothers & Co., Ltd.*, [1901] 1 Ch. 279.

In *Morgan v. Gray*, [1953] 1 Ch. 83 the court held that a bankrupt shareholder whose name remained on the register still retained his right to vote or tender a proxy at meetings of the corporation, there being no express provision to the contrary in the corporation's articles and the corporation not being in liquidation. He remained a member of the corporation in respect of his shares and was entitled to exercise (subject to the direction of the trustee in bankruptcy) the votes attributable to that status, notwithstanding that he no longer had any beneficial interest in the shares and that the corporation was entitled to pay any dividends to his trustee in bankruptcy.

Under the English *Companies Act*, a trustee in bankruptcy who has not obtained registration of the bankrupt's shares in his own name has no *locus standi* as a contributory to present a petition for the compulsory winding-up of the corporation: *In re H. L. Bolton Engineering Co.*, [1956] 1 Ch. 577.

The court may order the bankrupt to transfer to the trustee shares held in a foreign corporation: *In re Maguire* (1922), 2 C.B.R. 543.

Winding-up or bankruptcy of the corporation

If a winding-up order has been made, no transfers can be registered except with the sanction of the liquidator under the authority of the court: *Winding-up Act*, s.20.

If the corporation is being wound up under the *Bankruptcy and Insolvency Act*, on the other hand, transfers may be registered and new certificates issued in the ordinary form, signed by the proper officers, the trustee being bound to permit the use of the corporation's books and seal for that purpose: *Re Canadian Cereal & Flour Mills Co.* (1922), 51 O.L.R. 316. If, however, the shares are not fully paid, the question of contribution by the transferor should be dealt with before the transfer is accepted and registered.

Transmission by will or on an intestacy and transfers by executors and administrators

Subsections 51(2) and (7) of the federal Act provide that a private corporation must—and other corporations may—treat a person as a registered security holder if he furnishes the corporation with the required evidence that he is the executor, administrator, heir or legal representative of the heirs, of the estate of the deceased security holder. Subsection (7) provides for the type of information required to be deposited.

Where a shareholder dies, his shares, as personal estate, vest in his executors or administrators. The executors or administrators do not, however, automatically become shareholders (failing statutory provision to this effect) nor may they be registered as shareholders without their consent. It is necessary to determine on what evidence shares may be registered in the names of such personal representatives pursuant to a transmission on the death of a shareholder.

The Act follows in principle the provisions of s. 18 of *The Companies Clauses Act, 1845*, the effect of which was discussed in *Barton v. London & North Western Railway* (1889), 24 Q.B.D. 77 (C.A.) and may be summarized as follows. No effect need be given to the transmission, so far as the corporation is concerned, until the requirements of the section have been complied with. If the transmission is to persons as executors it must be so stated and their names must be given. Once the executors have been registered under the section they become shareholders and the corporation is not concerned with the character in which they hold the shares.

Where an executor has the legal right to shares registered in the name of the testator, he is entitled to have his name entered on the books of the corporation as ancillary to his legal title to the shares: *Scott v. Frank F. Scott (London) Ltd.*, [1940] Ch. 794 (C.A.).

On an application to enter a transfer to executors by transmission, the corporation is not called upon to examine the will with reference to the provisions of any particular trusts as to the ultimate disposal of the estate: *Simpson v. Molsons' Bank*, [1895] A.C. 270 at 281.

In jurisdictions where the governing Act forbids the entering on the register of notice of any trust, executors are entitled to have their names entered without any statement that they hold the shares in a representative capacity: *In re T. H. Saunders & Co.*, [1908] 1 Ch. 415; and should be so entered: *Barton v. London & North Western Railway, supra.*

It was held under the former Act that if executors so decide, they can require the corporation to recognize a transfer from the executors without first causing themselves to be registered as shareholders or complying with the requirements of the Act: *Deacon v. Central Manitoba Mines Ltd.*, [1934] 1 W.W.R. 45 (distinction between transmission and transfer explained); but it appears that this does not obviate the necessity of the directors satisfying themselves as to the status of the executors. Section 57(7) of the Act contemplates a direct transfer from the executors. The corporation need not examine the will to ascertain whether it confers authority to transfer the shares: *Barton v. North Staffordshire Railway* (1888), 38 Ch. D. 458, and see *Simpson v. Molsons' Bank*, [1895] A.C. 270 at 280. The notice acquired by the corporation by production of the probate is limited to notice of the names and addresses of the executors and the corporation is not entitled to assume that a transfer by the executors involves a breach of trust: *Grundy v. Briggs*, [1910] 1 Ch. 444. The will must, however, be examined where the testator was domiciled in the province of Quebec.

If there is more than one executor or administrator, all should join in any transfer of the shares held by them. The definition of a "person" in s. 2(1) includes the personal representatives of a deceased shareholder. If two executors are registered as shareholders one of them cannot make a valid transfer: *Barton v. North Staffordshire Railway* (1888), 38 Ch. D. 458.

In the event of an executor withdrawing his signature to a transfer, without giving any specific reason for so doing, the proper practice was stated by Eve J. in *Grundy v. Briggs*, [1910] 1 Ch. 444 at 449, to be to notify the executors that "unless within a limited time, and a strictly limited time, he took legal proceedings to prevent the company from proceeding to register the transfer, the company would, at the expiration of the time, register the transfer so lodged with them".

If the corporation registers a transfer made by a person who is not the executor, the true executor will be entitled to have the share register rectified and to recover from the corporation any dividends which may have been paid to the transferee: *Stuart v. Hamilton Jockey Club* (1910), 2 O.W.N. 673 and 1402 (C.A.); and where the transfer on the face of it shows that the transferor has no authority to deal with the shares, the corporation may not be able to rely on it in order to make the party propounding the transfer liable as warranting its genuineness.

Where ancillary letters of administration have been taken out in Ontario, the legal title to shares of a federal corporation having its head office in Ontario is in the Ontario administrators; it follows that a claim disputing the title of the administrators must be determined by an Ontario court: *Re Fenwick* (1915), 35 O.L.R. 29.

Foreign transmissions

Section 51(8) provides that if the laws of the jurisdiction governing the transmission of a security of a deceased holder do not require a grant of probate or letters of administration, a legal representative of the deceased holder is entitled (subject to any applicable law relating to the collection of taxes) to become a registered holder or to designate a registered holder if he deposits with the corporation the security certificate in question and reasonable proof of the governing laws relating to the deceased holder's interest in the security and of the right of the legal representative or person he designates to become the registered holder. In the absence of similar provisions, in the case of a dealing with shares by foreign executors or administrators, the taking out of ancillary letters probate or ancillary letters of administration or the re-sealing of the letters probate or letters of administration in the province where the head office of the corporation is situated, should be exacted: *A. G. v. New York Breweries Co.*, [1898] 1 Q.B. 205 (C.A.); affd [1899] A.C. 62 (H.L.). It has been held in Ontario, however, that executors derive their title, not from the letters probate—which are merely evidence—but from the will; and that before probate is issued they are clothed with their full title: *Re Green & Flatt* (1913), 29 O.L.R. 103. See also the observations of Idington J. in *Smith v. Levesque*, [1923] S.C.R. 578 at 580, 581. An administrator, on the other hand, derives his title purely from the grant of administration: *In re Thorpe* (1868), 16 Gr. 76. Even if *Re Green & Flatt* is to be relied on as authority for dispensing with ancillary letters probate, satisfactory evidence should be provided that there are no debts owing.

Estate tax and succession duty

Canada and the provinces formerly levied estate or succession duty and the relevant legislation provided that registration of transfers of shares of a deceased shareholder should not be made unless appropriate consents from the tax authorities concerned had been produced. While these provisions are no longer in force, there are a number of cases which are relevant both for constitutional and situs questions. These are discussed below.

By way of an example of such succession duty legislation, the Ontario *Succession Duty Act*, R.S.O. 1960, c. 386, s. 10, provided that no corporation, having its head office, principal place of business, register of transfers, or any place of transfer in Ontario, was to permit *inter alia*, the assignment or transfer of any property situate in Ontario in which the deceased at the time of his death had any beneficial interest, unless the consent in writing of the Treasurer was obtained; and no person in Ontario was without such consent *inter alia* to permit the transfer of any property in which the deceased had at the time of his death any beneficial interest. It will be noted that the application of the last-mentioned provision was not limited to property situate in Ontario (see *Warren v. Union Gas Co.*, [1943] 4 D.L.R. 668 (Ont. C.A.)) and where the corporation has registers in more than one jurisdiction, if the head office was in Ontario whether it be a federal or an Ontario corporation, the Ontario succession duty authorities required a consent to the transfer of the shares to be obtained under the provisions of the Ontario *Succession Duty Act*, whether the transfer was made on a register or branch register within or outside Ontario. See, however, *Re Russell*, [1942] O.R. 466, *infra*. Section 10 of the Ontario *Succession Duty Act* was *intra vires* in relation to shares of a federal corporation: *Christie v. British American Oil Co.*, [1947] O.R. 455; affd [1947] O.R. 842 (C.A.).

Where a provincially incorporated corporation has issued share certificates stated on their face to be transferable at a transfer agency either in the province of Quebec (the province of incorporation) or in the province of Ontario, if there is no liability for succession duty to the province of Quebec in respect of the shares, neither the corporation nor the transfer agent can make it a condition of transfer that a clearance should be furnished from the succession duty department of the province of Quebec, the certificates endorsed in blank being found in Ontario on the death of the registered owner: *Re Russell*, [1942] O.R. 466 (order of mandamus made under Ontario rule 629). No order of mandamus can be made against the transfer agent in Ontario in the case of shares of a foreign corporation, where, under the laws governing the corporation, a valid transfer cannot be effected without entry in a book to be kept in the state of incorporation: *Re Hatch & Fanny Farmer Candy Shops Inc.*, [1944] O.R. 586 (C.A.). It was further held that a statement in the share certificate that the shares were transferable in Toronto, could not constitute in law a contractual obligation on the part of the corporation or the transfer agent, either to the shareholder or a transferee, the statement being at variance with the powers of the corporation.

It should be noted that, upon a transmission owing to the death of the shareholder, shares of a corporation whose head office is outside the province may (under certain circumstances) be subject to succession duty. Thus the statute of Quebec, 4 Geo. V, c. 10, was held *intra vires* where it provided that taxation should attach to property outside the province if (1) the transmission is within the province, that is, the person to whom the property is transmitted is either domiciled or ordinarily resident within the province; and (2) the transmission is due to the death of a person domiciled within the province: *Burland v. The King; Alleyn v. Barthe*, [1922] 1 A.C. 215. Similarly under the Ontario *Succession Duty Act* the province had the right to tax the succession to Canadian shares and securities, the property of a British subject domiciled and resident in Ontario bequeathed to a beneficiary domiciled and resident in Ontario, notwithstanding that the shares and securities were in the United States at the time of the death: *A. G. Ont. v. Baby* (1926), 60 O.L.R. 1. See also *Treasurer of Ontario v. Blondé*, [1941] O.R. 227 at 238.

Situs of shares for estate tax and succession duty purposes

The question of the situs of shares is important in cases where the right to tax or the claim to tax is based on the local situation of the shares at the time of the death of the holder.

By virtue of its unrestricted taxing power, Parliament can impose a tax which is either direct or indirect and which relates to matters or persons either without or within its jurisdiction. However, in practice, until 1948 only property and persons within Canada were taxed and in administering the Act questions as to the situs of shares arose which were determined by the common law rules. The Act was amended in 1948 to provide that, for the purposes of the Act, shares in the capital stock of a corporation incorporated in Canada should be deemed to have a situs in Canada. Consequently from January 1, 1948 to January 1, 1959 (at which time the *Estate Tax Act* came into force) shares of both federal and provincial corporations had a situs for federal succession duty purposes in Canada regardless of the common law rules. The *Estate Tax Act* which applied in the case of any person dying on or after January 1, 1959, imposed a tax on all property wheresoever situate of all persons domiciled in Canada so that in the case of such persons no question as to the situs of shares arose. However, for the purpose of calculating deductions for provincial, gift and foreign taxes, questions of situs did arise and s. 9(8)(d) provided that for such purpose where the deceased was domiciled in Canada, shares of a corporation held by him were deemed to be situate in the province where he was domiciled at the time of his death, if any register of transfers or place of transfer was maintained by the corporation in that province for the transfer thereof, and otherwise in the place where the register of transfers or place of transfer nearest to the place where the deceased was ordinarily resident at the time of his death was maintained by the corporation for the transfer thereof. Where the deceased was domiciled outside of Canada, shares of a corporation held by him were, with minor exceptions, deemed to be situated in the place where the corporation was incorporated (s. 38(e)).

Under the *Constitution Act, 1867* the taxing authority of the provinces is restricted to "direct taxation within the province" and accordingly the provincial Succession Duty Acts must tax property, persons or events within the province. In the case of shares, the common law rules for determining situs are applicable and cannot be altered by the provinces so as to extend their power to tax: *The*

King v. National Trust Co., [1933] S.C.R. 670 at 673; *The King v. Williams*, [1942] A.C. 541 at 559; *The King v. Globe Indemnity Co. of Canada*, [1945] O.R. 190 at 196 (C.A.).

In *Re Jodrey* (1980), 8 E.T.R. 69 (S.C.C.), the Court considered whether a non-resident parent corporation, the shares of which were held by the testator's resident grandchildren, was "beneficially entitled" to the residue of the testator's estate which had been bequeathed to a wholly owned subsidiary corporation for purposes of Nova Scotia succession duty legislation. If so, the legislation imposed succession tax on the resident shareholders of a non-resident corporation. It was argued that the legislation was *ultra vires* the province as it imposed tax on property received by a corporation not resident in the province and as such was not a direct tax.

The Court concluded that the tax imposed was an *in personam* tax on a resident successor and hence *intra vires*. The legislation imposed on resident shareholder successors the same obligations imposed on resident successors, even though the property ultimately devolved by reason of death through the ownership of shares in a non-resident corporation. The tax was upon residents in the province measured by the benefit derived and not a tax on property outside the province.

In what follows, consideration is given to the situs of shares at common law for estate tax or succession duty purposes. As already indicated, the *Estate Tax Act* contained provisions establishing different rules as to determining situs for estate tax purposes.

Shares, being intangible property, have no real situs but rules have been developed ascribing to them a situs for succession duty and other purposes. The test under these rules for ascertaining the situs of shares for succession duty purposes, is where can the shares be effectively dealt with as between the shareholder and the corporation so that a transferee will become legally entitled to all the rights of a shareholder: *Brassard v. Smith*, [1925] A.C. 371 at 376; *Untermeyer Estate v. A.G. B.C.*, [1929] S.C.R. 84; *Erie Beach Co. v. A.G. Ont.*, [1930] A.C. 161; *The King v. Williams*, [1942] A.C. 541 at 558; *The King v. Globe Indemnity Co. of Canada*, [1945] O.R. 190 at 197 (C.A.).

No difficulty is encountered in applying this test to shares which are transferable on a register of transfers maintained by the corporation, provided there is only one such register of transfers. In cases where no transfer of the shares can be effected otherwise than by entry on the single register, the shares can only be dealt with in the jurisdiction in which the register is maintained and accordingly have their situs in such jurisdiction: *Untermeyer Estate v. A.G. B.C.*, *supra*; *Erie Beach Co. v. A.G. Ont.*, [1930] A.C. 161. In such cases, the location of the share certificate representing the shares, the residence or domicile of the shareholder, the country of incorporation and other factors have no bearing.

Where the deceased was domiciled in Ontario and had held shares in a corporation incorporated in Manitoba, the share register of which was maintained only in Manitoba, the situs of the shares was Manitoba. See *Minister of National Revenue v. Leckie*, [1967] S.C.R. 291. Similarly, where the deceased was domiciled in Ontario and had held shares in a Saskatchewan corporation, the situs of the shares was held to be in Saskatchewan notwithstanding that the deceased had brought the share register to Ontario and dealt with share transfers there. The shares could effectually only be transferred in Saskatchewan and a corporation could not be regarded as maintaining a share register where shares would not be effectively dealt with. Physical presence of the share register in another jurisdiction could have no effect. See: *Burton v. Minister of National Revenue*, [1969] S.C.R. 732.

Problems may arise where the corporation has established transfer offices in two or more jurisdictions at which the shares may be interchangeably transferred. "Interchangeably transferred" refers to the right of a shareholder to transfer the shares on any of the transfer registers, notwithstanding that he acquired the shares by transfer on a particular register. In the case of "book stock" where there are registers in different jurisdictions, the shares are not interchangeably transferable since they may only be transferred on the particular register at which they are from time to time registered. The shares of Canadian chartered banks were formerly in this category but shares of chartered banks no longer constitute book stock and are interchangeably transferable upon the different registers.

For some years there was uncertainty as to the rules to be applied to determine the situs of shares which were interchangeably transferable in two or more jurisdictions. However, the decisions of the Privy Council in *The King v. Williams*, [1942] A.C. 541 and *Treasurer of Ontario v. Blondé and Aberdein*, [1947] A.C. 24 have settled the law to a considerable extent.

It is now clear that in such a case, the situs of shares must be in a jurisdiction where a register of transfers is maintained, and the problem consists of determining which of the two or more jurisdictions is appropriate. If the share certificate, whether or not endorsed for transfer, is physically situate in a jurisdiction where there is a register of transfers, the shares will have their situs in that jurisdiction: *The King v. Williams, supra*. If the share certificate, however, is not physically located in a jurisdiction in which there is a register of transfers, a choice must be made on the basis of all the existing facts, the governing question being, which of the jurisdictions in which there is a register of transfers is most logically to be regarded as the place of transfer: *Treasurer of Ontario v. Blondé and Aberdein, supra*. In that case the testator was, at the date of his death, the registered holder of shares of a federal corporation and the testator and his wife were joint registered holders of shares in an Ontario corporation. Both the testator and his wife were domiciled and resident in Massachusetts, where the share certificates, none of which had been endorsed in blank, were situated. The head office of each corporation was in Ontario. Each corporation had duly appointed transfer agents in Toronto and New York. The shares in each corporation were listed and actively dealt in on the stock exchanges of Toronto and New York. It was held, adopting the test of convenience laid down in *The King v. Williams, supra*, that if it is possible on rational grounds to prefer one of the alternative places to the other as the place of transfer for the shares, the selection should be made accordingly. The fact that, under the law of New York, the shares were not situate in New York was held to be immaterial; and it was held that the New York transfer office of the Ontario corporation stood in all respects on a parity with the Ontario transfer office. In determining the situs of the shares the features to be taken into consideration were stated to be that (1) the shares were freely marketable both in New York and in Ontario; (2) the registered owners were domiciled and resident in Massachusetts; (3) probate in Ontario was not requisite to enable the executors of the testator to be registered on the New York register; and (4) there were clear advantages to the executors in choosing New York rather than Ontario as the place of transfer (*The King v. Globe Indemnity Co. of Canada*, [1945] O.R. 190 (C.A.) being referred to on this point). It was held that there were sufficient grounds (although there was no blank endorsement of the certificates) to enable a selection to be made between New York and Ontario, and that the shares were not, according to the law of Ontario, situate in Ontario, but in all the circumstances had a situs in New York.

Shares of a federal corporation were registered in the names of the plaintiff (resident in Manitoba) and the decedent as joint tenants with right of survivorship. The certificates, which stated on their face that the shares were transferable either at Montreal or Toronto, were in the possession of the decedent in Winnipeg at the date of death. The certificates were presented both at the office of a transfer agent in New York (established after the date of death) and at the office of the corporation's transfer agent in Toronto for transfer. The plaintiff was advised in both places that the shares could not be transferred without production of an Ontario Succession Duty release, but he refused to pay Ontario duty. The plaintiff having brought an action claiming a mandatory order directing the corporation to transfer or re-register the shares, it was held that the plaintiff having brought the certificates into Ontario and presenting them to the Toronto transfer agent had indicated the actual place where he would have the shares effectively dealt with, that the situs of the shares for succession duty purposes was in Ontario and that the refusal to record a transfer without the consent of the Treasurer of Ontario was well founded: *Christie v. British American Oil Co.*, [1947] O.R. 455; affd [1947] O.R. 842 (C.A.) (on appeal held that the situs of the shares for succession duty purposes had not been determined in the action, although Robertson C.J.O. was not to be understood as saying that a finding that the shares were situated in Ontario could not be supported upon the evidence given at the trial). Subsequently, the corporation's shares were subdivided and new certificates were issued in the joint names of the plaintiff and the decedent, transferable among other places at Winnipeg. The transfer agent there, on demand, refused to issue a new certificate in the plaintiff's name without an Ontario succession duty release. The shares were ultimately seized by the Ontario Treasurer and the plaintiff paid the duty demanded, but brought an action in Manitoba against the corporation claiming damages for wrongful refusal to transfer the shares to him. The trial judge dismissed the action and this was upheld by the Manitoba Court of Appeal, [1954] 1 D.L.R. 83 and the Supreme Court of Canada, [1954] S.C.R. 111 on the ground that the action was not properly constituted to determine the question of the situs of the shares; the plaintiff had chosen to pay the duty instead of moving against the seizure and therefore had not established that he had suffered any damage for which the corporation was responsible. The plaintiff argued that because the new certificates were transferable in Winnipeg the corporation was estopped from denying that the shares were properly transferable there. Kellock J. indicated that the material time as regards transferability was the date of death and that at that date the shares were situate and liable to duty in either Ontario or Quebec since these were the only places where they could have been effectively dealt with. Kerwin J. after quoting the statement on the certificates that the shares were transferable in a number of named cities, stated at p. 113:

> This means nothing more than that a transfer could be made in any of the named cities if the relevant law permitted it. It does not mean that the [corporation] was obliged to permit owners to transfer in any of these cities merely upon presentation of the certificate and a demand for such transfer. There is no basis for an estoppel because the [plaintiff] did not change his position by reason of the making of the statement quoted above in the new certificates.

Where the deceased shareholder of a British Columbia corporation had been domiciled in Nevada, the shares registered on the corporation's principal register in Vancouver but the share certificates held in Nevada, the situs of the shares was not British Columbia, despite the fact that the British Columbia Act required a transfer of shares of a deceased shareholder to be made only on the register kept in the registered office in British Columbia. The test for situs is to be at the moment of death and not after. See: *Minister of Finance for the Province of British Columbia v. First National Bank of Nevada*, [1975] 1 S.C.R. 525.

In the case of shares represented by bearer share certificates or bearer share warrants, the shares are usually transferable by delivery of the bearer share certificate or the bearer share warrant. Whether or not this is the case depends on the laws of the country of incorporation. Under this Act, bearer share certificates are not possible (except in the case of script or fractional shares) since a share certificate by virtue of s. 49(7) is required to state the name of the person to whom it was issued. However, it would appear that there is nothing in the Act to prevent the issue of bearer share warrants entitling the holder thereof on presentation to the corporation to shares therein specified. Such a bearer share warrant could have coupons attached for the payment of dividends. It will be observed in this regard that s. 49(1), which entitles a security holder to a security certificate complying with the Act or a non-transferable written acknowledgement of his right to obtain such a security certificate, is not phrased in terms which would prohibit the corporation from issuing bearer share warrants, which of course are transferable by delivery. In any such case, where the shares are transferable by delivery of a certificate or warrant, the shares may be effectively dealt with within the meaning of the rule in *Brassard v. Smith*, [1925] A.C. 371, by delivery of the certificate or warrant and accordingly have their situs where the certificate or warrant is physically situate; see *The King v. Williams*, [1942] A.C. 541.

It is arguable that in cases where the delivery of the share certificate by virtue of the section constitutes a valid transfer of the shares comprised therein, the shares may be effectively dealt with where the share certificate is situate as between the shareholder and the corporation, even though the corporation may treat the person in whose name the shares are registered, as being entitled to receive notice of and to vote at meetings of shareholders and to receive any payments in respect of the shares. It has been held, however, that shares which have been endorsed for transfer are not transferable by delivery of the certificate because no transfer of the shares is effective until entry thereof in the register of transfers, notwithstanding the common practice of stock exchanges to treat delivery of the certificate as delivery of the shares: *Re Brookfield Estate; Royal Trust Co. v. R.*, [1949] S.C.R. 329.

An apparent exception to this principle occurs in the case of "street certificates" which is the name customarily given to certificates which are registered in the name of a member of a stock exchange and endorsed in blank for transfer. In many cases, particularly where shares of speculative mining corporations are involved, certificates remain in street form and are passed from person to person without transfers ever being registered. In the case of street certificates, the holder's interest in the shares has been held to have a situs where the certificates are situate. The holder of such a certificate is not a shareholder of the corporation but is merely in a position to become a shareholder. The right to become a shareholder can be effectively dealt with by delivery of the street certificate and accordingly such right is treated as having a situs where the street certificate is physically situate: *The King v. Williams, supra*, at p. 557; *Re Brookfield Estate; Royal Trust Co. v. R., supra*. In the case of a street certificate it is pointed out that it is the right to become a shareholder, not the shares, that are taxed as having a situs within a particular jurisdiction.

It has been held in England that shares of South African corporations having duplicate registers in London, where the share certificates were held, were locally situated in England for the purpose of estate duty and that the fact that the power of transferring the shares in England was temporarily suspended due to post-war agreements, did not operate to change the location of the shares: *In re Ashcrott; Clifton v. Strauss*, [1927] 1 Ch. 313.

Registers of transfers and branch registers of transfers

Registration of the issue or transfer of a security in the central securities register, or in a branch securities register, is complete and valid registration for all purposes (s. 46(4)).

Lost, mutilated or destroyed certificates

Where share certificates are lost, the corporation and its transfer agent should be notified promptly of the loss, and a statement furnished indicating whether the certificates were endorsed or unendorsed and giving other available particulars of the loss. It is the practice of transfer agents in such event to notify promptly their co-transfer agents, if any, to place a note on their records in regard to the loss, and if the certificate is presented for transfer to notify, if possible, the person reporting the loss. The transfer agent does not assume any liability and does not undertake to stay the transfer. Should the lost certificate be endorsed in blank it is accordingly appropriate for the parties interested to have the corporation and its transfer agent restrained by a court of competent jurisdiction from dealing in any manner with such certificate.

Section 80 of the federal Act provides that where a security has been lost, apparently destroyed or wrongfully taken, if the owner fails to notify the issuer of that fact by written notice of his adverse claim within a reasonable time after becoming aware thereof, and if the issuer has registered a transfer of the security before receiving such notice, the owner is precluded from asserting against the issuer any claim to a new security. However, it would appear open to the owner to argue that the register should be rectified if a forged endorsement of the owner's signature were involved. Where there is a claim that a security has been lost, destroyed or wrongfully taken, the issuer is to issue a new security if the owner so requests before the issuer has notice that the security has been acquired by a bona fide purchaser, furnishes the issuer with a sufficient indemnity bond, and satisfies any other reasonable requirements of the issuer. Subsection (3) of s. 80 provides that if, after the issue of such a new security, a bona fide purchaser of the original security presents it for registration of transfer, the issuer is to register the same unless the registration would result in an over-issue in which case the provisions of s. 52 of the Act apply.

The by-laws of the corporation usually provide for the issuance of a certificate in lieu of a certificate lost, mutilated or destroyed on proof of the loss, mutilation or destruction, and the furnishing of a bond of a guarantee corporation indemnifying the corporation and its transfer agents and registrars against any liability which may arise by reason of the issuance of a new certificate in lieu of the certificate lost or destroyed. It is now usual for the transfer agent to require a bond unlimited as to amount in the case of the issuance of a new certificate in place of one alleged to be lost or destroyed.

In *Chartered Trust & Executor Co. v. Pagon*, [1950] O.R. 662, P., upon losing a share certificate endorsed in blank, notified the transfer agent, which made a "stop transfer" notation in its books, and received a new certificate upon giving the corporation and the transfer agent a bond of indemnity. The lost certificate was later presented for transfer, to the transfer agent, who by inadvertence, issued a new certificate. The court held that the transfer agent could not recover from P. under the bond of indemnity because the loss arose not as a result of issuing a duplicate certificate to P. but from the negligence of its officers and servants in accepting and acting upon the transfer of the lost certificate against which its books recorded a stop-over.

Custody of certificates after transfer

A certificate after transfer should be cancelled and a new certificate issued to the transferee; and if all the shares comprised in the certificate are not transferred, a fresh certificate for the balance is issued to the transferor. The corporation, however, is under no liability to the public at large for the safe custody of certificates for shares in its capital stock, and where a corporation by mistake returned a certificate, after transfer, to the transferor, whereby the latter was enabled fraudulently to raise money on the security of the shares, the person defrauded was held not entitled to recover from the corporation for the loss sustained: *Longman v. Bath Electric Tramways Ltd.*, [1905] 1 Ch. 646.

Chapter 7

BORROWING

Cross-references: Section 189;
Ontario Act, ss. 46-52, 184.

Introduction

The subject of corporate borrowing covers a very broad field. If all aspects of the law relating to borrowings by corporations were fully described, the discussion could continue almost without limit. The methods by which corporations borrow are many; the attributes of the debt instruments used are various; the remedies provided thereby for enforcement are numerous; the priority afforded by such instruments, whether secured or unsecured, is a matter for individual determination in all the circumstances and, in some cases, with reference to specific statutory provisions, for example, security taken pursuant to s. 427 of the *Bank Act*; the tax treatment of various kinds of "borrowings" may differ significantly. But all of this is beyond the scope of corporation law, as it is now generally understood. These subjects are more properly dealt with in discussions of corporate finance, securities law, banking law, creditors' and debtors' rights, personal property security law, real property law and the law of corporate taxation. Justice cannot be done to any of these subjects in a text dealing with corporation law. We leave, therefore, consideration of these important questions to other specialized texts dealing with such issues.

What will be discussed in this chapter are the aspects of the law related to corporate borrowing which are traditionally covered by corporation law statutes. Even this is not a small subject, since many aspects of corporation law generally affect the ability of a corporation to borrow.

Borrowing powers

Section 15(1) of the Act gives corporations all the capacity and, subject to the provisions of that Act, the rights, powers and privileges of a natural person (see Chapter 3). Since natural persons have the ability to borrow, so do corporations governed by the Act, subject to such restrictions as may be found in the Act or in the articles of incorporation. There are no restrictions in the Act limiting the forms of borrowing which a corporation may use. Accordingly, a corporation may borrow, with or without giving security, by means of (a) bills of exchange or promissory notes, (b) mortgages (of real or personal property), (c) the issue of bonds or debentures and (d) any other means that the law allows. It is no longer necessary, as it was under earlier corporation law statutes, to find express authorization for a particular form of borrowing somewhere in the corporation's incorporating documents. Further, s. 16(1) of the Act provides that it is not necessary for a by-law to be passed in order to confer any particular (for example, borrowing) power on the corporation or its directors. Pursuant to s. 16(2) of the Act, however, a corporation may not exercise any power, including a power to borrow, which it is restricted by its articles from exercising and must comply with any requirements contained in its articles which relate to or affect the manner in which such power is exercised.

In some cases it may be important to ascertain whether a transaction constitutes a borrowing or not. Thus, for example, overdrawing a corporation's bank account is a form of borrowing: see *Cunliffe Brooks & Co. v. Blackburn Building Society* (1884), 9 App. Cas. 857 at 865, 868. On the other hand a buying of goods on credit is not a borrowing. See *Kerr v. University Press Ltd.*, [1923] 2 W.W.R. 187 (Sask. C.A.) and *Re Red Deer Mill & Elevator Co.* (1907), 1 Alta. L.R. 237 and similarly the giving of a mortgage to secure existing debts is not borrowing: *Barthels, Shewan & Co. v. Winnipeg Cigar Co* (1909), 2 Alta. L.R. 21.

With respect to corporations not incorporated under the federal Act or a similar Act of a province, there may be doubt as to the power of the corporation to borrow money and, generally speaking, the governing statute and constating instruments must be examined with care. Thus, while every trading corporation has an implied power to borrow money for the purposes of its undertaking, it has been held that no such power exists for a non-trading corporation or certain public corporations such as railway corporations and waterworks corporations.

Authorization of borrowing by corporation

Section 189(1) of the Act provides that, unless the articles or by-laws or a unanimous shareholder agreement relating to a corporation otherwise provide, the corporation's articles are deemed to state that the directors may, without authorization of the shareholders, (i) borrow money on the corporation's credit, (ii) issue, reissue, sell or pledge debt obligations of the corporation, (iii) give a guarantee on behalf of the corporation to secure performance of an obligation of any person, except where such a guarantee is prohibited by s. 44 of the Act (concerning which, see Chapter 5), and (iv) mortgage, hypothecate, pledge or otherwise create a security interest in all or any property of the corporation to secure any or all of the corporation's obligations.

Accordingly, unless the articles, by-laws or a unanimous shareholder agreement otherwise provide, the directors may, without having obtained the approval of shareholders, effectively borrow, and in connection therewith, create any sort of debt obligation, on any terms and in any amount, with or without security. The previous practice of banks requiring a borrowing by-law to support the giving of credit to corporations has now generally been replaced by a certificate of non-restriction certifying that there are no restrictions on the corporation's power to borrow contained in its articles or by-laws or in any unanimous shareholders' agreement.

The corporation's directors are authorized by resolution to delegate their powers regarding the creation of corporation debt to a single director, to a committee of directors or to an officer of the corporation. This power to delegate may, however, be removed or restricted by the corporation's articles or by-laws or by a unanimous shareholder agreement: see s. 189(2).

When a corporation has upon the face of its constitution (that is, either by the statute or the statutory rules under which it is constituted) only a limited authority to borrow, the person dealing with such society or corporation must inquire or run the risk: *Chapleo v. Brunswick Permanent Benefit Building Society* (1881), 6 Q.B.D. 696 (C.A.), and where a corporation is incorporated under a public Act, the provisions of which forbid borrowing or buying on credit, no implied authority can arise. And, where directors of such a corporation have purchased goods on credit, they cannot be held liable or made to account for them on any principle: *Struthers v. Mackenzie* (1897), 28 O.R. 381.

If directors empowered under the articles to borrow up to a specified amount issue debentures when the liabilities of the corporation exceed that amount the debentures are void: *Re Pooley Hall Colliery Co.* (1869), 21 L.T. 690. See now ss. 52(2) of the Act, providing for a validation of overissued securities in certain cases. Directors may be personally liable on their implied representation that they had authority to issue valid securities where the securities are bad because the corporation has already exhausted its limited borrowing powers, even though this was not known to the directors: *Firbank's Executors v. Humphrey* (1886), 18 Q.B.D. 54 (C.A.).

The answer to the question whether the directors are liable on their representation of authority depends on whether the representation was one of fact or of law. If the representation is one of fact the directors are liable: *Richardson v. Williamson & Lawson* (1871), L.R. 6 Q.B. 276, where the power of the directors to borrow money depended on whether they had made a rule to do so and where in point of fact there was no such rule (as explained in

Beattie v. Lord Ebury (1872), L.R. 7 Ch. App. 777 at 801); *Cherry v. Colonial Bank of Australasia* (1869), L.R. 3 P.C. 24, where the directors in representing that they had power to borrow in effect represented that they had got the consent of a meeting of shareholders which was a prerequisite; *Weeks v. Propert* (1873), L.R. 8 C.P. 427, where the defendant knowing that the power of borrowing had been exercised represented that the directors had power to issue debentures binding on the corporation; *Firbank's Executors v. Humphreys, supra*; *West London Commercial Bank v. Kitson* (1884), 13 Q.B.D. 360 (C.A.). If, on the other hand, the representation is one of law the directors will not be liable; *Rashdall v. Ford* (1886), L.R. 2 Eq. 750; *Beattie v. Lord Ebury* (1872), L.R. 7 Ch. App. 777 at 802, (1875), L.R. 7 H.L. 102 at 130; *Struthers v. MacKenzie* (1897), 28 O.R. 381.

For examples of cases where the irregularity did not defeat the security see *Bank of Montreal v. Petrobuild Ltd.* (1981), 36 N.B.R. (2d) 375 and *Re Guaranteed Hardware Co.*, [1972] 3 O.R. 138 and *Re Rumford Holdings Ltd.* (1979), 100 D.L.R. (3d) 700 (Alta. T.D.). For an example of a case where irregularities were held to defeat the security see *Anderson Lumber Co. v. Canadian Conifer Ltd.* [1976] 3 W.W.R. 255; affd [1977] 5 W.W.R. 41 (Alta. C.A.).

Where action was taken by an officer of the corporation pursuant to a borrowing resolution and the majority shareholder had given notice at the same time both orally and in writing that the officer in question was not authorized, the Bank was held to be entitled to advance money in reliance on the borrowing resolution presently in its hands; the majority shareholder could not effectively countermand the borrowing resolution except by another resolution, see *Canadian Imperial Bank of Commerce v. Aizawa Holdings Ltd.* (1985), 63 A.R. 146 (Chambers). A mortgage which the governing act stated should not be created except with a sanction of a special resolution of the company previously given at a general meeting could be ratified by a subsequent meeting of shareholders: see *Thompson & Sutherland Ltd. v. Nova Scotia Trust Co.* (1971), 19 D.L.R. (3d) 59 (N.S.).

Procedure for exercising borrowing powers

It is often still a general practice for the directors, in organizing the corporation, to enact a by-law authorizing generally the borrowing of money by the corporation. Such a by-law commonly authorizes borrowing in such amounts and in such manner as the directors in their discretion think fit. Such a by-law is, however, not legally required since it usually repeats the provisions of the Act which empower the corporation to borrow. The corporation's bankers may also require that the directors pass a by-law, substantially in the form used by the particular bank, authorizing borrowings by the corporation from that bank. A number of banks now only require a certificate stating that there is no restriction or limit on the corporation's right to borrow.

Specific charge and floating charge

Where obligations involve more than a mere unsecured promise to pay and purport to give the holder the benefit of some security upon the assets of the corporation for the indebtedness represented by the obligations, the security may be conferred either by the obligation itself or by a covering trust deed. The security may be by way of specific mortgage or charge or by way of floating charge. It may also be by way of security interest in personal property granted in accordance with Provincial legislation dealing generally with personal property security.

A specific mortgage or charge attaches to specific parts of the corporation's property and, except insofar as the corporation is given under the provisions thereof the right to deal with such property, its power to do so ceases on the giving of the security. However, in *Stave Falls Lumber Co. v. Westminster Trust Co.*, [1940] 4 D.L.R. 382 (B.C. C.A.) where the trust deed specifically charged a logging corporation's timber licences and berths including standing timber, the court held that the trust deed permitted the corporation to carry on its business as a going concern; that it could, therefore, cut its standing timber for the purpose of carrying on its business and enter into a contract with another corporation for granting it cutting rights; and that moneys resulting from the sale were not impressed with a trust in favour of the bondholders. As to insurance moneys specifically charged, but which the trustee in its discretion was entitled to apply to sinking fund or general corporate purposes, on the trustee determining to apply them to general corporate purposes, they became the moneys of the corporation free from any trust in favour of the bondholders. It was further held that such moneys could be applied *inter alia* in reimbursing the trustee for fire insurance premiums and in making payment to the trust corporation in its corporate capacity on account of moneys owing to it by creditors of the corporation. A covenant to insure and to make the policies payable to the trustee will operate as an equitable assignment of a policy and the proceeds therefrom, even in the absence of a mortgage clause or a formal assignment: *Re Alliance Insurance Co. & Canada Trust Co.*, [1946] O.R. 298. Where a debenture charged certain assets, including equipment, it was held that certain trailers were not charged by the debenture. The use of the word "equipment" was too uncertain: see *Hythe Inn Ltd. (Receiver of) v. Canadian Imperial Bank of Commerce* (1986), 27 D.L.R. (4th) 220 (B.C. C.A.). Where a debenture covered chattels which might be added to or substituted for listed chattels, it was held that the charge covered subsequently purchased vehicles: see *Lite Enterprises Ltd. v. Atlantic Power Lines Ltd.* (1978), 24 N.B.R. (2d) 607.

A floating charge on the other hand confers an immediate equitable charge on the property present and future comprised in the charge. It does not prevent the corporation from dealing with and disposing of the assets which are subject to the charge in the ordinary course of business. If, however, certain events occur, the floating charge crystallizes and becomes a fixed charge on the types of assets which had been charged as they exist at the time of the crystallization. As to what produces a crystallization, see the quotations which follow and the notes below under the heading "Crystallization of floating charge."

The following judicial descriptions of a floating security may be quoted:

> A floating security is an equitable charge on the assets for the time being of a going concern. It attaches to the subject charged in the varying condition in which

it happens to be from time to time. It is of the essence of such a charge that it remains dormant until the undertaking charged ceases to be a going concern, or until the person in whose favour the charge is created intervenes. His right to intervene may of course be suspended by agreement. But if there is no agreement for suspension, he may exercise his right whenever he pleases after default.

Governments Stock & Other Securities Investment Co. v. Manila Railway, [1897] A.C. 81 at 86 per Lord Macnaghten:

. . . a floating charge . . . is ambulatory and shifting in its nature, hovering over and so to speak floating with the property which it is intended to affect until some event occurs or some act is done which causes it to settle and fasten on the subject of the charge within its reach and grasp:

Illingworth v. Houldsworth, [1904] A.C. 355 at 358 (H.L.) per Lord Macnaghten.

A floating security is not a future security; it is a present security, which presently affects all the assets of the company expressed to be included in it. On the other hand, it is not a specific security; the holder cannot affirm that the assets are specifically mortgaged to him. The assets are mortgaged in such a way that the mortgagor can deal with them without the concurrence of the mortgagee. A floating security is not a specific mortgage of the assets, plus a licence to the mortgagor to dispose of them in the course of his business, but is a floating mortgage applying to every item comprised in the security, but not specifically affecting any item until some event occurs or some act on the part of the mortgagee is done which causes it to crystallize into a fixed security. . . . This crystallization may be brought about in various ways. A receiver may be appointed, or the company may go into liquidation and a liquidator be appointed, or any event may happen which is defined as bringing to an end the licence to the company to carry on business:

Evans v. Rival Granite Quarries Ltd., [1910] 2 K.B. 979 at 999 (C.A.) per Buckley L.J.

The nature of a floating charge is fully discussed in *Gordon MacKay & Co. v. Capital Trust Corp.*, [1927] S.C.R. 374; and in the court below: *Gordon MacKay & Co. v. J. A. Larocque Co.* (1926), 59 O.L.R. 293 (C.A.). A floating charge need not cover all the assets of the corporation, but may include only certain specified assets: *In re Yorkshire Woolcombers Assn. Ltd.*, [1903] 2 Ch. 284 (C.A.), affd (*sub nom. Illingworth v. Houldsworth*) [1904] A.C. 355 (present and future book debts); *National Provincial Bank of England Ltd. v. United Electric Theatres Ltd.*, [1916] 1 Ch. 132 (furniture and loose effects which now are or may from time to time be placed upon or used in or about defined premises): *Hoare v. British Columbia Development Assn.* (1912), 107 L.T. 602 (charge of all rights and interests in and all profits derived from a certain arrangement).

Creation of floating charge

A floating charge may be created by apt words either in the debenture itself: *Re Farmers' Loan & Savings Co.; Debenture Holders' Case* (1899), 30 O.R. 337 (C.A.); *Johnston v. Wade* (1908), 17 O.L.R. 372 (C.A.), followed in *Gordon MacKay & Co. v. J. A. Larocque Co.* (1926), 59 O.L.R. 293 (C.A.); or in a covering trust deed: *National Trust Co. v. Trusts & Guarantee Co.* (1912), 26 O.L.R. 279.

It is not necessary that any special form of words should be used and in *In re Yorkshire Woolcombers Assn*, [1903] 2 Ch. 284 at 295, Romer L.J., in the Court of Appeal, said that a mortgage by a corporation which contains the following characteristics is a floating charge:

> (1.) If it is a charge on a class of assets of a company present and future; (2.) if that class is one which, in the ordinary course of the business of the company, would be changing from time to time; and (3.) if you find that by the charge it is contemplated that, until some future step is taken by or on behalf of those interested in the charge, the company may carry on its business in the ordinary way as far as concerns the particular class of assets I am dealing with.

Thus, in *Trusts & Guarantee Co. v. Abbott Mitchell Iron Co.* (1906), 11 O.L.R. 403, the mortgage of all the corporation's real estate and assets made to secure bonds provided that the trustees should permit the corporation to continue to carry on its business and that the corporation might pledge or mortgage material manufactured and unmanufactured. A subsequent clause provided that advances made by the trustees for bondholders should have priority over every other advance made to the corporation. In effect it was held that the foregoing provisions gave the trustees a floating charge on the material and that the corporation was entitled to create a specific charge thereon ranking in priority to the bondholders.

When a mortgage is made, not by a manufacturing corporation, but, for example, by a theatre corporation, where the chattels charged would not be changed with the same frequency as they would in the case of a manufacturing corporation, it may be more difficult to infer that the charge is floating and not specific. But where such a corporation operated a number of theatres and charged all the furniture, loose effects, plant, machinery, etc., upon various premises, present and future, and the mortgage contained a provision that the corporation would conduct its business in a proper manner, and the corporation had no power to let any of the premises mortgaged without the consent of the mortgagees, it was held that this was a charge upon a class of chattels, which, as to some of them would, and as to all of them might, necessarily be changed from time to time in the ordinary course of business. And, although the mortgage was not expressly in form a floating charge, it was held that it was not intended to interfere with the ordinary carrying on of the corporation's business and, as far as the chattels were concerned, created a floating charge only: *National Provincial Bank of England Ltd. v. United Electric Theatres Ltd.*, [1916] 1 Ch. 132. Astbury J. in that case remarked that if it had been intended that the charge should operate as a specific charge with regard to the chattels existing at the date of the mortgage a schedule of them might have been provided.

When a debenture set out that the interest thereon was "guaranteed by the capital and assets of the company invested in mortgages upon approved real estate," it was held that the intention was to secure payment of the principal and interest, to be secured on the capital and assets of the corporation, that the debentures were a charge on the assets and capital of the corporation and that on a winding-up they were entitled to rank ahead of unsecured claims: *Re Farmers' Loan & Savings Co.; Debenture Holders' Case* (1899), 30 O.R. 337

(C.A.). In *In re Panama, New Zealand & Australian Royal Mail Co.* (1870), L.R. 5 Ch. App. 318, where the corporation charged its "undertaking" with payment of the debentures issued, Giffard L.J. held that the use of the term implied that the business of the corporation was to continue and that the charge was therefore a floating one. See also *Johnston v. Wade* (1908), 17 O.L.R. 372 at 376 (C.A.), where the words used were "the company hereby charges with such payments its undertaking and all its property real and personal, rights, powers; and assets of every kind and description present; and future, including its uncalled capital."

Bonds and debentures

The term "debenture" is not a strictly technical term but is applied to a security for money, called on the face of it a debenture, and providing for the payment of a certain specified sum to the owner or bearer, with interest in the meantime. It may be applied to any instrument showing that the party making it owes money and is bound to pay it: *Bank of Toronto v. Cobourg, Peterborough & Marmora Railway* (1884), 7 O.R. 1 at 7. Any document which either creates a debt or acknowledges it is a debenture: *Levy v. Abercorris Slate Co.* (1888), 37 Ch. D. 260 at 264. See also *Acmetrack Ltd. v. Bank Canadian National* (1984), 48 O.R. (2d) 49 (C.A.), leave to appeal to Supreme Court of Canada refused (1984), 48 O.R. (2d) 49n.

A debenture may be a mere promise to pay or a promise to pay secured by mortgage or charge, either in the debenture itself or in a covering trust deed. See the observations of Lindley J. in *British India Steam Navigation Co. v. I.R.C.* (1881), 7 Q.B.D. 165 at 172, as to what various classes of instruments are entitled to be described as debentures; and *Edmonds v. Blaina Furnaces Co.* (1887), 36 Ch. D. 215 at 219 where Chitty J. said: "The term itself imports a debt — an acknowledgement of a debt — and, . . . generally, if not always, the instrument imports an obligation or covenant to pay. This obligation or covenant is in most cases at the present day accompanied by some charge or security."

This statement is quoted in *Re Shipman Boxboards Ltd.*, [1942] O.R. 118 at 121. An ordinary mortgage of freehold property is a debenture within the English *Companies Act*: *Knightsbridge Estates Trust Ltd. v. Byrne*, [1940] A.C. 613.

A debenture need not be under seal: *In re Fireproof Doors Ltd.*, [1916] 2 Ch. 142; *Biggerstaff v. Rowatt's Wharf Ltd.*, [1896] 2 Ch. 93 (C.A.). It is immaterial whether the document is styled a debenture by the corporation which issues it. If an instrument contains an acknowledgement of indebtedness, that is sufficient to constitute the instrument a debenture: *Lemon v. Austin Friars Investment Trust Ltd.*, [1926] Ch. 1 (C.A.); *R. v. Findlater*, [1939] 1 K.B. 594.

It has been stated that the terms "bonds" and "debentures" are used without any distinction of meaning in this country: *Johnston v. Wade* (1908), 17 O.L.R. 372 (C.A.). As applied to corporate obligations there is no legal distinction between the terms "bonds", "debentures" and "notes" and the fact that one or another of such terms appears in the designation of the obligation cannot be relied on as an indication of the security (if any) behind the obligation. Usually words are included in the title of the obligation to indicate generally the type of security. Apart from this there are also certain not very clearly defined distinctions observable in the general usage of the terms. The term "bond" is applied to government obligations which ordinarily are unsecured and to corporate obligations which are secured by a specific mortgage. Corporate obligations which are secured by a first mortgage on real estate are usually designated first mortgage bonds. An obligation may also be secured by a specific mortgage or charge on collateral security such as shares, bonds or other obligations of other corporations, in which case the obligation is usually called a collateral trust bond or debenture. The term "debenture" may be applied to any corporate obligation secured or unsecured as may the term "note", although the latter term is usually confined to unsecured obligations.

Debenture stock (which is most infrequent in Canada) is a term of loose meaning: *Scottish Widows' Fund & Life Assurance Society v. Canada Permanent Mortgage Corp.* (1929), 63 O.L.R. 637. It has been described as "borrowed capital consolidated into one mass for the sake of convenience." The corporation, as security for the whole amount to be borrowed, creates a mortgage or charge by means of a covering trust deed in favour of a trustee for the holders of the debenture stock, each of whom receives a certificate, entitling him to the sum therein specified, being a part of the whole indebtedness. Bonds or debentures are issued in fixed denominations, for example, $1,000, but debenture stock may be held in fractional amounts, for example, $800 or $1,250. The individual holders of debenture stock have no separate mortgage or charge. In this respect debenture stock differs from debentures, each of which may contain, and where there is no covering trust deed does contain, a separate charge. For particular purposes debenture stock differs from debentures in form rather than substance; and debenture stock will pass under a bequest of debentures in a will: *In re Herring; Murray v. Herring*, [1908] 2 Ch. 493 at 497.

Where, as is now usually the case, bonds are secured by trust deed, the distinction between bonds and debenture stock is largely technical, as the trust deeds securing the two kinds of security are in large part the same.

Debenture stock (subject to any express provision in the trust deed) is transferable in fractions, thereby differing from bonds which are only transferable as units. Trust deeds, however, usually provide that debenture stock is only transferable in multiples of a certain sum, for example, $100. There is also a difference in transfer procedure. On the transfer of registered debenture stock, the transferor delivers up his certificate and a new certificate is issued to the transferee, as on the transfer of shares. If all the debenture stock comprised in the certificate is not transferred, the transferor receives a new certificate for the balance not transferred. In the case of the transfer of bonds, on the other hand, the actual bond is handed over to the transferee who retains it. Debenture stock is not a common security in this country but in the past has been in the United Kingdom.

Bonds usually provide for payment at a fixed date, but they may be payable on a certain contingency, such as winding-up, wherein they differ from a promissory note or bill of exchange, which must be payable at a fixed or determinable future time, that is at a fixed time, or at a fixed period after the occurrence of a specified event which is certain to happen. See the *Bills of Exchange Act*, R.S.C. 1985, c. B-4, s. 23.

A bond or debenture under the corporate seal is a specialty debt which only becomes statute barred at the end of 20 years from maturity: *Toronto General Trust Corp. v. Central Ontario Railway Co.* (1903), 6 O.L.R. 534, affd (1904), 8 O.L.R. 604; *City of Ottawa v. Ottawa Electric Railway*, [1937] O.R. 358 (C.A.); *In re Atlantic & Pacific Fibre Importing & Manufacturing Co.*, [1928] Ch. 836.

Bonds are usually payable at a fixed place and must be presented there before payment can be enforced: *McDonald v. Great Western Railway* (1861), 21 U.C.Q.B. 223; *Osborne v. Preston & Berlin Railway* (1859), 9 U.C.C.P. 241; see also *Becher v. Corporation of Amherstburg* (1874), 23 U.C.C.P. 602 (no fixed place). And in an action for damages by way of interest from the date the bonds are due until they are actually paid, the corporation may set up by way of defence that the bonds were not presented at the particular place, for example, a bank, even if there were no funds in the bank at the time to meet the particular indebtedness: *Montreal City Bank v. Corporation of Perth* (1881), 32 U.C.C.P. 18. But it is otherwise if the corporation were sued by way of debt on the bonds: *Fellowes v. Ottawa Gas Co.* (1868), 19 U.C.C.P. 174; *Re Thomson & Victoria Railway* (1881), 9 P.R. 119. Want of presentation is not a valid objection if presentation would have been an idle gesture: *Montreal Trust Co. v. Abitibi Power & Paper Co.*, [1944] O.R. 515 at 523.

Where bonds are secured by trust deed creating a charge or where the bonds themselves contain a charge it is usual to insert a provision that all bonds of the series shall rank *pari passu*. Where this is not done and bonds are issued one after another in numerical order each bond ranks in priority of charge ahead of all the others subsequently issued: *Gartside v. Silkstone & Dodsforth Coal & Iron Co.* (1882), 21 Ch. D. 762.

The effect of a *pari passu* provision is that from the time when the security crystallizes there can be no priority amongst the bondholders: *In re Midland Express Ltd.*, [1914] 1 Ch. 41 at 49 (C.A.), approved and followed in *Wade v. Murray*, [1940] O.R. 239.

Trust deeds frequently provide for the issuance of bonds in different series with different rates of interest so that if all the bonds authorized are not immediately required to be issued bonds of a new series can be issued when desired at the then prevailing rate of interest.

When a corporation has issued a series of bonds, limited to a certain number, to rank *pari passu*, it cannot subsequently issue bonds to rank with the first series unless such power has been expressly reserved: *Re Hubbard & Co.* (1898), 68 L.J. Ch. 54. This general rule is subject, however, to the qualification that a corporation under certain circumstances may create a specific charge in priority to an earlier floating charge, so that bonds of a later issue secured by specific charge may have precedence over bonds of an earlier issue containing a floating charge only on such property.

Payment of the principal and interest of bonds issued by one corporation is sometimes collaterally secured by guarantee of another corporation. Thus, where a parent corporation desires to raise money by an issue of bonds of one of its subsidiary corporations, it may be necessary for the parent corporation to guarantee payment of the bonds in order to make them attractive to the public. The guarantee may be given by direct endorsement of the guarantor corporation made upon the bonds issued or by agreement, either embodied in the trust deed or in a separate trust agreement with the trustee of the bond mortgage. If the latter method is adopted, appropriate provisions are inserted in the agreement enabling the trustee to enforce the guarantee in the event of default and precluding individual bondholders from bringing separate actions.

Where the obligation of the guarantor on default was to "make payment of the bonds and interest coupons when they fall due," and upon non-payment of interest the principal became immediately due by the operation of the ordinary acceleration clause in the mortgage, a majority of the Supreme Court of Canada held that the surety also became liable for immediate payment of the principal moneys: *City of Three Rivers v. Sun Trust Co.*, [1923] S.C.R. 496.

Issuance of bonds after registration of a subsequent mortgage

Frequently, especially in the case of construction issues, all the bonds authorized are not immediately issued but are certified and delivered from time to time on compliance with the requirements of the trust deed in that regard, for example, against progress certificates of the architect in charge of the construction of a building. So far as the security against the corporation's lands is concerned, the situation is the same as in the case of an ordinary building loan and the bondholders will be protected in respect of further deliveries so long as the trustee has not received notice of a subsequent mortgage. Registration of a subsequent mortgage does not constitute notice: *Pierce v. Canada Loan Co.* (1894), 25 O.R. 671. See however *Acmetrack Ltd. v. Bank Canadian National*, *supra.* Where the security consists of ships see *The Benwell Tower* (1895), 8 Asp. M.L.C. 13. It will be observed that normal practice, however, is to make all the usual searches at the time of the second and subsequent issues.

Irregularity in issuance

Bonds must be issued in accordance with any requirements of the by-laws, and subject also to the provisions, if any, of the articles of the corporation. See, for example, *Anderson Lumber Co. v. Canadian Conifer Ltd.*, [1977] 5 W.W.R. 41 (Alta. C.A.); affg [1976] 3 W.W.R. 255 (Alta. T.D.) where debentures were held to be invalid as the articles of association required the authorization of a general meeting and this was never held. The holder of the debentures was deemed to know of the irregularity.

Where the issuance of bonds has been duly authorized, the form of the bonds may be left to be determined by the officers of the corporation without approval by a meeting of the board: *Reid v. Purity Farms Ltd.*, [1937] O.R. 248 (C.A.).

If bonds are irregularly issued the internal management rule applies, namely, that a bona fide holder for value without notice of the irregularity is protected: *Duck v. Tower Galvanizing Co.*, [1901] 2 K.B. 314; *Re Fireproof Doors Ltd.*, [1916] 2 Ch. 142; but if he has notice he will not be protected: *Davis's Case* (1871),

L.R. 12 Eq. 516; *Johnston v. Wade* (1908), 17 O.L.R. 372 (C.A.). In the absence of holding out a corporation would not be estopped by a forged bond: *Ruben v. Great Fingall Consolidated Co.*, [1906] A.C. 439.

Irregular and insufficient debentures for which a lender has bona fide advanced money may be evidence of an agreement on the part of the corporation to issue valid debentures, so that the holder may have a good equitable debenture on the principle laid down in *Re Strand Music Hall Co.* (1865), 3 De G. & Sm. 147, where Lord Justice Turner said: "I apprehend, however, that where this Court is satisfied that it was intended to create a charge, and that the parties who intended to create it had power to do so, it will give effect to that intention, notwithstanding any mistake which may have occurred in the attempt to effect it."

See also *In re Queensland Land & Coal Co.; Davis v. Martin*, [1894] 3 Ch. 181, where the debentures had been sealed and delivered to the lenders in blank as to the names of the obligees; and *In re Fireproof Doors Ltd.*, [1916] 2 Ch. 142, where the debentures had been irregularly sealed.

See also, *Royal Bank v. Cal Glass Ltd.* (1979), 9 B.L.R. 1 (B.C. S.C.); affd (1980), 22 B.C.L.R. 328 (B.C. C.A.) and *Canadian Pittsburgh Industries Ltd. v. Roberts & Hall Ltd.*, [1973] 2 W.W.R. 341 (Alta. T.D.).

Agreement to issue bonds

An agreement for consideration to issue debentures charging property constitutes a present charge of such property and the proposed debenture holder is thereby protected against an execution creditor who intervenes before the debentures are actually issued: *Simultaneous Colour Printing Syndicate v. Foweraker*, [1901] 1 K.B. 771; but in view of the statutory provisions relating to registration the principle stated in the above case may be of little practical assistance. So also if a winding-up occurs before the debentures are issued the lender will be secured: *Tailby v. Official Receiver* (1888), 13 App. Cas. 523; *Re Hampshire Land Co.*, [1896] 2 Ch. 743; *Pegge v. Neath & District Tramways Co.*, [1898] 1 Ch. 183; *Re New Durham Salt Co.* (1890), 7 T.L.R. 13; *Mercantile Investment & General Trust Co. v. River Plate Trust, Loan & Agency Co.*, [1892] 2 Ch. 303. But see *Re Hansard Publishing Union Ltd.* (1892), 8 T.L.R. 280 (C.A.).

An option to call at any time for a specific amount of the mortgage debentures of a given issue in satisfaction of a debt is a good equitable security while the issue remains unexhausted and may be exercised after judgment in a debenture holders' action: *Pegge v. Neath & District Tramways Co.*, [1898] 1 Ch. 183.

Sale of bonds if, as and when issued

Bonds are frequently sold before the trust deed is executed and registered; in such case the bonds are generally sold by an issuing house "if, as and when issued" and, if anything is paid by the purchaser before interim bonds or interim certificates or trustees' interim certificates for bonds actually secured by the trust deed are delivered, interim receipts are issued by the trust corporation which receives the money, the purchaser could be entitled under the receipt to the return of his money on a specified date if the bonds are not sooner available for delivery.

Where a corporation offers bonds for subscription and states the security offered and any bonds are taken up on the faith of such statement, the subscribers stand in equity in the same position as if the security had been actually issued. The following are illustrations.

A prospectus offered for subscription £20,000 of mortgage debentures "to be secured on the entire property of the Company". A applied for debentures on the terms of the corporation's prospectus and a resolution to allot was passed by the directors and notified to A, but no allotment took place. Afterwards a trust deed was executed charging certain property specified "in the schedule" in favour of the debenture holders, but no schedule was annexed. The court, in the subsequent winding-up of the corporation, held A was entitled to a charge on the entire property of the corporation: *Re New Durham Salt Co.* (1890), 2 Meg. 360, 35 Sol. J. 27.

A person subscribed and paid for debentures and received a provisional certificate certifying his title to receive the debentures so soon as the trust deed had been registered in India, and subsequently applied to and satisfied the court that the assets were in jeopardy. It was held that there had been a payment of money entitling the person who paid it to debentures and entitling him to the benefit of those debentures, if not to manual delivery of them, which gave him the actual right to be placed in the position of a debenture holder: *Thorn v. Nine Reefs Ltd.* (1892), 67 L.T. 93 (C.A.).

A lender took a promissory note from the corporation and an undertaking to issue to him debentures bearing interest at a specified rate and conferring a second charge on the corporation's undertaking. Having called for the debentures, he was held to be in equity a holder of second debentures and entitled to stand on the same footing in the distribution of the corporation's assets as if he were the legal holder of second debentures: *Pegge v. Neath & District Tramways Co.*, [1898] 1 Ch. 183.

In *Dey v. Rubber & Mercantile Corp.*, [1923] 2 Ch. 528 a scheme of arrangement involving an issue of debentures to certain creditors was approved by the court. It was held that as soon as the court sanctioned the scheme there was an obligation on the corporation to deliver sealed debentures and an obligation on individual creditors to receive them. They were debenture holders in equity and as such entitled to the rights of debenture holders.

The lender's right to assert the equity above mentioned, to have his security appropriated to him, will doubtless be subject to be defeated by non-compliance with any requirements of local laws as to registration. If the provisional certificate is to be regarded as an agreement to issue bonds it is in equity a charge created by the corporation. If the provisional certificate is a security, it will likewise be subject to any provincial requirements as to registration.

Pledge of bonds

It is not necessary that the directors should negotiate the bonds for cash. The issue or pledge of bonds to a creditor may be treated as a borrowing under a general borrowing power, and the reason for this is thus stated by Kay J. in *Howard v. Patent Ivory Manufacturing Co.* (1888), 38 Ch. D. 156 at 170:

> If you might not issue debentures to a creditor under a borrowing power it would come to this, that you would have to issue debentures to the bankers, or somebody else, who would advance the money, and then pay that money over to the creditor, or issue debentures to the creditor himself, he lending you money first and then you paying it back to him. Of course it is obvious that such a roundabout proceeding as that need not be resorted to, and the Court looks to the substance of the matter.

See also *Re The Real Property Act and Caveat No. 103969* (1922), 66 D.L.R. 691; *Venables v. Baring Brothers & Co.*, [1892] 3 Ch. 527; *Edelstein v. Schuyler & Co.*, [1902] 2 K.B. 144.

Where the act of incorporation gave the directors power to "issue and sell or pledge all or any of the . . . bonds for the purpose of raising money for the prosecution of the . . . undertaking", it was held that using bonds in the following manner was within the power. The corporation, a railway, made an agreement with contractors for the construction of part of its road, and deposited bonds to secure payment, and on the railway's default the bonds were delivered to the contractors at the rate of 50 cents on the dollar: *Winnipeg & Hudson's Bay Railway v. Mann* (1890), 7 Man. R. 81. See also *Re Inns of Court Hotel Co.* (1868), L.R. 6 Eq. 82 at 89, where the court held that debentures were not invalidated because they had been issued in part satisfaction of existing debts.

As to the rights of holders of bonds as collateral security where the terms of the issue itself do not authorize the use of the bonds by the corporation as collateral security for existing indebtedness, see *Re B.C. Portland Cement Co.* (1915), 22 D.L.R. 609; affd (1916), 27 D.L.R. 726 (B.C. C.A.).

A pledgee of bonds is entitled to call upon the trustee to enforce the security unless foreclosure is claimed: *Anderson v. McNair Lumber & Shingle Co.*, [1929] 2 D.L.R. 209 (B.C. C.A.). As to the rights of successive pledgees, see *Nova Scotia Central Railway v. Halifax Banking Co.* (1893), 21 S.C.R. 536. However, a pledge of a debenture may lead to an argument that the pledgee is obligated to realize on the pledge before enforcing the debenture and may in other respects be limited in enforcing the debenture held by way of pledge: *Seawater Products (Nfld.) Ltd. v. Royal Bank of Canada* (1980), 36 C.B.R. (N.S.) 21 (Nfld. S.C.) and *Harry D. Shields Ltd. v. Bank of Montreal* (1992), 7 O.R. (3d) 57 (Gen. Div.).

Bearer bonds and registered bonds

Bonds may be payable to bearer or the registered holder, or to bearer with power to register them and make them transferable thereafter (until withdrawn from the register) only on the register of transfers maintained by the trustee. They may also be made payable to the registered holder, but with coupons payable to bearer.

Canadian decisions now treat bearer debentures as negotiable instruments: *Young v. MacNider* (1895), 25 S.C.R. 272; *Parish of St. Cesaire v. McFarlane* (1887), 14 S.C.R. 738; *Eastern Townships Bank v. Municipality of Crompton*

(1871), 7 R.L. 446; *Jones v. Municipality of Albert* (1881), 21 N.B.R. 200. See also *Bechuanaland Exploration Co. v. London Trading Bank*, [1898] 2 Q.B. 658 where the secretary of the plaintiff corporation fraudulently took debentures from the safe and pledged them to the defendants for advances, and it was held that the defendants were entitled to hold them on the ground that they were negotiable instruments.

An instrument may be negotiable by estoppel from its own representations, for example, a deposit receipt of a bank "payable to order" and on its face declared to be negotiable: *Re Bennett; Provincial Treasurer v. Bennett*, [1936] 2 D.L.R. 291 (Man. C.A.).

A person taking a negotiable instrument in good faith and for value acquires a valid title even though the transferor is acting in fraud of the true owner: *London Joint Stock Bank v. Simmons*, [1892] A.C. 201; but if the taker of the instrument knows or has reason to know that the interest of the transferor is limited, he is not a purchaser in good faith for value without notice and is bound to inquire into the transferor's authority: *Sheffield (Earl) v. London Joint Stock Bank* (1888), 13 App. Cas. 333. The taker of the instrument may be put on inquiry by reason of the character of the transferor, for example, in *White v. Dominion Bank*, [1935] 1 D.L.R. 42 (Man. C.A.) where a trust corporation fraudulently pledged certain bonds registered in its name, which were held in trust for an estate, and there were indications in the instruments of hypothecation that the trust corporation was borrowing on the property of trust estates in its hands; it was held that the bank was put on inquiry and could not apply the proceeds of the bonds in reduction of the trust corporation's indebtedness to it.

Where, however, there was nothing suspicious in the securities themselves and the bank had no notice that the securities were not the property of the holder, other suspicious circumstances were held not to put the bank on inquiry: *McPherson v. Dominion Bank*, [1936] 1 D.L.R. 268 (Man. C.A.) distinguishing *White v. Dominion Bank, supra.*

A purchaser for value of stolen bearer bonds, without notice of the theft, acquires a good title, bearer bonds being negotiable instruments: *Garey v. Dominion Mfg. Ltd.* (1924), 56 O.L.R. 159. The law applicable is that of the country of the transfer. See also *Venables v. Baring Brothers & Co.*, [1892] 3 Ch. 527 (lender making advance on bearer bonds not known by him to have been stolen).

Where bonds are intended to pass by delivery, or to be negotiable, it is advisable to insert a clause that the principal moneys and interest will be paid without regard to any equities between the corporation and the original or any intervening holder, otherwise investors would have difficulty in dealing with a security which might be rendered valueless in their hands by the intervention of some latent equity. See *Mangles v. Dixon* (1852), 3 H.C.L. 702; *Athenaeum Life Assurance Society v. Pooley* (1858), 3 DeG. & J. 294; *Re Agra & Masterman's Bank* (1867), L.R. 2 Ch. App. 391; *Re Blakely Ordinance Co.* (1867), L.R. 3 Ch. App. 154.

Describing bonds as "bearer bonds", where they are stated on their face to be subject to the provisions of the trust deed securing them, an examination of which would have disclosed irregularities, does not make them negotiable to the extent that being termed first mortgage bonds they obtain a priority over any previous issue: *Re B.C. Portland Cement Co.* (1915), 22 D.L.R. 609; affd (1916), 27 D.L.R. 726 (B.C. C.A.).

As to the validity of a debenture not made payable to any particular named individual or corporation, see *Geddes v. Toronto Street Railway* (1864), 14 U.C.C.P. 513.

In the case of bearer bonds, if it is desired to be able to render them no longer negotiable, it may be provided that payment will be made "to the bearer, or if registered to the registered holder." On registration of the bearer as owner the bond ceases to be negotiable. It may also be provided that after registration the registered holder may have a transfer to bearer registered and in such case the bond again becomes negotiable.

A corporation will be bound to register as owner a person presenting a bearer bond for registration without production of any transfer: *Re Osler v. Toronto, Grey & Bruce Railway* (1881), 8 P.R. 506.

Contracts to subscribe for bonds; sale and purchase of bonds

Apart from statute, an agreement with the corporation to take up and pay for bonds is equivalent to an agreement to loan money and will not be enforced by decree of specific performance: *Dorchester Electric Co. v. The King* (1915), 24 D.L.R. 373; *South African Territories v. Wallington*, [1898] A.C. 309. The corporation's remedy against the subscriber is in damages. Under special circumstances general and substantial damages may be awarded: *General Securities Ltd. v. Don Ingram Ltd.*, [1940] S.C.R. 670.

Likewise, an action for specific performance of a contract by a corporation to issue its bonds to underwriters will not lie: *South African Territories v. Wallington, supra*; *Dickson v. Corson* (1927), 32 O.W.N. 152. Here again, the corporation's remedy against the underwriter is in damages.

The above rule—that specific performance will not lie—does not apply to an agreement to purchase outstanding bonds from the holder.

Where the subscription contract calls for payment by instalments and the subscriber is in default in payment of instalments and is unwilling to pay the balance owing he cannot recover the instalments paid: *Bass v. Clively* (1829), Taml. 80; *a fortiori* if the contract of subscription expressly provides that, upon default, previous instalments are liable to forfeiture. Where the corporation, in conformity with the subscription contract, has forfeited the bonds for non-payment of instalments, it cannot have specific performance; and apart from specific performance there is no right to recover further instalments: *Kuala Pali Rubber Estates v. Mowbray* (1915), 111 L.T. 1072 (C.A.). However, where the subscription contract is not specifically enforceable (by reason of there being no statutory provision as above applicable) on a distribution by a trustee for bondholders, bondholders who are in default in payment of instalments are entitled to a rateable distribution in respect of the advances actually made by them, without first being required to pay up the balance of their subscriptions: *In re Smelting Corp.; Seaver v. The Company*, [1915] 1 Ch. 472.

Where a corporation offers a bonus of its common shares to purchasers of bonds as an inducement to subscribe, such bonus is an essential consideration for the subscription and the illegality or nullity of the issue of common shares will avoid the subscription: *Dorchester Electric Co. v. The King* (1915), 24 D.L.R. 373. One method under which such a bonus can effectively be given is for the shares to be first issued to a vendor, or otherwise, in such manner that they are fully paid up, and then for the vendor or other person entitled to the shares to make them available for the purpose. See *Hood v. Caldwell* (1921), 50 O.L.R. 387; affd [1923] S.C.R. 488.

Where bonds are purchased subject to the approval of the purchaser's solicitor, such approval is a condition precedent to the agreement becoming binding on the purchaser: *Canada Investment v. Scotstown* (1915), 48 Que. S.C. 97.

Bonds secured by a charge on the corporation's land which gives a power, on default, of sale of the mortgaged property are an interest in land within s. 4 of the Statute of Frauds and contracts (including contracts of sale) relating to such bonds must be in writing: *Driver v. Broad*, [1893] 1 Q.B. 539; *McKinnon v. Doran* (1915), 34 O.L.R. 403; affd (1916), 35 O.L.R. 349; affd (1916), 53 S.C.R. 609.

In an action by the vendor of outstanding bonds against a defaulting purchaser for damages, the measure of the damages is the actual loss sustained, measured by the price which is afterwards obtained for the bonds which is the best price obtainable having regard to the condition of the market: *McKinnon v. Doran, supra.*

Where a resale of the bonds is contemplated the measure of damages may be the loss of the sale.

If there is a dispute as to the construction of bonds which contain the whole contract between the holder and the corporation, the court cannot, in determining the question, refer to the prospectus: *In re Tewkesbury Gas Co.*, [1911] 2 Ch. 279, [1912] 1 Ch. 1 (C.A.). The rights, if any, of the purchaser of such bonds must be asserted by way of a claim for rectification of the bonds, per Parker J. at p. 283. See also *Derwa v. Rio de Janeiro Tramway, Light & Power Co.* (1928), 62 O.L.R. 669, where the defendant corporation was organized under the laws of Canada, had its head office in Toronto, and carried on business in Rio de Janeiro, and its bonds and trust deed were construed according to the law of Ontario. In *Re Sapphire Petroleum Ltd.*, [1956] O.R. 581 (C.A.) the court rejected the contention that a prospectus could be looked at in the interpretation of a trust deed where the terms of the trust deed itself were not ambiguous.

However, where a corporation offers securities under a prospectus (the terms of the securities having already been settled), and the prospectus contains statements to the effect that the holders of the securities shall be entitled to certain benefits, an original subscriber on the terms of the prospectus can enforce the bargain as a collateral contract, although those statements do not appear in the securities: *Jacobs v. Batavia & General Plantations Trust Ltd.*, [1924] 2

Ch. 329 (C.A.). In the same case the plaintiff failed in respect of so much of his claim as related to securities acquired from others and not direct from the corporation. As to what it would be necessary to establish in order to succeed in respect of the latter securities, see the judgments of Warrington and Sargant L.JJ. in the same case.

Where an agent of the corporation induces a person to buy from it bonds, regular on their face but void in law by reason of non-compliance with the requirements of the Act, he is not in the absence of fraudulent intent liable in damages to the purchaser, merely on the ground of an implied representation that the bonds are legally valid; such a representation is one in point of law only: *Kavaner v. Bowhey*, [1928] 4 D.L.R. 907 (Alta. C.A.).

Transfer of bonds

Bearer bonds are transferable by delivery. For a discussion of Part VII of the federal Act dealing with transfers (*inter alia*) see Chapter 6, under the heading "Transfer provisions in Act." This Part of the Act is applicable to debt instruments as well as shares.

Where bonds are registered, transfer is effected by instrument in writing accompanied by delivery of the bond followed by registration in the name of the transferee or registration of a transfer to bearer. The trust deed prescribes the requisite formalities which are usually inserted in the body of the bond.

The liability of the obligor to the registered owner of bonds for the principal moneys can only be discharged by evidence that the registered owner has, in fact, duly executed a transfer thereof; a guarantee of the authenticity of the signature is not a defence as against the registered owner: *Racette v. The King*, [1942] S.C.R. 464. See, however, regarding interest on bonds registered as to principal, where such interest is payable by coupons which could have been cashed by anyone: *The King v. Racette*, [1948] S.C.R. 28.

Bonds are choses in action and the general rule is that the transferee of a chose in action stands in no better position than his transferor: *In re Rhodesia Goldfields, Ltd.*, [1910] 1 Ch. 239, and see *In re Goy & Co.; Farmer v. Goy*, [1900] 2 Ch. 149 at 153. As the effect of this rule would be most prejudicial to an innocent purchaser of bonds, acquiring them without knowledge of cross claims or equities of the corporation against his transferor, it is important to provide that bonds should be transferable free from any equities. Such a provision operates effectively notwithstanding that a winding-up has occurred or a judgment has been obtained in a debenture holders' action: *In re Goy & Co.; Farmer v. Goy, supra*. It was held, however, in *In re Palmer's Decoration & Furnishing Co.*, [1904] 2 Ch. 743, that the corporation could assert equities against an unregistered transferee. The debentures there in question contained the usual condition that "the principal moneys and interest hereby secured will be paid without regard to any equities between the company and the original or any intermediate holder" of the bond "and the receipt of the registered holder for such principal moneys or interest shall be a good discharge to the company therefor". Buckley J. said that the condition contemplated only equities as against a *registered* holder and did not protect a transferee who had not had himself registered. See also *In re Brown & Gregory Ltd.*, [1904] 1 Ch. 627; affd [1904] 2 Ch. 448 (C.A.), where the transferee under the circumstances was held not to be in the position of a bona fide purchaser for value.

In view of the foregoing decisions, the condition above referred to is now often amplified to read as follows:

> The principal moneys and interest hereby secured will be paid and registered bonds are to be transferable as aforesaid free from and without regard to any equities between the company and the original or any intermediate holder thereof, or any set-off or cross-claim, and the receipt of the registered holder for such principal moneys and interest shall be a good discharge to the company for the same.

Where securities were transferable by instrument in writing in common form either on the certificate itself or by separate instrument and the registered owner had executed the usual transfer and power of attorney, in some cases in blank, and new certificates were issued in the name of a nominee of the transferee, it was held that the beneficial ownership in or title to the securities was in the holder of the new certificates: *Secretary of State of Canada v. Alien Property Custodian for the United States*, [1930] Ex. C.R. 76.

Bonds registered in the names of two persons "and the survivor of them" on the death of one pass to the other, even though the deceased advanced the whole of the purchase price of the bonds: *Re Potter* (1926), 29 O.W.N. 327; *Webb v. Urquhart* (1926), 29 O.W.N. 400.

In Ontario the *Conveyancing and Law of Property Act*, R.S.O. 1990, c. C.34, provides as follows:

> 54.—(1) The bonds or debentures of a corporation made payable to bearer, or to any person named therein or bearer, may be transferred by delivery, and if payable to a person or order, after general endorsation thereof by such person, are transferable by delivery.
>
> (2) Any such transfer vests the property in the bond or debenture in the holder thereof and enables him to maintain an action thereon in the holder's own name.

Upon the death of the registered holder of debentures, the corporation recorded in the register the death of the testator, the fact that probate had been exhibited and that the plaintiff was the executor. Subsequently, the debentures having been duly appropriated to answer part of the plaintiff's share of residue, the plaintiff requested the corporation to register him in his own name as the holder of the debentures and not in his representative capacity. The corporation refused to register the plaintiff unless he executed a transfer of the debentures to himself in accordance with one of the conditions of the debentures requiring every transfer to be in writing. One of the conditions provided that a register should be kept, in which should be entered the names, etc., of the registered holders. It was held that, under the condition last mentioned, the corporation was bound to register the person who was legally entitled to the debentures; that upon the death of the testator, the registered holder, the property in the debentures legally devolved upon his executor, the plaintiff. The corporation accordingly was held bound to register the plaintiff with a clear title in his own name without reference to his representative character; what was involved was not a transfer but a transmission of the debentures: *Edwards v. Ransomes & Rapier Ltd.*, [1930] W.N. 180.

Use of trust deeds in borrowing

The only specific form of borrowing by a corporation which is dealt with in any detail by the Act is the issuance of debt obligations defined in s. 2(1) of the Act as including bonds, debentures and notes, whether secured or not, under a trust deed. It is usual for bonds or debentures issued by a corporation to be issued under a trust deed (or indenture) where they are intended to be widely held. This procedure carries with it important advantages. The trust deed will state in detail the obligations of the corporation and confer on the trustee the necessary powers and authorities to enable it to protect the rights and interests of the security holders by legal proceedings if necessary. Provisions are made for the administration of the trust, meetings of security holders and the procedure to be followed in various events when action is necessary. When, as is often the case, the security includes a specific charge on certain assets, the legal interest of the chargee is, by means of the trust deed, vested in the trustee. The trust deed is furthermore capable of registration in accordance with the requirements of statutes governing personal and real property security interests.

The procedure for the creation and authorization of securities secured by a trust deed is as follows. The directors pass a resolution creating the securities, authorizing the issuance of the securities proposed to be issued, defining their terms, appointing the trustee and approving the trust deed or a draft thereof. The validity of the trust deed is not affected by reason of the resolution approving a draft trust deed submitted, subject to such amendments, variations, additions and amplifications as designated officers may approve, and changes being made and so approved, where the trust deed as executed plainly carries out what in general terms is set out and authorized in the approved draft: *Montreal Trust Co. v. Abitibi Power Co.*, [1937] O.R. 939.

Part VIII of the Act, which deals with trust deeds, applies only when the bonds or other debt obligations issued or to be issued thereunder are part of a distribution to the public: see s. 82(2). When there is to be no distribution to the public, the Act establishes no requirements, presumably on the basis that those subscribing privately (i.e., non-publicly) for securities issued under trust deeds are able to look after their own concerns.

Trust deeds to secure bonds

The Director may exempt a trust indenture from the requirements of Part VIII, if the trust indenture, the debt obligations thereunder and the security interest affected thereby are governed by provincial or foreign law substantially equivalent to Part VIII, s. 82(3).

Trust deeds are discussed below under the following headings: Interest; Coupons; Income bonds; Currency in which moneys are payable; Redemption; Clogging the equity of redemption; and Sinking fund.

Interest

It is advisable for the trust deed to provide that interest shall be payable at the agreed rate both before and after maturity and before and after default, otherwise interest after maturity will only be allowed as damages and will be computed at the statutory rate which is 5 per cent per annum: R.S.C. 1985, c. I-18, s. 3; *Peoples Loan & Deposit Co. v. Grant* (1890), 18 S.C.R. 262; *Plenderleith v. Parsons* (1907), 14 O.L.R. 619. Where a rate higher than the statutory rate is contracted for it can be recovered: *Middleton v. Scott* (1902), 4 O.L.R. 459; *Pringle v. Hutson* (1909), 19 O.L.R. 652 (C.A.) but the provision must be specific. The words "until paid" or "fully paid and satisfied" are insufficient. These have been held to mean up to the day fixed for payment of principal, and not to carry the implication that subsequent interest is to be paid at the same rate: *Peoples Loan & Deposit Co. v. Grant, supra.* See also *Trusts & Guarantee Co. v. Continental Supply Co.*, [1932] 1 W.W.R. 921 (bonds and trust deed construed together) and *Wade v. Murray*, [1940] O.R. 239 (on construction of trust deed held that arrears of interest bore simple interest thereon at 7 per cent).

Where the trustee under a mortgage to secure bonds makes a declaration under an acceleration clause calling in the principal and interest, it has been held that interest at the rate provided for, and not at the statutory rate, was payable after the date of the declaration. The mortgagor by the interest coupon expressly promised to pay a specific sum of money on a specified date at a specified place, and the rate of interest was not affected in any way by default occurring within the period covered by the agreement for interest. The debt was not being detained any more after the declaration than before and it is only where the party is detaining the debt beyond the period during which the rate of interest is agreed upon that the statutory rate applies: *Eastern Trust v. Cushing Sulphite Fibre Co.* (1906), 2 E.L.R. 93, 3 N.B. Eq. 392; and to the same effect *Montreal Trust Co. v. Abitibi Power & Paper Co.*, [1944] O.R. 515 at 522.

Where judgment has been recovered for principal and interest, interest thenceforth ceases to be payable under the contract which is merged in the judgment: *Re European Central Railway* (1876), 4 Ch. D. 33 (C.A.); *Ex parte Fewings* (1884), 25 Ch. D. 338 (C.A.).

A covenant to pay interest may be so expressed as not to merge in a judgment, for example, a distinct covenant to pay interest so long as any part of the principal remains due either on the covenant or on a judgment: *Ex parte Fewings, supra*, at p. 355; or an independent covenant to pay interest so long as the principal sum or any part thereof shall remain due on the security of the indenture: *Popple v. Sylvester* (1882), 22 Ch. D. 98, 100.

Under the ordinary form of mortgage whereby the mortgaged premises are assigned to the mortgagee subject to a proviso for redemption if the mortgagor shall repay the loan with interest at an agreed rate, the corporation will not be allowed to redeem without paying interest at the agreed rate until payment even though judgment has been recovered on the covenant: *Economic Life Assurance Society v. Usborne*, [1902] A.C. 147. As pointed out in that case the rule in the case of redemption is different from that applicable where the mortgagee seeks to prove for subsequent interest, after a merger of the covenant by judgment, as a creditor in a winding-up (*Re European Central Railway, supra*) or in bankruptcy proceedings (*Ex parte Fewings, supra*).

In a winding-up a bondholder can only prove interest to the date of the winding-up: *In re Summerside Electric* (1908), 5 E.L.R. 129 at 139.

If the assets of a corporation are insufficient to pay in full the principal of the bonds and arrears of interest, the assets ought to be distributed rateably, according to the amounts due for principal and interest, although some of the bondholders have been paid interest down to a later date than others: *In re Midland Express Ltd.*, [1914] 1 Ch. 41 (C.A.) where there was no trust deed, so that the relationship of the bondholder and the corporation was that of mortgagee and mortgagor; followed in *Wade v. Murray*, [1940] O.R. 239 where the bonds were secured by a trust deed containing a *pari passu* clause. If there is a deficiency the court can direct payments on realization to be applied on account of principal, notwithstanding that the trust deed requires application of proceeds of realization towards payment first of interest and secondly of principal: *Smith v. Law Guarantee & Trust Society Ltd.*, [1904] 2 Ch. 569 (C.A.). In *Wade v. Murray, supra*, on an application by the trustee for advice and directions as to the proper distribution of proceeds of realization, Hogg J. declined to apply *Smith v. Law Guarantee & Trust Society Ltd., supra*, on the ground that that case was based solely on the construction and meaning of certain orders and that the decision was founded entirely upon the circumstances. It does not appear from the report of the *Wade* case what the express provisions, if any, of the trust deed were, in respect of the application of proceeds of realization. However, in the *Wade* case, while interest had been paid down to the same date on most of the bonds, there were small amounts of interest unpaid in respect of some coupons matured prior to such date, so that apparently the application of the *Smith* case would have prevented the rateable distribution of the proceeds in accordance with the rule laid down in *In re Midland Express Ltd.*, [1914] 1 Ch. 41 (C.A.). It is submitted that the *Smith* case is applicable when on a deficiency this is in the interests of the bondholders and no inequality as between holders of bonds and coupons would result. It would appear to be desirable to make specific provision in the trust deed that in the case of a deficiency the first amount payable is to be paid in repayment of principal and any balance is to be applied to the payment of interest. If the deficiency were applied only to the interest amount, income tax would appear to be chargeable on the entire amount of interest paid.

The holder of an uncashed cheque representing interest on registered debentures is a secured creditor for such interest even though he has refrained from cashing the cheque at the request of the corporation: *In re Defries & Sons Ltd.*, [1909] 2 Ch. 423. It is now usual, however, to introduce special provisions in the trust deed under which the corporation covenants not to extend or assent to the extension of time for payment of any coupons or interest and such coupons or interest, in case time for payment is extended, are not to be entitled to the benefit of the security in case of default, except subject to prior payment of all bonds, and of matured coupons and interest thereon, payment of which has not been extended.

Independently of statute or contractual stipulations there is no general rule of law which compels a corporation to charge interest on money borrowed for construction purposes against revenue and prohibits it from charging such interest during construction to capital account: *Hinds v. Buenos Ayres Grand National Tramways Co.*, [1906] 2 Ch. 654.

Coupons

It is usual to make the interest on bonds payable by coupons to bearer, and where this is done such coupons are negotiable securities: *Toronto General Trusts v. Central Ontario Railway* (1905), 10 O.L.R. 347 (C.A.); *McKenzie v. Montreal & Ottawa Railway* (1878), 29 U.C.C.P. 333 (C.A.); *Connolly v. Montreal Park & Island Railway* (1901), 20 Que. S.C. 1 (C.A.). As to the nature of a coupon, see *McKenzie v. Montreal & Ottawa Railway* (1877), 27 U.C.C.P. 224. Coupons on bonds secured by a trust deed partake of the nature of a specialty and are barred in 20 years: *Toronto General Trusts Corp. v. Central Ontario Railway* (1903), 6 O.L.R. 534; affd (1904), 8 O.L.R. 604.

A coupon detached from the bond to which it relates does not lose the benefit of the mortgage lien: *Trusts & Guarantee Co. v. Grand Valley Railway* (1919), 44 O.L.R. 398 at 412 (C.A.). The holder of detached coupons can sue on them without being at the same time holder of the bond: *McKenzie v. Montreal & Ottawa Railway, supra.* The holder, however, takes subject to the terms of the trust deed, for example, that no action shall be brought except by the trustee: *Levis County Railway v. Fontaine* (1904), 13 Que. K.B. 523 (C.A.). See also as to detached coupons *Derwa v. Rio de Janeiro Tramway Light & Power Co.* (1928), 62 O.L.R 669 at 681. In the same case, *semble*, that if there is any ambiguity in the coupons, the bonds and perhaps even the trust deed may be looked at for an explanation.

As to the circumstances under which the acquisition and payment of coupons will have the effect of preserving the lien and the right to rank with the bond for interest payments, see *Trusts & Guarantee Co. v. Grand Valley Railway, supra*, and cases cited.

Some of the older decisions do not appear to be consistent on the question whether interest on interest should be allowed in respect of overdue coupons. See *Jones v. Municipality of Albert* (1881), 21 N.B.R. 200 (not allowed); *Desrosiers v. Montreal, Portland & Boston Railway* (1883), 28 L.C.J. 1 (interest allowed under the Quebec Civil Code); *London & Canadian Loan & Agency Co. v. Rural Municipality of Morris* (1890), 7 Man. R. 128 (compound interest allowed). In Ontario the question appears to be settled, simple interest being allowed in *Wade v. Murray*, [1940] O.R. 239 and *Montreal Trust Co. v. Abitibi Power & Paper Co.*, [1944] O.R. 515.

Income bonds

Bond interest is payable whether there are profits or not unless it is expressly provided that interest shall be payable out of profits only. Such bonds are called "income bonds". Where interest is payable out of net profits only, the corporation is not entitled to carry the net profits forward, but must set aside out of net profits so much as is necessary for the maintenance of the security and use the balance in payment of interest on the bonds: *Heslop v. Paraguay Central Railway* (1910), 54 Sol. J. 234.

Noteholders were entitled, in addition to a fixed rate of interest, to receive a proportion of the profits whenever the profits of the corporation available to pay a specified dividend in respect of any year should exceed the amount required to pay a specified dividend on its shares. The directors applied the whole profits of one year, after payment of interest on the corporation's debentures and the fixed rate of interest on the notes, in reduction of a previous debit balance in profit and loss. It was held that the directors were entitled to do so and that the words "available for dividend" meant "available for dividend after making any reserve or other similar application which the directors, in good faith, acting on behalf of the company, think it is their duty to make in the interests of the company": *Long Acre Press, Ltd. v. Odhams Press, Ltd.*, [1930] 2 Ch. 196.

Currency in which moneys are payable

Bonds and coupons frequently provide for payment in one of several currencies at the holder's option at a fixed or defined rate of exchange.

A bond provided for payment of $1,000 in lawful money of Canada at London, England, and continued "The principal and interest of this bond shall be payable there at the fixed rate of exchange of $\$4,86^{2/3}$ for the pound sterling." The interest coupon stated the corporation "will pay to the bearer on the first day of July, 1920, of lawful money of Canada at the fixed rate of exchange of $\$4,86^{2/3}$ for the pound sterling at . . . in London, England . . .". There was no amount specified in the text of the coupon though a blank space was left for it in the form provided. In the margin were the words and figures "$25 or £5 2s. 9d." and beneath "1st July, 1920" and still lower "Interest coupon No. 21". Payment at the place specified of £5 2s. 9d. (the amount specified in the coupon as the equivalent of $25) was held to be a satisfaction of the obligation. The holder was not entitled to receive $25 in Canadian currency: *Brown v. Alberta & Great Waterways Railway* (1921), 59 D.L.R. 520 (Alta. C.A.).

Where a coupon expressed a promise to pay 12.50 francs to the bearer at designated banks in Paris, Brussels or Toronto, as half-yearly interest on the corporation's 5 per cent gold bond, but nowhere in the coupons, the bonds or the trust deed was there any direct promise or expression of any obligation to pay otherwise than in francs, and coupons were presented for payment in Toronto, tenders of (1) notes of the Bank of France (legal tender in France) to the amount of the face value of the coupons, (2) notes of the National Bank of Belgium (legal tender in Belgium) to a like amount, (3) the equivalent in Canadian money of the face value of the coupons at the day's rate of exchange for French francs, and (4) the equivalent in Canadian money of the face value of the coupons at the day's rate of exchange for Belgian francs, were held to be sufficient: *Derwa v. Rio de Janeiro Tramway Light & Power Co.* (1928), 62 O.L.R. 669.

A creditor, in respect of a debt payable in a foreign country in foreign currency, is entitled at common law to recover the equivalent in English currency at the rate of exchange current at the date when the debt became payable in the foreign country: *Madeleine Vionnet & Cie v. Wills*, [1940] 1 K.B. 72 (C.A.), following *In re British American Continental Bank Ltd.; Credit Generale Liegeois' Claim*, [1922] 2 Ch. 589; and see *The Custodian v. Blucher*, [1927] S.C.R. 420. If the action is on the covenant the date for conversion is the due date: *In re Chesterman's Trusts*, [1923] 2 Ch. 466 at 479 (C.A.). Where, however, the judgment does not include a judgment on the covenant, and an application is made for an accounting to ascertain the amount to which the plaintiff and the bondholders are entitled out of the proceeds of realization, the date for conversion is the date of the Master's certificate: *Montreal Trust Co. v. Abitibi Power & Paper Co.*, [1944] O.R. 515 at 524. In the same case it was further held that the credit, to which the mortgagor corporation was entitled on taking the account in respect of moneys paid to the plaintiff in Canadian funds on account of principal under orders of the court, was the amount by which the principal indebtedness would have been reduced had the stipulated foreign currency been purchased on the respective dates and the proceeds paid to the plaintiff.

In some provinces, for example, Ontario, the common law rule has been statutorily amended. In Ontario, the statutory rule fixes the date of satisfaction of the relevant Canadian judgment as the date for conversion: see *Courts of Justice Act*, R.S.O. 1990, c. C. 43, s. 121.

Where bonds are payable in one of two currencies at the holder's option, in the absence of any restriction or limitation in the governing provisions, the option continues after the maturity date of the bonds; where bonds are called for redemption, with the concurrent condition of surrender of the bonds for payment, default arises on the date when payment is refused; there is no duty on the bondholder to present his bonds for redemption on any particular day: *Gatineau Power Co. v. Crown Life Insurance Co.*, [1945] S.C.R. 655 and cases cited.

Where the sum expressed to be payable on a debenture was "five hundred dollars ($500) of lawful money of the Dominion of Canada or £102 14s. 10d., its sterling equivalent, at the rate of $4.86^{2/3}$ to the one pound sterling" at any branch of a specified bank at various places in Canada, the City of New York or London, England, at the holder's option, and the debenture was presented for payment in Canada and payment of £102 14s. 10d. or its equivalent in Canadian money at the current rate of exchange was demanded, it was held that payment of $500 discharged the obligation: *Royal Trust Co. v. Oak Bay*, [1934] 4 D.L.R. 697. The insertion of the words "its sterling equivalent" indicated that the amount of English money was to be of the same value as the amount in Canadian dollars; and the purpose of inserting the words "at the rate of $4.86^{2/3}$" was to fix the rate of exchange.

Where the contract is to pay a specified number of dollars at a specified place, but the term "dollar" is not qualified so as to make it clear whether United States dollars or Canadian dollars are intended, *prima facie* the place of payment will govern as to the currency in which the debt is to be discharged: *Adelaide Electric Supply Co. v. Prudential Assurance Co.*, [1934] A.C. 122 at 152, 156. In *Broken Hill Proprietary Co. v. Latham*, [1933] Ch. 373 and 393 (C.A.) Maugham J. held that where a trust deed securing debentures provided for payment of a specified number of pounds in Australia or London at the holder's option, payment to debenture holders who elected to be paid in London must be in sterling. The decision of Maugham J. was approved in the *Adelaide Electric Supply* case and the contrary decision of the Court of Appeal overruled. The *Adelaide Electric Supply* case was applied and followed in *Auckland Corporation v. Alliance Insurance Co.*, [1937] A.C. 587 and considered in *National Bank of Australasia Ltd. v. Scottish Union & National Insurance Co.*, [1952] A.C. 493 at 511. In *Corporation des Obligations Municipales v. Ville de Montreal Nord* (1922), 61 D.L.R. 542 interest coupons of a Canadian corporation were made payable in the United States and the character of the money in which payment was to be made was not specified. A holder of such coupons was held to be entitled to be paid in United States currency. In an action brought in Quebec after payment in United States currency had been refused, judgment was given for an amount in Canadian currency equal to what such holder would have received in the United States when it was due. The above rule, however, is one of construction and the presumption that the currency of the place of payment is intended is rebuttable: *Weiss v. State Life Insurance Co.*, [1935] S.C.R. 461. The statute governing the powers of the obligor may exclude the creation of an obligation payable in a foreign currency: *Saskatoon v. London & Western Trusts Co.*, [1934] 1 D.L.R. 103 (Sask. C.A.).

Where the obligation is expressed in units of a foreign currency and the place of payment is not the country to which the units of foreign currency belong, it is to be satisfied by payment in whatever at the date of repayment is legal tender and legal currency in the foreign country whose currency was lent: *In re Chesterman's Trusts; Mott v. Browning*, [1923] 2 Ch. 466 (C.A.); *Pyrmont Ltd. v. Schott*, [1939] A.C. 145 at 157, 158. If there is a market at the place of payment for the sale and purchase of the foreign currency, then the measure of damages for failure to deliver the agreed amount of foreign currency is the sum which it would have cost the payee at the place of payment to obtain for himself such amount of foreign currency: *Marrache v. Ashton*, [1943] A.C. 311 (currency regulations and restrictions imposed by the foreign government disregarded).

The expression "gold bond" has no well-defined commercial meaning; a bond so described is not necessarily a promise to pay in gold coin: *Derwa v. Rio de Janeiro Tramway Light & Power Co.* (1928), 62 O.L.R. 669. Such an obligation is not in current use.

A contract to pay to a bondholder a specified sum in London in sterling in gold coin of the United Kingdom of or equal to the standard of weight and fineness existing on a specified date, entitled the bondholder to payment of such sum in sterling as represented the gold value (market value in London) of the nominal amount of each respective payment, such value to be ascertained in accordance with the standard of weight and fineness existing on the specified date: *Feist v. Société Intercommunale Belge d'Electricité*, [1934] A.C. 161. In that case the question was treated as one of construction based on the surrounding circumstances at the date of the contract. The facts that at the date of the contract English currency was inconvertible and that gold was not obtainable were considered as leading to the surmise that the parties did not contemplate the settlement of the obligation in gold and that it was to protect the bondholders against England going off the gold standard that the gold clause was inserted. But since the decision in *R. v. International Trustee for the Protection of Bondholders Aktiengesellschaft*, [1937] A.C. 500, it is not possible to confine the decision in the *Feist* case to contracts not only containing a gold clause but also possessing indications in the same sense as those which were contained in the *Feist* case: *New Brunswick Railway v. British & French Trust Corp.*, [1939] A.C. 1 at 18. However, such construction will not be adopted unless the gold clause obligation is expressed in clear language. In the last cited case, the obligation was to pay a specified sum in "sterling gold coin of Great Britain of the present standard of weight and fineness . . . with interest thereon" at a specified rate. The coupon provided for payment of a definite sum, namely, "£2 10s., stg." but contained no reference to gold. While the principal obligation was construed in accordance with the *Feist* case, it was held that this construction was inapplicable to the interest payments.

Federal legislation was enacted in 1937 (*The Gold Clauses Act*, 1937, c. 33) designed to relieve obligors from the effect of the gold clause in obligations payable in money of Canada, or obligations governed by the law of Canada and payable in Canada or elsewhere in money other than money of Canada.

This legislation was considered in *New Brunswick Railway v. British & French Trust Corp., supra,* where an action had been brought in England by a bondholder claiming payment there of an obligation, containing a gold clause, providing for payment in London. The obligation had matured and payment, on what was held to be the true construction, had been repudiated before the coming into force of the Act. It was held by the House of Lords that the Act, upon its proper construction, did not affect the rights of an English creditor suing in England.

The defects disclosed in the 1937 legislation were remedied by new legislation passed in 1939. The federal *Gold Clauses Act* was, however, repealed in its entirety with effect from December 1, 1983: S.C. 1980-81-82-83, c. 159, Sch. item 29. *The Gold Clauses Act*, R.S.O. 1980, c. 189, was formerly applicable to obligations governed by the law of Ontario. It has also now been repealed with effect from November 4, 1986: S.O. 1986, c. 44.

In *Treseder-Griffin v. Co-operative Insurance Society Ltd.*, [1956] 2 Q.B. 127 (C.A.) a gold clause in a domestic contract (a lease between two parties residing in England) was held invalid.

Redemption

Bonds may be perpetual or may be payable on demand or may mature at a specified date or in instalments, a fixed amount falling due annually over a period of years; or the principal may be made to fall due in certain events.

Commonly the trust deed reserves the right to the corporation to redeem bonds in whole or in part at a specified premium on specified notice, and provides that in the case of a partial redemption, the particular bonds to be redeemed are to be selected by lot or in such other manner as the trustee may deem equitable. Money deposited with the trustee by the corporation for the redemption of bonds on the exercise of such right in accordance with the provisions of the trust deed, ceases to be under the control of the corporation and the corporation cannot by subsequent instructions require the trustee to deal otherwise with the money unless the trust deed so provides: *Re Brantford Grinding Wheel Co.* (1931), 40 O.W.N. 284.

Where bonds are expressed to be "redeemable" at a certain date, it means that the corporation may redeem them if it so desires, but is not obliged to do so: *Morrison v. Chicago & North West Granaries Co.*, [1898] 1 Ch. 263.

A covenant to pay, without specifying a time for payment, creates either a present liability to pay, or, at the least, a liability to pay on demand. A covenant to pay on or before a certain day creates a liability to pay on the day named with an option of earlier payment. A covenant to pay on or after a certain day gives an option to pay on the date named but creates no liability until after the day is passed, and possibly not even then, until demand is made: *In re Tewkesbury Gas Co*, [1911] 2 Ch. 279. In that case the bonds contained a covenant for redemption "on or after" a certain date, with a further provision that the particular bonds to be paid off would be determined by ballot. The corporation failed to hold any ballot and, the date for payment having passed, one of the bondholders demanded payment and upon the corporation's refusal commenced an action to enforce the security. The court held that the principal moneys were presently due and payable and that the sentence in the debenture regarding balloting was void for repugnancy and could not defeat the corporation's liability to pay.

Where the principal is made to fall due on the occurrence of a certain event, for example, a winding-up, the corporation or the guarantors of the bonds are entitled to redeem on such event occurring, and the bondholders, in the absence of other provisions in the bonds, have no option to refuse redemption: *Consolidated Goldfields of South Africa v. Simmer & Jack East Ltd.* (1913), 82 L.J. Ch. 214.

The application by the trustee of sinking fund moneys in the purchase of bonds of the corporation to be held in a sinking fund under the trust deed amounts to a redemption of the bonds: *Dominion Telegraph Securities Ltd. v. M.N.R.*, [1947] S.C.R. 45 at 54, 63.

Clogging the equity of redemption

The ordinary rule of "once a mortgage always a mortgage" and the principle that any stipulation which restricts or clogs the equity of redemption is void applies to mortgages by a corporation. Thus, where a corporation to secure a loan pledged its debenture stock with an option to the pledgee to purchase at 40 per cent within 12 months, the loan to become due on 30 days' notice by either side, it was held the option was void on the lender endeavouring to exercise it within the 12 months and before a notice of redemption had been given by the corporation. The corporation was entitled to redeem on payment of principal, interest and costs: *Samuel v. Jarrah Timber Wood Paving Corp.*, [1904] A.C. 323. But where the stipulation by the mortgagee is a collateral contract, though contemporaneous, in substance independent of the security, and not unfair, the court will enforce the bargain of the parties: *Kreglinger v. New Patagonia Meat*

& Cold Storage Co., [1914] A.C. 25. In that case the lenders advanced money to the borrowers upon the security of a floating charge over all their property present and future, and agreed not to demand redemption for a period of five years, but the borrowers were to be at liberty to repay the debt at an earlier period on giving notice. The agreement also contained a provision that the borrowers should not sell any sheepskins to any purchasers other than the lenders for a period of five years from the date of the agreement, so long as the lenders were willing to purchase the same at an agreed price. The loan was paid off before expiration of the five years. It was held that the option of purchasing the sheepskins was not terminated but continued for the period of five years. So also a bargain for the payment to debenture stockholders of an additional sum on the winding-up of the corporation, is valid, if fairly made, as it is neither in the nature of a penalty clogging the equity of redemption, nor is it inconsistent with or repugnant to the contractual and equitable rights of the corporation to redeem: *In re Cuban Land & Development Co.*, [1921] 2 Ch. 147.

Quaere, whether the doctrine against clogging the equity of redemption applies to debentures secured by a floating charge: *De Beers Consolidated Mines Ltd. v. British South Africa Co.*, [1912] A.C. 52 at 68, per Lord Atkinson.

A postponement of the contractual right of redemption is not a clog on the equity of redemption: nor will it be invalid as offending the rule against perpetuities: *Knightbridge Estates Trust Ltd. v. Bryne*, [1940] A.C. 613.

Sinking fund

Bonds for a fixed term of years are not redeemable before maturity at the option of the corporation without the consent of the holders unless the trust deed so provides. Where, as an alternative to making a fixed portion of the bond indebtedness repayable annually (which can be accomplished by means of the issue of serial or instalment bonds), it is desired to obligate the corporation to retire annually a proportion of its bonds, the trust deed will include clauses providing for the creation of a sinking fund and the retirement of a certain principal amount of bonds annually by purchase at or below the redemption price, or by drawings in the event of sufficient bonds not being obtainable by purchase to exhaust the sinking fund moneys or by drawings in the first instance. There is great variety in sinking funds, the terms depending largely on the particular circumstances. Thus, where the assets are of a wasting nature, for example, where the security consists in part of gas or oil wells, the sinking fund is calculated to provide against depletion; where the security consists of an office building, the sinking fund should be sufficient to reduce the amount of bonds outstanding at maturity to a figure which will permit refunding.

The existence of an adequate sinking fund is also of assistance in ensuring a market for the bonds by reason of the purchases for sinking fund and the calling of bonds where the purchases cannot be effected. The common provision that the corporation itself may purchase bonds and tender them to the trustee in satisfaction of the sinking fund payments at the premium which would be payable on redemption is capable of abuse. It is usually considered to be a fairer provision, either to permit the corporation to purchase bonds at prices not greater than the redemption price and tender bonds to the trustee in competition with other bondholders for purchase for the sinking fund, or to permit the corporation to tender bonds at the cost to the corporation (not exceeding the redemption price) on account of sinking fund payments.

Where the trust deed provides for a sinking fund to be applied in the purchase of bonds which are offered for redemption at the lowest price, the lowest price means the lowest average price obtainable. And if the trustee, by paying a higher price for a block of bonds, which will exhaust the moneys at its disposal, will be enabled to redeem a larger number of bonds than if it had accepted a lower tender for a small block and had had to pay more for the balance required to exhaust the moneys in its hands, then the trustee is entitled to reject such lower tender: *National Trust v. Whicher*, [1912] A.C. 377.

On the construction of a sinking fund provision and the acts of the parties with reference to the question whether a payment had in fact been deposited in a sinking fund account, see *Stave Falls Lumber Co. v. Westminster Trust Co.*, [1940] 4 D.L.R. 382 (B.C. C.A.) 396.

Interest paid to the trustee in respect of bonds acquired for and held in a sinking fund is not a deductible expense for income tax purposes: *Dominion Telegraph Securities Ltd. v. M.N.R.*, [1947] S.C.R. 45; bonds so acquired and held cease to be outstanding obligations of the corporation and their acquisition amounts to a redemption, per Kellock J. at p. 54 and Estey J. at p. 63.

In *Re Sapphire Petroleums Ltd.*, [1956] O.R. 581 (C.A.) the trust deed provided that debentures purchased by the corporation and debentures redeemed by the corporation prior to maturity were to be credited against sinking fund requirements. The debentures were convertible into shares of the corporation. It was held that debentures which had been converted had not been redeemed within the meaning of the trust deed and could therefore not be tendered in satisfaction of sinking fund requirements.

Registration requirements

It is not within the scope of this work to discuss in any detail the requirements of registration. These are governed by provincial law and are applicable in the various places where the corporation in question owns property or carries on business.

Careful consideration must be given to these registration requirements, as without proper registration, the security afforded by the trust deed may be set aside for the benefit of other creditors.

Position, powers and duties of the trustee

Where bonds are secured by a covering trust deed a trustee is therein appointed, in whom the title to the assets specifically charged is vested or to whom they are charged. The Act requires that, when the debt obligations issued or to be issued under a trust indenture are part of a distribution to the public, at least one of the trustees must be a corporation incorporated in Canada and authorized to carry on the business of a trust corporation: see s. 82(3).

Under the *Ontario Business Corporations Act*, the only requirement is that at least one of the trustees be resident or authorized to do business in Ontario: see s. 46(3). In Ontario, however, the *Loan and Trust Corporations Act*, R.S.O. 1990, c. L-25, s. 213(1) prohibits any person other than a registered corporation from conducting, undertaking or transacting in Ontario the business of a trust corporation, which is defined as a corporation incorporated or operated for the purpose of acting as a trustee, bailee, agent, executor, etc. (s. 1). In *Montreal Trust Co. v. Abitibi Power Co.*, [1937] O.R. 939, the validity of a bond mortgage was attacked by the liquidator on the ground, among others, that a New York bank, which had been appointed "authenticating trustee" to perform certain designated duties either separately or in conjunction with the Canadian trustee in whose favour the mortgage and charge had been given, was not a proper trustee. Kingstone J., in upholding the validity of the trust deed, considered that the *Loan and Trust Corporations Act* had to do with the activities of the corporation as such and not an isolated contract and that the ordinary operation and general character of the corporation's business must determine whether it was within the prohibition or not, following *Euclid Avenue Trusts Co. v. Hohs* (1911), 23 O.L.R. 377, (1911), 24 O.L.R. 447 (C.A.); and that in any event, even if the New York bank did offend against the statute, that did not of itself invalidate the mortgage. It would seem that s. 16(3) of the Act, which provides that acts of a corporation are not invalid by reason only that they are contrary to the Act, may also have the effect of ensuring the validity of security held under a trust indenture in such a situation.

Generally, the obligations of the trustees must be determined in accordance with the laws of the province in which the trust deed is executed; if the mortgaged premises are situated in that province, the mortgagor corporation is, at the time of the entering into of the contract, resident there and the bulk of the provisions are to be performed there, although the trustees are resident in a foreign country: *Harris Investments Ltd. v. Smith*, [1934] 1 D.L.R. 748 (B.C. C.A.).

A trustee for bondholders stands in the same position as any other trustee. The bondholders are entitled to be put in full possession of all information concerning the trust estate in the possession of the trustee: *In re Magadi Soda Co.* (1925), 94 L.J. Ch. 217.

A provision permitting the trustee to delegate powers is commonly inserted; such a provision is limited to individual instances and does not permit one co-trustee to delegate to the other all his powers and duties: *Harris Investments Ltd. v. Smith, supra.*

Where discretionary powers are vested in a corporate trustee, it has been held that they must be exercised by the board of directors and cannot be delegated to an executive officer: *Re Wilson*, [1937] O.R. 769 (C.A.). That was a case where a trustee had been guilty of neglect and default and relied on a clause in a will providing that, in respect of certain matters left to the discretion of the trustee, its decision should be final. It was alleged by the trustee that the discretion had been exercised by its general manager, but its board of directors had not purported to delegate to such officer the discretion in question. It was held that the beneficiaries were entitled to the benefit of the judgment of the board of directors of the trustee, in respect of the exercise of discretion involved and that the attempted exercise of such discretion by the general manager was nugatory. However, it may be questioned whether a corporate trustee might not be held in fact to have exercised its discretion, even in the absence of an express power of delegation in the trust deed, if the trustee exercised a discretionary power, either through its trust officer or some other officer duly authorized by the board to carry out the duties imposed on the trustee in the execution of the trusts. It is submitted that the answer to any such question should depend on the circumstances and that cases may arise where the discretion of the trustee can be properly and effectively exercised by a duly authorized officer. It may be, therefore, that the rule laid down in *Re Wilson* will be subject to some qualification. See *In re City Equitable Fire Insurance Co.*, [1925] Ch. 407 at 426 (C.A.). In view of the express provisions for delegation now invariably inserted in trust deeds, the question may not, however, arise.

In the case of a trustee under a trust indenture pursuant to which debt obligations are being issued to the public, to whom the Act applies, there are a number of statutory requirements which must be complied with. No person having a material conflict of interest between his role as trustee and his role in any other capacity may be appointed a trustee; when a trustee previously appointed becomes aware that a material conflict of interest exists, it has 90 days either to eliminate the conflict or resign; a trustee who does not take appropriate action in the face of a material conflict may be replaced on an application to the court by any interested person; the Act expressly provides that the existence of a material conflict of interest has no effect on the validity of a trust indenture and the debt obligations issued thereunder: see s. 83 of the Act.

Section 91 of the Act also requires that those trustees to whom the Act applies act honestly and in good faith with a view to the best interests of the holders of the debt obligations and exercise the care, diligence and skill of a reasonably prudent trustee. Such trustees are permitted, however, to rely on certain statements made by others in fulfilling their responsibilities: see s. 92. Trustees of trust indentures to which the Act does not apply are, as indicated, subject to the traditional obligations imposed on trustees by equity. Those to whom the Act applies are subject to those same obligations except to the extent that they are modified by the Act.

It is now the universal practice to embody in the trust deed elaborate provisions for the protection of the trustee, defining its duties, rights and powers and exonerating it from liability. For an illustration of the importance of these trustee relief provisions see *Stothers v. Toronto General Trusts Corp.* (1919), 44 O.L.R. 432 (C.A.). However, the Act renders ineffective any attempt to relieve a trustee, to whom the Act applies, from its obligations of honesty and good faith and to exercise the care, diligence and skill of a reasonably prudent trustee established under the Act: see s. 93.

A provision exonerating the trustee from "the consequences of any mistakes or oversight or error of judgment or forgetfulness or want of prudence", will not relieve a trustee from liability for a wilful breach of trust, that is, wilfully or knowingly acting contrary to his duty; but will protect a trustee in respect of an omission occurring in the honest exercise of his powers: *In re Trusts of Leeds City Brewery Ltd.'s Debenture Stock Trust Deed; Leeds City Brewery Ltd. v. Platts*, [1925] Ch. 532n (C.A.). In that case a provision for indemnification of the trustee against claims in respect of anything done or omitted without his wilful default was also considered and Lord Sterndale M.R. expressed the view that such provision and the one above mentioned were designed to protect trustees in anything that they might do honestly, except in cases where they were wilfully or knowingly acting contrary to their duty. In that case the further question was raised, but not decided, whether, in an action against trustees of a bond mortgage for breach of trust, the action could be brought by the corporation without the bondholders being parties.

In Ontario, if it appears to the court that the trustee has acted honestly and reasonably and ought fairly to be excused for the breach of trust, the court may relieve the trustee from personal liability: the *Trustee Act*, R.S.O. 1990, c. T.23, s. 35.

Under such a provision the trustee, in order to become entitled to relief, must not only prove that he has acted honestly and reasonably but also show that under all the circumstances he ought fairly to be excused: *National Trustees Co. of Australasia v. General Finance Co. of Australasia*, [1905] A.C. 373 at 381. In that case it was held that it was no defence that the trustee had acted upon erroneous advice of its solicitors and that it was a material circumstance that the trustee was a trust corporation receiving remuneration for its services. See also *Whicher v. National Trust Co.* (1910), 22 O.L.R. 460 at 466, 483 (C.A.), reversed by the Judicial Committee of the Privy Council upon the facts of the case without an expression of opinion on this point (*sub nom. National Trust Co. v. Whicher*) [1912] A.C. 377. It is now common to provide in trust deeds that trustees may take legal advice and will be protected in acting thereon. Where any question of difficulty arises, trustees may properly take legal advice under such a clause.

An alternative available to trustees in Ontario is to make an application to the court for advice under s. 60 of the *Trustee Act*. See *Re Brandon Shoe Co.* (1924), 26 O.W.N. 27. If the trustee acts in accordance with the order it is protected: *Stothers v. Toronto General Trusts Corp., supra*. For the form of order see *Strothers v. Toronto General Trusts Corp.* at p. 471. The court usually requires a bondholder to be served and appoints a separate solicitor to represent the bondholders, but whether, in any particular case, it is necessary to serve a bondholder would appear to be a matter for the discretion of the court. In *Stothers v. Toronto General Trusts Corp., supra* (and see *Re Ontario & West Shore Railway* (1911), 2 O.W.N. 1041 at 1042) an order was made that one guarantor municipality should represent all municipal corporations interested, but no bondholder was required to be served.

A trustee may be placed in a very embarrassing position if it is called upon to act in pursuance of a resolution which has been passed by a majority of the bondholders, but which is attacked as illegal by a minority. The proper course for the trustee in such a case in Ontario is to make an application to the court for advice under s. 60 of the *Trustee Act*, and also in the action, if one is pending.

Such course is further advisable where a resolution providing for a reorganization of the corporation is being attacked, for if the trustee takes no action the minority, by blocking the reorganization, will succeed in their aim, whether their contentions are well founded or not. An order of this kind was made in *O'Brien v. British America Nickel* (Middleton J., April 21, 1921, unreported), the trustee being directed to carry out the scheme of reorganization upon taking security by way of indemnification, which was to be available for the protection of the dissentient bondholder in the event his action was successful.

There is a dearth of authority as to the duties of the trustee on an application to the court to sanction a scheme, where a contest develops, either between different classes of creditors or within a class, and the scheme is opposed. Where a petition by the liquidator for the sanctioning of an arrangement was supported by the holders of second debentures and by the holders of a substantial amount of first debentures, but was opposed by two holders of first debentures, Lindley L.J. in the course of the argument observed that the liquidator seemed to be a person who should stand neutral and let the persons interested argue the question: *In re Alabama, New Orleans, Texas & Pacific Junction Railway*, [1891] 1 Ch. 213 at 233 (C.A.); and Fry L.J. in the same case at p. 248 said:

> Where a class of persons divides itself into two, and the liquidator or receiver or trustee is alike the liquidator, receiver or trustee for all of them, and where both those classes appear in their own proper persons, I doubt the propriety of the liquidator, receiver, or trustee taking a strong part on one side or the other.

In *Montreal Trust Co. v. Abitibi Power & Paper Co.*, [1938] O.R. 81 at 92, McTague J. commended the action of the trustee in adopting the position that it was trustee for all the bondholders and not merely those in favour of the plan, which was opposed by other bondholders. On the other hand the observations of Maugham J. in *In Re Dorman, Long & Co.*, [1934] Ch. 635 at 671, indicate that it is the privilege, and possibly the duty, of the trustee to make available to the bondholders its opinion on the merits of a proposed plan. He also stated that the question of the duties of trustees was not a technical matter and that, the greater the complexity of a proposed scheme, the more necessary it is to the bondholders to have the assistance of independent trustees and the more useful their advice is likely to be.

It is submitted that, whatever may be the strict legal obligations of the trustee, it is entitled to participate in the negotiation of a plan and to endeavour to have any defects or inequitable provisions removed; to recommend a plan for adoption by the bondholders if it considers the plan to be in their interests; and to advocate the rejection of a plan which it considers to be contrary to such interests. If, on the other hand, the plan is of such a nature and the circumstances are such that the bondholders are in as good a position as the trustee to form an opinion whether the plan is one which is advantageous to them to adopt, there may be no necessity for the trustee to express its views to the bondholders before the meeting at which the plan is to be considered. If the plan has been approved at the meeting by the requisite majority, but is opposed on an application to the court to have the plan sanctioned, there is no doubt the trustee should not take an active part in either supporting or opposing the application. There seems to be no reason, however, against the trustee making available to the court its own views as to the advantages or disadvantages of the plan, and the same principle would seem to be applicable even if the application to the court for the sanction of the plan is unopposed.

The trustee is responsible for the conduct of the trust and cannot divest itself entirely of such responsibility by calling bondholders' meetings. The trustee must protect to the best of its ability the security it has taken for the bondholders, and therefore may bring an action to enforce the trusts of the mortgage: *Hatherton v. Temiscouata Railway* (1897), 12 Que. S.C. 481. Where the issuing house had disappeared, the majority of the bonds were held in small amounts and no record was available to the trustee of the names and addresses of the bondholders, Murphy J. in *National Trust Co. v. Vancouver Kraft Co.*, [1938] 2 D.L.R. 791, held that the trustee was not open to criticism in proceeding to enforce the security without calling a bondholders' meeting.

Prior to instituting enforcement or other appropriate proceedings in the event of actual or threatened default, a trustee will normally attempt by negotiation with the corporation to have the default cured or prevented. It may also if circumstances permit put the matter before a bondholders' meeting with a view to obtaining the views of the bondholders.

Within 30 days of becoming aware of any default arising under the trust indenture, a trustee to whom the Act applies (i.e., one appointed under a trust indenture pursuant to which debt obligations are being issued to the public) is required to give notice to the bondholders of the default unless it has been cured by that date or unless the trustee reasonably believes that it is in the best interests of the bondholders to withhold such notice and so informs the issuer or guarantor of the bonds in writing: see s. 90. In many cases, the trust indenture itself will impose more stringent obligations on a trustee both to report defaults to bondholders and to take action in respect thereof.

The rule as to a trustee purchasing bonds of the issue under which it is trustee is stated in *In re Magadi Soda Co.*, (1925), 94 L.J. Ch. 217. Modern trust deeds expressly permit the trustee to purchase and deal in the bonds. A trustee for bondholders may become a purchaser as such trustee on the sale of the mortgaged assets: *Royal Trust Co. v. Baie des Chaleurs Railway* (1907), 13 Ex. C.R. 1.

As to the custody of title deeds, there is no implied covenant on the part of a mortgagee to take reasonable care of them during the continuance of the security: *Gilligan v. National Bank Ltd.*, [1901] 2 Ir. 513. It will be observed that personal property security legislation in Ontario and other provinces requires a secured party to use reasonable care in the custody and preservation of collateral in its possession.

A trustee is not liable to the bondholders for loss through failure of a bank in which redemption moneys are deposited in accordance with the trust deed: *Van Horne v. Montreal Trust Co.* (1924), 62 Que. S.C. 436.

As to the responsibility of trustees where agents employed by them have taken illegal commissions, see *Toronto General Trusts v. Robins* (1911), 19 O.W.R. 212.

As to effect of payment to a "fiscal agent" of the mortgagee, see *London & Western Trust Co. v. Sale*, [1937] O.W.N. 110 (C.A.).

Remuneration

The corporation should covenant to pay the trustee's reasonable remuneration, and the trust deed should also provide that this is to be paid out of the mortgaged assets; otherwise the trustee may fail to obtain priority over the bondholders for its remuneration out of proceeds paid into court on the sale of the assets in a debenture holders' action: *In re Accles, Ltd.* (1902), 51 W.R. 57. A provision in the trust deed that the trustees may retain their remuneration out of the moneys to arise under the primary trust for conversion will give the trustees priority over the bondholders: *In re Piccadilly Hotel Ltd.*, [1911] 2 Ch. 534. To the same effect is the decision in *In re City Housing Trust Ltd.*, [1942] Ch. 262. If the assets are deficient the following will rank ahead of the trustee's remuneration: (1) costs of realization; (2) costs, including remuneration, of the receiver: *In re Glyncorrwg Colliery Co.*, [1926] Ch. 951 (trustees entitled under trust deed to hold proceeds in first place to pay or retain the costs and expenses, including their own remuneration, incurred in or about the execution of the trusts). It is important that the remuneration should be expressed to continue until the assets are realized: *In re Piccadilly Hotel Ltd., supra.*

Where a receiver is appointed, the services of the trustee in the ordinary course of things come to an end and remuneration will not be continued: *In re Locke & Smith, Ltd.*, [1914] 1 Ch. 687. But the mere appointment of a receiver does not discharge the trustee and the question whether the trustee's remuneration continues after the appointment of a receiver is a question of the proper construction of the provisions of the trust deed: *Simpson Balkwill & Co. v. Canadian Credit Men's Trust Assn. Ltd.* (1922), 70 D.L.R. 731. And see *In re Anglo-Canadian Lands (1912) Ltd.*, [1918] 2 Ch. 287, distinguishing *In re Locke & Smith Ltd., supra.*

Where the trust deed provided for the payment of a yearly sum to the trustees for their services as trustees during the continuance of the security, it was held that, notwithstanding the appointment of a receiver under a prior trust deed, the sale of the corporation's property, the payment off of the first mortgage debentures and the payment into court of the balance of the proceeds, the trustees were entitled to their remuneration during the continuance of the security: *In re British Consolidated Oil Corp.*, [1919] 2 Ch. 81.

Trust deeds now usually contain provisions that the remuneration of the trustee shall continue until the trusts thereunder have been completely performed notwithstanding that proceedings have been taken to enforce the trusts and a receiver, or receiver and manager, has been appointed.

The factors to be taken into account by the court in determining the remuneration of the trustee are set out in *Toronto General Trusts Corp. v. Central Ontario Railway* (1905), 6 O.W.R. 350 at 354, as (1) the magnitude of the trust; (2) the care and responsibility springing therefrom; (3) the time occupied in performing its duties; (4) the skill and ability displayed; and (5) the success which has attended its administration. But a trustee who has done nothing cannot claim remuneration on the basis of the magnitude of the trust and the responsibility involved: *Re Benson-Hines London Hotel Co., Ex parte Weir*, [1926] 4 D.L.R. 776. For further decisions on remuneration of the trustee, see *Hanson v. Montreal Park & Island Railway* (1902), 5 Que. P.R. 355; *Royal Trust Co. v. Atlantic & Lake Superior Railway* (1908), 13 Ex. C.R. 42 at 60; *National Trust Co. v. Vancouver Kraft Co.*, [1938] 2 D.L.R. 791.

A trustee may sue the corporation for its own remuneration without obtaining authorization from the bondholders: *Hatherton v. Temiscouata Railway* (1897), 12 Que. S.C. 481.

Apart from agreement, where the trustee advances moneys in payment of a prior mortgage, he is entitled to be subrogated to the rights of the mortgagee in respect of such payments and to charge interest at the same rate as is payable under the prior mortgage; on other moneys advanced he is only entitled to charge interest at the legal rate: *In re Seibel Estate*, [1931] 2 W.W.R. 581. A trustee, however, is not entitled to reimbursement, as against the bondholders, where expenditures have not been made wholly in the interests of the bondholders (the trustee having acquired an interest in the mortgaged premises and the expenditure having been made after the acquisition of that interest) or where expenditures have been made voluntarily: *Vermont Loan & Trust Co. v. Ennis*, [1933] 2 W.W.R. 397 (Sask. C.A.).

The federal Act contains a number of statutory requirements in respect of a trustee. These may be summarized as follows:

A holder of debt obligations issued under a trust indenture may, on payment to the trustee of a reasonable fee, require the trustee to furnish, within 15 days after delivery of the required statutory declaration, a list setting out the names and addresses of the registered holders of the outstanding debt obligations, the principal amount owned by each such holder and the aggregate principal amount of debt obligations outstanding, as shown on the trustee's records on the date the statutory declaration is delivered to the trustee; the issuer of such debt obligations is required to furnish the trustee with the information required to enable the trustee to comply with the foregoing provisions on demand by the trustee; the statutory declaration is to contain the name and address of the person requiring the trustee to furnish the list (if the person is a corporation, the address for service thereof) and that the list will not be used except as permitted. If the person requiring a list is a corporation, the statutory declaration is to be made by a director or officer of the corporation concerned. This list may not be used by any persons except in connection with an effort to influence the voting of the holders of the debt obligations, an offer to acquire debt obligations, or any other matter relating to the debt obligations or the affairs of the issuer or guarantor thereof; an offence is provided for contravention of this provision. See s. 85.

Section 89 provides that, on demand of the trustee, the issuer or guarantor of debt obligations or trust indenture is to furnish the trustee with evidence in such form as the trustee may require as to compliance with any condition relating to any action required or permitted to be taken by the issuer or the guarantor under the trust indenture and that a certificate of compliance with respect to all requirements contained in the trust deed is to be furnished to the trustee at least once in every 12-month period, beginning on the date of the trust indenture and on any other term of the demand of the trustee. Such certificate relates to requirements that, if not complied with, would constitute an event of default with the giving of notice, lapse of time or otherwise or if there has been such failure then particulars.

Evidence of compliance in certain cases is required to be made by a statutory declaration or a certificate by a director or officer of the corporation stating the conditions in the indenture have been complied with and in appropriate circumstances the opinion of a legal counsel and/or of an auditor or accountant that the conditions have been complied with. The certificate is to state (a) that the person giving the evidence has read and understands the conditions of the trust indenture, (b) the nature and scope of the examination or investigation on which he bases the certificate, statement or opinion and (c) that he has made such examination or investigation necessary to enable him to make the statements or give the opinion contained or expressed therein. Such evidence of compliance is to be furnished in the case of the issue, certification and delivery of debt obligations under the trust indenture, the release and substitution of property subject to the security interest constituted by the trust indenture or the satisfaction and discharge of the trust indenture. Evidence of compliance with the provisions of the indenture may also be required by the trustee in the case of any act to be done by the trustee at the request of the issuer or guarantor. See ss. 86-88.

Replacement

The trust deed usually provides for the resignation of the trustee and the substitution of a new trustee. A new trustee can be appointed by a judge of the Ontario Court, General Division, under the *Trustee Act* on originating notice: *Re Imperial Steel Corp.* (1925), 28 O.W.N. 242; affd [1925] S.C.R. 703. See also *Harrisburg Trust Co. v. Trusts & Guarantee Co.* (1914), 6 O.W.N. 110, where it was held that the court had the power to make the appointment as a matter of inherent jurisdiction as well as under the *Trustee Act.* In any case, the trust deed usually confirms that the court has the power of appointment. The trust deed often also provides that the bondholders may remove the trustee and replace it with a new trustee.

An effective notice to the original trustee will not be displaced by a change of trustees: *Slattery v. Slattery,* [1945] O.R. 811 (C.A.).

When security enforceable

Default

The security may become enforceable under the provisions of the trust deed or independently thereof. It will become enforceable under the trust deed if any of the events of default therein specified occur, for example, non-payment of principal or interest, failure to pay taxes, suffering an execution to be levied against the mortgaged premises, etc., and if any period of grace therein provided for following a particular default has expired. Independently of any provision in the trust deed the security becomes enforceable, so far as the mortgage of the corporation's undertaking is concerned, if the corporation ceases to carry on its business: *Hodson v. Tea Co.* (1880), 14 Ch. D. 859 (appointment of a receiver); *In re Crompton & Co.*, [1914] 1 Ch. 954 (resolution for voluntary winding-up for purpose of reconstruction); *Wallace v. Universal Automatic Machines Co.*, [1894] 2 Ch. 547 (C.A.) (compulsory winding-up); *Trusts & Guarantee Co. v. Drumheller Power Co.*, [1924] 2 D.L.R. 787 (ceasing to carry on its ordinary business by selling its assets and forming itself into a holding corporation). As to enforcement when the security is in jeopardy, see below.

Many trust deeds expressly provide that no enforcement rights or only very limited rights of enforcement exist for bondholders otherwise than pursuant to the terms of the trust deed. In such cases, enforcement will be permitted only in accordance with the terms of the trust deed. The result in most cases is a severe limitation on the ability of an individual bondholder to enforce his security.

If the trust deed calls for payment at a specified place, for example, at the registered office of the corporation, there is no default unless the bondholder presents himself at that place and demands payment so that the obligation to pay may be discharged: *Re Escalera Silver Lead Mining Co.* (1918), 25 T.L.R. 87. But if the place of payment is the office of the trustee, a demand for payment is unnecessary: *Royal Trust Co. v. Penny Spruce Mills Ltd. & Montreal Trust Co.* (1959), 21 D.L.R. (2d) 656 (B.C. C.A.). In that case, Davey J.A. after referring to *Re Escalera Silver Lead Mining Co.*, *supra*, and cases to the same effect said at p. 658:

> The reasoning upon which those cases rest is stated by Warrington J. in *Re Escalera Silver Lead Mining Co.*, *supra.* It is this: A debtor is obliged to pay the debt at no place but the place stipulated by the contract; that since the debtor can pay no one but the creditor or his agent, he cannot be required to perform his obligation unless the creditor or his agent presents himself at the nominated place to receive payment. That is why demand at the place of payment, when a place is stipulated, is necessary to put the debtor in default.
>
> That reasoning is not applicable to the case at bar, for the trust deed stipulated the place of payment to be the registered office of the Trustee, 203 Bank of Nova Scotia Building, Edmonton, Alberta.' That is where the appellant had to pay the debt, and it could always find the trustee there in order to do so. No demand was therefore necessary to enable the debtor to discharge the obligation.

If more than one place is named for payment, for example, at a specified bank or at the head office of the corporation, then it is for the person to whom payment is to be made to fix the place of payment, and unless he has done so there is no default: *Thorn v. City Rice Mills* (1889), 40 Ch. 357 at 359; *Trusts & Guarantee Co. v. Drumheller Power Co.*, [1914] 2 D.L.R. 208.

Whether there has been default in payment is a question to be determined on the wording of the trust deed. In *In re Harris Calculating Machine Co.*, [1914] 1 Ch. 920 at 922, the conditions endorsed on the debentures were as follows:

> (3) The principal moneys hereby secured shall immediately become payable . . . if the registered holder shall serve notice in writing upon the company requiring

> payment of the principal moneys and interest (if any) and the company has made default . . . for three days after such service.
>
> (12) The principal moneys . . . will be paid at Lloyds Bank Limited, 222, Strand, W.C., or other the company's bankers for the time being, on presentation of this debenture, which may be surrendered on payment.

A bondholder gave notice to the corporation requiring payment of principal and interest within three days, but neither principal nor interest was paid, and the bondholder then commenced a debenture holders' action, claiming the usual relief. The defence stated in general terms that the money was not due as there had been no demand at Lloyds Bank. It was held that there had been default in payment of interest under condition 3 and that, therefore, compliance with condition 12 as to presentation for payment was unnecessary in order to render the principal payable.

If presentation is requisite it is a condition precedent and should be pleaded in defence: *In re Harris Calculating Machine Co., supra.*

Jeopardy

The security may also become enforceable in another type of situation. If, for example, judgments have been recovered against the corporation and executions are likely to issue, the bondholders are entitled to have a receiver appointed even though the corporation is not in default: *Grigson v. Taplin & Co.* (1915), 85 L.J. Ch. 75; *In re London Pressed Hinge Co.*, [1905] 1 Ch. 576; *Trusts & Guarantee Co. v. Drumheller Power Co.*, [1924] 2 D.L.R. 787; or where the corporation proposed to distribute its reserve fund, which was practically its only asset, among the shareholders; *Tilt Cover Copper Co.*, [1913] 2 Ch. 588; or where a winding-up petition is pending: *In re Victoria Streamboats, Ltd.; Smith v. Wilkinson*, [1897] 1 Ch. 158; or where a writ has been issued, other proceedings are threatened and the operations of the corporation are at a standstill: *In re Newport Constructions Co.; Barclays Bank, Ltd. v. The Company*, [1948] W.N. 64.

This is called the doctrine of "jeopardy", and the principle on which the court intervenes is that the bondholders need not stand by and see the assets seized by unsecured creditors. It is not sufficient for the plaintiff merely to show that the proceeds of the assets if realized would be insufficient to pay off the bonds: *In re New York Taxicab Co.*, [1913] 1 Ch. 1; but see *Braunstein v. Marjorlaine Ltd.* (1914), 58 Sol J. 755, where, however, there were other circumstances present. The power of the court to appoint a receiver and manager on the ground of jeopardy is not dependent on the provisions of the trust deed. Whether a case of jeopardy has been made out depends on the circumstances of each case. The applicant must prove some peril to the property: *Eastern Trust Co. v. Nova Scotia Steel & Coal Co.* (1926), 59 N.S.R. 123, [1927] 1 D.L.R. 421 (N.S. C.A.). In that case the appointment of a receiver on the ground of jeopardy was refused. Proof of non-payment of interest, losses in the past, curtailment of operations in the steel department and the closing down of one of several plants, were regarded as insufficient grounds. Carroll J., whose judgment was affirmed on appeal, in contrasting the case with that of the

Dominion Steel Company, where a receiver and manager had been appointed, said at p. 126:

> In that case, however, it was abundantly proven that the company was no longer able to carry on; its credit was gone; it could not get funds to carry on its business, and it was faced with the immediate prospect of having to close down with outstanding contracts unfilled. It was in a state of suspended animation. It was a case in which the business of the company had come to an end. That is not the case here. Here we have a going concern, a live corporation, operating the property, which property is not threatened by creditors.

A mortgagee is entitled as of right to a receiver, although judgment creditors may already have had one of their own appointed: *Allan v. Manitoba & Northwestern Railway* (1894), 10 Man. R. 106.

Remedies on security becoming enforceable

On the security becoming enforceable by reason of default or jeopardy the trustee or the bondholders (to the extent that independent action by bondholders is not precluded by the trust deed) have the remedies of a mortgagee. These remedies include an action on the covenant for payment (*Allan v. Manitoba & Northwestern Railway* (1894), 10 Man. R. 106) and an action to enforce the security; in the latter type of action a receiver or receiver and manager may be appointed by the court. As to the relative rights of the trustee and the bondholders to take enforcement proceedings, see the notes under the heading "Persons entitled to enforce security" in this chapter.

Certain other remedies may in particular cases be considered. The trust deed may provide in the event of default for the appointment of a receiver or receiver and manger or for possession and sale independently of proceedings in the courts. Proceedings for the winding-up of the corporation or in bankruptcy may also be taken. These courses of action are considered below.

In certain circumstances it may be desirable to canvass the possibility of a reorganization prior to or following the institution of enforcement proceedings. See the notes under the heading "Reorganization with or without a sale," in this chapter.

Action to enforce the security

Such a proceeding is a mortgagees' action and is subject only to the laws and the rules of practice in force in the province in which the action is pending; the right to proceed with the action may be suspended by provincial legislation imposing a general moratorium or one limited to a special class of action or suitor or to one particular action or suitor; so far as provincial jurisdiction under the head of property and civil rights is concerned it is immaterial that a winding-up has intervened and that leave to proceed has been granted under s. 21 of the *Winding-up Act*: *Abitibi Power & Paper Co. v. Montreal Trust Co.*, [1943] A.C. 536.

Where the action is based on default, default must be pleaded in the statement of claim: *Royal Trust Co. v. Penny Spruce Mills Ltd.* (1959), 21 D.L.R. (2d) 656 at 659 (B.C. C.A.).

The usual and proper course in Ontario, in most cases, is to bring an action against the corporation to have the trusts of the trust deed carried into execution, to have a receiver and manager appointed, to have it declared that the trustee is entitled to a mortgage and charge on the property and assets covered by the trust deed, to have the mortgage and charge enforced by sale, and for an order directing the taking of the necessary accounts and enquiries. Forthwith after action has been commenced an application is made to the court on motion for the appointment of a receiver and manager.

Sometimes the corporation instructs counsel to consent to judgment, in which case the motion is turned into a motion for judgment and judgment is pronounced in the appropriate form. This procedure is now less frequently followed than heretofore; it is undesirable, where, as may often be the case, a compromise or arrangement is eventually effected between the corporation and the bondholders; moreover, it is often more convenient for other reasons to avoid an immediate judgment. In England the court is averse to declaring a charge in cases where the motion for the appointment of receiver and manager is treated as the trial of an action, except where it is absolutely clear that an indefeasible charge has been created or the plaintiff has proved his title to a charge apart from consent, as on a hearing or motion for judgment in default of defence: *In re Gregory Love & Co.; Francis v. The Company*, [1916] 1 Ch. 203 at 209; and similarly in *Marwick v. Lord Thurlow*, [1895] 1 Ch. 776; *In re Crigglestone Coal Co.; Stewart v. Crigglestone Coal Co.*, [1906] 1 Ch. 523.

Where a loan secured by a floating charge is made payable on demand the cases have held that a reasonable period of time is necessary in order for payment to be demanded and the security cannot be realized or if realized damages may be awarded: *Jeannette B.B.Q. Ltée v. Caisse Populaire de Tracadie Ltée.* (1989) 100 N.B.R. (2d) 374 at 400 (Q.B.), varg on reconsideration (1989), 100 N.B.R. 374, vard (1991), 82 D.L.R. (4th) 548 (N.B. C.A.); *Mister Broadloom Corp. (1968) v. Bank of Montreal* (1983), 44 O.R. (2d) 368 (C.A.) (leave to appeal to the Supreme Court of Canada refused (1984), 3 O.A.C. 320); *Whonnock Industries Ltd. v. National Bank of Canada* [1987] 6 W.W.R. 316 (B.C. C.A.) (leave to appeal to S.C.C. refused [1988] 2 W.W.R. lxvii), such period may be varied either implied or expressly; see *Four-K Western Equipment Ltd. v. Canadian Imperial Bank of Commerce* (1983), 46 C.B.R. (N.S.) 146 (B.C. S.C.).

The same person cannot be both a plaintiff and a defendant in the same action: *Neale v. Turton* (1827), 4 Bing. 149 at 151; *Wavell v. Mitchell*, [1891] W.N. 86; *In re Phillips*, [1931] W.N. 271 (disapproving the procedure allowed in *In re Abercrombie's Will Trusts*, [1931] W.N. 109). Accordingly, it is submitted that in a case where the trustee bringing an action to enforce the security of a trust deed is also trustee under one or more subsequent trust deeds covering the same property, the proper course is to have one or more holders of each class of junior securities appointed to represent all the holders of that class and to have such persons, and not the trustee, added as defendants: *In re Phillips, supra.* The same procedure should be followed where a trustee occupies a position prejudicial to the interest of the bondholders. See *Payne v. Parker* (1865), L.R. 1 Ch. App. 327; *Farmers' Loan & Trust Co. v. Northern Pacific Railway* (1895), 70 Fed. 423. On the other hand it may be noted that in the proceedings brought by the trustee in 1924 for the enforcement of the trust deed securing the first income bonds of *British America Nickel Corp.* (unreported), the same trust corporation as trustee for the holders of two series of junior bonds was added as a defendant in the Master's office. No objections to this course were raised. It was stated by Sargant L.J. in *Hardie & Lane Ltd. v. Chiltern*, [1928] 1 K.B. 663 at 699, that "it is incorrect to make any individual a defendant twice over because he happens to fill two capacities or has two different interests. The case often arises in actions in relation to trusts and the practice to the contrary is, in my experience, invariable." If the trustee has a material conflict of interest, he is required to resign or eliminate the conflict within 90 days, failing which he may be removed by court order: s. 83.

Under the usual form of trust deed, the trustee is the proper plaintiff; but where the trustee refuses to take the initiative, any bondholder can, after any conditions precedent in the trust deed have been complied with, bring a class action to enforce the trust: *Shaughnessy v. Imperial Trusts Co.* (1904), 3 N.B. Eq. 5; *Perron v. L'Eclaireur & Nadeau* (1933), 57 Que. K.B. 445 (C.A.) (failure of trustee to act after notice prescribed by trust deed). Even where the necessary request of bondholders (to make the taking of action by the trustee imperative) has not been made, bondholders may be entitled to bring a class action where the circumstances warrant: *Re Imperial Steel Corp.* (1925), 28 O.W.N. 242; affd [1925] S.C.R. 703.

As to bondholders' actions to enforce the security see further the notes under the heading "Persons entitled to enforce security" in this chapter.

In *In re The Services Club Estate Syndicate Ltd.*, [1930] 1 Ch. 78, Maugham J. stated the practice in England to be settled that, where an action is brought by the trustees of a covering deed, the court is accustomed to give the conduct of the action to someone else merely because the trustees are accounting parties.

Where the trustee is plaintiff, it is entitled to judgment for the full amount of the bonds and interest; the corporation is not entitled to take the position that the only bonds which it is called upon to pay are those which may be proved within a time to be fixed by the court, for there is nothing to justify the court in compelling bondholders to prove their claims by a fixed time or lose them: *Toronto General Trusts Corp. v. Lake Superior Corp*, [1935] O.W.N. 325 (C.A.).

As to the considerations by which the court will be guided in making an order directing the sale of the assets in an action to enforce the trust of the trust deed, see *Montreal Trust Co. v. Abitibi Power & Paper Co. Ltd.*, [1940] O.W.N. 307 (leave to appeal refused by McTague J.A.).

The remedy of foreclosure may be granted in an action by debenture holders having a charge where the security is deficient and there is no covering trust deed: *Sadler v. Worley*, [1894] 2 Ch. 170 (property charged included leaseholds and uncalled capital); but foreclosure will not be ordered in the absence of any one debenture holder: *In re Continental Oxygen Co.*, [1897] 1 Ch. 511 (where an order for sale of the property was made). All holders of debentures ranking after the mortgage must be made parties: *Westminster Bank Ltd. v. Residential Properties Improvement Co.*, [1938] Ch. 639.

The usual acceleration clause, whereby in the event of default for a stated period the whole principal sum becomes due, is a cumulative provision and does not interfere with the right of foreclosure which becomes immediately exercisable on the occurrence of default: *Farmers Loan & Trust v. Nova Scotia Central* (1891), 24 N.S.R. 542.

If there is a covering trust deed with a power of sale only, there can be no foreclosure: *Schweitzer v. Mayhew* (1862), 31 Beav. 37; or where the security is in the form of a trust for sale: *Paton v. Wilkes* (1860), 8 Gr. 252 at 257; and see *Locking v. Parker* (1872), L.R. 8 Ch. App. 30; *Sampson v. Pattison* (1842), 1 Hare 533; *Jenkins v. Ross* (1857), 5 De G. & Sm. 107. But where a mortgage in favour of a trustee to secure bonds contained no trust for sale, and although called a trust deed was essentially a mortgage, it was held that the trustee was entitled to foreclosure: *Michigan Trust Co. v. Canadian Puget Sound Lumber Co.*, [1918] 3 W.W.R. 273 (B.C. C.A.); and in *In re Corporate Equitable Property Society Ltd.*, [1940] W.N. 208, where there was a covering trust deed containing a charge, Bennett J. considered that, in view of the decision in *Sadler v. Worley, supra*, there was no reason why debenture stockholders and their trustees should not be able to obtain a decree of foreclosure.

If the assets are insufficient to pay the bonds in full the plaintiff is entitled to costs as between solicitor and client: *In re New Zealand Midland Railway*, [1901] 2 Ch. 357 (C.A.); but not if enough is realized to pay the bonds in full: *In re Queen's Hotel Co.; Cardiff, Ltd.*, [1900] 1 Ch. 792. The principle that, where the assets are insufficient, the plaintiff is entitled to costs as between solicitor and client, will be applied to a trustee for bondholders who is the plaintiff and to individual bondholders added as parties defendant in the interests of the class; such individual defendants will be entitled to party and party costs only, unless it is established that the assets will be insufficient; a liquidator defendant is entitled only to party and party costs and even such costs can only be awarded with the consent of the other parties: *Montreal Trust Co. v. Abitibi Power & Paper Co.*, [1943] 4 D.L.R. 207.

Where the assets are insufficient, the order in which they are to be applied is (1) the plaintiff's costs of realization; (2) the amount due the receiver and manager including his remuneration; (3) the costs, charges and expenses of the trustee; (4) the costs of the plaintiff; and (5) the bondholders: *Batten v. Wedgewood Coal & Iron Co.* (1884), 28 Ch. D. 317; *In re London United Breweries Ltd.*, [1907] 2 Ch. 511; *In re Glyncorrwg Colliery Co.*, [1926] Ch. 951.

An acceleration clause is recognized as effectual by the courts: *Wallingford v. Mutual Society* (1880), 5 App. Cas. 685. See also *Re Brandon Shoe Co.* (1924), 26 O.W.N. 27 (in events which happened due date not accelerated).

Appointment of a receiver or receiver and manager under the trust deed

The trust deed frequently provides in the event of default for the appointment in writing by the trustee of a receiver or a receiver and manager. The bondholders themselves may have the power under the trust deed to appoint a receiver or a receiver and manager and, subject to the provisions of the trust deed, they have the right in a bondholders' action to seek such an appointment from the court. Note that under the Ontario Act, a trustee may not act as the receiver, but under the federal Act this is permissible.

Possession and sale

The trustee for bondholders may, if the right is given by the trust deed, enter and take possession and sell in the event of default but this remedy is not usually resorted to as a court sale is considered preferable, and if the corporation has been carrying on a business and the corporation's undertaking is covered by the charge, an action to enforce the trusts for sale and for the appointment of a receiver is usually brought.

In *Wade v. Crain* (1915), 35 O.L.R. 402 (C.A.); affd (1917), 55 S.C.R. 208 an unpaid vendor of lands whose agreement permitted him on default of the purchaser to enter and take possession, on default occurring took possession not only of the lands but also of certain chattels which were claimed in an action by the liquidator. The vendor attempted to justify the taking of the chattels under the terms of a charge conferred by bonds of which he held some $24,000 out of an issue of $100,000. The Court of Appeal held that the attempted justification failed and that in the absence of the other bondholders who were not before the court there should be no adjudication on the right to prove on the bonds in the winding-up.

Winding-up petition

A bondholder may, if principal or interest is due and unpaid, file a winding-up petition: *Re Borough of Portsmouth Tramway Co.*, [1892] 2 Ch. 362; and a bondholder who has brought an action and obtained the appointment of a receiver is not thereby disentitled from petitioning to wind up. A bondholder whose principal or interest is not due is not a creditor entitled to petition for a winding-up order: *In re Melbourne Brewery & Distillery*, [1901] 1 Ch. 453.

Sometimes in order to obviate proceedings by the bondholders and to save expense, the bondholders, if the corporation is in liquidation, make an arrangement with the liquidator whereby he sells the assets and pays the claim of the bondholders out of the proceeds. In such a case the bondholders do not lose their prior claim on the proceeds by abandoning their lien as against the purchaser of the assets nor by failing to value their security: *Re St. John River Log Driving Co.*, [1927] 3 D.L.R. 800 (N.B. C.A.) (leave to appeal was granted but not proceeded with). The bondholders must, of course, prove their claim in the liquidation after the sale if the foregoing procedure is adopted.

See further the notes to ss. 11-12 of the *Winding-up Act*, in chapter 20.

Reorganization with or without a sale

Upon the security becoming enforceable it may become clear prior to or following the institution of enforcement proceedings that a satisfactory sale of the mortgaged premises cannot be effected for cash. In such circumstances it may become necessary to attempt to bring about a reorganization under which the mortgaged premises will be sold for securities of another corporation (which may be a corporation specially formed for the purpose) which will be distributed to the bondholders, or the bondholders will accept new securities of the existing corporation in lieu of their bonds or agree to some modification of their existing securities.

Where the trust deed contains adequate provisions enabling a stated majority at a meeting of the bondholders to consent to what is proposed, such provisions will frequently be utilized to effect a reorganization. Frequently as part of the scheme of reorganization a compromise or arrangement will also be effected between the corporation and its shareholders under s. 192 of the Act or, in the case of corporations incorporated under the corporation statute of one of the provinces, under the similar provisions of such statutes; such a reorganization requires the co-operation of the shareholders and possibly of other creditors as well as the requisite approval of the court. For a discussion of the operation and effect of such majority provisions contained in the trust deed, see the notes under "Distinction between a compromise and a modification of bondholders' rights" in this chapter.

If, on the other hand, the majority provisions are defective or inadequate, or if, as is sometimes the case, the trust deed contains no such provisions, a reorganization may be effected under the *Companies' Creditors Arrangement Act* or in some circumstances, under the *Bankruptcy and Insolvency Act.* These Acts may be resorted to when the rights of unsecured and secured creditors are also dealt with as part of the scheme of reorganization, or where a compromise or arrangement between the corporation and its shareholders is at the same time effected under s. 192 of this Act or similar legislation of the provinces. See *Bargain Harold's Discount Ltd. v. Paribas Bank of Canada* (1992), 7 O.R. (3d) 362 (Gen. Div.).

A trust deed ordinarily by implication confers on the trustee or a majority of the bondholders the right to consent to a modification of rights under a proposal under the *Bankruptcy and Insolvency Act.*

Effect of winding-up on enforcement proceedings

The mere fact that the corporation has gone into liquidation does not prevent a bondholder from bringing an action to enforce his security: *In re Longdendale Cotton Spinning Co.* (1878), 8 Ch. D. 151; *Imperial Paper Mills v. Quebec Bank* (1910), 2 O.W.N. 1500 at 1502.

After a winding-up order has been made, no action may be commenced or proceeded with except with the leave of the court. Such leave does not alter the nature of the proceeding which remains a mortgagees' action subject only to the laws and the rules of practice from time to time in force in the province where the action is pending: *Abitibi Power & Paper Co. v. Montreal Trust Co.*, [1943] A.C. 536 at 547.

If a mortgagee has already commenced an action and a winding-up intervenes, he should have leave to proceed except under special circumstances, or unless the same relief is given to him in the winding-up as he would obtain in the action: *In re David Lloyd & Co.* (1877), 6 Ch. D. 339 (C.A.). Where the bondholders make no claim in the winding-up and their security is deficient, leave to proceed is *ex debito justitiae*: *Abitibi Power & Paper Co. v. Montreal Trust Co.*, [1943] A.C. 536 at 547. Leave to bring an action will usually be granted as a matter of course, per Meredith C.J. in *Re Brampton Gas Co.* (1902), 4 O.L.R. 509 at 518; *Capital Trust Corp. v. Yellowhead Pass Coal Co.* (1916), 27 D.L.R. 25 (Alta. C.A.); *Re Canadian Western Steel Corp.* (1922), 51 O.L.R. 615 (an appeal was disposed of on other grounds). In *Re Martin International Trap Rock Co.* (1915), 8 O.W.N. 599, on a motion for leave to proceed to enforce a mortgage, a winding-up having intervened, Lennox J. made an order allowing the applicants to proceed to enforce their mortgage after the expiration of three months, subject to the right of the liquidator or an unsecured creditor or a shareholder to apply for an extension of time. The judge held that he had a discretion to refuse leave to proceed, adopting the reasoning of Kay J. in *In re Henry Pound* (1889), 1 Megone 279, and not following *In re David Lloyd & Co.* (1877), 6 Ch. D. 339 (C.A.).

Re Martin International Trap Rock Co., *supra*, appears to be in conflict with an earlier decision, *In re British Columbia Tie & Timber Co.* (1908), 14 B.C.R. 81, where Clement J., following *In re David Lloyd & Co.*, dismissed a motion by a liquidator for an order to restrain a mortgagee in possession from proceeding to sell, and thought that as the mortgagee's action did not come within any one of the classes of "proceeding" specified in s. 22 of the *Winding-up Act*, s. 21 should not be extended to cover any proceeding outside those classes. But *quaere*, whether this decision is good law. See also the notes to the *Winding-up Act*, s. 21 in chapter 21.

Prima facie a mortgagee is entitled to possession of the assets mortgaged to him and a liquidator ought not, by taking possession, to interfere with the security: *Shortreed v. Raven Lake Portland Cement Co.* (1909), 13 O.W.R. 720. It was held in the same case that if the parties could not agree on what was specifically covered by the mortgage the plaintiff might have leave to bring action, or an issue might be directed for this purpose.

Where the trustee for bondholders is in possession, the liquidator has no right to dispossess the trustee until the secured debt is paid: *Three Rivers Bucket & Box Factory v. Beliveau* (1921), 30 Que. K.B. 389.

In England, if the liquidator is in possession at the time when an application to appoint a receiver is made, or if there is a winding-up at the time the receiver is appointed by the court or afterwards, the court will usually appoint the liquidator to act as receiver in order to avoid unnecessary expense: *Perry v. Oriental Hotels Co.* (1870), L.R. 5 Ch. App. 420; *In re Henry Pound, Son & Hutchins* (1889), 42 Ch. D. 402 at 419 (C.A.); but this is only a *prima facie* rule of practice which may easily be displaced: *British Linen Co. v. South American & Mexican Co.*, [1894] 1 Ch. 108 at 118 (C.A.). Where debenture holders have secured the appointment of a receiver, their right to have a receiver is not taken away by the winding-up and the receiver ought not to be displaced without some strong reason for doing so: *In re Joshua Stubbs, Ltd.*, [1891] 1 Ch. 187;

Strong v. Carlyle Press, [1893] 1 Ch. 268. The court will not appoint the liquidator receiver where the receiver has been appointed by the debenture holders themselves under power to do so: *In re Henry Pound, Son, & Hutchins* (1889), 42 Ch. D. 402 at 419 (C.A.); unless the power has not been exercised *bona fide*: *Re Maskelyne British Typewriter Ltd.*, [1898] 1 Ch. 133 (C.A.).

Where a majority of the debenture holders under a power contained in the debentures had appointed the liquidator of the corporation as receiver and an application was subsequently made for the appointment of another receiver, Britton J. in *Re Civil Service Co-operative Supply Assn.* (1916), 10 O.W.N. 143 was of the opinion that the majority of the debenture holders could appoint another receiver in place of the liquidator and that the court was not debarred from appointing another person because of the former action of the majority. See also *Bank of Montreal v. Maritime Sulphite Fibre Co.* (1901), 2 N.B. Eq. 328, where the liquidators, under a winding-up order granted subsequently to the appointment of a receiver, disputed the validity of the mortgage and the extent of the property covered and the court held that the receiver (who had been appointed before the winding-up order, but after the application to wind up) should not be discharged, but the order appointing the receiver was varied and confined to the property described in the mortgage.

Effect of bankruptcy on enforcement proceedings

The *Bankruptcy and Insolvency Act* changes the position of secured creditors in a number of ways. Under section 50 of that Act a proposal may be made by an insolvent person, a receiver, a liquidator, a bankrupt or the trustee of a bankrupt. The proposal may be made to the creditors generally or as separated into classes and may also be made to secured creditors in respect to any class or classes of secured claims; the proposal must be made to all secured creditors in respect to secured claims of a particular class; these secured claims are included in the same class if the interests of the creditors holding those claims are sufficiently similar to give them a commonality of interest taking into account the nature of the debt, the nature and priority of the security, the remedies available, the treatment of claims under the proposal and to the extent to which the claims will be paid and such further criteria as may be prescribed; the court is given power to determine classes of secured claims appropriate to a proposal. A secured creditor will then be bound by a proposal accepted by its class of secured creditors.

Part XI of the Act (sections 243 to 252) is new and contains a number of provisions relating to secured creditors and receivers. A secured creditor who intends to enforce a security on substantially all of the inventory, accounts receivable or other property is required to send to the insolvent person in prescribed form and manner a notice of such intention and the security is not to be enforced until the expiry of 10 days after the sending of the notice unless the insolvent person consents to an earlier enforcement of the security, which consent cannot be given prior to the sending of the notice in question.

A receiver must as soon as possible and not later than 10 days after becoming a receiver by appointment or otherwise send notice to the Superintendent and to the trustee or to the insolvent person and all creditors of the insolvent person that the receiver has ascertained. The receiver under section 247 is required to act honestly and in good faith and to deal with the property of the insolvent person or the bankrupt in a commercially reasonable manner. Power is given to the court in section 248 to make an order with respect to the secured creditor or receiver who is failing or has failed to carry out any duty imposed by the Act.

It will be observed that section 69 of the Act provides for a stay against certain rights of a secured creditor or under a security agreement while a proposal is under consideration. There is an exception in the case of a secured creditor who has taken possession of secured assets of the insolvent for the purpose of realization before notice of intention under section 50.4 was filed to make a proposal or in the case of a secured creditor who has given notice of intention under section 244(1) to enforce that creditor's security against the insolvent person more than 10 days prior to the time the notice of intention under section 50.4 was filed. Section 50.4 deals with the filing of a notice of intention to make a proposal by an insolvent and the furnishing of certain information in connection therewith.

Under section 69.4 the court is empowered to relieve a secured creditor from the operation of s. 69 if the court is satisfied that the creditor is likely to be materially prejudiced by the delay or such relief is otherwise equitable.

Persons entitled to enforce security

As a general rule and subject to the provisions of the trust deed, the bondholders themselves have the right on default to enforce the security in the absence of a contrary provision in the trust deed; the action may be brought by a bondholder suing on behalf of himself and all other bondholders, making the trustee a co-defendant with the corporation, and the same is the case where the security is contained partly in the bonds and partly in the trust deed: *Shaughnessy v. Imperial Trusts Co.* (1904), 3 N.B. Eq. 5; *Perron v. L'Eclaireur & Nadeau* (1933), 57 Que. K.B. 445 (C.A.). See also *Downer v. Boughner* (1930), 66 O.L.R. 279 (action to set aside assignment to another bondholder of a prior mortgage) where Wright J. citing *Duke of Bedford v. Ellis*, [1901] A.C. 1 at 8 and *Markt & Co. v. Knight Steamship Co.*, [1910] 2 K.B. 1021 at 1027 (C.A.) said at p. 283:

> My view is that these authorities establish the right of the plaintiff . . . to bring the action on behalf of all the bondholders . . . There is here a community of interest, a community of grievance, and the relief sought is in its nature beneficial to all the bondholders. If the conveyance is set aside, the bondholders, through their trustees . . . will be entitled to redeem; and, if the property is sold, the bondholders will share ratably in the proceeds.

Where the action is brought by a bondholder on behalf of himself and other members of the class it is important that no defences should be open to the corporation as against that particular bondholder, for example, counterclaim: *Huggons v. Tweed* (1879), 10 Ch. D. 359 (C.A.). Where a person suing on behalf of himself and others is disentitled to sue on his own behalf he cannot do so on behalf of others interested: *Dillon v. Township of Raleigh* (1887), 13 O.A.R. 53.

The plaintiff may discontinue after judgment if he has no notice that any other bondholder claims to have the benefit of the judgment: *In re Alpha Co.*, [1903] 1 Ch. 203.

Where a debenture holder's action has been begun by a person some of whose dealings in relation to the affairs of the corporation appear to require investigation, the court may give the conduct of the action to an independent person: *In re The Services Club Estate Syndicate Ltd.*, [1930] 1 Ch. 78.

In Quebec, notwithstanding a provision in the trust deed that any proceedings taken by an individual bondholder are to be for the equal benefit of all, a bondholder may maintain an action for the amount due to himself: *Perron v. L'Eclaireur & Nadeau* (1933), 57 Que. K.B. 445 (C.A.).

It is usual, however, for the trust deed to curtail the right of the bondholders to take proceedings, unless the trustee refuses to do so, and in every case its terms must be looked at to ascertain the bondholders' rights in this regard. In *Levis County Railway v. Fontaine* (1904), 13 Que. K.B. 523 (C.A.), the trust deed provided that "any proceeding for the purpose of enforcing any of the rights resulting from said bonds or from this mortgage shall only be initiated by the trustee in its own name". It was held that such a provision deprived the bondholders of the right of suit and was binding on a person who had acquired interest coupons which were deemed to be subject to the covenants contained in the bonds.

The trust deed may preclude a bondholder from taking proceedings to enforce the security until certain conditions have been satisfied. It is a matter to be determined on the construction of the provisions of the trust deed whether the conditions apply to the particular proceedings taken by the bondholder: *Stoddart v. Shields Lumber Co.* (1920), 53 D.L.R. 322 (B.C. C.A.).

If the power to enforce the security is, by the trust deed, vested in the trustee subject to conditions which have been performed, the trustee is the proper plaintiff, even in a suit for foreclosure: *Michigan Trust Co. v. Canadian Puget Sound Lumber Co.*, [1918] 3 W.W.R. 273 (B.C. C.A.).

It is not a defence to an action by a trustee to enforce the provisions of the trust deed where foreclosure is not claimed that the trustee has been required to act at the instance of a pledgee of the bonds: *Anderson v. McNair Lumber & Shingle Co. Ltd.*, [1929] 2 D.L.R. 209 (B.C. C.A.).

In *Stoddart v. Shields Lumber Co.*, *supra*, the conditions in the trust deed restricting bondholders from taking enforcement proceedings were held not to be an obstacle to the plaintiff's right of recovery against a guarantor of the bonds. A guarantee can be and often is framed so as to give the guarantor the same protection against actions by individual bondholders as is conferred by the conditions above mentioned.

A trust deed provided that "no action shall be taken under this debenture except with the consent in writing of a majority of the debenture holders." A bondholder was held to be precluded from bringing an action to recover principal and interest without obtaining such consent: *Pethybridge v. Unibifocal Co.*, [1918] W.N. 278. See the following cases involving actions by bondholders to enforce their securities: *Hope v. Croydon & Norwood Tramways Co.* (1887), 34 Ch. D. 730; *Rogers & Co. v. British & Colonial Colliery Supply Assn.* (1898), 68 L.J.Q.B. 14; *Laliberte v. La Rue*, [1931] S.C.R. 7.

On the other hand in *Cleary v. Brazil Railway* (1916), 85 L.J.K.B. 32, where the trust deed contained a provision to the effect that no bondholder should have the right to institute any suit or proceeding for the execution of the trusts of the trust deed, this was held not to disentitle a bondholder from suing for arrears of interest on the covenant contained in the bond and the coupons attached.

The customary clause of a trust deed that the trustee is authorized to institute proceedings for the enforcement of the security or the trusts upon request from the bondholders, does not mean that the trustee is not empowered to bring suit in the absence of such authorization: *Hatherton v. Temiscouata Railway* (1897), 12 Que. S.C. 481.

The usual clause in a trust deed authorizing the trustee to take proceedings on requisition of the bondholders will not prevent the trustee from suing for its remuneration without having first obtained authorization from the bondholders: *Hatherton v. Temiscouata Railway, supra.*

As a general rule, a trustee who takes proceedings to enforce the security of a trust deed will represent the holders of the bonds secured by the trust deed for all purposes of the action without it being necessary to join or add any of such holders as parties. See Ontario Rule 9.01 and *Michigan Trust Co. v. Canadian Puget Sound Lumber Co.*, [1918] 3 W.W.R. 273 (B.C. C.A.).

As to the parties where the trustee occupies a position prejudicial to the interest of the bondholders whom it represents, see the notes under "Action to enforce the security," in this chapter and see s. 83 of the federal Act.

The court will not permit a plaintiff in a bondholders' action, who has obtained the appointment of a receiver, to be attacked pending the continuance of the proceedings by misleading and untrue statements such as published interviews suggesting to the public that his action was improper: *H.W. Dillon & Sons Ltd. v. The Company; In re Sir Robert Thomas*, [1930] W.N. 156.

Receivers

Receivers or receivers and managers may be appointed by the trustee or by the bondholders, where the trust deed or the bonds so provide, or by the court in an enforcement action.

The law applicable to receivers and receiver-managers is a subject to which entire texts are devoted. As a result, any detailed consideration of this subject is beyond the scope of this work. What can usefully be included here, however, is a discussion of the provisions included in Part IX of the Act that deal with receivers and receiver-managers (ss. 94-101) and a brief summary of some of the more important principles.

The Act is different from most of its provincial counterparts in dealing expressly with this subject. Generally, corporation statutes do not address this subject and receivership law is governed by judicature acts and the common law. According to the report of the Dickerson Committee, in its "Proposals for a New Business Corporations Law for Canada" (1971), the draft Act which was prepared, on which the Act is substantially based, included provisions dealing with receivers and receiver-managers for two reasons. First it was thought desirable to clarify the ability of a receiver to take over the assets of or to administer the corporation in question. Second, the existence of these provisions makes the law applicable to receivers of corporations incorporated under the Act uniform across Canada, at least to the rather limited extent that the Act deals with the subject: see page 66 (Vol. I). The second point seems to have been directed particularly at receivers appointed in Quebec in respect of corporations incorporated under the Act, since the provisions included in the Act are generally consistent with the position at common law.

Receivers and receiver-managers may be appointed by the court upon application of an interested person or may be privately appointed by a creditor pursuant to the authority granted to it in its debt instrument. Part IX of the Act deals with receivers and receiver-managers of both kinds.

Part IX of the Act begins by quite simply stating the functions of receivers and receiver-managers. A receiver of any of a corporation's property may, subject to the rights of any secured creditor, receive the income from the property, pay associated liabilities and realize the security interest of those on behalf of whom it has been appointed; it may not carry on the corporation's business without the permission of the court (s. 94). A receiver who is also appointed receiver-manager of the corporation may also carry on the corporation's business to the extent necessary to protect the security interest of those on whose behalf it was appointed (s. 95). Since court-appointed receivers and receiver-managers are not appointed on anyone's behalf, these statements of function would seem to apply only in the case of private appointments.

If a receiver-manager is appointed, either by a court or privately, the corporation's directors may not exercise those powers that the receiver-manager is authorized to exercise so long as the receiver-manager is in place (s. 96). Generally, such a provision will not prevent the directors of the corporation from bringing an action seeking relief as a result either of the receiver-manager's allegedly improper appointment or its allegedly improper conduct while in office: *Golden West Restaurants Ltd. v. Canadian Imperial Bank of Commerce*, [1989] 5 W.W.R. 471 (Sask. Q.B.); affd [1990] 3 W.W.R. 287 (Sask. C.A.).

A privately appointed receiver or receiver-manager must act honestly and in good faith and must deal with the corporation's property in its possession or control in a commercially reasonable manner. Such a receiver or receiver-manager must also comply with the terms of the instrument pursuant to which it is appointed and any directions of the court. A court-appointed receiver or receiver-manager must act in accordance with the court's directions. A court-appointed receiver or receiver-manager which failed to meet the standards expressly imposed by the Act on privately appointed receivers and receiver-mangers would quickly be directed to do so by the courts. Specific provision is made in the Act for the court to make any order it thinks fit including directions on any matter relating to the duties of the receiver or receiver-manager: (ss. 97-100).

The Act also contains certain specific requirements imposed on all receivers and receiver-managers of corporations subject to the Act. Any receiver or receiver-manager must notify the Director under the Act immediately of his appointment and discharge, take custody and control of the corporation's property as directed by his appointment, open and maintain a separate bank account in his name as receiver or receiver-manager, keep detailed accounts of all transactions, keep account of administration for inspection by the directors of the corporation during usual business hours, prepare financial statements of his administration every six months and prepare a final account of his administration on completion of duties (s. 101).

In the many other aspects of receivership law not dealt with in the Act, the developed law concerning receivers and receiver-managers will be applicable. For instance, the Act says nothing about when a court should appoint a receiver or receiver-manager or what the powers and duties of a court-appointed receiver or receiver-manager should be nor does it deal with the question of whether a privately appointed receiver or receiver-manager is the agent of the creditor or the debtor corporation. In connection with these and many other issues, the usual rules apply.

Receivers appointed under power

Receivers or receivers and managers may be appointed by the trustee or by the bondholders, where the trust deed or the bonds so provide, or by the court in an enforcement action. Very different consequences flow from the two modes of appointment. As to the appointment of receivers by the court, see the next heading "Receivers appointed by court".

Trust deeds securing bonds now almost invariably provide that the trustee may, in the event of default, appoint a receiver and, on such appointment, the instrument itself must be referred to for the powers and duties of the receiver. Such power must be exercised *bona fide*, otherwise the court will appoint its own receiver: *Re Maskelyne British Typewriter Ltd.*, [1898] 1 Ch. 133 (C.A.). The appointment of a receiver by debenture holders under their debentures does not necessarily prevent the court from appointing a receiver: *In re "Slogger" Automatic Feeder Co.*, [1915] 1 Ch. 478. A receiver appointed under an instrument is to act in accordance with that instrument and any direction of a court (s. 98).

Unless the power is expressly made exercisable on the property of the corporation becoming in jeopardy, the bondholders must resort to the court if a receiver is desired to be appointed on those grounds.

Unless the trust deed states, as it ought, that the receiver is to be deemed the agent of the corporation (see for example *Peat Marwick Ltd. v. Consumers' Gas Co.* (1980), 29 O.R. (2d) 336 (Ont. C.A.), he will be deemed to be the agent of the bondholders or the trustee, who will be liable for any default on his part: *Re Vimbos Ltd.*, [1900] 1 Ch. 470; *Robinson Printing Co. v. Chic Ltd.*, [1905] 2 Ch. 123 (debenture holders held to be personally liable for debts incurred by the receiver). If the receiver is the agent of the bondholders he can claim remuneration from them: *Deyes v. Wood*, [1911] 1 K.B. 806 (C.A.). It is now the practice to use apt words making the receiver the agent of the corporation and expressly excluding any liability of the bondholders not only to the receiver for his remuneration and expenses, but also to anyone having any dealings with the receiver: *Cully v. Parsons* (1924), 93 L.J. Ch. 42. See *Central London Electricity Co. v. Berners*, [1945] W.N. 51 (undertaking given by receiver on behalf of bondholders without authority).

A receiver appointed under a debenture which provides that the receiver is to be the agent of the corporation and confers upon the receiver express power to get in the property charged, can bring an action in the corporation's name for that purpose: *M. Wheeler & Co. v. Warren*, [1928] Ch. 840 (C.A.).

But even where the receiver is the agent of the bondholders he is for some purposes the agent of the corporation, at all events so far as is necessary to enable him to exercise the powers conferred on him by the debentures: per Warrington J. in *Robinson Printing Co. v. Chic Ltd.*, [1905] 2 Ch. 123 at 132.

A receiver will be liable to a trustee in bankruptcy for conversion of the assets of which he has taken possession as receiver where the security has been set aside as fraudulent; but if the trustee has elected to treat the receiver as a trespasser he cannot require the receiver to account for profits realized in the completion of contracts as damages: *In re Simms; Ex parte Trustee*, [1934] Ch. D. 1 (C.A.).

Where the receiver is expressly stated to be the agent of the corporation there is no personal liability of the receiver or trustee for debts incurred in carrying on the business: *Owen v. Cronk*, [1895] 1 Q.B. 265 (C.A.); *Gosling v. Gaskell*, [1897] A.C. 575.

A receiver and manager, even though appointed under a power contained in the debenture which provides that he is to be deemed to be an agent of the corporation, will be deemed to be in possession of the mortgaged premises so as to be subject to liability as an "occupier" thereof under the provisions of a statute imposing liability on an occupier: *Meigh v. Wickenden*, [1942] 2 K.B. 160.

On the making of a winding-up order the receiver ceases to be an agent of the corporation: *Gosling v. Gaskell, supra.* If in such circumstances a receiver desires to realize the property, he acts as agent of the debenture holders: *In re Courts (Emergency Powers) Act, 1939; In re Brown & Co. (General Warehousemen) Ltd.*, [1940] Ch. 961. The trustee for the bondholders upon the corporation going into liquidation does not become liable on the contracts of the receiver in the absence of any authorization, express or implied, constituting the receiver the agent of the trustee: *Gosling v. Gaskell, supra.* Similarly, on the commencement of a voluntary liquidation, the right of the receiver to bind the corporation ceases; if he thereafter makes a contract without purporting to act for any principal and not being thought by the other party to be acting for a principal, he will be personally liable: *Thomas v. Todd*, [1926] 2 K.B. 511.

While the winding-up of the corporation puts an end to the agency of a receiver appointed under powers contained in the trust deed, which provides that the receiver is to be deemed the agent of the corporation, the winding-up does not terminate the powers of the receiver: *Gough's Garages Ltd. v. Pugsley*, [1930] 1 K.B. 615 at 621, 626.

In *Re B. Johnson & Co. (Builders)*, [1955] 1 Ch. 634, the Court of Appeal considered the difference between a receiver, with ancillary powers of management, for the debenture holders and a person charged with the duty of managing the affairs of the corporation for the corporation's benefit. At page 662 Jenkins L.J. said:

> The duties of a receiver and manager for debenture holders are widely different from those of a manager of the company. He is under no obligation to carry on the company's business at the expense of the debenture holders. Therefore he commits no breach of duty to the company by refusing to do so, even though his discontinuance of the business may be detrimental from the company's point of view. Again, his power of sale is, in effect, that of a mortgagee, and he therefore commits no breach of duty to the company by a bona fide sale, even though he might have obtained a higher price and even though, from the point of view of the company, as distinct from the debenture holders, the terms might be regarded as disadvantageous . . . in the absence of fraud or *mala fides* . . ., the company cannot complain of any act or omission of the receiver and manager, provided that he does nothing that he is not empowered to do, and omits nothing that he is enjoined to do by the terms of his appointment.

Receivers appointed by court

Status

In an enforcement action the court may appoint a receiver or a receiver and manager and in such case he is to act in accordance with the directions of the court (s. 97). See s. 100 of the Act for directions that may be given. As to the procedure, see the notes under the heading "Procedure for appointment of receiver by the court" below. When, as is usually the case, the business of the corporation is included in the charge, the court will appoint the receiver to act as manager of the business. The procedure in Ontario is set out in Rule 41 of the Rules of Civil Procedure.

It is the settled rule in England that one of the parties is not to be appointed receiver without the consent of the other party unless a very special case is made: *In re Lloyd; Allen v. Lloyd* (1879), 12 Ch. D. 447 at 451 (C.A.). In *Eastern Trust Co. v. Nova Scotia Steel & Coal Co.*, [1938] 4 D.L.R. 808 the court criticised the appointment of the trustee as receiver. Under the Ontario Act a trustee may not act as a receiver (s. 50) but this would appear to be admissable under the federal Act.

A receiver and manager is empowered to carry on the business of the corporation for the purpose of realization. It is its primary duty to preserve and carry on the undertaking as a going concern: *National Trust Co. v. Dominion Iron & Steel Co.*, [1927] 3 D.L.R. 1063 (N.S. C.A.). A receiver and manager will not be authorized to make large expenditures where this is not clearly beneficial to the estate. See *Ritchie v. Central Ontario Railway* (1904), 7 O.L.R. 727. While a receiver ought to obtain the authorization of the court before making large expenditures, yet where such expenditures have been made without authorization but in good faith and have resulted in benefit to the property, such expenditures should be approved by the court: *Georgia Investments Co. v. Stratford Realty Co.* (1937), 18 C.B.R. 253.

The receiver will not be directed to manage the business unless the latter is by express terms or by implication included in the security: *Whitley v. Challis*, [1892] 1 Ch. 64 (C.A.). The business of the corporation will be included in the security if the latter covers the "goodwill" of the corporation, and it is important that the trust deed should so provide. The word "property" may be sufficient to include the goodwill or business of the corporation: *Salter v. Leas Hotel Co.*, [1902] 1 Ch. 332. In *Peek v. Trinsmarin Iron Co.* (1876), 2 Ch. D. 115, *Makins v. Percy Ibbotson & Sons*, [1891] 1 Ch. 133 and *Edwards v. Standard Rolling Stock Syndicate*, [1893] 1 Ch. 574, receivers and managers were appointed where the charge did not in terms include the goodwill.

The duty of the receiver is to take possession of and protect the assets of the corporation comprised in the charge: *In re Manchester & Milford Railway* (1880), 14 Ch. D. 645 (C.A.). He is responsible for negligence in administering the estate and reasonable care and ordinary business control are required: *Plisson v. Duncan* (1905), 36 S.C.R. 647.

The position of a receiver and manager appointed by the court is thus described by Haldane L.C. in *Parsons v. Sovereign Bank of Canada*, [1913] A.C. 160 at 167:

> A receiver and manager appointed, as were those in the present case, is the agent neither of the debenture-holders, whose credit he cannot pledge, nor of the company, which cannot control him. He is an officer of the Court put in to discharge certain duties prescribed by the order appointing him. . . .

See also as to the status of a receiver and manager as an officer of the Court, Cairns L.J. in *Garden v. London Chatham & Dover Railway (No. 1)* (1867), L.R. 2 Ch. App. 201 at 211.

The receiver is not the agent or manager of the corporation and cannot make contracts on which the corporation will be liable: *Moss Steamship Co. v. Whinney*, [1912] A.C. 254; he is a principal and not an agent, per Vaughan Williams L.J. in *In re Glasdir Copper Mines*, [1906] 1 Ch. 365 (C.A.). It follows that he is personally liable on all contracts, except in cases where there is a special stipulation to the contrary; and he must look to the assets for indemnity against the liability so incurred: *Burt, Boulton & Hayward v. Bull*, [1895] 1 Q.B. 276 (C.A.); *Boehm v. Goodall*, [1911] 1 Ch. 155; *Johnston v. Courtney*, [1920] 2 W.W.R. 459 (B.C. C.A.) (no liability of a party for receiver's expenses).

Neither the plaintiff in an action to enforce the security nor the bondholders are chargeable with interest on moneys in the hands of the receiver and manager from time to time; if a liquidator considers that excessive amounts are being retained by the receiver and manager his remedy is to apply to the court to direct its officer accordingly: *Montreal Trust Co. v. Abitibi Power & Paper Co.*, [1944] 3 D.L.R. 505.

As to the receiver's right to be indemnified out of the estate, see *In re Glasdir*

Copper Mines, [1906] 1 Ch. 365 (C.A.); *Strapp v. Bull*, [1895] 2 Ch. 1 (C.A.); *In re British Power Traction & Lighting Co.*, [1907] 1 Ch. 258.

A contract for sale of property in a bondholders' action entered into by a receiver should contain a clause stating the date by which the approval of the court must be obtained. Where such a contract is made subject to the approval of the court, but no date is fixed for obtaining such approval, it must be obtained before the date fixed for closing and, where the receiver allowed the date of closing to go by and the purchasers repudiated and a year later the receiver applied for approval of the conditional contract, it was held that the purchasers were entitled to repudiate and to be repaid the deposit: *In re Sandwell Park Colliery Co.*, [1929] 1 Ch. 277.

When the receiver desires to appoint an agent to find a purchaser he should apply to the court for leave. If the receiver has not done so, the agent is not entitled to any commission but the court has a discretion to award the agent such commission as it considers just: *In re National Flying Services Ltd.; Cousins v. The Company*, [1936] Ch. 271.

Where a receiver desires to obtain the direction of the court, he should ask the person who has the conduct of the proceedings, the plaintiff, to make the application: *Windschuegl v. Irish Polishes Ltd.*, [1914] 1 Ir. 33.

One who secures the appointment of a receiver is not liable for his acts: *Bottoms v. Pacific Northwest Lumber Co.*, [1929] 4 D.L.R. 415. A receiver is not liable for rent in respect of the corporation's leasehold property: *Hay v. Swedish & Norwegian Railway* (1892), 8 T.L.R. 755; *Hand v. Blow*, [1901] 2 Ch. 721; *In re Westminster Motor Garage Co.* (1914), 84 L.J. Ch. 753.

As to the position of the receiver in relation to contracts made by the corporation, see the next heading, below.

As to appointment of a receiver by the court at the instance of a legal mortgagee, see *Manufacturers' Life Insurance Co. v. Hanson*, [1924] 2 D.L.R. 692 at 701 (Alta. C.A.).

Effect of appointment on the corporation

The appointment of a receiver by the court leaves the corporation in existence, but deprives the corporation of all power to enter into contracts, or to alienate, pledge or otherwise dispose of the assets of which the receiver is put in possession. The corporation's powers are in abeyance: *Moss Steamship Co. v. Whinney*, [1912] A.C. 254. In *Re Hat Development Ltd.* (1988), 71 C.B.R. (N.S.) 264 (Q.B.), affd (1989), 65 Alta. L.R. (2d) 374 (C.A.), it was held that such appointment (pursuant to the Alberta Act) deprived the directors of their power to create trust deeds incurring further indebtedness.

The appointment of a receiver will ordinarily operate as a dismissal of the corporation's servants: *Reid v. Explosives Co.* (1887), 19 Q.B.D. 264; *Rolfe v. Canadian Timber & Saw Mills Co.* (1906), 12 B.C.R. 363; *Toronto-Dominion Bank v. Leonard Industries Ltd. et al.*, [1984] 1 W.W.R. 120 (Sask. Q.B.).

The appointment of a receiver does not necessarily put an end to all the corporation's trading contracts. As the receiver is appointed to manage the corporation's business, he is at liberty to continue with a contract or repudiate it: *Parsons v. Sovereign Bank of Canada*, [1913] A.C. 160. If the repudiation of a contract would destroy the goodwill of the corporation, which it is the duty of the receiver to preserve, the court will not permit the repudiation: *In re Newdigate Colliery Ltd.*, [1912] 1 Ch. 468 (C.A.). However, if the contract does not affect the corporation's goodwill, the court will grant leave to disregard it: *In re Great Cobar Ltd.*, [1915] 1 Ch. 682.

In certain circumstances a customer of the corporation may be able to set off damages sustained by the cancellation of his contract with the corporation: *Forster v. Nixon's Navigation Co.* (1906), 23 T.L.R. 138; *Parsons v. Sovereign Bank of Canada, supra.* In the latter case a receiver delivered goods to a customer of the corporation under a contract made by the corporation before his appointment, assigned the amounts due for such goods to a bank, and afterwards cancelled the contract made by the corporation. Notice of the assignment to the bank was not given to the customer until after the contract had been cancelled. In an action brought by the bank against the customer to recover the debt so assigned the customer was entitled to set off damages sustained by the cancellation of the contract.

Where, at the commencement of a receivership, bondholders held interim certificates which were exchangeable for definitive bonds, the corporation in receivership was ordered to deliver such bonds and the receiver and manager was directed to co-operate with it in this connection: *National Trust Co. v. Barcelona Traction, Light & Power Co.; Ex parte Westminster Bank Ltd.*, [1951] O.R. 530 (C.A.).

Effect of appointment on prior encumbrances

A prior mortgagee requires leave to take proceedings to displace a second mortgagee and its receiver. See *Trusts & Guarantee Co. v. Grand Valley Railway* (1914), 5 O.W.N. 848. And a prior mortgagee cannot sue the receiver without leave: *Trusts & Guarantee Co. v. Oakwood Clubs* (1931), 40 O.W.N. 581.

Where a receiver had been appointed by the court and a prior mortgagee, purporting to act under a power of sale contained in the mortgage, advertised the property for sale, without making an application to the court for leave, an order was made by Wright J. staying the sale; but on appeal the order was set aside on the ground that the mortgagees were not affected by the receivership order: *Watson v. Imperial Steel Corp.* (1925), 29 O.W.N. 11 and 81 (C.A.).

A prior mortgagee is not entitled to attack as improper the appointment of a receiver by the court in an action to enforce a second bond mortgage; if the corporation and the second mortgagee are satisfied with the conduct of the receiver the prior mortgagee cannot complain: *Trusts & Guarantee Co. v. Grand Valley Railway, supra.*

When a prior mortgagee applies to the court for leave to take possession, notwithstanding the appointment of a receiver in an action brought on behalf of junior debenture holders, he is not entitled to any rents collected by the receiver prior to such application: *In re Metropolitan Amalgamated Estates Ltd.*, [1912] 2 Ch. 497.

Procedure for appointment of receiver by the court

As soon as the writ in an action to enforce the security has been issued and served an application may be made to the court for the appointment of a receiver or receiver and manager.

Except under exceptional circumstances a receiver ought not to be appointed *ex parte*: *In re Connolly Bros. Ltd.*, [1911] 1 Ch. 731 (C.A.); *Trusts & Guarantee Co. v. Drumheller Power Co.*, [1924] 2 D.L.R. 208.

A receiver cannot be appointed on an originating motion: *Re Imperial Steel Corp.* (1925), 28 O.W.N. 242; affd [1925] S.C.R. 703.

Where a winding-up order has been made, leave to commence or continue proceedings must be obtained: *Winding-up Act*, s. 21.

The practice in Ontario of appointing a receiver and manager for, an indefinite period was criticized by Robertson C.J.O. in *National Trust Co. v. Barcelona Traction, Light & Power Co.; Ex parte Westminster Bank Ltd.*, [1951] O.R. 530 at 551 (C.A.).

The order usually requires the receiver and manager to give security to be fixed by the Master. It is usually desirable that the order should permit the receiver and manager to act at once and before giving security. Where it is referred to a referee to appoint a receiver, it is his duty to take security unless the court has dispensed with security: *Toronto Packing Co. v. Abrams* (1922), 21 O.W.N. 29; Ontario rule 461.

Where the receiver and manager is appointed with remuneration he is bound to pay the reasonable expenses of furnishing security, but he will be allowed such expenses if appointed without remuneration: *Harris v. Sleep*, [1897] 2 Ch. 80 at 82 (C.A.). In Ontario, the *Loan and Trust Corporations Act* provides that when a trust corporation is authorized to execute the office of receiver and the Lieutenant-Governor in Council approves of such corporation, no security is required for the due performance of its duties as such receiver unless otherwise ordered.

As to the accounts and enquiries directed to be made by the judgment in an enforcement action appointing a receiver, see *In re Burradon & Coxlodge Coal Co.*, [1929] W.N. 15.

Liens and claims having priority over bondholders

There are a number of claims which may rank ahead of the claim by bondholders; care must be taken to ensure that such claims are paid.

Compromises and modification of rights of bondholders

Applicable provisions of trust deed

It is usual for the trust deed to contain provisions enabling a stated majority at a meeting of bondholders to consent by extraordinary resolution to a compromise of their rights or to a modification of the terms of their security, which consent if properly obtained will bind a dissentient minority.

Whether the particular thing proposed to be effected is within the terms of the power conferred upon the majority under the trust deed, is a question of construction of the trust deed, and such power must be strictly construed. As a result of the litigation which has arisen upon the construction of majority clauses, there has been a progressive elaboration of such provisions and it is not uncommon to find set out in a modern Canadian trust deed many powers exercisable by extraordinary resolution and designed to permit the modification of the security in specified ways. The standard majority provisions authorize the bondholders by extraordinary resolution to sanction *inter alia* (1) any scheme of reorganization; (2) an amalgamation, sale or lease of the undertaking; (3) the acceptance by the trustee in satisfaction for the sale of the mortgaged premises of shares or securities of any other corporation formed or to be formed and the distribution thereof among the bondholders; (4) the release of the mortgaged premises in whole or in part; (5) compromises or arrangements with creditors secured or otherwise; and (6) any modification, alteration or compromise of the rights of the bondholders against the corporation or its property.

In the absence of anything in the bond mortgage giving a majority of the bondholders power to delegate, the appointment of a committee with power to modify the security is *ultra vires*: *British America Nickel Corp. v. M.J. O'Brien Ltd.*, [1927] A.C. 369.

It is now usual in the trust deed to give power to the bondholders by extraordinary resolution to appoint a committee to exercise on behalf of the bondholders such of the powers of the bondholders exercisable by extraordinary resolution as may be specified in the resolution, the bondholders also being empowered in the resolution making such appointment to provide for payment of the expenses and remuneration of the committee.

In *Downer v. Boughner* (1930), 66 O.L.R. 279, the defendant, who was a bondholder, had been appointed a member of a committee of the bondholders, the appointment of which had been authorized at a meeting of the bondholders for the purpose of carrying out a scheme for reorganization. The defendant had previously contracted with the holder of a prior mortgage to take an assignment thereof and had made a payment on account. The actual assignment was made by instrument dated subsequent to the date of the appointment of the defendant as a member of the committee. In an action brought by the bondholders, who contended that the defendant, by virtue of his appointment as one of the committee, was in effect a trustee and as such was precluded from taking the assignment without disclosing the transaction to the other bondholders, Wright J. said there was no fiduciary relationship of the defendant to the other bondholders and held that he was not precluded from taking an assignment of the mortgage which he had previously contracted to take.

In the *British America Nickel* case, *supra*, the Ontario Court of Appeal, whose judgment ((1925), 57 O.L.R. 536) was affirmed, held that the power to consent to a prior charge had been exhausted by its previous exercise on another occasion. The Judicial Committee did not deal with this point in its judgment. The bond mortgage contained, *inter alia*, "(d) Power to accept any other securities of the corporation in lieu of the bonds hereby secured, or to consent to an issue of securities of the corporation constituting a prior charge to these presents and to the bonds hereby secured." Prior to the scheme under attack, the power to consent to a prior charge had been exercised, and it was held that the power could not again be exercised, so as to permit the discharge of the charge previously authorized and the substitution therefor of a mortgage or charge for a larger amount, the additional moneys or bonds to be appropriated and used for paying or securing liabilities not covered by the mortgage or charge to be discharged. The power was therefore exhausted prior to the proposed scheme. It has now become usual to stipulate expressly that the specified powers may be exercised from time to time and are not to be exhausted by being exercised.

Procedure at meetings

The requirements as to the amount of bonds required to be represented and the number of affirmative votes required to be cast at a meeting of bondholders in order to pass a resolution as an extraordinary resolution should be expressly set out in the trust deed. A common provision requires representation in person or by proxy of a majority in value of the outstanding bonds and the carrying of the resolution by a majority consisting of not less than three-fourths of the votes given on a poll. It is also usual to provide that if a quorum is not present at the meeting, the meeting may be adjourned to a later date or that the meeting is automatically to stand adjourned for a specified number of days, that notice of such adjourned meeting (although not necessarily of its purposes) is to be given and that the bondholders present and voting at the adjourned meeting are to be a quorum and may transact the business for which the meeting was originally convened. Where a meeting has been adjourned for lack of a quorum and notice of the adjourned meeting has been duly given in accordance with the trust deed, which prescribed that a majority of the bondholders present at the adjourned meeting should constitute a quorum, a resolution duly passed at the last of two further adjourned meetings was held to be valid, notwithstanding that such further meetings were held without formal notice, on the ground that such further meetings were in fact only continuations of the first adjourned meeting: *Re Argyle Motor Service Ltd.*, [1932] 1 D.L.R. 81 (N.S. C.A.).

In the Canadian case of *British America Nickel Corp. Ltd. v. M.J. O'Brien Ltd.*, [1927] A.C. 369, the Privy Council held that the majority must exercise their franchise for the purpose of benefiting the class as a whole and not merely individual members only, and that their duty is to look to the difficulties of the bondholders as a class and not to give any one of the bondholders a special personal advantage, not forming part of the scheme to be voted for, in order to induce him to assent. *Quaere* whether this decision is still good law. This decision goes further than the English decision in which it has been stated that, although the powers of the majority must be exercised *bona fide* and the court will relieve against unfairness (*Re New York Taxicab Co.*, [1913] 1 Ch. 1), oppression or bribery, each bondholder may vote in favour of his individual interests, even where they are peculiar to himself and are not shared by the other bondholders and even where special provision is made for such interests, provided that it is made openly: *Goodfellow v. Nelson Line Liverpool Ltd.*, [1912] 2 Ch. 324.

If the notice convening the meeting to consider an extraordinary resolution has been given in accordance with the provisions of the trust deed and the resolution is within the powers conferred upon the majority by the trust deed and has been duly passed by the requisite majority, it is immaterial whether or not every bondholder was present or whether any bondholder did not actually receive notice of the meeting. If the bonds or any of them are or may be in bearer form, it is customary to provide in the trust deed that notice to the holders of such bonds shall be given by advertisement and if it is provided that notice is to be given in such manner and such notice is given, such notice is sufficient: *In re Alabama, New Orleans, Texas & Pacific Junction Railway*, [1891] 1 Ch. 213 at 238 (C.A.); *Follit v. Eddystone Granite Quarries*, [1892] 3 Ch. 75 at 84; *In re Empire Mining Co.* (1890), 44 Ch. D. 402 at 410. It is also immaterial whether some bondholders who had notice of the meeting did not attend: *In re Empire Mining Co., supra.*

Dissentient bondholders, although bound by the terms of an extraordinary resolution authorizing the creation of prior lien bonds for the purpose of raising money by loan, are entitled to contest the priority of the holders of such prior lien bonds by reason of the authority conferred on the corporation not being complied with: *Re B.C. Portland Cement* (1915), 22 D.L.R. 609; affd (1916), 27 D.L.R. 726 (B.C. C.A.). In that case new bonds were issued and delivered to creditors as collateral security for the corporation's indebtedness to them. Such creditors in respect of those bonds were held in the circumstances to rank after the bonds of the first issue.

Powers contained in the trust deed, giving a majority the right, by extraordinary resolution, to cut down or alter the rights of the minority, cannot be exercised against the minority at a meeting, the notice of which states that the rights of the minority will not be interfered with: *Jamieson v. Hotel Renfrew* (Trustees of), [1941] 4 D.L.R. 470 at 478.

The duty of the chairman at a meeting of bondholders is to ascertain the sense of the meeting and where he failed to exercise his power to demand a poll when, if he had done so and he had used the instruments of proxy in the manner thereby directed, the resolution could not have been carried, it was held that the resolution was not properly carried on a show of hands: *Second Consolidated Trust Ltd. v. Ceylon Amalgamated Tea & Rubber Estates Ltd.*, [1943] W.N. 186. It is usually provided in the trust deed that an extraordinary resolution may be passed only on a poll and not by a show of hands.

Where bondholders bring an action to impeach the validity of a resolution passed by a majority, they should sue on behalf of themselves and all other bondholders and some one should be made a party to defend on behalf of or as representing the majority: *Northern Assurance Co. v. Farnham United Breweries*, [1912] 2 Ch. 125.

Where a scheme of reorganization was set aside by reason of a defective notice of meeting, the bond issue created in pursuance of the scheme was also set aside: *Pacific Coast Mines v. Arbuthnot*, [1917] A.C. 607. For the terms of the order and indemnification of the trustee in that case see (1916), 9 W.W.R. 1208 at 1229, 1237 (Clement J.); and to the same effect see *Re B.C. Portland Cement Co.* (1915), 22 D.L.R. 609; affd (1916), 27 D.L.R. 726 (B.C. C.A.).

Distinction between a compromise and a modification of bondholders' rights

The English decisions relating to the construction of majority provisions have drawn a distinction between a compromise and a modification of the rights of bondholders. A scheme is a compromise where there is some question in controversy between two or more persons of the ascertainment of their rights or some difficulty in the enforcement of those rights: *Sneath v. Valley Gold Co.*, [1893] 1 Ch. 477 (C.A.). In that case, a special resolution of debenture holders was passed with regard to the exchange of debentures of a corporation for ordinary shares in a new corporation, which had taken over the assets of the original corporation upon the property of which the debentures were a first charge. This arrangement was held to be a compromise within the meaning of the applicable clause in the trust deed, on the ground that, unless the scheme as proposed by the resolution was effected, the debenture holders would lose their security entirely, and there was a difficulty, controversy or dispute which could not be overcome unless the terms of the resolution were carried out. Such a difficulty, controversy or dispute is a condition precedent to carrying out a compromise, but that is not to say that there must have already been litigation.

On the other hand, in *Mercantile Investment & General Trust Co. v. International Co. of Mexico*, [1893] 1 Ch. 484n (C.A.), where it was sought to give effect to a resolution of the same nature, the court held that it was *ultra vires* and not binding upon the dissentient minority because there was no apparent difficulty in enforcing the rights of the debenture holders against the corporation or its property. In the absence of any difficulty, the transaction was held to amount to an extinction of the debenture holders' rights. Subsequently, the case was reopened and sanction given to the scheme as a compromise of the debenture holders' rights because difficulties which had subsequently arisen were brought to the attention of the court: *Mercantile Investment & General Trust Co. v. River Plate Trust, Loan & Agency Co.*, [1894] 1 Ch. 578.

A modification of the rights of the bondholders, if sanctioned by the requisite majority acting under the terms of the trust deed, does not involve the proof of difficulties as a condition precedent: *Northern Assurance Co. v. Farnham United Breweries*, [1912] 2 Ch. 125, where Joyce J. held that, though there was no evidence of any difficulty, redeemable debentures might by extraordinary resolution be converted into irredeemable debentures, power to do this being expressly given by the trust deed. Thus, on the construction of majority clauses the courts have upheld as a modification of rights the creation of a prior charge: *Follit v. Eddystone Granite Quarries*, [1892] 3 Ch. 75; the exchange of debenture stock for debenture stock in another corporation: *Re W. H. Hutchison & Sons Ltd.* (1915), 31 T.L.R. 324; the conversion of redeemable debentures payable at a fixed date into irredeemable debentures: *Northern Assurance Co. v. Farnham United Breweries, supra*; an arrangement whereby a principal payment due under debentures was waived: *In re Joseph Stocks & Co.*, [1912] 2 Ch. 134n; the conversion of guaranteed debentures into non-guaranteed debentures: *Goodfellow v. Nelson Line Liverpool Ltd.*, [1912] 2 Ch. 324.

An exchange of debentures, secured by a trust deed, for preference shares may be construed as a compromise if difficulties can be shown, but being an extinction of the debenture holders' rights against the property of the corporation it cannot be sustained as a modification of their rights: *Mercantile Investment & General Trust Co. v. International Co. of Mexico*, [1893] 1 Ch. 484n (C.A.); *Sneath v. Valley Gold Co.*, [1893] 1 Ch. 477 (C.A.). But where, pursuant to the express provisions of the trust deed, bonds are exchanged for bonds or shares in another corporation, such a transaction has been upheld upon the construction of the provisions contained in the trust deed as a modification of rights: *In re W. H. Hutchinson & Sons Ltd.* (1915), 31 T.L.R. 324; *Spicer v. Hillingdon* (1908), Times newspaper May 14, p. 18; *In re Buenos Aires Port & City Tramways* (1920), 89 L.J. Ch. 597 and cases cited in the preceding paragraph. In *National Trust Co. v. Maritime Coal Co.*, [1930] 2 D.L.R. 309, Carroll J., upon a consideration of the *Mercantile Investment* and *Sneath v. Valley Gold* cases, *supra*, held that a scheme whereby the claims of bondholders were released upon payment by the corporation to the bondholders of approximately 50 per cent of the par value of the bonds in cash, together with delivery to the trustee under the trust deed of a number of preference shares of the corporation, was not a compromise, since there were in fact no difficulties, nor any pressing necessity to preserve the bondholders' security. He held that the scheme was a modification of the bondholders' rights, since, although the rights of the bondholders against the property of the corporation were probably extinguished, as preferred shareholders they had certain rights against the corporation or its property and a right to share in the corporation's profits. The term "modification" as used in the trust deed was accordingly held to include such a change of rights as had been proposed. It will be noted that the customary practice is to convene a meeting of bondholders for the modification, alteration, abrogation, compromise or arrangement of the rights of the bondholders against the corporation.

Chapter 8

DIRECTORS

Cross references: Sections 6 (1)(e), 18;
Ontario Act, ss. 115-137.

Number of Directors; Power to Manage

Subject to the provisions of any unanimous shareholder agreement the directors are to manage the business and affairs of a corporation (s. 102(1)).

Under s. 6(1)(e) of the Act, the articles of incorporation are to set out the number of directors or the minimum and maximum number of directors of the corporation. It will be noted that under s. 102(2) of the Act, a corporation may have one or more directors but if any of its issued securities are or were part of a distribution to the public and remain outstanding and are held by more than one person, the corporation is to have at least three directors, at least two of whom are not to be officers or employees of the corporation or its affiliates. Similar provisions are contained in the Ontario Act except that s. 115(3) of that Act provides that in the case of a corporation that is an offering corporation (as defined), at least one third of the directors are not to be officers or employees of the corporation itself or any of its affiliates.

The Act provides in s. 114(2) that subject to the articles or by-laws, a majority of the directors or of the minimum number of directors required by the articles constitutes a quorum and notwithstanding any vacancy, the directors in office, so long as they constitute a quorum, may exercise all the powers of the directors. The similar provision in the Ontario Act is s. 126(3) which provides that a quorum cannot be less than two fifths of the number of directors or the minimum number of directors and s. 126(4) which states that where a corporation has fewer than three directors, all the directors must be present to constitute a quorum.

It has been held in England that where the articles provide for a minimum number of directors and the number falls below the minimum, the continuing directors cannot legally act; *Re Alma Spinning Co.; Bottomley's Case* (1880), 16 Ch. D. 681. It has been held, however, that if the articles permit the continuing directors to act notwithstanding any vacancy in their number, their acts are valid even though their number has fallen below the minimum: *In re Scottish Petroleum Co.* (1883), 23 Ch. D. 413; *In re Bank of Syria*, [1901] 1 Ch. 115 (C.A.). The doctrine of the last two cases does not apply, however, if the minimum number of directors was never elected: *In re Sly, Spink & Co.*, [1911] 2 Ch. 430. In *Re Nutter Brewery Ltd.* (1909), 1 O.W.N. 400, Clute J. said at p. 403 that he was strongly inclined to the view that, if the board of a federal corporation consisted of five directors and only three were elected, the board was never validly constituted.

Having regard to the foregoing authorities, it would appear important, as regards corporations incorporated under the Act, to elect at annual meetings of shareholders the full authorized number of directors. As to the filling of vacancies on the board, see the notes under the heading "Filling vacancies" in this chapter.

Where the articles of a corporation provided that the directors should not act if their number fell below two, except for the purpose of filling vacancies, the court held that the appointment of a director made by a lone director, all the others having resigned, was valid: *Macson Development Co. v. Gordon* (1959), 19 D.L.R. (2d) 465 at 469.

Where the by-laws provide for a board of seven with a quorum of four and four directors cease to be qualified, the remaining three have no power to fill vacancies: *Sovereen Mitt, Glove & Robe Co. v. Whitside* (1906), 12 O.L.R. 638 (C.A.). Where there is no quorum under the by-laws, no business can be carried on by the remaining directors: *Sovereen Mitt, Glove & Robe Co. v. Whitside, supra*; *Manes Tailoring Co. v. Willson* (1907), 14 O.L.R. 89 at 96, where the number of the board was reduced without carrying out the necessary proceedings in that regard. See also *Toronto Brewing & Malting Co. v. Blake* (1882), 2 O.R. 175; *Twin City Oil Co. v. Christie* (1909), 18 O.L.R. 324. But the presence on the board of directors of some who are not qualified at the time of their election is not sufficient to invalidate the acts of the board if done by a legal quorum of properly elected directors: *Morden Woollen Mills Co. v. Heckels* (1908), 17 Man. R. 557 (C.A.).

It will be noted that s. 116 of the Act provides that an act of a director or an officer is valid notwithstanding an irregularity in his election or appointment or a defect in his qualification. Notice of directors in prescribed form (Form 6) is to be sent to the Director by the incorporators at the time of filing articles of incorporation (s. 106(1)). Within 15 days after any change is made among the directors, a corporation is required to send to the Director a notice in prescribed form (Form 6) setting out the change which form is to be filed by the Director (s. 113(1)). Section 106(2) provides that each director named in the first notice will hold office from the date of the issue of the certificate of incorporation until the first meeting of shareholders. A vacancy in the directors may be filled by directors except in the case of a vacancy arising from an increase in the number or minimum number of directors or from a failure to elect the number of directors required by the articles (s. 111(1)). Section 106(6) provides that if directors are not elected at a shareholders' meeting, the incumbent directors continue in office until their successors are elected.

It will further be noted that s. 253(2) provides that a director named in a notice sent by a corporation under s. 113 and filed by the director is presumed for the purposes of the Act to be a director of the corporation. A similar provision appears in s. 262(3) of the Ontario Act. Assuming therefore that a director has been named in such a notice upon his election and then resigns, if a notice is not sent he is presumed for the purposes of the Act to be a director and certain liabilities may continue to attach to him in that regard.

Where the board has been reduced below the statutory minimum or there is no quorum under the by-laws, a meeting of shareholders may be convened for the purpose of filling the vacancies. See *Sovereen Mitt, Glove & Robe Co. v. Whitside* (1906), 12 O.L.R. 638 (C.A.).

Organizational meeting

It is provided in s. 104(1) that, after issue of the certificate of incorporation, the directors are to meet to (i) make by-laws; (ii) adopt forms of securities certificates and corporate records; (iii) authorize the issue of securities; (iv) appoint officers; (v) appoint an auditor to hold office until the first annual meeting of shareholders; (vi) make banking arrangements; and (vii) transact any other business. The meeting may be called by either an incorporator or director by giving not less than five days' notice (s. 104(3)). The requirement to hold an organizational meeting does not apply where a certificate of amalgamation or a certificate of continuance has been issued to the corporation (s. 104(2)).

It would appear that the directors named in the articles are not provisional directors and have all the powers of permanent directors. They hold office until the first meeting of shareholders (s. 106(2)). Under former federal Acts there were provisions for the appointment of "first or provisional" directors and there were certain restrictions on their powers which could be ascertained only by construing the words of the governing statute: *Selkirk v. Windsor* (1910), 21 O.L.R. 109; affd 22 O.L.R. 250; *Monarch Life Assurance Co. v. Brophy* (1907), 14 O.L.R. 1 (C.A.).

Powers of provisional directors

The question of the powers of provisional directors was considered in *Re North Simcoe Ry. and Toronto* (1875), 36 U.C.Q.B. 101. Gwynne J. at p. 119, there expressed the opinion that the powers of provisional directors were confined to putting the act of incorporation into operation until the amount of share capital necessary to enable the corporation to elect regular directors was subscribed, whereupon the duties of the provisional directors ceased. This case was affirmed on appeal, but the question of the powers of provisional directors was not in issue on the appeal. See also *In re London, Huron & Bruce Ry. and Township of E. Wawanosh* (1875), 36 U.C.Q.B. 93.

Where an Act creating a corporation required that it should not commence operations until 50 per cent of its capital had been paid up, it was held that this did not prevent the provisional directors from proceeding to allot shares and collect calls or do any other act within their power short of actual operation of the corporation: *North Sydney Mining & Transportation Co. v. Greener* (1898), 31 N.S.R. 41.

The provisional directors cannot make a contract for hire of services of a medical examiner for the whole duration of the corporation's existence: *Lebel v. Security Life Insurance Co.* (1915), 47 Que. S.C. 238.

In *Johnston v. Wade* (1908), 17 O.L.R. 372, MacMahon J. the trial judge, whose decision was affirmed by the majority of the Court of Appeal, thought provisional directors, under the relevant section of the Ontario Act, had the full powers of permanent directors.

As to the powers of provisional directors under the *Bank Act* as it stood at the date of the decisions, see *Re Monarch Bank of Canada* (1910), 22 O.L.R. 516; *Re Monarch Bank of Canada* (1914), 32 O.L.R. 207 (C.A.).

The provisional directors of a corporation acquire no rights or interests in the charter capable of sale; corporation charters are *extra commercium* and where a corporation is incorporated by special Act there is the further rule that it is a matter of public policy that Acts of the legislature should not be the subjects of purchase and sale: *Vipond v. Robert* (1908), 17 Que. K.B. 403. It will be noted that while the charter itself cannot be sold if all the shares are sold to another group, in effect a sale of the "charter" has taken place.

Where, however, the Act did not contain the word "provisional" or indicate that the authority of the first directors was temporary or limited, it was held that a corporation was bound by a contract for the sale of land signed on its behalf by one of those named in the letters patent as "provisional" directors who had represented himself, with the acquiescence and knowledge of the other provisional directors, to be its general manager: *Muldowan v. German Canadian Land Co.* (1909), 19 Man. R. 667.

Where directors were described as provisional but the statute provided that they were to be directors until replaced by others duly elected in their stead and where no proceedings had been taken to organize the corporation, it was held that the directors could defend an action on behalf of the corporation: *Campbell v. Taxicabs Verrals Ltd.* (1913), 27 O.L.R. 141.

Provisional directors must proceed regularly in the manner prescribed by the Act, and if they meet without proper notice having been given or attempt to transact business without a quorum, their acts will be invalid: *McLaren v. Fisken* (1881), 28 Gr. 352. See also *Exchange Auto Parts Ltd. v. Furby* (1963), 41 W.W.R. 678, 38 D.L.R. (2d) 630 (Man. C.A.) dealing with the power of provisional directors to institute proceedings on behalf of the corporation.

The functions of the first directors come to an end upon the election of the permanent directors: *MacDonald v. McBeth* (1862), 11 U.C.C.P. 224 at 228, and they can then no longer bind the corporation: *North Sydney Mining & Transportation Co. v. Greener* (1898), 31 N.S.R. 41. Apparently the provisional directors are not entitled to lay down their office before the election of permanent directors. Where a special Act made certain persons first directors "to continue in office until the first ordinary meeting held after the passing of the Act", it was held that the Act imposed upon such persons the statutory obligation of continuing as directors until the first ordinary meeting: *In re South London Fish Market Co.* (1888), 39 Ch. D. 324 (C.A.). Section 119(2) of the Ontario Act provides that no director named in the articles may resign his office unless at the time the resignation is to be effective his successor is elected or appointed. It will be noted that there is no comparable provision under the federal Act.

Qualifications of directors

Section 105(1) provides that certain persons falling within certain categories are disqualified from being directors: (a) anyone less than 18 years of age; (b) anyone who is of unsound mind and so found by a court in Canada or elsewhere; (c) a person who is not an individual; or (d) a person who has the status of a bankrupt. In addition, subs. (3) of s. 105 provides that a majority of the directors of a corporation must be resident Canadians. However, this is reduced to one-third in the case of a holding corporation earning, in Canada directly or through its subsidiaries, less than 5 per cent of the consolidated gross revenues of the holding corporation and its subsidiaries as shown in the most recent financial statements (s. 105(4)). The provisions under the Ontario Act are broadly similar but it will be noted that a non-resident corporation is not required to have a minority of resident Canadians as directors (s. 118(3)). A non-resident corporation is defined in s. 1(1) of the Ontario Act as a corporation incorporated in Canada prior to April 27, 1965 and that is not deemed to be resident in Canada for the purposes of the *Income Tax Act* (Canada) by s. 250(4) of that Act which deems such a company to be resident in Canada if at any time in a taxation year it was resident in Canada or carried on business in Canada. A company at common law is ordinarily resident where its directors meet and conduct business.

The term "resident Canadian" is defined in s. 2(1) of the federal Act as an individual who is a Canadian citizen ordinarily resident in Canada, a Canadian citizen not ordinarily resident in Canada who is prescribed under s. 11 of the Regulations of the federal Act, or a permanent resident within the meaning of the *Immigration Act* ordinarily resident in Canada not more than one year after the time at which he first became eligible to apply for Canadian citizenship. The class of persons prescribed in s. 11 are (i) persons who are full-time employees of the federal government or of a province, of an agency thereof, or of a federal or provincial Crown corporation; (ii) full-time employees of a corporation, more than 50 per cent of the voting shares of which are beneficially owned or over which control or direction is exercised by resident Canadians or where a majority of the directors are resident Canadians or a subsidiary of such a corporation where the principal reason for the residence of the employee outside Canada is to act as such; (iii) persons who are full-time students at a university or other educational institution recognized by the educational authorities of a majority of the provinces of Canada and who have been resident outside of Canada for less than 10 consecutive years; (iv) persons who are full-time employees of an international association or organization of which Canada is a member or (v) persons who were at the time of reaching their 60th birthday ordinarily resident in Canada and have been resident outside Canada less than 10 consecutive years.

It will be noted that under the former Act there was no limitation as to age and that in certain circumstances a limited corporation might act as a director of a corporation registered under the *English Companies Act, 1862*: *Re Bulawayo Market & Offices Co.*, [1907] 2 Ch. 458.

Under the British Columbia *Companies Act* at least one director must be ordinarily resident in the province and a similar provision is found in the *Business Corporations Act* of Saskatchewan. The former provision in Alberta requiring a majority of the directors to be resident in Alberta has now been changed to the requirement that a majority of the directors be resident in Canada. It may be that these requirements are invalid under the Charter of Rights, compare *Andrews v. Law Society (British Columbia)*, [1989] 1 S.C.R. 143 (S.C.C.).

If a person is elected in contravention of the provisions of s. 105, it would appear that he would not become a director *de jure*. It will be observed that directors are only to transact business if a majority of the directors present are resident Canadians, unless it is a corporation of the kind referred to in s. 105(4) (s. 114(3)). There is an exception for certain telephone meetings or if the resident Canadian director (who is unable to be present and who would have formed part of the required majority) approves in writing the business to be transacted at the meeting. It would appear that the business transacted at a meeting of the board with a non-Canadian majority of directors may be valid but the participating directors and the corporation itself have probably committed an offence pursuant to the provisions of s. 251 of the federal Act. See *Jenner's Case* (1878), 7 Ch. D. 132 (C.A.); *In re Percy & Kelly Nickel Cobalt & Chrome Iron Mining Co.; Hambley's Case* (1877), 5 Ch. D. 705; *Premier Trust Co. v. McAlister*, [1933] O.R. 195 at 202 (purported appointment nugatory).

Share qualification

No share qualification is necessary for a director unless the articles so prescribe (s. 105(2)). The former provisions required that a director be a shareholder and if the by-laws so provided owning shares of the corporation "absolutely in his own right". If the quoted words appear in the articles it would appear that the person must be the beneficial owner of the qualifying shares in question (see *Ritchie v. Vermillion Mining Co.* (1902), 4 O.L.R. 588 at 597 (C.A.), per Maclennan J.A.; *Philipps v. Cameron Copper Mines Ltd.*, [1959] Que. S.C. 433; *Premier Trust Co. v. McAlister*, [1933] O.R. 195 at 202).

If the words used are "in his own right" it will be sufficient if he holds them as a nominee for a third party: see *Pulbrook v. Richmond Mining Co.* (1878), 9 Ch. D. 610. It was there said that a man holds in his own right if he is registered without any qualification. Although this decision was questioned in the Court of Appeal in England in *Bainbridge v. Smith* (1889), 41 Ch. D. 462 at 470, it was followed in *Cooper v. Griffin*, [1892] 1 Q.B. 740, *Howard v. Sadler*, [1893] 1 Q.B. 1 and *Sutton v. English & Colonial Produce Co.*, [1902] 2 Ch. 502. See also *Commercial Loan and Trust Co. v. Macaw*, [1923] 1 D.L.R. 744 at 748 (Man. C.A.).

For a discussion of share qualification requirements see *Fremont Canning Co. v. Wall*, [1941] O.R. 379 (C.A.).

The subsequent obtaining of qualification shares will not validate the original appointment: *Channel Collieries Trust Ltd. v. Dover, St. Margaret's & Martin Mill Light Ry. Co.*, [1914] 2 Ch. 506 at 511 (C.A.).

It has been held in Quebec that it is not necessary for the qualification of a director that he should have been actually registered as a shareholder; if his subscription for the requisite number of shares has been accepted that is enough: *Alley v. Trenholme* (1893), 3 Que. S.C. 163; but see *Spencer v. Kennedy*, [1926] Ch. 125, where the court held that actual registration as a shareholder was necessary before an appointment as a director would be valid. See also *Re Haggert Bros. Manufacturing Co.; Peaker & Runions' Case* (1892), 19 O.A.R. 582 at 587.

Vacation of office

The general form of by-law will usually provide that the office of a director shall *ipso facto* be vacated if (i) he becomes bankrupt or suspends payment of his debts generally or compounds with his creditors or makes an authorized assignment or is declared insolvent; (ii) he is found to be a mentally incompetent person; (iii) he resigns his office by notice in writing to the corporation which resignation will be effective at the time received by the corporation or any time specified in the notice, whichever is later; (iv) he dies; or (v) he is removed from office by the shareholders.

A by-law may also contain other grounds for the vacation of the office of a director. For example, if he accepts or holds any office in the corporation except certain specified offices; if he absents himself from meetings of the directors during a specified period without special leave of absence; or if he is concerned or interested in or participates in the profits of any contract with the corporation. There are, of course, other grounds which could be included.

Section 108(1) of the Act provides that a director of a corporation ceases to hold office when (i) he dies or resigns; (ii) he is removed under the provisions of s. 109 (a resolution passed at a special meeting of the shareholders); or (iii) he becomes disqualified under s. 105(1). The resignation of a director becomes effective when the resignation in writing is sent to the corporation or at the time specified in the resignation whichever is later (s. 108(2)). See also the cases referred to under the heading "Resignation", below.

It will be observed that s. 116 provides that an act of a director is valid notwithstanding an irregularity in his appointment or a defect in his qualification. Presumably when s. 108 and s. 116 are read together, a director may act if he was never properly qualified but, if he was qualified and ceased to be qualified following his election, he is no longer a director.

Where the grounds of disqualification include bankruptcy or insolvency, disqualification may be based on admissions of insolvency without any definite act of insolvency from which the insolvency dates: *London & Counties Assets Co. v. Brighton Grand Concert Hall Ltd.*, [1915] 2 K.B. 493 (C.A.); *James v. Rockwood Colliery* (1912), 106 L.T. 128 (request to corporation to accept a composition).

If the by-laws provide that a director who accepts or holds any office or place of profit in the corporation shall vacate his office and a director is elected or appointed an officer of the corporation, such election or appointment is valid but his position as a director is automatically terminated: *Iron Ships Coating Co. v. Blunt* (1868), L.R. 3 C.P. 484; *Eales v. Cumberland Black Lead Mine Co.*

(1861), 6 H. & N. 481. A trustee of a debenture trust deed nominated and paid by the corporation is within the prohibition: *Astley v. New Tivoli Ltd.*, [1899] 1 Ch. 151. And where a director is appointed managing director at a remuneration, he will not only automatically vacate his office, but will also be disentitled to recover his salary from the corporation if the necessary procedure for validating his remuneration has not been followed: *Claudet v. Golden Giant Mines Ltd.* (1909), 15 B.C.R. 13 (C.A.).

Voluntary and deliberate absence only is covered by such a provision, vacating the office of an absent director, which does not apply to absence due to illness: *Mack's Claim*, [1900] W.N. 114. Time does not begin to run until the director has failed to attend a meeting at which he ought to have been present: *In re London & Northern Bank; McConnell's Claim*, [1901] 1 Ch. 728.

Where the board of directors of a corporation passed a resolution in the absence of P., who was a director, excluding P. from the board for his absence from board meetings and subsequently elected another director, the court held that, although the articles of association did not require a director to hold a share qualification and although they conferred on directors a right not to specified remuneration but to such sums as the corporation in general meeting prescribed, P. had a sufficient proprietary interest in the matter to enable him to pursue an action for relief by way of declaration and injunction against his exclusion from the board and the appointment of a successor: *Hayes v. Bristol Plant Hire Ltd.*, [1957] 1 All E.R. 685 applying *Pulbrook v. Richmond Mining Co., supra.*

Directors who are members of a partnership firm which supplies goods to the corporation at a profit, become disqualified under a provision providing for vacation of office if a director is concerned or interested in or participates in the profits of a contract with the corporation. Where such contracts were in violation of the provisions of the Alberta Companies Ordinance art. 57, Table "A", it was held that they could not be ratified by a majority of the shareholders however great: *Theatre Amusement Co. v. Stone* (1915), 50 S.C.R. 32; a unanimous vote of the shareholders alone would suffice, per Anglin J. at p. 37.

Anyone who is a shareholder in another corporation which contracts with the corporation is "interested in the contract": *Todd v. Robinson* (1884), 14 Q.B.D. 739 (C.A.); *Dimes v. Grand Junction Canal Co.* (1852), 3 H.L.C. 794; *Whiteley v. Barley* (1888), 21 Q.B.D. 154 (C.A.); *Transvaal Lands Co. v. New Belgium (Transvaal) Land & Development Co.*, [1914] 2 Ch. 488 at 497 (C.A.).

Where a director becomes disqualified by some act, such as being secretly interested in a contract, the board have no power to condone such act, but it has been held that the disqualification continues only so long as the contract continues, and the director's subsequent re-election may be valid: *Re Bodega Co. Ltd.*, [1904] 1 Ch. 276.

Resignation

In the absence of any provision in the by-laws making acceptance of resignation necessary, a resignation does not require acceptance to become effective: *Glossop v. Glossop*, [1907] 2 Ch. 370; *Richards & Co. (Trustee of) v. Coulson*, [1937] O.R. 456 at 568; *Re Neokratine Safety Explosive Co. of New South Wales Ltd.* (1891), 12 N.S.W. Eq. 269; *Transport Ltd. v. Schonberg* (1905), 21 T.L.R. 305; *Macson Development Co. v. Gordon* (1959), 19 D.L.R. (2d) 465 at 468; *Molyneux v. Hamm*, [1957] Que. S.C. 108 at 112. Where under the by-laws a director is entitled to resign and the effectiveness of his resignation does not depend on acceptance by the corporation, the directors are bound to accept the resignation: *Glossop v. Glossop, supra*; *Commercial Loan & Trust Co. v. Macaw*, [1923] 1 D.L.R. 744 at 748 (Man. C.A.).

A resignation tendered orally is effective if accepted by the corporation. Thus, where the articles provided that the office of a director should be vacated if by notice in writing to the corporation he resigned his office, and directors at the annual meeting verbally offered to resign and their resignations were accepted by the meeting, it was held that they had ceased to be directors: *Latchford Premier Cinema Ltd. v. Ennion*, [1931] 2 Ch. 409.

A valid resignation cannot be withdrawn without the consent of the other directors: *Glossop v. Glossop, supra.*

If a director has resigned and his resignation has been accepted by the board, he is not liable for the statements in a report in the drawing up of which he has taken no part even if he knew that his name appeared in the report as a director: *In re National Bank of Wales Ltd.*, [1899] 2 Ch 629; affd (*sub nom. Dovey v. Cory*) [1901] A.C. 477 at 488. While the resignation of a director will not rid him of an existing liability for misfeasance, no new liability can arise after his resignation has been delivered to the corporation: *Richards & Co. (Trustee of) v. Coulson*, [1937] O.R. 456 at 568 (C.A.).

The mere resignation of a director, to take effect contemporaneously with the execution of a contract between the corporation and the directors, advantageous to the latter, will not assist the director as regards failure to comply with the fiduciary liability to make full disclosure to the corporation: *Denman v. Clover Bar Coal Co.* (1913), 48 S.C.R. 318.

A Director who resigns is entitled to submit to the corporation a written statement giving the reasons for his resignation and such notice is required to be sent to every shareholder entitled to receive notice of a meeting of shareholders and to the Director, unless the statement is included in or attached to a management proxy circular required by s. 150 (see s. 110(3)). It will be observed that by virtue of s. 110(4), no corporation, or person acting on its behalf, incurs any liability by reason only of circulating such a statement in compliance with the Act. Section 119(2) of the Ontario Act provides that no director named in the articles may resign his office unless at the time the resignation is to be effective his successor is elected or appointed. It will be noted that there is no comparable provision under the federal Act.

It will be observed that s. 113 of the Act requires a corporation to send to the Director a notice in prescribed form (Form 6) setting out the change within 15 days after such change and the Director is to file the notice. It will further be noted that s. 262(3) provides that a director named in a notice sent by a corporation under s. 113 and filed by the Director, is presumed for the purposes of this Act to be a director of the corporation. A similar provision appears in s. 262(3) of the Ontario Act. Assuming therefore that a director has been named in such a notice upon his election and then resigns, if a notice is not sent he is presumed for the purposes of the Act to be a director and certain liabilities may attach to him in that regard. While a presumption can ordinarily be rebutted, certain presumptions cannot. In *Laprise v. Julio's Pizza & Spaghetti Parlour* (1986), 62 C.B.R. (N.S.) 36 (Ont. Prov. Ct.) an action was brought against a director for unpaid wages, and despite the fact that no change of notice of directors was filed, the defence was raised that the director had resigned more than six months previously to the claim arising; it was held that the *Corporations Information Act* (Ontario) only made the certificate *prima facie* evidence of the status of the director and the actual date of the resignation was treated as governing. However, s. 261(3) of the Ontario *Business Corporations Act*, 1982 was not apparently cited to the court and the decision does not deal with the question of presumption.

Challenging status of directors

An individual shareholder has a right of action for a declaration that directors are disqualified in pursuance of a provision of the articles of association: *Theatre Amusement Co. v. Stone* (1914), 50 S.C.R. 32.

Where it is alleged that directors were not properly elected, a shareholder may bring a class action on behalf of all the shareholders against the corporation and the directors in question to restrain such directors from acting: *Channel Collieries Trust Ltd. v. Dover, St. Margaret's & Martin Mill Light Ry.*, [1914] 2 Ch. 506 (C.A.). It is necessary that the directors whose election is attacked should be joined as defendants: *Fremont Canning Co. v. Wall*, [1941] O.R. 379 (C.A.).

One director may be estopped from denying the qualification of another: *Kiely v. Smyth* (1879), 27 Gr. 220 at 222.

The eligibility of directors should not be enquired into in a collateral way, for example, by a secretary of the corporation refusing to give up the corporation's books and setting up that the directors who displaced him were ineligible or not properly elected: *Modstock Mining Co. v. Harris* (1902), 40 N.S.R. 336.

And where a corporation brought action against its former secretary to compel delivery up of books belonging to the corporation to a new secretary appointed by it, and the defendant pleaded he was still secretary as the directors who appointed the new secretary had not been duly elected, it was held that the defence set up was not a proper way of testing the election of directors which should have been done by a motion to stay or setting aside the proceedings on the ground that they were not properly authorized: *Austin Mining Co. v. Gemmell* (1886), 10 O.R. 696 (C.A.).

A qualified director may bring an action in his own name against the other directors for an injunction to restrain them from wrongfully excluding him: *Pulbrook v. Richmond Mining Co.* (1878), 9 Ch. D. 610 followed in *Hayes v. Bristol Plant Hire Ltd.*, [1957] 1 All E.R. 685.

It is necessary to stipulate the directors intended to be elected by management in the proxy statement. If this is changed without suitable reason, for example, the death of a nominee, an application may be made for a determination that the election of the substituted director is improper. If a meeting of the shareholders fails to elect the number or maximum number of directors required by reason of the disqualification, incapacity or death of any candidate, the directors elected may exercise all the powers of the directors if they constitute a quorum (s. 106(7)).

In *Manitoba Metis Federation Inc. v. Spence* (1984), 26 Man. R. (2d) 313, 8 D.L.R. (4th) 138 (C.A.) allegations of irregularities in an election of a vice-president and a director were made. The Court of Appeal held that the election had been irregular, but that it was fair and reasonable for the federation in effect to pay the costs of all contenders for the position. Also In *Re Prudential Group Syndicate Ltd.* (1984), B.C. Corps L.G. 78,245 where the holders of all shares but three, had presented to the directors of the corporation resolutions in writing whereby such shareholders had agreed to increase the number of directors by three and to appoint themselves to such positions. The directors refused to accept the instructions and in an action it was held that they were justified as the proposed procedure was improper.

Increase or decrease in number of directors (s. 112)

The articles of incorporation may be amended from time to time to increase or decrease the number or the maximum or minimum number of directors (ss. 112(1), 173(1)(m)). The change is authorized by a special resolution of the shareholders and at the same meeting where an amendment is so authorized, the shareholders are entitled to elect an additional number of directors authorized by any increase and if they so do the articles are deemed to be amended as of the date of adoption by the shareholders of the amendment to the articles so that the election of directors would be effective as of such date (s. 112(2)). It will be observed that no decrease in the number of directors is to shorten the term of an incumbent director (s. 112(1)), so that if it is desired to decrease the number of the board and there would be more directors than would be authorized following the reduction, resignations would have to be obtained prior to the reduction. In addition, special provision is made for cumulative voting pursuant to s. 107.

Under the old Act the change in the number of directors was made by by-law or, in the case of an Ontario corporation, by a special resolution.

It will be noted that where there is an increase in the number of directors, the additional directors must be elected by the shareholders at a meeting called for that purpose and the directors cannot fill a vacancy resulting from an increase in the minimum number of directors or from a failure to elect the minimum number of directors required by the articles (s. 111(1)). In addition, the articles may provide that a vacancy among the directors may only be filled by the shareholders (s. 111(4)).

Until the new board is properly constituted, the old board can act: *In re Sims Packing Co.* (1924), 4 C.B.R. 367 (execution of assignment under the *Bankruptcy Act* authorized by resolution of the old board).

Effect of non-compliance with s. 112

It is necessary to consider the effect of non-compliance with a provision such as s. 112, first between the corporation and its shareholders and then between the corporation and outsiders.

So far as the shareholders are concerned, until the requirements of the section have been complied with, the change is ineffective. Thus, an election of an increased board without compliance with the section is void and confers no right on those elected to hold office: *Sherker v. Rudner* (1911), 39 Que. S.C. 44 (C.A.) where it was held that an action lay in the nature of *quo warranto* proceedings under the appropriate statutory provisions to oust the director so irregularly elected, and that a shareholder present at the meeting and not objecting could bring the action. And where, at an annual meeting, a resolution was passed purporting to elect a number of directors greater than the number provided for in the letters patent, and the provisions of the section corresponding to a predecessor of s. 112 had not been complied with, the resolution was *ultra vires* and the election was quashed in an action brought by a shareholder for that purpose: *McKenna v. Spooner Oils Ltd.*, [1934] 1 W.W.R. 255 (as to shareholders bringing actions for breach of this and other statutory requirements see the notes to Chapter 16. See also *Christopher v. Noxon*, (1884), 4 O.R. 672 (resolution for forfeiture of shares); *Re Carpenter Ltd.; Hamilton's Case* (1916), 35 O.L.R. 626 (invalid allotment); *Manes Tailoring Co. v. Willson* (1907), 14 O.L.R. 89 at 96 and *Clary v. Golden Rose* (1912), 4 O.W.N. 1491, both cases involving the validity of a reduction in the number of directors.

An outsider dealing with the corporation, who has no notice of any irregularity, is not, however, bound to enquire into the regularity of compliance with a section such as s. 112: *Re W. N. McEachren & Sons Ltd.; McGibbon v. Imperial Trust Co.*, [1933] O.R. 349 at 361 (C.A.); *Gray v. Yellowknife Gold Mines Ltd. (No. 1)*, [1945] O.R. 688 at 716 (Hope J. reversed in part [1947] O.R. 928 on grounds not affecting the decision on this point). In *Re W. N. McEachren & Sons Ltd.*, *supra*, the letters patent provided for a board of three directors. The corporation had purported to increase the board to five at a special general meeting of shareholders. There was no evidence that the requirements of the section of the *Ontario Companies Act* under which the corporation was incorporated which corresponded to s. 112 had been complied with. The Court of Appeal held that the corporation could not escape liability under an agreement, executed under its seal, on the ground that its directors who had authorized such execution had not been regularly elected.

Prior to the enactment of s. 112, some question existed as to whether the shareholders could increase the board and elect directors at the same meeting without holding an extraordinary general meeting. See *Charter Oil Co. v. Beaumont* (1967), 62 W.W.R. 617, 65 D.L.R. (2d) 112 (B.C. C.A.) and *Western Mines Ltd. v. Shield Development Co.*, [1976] 2 W.W.R. 300, 65 D.L.R. (3rd) 307 (B.C. S.C.).

Where, however, the section provides that a by-law increasing the board is not valid until filed with the Department and published in the *Canada Gazette*, as was the case under s. 104 of the Act of 1927, an outsider dealing with the corporation is bound to satisfy himself not only that the by-law has been regularly passed, but that it has been so filed and published: *Bank of Montreal v. Guaranty Silk Dyeing & Finishing Co.*, [1935] O.R. 493 at 517, per Masten J.A.

Election of directors; Removal; Vacancies

Procedure for election

The election of directors is governed by the law of the corporate domicile: *National Trust Co. v. Ebro Irrigation & Power Co.*, [1954] O.R. 463.

Section 106(3) requires that the board of directors be elected by the shareholders. In view of this requirement, it is doubtful whether it would be legal for a corporation incorporated under the Act to bind itself by agreement, or to pass a by-law providing that one or more directors should be appointed by a named individual or by some outside body. In any event, it is doubtful whether a contract by a corporation to elect as directors nominees of an outside body will be specifically enforced: *Plantations Trust Ltd. v. Bila Rubber Lands Ltd.* (1916), 114 L.T. 676; see also, as to an agreement by a corporation that a shareholder shall have the right of appointing or nominating a director of the corporation: *British Murac Syndicate Ltd. v. Alperton Rubber Co.*, [1915] 2 Ch. 186. As to agreements by shareholders to vote in a particular way see the notes under the heading "Voting" in Chapter 10. It would be permissible for the articles to provide for different classes of directors to be elected by different classes of shareholders, similar to provisions in a shareholders' agreement in that regard.

Unless the election is pursuant to a resolution in writing signed by all the shareholders, the election must take place at a general meeting which by virtue of s. 132(1) must be held within Canada as provided in the by-laws or in the absence of such provision as determined by the directors. A meeting may be held outside of Canada if all the shareholders entitled so agree and the shareholder who attends such a meeting is deemed to have agreed to its being held outside Canada, except where his attendance is for the express purpose of objecting to the transaction of any business on the grounds that the meeting is not lawfully held (s. 132(2)).

In practice the directors may be elected at the annual meeting and such an election is valid notwithstanding that financial statements had not been mailed to the shareholders prior to the meeting as required by s. 121: *Watt v. Commonwealth Petroleum Ltd.*, [1938] 4 D.L.R. 701 (Alta. C.A.).

Directors may be elected for a term expiring not later than the close of the third annual meeting of shareholders following the election and not all directors elected at a meeting of shareholders need hold office for the same term. If a director is not elected for an expressly stated term, he ceases to hold office at the close of the first annual meeting of the shareholders following his election (see s. 106(3), (4), and (5)).

Notwithstanding a statutory provision requiring directors to be elected by ballot, an election by unanimous vote without ballot will be valid if no more than the necessary number of directors are nominated: *Morden Woollen Mills Co. v. Heckels* (1908), 17 Man. R. 557 (Man. C.A.) and where the number of qualified shareholders is the same as that of the board, no formal election is necessary: *Kiely v. Kiely* (1878), 3 O.A.R. 438. It is advisable that the by-laws should provide that the election of directors need not be by ballot unless demanded.

In *Doig v. Mathews* (1916), 25 D.L.R. 732, an interim injunction was refused where an election of directors was attacked on the ground that there was an insufficient quorum under the articles, without counting shareholders present who were disqualified from voting, owing to their being in arrears in respect of calls.

Cumulative voting

Under s. 107 of the federal Act, the articles may provide for cumulative voting in the election of directors, that is, that every shareholder will have for this purpose the number of votes attached to his shares multiplied by the number of directors to be elected and that such votes may be cast for one candidate or distributed amongst several candidates. Where cumulative voting is provided for in the articles, a fixed number of directors must be provided for rather than a minimum and a maximum. Section 107 provides a code for the election of directors by cumulative voting. It should be noted that (a) a separate vote of shareholders is required for each candidate nominated as a director, unless a resolution is passed unanimously permitting two or more persons to be elected by a single resolution; (b) if a shareholder has voted for more than one candidate without specifying the distribution of his votes among the candidates, he is deemed to have distributed his votes equally among the candidates for whom he voted; (c) if the number of candidates is greater than the number of positions to be filled, the candidates receiving the least number of votes are to be eliminated until the number of candidates remaining equals the number of positions to be filled; (d) each director is to cease to hold office at the close of the first annual meeting of shareholders following his election; and (e) a director may not be removed from office nor may the board be decreased if the votes cast against this would be sufficient to elect him and such votes could be voted cumulatively at an election at which the same number of votes were cast and the number of directors required by the articles were then being elected.

Failure to elect directors (s. 106(6))

Where no election of directors has effectively been made at the proper time, which will ordinarily be at the annual meeting, such election may take place at a subsequent special meeting of the shareholders called for that purpose. Section 111(2) provides that if there is no quorum of directors or if there has been a failure to elect the minimum number of directors required by the articles, the directors then in office are to forthwith call a special meeting of shareholders to fill the vacancy. If they fail to do so, or if there are no directors then in office, the meeting may be called by any shareholder. Section 111(3) provides for the election of a director to fill a vacancy where a director representing a class is concerned. The shareholders would also be entitled to requisition a meeting pursuant to the provisions of s. 143, regarding which see the discussion in Chapter 10. In addition to the foregoing, an action presumably would appear to be possible under the provisions of s. 239 and it should be noted that the court has the power under s. 241(3) to make an order appointing directors in place of, or in addition to, all or any of the directors then in office.

It would appear that a meeting must be convened in accordance with the by-laws of the corporation: see *Austin Mining Co. v. Gemmel* (1886), 10 O.R. 696 (C.A.); see also *Sovereen Mitt, Glove & Robe Co. v. Whitside* (1906), 12 O.L.R. 638, and *Christopher v. Noxon* (1884), 4 O.R. 672.

It should be noted that s. 106(6) provides that where directors are not elected at the proper time the retiring directors shall continue in office until their successors are elected. Accordingly, directors, who would retire in the event a new election was duly proceeded with, will remain in office notwithstanding that their term of office has expired and that the shareholders have failed to elect a new board. See *Re W. N. McEachren & Sons Ltd.*, [1933] O.R. 349 (C.A.) 360; *Gold-Rex Kirkland Mines v. Morrow*, [1944] O.R. 415 at 418. See also *Majich v. Krancevic*, [1958] Que. P.R. 64 (Que. S.C.) and [1958] Que. P.R. 69 (C.S. Qué.) where, under a provision in the *Quebec Companies Act, 1941* similar to the provision under discussion, the court refused to grant *quo warranto* for the removal of directors merely on the ground that it was more than a year since they had been elected. The shareholders then applied for a writ of mandamus seeking the holding of a meeting and an election of directors, but the court refused to grant the application as no notice or demand for the convocation of a meeting had been given as required by the *Quebec Companies Act, 1941*, c. 276, ss. 96 and 220: *Majich v. Croatian Home of Noranda Inc.*, [1958] Que. S.C. 525.

Apart from statute or by-law, it would seem to be implied that the directors of the corporation should hold office until their successors are duly elected and qualified. This is an application of the rule in respect of ordinary trustees.

Where an election of directors is not held and a vacancy occurs while the directors continue in office by virtue of s. 106, it would appear they have power to fill the vacancy if a quorum remains in office (see s. 111(1)). This result would not follow, however, if the vacancy resulted from an increase in the number or minimum number of directors or a failure to elect the number or minimum number of directors required by the articles, but see s. 106(7).

In the case of corporations incorporated by memorandum and articles, a common form of article provides that, if at any meeting at which an election of directors ought to take place, the places of the retiring directors, or some of them, are not filled up, the retiring directors, or such of them as have not had their place filled up, shall, if willing to act, be deemed to have been re-elected. Under such an article, if a retiring director is not re-elected and his place is not filled up at the same meeting, he retains office since by the article he is deemed to have been re-elected; the operation of such an article is not limited to cases of accidental omission to fill the places of retiring directors: *Holt v. Catterall* (1931), 47 T.L.R. 332; followed in *Grundt v. Great Boulder Proprietary Mines Ltd.*, [1948] Ch. 145 (C.A.) where a somewhat similar article was under consideration.

Removal of directors

An election of directors before the term of office of their predecessors has expired is apparently a nullity, and mandamus will lie to compel the corporation to proceed to another election on the day fixed by the charter: *The Queen v. Bank of Upper Canada* (1849), 5 U.C.Q.B. 338 (C.A.). In that case Robinson C.J. seemed to be of the opinion that *quo warranto* would be a proper proceeding where the object was not to call in question by what right an officer of a corporation pretends to hold office, but whether the corporation itself had not, as a body, acted in disregard of the provisions of its charter.

A corporation whose directors are appointed for a definite period has no inherent power to remove them before the expiration of their term: *Re Imperial Hydropathic Hotel Co., Blackpool v. Hampson* (1882), 23 Ch. D. 1 (C.A.).

If the by-laws provide that the directors shall hold office for one year and until their successors are appointed, the shareholders cannot themselves pass another by-law providing that the appointment is terminable by resolution. They must wait until the next annual meeting and put in a new set of directors who will pass a new by-law: *Stephenson v. Vokes* (1896), 27 O.R. 691.

In the absence of any provision for recall in the statute or by-laws, the directors cannot be ousted during the term for which they were elected: *London Finance Corp. v. Banking Service Corp.*, [1925] 1 D.L.R. 319 at 323.

Except in certain cases where cumulative voting is concerned, the shareholders of a corporation may, by ordinary resolution at a special meeting, remove any director or directors from office unless that director is elected on behalf of a class or series of shares in which case only the shareholders of that class of shares may so vote to remove that director (s. 109). The vacancy may be filled by the directors or by the shareholders. Ordinarily where removal of directors is sought at the shareholders' meeting the replacement director would be stipulated in the material circulated to the shareholders.

In *Weremchuk v. Allan* (1985), 29 B.L.R. 242, 62 B.C.L.R. 273 (C.A.) a vacancy had arisen on the board of directors of a credit union and, because one board member left the meeting, a resolution was passed appointing A to the board, but following the meeting notice of intention to rescind the appointment was given to the secretary. The person elected was advised unofficially and at a subsequent meeting, but, in the absence of a quorum, a resolution was adopted rescinding the appointment of A and appointing B. The court found that the rescission was invalid because of the absence of a quorum and the board was directed to reconsider the motion to rescind. It was pointed out that a board of directors generally has power to rescind decisions before they are acted upon. Since there was no formal notification to B, B's appointment was accordingly inchoate pending the outcome of the rescission vote. See also *Homestead Development Ltd. v. Lehman Resources Ltd.* (1988), 40 B.L.R. 1 (B.C. S.C.).

Where the letters patent of a corporation provided that directors might be removed "by a three-fifths vote . . . at a special general meeting" of shareholders, the Ontario Court of Appeal held that the necessary majority was three fifths of the shares represented and voted at a meeting regularly constituted and not three fifths of all the issued shares: *Noble v. Cameron*, [1955] O.R. 608.

Where the letters patent authorize shareholders to depose directors, the notice of the meeting called for this purpose must clearly disclose what is intended to be done and not be so framed as to lead shareholders to believe that it is only intended to fill vacancies: *Milot v. Perrault* (1886), 12 Que. L.R. 193.

Where a director receives notice or otherwise learns of a meeting of shareholders called for the purpose of removing him from office or at which another person is to be appointed or elected to fill the office of director whether because of his resignation or removal or because his term of office has expired or is about to expire, he is entitled to submit to the corporation a written statement giving the reasons for his opposing any proposed action or resolution and this is to be circulated by the corporation to the shareholders (s. 110(2), (3)). Where a special resolution was passed removing a director and there was a failure to file a copy of the resolution, it was held that, while the corporation was subject to a penalty, the resolution itself was valid without the necessity of filing: *Dorey v. Bondeco Automotive Industries Ltd.* (1978), 30 N.S.R. (2d) 620, 49 A.P.R. 620 (N.S. T.D.).

See *Smith v. First Merchant Equities Inc.* (1988), 50 D.L.R. (4th) 369 (Sask. Q.B.) where it was held that the proxy material sent gave sufficient reasons in considering the removal of a director. Further details were held to be unnecessary.

Filling vacancies

The power of the continuing directors to fill a vacancy under a provision such as that contained in s. 111(1) is limited to filling it for the remainder of the term of the director whose office has been vacated.

The by-laws commonly provide that the directors' term of office is to be from the meeting at which they are elected until the annual meeting next following or until their successors are appointed. The provisions of s. 106(5), requiring annual election and retirement of directors then in office, which apply in the absence of election for a stated term, when read in conjunction with s. 106(6), which provides that the retiring directors are to continue in office until their successors are elected, appear to have the same result. Even if the directors' term of office is stated to be one year from the meeting at which they are elected, the directors' term of office does not necessarily end on the expiration of a year from election or on the date when the annual meeting ought to be held.

If a director's term of office is for one year or until his successor is elected, or if he is required to retire at the annual meeting although eligible for re-election, or if he is required to retire in rotation at the annual meeting as being a member of a class due for retirement, and if the shareholders fail to re-elect him or to elect a successor at the annual meeting, it would appear that the directors cannot thereafter fill the vacancy (see s. 111(1)).

A vacancy which can be filled is any vacancy not occurring by effluxion of time, that is, occurring by death, resignation or bankruptcy: *York Tramways Co. v. Willows* (1882), 8 Q.B.D. 685 at 694; or arising otherwise than by retirement in rotation: *Munster v. Cammell Co.* (1882), 21 Ch. D. 183. Such a vacancy can be filled by the directors notwithstanding that a meeting of shareholders has subsequently been held which failed to fill the vacancy. It appears, however, that it also can be filled by a meeting of the shareholders.

Even if the provisions of the governing Act authorizing directors to fill vacancies do not contain the qualifying words "so long as a quorum of directors remains in office", if less than the quorum under the by-laws is in office the remaining directors cannot fill vacancies: *Sovereen Mitt, Glove & Robe Co. v. Whitside* (1906), 12 O.L.R. 638, 670, and cases cited.

In *Channel Collieries Trust v. Dover, St. Margaret's & Martin Mill Light Ry.*, [1914] 2 Ch. 506 (C.A.) it was held that where two of the board of three ceased to be directors, the sole remaining director could by appointment complete the board. This was a case under the *Companies Clauses Consolidation Act, 1845*, s. 89 of which provided that the remaining directors, if they thought proper to do so, might elect some other shareholder in the place of the directors. Lord Cozens Hardy M.R. pointed out that it is common for a corporation to have a board of directors which is merely the quorum and therefore, unless the continuing directors can fill up the vacancy, the corporation would be at a deadlock and nothing could be done except by the intervention of the court in the manner suggested by Mellish L.J. in *Macdougall v. Gardiner* (1875), 1 Ch. D. 13 (C.A.). It should be noted, however, that the *Companies Clauses Consolidation Act* contained no provision corresponding to s. 106(7) of this Act.

Apparently the power to complete the board, given to directors by s. 111(1), would not deprive a special meeting of the corporation of the power to elect directors where there are no directors, or where the directors do not think fit to exercise their power: *Isle of Wight Ry. v. Tahourdin* (1884), 25 Ch. D. 320 (C.A.); and see *Barron v. Potter*, [1914] 1 Ch. 895 at 903, where Warrington J. said that this "principle [is] founded on plain common sense". See also s. 111(2).

Where the articles gave the directors powers to appoint "any other qualified person" to fill a vacancy, it was held that the articles meant a person actually holding the necessary share qualification, and that the persons appointed were not qualified until their actual registration as shareholders: *Spencer v. Kennedy*, [1926] Ch. 125.

Where there has been an increase in the number of the board of directors the new places on the board should be filled by the shareholders and not by the directors. See the notes, *supra*, under the heading "Increase or decrease in numbers of directors" in this chapter. See also s. 111(1).

Officers appointed by the directors

Section 121 provides that, subject to the provisions of the articles, the by-laws or any unanimous shareholder agreement, the directors may designate the offices of the corporation, appoint as its officers persons of full capacity, specify their duties and delegate to them powers to manage the affairs and business of the corporation except to do matters referred to in s. 115(3). In addition the section provides that a director may be appointed to any office of the corporation and two or more offices of the corporation may be held by the same person. As to the appointment of officers generally, see the notes in Chapter 3, (which includes a discussion on the authority of such officers).

Regularity of elections

Procedure

A director or officer whose election is obtained by trick or artifice cannot be considered a bona fide director or officer, but where shares have been actually purchased and paid for, the fact of their being purchased with a view to influencing the election is not material: *Toronto Brewing & Malting Co. v. Blake* (1882), 2 O.R. 175.

Where a meeting of shareholders was called for twelve o'clock, opened by the shareholders present at one minute after twelve, and having elected a board of directors adjourned at ten minutes after twelve, the meeting was held to be a fraud on an absent majority shareholder (who had signified his intention to be present but was delayed): *Armstrong v. McGibbon* (1906), 15 Que. K.B. 345 (Que. C.A.).

Failure to notify all the shareholders will nullify the election unless all the shareholders attend in person or by proxy, even though an absolute majority of the shareholders vote for the directors elected: *Milot v. Perrault* (1886), 12 Que. L.R. 193. Improper rejection of proxies is a ground for setting aside an election of directors: *Kelly v. Electrical Construction Co.* (1908), 16 O.L.R. 232 at 240; so also the fact that shareholders not entitled to vote because in arrears in respect of calls have been permitted to vote: *Armstrong v. McGibbon, supra.*

Where candidates for the board of directors acted as scrutineers and exercised their discretion as to the right of certain voters to vote, it was held that the duty of the scrutineers was so plainly in conflict with their interest as candidates that they were disqualified from acting, and the election was set aside: *Dickson v. McMurray* (1881), 28 Gr. 533 (Ont. Ch.).

Attacking an election

In Ontario an action is usually brought to set aside an election on the ground of irregularity and this must *prima facie* be brought in the name of the corporation: *Kelly v. Electrical Construction Co.* (1908), 16 O.L.R. 232. Under the then British Columbia Act it was held that one shareholder cannot sue even though he brings the action on behalf of himself and all other shareholders: *Fraser River Mining & Dredging Co. v. Gallagher* (1896), 5 B.C.R. 82 (C.A.). In *Watt v. Commonwealth Petroleum Ltd.*, [1938] 4 D.L.R. 701, it was held by the Alberta Court of Appeal that a shareholder had shown no cause of action to set aside an election on the ground of irregularities, where he had not invited the corporation to take steps to set aside the election and there was no suggestion that the majority were not willing to confirm the election and there was no suggestion of fraud. But where the corporation was a party defendant and all necessary parties were before the court, Mulock C.J. held that it was proper to dispose of the case on its merits and set aside an irregular election of directors conditionally on the plaintiffs obtaining authority to use the name of the corporation as plaintiff and amending their statement of claim, the existing directors to continue in office until the election of their successors: *Kelly v. Electrical Construction Co.*, *supra*. Where directors are improperly elected and act as such against the wishes of a majority of the shareholders, the majority are entitled to use the name of the corporation in an action to set aside the election: *Colonial Assurance Co. v. Smith* (1912), 4 D.L.R. 814.

Such an action will only be stayed if it appears that the holders of a majority of the shares are opposed: *Pender v. Lushington* (1877), 6 Ch. D. 70 at 79, 80 (corporation named as co-plaintiff); *Harben v. Phillips* (1883), 23 Ch. D. 14 (C.A.). In the latter case, the action having been brought by the plaintiff and all other shareholders except the defendants, making the corporation a co-plaintiff and an injunction having been granted, *inter alia*, restraining the defendants from acting as directors, on appeal the order for an injunction was discharged and the appeal directed to stand over until a meeting of the shareholders to ascertain their views had been held. In *Fremont Canning Co. v. Wall*, [1941] O.R. 379 (C.A.) a shareholder, suing on behalf of all shareholders other than the defendant, asked for a declaration that certain persons named were in fact the directors of the defendant corporation. Robertson C.J.O., with whom Gillanders J.A. agreed, held that the declaration asked for was not a declaration of right within the meaning of s. 15(b) of *The Judicature Act*, R.S.O. 1937, c. 100 (now R.S.O. 1990, c. C.43, s. 97), and that in any event the question of the right of two persons named, whose qualification as directors was denied, could not be determined in their absence. Apart from the failure to join such persons, the judgment does not suggest that the action, brought on behalf of a shareholder and others, was improperly constituted.

If the basis of attack is that the directors elected were not qualified, a shareholder is entitled to bring an action on behalf of himself and all other shareholders against the corporation and the directors for an injunction restraining directors, not being qualified, from acting: *Channel Collieries Trust v. Dover St. Margaret's & Martin Mill Light Ry.*, [1914] 2 Ch. 506 (C.A.).

As to the relief claimed in such an action, see *Tough Oakes Mines Ltd. v. Foster* (1917), 39 O.L.R. 144 at 145.

Where in a disputed election the real issue was whether a trusted agent of the corporation was to be permitted to sell his own property to the corporation without disclosing the extent of his interest, and it was doubtful whether the facts of the case were understood by the shareholders who gave their proxies to the agent and his associates, with the result that a large majority of the votes were cast in favour of the agent and his associates, an action by the latter for a declaration that they were validly elected directors was dismissed, thereby making necessary an entirely new election: *Dominion Royalty Corp. v. Holborn* (1932), 41 O.W.N. 288.

If the election of directors is *ultra vires* (as opposed to an irregularity in an election), for example, where a number of directors in excess of that provided for the letters patent has been elected without complying with s. 87, acquiescence in the election will not preclude a shareholder from attacking it: *Sherker v. Rudner*

(1911), 39 Que. S.C. 44 (C.A.); *McKenna v. Spooner Oils Ltd.*, [1934] 1 W.W.R. 255.

So also a minority can sue where it is charged that the directors who control a majority of the shares have brought about their election by fraudulent means: *Davidson v. Grange* (1854), 4 Gr. 377 (C.A.). Similarly, where directors have become disqualified under the articles by contracting with the corporation at a profit, any shareholder has a right of action for a declaration of such disqualification: *Theatre Amusement Co. v. Stone* (1915), 50 S.C.R. 32.

It appears that slight irregularities in matters of form will not render an election void which has otherwise been fairly held. Where all subscribers to the memorandum of association concurred in the appointment of the first directors, the fact that they did not meet together for the purpose of coming to their determination did not invalidate their act; and also a resolution, passed at a general meeting at which an election to fill vacancies might have been held, authorizing the existing directors to continue in their offices was held tantamount to a re-election of them: *Great Northern Salt & Chemical Works; Ex parte Kennedy* (1890), 44 Ch. D. 472; and see the remarks of Lindley L.J. in *Re George Newman & Co.*, [1895] 1 Ch. 674 (C.A.).

In Ontario it has been held that *quo warranto* will not lie where the election of directors is attacked in the case of an ordinary trading corporation: *The Queen v. Hespeler* (1854), 11 U.C.Q.B. 222 (C.A.); see also *In re Albert Mining Co.* (1873), 15 N.B.R. 29 (N.B. S.C.). It might seem, however, that if the corporation were exercising functions of a semi-public nature and had objects of public concern *quo warranto* proceedings could be taken: *Re Moore & Port Bruce Harbour Co.* (1857), 14 U.C.Q.B. 365. This procedure is permissible in Quebec: *Sherker v. Rudner* (1911), 39 Que. S.C. 44 (C.A.); *Gilbert v. Hall* (1886), M.L.R. 2 Q.B. 374; *Armstrong v. McGibbon* (1906), 15 Que. K.B. 345 (C.A.).

In *Re Moore & Port Bruce Harbour Co., supra*, at 367, the right to proceed by way of mandamus was also discussed, and it was considered that it should be confined to cases in which the election had been merely colourable and altogether void and not to cases where votes had been improperly received or rejected, or where exception had been taken to the candidate's qualification; and the fact that an election was not attacked for eight months was considered as a ground for refusing relief.

As to the right to proceed by mandatory injunction see *Toronto Brewing & Malting Co. v. Blake* (1882), 2 O.R. 175; *Gilman v. Robertson* (1884), 7 L.N. 353, M.L.R. 1 S.C. 5.

Directors *de facto*

Although his election as a director may have been defective or irregular, a person may act in the capacity of director in which event he is said to be a director *de facto*.

Persons publicly exercising the functions of directors of corporations have been held to be directors to the extent that their acts are deemed valid in respect of third persons who are not aware of their lack of status or are binding on the corporation so far as the rights of third parties who are unaware of the true position are concerned: *R. v. Bedford Level* (1805), 6 East 368; *Re County Life Assurance Co.* (1870), L.R. 5 Ch. App. 288; *Mahony v. East Holyford Mining Co.* (1875), L.R. 7 H.L. 869 (H.L.); *County of Gloucester Bank v. Rudry Merthyr Steam & House Coal Colliery Co.*, [1895] 1 Ch. 629 (C.A.); *Macdonald v. Drake* (1906), 16 Man. R. 220 (C.A.) at 226.

Thus, a corporation cannot escape liability on an agreement under its corporate seal with an outsider on the ground that its directors were not regularly elected: *Re W. N. McEachren & Sons Ltd.*, [1933] O.R. 349 (C.A.) at 361; *Gray v. Yellowknife Gold Mines Ltd. (No. 1)*, [1945] O.R. 688.

The rule is different as regards acts affecting only the shareholders of the corporation *inter se*, for example, the validity of an allotment of shares.

Section 116 of the federal Act provides that an act of an officer or director is valid notwithstanding an irregularity in his election or appointment or a defect in his qualification. Such statutory provisions and similar provisions in the articles in common form have been held to be effective as between the corporation and its shareholders: *Dawson v. African Consolidated Land & Trading Co.*, [1898] 1 Ch. 6; *British Asbestos Co. v. Boyd*, [1903] 2 Ch. 439 (validity of meeting of shareholders); *Alberta Improvement Co. v. Peverett* (1914), 7 W.W.R. 757 (Sask. C.A.). Such provisions protect acts both with regard to insiders and outsiders and are available to directors if there is good faith: *Channel Collieries Trust Ltd. v. Dover St. Margaret's & Martin Mill Light Ry.*, [1914] 2 Ch. 506 (C.A.) at 512, 515. The section is designed to avoid questions being raised as to the validity of transactions where there has been a slip in the appointment of a director and cannot be invoked to override the substantive provisions relating to such appointments: *Morris v. Kanssen*, [1946] A.C. 459.

The election of new directors by *de facto* directors (they being improperly appointed) was held under the corresponding provision of the Alberta Act to be valid in *Oliver v. Elliott* (1960), 30 W.W.R. 641, 23 D.L.R. (2d) 486 (Alta. T.D.).

A director *de facto* is, like an executor *de son tort*, subject to the burdens of the office, but not entitled to any of its benefits: *Macdonald v. Drake* (1906), 16 Man. R. 220 (C.A.). When directors assume their fiduciary office they become liable in all respects as though rightly appointed and they cannot be heard to criticize the regularity of their appointment: *Re Owen Sound Lumber Co.* (1915), 34 O.L.R. 528; vard (1917), 38 O.L.R. 414 (C.A.).

The principle has also been applied to other agents of a corporation, and in any case where a person holds himself out as an agent or official of a corporation and the circumstances are such that in law the corporation could repudiate such person, or take proceedings to restrain him but has not done so, then his acts within his apparent authority will bind the corporation as regards persons ignorant of his true position, even though his assumption of authority is entirely unwarranted: *Mahony v. East Holyford Mining Co., supra*; and see *Allen v. Ont. & Rainy River Ry.* (1898), 29 O.R. 510 (C.A.).

De facto directors not only have the power but the duty to convene a general meeting of shareholders for the purpose of properly constituting the board: *Streit v. Swanson*, [1946] O.R. 565.

Prima facie the corporation alone may bring an action to restrain a *de facto* director irregularly elected from acting as a director or representing himself as such. An individual shareholder has no such right: *Foss v. Harbottle* (1843), 2 Hare 461; *Kelly v. Electrical Construction Co.* (1908), 16 O.L.R. 232. See further the cases in the notes under the heading "Attacking an election" in this chapter. Nor can the right of *de facto* directors to act as directors be questioned collaterally by a defendant in an action brought against him by the corporation: *Austin Mining Co. v. Gemmell* (1886), 10 O.R. 696 (C.A.).

In an action for an accounting brought by a corporation against its president the onus of proof is on the defendant who alleges that the corporation's board of directors is incomplete: *Temiscouata Ry. v. Macdonald* (1900), 3 Que. P.R. 462.

Indemnification of directors (s. 124)

Section 124 provides that, except in respect of an action by or on behalf of the corporation to procure a judgment in its favour, a corporation may indemnify a director or officer, or a former director or officer or a person who acts or acted at a corporation's request as a director or officer of a corporation of which the corporation was or is a shareholder or creditor against all costs, charges and expenses including amounts to settle an action reasonably incurred by him in respect of any civil, criminal or administrative action or proceeding to which he is made a party by reason of having been a director or officer if the director or officer acted honestly and in good faith with a view to the best interests of the corporation and in the case of a civil or administrative action or proceeding enforced by a monetary penalty if he had reasonable grounds for believing that his conduct was lawful. Where the corporation is a plaintiff under subs. (2), with the approval of a court, the corporation may indemnify the defendant subject to the same conditions as in s. 124(1). In addition if the director is qualified for relief and was substantially successful on the merits in his defence of the action proceeding then he is entitled by virtue of subs. (3) as of right to indemnity. The corporation may under subs. (4) purchase and maintain insurance for the benefit of any potential defendant against any such liability except where the liability relates to the failure to act honestly and in good faith with a view to the best interests of the corporation. An application to approve an indemnity under the section may be made to court by a corporation or any person referred to in s. 124 (see s. 124(5)) and notice of the application is to be given to the Director pursuant to subs. (6). The court may order a notice to be given to any interested person and such person is entitled to appear and be heard in person or by counsel (subs. (7)). In construing a similar provision under the British Columbia Act it was held in *Denton v. Equus Petroleum Corp.* (1986), 33 B.L.R. 314 (B.C. S.C.) that the costs of illegal expenses incurred in the course of a criminal investigation were not covered by the statute and a simple statement that the director believed that his conduct was lawful was not sufficient without setting out the grounds. In that case no charge was actually laid, but allegations were made against the director by fellow members of the board of the corporation in question and there was a substantial period of investigation. It is submitted that the case was wrongly decided and that the costs should have been reimbursed and that this constituted an administrative action or proceeding in that it was an investigation to see whether criminal charges should be laid. In *Balestreri v. Robert* (1985), 30 B.L.R. 283, [1985] C.S. 1038 (Que. S.C.) a director was held not to be entitled to indemnity since he was found not to have acted in good faith and therefore not entitled to indemnity. In *Prime Resources Group Inc. v. Pezim* (1991), 1 B.L.R. (2d) 140 (B.C. S.C.), an order under the comparable provision of the British Columbia Act was granted permitting the corporation to indemnify three directors for legal fees incurred in defending proceedings under the Securities Act. The Commission's findings did not reveal deceit or fraudulent intent. Where a director impugned the exercising of proxies in the election of a new nominee as director, indemnity was denied under the Ontario Act. Although the director acted in good faith and on the advice of corporate counsel, he had been acting in his own interests and not in the interests of the corporation. See: *Blair v. Consolidated Enfield Corp.* (unreported), Ont. Ct. Gen. Div., Carruthers, J. October 28, 1992.

Quite apart from the statutory indemnification, on the ordinary principles of the law of agency an officer of a corporation is entitled to be indemnified against all liabilities and expenses incurred by him in pursuance of his duties: *In re Famatina Development Corp.*, [1914] 2 Ch. 271 (C.A.) (engineer entitled to the costs of his successful defence to an action for alleged libel in a report he was employed to make).

A provision in the articles to relieve directors from claims by the corporation for loss arising from their negligence, not dishonesty, will be valid: *In re Brazilian Rubber Plantations & Estates Ltd.*, [1911] 1 Ch. 425. A provision in the articles exonerating directors except in case of wilful neglect or default is also valid: *In re City Equitable Fire Insurance Co.*, [1925] Ch. 407 (C.A.). Negligence is not willful unless the officer knows that he is committing and intends to commit a breach of his duty or is recklessly careless in the sense of not caring whether his act or omission is or is not a breach of duty: ibid. at 434, 523, 525. But where an article provided that directors should be indemnified against costs, losses and expenses incurred by them in or about the discharge of their duties except such as might happen from their own willful or wrongful act or default, directors were held not to be protected from negligence resulting in loss to the corporation: *In re City of London Insurance Co.* (1925), 41 T.L.R. 521.

The by-laws usually provide that the directors shall be paid out-of-pocket disbursements, including travelling expenses actually and properly incurred by them in connection with the affairs of the corporation, and such a by-law ratified by the shareholders will entitle a director to recover travelling expenses. But if payment of travelling expenses is not authorized by the by-laws, a director is not entitled to be reimbursed therefor as he is impliedly bound to pay his travelling expenses out of his remuneration: *Young v. Naval, Military & Civil Service Co-operative Society of South Africa*, [1905] 1 K.B. 687.

Travelling expenses, incurred by a director who has been abroad on his private affairs, on returning to Canada to attend a directors' meeting are not deductible for income tax purposes: *Bahamas General Trust Co. v. Provincial Treasurer of Alberta*, [1942] 1 D.L.R. 169 (Alta. T.D.).

The by-law should be comprehensive in its terms, as otherwise it may be found that certain disbursements are not covered; for example, in *Marmor Ltd. v. Alexander*, [1908] S.C. 78, it was held that expenses incurred by a director in travelling to attend meetings were not covered by an article providing for indemnification of directors for expenses incurred "in the execution of their respective offices". A director is, of course, entitled to be reimbursed for money properly spent on the corporation's behalf. See *Benor v. Canadian Mail Order Co.* (1907), 10 O.W.R. 899 (Ont. K.B.).

See also the notes under the headings "Remuneration of directors" and "Personal liability of directors" in this chapter.

Status of directors and its consequences

Position of directors

A corporation must act by agents, and usually the persons by whom it acts are termed directors. The Act does not define the exact position of directors.

Directors have been described as mere trustees or agents of the corporation; trustees of the corporation's money and property; agents in the transactions which they enter into on behalf of the corporation: *Great Eastern Ry. v. Turner* (1872), L.R. 8 Ch. App. 149 at 152.

Directors have also been described as managing partners of the corporation: *Automatic Self-Cleansing Filter Syndicate Co. v. Cuninghame*, [1906] 2 Ch. 34. When, however, they are referred to as agents, trustees or managing partners, "it is essential to recollect that such expressions are not exhaustive of the powers or responsibilities of those persons, but only as indicating useful points of view from which they may for the moment and for the particular purpose be considered . . . . It is not meant that they belong to the category but that it is useful for the purpose of the moment to observe that they fall *pro tanto* within the principles which govern that particular class": *Re Imperial Hydropathic Hotel Co.; Blackpool v. Hampson* (1882), 23 Ch. D. 1 at 12. Their position is a statutory one which is similar in varying respects to those of agents, trustees and managing partners and is clearly of a fiduciary nature: *Regal (Hastings) Ltd. v. Gulliver*, [1942] 1 All E.R. 378 at 387 (H.L.).

It has also been said that the true position of directors is that they are really commercial people managing a trading corporation for the benefit of themselves and of all the other shareholders in it, per Jessel M.R., in *In re Forest of Dean Coal Mining Co.* (1878), 10 Ch. D. 450 at 452. In *In re City Equitable Fire Insurance Co.*, [1925] Ch. 407 at 426-27 (C.A.), Romer J., made the following observations with regard to the position and duties of directors:

> It has sometimes been said that directors are trustees. If this means no more than that directors in the performance of their duties stand in a fiduciary relationship to the company, the statement is true enough. But if the statement is meant to be an indication by way of analogy of what those duties are, it appears to me to be wholly misleading. I can see but little resemblance between the duties of a director

> and the duties of a trustee of a will or of a marriage settlement. It is indeed impossible to describe the duty of directors in general terms, whether by way of analogy or otherwise. The position of a director of a company carrying on a small retail business is very different from that of a director of a railway company. The duties of a bank director may differ widely from those of an insurance director, and the duties of a director of one insurance company may differ from those of a director of another. In one company, for instance, matters may normally be attended to by the manager or other members of the staff that in another company are attended to by the directors themselves. The larger the business carried on by the company the more numerous, and the more important, the matters that must of necessity be left to the managers, the accountants and the rest of the staff. The manner in which the work of the company is to be distributed between the board of directors and the staff is in truth a business matter to be decided on business lines . . .
>
> In order, therefore, to ascertain the duties that a person appointed to the board of an established company undertakes to perform, it is necessary to consider not only the nature of the company's business, but also the manner in which the work of the company is in fact distributed between the directors and the other officials of the company, provided always that this distribution is a reasonable one in the circumstances, and is not inconsistent with any express provisions of the articles of association. In discharging the duties of his position thus ascertained a director must, of course, act honestly; but he must also exercise some degree of both skill and diligence.

By s. 102(1) of the Act the management of the corporation is vested in the directors. They are entitled to manage the corporation without interference by the shareholders and, in the absence of illegality, fraud or oppression of minority shareholders' interests, the courts will not interfere in this management.

It will be noted that s. 122 of the Act now provides that every director and officer of a corporation in exercising his powers and discharging his duties is required to act honestly and in good faith with a view to the best interests of the corporation and to exercise the care, due diligence and skill that a reasonably prudent person would exercise in comparable circumstances; every director and officer is required to comply with the Act, the regulations, the articles, by-laws and any unanimous shareholder agreement. Subject to the provisions of a unanimous shareholder agreement no provision in the articles or any contract, by-law or resolution relieves any director or officer from the duty to act in accordance with the Act or the regulations or relieves him from liability for a breach thereof (s. 122(3)).

A single director is entitled to maintain an action in respect of his individual rights as such: *Pulbrook v. Richmond Consolidated Mining Co.* (1878), 9 Ch. D. 610 at 612 (where Jessel M.R. pointed out that these rights include a right to take a part in the corporation's management and to be present and vote at the meetings of the board of directors); *Howard v. Dench*, [1942] 2 D.L.R. 177 (B.C. C.A.) (a director is entitled to an order restraining his wrongful exclusion from taking part in the management); *Hayes v. Bristol Plant Hire Ltd.*, [1957] 1 All E.R. 685 at 687 (right of a director to an order restraining his exclusion from the board).

There is no legal objection to a person who is employed in a managerial capacity also being a director: *Bashforth v. Provincial Steel Co.* (1913), 10 D.L.R. 187 at 189 (Ont. H.C.).

An agreement between the three shareholders of a corporation, providing that a decision at a meeting of shareholders or directors had to be unanimous, was held to be void. The directors of a corporation have a duty to decide matters affecting the welfare of the corporation in accordance with their best judgment and this was impossible under the terms of the agreement: *Atlas Development Co. v. Calof* (1963), 41 W.W.R. 575 (Man. Q.B.). However, if the agreement in question had constituted a unanimous shareholder agreement it presumably would have been upheld.

In two cases it has been held that arson by a director or an officer of a corporation will preclude recovery by the corporation under a fire insurance policy. See *Direct Investments Ltd. v. Dominion Insurance Corp.* (1968), 68 D.L.R. (2d) 278 (Ont. H.C.); *Siountres v. United States Fire Insurance* (1982), 128 D.L.R. (3d) 493 (Ont. H.C.). It is suggested, however, that these decisions would not be applicable in a corporation of any size. For example, in *TransCan. Resources Ltd. v. Bobella* (1983), 127 A.P.R. 51 (Nfld.) it was held that knowledge by directors of an unregistered assignment of a security which was subsequently given to the corporation itself did not fix the corporation with notice of the prior assignment and the assignment to the corporation was valid.

In *Osborne v. Kane* (1977), 19 N.B.R. (2d) 316 (Q.B.), the plaintiff had agreed to go into business with the defendants and a corporation was formed for that purpose. The plaintiff contributed cash and the defendants were to contribute goods and expertise. The business failed and the plaintiff sued the other directors alleging a breach of their agreement to provide expertise and claiming repayment of the money he had invested. It was held in dismissing the action that the plaintiff had failed to establish that the defendants' failure to give expert advice was a cause of the loss.

The position of directors will now be considered under a number of sub-headings dealing with various aspects of that position and the consequences which flow therefrom. It must be kept in mind, however, that the position must be looked at as a whole and that in any particular case the courts are basically concerned with the overall concept of the directors' position and the consequences which flow therefrom rather than with any particular aspect thereof.

Directors as agents

The rule that directors are agents in the transactions which they enter into on behalf of the corporation is established by numerous decisions. "The company itself cannot act in its own person for it has no person; it can only act through directors, and the case is, as regards those directors, merely the ordinary case of principal and agent. Wherever an agent is liable those directors would be liable; where the liability would attach to the principal, and the principal only, the liability is the liability of the company": *Ferguson v. Wilson* (1866), L.R. 2 Ch. App. 77 at 89.

A sole governing director of a corporation may, as agent and on behalf of the corporation, enter into a contract of service with himself: *Lee v. Lee's Air Farming Ltd.*, [1960] 3 W.L.R. 758 (P.C.).

Directors as trustees for the corporation

Directors are trustees for the corporation of the corporation's property: *In re Sharpe, Masonic & General Life Assurance Co. v. Sharpe*, [1892] 1 Ch. 154 (C.A.); *In re Forest of Dean Coal Mining Co.* (1878), 10 Ch. D. 450; but are not as such trustees of the corporation's property within the meaning of s. 2(42) (definition of trustee) or s. 390 (breach of trust) of the Criminal Code: *Ex parte Giroux*, [1926] 2 D.L.R. 900 (Que. C.A.). They cannot use the corporation's property for their own benefit: *Pure Canadian Silver Black Fox Co. v. Morrison* (1915), 24 D.L.R. 915; *McGill Shipbuilding & Transportation Co. v. Canadian Bank of Commerce*, [1925] 2 D.L.R. 1183 (N.S. C.A.) (scheme to pay off personal indebtedness of directors with corporation's assets; creditor put on enquiry).

A director is also accountable for any profit he realizes from any dealing with property of the corporation. Thus, a director who purchased property of the corporation for his own benefit on a sale thereof by a mortgagee was held to be a trustee thereof for the corporation and accountable for any profit realized on the resale thereof: *Re Iron Clay Brick Manufacturing Co.* (1889), 19 O.R. 113. And a director who took from a third party, to secure a debt, a mortgage on property which he knew belonged in equity to the corporation was held liable to account for the corporation for the proceeds he received from the sale of the property: *N. Rattenbury Ltd. v. Winchester*, [1950] 3 D.L.R. 826; affd [1953] 3 D.L.R. 660 (P.E.I. C.A.).

And where the managing director of a corporation devoted time to, and utilized the corporation's funds and resources in, the preliminary development of a property of a sort which the corporation might develop in the course of its business and then took a lease of the property in his own name, he was held to be a trustee of the lease for the corporation: *Natural Sodium Products Ltd. v. Holland*, [1946] 1 W.W.R. 605.

Directors are not bound to invest the corporation's funds in trustee securities, and may invest them in the name of a sole trustee: *Burland v. Earle*, [1902] A.C. 83 P.C.

As trustees the conduct of directors is to be considered with reference to the particular business they are appointed to manage, but it has been repeatedly held that directors who had misapplied funds were liable for "breach of trust": *Faure Electric Accumulator Co.* (1889), 40 Ch. D. 141; *In re Sharpe Masonic & General Life Assurance Co. v. Sharpe*, [1892] 1 Ch. 154 (C.A.). See *Smith v. Anderson* (1880), 15 Ch. D. 247 at 275; *Therien v. Brody* (1893), 4 Que. S.C. 23. Where a director of a construction corporation knowingly misused moneys which, by the relevant *Mechanics' Lien Act*, constituted a trust fund for the benefit of his workmen, he was held personally liable: *Scott v. Riehl* (1959), 15 D.L.R. (2d) 67. See also *Air Canada v. M & L Travel Ltd.* (1991), 2 O.R. (3d) 184, 77 D.L.R. (4th) 536 (C.A.); leave to appeal to S.C.C. granted.

Where there has been some misapplication of the funds of the corporation to purposes which are *ultra vires* of the corporation, this is regarded as a breach of trust for which the directors guilty of it will be held personally liable: *Stringers' Case* (1869), L.R. 4 Ch. App. 475.

Where a director has made himself liable for a breach of trust he is bound to reimburse the corporation: *Joint Stock Discount v. Brown* (1869), L.R. 8 Eq. 381. The director may also be liable to outsiders: *Brenes & Co. v. Downie*, [1914] S.C. 97 (Scot.); *National Trust Co. Ltd. v. Gilbart & Gilbart*, [1921] 1 W.W.R. 359 (Sask. C.A.).

Generally speaking, acts of the directors within the scope of the powers of the corporation, although impeachable by the corporation as a breach of trust, are binding on the corporation as against strangers who act in good faith and without the knowledge or notice of the breach of trust: *Sun Trust Co. v. Bégin*, [1937] S.C.R. 305 per Duff C.J.C. at 312.

The doctrine that a director is a trustee of the corporation's property has no application to the case of a director paying off a creditor and taking up from him a security irregularly issued: *In re Bank of Syria; Owen & Ashworth's Claim; Whitworth's Claim*, [1901] 1 Ch. 115 at 121 (C.A.).

Directors as trustees for the shareholders

At common law, in ordinary cases no fiduciary relationship exists between the directors and the shareholders of the corporation as such: *Percival v. Wright*, [1902] 2 Ch. 421; *Duff v. Rudolph & Lunenburg Gas Co.*, [1929] 4 D.L.R. 813. The directors are not trustees for shareholders individually: *Percival v. Wright*, *supra*.

A director of a corporation owes no duty to a shareholder, whose shares he is purchasing, to disclose all information that might affect the value of the shares unless special circumstances exist: *Duff v. Rudolph & Lunenberg Gas Co.*, *supra*. In that case it was held that, in the absence of special circumstances, a director of a corporation is free to purchase shares in the corporation of which he is a director.

Ordinarily no trust rests upon the directors in favour of the other shareholders as to the transfer of the directors' shares; the directors have the power under ordinary circumstances to consent to a transfer of their own shares where the consent of the directors is required. A director is not a trustee for the general body of the shareholders so as to be unable to deal with his shares in a manner prejudicial to the interests of his *cestuis que trustent*, but is as free to deal with his shares as any other person: *Re National Provincial Marine Co.; Gilbert's Case* (1870), L.R. 5 Ch. App. 559; *In re Cawley & Co.* (1889), 42 Ch. D. 209 at 233; *Thompson v. Canada Fire & Marine Insurance Co.* (1885), 9 O.R. 284 (C.A.). Apparently the same applies to qualification shares: *Commercial Loan & Trust Co. v. Macaw*, [1923] 1 D.L.R. 744 (Man. C.A.) (transfer of his qualification shares by a director, who at the same time resigned, upheld against the liquidator).

But if the directors are guilty of keeping the shareholders in the dark as to the state of the corporation's affairs, until the directors have transferred their shares for the purpose of getting rid of their own liability thereon, the court will interfere to declare the transfer invalid: *Murray v. Bush* (1872), L.R. 6 H.L. 37.

In *Teck Corp v. Millar*, [1973] 2 W.W.R. 385 (B.C. S.C.) the directors were held entitled to issue shares to a third party, thus defeating the objectives of the majority shareholders prior to such issue, if the directors honestly and on reasonable grounds decided that the corporation's best interests required such an issue.

Under special circumstances the shareholders may be entitled to set up that a fiduciary relationship has been established and to treat the directors as trustees for them. See for example: *Vladi Private Islands Ltd. v. Haase* (1990), 253 A.P.R. 323 (N.S. C.A.) where the court refused to strike out a statement of claim in which both a derivative action and a personal class action had been commenced, the latter based on an alleged breach of fiduciary duty. So where directors of a corporation were approached with a view to effecting a merger to be carried out by a sale of the assets of the corporation of which they were directors, and the directors secured the consent of the majority of the shareholders and surreptitiously acquired shares of the new corporation for their own profit, it was held that the directors became the agents, in the transaction, of the shareholders, and that the latter were entitled to treat the directors as trustees for them of the profit made: *Allen v. Hyatt* (1914), 17 D.L.R. 7 (P.C.). See also *Gadsden v. Bennetto* (1913), 9 D.L.R. 719 (Man. C.A.) where directors, having conspired to dispose of the corporation's property and make a secret profit, acquired shares at an undervalue from the shareholders by suppressing the terms of the offer received for the corporation's property, and were held to be trustees for the shareholders of the profits made. It was also held in the same case that where a committee of the directors is appointed for the purpose of disposing, not only of the property of the corporation, but also of the shares belonging to individual shareholders, the responsibility of the members of the committee is different from that of ordinary directors, they being confidential agents of the shareholders as well as of the corporation.

The common law provision has been virtually abolished for public companies because of the provisions of the Act dealing with insider trading — see Chapter 9. See also *Green v. Charterhouse Group Canada Ltd.*, [1973], 2 O.R. 677.

Directors as trustees for the corporation's creditors

The directors are not trustees for the corporation's creditors: *Poole, Jackson & White's Case* (1878), 9 Ch. D. 322 (C.A.); *Wilson v. Bury* (1880), 5 Q.B.D. 518 (C.A.); *Ferguson v. Wilson* (1866), L.R. 2 Ch. App. 77; *Bank of Toronto v. Cobourg, Peterborough & Marmora Ry.* (1885), 10 O.R. 376 (C.A.); *A.G. Can. v. Standard Trust Co. of New York*, [1911] A.C. 498 (P.C.).

Fiduciary position of directors

It is a director's duty to give his whole ability, business knowledge, exertion and attention to the best interests of the shareholders who have placed him in that position: *Re Iron Clay Brick Manufacturing Co.* (1889), 19 O.R. 113 at 123. Directors, by reason of their fiduciary obligations, in the exercise of their powers are bound to act with the utmost good faith for the benefit of the corporation: *Sun Trust Co. v. Bégin*, [1937] S.C.R. 305 at 307.

Directors are trustees of the powers vested in them and must act not only not *mala fide* but *uberrimae fidei*; their powers can be exercised only for the purposes for which they were intended and not for the directors' own advantage: *Legion Oils Ltd. & Boyd v. Barron* (No. 2) (1956), 2 D.L.R. (2d) 505.

There have been a number of cases dealing with the position of directors and officers who have left the employ of a corporation and commenced work for another corporation. It has been held in such cases that a director or senior officer is precluded from obtaining for himself secretly any property or business advantage belonging to the corporation or for which he had been negotiating. See *Canadian Aero Service Ltd. v. O'Malley*, [1974] S.C.R. 592; see also *DCF Systems Ltd. v. Gellman* (1978), 5 B.L.R. 98 (Ont. H.C.); *W. J. Christie & Co. v. Greer* (1981), 14 B.L.R. 146 (Man. C.A.); *Dominion High-Rise Ltd. v. Night-Hawk Cleaning & Supply Co.* (1982), 37 O.R. (2d) 148 (Ont. Co. Ct.); *Moore International (Can.) Inc. v. Carter* (1982), 40 B.C.L.R. 322 (S.C.); *57134 Manitoba Ltd. v. Palmer* (1989), 37 B.C.L.R. (2d) 50, 44 B.L.R. 94 (C.A.); *Resfab Manufacturier de Ressort Inc. v. Archambault* (1985), 10 C.P.R. (3d) 102, [1986] R.D.J. 32 (Que. C.A.); *Lacey v. Stoyles* (1986), 178 A.P.R. 181 (Nfld. T.D.); *Roper v. Murdoch* (1987), 14 B.C.L.R. (2d) 385, 39 D.L.R. (4th) 684 (S.C.); *Commercial Transport (Northern) Ltd. v. Watkins* (1983), 22 B.L.R. 249 (Ont. H.C.); *J & P Gourmet House Ltd. v. Li* (1991), 39 C.P.R. (3d) 519 (B.C. S.C.). Senior officers of a corporation are treated in the same manner as directors: see *Lake Mechanical Systems Corp. v. Crandell Mechanical Systems Inc.* (1985), 9 C.C.E.L. 52, 31 B.L.R. 113 (B.C. S.C.). It should be noted, however, that a fiduciary duty is only imposed on officers and managers with the power and ability to guide and direct affairs of the corporation; an ordinary employee will not be subject to such requirements. However, they may not take with them documents belonging to their former employer. See *R. W. Hamilton Ltd. v. Aeroquip Corp.* (1988), 40 B.L.R. 79, 65 O.R. (2d) 345 (Ont. H.C.).

Directors are fiduciary donees of their powers. The following cases exemplifying this principle relate to the powers indicated: Making calls on shares: *Alexander v. Automatic Telephone Co.*, [1899] 2 Ch. 302, [1900] 2 Ch. 56 (C.A.). Issuing and allotting shares: *Punt v. Symons & Co.*, [1903] 2 Ch. 506; *Madden v. Dimond* (1905), 12 B.C.R. 80 (C.A.); *Martin v. Gibson* (1908), 15 O.L.R. 623 (Ch. Div.); *Piercy v. Mills & Co*, [1920] 1 Ch. 77; *Smith v. Hanson Tire & Supply Co.*, [1927] 3 D.L.R. 786 (Sask. C.A.); *C. E. Plain Ltd. (Trustee of) v. Kenley & Royal Trust Co.*, [1931] O.R. 75 (C.A.); *Hebb v. Mulock & Newmarket Era & Express Ltd.*, [1945] O.R. 727 at 737 (C.A.). For a discussion of the validity of the issue of shares by the directors, see Chapter 5. Permitting transfers of unpaid shares: *Re Peterborough Cold Storage Co.* (1907), 14 O.L.R. 475. Forfeiting shares: *Blisset v. Daniel* (1853), 10 Hare 493. Adding new directors to the board: *Legion Oils Ltd. & Boyd v. Barron* (No. 2) (1956), 2 D.L.R. (2d) 505; *Olson v. Phoenix Industrial Supply Ltd.*, [1984] 4 W.W.R. 498 (Man. C.A.). See also *Exco Corp v. N.S. Savings & Loan Co.* (1987), 35 B.L.R. 149, 78 N.S.R. (2d)

91 (N.S. T.D.) and *Teck Corp. v. Millar*, [1973] 2 W.W.R. 385, 33 D.L.R. (3d) 288 (B.C. S.C.).

If a director makes a secret profit in breach of trust it is a fraud in equity and it is immaterial whether the director in question believes he is entitled in law to retain the profits except possibly as to the question of punitive damages: *D'Amore v. McDonald*, [1973] 1 O.R. (2d) 370 (C.A.). The powers of directors must be exercised *bona fide* for the corporation's benefit: *Madden v. Dimond*, *supra*; *Rudolph v. Macey* (1906), 3 W.L.R. 52 (B.C. C.A.). So also they must not sell the corporation's property at an undervaluation: *Daniel v. Gold Hill Mining Co.* (1899), 6 B.C.R. 495; *Boyle v. Rothschild* (1907), 10 O.W.R. 696.

The fiduciary position of a director bars him from acknowledging on behalf of the corporation a debt due to himself by the corporation: *Re Transplanters (Holding Company) Ltd.*, [1958] 2 All E.R. 711.

Ignorance of the director that he is acting in breach of the fiduciary relationship will have effect on the measure of relief which will be exacted against him. See *In re Bulmer; Ex parte Greaves*, [1937] 1 Ch. 499 (C.A.).

The fiduciary relationship is with the corporation only and does not extend to a stranger with whom the corporation is dealing; for example, a person with whom the corporation enters into a contract to act as agent: *Bath v. Standard Land Co.*, [1911] 1 Ch. 618 (C.A.) 625 at 642. The director's duty to account is to the corporation and no fiduciary duty is owed to the individual shareholders or to the creditors of the corporation: *Western Finance Co. v. Tasker Enterprises Ltd.*, [1981] 1 W.W.R. 323 (Man. C.A.).

If the directors have abused their position so as to obtain an advantage at the expense of the corporation, it is for the corporation or its shareholders to complain, and not for an outsider. Debenture holders, who had obtained their debentures after certain directors of the corporation had caused debentures to be issued to themselves at a discount of 25 per cent in satisfaction of their claims against the corporation, were held to have no status to attack the issue made to the directors as being invalid because of the discount; the transaction was not *ultra vires* nor was it void, and could only be complained of as unfair by the corporation or a corporator: *Bank of Toronto v. Cobourg, Peterborough & Marmora Ry.* (1885), 10 O.R. 376 (C.A.). See also *Greenstreet v. Paris* (1874), 21 Gr. 229 (Ont. Ch.).

When a director had been induced to transfer his shares in the corporation without valuable consideration, under threat of criminal prosecution for misfeasance, he was entitled to recover the shares or their value as having been obtained under compulsion and was not *in pari delicto* in stifling a criminal prosecution by transferring his shares under such circumstances: *Stoltze v. Fuller*, [1939] S.C.R. 235.

See also *F. R. Diesel Electric Co. v. Farkas* (1985), B.C. Corps. L.G. 78 at 309 (B.C. S.C.); *Canada Trust Co. v. Lloyd*, [1968] S.C.R. 300; where equitable relief was granted against directors who improperly withdrew funds from a corporation in 1921, interest being allowed to the date of judgment in 1964. It was held that the delay of 43 years should not prevent the granting of equitable relief since the directors had since 1921 enjoyed the benefits of the moneys they had taken without colour of right or mistaken belief in their entitlement so to do or other factors which might warrant some relaxation of equitable rules.

Green v. Charterhouse Group Canada Ltd., [1973] 2 O.R. 677 involved the liability of directors pursuant to the Ontario *Securities Act* (which provided for liability where a material fact was not disclosed and securities were traded). In that case, the parties had entered into a buy/sell agreement with respect to the shares in question. One defendant had been approached by a third party who proposed a take-over bid of the corporation. The plaintiff advised the other parties to the buy/sell agreement that he wished to sell his shares and was told to wait because they might become more valuable. The shares were purchased under the buyer/seller agreement and subsequently, the third party made a successful takeover bid and the value of the shares of the corporation increased substantially. The plaintiff sued, alleging that the defendants as insiders had made use of specific and confidential information to their benefit. The action was dismissed. It was pointed out that the information concerning the possible takeover was quite uncertain and certainly not specific and confidential. The defendants had warned the plaintiff that the value of the shares might increase and the evidence showed that the defendants had reluctantly purchased the shares to safeguard the value of their own holdings and to prevent dumping in the open market of a large shareholding. See also *Bell v. Source Data Control Ltd.* (1988), 66 O.R. (2d) 78, 53 D.L.R. (4th) 580 (C.A.); *Norcen International Ltd. v. Suncor Inc.* (1988), 91 A.R. 81 (Q.B.) and *Alta. Treasury Branches v. Hat Development Ltd.* (1988), 64 Alta. L.R. (2d) 17, 71 C.B.R. (N.S.) 264 (Alta. Q.B.); affd (1989), 65 Alta. L.R. (2d) 374 (Alta. C.A.).

See also *Northern & Central Gas Corp. v. Hillcrest Collieries Ltd.*, [1976] 1 W.W.R. 481, 59 D.L.R. (3rd) 533 (Alta. T.D.) which discusses the duty of directors pursuant to certain warranties. In addition to damages, the sale of certain property was set aside as the directors did not act *bona fide* and were in breach of their fiduciary duties to the vendor. See also *Roberts v. Pelling*, [1982] 2 W.W.R. 185, (*sub. nom* Pelling v. Pelling) 16 B.L.R. 150 (B.C. S.C.); *Dusik v. Newton* (1985), 62 D.C.L.R. 1; affg in part (1983), 50 B.C.L.R. 321 (B.C. C.A.) for the duty of a director to inform a shareholder of a proposed sale of shares of corporation. *Imperial Trust Co. v. Canbra Foods Ltd.* (1987), 50 Alta L.R. (2d) 375, 78 A.R. 267 (Q.B.); *Angus v. R. Angus Alberta Ltd.*, [1988] 3 W.W.R. 737, 39 B.L.R. 1 (Alta. C.A.), additional reasons at (November 10, 1988), Doc. No. Edmonton Appeal 19125 (Alta. C.A.), application for rehearing refused (September 16, 1988), Doc. No. Edmonton Appeal 19125 (Alta. C.A.); *Hoffman Products Ltd. v. Karr* (1989), 70 O.R. (2d) 789 (Ont. H.C.), leave to appeal to Ont. Div. Ct. refused (1990), 72 O.R. (2d) 797 (Ont. H.C.).

In order to obtain an interim injunction to enforce the fiduciary obligations of a former senior employee, officer and director, it must be demonstrated that there would be irreparable harm if the injunction were not granted and the balance of convenience must be in favour of those seeking the injunction: see *Ainley & Associates Ltd. v. Tatham* (1989), 46 B.L.R. 104 (Ont. H.C.).

For a general discussion of the duties and liabilities of directors and officers see *Carlson v. Trans-Pac Industries Corp.* (1989), 43 B.L.R. 192 (B.C. S.C.) affd (1990), 2 B.L.R. (2d) 70 (B.C. C.A.).

A travel agency had agreed to keep moneys owing to an airline from tickets sold in a trust fund and to remit according to a schedule. The moneys in question were not kept in a trust fund and were intermingled with other funds. The controlling directors then drew on what should have been trust funds for general expenses of the corporation and for their own benefit. The airline was held to be entitled to judgment against the directors since the breach of trust was expressly induced by the directors, they had to bear personal liability for that breach: see *Air Canada v. M & L Travel Agency Ltd.* (1991), 2 O.R. (3d) 184, 77 D.L.R. (4th) 536 (C.A.); leave to appeal to S.C.C. granted (1991), 85 D.L.R. (4th) xiii (note). See also *China Software Corp. v. Leimbigler* (1989), 27 C.P.R. (3d) 215 (B.C. S.C.).

Cases held to involve abuse of the fiduciary position of directors

It is incumbent upon a director to assume no part which would be inconsistent with a proper, free and independent discharge of his duties in that respect. No one occupying a fiduciary relationship can be permitted to do an act on his own personal behalf which might or could be construed to be inconsistent with the fiduciary character which he held at the time: *Re Iron Clay Brick Manufacturing Co.* (1889), 19 O.R. 113; *Natural Sodium Products Ltd. v. Holland*, [1946] 1 W.W.R. 605. So where a director was to be paid a commission of 12 1/2 per cent on sales of the corporation's shares, and made an arrangement with another person whereby the latter was to sell on a 5 per cent commission, which was held to be a fair commission, the director was held liable to account to the corporation for the difference: *Stickney v. Buckel* (1905), 6 O.W.R. 751.

Where a director had irregularly and illegally caused shares (which he subsequently sold) to be issued to himself, it was held that in equity they remained the property of the corporation and that the director was bound to account to the corporation and pay the amount he received therefor and, the shares having been sold for less than par, that he was bound to pay such further sum as was necessary to refund the corporation's capital to the extent to which he had depleted it: *McGuire & Forester Ltd. v. Cadzow*, [1933] 1 D.L.R. 192 (Alta. C.A.).

Where directors of a corporation, in the course of their duties as such in negotiating with the guarantor of bonds, personally acquired from the guarantor the controlling shares of the corporation at no cost and a mortgage on the corporation's property at less than face value, it was held that this was a breach of their fiduciary duty, that they must surrender the shares to the corporation and that the mortgage must be treated as security only for the amount they had paid with interest at 5 per cent per annum: *Zwicker v. Stanbury*, [1953] 2 S.C.R. 438.

Where the directors of the plaintiff corporation, pursuant to a scheme to defraud that corporation, issued shares to the defendant corporation in which they were interested, the court declared the issuance fraudulent and void, directed the surrender and cancellation of the outstanding share certificates which had not been transferred by the defendant to third parties, and directed the removal of the defendant's name from the register. The directors of the plaintiff corporation were held liable to that corporation for the value of the shares transferred by the defendant, the value being fixed at par less the discount which the issuing corporation's letters patent allowed it to pay, notwithstanding that the market value of the shares was less than that amount. The defendants were allowed to get in and return to the corporation for cancellation as many of these shares as they could, credit being given at par less the discount: *Signal Hill Oils Co. v. London Oil Securities*, [1927] 3 D.L.R. 984 (Alta. T.D.).

Where a majority of the directors of a parent corporation and of a subsidiary corporation (of which there were minority shareholders) were common to the two corporations, the common directors were substantial shareholders of the parent corporation but had only a nominal share interest in the subsidiary, and certain transactions purported to be authorized by the two boards were carried out which were to the advantage of the parent corporation and to the detriment of the subsidiary, the court set such transactions aside: *Gray v. Yellowknife Gold Mines Ltd.* (No. 1), [1947] O.R. 928 (C.A.) (shares of a third corporation acquired by the parent corporation from the subsidiary declared to be the property of the subsidiary and ordered to be transferred to it); and *Gray v. Yellowknife Gold Mines Ltd.* (No. 2), [1947] O.R. 994 (C.A.) (option granted by subsidiary on its treasury shares to parent corporation declared invalid and issuance of shares to parent corporation under such option set aside).

Passive conduct on the part of a director may amount to a breach of his duty: *Scottish Co-operative Wholesale Society Ltd. v. Meyer*, [1959] A.C. 324. In that case three of the five directors of a subsidiary corporation were also directors of the parent corporation and though they were aware of the parent's policy to destroy the subsidiary by diverting business from the subsidiary to the parent, they did not advise their two co-directors and did nothing to save the subsidiary. The House of Lords held that this inaction on the part of the three directors amounted to a breach of their duties.

Directors are not at liberty to sacrifice the interests of the corporation and, while ostensibly acting for the latter, divert in their own favour business which would properly belong to the corporation they represent. Thus, where directors, while still retaining their position as such, and still actually acting as managers of the corporation, negotiated for a contract on their own behalf in exactly the same manner as they had always acted for the corporation, and caused such contract to be made and to be taken over by a new corporation formed by them, and thereafter used their voting power as shareholders to ratify and approve what was done and to release all claims against themselves as directors, it was held that the directors must be regarded as holding the benefit of such contract on behalf of the corporation, and that the transaction could not be regularized by resolutions of the shareholders controlled by votes of the directors: *Cook v. Deeks*, [1916] 1 A.C. 554 (P.C.), and see *Leavens v. Great West Permanent Loan Co.* (No. 2), [1927] 3 W.W.R. 486; *Kendall v. Webster* (1910), 15 B.C.R. 268 (C.A.).

Directors may stand in a fiduciary relationship as regards future subscribers for shares where new shareholders are brought into the corporation: *In re Hess*

Manufacturing Co. (1894), 23 S.C.R. 644. In such cases where a director has committed a breach of his fiduciary obligations by failure to make proper disclosure in respect of a contract entered into with the corporation, future subscribers will not be bound: *Denman v. Clover Bar Coal Co.* (1913), 48 S.C.R. 318. See also *Crawford v. Bathurst Land & Development Co.* (1916), 37 O.L.R. 611; affd (1918), 42 O.L.R. 256; revd (*sub nom.* Fullerton v. Crawford) (1919), 59 S.C.R. 314.

Where a managing director had abused his powers of management for his private advantage, he was liable to indemnify the corporation in respect of a liability imposed upon it by such abuse of his powers: *Eastern Shipping Co. v. Quah Beng Kee*, [1924] A.C. 177 (P.C.). See also *Regal (Hastings) Ltd. v. Gulliver*, [1942] 1 All E.R. 378 (H.L.).

Where the manager of a corporation used its moneys to purchase property which he turned over to another corporation, of which he was also managing director, the first corporation was held entitled to a lien on the property: *Northern Creameries Ltd. v. Rossington Produce Co.* (1922), 66 D.L.R. 548 (Alta. C.A.).

Cases held not to involve abuse of the fiduciary position of directors

Prima facie a director may act as a director of a rival corporation: *London & Mashonaland Exploration Co. v. New Mashonaland Exploration Co.*, [1891] W.N. 165 approved in *Bell v. Lever Bros. Ltd.*, [1932] A.C. 161 at 195 (H.L.). A director, to whom shares of a subsidiary corporation have been transferred by the parent corporation in order to qualify him, is not accountable to the parent corporation for remuneration received as a director of the subsidiary corporation: *In re Dover Coalfield Extension Ltd.*, [1908] 1 Ch. 65 (C.A.).

Where, however, there are interlocking directorates and a person is a director of two corporations which enter into transactions with one another, such person owes a fiduciary duty to each of them; *Gray v. Yellowknife Gold Mines Ltd.* (No. 1), [1947] O.R. 928 (C.A.); *Gray v. Yellowknife Gold Mines Ltd.* (No. 2), [1947] O.R. 994 (C.A.).

In the absence of agreement there is no duty or obligation cast on the directors to pledge their own credit for the benefit of the corporation: *Christopher v. Noxon; Re Ingersoll Gas Co.* (1884), 4 O.R. 672 at 682.

If directors *bona fide* and reasonably believe that they are acting in the corporation's interest, they are not liable for breach of trust because in so acting they are also pursuing their own interest: *Hirsche v. Sims*, [1894] A.C. 654 at 660 (P.C.); *Lagunas Nitrate Co. v. Lagunas Syndicate*, [1899] 2 Ch. 392 (C.A.).

Where, with full knowledge that an individual was the majority shareholder and a director of two other corporations, a corporation appointed that individual as its managing director and entered into an arrangement with the two other corporations which was successful for all concerned with the result that the managing director derived a profit therefrom by reason of his interest in the other two corporations, the British Columbia Court of Appeal held that he was not accountable for such profit; the corporation which appointed him as managing director had no right to demand that he would favour its interests at the expense of the other corporations and could only demand that he act within the scope of his authority under the arrangement (which he did) and fairly towards both sides in all matters involving a conflict of interest: *Atkins & Durbrow Ltd. v. Bell* (1957), 10 D.L.R. (2d) 484 (B.C. C.A.). See also *Can. Plastic Containers Ltd. v. Farkas* (1973), 12 C.P.R. (2d) 77 (Ont.); *Misener v. H.L. Misener & Son Ltd.* (1977), 21 N.S.R. (2d) 92, 77 D.L.R. (3rd) 428 (Ont. C.A.); *Molchan v. Omega Oil & Gas Ltd.* (1985), 40 Alta. L.R. (2d) 251, [1986] 1 W.W.R. 398 (Alta. C.A.), (affd on other grounds [1988] 3 W.W.R. 1, 57 Alta. L.R. (2d) 193 (S.C.C.); application for rehearing denied (1988), 49 D.L.R. (4th) vii (note) (S.C.C.); *Martin v. Columbia Metals Corp. Ltd* (1980), 12 B.L.R. 72 (Ont. H.C.). See also *Abbey Glen Property Corp. v. Stumborg* (1981), 37 A.R. 212 (Q.B.) where directors who had been ordered to account for profits due to a breach of fiduciary duty were entitled to deduct certain fees for management. See also *Victorov v. Davison* (1988), 20 C.P.R. (3d) 481 (Ont. H.C.); *Peso Silver Mines Ltd. v. Cropper*, [1966] S.C.R. 673 (S.C.C.).

Secret profits and commissions

Directors are trustees (in the strictest sense) for the corporation of secret profits and will be bound to return them even though the corporation is no worse off as a result of such profits having been made: *Ruethel Mining Co. v. Thorpe* (1907), 9 O.W.R. 942; affd (1907), 10 O.W.R. 222.

It is a breach of the fiduciary relationship for the directors to make a secret profit at the expense of the shareholders: *Gadsden v. Bennetto* (1913), 9 D.L.R. 719 (Man. C.A.); *Crawford v. Bathurst Land & Development Co.* (1916), 37 O.L.R. 611, (1918), 42 O.L.R. 256; but see the same case (*sub nom. Fullerton v. Crawford*) (1919), 59 S.C.R. 314, where the judgment below was reversed by a majority of the Supreme Court of Canada. See also *Zwicker v. Stanbury*, [1953] 2 S.C.R. 438, referred to above under the heading "Cases held to involve abuse of the fiduciary position of directors" in this chapter.

There are a considerable number of cases dealing with the question of secret profits: see *L. A. Brown Ltd. v. Brown* (1969), 1 N.B.R. (2d) 836 (C.A.) where a trustee of a bankrupt corporation successfully sued a director who had purchased land as an agent for the corporation and took title in his own name. He was held liable for the profit on resale of the land to the corporation. In this particular case the shareholder held 97 of 100 issued shares of the capital of the corporation and was its president and director and one of three shareholders; where the profit was alleged to represent payment for work done and there was no substantiating evidence, the trustee in bankruptcy was held entitled to recover amounts paid. See also *Brown v. Gentleman*, [1971] S.C.R. 501, 15 C.B.R. (N.S.) 274. Where a director of a corporation made unauthorized loans to two other corporations under his control and one of those corporations had subscribed for shares of another corporation which were partly paid, a call was made on the shares and the shares were forfeited on failure to pay the call. The court held that the shares were properly forfeited but the director should not be allowed to profit from the breach of trust by setting up the separate identities of himself and his corporations as a shield: *Fern Brand Waxes Ltd. v. Pearl*, [1972] 3 O.R. 829, 29 D.L.R. (3rd) 662 (C.A.). See also *Abbey Glen*

Property Corp. v. Stumborg, [1978] 4 W.W.R. 28, 4 B.L.R. 113 (Alta C.A.); *Sigurdson v. Langridge* (1977), 26 C.B.R. (N.S.) 44, 9 A.R. 72 (Alta. T.D.); *Redekop v. Robco Construction Ltd.* (1978), 7 B.C.L.R. 268, 89 D.L.R. (3d) 507 (B.C. S.C.); *Re Weber Feeds Ltd. (Trustee) v. Weber* (1979), 30 C.B.R. (N.S.) 97 (Ont. C.A.); revg (1978), 3 B.L.R. 107; *MacMillan Bloedel Ltd. v. Binstead* (1983), 22 B.L.R. 255, 14 E.T.R. 269 (B.C. S.C.); *Bottoms v. Brent Petroleum Industries Ltd.* (1984), 17 E.T.R. 48 (B.C. S.C.); *Kremlin Canada Inc. v. Turner* (March 1, 1990), Doc. No. CA 26189 (Ont. C.A.); leave to appeal to S.C.C. refused (*sub nom.* Turner v. Kremlin Canada Inc.) (1990), 44 O.A.C. 80 (note), 126 N.R. 158 (note) (S.C.C.); *Jiffy People Sales (1966) Ltd. v. Eliason* (1975), 58 D.L.R. (3d) 439, 21 C.P.R. (2d) 209 (B.C. S.C.).

Any profits accruing from a wrongful use by directors of the corporation's property for their own benefit must be accounted for by them to the corporation: *Pure Canadian Silver Black Fox Co. v. Morrison* (1915), 24 D.L.R. 915.

In *Regal (Hastings) Ltd. v. Gulliver*, [1942] 1 All E.R. 378 (H.L.) directors had subscribed for shares in a subsidiary corporation at par which they sold shortly afterwards at a profit. The directors obtained the shares by reason only of the fact that they were directors of the parent corporation and that they were in a position to utilize their knowledge acquired as such. On the other hand, the parent corporation was not in a position to subscribe for the shares and the directors in taking up the shares acted in good faith, intending to act in the interests of the parent corporation. The directors were held to be liable by reason of their fiduciary relationship to the parent corporation to account for the profit realized upon the resale of the shares.

Where a director has wrongfully diverted the corporation's funds to his own use, the corporation is entitled, notwithstanding the consent of his co-directors, to claim the funds and interest thereon: *Rogers Hardware v. Rogers* (1913), 10 D.L.R. 541; but apparently not compound interest: *Saskatchewan Land & Homestead Co. v. Moore* (1915), 7 O.W.N. 684; revd in part (1915), 8 O.W.N. 525.

Where a director is held liable to account, the corporation has the option of claiming the property itself, or its highest value whilst held by the director, and the latter is not released by proof that he paid for the property a sum which, at the time he bought it, was its then full market value: *Eden v. Ridsdales Railway Lamp & Lighting Co.* (1889), 23 Q.B.D. 368 (C.A.); *Re Iron Clay Brick Manufacturing Co.* (1889), 19 O.R. 113, 121. However, when the directors have not been guilty of moral fraud, the rule is not to be pressed too harshly; thus, where directors had improperly allotted shares to themselves at an undervalue, they were held liable to account for the profits they had made on the shares which they sold, but, as to the shares which they retained, the proper measure of damages was not the highest value at which small lots of shares had been sold, but the market value as of the date of allotment: *Shaw v. Holland*, [1900] 2 Ch. 305 (C.A.).

When a director is held liable to account and the profit takes the form of paid-up shares in the corporation, insofar as they have not passed into the hands of innocent purchasers for value, the certificates may be ordered to be cancelled: *Proprietary Mines Ltd. v. MacKay*, [1939] O.R. 461 (C.A.); affd (*sub nom.* MacKay v. Proprietary Mines Ltd.) [1941] 1 D.L.R. 240 (S.C.C.). In the same case, regarding shares of another corporation which it was held that the director had acquired on behalf of the corporation, the director was ordered to transfer the same to the corporation or account for them; and as to shares in the corporation for which the director was ordered to account in excess of those represented by certificates ordered to be cancelled, a reference was directed to the Master to inquire and report the amounts properly payable by the director in respect thereof. As to the basis of determining the value of shares not returned to the corporation in respect of which a director has been ordered to account, see *Crown Reserve Consolidated Mines Ltd. v. MacKay*, [1941] 3 D.L.R. 461 (Ont. C.A.).

Where a director was ordered to pay damages to the corporation for having caused it to sell certain assets to another corporation at an undervalue, thereby making a profit, no fraud or negligence necessarily being involved, the measure of damages was held to be the amount by which the director benefited in the transaction: *Crown Reserve Consolidated Mines Ltd. v. Mackay, supra.*

In an action to make directors account for profits, the corporation should be made a party to the proceedings: *Meyers v. Cain* (1905), 6 O.W.R. 834.

A director cannot plead the Statute of Limitations where the claim is for fraudulent breach of trust or is to recover trust property or the proceeds: *Saskatchewan Land Co. v. Moore* (1914), 5 O.W.N. 183; vard (1914), 6 O.W.N. 100. However, where the claim against directors is in respect of moneys received as a bribe which was never reduced into possession as the property of the corporation, the directors are constructive trustees only and the claim will be barred by the Statute of Limitations: *Clarkson v. Davies*, [1923] A.C. 100 at 110 (P.C.), following *Taylor v. Davies*, [1920] A.C. 636.

Where strangers actively participate with a director in conduct which constitutes a breach of the director's fiduciary obligations to a corporation, they may be liable as constructive trustees to account to the corporation for their own-as well as the director's-profits: *Canada Safeway Ltd. v. Thompson*, [1951] 3 D.L.R. 295 (B.C. S.C.). In that case the president and managing director of the plaintiff corporation bought shares of another corporation in conjunction with the defendants. The shares were subsequently sold at a profit to the plaintiff corporation and in an action for an accounting against the defendants, the court held that they, having fraudulently assisted in the concealment of the director's breaches of his duty, had become constructive trustees and were liable to account to the plaintiff for the profits they had made on the shares and additionally were jointly and severally liable to the plaintiff for the profit the director had made on the sale.

Termination of fiduciary relationship

Upon the appointment of a liquidator for a corporation which is being wound up under the *Winding-up Act*, the fiduciary relationship between the directors and the corporation is at an end unless their powers as directors have been continued as provided by s. 31 of that Act: *Chatham National Bank v. McKeen*

(1895), 24 S.C.R. 348 (S.C.C.). See also *Holmested v. Annable* (1914), 18 D.L.R. 3; *Cook v. Deeks*, [1916] 1 A.C. 554 at 559 (P.C.).

A director is not precluded from purchasing the corporation's property after the fiduciary relationship has come to an end: *Chatham National Bank v. McKeen*, *supra*. Thus, where the corporation was in liquidation and had practically refused an extension of a lease, the directors were held entitled to obtain an extension personally and for their own benefit: *Boston Shoe Co. v. Frank* (1915), 48 Que. S.C. 66 (Que. C.A.). Possibly the same result follows on the appointment of a receiver and manager in a bondholders' action: *Parsons v. Sovereign Bank of Canada*, [1913] A.C. 160 at 166 (P.C.).

Contracts of directors with the corporation

This topic is dealt with under the following subheadings: General rule; Cases within the rule; Cases outside the rule; Sanction of contracts by shareholders; Statutory provisions affecting rule; Provisions of by-laws or articles; Director voting on contract; Disclosure; Sales by the directors to the corporation; Action to set aside contract or to compel accounting.

General rule

The right of a director to contract with the corporation under the general law is of the narrowest description. Such disability is due to the fiduciary character of the relationship of a director to the corporation. The general rule was stated in *North-West Transportation Co. v. Beatty* (1887), 12 App. Cas. 589 at 593 (P.C.), as follows:

> On the other hand, a director of a company is precluded from dealing, on behalf of the company, with himself, and from entering into engagements in which he has a personal interest conflicting, or which possibly may conflict, with the interests of those whom he is bound by fiduciary duty to protect; and this rule is as applicable to the case of one of several directors as to a managing or sole director.

Some years earlier in *Aberdeen Railway v. Blaikie Bros.* (1854), 1 Macq. H.L. 461 it was laid down by Lord Cranworth L.C. that, as directors have duties of a fiduciary nature towards their principal (the corporation) which they are bound to discharge, they cannot be allowed to enter into engagements in which they have or can have a personal interest, conflicting or which possibly may conflict with the interest of those whom they are bound to protect, and he added "So strictly is this principle adhered to that no question is allowed to be raised as to the fairness or unfairness of a contract so entered into".

If the rule is infringed, the contract is voidable at the option of the corporation and the director is liable to account for any profits: *Transvaal Lands Co. v. New Belgium (Transvaal) Land & Development Co.*, [1914] 2 Ch. 488 (C.A.).

Cases within the rule

Where there is no by-law, article, charter provision or statutory provision authorizing the directors to enter into contracts with the corporation no question of the fairness or unfairness of the contract can arise, and unless the contract is sanctioned by the shareholders the profit arising therefrom can be recovered: *In re Cardiff Preserved Coal Co.* (1862), 32 L.J. Ch. 154; *Imperial Mercantile Credit Assn. v. Coleman* (1871), L.R. 6 Ch. App. 558 at 567; *Parker v. McKenna* (1874), L.R. 10 Ch. App. 96; *Roray v. Howe Sound* (1915), 22 D.L.R. 855 (B.C. C.A.); *Huggard v. Prudential Life Insurance Co.*, [1924] 1 W.W.R. 642 (Man. C.A.) (directors not entitled to overriding commission on sale of shares in absence of express provision by shareholders).

It is immaterial that the terms of the contract are the best that could be obtained: *Madden v. Dimond* (1905), 12 B.C.R. 80 (C.A.); or "whether the profit would or should otherwise have gone to the plaintiff, or whether the profiteer was under a duty to obtain the source of the profit for the plaintiff, or whether he took a risk or acted as he did for the benefit of the plaintiff, or whether the plaintiff has in fact been damaged or benefited by his action," per Lord Russell of Killowen in *Regal (Hastings) Ltd. v. Gulliver*, [1942] 1 All E.R. 378 (H.L.), at 386.

The duty extends to disclosure of an interest in property on the security of which the corporation is proposing to make a loan to an outsider: *Canadian Guaranty Trust v. Young*, [1933] 1 D.L.R. 256 (Man. C.A.).

A director will be held to be contracting with the corporation within the meaning of the rule where he is a shareholder in another corporation, whether beneficially or as a trustee, and without regard to the quantum of his holdings: *Transvaal Lands Co. v. New Belgium (Transvaal) Land & Development Co.*, [1914] 2 Ch. 488 (C.A.). If the director owns substantially all the shares of a corporation which he makes use of as vendor of assets to the corporation of which he is a director, he will be identified as vendor with the vendor corporation: *Patton v. Yukon Consolidated Gold Corp.*, [1934] O.W.N. 321 (C.A.).

The rule is also applicable where a person is a director of two corporations which enter into transactions with each other, as such person has fiduciary duties to both corporations: *Gray v. Yellowknife Gold Mines Ltd. (No. 1)*, [1947] O.R. 928 (C.A.); and *Gray v. Yellowknife Gold Mines Ltd. (No. 2)*, [1947] O.R. 994 (C.A.).

If the director has been instructed to sell, as advantageously as possible, securities belonging to the corporation and he sells to a corporation in which he has an interest without disclosing the fact, he is accountable for the profits made by such corporation on the re-sale of the securities less the amount of commission which would have been payable at the ordinary rates of brokerage: *Re International Equities Ltd.; Ex parte Bulmer*, [1943] 4 D.L.R. 635 and 806. On the other hand, where a director had not contracted with the corporation directly, but at the instance of the other members of the board agreed to find subscribers for shares in a subsidiary, and such subscribers were corporations in which the director had a minority interest as a shareholder, the director was exonerated from liability to account for profits made by such corporations on the re-sale of the shares, no part of such profits having been distributed or received by him: *Regal (Hastings) Ltd. v. Gulliver*, [1942] 1 All E.R. 378 (H.L.), at 382, 390.

In *Atkins & Durbrow Ltd. v. Bell* (1957), 10 D.L.R. (2d) 484 (B.C. C.A.),

D corporation, with full knowledge that B was the majority shareholder and a director of two other corporations, appointed B its managing director and entered into an arrangement with the two other corporations which was successful for all concerned with the result that B derived a profit therefrom by reason of his interest in the other two corporations. In an action brought by D corporation against B for breach of trust, the British Columbia Court of Appeal held that B was not liable and that D corporation had no right to demand that he would favour its interests at the expense of the other two corporations and could only demand that he act within the scope of his authority under the arrangement (which he did) and fairly towards both sides in all matters involving a conflict of interest.

The rule applies in the case of a purchase by a director or by a syndicate in which the director is interested as in the case of other contracts between the director and the corporation: *Roxborough Gardens of Hamilton Ltd. v. Davis* (1920), 46 O.L.R. 615 (C.A.); *Ferguson v. Wallbridge*, [1935] 3 D.L.R. 66 at 74 (P.C.).

The rule also applies in the case of a director who acts as the corporation's solicitor, in respect of a claim for legal services: *Cradock v. Piper* (1850), 1 Macn. & G. 664; *Re Corsellis* (1887), 34 Ch. D. 675 (C.A.); *Re Barber* (1887), 34 Ch. D. 77; *Re Mimico Sewer Pipe Co.* (1895), 26 O.R. 289; *Huggard v. Prudential Life Insurance Co.*, [1924] 1 W.W.R. 642 (Man. C.A.). Thus, in *Cape Breton Cold Storage Co. Ltd. v. Rowlings*, [1929] S.C.R. 505, a director and officer of the corporation acted as solicitor, although not formally appointed as such, in a number of matters and was consulted by his fellow directors, who were aware of his so acting, and by the officers of the corporation. He was paid substantial amounts on account of his legal services and sued on an account for legal services rendered. It was held that he could not succeed as he was seeking to recover for services rendered under a contract which, by the principle above referred to, was incapable of being enforced. See, however, *Boland v. Irvin Porcupine Gold Mines Ltd.*, [1948] O.W.N. 181; affd [1948] O.W.N. 483 where the principle laid down in *Cape Breton Cold Storage Co. Ltd. v. Rowlings, supra*, was held not to be applicable in the case of an Ontario corporation, and the principle (payment to a director at the ordinary market price for a service rendered by him otherwise than *qua* director may be made without a by-law) laid down in *Fullerton v. Crawford* (1919), 59 S.C.R. 314 at 346-47, was applied.

The issuing of debentures to the corporation's bankers as security for an overdraft that has been personally guaranteed by the directors is an arrangement in which directors are interested within the meaning of the common form of article permitting contracts, arrangements or dealings with the corporation but prohibiting voting thereon if the director is interested: *Victors Ltd. (in liquidation) v. Lingard*, [1927] 1 Ch. 323. It is not unusual to make express provision for such transactions in the by-laws and s. 120(5)(a) of the federal Act now expressly protects such transactions.

In *Export Brewing & Malting Co. v. Dominion Bank*, [1937] 3 D.L.R. 513 (P.C.), the Judicial Committee of the Privy Council held that directors, who were the principal stockholders in the corporation, had no power without a resolution of the stockholders to enter into an agreement pledging the assets of the corporation as security for their personal obligations. The rule was also applied in *Abana Mines v. Wall* (1935), 58 Que. K.B. 352 (Que. C.A.) where the president of the corporation had an undisclosed personal interest in a promissory note issued by the corporation.

Cases outside the rule

No question of conflict of interest arises where a director subscribes for bonds or shares of the corporation on the same terms as the public: *Campbell's Case* (1876), 4 Ch. D. 470; and the application of the general rule may be excluded, as, for example, in the case of the employment of a director as manager where the appointment was more in the interests of the corporation than the appointment of an outsider: *Van Hummel v. International Guarantee Co.* (1913), 10 D.L.R. 306 at 311. Moreover, as indicated below, the operation of the rule may be excluded or qualified by applicable provisions of the governing statute, by-laws or articles and a contract between a director and the corporation, otherwise voidable, may be ratified by the shareholders.

Sanction of contracts by shareholders

A general meeting of the shareholders can sanction a contract in which a director is interested, in which event the director will be protected: *Dunne v. English* (1871), L.R. 18 Eq. 524; *Morison v. Thompson* (1874), L.R. 9 Q.B. 480; *N.W. Transportation Co. v. Beatty* (1887), 12 App. Cas. 589; *Grant v. United Kingdom Switchback Railway* (1889), 40 Ch. D. 135 (C.A.); *Eden v. Ridsdales Railway Lamp & Lighting Co.* (1889), 23 Q.B.D. 368 (C.A.); *A.G. Can. v. Standard Trust Co.*, [1911] A.C. 498 (P.C.); *Van Hummell v. International Guarantee Co.* (1913), 10 D.L.R. 306; *Armstrong Trading Co. v. Grenan* (1921) 59 D.L.R. 356 (Man. C.A.); *Huggard v. Prudential Life Insurance Co., supra*; *Regal (Hastings) Ltd. v. Gulliver*, [1942] 1 All E.R. 378 at 389 (H.L.). In *Canada Safeway Ltd v. Thompson*, [1951] 3 D.L.R. 295 at 321, Manson J. expressed the view that nothing less than a unanimous resolution of the shareholders after full disclosure would enable a director to avoid accountability for profits. See *Earle v. Burland* (1900), 27 O.A.R. 540 at 561 per Moss J.A. See further the qualification in the following paragraph.

A contract in which a director is interested may be adopted by the corporation provided that its adoption is not brought about by unfair or improper means, and is not illegal or fraudulent or oppressive towards those shareholders who oppose it: *North-West Transportation Co. v. Beatty* (1887), 12 App. Cas. 589. In such a case a director has a perfect right to acquire sufficient shares to give him a majority, and to exercise his voting power in such a manner as to secure election of directors who will support the transaction and to ratify the proceedings at a shareholders' meeting: ibid. See also *Christopher v. Noxon* (1884), 4 O.R. 672. *Quaere* whether a majority of the contributories in a winding-up can ratify a contract which is invalid by reason of interested directors having voted thereon: *Ferguson v. Wallbridge*, [1935] 3 D.L.R. 66 at 80 (P.C.).

The notice of meeting should set out particulars of the directors' interest:

Kaye v. Croydon Tramways Co., [1898] 1 Ch. 358 (C.A.); *Tiessen v. Henderson*, [1899] 1 Ch. 861; *Normandy v. Ind, Coope & Co.*, [1908] 1 Ch. 84; *McDougall v. Black Lake Asbestos & Chrome Co.* (1920), 47 O.L.R. 328 at 334; *Irvin v. Irvin Porcupine Gold Mines Ltd. & Mulliette*, [1940] O.W.N. 315.

Where directors, by reason of being interested, are prohibited by the articles from voting as directors, such prohibition will not prevent them from voting as shareholders; and where the directors had power under the articles to fix their own salaries but were unable, by reason of being interested, or were unwilling to exercise such power, the corporation in general meeting can exercise such power: *Great Western Garment Co. v. M.N.R.*, [1948] 1 D.L.R. 225 and cases cited at p. 231.

If the contract is prohibited by statute, the prohibition renders the contract void even though a penalty is also imposed: *Montreal Trust Co. v. Canadian National Railway*, [1939] A.C. 613 (P.C.) (s. 121 of the *Railway Act*, R.S.C. 1927, c. 170).

Statutory provisions affecting rule

Section 120 provides that a director or officer of a corporation who is a party to a material contract or proposed material contract with the corporation or is a director or officer of or who has a material interest in any person who is a party to a material contract or proposed material contract with the corporation is to disclose in writing to the corporation or to request to have entered in the minutes of directors' meetings the nature and extent of his interest. This disclosure in the case of a director is to be made at a meeting at which a proposed contract is first considered or at the first meeting after he becomes so interested or after he becomes a director. In the case of an officer who is not a director, the disclosure is to be made forthwith after he becomes aware that the contract or proposed contract is to be considered or has been considered at a meeting of the directors or forthwith after he becomes interested or becomes an officer as the case may be. If the material contract or proposed material contract is one that in the ordinary course of the corporation's business would not require approval by the directors or shareholders, a director or officer is to disclose in writing to the corporation or request to have entered into the minutes of meetings of directors the nature and extent of his interest forthwith after he becomes aware of the contract or proposed contract.

An interested director is not to vote on any resolution to approve the contract unless it is: (1) an arrangement by way of security for money lent or obligations undertaken by him for the benefit of the corporation or an affiliate; (2) one relating to his remuneration as a director, officer, employee or agent of the corporation or an affiliate; (3) for an indemnity or insurance pursuant to s. 124 relating to directors' indemnities; or (4) a contract with an affiliate (s. 120(5)).

Section 120(6) provides that a general notice to the directors that the person concerned is a director or officer or has a material interest in a person and is to be regarded as interested in a contract made with that person is a sufficient declaration of interest in relation to any contract so made. Section 120(7) provides that a material contract between a corporation and one or more of its directors or officers or between a corporation and another person of which a director or officer of the corporation is a director of officer or in which he has a material interest is neither void or voidable by reason only of that relationship or by reason only that a director with an interest in the contract was present at or is counted to determine the presence of a quorum at a meeting of directors or a committee of directors that authorized the contract, if the director or officer disclosed his interest in accordance with the provisions of s. 120 and the contract was approved by the directors or the shareholders and was reasonable and fair to the corporation at the time it was approved.

It will be obvious that there may be considerable difficulty in determining whether a contract is reasonable and fair. Where there is failure to disclose an interest in the material contract in accordance with the provisions of s. 120, s. 120(8) provides that a court may, on the application of a corporation or a shareholder, set aside the contract on such terms as it thinks fit.

As to what is involved in a declaration of interest of the sort called for in the section, see the notes under the heading "Disclosure" in this chapter.

A director who is interested in a contract or proposed contract is prohibited from voting in respect thereof, subject to the exceptions specified in s. 120(5). Paragraph (a) of that subsection excepts contracts to give directors security for advances or by way of indemnity. See *In re Cleadon Trust Ltd.*, [1939] 1 Ch. 286 at 299 (C.A.), (similar provisions of corporation's articles considered).

Since the enactment of a statutory provision it is submitted that a corporation cannot by the provisions of its by-laws override the requirements as to disclosure contained in the statute. See *Gray v. Yellowknife Gold Mines Ltd.* (No. 1), [1947] O.R. 928 at 988 (C.A.). The decisions indicate that it was possible in the articles of association to override the rule applicable under the common law. See *Imperial Mercantile Credit Assn v. Coleman* (1871), L.R. 6 Ch. App. 558 at 568, 570; *Costa Rica Ry. v. Forwood*, [1900] 1 Ch. 756, [1901] 1 Ch. 746, 757, 758; *Transvaal Lands Co. v. New Belgium (Transvaal) Land & Development Co.*, [1914] 2 Ch. 488 at 504 (C.A.). As to the distinction between articles of association and by-laws in this regard see *Gray v. Yellowknife Gold Mines Ltd.* (No. 1), *supra*, at 988.

The corporation may be estopped from claiming under the section to set aside a transaction with a director: *Beaver Dam Mining Co. v. Larson* (1927), 32 O.W.N. 143 at 145; affd (1927), 33 O.W.N. 19 (C.A.).

Provisions of by-laws or articles

In the absence of such statutory provisions as the above, the by-laws or articles commonly either expressly authorize directors to enter into contracts with the corporation subject to their making full disclosure of their interest and refraining from voting, or confer an implied authorization by providing that such directors shall not vacate their office by reason of being interested in contracts with the corporation provided they make full disclosure and refrain from voting. See *Costa Rica Ry. Co. Ltd. v. Forwood*, [1900] 1 Ch. 756, [1901] 1 Ch. 746. As to what constitutes compliance with the conditions of such a by-law or article, see *Imperial Mercantile Credit Assn. (Liquidators of) v. Coleman* (1873), L.R. 6 H.L. 189.

The onus lies on the director to show that he has complied with the conditions of such a by-law or article: *Gray v. New Augarita Porcupine Mines Ltd.*, [1952] 3 D.L.R. 1 at 14 (P.C.).

Unless it is expressly stated that the director is not disqualified from contracting with the corporation by reason of being a shareholder in another corporation, the general rule applies: *Transvaal Lands Co. v. New Belgium (Transvaal) Land & Development Co.*, [1914] 2 Ch. 488 (C.A.). If the provisions of the by-law authorizing the contract are not complied with, the contract is voidable as if no such by-law existed: ibid. However, if the contract has been ratified by the shareholders and the transaction is free from fraud it will stand, even though interested directors have voted as shareholders in favour of such ratification: *Ferguson v. Wallbridge*, [1934] 2 D.L.R. 270 (B.C. C.A.). On the appeal to the Judicial Committee of the Privy Council ([1935] 3 D.L.R. 66 at 80) which was dismissed on the ground that the action was not properly constituted, it was pointed out that there is a distinction between the powers of majorities of shareholders in a going concern and contributories in a winding-up to ratify a contract which is not binding on the corporation in the absence of ratification.

Except so far as authorized by the articles, by-laws or governing statute the board of directors cannot make a binding contract with any other corporation in which a member of the quorum of their board is interested. If the latter corporation has notice of the irregularity the former may obtain rescission of the transaction, even after completion, if rescission is still possible. If the agents of a purchasing corporation are also agents of a selling corporation, the former is fixed with notice of anything of which its purchasing agents had notice: *Transvaal Lands Co. v. New Belgium (Transvaal) Land & Development Co., supra*; *Roxborough Gardens of Hamilton v. Davis* (1920), 46 O.L.R. 615 (C.A.).

Where the articles of a corporation imposed the penalty of disqualification on directors contracting with the corporation at a profit, the consequences of an infraction of the article were held to be not only disqualification of the offending directors but the giving of a right of action to any shareholder for a declaration of such disqualification and an account of the moneys improperly received. Nor could such a contract be ratified by a majority of the shareholders as the matter was not merely one of internal management: *Theatre Amusement Co. v. Stone* (1915), 50 S.C.R. 32.

The usual form of by-law provides that any contract may be submitted for approval or ratification at any annual or general or special meeting of the shareholders called for the purpose and subject to the provisions of s. 120 such contract may be approved by a resolution passed by a majority of the votes cast at any such meeting and in such case shall be valid and binding upon the corporation and upon all the shareholders as though it had been approved, ratified and confirmed by every shareholder of the corporation. The by-law will also usually provide that (a) no director or officer is to be disqualified by his office from or vacate his office by reason of holding any office or place of profit under the corporation or under any body corporate in which the corporation shall be a shareholder or by reason of being otherwise in any way directly or indirectly interested in or contracting with the corporation and (b) no director or officer is liable to account to the corporation or any of its shareholders or creditors for any profit realized by or from any such contract or arrangement by reason of any fiduciary relationship. He is required to disclose the nature and extent of his interest as set out in the Act and is not to vote on the resolution but may be counted to determine the presence of a quorum at the meeting of directors where such a vote is being taken.

It will be observed that s. 120(7) provides that an agreement is neither void nor voidable by reason of a director or an officer of the corporation having an interest in the contract, if he disclosed his interest in accordance with the provisions of the Act and the contract was approved by the directors or shareholders and was reasonable and fair to the corporation at the time it was approved. It will be observed that opinions may defer as to whether a contract is reasonable and fair to a corporation at the time of approval and therefore the provisions as suggested in the by-laws are of crucial importance for the protection of directors. It is also suggested that so long as the provisions in the by-laws are in amplification of rather than a contradiction of the terms of the Act the terms of the by-law would govern.

Director voting on contract

Under the general principles of equity a director cannot vote in respect of a contract in which he is interested: *Wade v. Kendrick* (1905), 37 S.C.R. 32 at 53. As to the statutory provisions affecting this rule and whether a director interested in a contract can be counted towards making a quorum of the board for the purpose of the consideration of that contract, see the notes under the heading "Quorum" in this chapter.

It is not necessary in order to vitiate a contract or arrangement between a director and his corporation that the director should actually record his vote, where several directors are interested in similar contracts and by arrangement each votes in favour of the other's contract: *Thorpe v. Tisdale* (1909), 13 O.W.R. 1044 at 1049. Where a director of a corporation was only interested as attorney for a person who was not a director, he was disqualified from voting in respect of a transaction between such person and the corporation: *Re Clark, Shimmin v. Clark*, [1932] 3 D.L.R. 702 at 706 (B.C. C.A.).

If several directors are interested in what is in reality one transaction, a quorum cannot be obtained by splitting the resolution into parts and taking a vote on each part separately: *In re North Eastern Insurance Co.* [1919] 1 Ch. 198. See also *Zimmerman v. Andrew Motherwell of Canada Ltd. (Trustee of)* (1923), 54 O.L.R. 342; affd [1925] 3 D.L.R. 953 (P.C.) where on the facts the director was held not to be disqualified.

Disclosure

The expression "declare his interest" means that the director must declare the nature of his interest; the requirement is not satisfied by the mere declaration of the existence of an interest: *Liquidators of Imperial Mercantile Credit Assn v. Coleman* (1873), L.R. 6 H.L. 189 at 200.

There must be full disclosure by the director of his interest: *Costa Rica Ry. v. Forwood,* [1900] 1 Ch. 756; [1901] 1 Ch. 746 (C.A.). If there is full disclosure and assent by the corporation the director can retain his profit: *A.G. Can. v. Standard Trust Co.*, [1911] A.C. 498 (P.C.); *Bennett v. Havelock Electric Light & Power Co.* (1910), 21 O.L.R. 120; revd (1912), 25 O.L.R. 200 (C.A.).

There is no precise formula to be used by a director in disclosing his interest, the amount of detail required depending in each case upon the nature of the contract and the context in which it arises. It can rarely be sufficient for a director to say "I must remind you that I am interested" and nothing more, unless there is some special provision in a corporation's by-laws or articles that makes such a general warning sufficient. The declaration must inform his fellow directors fully, if this is material to their judgment, not only that he has an interest but what it is and how far it goes: *Gray v. New Augarita Porcupine Mines Ltd.*, [1952] 3 D.L.R. 1 at 14 (P.C.). In that case a director stood to gain a great deal by a settlement with the corporation, but only he had the means of knowing how much he would gain. The Judicial Committee of the Privy Council held that it was imperative that his disclosure fully inform his fellow directors of the real state of affairs and that having failed to do so, he was liable to account for all profit that he made by the settlement.

The duty to make full and complete disclosure is a fiduciary burden which cannot be discharged by resigning from the board on the understanding that the resignation is to be contemporaneous with the formal execution of the contract: *Denman v. Clover Bar Coal Co.* (1913), 48 S.C.R. 318 (S.C.C). Though the contract be declared not binding on the corporation the director may be awarded compensation on a *quantum meruit* basis for the services rendered the corporation on the faith of the contract set aside: ibid. The duty to disclose may extend not only to present but to future shareholders where it is intended to bring in new shareholders by issuing shares to the public: ibid. See also *Re Hess Manufacturing Co.* (1894), 23 S.C.R. 644.

Directors may lend money to the corporation and take security therefor and enforce payment as ordinary creditors, but such contracts must be made with the utmost good faith and are subject to the severest scrutiny: *Neelon v. Town of Thorold* (1891), 20 O.R. 86, (1894), 22 S.C.R. 390.

Where an interested director has made disclosure of his interest in a transaction and the directors have applied their minds to the facts, neither the interested director nor those who voted for the transaction are liable for loss sustained in the absence of fraud, negligence or improvidence in entering into the transaction: *Canadian Guaranty Trust Co. v. Young*, [1933] 1 D.L.R. 256 (Man. C.A.).

Sales by directors to the corporation

Where a director sells property, which is his own in law and in equity, to a corporation under a contract which is voidable under the rule dealt with above, the corporation can set the contract aside and the parties will be remitted to their original rights. However, if the corporation claims an interest in such property by reason of the transaction, it can do so only by affirming the contract which thus becomes validated. Moreover, if rescission is no longer possible the corporation cannot make the director take less than the price agreed: *Burland v. Earle*, [1902] A.C. 83 (P.C.); *Cook v. Deeks*, [1916] 1 A.C. 554 at 563; *Ruethel Mining Co. v. Thorpe* (1907), 9 O.W.R. 942; affd (1907), 10 O.W.R. 222. As to what conduct will amount to ratification, see *Gunning v. Lusby*, [1925] 1 D.L.R. 101 (P.C.).

Where the director is dealing with property which, though his own in law, was originally acquired by him under circumstances which made it in equity the property of the corporation, the corporation can in such a case treat the profit on the resale to it as acquired on its behalf and make the director account for it. This rule only applies when the fiduciary relationship exists at the time of the acquisition of the property by the director: *Jacobus Marler Estates, Ltd. v. Marler* (1916), 85 L.J.P.C. 167n.

Even where the corporation is not entitled to treat the property itself or the director's profit on the resale as acquired on the corporation's behalf, and is unable to restore the agent to his original position and has accordingly lost the right to repudiate the transaction, it may still have a remedy in damages against the director for negligently allowing the corporation to purchase the property at the price specified. The measure of damages is the difference between the market value and the price paid if the property has a market value; if it is specific property having no market value the measure of damages will be the corporation's loss in the whole transaction, and the court will fix a proper price between vendor and purchaser and estimate the damages on the basis of such price: *Jacobus Marler Estates Ltd. v. Marler, supra.*

Action to set aside contract or to compel accounting

An action to set aside a contract between a director and the corporation or to make a director account for profits should primarily be brought by the corporation itself, or at any rate the corporation should be a party: *Bennett v. Havelock Electric Light & Power Co.* (1910), 21 O.L.R. 120 at 125; *Meyers v. Cain* (1905), 6 O.W.R. 834; except where the persons against whom relief is claimed control the majority of the shares of the corporation and will not permit the action to be brought in the name of the corporation: *Burland v. Earle*, [1902] A.C. 83 at 93 (P.C.); and see *Shaw v. Union Trust Co.* (1915), 35 O.L.R. 146; *Cook v. Deeks*, [1916] 1 A.C. 554; *Houston v. Victoria Machinery Depot Ltd.*, [1924] 2 D.L.R. 657 (apparent that application to corporation to authorize suit would be futile); *Zwicker v. Stanbury*, [1953] 2 S.C.R. 438. A minority shareholder may be disqualified by his conduct from suing: *Gray v. Yellowknife Gold Mines Ltd.* (No. 1), [1947] O.R. 928 at 949 (C.A.), and cases cited. See further the notes to Chapter 15.

The court may, however, in a proper case, amend the pleadings or treat them as amended, so as to enable relief to be given where the corporation has not been made a party: *Allen v. Hyatt* (1914), 17 D.L.R. 7 (P.C.). See also *Johnston v. Carlin* (1914), 20 B.C.R. 520 (C.A.) where the court was equally divided on the question whether it was necessary for a shareholder to make a formal request to the corporation before he brought an action in his own name; *Rumford v. Hinton* (1922), 52 O.L.R. 47 (C.A.) where it was held that the plaintiff had no status *qua* shareholder to maintain a class action; and *Gunning v. Lusby*, [1925] 1 D.L.R. 101 (P.C.) where it held that plaintiffs in a representative action cannot sue on behalf of persons who object to being represented by them.

An outsider has no status to attack a sale by the corporation to directors which would be effective if approved by all the shareholders: *Grammas v. Kensington Cafe Ltd.*, [1919] 3 W.W.R. 301 (Man. K.B.).

See also the discussion in Chapter 16.

Powers conferred on directors by the act

In addition to the general authority implied by s. 102(1), which provides that the business and affairs of the corporation shall be managed by the board, s. 103(1) of the Act gives to the directors the power by resolution, to make, amend, or repeal any by-laws that regulate the business or affairs of the corporation. Questions relating to the internal management of a corporation are governed by the law of the corporate domicile: *National Trust Co. v. Ebro Irrigation & Power Co.*, [1954] O.R. 463 (H.C).

The directors can do anything that the corporation can do, and if the question arises whether a particular transaction is within the powers of the directors, it is simply necessary to examine the statute, articles and by-laws to see if there is an express provision requiring the authority of a general meeting of the shareholders. If there is not, the directors will have ample power: *Re Patent File Co.* (1871), L.R. 6 Ch. App. 83; *Re Pyle Works (No. 2)*, [1891] 1 Ch. 173; *Commercial Rubber Co. v. St. Jerome* (1908), 17 Que. K.B. 274; *Quebec & Lake St. John Railway v. Kennedy* (1913), 48 S.C.R. 520 at 530; *Mid-West Collieries Co. v. McEwen*, [1925] S.C.R. 326; *Sherwood v. Coleraine Quebec Asbestos Ltd.*, [1955] Que. S.C. 50 at 53. However, it will be noted that any by-law or amendment or repeal made pursuant to s. 103(1) is required to be submitted to the shareholders at the next meeting of shareholders and the shareholders may confirm, reject or amend the by-law in question. The by-law, amendment or repeal is effective from the date of the resolution of the directors until confirmed or confirmed as amended by the shareholders or until it ceases to be effective upon rejection, and where the by-law is confirmed or confirmed as amended it continues in effect in the form in which it was confirmed, but if rejected or if the directors do not submit a by-law, amendment or repeal to the shareholders the by-law, amendment or repeal ceases to be effective and no subsequent resolution of the directors to make, amend or repeal a by-law having substantially the same purpose or effect is effective until confirmed or confirmed as amended by the shareholder. The shareholders may by their own motion make a proposal to amend, make or repeal a by-law (s. 103(5)). The question as to when the by-law ceases to be effective is not entirely clear. Presumably it would be from the date of the next annual or specific meeting of shareholders after its enactment or possibly as from the date of the notice calling such meeting if the confirmation was not proposed in such notice. The situation might well be different in a closely held corporation as opposed to a corporation with many shareholders.

The articles of association constitute a contract between the corporation and the shareholders: *Theatre Amusement Co. v. Stone* (1915), 50 S.C.R. 32 at 37. See *Rayfield v. Hands*, [1958] 2 All E.R. 194 for a review of English case law on the nature of the contractual relations established by the memorandum and articles of association both as between the corporation and the members thereof and as between the members *inter se*.

In the case of a corporation incorporated by memorandum and articles, where the latter provide that the management of the business of the corporation shall be vested in the directors and delegate to them power to do everything which may be done by the corporation except in general meeting, such delegation is not limited to the management of the business of the corporation: *Campbell v. Rofe*, [1933] A.C. 91.

It will be noted that s. 110(1) provides that a director is entitled to receive notice of and to attend and be heard at any meeting of shareholders.

A number of the powers of the directors are dealt with elsewhere in the comment under other sections of the Act relating thereto, as follows:

Contracts, see Chapter 3.
Allotment of shares, see Chapter 5.
Declaration and payment of dividends, see Chapter 5.
Transfer of shares, see Chapter 6.
Exercise of borrowing powers, see Chapter 7.

As the powers of management are given to the directors, the management of the business cannot (in the absence of statutory provision or a unanimous shareholder agreement) be exercised by the shareholders, nor can the directors be overruled or controlled by the shareholders: *Quebec Agricultural Implement Co. v. Hébert* (1874), 1 Que. L.R. 363; *Cann v. Eakins* (1891), 23 N.S.R. 475 (C.A.); *Dunsmuir v. Colonist Printing & Publishing Co. (No. 2)* (1902), 9 B.C.R. 290; *Automatic Self Cleansing Filter Syndicate Co. v. Cuninghame*, [1906] 2 Ch. 34; *Re Hydro-Electric Power Commission of Ontario and Thorold & Pelham (Townships)* (1924), 55 O.L.R. 431 at 435 (C.A.); *John Shaw & Sons (Salford) Ltd. v. Shaw*, [1935] 2 K.B. 113 (C.A.). Thus a resolution of the shareholders to pay preference dividends by weekly payments in advance is invalid, being an interference by the corporation with the management of the business of the corporation entrusted to the directors: *Scott v. Scott*, [1943] 1 All E.R. 582.

Since under the federal Act and most, if not all, of the provincial Acts a shareholder who is entitled to vote at an annual meeting may make a proposal to make, amend, or appeal a by-law the old cases listed below which exclude the power of the shareholders to deal with by-laws except by way of considering by-laws previously passed by the directors would appear to be no longer good law in those jurisdictions: *Stephenson v. Vokes* (1896), 27 O.R. 691 at 696; *Dunsmuir v. Colonist Printing & Publishing Co.* (1902), 9 B.C.R. 290; *Beaudry v. Read* (1907), 10 O.W.R. 622 at 625 (Ont. K.B.); *Kelly v. Electrical Construction Co.* (1908), 16 O.L.R. 232; *Cann v. Eakins* (1891), 23 N.S.R. 475 (C.A.); *Colonial*

Assurance Co. v. Smith (1912), 4 D.L.R. 814; *Fox Selkirk Land & Investment Co. Ltd.* (1912), 8 D.L.R. 945 at 947; *Re Good & Jacob Y. Schantz & Co.* (1911), 23 O.L.R. 544 (C.A.).

Where directors of a corporation act within their powers they can bind the corporation under a contract without authorization by the shareholders: *Quebec & Lake St. John Railway v. Kennedy* (1913), 48 S.C.R. 520 at 530.

If the shareholders are dissatisfied with acts of the directors they can appoint a new board at the next election of directors, or appeal to the courts if the directors are committing a breach of trust. See *Taylor v. Chichester Railway* (1867), L.R. 2 Ex. 356; *John Shaw & Sons (Salford) Ltd. v. Shaw*, *supra*, at 134.

Majority shareholders may enter into an agreement to combine their interests and voting powers to secure control of a corporation by the election of certain directors and the appointment of certain officers: *Ringuet v. Bergeron* (1960), 24 D.L.R. (2d) 449 (S.C.C.).

Quaere as to the legality of an agreement between individuals which will control the statutory rights and powers of the shareholders by providing that no by-laws, resolutions or proceedings are to be passed or taken without the unanimous consent of all shareholders and directors; in any event such an agreement must be proved in the clearest manner: *Berkinshaw v. Henderson* (1909), 14 O.W.R. 833 (C.A.).

The powers of the directors are vested in them collectively and must be exercised at the regular meetings of the board, or as provided by the by-laws, and not by the directors acting individually: *Schmidt v. M. Beatty & Sons Ltd.* (1916), 10 O.W.N. 230; *Standard Construction Co. v. Crabb* (1914), 7 W.W.R. 719; *Bent v. Arrowhead Lumber Co.* (1909), 18 Man. R. 632 (Man. C.A.); *Swayze v. Grobb* (1915), 8 O.W.N. 316 (H.C.); *Almon v. Law* (1894), 26 N.S.R. 340 (C.A.). See further, *infra*, under the heading "Exercise of powers" in this chapter.

Examples of powers

The following are examples of powers which the directors may exercise under their general authority.

Appointments

Even without express power, it is the right of the directors to appoint necessary officers and agents and to provide for the manner of their payment: *Falkiner v. Grand Junction Ry.* (1883), 4 O.R. 350. And although the directors may go out of office and new directors be elected at the end of each year, they may engage managers and other officials for terms extending over a much longer period: *Howarth v. Singer Manufacturing Co.* (1893), 8 O.A.R. 264 at 270. As to the appointment of agents and officers, see the notes to Chapter 3, *supra*.

Power to compromise

The directors, being the active representatives of the corporation, may in a proper case exercise a power of compromise: *Bath's Case* (1878), 8 Ch. D.

334 (C.A.); *Dixon v. Evans* (1872), L.R. 5 H.L. 606 (bona fide compromise of disputed claim).

Arrangements with creditors

The directors of a corporation have the right to assign the property of the corporation to a trustee for the benefit of the corporation's creditors without the formal sanction of the whole body of shareholders: *Hovey v. Whiting* (1886), 14 S.C.R. 515; *In re Pacific Coast Coal Mines & Hodges*, [1926] 4 D.L.R. 759 (B.C. C.A.) (assignment in bankruptcy where it was alleged that the board had been irregularly elected); see also *Re Olympia Co.* (1915), 25 D.L.R. 620 (Man. C.A.).

The directors have unlimited powers over the property of the corporation and may deal with it so as to pay the just debts of the corporation: *Hovey v. Whiting*, *supra*, per Ritchie C.J. at p. 520. Directors may, without the sanction of the shareholders, make an acknowledgement of the corporation's insolvency for the purpose of a winding-up: *Re Manitoba Commission Co.* (1912), 2 D.L.R. 1.

Raising money

As to the exercise of the borrowing powers of a corporation, see the notes to Chapter 7.

In *Merchants' Bank of Canada v. Hancock* (1884), 6 O.R. 285 at 290, it was held that the directors of a trading corporation could raise money required for carrying on the corporation's business on the security of warehouse receipts. In the case of a bank, it has been held that the directors of a corporation may take such steps as seem necessary to protect its interest and to obtain advances: *Re Ontario Bank* (1910), 21 O.L.R. 1; affd (*sub nom. McFarland v. Bank of Montreal*) [1911] A.C. 96.

Where the articles authorized the directors to do such acts as were not by the Act or by the articles required to be exercisable or done by the corporation in general meeting, the directors in the absence of such requirement were held entitled to enter into a mortgage on behalf of the corporation: *Australian Auxiliary Steam Clipper Co. v. Mounsey* (1858), 27 L.J. Ch. 729.

Contracts

As to the power of directors to enter into contracts on behalf of the corporation, see the notes to Chapter 3, *supra.*

Remuneration of directors, officers and employees

Section 125 enables the directors to fix the remuneration of directors, officers and employees of the corporation.

The view has been expressed that the predecessor to s. 125 required the remuneration to be fixed by the directors; and that this could not be done by the shareholders: *Wilson v. Woollatt* (1928), 62 O.L.R. 620 at 624 (C.A.); affd (*sub nom. Woollatt v. Western Racing Association*) [1929] S.C.R. 483. In that case under the circumstances it was held that a resolution fixing the remuneration should be assumed to have been duly passed and the claim for remuneration was allowed with compound interest.

If the directors' resolution fixing the remuneration is ambiguous it will be construed *contra proferentem*: *Burland v. Earle*, [1902] A.C. 83 at 101 (P.C.) (managing director); but in the same case, where the secretary ceased to hold that office and was appointed vice-president, the resolution making no mention of salary, but continued to do the same class of work as before and was allowed to draw his former salary, it was held that the inference might fairly be drawn that he was intended to retain his salary, although there was a shifting in the offices.

As to the construction of a by-law appointing a general manager, which provides for the entering into of an agreement with respect to his remuneration, see *Warren v. Superior Engravers Ltd.*, [1941] 1 D.L.R. 323 (Ont. C.A.).

An officer, who is not also a director, who has rendered services without his remuneration being fixed, is entitled to bring action on a *quantum meruit* basis: *Bill v. Darenth Valley Ry.* (1856), 1 H. & N. 305. See also *E. B. M. Co. v. Weinfield* (1939), 66 Que. K.B. 60, where in the circumstances it was held that no resolution of the board was required authorizing the retention of advocates claiming remuneration for their services.

The remuneration of directors generally, as well as the right of an officer, who is also a director, to remuneration for services rendered not as a director but in some other capacity is considered below under the heading "Remuneration of directors".

Where an officer is to be entitled to a percentage of the profits of the corporation, the term "profits" should be defined in the contract or resolution providing for his remuneration. In the absence of such definition the term will not include profit on the sale of the whole undertaking in a winding-up, but may include the profit on the sale of an asset while the corporation is a going concern: *Fromes v. Bultfontein Mining Co.*, [1891] 1 Ch. 140; and this will be so although such profits are not in the form of money and are only turned into money upon subsequent realization in a winding-up: *In re Spanish Prospecting Co.*, [1911] 1 Ch. 92 (C.A.).

It should be noted that where there is an employment not to be performed within a year the Statute of Frauds may apply: *Cameron v. Gallagher-Holman Ltd.*, [1924] 1 D.L.R. 242 (Man. K.B.). Where the contract of employment is such that the whole contract may possibly be performed within a year, even though the parties contemplated that performance might and probably would extend beyond the year, and there is no express stipulation to the contrary, the Statute of Frauds does not apply: *Campbell v. Business Fleets Ltd.*, [1954] O.R. 87 (C.A.).

An officer may effectively reduce his salary by expressly accepting the sums from time to time paid him in full satisfaction of his remuneration; as to the acts of an officer from which such reduction will be inferred, see *Warren v. Superior Engravers Ltd.*, [1941] 1 D.L.R. 323 at 330, 332 (Ont. C.A.).

It will be apparent that in the case of a large corporation the directors will not ordinarily set the salaries payable to employees other than senior management executives.

Other examples

The directors may accept a conditional bonus granted by a municipality and give a hypothec as security: *Commercial Rubber Co. v. St. Jerome* (1908), 17 Que. K.B. 274 (P.C.); they may defend an action in the name of the corporation: *Campbell v. Taxicabs Verrals Ltd.* (1913), 27 O.L.R. 141 (Ont. H.C.); contract a hypothec which will be binding on the corporation: *Savaria v. Paquette* (1901), 20 Que. S.C. 314; select investments for the corporation subject to the control of a general meeting: *Burland v. Earle*, [1902] A.C. 83 (P.C.); sell all the corporation's lands, if such sale is in their honest opinion advisable: *Ritchie v. Vermillion Mining Co.* (1901), 1 O.L.R. 654 at 657, per Street J. whose judgment was affirmed (1902), 4 O.L.R. 588 (C.A.); *Sherwood v. Coleraine Quebec Asbestos Ltd.*, [1955] Que. S.C. 50. The sale of all or substantially all the assets or undertaking of a corporation must be authorized by the shareholders (s. 189(3)-(8)).

It is not beyond the powers of directors of a bank to authorize by resolution a subscription to a hospital: *Hamilton v. Bank of Montreal* (1929), 67 Que. S.C. 539.

A corporation as assignor in a deed of assignment covenanted that certain mortgages were good and valid charges on lands, and that the corporation had not done or permitted any act, etc., whereby the mortgages had become released or discharged in part or in entirety. It appeared that certain of the lands comprised in these mortgages had been sold for taxes. It was held that the covenant was not *ultra vires* of the corporation or of the directors; and that the plaintiffs were entitled thereunder to recover the value of the lands so sold: *Real Estate Investment Co. v. Metropolitan Building Society* (1883), 3 O.R. 476.

Termination of powers

The powers of directors cease on the appointment of a liquidator under the *Winding-up Act*, R.S.C. 1985, W-11, s. 31, except insofar as the court or the liquidator sanctions the continuance of such powers. See *Chatham National Bank v. McKeen* (1895), 24 S.C.R. 348 (S.C.C.). The winding-up provisions of provincial Acts generally contain a similar section, as for example, s. 221(1)(c) of the Ontario Act.

Under the *Bankruptcy and Insolvency Act*, on the other hand, an assignment or receiving order has not the effect of terminating the directors' powers. Meetings may be held and by-laws passed: *Re Canadian Cereal & Flour Mills Co.* (1922), 51 O.L.R. 316. This decision was followed in *National Trust Co. v. Ebro Irrigation & Power Co.*, [1954] O.R. 463 (H.C.) where a foreign court had purported to adjudge a Canadian corporation bankrupt.

Ratification of acts beyond the powers of the board

Acts which are *ultra vires* of the board, but not beyond the powers of the corporation, may be ratified by the shareholders: *Adams v. Bank of Montreal* (1899), 8 B.C.R. 314, (1901), 32 S.C.R. 719. See also *National Land & Loan Co. v. Rat Portage Lumber Co.* (1917), 36 D.L.R. 97 (Man. K.B.). There can be no ratification where an act is illegal or where the corporation is not fully informed: *Rountree v. Sydney Land & Loan Co.* (1908), 39 S.C.R. 614; *Hereford Ry. v. The Queen* (1894), 24 S.C.R. 1 at 12 (S.C.C.).

Where a director was procuring a meeting of the shareholders to be called for the purpose of confirming acts on his part alleged to be illegal, a motion for an injunction to restrain him from so doing was dismissed, it not having been made clear that the acts complained of were *ultra vires* of the corporation: *McClure v. Langley* (1916), 10 O.W.N. 32.

Where individual directors professing to act on behalf of the corporation enter into an arrangement which is not in the ordinary course of its business, the corporation is not bound unless it ratifies it: *Hamilton & Port Dover Railway v. Gore Bank* (1873), 20 Gr. 190 at 194; *Reuter v. Electric Telegraph* (1856), 6 E. & B. 341. See also *Houghton & Co. v. Nothard, Lowe & Wills Ltd.*, [1928] A.C. 1. But such acts of directors may be ratified expressly or by acquiescence. If the corporation elects to repudiate it should make known its election promptly, so that the person with whom its agent has dealt may remain as short a time as possible subject to an unequal bargain. If it delays after the lapse of sufficient time for enquiry and deliberation, it will be taken to have acquiesced, and even slight acts referable to the contract will be deemed an adoption of it: *Conant v. Miall* (1870), 17 Gr. 574 at 580.

Delegation

In the absence of any express or implied power enabling them to do so the directors cannot delegate their powers: *Cobb v. Becke* (1845), 6 Q.B. 930; *Saskatchewan Land Co. v. Moore* (1914), 5 O.W.N. 183; vard (1914), 6 O.W.N. 100.

The rule applies not only to a general delegation to an executive committee: *Monarch Life Assurance Co. v. Brophy* (1907), 14 O.L.R. 1 (C.A.); and to such a delegation to the president: *Tanguay v. Royal Paper Mills* (1907), 31 Que. S.C. 397; but also to a delegation of such powers as are expressly given to the board by the governing Act: *Re Bolt & Iron Co.; Hovenden's Case* (1884), 10 P.R. 434; *In re Leeds Banking Co.; Howard's Case* (1866), L.R. 1 Ch. App. 561 (allotting shares); *Re Pakenham Pork Packing Co.* (1906), 18 O.L.R. 100 (C.A.) (allotting shares); *Twin City Oil Co. v. Christie* (1909), 18 O.L.R. 324 (allotting shares); *Provident Life Insurance & Investment Co. v. Wilson* (1865), 25 U.C.Q.B. 53 (C.A.) (making calls).

Nor can the directors by contract with a manager deprive themselves of the right of control and management: *Horn v. Faulder (Henry) & Co.* (1908), 99 L.T. 524. Section 115 of the Act provides for delegation to a committee or to a managing director. For comment on this provision, and the limitations applicable thereto, see below. The administration of the business of the corporation may be delegated to an employee, subject only to such direction and control as it is the duty of the directors to exercise: *Montreal Public Service*

Co. v. Champagne (1917), 33 D.L.R. 49 (P.C.); and see *Mid-West Collieries Co. v. McEwen*, [1925] S.C.R. 326 at 330; and shareholders will be bound by an agreement approved in good faith by a majority, that the corporation's management shall be left entirely to one person: *Waschysyn v. Kildonan Ice & Fuel Co.*, [1937] 2 D.L.R. 653 at 659 (Man. C.A.). But see *Baird v. District Registrar of Titles*, [1938] S.C.R. 25 (S.C.C.).

On the other hand, it has been held in Quebec that it is only ministerial acts or acts of administration that can be delegated and not the discretionary powers of the board of directors: *Tanguay v. Royal Paper Mills* (1907), 31 Que. S.C. 397; and in *Re Wilson; Capital Trust Corp. v. Wilson*, [1937] O.R. 769 (C.A.) under the particular circumstances of the case, it was held that discretionary powers vested in a trust corporation under a will must be exercised by the board of directors and could not be delegated. The decision does not lay down any general rule except, possibly, as to trustees, and Masten J.A., in delivering the judgment of the court, stated at p. 780 that the statements respecting the application of the principle of law discussed did not relate in any way to the powers which in other circumstances and for other purposes are conferred on the directors by the Act or by common law, as to which see the judgment of Romer J. in *In re City Equitable Fire Insurance Co.*, [1925] Ch. 407, 426 (C.A.). In any event, so far as outsiders dealing with the corporation are concerned, they may rely on the rule of indoor management: *McKnight Construction Co. v. Vansickler* (1915), 51 S.C.R. 374 at 383; *Dorval Equipment Co. v. Franki Compressed Pile Co.*, [1953] Que. Q.B. 787 (C.A.); *Cobetto v. Belanger Bowling Alley & Restaurant*, [1955] Que. S.C. 301.

Where two of the three directors of a corporation entered into an agreement whereby they would agree on questions of the management of the corporation and in case of disagreement would refer the disputed matter to an arbitrator whose decision would govern, the court held that the agreement contravened the Act and was invalid: *Motherwell v. Schoof*, [1949] 4 D.L.R. 812 at 818.

Board committees (s. 115)

The directors in the absence of express authority cannot delegate to a committee of their number the supervision of the corporation's affairs generally: *Monarch Life Assurance Co. v. Brophy* (1907), 14 O.L.R. 1 (C.A.); *Tanguay v. Royal Paper Mills* (1907), 31 Que. S.C. 397.

Section 115 provides that directors of a corporation may appoint a managing director, who is a director and who is a resident Canadian, or a committee of directors and delegate to such managing director or committee any of the powers of the directors. A majority of the members of such committee must be resident Canadians except in the case of a holding corporation as set out in s. 105(4). It is provided in s. 115(3) that no managing director or a committee of directors has power to: (i) submit to the shareholders any question or matter requiring the approval of the shareholders; (ii) fill a vacancy among the directors or the office of auditor; (iii) issue securities except in the manner and on the terms authorized by the directors; (iv) declare dividends; (v) purchase, redeem or otherwise acquire shares issued by the corporation; (vi) pay a commission in respect of the sale of the shares; (vii) approve a management proxy circular; (viii) approve a take-over bid circular or directors' circular; (ix) approve any financial statements which are to be laid before the shareholders; or (x) adopt, amend or appeal any by-laws.

It will be noted that the committee as appointed has substantial limits on its authority and is not equivalent to an executive committee as could be created under the former federal Act.

A corporation may, and often will, have a number of committees, including an audit committee (as to which, see Chapter 11), a compensation committee and a nomination committee and in addition, can have an executive committee subject to the limits on its authority as above set out.

The usual provision in the by-laws states that the committee may meet for the transaction of business, adjourn or otherwise regulate its meetings as it sees fit and may from time to time adopt, amend or repeal rules or procedures in this regard. This is, of course, subject to the provisions of the Act and any other provisions of the by-laws of the corporation in question. Thus, in the case of *Baird v. District Registrar of Titles*, [1938] S.C.R. 25 (S.C.C.) it was held that the executive committee was acting within the scope of its authority in passing a resolution which provided that any one of certain designated persons was authorized to sign as an authorized signing officer with one of two designated officers and that all documents so executed should be binding on the corporation without any further authorization.

Should the directors delegate their powers to a committee without fixing a quorum of the committee, all of the members of the latter must be present to give effect to what they do, though unanimity may not be necessary. Such a committee has no power to appoint other members either in addition or to fill a vacancy: *Re Liverpool Household Stores Assn.* (1890), 59 L.J. Ch. 616; *Cook v. Ward* (1877), 2 C.P.D. 255 (C.A.).

Where under a general authority, conferred pursuant to the provisions of the Ontario Act, the directors appointed an executive committee to attend to the necessary business which might arise between the meetings of the board and to confer and advise with the managers in the best interests of the corporation and to report their actions and recommendations to the board for final adoption, it was stated that, except in necessary matters of business which might arise between the meetings of the board, the committee had only authority to report their actions and recommendations to the board for final adoption: *Re Henderson Roller Bearing Manufacturing Co.* (1908), 11 O.W.R. 526.

In jurisdictions where corporations are incorporated by memorandum and articles, the latter commonly provide for executive committees.

Where the articles of the corporation enabled the board of directors to appoint a committee of their own number and to delegate to any such committee all or any of the powers of the board, and one of the directors was appointed a committee with all the powers of the board, it was held that the delegation was valid and that a committee in such a case need not consist of more than one person: *Re Taurine Co.* (1884), 25 Ch. D. 118 (C.A.).

Where under the articles directors can delegate any of their powers to committees consisting of such member or members of their body as they think fit, " a committee of one so named is tantamount to naming one as managing director": *Mid-West Collieries Co. v. McEwen*, [1925] S.C.R. 326 at 332 (S.C.C.).

Exercise of powers

Meetings of directors

The directors must (unless otherwise authorized by the governing Act) act at regularly constituted meetings, and where the meetings are not held on definitely fixed days due notice must be given to all the directors: *Harben v. Phillips* (1883), 23 Ch. D. 14 (C.A.); *O'Dell v. Boston & Nova Scotia Coal Co.* (1896), 29 N.S.R. 385; *Young v. Consumers' Cordage Co.* (1896), 9 Que. S.C. 471; *First Natchez Bank v. Coleman* (1903), 2 O.W.R. 358 (C.A.); *Harris v. English Canadian Co.* (1905), 3 W.L.R. 5 (B.C. S.C.); *Re Cardiff Coal Co.* (1911), 18 W.L.R. 165; *Gray & Farr Co. v. Carlile*, [1932] 1 D.L.R. 391 (Alta. C.A.) (provision in the articles for adoption of a resolution by the signatures of all the directors without a meeting); *Guthrie v. West Indian Lime-Oil Sales Co.*, [1956] Que. Q.B. 229 (C.A.) (express power in by-laws for directors to sign resolutions without meeting). Section 117 of the Act provides that a resolution in writing signed by all the directors entitled to vote on that resolution at a meeting of directors or a committee thereof is as valid as if passed at a meeting of directors or a committee of directors as the case may be; a copy of every such resolution is to be kept with the minutes of the proceedings of the directors or committee of directors.

With the consent of the directors a meeting may be held under any circumstances, but a casual meeting of two directors cannot be converted into a board meeting at the option of one director: *Barron v. Potter*, [1914] 1 Ch. 895.

If the chairman is to have a casting vote at meetings the by-laws or the statute must so provide: *Toronto Brewing & Malting Co. v. Blake* (1882), 2 O.R. 175, per Proudfoot J., at 184. The by-laws may exclude the right of the presiding officer to a casting vote. See *Fremont Canning Co. v. Wall*, [1941] O.R. 379 at 398 (C.A.).

In the absence of some express limitation in the charter or by-laws, for example, where the by-laws provide for a chairman of the board who is to preside at meetings of directors, it is the duty and right of the president to preside at all meetings: *Fremont Canning Co. v. Fine Foods, supra*, at 390.

An agreement on the part of two of the three directors of a corporation that they would agree on questions of the management of the corporation and, in case of disagreement, would refer the matter to an arbitrator whose decision would govern was held to contravene the Act and to be invalid: *Motherwell v. Schoof*, [1949] 4 D.L.R. 812 at 818.

As to the effect of the presence of strangers at a meeting in the face of objection thereto by one of the directors, see *Harris v. English Canadian Co.* (1905), 3 W.L.R. 5.

In an action for wrongful exclusion from meetings, brought by a director, the corporation must prove the regulation under which he is excluded: *Boak v. Woods*, [1926] 1 D.L.R. 1186 (B.C. C.A.).

Section 123 provides that a director present at any meeting of directors or committee is deemed to have assented to any resolution passed or action taken at such meeting unless (i) he requests his dissent be or his dissent is entered in the minutes of the meeting, (ii) he sends written dissent to the secretary of the meeting before the meeting is adjourned or (iii) he sends his dissent by registered mail or delivers it to the registered office immediately after adjournment of the meeting. If he is not present at the meeting where a written resolution was passed or action is taken, the director is deemed to have consented thereto unless, within 7 days after he becomes aware of the resolution, he causes his dissent to be placed with the minutes of the meeting or sends his dissent by registered mail or delivers it to the corporation. A director voting for or consenting to a resolution is not entitled to dissent thereto.

Section 123(4) of the Act provides that a director is not liable under s. 118 (issuance of shares, improper purchase redemption or other acquisition of shares, improper commissions, dividends or financial assistance, or payment of an indemnity or to a shareholder contrary to the Act), s. 119 (liability of directors for wages) or s. 122 (duty of care) if he relied in good faith on financial statements of the corporation represented to him by an officer of the corporation or in a written report of the auditor to fairly reflect the financial condition of the corporation or on the report of a lawyer, accountant, engineer, appraiser or other person whose profession lends credibility to a statement made by him.

Directors' meetings are discussed below under the following subheadings: Notice of directors' meetings; Notice of business; Personal attendance; Quorum; Resolutions; By-laws; Minutes; Irregularities.

Notice of directors' meetings

The by-laws or articles usually provide for a minimum amount of notice of directors' meetings. The time specified in such a by-law or article should be reasonable: *Madden v. Dimond* (1905), 12 B.C.R. 80 at 90 (C.A.). If the by-laws or articles do not specify a minimum time, notice must be given a reasonable time prior to the meeting of the board: *In re Homer District Consolidated Gold Mines; Ex parte Smith* (1888), 39 Ch. D. 546. However, if all the directors are present, insufficiency of notice will be immaterial: *Browne v. La Trinidad* (1888), 37 Ch. D. 1 (C.A.). The by-laws commonly provide that meetings may be held without formal notice if all the directors are present or those absent have signified their consent to the meeting being held in their absence. A letter from the president of the corporation purporting to waive notice on behalf of the absent directors is not a signification of consent within the meaning of such a by-law: *Canadian Ohio Motor Car Co. v. Cochrane* (1915), 7 O.W.N. 698.

The by-laws sometimes provide that for the first meeting of directors held after the annual meeting for the election of officers no notice is required.

It has been held that notice must be given to a director who has indicated verbally that he cannot attend a meeting on the basis that he may change his mind: *In re Portuguese Consolidated Copper Mines Ltd.* (1889), 42 Ch. D. 160

at 168 (C.A.), per Lord Esher M.R.; *Young v. Ladies' Imperial Club Ltd.*, [1920] 2 K.B. 523 (C.A.); but if the giving of the notice to the absent director can have no possible result, such notice to him is unnecessary: *Halifax Sugar Refining Co. v. Francklyn* (1890), 59 L.J. Ch. 591; *Windsor v. Windsor* (1912), 3 D.L.R. 456 (meetings held in England and directors who were not notified absent in America). In *Young v. Ladies' Imperial Club, supra*, at 528, Lord Sterndale M.R. was inclined to the view that illness of the person entitled to notice, so dangerous that it was impossible for him to be moved, would also be an exception even though he might not be at a distance.

While in the ordinary case, subject to the exceptions above noted, a meeting of directors will be invalid if one of the directors entitled to take part has not been notified, different considerations arise if the business to be transacted is such that the particular directors who have not been summoned would not be entitled to vote. In *John Shaw & Sons (Salford) Ltd. v. Shaw*, [1935] 2 K.B. 113 (C.A.), the articles provided for two classes of directors, permanent and ordinary; the ordinary directors were to have no right to vote in respect of certain matters and three of them, specially named, were to have no right to deal with a specified matter which was included in the matters as to which the ordinary directors' right of voting was excluded. Action was taken in respect of such specified matter at a board meeting to which none of the ordinary directors were summoned. Greer L.J. held that it was unnecessary to summon the ordinary directors because, if they had been summoned and had attended, they could have been directed by the permanent directors to retire and could not have refused. Slesser L.J., on the other hand, took the view that the ordinary directors, other than the named individuals, were entitled to be present and influence the minds of the permanent directors, even though they might not vote; and that, such ordinary directors not having been summoned, the action taken by the permanent directors was ineffective. The third member of the court, Roche L.J., did not agree with the affirmative conclusion of Slesser L.J., on the point, on the ground that the requisite information which might have a bearing on the right of the ordinary directors to be summoned was not before the court.

Five of nine provisional directors of a railway corporation being a quorum, four of them met at Winnipeg pursuant to a valid notice under the statute, and adjourned to a day named, when six met at Toronto in alleged pursuance of adjournment but without proper notice under the statute. It was held that the meeting of the six directors did not constitute a duly organized meeting of directors, though had all the directors who were at the meeting at Winnipeg attended pursuant to the adjournment it might have cured the irregularity: *McLaren v. Fisken* (1881), 28 Gr. 352.

Where a bare majority of the directors call a directors' meeting at a time that does not reasonably permit of the attendance of a full board and, not acting *bona fide* in the corporation's interests but for the purpose of retaining themselves in office and improperly controlling the vote at shareholders' meetings pending, improperly issue shares to themselves, the parties to whom the shares are issued will be restrained from voting them at the meetings: *Glace Bay Printing Co. v. Harrington* (1910), 45 N.S.R. 268 (T.D.).

A resolution passed at a meeting notice of which has not been given to all the directors, may be ratified at a subsequent meeting within a reasonable time: *Lytton Gold Mines Ltd. v. Munro* (1934), 49 B.C.R. 18, and cases cited.

A director may waive notice of a meeting of directors in any manner whatsoever and his attendance constitutes a waiver of notice unless he attends for the purpose of objecting to the transaction of business on the ground that the meeting is not properly called (s. 114(6)).

Notice of an adjourned meeting of directors is not required to be given if time and place of the adjourned meeting is announced at the original meeting of directors.

Notice of business

Notice of the business to be transacted at a directors' meeting, as distinguished from notice of the holding of the meeting, is not necessary unless required by the governing act. Thus in s. 114(5) a notice of meeting of directors need not specify the purpose of or business to be transacted unless the by-laws otherwise provide or a matter referred to in s. 115(3) is to be dealt with at the meeting in question. These are as follows: (i) any submission to the shareholders of any question or matter requiring their approval; (ii) any filling of a vacancy among the directors or in the office of auditor; (iii) the issuance of security except as may have previously been authorized by the directors; (iv) a declaration of dividends; (v) the purchase, redemption or other acquisition of shares issued by the corporation; (vi) payment of a commission on the purchase of shares or to anyone agreeing to procure purchasers for such shares as set out in s. 41; (vii) approving a management proxy circular; (viii) approving a take-over bid circular or directors circular; (ix) approving financial statements to be circulated to the shareholders; or (x) the adoption, amendment or repeal of any by-law. There is no restriction in the Ontario Act similar to s. 114(5).

The common law rule was that directors at meetings of the board could deal with all the affairs of the corporation requiring their attention, whether ordinary or not, and previous notice of special business was not a necessary condition of the proceedings being valid unless special provision to that effect was made in the charter or by-laws. In the case of extraordinary or special business it might be very prudent and right to give notice of it, but it was not legally necessary to do so: *La Compagnie de Mayville v. Whitley*, [1896] 1 Ch. 788 (C.A.). The contrary opinion which had been previously expressed by Robertson J. in *Waddell v. Ontario Canning Co.* (1889), 18 O.R. 41, is not likely to be followed in Canada.

Personal attendance

Unles there is statutory or other authority the directors must meet in person: see *Harris v. English Canadian Co.* (1905), 3 W.L.R. 5 (B.C. S.C.). A director's vote cannot be cast by proxy at a meeting of the board: *Re Portuguese Consolidated Copper Mines Ltd.* (1889), 42 Ch. D. 160 at 165; *McGuire & Forester Ltd. v. Cadzow*, [1933] 1 D.L.R. 192 (Alta. C.A.). Regarding a corporation incorporated by memorandum of association where the articles authorized a method of procedure by the directors other than attending a regular meeting, see *Gray & Farr Co. v. Carlile*, [1932] 1 D.L.R. 391. In *Re Associated Color Laboratories Ltd.* (1970), 73 W.W.R. 566, 14 C.B.R. (N.S.) 35 (B.C. S.C.) it was held that the articles did not contemplate telephone meetings since they specifically provided for appointment of an alternate director in the place of an absent director and for the validity of any resolution in writing signed by all the directors.

If so provided by the by-laws a director may, if all the directors consent, participate in a meeting of directors or a committee by telephone or other communication facility which permit all persons participating in the meeting to hear each other and the director participating in such a manner is deemed for the purposes of this Act to be present at the meeting in question (s. 114(9)). It is usual to obtain a consent to such meetings from each director upon his election or appointment.

Quorum

The by-laws generally fix the quorum of the directors, this being expressly provided for in s. 114(2). The Act provides that, subject to the provisions of the articles or by-laws, a majority of the number of directors or minimum number of directors set out in the articles is a quorum for any meeting of directors and notwithstanding any vacancy among the directors a quorum may exercise all the power of the directors. In the absence of any requirement of the governing Act it would appear that the by-laws may provide for a quorum of as few as two directors even where the number of directors is large. One director cannot constitute a meeting: *Re D. & S. Drug Co.* (1916), 10 W.W.R. 612; revd on other grounds (1917), 31 D.L.R. 643; while that decision seems consistent with the general rule that at least two persons must be present to constitute a meeting, it has been held in England that a quorum of directors may be one: *In Re Fireproof Doors, Ltd.*, [1916] 2 Ch. 142. It will be observed that under s. 114(8) if there is only one director of a corporation, that director may constitute a meeting by himself. Under the Ontario Act (s. 126(3)), unless the articles or by-laws otherwise provide, a majority of the directors or minimum number of directors constitutes a quorum, but in no case may a quorum be less than two fifths of the board.

It is provided in the Act that a majority of the directors present must be resident Canadians and directors are not to transact business at a meeting unless this requirement has been met. There is an exception for a holding corporation pursuant to s. 105(4) and s. 114(3) and in addition business may be transacted if a resident Canadian director who is unable to be present approves, in writing or by telephone or some other communication facility, of the business transacted at the meeting and a majority of resident Canadian directors would have been present had the director been present at the meeting. It will be noted that the requirement of a majority of resident Canadians applies also to meetings of a committee of directors (s. 115(2)). Note the exception from the requirement of resident Canadian directors under the Ontario Act for non-resident corporations (as defined) s. 118(3), s. 126(6).

Where the by-laws do not fix the quorum, it would appear that a majority of the directors is necessary to constitute a quorum: *York Tramways Co. v. Willows* (1882), 8 Q.B.D. 685; although it has been held that a lesser number established by the practice of the directors may be sufficient: *Lyster's Case* (1867), L.R. 4 Eq. 233.

In *International Mining Syndicate v. Stewart* (1914), 48 N.S.R. 172, it was held that two out of four provisional directors constituted a quorum, where one forfeited his shares and the other refused to attend, having acquired interests adverse to the corporation.

Where a quorum is present at a meeting, a majority of those present and constituting the quorum may validly act for the corporation: *Withnell v. Gartham* (1795), 6 T.R. 388; *Rex v. Bower* (1823), 1 B. & C. 492; *Cortis v. Kent Water Works* (1827), 7 B. & C. 314.

The Act now provides that (i) where a director has disclosed his interest and refrained from voting or otherwise complied with the requirements of s. 120 and (ii) if the contract was approved by the directors or the shareholders of the corporation and was reasonable and fair to the corporation at the time it was approved, the interested directors may be counted to determine the presence of a quorum at the meeting of directors or committee of directors in question that authorized the contract. The common law rule was that directors disentitled from voting by reason of being interested in a contract before the meeting for its consideration could not be counted towards making a quorum: *Yuill v. Greymouth Point Elizabeth Railway & Coal Co.*, [1904] 1 Ch. 32; *Re D. & S. Drug Co.; Donald's Claim* (1916), 10 W.W.R. 612, revd on other grounds (1917), 31 D.L.R. 643; but the presence, on the board of directors, of three who were not qualified by reason of being in arrears in respect of unpaid calls at the time of their election, was held not sufficient to invalidate the acts of the board done by a legal quorum of properly elected directors: *Morden Woollen Mills Co. v. Heckels* (1908), 17 Man. R. 557 (Man. C.A.). A resolution passed by four directors of whom three are interested, a quorum being fixed at two, will not bind the corporation and a contract based upon such resolution will be invalid until ratified: *Ferguson v. Wallbridge*, [1935] 3 D.L.R. 66 at 74 (P.C.).

Semble directors, interested adversely to the corporation, may be asked to retire while the matter in respect of which such interest exists is being discussed: *Yuill v. Greymouth Point Elizabeth Railway & Coal Co.*, *supra*; as to whether this applies to directors who, though not being adversely interested, are otherwise disentitled to vote, see the conflicting views of Greer L.J. and Slesser L.J. in *John Shaw & Sons (Salford) Ltd. v. Shaw*, [1935] 2 K.B. 113 (C.A.).

Where the five directors of a corporation were the only shareholders, and at a meeting at which all were present, headed in the minutes as a board meeting, authorized a contract in which they were personally interested, the contract having been assented to by all the shareholders, they were assumed to have waived all formalities and to have constituted the meeting a general meeting of shareholders: *In re Express Engineering Works Ltd.*, [1920] 1 Ch. 466 (C.A.).

Where an act which could only be done at a shareholders' meeting was done in a meeting described as a meeting of directors, at which two out of the three shareholders were present, the third shareholder having been a consenting party thereto, the corporation was held to be bound: *McGuire & Forester Ltd. v. Cadzow*, [1933] 1 D.L.R. 192 (Alta. C.A.).

The acts of directors at meetings where there is not a quorum are voidable by the corporation, subject, of course, to the rule in the *Turquand* case discussed under the heading "Irregularities," below, where it applies. That rule does not apply where the person relying on the contract is the representative of an officer who was making a secret profit out of the transaction: *Abana Mines v. Wall* (1935), 58 Que. K.B. 352 (Que. C.A.).

Resolutions

The formal acts of the directors at meetings of the board are expressed in the form of resolutions or by-laws.

The distinction between a resolution and a by-law is that a "resolution applies to a single act of the corporation, while a by-law is a permanent continuing rule, which is to be applied to all future occasions": *Mackenzie v. Maple Mountain Mining Co.* (1910), 20 O.L.R. 615 (C.A.), per Osler J.A., at 618. This seems, however, an over-simplification. Thus, a borrowing by-law enacted under s. 63 may be a general by-law authorizing a series of borrowings and thus establishing a "general continuing rule". It may on the other hand simply authorize one specific borrowing.

For other cases discussing the distinction between a resolution and a by-law, see *Manes Tailoring Co. v. Willson* (1907), 14 O.L.R. 89 at 96 (Ont. Ch. Div.), and *Denault v. Stewart; Denault & Co.* (1918), 54 Que. S.C. 209.

It was held in *Mackenzie v. Maple Mountain Mining Co., supra*, that while a resolution is not necessarily a by-law, a by-law may be enacted in the form of a resolution, where the object to be accomplished is the subject of a by-law, that is, a rule of law of the corporation for its government. One test is whether the corporation itself has treated the resolution as a by-law: *St. Vital Investment v. Halldorson* (1921), 56 D.L.R. 418 at 426 (Man. C.A.).

By-laws

Under s. 103, unless otherwise provided by the articles, by-laws or a unanimous shareholder agreement, the directors may by resolution make, amend or repeal any by-laws to regulate the business or affairs of a corporation; such by-law, amendment or repeal is to be submitted to the shareholders at the next meeting of shareholders and may by ordinary resolution be confirmed, rejected or amended at that time. A by-law or amendment or repeal is effective from the date of the resolution of the directors until it is confirmed or amended by the shareholder at which point it continues in effect in the form which it was confirmed or amended. If it was rejected by the shareholders or if it is not submitted by the directors to the shareholders at the appropriate meeting, the by-law, amendment or repeal ceases to be effective and no subsequent resolution of the directors with respect to the same or substantially the same matters is effective until confirmed or confirmed as amended by the shareholders. A shareholder entitled to vote at an annual meeting of shareholders is entitled to make a proposal to make, amend or repeal any by-law.

The general by-laws are not instruments within the meaning of Consolidated Rule 604 (Ontario) (now Ontario Rules of Civil Procedure, R 14.05(3)(d)) providing for the determination on originating notice of rights depending upon the construction of any deed, will or other instrument: *Re Fine Foods of Canada Ltd.*, [1939] O.R. 401. As to the effect to be given to a recital in a by-law, see *Hammond v. Bank of Ottawa* (1910), 22 O.L.R. 73 at 80 (C.A.).

A valid by-law may operate as a contract between the shareholders and the corporation: *Erie Co-operative Co. v. Taylor* (1924), 27 O.W.N. 16; *Rands v. Hiram Walker, G. & W. Ltd.*, [1936] O.R. 488; *Kamouraska Telephone Co. v. Houle* (1918), 27 Que. K.B. 400; but can have no effect as a law upon other persons; *Lynch v. Wm. Richards Co. Ltd.* (1900), 37 N.B.R. 549 at 557; and must not work unequally towards members of any one class affected by it: *North-West Electric Co. v. Walsh* (1899), 29 S.C.R. 33 at 49; *Re Good & Jacob Y. Shantz Son & Co.* (1911), 23 O.L.R. 544 at 552 (C.A.).

Minutes

Records must be kept of minutes of meetings of directors and resolutions (s. 20(2)). Section 22 provides that records required to be kept by the Act may be in a binder or loose-leaf form or a photographic film form, or may be recorded under any system of mechanical or electronic data processing or other information storage device capable of reproducing any required information in intelligible written form within a reasonable time.

Although there were no minutes of a resolution the court may accept parol evidence as to what took place at a meeting and presume that a resolution was passed or other action taken: *In re Pyle Works* (No. 2), [1891] 1 Ch. 173 at 184; *North West Battery Co. v. Hargrave* (1913), 15 D.L.R. 193 (Man. K.B.); *Boston Shoe Co. v. Frank* (1915), 48 Que. S.C. 66 (Que. C.A.); *McCammon v. Westport Manufacturing & Plating Co.* (1916), 9 O.W.N. 397; *In re Fireproof Doors, Ltd.*, [1916] 2 Ch. 142; *Classic Hosiery Co. v. Fillis* (1920), 18 O.W.N. 17; *Wilson v. Woollat* (1928), 62 O.L.R. 620 (C.A.) and cases cited at pp. 626 and 726; *Fancy v. Dealers Security Ltd.* (1932), 41 O.W.N. 500 (C.A.). But see *Claudet v. Golden Giant Mines Ltd.* (1909), 15 B.C.R. 13 where the trial court held that minutes re-transcribed into the minute book from transcribed shorthand notes taken by a deceased person were not admissible to prove what transpired at a directors' meeting. If, however, the minutes have been re-transcribed by the same person who took the shorthand notes, or had been confirmed, it is suggested that the minutes would have been admissible. The case was reversed on appeal but on other grounds.

In *McLaws v. Walker* (1988), 29 B.C.L.R. (2d) 219 (B.C. S.C.) it was held that, pursuant to the provisions of the British Columbia Act, the court had power to rectify errors in the conduct of the business of a corporation and acts of directors at a meeting improperly adjourned can be set aside. Recording of the acts of the directors in the minutes does not prevent the court from exercising its power.

In the absence of any statutory provision, a certified copy of a resolution of the board of directors does not require the seal of the corporation to be affixed:

Re Ford and Reliance Shoe Co., [1937] O.W.N. 295 (C.A.). Under s. 29 of the *Evidence Act*, R.S.O. 1990, c. E.23 where the original record could be received in evidence, a proceeding of any corporation created by charter or statute in Ontario purporting to be certified under the seal of the corporation and the hand of the presiding officer or secretary thereof, is to be receivable in evidence without proof of the seal of the corporation, or of the official character of the person or persons appearing to have signed the same, and without further proof thereof. A similar provision appears in s. 24 of the *Canada Evidence Act*, R.S.C. 1985, c. C-5.

Irregularities

As to the regularity of proceedings at meetings of directors, it should be remembered that persons dealing with a corporation are not presumed to have notice of the articles (s. 18(a)); they are not bound to inquire into the regularity of its "indoor management". They may presume that its internal management is regular, and, for example, one lending to a corporation which has power to borrow with the sanction of a general meeting is not put on inquiry as to whether that sanction has been given in the prescribed way: *Royal British Bank v. Turquand* (1856), 6 E. & B. 327; *Bargate v. Shortridge* (1855), 5 H.L. Cas. 297; *Montreal & St. Lawrence Light & Power Co. v. Robert*, [1906] A.C. 196; *Goulet v. Hydraulic Co. of Portneuf* (1917), 52 Que. S.C. 58; *Jackson v. Cannon* (1903), 10 B.C.R. 73 (C.A.); *The King v. Canada West Manufacturing Ltd.*, [1950] 2 D.L.R. 671; *Bank of Nova Scotia v. LeBlanc*, [1954] 2 D.L.R. 579 (N.B. C.A.). See further as to the rule in *Royal British Bank v. Turquand, supra*, the notes to Chapters 3 and 7.

Where directors have acted irregularly and there is notice of the irregularity in the proceedings, the rule in the *Turquand* case does not apply: *Howard v. Patent Ivory Manufacturing Co.* (1888), 38 Ch. D. 156. Nor does the rule apply as between the corporation and an officer thereof: *Courchêne v. Viger Park Co.* (1915), 23 D.L.R. 693 (Que. C.A.); and see *John Shaw & Sons (Salford) Ltd. v. Shaw*, [1935] 2 K.B. 113 (C.A.).

A director, who takes part in irregular proceedings, may be estopped from setting up the irregularity: *Gray v. Yellowknife Gold Mines Ltd.* (No. 1), [1945] O.R. 688 (director solicitor for corporation). A director, however, who has paid off a creditor and taken an assignment of a security irregularly given, is entitled to stand in the shoes of the creditor: *In re Bank of Syria; Owen & Ashworth's Claim; Whitworth's Claim*, [1901] 1 Ch. 115 at 121 (C.A.).

The notice of the irregularity may be actual or constructive: *Irvine v. Union Bank of Australia* (1877), 2 App. Cas. 366. As between corporations, the mere fact that they have directors in common is not sufficient to impute to one corporation notice of the existence of facts within the knowledge of the other corporation: *J. D. McArthur Co. v. Alberta & Great Waterways Railway*, [1924] 2 D.L.R. 118 (Alta. C.A.). The same rule applies where two corporations have the same secretary: *In re Fenwick Stobart & Co.*, [1902] 1 Ch. 507; or the same manager: *Edmonton Portland Cement Co. v. Duplessis* (1917), 55 S.C.R. 623 (S.C.C.). In order to make the notice effective it must have been the duty of the officer to communicate it to his corporation: *Young v. David Payne & Co.*, [1904] 2 Ch. 608 (C.A.); *In re Fenwick Stobart & Co., supra.*

Subject to the effect of the rule in *Royal British Bank v. Turquand*, an act done by a majority of the directors informally and privately is not, in the absence of express authorization, binding on the corporation. Thus, where the secretary had fixed the seal of a corporation to a bond after obtaining the authority of two directors privately, and the promise of the third to sign an authorization, it was held that the bond was void: *D'Arcy v. Tamar, Kit Hill and Callington Ry.* (1867), L.R. 2 Ex. 158; *Re County Life Assurance Co.* (1870), L.R. 5 Ch. App. 288; *In re Haycraft Gold Reduction Co.*, [1900] 2 Ch. 230; *Paul v. Kobold* (1905), 2 W.L.R. 90 at 95. And where the articles of association authorize a method of procedure by the directors other than at a regular meeting, there is by implication a denial of any other informal method: *Gray & Farr Co. v. Carlile*, [1932] 1 D.L.R. 391 at 395 (provision for adoption of a resolution by the signatures of all the directors without a meeting).

The provisions of s. 18 should be reviewed where a question of internal management is concerned. See the notes on Chapter 3.

Remuneration of directors

This topic is dealt with under the following subheadings: Right to remuneration; Requirement of a by-law; Remuneration for services rendered in other capacities; Apportionment; Payments not justifiable as remuneration; Gratuities and remuneration for past services; Compensation for loss of office; Remuneration out of capital; Remuneration by issue of paid-up shares; Waiver and forfeiture of remuneration; Misconduct; Directors as restricted creditors in bankruptcy. Travelling expenses incurred by directors are discussed in the notes under the heading "Indemnification of directors" in this chapter.

Right to remuneration

Prima facie directors of a corporation are not entitled to remuneration in the absence of statutory authority: *Hutton v. West Cork Railway* (1883), 23 Ch. D. 654 at 672 (C.A.); *Birney v. Toronto Milk Co.* (1902), 5 O.L.R. 1 (Ont. C.A.); *Beaudry v. Read* (1907), 10 O.W.R. 622 (Ont. K.B.); *Re Queen City Plate Glass Co.; Eastmure's Case* (1910), 1 O.W.N. 863; *Re Solicitors* (1913), 27 O.L.R. 147 at 258 (C.A.); *Roray v. Howe Sound* (1915), 22 D.L.R. 855 (B.C. C.A.); or in the absence of the sanction of the shareholders: *Minister of Rys. & Canals v. Quebec Southern Ry.; Hodge & White's Claim* (1908), 12 Ex. C.R. 11. See also *Public Trustee v. Toronto Humane Society* (1987), 60 O.R. (2d) 236, 27 E.T.R. 40 (Ont. H.C.) where directors of charitable corporations are not entitled to be paid as employees in the absence of special provision or court order.

Where a person has accepted the office of director of a corporation and has acted as such, there may be inferred an agreement between him and the corporation, on his part that he will serve the corporation on the terms as to qualification and otherwise contained in the articles of association, and on the part of the corporation that he shall receive the remuneration and benefits provided by the articles for the directors: *Re Anglo Austrian Co.; Isaac's Case*, [1892] 2 Ch. 518.

The amount of remuneration to be paid to directors is a matter of internal management: *Burland v. Earle*, [1902] A.C. 83 (P.C.); *Normandy v. Ind, Coope & Co.*, [1908] 1 Ch. 84. A corporation may vary the remuneration of directors and discriminate between directors: *Foster v. Foster*, [1916] 1 Ch. 532.

Directors cannot retain a bonus agreed upon between some of them, but which has not been duly authorized by a meeting of the board: *Gray & Farr Co. v. Carlile*, [1932] 1 D.L.R. 391 (Alta. C.A.); or remuneration fraudulently voted in order to deprive minority shareholders of the profits of the corporation: *Nolan v. Parsons*, [1942] O.R. 358 (C.A.).

If a director withdraws sums in excess of the authorized remuneration, he is guilty of a breach of trust: *Re Bolt & Iron Co.* (1888), 14 O.R. 211; affd (1890), 16 O.A.R. 397.

A director receiving remuneration from one corporation is not accountable therefor to another corporation which provided his qualification shares: *In re Dover Coalfield Extension Ltd.*, [1908] 1 Ch. 65 (C.A.).

A director who has not been validly appointed is not entitled to recover on a *quantum meruit*: *Woolf v. East Nigel Gold Mining Co.* (1905), 21 T.L.R. 660; *Harrigan v. McLeod* (1915), 21 D.L.R. 509 (N.S. C.A.).

Where a director has vacated his office under a provision of the articles he is not entitled to remuneration for his services during the period between such vacation of office and his re-election and the corporation will be entitled to recover from him fees paid during such period under the mistake of fact that he was a director: *In re Bodega Co.*, [1904] 1 Ch. 276.

Requirement of a by-law

The subject of remuneration of directors is usually dealt with in the by-laws; a standard provision is that such remuneration may be set from time to time by the board of directors and such remuneration is in addition to the salary paid to an employee of the corporation who is also a member of the board of directors; the board of directors may also award special remuneration to any director undertaking special services on the corporation's behalf other than the routine work ordinarily required of a director by the corporation and the confirmation of any such resolution or resolutions by the shareholders is not required. The standard provision in the by-laws also provides that a director is entitled to be paid his travelling and other expenses properly incurred by him on behalf of the corporation.

Where the statute so requires, directors are not entitled to remuneration for their services as such in the absence of a by-law authorizing the remuneration: *Birney v. Toronto Milk Co.* (1903), 5 O.L.R. 1 at 5 and 6 (Ont. C.A.); *Beaudry v. Read* (1907), 10 O.W.R. 622 at 625 (Ont. K.B.); *Re Queen City Plate Glass Co.; Eastmure's Case* (1910), 1 O.W.N. 863. See also *D'Amore v. McDonald*, [1973] 1 O.R. (2d) 370 (C.A.).

It would not appear that under the present Act a by-law is required per se for remuneration of directors or officers. See s. 125 of the federal Act which provides that the directors of a corporation may fix the remuneration of directors, officers or employees of a corporation subject to the provisions of the articles, by-laws or any unanimous shareholder agreement; however, where the governing Act requires a by-law a resolution will not suffice: *Gardner v. Canadian Manufacturer Publishing Co.* (1900), 31 O.R. 488 at 493; *Birney v. Toronto Milk Co., supra*; *Bartlett v. Bartlett Mines Ltd.* (1911), 24 O.L.R. 419 (Ont. Dist. Ct.). But where a by-law authorized the directors to fix the salary of the officers, including such officers as might be directors and the directors passed a resolution recommending that the salary of the president and manager be fixed at a stated amount and at a meeting of the shareholders held the same day the recommendation of the directors was ratified, a resolution of the directors fixing the salary was assumed to have been duly passed: *Wilson v. Woollatt* (1928), 62 O.L.R. 620 (C.A.); affd (*sub nom. Woollatt v. Western Racing Assn.*), [1929] S.C.R. 483. It will be noted that federal legislation governing banks, insurance companies and trust and loan companies require directors' remuneration to be fixed by by-law and that no remuneration is to be paid in the absence of a by-law.

The director, to recover remuneration, must bring himself within the provisions of any applicable by-law: *Re Bolt & Iron Co.; Livingstone's Case* (1889), 16 O.A.R. 397; *Burland v. Earle*, [1902] A.C. 83 at 101 (P.C.); *Cameron v. Gallagher Holman Ltd.*, [1924] 1 D.L.R. 242 at 245 (Man. K.B.); *Warren v. Superior Engravers Ltd.*, [1941] 1 D.L.R. 323 (Ont. C.A.); *Allish v. Allied Engineering of B.C. Ltd.* (1957), 9 D.L.R. (2d) 688 (B.C. C.A.).

The by-law may be general in its terms and authorize the board of directors to determine the amount of the remuneration: *Mackenzie v. Maple Mountain Mining Co.* (1910), 20 O.L.R. 615 (C.A.); *Hood v. Caldwell*, [1923] S.C.R. 488 at 494. A director will be bound by the provisions of such a by-law: *Marks v. Rocsand Co. Ltd.* (1921), 49 O.L.R. 137 (C.A.), and similarly as regards the provisions of the articles: *Re J. C. Harris Groceterias Ltd.*, [1940] 2 D.L.R. 257 (N.S. C.A.); *Allish v. Allied Engineering of B.C. Ltd., supra.*

If the by-laws will not support the director's claim for remuneration a contract to pay remuneration as on a *quantum meruit* basis will not generally be implied: *Re Queen City Plate Glass Co.; Eastmure's Case* (1910), 1 O.W.N. 863; *Marks v. Rocsand Co. Ltd., supra.* However, in *Denman v. Clover Bar Coal Co.* (1913), 48 S.C.R. 318 (S.C.C.) a director was held entitled to be allowed for his services as general manager on the basis of a *quantum meruit.*

Where payment is to be made "at such time as the directors may determine" a determination of the time for payment is requisite to entitle a director to sue for his remuneration: *Caridad Copper Mining Co. v. Swallow*, [1902] 2 K.B. 44 (C.A.) (directors entitled to postpone payment indefinitely).

Where the by-laws provide for payment of such sums by way of remuneration for services as may be determined by the corporation at a general meeting, and the remuneration is so determined to a specified date only, remuneration cannot be recovered for services rendered subsequently: *Re Bolt & Iron Co.; Livingstone's Case* (1889), 16 O.A.R. 397.

When the by-laws give the directors power to fix the remuneration of all officers and to appoint a general manager, the directors' powers extend to appointing and fixing the remuneration of a managing director: *Re Crescent Silver Cobalt Mines Ltd.; Ex parte Barber*, [1934] O.W.N. 558.

Remuneration for services rendered in other capacities

A distinction may be drawn between remuneration for services rendered in the ordinary course of the duty of a director and services rendered in some other capacity. There were a number of decisions, not entirely consistent, on the validity of this distinction under a provision of a former Ontario Act which required the passing or confirmation by a general meeting of a by-law for the remuneration of the president or of any director. It was eventually held by the Ontario Court of Appeal, however, that even under such a provision a director or president might be entitled to remuneration for services outside the ordinary scope of the duties of such office although such remuneration was not authorized by a by-law so passed or confirmed: *Fremont Canning Co. v. Wall*, [1941] O.R. 379 (C.A.); *Boland v. Irvin Porcupine Gold Mines Ltd.*, [1948] O.W.N. 181 and 483 (C.A.); *Re Arton Lumber Co.* (1960), 32 W.W.R. 516 (B.C. S.C.).

In the *Fremont Canning Co.* case the directors, pursuant to a by-law authorizing them to fix the remuneration of all officers, approved an agreement appointing the president as general manager for a fixed term and for a fixed remuneration with duties distinct from those he performed as president. After the expiration of the agreement the president continued to perform services as general manager, receiving the salary which had been approved by the board, and it was held that the president was thus placed in the position of an employee on a yearly salary basis and entitled to retain the amounts paid him as such. It should be noted that in this case the original appointment and remuneration had been authorized pursuant to a general by-law and that the action of the directors had been confirmed by the shareholders. In this case and in *Premier Trust Co. v. McAlister*, [1933] O.R. 195 at 205, the action was by the corporation for recovery of money paid. These cases should be contrasted with *Cape Breton Cold Storage Co. v. Rowlings*, [1929] S.C.R. 505 (S.C.C.) where a director was held not entitled to recover for services as a solicitor because there was no retainer or other contract of employment and the services were such as a director substantially interested in the corporation might well render without remuneration.

In *Boland v. Irvin Porcupine Gold Mines Ltd.*, *supra*, a director was held entitled to recover for professional services rendered to the corporation as its solicitor, although never formally appointed as such, because the directors knew of, acted on and received the benefit of such services.

In *Craven-Ellis v. Canons Ltd.*, [1936] 2 K.B. 403 (C.A.) a director was allowed compensation on a *quantum meruit* basis for services performed as an estate agent although the contract providing for his remuneration for such work was void. See also *Re Eric Petersen Construction Ltd.* (1967), 10 C.B.R. (N.S.) 254, 60 W.W.R. 103 (B.C. S.C.); *Flame Bar-B-Q Ltd. v. Hoar* (1978), 22 N.B.R. (2d) 595; revd on other grounds (1979), 27 N.B.R. (2d) 271 (N.B. C.A.). See also *Lorenc v. Koteles* (1981), 14 Man. R. (2d) 427 (Q.B.) where a president used some funds of the charitable corporation to reimburse himself for loss of income because of time spent for the corporation and also to retain counsel for the corporation. The actions were not authorized by the board of directors and were held to be improper.

The following cases, in which the decision was not based upon the former provisions of the Ontario Act above mentioned or similar legislation, may be referred to.

Held not entitled to remuneration:

Burland v. Earle (1900), 27 O.A.R. 540, 563; vard, [1902] A.C. 83, 101 (P.C.) (remuneration claimed by president not provided for by a by-law and not covered by a directors' resolution).

Cameron v. Gallagher Holman Ltd., [1924] 1 D.L.R. 242 (Man. K.B.) (managing director not entitled to remuneration for his services as manager as by-law required such remuneration to be determined by the directors and they had not passed a resolution).

Huggard v. Prudential Life Insurance Co., [1923] 1 W.W.R. 555; affd, [1924] 1 W.W.R. 642 (Man. C.A.) (director claiming under a contract entitling him to commission on sales of shares and by way of solicitor's fees).

Menzies v. Tyndall Quarries Co., [1926] 4 D.L.R. 350 (director claiming as mill manager and representative; no by-law and resolution of board only provided for salaries of directors; requirement of a by-law held to be imperative).

Re J. C. Harris Groceterias Ltd. [1940] 2 D.L.R. 257 (N.S. C.A.) (director acting as manager and as clerk; no appointment or fixing of salary by directors in accordance with articles).

Allish v. Allied Engineering of B.C. Ltd. (1957), 9 D.L.R. (2d) 688 (B.C. C.A.) (director claiming remuneration as manager, no resolution of board fixing salary as required by the articles).

Held entitled to remuneration:

Burland v. Earle (1900), 27 O.A.R. 540, 563; vard, [1902] A.C. 83, 101 (P.C.) (remuneration claimed by vice-president not provided for under a by-law but deemed to have been covered by a directors' resolution).

Durost v. Home Mixed Fertilizers Ltd., [1942] 4 D.L.R. 241 (N.B. C.A.) (director held entitled to remuneration under implied contract for services performed as a subordinate, no by-law having been passed under the *New Brunswick Companies Act, 1916*, c. 14, s. 90(b) and the director having refused to accept the remuneration voted to him after the performance of the services).

Anderson v. Herbert Paint & Varnish Co., [1928] 1 D.L.R. 417 (Alta. T.D.) (remuneration for services as secretary-treasurer and bookkeeper fixed by agreement with general manager; officer became a director after commencement of employment; defence based on article requiring remuneration of directors to be determined in general meeting, which was held not to be applicable).

Dufour v. Dufour-Wilson Motors Ltd., [1949] 2 W.W.R. 593 (remuneration of three directors as general manager, secretary-treasurer and plant foreman respectively covered by a directors' resolution).

Re Arton Lumber Co. (1960), 32 W.W.R. 516 (B.C. S.C.) (directors held to be entitled to remuneration under an implied contract for services performed as subordinates).

Apportionment

Where the remuneration is fixed at a certain sum "per annum" or "in each year" a director can only recover for each complete year: *In re Central de Kaap Gold Mines* (1899), 69 L.J. Ch. 18; *Salton v. New Beeston Cycle Co.*, [1899] 1 Ch. 775; *Inman v. Ackroyd*, [1901] 1 K.B. 613; *In re London & Northern Bank; McConnell's Claim*, [1901] 1 Ch. 728; *Moriarty v. Regent's Garage*, [1921] 2 K.B. 766 (C.A.). Where the remuneration was "for each year" requiring service for a full year, the director was, however, held entitled to his remuneration notwithstanding that the corporation went into liquidation before the year expired: *In re Shaws Bryant & Co.*, [1901] W.N. 124. Where the remuneration is fixed "at the rate of" so much per annum a director will be entitled to remuneration for a broken portion of a year served: *Moriarty v. Regent's Garage*, *supra*, per Younger L.J., at 786.

Payments not justifiable as remuneration

Where the remuneration is not justifiable for the services rendered or by the state of the corporation's business, directors cannot vote the president a salary in order to permit him to acquire shares and gain control of the corporation: *Giguère v. Colas* (1915), 48 Que. S.C. 198; or vote to themselves remuneration with a view to compelling a minority shareholder to sell to them his shares at a low price, the appropriation of moneys in this way being deemed to be fraudulent: *Nolan v. Parsons*, [1942] O.R. 358 at 363 (C.A.). So also where there is no bona fide purpose of remuneration, but the intention on the part of the directors is to vote all the profits of the corporation to themselves for past service in capacities to which they had never been appointed, such action will not be upheld: *Gardner v. Canadian Manufacturing Publishing Co.* (1900), 31 O.R. 488. See also *Cook v. Hinds* (1918), 42 O.L.R. 273 (C.A.) judgment of Lennox J.

Gratuities and remuneration for past services

A corporation may vote gratuities to the directors where this is done as incidental to the carrying on of the corporation's business: *Hutton v. West Cork Ry.* (1883), 23 Ch. D. 654 at 671-2 (C.A.); *Hampson v. Price's Patent Candle Co.* (1876), 45 L.J. Ch. 437; but not gifts to directors when the corporation's capital is impaired: *Crawford v. Bathurst Land & Development Co.* (1916), 37 O.L.R. 611 at 638; affd (1918), 42 O.L.R. 256, per Riddell and Rose JJ. This case was reversed by the Supreme Court of Canada, by a majority of three to two ((1919), 59 S.C.R. 314), but the judgments of the majority on this head went on the ground of personal disqualification of the plaintiff to bring the action and acquiesence; and it is submitted that the above qualification to the rule is settled by the decisions mentioned in the judgments in the above case. See also the judgment of Rose J. in *Cook v. Hinds* (1918), 42 O.L.R. 273 at 301

(C.A.); and *Re Continental Publishing Co.* (1924), 25 O.W.N. 610 (gratuity not payable out of capital).

A gift by a corporation to one of its directors or his widow cannot be supported unless specially authorized by the instrument regulating the corporation or by a meeting of the shareholders specially called for the purpose of approving the gift: *In re Lee, Behrens, & Co.*, [1932] 2 Ch. 46.

On the other hand creditors have no status to attack payments made by a corporation for insurance premiums on the lives of directors, the corporation being in good circumstances at the time of such payments, where the agreement between the corporation and the directors provided that the proceeds of the policy on the life of the first director to die were to be applied in purchasing the deceased director's shares which were to be divided among the surviving directors: *Payne v. Nancekivell* (1934), 15 C.B.R. 471. The court indicated that the agreement was *ultra vires* and would have been vulnerable to attack by shareholders.

The Act does not deal with the question of granting remuneration for past services, but this may be done, at any rate where all the shareholders agree: *In re Dorenwends Ltd.* (1924), 55 O.L.R. 413 (C.A.); *Bartram v. Birtwhistle* (1908), 15 O.L.R. 634 (C.A.), where a grant by the shareholders at an annual meeting to the treasurer of the corporation for his services during the past 30 years was upheld. This is a matter of internal economy, per Boyd C., at p. 636.

On the construction of the memorandum the grant of a pension by way of gratuity to a retired secretary of a club was held *intra vires*: *Cyclists' Touring Club v. Hopkinson*, [1910] 1 Ch. 179. A corporation constituted by Act of Parliament can pay pensions or superannuation allowances for employees retiring by reason of age, infirmity or otherwise, notwithstanding that it has no express power: *Wimbledon & Putney Commons Conservators v. Tuely*, [1931] 1 Ch. 190.

A corporation cannot, however, expend its funds in payments to the directors for past services where it has transferred its undertaking to another corporation and is being wound up: *Hutton v. West Cork Ry.* (1883), 23 Ch. D. 654 (C.A.). Where the business of the corporation had ceased, gratuities were held to be invalid in the absence of due ratification by the shareholders: *Lumbers v. Fretz* (1928), 62 O.L.R. 635; affd (1928), 63 O.L.R. 190 (C.A.). See also *Stroud v. Royal Aquarium* (1903), 89 L.T. 243; *Warren v. Lambeth Waterworks* (1904), 21 T.L.R. 685. Where the articles of association authorized the payment, a bonus and salary for services rendered voted at a meeting at which all the shareholders were present could not be recovered back: *Macdonald Bros. v. Godson* (1916), 31 D.L.R. 363 (B.C. C.A.). See also *Cook v. Hinds* (1918), 42 O.L.R. 273 (C.A.), a case of remuneration for past services in which the judgment, however, went on other grounds.

Where, however, shares had been issued in satisfaction of a claim for arrears of salary of the general manager held to be unenforceable and invalid, the court, in setting aside the transaction, applied the rule that real consideration is requisite to support the issuance of fully paid shares: *Warren v. Superior Engravers Ltd.*, [1941] 1 D.L.R. 323 at 333 (Ont. C.A.). In that case the shareholders had refused to approve a by-law for the allotment of the shares.

Compensation for loss of office

Upon the termination of a corporation's undertaking by amalgamation or sale of assets the directors are sometimes given compensation for the loss of their positions. Full and complete disclosure to the parties interested of all the main facts is a necessary basis of such compensation: *Clarkson v. Davies*, [1923] A.C. 100 (P.C.) but, as was pointed out in that case at p. 110, such a transaction is not *ultra vires* and if unauthorized is capable of ratification.

Remuneration out of capital

In England, if the articles authorize it remuneration may be paid out of capital, there being no general presumption that directors' fees are to be paid out of profits only: *Re Lundy Granite Co.* (1872), 26 L.T.N.S. 673, and directors can sue for the fees to which they are entitled: *Nell v. Atlanta Co.* (1894), 11 T.L.R. 407.

However, in *Re Publishers' Syndicate; Paton's Case* (1903), 5 O.L.R. 392 at 406 (C.A.), Maclaren J.A. laid down the proposition that the remuneration of directors for their trouble as such can only be given out of the assets properly divisible among the shareholders themselves and not out of capital, citing *In re George Newman & Co.*, [1895] 1 Ch. 674 (C.A.), which was, however, a case involving gifts to directors: see per Lindley L.J., at p. 686. Moreover, in the *Publishers' Syndicate* case it did not appear that any services had been rendered and the statutory requirement of a by-law authorizing the remuneration had not been complied with. The case is accordingly not decisive on the question of the legality of the payment of remuneration out of capital where the corporation's by-laws authorize such payment. Probably such payment will be upheld provided sufficient assets remain to pay all creditors' claims in full. The result will be different if the corporation is insolvent: *Re Continental Publishing Co.* (1924), 25 O.W.N. 610.

In *Wilson v. Woollatt* (1928), 62 O.L.R. 620 (C.A.); affd (*sub nom. Woollatt v. Western Racing Assn.*), [1929] S.C.R. 483 it was contended that a bonus was not properly payable because the capital was impaired, but it was held that there was a substantial surplus over the par value of the issued shares.

In *Allish v. Allied Engineering of B.C. Ltd.* (1957), 9 D.L.R. (2d) 688 (B.C. C.A.), the British Columbia Court of Appeal dismissed a corporation's claim for moneys paid to its managing director under an informal arrangement on the basis that the payments were not made out of capital, that they were within the power of the corporation and that the shareholders knew the material facts and had impliedly approved the payments as made.

Remuneration by issue of paid-up shares

The issuing by a corporation of paid-up shares is a legitimate mode of paying a debt. See *Gardner v. Iredale*, [1912] 1 Ch. 700; and in *Beaudry v. Read* (1907), 10 O.W.R. 622 (Ont. K.B.), Riddell J. was apparently of the opinion that the issuing of paid-up shares to directors by way of remuneration was unobjectionable provided the requirements of the governing statute were complied with (which was not so in that case). A corporation may, with the unanimous consent of the shareholders, award remuneration in the form of paid-up shares by applying in that manner surplus available for distribution by way of dividend: *In re Dorenwends Ltd.* (1924), 55 O.L.R. 413 (C.A.).

Waiver and forfeiture of remuneration

Directors can by resolution postpone their right to remuneration not yet due: *In re London & Northern Bank; McConnell's Claim*, [1901] 1 Ch. 728; but see *In re Central de Kaap Gold Mines* (1899), 69 L.J. Ch. 18. Directors are entitled to "remuneration for their services", or "remuneration as directors", notwithstanding that they may also be receiving remuneration as receivers and managers in a debenture holders' proceeding: *In re South Western of Venezuela Ry.*, [1902] 1 Ch. 701. See also *Victoria Fire Insurance Co. v. Thomson* (1882), 32 U.C.C.P. 476. Nor is a directors' remuneration affected because his duties have diminished: *In re Consolidated Nickel Mines*, [1914] 1 Ch. 883; nor because there has been a shifting of duties, if it is clear that there was an intention that his remuneration should nevertheless continue: *Burland v. Earle*, [1902] A.C. 83 at 101 (P.C.); but where a director holds office not under an independent contract but on the terms of the articles or by-laws, the effect of liquidation is to terminate his contract of service since his employment is limited to the active life of the corporation, and no damages are recoverable for such termination: *In re T. N. Farrer Ltd.*, [1937] 1 Ch. 352.

Misconduct

The rule as regards forfeiture of the right to remuneration in the event of misconduct is that, where the duties are severable, the agent, employee or director is entitled to remuneration in all cases where he has been honest but is not entitled to it in instances where he has been dishonest: *Nitedals Taendstikfabrik v. Bruster*, [1906] 2 Ch. 671; but, where the duties are inseparable, unfaithfulness even without fraud in the performance of any one of them will disentitle him to any remuneration. In *Cook v. Hinds* (1918), 42 O.L.R. 273 (C.A.), it was held that the duties of directors who were also managers and general superintendents of the corporation's business were not severable so as to entitle them to remuneration in respect of their services as managers and superintendents where they had been guilty of diverting business from the corporation, but this finding may perhaps depend on the peculiar facts of that case.

Misconduct on the part of an employee who is also a director does not disentitle him to salary previously earned: *Canada Bonded Attorney & Legal Directory v. Leonard-Parmiter Ltd.* (1918), 42 O.L.R. 141 (C.A.).

Directors as restricted creditors in bankruptcy

The *Bankruptcy and Insolvency Act* provides as follows:

140. Where a corporation becomes bankrupt, no officer or director thereof is entitled to have his claim preferred as provided by section 136 in respect of wages, salary,

commission or compensation for work done or services rendered to the corporation in any capacity.

Personal liability of directors

This topic is discussed under the following sub-headings: Standard required of directors; Breach of trust — misfeasance; Negligence; Non-intervention in corporation's affairs; Breach of warranty of authority; Dividends; Other statutory liabilities; Liability in tort; Contribution; Criminal liability; Liability for amounts withheld from employees pursuant to the *Income Tax Act.*

Standard required of directors

Under the federal Act, every director and officer of a corporation in exercising his powers and discharging his duties is required to act honestly and in good faith with a view to the best interests of the corporation and is also required to exercise the care, diligence and skill that a reasonably prudent person would exercise under comparable circumstances. In addition, every such person is to comply with the requirements of the Act, regulations, articles, by-laws and any unanimous shareholder agreement. Except as provided by any unanimous shareholder agreement, no provision in any contract or resolution, the articles or by-laws relieves a director or officer from the duty to act in accordance with the Act or the regulations or relieves him from any liability for breach thereof. See s. 122.

The rule at common law was somewhat different, directors being bound to use fair and reasonable diligence in the management of the corporation's affairs, and to act honestly, but not bound to do more: *Re Forest of Dean Coal Mining Co.* (1878), 10 Ch. D. 450 at 452; *Prefontaine v. Grenier*, [1907] A.C. 101 at 111; *Stavert v. Lovitt* (1908), 42 N.S.R. 449 (C.A.); *Re Owen Sound Lumber Co.* (1917), 38 O.L.R. 414 at 421, 422 (C.A.); *Northern Trust Co. v. Butchart* (1917), 35 D.L.R. 169; *In re City Equitable Fire Insurance Co.*, [1925] Ch. 407 (C.A.); *Western Ontario Natural Gas Co. v. Aikens*, [1946] O.R. 661 at 688.

"If directors act within their powers; if they act with such care as is reasonably to be expected from them, having regard to their knowledge and experience — and if they act honestly for the benefit of the company they represent, they discharge their equitable as well as their legal duty to the company": *In re National Bank of Wales*, [1899] 2 Ch. 629, per Lindley M.R., in the Court of Appeal adopting the statement of the law laid down in *Lagunas Nitrate Co. v. Lagunas Syndicate*, [1899] 2 Ch. 392 (C.A.).

In *Scottish Co-operative Wholesale Society Ltd. v. Meyer*, [1959] A.C. 324, the House of Lords held that directors' misconduct of the affairs of a corporation might take the form of passive conduct, neglect of its interests and concealment from the minority of knowledge that it was material for the corporation to know. Lord Keith said at p. 363:

> But I cannot think that where directors, having power to do something to save a company, lie back and do nothing, they are not conducting the affairs of the company, perhaps foolishly, perhaps negligently, perhaps with some ulterior object

in view. They are certainly conducting the affairs of the company in breach of their duty as directors.

A director is not bound to bring any special qualifications to his office: *In re Brazilian Rubber Plantations & Estates Ltd.*, [1911] 1 Ch. 425. As was stated by Romer J. in *In re City Equitable Fire Insurance Co.*, [1925] Ch. 407 at 428 (C.A.); "A director need not exhibit in the performance of his duties a greater degree of skill than may reasonably be expected from a person of his knowledge and experience. A director of a life insurance company, for instance, does not guarantee that he has the skill of an actuary or of a physician."

Breach of trust — misfeasance

Particular acts of directors may constitute breaches of trust or misfeasance for which they will be liable to the corporation. Misconduct involving misapplication of funds or property of the corporation is generally termed "breach of trust", whereas the word "misfeasance" characterizes other breaches of duty which do not involve such misapplication but result in pecuniary loss to the corporation.

The liability of a director for breach of trust is discussed under the heading "Fiduciary position of directors" in this chapter. See also the notes on "Contracts of directors with the corporation" in this chapter.

Where a director arranged with a shareholder to stop payment on the cheque issued by the shareholder in payment of his shares, the court held that this conduct was "an active breach of duty — in other words, misfeasance": *Re Lake Ontario Navigation Co., Hutchinson's Case* (1909), 13 O.W.R. 1037. Section 124 of the *Winding-up Act, infra*, provides a summary procedure against directors who have been guilty of any misfeasance or breach of trust.

Directors who accept and hold their qualification shares in trust for the promoters, to whom they hand blank transfers, are guilty of misfeasance: *In re London & South Western Canal Ltd.*, [1911] 1 Ch. 346.

Directors have a wide discretion, and while acting honestly within it cannot be charged with misfeasance. Thus, when a director was cognizant that money had been improperly paid on the formation of a corporation, but took no steps to recover the money for the corporation, it was held that he was not liable for misfeasance: *Re Forest of Dean Coal Mining Co.* (1878), 10 Ch. D. 450. Similarly when in their discretion directors allowed calls to remain unpaid they were not held liable: *Re Liverpool Household Stores Assn.* (1890), 59 L.J. Ch. 616.

A director who does not really exercise his judgment will be liable: *In re New Mashonaland Exploration Co.*, [1892] 3 Ch. 577. Where the alleged misfeasance is neither *ultra vires*, nor fraudulent nor dishonest, failure on the part of the directors really to exercise their judgment as such and actual loss or damage to the corporation must be shown: ibid.

A director is not liable for a fraud committed by his co-directors or by any other agents of the corporation unless it has been expressly authorized or tacitly permitted by him: *Cargill v. Bower* (1878), 10 Ch. D. 502.

An innocent director is not liable for the fraud of a co-director in issuing to the shareholders false and fraudulent reports. A director is not bound to examine minutely each of the corporation's books, nor is the doctrine of constructive notice to be so extended as to impute to him a knowledge of the contents of the books: *Land Credit Co. of Ireland v. Lord Fermoy* (1870), L.R. 5 Ch. App. 763; *Re Denham & Co.* (1884), 25 Ch. D. 752; *Re H. J. Logan Co.*, [1926] 2 D.L.R. 946.

Directors will not be personally liable when they have been misled by misrepresentation or concealment by the regularly authorized executive officers of the corporation where there was no reason to doubt their fidelity: *Rance's Case* (1871), L.R. 6 Ch. App. 104 at 118; *Prefontaine v. Grenier*, [1907] A.C. 101 at 190; *Prudential Trust Co. v. McQuaid* (1919), 45 D.L.R. 346 (Alta. C.A.). Thus they are not bound to verify the calculations of the corporation's auditors: *Dovey v. Cory*, [1901] A.C. 477 at 486 (P.C.). See also s. 123(4) of the Act.

Nor will directors or officers be liable where they have, in good faith, done something irregularly (e.g., allotted shares) which has been adopted by the corporation: *Imperial Bank v. Dennis* (1926), 59 O.L.R. 20. See also *Pavlides v. Jensen*, [1956] 1 Ch. 565; *Crown Trust Co. v. Ontario* (1988), 64 O.R. (2d) 774; *Daniels v. Daniels*, [1978] Ch. 406 and *Prudential Assurance v. Newman Industries (No. 2)*, [1980] 2 All E.R. 841.

For the liability of directors in respect of misrepresentations in a prospectus, see the notes to Chapter 13.

Negligence

Directors will be liable for acts of gross negligence: *Northern Trust Co. v. Butchart* (1917), 35 D.L.R. 169; *Stavert v. Lovitt* (1908), 42 N.S.R. 449 (C.A.); *Cushing Sulphite Fibre Co. v. Cushing* (1906), 37 N.B.R. 313 (C.A.); but a mere default of judgment or error in a matter of discrimination is not negligence, and directors were held not liable for an improvident loan to one of themselves: *Turquand v. Marshall* (1869), L.R. 4 Ch. App. 376. It was said in that case that whatever may have been the amount lent to anybody and however ridiculous and absurd the conduct of the directors might seem, it was the misfortune of the corporation that they trusted such unwise directors, and that to fix them with liability something more must be alleged, as for instance that the lending was fraudulent and improper.

In the discharge of the particular duties which they have assumed directors are bound to take reasonable care, and failure to exercise such care constitutes negligence. On this point Romer J. made the following observations in *In re City Equitable Fire Insurance Co.*, [1925] Ch. 407 at 427 (C.A.).

> It has been laid down that so long as a director acts honestly he cannot be made responsible in damages unless guilty of gross or culpable negligence in a business sense. But as pointed out by Neville J. in *In re Brazilian Rubber Plantations and Estates Ltd.*, [1911] 1 Ch. 425, 437, one cannot say whether a man has been guilty of negligence, gross or otherwise, unless one can determine what is the extent of the duty which he is alleged to have neglected. For myself, I confess to feeling some difficulty in understanding the difference between negligence and gross

> negligence, except in so far as the expressions are used for the purpose of drawing a distinction between the duty that is owed in one case and the duty that is owed in another. If two men owe the same duty to a third person, and neglect to perform that duty, they are both guilty of negligence, and it is not altogether easy to understand how one can be guilty of gross negligence and the other of negligence only. But if it be said that of two men one is only liable to a third person for gross negligence, and the other is liable for mere negligence, this, I think, means no more than that the duties of the two men are different. The one owes a duty to take a greater degree of care than does the other: see the observations of Willes J. in *Grill v. General Iron Screw Collier Co.* (1866), L.R. 1 C.P. 600, 612. If, therefore, a director is only liable for gross or culpable negligence, this means that he does not owe a duty to his corporation, to take all possible care. It is some degree of care less than that. The care that he is bound to take has been described by Neville J. in the case referred to above as "reasonable care" to be measured by the care an ordinary man might be expected to take in the circumstances on his own behalf. In saying this Neville J. was only following what was laid down in *Overend & Gurney Co. v. Gibb* (1872), L.R. 5 H.L. 480, 486 as being the proper test to apply, namely: "Whether or not the directors exceeded the powers entrusted to them, or whether if they did not so exceed their powers they were cognisant of circumstances of such a character, so plain, so manifest, and so simple of appreciation, that no men with any ordinary degree of prudence, acting on their own behalf, would have entered into such a transaction as they entered into?".

If directors adopt a system of doing business which ignores a factor which by statute ought to be a part of that system (e.g., the obligation to keep corporation funds and trust funds distinct) that will constitute such negligence as will impose liability if loss is shown to have resulted: *Re Dominion Trust Co.; Directors' Case* (1917), 32 D.L.R. 63 (B.C. C.A.); *Scott v. Riehl* (1958), 15 D.L.R. (2d) 67 (B.C. S.C.).

See also the notes under the heading "Standard required of directors" in this chapter.

A claim against directors based on negligence may be barred by lapse of time: *Canadian Guaranty Trust Co. v. Young*, [1933] 1 D.L.R. 256 (Man. C.A.).

Non-intervention in corporation's affairs

A director is not bound to take any definite part in the conduct of the corporation's business: *In re Brazilian Rubber Plantations & Estates Ltd.*, [1911] 1 Ch. 425, and a director who takes no part in the negligent or *ultra vires* acts of the board will escape liability: *Re Dominion Trust Co.; Directors' Case, supra.* It will be noted that under s. 123(3) a director who is not present at the meeting where a resolution was passed or action taken is deemed to have consented thereto unless within 7 days after he becomes aware of the resolution he causes his dissent to be placed with the minutes of the meeting or sends his dissent by registered mail or delivers it to the registered office of the corporation. So far, however, as he does participate, he must exercise reasonable care: *In re Brazilian Rubber, supra.*

A director is not bound to attend any meeting of the board, but gross inattention to the business of the directors may amount to a breach of trust.

An ordinary director who only attends at the board occasionally cannot be expected to devote as much time and attention to the business as the sole managing partner of an ordinary partnership: *In re Forest of Dean Coal Mining Co.* (1878), 10 Ch. D. 450 at 452; *Marzetti's Case* (1880), 28 W.R. 541; *Re Faure Electric Accumulator Co.* (1889), 40 Ch. D. 141; *Sheffield & South Yorkshire Permanent Building Society v. Aizlewood* (1890), 44 Ch. D. 412; *Marquis of Bute's Case*, [1892] 2 Ch. 100; *In re National Bank of Wales Ltd.*, [1899] 2 Ch. 629 (C.A.).

Directors who were only present at a directors' meeting which confirmed the minutes of the meeting at which an improper application of funds was resolved upon cannot be thereby held to concur in the improper application: *In re Lands Allotment Co.*, [1894] 1 Ch. 616 (C.A.).

Similarly, where a director did not authorize or direct the payment out of the corporation's moneys in illegal commissions, except in one instance where he joined in signing a cheque "on account of commission," he was held to be liable only for the amount of such cheque: *Re Monarch Bank of Canada* (1910), 22 O.L.R. 516.

See also the cases discussed in the notes under the heading "Standard required of directors", in this chapter.

Breach of warranty of authority

Directors who act in excess of their authority are in some cases held liable to those with whom they deal on the ground of implied warranty of their authority: *Firbanks Executors v. Humphreys* (1886), 18 Q.B.D. 54 (C.A.); *Chapleo v. Brunswick Permanent Benefit Building Society* (1881), 6 Q.B.D. 696 (C.A.).

If directors represent that they have authority to enter into a transaction, where as a matter of fact they have not, and the party to whom the representation is made, acting upon it, incurs loss, he may sue the directors for damages: *Firbanks Executors v. Humphreys, supra*; *Whitehaven Joint Stock Banking Co. v. Reed* (1886), 54 L.T. 360 (C.A.); *Weeks v. Propert* (1873), L.R. 8 C.P. 427; *Looker v. Wrigley* (1882), 9 Q.B.D. 397.

The misrepresentation must be one in point of fact. If the misrepresentation is in point of law, that is, if the person who deals with the agent is fully aware in point of fact what the extent of the authority of the agent is, but makes a mistake as to whether that authority is sufficient in point of law or not, the agent will not be liable, per Mellish L.J., in *Beattie v. Lord Ebury* (1872), L.R. 7 Ch. App. 777 at 802.

Thus, where directors had bought goods on the credit of the corporation which by its act of incorporation it had no power to buy, they were held not liable on a warranty of authority or otherwise, the representation being one of law and not of fact: *Struthers v. Mackenzie* (1897), 28 O.R. 381. So also, where the statute expressly took away the power of pledging the credit of a co-operative association, the directors were not liable on an implied warranty that the directors had authority or the association had power to purchase goods on credit: *MacDonald-Crawford Ltd. v. Burns*, [1924] 2 D.L.R. 977 (Sask. C.A.) and cases cited.

As to the personal liability of directors who fail to make it clear in executing a contract that they do so as agents on behalf of the corporation, see the notes in Chapter 3.

Dividends

As to the liability of directors in the event of wrongful payment of dividends, see the notes to s. 42 of the Act and s. 124 of the *Winding-up Act*.

Other statutory liabilities

Section 118(1) provides that a director voting for or consenting to resolutions authorizing the issue of a share under s. 25 for a consideration other than money are jointly and severally liable to the corporation to make good any amount by which the consideration received is less than the fair equivalent of the money that the corporation would have received if the share was issued for money on the date of the resolution; he is not liable, however, by virtue of subs. (6), if he proves that he did not know and could not reasonably have known that the share was issued for a consideration less than the fair equivalent of the money that the corporation would have received if the share had been issued for money. An action to enforce liability under s. 118(1) must be commenced within two years of the date of the resolution authorizing the action complained of.

In addition to the liabilities for certain wages, as to which see heading "Liability of directors for wages", and as to the liability for the issuance of shares, directors may also be liable with respect to the purchase, redemption, or other acquisition of shares contrary to the provisions of ss. 34 to 36, a commission payable on the issue of shares contrary to s. 41, the payment of a dividend contrary to s. 42, the giving of financial assistance contrary to s. 44, a payment of an indemnity contrary to s. 124 or a payment to a shareholder contrary to s. 190 or s. 241 (s. 118(2)). In each such case the directors are jointly and severally liable to restore to the corporation any amount so distributed or repaid not otherwise recovered by the corporation. By virtue of subs. (3) a director who has satisfied a judgment rendered under this section is entitled to contribution from the other directors who voted for or consented to the unlawful act on which the judgment is founded. In addition, a director may apply to a court for an order compelling a shareholder or other recipient to pay or deliver to the director any money or property paid or distributed to the shareholder or other recipient contrary to the sections in question. A court under s. 118(5) may make such an order, or order a corporation to return or issue shares to a person from whom the corporation has purchased, redeemed or otherwise acquired them, or make any further order that it may think fit. The basic test in the Act is that a corporation may not make a payment of the type referred to if it is or would, after the payment in question, be unable to pay its liabilities as they become due or if the realizable value of its assets would, after the payment, be less than the aggregate of its liabilities and stated capital, or in some cases, the amount required for payment on redemption or liquidation of shares ranking prior to the holders of the shares to be purchased or redeemed. It will be observed that a reduction of capital pursuant to s. 38 of the Act is not specifically dealt with under s. 118, although subs. (6) of s. 38 provides that the section does not affect any liability arising under s. 118.

Liability in tort

Directors may also be liable to outsiders for their own wrongs, for example, fraud: *Re Traders' Trust Co. & Kory* (1916), 26 D.L.R. 41; *Parker v. McQuesten* (1868), 32 U.C.Q.B. 273. See also *Ontario Bank v. Merchants Bank of Halifax* (1900), 5 Que. P.R. 392 (director of warehousing corporation not liable for failure to inform holder of warehouse receipt of disappearance of goods, in absence of any allegation of fault of director in respect thereof).

A director may be held liable for the acts of the corporation if fraud on the part of the corporation in which he has participated and loss or damage to the plaintiff attributable to such fraud (which loss may include a benefit accruing to the director from such fraud) are shown: *McLaughlin v. Solloway Mills*, [1936] S.C.R. 127 at 138; vard (*sub nom. Solloway v. McLaughlin*) [1938] A.C. 247; and see *Solloway v. Johnson*, [1934] A.C. 193 at 207.

Directors who are parties to a fraud or the commission of any other wrong are personally liable on the general principle that a servant or agent who commits a wrong is liable for damages resulting therefrom as well as his principal: *Scott v. Riehl* (1959), 15 D.L.R. (2d) 67 (B.C.) (misappropriation of trust fund by director); *Briess v. Woolley*, [1954] A.C. 333 (fraudulent misrepresentation of corporation's trading accounts by director).

Directors, however, are not responsible for the tortious acts of the corporation unless such acts are expressly directed by them: *Rainham Chemical Works v. Belvedere Fish Guano Co.*, [1921] 2 A.C. 465 at 476; *Northern Electric Co. v. Burkholder*, [1935] 4 D.L.R. 598 at 619. If directors are to be made liable as principals the agency of the corporation must be established and will not be inferred from the fact that they are the sole directors and shareholders: *British Thomson-Houston Co. v. Sterling Accessories Ltd.*, [1924] 2 Ch. 33, 38. Directors have been held personally liable where they knowingly pursued a course of action which constituted copyright infringement, see: *Apple Computer Inc. v. Mackintosh Computers Ltd.* (1986), 28 D.L.R. (4th) 178 (F.C.T.D.), affd on other grounds [1990] 2 S.C.R. 209 and for the liablity of executives in respect of injuries suffered by an employee who slipped on a snow covered sidewalk see: *Berger v. Willowdale* (1983), 145 D.L.R. (3d) 247 (Ont. C.A.). In certain circumstances, directors may be personally sued for negligent or fraudulent misrepresentation. See for example: *Toronto Dominion Bank v. Leigh Instruments Ltd. (Trustee of)* (1991), 40 C.C.E.L. 262 (Ont. Div. Ct.), affg December 21, 1990, Ont. Ct. Gen. Div., where it was alleged that the directors knew that the financial condition of the corporation had deteriorated and either personally made representations contained in commitment letters or alternatively owed an independent duty to the bank to disclose such facts, the statement of claim was not dismissed as against the defendant directors in their personal capacity.

Thus, in *Schmiechel v. Lane*, [1983] 3 W.W.R. 30; affd [1983] 5 W.W.R. 151 (Sask. C.A.) it was held that the general rule that directors or servants of a corporation acting within a scope of their authority are not liable in tort for inducing or procuring a breach of contract by their employer is subject to an exception where some of the directors conspire prior to a board meeting to induce the board as a whole wrongfully to break a contract by dismissing one of the corporation's servants. The general rule that directors or employees of a corporation acting within a scope of their authority are not liable in tort for inducing or procuring a breach in contract by the corporation is not the case where there is *mala fides*, fraud or a lack of *bona fides*. See *Gravelbourg Savings & Credit Union Ltd. v. Heritage Motors Ltd.* (1982), 19 Sask. R. 178 (Sask. Q.B.). See also *Oceatain Investments Ltd. v. Canadian Commercial Bank* (1983), 51 A.R. 364 (Ont. Q.B.); *Schouls v. Canadian Meat Processing Corp.* (1983), 41 O.R. (2d) 600, 1 C.C.E.L. 209 (Ont. H.C.); *McFadden v. 481782 Ontario Ltd.* (1984), 47 O.R. (2d) 134, 5 C.C.E.L. 83 (Ont. H.C.); *Kepic v. Tecumseh Road Builders* (1985), 29 B.L.R. 85 (Ont. H.C.) (judgment varied on other grounds in the Court of Appeal (1987), 18 C.C.E.L. 218); *Morgan v. Saskatchewan* (1985), 31 B.L.R. 173, 43 Sask. R. 129 (Sask. C.A.); *Apple Computer Inc. v. Mackintosh Computers Ltd.*, [1990] 2 S.C.R. 209, 36 F.T.R. 159 (S.C.C.); *Beamish v. Solnick* (1980), 10 B.L.R. 224 (Ont. H.C.); *Einhorn v. Westmount Investments Ltd.* (1970), 73 W.W.R. 161, 11 D.L.R. (3rd) 509 (Sask. C.A.); *Regina v. Rosen*, [1985] 1 S.C.R. 83; and *Henry Electric Ltd. v. Farwell* (1985), 60 B.C.L.R. 105; affd 5 B.C.L.R. (2d) 273 (C.A.).

Contribution

In cases of breach of trust, not involving fraud, a director who has been required to make compensation to the corporation is entitled to contribution from co-directors or others who were parties to the wrongful act: *Ashurst v. Mason* (1875), L.R. 20 Eq. 225 (contribution in respect of calls paid by a director on shares purchased and transferred to a director in trust for the corporation); *Ramskill v. Edwards* (1886), 31 Ch. D. 100 (contribution in respect of amount paid by director representing loss to corporation on *ultra vires* loan). There is no right of contribution when the transaction was fraudulent: *Moxham v. Grant*, [1900] 1 Q.B. 88 at 93, 95 (C.A.).

The liability to make contribution survives to the estate of a deceased director: *Ramskill v. Edwards, supra.*

Criminal liability

As to the criminal liability of directors, see *R. v. Hendrie* (1906), 11 O.L.R. 202 (C.A.), where it was held that more than mere acquiescence was required to make them parties to the offence of keeping a common betting-house under the Criminal Code. In *R. v. Hays* (1907), 14 O.L.R. 201 (C.A.) the court quashed the conviction of a director for omitting to do an act required by an Act of the Parliament of Canada on the ground that the omission, that is, default in filing returns, was not his but the corporation's.

As to the criminal liability of directors for a prospectus false in a material respect under s. 400 of the Criminal Code, see the notes in Chapter 13. Under

s. 328(e) of the Criminal Code theft may be committed by directors against a corporation. Theft is defined by s. 322(1) of the Criminal Code.

As to liability of directors for pollution caused by the corporation, see *R. v. Bata Industries Ltd.* (1992), 9 O.R. (3d) 329 and *R. v. Amoco Fabrics & Fibres Ltd.* (1992), 73 C.C.C. (3d) 558 (Prov. Div.). In *R. v. Varnicolor Chemical Ltd.* (1992), 9 C.E.L.R. (N.S.) 176 (Ont. Prov. Div.), a prison sentence was imposed on "the only officer and director to take an active part in the operations and management of that company". In addition there are numerous provincial statutes imposing criminal or other liability on directors.

Liability for amounts withheld from employees pursuant to the Income Tax Act

Section 227.1 of the *Income Tax Act* (Canada) provides that where a corporation has failed to deduct or withhold an amount as required under the Act or has failed to remit such amount, the directors of the corporation at the time the corporation was required to deduct, withhold, remit or pay the amount are jointly and severally liable together with the corporation to pay that amount and any interest or penalties relating thereto. Subsection (2) of that provision states that a director is not liable unless a certificate for the amount of the corporation's liability has been registered in the Federal Court of Canada under s. 223 of the *Income Tax Act* and execution for such amount has been returned unsatisfied in whole or in part, or if the corporation has commenced liquidation or dissolution proceedings, or has been dissolved and a claim for the amount of the corporation's liability has been proved within six months after the earlier of the date of commencement of the proceedings and the date of dissolution, or the corporation has made an assignment or a receiving order has been made against it under the *Bankruptcy and Insolvency Act* and a claim for the amount of the corporation's liability referred to in question has been proved within six months after the date of the assignment or receiving order. The action to recover an amount payable by a director pursuant to this provision must be commenced within two years after he last ceased to be a director of the corporation involved (s. 227.1(4)). The amount recoverable is the amount remaining unsatisfied after execution (subs. (5)) and the director is entitled to the same preference as the Crown would have had in respect of any amount paid (subs. (6)); in addition, he is entitled to contribution from the other directors (subs. (7)).

Subsection (3) of s. 227.1 provides that a director is not liable for failure to withhold or remit if he has exercised the degree of care, diligence and skill to prevent the failure that a reasonably prudent person would have exercised in comparable circumstances. There have been a number of cases pursuant to this provision, for example, *McCullough v. MNR* (1989), 89 D.T.C. 466, [1989] C.T.C. 2236 (T.C.C.), *DeWitt v. MNR*, [1990] 90 D.T.C. 1027, 1 C.T.C. 2098 (T.C.C.) and *Clarke v. M.N.R.* (1990), 3 C.B.R. (3d) 213 (T.C.C.), for illustrations of cases where there was held to be no liability on directors. If a certificate is given by the chief financial officer of a corporation that all amounts due have been withheld and remitted and such certificate is presented at each directors' meeting, it would appear that this should be sufficient to relieve the director from liability under the provisions of subs. (3).

Liability of directors for wages (s. 119)

Under s. 119 of the Act the directors of a corporation are made personally liable to a prescribed extent for wages payable to employees while the directors are in office.

The section is *intra vires*: *Schumacher v. Moore*, [1934] 4 D.L.R. 585 (Man. C.A.) applying *Reference re s. 110 Dominion Companies Act*, [1934] S.C.R. 653 and following the opinion expressed by Richards J.A. in *Macdonald v. Drake* (1906), 16 Man. R. 220 (Man. C.A.) that the section is a limited exception from the exemption from liability of shareholders granted by s. 45.

It will be observed that s. 113 of the Act requires a corporation to send to the Director a notice in prescribed form (Form 6) setting out the change within 15 days after such change and the Director is to file the notice. It will further be noted that s. 253(2) provides that a director named in a notice sent by a corporation under s. 113 and filed by the Director is presumed for the purposes of this Act to be a director of the corporation. A similar provision appears in s. 262(3) of the Ontario Act. Assuming therefore that a director has been named in such a notice upon his election and then resigns, if a notice is not sent he is presumed for the purposes of the Act to be a director and certain liabilities may attach to him in that regard. While a presumption can ordinarily be rebutted, certain presumptions cannot. In *Laprise v. Julio's Pizza & Spaghetti Parlour* (1986), 62 C.B.R. (N.S.) 36 (Ont. Prov. Ct.) an action was brought against a director for unpaid wages, and despite the fact that no change of notice of directors was filed the defence was raised that the director had resigned more than six months previously to the claim arising; it was held that the *Corporations Information Act* (Ontario) only made the certificate *prima facie* evidence of the status of the director and the actual date of the resignation was treated as governing. However, s. 261(3) of the *Ontario Business Corporations Act, 1982* was not apparently cited to the court and the decision does not deal with the question of presumption.

Object of section

The object of the section is to give employees of the classes named a guarantee against the loss of their wages in case of the insolvency of the corporation by making the directors sureties for payment by the corporation: *Welch v. Ellis* (1895), 22 O.A.R. 255 at 262; *Guenard v. Coe* (1914), 17 D.L.R. 47 (Alta. C.A.); *Mulligan v. Lancaster*, [1937] 1 D.L.R. 414 at 416 (Alta. C.A.).

In *Darrah v. Wright* (1914), 7 O.W.N. 233 and *Pilote v. Leclerc* (1917), 52 Que. S.C. 127, the section was said to be penal and therefore to be construed strictly, but in *Macdonald v. Drake*, *supra*, and *Dallaire v. Leclerc* (1918), 53 Que. S.C. 201 the opposite view was taken and in *Lee v. Friedman* (1910), 20 O.L.R. 49 at 56, Riddell J. stated that it was penal as regards the directors but highly remedial as regards employees.

In *Young v. Dannecker* (1926), 30 O.W.N. 394; affd (1927), 31 O.W.N. 205, Kelly J. held that the statute must be interpreted strictly and the claimant's case clearly made out and dismissed an action on the ground that there was no positive evidence that the claimants contracted with or were engaged by any representative of the corporation to whom the corporation's records gave authority to act for it in such matters.

De facto directors are liable under the section: *Macdonald v. Drake, supra.*

Persons entitled to benefit of s. 119

It is difficult to reconcile all the cases as to the classes of persons who are entitled to the benefit of the section which under the former Act were "clerks, labourers, servants and apprentices" and under the present s. 119(1) are "employees". There appears to be no limitation with respect to the term "employee" which is not defined and presumably would include all employees of whatever kind up to and including the president and other executives of the corporation in question. However, until cases are available with respect to the interpretation of the word "employee", it has been thought useful to retain references to the authorities on the old provision. In this regard it should be noted there may very well be a difference in the terms "wages" and "salary", and since the term "wages" is used, not "salary" this may affect the class of employee who is entitled to claim pursuant to the section. It will be noted that s. 119(1) provides liability for "all debts not exceeding 6 months' wages" and it might be argued that a debt not constituting a wage would be owing by a director as long as it did not exceed the amount in question. The same wording was used under the former provision; the authorities under that section indicating that wages alone can be claimed from him.

Labourers of all kinds, engineers, foremen, shipping and office clerks, and others of that class are within the old section: *Fee v. Turner* (1904), 13 Que. K.B. 435 at 447 per Hall J.; *Welch v. Ellis* (1895), 22 O.A.R. 255, where Maclennan J.A. considered that only the humblest class of wage earners was covered, was a decision on the corresponding section of the *Ontario Companies Act*, which, as then in effect, omitted the word "clerk". There a contractor's foreman, who hired and dismissed men, received and disbursed money for wages, and who did no manual labour was held not to be a labourer, servant or apprentice. For other decisions on the Ontario section when it did not contain the word "clerk", see *Herman v. Wilson* (1901), 32 O.R. 60 (a manager of a mining corporation held not to be within the section); *Ryan v. Wills* (1918), 43 O.L.R. 624 (a motion picture actress held not within the section); *Domanski v. Wilson*, [1935] O.R. 400 (C.A.) (a manager of a corporation held not within the section even though he did a certain amount of manual labour).

A director who is an employee is precluded from suing the other directors under the section, for it is not the intention of the section that the members of the board should be jointly and severally liable to each other for work which a director performs as a clerk, labourer, servant or apprentice: *Mulligan v. Lancaster*, [1937] 1 D.L.R. 414 (Alta. C.A.).

The word "labourer" includes a person actually performing manual work at a daily wage, although he is also entrusted with the supervision of other workmen, and to that extent is a boss or foreman: *Fee v. Turner* (1904), 13 Que. K.B. 435; also a miner paid at the rate of so much a car, but otherwise working as a daily labourer, being under the direction of a pitboss: *Crew v. Dallas* (1908), 9 W.L.R. 598.

The word "clerk" includes a bookkeeper working under instruction from a general manager, but not an auditor working under a contract, much, if not all, of whose work could be done by his employees: *Re Yellowhead Pass Coal & Coke Co.*, [1917] 2 W.W.R. 985. The cases under s. 72 of the *Winding-up Act, infra*, are also in point as to the meaning of the term "clerk". The earlier cases are collected in *Re Parkin Elevator Co.; Dunsmoor's Claim* (1916), 37 O.L.R. 277 at 287 to 290 (C.A.).

The word "servant" includes a mine superintendent with a restricted authority, and a mine physician who looked solely to his remuneration from the corporation for his livelihood and was under the obligation to attend anyone connected with the corporation when occasion arose: *Re Yellowhead Pass Coal & Coke Co.*, [1917] 2 W.W.R. 985; also a "mine manager": *Crowder v. Coleman*, [1924] 1 D.L.R. 849 (Alta. C.A.); and a mining engineer during the period when he devoted all his time to the corporation's work, entirely on the corporation's premises, as superintendent of construction on a monthly hiring and under the direction of the managing director, but not during the period when he was at liberty to perform and did perform work for others and was not under the supervision of any directors or officers: *Stevens v. Spencer*, [1930] 3 D.L.R. 993 (Alta. C.A.); but a field manager of a mining corporation, who was a director, was held not to be a servant and a doubt was expressed whether in view of the facts the result would have been different if he had not been a director: *Mulligan v. Lancaster*, [1937] 1 D.L.R. 414 (Alta. C.A.).

Newspaper reporters having no formal contract, not being exclusively employed by the newspaper, whose services were of a particular class and in respect of which no control was exercised, were not servants within the meaning of s. 209 of the *Companies (Consolidated) Act, 1908*: *In re Ashley & Smith*, [1918] 2 Ch. 378.

See also as to the meaning of labourers, servants, and apprentices the following cases: *Nowlan v. Ablett* (1835), 2 C.M. & R. 54; *Riley v. Warden* (1848), 2 Ex. 59; *Sleeman v. Barrett* (1864), 2 H. & C. 954; *Nicoll v. Greaves* (1864), 33 L.J.C.P. 259; *Lawlor v. Linden* (1876), Ir. R. 10 C.L. 188; *Hunt v. Great Northern Ry.*, [1891] 1 Q.B. 601 (train guard not a workman); *Jones v. Stadler* (1934), 72 Que. S.C. 1 (does not include secretary-treasurer).

Claim must be for wages

The plaintiff's claim must be for wages. Expending money for the corporation at its request in payment of wages and other services does not create a debt for wages within the section: *Herman v. Wilson* (1901), 32 O.R. 60; but leaving wages undrawn at the request of the corporation does not affect the claim as being one for wages: *George v. Strong* (1910), 15 O.W.R. 99.

As to the distinction between "wages" and "salary", see *Gordon v. Jennings* (1882), 51 L.J.Q.B. 417; *Moriarty v. Regent's Garage*, [1921] 1 K.B. 423 at 445.

There must be actual services. If the plaintiff has only held himself in readiness to perform them, that is not enough: *Mullen v. Millar* (1924), 56 O.L.R. 345 (C.A.).

An allowance for travelling expenses has been held within the section: *Pukulski v. Jardine* (1912), 26 O.L.R. 323; but in *Darrah v. Wright* (1914), 7 O.W.N. 233, Lennox J. disallowed travelling expenses.

There has been som question whether the liability included termination or severance pay. The matter has now been settled by the Supreme Court of Canada in *Crabtree (Succession de) c. Barrette*, [1991] R.J.Q. 1193 (C.A.) where the Court held that the claim under the federal Act did not include such amounts. It was pointed out, however, that where the governing statute used broader language, the liability might well include this amount as well as others: see *Meyers v. Walters Cycle Co.* (1990), 85 Sask. R. 222 (C.A.). For an overview of earlier cases see *Schwartz v. Scott*, [1985] C.A. 713, 32 B.L.R. 1 (Que. C.A.) where an action was commenced by employees to recover wages and other sums from the directors and at trial a claim for severance pay was rejected on the basis that it did not constitute wages. On appeal it was held that severance pay should be included since claims for all debts were covered subject to the maximum of six months' wages. It will be observed that in *Mesheau v. Campbell* (1982), 39 O.R. (2d) 702, 141 D.L.R. (3d) 155 (C.A.) the court held that a claim for damages for wrongful dismissal would not be included within the provision as such a claim constitutes unliquidated damages rather than a debt. See also *Crabtree (Succession de) c. Barrette, supra.* In *Mills-Hughes v. Raynor* (1985), 10 C.C.E.L. 180, 32 B.L.R. 118 (Ont. H.C.) it was held that a claim for bonus, statutory severance and termination pay were not debts for services performed but arose by statute after termination of the employment and the directors were not liable. However, on appeal, vacation pay which accrued to employees was to be held in trust and constituted a debt due for services rendered. See also *Vopni v. Groenewald* (1991), 84 D.L.R. (4th) 366 (Ont. Gen. Div.). The balance of the claims for termination and severance payments and bonus constituted either a statutory benefit or were dependent on making profit and in either case were either not debts or not payable. See the Ontario Court of Appeal decision reported at (1988) 19 C.C.E.L. 6. An independent contractor was held not to be an employee and accordingly not entitled to sue under the similar provision of the Ontario Act. See *Kornblum v. Dye* (1986), 59 C.B.R. (N.S.) 219 (Ont. Dist. Ct.).

Judgment against corporation

The recovery of a judgment against the corporation is a condition precedent to the right to sue the directors (unless sub-paragraph (a) of subs. (2) applies) and is for that purpose conclusive of its validity as against the directors until set aside in a proper proceeding: *Derbach v Shaw*, [1933] 4 D.L.R. 461 at 463 (Man. C.A.). The judgment is not open to collateral attack by the directors, in the action by the wage-earners against them, for irregularity in the absence of fraud: *Lee v. Friedman* (1910), 20 O.L.R. 49 at 55; even though the judgment is clearly voidable: *Stevens v. Spencer*, [1930] 3 D.L.R. 993 (Alta. C.A.); it will be observed that the directors are not precluded from raising defences which might have but were not raised in the earlier action against the corporation pursuant to the Alberta Act: *Feuchter v. Smolek* (1983), 46 A.R. 58 (Ont. Q.B.). But a motion for summary judgment against directors was refused when the judgment against the corporation was by default: *Rogers v. Wood* (1912), 2 D.L.R. 914. The judgment against the corporation, being *res inter alios acta*, the plaintiff must prove in the action against the directors, his claim, his recovery of judgment against the corporation and that the corporation had no assets to satisfy the judgment against it: *Mullen v. Millar* (1924), 56 O.L.R. 345 at 347 (C.A.); *Derbach v. Shaw, supra.*

The plaintiff's claim being on the original debt and not on the judgment against the corporation, the directors may set up such defences as that the plaintiff does not come within the class of persons who are entitled to recover under the section: *Guenard v. Coe* (1914), 17 D.L.R. 47 (Alta. C.A.); *Darrah v. Wright* (1914), 7 O.W.N. 233; or may deny the employment by the corporation, the performance of services and that any moneys were owing by the corporation: *Derbach v. Shaw, supra.* See also *Hurtubise v. Berthiaume*, [1987] R.J.Q. 678.

Since the liability of the directors is several as well as joint, the plaintiff is entitled to sue the directors separately as well as jointly, and is not bound to join them all as defendants: *Reuckwald v. Murphy* (1914), 32 O.L.R. 133 (C.A.).

Where a number of plaintiffs were suing in one action against the directors, they were required to elect whether one of them, and if so which, would proceed with the action: *Herbert v. Evans* (1909), 13 O.W.R. 682. But see *Risler v. McTeer*, [1919] 1 W.W.R. 746, where the claims of a number of wage-earners were permitted to be joined under Alberta rule 15 as involving the same series of transactions.

The plaintiff will not be prejudiced by the fact that in his suit against the corporation he has included a claim on a note as well as one for wages: *Williams v. Graham* (1916), 34 W.L.R. 855 (Man. C.A.).

Execution unsatisfied

The execution must be returned unsatisfied in whole or in part. This means a formal return made in strict compliance with the rules: *Crowder v. Coleman*, [1924] 1 D.L.R. 849 (Alta. C.A.). Thus, in *Pearce v. McKeever*, [1989] 1 W.W.R. 245, 62 Alta. L.R. (2d) 312 (Alta. C.A.) an order pursuant to the *Employment Standards Act* was issued directing the corporation to pay the amount in question. The order was filed with the court making it enforceable as a judgment on the court. No writ of execution had been issued and the employee sued the directors. It was held that, under the comparable provision of the Alberta Act, no liability could be imposed without an execution against the corporation being returned unsatisfied. The steps taken in the instant case did not amount to an execution.

It is sufficient compliance with the section that the execution is placed in the hands of the sheriff of the county in which the head office of the corporation is situated: *Pukulski v. Jardine* (1912), 26 O.L.R. 323. It is enough to satisfy the statute that a fair and bona fide attempt has been made to collect the amount of the judgment from the corporation and that a bona fide return has been made that there are no assets of the corporation to satisfy it: *Brice v. Munro* (1885), 12 O.A.R. 453 at 464, 468 (Ont. C.A.). A purely formal return without a serious attempt to discover goods or to realize upon them is insufficient: *Grills v. Farah* (1910), 21 O.L.R. 457; *Piroth v. Kalinocha*, [1986] 2 W.W.R. 88, 43 Sask. R. 166 (Sask. Q.B.); and where an execution against the corporation has been returned unsatisfied and a formal return of *nulla bona* has been made by the sheriff without any bona fide attempt to ascertain whether or not there were assets available to satisfy the execution and there were in fact exigible assets sufficient to satisfy the claim the return is not such a return as is contemplated by the section: *Stevens v. Spencer*, [1930] 3 D.L.R. 993 (Alta. C.A.). In that case, the rules provided that every writ of *fieri facias* should be issued against both the goods and lands of the debtor and that the sheriff, in addition to making it appear to the court in what manner he had executed the writ, must return the writ to the court. The sheriff's certificate made no mention of lands and the writ was not returned to the court. It was held that there had not been a return to the execution contemplated by the section.

Effect of winding-up

Under sub-paragraphs (b) and (c) of s. 119(2), suit and an unsatisfied execution are unnecessary if the corporation has gone into liquidation and dissolution proceedings or has dissolved or has made an assignment under the *Bankruptcy and Insolvency Act* or a receiving order has been made against it under the *Bankruptcy and Insolvency Act* and a claim for the debt has been duly filed and proved within six months after the earliest of the date of commencement of liquidation and dissolution proceedings and the date of dissolution or the date of the assignment or receiving order.

In the event of a winding-up supervening, a plaintiff, where a judgment and execution are preliminary conditions to suing the directors, should apply for leave to sue the corporation and issue execution: *Re Lake Winnipeg Transportation Co.; Paulson's Claim* (1891), 7 Man. R. 602; *Risler v. Alberta Newspapers Ltd.* (1919), 14 Alta. L.R. 460.

If the execution is already in the sheriff's hand, s. 21 of the *Winding-up Act* does not prevent the making of a return of *nulla bona* after the winding-up order: *Puklaski v. Jardine, supra*. As to what return is sufficient where the corporation has become bankrupt see *Crowder v. Coleman*, [1924] 1 D.L.R. 849 (Alta. C.A.). A creditor cannot issue execution against a corporation in liquidation without leave, and if he does the execution will be a nullity: *Pilote v. Leclerc* (1917), 52 Que. S.C. 127.

A workman is not entitled to his remedy against the directors when, having obtained judgment before the winding-up, he neglects to execute it before the corporation goes into liquidation and fails to get leave to issue execution afterwards: *Pilote v. Leclerc* (1917), 52 Que. S.C. 127. On the other hand, the Quebec Superior Court held in *Dallaire v. Leclerc* (1918), 53 Que. S.C. 201, that the plaintiff need not show a return of *nulla bona* if the corporation's inability to satisfy the claim appeared from the fact that it had gone into liquidation and that there had been a sale by the liquidator. It was further held that a delay of nine days by the plaintiff was not negligence on his part which the directors could set up as sufficient ground for a non-suit unless they were prejudiced thereby. It was held that the winding-up did not put an end to the directors' powers, but only suspended their exercise, so that the directors did not cease to be such on the occurrence of the liquidation. The fact that the corporation is in liquidation does not relieve the plaintiff from first suing the corporation, which he could do with leave: *Leclerc v. Beaulieu* (1924), 63 Que. S.C. 90.

Where a corporation goes into bankruptcy it continues in existence and directors do not cease to be such in the absence of evidence of their resignation or any act of theirs or of the corporation terminating their office: *Davey v. Gibson* (1929), 64 O.L.R. 627.

See also the discussion on these questions in Chapter 24.

Other requirements

A director is not liable under s. 119 unless he is sued while he is a director or within two years after he ceased to be a director and is only liable for the balance remaining unsatisfied after execution and only for wages that become due during the time he was a director. He is entitled to contribution against other directors who are liable for the claim and is entitled to the same priority or preference as the employee would have been entitled to upon the payment of the liability and where judgment has been obtained he is entitled to an assignment of the judgment, see subss. 119(3)-(6).

It may be noted that under the employment standards legislation of a number of provinces, such as the Manitoba *Payment of Wages Act*, the Director of the Employment Standards Branch of the government may issue a payment order against the corporation and/or its directors. The directors are obliged to comply with any such order without any benefit from the type of condition precedent to liability that exists under s. 119.

Chapter 9

INSIDER TRADING

Cross references: Ontario Act, s. 138;
Ontario Securities Act, ss. 106-121.

General

Under the federal Act and the Acts of certain of the provinces, "insiders" of a corporation, with certain exceptions, are required to file reports with respect to their trading in shares and other securities of the corporation. Additional provisions of importance relating to "Insider Trading and Self-Dealing" are contained in the Securities Acts of the various provinces which should be consulted where a public or "reporting issuer" corporation is concerned. Failure to comply with the provisions of these Acts can result in substantial liabilities and penalties.

The insider trading provisions contained in Part XI of the Act relate to a "distributing corporation" which is defined in s. 126(1) to mean a corporation any of the issued securities of which are or were part of a distribution to the public and remain outstanding and are held by more than one person. A "share" for purposes of Part XI means a share carrying voting rights under all circumstances or by reason of the occurrence of an event that has occurred and is continuing, and includes a security currently convertible into such a share and currently exercisable options and rights to acquire such a share or such a convertible security.

The term "insider" is defined (except for the purposes of s. 131) as a director or officer of a distributing corporation, a distributing corporation that purchases or otherwise acquires shares issued by it (except on a redemption of redeemable shares) or shares issued by any of its affiliates, or a person who beneficially owns more than 10 per cent of the shares of a distributing corporation or who exercises control or direction over more than 10 per cent of the votes attached to shares of a distributing corporation (hereinafter referred to as "a 10 per cent shareholder"). However, shares owned by an underwriter under an underwriting agreement during the course of a distribution to the public are excluded during such period. An "officer" is defined to mean the chairman, president, vice-president, secretary, treasurer, comptroller, general counsel, general manager, managing director or any other individual who performs similar functions and, in addition, each of the five highest paid employees of a distributing corporation (including any of the foregoing). Additional rules are provided in s. 126(2) to determine who are insiders and the ownership of securities of the corporation as follows: a director or an officer of a body corporate that is itself an insider of a distributing corporation is deemed to be an insider of the distributing corporation; a director or an officer of a body corporate that is a subsidiary of a distributing corporation is deemed to be an insider of its holding distributing corporation; a person is deemed to own beneficially shares beneficially owned by a body corporate controlled by him directly or indirectly; a body corporate is deemed to own beneficially securities beneficially owned by its affiliates; and the acquisition or disposition by an insider of an option or right to acquire a share is deemed a change in the beneficial ownership of the share to which the option or right to acquire relates.

For the purposes of Part XI, if a body corporate becomes an insider of or enters into a business combination with a distributing corporation, a director or officer of such body corporate or a 10 per cent shareholder is deemed to have been an insider of the distributing corporation for the previous 6 months or for such shorter period as he was a director, officer or such a shareholder of the body corporate; and, if a distributing corporation becomes an insider of, or enters into a business combination with, a body corporate, a director or officer of the body corporate or a 10 per cent shareholder is deemed to have been an insider of the distributing corporation for the previous 6 months or for such shorter period as he was a director, an officer or such a shareholder of the body corporate (s. 126(3)). A "business combination" is defined as meaning an acquisition of all or substantially all the property of one body corporate by another, or an amalgamation of two or more bodies corporate (s. 126(4)).

Unless he has filed or has been exempted from filing an insider report under the *Canada Corporations Act* or under the regulations, a person who is an insider of a body corporate on the day on which it is continued as a corporation under the Act is required, within ten days after the end of the month in which such day occurs, to send to the director an insider report in prescribed form, if the corporation is a distributing corporation (s. 127(1)). A person who becomes an insider is required within ten days after the end of the month in which he became an insider to send a similar report to the director (s. 127(2)).

In *Sparling v. Quebec (Caisse de dépôt et placement du Quebec)*, [1988] 2 S.C.R. 1015, 41 B.L.R. 1 (S.C.C.) the Caisse was an agent of the Crown in right of Quebec and owned more than 10 per cent of the shares of a publicly traded corporation governed by the federal Act; accordingly, it was an insider of the corporation. It refused to file an insider report contending that by virtue of Crown immunity it was exempt from the provisions of the Act. The Supreme Court of Canada held that the insider trading provisions of the federal Act were applicable to the Caisse and that accordingly, it was required to file insider reports.

A person who is deemed to have been an insider under s. 126(3) is required, within ten days after the end of the month in which he is so deemed to have become an insider, to file the insider reports for the deemed period that he would have been required to file had he been otherwise an insider for such period (s. 127(3)). Subsequent reports by an insider are to be made in prescribed form within ten days following the end of the month in which there is any change in his interest in securities of a distributing corporation (s. 127(4)).

A report of a person that includes securities deemed to be beneficially owned (by virtue of s. 126(2)(c)) by that person is deemed to be a report of the body corporate that owns the securities and the body corporate is not required to file a separate report (s. 127(5)). Similarly, a report of a body corporate that included securities deemed to be beneficially owned (by virtue of s. 126(1)(d)) by the body corporate is deemed to be a report of an affiliate and the affiliate is not required to file a separate report (s. 127(6)).

A report of a person that includes securities deemed beneficially owned by that person is required to disclose separately the number or amount of the securities owned by a body corporate and the name of the body corporate (s. 127(7)).

Upon an application by or on behalf of an insider the Director may make an order on such terms as he thinks fit exempting the insider from any of the requirements of s. 127, which order may have retrospective effect (s. 127(8)).

A person who without reasonable cause fails to comply with s. 127 is guilty of an offence and is liable on summary conviction to a fine not exceeding $5,000 or to imprisonment for a term not exceeding six months or to both; if such person is a body corporate, any director or officer who knowingly authorizes, permits or acquiesces in such failure is also guilty of an offence and liable on summary conviction to the same penalties, whether or not the body corporate has been prosecuted or convicted (s. 127(9), (10)).

A corporation that proposes to purchase or otherwise acquire its own shares other than by means of a redemption under s. 36 is required to give notice of the same to the Director in the prescribed manner (s. 128).

The Director is to summarize in a periodical available to the public the information contained in insider reports filed with him under ss. 127 and 128 and the particulars of any exemptions granted from the above filing requirements and the reasons therefor (s. 129).

An insider is prohibited from knowingly selling, directly or indirectly, a share of the distributing corporation or any of its affiliates if he does not own a share of the distributing corporation or any of its affiliates or has not fully paid for the shares to be sold; this provision does not apply to an insider selling a share he does not own if he owns another share convertible into the share sold or an option or right to acquire the share sold and, within ten days after the sale, he exercises the conversion privilege, option or right and delivers the share so acquired to the purchaser or transfers the convertible share, option or right to the purchaser (s. 130(1), (3)). An insider is also prohibited from directly or indirectly buying or selling any put or call with respect to a share of the corporation or any of its affiliates (s. 130(2)). Penalties are provided in s. 130(4) for a breach of the foregoing provisions.

An insider (as defined below) who, in connection with a transaction in a security of the corporation or any of its affiliates, makes use of any specific confidential information for his own benefit or advantage that, if generally known, might reasonably be expected to affect materially the value of the security, is liable to compensate any person for any direct loss suffered by that person as a result of the transaction, unless the information was known or in the exercise of reasonable diligence should have been known to that person and is also accountable to the corporation for any direct benefit or advantage received or receivable by him as a result of the transaction (s. 131(4)). An action to enforce any right given by this provision must be commenced within two years after discovery of the facts that gave rise to the cause of action or, where the transaction is required to be reported under the insider provisions, within two years from the time of reporting in compliance with such provisions (s. 131(5)). For the purposes of s. 131 "insider" means the corporation, an affiliate of the corporation, a director or an officer of the corporation, a person who beneficially owns more than 10 per cent of the shares of the corporation or who exercises control or direction over more than 10 per cent of the votes attached to the shares of the corporation, a person employed or retained by the corporation or a person who receives specific confidential information from any of the foregoing or from those deemed to be insiders under s. 131(2), or such a person who has knowledge that the person giving the information is a person so described (s. 131(1)). If a body corporate becomes an insider of, or enters into a business combination with, a corporation or vice versa, a director or officer of the one is deemed to have been an insider of the other for the previous six months or for such shorter period as he was such a director or officer; for the foregoing purpose, "business combination" means an acquisition of all or substantially all the property of one body corporate by another or an amalgamation of two or more bodies corporate (s. 131(2), (3)).

In *Green v. Charterhouse Group Canada Ltd.* (1976), 12 O.R. (2d) 280, 68 D.L.R. (3d) 592 (C.A.) a controlling group of shareholders had knowledge of a possible takeover and notified a shareholder, desiring to sell his shares, in general terms of this possibility. It was held that the notification in general terms was not sufficient to excuse the defendants in an action under the *Securities Act* (Ontario) but the evidence showed that the confidential information was not the main force motivating the defendants. In fact, the shares in question were acquired reluctantly; in other words, the information in question was not made use of and accordingly, there was no liability. See also *NIR Oil Ltd. v. Bodrug* (1985), 38 Alta. L.R. (2d) 321, 18 D.L.R. (4th) 608 (Alta. C.A.); *Re Royal Trustco Ltd. v. Ontario Securities Commission* (1983), 42 O.R. (2d) 147, 21 B.L.R. 236 (Ont. Div. Ct.). See also the comment in Chapter 8.

Chapter 10

SHAREHOLDERS' MEETINGS

Cross-references: Ontario Act, ss. 92-114.

Meetings of shareholders

The will of the shareholders of a corporation is expressed, subject to the express provisions of the Act and to the legal principles hereinafter mentioned, by resolutions duly passed at properly constituted shareholders' meetings. The role of the shareholders in connection with the day to day management of the affairs of the corporation, having regard to the broad powers of management now conferred on the directors, is now relatively restricted. The shareholders in general meeting do, however, possess certain important powers. By reason of the fact that they are entitled to elect the directors, they have an indirect control over the general policy of the corporation. Moreover, the Act confers on them the exclusive functions of appointing auditors and confirming by-laws passed by the directors and certain other functions.

There was formerly some question as to the effect of the consent of all of the shareholders expressed otherwise than at a meeting of shareholders. However, the matter has now been put to rest by the provisions of s. 142, which states that a resolution in writing signed by all of the shareholders entitled to vote on that resolution at a meeting of the shareholders is as valid as if it had been passed at a meeting of the shareholders and a resolution in writing dealing with matters required by the Act to be dealt with at a meeting of shareholders and signed by all the shareholders entitled to vote at that meeting satisfies all of the requirements of the Act relating to the meetings of shareholders. A copy of such resolutions are to be kept with minutes of the meetings of shareholders; there is, however, an exception to proceeding by way of signature where a written statement is submitted by a director under s. 110(2) or by an auditor under s. 168(5). Section 110(2) provides that a statement may be given by a director who has resigned, who receives a notice or otherwise learns of a meeting of shareholders called to remove him from office or receives a notice or otherwise learns of a meeting of directors or shareholders in which another party is to be elected or appointed to fill the office of director, whether because of his resignation or removal or because his term of office has expired or is about to expire. Such statement is to be given to the corporation setting out the reasons for his resignation or the reasons why he opposed any proposed action or resolution. Section 168(5) contains a similar provision in the case of an auditor.

A shareholder, in addition to attending a meeting in person, may also do so by proxy and if a corporation has 15 or more shareholders, the corporation is required-concurrently with giving a notice of meeting of the shareholders-to send a form of proxy in prescribed form to each shareholder who is entitled to receive notice of the meeting and must give a management circular proxy in prescribed form.

If the company is being wound up under the *Bankruptcy and Insolvency Act*, the regulations of the charter and by-laws as to meetings of directors and shareholders and the passing of by-laws and resolutions continue to apply: *Re Canadian Cereal & Flour Mills Co.* (1921), 51 O.L.R. 316 (S.C.). This decision was followed in *National Trust Co. v. Ebro Irrigation & Power Co.*, [1954] O.R. 463 (H.C.), where a foreign court had purported to adjudge a Canadian company bankrupt.

Annual meetings

In s. 133(a) it is provided that the directors of a company are to call an annual meeting of the shareholders not later than 18 months after the company comes into existence and subsequently not later than 15 months after holding the last proceeding annual meeting.

It is customary to elect directors at the annual meeting: *Watt v. Commonwealth Petroleum Ltd.*, [1938] 4 D.L.R. 701 (Alta. C.A.). It was pointed out in that case at p. 706 that an election of directors at a meeting called as an annual meeting was valid notwithstanding that financial statements had not been mailed to the shareholders prior to the meeting as required by what is now s. 159. It is no longer required to approve the accounts at the annual meeting.

Under s. 155 the accounts therein specified are to be laid before the annual meeting and under s. 162 the auditors are to be appointed at such meeting.

Formerly it was common practice at an annual meeting to ratify the acts of the directors during the period subsequent to the preceding annual meeting and to have the notice of meeting provide for such ratification. This is still often done in a case where no proxy solicitation requiring a management proxy statement is required. However, if a management proxy statement is required, a management proxy circular statement must give details of what has been done and obviously this is impractical; accordingly, the former practice has now been discontinued. Section 144 provides that if for any reason it is impractical to call a meeting of the shareholders in the manner prescribed in the Act, the court on the application of a director or shareholder entitled to vote or of the Director may order a meeting to be called, held and conducted in such manner as the court directs.

In *Mayr v. St. Lawrence Corp.*, [1950] Que. K.B. 635 a majority of the Quebec Court of Appeal (Barclay and McDougall JJ. dissenting) held that the shareholders of a company might proceed by way of mandamus both to set aside and declare illegal, on the ground that insufficient notice was given, annual and special general meetings of shareholders and, in the same proceedings, compel the directors to call new meetings after giving proper notice. At p. 652 McDougall J. expressed the view that s. 100 of the federal Act not only provided an equally convenient, beneficial and effectual remedy as a writ of mandamus, but provided an express remedy to meet the very situation that arose in that case. Furthermore, he pointed out that the fact the legislature saw fit to insert s. 100 indicated that it considered the rights and obligations between shareholders and corporation as private rights and obligations, for if the holding of an annual meeting were a public duty s. 100 would not be necessary as mandamus would lie.

Where the by-laws provide that the annual meeting is to be held on a specified date in each year and the time for the annual meeting is allowed to go by without the meeting having been held, it may be that the irregularity can be cured by holding a special and annual meeting, giving notice of such meeting in the usual way and stating the date, time and place for holding the same and the business to be transacted thereat. At such meeting a resolution might be passed to the effect that, notwithstanding the provisions of the by-laws specifying the date of the annual meeting, the shareholders approve of the delay in holding the meeting and approve of the meeting having been held when it is held.

It may be, however, having regard to the express requirements of s. 133(a), that if the annual meeting is not held in the calendar year next following that in which the last annual meeting was held, or if the meeting is not held within 15 months after the last annual meeting, an order of the court under s. 144 is requisite, or the meeting may be requisitioned by shareholders holding the stipulated number of issued shares of the corporation.

The annual meeting may be held on a public holiday in the absence of specific statutory prohibition: *Nesbitt, Thomson & Co. v. McColl Frontenac Oil Co.* (1938), 43 Que. P.R. 138.

Special meetings

The directors may at any time call a special meeting of the shareholders for the transaction of any business the general nature of which is specified in the notice of the meeting (s. 133(b)). The by-laws frequently permit such meetings to be summoned by designated officers. For the distinction between general and special meetings, see *Austin Mining Co. v. Gemmel* (1886), 10 O.R. 696 at 706 (C.A.).

Subsections (1) to (6) inclusive of s. 143 contain provisions for the holding of a meeting on the requisition of shareholders. The requisitionists must hold, at the date of the deposit of the requisition, not less than 5 per cent of the issued shares of the corporation of the class or classes which, at that date, carry the right of voting at the meeting to be called (subs. (1)). The requisition must state the business to be transacted at the meeting, must be signed by the requisitionists in one or more documents of like form and must be sent to each director and to the registered office of the corporation. It is not necessary, where more than one document embodying the requisition is signed, that the documents should be in identical terms: *Fruit & Vegetable Growers' Assn. Ltd. v. Kekewich*, [1912] 2 Ch. 52.

Upon receiving such requisition, the directors are to call a meeting of the shareholders to transact the business stated in the requisition unless the directors themselves have called a meeting of shareholders and have given notice under s. 135 or a record date has been fixed under s. 134(2) for a shareholder entitled to receive notice of meeting or if the business of the meeting as stated in the requisition includes matters in s. 137(5)(b) to (e) (inclusive) namely, a proposal to enforce a personal claim or address a personal grievance or primarily for the purpose of promoting general economic, political, racial, religious, social or similar causes, a proposal that was included by the corporation at the shareholders' request in a management proxy circular relating to a meeting of shareholders held within two years preceding the receipt of such request and the shareholder failed to present the proposal in person or by proxy at the meeting or substantially the same proposal had been submitted in a management proxy circular or a dissident's proxy circular relating to a meeting of the shareholders within two years preceding the receipt of shareholders' request and the proposal was defeated, or the rights to submit a shareholder proposal are being abused to secure publicity; the meeting is to be called as nearly as possible in the manner in which meetings are to be called pursuant to the by-laws and Parts XII and XIII of the federal Act (s. 143(5)).

For an example of a case in which the court found that the proposal was primarily for the purpose of promoting political, racial or similar causes see *Varity Corp. v. Jesuit Fathers of Upper Canada* (1987), 59 O.R. (2d) 459; affd (1987), 60 O.R. (2d) 640 (C.A.).

In *Nalcap Holdings Inc. v. Kelvin Energy Ltd.*, [1988] R.J.Q. 2762 (S.C.), the court had no jurisdiction to call a special meeting where the 21-day period had not yet elapsed. For an example of a case where a court order was granted see *Re Canadian Javelin Ltd. and Boon-Strachan Coal Co.* (1976), 69 D.L.R. (3d) 439 (Que. S.C.); in that case there were two parallel boards of directors and criminal charges had been laid against the person who had previously been the directing force. The court's judgment, which was under appeal, had confirmed one of the boards but it was evident that the board did not feel ready to ask the shareholders for a mandate. The court ordered a disinterested person to conduct the meeting and pointed out that the word "impractical" did not mean impossible. See also *Athabaska Holdings Ltd. v. ENA Data Systems Inc.* (1980), 30 O.R. (2d) 527, 116 D.L.R. (3d) 318 (Ont. H.C.). Thus, in a case under the Ontario Act where there was a legitimate dispute as to which members had authority to act and thus to call meetings, the court ordered a meeting to be held and also to determine the issues to be discussed at that meeting. See *Croatian Peasant Party of Ontario, Canada v. Zorkin* (1981), 38 O.R. (2d) 659 (Ont. H.C.). See also *B. Love Ltd. v. Bulk Steel & Salvage Ltd.* (1982), 40 O.R. (2d) 1 (Ont. H.C.) (giving additional reasons for the judgment as reported in (1982), 38 O.R. (2d) 691 (Ont. H.C.)). Under the circumstances of this case the court dispensed with the quorum requirements in the corporation's by-laws. In *Trans-Mountain Pipe Line Co. v. Inland Natural Gas Co.* (1983), 49 B.C.L.R. 126, B.C. Corps. L.C. 78, 214 (C.A.) the court held in an application for an injunction to restrain a meeting of shareholders that there must be a very strong case to justify a court in restraining any meeting of shareholders.

If the directors do not — within 21 days from the date of the deposit of the requisition — proceed to call the meeting, any requisitionist may do so (s. 143(4)).

Joint holders of shares must all sign the requisition unless the by-laws otherwise provide: *Patent Wood Keg Syndicate v. Pearse*, [1906] W.N. 164.

A trustee in bankruptcy of a shareholder in a private company, who has not caused himself to be registered as the holder of the shares, is not entitled to serve a requisition: *Re Fox Johnson & Co.*, [1942] 2 D.L.R. 784 at 789 (Ont. H.C.).

Where by statute the holders of a specified proportion of the shares of the company have a right to call a special meeting, it is not open to the directors further to limit that right: *Austin Mining Co. v. Gemmel* (1886), 10 O.R. 696, 705 (C.A.); *Re Cambrian Peat & Fuel Co.* (1875), 23 W.R. 405. The proportion is to be reckoned on the amount of shares subscribed for, not on the amount paid: *Purdom v. Ontario Loan & Debenture Co.* (1892), 22 O.R. 597 (H.C.).

Under similar statutory provisions it has been held that the holders of the requisite proportion of shares are competent to convene a special meeting for the election of directors, where no annual general meeting has been held, or where, if held, no election has taken place: *Austin Mining Co. v. Gemmel* (1886), 10 O.R. 696 at 703 (C.A.); or where there is no quorum of directors remaining in office: *Sovereen Mitt, Glove & Robe Co. v. Whitside* (1906), 12 O.L.R. 638 (C.A.). Where the meeting is held for the purpose of electing directors to replace existing directors, no election having been held at the proper time, it is sufficient for the notice to specify the election of directors as the business to be transacted at the meeting without stating that it is proposed to remove the existing directors; the latter hold office until their successors are elected (s. 89): *Gold-Rex Kirkland Mines Ltd. v. Morrow*, [1944] O.R. 415, 418 (H.C.). Where, the directors having failed to call the meeting pursuant to requisition, the requisitionists themselves call the meeting, and the notice is defective, the requisitionists may call a further meeting and send out a fresh notice calling it; no new requisition is necessary: *Gold-Rex Kirkland Mines Ltd. v. Morrow*, *supra*.

During the period of 21 days specified in s. 143(3) the board only can call the meeting; the secretary cannot do so on his own responsibility: *In re State of Wyoming Syndicate*, [1901] 2 Ch. 431. In that case the point was raised but not decided whether, after the expiration of the 21-day period, the requisitionists could call the meeting by notices signed by the secretary.

Where the directors, or failing them the shareholders, have power to call a general meeting, the court will not interfere to compel the directors to summon a meeting: *MacDougall v. Gardiner* (1875), 1 Ch. D. 13 (C.A.); but now the court is expressly given power under s. 104 to order a meeting of shareholders to be called under the circumstances specified in the section. Where provisions enabling shareholders by requisition to require a meeting of shareholders to be held have not been invoked, the court will not, in an action against *de facto* directors only, grant an interlocutory mandatory order requiring them to convene a meeting because-as the corporation is not before the court-there is no party that the court can order to do a corporate act; it would appear that shareholders are entitled to proceed by way of requisition in the case of *de facto* directors: *Streit v. Swanson*, [1946] O.R. 565 (H.C.).

The shareholders of a corporation had requisitioned a general meeting to increase the number of directors and to pass a resolution preventing the issue of shares without the prior approval of shareholders. At the same time an interlocutory injunction was sought to prevent the entering into of any agreement or the issue of any shares before the holding of the general meeting which had been requisitioned. The court dismissed the application saying that the fact that the requisition had been made in no way restricted the powers of the directors to manage the corporation. They were entitled to make agreements and issue shares provided that the purpose of their action was to serve the best interests of the corporation and no improper motive prompted such action: *Shield Development Co. v. Snyder*, [1976] 3 W.W.R. 44 (B.C. S.C.).

It is not proper to bring before a special general meeting a resolution for the removal of a director where that matter is not covered by the terms of the requisition and where the directors have not convened the meeting for that particular purpose: *Ball v. Metal Industries Ltd.* (1957), S.L.T. 124.

Meetings called upon order of the court

As to the power of the court to call an annual meeting under s. 144(1) see the notes under the heading "Annual meetings", above.

Section 144(1) also provides that if for any reason it is impracticable to call a meeting of shareholders in any manner in which such meetings may be called or to conduct the meeting in the prescribed manner, the court may order a meeting to be called and may give such consequential directions as it thinks expedient. The court has the power to order the quorum required by the by-laws or by the Act be varied or dispensed with (s. 144(2)).

The articles of a corporation incorporated in British Columbia required the presence of not less than two shareholders at any general meeting of shareholders. One of the only two shareholders petitioned the court for an order convening the annual general meeting and directing that the presence in person of one shareholder of the corporation holding a majority of its shares should be deemed to be a sufficient quorum for the transaction of business. The petition was dismissed and the court indicated that it had no power to make such an order. It will be noted that the provisions of the Act in question did not include the power to order the quorum required by the by-laws or the Act to be varied or dispensed with. See *Re Cowichan Leader Ltd.* (1963), 45 W.W.R. 57, 42 D.L.R. (2d) 111 (B.C. S.C.).

In *Commonwealth International Leverage Fund Ltd. v. Zimmerman* (1966), 58 D.L.R. (2d) 160 (P.E.I.C.A.) the court held that it was not impractical to hold a meeting where an injunction had been granted against the holding of the original meeting and the court proceedings with respect thereto were still in progress. It was pointed out that the corporations involved could call fresh meetings if the court order was regarded as terminating the original meetings.

The cases in which the section may be invoked are, in practice, of infrequent occurrence having regard to the ability of the holders of 5% of the issued shares to cause a meeting to be convened on requisition under s. 143. See the notes under the heading "Special meetings", above.

The *English Companies Act, 1948*, contains a similar provision (s. 135) which was construed in *Re El Sombrero Ltd.*, [1958] 1 Ch. 900. In that case the two directors of a corporation held 50 shares each and the only other shareholder

900 shares. No annual meetings had been held and no annual returns filed. The articles of association provided that the quorum for general meetings was two members present in person or by proxy and that if, within half an hour from the time appointed for a meeting, a quorum was not present the meeting was dissolved. The majority shareholder requisitioned an extraordinary general meeting for the purpose of removing the two directors. The directors deliberately did not attend the meeting with the result that it was dissolved under the provision in the articles. The court held that the case was one in which it ought to exercise its discretion under the section because otherwise it would be depriving the majority shareholder of his statutory right to remove the directors and because the directors had failed to perform their statutory duty to call an annual general meeting. The court indicated that in determining whether it is "impracticable" to conduct a meeting in the prescribed manner, it was necessary to examine the circumstances of the particular case and decide whether, as a practical matter, the desired meeting could be conducted. It was also held that the court had jurisdiction to intervene notwithstanding that the application under the section was opposed by some shareholders.

A similar provision in the Ontario Act (s. 106) was considered by the Ontario Court of Appeal in *Re Morris Funeral Service Ltd.*, [1957] O.W.N. 161 (C.A.). In that case the board of directors of the corporation was divided into two factions. The controlling shares were held by the executors of an estate who included representatives of the two factions. One of the factions had obtained an order under the section convening a meeting of shareholders for the removal of directors with special provisions as to quorum at the meeting which, as the controlling shares could not be voted at the meetings because of disagreement among the executors, would permit that faction to control the meeting. There had been no breaches of duty on the part of the directors sought to be removed. On an appeal from the order, the court reviewed the English authorities and noted that in each of them "the court was requested to remove some obstacle making it impracticable for the shareholders as a whole, or for an overwhelming majority thereof, to call or conduct a meeting in accordance with the requirements in that behalf of the company's Articles of Association" (Aylesworth J.A. at p. 164). The court held that its powers under the section were discretionary, but that the section could not be invoked successfully (except in extraordinary circumstances which were not present here) for the express and sole purpose of placing in control of the corporation's directorate and affairs one of two or more contending factions among the shareholders. The order convening the meeting was accordingly set aside. See also *Re British International Finance (Canada) Ltd.; Charlebois v. Bienvenu*, [1968] 2 O.R. 217, 68 D.L.R. (2d) 578 (C.A.); in that case the applicants had been directors of a corporation and were not elected as directors at an annual general meeting. The applicants claimed that the election was invalid and applied for an order of the court directing a meeting to be called, held and conducted in such manner as the court thought fit. The Court of Appeal held that the section in the Act applied to situations when it was impractical to call a meeting of shareholders and where it was impractical to conduct the meeting in the manner prescribed; the provision was not wide enough to sanction an order calling or conducting a meeting to achieve the purpose beyond the powers of a meeting of shareholders called in any other way. The proposed election of directors was beyond the powers of the shareholders, but apart from the power of the shareholders to remove directors by a two-thirds vote, it was not competent for the corporation to hold what, in effect, amounted to a second election within the year. If the purported election was invalid then the board previously elected remained in office, but if it were valid then the board so elected was still in office with the term not having expired.

However, in *Re Routley's Holdings Ltd.*, [1960] O.W.N. 160, 22 D.L.R. (2d) 410 (C.A.) the directors were in breach of their statutory duty in that they had failed to call an annual meeting for over five years and, when such a meeting was finally held, had failed to conduct it in a lawful manner. On an application under a predecessor of s. 106 the court distinguished the *Morris Funeral Service* case on the grounds that in that case the directors had not been in breach of their statutory duties, the sole purpose of the proposed meeting had been to place one faction in control of the corporation; the applicants for the orders had not availed themselves of other procedures open to them, and the assistance of the court was being sought to give the applicants for the order an advantage to which they were not entitled. In the *Routley's Holdings* case the court found there were no means available to the applicants, short of an order of the court, which would provide any assurance that the business of the meeting would be properly conducted. It accordingly directed that an annual meeting be held and that the quorum requirements set out in the by-laws be altered so that the meeting would not in the circumstances which existed prove to be abortive.

Under the former Ontario Act meetings of the shareholders, the board of directors and the executive committee were to be held subject as therein provided at the place where the head office of the corporation was situate. In *Re Routley's Holdings Ltd.*, [1960] O.W.N. 160 the Ontario Court of Appeal held that the word "place" in the Act had geographical significance and ordered the annual meeting of the shareholders to be held at a place in the municipality in which the head office was situate other than the head office; further, it was held that the provision of the Ontario Act under which the order was made afforded the court ample authority to direct the holding of a meeting at a place other than the head office.

In Re Pall Mall Building Society's Deed of Dissolution, [1947] W.N. 143, where the register of members had been destroyed by enemy action so that the names and addresses of a large number of members were unknown, publication of a notice of meeting in an appropriate newspaper was directed, notices being directed to be sent in the usual manner where the names and addresses of members were known.

In a review of an election by the court, s. 145 provides that a corporation or a shareholder or a director may apply to a court to determine any controversy with respect to an election or appointment of a director or auditor of the corporation; on such application the court may make any order that it thinks fit including an order restraining a director or auditor whose election or appointment is challenged from acting, pending the determination of the dispute, an order declaring the result of the disputed election or appointment, an order requiring a new election or appointment and including in the order directions for the management of the business and the affairs of the corporation until a new election is held or appointment made and an order determining voting rights for shareholders or persons claiming to be shareholders.

Pooling agreements and unanimous shareholder agreements

Section 146(1) provides that a written agreement between two or more shareholders may provide that in exercising voting rights the shares held by them shall be voted as therein provided. Section 146(2) provides that an otherwise lawful written agreement amongst all the shareholders of a corporation or among the shareholders and a person who is not a shareholder that restricts, in whole or in part, the powers of directors to manage the business affairs of the corporation is valid. A declaration by the person who is the beneficial owner of all the shares of the corporation which so restricts the powers of the directors is deemed to be a unanimous shareholder agreement under s. 146(3). A unanimous shareholder agreement will bind a transferee of shares unless the transferee has no actual knowledge of it or if there is no reference thereto on the certificate that was transferred to him (s. 146(4)).

It will be noted that pursuant to s. 146(5) a shareholder who is a party to a unanimous shareholder agreement has all the rights, powers and duties of a director of the corporation to which the agreement relates to the extent that the agreement restricts the powers of directors to manage the business and affairs of the corporation and the directors are thereby relieved of their duties and liabilities including liabilities under s. 119 to the same extent. For discussion of this type of agreement and voting trusts see Chapter 6.

Summoning of meetings

Ordinarily the summoning of meetings should be authorized by resolution of the board; the consent of a quorum of directors as individuals will not suffice: *In re Haycraft Gold Reduction & Mining Co.*, [1900] 2 Ch. 230; but the directors as a board may, before the meeting, ratify an unauthorized notice sent out by an official of the corporation and purporting to have been given under their authority: *Hooper v. Kerr, Stuart & Co.* (1900), 83 L.T. 729. Resolutions passed at a meeting summoned by a board of *de facto* directors are not invalid: *Boschoek Proprietary Co. v. Fuke*, [1906] 1 Ch. 148. The by-laws often provide for meetings to be summoned by designated officers. As to notices given by unauthorized persons, see *In re Haycraft Gold Reduction & Mining Co., supra*; *Re State of Wyoming Syndicate*, [1901] 2 Ch. 431; *Courchêne v. Viger Park Co.* (1915), 23 D.L.R. 693 (Que. C.A.).

In *Wood v. Pan-American Investments Ltd.* (1961), 28 D.L.R. (2d) 703 (B.C. S.C.) the articles of association required a meeting of shareholders to be authorized by a director's resolution or by a shareholder's requisition. The corporation in question had three directors and two directors authorized the sending of the notice, but without a meeting of the board. An injunction was granted to the third director against the holding of the meeting. The failure to hold the directors' meeting was not a mere irregularity and it was pointed out that the notice did not state the nature of the business to come before the general meeting of shareholders. The plaintiff did not have an opportunity as a director to lay before the board his views as to matters to be brought before such meeting.

A purported annual meeting called by a minority shareholder of the corporation, who did not act in good faith after the resignation of all of the directors, is a complete nullity for want of formality; the proper procedure, if it is not clear what is the wish of the majority of shareholders, is to order a meeting to be convened under court order. See *South Shore Development Limited v. Snow*, [1973] 4 N.S.R. (2d) 601 (N.S. T.D.).

The correct procedure is for the notice to state that it is given "by order of the board," unless the by-laws provide for the summoning of meetings by a designated officer, for example, the president. The corporation may take advantage of an irregularity as against its secretary-treasurer: *Courchêne v. Viger Park, supra.*

A court is very reluctant to enjoin shareholders from holding a meeting of the corporation, as such a meeting is the only way the shareholders can interfere, if the majority of them think that the course taken by the directors, in a matter which is *intra vires* of the directors, is not for the benefit of the corporation: *Isle of Wight Railway v. Tahourdin* (1884), 25 Ch. D. 320 (C.A.) (injunction refused); *Harben v. Phillips* (1883), 23 Ch. D. 14 (C.A.) (injunction refused upon directors who were improperly appointed undertaking to act in a certain manner until a shareholders' meeting was held); *McDougald v. Wilson*, [1933] 3 D.L.R. 111 (Que. S.C.) (injunction refused).

In the absence of express authority in the by-laws or articles the directors have no power to postpone, as opposed to adjourning, a meeting of shareholders properly convened: *Smith v. Paringa Mines Ltd.*, [1906] 2 Ch. 193.

The summoning of meetings is dealt with below under the following headings: Place of meetings; Contents of notice; Length of notice; Right to receive notice; Waiver of notice; Proxies and proxy solicitation.

Place of meetings

Section 132 provides that shareholders' meetings are to be held at the place within Canada set out in the by-laws or, if the by-laws make no such provision, in such place within Canada as determined by the directors; a meeting of shareholders of the corporation may be held outside of Canada if all the shareholders entitled to vote so agree and a shareholder attending a meeting is deemed to have so agreed except where he attends a meeting for the express purpose of objecting to the transaction of any business on the ground that the meeting is not lawfully held.

A meeting outside the place authorized under the Act or the articles was held to be improperly called. See *Upper Canada Resources Ltd. and Minister of Consumer and Commercial Relations* (1978), 20 O.R. (2d) 100 (Ont. H.C.).

Contents of notice

A notice of the time and place of a meeting of the shareholders is to be sent not less than 21 days and no more than 50 days prior to the meeting to each shareholder entitled to vote at the meeting, to each director and to the auditor of the corporation. Where a record date has been fixed for receiving notice of a meeting pursuant to s. 134(2), no notice need be sent to the shareholders not registered on the record date, but failure to receive notice does not deprive a shareholder of the right to vote at the meeting.

In the case of an adjourned meeting, if the adjournment is for less than 30 days it is not necessary, unless otherwise provided in the by-laws, to give notice of the adjourned meeting otherwise than by announcement at the earlier meeting that it is adjourned. If there is an adjournment or adjournments for an aggregate of 30 days or more, then notice of the adjournment is to be given for the original meeting, but unless it has been adjourned by one or more adjournments for a period greater than 90 days it is not necessary to solicit proxies for such adjourned meeting (s. 135(3), (4)).

All business to be transacted at a special meeting of shareholders and all business transacted at an annual meeting of shareholders except consideration of the financial statements, the auditors report, the election of directors and reappointment of the incumbent auditor is deemed to be special business. The notice of a meeting at which special business is to be transacted is to state the nature of that business in sufficient detail to permit the shareholder to form a reasoned judgment thereon and to set out the text of any special resolution to be submitted to the meeting (s. 135(5), (6)).

It was proposed to pass two special resolutions dealing with matters about which the directors had received detailed reports which were not put before the members, the members being told that they should repose confidence in the judgment of directors. It was held that the resolutions were not properly passed and an injunction should be issued to restrain any action pursuant thereto pending the trial of an issue. The principle of full disclosure was to be broadly applied and was not to be limited to cases of gain to the directors or oppression of the minority shareholders. See *Rudkin v. B.C. Auto Assn.* (1969), 20 W.W.R. 649 (B.C. S.C.). Thus, where a proxy form and a letter setting out the purpose of the meeting accompany the notice of meeting they are to be read together so that any deficiencies in the notice may be made good in the accompanying documents set out by the requisition for a meeting. See *Dalex Mines Ltd. (N.P.L.) v. Schmidt*, [1973] 5 W.W.R. 357, 38 D.L.R. (3d) 17 (B.C. S.C.).

Thus in *Wotherspoon v. Canadian Pacific Ltd.* (1979), 22 O.R. (2d) 385 where a meeting was called to consider the sale of the assets, the notice was held to be defective in that there had been no inclusion of the appraiser's report and any action done in reliance of the proceedings of the defective meeting was held to be *ultra vires*. On appeal, however, reported at (1982), 35 O.R. (2d) 449, the court held that it was unreasonable to suggest that the notice was defective and was improper unless accompanied by 128 pages of appraisal reports. It was also held that even if the meeting had been improper the action taken would have been invalid rather than *ultra vires*. The judgment of the Court of Appeal was affirmed on this point by the Supreme Court of Canada, [1987] 1 S.C.R. 952, 39 D.L.R. (4th) 169. In such cases it is now the practice to include a summary of the appraisal report.

Section 137 provides that any shareholder entitled to vote at an annual meeting may submit to the corporation notice of any matter he proposes to raise at the meeting and discuss at the meeting any matter in respect of which he could have proposed to raise. Where a notice is issued by a majority shareholder which fails to state the purpose of the meeting, the directors are entitled to ignore the notice. See: *Pahl v. Potential Marketing Inc.* (1990), 88 Sask. R. 81 (Q.B.). The corporation soliciting proxies is to set out the proposal so raised in the management proxy circular or to attach the proposal to such circular. The shareholder is entitled upon request to the corporation to include in the management proxy circular or to attach thereto a statement of not more than 200 words in support of the proposal that he is making together with his name and address. The proposal may include nominations for the election of directors if the proposal is signed by one or more holders of shares aggregating not less than 5 per cent of the total number or of the shares or of the class of shares entitled to vote at the meeting and to which the proposal is to be presented, but this provision does not preclude a nomination being made at a meeting of shareholders; it is provided that no corporation or person acting on its behalf incurs any liability by reason only of circulating a proposal or statement of compliance with the section; a corporation is not required to circulate the proposal or supporting statement if the proposal is not submitted to the corporation at least 90 days prior to the anniversary date of the previous annual meeting of shareholders or it clearly appears that the proposal is primarily for the purpose of enforcing a personal claim or redressing a personal grievance of the shareholder against the corporation, its directors, officers or security holders or primarily to promote general economic, political, racial, religious, social or similar causes; or if the corporation at the shareholders' request included a proposal in the management proxy circular relating to a meeting of shareholders within two years preceding the receipt of such request and the shareholder failed to present the proposal in person or by proxy at the meeting or if it was submitted, either in a management or dissident's proxy circular, the proposal was defeated or if the rights conferred by the section in question are being abused to secure publicity.

A corporation refusing to include a proposal and management proxy circular is to notify the shareholder within ten days after receiving the proposal of its intention to omit the proposal and is to send to the shareholder a statement of the reasons for the refusal. The shareholder may then apply to a court to restrain the holding of the meeting at which the proposal is sought to be presented; the court may make any further order it thinks fit. An application may also be made by the corporation or any person claiming to be grieved by a proposal for an order permitting the corporation to omit the proposal from the management proxy circular and the court if it is satisfied that one of the exemptions applies may make such order as it thinks fit. Notice of any application to the court is also to be given to the Director and the Director is entitled to appear and be heard in person or by counsel (s. 137(7) - (10)).

A notice that a meeting will be held at a specified time and place, but dependent upon a certain contingency, is not a good notice: *Alexander v. Simpson* (1889), 43 Ch. D. 139 (C.A.). Where the actual holding of the meeting is not contingent on any event, the notice is valid even if the business to which it refers is contingent: *Tiessen v. Henderson*, [1899] 1 Ch. 861; *Re North of England Steamship Co.*, [1905] 2 Ch. 15 (C.A.), and the issuance of a notice in anticipation of the passing of a statute which provides for the holding of the meeting in respect of which the notice issued is valid, where the statute has actually become law by the hour specified in the notice for the meeting: *Pacific Coast Coal Mines Ltd. v. Arbuthnot*, [1917] A.C. 607 at 617.

A notice summoning a meeting for a specified hour or so soon thereafter as another meeting convened for the same day and place has been concluded is a sufficient specification of the time of the meeting: *Carruth v. Imperial Chemical Industries Ltd.*, [1937] A.C. 707 at 760 (H.L.).

A notice must be full and not misleading: *Baillie v. Oriental Telephone & Electric Co.*, [1915] 1 Ch. 503 (C.A.). The omission of a material fact may result in the notice being misleading: *Normandy v. Ind. Coope & Co.*, [1908] 1 Ch. 84, as may the generality of the words used in the notice: *Marks v. Rocsand Co.* (1920), 48 O.L.R. 224 (Ont. H.C.). However, it is not necessary that a notice give full details of the business to be transacted; a fair, candid and reasonable explanation of the purpose for which the meeting is convened is sufficient: *Kaye v. Croydon Tramways Co.*, [1898] 1 Ch. 358 (C.A.).

A notice calling a shareholders' meeting is not to be construed with excessive strictness but should be read and construed as an ordinary businessman would read and construe it: *Alexander v. Simpson* (1889), 43 Ch. D. 139 (C.A.); *Henderson v. Bank of Australasia* (1890), 45 Ch. D. 330 at 337; *Irvin v. Irvin Porcupine Gold Mines Ltd.*, [1940] O.W.N. 315 at 316 (H.C.); *Choppington Collieries Ltd. v. Johnson*, [1944] 1 All E.R. 762 at 763 (C.A.).

The failure to specify the business with clearness and accuracy will invalidate the notice and render the meeting irregular: *Wills v. Murray* (1850), 4 Ex. 843; *Re Silkstone Colliery Co.* (1875), 1 Ch. D. 38; *Kaye v. Croydon Tramways Co.*, [1898] 1 Ch. 358 (C.A.); *Lumbers v. Fretz* (1928), 62 O.L.R. 635 (H.C.); affd (1928), 63 O.L.R. 190 (C.A.) (failure to refer to voting of remuneration to directors). In these cases the notice dealt with one item of business only and it was found defective.

Where the notice includes two items of business and one of them turns out to be *ultra vires*, the notice is not invalid as regards the other item: *Cleve v. Financial Corp.* (1873), L.R. 16 Eq. 363; *Thomson v. Henderson's Transvaal Estates Ltd.*, [1908] 1 Ch. 765 (C.A.).

Business cannot be transacted at a meeting foreign to the objects specified in the notice, but if it is, this will not render the whole meeting irregular: *Re British Sugar Refining Co.* (1857), 3 K. & J. 408.

If the notice is misleading the holding of the meeting will be restrained: *Jackson v. Munster Bank* (1884), 13 L.R. Ir. 118; and the court will restrain the directors from acting on resolutions passed on insufficient notice until confirmed at a properly called meeting: *Kaye v. Croydon Tramways Co., supra*; *Pelech v. Ukrainian Mutual Benefit Assn.*, [1940] 4 D.L.R. 342 at 346 (Man. K.B.).

Directors may employ the corporation's officers and funds for the purpose of putting their recommendations before the shareholders in an explanatory circular accompanying a notice, and it is not incumbent on the directors in so doing to put forward the arguments of the dissentient shareholders as long as there is no fraud involved: *Campbell v. Australian Mutual Provident Society* (1908), 24 T.L.R. 623.

Where special business is intended to be dealt with it is not enough to give a general notice of an annual meeting, and notice of the nature of such special business must be given: *McDougall v. Black Lake Asbestos & Chrome Co.* (1920), 47 O.L.R. 328 (Ont. H.C.).

Relevant and legitimate amendments may be proposed to any resolution coming within the scope of the notice: *Henderson v. Bank of Australasia* (1890), 45 Ch. D. 330 at 346 (C.A.). Where notice was given of intention to fix the directors' remuneration and the only change was to reduce the remuneration from that set forth in the notice of meeting, the amendment did not invalidate the resolution: *Torbock v. Lord Westbury*, [1902] 2 Ch. 871. Where a meeting has been called to consider an agreement, a shareholder cannot object to a resolution approving the agreement with some modifications not making it more onerous on the corporation: *Wright's Case* (1871), L.R. 12 Eq. 331 at 341. See also *Betts & Co. v. MacNaghten*, [1910] 1 Ch. 430 (where articles required general notice of special business to be specified). Where the notice sets out that it is proposed to remove any of the directors, all may be removed: *Isle of Wight Railway v. Tahourdin* (1884), 25 Ch. D. 320 (C.A.).

Where an Act passed for the purpose of validating an *ultra vires* agreement so provided "subject to the same being adopted by a resolution passed by 75 per cent of the shareholders present personally or by proxy at any meeting . . . called for that purpose," it was held that a notice of the meeting was bad which did not put the shareholders in a position in which each of them could have judged for himself whether he would consent to the proposals coming before the meeting: *Pacific Coast Coal Mines, Ltd. v. Arbuthnot*, [1917] A.C. 607 (P.C.). It was further held that the conditions of the Act must be literally complied with to render such agreement *intra vires* and such fulfilment could not be inferred from acquiescence. See also the observations of Viscount Haldane, at p. 618, as to the necessity for full notice to shareholders who had given proxies at dates prior to the agreement sought to be ratified. See also *Zimmerman v. Trustee of Andrew Motherwell of Canada Ltd.* (1923), 54 O.L.R. 342 (Ont. C.A.) (notice specifying object of borrowing money need not specify other provisions of by-law); and the same case on appeal to the Judicial Committee of the Privy Council, [1925] 3 D.L.R. 953.

A notice convening a shareholders' meeting for the purpose of confirming a contract in which directors of the corporation are interested must give sufficient particulars as to that interest to allow the shareholders to know precisely that about which they are to vote: *Kaye v. Croydon Tramways Co.*, [1898] 1 Ch.

358 (C.A.); *Tiessen v. Henderson*, [1899] 1 Ch. 861; *Normandy v. Ind, Coope & Co.*, [1908] 1 Ch. 84; *Marks v. Rocsand Co.* (1920), 48 O.L.R. 224 (Ont. H.C.). The names of the directors interested in the contract to be ratified must be given in the notice: *Irvin v. Irvin Porcupine Gold Mines Ltd.*, [1940] O.W.N. 315 (H.C.).

Length of notice

Section 135(1) provides that the notice of a meeting of shareholders is to be sent not less than 21 days and no more than 50 days before the meeting. The comparable provision in the Ontario Act is s. 96, where in the case of an offering corporation the notice is to be sent not less than 21 days but for any other corporation not less than 10 days and in either case not more than 50 days prior to the meeting. Not less than so many days means clear days; that is, the time must be reckoned excluding both the day of mailing and the day of the meeting: *R. v. Justices of Shropshire* (1838), 8 Ad. & E. 173; *In re Railway Sleepers Supply Co.* (1885), 29 Ch. D. 204; *R. v. Turner*, [1910] 1 K.B. 346 at 359 (C.A.); *Ashton v. Powers* (1922), 51 O.L.R. 309 (H.C.); *Blitt v. Congregation Ajudath Acham* (1926), 64 Que. S.C. 303 (at least three days' notice); *In re Hector Whaling Ltd.*, [1936] 1 Ch. 208.

In the absence of any applicable provision as to length of notice only reasonable notice is required: *John Morley Building Co. v. Barras*, [1891] 2 Ch. 386 (two days' notice of meeting of subscribers to memorandum of association held sufficient).

When special notices have been sent to each of the shareholders individually an omission literally to comply with the regulations, where these require advertising, will not make the notice defective: *Re British Sugar Refining Co.* (1857), 3 K. & J. 408.

A notice served by post is to be deemed to have been received when the registered letter containing it would be delivered in the ordinary course of post (s. 253). Accordingly, if a specified number of days' notice is required, when notice is given by post it is necessary to allow a sufficient margin of time for the delivery of the letter in computing the interval between the date of service and the date of meeting: *Ashton v. Powers, supra*.

The operation of s. 253 is excluded in the case of s. 135 by providing not for a definite number of days' notice, but for the sending of a notice a certain number of days before the date of the meeting.

In a case pursuant to the British Columbia Act meetings of four corporations were involved, three corporations had given 20 days' notice and one corporation had given 19 days' notice. The Act required 21 days' notice but it was held that the meetings were validly held and that the failure to give the required notice had not been intentional. In addition there was no evidence that any shareholder was affected by the defective notice or had complained of it. The corporations should not be put to the expense of another meeting in the circumstances. See *New Frontier Petroleum Inc. v. Oneida Resources Corp.* (1981), 34 B.C.L.R. 53 (B.C. S.C.). Thus, in a case where the notice was short by one day, an objecting shareholder was held to have waived his right to object by attending the meeting: *Moco Management Ltd. v. Llernam Holdings Ltd.* (1985), 68 B.C.L.R. 128 (B.C. S.C.). In *United States Precious Metals Inc. v. Ruskin Developments Ltd.* (1986), 8 B.C.L.R. (2d) 258 (B.C. C.A.), a notice was mailed for an annual meeting one day short of the notice required by the Act. The plaintiff obtained an *ex parte* injunction restraining the holding of the meeting as he had acquired a large number of the shares of the corporation intending to vote them at the annual meeting. The corporation obtained an order validating the original notice and vacating the injunction. The balance of convenience was held to be in favour of the corporation holding the meeting.

Where a notice was required to be published once a week for four successive weeks before a specified date, it was held that the notice must be published during a period commencing not less than 28 days prior to the specified date: *Re Kyro River Improvement Co.* (1929), 64 O.L.R. 225 (C.A.); but where the requirement was publication "for not less than three consecutive weeks before the day appointed" it was held that it was not necessary that three weeks should elapse between the publication of the first notice and the day of the meeting: *Portland & Lancaster Steam Ferry Co. v. Pratt* (1850), 7 N.B.R. 17 (C.A.).

If a meeting has been called on insufficient notice an injunction may be obtained restraining the holding of the meeting: *Ashton v. Powers, supra.* In *Mayr v. St. Lawrence Corp.*, [1950] Que. K.B. 635 a majority of the Court of Appeal held that mandamus was a proper remedy for shareholders seeking to set aside annual and special general meetings of shareholders on the ground that insufficient notice had been given and to compel the directors to call new meetings on proper notice.

Where directors of a corporation are proceeding to call a meeting at an early date to prevent some of the shareholders from exercising their voting power, they will be restrained by the court: *Cannon v. Trask* (1875), L.R. 20 Eq. 669.

Right to receive notice

Section 135(1) of the Act provides that the notice is to be given to every shareholder entitled to vote at the meeting in question, to each director and to the auditor of the company.

However, the by-laws or articles commonly provide that accidental omission to give notice or non-receipt thereof does not invalidate a meeting.

The by-laws of a corporation may restrict the giving of notice: *R. v. Bird* (1811), 13 East 367. In England the articles frequently dispense with notice to non-resident members and on the construction of such an article it was held that members who had no registered address and had not furnished the corporation with any address in the United Kingdom for the service of notices were not entitled to receive notices of general meetings: *Dickson v. Halesowen Steel Co.*, [1928] W.N. 33. Even in the absence of an article dispensing with notice to non-resident members, it was held in *In re Union Hill Silver Co.* (1870), 22 L.T. 400, that s. 52 of the *English Companies Act, 1862*, requiring seven days' notice of general meetings to be served on every member did not apply as regards members resident in the United States as such members could not have received the notice in the ordinary course of post. In *In re Newcastle United*

Football Co., [1932] W.N. 109, a resolution was held to be validly passed, although two shareholders resident outside the jurisdiction had not received the requisite 21 days' notice of the meeting. These decisions were approved in *In re Warden & Hotchkiss Ltd.*, [1945] Ch. 270 (C.A.).

It is not usual for the by-laws to contain special provisions for the giving of notices to shareholders whose addresses are outside of Canada. The common provision requiring notices of any meeting to be mailed a specified number of days before the meeting gives rise to no difficulty, as no time need be allowed to permit the notice to reach the shareholders in the ordinary course of post.

In the case of *Miller v. F. Mendel Holdings Ltd.*, [1984] 30 Sask. R. 298, 2 W.W.R. 683 (Sask. Q.B.), the Saskatchewan Act provided that every shareholder was to receive notice of meetings and to have one vote unless the articles otherwise provided. The articles of the particular corporation limited the right to vote to one class of shares but the court held that the right to receive notice of meetings and by implication to attend the meeting was not affected since non-voting shareholders would be able to participate in discussions in an attempt to persuade voting shareholders to their view. It will be noted that the federal Act is worded differently.

Where the giving of notice to shareholders resident in enemy countries is forbidden by statute, their right to receive notice is suspended and a resolution passed at a meeting, notice of which was not given to such shareholders, will be effective: *In re Anglo-International Bank Ltd.*, [1943] Ch. 233 (C.A.).

Apart from special provisions in the charter or by-laws, holders of preferred shares with no right to vote are not entitled to notice of meetings: *In re Mackenzie & Co.*, [1916] 2 Ch. 450.

The directors cannot disregard the provisions of the corporation's by-laws as to notice of meetings of shareholders: *Canada Furniture Co. v. Banning* (1918), 39 D.L.R. 313 (Man. K.B.).

Apart from special provision in the statute or governing regulations, the executors of a deceased shareholder, who have not themselves become registered as shareholders, are not entitled to notice; nor need a notice be sent directed to the deceased shareholder at his registered address: *Allen v. Gold Reefs of West Africa Ltd.*, [1900] 1 Ch. 656 (C.A.).

If all the shareholders are actually present at a meeting, whether with or without notice, the want of notice will be excused unless objection is taken at the time: *Re British Sugar Refining Co.* (1857), 3 K. & J. 408.

An exception to this general statutory rule in s. 135 applies where a record date has been fixed for determining shareholders entitled to receive notice of a meeting of shareholders. The record date is not to precede by more than 50 days or by less than 21 days the date on which the meeting is to be held; if no record date is fixed, the record date for determination of shareholders entitled to receive notice of the meeting of shareholders is to be at the close of business on the day immediately preceding the day on which the notice is given or, if no notice is given, the day on which the meeting is held; if a record date is fixed unless notice of the record date is waived in writing by every holder of a share of the class or series affected whose name is set out in the securities register, not less than seven days before the date so fixed it is to be advertised in a newspaper, published or distributed in the place where the corporation has its registered office and in each place in Canada where a transfer of its shares may be recorded and by written notice to each stock exchange in Canada in which the shares of the corporation are listed for trading (s. 134(2) - (4)).

Waiver of notice

Section 136 provides that a shareholder or any other person entitled to attend a meeting of shareholders may in any manner waive notice of a meeting of shareholders and attendance of any such person at a meeting of shareholders is a waiver of notice of the meeting unless he attends such meeting for the express purpose of objecting to the transaction of any business on the ground that the meeting is not lawfully called.

Section 138 of the Act provides that a corporation is to prepare a list of shareholders entitled to receive notice of the meeting arranged in alphabetical order and showing the number of shares held by each such shareholder; if no record date is fixed then the list is to be prepared on the close of business of the day immediately preceding the day on which the notice is given or where there is no notice on the day on which the meeting is held; if a record date has been fixed under s. 134(2) not later than ten days after such date; where a record date has been fixed the person named in the list is entitled to vote the shares in his name at the meeting to which the list relates, except to the extent he has transferred the ownership of any of his shares after the record date and the transferee produces properly endorsed share certificates or otherwise establishes ownership of the shares and demands not later than ten days prior to the meeting or such shorter period before the meeting as the by-laws of the corporation may provide that his name be included in the list before the meeting, in which case the transferee is entitled to vote his shares at the meeting; where no record date is fixed the person named in the list is entitled to vote the shares shown opposite his name unless there has been a transfer and similar evidence is given by the transferee as in the case where a record date has been fixed; a shareholder may examine such list during usual business hours at the registered office of the corporation or at the place where its central security register is maintained and at the meeting of the shareholders for which the list was prepared (s. 138).

In the absence of statutory provision, all the shareholders being present may waive notices and formalities: *In re Express Engineering Works Ltd.*, [1920] 1 Ch. 466 (C.A.); *In re Oxted Motor Co.*, [1921] 3 K.B. 32; and apparently a shareholder personally present can waive notice as regards himself: *Re Excel Footwear Co., Ex. parte Nova Scotia Trust Co.*, [1923] 3 D.L.R. 212 (N.S. C.A.).

Where some shareholders are present by proxy, a defective notice is not cured unless the authority conferred by the proxy is wide enough to cover the business transacted at the meeting: *Marks v. Rocsand Co.* (1920), 48 O.L.R. 224 at 228 (H.C.), (1921), 49 O.L.R. 137 (C.A.).

Proxies and proxy solicitation

A shareholder entitled to vote at a meeting of shareholders may, by means of a proxy, appoint a proxyholder or one or more proxyholders, who need not be shareholders, to attend and act at the meeting in the manner and to the extent authorized, and with the authority conferred, by the proxy. "Proxy" is defined to mean a completed and executed form of proxy by means of which a shareholder appoints a proxyholder to attend and act on his behalf at a meeting of shareholders. A proxy is to be executed by the shareholder or his attorney authorized in writing and is valid only at the meeting in respect of which it is given or any adjournment thereof. In addition to revocation in any other manner permitted by law, a shareholder may revoke a proxy by depositing an instrument in writing executed by the shareholder or by his attorney authorized in writing either at the registered office of the corporation at any time up to and including the last business day preceding the day of the meeting, or any adjournment thereof, at which the proxy is to be used or with the chairman of such meeting on the day of the meeting, or adjournment thereof. The directors may specify in a notice calling a meeting of shareholders a time, not exceeding 48 hours, excluding Saturdays and holidays, preceding the meeting or an adjournment thereof before which time proxies to be used at the meeting must be deposited with the corporation or its agent (s. 148).

In the case of a corporation which has 15 or more shareholders (joint shareholders being counted as one shareholder), certain additional requirements are to be met unless an order is obtained from the Director exempting compliance with such requirements. The management of such corporation is required, concurrently with giving notice of a meeting of shareholders, to send a form of proxy in prescribed form to each shareholder who is entitled to notice of the meeting (s. 149). Where a solicitation of proxies is made by or on behalf of the management of a corporation, a management proxy circular in prescribed form either as an appendix to, or a separate document accompanying, the notice of meeting is to be sent to each shareholder whose proxy is solicited and to the auditor of the corporation; in the case of any other solicitation, the person making the solicitation must send to each shareholder whose proxy is solicited, the auditor of the corporation and the corporation, a dissident's proxy circular in prescribed form stating the purposes of the solicitation. The term "solicitation" as defined in s. 147 includes among other things a request for a proxy and the sending of a form of proxy to a shareholder pursuant to s. 149. A copy of a management proxy circular or dissident's proxy circular is to be sent to the Director together with a copy of the notice of meeting, form of proxy and any other documents for use in connection with the meeting (s. 150(2)). A shareholder had sent a letter addressed to other shareholders complaining about the management of the corporation and proposing changes. In an application to court it was held that this was not a solicitation for proxies and accordingly no information circular was required: *Western Mines Ltd. v. Sheridan*, [1976] W.W.D. 29 (B.C. S.C.).

It will be observed that the proxy solicitation provisions are not applicable if the corporation has fewer than 15 shareholders; in a similar provision under the Ontario Act this was interpreted to mean shareholders entitled to vote and not all shareholders, that is where a corporation had 15 preference shareholders, none of whom were entitled to vote and 11 common shareholders, it was held that the corporation had fewer than 15 shareholders and therefore no exempting order was required: *Re Frontier Acceptance Corp.*, [1969] 2 O.R. 302 (Ont. H.C.).

The regulations set out detailed instructions with respect to the form of proxy: the contents of the management proxy circular, the contents of a dissident's proxy circular, the date of the proxy circular and of the information and the financial statements contained in the proxy circular. The more important of these may be summarized as follows:

1. The form of proxy should indicate in boldfaced type whether it is solicited by or on behalf of the management of the corporation and is likewise to indicate that a shareholder may appoint a proxyholder other than any person designated on the form to attend and act on his behalf and is to contain instructions as to the manner in which the shareholder may do so. A means of designating another person as proxyholder is to be given, and a form of proxy is to provide a means for the shareholder to specify that the shares registered in his name are to be voted for or against each matter or group of related matters identified in the notice of meeting and management proxy circular, a dissident's proxy circular or a proposal under s. 137 of the Act, other than appointment of an auditor and the election of directors. If such choice is not provided, the form of proxy may confer authority if the form of proxy or the circular states in boldfaced type how the proxyholder will vote the shares in respect of each matter or group of related matters. The proxy is to provide a means for the shareholder to specify that the shares registered in his name shall be voted or withheld from voting, in respect of the appointment of an auditor or election of directors. The proxy or the circular is to state that the shares voted represented by the proxy will be voted or withheld from voting and that on any ballot that may be called, if the shareholder specifies a choice with respect to any matter to be acted upon, the shares will be voted accordingly. Discretionary authority in respect of amendments to matters identified in the notice of meeting or other matters that may properly come before the meeting, may be conferred by a form of proxy if the person by or on whose behalf the solicitation is made is not aware within a reasonable time prior to the solicitation that the amendments or other matters are to be presented at the meeting, and if the form of proxy or circular states specifically that it confers such discretionary authority. The form of proxy is not to confer authority in respect of the appointment of an auditor or the election of a director unless a bona fide proposed nominee is named in the form of proxy or circular in question or a proposal under s. 137 of the Act (ss. 32 - 34 of the Regulations).
2. The management proxy circular is to contain the following information: a statement of the right of the shareholder to revoke a proxy and the method by which such right of revocation may be exercised; a statement in boldfaced type that the solicitation is made by or on behalf of the management of the corporation; the name of any director of the corporation who has informed

the management in writing that he intends to oppose any action intended to be taken by the management and the action that he intends to oppose; the method of solicitation if otherwise by mail and if the solicitation is made by specially engaged employees or agents, the material features of any contract or arrangement for solicitation, the parties to such contract or arrangements, and the cost or anticipated costs thereof; the name of the person by whom the cost of solicitation will be borne; the number of shares of each class of shares of the corporation entitled to be voted and the number of votes to which each share of each such class is entitled; if the corporation has constrained share provisions, the general nature thereof; if the proceeds of an issue of securities were used for a purpose other than that stated in the document under which the securities were issued, the date of the document, the amount and designation of securities so issued and details of the use made during the financial period of the proceeds in question; details of any financial assistance given by a corporation since the beginning of its last completed financial year to a shareholder of a corporation or any of its affiliates (not a director, officer or employee) or to an associate of any such shareholder, or to any person in connection with a purchase of shares issued or to be issued by the corporation, if the giving of the assistance was material to the corporation or any of its affiliates or to the recipient; if indemnification is paid or becomes payable to the directors or officers, the amounts so paid or payable, the name and title of the individual indemnified or to be indemnified under s. 124 of the Act and the circumstances giving rise thereto; if insurance for the directors or officers is to be purchased the amount or approximate amount of premium paid by the corporation in respect of the directors as a group and the officers as a group; the aggregate amount of premiums paid by the individuals in each such group, the total amount of insurance purchased for each such group and a summary of any deductibility or co-insurance clause or other provision in the insurance contract that exposes the corporation to liability in addition to the payment of premiums; details of any action brought or taken under ss. 239 or 241 of the Act to which the corporation is a party, the name of each person who, to the knowledge of the directors or officers of the corporation, beneficially owns or exercises control or direction over shares carrying more than 10 per cent of the votes attaching to shares of the corporation, the approximate number of the shares so owned, controlled or directed by each such person and the percentage of voting shares of the corporation represented by the number of shares so owned, controlled or directed; if there is a change in effective control of the corporation since the beginning of its last financial year, the name of the person who, to the knowledge of directors or officers of the corporation, acquired control, the date and description of the transaction in which control was acquired and the percentage of shares entitled to be voted now owned or controlled or directed by that person; the percentage of votes required for the approval of any matter that is to be submitted to a vote of shareholders at the meeting other than the election of directors or the appointment of an auditor; if a new auditor is proposed to be appointed, his name and the name of any previous auditor appointed within the preceding five years and the date of his appointment. If directors are to be elected, a statement of the right of any class of shareholders to elect a specified number of directors or to accumulate their votes or of any conditions precedent to the exercise thereof; in tabular form if directors are to be elected, the name of the nominee, the time when his term of office will expire and all other major positions and offices with the corporation or any significant affiliates personally held by him; the present principal occupation or employment of each such person, similar information during the preceding five years, unless he is now a director and was elected to his present term of office by a vote of shareholders at a meeting the notice of which was accompanied by a proxy circular containing that information; if a person to be elected is or has been a director of the corporation, the period or periods during which he has so served, the approximate number of shares of each class, or the corporation and if the corporation's holding body corporate beneficially owned over which control or direction is exercised by each such person and if more than 10 per cent of the votes attached to shares of any class of the corporation or its holding body corporate are beneficially owned or subject to control or direction by any such person or his associates, the approximate number of each class of shares so owned, controlled or directed by the associates and the name of each associate; the name and details of any contract arrangement or understanding between any proposed management nominee and any other person except the directors and officer of the corporation acting solely in their capacity as such, pursuant to which the nominee is to be elected including the name of the other person; if action is to be taken with respect to the election of directors, any bonus, profit sharing or plan of remuneration in which any director of such corporation will share, any pension or retirement plan of the corporation in which any director or officer will participate, the granting to any director or officers of the corporation of any option or right to purchase any securities other than rights issued rateably to all shareholders or to all shareholders resident in Canada, a statement of executive remuneration in prescribed form, details of the largest aggregate amount of debt outstanding at any time since the beginning of the last completed year of each director and officer of the corporation or any proposed nominee, including any associate, which shall specify the nature of the debt, details of the transaction in which it was incurred, the amount presently outstanding and the rate of interest paid or charged, but not amounts in the ordinary course of business or if the aggregate debt does not exceed $10,000 at any time during the period; the details including the approximate amount of any material interest of any director or officer or proposed nominee or any 10 per cent shareholder or any associate or affiliate of any of the foregoing persons in any transaction or proposed transaction that has materially affected or will materially affect the corporation or any of its affiliates; certain items need not be listed, for example, where the transaction is in the ordinary course of business; details of any agreement or arrangement as specified, details of any material interest of any director, officer, proposed nominee or any associate in any matter to be acted on at the meeting other than the election of directors or appointment of an auditor; prescribed details with respect to the authorization or issue of securities if to be authorized at the meeting in question; if the meeting is to modify rights attaching to any securities of the corporation, then certain prescribed information is to be given, including any information material to the proposed modification or exchange; similarly with respect to an amalgamation; a statement of the right of dissent under s. 190 if such exist; actions to be taken with respect to any matter other than the approval of financial statements, the substance of each such matter or group of related matters to the extent not previously referred to and sufficient details as to permit shareholders to form a reasoned judgment concerning the matter; if such matter is not required to be submitted to a vote of shareholders, the reason for so submitting it and the action intended to be taken by management in the event of a negative vote by the shareholders. And lastly, a statement signed by an officer or director of the corporation that the contents and the sending of the circular has been approved by the directors (s. 35 of the Regulations).

3. A circular sent to the Director is to be accompanied by a statement signed by a director or officer that a copy of the circular has been sent to each director, to each shareholder entitled to a notice of the meeting to which the circular relates and to the auditor of the corporation (s. 36 of the Regulations). Detailed rules are also given with respect to the contents of a dissident's proxy circular (ss. 37 - 41 of the Regulations). The date of proxy circular is to be not more than 30 days prior to the day in which it was first sent to a shareholder of the corporation and the information other than financial statements required to be contained in it shall be given as of the date of the circular (s. 42 of the Regulations). The financial statements whether they accompany or form part of the circular, are to be prepared in accordance with the prescribed manner, and if not reported on by the auditor of the corporation are to be accompanied by a report of the chief financial officer of the corporation stating that financial statements have not been audited but have been prepared in accordance with the requirements of Part V of the Regulations passed under the federal Act (s. 43 of the Regulations).

If a form of proxy, management proxy circular or dissident's proxy circular contains an untrue statement of a material fact or omits to state a material fact required therein or necessary to make a statement contained therein not misleading, an interested person or the Director may apply to the court for an appropriate remedy; notice of any such application by an interested person is to be given to the Director (s. 154).

A person who solicits a proxy and is appointed proxyholder is to attend in person or cause an alternative proxyholder to attend the meeting and to comply with the directions of the shareholder who appointed him. A proxyholder, or an alternate proxyholder, has the same rights as the shareholder who appointed him to speak at a meeting of shareholders in respect of any matter, to vote by way of ballot at the meeting and, except where a proxyholder or an alternate has conflicting instructions from more than one shareholder, to vote at such a meeting in respect of any matter by way of any show of hands (s. 152).

Shares of a corporation that are registered in the name of a registrant or his nominee and not beneficially owned by the registrant are not to be voted unless the registrant, forthwith after receipt of the notice of meeting, financial statements, management proxy circular, dissident's proxy circular and any other documents, other than the form of proxy, sent to shareholders by or on behalf of any person for use in connection with the meeting, sends a copy thereof to the beneficial owner together with, unless the registrant has already received the same, a written request for voting instructions. "Registrant" is defined in Part XII to mean a securities broker or dealer required to be registered to trade or deal in securities under the laws of any jurisdiction. If voting instructions are not received from the beneficial owner the registrant is not to vote or appoint a proxyholder to vote the shares, but if voting instructions are received the shares are to be voted in accordance therewith. If requested by the beneficial owner, the registrant is required to appoint him or his nominee as proxyholder (s. 153).

In the case of *Brown v. Duby* (1980), 28 O.R. (2d) 745, 11 B.L.R. 129 (Ont. H.C.) shareholders of a federally incorporated corporation were dissatisfied with management and sent letters to shareholders in the United States asking them to withhold proxies from management until the dissidents could provide proxy material. The letter was in conformity with U.S. law. In an application by the corporation for an interlocutory injunction restraining the defendants from soliciting proxies without a dissident's proxy circular it was held that the application should be dismissed. While the corporation had established a *prima facie* case of solicitation which required a proxy circular the remedy of an injunction was not appropriate. The object of the provisions in question was to benefit and protect the shareholders and ample time remained within which to make a full presentation to the shareholders prior to the next annual meeting.

Procedure at meetings

Meetings of shareholders are to be governed by the same rules as to procedure as apply to parliamentary and municipal bodies except where the statute or by-laws otherwise provide: *Lumbers v. Fretz* (1928), 62 O.L.R. 635 at 650 (H.C.); affd (1928), 63 O.L.R. 190 (C.A.).

Procedure at meetings is discussed under the following headings: Admission; Chairman; Quorum; Right of discussion; Resolutions; Voting; Proxies; Show of hands; Poll; and Adjournment.

Admission

Shareholders (holding shares of a class carrying rights of attendance at the meetings) or their proxies or in the case of corporate shareholders their authorized representatives (s. 140(2)) arc entitled to be admitted.

Under s. 148(1) a proxy need not be a shareholder. An authorized representative appointed under s. 140(2) need not himself be a shareholder. See the material under the heading "Proxies", below. Under the Ontario Act (s. 110(1)) a proxy need not be a shareholder.

There is no objection to the presence at the meeting of the secretary or other officials of the company, scrutineers and others who may have duties to perform in connection with the meeting, notwithstanding that they may not be shareholders. Representatives of the press may be admitted if the shareholders present approve; ordinarily this will be decided by the chairman.

Chairman

The by-laws usually provide that the president, or in his absence the vice-president, is to preside at meetings of shareholders. Where the by-laws require the president to preside, the shareholders cannot elect another chairman if the president is present: *Re Lemay Ltd.* (1924), 26 O.W.N. 443 (H.C.).

Subject to any express provisions of the charter or by-laws, it is the duty and right of the president to preside at all meetings including meetings of the shareholders: *Freemont Canning Co. v. Wall*, [1941] O.R. 379 at 409 (C.A.), where Masten J.A. said that such conclusion was entirely consistent with the provisions of the by-laws giving the president general charge and control of the business and affairs of the corporation, which phrase in his opinion included the business of the annual meeting of shareholders. The by-laws in that case did not expressly provide that the president should be chairman at meetings of shareholders. In the same case, at p. 405, Robertson C.J.O. said:

> It may well be that if the president, or anyone else who may be chairman, should so conduct himself as chairman as to prevent the shareholders transacting the proper business of the meeting in a lawful manner, as, for example, by ordering an adjournment against the wishes of the meeting, the majority of shareholders present may oust him and appoint another chairman in his place.

An action brought by shareholders in their own behalf for a declaration that the president wrongfully refused to accept the nomination of another person to act as chairman cannot succeed: *Freemont Canning Co. v. Wall*, *supra*, at 403.

It is the duty of the chairman to see that the proceedings are conducted in an orderly manner and to see that the sense of the meeting is properly ascertained with regard to any question which is properly before it: *National Dwellings Society v. Sykes*, [1894] 3 Ch. 159, 162; *Bluechel & Smith v. Prefabricated Buildings Ltd.*, [1945] 2 D.L.R. 725 at 729 (B.C. S.C.). When the views of the minority have been heard the chairman, with the approval of the meeting, may declare the discussion closed and put the question to the vote: *Wall v. London & Northern Assets Corp.*, [1898] 2 Ch. 469 (C.A.).

The chairman will not be permitted to defeat the purpose for which the meeting was called by stopping the meeting or refusing or failing to act: *National Dwellings Society v. Sykes*, [1894] 3 Ch. 159 (stopping the meeting, declaring the meeting dissolved and leaving the chair); *Catesby v. Burnett*, [1916] 2 Ch. 325 (leaving the chair); *Spurr v. Albert Mining Co.* (1874), 15 N.B.R. 260 (C.A.) (refusal to put a motion to the meeting); *Gray v. Yellowknife Gold Mines Ltd. (No. 1)*, [1946] O.W.N. 938 at 945 (H.C.) (failing to take action on a pending motion). Under such circumstances the shareholders may appoint another chairman and proceed with the meeting. See also *Re United Canso Oil & Gas*

Ltd. (1980), 41 N.S.R. (2d) 282, 12 B.L.R. 130 (N.S. T.D.). As to the position with regard to adjournment, see under the heading "Adjournment" below. See also *Re Bomac Batten Ltd. and Pozhke* (1983), 43 O.R. (2d) 344, 23 B.L.R. 273 (Ont. H.C.).

The chairman has *prima facie* authority to decide all questions which necessarily require decision at the meeting; his decision will be deemed to be correct unless proved to be wrong; a shareholder, however, is entitled to have the correctness of the chairman's decision determined by the court: *In re Indian Zoedone Co.* (1884), 26 Ch. D. 70 (C.A.); *Henderson v. Bank of Australasia* (1890), 45 Ch. D. 330 (C.A.). As to the necessity of stating objections to the chairman at the meetings before he renders his decision, see *McCoubrey, Re* (1924), 5 C.B.R. 248 (Alta. T.D.) (meeting of creditors). See also s. 257(2) as to the presumption of the validity of proceedings duly entered in the minutes.

The decision of the chairman as to who is entitled to vote is in the nature of a judicial act; accordingly if he acts in good faith and without malice, he is entitled to be protected against liability in damages for refusing to accept votes tendered in person or as proxy by a shareholder on the mistaken ground that he was an alien enemy: *Bluechel & Smith v. Prefabricated Buildings Ltd.*, [1945] 2 D.L.R. 725 (B.C. S.C.). But if he does not proceed in a judicial manner and assumes, without making inquiries, that the seal of a corporate shareholder was illegally affixed to a proxy and rejects the proxy, with the result that minority interests with which he is identified remain in control of the corporation, the court will intervene to right the wrong on the authority of *Pender v. Lushington* (1877), 6 Ch. D. 70: *Johnson v. Hall* (1957), 10 D.L.R. (2d) 243 (B.C. S.C.). See also *Exco Corp. v. N.S. Savings & Loan Co.* (1987), 78 N.S.R. (2d) 91, 35 B.L.R. 149 (N.S. T.D.).

Where the articles provide that no objection shall be made to the validity of any vote except at the meeting at which the vote is tendered, and that votes not disallowed at the meeting shall be deemed valid for all purposes, the decision of the chairman as to the validity of proxies is final and cannot be reviewed in the absence of bad faith or fraud: *Wall v. London & Northern Assets Corp.*, [1899] 1 Ch. 550; *Wall v. Exchange Investment Corp.*, [1926] 1 Ch. 143 (C.A.). As to the conclusiveness of the chairman's declaration of the result of a vote under statutory provisions making a declaration by the chairman that a resolution has been carried, unless a poll is demanded, conclusive evidence of the fact, see *In re Hadleigh Castle Gold Mines*, [1900] 2 Ch. 419; *Arnot v. United African Lands Ltd.*, [1901] 1 Ch. 518 (C.A.); *In re Caratel (New) Mines Ltd.*, [1902] 2 Ch. 498.

However, some matters relating to the conduct of the meeting are under the control of those present who may decide, for example, whether notices, resolutions, minutes and accounts are to be read or taken as read; whether representatives of the press or other persons, not entitled to be summoned to the meeting, are to be permitted to be present; whether and when discussion is to be terminated. While, if necessary, a vote must be taken, if no objection is made the assent of the meeting will be assumed: *Carruth v. Imperial Chemical Industries Ltd.*, [1937] A.C. 707 at 761, 767 (H.L.).

The chairman has no casting vote at common law in the case of an equality of votes: *Nell v. Longbottom*, [1894] 1 Q.B. 767 at 771. Under the standard form of by-law the chairman is generally given the right to exercise a casting vote, but this provision is intended only as a means of dealing with occasional or frequent tie votes rather than a settled condition: *Re Citizen's Coal & Forwarding Co.*, [1927] 4 D.L.R. 275 (Ont. Co. Ct.). For a chairman to use his casting vote as the means of giving himself control of the corporation is a breach of his duty as a director: *Re Bondi Better Bananas Ltd. & Vallario*, [1951] O.R. 410 at 421 (H.C.). There is no provision in the present federal Act as there was in the preceding federal Act giving the chairman a casting vote and s. 141(1) provides that, unless the articles otherwise provide, each share of the corporation entitles the holder thereof to one vote at a meeting of shareholders. It is not clear whether a casting vote is a mere incident of the holding of a meeting in which case it would seem to be within the powers of the directors to pass a by-law pursuant to s. 103(1) which refers to any by-law regulating the business affairs of the corporation or whether the provision for a casting vote should be inserted in the articles. The better view appears to be that it is a matter of administration and accordingly can be dealt with in the by-laws unless prohibited in the articles. It will be noted, however, that it was felt necessary in the Ontario Act to make specific provision with respect to this question (s. 97). Under s. 97(a) of the Ontario Act the chairman is not entitled to a second or casting vote at any general meeting unless the articles, by-laws or a unanimous shareholder agreement otherwise provide.

The chairman should call the meeting to order promptly at the appointed hour, however, when the business of the meeting had been completed and the meeting dissolved within ten minutes after the appointed hour, the proceedings were invalidated at the instance of the holder of a majority of the shares who had signified his intention to be present and then arrived and found the meeting concluded: *Armstrong v. McGibbon* (1906), 15 Que. K.B. 345 (C.A.).

When a committee of two has been appointed to pass on ballots and proxies, the chairman is not justified in acting upon the report only of one of the two: *Dominion Royalty Corp. v. Holborn* (1932), 41 O.W.N. 288 (H.C.).

Quorum

Section 139(1) of the Act now provides that unless otherwise set out in the by-laws, a quorum of shareholders is the presence of the holders of a majority of the shares entitled to vote at the meeting in persons or represented by proxy, irrespective of the number of persons actually present at the meeting. Subsection (3) of s. 139 provides that if a quorum is not present at the opening of the meeting of shareholders, the shareholders present may adjourn the meeting to a fixed time and place but may not transact any other business. It is normal for the by-laws to provide for the required quorum at a meeting of the shareholders.

The provisions in respect of the quorum should be adapted to the circumstances. For example, in the case of a corporation with a large number of shareholders, a stipulation that the holders of 25 per cent (or some lesser figure) of the shares entitled to vote at the meeting is sufficient to constitute a quorum would be usual and proper; in the case of a corporation with a small number of shareholders the representation of 51 per cent of the shares is not uncommon. It is desirable to provide that for the purposes of choosing a chairman or adjourning a meeting the presence of two shareholders in person is sufficient.

At common law a meeting must consist of more than one person: *Sharp v. Dawes* (1876), 2 Q.B.D. 26 (C.A.); *In re Sanitary Carbon Co.*, [1877] W.N. 223; *Re Primary Distributors Ltd.*, [1954] 2 D.L.R. 438 (B.C. S.C.); but where one person held all the shares of a class it was held that the provision for a meeting of the holders of shares of that class in the memorandum and articles must be construed so as to be applicable to the case of a single shareholder: *East v. Bennett Bros. Ltd.*, [1911] 1 Ch. 163; applied in *Re Woodward; Ex parte Totten*, [1940] O.R. 387 where the Ontario Court of Appeal held that one creditor alone, if there is but one creditor, may hold a meeting as provided by the *Bankruptcy and Insolvency Act* to appoint a new trustee.

These questions have now been put to rest by the provisions of s. 139(4) which provides that if a corporation has only one shareholder or only one holder of any class or series of shares, the shareholder present in person or represented by proxy constitutes a meeting. It will be observed that s. 139(2) provides that if a quorum is present at the opening of a meeting of the shareholders, the shareholders present may, unless the by-laws otherwise provide, proceed with the business of the meeting notwithstanding that the quorum is not present throughout the meeting. It may be questioned whether the section will enable a particular item of business to be pursued if a quorum was not present for the transaction of that particular business.

If the by-laws provide for a quorum to be present in person or by proxy and also provide that a proxy need not be a shareholder, it would appear that proxies who are not shareholders should be counted to make up the number of shareholders requisite to constitute a quorum. See *Ernest v. Loma Gold Mines Ltd.*, [1897] 1 Ch. 1 at 8 (C.A.).

Where the articles of a corporation provided that no business should be transacted at any general meeting unless a quorum was present when the meeting proceeded to business, the court held that there was compliance with the article if there was a quorum present when the meeting proceeded to consider the business for which it was convened although, because of the withdrawal of a member from the meeting before the vote was taken, there was no quorum present when the meeting voted on that business: *In re Hartley Baird Ltd.*, [1955] 1 Ch. 143. Having regard to that decision, it may be desirable to provide in the by-laws that no business is to be transacted at a meeting unless a quorum is present at the time of the transaction of such business.

In the absence of a quorum no business can be transacted: *Howbeach Coal Co. v. Teague* (1860), 5 H. & N. 151 and see *Armstrong v. McGibbon* (1906), 15 Que. K.B. 345 (C.A.). Failing a quorum, a meeting is a nullity: *Lumbers v. Fretz* (1928), 63 O.L.R. 190 (C.A.).

However, the corporation, as against an outsider, may be precluded from setting up the irregularity, for example, in the case of bonds in the hands of a bona fide holder which are valid on their face but authorized by a resolution invalid for want of a proper quorum: *In re Fireproof Doors Ltd.*, [1916] 2 Ch. 142.

Where a corporation has furnished a vendor of property with a copy of a resolution of directors authorizing the purchase, purporting to be regular, the corporation cannot afterwards claim that the resolution was passed at a meeting at which there was no quorum present: *Montreal & St. Lawrence Light & Power Co. v. Robert*, [1906] A.C. 196 (P.C.).

Montreal Trust Co. v. Oxford Pipe Line Co., [1942] O.R. 490 (C.A.) was decided at a time when the Ontario Act contained no provision relating to a quorum. In that case there was no by-law prescribing the quorum at meetings of shareholders. The Court of Appeal held that the Act did not require any particular number of shares to be represented in order to form a quorum for the passing of the resolution in question (a resolution for winding-up) and that, as neither the charter nor the by-laws contained any requirement as to quorum, the percentage of shares represented had no bearing and if only two shareholders should attend there was a quorum.

Shareholders who are not entitled to vote may possibly assist in forming a quorum: see *Doig v. Mathews* (1915), 25 D.L.R. 732 (B.C. S.C.) and cases cited; *Doig v. Port Edward Townsite Co.* (1916), 22 B.C.R. 418 (S.C.).

In *Re Barsh et al. and Feldman* (1986), 54 O.R. (2d) 340, the by-laws of the corporation called for all three shareholders to be present for meetings. The corporation having only three shareholders, all of whom held equal amounts of shares, two of the shareholders applied for an order varying the quorum requirements to allow two shareholders to have a meeting without the third. The application was dismissed. It was pointed out that the quorum provisions were meant to ensure that no corporate action could be taken without the consent of all three shareholders and if the consent of the third shareholder was not obtainable a winding-up of the corporation would constitute an appropriate remedy. Where some, but not all, of the trustees of an estate were present at a shareholders' meeting the court held that such co-trustees could form part of the quorum. See *Cohen-Herrendorf v. Army & Navy Department Store Holdings Ltd.* (1986), 55 Sask. R. 134 (Sask. Q.B.).

Right of discussion

Shareholders are entitled to a fair hearing at the meetings of the corporation *Const v. Harris* (1823), Turn. & R. 496.

As to the right of a shareholder to speak at a meeting, see *Wall v. London & Northern Assets Corp.*, [1898] 2 Ch. 469 (C.A.).

A speech by a shareholder at a meeting of the corporation defamatory of the directors is privileged where it is in reference to matters which affect the corporation's interests: *Parsons v. Surgey* (1864), 4 F. & F. 247. The presence of reporters does not in itself destroy the privilege although it may be lost if the public or press are present at the meeting at the express invitation of the shareholder publishing the defamatory matter: *Pittard v. Oliver*, [1891] 1 Q.B. 474.

A circular sent by a shareholder to other shareholders of the company is privileged in the absence of malice although it contains libellous matter: *Quartz Hill Gold Mining Co. v. Beall* (1882), 20 Ch. D. 501. And likewise a report containing defamatory statements sent by the directors to all the shareholders is privileged, in the absence of malice, it being the duty of the directors to inform the shareholders: *Lawless v. Anglo-Egyptian Cotton & Oil Co.* (1869), L.R. 4 Q.B. 262, followed in *Harper v. Hamilton Retail Grocers' Assn.* (1900), 32 O.R. 295 (C.A.).

A report to a newspaper of the proceedings of a general meeting is not, however, privileged: *Davison v. Duncan* (1857), 7 E. & B. 229.

A notice published in a newspaper by a former manager of the corporation containing defamatory statements regarding the directors constituted a libel on the corporation as it reflected disastrously on the credit and standing of the corporation: *Owen Sound Building & Savings Society v. Meir* (1893), 24 O.R. 109, see also *Safeway Stores Ltd. v. Harris* (1948), 56 Man. L.R. 146 (C.A.). In *Liverpool Household Stores v. Smith* (1887), 37 Ch. D. 170 (C.A.), an injunction to restrain the publication in a newspaper of future articles reflecting unfavourably on a corporation was refused because of the difficulty on an interlocutory application of determining whether the material was libellous.

Resolutions

Matters coming before a shareholders' meeting for determination are ordinarily dealt with by the moving and seconding of resolutions which are debated and then put to the vote of the meeting. The vote is ordinarily taken by a show of hands, but this may be followed by a poll; see the notes under the headings "Show of hands" and "Poll" below.

A resolution will be passed only if a majority of the votes cast are in its favour. In certain instances under this Act more than a simple majority of the votes cast is required for effective shareholders' approval of a particular course. A resolution which is inconsistent with the requirements of the governing instruments is invalid: *Quin & Axtens v. Salmon*, [1909] A.C. 442 (H.L.).

Where business is of such a nature as to require a special majority at a shareholders' meeting, the governing legislation will ordinarily also require that the meeting be called for the purpose of dealing with that business and may prescribe further formalities in connection with the meeting.

Voting

The *Interpretation Act* provides that in every federal Act, unless the contrary intention appears, words making any association or number of persons a corporation or body politic and corporate shall vest in a majority of the members of the corporation the power to bind the others by their acts. A similar provision appears in the Interpretation Acts of the provinces; see *Noble v. Cameron*, [1955] O.R. 608 (C.A.) for a discussion of the Ontario provision.

Section 140(1) of this Act, however, provides that in the absence of other provisions in that behalf in the articles, each share of a corporation entitles the holder thereof to one vote at a meeting of shareholders. It will be noted that a series of shares may be issued with more than one vote per share and there may also be provisions for cumulative voting for directors. Thus, in *Jacobsen v. United Canso Oil & Gas Ltd.*, [1980] 6 W.W.R. 38, 11 B.L.R. 313 (Alta. Q.B.) a by-law limited shareholders to no more than 1,000 votes regardless of the number of shares actually held. There was only one class of shares and the by-law was held to be invalid as contravening the provisions of the federal Act. In *Re Marshall and Marshall Boston Iron Mines Ltd.* (1981), 129 D.L.R. (3d) 378 (Ont. H.C.) there was an application for an order requiring the chairman of an adjourned general meeting of shareholders to count votes of escrowed shares according to the directions of the beneficial owners rather than the registered owners. The application was dismissed and it was held that the chairman was not required to go beyond the share register and was entitled to rely on votes as cast by the registered owners.

As to the general rule that the vote of the majority at shareholders' meetings will bind the minority and as to the exceptions to that rule, see the notes under the heading "Rights of majority and minority shareholders" in this chapter.

Persons whose names appear without qualification on the register as shareholders are entitled to vote, and it is not necessary that they should be beneficial owners of the shares, and the presiding officer may not adjudicate on the right to vote as between persons so registered and other persons claiming the shares: *Tough Oakes Mines Ltd. v. Foster* (1917), 39 O.L.R. 144 (H.C.). An agreement for disposal of shares, as for example an agreement to give them as a bonus with preference shares when offered by the corporation, does not deprive the registered holder of the ownership or the right of voting: *London Finance Corp. v. Banking Service Corp.*, [1925] 1 D.L.R. 319 at 323 (H.C.).

The question of beneficial ownership cannot be entered into and an action lies to compel the directors to record a vote where the shareholder is improperly deprived of his right: *Pender v. Lushington* (1877) 6 Ch. D. 70.

A shareholder may be restrained from voting in respect of shares held through an irregular transaction, but the court must be shown that the share issue (or acquisition) in question was irregular. This can only be done if the shareholder is a party. See *Re Dominion Jubilee Corporation* (1978), 21 Nfld & P.E.I.R. 334, 56 A.P.R. 334 (Nfld. T.D.).

Where shares were allotted and issued by a petroleum corporation in consideration of the sale of properties to it, and the sale agreement provided that the shares were to be placed "in escrow" with a chartered bank or trust corporaton and a licence issued by the provincial Securities Act authorities with regard to the sale of the corporation's shares to the public contained a similar escrow provision, it was held that the vendor of the properties was entitled to vote the escrowed shares; it was considered doubtful that the use of the word "escrow" in the sense above indicated was proper but in any case the party to whom the shares had been issued became a shareholder immediately the shares were allotted and issued and its status as such shareholder established its right to vote: *Sasko-Wainwright Oil & Gas Ltd. v. Old Settlers Oils Ltd.* (1957), 7 D.L.R. (2d) 393 (Alta. C.A.).

During a state of war an alien enemy is not entitled to vote in respect of shares of an English corporation: *Robson v. Premier Oil & Pipe Line Co.*, [1915] 2 Ch. 124 at 136; or in respect of shares of a Canadian corporation; *Bluechel & Smith v. Prefabricated Buildings Ltd.*, [1945] 2 D.L.R. 725 at 729 (B.C. S.C.).

There is nothing to prevent a shareholder from transferring some of his shares to nominees to increase his voting power on a show of hands: *Re Stranton Iron & Steel Co.* (1873), L.R. 16 Eq. 559.

A shareholder's vote is a right of property, and he may use it as he pleases, whether his motive be proper or improper: *Pender v. Lushington, supra.* "Unless otherwise provided by the regulations of the company, a shareholder is not debarred from voting or using his voting power to carry a resolution by the circumstances of his having a particular interest in the subject matter of the vote": *Burland v. Earle*, [1902] A.C. 38 at 94 (P.C.). Thus, where a Director who held half the shares in a corporation made a contract to sell a ship of his own to the corporation and cast his own vote in favour of the contract, it was held that the contract, though voidable, had been adopted, and was binding on the corporation: *North-West Transportation Co. v. Beatty* (1887), 12 App. Cas. 589 (P.C.). It will be noted that it was pointed out that acquisition of another ship was essential for the efficient conduct of the business of the corporation, that the ship was well-adapted for that purpose, that it was not within the power of the corporation to acquire any other ship equally well-adapted for its business and that the price agreed to be paid was not excessive or unreasonable. Accordingly, it was not oppressive or unfair for the director to vote in favour of the contract. The rule was quoted and applied in *Macdonald Bros. v. Godson* (1916), 31 D.L.R. 363 at 367 (B.C. C.A.), and in *Western Ontario Natural Gas Co. Ltd v. Aikens*, [1946] O.R. 661 at 692. In *Central Gas Utilities Ltd. v. Canadian Western Natural Gas Co.* (1965), 53 W.W.R. 705 (Alta. C.A.) it was held that a director who cannot vote at a directors' meeting to approve a transaction because of his interest therein may nevertheless vote as a shareholder in a general meeting called to affirm or disaffirm an agreement.

There are, however, certain limitations on the rule that a shareholder may use his vote as he pleases. In certain circumstances a shareholder must exercise his vote as a member of a class; cf. *British America Nickel Corp. v. M.J. O'Brien Ltd.*, [1927] A.C. 369 (P.C.) and see the particular headings in Chapter 12. In addition a majority of shareholders will not be allowed to commit a wrongful act against the minority; in this connection see the notes under the heading "Rights of majority and minority shareholders," *infra.* Then too, a shareholder may not use his voting power to commit a breach of trust (i.e., vest the funds or the property of the corporation in himself): *Cook v. Deeks*, [1916] 1 A.C. 554 (P.C.); nor, if he is implicated in a breach of trust, in a matter connected with the breach: *Leavens v. Great West Permanent Loan Co. (No. 2)*, [1927] 3 W.W.R. 486 (Man. K.B.).

In certain circumstances the court will grant an interlocutory injunction restraining the voting of shares. Thus, in *Foster v. Oakes* (1916), 10 O.W.N. 210 (H.C.) the ownership of large blocks of the corporation's capital stock was the subject of pending litigation in Ontario and elsewhere, the registered owners of such shares had no beneficial interest therein and, if an injunction were not granted, persons having substantial beneficial interests in the corporation would be exposed to the risk of having these interests dealt with or interfered with by the votes or other acts of those who had no beneficial interest in the shares. In *Cameron v. Blair Holdings Corp. Ltd.*, [1955] O.W.N. 61 (C.A.) escrowed shares representing control of Stanwell Oil & Gas Ltd. had been issued to Blair Holdings under an agreement between Stanwell and Blair Holdings which both these corporations agreed should be rescinded; the persons who had acquired the escrowed shares did not deny the facts on the basis of which rescission was claimed; and in a class action brought by minority shareholders of Stanwell an interlocutory injunction was granted restraining the voting of the escrowed shares on the ground that it would plainly be inequitable that persons who possess voting powers attached to shares issued under an agreement which both parties thereto said should be rescinded should continue to occupy and control the affairs and destiny of the corporation pending the final determination of the issues in the action.

An agreement by a shareholder to vote in a particular manner is legal and a threatened breach of such agreement may be restrained by injunction: *Greenwell v. Porter*, [1902] 1 Ch. 530. In that case an interlocutory injunction was granted restraining the defendants who were shareholders and directors of the corporation from voting against the election of a certain director contrary to an agreement that they had entered into to vote for him. The *Greenwell* case was referred to in *Waschysyn v. Kildonan Ice & Fuel Co.*, [1937] 2 D.L.R. 653 at 658 (Man. C.A.), and *Motherwell v. Schoof*, [1949] 4 D.L.R. 812 at 817 (Alta. S.C.). In the latter case the court held that certain provisions in an agreement entered into by two of the three directors (in effect in their capacity as shareholders) limiting the number of directors to three were valid.

Where a majority of the shareholders of a corporation agreed to vote unanimously at all shareholders' meetings and to use their voting power to elect one another as directors and to secure their appointment as officers of the corporation, a majority of the Supreme Court of Canada held that the agreement was valid: *Ringuet v. Bergeron*, [1960] S.C.R. 672, 24 D.L.R. (2d) 449 (S.C.C.). At p. 458, Judson J. said:

> There is nothing illegal or contrary to public order in an agreement for achieving these purposes. Shareholders have the right to combine their interest and voting powers to secure such control of a company and to ensure that the company will be managed by certain persons in a certain manner. . . . The fact that [such an] agreement may potentially involve detriment to the minority does not render it illegal and contrary to public order. If there is such injury, there is a remedy available to the minority shareholder who alleges a departure from the standards required of the majority shareholders and the directors. The possibility of such injurious effect on the minority is not a ground for illegality.

An executor, administrator, committee, guardian or trustee may vote in respect of any shares registered in his name. Where there are several executors all must concur in voting the shares of the estate they represent: *Lumbers v. Fretz* (1928), 62 O.L.R. 635 at 650 (H.C.); affd (1928), 63 O.L.R. 190 (C.A.).

If an executor acquires in his personal capacity sufficient shares in the corporation to take away the majority control from the holding of the estate which he represents, he should relinquish his trust: *Rose v. Rose* (1914), 7 O.W.N. 416 (C.A.).

It has been held that executors, though not registered as shareholders, are entitled to raise the rights of dissentient shareholders on a reconstruction: *Llewellyn v. Kasintoe Rubber States Ltd.*, [1914] 2 Ch. 670 (C.A.).

A bankrupt shareholder whose name remains on the register may vote or tender a proxy at meetings of the corporation providing the corporation is not in liquidation and there are no express provisions to the contrary in the corporation's by-laws. He remains a member in respect of his shares and is entitled to exercise (subject to the direction of the trustee in bankruptcy) the votes attributable to those shares, notwithstanding that he no longer has any beneficial interest in the shares and that the corporation is entitled to pay any dividends to his trustee in bankruptcy: *Morgan v. Gray*, [1953] 1 Ch. 83.

The rights of a mortgagee of shares or other person holding shares as collateral security depends on registration as a shareholder. If the mortgagee or person holding the shares as collateral security is entered on the books of the corporation as the holder of the shares he is entitled to vote, unless he is described on the books as representing a named mortgagor or person giving such collateral security. In the latter event such mortgagor or other person is entitled to exercise the voting rights.

Trustees for bondholders, holding as security specifically mortgaged shares in a subsidiary corporation, are, unless the trust deed otherwise provides, entitled to vote the shares even before default: *Siemens Bros & Co. v. Burns*, [1918] 2 Ch. 324 at 356 (C.A.). If the mortgagee has, however, agreed to vote the shares in accordance with the mortgagor's direction, he is bound to do so and the court will enforce the agreement by mandatory injunction: *Puddephatt v. Leith*, [1916] 1 Ch. 200.

Joint holders must concur in voting, unless the by-laws provide otherwise, as, for example, the common form which is to the effect that the person first named in the register shall exercise the voting power: *Lumbers v. Fretz* (1928), 62 O.L.R. 635 at 649 (H.C.); affd (1928), 63 O.L.R. 190 (C.A.).

Joint holders of shares by virtue of their property therein are entitled to have their shares entered on the register, for example, in the reverse order as to part of the shares, so as to enable them to exercise their voting power in the event of one of them being unable to be present in person at meetings: *Burns v. Siemens Bros. Ltd. (No. 2)*, [1919] 1 Ch. 225.

Under s. 140(4) of the Act any one of two or more joint holders present at a meeting may, in the absence of the other or others vote thereon; but if more than one are present or represented by proxy, they are to vote together on the shares jointly held.

Semble, if shares are registered in the name of a partnership firm, the partners are joint holders: *In re Glory Paper Mills Co.; Dunster's Case*, [1894] 3 Ch. 473 (C.A.), 482.

As to voting in person by a partner where shares are registered in the name of a partnership, see *Gray v. Yellowknife Gold Mines Ltd. (No. 1)*, [1946] O.W.N. 938 at 945 (H.C.).

Proxies

Section 148 of the Act provides that a shareholder entitled to vote at a meeting of shareholders may by means of a proxy appoint a proxyholder or one or more alternate proxyholders who need not be shareholders to attend and act at the meeting in the manner and to the extent authorized by the proxy and with the authority conferred thereby; the proxy is to be executed by the shareholder or by his attorney authorized in writing and is valid only at the meeting in respect of which it is given or any adjournment thereof. The shareholder may revoke a proxy by depositing an instrument in writing executed by him or his attorney authorized in writing at the registered office of the corporation at any time up to and including the last business day preceding the day of the meeting or an adjournment thereof in which the proxy is to be used or with the chairman of the meeting on the day of the meeting or an adjournment thereof or in any other manner permitted by law; the directors may specify in a notice calling a meeting of shareholders a time not exceeding 48 hours including Saturdays and holidays preceding the meeting or an adjournment thereof before which time the proxy that is to be used at the meeting must be deposited with the corporation or its agent (s. 148(2) - (5)).

Where a corporation has 15 or more shareholders, the management of the corporation must send a form of proxy in prescribed form to each shareholder entitled to receive notice of the meeting (s. 149) and no person may solicit proxies unless a management proxy circular or dissident's proxy circular, each in prescribed form, accompanies the material. See s. 150. Provision is made in s. 151 to obtain an exempting order from the requirements of soliciting proxies or from providing a management circular, or dissident's proxy circular. An application is to be made to the Director who may make an order on such terms as he thinks fit. The order may have a retrospective effect.

Section 152 provides that a person soliciting a proxy and who is appointed proxyholder shall attend in person or cause an alternative proxyholder to attend the meeting in respect of which the proxy is given and comply with the direction of the shareholder who appointed him; such proxyholder or alternate has the same rights as the shareholder who appointed him to speak at the meeting of the shareholders with respect to any matter, to vote by ballot and except where a proxyholder or alternate proxyholder has conflicting instructions from more than one shareholder to vote by way of show of hands.

There was no common law right to vote by proxy: *Harben v. Phillips* (1883), 23 Ch. D. 14 (C.A.), at 32, 35; *Howard v. Hill* (1889), 37 W.R. 219; *McLaren v. Thomson*, [1917] 2 Ch. 261 at 263 (C.A.).

In the absence of any by-laws imposing regulations nothing more is necessary to a proxy than its valid execution by the shareholder: *Kelly v. Electrical Construction Co., supra.*

A provision in the articles to the effect that an instrument appointing a proxy is to be as nearly as possible "in the following form" and specifying a form applicable to voting at a particular meeting has been held to be directory only, so as not to invalidate an instrument of proxy authorizing voting at any meeting: *Isaacs v. Chapman* (1916), 32 T.L.R. 237 (C.A.).

The Ontario Act formerly provided that a proxy was not to contain anything but the appointment of a proxy or the revocation of a former proxy. Under this earlier provision, it was held that notations on an instrument of proxy as to when proxies were to be filed and that those persons whose names were printed in the form would vote in a particular manner invalidated the instrument: *Re National Grocers Co.*, [1938] O.R. 142; *Re Langley's Ltd.*, [1938] O.R. 123 (C.A.); so also where the instrument contained a statement indicating the number of shares held and the words "subject to the attached restrictions" (which purported to control the purposes for which the shares might be voted) appeared under the signature: *Montreal Trust Co. v. Oxford Pipe Line Co.*, [1942] O.R. 490 at 497 (C.A.).

A proxy may be signed and delivered in blank and filled in afterwards by any person properly authorized to do so: *Sadgrove v. Bryden*, [1907] 1 Ch. 318.

In *Re United Canso Oil & Gas Ltd.* (1980), 41 N.S.R. (2d) 282, 21 B.L.R. 130 (N.S. T.D.) the by-laws required that a proxy be in writing and signed by the shareholder. It was held in that case that a mechanically produced signature was sufficient.

Beatty v. First Exploration Fund (1987) & Co. (1988), 25 B.C.L.R. (2d) 377, 40 B.L.R. 90 (B.C. S.C.) involved an allegation that faxed proxies and proxies delivered to the chairman before the commencement of voting on a resolution, but after the commencement of the meeting, should be counted in the voting. The court held that the faxed proxy was valid as it was signed and in writing as required. A faxed proxy was, in fact, a photocopy of the original proxy including the signature. There was no greater opportunity for fraud with respect to the faxed proxy than with respect to an original proxy. It was also held that because the notice of meeting and proxy did not refer to the restrictions stated in the information circular as to the delivery of proxies not less than 24 hours prior to the meeting or to the chairman prior to the commencement of the meeting, the restrictions were invalid and that the common law rule that proxies could be delivered up to the time of voting should prevail. The judgment on this latter point would seem to be open to some question.

In *Canadian Express Ltd. v. Blair* (1990), 46 B.L.R. 92 (Ont. H.C.) the shareholder struck out the name of management designee on a proxy and put in a different person as his proxy. It was held that the new proxy had full authority to vote in his discretion on any matter coming before the meeting as if the shareholder were present and was not bound to vote for slate of management designees for directors. The form supplied by management is effectively converted to unsolicited shareholder proxies oncc the names of the proposed management proxyholders are deleted and the names of the shareholders designees are inserted. However, see *Value Investment Corp. v. Caldwell Gundy Inc.* (1989), 44 B.L.R. 142 (B.C. S.C.) where a modified proxy was held to be invalid.

Where the articles of a corporation give the alternative right to vote personally or by proxy and there is nothing in the articles to take away the alternative right to vote personally when proxies have been given, when a shareholder attends the meeting and votes personally his vote must be accepted, and a proxy previously given by him rejected, even if the proxy has not been validly revoked in accordance with the articles: *Cousins v. International Brick Co.*, [1931] 2 Ch. 90 (C.A.). See also *Mercator Enterprises Ltd. v. Harris* (1978), 29 N.S.R. (2d) 691, 45 A.P.R. 691 (N.S. C.A.), where it was held that where a shareholder who was appointed a proxy attends a meeting he can vote in person and his right to do so is paramount to the right of the proxyholder. His presence at the meeting does not revoke the instrument of proxy but if the shareholder votes before the proxy he impliedly revokes the proxy.

In *Goldhar v. D'Aragon Mines Ltd.* (1977), 15 O.R. (2d) 80, 1 B.L.R. 204 (Ont. H.C.) shareholders had requisitioned a meeting pursuant to the Ontario Act to remove existing directors and electing others in their place. The corporation mailed out an information circular and form of proxy to shareholders in response to such requisition, the information circular provided that if the resolution removing the directors was passed management nominees named on the form of proxy intended to vote shares represented by proxies held by them to re-elect the existing board. It was held that the form of proxy was null and void as it was unfair and did not permit shareholders to exercise a choice of nominating the existing board or electing a new one.

In *U.S. Gold Corp. v. Atlanta Gold Corp.* (1989), 43 B.C.L.R. (2d) 71, 46 B.L.R. 229 (B.C. C.A.); application for rehearing refused (unreported), January 23, 1990, the chairman of the meeting ruled that proxies which were undated were not allowed. The dissident shareholder challenged this ruling in court and was unsuccessful, but on appeal it was held that the technical defect should have been rectified by the court of first instance as there was no doubt that the proxies, if not allowed, would have effectually disfranchised the shareholders involved.

Apart from special provisions in the by-laws, an instrument of proxy need not be given to a single person only, but may be given to several persons, notwithstanding that in the case of equal division among the persons appointed as proxies the vote of the shareholder may be lost: *Nesbitt, Thomson & Co. v. McColl Frontenac Oil Co.* (1938), 43 Que. P.R. 138.

Directors may, at the corporation's expense, send out forms of proxy in which the directors are named accompanied by stamped envelopes for the return of the forms: *Peel v. London & N.W. Ry.*, [1907] 1 Ch. 5 (C.A.); *Campbell v. Australian Mutual Provident Society* (1908), 24 T.L.R. 623. Proxies need not be sent to all shareholders if there is no sinister motive (i.e., to gain support) in selecting those to whom the proxies are sent: *Wilson v. London, Midland & Scottish Ry.*, [1940] 1 Ch. 169 at 393.

The chairman is entitled to decide on the validity of proxies and his decision will be presumed to be right until the contrary is shown, but if the question is brought before the court it can decide whether the chairman was right or wrong: *In re Indian Zoedone Co.* (1884), 26 Ch. D. 70 (C.A.). In deciding on the validity of proxies the chairman must proceed in a judicial manner: *Johnson v. Hall* (1957), 10 D.L.R. (2d) 243 (B.C. S.C.). The fact that an invalid form of proxy has been recognized by the chairman at previous meetings will not raise an estoppel as amongst shareholders: *Montreal Trust Co. v. Oxford Pipe Line Co.*, [1942] O.R. 490 at 498 (C.A.). See the material under the subheading "Chairman" in this chapter.

See also on proxies: *Pacific Coast Mines Ltd. v. Arbuthnot*, [1917] A.C. 607 at 618 (P.C.) (notice to shareholders, including those who gave proxies, should have given more details); *Marks v. Rocsand* (1920), 48 O.L.R. 224 at 228 (where some shareholders are present by proxy, a defective notice is not cured unless the authority conferred by the proxy is wide enough to cover the business transacted at the meeting); *Lumbers v. Fretz* (1928), 62 O.L.R. 635 (H.C.); affd 63 O.L.R. 190 (C.A.) (improper use of proxies where shareholders not given information to enable them to decide whether or not they should attend in person).

In *Patten v. Outerbridge* (1982), 37 Nfld. & P.E.I.R. 318, 104 A.P.R. 318 (Nfld. T.D.) a proxyholder voted against an amendment to a motion at the annual meeting of the corporation. It was argued that the proxy was specific and not general and therefore could not be voted on motions beyond those specified. The court held that the amending motions were contrary to the proxy instructions and therefore the proxyholder could vote against the amending motions.

See *Value Investment Corp. v. Caldwell Gundy Inc.* (1989), 44 B.L.R. 142 (B.C. S.C.) where a dissident group of shareholders had altered a management proxy for use as a dissident proxy and this afforded no space for an alternate proxyholder or choice to vote for or against a resolution. The chairman of the meeting ruled that the dissident proxy was invalid and the chairman's ruling was upheld since the modified proxy did not conform with the British Columbia Act.

See also *Garvie v. Axsmith*, [1962] O.R. 65, 31 D.L.R. (2d) 65 (Ont. H.C.) where the notice of meeting called for the purpose of approving an agreement for the purchase of the assets of another corporation was set aside on the basis that insufficient information was set out in the materials sent out with the notices as to the method of valuation of the two corporations concerned. Such particulars should be given as would permit the shareholders to exercise an intelligent judgment on the proposal. In *Garvie v. Axsmith, supra*, it was also held that the use of a proxy form with the name of the proxyholder printed thereon was not sufficient to invalidate the notice of the meeting nor to invalidate the form of proxy.

See also *Canadian Express Ltd. v. Blair* (1990), 46 B.L.R. 92 (Ont. H.C.); under a similar provision under the British Columbia Act the court ordered the appointment of an independent chairman to conduct the annual general meeting where there was a dispute as to the voting rights of certain shares which were alleged to have been improperly allotted by the directors. It was noted that there had to be a strong case to authorize and justify interference with the conduct of an annual general shareholders' meeting. See *Allied Cellular Systems Ltd. v. Bullock* (1990), 49 B.L.R. 306; leave to appeal to C.A. refused, 21 A.C.W.S. (3d) 1146 (B.C. C.A.).

In the absence of a requirement in the governing statute or regulations that a proxy must be a shareholder, a proxy need not himself be a shareholder: *Colonial Assurance Co. v. Smith* (1912), 4 D.L.R. 814 at 817 (Man. K.B.).

If one corporation holds shares in another it may exercise its vote by proxy: *In re Indian Zoedone Co.* (1884), 26 Ch. D. 70 (C.A.).

Under s. 140(2), (3) a company may by resolution of its directors authorize such person as it thinks fit to act as its representative at any meeting of shareholders of any corporation in which it holds shares. A person so authorized is entitled to exercise the same powers on behalf of the corporation which he represents as it could itself exercise if it were an individual shareholder. Thus he can be taken into account for determining whether there is a quorum: *In re Kelantan Coco Nut Estates Ltd.*, [1920] W.N. 274. The representative need not be a shareholder of the corporation. It is customary to require at the meeting submission of a certified copy of the resolution passed under s. 140(2). The right to vote depends on whether such a resolution was in fact passed and not upon the evidence offered: *Colonial Gold Reef Ltd. v. Free State Rand Ltd.*, [1914] 1 Ch. 382 at 388.

In the absence of a statutory provision such as that contained in s. 140(2), a corporation cannot vote by merely acting through an authorized agent, but must deposit a signed proxy: *Re Carrie*, [1936] 1 D.L.R. 455 (Ont. H.C.).

In the absence of any contrary provision in the by-laws or the governing statute, an instrument of proxy signed by a corporation need not be under its corporate seal: *Re McCoubrey*, [1924] 4 D.L.R. 1227 at 1241; and such a provision in the articles of an English corporation will only be applied to corporations having a common seal according to English law: *Colonial Gold Reef Ltd. v. Free State Rand Ltd., supra.*

Where instruments of proxy are required to be lodged a certain number of hours before a meeting or adjourned meeting, it is not a compliance with the requirements to lodge them the specified number of hours before a poll is taken: *Shaw v. Tati Concessions Ltd.*, [1913] 1 Ch. 292. Where proxies are required by the articles to be lodged a certain time before the day for holding the meetings at which the person named therein proposes to vote, proxies lodged between the date of the original meeting and the adjournment thereof are invalid, for the adjourned meeting is in law merely a continuation of the original meeting: *McLaren v. Thomson*, [1917] 2 Ch. 261 (C.A.); *Jackson v. Hamlyn*, [1953] 1 Ch. 577.

The shareholders or their proxies must personally attend and vote. A vote cannot be taken by means of polling papers in the absence of statutory or other authority entitling the shareholders to vote in this manner: *McMillan v. Le Roi*, [1906] 1 Ch. 331. *Quaere*, whether a by-law containing such a provision would be valid under this Act.

Questions which may arise in respect of the validity of instruments of proxy include the following, the views expressed being subject to the applicable statutory provisions and to the by-laws and resolutions of the particular corporation.

If an instrument of proxy given by a partnership is signed with the partnership name, for example, "Jones & Co.", it should be treated as valid. If, on the other hand, the signature is the firm name *per* the person who signs on behalf of the firm, the instrument should be treated as subject to verification of authority to sign. In *Re United Canso Oil & Gas Ltd.* (1980), 41 N.S.R. (2d) 282, 12 B.L.R. 132 (N.S. T.D.) it was held that in the case where the corporation's by-laws required that a proxy be in writing and signed by the shareholder, a mechanically produced signature was sufficient. See also *Re Bomac Batten Ltd. and Pozhke* (1983), 43 O.R. (2d) 344, 23 B.L.R. 273 (Ont. H.C.).

Instruments of proxy are frequently lodged on behalf of corporations signed by one officer only. Unless there is an express requirement that such instruments are to be executed under seal, the instrument should be accepted as valid subject to verification of authority.

Instruments of proxy, where the shares are registered in more than one name, should be signed by all the registered holders, unless the holding is a joint holding and the by-laws provide that the signature of one joint holder is sufficient and this is not prohibited by the governing statute.

In the case of shares registered in the names of executors or trustees, the signature of all are requisite in the absence of authority of one or less than all to sign.

If an instrument is signed with an "X" by an individual it is customary to accept the signature as valid if it is witnessed. An instrument signed but not witnessed should be accepted as valid, at any rate unless the by-laws expressly provide otherwise; the same applies to an undated instrument (which, by virtue of s. 32(2) of the Regulations, is deemed to bear the date on which it is mailed).

Sometimes more than one instrument is filed in respect of the same holding (not being a nominee holding). If both instruments are dated, the one of later date should be accepted. If neither instrument is dated, or if one is dated and the other not, it is a question of fact as to which instrument is to prevail.

If there are alterations on the instrument, unless these are initialled, the instrument should be accepted subject to verification. If the name of the proxy has not been filled in the instrument should be rejected.

When a nominee holds shares for more than one beneficial owner and certain of the beneficial owners instruct their shares to be voted in one way and others in a different way, it may be that instruments of proxy will be lodged directing a specified number of shares to be voted in favour of a proposal and a specified number of shares to be voted against, or that a proxy will be appointed in respect of one block of shares different from the proxy appointed in respect of another block. Subject to the provisions of the governing statute, it is considered doubtful whether a registered holder can legally split the voting power as between different parts of the same holding. However, in practice this is permitted. See also ss. 152(2) and 153(4) of the federal Act which seem to sanction this procedure. The same question may arise in another way subsequently to an instrument of proxy being lodged. For example, a broker, in accordance with instructions from his clients, may signify a wish that some of the shares of which he is the registered holder and with respect to which he has appointed a proxy should be voted for and others against the proposals. In such a case it is customary to issue two ballots, one with respect to part of the holdings and the other with respect to the balance.

It should be noted that if a form of proxy, management proxy circular or dissident's proxy circular contains an untrue statement of a material fact or omits to state a required material fact or omits information which makes a statement contained in the proxy misleading, an order may be obtained to restrain the solicitation, the holding of the meeting, or the implementation or action on resolutions passed at the meeting to which the proxy relates; to correct the proxy; or to adjourn the meeting. Such application may be made by any "interested party" or by the Director. See s. 154 of the Federal Act.

Show of hands

In the first instance the votes of the shareholders present are usually taken by a show of hands without regard to the number of shares or proxies held by the voters. This is in accordance with the common law rule as to voting at meetings and unless there is a provision to the contrary in the governing Act, the charter or the by-laws, this rule will prevail: *In re Horbury Bridge Coal, Iron & Waggon Co.* (1879), 11 Ch. D. 109 at 115 (C.A.). If a poll is then demanded it is taken in the manner prescribed by the by-laws.

In *Carruth v. Imperial Chemical Industries Ltd.*, [1937] A.C. 707 (H.L.) at 755, Lord Blanesburgh suggested that there could be no valid demand for a poll unless there had first been a valid show of hands, and see s. 141(1) which provides that, unless the by-laws otherwise provide, voting at a meeting of shareholders is to be by show of hands except when a ballot is demanded by a shareholder or proxyholder entitled to vote at a meeting; if a ballot is demanded before the vote on a show of hands is taken, it would appear that unless there is some provision in the by-law there is no necessity of having a show of hands.

It will be noted under s. 152(3) that where the chairman of a meeting of shareholders declares to the meeting that if a ballot is conducted, the total number of votes attaching the shares represented at the meeting by proxy required to be voted against what to his knowledge will be the decision of the meeting in relation to a matter or group of matters is less than five per cent of all the votes that might be cast at the meeting on such a ballot, unless a shareholder or proxyholder demands a ballot, the chairman may conduct the vote in respect of that matter or group of matters by a show of hands and a proxyholder or alternate may vote in respect of that matter or group of matters by a show of hands.

On a show of hands, a person holding proxies, if he is a shareholder, has one vote, but only one for himself and all the shareholders whom he represents; if a person who is not a shareholder, being permitted under the governing Act or the corporation's regulations to act as a proxy, represents only one person, namely, the absentee for whom he votes, apparently he can vote on a show of hands: *Ernest v. Loma Gold Mines Ltd.*, [1897] 1 Ch. 1 (C.A.). Where the vote is on a show of hands a shareholder representing an absent shareholder as proxy votes only for himself. Consequently his vote will not operate as an estoppel against the absent shareholder. See *McKenna v. Spooner Oils Ltd.*, [1934] 1 W.W.R. 255 (Alta. T.D.).

Poll

The right to demand a poll is incident to an election at a public meeting: *Campbell v. Maund* (1835), 5 Ad. & El. 865, and may be exercised by any shareholder in the absence of provision to the contrary. As to counting joint holders where the articles provide that a poll can only be demanded by a specified number of members, see *Cory v. Reindeer Steamship Ltd.* (1915), 31 T.L.R. 530. A provision that a poll shall be taken if demanded is imperative: *Anthony v. Seger* (1789), Hagg. Con. Cas. 9. The meeting is regarded as continuing until the poll is taken: *R. v. Wimbledon* (1882), 8 Q.B.D. 459; *Shaw v. Tati Concessions Ltd.*, [1913] 1 Ch. 292; *Holmes v. Keyes*, [1959] 1 Ch. 199 (where there was a poll on a resolution for the election of directors, held by the Court of Appeal that there was no election until the result of the poll was ascertained).

As to whether there must be a show of hands before a poll is demanded see the notes under the heading "Show of hands" above.

The voting power of shares arises only when a poll is demanded: *Montreal Trust Co. v. Oxford Pipe Line Co.*, [1942] O.R. 490 at 499 (Ont. C.A.). On a poll, one vote is counted for each share which the person voting holds or represents by proxy (unless there are other voting rights attached to the shares voted).

For the purposes of taking a poll it is customary to appoint scrutineers to compute the votes and report to the chairman. In the absence of any special regulations as to the appointment of scrutineers, the meeting usually appoints them by resolution although sometimes the scrutineers are appointed by the chairman with the approval of the meeting. Scrutineers need not be shareholders.

The function of the scrutineers is judicial. Where an election of directors is being held, a director who is a candidate is not entitled to act as scrutineer, and if he does the election may be set aside: *Dickson v. McMurray* (1881), 28 Gr. 533 (Ont. Ch.). It is only the corporation, however, which has a cause of action to set aside an election of directors by reason of informalities and irregularities: *Watt v. Commonwealth Petroleum Ltd.*, [1938] 4 D.L.R. 701 (Alta C.A.).

As to the manner of taking a poll it is usual to require every person who desires to vote to sign a ballot and mark it, as the case may be, "for" or "against" the resolution. The shares held and represented by proxy by the person signing the ballot are noted at the foot of the ballot by the scrutineers and when the scrutineers have computed the votes for and against they report to the chairman who declares the result.

When the person in whose favour instruments of proxy are made out signs a voting paper "for self and proxies", the vote is good for himself and the persons who appointed him their proxy, in the absence of any express provision in the by-laws or articles as to the mode of voting: *Foerster v. Newlands (West Griqualand) Diamond Mines Ltd.* (1902), 18 T.L.R. 497.

It is customary for the by-laws to provide that if a poll is demanded on the election of a chairman or the question of adjournment it is to be taken forthwith and that if a poll is demanded on any other question it is to be taken in such manner and either at once or later in the meeting or after adjournment as the chairman directs. In such a case the chairman may direct the poll to be taken then and there: *Chillington Iron Co., Re* (1885), 29 Ch. D. 159. See *Re Horbury Bridge, Coal, Iron & Waggon Co.* (1879), 11 Ch. D. 109; *R. v. D'Oyly* (1840), 12 Ad. & El. 139; and *Jackson v. Hamlyn*, [1953] 1 Ch. 577.

Where the articles of a corporation provide that a meeting may be adjourned by the chairman for the purpose of taking a poll he has an absolute discretion to determine whether or not to direct an adjournment for this purpose: *Legion Oils Ltd. & Boyd v. Barron (No. 2)* (1956), 2 D.L.R. (2d) 505 at 510 (Alta. T.D).

The Ontario Act formerly provided that a poll was to be taken in such manner as the by-laws prescribed and, failing this, as the chairman might direct. Doubt has been expressed that under such a provision the chairman may postpone the taking of a poll to a later date and the view has been expressed that in the absence of such considerations as the shareholders requiring time to consider the question before the meeting before voting or the difficulty of taking a poll due to the number of shareholders in attendance at the meeting, the poll should be taken immediately: *Gray v. Yellowknife Gold Mines et al. (No. 1)*, [1946] O.W.N. 938 at 944 (Lennox, Assistant Master).

Adjournment

Where notice of a meeting has once been given, the directors cannot in the absence of special provisions in the articles by a further notice postpone the meeting: *Smith v. Paringa Mines Ltd.*, [1906] 2 Ch. 193.

The chairman has no power to adjourn a meeting at his own will and if he wrongfully adjourns the meeting, the shareholders may select a new chairman and proceed with the business of the meeting: *National Dwellings Society v. Sykes*, [1894] 3 Ch. 159. See also *Re Bomac Batten Ltd. and Pozhke* (1983), 43 O.R. (2d) 344, 23 B.L.R. 273 (Ont. H.C.). But if a meeting is properly adjourned members who remain behind cannot validly proceed with the business of the meeting: *R. v. Gaborian* (1809), 11 East 77. The declaration of the chairman adjourning a meeting is binding until it is successfully challenged; and by participating at the meeting, reconvened pursuant to adjournment, shareholders are deemed to have waived any irregularity: *Gray v. Yellowknife Gold Mines (No. 1)*, [1946] O.W.N. 938 at 940 (H.C.).

Where the chairman may with the consent of the members present at any meeting adjourn the same, he may in his discretion refuse to adjourn the meeting, notwithstanding that a majority of those present desire an adjournment: *Salisbury Gold Mining Co. v. Hathorn*, [1897] A.C. 268 (P.C.).

An adjourned meeting is only a continuation of the original meeting: *Spencer v. Kennedy*, [1926] Ch. 125 at 135; even where for the purpose of confirming a special resolution the statute requires the meeting to be held within a specified time: *Neuschild v. British Equatorial Oil Co.*, [1925] Ch. 346. Accordingly, even though the chairman has vacated the chair on his motion to adjourn, he is entitled to preside at the adjourned meeting as chairman: *Dominion Royalty Corp. v.*

Holborn (1932), 41 O.W.N. 288 (H.C.). Section 144 of the *English Companies Act, 1948* provided that a resolution passed at an adjourned meeting was passed on the date it was in fact passed and not at an earlier date.

The business which may come before the adjourned meeting is limited to the business which could have come before the original meeting: *Christopher v. Noxon* (1884), 4 O.R. 672 (H.C.); *McLaren v. Thomson*, [1917] 2 Ch. 261 (C.A.). Nor need notice be given of a regularly adjourned meeting: *Wills v. Murray* (1850), 4 Ex. 843; *Scadding v. Lorant* (1851), 3 H.L.C. 418 (H.L.); *The Queen v. Grimshaw* (1847), 10 Q.B. 747 at 752. The meeting, however, must be adjourned to reassemble at a definite place, date and time. If, as is sometimes done, the meeting is merely adjourned to reassemble at the call of the chairman, a new notice is necessary. If notice of the adjourned meeting is required, and the notice of the adjourned meeting is not in proper form, action taken at the adjourned meeting will be ineffective: *Robert Batcheller & Sons, Ltd. v. Batcheller*, [1945] 1 Ch. 169.

Rights of majority and minority shareholders

Supremacy of the majority

The will of the majority of the shareholders of a corporation is the will of the corporation, and whatever the corporation has power to do, a majority of shareholders may cause to be done against the will of a minority: *Australian Auxiliary Steam Clipper Co. v. Mounsey* (1858), 4 K. & J. 733 at 740; *In re Horbury Bridge, Coal, Iron & Waggon Co.* (1879), 11 Ch. D. 109 (C.A.), unless, of course, there is some express provision to the contrary which is applicable to the particular corporation.

This principle of the supremacy of the majority is embodied in the *Interpretation Act*, which provides that in every federal Act, unless the contrary intention appears, words making any association or number of persons a corporation or body politic and corporate shall vest in a majority of the members of the corporation the power to bind the others by their acts. A similar provision appears in the Interpretation Acts of the provinces; see *Noble v. Cameron*, [1955] O.R. 608 (Ont. C.A.) for an examination of the Ontario provision.

Generally speaking, a person when he acquires shares in a corporation may be said to agree to submit himself to the decision of the majority at shareholders' meetings on all matters which are within the competence of such meetings. Thus, it has been held that at any meeting of shareholders the majority, in the absence of express provisions to the contrary, will bind the minority: *In re Horbury Bridge, Coal, Iron & Waggon Co., supra*; *Patrick v. Empire Coal & Tramway Co.* (1907), 3 N.B. Eq. 571, 4 E.L.R. 98 (N.B. S.C.); *Noble v. Cameron, supra*.

Such majority must, however, be a bona fide majority: *Davidson v. Grange* (1854), 4 Gr. 377 (C.A.), and must proceed regularly and with *bona fides*: *Harben v. Phillips* (1883), 23 Ch. D. 14 (C.A.); *Henderson v. Bank of Australasia* (1890), 45 Ch. D. 330; and thus minorities are, as will appear below, entitled to protection against the wrongful acts of majorities.

The rule as to the supremacy of the majority has an important application as regards litigation in respect of wrongs alleged to be done the corporation.

If the corporation as represented by the majority considers that a wrong has been done it which warrants suit, it can, and presumably will, sue. If on the other hand the corporation, as so represented, does not consider that it has been wronged, there will ordinarily be no question of suit. The courts have accordingly determined that the corporation is ordinarily the proper plaintiff in respect of any wrong allegedly done to it and they will ordinarily not interfere or permit interference in what is a matter of internal management by allowing individual shareholders to sue in respect of such wrongs. This principle governs both where the majority has lawfully approved and where it might lawfully approve the acts complained of.

The principle referred to above is known as the rule in *Foss v. Harbottle* (1843), 2 Hare 461, 67 E.R. 189. In that case minority shareholders sued certain of the directors for alleged wrongful acts after the majority of the shareholders at a general meeting had resolved that no action should be taken in respect of such acts. It was held that the particular acts of the directors could be confirmed by the majority of the shareholders and that in the circumstances the court should not interfere. This is the basis for the principle that the court is reluctant to interfere in matters relating to the internal management of corporations.

The rule in *Foss v. Harbottle* was summarized by Jenkins L.J. in *Edwards v. Halliwell*, [1950] 2 All E.R. 1064 at 1066 (C.A.), as follows:

> The rule in *Foss v. Harbottle* (1), as I understand it, comes to no more than this. First, the proper plaintiff in an action in respect of a wrong alleged to be done to a company or association of persons is *prima facie* the company or the association of persons itself. Secondly, where the alleged wrong is a transaction which might be made binding on the company or association and on all its members by a simple majority of the members, no individual member of the company is allowed to maintain an action in respect of that matter for the simple reason that, if a mere majority of the members of the company or association is in favour of what has been done, then *cadit quaestio*. No wrong has been done to the company or association and there is nothing in respect of which anyone can sue. If, on the other hand, a simple majority of members of the company or association is against what has been done, then there is no valid reason why the company or association itself should not sue. In my judgment, it is implicit in the rule that the matter relied on as constituting the cause of action should be a cause of action properly belonging to the general body of corporators or members of the company or association as opposed to a cause of action which some individual member can assert in his own right.

It will be observed that the rule in *Foss v. Harbottle* is concerned with wrongs alleged to have been done to the corporation or association. When the rights invaded are not the rights of the corporation or association but the rights of the individual members thereof, the rule has no application: *Edwards v. Halliwell*, [1950] 2 All E.R. 1064 (C.A.). See the discussion on these matters in Chapter 16.

Individual shareholder's rights

Apart from his rights as one of the majority or minority, which is discussed in Chapter 16, a shareholder has a number of rights in his individual capacity which he may enforce by action regardless of the wishes of the majority.

Perhaps the most important of the rights appertaining to his status as a shareholder is the right to insist that the corporation observe all the provisions governing it: *Salmon v. Quin & Axtens Ltd.*, [1909] 1 Ch. 311 (C.A.), [1909] A.C. 442; *Smith v. Humbervale Cemetery Co.* (1915), 33 O.L.R. 452 at 459 (C.A.), and cases cited. In the *Smith* case a single shareholder was granted an injunction restraining the corporation from doing an *ultra vires* act.

A shareholder of a corporation whose property interests or rights are injured by *ultra vires* acts committed through breach of the criminal law is entitled to relief, including an injunction, against the corporation: *Kozlowski v. Workers' Benevolent Society*, [1934] 1 D.L.R. 237 at 243, per Trueman J.A.

In *Theatre Amusement Co. v. Stone* (1915), 50 S.C.R. 32 (S.C.C.), it was held that a single shareholder was entitled to succeed in an action against the corporation and the directors for breach of the statutory articles (as to vacating the office of director). At p. 36, Duff J. said:

> The articles of association are binding upon the company, the directors and the shareholders, until changed in accordance with the law. So long as they remain in force, any shareholder is entitled, unless he is estopped from taking that position by some conduct of his own, to insist upon the articles being observed by the company, and the directors of the company. This right he cannot be deprived of by the action of any majority. In truth, the articles of association constitute a contract between the company and the shareholders which every shareholder is entitled to insist upon being carried out.

Where the contributions of members of a trade union had been increased contrary to the rules of the trade union (which correspond to the articles of a corporation: *Cotter v. National Union of Seamen*, [1929] 2 Ch. 58), the Court of Appeal held that two members of the union were entitled to a declaration that the increase was invalid on the ground that the personal and individual rights of membership of each of them had been invaded by the invalid increases: *Edwards v. Halliwell*, [1950] 2 All E.R. 1064 (C.A.).

The Act confers a number of individual rights on shareholders and if these rights are breached, the shareholder may sue to restrain the violation of his rights or for other relief.

If a shareholder's share carries a vote but the corporation refuses to record his vote, an individual right is infringed: *Pender v. Lushington* (1877), 6 Ch. D. 70 where Jessel M.R. stated at p. 80:

> This is an action by Mr. *Pender* for himself. He is a member of the company, and whether he votes with the majority or the minority he is entitled to have his vote recorded—- an individual right in respect of which he has a right to sue. That has nothing to do with the question like that raised in *Foss v. Harbottle* and that line of cases. He has a right to say, "Whether I vote in the majority or minority, you shall record my vote, as that is a right of property belonging to my interest in this company, and if you refuse to record my vote I will institute legal proceedings against you to compel you."

In the absence of a provision to the contrary, a shareholder has the right to demand a poll at a shareholders' meeting; see the notes under the heading "Poll" in this chapter.

A shareholder has the right to bring an action against the corporation for a dividend which has been declared and is payable: *In re Severn & Wye & Severn Bridge Ry.*, [1896] 1 Ch. 559.

The right to inspect certain books of the corporation is a right attaching to a shareholder in his individual capacity: *Cooper v. Premier Trust Co.*, [1945] O.R. 35 at 43 (C.A.).

Section 190 of the Act gives the holder of shares of any class of a corporation the right to dissent by following a prescribed procedure if certain matters of a fundamental nature are authorized, such as an amendment to change or remove any provisions restricting or restraining the issue, transfer or ownership of shares of any class, an amendment to the articles to change, remove or add any restriction on the business or businesses that the corporation may carry on, an amalgamation, the continuance under the laws of another jurisdiction, or the sale, lease or exchange of all or substantially all of its property. In such event an offer is to be made to the dissenting shareholder by the corporation for payment for his shares at the fair value thereof. An application may be made to the court either by the corporation or the shareholder to determine the fair value for the shares of any dissenting shareholder. Some question may arise under the provisions of the federal Act as to whether a shareholder is entitled to sue to restrain a course of action which would otherwise be regarded as improper if he is entitled to follow the process for dissent set out in s. 190. This matter is discussed in Chapter 16.

A shareholder has a right to share proportionately in a distribution of assets on a surrender of the charter of the corporation or as incidental to a liquidation.

Chapter 11

FINANCIAL STATEMENTS AND AUDITORS

Section 155. Annual financial statements
Section 156. Exemption
Section 157. Consolidated statements
Section 158. Approval of financial statements
Section 159. Copies to shareholders
Section 160. Copies to director
Section 161. Qualification of auditor
Section 162. Appointment of auditor
Section 163. Dispensing with auditor
Section 164. Ceasing to hold office
Section 165. Removal of auditor
Section 166. Filling vacancy
Section 167. Court appointed auditor
Section 168. Right to attend meeting
Section 169. Examination
Section 170. Right to information
Section 171. Audit committee
Section 172. Qualified privilege (defamation)

Cross-references: Ontario Act, ss. 148-160.

FINANCIAL STATEMENTS

By s. 20 of the federal Act, every corporation is required to prepare and maintain adequate corporate records, and if they are kept at a place outside Canada a copy must be kept in Canada adequate to enable directors to ascertain the financial position of the corporation with reasonable accuracy on a quarterly basis. See the comment in that section in Chapter 4. There are many other statutes, both provincial and federal, requiring corporations to prepare and retain records of various kinds. Section 155 requires the directors of a corporation to place before the shareholders at every annual meeting comparative financial statements in prescribed form relating to the period that began immediately after the end of the last completed financial year and ended not more than six months before the annual meeting (if the annual meeting is the first one, the period begins from the date of incorporation), the financial statements for the immediately preceding financial year, the report of the auditor and any further information respecting the financial position of the corporation and the results of its operation required by its articles, by-laws or any unanimous shareholder agreement. It will be noted that the statements for the immediately preceding financial year may be omitted if the reason for the omission is set out in the financial statements or in a note thereto to be placed before the shareholders at an annual meeting.

Section 157 provides that a corporation is to keep at its registered office a copy of the financial statements of each of the subsidiaries and of each body corporate the accounts of which are consolidated in the financial statements of the corporation. These statements are open for examination by shareholders of a corporation, their agents and legal representatives on request. However, a corporation may, within 15 days of a request for such examination, apply to a court for an order barring the right of any person to make such examination and the court may, if it is satisfied that such examination will be detrimental to the corporation or to a subsidiary, bar such right and make any further order it thinks fit. Notice of the application is to be given to the Director as well as the person requesting the examination.

Section 156 provides that a corporation may apply to the Director for an order authorizing the corporation to omit from its financial statements any prescribed item or to dispense with the publication of any particular prescribed financial statement and the Director may, if he reasonably believes that such a disclosure of the information contained therein will be detrimental to the corporation, permit such omission on such reasonable conditions as he thinks fit.

There have been a number of cases dealing with the grounds for exemption from filing certain information with the department or releasing it to the shareholders. In *Re Armco Can Ltd. and Minister of the Department of Consumer and Corporate Affairs* (1975), 8 O.R. (2d) 741 (C.A.), there was an application for exemption from supplying the figures for sales and gross revenue. The court held that the applicant must satisfy the requirement that it would be seriously, unfairly and adversely affected. If this were done, the applicant should be granted an exemption unless those opposing the application satisfy the court that there is a need for a disclosure in the public interest which overbalances the detriment to the applicant. This initial burden can be satisfied if it is shown that the corporation is subject to unfair disclosure with respect to its competitors, either because its competitors are not required to make any disclosure or the disclosure required of competitors is not as revealing as would be the disclosure by the corporation. A common instance of inequitable disclosure arises where a corporation has a single product and to disclose gross or sales revenue and expenses would reveal its margin of profit as contrasted with a multinational conglomerate the revenue of which is drawn from sales of a wide variety of products. In the particular case, the Minister alleged that there were interested groups and that the information requested should be given. The four groups were corporation shareholders, customers, suppliers, employees and creditors; governmental agencies regulating the economy; private consulting firms; and potential competitors. This allegation was rejected and it was held that the general public interest in adequate disclosure by all Canadian corporations of appreciable size would not override the detriment to the applicant and accordingly the application for exemption was granted. In the present case, the applicant was one of eight corporations in the field, six of whom were not required to file, one of whom sold more than timber products; the applicant was the only one selling only timber products and, therefore, was held to be disadvantaged by the disclosure. See also *Re A.E. Ames & Co.*, [1972] 3 O.R. 405, where the Court of Appeal held that an application for exemption from filing financial statements would be refused. Under the Act, disclosure was the rule and exemption was the exception. In a federally incorporated corporation disclosure was one of the necessary incidents of business subject to the right to apply for and obtain an exemption. It was noted that there were two competitor corporations who were federally incorporated and who had filed the returns in question. For examples of a single-product corporation being granted an exemption, see *Re St. Lawrence Starch Co.*, [1972] 1 O.R. 293; *Re Firth Brown Steels Ltd.*, [1972] 3 O.R. 66 (C.A.); *Re Maher Shoes Ltd.*, [1967] 2 O.R. 684. Where a corporation offering securities to the public is involved, however, the rule is much stricter. Thus, in *Re Niagara Wire Weaving Co.*, [1971] 3 O.R. 633 (C.A.) it was held that the Securities Commission in Ontario, in considering an application exempting the disclosure of sales and gross operating revenue, should examine the relevant facts affecting the applicant and place either on the side of benefit of the shareholders or on the side of detriment to the shareholders. In such a procedure the court suggested that if the commission did not consider that the applicant itself had made out a case for exemption, some effort should be made to ascertain the views of shareholders. Subsequently, the commission made an order permitting the nondisclosure of sales of gross operating revenue, subject to the condition that the applicant submit to its next annual meeting of shareholders a resolution ratifying this omission and if this resolution was not carried by at least 90 per cent of the votes cast, the information was to be disclosed at the annual meeting. The court held in *Re Niagara Wire Weaving Co. (No. 2)*, [1972] 3 O.R. 129 that the matter should be remitted to the commission which should strike out the condition since it was an unlawful delegation to the shareholders to make the decision which ought to have been made by the commission itself. The court pointed out that it was one thing to say it was prudent for the commission on making an order to ascertain the wishes of the shareholders prior to making the order, but quite another thing to order that the information could be omitted unless sometime in the future a certain proportion of shareholders might vote otherwise. For example, there might be a material increase in the number of shares held by customers or competitors of the corporation who had ulterior motives in obtaining information as to the applicants' sales.

Re Denison Mines Ltd. v. Ontario Securities Commission (1981), 32 O.R. (2d) 469 (Div. Ct.) involved an appeal from a decision of the Ontario Securities Commission requiring the publication of segmented information by industry and geographic area in accordance with the requirements of the *Ontario Securities Act*, very similar to s. 155 of the federal Act. The segmented information was required by the Regulations which referred to the handbook of the Canadian Institute of Chartered Accountants. It was held that the reference in the Regulations to the requirements of the CICA was not an improper delegation of authority but rather an incorporation by reference and was valid. In addition, the Act provided that an exemption could be made by the commission if satisfied in the circumstances of the particular case that there was adequate justification for so doing. The court held that unless it is demonstrated that the commission had made a plain and vital mistake the court should not interfere with the discretion of the commission. This decision would appear to be applicable to s. 156 of the federal Act.

Financial statements are not to be issued, published or circulated unless they are approved by the directors of the corporation evidenced by the signature of one or more directors thereto and accompanied by the report of the auditor of the corporation, if any (s. 158(2)).

Directors who sign a balance sheet in pursuance of s. 158 do not sign in their personal capacity but on behalf of all the directors as a statement to the shareholders of the corporation's assets and liabilities: *John Shaw & Sons (Salford) Ltd v. Shaw*, [1935] 2 K.B. 113 (C.A.). Such signature is not, by reason of the directors' interest in the matter, a sufficient acknowledgement of a sum shown in the balance sheet to be owing to directors for their fees or of a debt due to a director to defeat the operation of the Statute of Limitations: *In re Coliseum (Barrow) Ltd.*, [1930] 2 Ch. 45; *Re Transplanters (Holding Company) Ltd.*, [1958] 2 All E.R. 711; nor is a balance sheet signed by two directors and approved by the shareholders an account stated between the corporation as creditor and the directors who sign the balance sheet so as to involve a fresh promise to pay any amounts therein stated to be owing to them: *John Shaw & Sons (Salford) Ltd. v. Shaw, supra*. However, a balance sheet presented at a corporation's annual general meeting at which a creditor was present in his capacity as a shareholder is a sufficient acknowledgement of the corporation's indebtedness to the creditor to defeat the statute, the creditor having proven that the total amount shown in the balance sheet as due to creditors included, although it did not specify, the amount due to him: *Jones v. Bellegrove Properties Ltd.*, [1949] 2 K.B. 700 (C.A.).

Copies of such financial statements are to be sent to each shareholder not less than 21 days prior to the annual meeting of shareholders or before the signing of the resolution under s. 142(1)(b) in lieu of the annual meeting except in the case of a shareholder who has informed the corporation in writing that he does not wish a copy of the documents in question. "Not less than" has the same meaning as "at least": *In re Hector Whaling Ltd.*, [1936] 1 Ch. 208. In that case it was also held that a provision in the articles that the day of service of a notice is to be counted in the relevant number of days must be disregarded.

A copy is to be sent to the Director if any of the securities of the corporation that are or were part of a distribution to the public remain outstanding and are held by more than one person or if the gross revenues of the corporation exceed $10,000,000 or if the assets exceed $5,000,000. It will be observed that by virtue of s. 160(2), the gross revenues and assets of the affiliates are to be included in computing the $10,000,000 and $5,000,000 figures respectively.

An exemption order from the deemed inclusion under s. 160(2) may be applied for (s. 160(3)). If interim financial statements are sent or required to be filed with or sent to a public authority or stock exchange the corporation is to send copies to the Director (s. 160(4)).

It will be observed that under s. 160(5) a subsidiary corporation is not required to comply with the section if the financial statements of its holding corporation are in consolidated or combined form and include the accounts of the subsidiary and such statements are included in the document sent to the Director by the holding corporation in compliance with the section. It will be noted that because of the definition of the word "corporation" in s. 2(1) of the Act, both the subsidiary and its parent must be federal corporations.

In *Mayr v. St. Lawrence Corp.*, [1950] Que. K.B. 635 a majority of the Court of Appeal held that shareholders of a corporation were entitled to proceed by way of mandamus to compel the directors to supply reports and statements of the operation of the corporation and its subsidiaries; but see the dissenting judgements at pp. 647 and 649.

It would appear that the omission altogether from the accounts of any asset or reserve is not permissible under the Act. A conservative statement of the financial position of the corporation reflected in the valuation of an asset may result in what is in effect a secret reserve. As pointed out by Buckley J. in *Newton v. Birmingham Small Arms Co.*, [1906] 2 Ch. 378 at 387, "assets are often by reason of prudence estimated and stated to be estimated at less than their probable real value". *Young v. Brownlee & Co.*, [1911] S.C. 677 (Court of Sess.) indicates that it is not illegal for directors to make a low valuation of stocks or other assets in order to create a reserve in view of future or contingent liabilities, since the matter is *prima facie* within the discretion of the directors acting upon a sound and honest consideration of the whole facts. The practice of setting up secret reserves was criticized by Wright J. in the judgment at the trial in *R. v. Kylsant* (1931), 48 T.L.R. 62.

Article V of the Regulations passed under the federal Act (ss. 44-47) sets out detailed requirements for the financial statements in certain particulars. The financial statements are to be prepared in accordance with the standards from time to time established by the Canadian Institute of Chartered Accountants and the auditors' report is to be prepared in accordance with standards of such institute.

It will be observed that the financial statements are required to include at least a balance sheet, a statement of retained earnings, an income statement and statement of changes in financial position although they need not be designated by such names. Where a corporation carries on a business composed of various branches which are diversified and if the corporation sends its financial statements to the Director pursuant to s. 160(1) of the Act, the financial statements are to disclose separately or in a schedule, a summary of financial information for each class of business the revenue from which is 10 per cent or more of the corporation's total revenues for the period in question. Such disclosure is to contain a note stating that the directors of the corporation have determined its classes of business at a meeting of directors which classes have been recorded in minutes of that meeting; such classes are to be determined in accordance with the Statistics Canada Standard Industrial Classification Code or if not, then a description of the basis used to determine such classes of business; the foregoing does not apply to a corporation disclosing segmented information in accordance with the standards existing from time to time of the Canadian Institute of Chartered Accountants.

See also Chapter 13 for a discussion of certain requirements relating to contents of financial statements pursuant to provincial securities legislation.

Audit Committee

Section 171 of the Act provides that a corporation described in s. 102(2) must, and any other corporation may, have an audit committee composed of not less than three directors of the corporation, a majority of whom are not officers nor employees of the corporation or any of its affiliates. It will be observed that the wording by referring to s. 102(2) is somewhat confusing since that section refers to both ordinary corporations and corporations any of the issued securities of which are or were part of a distribution to the public and remain outstanding and are held by more than one person. While it is obvious that what is meant is a corporation of this latter type, the wording is not clear and it will be observed that the Ontario Act in s. 158(1) provides that a corporation that is an offering corporation must and any other corporation may have an audit committee. The audit committee is to review the financial statements of the corporation before such financial statements are approved by the directors. The corporation's auditor is entitled to receive notice of every meeting of the audit committee and, at the expense of the corporation, may attend and be heard at such meeting and if so requested by a member of the audit committee is to attend every meeting of the committee held during the auditor's term of office. Meetings of the audit committee may be called by either the auditor or a member of the audit committee. There is a duty to inform the audit committee and the auditor if any director or officer of the corporation becomes aware of any error or misstatement in a financial statement reported on by the auditor or any former auditor; if such auditor or former auditor is notified or becomes aware of an error or misstatement, which in his opinion is material, he is required to report the same and inform each director accordingly. In such case, the directors are to prepare and issue revised financial statements or otherwise inform the shareholders and, if required to file statements with the Director under s. 160, the corporation is to inform the Director of the error or misstatement in the same manner as the shareholders.

Section 171(2) provides that a corporation may apply to the Director for an order authorizing the corporation to dispense with an audit committee and the Director may, if satisfied the shareholders will not be prejudiced by such an order, permit the corporation to dispense with the same on such reasonable conditions as he thinks fit.

Auditors (ss. 161-172)

Statutory provisions

At the organization meeting, the directors are to appoint an auditor to hold office until the first annual meeting of shareholders (s. 104(1)); thereafter, the shareholders of the corporation by ordinary resolution at the first annual meeting of shareholders and at each succeeding annual meeting, are to appoint an auditor to hold office until the close of the next annual meeting (s. 162). Under s. 161(1) an auditor is disqualified from being appointed as such if he is not independent of the corporation, its affiliates or the directors or officers of such corporation or its affiliates. It will be observed under s. 161(2) that independence is a question of fact and that a person is deemed not to be independent if he or his business partner is a business partner, director, officer or employee of the corporation or any of its affiliates or a business partner of any director, officer, employee of any such corporation or any of its affiliates, or beneficially owns or controls, directly or indirectly, a material interest in the securities of the corporation or any of its affiliates or has been a receiver, receiver-manager, liquidator or trustee in bankruptcy of the corporation or any of its affiliates within two years of his proposed appointment as auditor of the corporation; if an auditor becomes disqualified, he is to resign forthwith after becoming aware of his disqualification (s. 161(3)) and an interested person may apply to a court for an order declaring an auditor to be disqualified and the office of auditor to be vacant (s. 161(4)). However, an interested person may also apply to a court for an order exempting an auditor from disqualification and the court may, if it is satisfied that an exemption will not unfairly prejudice the shareholders, make an exemption order under such terms as it thinks fit which order may have retrospective effect (s. 161(5)).

It will be observed that under the definitions in s. 2(1), the word "auditor" includes a partnership of auditors.

Upon the appointment of an auditor, while there is no statutory requirement, it is customary to give written notice of their appointment. It will be observed that pursuant to s. 149(9) of the Ontario Act, there is a requirement to give notice in writing to an auditor of his appointment forthwith after the making of the appointment.

In theory at least, an auditor is not required to be professionally qualified although it would be unusual (and indeed imprudent) for a board of directors to make such an appointment. It will be observed that if the corporation is not required to file its financial statements with the Director pursuant to s. 160, the appointment of an auditor may be dispensed with by unanimous approval of the shareholders, including those not otherwise entitled to vote; which resolution is valid only until the next succeeding annual meeting of the shareholders; a wholly owned subsidiary of a holding body corporate may apply to the Director for an order exempting the corporation from appointing an auditor in such circumstances as may be prescribed (s. 163).

If there is a vacancy in the position of auditor it may be filled, depending on the circumstances, by the directors (s. 166(1)), the shareholders or by court order. Directors may act if there is a quorum or unless the articles of the corporation provide that a vacancy may be filled only by a vote of the shareholders. The shareholders may fill the vacancy if there is no quorum of directors (see s. 166(2)) or by resolution at a special meeting at which an auditor in office has been removed (s. 165). The court may, on application of any shareholder or the Director, appoint an auditor who holds office until an auditor is appointed by the shareholders, but this provision is not applicable if the shareholders have resolved not to appoint an auditor pursuant to s. 163 (see s. 167).

An auditor ceases to hold office when he dies, resigns or is removed by vote of the shareholders pursuant to s. 165; his resignation becomes effective at the time of sending a written resignation to the corporation or at the time specified in the resignation, whichever is later (s. 164).

An auditor of the corporation is to make the examination which in his opinion is necessary to enable him to report in the prescribed manner on the financial statements required by the Act to be placed before the shareholders except those of the immediately preceding year. He may rely on the report of an auditor of another corporation or an unincorporated business, the accounts of which are included in whole or in part in the financial statements of the corporation in question, and this is applicable whether the financial statements to be reported on are in consolidated form or not (s. 169). In connection with the performance of his duties, the present or former directors, officers, employees or agents of the corporation are to furnish to the auditor such information and explanation, and access to records, documents, books, accounts and vouchers of the corporation or any of its subsidiaries as are, in the opinion of the auditor, necessary to enable him to make the examination and report required and that they are reasonably able to furnish on demand. The directors of the corporation are to obtain from the present or former directors, officers, employees or agents of any subsidiary of the corporation, the information and explanations that they are reasonably able to furnish and that are in the opinion of the auditor necessary to enable him to make the required examination and report and to furnish the auditor with the information and explanations so obtained (s. 170).

An appointment of an auditor under what is now s. 167 should not be made without notice of the application for the appointment being given to the corporation, especially where on such appointment the validity of the annual meeting may be considered and there is pending litigation: *Manson v. Prince Rupert Dry Dock & Engineering Co.* (1920), 28 B.C.R. 58.

Under the corresponding provisions of the English Act to s. 161, an auditor appointed to fill the office of auditor is — but an auditor appointed *ad hoc* for some limited purpose is not — an officer of the corporation within the meaning of the English Act and a public officer of a public corporation within the meaning of the *Larceny Act, 1861*: *R. v. Shacter*, [1960] 2 W.L.R. 258 (C.A.) following the earlier cases of *In re London & General Bank*, [1895] 2 Ch. 166 (C.A.); *In re Kingston Cotton Mills Co.*, [1896] 1 Ch. 6 (C.A.); *In re Western Counties Steam Bakeries & Milling Co.*, [1897] 1 Ch. 617 (C.A.).

The words "the shareholders" in what is now s. 169 do not mean "all the shareholders" but "the shareholders assembled at the general meeting" and auditors fulfil their duties when they send their report to the secretary of the corporation leaving the secretary or the directors to carry out the statutory duty of calling a general meeting of the shareholders: *In re Allen, Craig & Co. (London) Ltd.*, [1934] Ch. 483.

Where auditors are simply appointed by resolution without any special terms or conditions imposed by by-law or agreement their duties are confined to the statutory duties imposed by s. 169 and are different from those which may exist where a special investigation is undertaken under the terms of a special contract: *Guardian Insurance Co. v. Sharp et al.*, [1941] 2 D.L.R. 417 at 423 (S.C.C.), and to the same effect *International Laboratories Ltd. v. Dewar et al.*, [1933] 3 D.L.R. 665 at 696 (Man. C.A.).

By-laws will be void which forbid the auditors to disclose to the shareholders information which is material to a report as to the true state of the corporation's affairs: *Newton v. Birmingham Small Arms Co. Ltd.*, [1906] 2 Ch. 378.

The court will not enforce the auditors' right of access to the books by mandatory injunction in an interlocutory application without any steps having been taken to ascertain what the wishes of the shareholders are as regards the continuance of the auditors' appointment: *Cuff v. London & County Land & Building Co. Ltd.*, [1912] 1 Ch. 440 (C.A.); nor in Alberta can such right be enforced against the directors by originating summons: *Baldwin v. Bowden* (1912), 6 D.L.R. 520.

An auditor may be regarded as an agent of the shareholders for the purpose of carrying out his statutory duty of conducting the audit, but he is not such an agent in so far as his knowledge of fraudulent representations made by the directors is imputed to the shareholders: *Spackman v. Evans* (1868), L.R. 3 H.L. 171 at 196 and 236. Apart from any special contract an auditor of a corporation is not an agent of the corporation: *Re Transplanters (Holding Company) Ltd.*, [1958] 2 All E.R. 711 at 714. In that case it was held that one cannot spell out of the relation between an auditor and the corporation any authority to do more than to perform the duties laid on him as auditor by the *Companies Act, 1948*; and that, as a result, in signing his certificate to a balance sheet an auditor is not acting as an agent of the corporation so as to constitute the balance sheet an acknowledgement of indebtedness to creditors under the Statute of Limitations.

Other rights of auditors

While the auditor is entitled to receive notice of every meeting of shareholders at the expense of the corporation, to attend and to speak thereat on matters relating to his duties as auditor as such; if a director or shareholder of a corporation gives written notice not less than ten days prior to the meeting of shareholders to an auditor or former auditor, he must attend the meeting at the expense of the corporation and answer questions relating to his duties as auditor; where such a notice is sent to an auditor a copy thereof is to be sent to the corporation (s. 168).

It will be observed that any oral or written statement or report made under the Act by any auditor or former auditor of the corporation has qualified privilege (s. 172); in other words, the auditor or former auditor is not ordinarily liable for defamation; it will be observed, however, that certain matters will defeat a claim for qualified privilege. Thus, a proof of malice in a speaker may defeat a claim of qualified privilege as may such matters as unjustifiably wide publication, which can include a communication or report for the news media generally or purely baseless allegations.

Change of auditors

Where an auditor resigns, receives a notice or otherwise learns of a meeting of shareholders called for the purpose of removing him from office, or receives notice or otherwise learns of a meeting of directors or shareholders at which another person is to be appointed to the office of auditor, whether because of the resignation or removal of the incumbent auditor or because his term of office has expired or is about to expire, or receives a notice or otherwise learns of a meeting of shareholders at which it is proposed to dispense with the appointment of an auditor, he is entitled to submit to the corporation a written statement of reasons for his resignation or why he opposes any proposed action or resolution; the corporation is to send forthwith a copy of such statement to every shareholder and to the Director unless the statement is included or attached to a management proxy circular as required by s. 150; no person is to accept appointment or consent to be appointed as auditor of a corporation if he is replacing an auditor who has resigned, been removed or whose term of office has expired or is about to expire until he has requested and received from that auditor a written statement of the circumstances and the reason why in that auditor's opinion he is to be replaced; if no reply is received within 15 days after making such request, such new person may be appointed as the auditor of the corporation; unless no reply is received an appointment as an auditor of a person who has not complied with the above requirements is void (ss. 168(5)-(9)).

Duties of auditors

The Act does not lay down any rules as to the amount of care and skill which the auditors must bring to the performance of their duties. What they have to do in order to form their opinion or to ascertain the truth of the facts to which they certify will be determined by the general rules governing the duties of auditors, whether derived from the ordinary law or the terms of their employment.

The duties of auditors are stated by Lindley L.J. in *In re London & General Bank (No. 2)*, [1895] 2 Ch. 673 at 682 (C.A.), as follows:

> It is no part of an auditor's duty to give advice, either to directors or shareholders, as to what they ought to do. An auditor has nothing to do with the prudence or

imprudence of making loans with or without security. It is nothing to him whether the business of a company is being conducted prudently or imprudently, profitably or unprofitably. It is nothing to him whether dividends are properly or improperly declared, provided he discharges his own duty to the shareholders. His business is to ascertain and state the true financial position of the company at the time of the audit, and his duty is confined to that. But then comes the question, How is he to ascertain that position? The answer is, By examining the books of the company. But he does not discharge his duty by doing this without inquiry and without taking any trouble to see that the books themselves shew the company's true position. He must take reasonable care to ascertain that they do so. Unless he does this, his audit would be worse than an idle farce. Assuming the books to be so kept as to shew the true position of a company, the auditor has to frame a balance-sheet shewing that position according to the books and to certify that the balance-sheet presented is correct in that sense. But his first duty is to examine the books, not merely for the purpose of ascertaining what they do shew, but also for the purpose of satisfying himself that they shew the true financial position of the company. This is quite in accordance with the decision of Stirling, J. in *Leeds Estate Building and Investment Co. v. Shepherd* ((1887), 36 Ch. D. 787). An auditor, however, is not bound to do more than exercise reasonable care and skill in making inquiries and investigations. He is not an insurer; he does not guarantee that the books do correctly shew the true position of the company's affairs; he does not even guarantee that his balance-sheet is accurate according to the books of the company. If he did, he would be responsible for error on his part, even if he were himself deceived without any want of reasonable care on his part, say, by the fraudulent concealment of a book from him. His obligation is not so onerous as this. Such I take to be the duty of the auditor: he must be honest — i.e., he must not certify what he does not believe to be true, and he must take reasonable care and skill before he believes that what he certifies is true. What is reasonable care in any particular case must depend upon the circumstances of that case. Where there is nothing to excite suspicion very little inquiry will be reasonably sufficient, and in practice I believe business men select a few cases at haphazard, see that they are right, and assume that others like them are correct also. Where suspicion is aroused more care is obviously necessary; but, still, an auditor is not bound to exercise more than reasonable care and skill, even in a case of suspicion, and he is perfectly justified in acting on the opinion of an expert where special knowledge is required.

Lopes L.J. in *In re Kingston Cotton Mills Co. (No. 2)*, [1896] 2 Ch. 279 (C.A.) said at p. 288:

It is the duty of an auditor to bring to bear on the work he has to perform that skill, care, and caution which a reasonably competent, careful and cautious auditor would use. What is reasonable skill, care and caution must depend on the particular circumstances of each case. An auditor is not bound to be a detective, or, as was said, to approach his work with suspicion or with a foregone conclusion that there is something wrong. He is a watch-dog, but not a blood-hound. He is justified in believing tried servants of the company in whom confidence is placed by the company. He is entitled to assume that they are honest, and to rely upon their representations, provided he takes reasonable care. If there is anything calculated to excite suspicion he should probe it to the bottom; but in the absence of anything of that kind he is only bound to be reasonably cautious and careful.

In the same case Lindley L.J., at p. 284, said:

> I protest, however, against the notion that an auditor is bound to be suspicious as distinguished from reasonably careful.

The rules laid down in *In re London & General Bank (No. 2), supra*, and *In re Kingston Cotton Mills Co. (No. 2), supra*, were adopted by the Supreme Court of Canada as applicable to auditors engaged to make the statutory audit required under the former Act: *Guardian Insurance Co. v. Sharp et al.*, [1941] 2 D.L.R. 417 at 423 and 430.

In *Fomento (Sterling Area) Ltd. v. Selsdon Fountain Pen Co.*, [1958] 1 All E.R. 11 (a case dealing with the duties of an auditor employed to determine, pursuant to the provisions of an agreement, the amount of royalties payable under certain patents) Lord Denning said at p. 23:

> What is the proper function of an auditor? It is said that he is bound only to verify the sum, the arithmetical conclusion, by reference to the books and all necessary vouching material and oral explanations; and that it is no part of his function to inquire whether an article is covered by patents or not. I think this is too narrow a view. An auditor is not to be confined to the mechanics of checking vouchers and making arithmetical computations. He is not to be written off as a professional "adder-upper and subtractor". His vital task is to take care to see that errors are not made, be they errors of computation, or errors of omission or commission, or downright untruths. To perform this task properly, he must come to it with an inquiring mind — not suspicious of dishonesty, I agree — but suspecting that someone may have made a mistake somewhere and that a check must be made to ensure that there has been none. I would not have it thought that *Re Kingston Cotton Mill Co. (No. 2)* relieved an auditor of his responsibility for making a proper check. But the check, to be effective, may require some legal knowledge, or some knowledge of patents or other specialty. What is he then to do? Take, for instance, a point of law arising in the course of auditing a company's accounts. He may come on a payment which, it appears to him, may be unlawful, in that it may not be within the powers of the corporation, or improper in that it may have no warrant or justification. He is, then, not only entitled but bound to inquire into it and, if need be, to disallow it: see *Roberts v. Hopwood*, ([1925] A.C. 578 at p. 605), *Re Ridsdel, Ridsdel v. Rawlinson* ([1947] 2 All E.R. 312 at p. 316). It may be, of course, that he has sufficient legal knowledge to deal with it himself, as many accountants have, but, if it is beyond him, he is entitled to take legal advice on the principle stated in *Bevan v. Webb* ([1901] 2 Ch. 59 at p. 75) that
>
> > permission to a man to do an act, which he cannot do effectually without the help of an agent, carries with it the right to employ an agent.
>
> So also, with an auditor who is employed for the purpose of checking the royalties payable. It is part of his duty to use reasonable care to see that none has been omitted which ought to be included. He is not bound to accept the *ipse dixit* of the licensee that there are no other articles which attract royalty. He is entitled to check the accuracy of that assertion by inquiring the nature of any other articles, which, it appears to him, may come within the patented field. If he cannot be sure, of his own knowledge, whether they attract royalty or not, he can take the advice of a patent agent, just as, within the legal sphere, he can take the advice of a lawyer.

The duty of an auditor is verification not detection: *In re City Equitable Fire Insurance Co.*, [1925] Ch. 407 at 520 (C.A.). In *Renfrew (County) v. Lockhart*, [1933] O.W.N. 627 (C.A.) Middleton J.A. said at p. 632 "an auditor is bound to be on the alert, but he is not bound to approach the task of auditing in the belief that there is concealed fraud which he has to discover".

The terms of the contract under which the auditors are performing their duties limiting the scope of the audit are material in determining the extent of their duties: *International Laboratories Ltd. v. Dewar et al.*, [1933] 3 D.L.R. 665 at 666, 683, 698 (Man. C.A.); *Jamieson, Austin & Mitchell Ltd. v. Battrum*, [1934] 1 W.W.R. 324 at 326. It will also be material in determining the extent of the duties of auditors whether they are reporting on the accounts of a corporation to a few shareholders who are also directors and hold every pecuniary interest in the corporation or whether the corporation has a large number of outside shareholders: *Pendlebury's Ltd. v. Ellis Green & Co.* (1936), 94 Accountant 508.

If the balance sheet fails to show the true financial position of the corporation, and the corporation suffers damages thereby, the onus is on the auditors of showing that the damage is not the result of their breach of duty: *Re Republic of Bolivia Exploration Syndicate Ltd. (No. 2)*, [1914] 1 Ch. 319. Auditors will be exonerated from liability if they adequately draw the corporation's attention to wrongful payments made by it: ibid.

There is no duty on the auditors to take stock, but it may be their duty to call for explanations and demand particulars of items lumped together on the stock sheets: *Henry Squire, Cash Chemist Ltd. v. Ball, Baker & Co.* (1911), 28 T.L.R. 81 (C.A.).

It is the duty of auditors in general to satisfy themselves of the actual existence and safe custody of the corporation's securities. Auditors should only accept a certificate of the possession of securities belonging to the corporation from a reputable, trustworthy and responsible person, be that person a bank or an individual. While an auditor should not ordinarily accept such a certificate from the corporation's brokers without drawing attention to the fact of the securities being in such custody, accepting such a certificate, under the circumstances, did not amount to "wilful neglect or default" within the meaning of an article protecting auditors against liability except for such neglect or default: *In re City Equitable Fire Insurance Co.*, [1925] Ch. 407 (C.A.).

Nor will auditors who are performing a statutory audit be held negligent for failing to examine duplicate deposit slips where there is nothing to arouse suspicion: *Guardian Insurance Co. v. Sharp et al.*, [1941] 2 D.L.R. 417 (S.C.C.).

See also on the duties of auditors the Annotations in (1912), 6 D.L.R. 522 and [1933] 1 D.L.R. 172, the judgment of Hodgins J.A. in *Re Owen Sound Lumber Co.* (1917), 38 O.L.R. 414 (C.A.) and the case of *Whitehouse v. Jordan*, [1980] 1 All. E.R. 650.

As to the liability, if any, of auditors for passing sums paid prior to the audit which by reason of want of authority in the regulations of the corporation or non-compliance with some statutory provision ought not to have been paid, see *In re Republic of Bolivia Exploration Syndicate*, [1914] 1 Ch. 139 at 172 and cases cited. See also *Blue Band Navigation Co. v. Price Waterhouse & Co.*, [1934] 3 D.L.R. 404 at 433 (B.C. C.A.), where Macdonald J.A. said that it is at least doubtful that auditors must decide whether or not certain acts are *ultra vires.*

Liability of auditors

If any loss is caused to the corporation from the neglect of their duties auditors may be personally liable: *Leeds Estate Building & Investment Co. v. Shepherd* (1887), 36 Ch. D. 787; and they may be made liable on a misfeasance summons under s. 125 of the *Winding-up Act*: *In re Kingston Cotton Mills Co. (No. 2)*, [1896] 2 Ch. 279 (C.A.).

It was formerly the law that auditors were not liable for negligence to third parties with whom no contractual or fiduciary relationship existed. As a result of the decision in *Hedley Byrne & Co. v. Heller & Partners Ltd.*, [1964] A.C. 465 the former authorities were overruled. In that case a banker gave a favourable reference with respect to a client but stipulated that this was "without responsibility". The House of Lords held that a negligent, albeit honest, misrepresentation, whether spoken or written, might give rise to an action for damages as, apart from any contract or fiduciary relationship, the law will imply a duty of care when a party seeking information from a party possessed of a special skill trusts him to exercise due care and such party knew or ought to have known that reliance was being placed on his skill and judgment. In the present case, however, since there was an express disclaimer of responsibility, no such duty would be implied.

Two recent decisions in England indicate the limits on the responsibility of an auditor. In *Caparo Industries plc v. Dickman and others*, the plaintiff owned shares in a public corporation whose audited accounts showed profits substantially less than those anticipated. The plaintiff purchased further shares and later in the year made a successful take-over bid for the corporation in question. Following the take-over, the plaintiff commenced an action against the auditor of the corporation alleging that the accounts were inaccurate and misleading and that while the accounts showed a substantial profit there was in fact a substantial loss. A preliminary issue was directed as to whether the auditor owed a duty of care to the plaintiff either as a shareholder or a potential investor. The decision in the House of Lords [1990] 1 All E.R. 568 held that the auditor of a public corporation's accounts owed no duty of care to the public at large who relied on the accounts to buy shares in the corporation nor was there any duty of care to an individual shareholder wishing to buy more shares since an individual shareholder was in no better position than a member of the public at large and the auditor's statutory duty to prepare accounts was owed to the body of shareholders as a whole. The purpose for which accounts were prepared and audited was to enable the shareholders as a body to exercise informed control of the corporation and not to enable individual shareholders to buy shares with a view to profit.

Similarly, in *James McNaughton Papers Group Ltd. v. Hicks Anderson & Co.*, [1991] 2 W.L.R. 641, a decision of the English Court of Appeal, it was held that there was no duty of care by the auditor to a proposed purchaser in the following circumstances: negotiations were underway for the take-over of certain corporations by the plaintiff; the draft accounts for the group were submitted to the purchaser and were labelled as final drafts showing an amount as the loss for the year; an official of the purchaser queried the auditor with respect to the accounts and in response to a question, the auditor indicated that the group was breaking even or doing marginally worse. After the take-over had been completed, a number of errors in the accounts were discovered and the purchaser claimed against the auditors for negligence. It was held that it could not be said that there was any general principle of liability and that each individual case must be examined in the light of the concepts of foreseeability, proximity and fairness. In giving judgment for the auditor, it was pointed out that the accounts were produced for the selling group and were merely draft accounts although they were marked "final draft". The answer given by the auditor to the purchaser was a very general one and it was not possible in the view of the court to attribute to the auditor the knowledge that the purchaser would rely on the answer without any further inquiry or advice. Accordingly, the court held that there was no duty of care owed by the auditor to the plaintiff.

The case law in Canada would seem to be quite different from that in England. The leading case is the decision by the Supreme Court of Canada in *Haig v. Bamford et al.*, [1977] 1 S.C.R. 466. In that case auditors prepared audited financial statements which were used or intended to be used for the purpose of attracting a new investor to the corporation. The plaintiff was shown the statements and invested in the corporation in reliance thereon. These statements were in error but the auditors did not know the plaintiff at the time the statements were prepared nor did they know that the particular plaintiff would be shown the statements. The court held that actual knowledge of the specific plaintiff was not necessary to impose liability on the auditor. It discussed the two remaining choices, namely, the foreseeability of the use of the audited financial statement by the plaintiff and reliance thereon and actual knowledge of the limited class that will use and rely on the statement. While no specific ruling was made, liability was imposed on the auditors and it was plain that the court leaned towards the second choice. Accordingly, the laws that currently exist in Canada should be regarded as requiring that auditors have actual knowledge of the limited class that will use and rely upon the audited statements and anyone who might ultimately act and rely on such statements will not automatically be within this class. See also *Dupuis v. Pan American Mines Ltd.* (1979), 7 B.L.R. 288 (Que.); *B.D.C. Ltd. v. Hofstrand Farms Ltd.*, [1986] 1 S.C.R. 228. In *Kuziw v. Abbott* (1984), 26 Man. R. (2d) 139; affd (1984), 40 Man. R. (2d) 241, the trial judge indicated that the test was: did the public accountant prepare or provide information upon which, to his knowledge, the plaintiff or that class of persons to which the plaintiff belonged, intended to rely? The action was dismissed. Two recent cases in British Columbia, *Surrey Credit Union v. Willson*, [1990] 6 W.W.R. 578 (appeal dismissed June 12, 1991) and *Kripps v. Touche Ross* (1990), 52 B.C.L.R. (2d) 291, involved suits by purchasers of securities from financial institutions which later went into receivership or liquidation. In both cases, it was held as a preliminary matter that the security holders were of a class that was foreseeable, and accordingly, the question of liability for negligence was to be determined. It will be noted that the securities in both cases were offered pursuant to prospectuses and the consent of the auditors to the use of their audited financial reports was given.

In *Roman Corp. v. Peat Marwick Thorne* (1992), 11 O.R. (3d) 248, a claim against the auditors of a group of corporations at the instance of a controlling shareholder was struck out. The court noted that the claim was made under three headings: (i) breach of contract; (ii) negligence and (iii) breach of fiduciary duty. The court held that despite the appointment of the auditors by the shareholders there was no contract and the auditor owned no duty to any individual shareholder (even a controlling shareholder), but rather to the collective body of shareholders. As to the claim in negligence, there might have been a wrong against the corporation but not against the plaintiff shareholder. Any suit for negligence against an auditor must be brought by the corporation itself or by a derivative action. The court also held that there was no basis for any claim of fiduciary relationship by the shareholder.

In New Zealand the case of *Scott Group Ltd. v. McFarlane et al.*, [1978] 1 N.Z.L.R. 553 (C.A.) involved the take-over of a public corporation by the plaintiff in reliance on audited financial statements prepared by the defendants. At the time of preparation of the statements, the auditors had no knowledge that the plaintiff or anyone else was planning a take-over. The statements contained substantial inaccuracies. The court held that the auditors were liable and Woodhouse J., at p. 575, suggested that the auditors must "be taken to have accepted not merely a direct responsibility to the shareholders but a further duty to those persons whom they can reasonably foresee will need to use and rely upon them when dealing with the corporation or its members in significant matters affecting the corporation's assets and business". The other judge, holding the auditors to be liable, indicated that the evidence disclosed a plain risk of a take-over and the virtual certainty that in such an event the accounts will be relied on by an offeror. A corporation purchasing all or a majority of the shares would be more directly and closely affected than, for instance, an ordinary purchaser of shares on the stock market. He held that there was no need to express an opinion on the perhaps unusual case of an ordinary market purchaser who first made a careful study of the audited accounts or even on the case of a quite unforeseeable take-over. No judge in that case held that an ordinary shareholder or creditor of the corporation could sue the auditors successfully.

It is hoped that the Supreme Court of Canada will be given an early opportunity to settle the law in Canada which at the present time would appear to be in a state of some uncertainty. It will be noted that there may be a difference between the auditors and auditors' liability where audited statements are used in a prospectus or other document with the consent of the auditor for the purpose of selling or issuing securities of the corporation in question and ordinary financial statements. If the foreseeability test is found to be the basis of liability for an auditor and it is necessary for a shareholder to review the financial statements before deciding to purchase shares and he would have not decided to do so but for such statements, there would appear to be no question of his ability to sue under the present law in Canada. Suppose, however, that a shareholder purchases shares based on research of a stockbroker whose analysts reviewed the financial statements in question: would or should this make a difference to any final outcome?

It will be noted that the damages due to the shareholders are basically the same as those due to the corporation in question divided amongst the shareholders on a *pro rata* basis according to their share interests. It may be questioned whether the auditors should be liable for double damages to both the corporation and the shareholders.

In an action against auditors for breach of their duty, which is an action in damages for negligence, damages must be alleged and proved and the damages must be such as flow from the default of the auditors: *Renfrew (County) v. Lockhart et al.*, [1933] O.W.N. 627 at 629, 634 (C.A.). For other illustrations of the point that the damages suffered by the corporation must flow from the default of the auditors, see *Henry Squire, Cash Chemist Ltd. v. Ball, Baker & Co.* (1911), 28 T.L.R. 81 (C.A.); *International Laboratories Ltd. v. Dewar*, [1933] 3 D.L.R. 665 at 705 (Man. C.A.); *Diamond T. Montreal Ltd. v. Ross & Wadsworth* (1939), 35 Canadian Chartered Accountant 205 (Que. S.C.); *Guardian Insurance Co. v. Sharp*, [1941] 2 D.L.R. 417 at 427 (S.C.C.).

In *International Laboratories Ltd. v. Dewar, supra*, it was held that some of the items of loss were due to the negligence of the corporation. Similar findings were made in *Guardian Insurance Co. v. Sharp et al., supra*, and *McBride's Ltd. v. Rooke*, [1942] 3 D.L.R. 81 at 94 (Sask. C.A.) (corporation recovered from auditors amount of an employee's defalcations subsequent to auditor's negligent failure to discover thefts and warn the corporation but did not recover amounts of fees paid to the auditors for their services and fees paid to another firm for conducting a special audit).

Auditors will not be liable if the loss was directly due to the negligent methods of the officers of the corporation and not to anything done or omitted by the auditors: *Jamieson, Austin & Mitchell Ltd. v. Battrum*, [1934] 1 W.W.R. 324. See also *Re S. P. Catterson & Son* (1937), The Accountant, vol. 96, at 308, where, the faulty system of accounting having been drawn to the attention of the directors by the auditors, it was held that the auditors were not negligent in failing to detect defalcations; *Pendlebury's Ltd. v. Ellis Green & Co.* (1936), 94 Accountant 508, where lack of a proper internal check had been brought to the notice of directors.

It will be noted that in recent cases, fraudulent activities or improper conduct of officers of the corporation will not necessarily excuse the auditor. Thus, in two Australian cases, a finding of contributory negligence was held to be ineffective to excuse the auditor or, indeed, that such a finding could be made at all. It was pointed out that if, as where the audit is of a public corporation, the audit contract is found to impose a duty to be exercised so as to safeguard the interests of shareholders, it was difficult to see how the conduct of any servant or director could constitute the relevant negligence so as to defeat the claim against the auditor whose duty is to check the conduct of such persons and where appropriate, to report it to the shareholders. See *Pacific Acceptance Corporation Ltd. v. Forsyth et al.* (1967), 92 W.N. 29 (N.S.W.) and *Simonius Vischer & Co. v. Holt & Thompson*, [1979] 2 N.S.W.L.R. 332 (C.A.). See also *Revelstoke Credit Union v. Miller et al.*, [1984] 2 W.W.R. 297 (B.C. S.C.) and *West Coast Finances Ltd. v. Gunderson et al.*, [1974] 2 W.W.R. 428 (reversed on other grounds, [1975] 4 W.W.R. 501 (B.C. C.A.)). In these cases the courts refused to follow the Australian cases referred to above. See also *Coopers & Lybrand v. H.E. Kane Agencies Ltd.* (1985), 17 D.L.R. (4th) 695 (N.B. C.A.) (varg (1983), 23 C.C.L.T. 233, where contributory negligence was held to apply in a claim against auditors); *Harvey Credit Union Ltd. v. G.H. Ward & Partners* (1981), 128 D.L.R. (3d) 656 (Ont. H.C.).

The auditors are entitled to rely upon the efficiency of a system of internal control provided by the management: *Sharp v. Guardian Insurance Co.*, [1940] 2 D.L.R. 512 at 513, 534 (Que. C.A.), and cases cited; affd (*sub nom. Guardian Insurance Co. v. Sharp et al*), [1941] 2 D.L.R. 417 (S.C.C.).

Negligence of officers of the corporation will not relieve auditors from their contractual obligations: *McBride's Ltd. v. Rooke*, [1942] 3 D.L.R. 81 at 94 (Sask. C.A.).

Upon discovery of an irregularity it is the duty of the auditors at once to report the true facts to the corporation and they will be responsible for any loss which results from their failure so to report at the time they acquire the information: *Canadian Woodmen of the World v. Hooper* (1932), 41 O.W.N. 328, [1933] 1 D.L.R. 168 (C.A.). In the same case it was held that the auditors are not entitled to compel a realization of collateral securities lodged with the corporation by other parties liable to it in respect of the irregularity but that they are entitled to have these securities taken into consideration in ascertaining the amount of the loss if they are realized. See also ss. 171(7) and 171(8) referred to above.

In the last mentioned case the Master found on a reference that the plaintiff was in no worse position, as regards the rights which it could enforce to recoup its loss, at the time when the auditors disclosed the true situation than it had been at the time when the auditors should have done so, and that, accordingly, the plaintiff had not suffered any damage. However, the Court of Appeal held, following the principle laid down in *Village of Brighton v. Auston* (1892), 19 O.A.R. 305, that if no substantial damage could be proved the plaintiff was at all events entitled to nominal damages, and directed judgment to be entered in favour of the plaintiff for one dollar and the costs of the action not dealt with by the prior order of the Court of Appeal and for the costs of the appeal: *Canadian Woodmen of the World v. Hooper*, [1935] O.W.N. 113 (C.A.).

The auditors of a corporation questioned an advance made by it to a syndicate and the president of the corporation, who was at the time a man of substantial means, guaranteed the advance; the auditors disclosed the guarantee in their report and the circumstances surrounding it were fully explained by the president at a shareholders' meeting which adopted the report; it was held that the auditors were not under the circumstances guilty of negligence so as to make them liable to the corporation for the loss arising out of the advances to the syndicate; and it was held (per McPhillips J.A.) that no claim for damages could lie against the auditors until proceedings to recover the debt had been taken against the syndicate: *Blue Band Navigation Co. v. Price Waterhouse & Co.*, [1934] 3 D.L.R. 404 (B.C. C.A.).

Where it appeared that the shareholders would not have taken proceedings to recover unauthorized payments if these had been brought to their attention, there was no damage to the corporation: *In re Republic of Bolivia Exploration Syndicate*, [1914] 1 Ch. 139 at 176.

An auditor may set up the Statute of Limitations as a defence to a claim made against him: *Leeds Estate Building & Investment Co. v. Shepherd* (1887), 36 Ch. D. 787 at 809.

As to the prescription period in Quebec in respect of a claim against auditors, see *Guardian Insurance Co. v. Sharp*, [1938] 4 D.L.R. 811 (revd on other grounds (*sub nom. Sharp v. Guardian Insurance Co.*), [1940] 2 D.L.R. 512 (Que. C.A.)). The question of prescription was not considered on the further appeal to the Supreme Court of Canada: *Guardian Insurance Co. v. Sharp et al.*, [1941] 2 D.L.R. 417 at 427.

Where, in a contract between the corporation and an officer, it is provided that the latter's remuneration is to be ascertained by the auditors' certificate as to net profits, if the certificate of the auditors is based on a wrong principle, it is not conclusive and binding upon the parties: *Johnston v. Chestergate Hat Mfg. Co.*, [1915] 2 Ch. 338.

Directors are not bound to test the accuracy of auditors' accounts: *Dovey v. Cory*, [1901] A.C. 477.

Chapter 12

FUNDAMENTAL CHANGES

Section 173. Amendment of articles
Section 174. Constraints on shares
Section 175. Proposal to amend
Section 176. Class vote
Section 177. Delivery of articles
Section 178. Certificate of amendment
Section 179. Effect of certificate
Section 180. Restated articles
Section 181. Amalgamation
Section 182. Amalgamation agreement
Section 183. Shareholder approval
Section 184. Short form amalgamations
Section 185. Filing of articles
Section 186. Effect of certificate
Section 187. Continuance (import)
Section 188. Continuance (export)
Section 189. Borrowing powers, etc
Section 190. Dissents
Section 191. Reorganizations
Section 192. Arrangements

Cross-reference: *Companies' Creditors Arrangement Act*, R.S.C. 1985, c. C-36. Ontario Act, ss. 42(2)-(4), 168-186.

General

Part XV (ss. 173-192) of the Act is entitled "Fundamental Changes". Though the origin of the term is unclear, its meaning is not. It is the term given to those changes or alterations to the powers, objects, share capital, structure or nature of the business of a corporation that are so fundamental as to require an amendment to the articles of the corporation itself. Such changes affect the "very life-blood" of its existence. Under the former Act such changes would usually have required that the corporaton obtain supplementary letters patent.

There are many reasons why a modern corporation may wish to undertake a fundamental change. It may wish to have a new name, more appropriate for its current business or operations. It may wish to move the geographical location of its head office. Sometimes the capital structure of the corporation is no longer suitable and it is necessary to alter the rights attaching to all or some of the existing shares. In other cases, new capital is required which can only be obtained on condition that the rights of existing shareholders are modified. All such changes require that the company amend its articles.

Alternatively, it may be desirable to combine the corporaton with a related corporation to take advantage of business or tax considerations. This can be done by amalgamating the corporations pursuant to the enabling provisions found in the Act. As well, amalgamations can be used to implement various complex reorganizations of corporations including take-over bids: see, for example, *Neonex International Ltd. v. Kolasa*, [1978] 2 W.W.R. 593, 3 B.L.R. 1, 84 D.L.R. (3d) 446 (B.C. S.C.) or *Palmer v. Carling O'Keefe Breweries of Canada Ltd.* (1987), 37 B.L.R. 316 (Ont. H.C.).

Even more complex reorganizations may require the use of the arrangement procedure. Thus, arrangements may be used to reorganize corporations that are in financial difficulty, such as Dome Petroleum: *Savage v. Amoco Acquisition Co.* (1988), 59 Alta. L.R. (2d) 260. Alternatively, arrangements can be used to implement tax effective reorganizations of solvent corporations: see *Re Canadian Pacific Ltd.* (1990), 72 O.R. (2d) 545 and (1990), 73 O.R. (2d) 212.

Sometimes it is desirable to allow a corporation incorporated under the laws of another jurisdiction to take advantage of the provisions of the Act. Alternatively, some other legal jurisdiction may offer a corporate statute that fulfils a particular corporate need. In such cases, the continuance provisions of the Act come into play. Continuances, either importing a corporation under the Act or exporting a corporation to another jurisdiction, facilitate the ability to take advantage of different laws of other jurisdictions.

Other situations that are categorized as fundamental changes include the possible sale or lease of all or substantially all the property of the corporation.

Such a transaction would clearly constitute a fundamental change in the nature and scope of the corporation's business.

There are, however, constraints on the fundamental changes that can be effected by a corporation. The constraints are both procedural and substantive. Although a corporation has the rights, privileges and powers of a natural person it is still subject to the Act (s. 15(1)). No fundamental change can be made unless the steps prescribed in the statute have been strictly followed. As well, the Act provides remedies for shareholders who do not agree with certain proposed fundamental changes. These remedies include the right of a shareholder to "dissent" from the change and be paid the fair value of the shares held by such shareholder. (See the discussion under the heading "Right to dissent", *infra*, and in Chapter 16.) Note also that a corporation cannot, by altering its articles, justify a breach of contract: *Baily v. Equitable Life Assurance Co.*, [1904] 1 Ch. 374 at 385 (C.A.); *Southern Foundries (1926) Ltd. v. Shirlaw*, [1940] A.C. 701 at 726, 740, 741.

The procedure to amend the constitution of a corporation under the Act is similar to the procedure used to obtain supplementary letters patent under the former Act. Generally, fundamental changes must be authorized by a special resolution, which needs a two-thirds majority of the votes cast by shareholders entitled to vote on such resolution (see Chapter 10 "Shareholders' Meetings"). In some cases, other requirements must be met and perhaps even the sanction of a court obtained.

Amendment of articles

Section 173(1) provides that the articles of a corporation must be amended by a special resolution. It also specifies that articles of amendment are necessary for (a) a change of name; (b) a change in the place where the registered office is located; (c) a change of the business or businesses that the corporation may carry on (if such business or businesses are set out in the articles); (d) a change in the maximum number of shares of all or any classes that the corporation is authorized to issue; (e) the creation of new classes of shares; (f) a change to the stated capital; (g) changes to the designation of all or any shares, or additions to, changes in or removal of any rights, privileges, restrictions and conditions (including rights to accrued dividends) in respect of all or any of its shares; (h) changes to shares of any class or series into a different number of shares or into the same or a different number of other classes or series; (i) division of a class of shares into series, and fixing the number of shares in each series and the rights, privileges, restrictions and conditions thereof; (j) authorization to the directors to make a division of any class of unissued shares into series and to fix the number of shares in each series and the rights, privileges, restrictions and conditions thereof; (k) authorization to the directors to change the rights, privileges, restrictions and conditions attached to unissued shares of any series; (l) any action to revoke, diminish or enlarge any authority conferred under (j) or (k) above; (m) any increase or decrease in the number of directors or the minimum or maximum number of directors (subject to the provisions of s. 107, which deals with cumulative voting, and s. 112 which provides that no decrease may shorten the term of an incumbent director); (n) any action to add, change or remove restrictions on the issue, transfer or ownership of shares, or (o) adding, changing or removing any other provision that is permitted by the Act to be set out in the articles. In addition, articles of amendment may be ordered by a court under s. 191, see *infra,* and s. 241, as to which see Chapter 16. As to articles of amalgamation, see *infra.*

Change of name

A corporation may amend its articles to change its name to any other name (s. 173(1)(a)). The directors of a corporation designated by a number (s. 11(2)) may, without shareholder approval, cause the corporation to amend its articles to adopt a verbal name (s. 173(3)).

All changes of names must still comply with the rules governing corporate names set out in ss. 10 and 12 (see Chapter 2). The articles of amendment changing the name must be filed together with a Canada-based NUANS search report made within the previous 90 days.

Change of registered office

Similarly, a corporation may amend its articles changing the place within Canada in which its registered office is situated (s. 173(1)(b)). That is, a corporation may not move its registered office to a new municipality or geographic township without specific authorization. The corporation may, however, move its office to a new address *within* the designated municipality or township without filing articles. It will be noted that the comparable provision under the Ontario Act requires a special resolution to change the place where its registered office is to be situate; a certified copy of the special resolution is to be filed with the Director (s. 14(4), (5)). Articles of amendment for this purpose may be obtained under the Ontario Act by virtue of s. 168(1)(b).

Change of business

Most corporations now do not have specific objects, clauses or powers in their articles or by-laws (s. 15, s. 16(1)) (see Chapter 3). However, if it is necessary or desirable to add, change or remove any restrictions upon the corporation's business activities, then an amendment to the articles is required.

Because a change of business, like other fundamental changes, gives rise to the dissent remedy to dissatisfied shareholders, it is normal practice to omit any reference to permitted or restricted business in the articles. This enables the corporation to carry on any business (other than those prohibited by s. 3(4)), and to change that business at any time without reference to the shareholders. A corporation is, however, restrained from certain sales, leases or exchanges of assets of its business without shareholder approval (see commentary on s. 189 below).

Changes to share capital

It is possible to increase or decrease the authorized share capital of a corporation in many ways, all of which require an amendment to the articles. Perhaps the simplest cases are changes to the number of shares the corporation is authorized to issue. For example, changing the authorized shares from a fixed to an unlimited number (s. 173(1)(d)). It is quite common for private corporations to be initially incorporated with an unlimited number of shares; this gives flexibility to the directors in issuing shares. In some private corporations, this may be unwise. It may be preferable to restrict the number of authorized shares to those issued to a particular group of shareholders who then have the ability to vote on the creation of additional shares.

It may be desirable to create additional classes or change the terms and conditions of existing shares (ss. 173(1)(e) and (g)), or to change the shares of any class or series into a different number of shares of the same class or series, or into the same or a different number of shares of other classes or series (s. 173(1)(h)). The provisions enable transactions such as stock splits and stock consolidations and allow a corporation great flexibility in amending share conditions. See Chapter 5 for a discussion on share capital.

It is also possible to divide an issued or unissued class of shares into series and to fix the number of shares in each series and the rights and conditions attaching to each series (s. 173(1)(i)). It is also possible to authorize the directors to divide an authorized, but unissued, class of shares into series, to fix the number of shares in such series and the rights and conditions thereof. As well, the directors can be authorized to amend or change the rights and restrictions attached to unissued shares of any series (s. 173(1)(j)).

Thus, the directors can be given substantial powers with respect to the corporation's share capital. Such powers can be used in many different ways. For example, directors of public corporations could discourage unwelcome take-over bids (see Chapter 13). Alternatively, this power given to directors could provide flexibility for corporations that may themselves wish to make an acquisition where time may be limited.

Class votes

Section 176 describes the circumstances in which a class, or in some cases, a series of shares will be entitled to a separate vote as a class (or series, as the case may be) on a proposed amendment to the articles whether or not such shares are otherwise entitled to vote. Each class or series entitled to vote on the proposed amendment must approve it by a special resolution; the failure to obtain such approval of any class or series entitled to vote thereon will cause the proposed amendment to fail.

A separate class vote will be triggered by a proposal to amend the articles to: (a) increase or decrease any maximum number of authorized shares of such class, or increase any maximum number of authorized shares of a class having rights or privileges equal or superior to the shares of such class; (b) effect an exchange, reclassification or cancellation of all or part of the shares of such class; (c) add, change or remove the rights, privileges, restrictions or conditions attached to the shares of such class and, without limiting the generality of the foregoing, (i) remove or change prejudicially rights to accrued dividends or rights to cumulative dividends, (ii) add, remove or change prejudicially redemption rights, (iii) reduce or remove a dividend preference or a liquidation preference, or (iv) add, remove or change prejudicially conversion privilege, options, voting, transfer or pre-emptive rights, or rights to acquire securities of a corporation, or sinking fund provisions; (d) increase the rights or privileges of any class of shares having rights or privileges equal or superior to the shares of such class; (e) create a new class of shares equal to or superior to the shares of such class; (f) make any class of shares having rights or privileges inferior to shares of such class equal or superior to the shares of such class; or (g) effect an exchange or create a right of exchange of all or part of the shares of another class into shares of such class; or (h) constrain the issue, transfer or ownership of the shares of such class or change or remove such constraint.

It is possible to limit the right to a class vote in the case of amendments described in paragraphs (a), (b) and (e) above by so providing in the articles. On the other hand, it is not possible to amend the rights of existing shares, create new shares, or otherwise reorganize share capital, except in accordance with the above.

It can be seen that, in many cases, the right to a class vote occurs where a change to an existing class of shares, or the creation of a new class of shares, results in new shares with rights or privileges "equal or superior to" the class of shares which is given the separate vote. Unfortunately there are no cases on the meaning of the phrase "having rights or privileges equal or superior to". It seems logical that the phrase must refer to the rights or privileges of the particular class of shares considered as a whole and not to one particular term or condition of a share — since it is hard to envisage a situation where a particular class of shares does not have at least one of its terms (right to vote, dividend entitlement, participation in profits, participation on dissolution or liquidation and so on) that is the same as at least one of the terms of another class of shares. The problem with this analysis is that it is often difficult to decide when a class vote should occur. The decision might involve the directors of a corporation in complex valuation issues, weighing the merits of, say, the absence of a right to vote compared to enhanced dividend entitlement. Where the shares are publicly traded, the answer to this question may be easy to obtain. But in some public, and most private corporations, there is considerable scope for legitimate differing views of the value of a particular right or privilege attaching to a share. Accordingly, unless the situation is very clear cut, it is advisable to obtain a separate class vote for any proposed amendment to articles that affects share rights where there is more than one class of issued shares.

Certain English decisions indicate that the courts will distinguish between the legal and the commercial effect of alterations in share capital and require the consent of the holders of shares of a particular class thereto only if the rights of such holders are varied or affected in the strict legal sense.

In *Greenhalgh v. Arderne Cinemas Ltd. (No. 1)*, [1946] 1 All E.R. 512, the corporation had two classes of ordinary shares, the one being ordinary shares of 10s. each and the other being ordinary shares of 2s. each. Under the articles, each share entitled the holder to one vote, and the rights attached to any class could be varied with the sanction of an extraordinary resolution passed at a separate general meeting of the holders of the shares of that class. The corporation took steps to subdivide the ordinary shares of 10s. each into ordinary shares of 2s. each, ranking equally as to voting and otherwise with the original shares of that class, but did not convene a class meeting of the holders of the original shares in connection with the subdivision. The effect of the subdivision was that the plaintiff, a holder of the original shares, lost voting control of the corporation. The Court of Appeal held that the rights of the holders of the original shares had not as a matter of law been varied and that a meeting of the holders of shares of that class in connection with the subdivision had not been necessary. The position of the holders of the original shares had been altered but their legal rights and in particular their voting rights had not been varied.

See also *In re John Smith's Tadcaster Brewery Co.*, [1953] 1 Ch. 308 where the voting rights attached to the preference shares would be diluted by the proposed creation and issuance of additional ordinary shares. The Court of Appeal held that the increase of capital need not be sanctioned by the holders of the preference shares.

An agreement provided that the plaintiff was in certain events entitled to the allotment and issuance of 40,000 fully paid and non-assessable shares of the capital stock of the defendant corporation. After the agreement was entered into, but before such entitlement arose, the corporation by supplementary letters patent changed its authorized capital so that each shareholder was entitled to only one share for every four held. In construing the agreement the Ontario Court of Appeal held that the words "capital stock" in the agreement meant issued capital and accordingly the plaintiff was in no different position than the holders of any issued shares and was entitled only to one share for each four shares provided for in the agreement, that is, 10,000 shares: *St. Michael Uranium Mines Ltd. v. Rayrock Mines Ltd.* (1958), 15 D.L.R. (2d) 609 (reversing the decision of Ferguson J, [1957] O.R. 589).

The holders of a series of shares are entitled to vote separately as a series if, but only if, that series is affected by a proposed amendment differently from other series of shares of the same class (s. 176(4)).

In voting, the power to alter the articles must be exercised *bona fide* for the benefit of the corporation as a whole: *Allen v. Gold Reefs of West Africa Ltd.*, [1900] 1 Ch. 656 (C.A) 671; *Brown v. British Abrasive Wheel Co.* (1919), 88 L.J. Ch. 143; *Sidebottom v. Kershaw, Leese & Co.*, [1920] 1 Ch. 154 at 163 (C.A.). It is for the shareholders, acting in good faith, and not for the court, to determine whether an alteration is for the benefit of the corporation; if, however, the action of the majority of the shareholders is so oppressive that they cannot be considered to have been acting in good faith, or their decision is such that no reasonable person could consider it for the benefit of the corporation, or if they had no reasonable ground for coming to their decision, then the resolution may be set aside: *Shuttleworth v. Cox Bros. & Co. (Maidenhead)*, [1927] 2 K.B. 9 (C.A.).

In *Greenhalgh v. Arderne Cinemas*, [1950] 2 All E.R. 1120 at 1126 (C.A.),

Evershed M.R. summarized the principles emerging from the English authorities as follows:

> In the first place, it is now plain that "*bona fide* for the benefit of the company as a whole" means not two things but one thing. It means that the shareholder must proceed on what, in his honest opinion, is for the benefit of the company as a whole. Secondly, the phrase, "the company as a whole", does not (at any rate in such a case as the present) mean the company as a commercial entity as distinct from the corporators. It means the corporators as a general body. That is to say, you may take the case of an individual hypothetical member and ask whether what is proposed is, in the honest opinion of those who voted in its favour, for that person's benefit.
>
> I think the thing can, in practice, be more accurately and precisely stated by looking at the converse and by saying that a special resolution of this kind would be liable to be impeached if the effect of it were to discriminate between the majority shareholders and the minority shareholders so as to give to the former an advantage of which the latter were deprived. When the cases are examined in which the resolution has been successfully attacked, it is on that ground that it has fallen down. It is, therefore, not necessary to require that persons voting for a special resolution should, so to speak, dissociate themselves altogether from the prospect of personal benefit and consider whether the proposal is for the benefit of the company as a going concern. If, as commonly happens, an outside person makes an offer to buy all the shares, *prima facie*, if the corporators think it is a fair offer and vote in favour of the resolution, it is no ground for impeaching the resolution because they are considering the position of themselves as individual persons.

See also the discussion in Chapter 10, "Shareholders' Meetings".

Constrained shares (see the discussion in Chapter 5) are limited in their rights to a class vote. For example, s. 176(2) provides that the separate class vote rules do not apply in respect of a proposal to add a right or privilege to convert existing shares into constrained shares that have otherwise identical rights or privileges. As well, it is possible to create a new class of constrained shares, otherwise containing terms equal to an existing class of shares, without triggering a class vote.

Changes to shares — effect on stated capital

As noted in Chapter 5, there are detailed rules which assist in determining the stated capital attributable to a class or series of shares. For example, s. 39(4)(a) provides that where articles of amendment change or convert shares of one class or series into shares of another class or series, the corporation must: (a) deduct from the stated capital account maintained for the class or series of shares converted or changed an amount equal to the result obtained by multiplying the stated capital of the shares of that class or series by the number of shares of that class or series converted or changed, divided by the number of issued shares of that class or series immediately before the conversion or change; and (b) add the result obtained under paragraph (a) and any additional consideration received pursuant to the conversion or change to the stated capital account maintained or to be maintained for the class or series of shares into which the shares have been converted or changed.

Accordingly, where changes to share capital are effected by articles of amendment, any consequential changes to the stated capital of such shares are governed by the Act.

Changes to stated capital

Section 173(1)(f) provides that the articles may be amended to "reduce or increase" stated capital, which, for purposes of the amendment is deemed to be set out in the articles.

This provision is both curiously drafted, and perhaps redundant. The curious drafting relates to the phrase "which, for purposes of the amendment is deemed to be set out in the articles". This phrase is meant to deal with the fact that articles of incorporation (s. 6 in the Act) do not require the stated capital to be set out therein. It is therefore incongruous to file articles to "amend" stated capital in circumstances where the stated capital is not set out in the articles.

But there is a more substantive issue. Changes to stated capital are dealt with elsewhere in the Act. For example, s. 38 provides that, subject to certain solvency tests, a corporation may, by special resolution, reduce its stated capital for any purpose, including certain purposes specifically set out in s. 38.1(1). Though not quite so explicit, s. 26(5) implies that a corporation can add amounts to its stated capital. As well, subs. 26(2) and (3) deal with additions to stated capital on the issuance of shares. See Chapter 5.

Thus, the Act appears to contain a complete scheme dealing with changes to stated capital without having to resort to s. 173(1)(f). Accordingly, it seems unlikely that there would be many practical instances where a corporation would go to the additional trouble of amending its articles when it can accomplish the same result by other means. Therefore, it seems that s. 173(1)(f) is essentially a redundant procedure.

The alternative view is that articles of amendment are required to implement *all* changes to stated capital and provisions such as those found in ss. 26(5) and 38 are preliminary steps in the process.

It would not appear that this alternative view is correct. First, it seems clear that articles are not an appropriate place to deal with stated capital. As discussed in Chapter 5, stated capital can be changed by the issuance of additional shares or redemption or purchase for cancellation of issued shares. Such changes are not required to be set out in the articles — nor is the initial stated capital required to be set out therein (s. 6). It seems, therefore, incongruous to argue that a particular change to stated capital must be set out in the articles.

Second, s. 177(2) provides that if an amendment to the articles results in a reduction of stated capital, then the solvency and creditor protection provisions of subss. 38(3) and (6) apply. If a reduction of capital under s. 38 was just an ancillary or preliminary step to a reduction of stated capital via articles of amendment pursuant to s. 173(1)(f), s. 177(2) would be totally unnecessary. Therefore, it seems clear that s. 173(1)(f) must be an alternative procedure to implement changes to stated capital.

The cases under the English Act have laid down the following principles: where there are several classes of shares *prima facie* the reduction should be *pari passu*: *Bannatyne v. Direct Spanish Telegraph Co.* (1887), 34 Ch. D. 287 (C.A.). If, however, preference shares are entitled to priority as to capital the reduction should be effected upon the other classes: *In re Agricultural Hotel Co.*, [1891] 1 Ch. 396; *In re London & New York Investment Corp.*, [1895] 2 Ch. 860. The rule is that, where there are different classes of shares, the loss of capital should fall on those classes which, according to the constitution of the corporation, are the proper ones to bear it: *In re Floating Dock Co., Ltd.*, [1895] 1 Ch. 691. But a reduction may be sanctioned which alters the rights of different classes of shareholders: *In re Welsbach Incandescent Gas Light Co., Ltd.*, [1904] 1 Ch. 87; or differentiates between different groups of shareholders: *British & American Trustee & Finance Corp. v. Couper*, [1894] A.C. 399 (the corporation had power under its articles to reduce capital by paying off capital).

Under this Act where there are different classes of shares and the proposed reduction alters the rights of the holders of preferred shares or other shares having special rights it would appear necessary in effecting the reduction to obtain the approval of the holders of shares of such class under the applicable share provisions or to proceed by way of arrangement or compromise under s. 192.

As noted in Chapter 5, s. 39(4) provides the rules for adjusting stated capital accounts when issued shares are converted or changed into shares of another class or series. The basic rule is, as one would expect, that the stated capital is removed from the former class or series, and credited to the class or series into which the former shares were converted or changed.

Changes to directors

Any changes to the fixed number of directors of a corporation or to the stated minimum and maximum number of directors must be made by amending the articles. There are two additional constraints. First, if the articles provide for cumulative voting (see Chapter 8) the number of directors may not be decreased if the votes cast against the motion would be sufficient to elect a director under cumulative voting procedures. Second, no amendment may shorten the fixed term of an incumbent director.

There are many examples of situations where a corporation may wish to change the number of directors. Perhaps the most common in the case of a private corporation is where an existing director has retired or passed away, and it is felt that there is no suitable replacement, yet the articles provide for a fixed number of directors. In other situations, the articles may provide for a fixed number of directors, or a minimum or maximum number of directors, that no longer suit the current needs of the corporation.

In most cases, it is better to incorporate the company with a flexible board with a reasonably broad range of maximum and minimum number of directors.

Change to restrictions on shares

An amendment to add, change or remove restrictions on the issue, transfer or ownership of shares under s. 173(1)(n) to create or amend the articles of a "constrained share company" under s. 174 requires a special resolution. See the discussion in Chapter 5 on constrained share corporations.

Conversion of a private company into a public company and vice versa

The combined effect of ss. 173(1)(n) and (o) makes it plain that conversion of a private corporation into a public corporation and vice versa can be accomplished by articles of amendment.

Revocation of amendments to articles

Section 173(2) provides that the directors of a corporation may revoke the resolution before it is acted upon without the further approval of the shareholders, provided that the special resolution effecting the amendment to the articles authorizes such revocation.

Procedure for amendments to articles

Section 175 deals with the procedure to amend articles. A proposal to amend the articles may be made by a director or by a shareholder who is entitled to vote at an annual meeting of shareholders (see commentary on s. 137 in Chapter 10 which describes the procedure for a proposal to be made by a shareholder).

The notice of the meeting at which a proposal to amend the articles is to be considered must set out the proposed amendment. If applicable, it should state that dissenting shareholders are entitled to be paid the fair value of their shares in accordance with s. 190. However, failure to make that statement does not invalidate the amendment (s. 175(2)).

Section 176 provides that each class (and series) of shares is entitled to vote separately as a class (or series) on certain proposals to amend the articles, whether or not such shares are otherwise entitled to vote. Generally, a separate class (or series) vote is given in circumstances where the rights of the class (or series) would be adversely affected or impaired by the amendment. See the discussion on "Class votes" in this chapter.

Under s. 177, after an amendment to the articles has been adopted by shareholders, articles of amendment must be delivered to the Director. The articles of amendment must be in the form prescribed by regulation (Form 4). By virtue of s. 262(2) the articles must be in duplicate, signed by an officer or director of the corporation.

Section 178 states that upon receipt of the articles of amendment, the Director must issue a certificate of amendment. More specifically, the Director endorses on the articles the word "filed" and the date of filing, issues duplicate certificates of amendment to which are attached one of the copies of the articles of amendment. One copy of the certificate is filed by the Director and the other is sent to the corporation. Finally, the Director publishes a notice in the *Canada Gazette*. See also Chapter 17 for a discussion of correction of errors in the articles.

The extent of the Director's powers to refuse a certificate was explored by the Ontario Court of Appeal in *Re Canada Business Corporations Act* (1991), 3 O.R. (3d) 336. In that case it was argued that the Director could refuse to accept articles of amalgamation and refuse to issue a certificate of amalgamation unless the amalgamating corporations established that the proposed amalgamation would not adversely affect shareholders of the amalgamating corporations. These arguments were rejected. The court found that the Director had powers to reject an amalgamation, but only for failure to satisfy the Director with respect to the specific matters set out in subss. 185(2) and (3). (These matters are discussed, *infra*, under "Amalgamations".) Presumably, similar restrictions would apply to limit the Director's powers to refuse to issue a certificate of amendment.

The amendment becomes effective on the date shown in the certificate and the articles of the company are amended accordingly (s. 179(1)). There is no statutory provision or formal procedure specifying a time of day when an amendment becomes effective; conversely, however, there are no restrictions against multiple consecutive amendments to the articles of a company occurring on the same day. There is authority for the proposition that "judicial acts", such as issuing writs, etc., are effective from the first moment of the day on which they were issued. See *Dini v. Fauquier* (1904), 8 O.L.R. 712 (Div. Ct.) and *Converse v. Mitchie* (1865), 16 U.C.C.P. 167 (C.A.). It seems doubtful, however, whether the filing of articles could be considered judicial acts and accordingly it seems unlikely that the principle in these cases would apply to the filing of articles of amendment. In cases where the effective time of day of amendments to articles is important, it is normally determined in the appropriate implementing resolutions, together with the notes made by the individuals actually filing the articles with the office of the Director. See also the discussion in Chapter 2.

Restated articles

Section 180 provides a mechanism for consolidation of all amendments to the articles, so that it is not necessary to review a number of documents to ascertain all the provisions in the articles of a corporation.

No special resolution or other approval of shareholders is required for the directors to file the restated articles. The directors are authorized to file restated articles at any time. They would normally do so when there have been a number of amendments to the articles, and it has become desirable to have all such amendments incorporated into one simple document. In addition, the Director may, where reasonable, direct that restated articles be filed. It is understood that the Director has no specific policy when to direct a restatement of articles and that no such direction has, in fact, been given. Presumably the Director could intervene where having the articles of a corporation in a large number of different parts might cause serious practical problems for shareholders or creditors of the corporation.

Duplicate restated articles in the prescribed form (Form 7) are sent to the Director. The restated articles, signed by a director or authorized officer, must set out the original articles of incorporation as well as the restated articles continuing all amendments (other than deleted provisions, which are omitted). All provisions normally found in the articles must be included in the restated articles, that is, registered office, directors, powers if any, and so on. The information should be current as at the date of the restated articles.

Upon receipt of restated articles, the Director issues a restated certificate of incorporation following the procedures set out in s. 262, see Chapter 17. The effective date of the restated articles is the filing date shown thereon, and from that date the restated articles supersede the original articles of incorporation and all amendments thereto to date.

Amalgamations

General

The general understanding of the term "amalgamation" among the business community, and in early corporate law, was a combination of interests of two or more corporations. This could include the sale of assets from one corporation to another, or from two or more corporations to a new corporation formed for that purpose. It could also include share acquisitions, again either of one corporation by another, or by two or more corporations by a new corporation.

Apart from statute, the term "amalgamation" is loosely applied to various forms of mergers of two or more corporations. It would appear from the older cases that an amalgamation always involved in substance the acquisition by one corporation of the assets, or a substantial part of the assets, of another corporation, under transactions of varying types, one result of which is that shares or securities of the first corporation come into the hands of shareholders of the second corporation. Thus, in *Seaboard Life Insurance Co. v. British Columbia AG* (1986), 5 B.C.L.R. (2d) 375, where Corporation A acquired the shares of Corporation B, shareholders of Corporation B becoming shareholders of Corporation A or selling their shares to Corporation A in accordance with the terms of the agreement, which also provided for the transfer of all the business and assets of the Corporaton B to Corporation A, the question arose as to whether the transfers of land owned by Corporation B to Corporation A required the payment of fees under the *Land Titles Act* based on value or a nominal fee for a change of name. It was held that the transaction between the two corporations was properly characterized as an amalgamation within the meaning of the *Land Titles Act* and nominal fees only were payable. In *Neonex International Ltd. v. Kolasa*, [1978] 2 W.W.R. 593 (B.C.), it was held that once a certificate of amalgamation had been issued, no complaints could be raised to prevent the amalgamation from proceeding as there was no way an amalgamation could be undone (*sed quaere*). However, if the corporation is not carrying on active business it has been held that an amalgamation can be annulled: *MSL Properties Ltd. v. Canada Place Inc.* (1987), 39 B.L.R. 40 (Man.). See the heading Effect of Amalgamation, *supra*.

It will be noted that a merger under Delaware law results in the creation of a new corporation with the result that there is a deemed acquisition of control of the business carried on by a Canadian subsidiary of one of the merging parties, with the result that the transaction is, or may be, reviewable under the *Investment Canada Act*: *Dow Jones & Co. v. Canada (Attorney-General)*, (1981) 122 D.L.R. (3d) 731 (F.C.A.).

However, the amalgamations now dealt with are those made pursuant to ss. 181-186 of the Act. These are sometimes referred to as "statutory amalgamations". Such amalgamations have been a feature of provincial corporate law for many years, the first being Quebec in 1941. Such a procedure was also provided for in the former federal Act as part of the 1965 amendments thereto.

Under these statutes, an amalgamation could be effected by following the prescribed statutory procedure where two or more corporations incorporated under the same governing legislation could enter into a joint agreement prescribing the terms and conditions of amalgamation and the method of bringing it into effect. This agreement would then be submitted to separate meetings of the shareholders of each corporation. Upon approval by the prescribed vote of the shareholders of each corporation, a joint application would be made for letters patent, or supplementary letters patent, confirming the agreement. Upon the issuance of such letters patent, the corporations became amalgamated and formed one corporation.

As at the date hereof, all jurisdictions in Canada, including the two territories, have enacted legislation providing for amalgamations between corporations governed by the laws of such jurisdiction. Under the laws of all of these jurisdictions, as it now reads, the amalgamated corporation is a continuation of and one and the same corporation as each and all of the amalgamating corporations.

Procedure

There are three basic procedural steps which generally must occur to complete an amalgamation. There must be an amalgamation agreement (s. 182), usually followed by shareholder approval (s. 183), and finally, filing of articles of amalgamation (s. 185).

The amalgamation agreement must generally follow the prescribed form (Form 47) and must set out the provisions that are required to be included in articles of incorporation under s. 6 of the Act, the name and address of each proposed director of the amalgamated corporation, the manner in which the shares of such amalgamating corporation are to be converted into shares or other securities of the amalgamated corporation, or if they are not to be so converted, the amount of money or securities of any body corporate that the holders of such shares are to receive in addition to or instead of securities of the amalgamated corporation, the manner of payment of money in respect of the issue of fractional shares, whether the by-laws of the amalgamated corporation are to be those of one of the amalgamating corporations and, if not, a copy of the proposed by-laws and details of any arrangements necessary to perfect the amalgamation and to provide for the subsequent management and operation of the amalgamated corporation (s. 182(1)). If shares of one of the amalgamating corporations are held by or on behalf of another of the amalgamating corporations the amalgamation agreement must provide for the cancellation thereof upon the amalgamation, without any repayment of capital. Such shares may not be converted into shares of the amalgamated corporation (s. 182(2)).

The amalgamation agreement is then submitted by the directors of each amalgamating corporation to meetings of the shareholders of such corporations for approval (s. 183(1)). For comment on the contents of the material to be sent to shareholders, see *Re Universal Explorations Ltd and Petrol Oil & Gas Co.* (1982), 17 B.L.R. 135 (Alta. C.A.).

The proposed amalgamation must be approved by a special resolution of the shareholders of each amalgamating corporation. Each share of the amalgamating corporations carries by statute the right to vote on such a resolution, whether or not it is otherwise entitled to vote.

As well, a proposal to amalgamate is, in some circumstances, subject to a separate vote of each class, and in some cases, series of the shares of each amalgamating corporation. These provisions, requiring approval by a special resolution of each relevant class or series, are operative in favour of the holders of a particular class or series of shares of an amalgamating corporation where the amalgamation agreement contains a provision which, if contained in a proposed amendment to the articles, would entitle such holders to a separate vote under s. 176. See the discussion under "Class votes" in this chapter.

As well as a vote, *seriatim* of each class or series entitled to vote, there must also be a combined vote of all shares of all classes. That is, a particular proposed amalgamation may require many separate votes; failure to obtain a special resolution in any vote will mean the amalgamation has not been adopted.

An amalgamation agreement is considered adopted when all relevant holders of shares of each amalgamating corporation have passed a special resolution approving it. However, the agreement may (but need not) provide that the amalgamation may be terminated by the directors of an amalgamating corporation, notwithstanding shareholder approval. Such a clause in an agreement provides protection against unanticipated negative consequences of an amalgamation. For example, an amalgamation may receive the necessary shareholder approvals but a large number of shareholders may exercise their dissent rights such that the amalgamated corporation would be financially impaired if the amalgamation proceeded.

Once the amalgamation has been adopted by shareholders, assuming the directors do not elect to terminate the proceedings, two executed copies of articles of amalgamation in the prescribed Form 9 are sent to the Director, together with a notice of registered office of the amalgamated corporation and a notice of directors. The executed articles must have attached thereto the statutory declaration of an officer or director of each amalgamating corporation. Such declaration must establish to the satisfaction of the Director that certain financial solvency tests are met and creditors are protected. More specifically, the declaration must show that each amalgamating corporation and the amalgamated corporation will be able to meet its debts as they become due, and that the realizable value of the assets of the amalgamated corporation is at least equal to the aggregate of the liabilities and stated capital of all classes. This test is the same as the test for the payment of dividends (s. 42). The declaration must also show either that no creditor will be prejudiced by the amalgamation, or, the alternative, that all known creditors have been given adequate notice and none has made an objection on substantive grounds (s. 185(2)).

Depending on the nature of the amalgamation and the financial status of the amalgamating corporations, it may be easy to satisfy the Director that no creditors would be prejudiced by the amalgamation (s. 185(2)(b)(i)) by a simple statement to that effect.

On the other hand, there may be issues concerning the security and/or credit risk to one or more creditors. In such case, it will be necessary to give all creditors notice of the amalgamation.

Creditors are deemed to have been given adequate notice if a notice in writing has been sent to each creditor with a claim in excess of $1,000, and a notice is published once in a newspaper published or distributed in the place where the corporation has its registered office and reasonable notice is given in each province where the corporation carries on business. The notice must specify that the corporation intends to amalgamate, give the names of the other amalgamating corporations, and state that a creditor may object to the amalgamation within 30 days from the date of the notice (s. 185(3)).

Upon the receipt of the foregoing material, the Director is to issue a certificate of amalgamation following the procedure set out in s. 262.

It has been established that the Director has the discretion to refuse to issue a certificate but only within the limits of the matters set out in subss. 185(2) and (3): *Re Canada Business Corporations Act* (1991), 3 O.R. (3d) 336 (Ont. C.A.). That is, the Director's powers are limited to ensuring compliance by the amalgamating corporations with the solvency requirements and ensuring the protection of creditors' rights. In particular, the Director's powers do not extend to the protection of shareholders. Shareholders have available to them the dissent right (see discussion under "Right to dissent" in this chapter) and, in extreme cases, the oppression remedy (see *infra* and Chapter 16 under the heading "Statutory remedies").

Short-form amalgamations

Section 185 provides for a simplified procedure which can be used in the case of a vertical or horizontal short-form amalgamation.

A vertical short-form amalgamation (s. 184(1)) can occur upon the amalgamation of a holding corporation and one or more of its wholly owned subsidiary corporations. A holding corporation is one that controls another corporation, the subsidiary (s. 2(4)). In order to complete a vertical short-form amalgamation the holding corporation must own all the shares of the subsidiary. All corporations that are parties to the amalagamation must be incorporated under the federal Act.

Procedurally, a vertical short-form amalgamation is simpler than a normal amalgamation. No amalgamation agreement is required and approval need only be given by resolution of the directors of each amalgamating corporation. These resolutions must provide that the shares of any amalgamating subsidiary are cancelled, that the articles of amalgamation are the same as the articles of incorporation of the holding corporation, and that no securities be issued in connection with the amalgamation.

A horizontal short-form amalgamation is similar, except that it must occur between two or more wholly owned subsidiaries of the same holding body corporate. (Note that it is necessary only that the subsidiaries be incorporated under the federal Act.) This form of amalgamation also does not require shareholder approval, but must be approved by resolution of the directors of each amalgamating corporation. No amalgamation agreement is required. The directors' authorizing resolution must provide that the shares of all but one of the amalgamating subsidiaries are cancelled without payment, the articles of amalgamation must be the same as the articles of the corporation whose shares survive and that the stated capital of the corporation whose shares are cancelled is added to the stated capital of the shares of the corporation whose shares survive. Where there is more than one class of shares that survive, the Act does not provide any rules allocating stated capital between the classes.

Although the Act does not require an amalgamation agreement for a short-form amalgamation, it is the usual practice to set out in the authorizing resolutions those matters which would otherwise be dealt with in an amalgamation agreement or if desired an amalgamation agreement can be entered into.

Effect of amalgamation

Section 190(1) of the Act provides that a holder of shares may dissent if a corporation resolves to amalgamate with another corporation except in the case of a vertical or horizontal short-form amalgamation. However, the question arises as to whether a holder of shares in a squeeze-out amalgamation is limited to his right to dissent or can he bring an application pursuant to s. 241 of the Act which provides that a complainant, which includes a present or past registered or beneficial owner of a security of a corporation, may apply to the court and if the court is satisfied that any act of the corporation is oppressive or unfairly prejudicial to or unfairly disregards the interests of any security holder the court may make an order to rectify the matters complained of. The court is given power in subs. (3) to make an order restraining the conduct complained of or other relief including an order compensating an aggrieved person. Thus, in *Carlton Realty Co. v. Maple Leaf Mills Ltd.* (1978), 22 O.R. (2d) 198 and *Alexander v. Westeel Roscoe Ltd.* (1978), 22 O.R. (2d) 211 a squeeze-out amalgamation was involved whereby minority shareholders were to be given non-voting preference shares in the amalgamated corporation which proposed to redeem the same forthwith following the amalgamation. The first case involved a corporation incorporated under the laws of Ontario and it was held that the applicant shareholders had a property right in their shares which could not be taken without their consent to a sale and where a sufficient case to cast doubt on the corporation's right to proceed in the manner proposed, an interlocutory injunction would issue. The second case was under the predecessor Act of the present federal Act and the same conclusion was reached. It will be observed that an action to prevent the amalgamation must be made prior to the amalgamation, being prior to articles of amalgamation being issued. See *Neonex International Ltd. v. Kolasa*, [1978] 2 W.W.R. 593 (B.C.) where there was an application to fix a fair value of shares held by dissenting shareholders. It was pointed out that the amalgamation was an accomplished fact and that no application had been made for relief under the predecessor to s. 241. See also

Re Yokohama Enterprises Inc. and Mascot Entertainment Inc. (1984), 56 B.C.L.R. 132.

In the case of a take-over bid under s. 194 and following, s. 206 gives a specific right to acquire the minority shares when the offer is accepted by not less than 90 per cent of the shares in question. However, in an amalgamation of the type under discussion, since no such specific right is given, it is submitted that the point would probably be decided in favour of the shareholder opposing the amalgamation. See also *Burdon v. Zeller's Ltd.* (1981), 16 B.L.R. 59 (Que.).

It is suggested that two recent cases indicate that the remedy of an injunction against a proposed statutory amalgamation squeeze out would be available. In the case of *Brant Investments Ltd. v. Keeprite Inc.* (1991), 3 O.R. (3d) 289 (Ont. C.A.) it was held that a shareholder could apply both for an oppression remedy under what is now s. 241 as well as bringing an action for the fair value of his shares pursuant to what is now s. 190 as a dissenting shareholder. It was held that in the facts of the case there was no oppression and the fair value of the shares was fixed by the court. A court has power under s. 241(3) to restrain the conduct complained of and in *Palmer v. Carling O'Keefe Breweries of Canada Ltd.* (1989), 41 B.L.R. 128 (Ont. Div. Ct.) the court suggested that an order to set aside the amalgamation was available but it was not prepared to make such an order as there were many changes in the 18 months which had elapsed since the amalgamation and there would be most unfortunate tax consequences. While in theory an amalgamation might be able to be "undone" the issue of securities or debt or the acquisition of assets might well make this impossible from a practical point of view and there is some question whether an amalgamation once completed can be undone, *c.f. Ruskin v. Canada All-News Radio Ltd.* (1979), 7 B.L.R. 142 (Ont. H.C.). However, if an application for injunction is brought immediately after the notice of the proposed meeting is received, it would appear that the Court can grant an injunction against the proposed amalgamation and that the existence of the valuation remedy would not debar the applicant. It may be, however, that in a case where there were good business reasons for the statutory amalgamation squeeze out a Court would be reluctant to interfere with the business judgment of the directors by prohibiting the proposed amalgamation, and might grant some other form of relief contemplated by s. 241(3): see *General Accident Assurance Co. of Canada v. Lornex Mining Corp.* (1988), 40 B.L.R. 299 (Ont. H.C.). On the other hand it is doubtful in the ordinary case that there can be good business reasons which would justify confiscation of the interests of the minority shareholders. The mere saving of expense would not appear to be sufficient.

While the Securities Acts of various provinces (or policies issued thereunder) may permit squeeze-out amalgamations, it is suggested that this is not relevant in interpreting the rights of a shareholder under the federal Act. However, see *General Accident Assurance Co. of Canada v. Lornex Mining Corp.* (1988), 40 B.L.R. 299 (Ont.), where an application for injunction against a corporate reorganization was refused since it was held, on the basis of the material before the court, that the applicant had failed to establish that the proposed organization was oppressive, unfairly prejudicial or unfairly disregarded the rights of the minority shareholders. The court also pointed out the existence of the dissent remedy. Although the matter is by no means clear, it is suggested that this case may have been incorrectly decided. See also *Re Ripley International Ltd.* (1977), 1 B.L.R. 269 (Ont.).

Section 181 provides that the amalgamating corporations continue as one corporation. This provision has two important substantive implications. First, the corporations in question must be incorporated under or otherwise subject to the Act. Second, they continue as one. These topics are explored below.

An amalgamation under the federal Act can only occur between corporations subject to the Act (but see the discussion under "Arrangements", in this chapter). Thus, if it is desired to amalgamate two or more corporations using the procedure in the Act, it is first necessary that all amalgamating corporations be subject to the Act. If any such corporations are governed by different legislation, it may be possible to continue such corporations under the Act to facilitate the amalgamation. See the discussion under "Continuance" in this chapter.

Upon an amalgamation, the amalgamating corporations "continue" as one (s. 181). Section 186 governs some of the legal consequences of an amalgamation. On the date of the amalgamation certificate, the amalgamating corporations are amalgamated and continue as one, with all of the property of each amalgamated corporation becoming the property of the amalgamated corporation. All liabilities, claims, causes of action and legal proceedings by or against any amalgamating corporation (whether civil, criminal or administrative) may be continued against or by the amalgamated corporation. Convictions, rulings, orders and judgments made by or against any amalgamating corporation continue in force by or against the amalgamated corporation (s. 186(a)-(f)). Section 186(g) states that the articles and certificate of amalgamation are deemed to be the articles and certificate of incorporation, respectively. This provision is not substantive — it does not mean that an amalgamation is the legal equivalent of incorporation. Rather, the provision is procedural, and is essentially the equivalent of the restatement provisions of s. 180. As such it obviates the need, after amalgamation, to refer back to the articles of the amalgamating corporations to obtain the information usually found in the articles.

The jurisprudence makes it clear that the amalgamated corporation is one and the same entity as all the amalgamated corporations. In the case of *R. v. Black and Decker Manufacturing Co. Limited*, [1975] 1 S.C.R. 411 (S.C.C.), the Supreme Court of Canada determined that the amalgamation of corporations under the former Act did not involve the "death by suicide or the mysterious disappearance" of the amalgamating corporations. Instead, the relevant statutory scheme provided that each amalgamated corporation was "continued" within the amalgamated corporation, finding "security, strength and . . . survival in that union". Accordingly a prosecution against the amalgamated corporation for an offence by one of the amalgamating corporations could be brought. The *R. v. Black and Decker* case has been followed throughout Canada and it is beyond doubt that the same principles apply to amalgamations under the Act. For example, in *Re Canada Business Corporations Act* (1991), 3 O.R. (3d) 336, the

Ontario Court of Appeal assumed, without discussion, that upon an amalgamation under the Act the amalgamating corporations continued as one corporation. Similarly, amalgamations under the laws of Ontario and British Columbia, which have similar provisions, have been interpreted in the same manner by the courts. See *Witco Chemical Co. v. Oakville (Town)*, [1975] 1 S.C.R. 273; *Re Koch Transport Ltd. and Class Freight Lines Ltd.* (1982), 135 D.L.R. (3d) 695 (Ont.); *R. v. Mercantile Distributing Ltd.* (1975), 6 W.W.R. 187 (B.C. S.C.). See also Graham Turner "Amalgamations and Continuations", 36 Canadian Tax Journal, 1479 for a discussion of these issues, and *Loeb Inc. v. Cooper* (1991), 5 O.R. (3d) 259 (Ont. Gen. Div.); and *Re Manco Home Systems Ltd.* (1990), 78 C.B.R. (N.S.) 109 (B.C. C.A.).

Thus, the legal position of an amalgamation under the Act, with the continued existence of each amalgamating corporation, is somewhat different from the position that occurs under the laws of some foreign jurisdictions where a "merger" results in the cessation of one or more merging corporations, resulting in the creation of a new entity. For Canadian income tax purposes also, a new corporation is created upon an amalgamation (s. 87 of the *Income Tax Act* (Canada)).

There are few substantive issues that turn on whether there is, or is not, a new corporation created upon an amalgamation since, as noted, s. 186 contains detailed rules that flow through the assets, rights, liabilities and responsibilities of the amalgamating corporations to the amalgamated corporation. Some issues are not completely dealt with, such as the relative position of secured creditors of amalgamating corporations *vis-à-vis* property acquired post-amalgamation by the amalgamated corporation. Such matters are usually dealt with by having a special provision in the appropriate contract dealing with the effects of an amalgamation. It is usual to provide that the consent of the contracting counterparty must be obtained upon an amalgamation. Note in s. 179(e) of the Ontario Act that the amalgamated corporation is deemed to be the litigant in any civil action involving an amalgamating corporation.

Continuance

Canada has 13 different legal jurisdictions which allow for the formation of corporations. These are the federal, the ten provincial and the two territorial jurisdictions. Though many of the basic legal doctrines governing corporations are common to all, there are subtle, but important, differences between the laws of the different jurisdictions. There may be circumstances in which it is desirable for a corporation, incorporated under the laws of one Canadian jurisdiction, to seek to take advantage of the laws of another Canadian jurisdiction. This process is accomplished by the continuance provisions of the relevant Act. All jurisdictions provide for this, with the exception of Quebec.

In fact, the continuance provisions of the federal Act are not limited to continuances between corporations governed by the laws of a Canadian jurisdiction. It is possible to continue any corporation, wherever incorporated, under the Act, provided the incorporating jurisdiction has provisions which allow such continuance. It is also possible, subject to obtaining the consent of the Director, to continue a corporation subject to the Act in any jurisdiction, including jurisdictions outside Canada.

Section 187 of the Act deals with imports, that is, the transfer of a corporation incorporated under the laws of another jurisdiction to be a corporation governed by the Act. The process consists of essentially two steps. The corporation's own jurisdiction must have a procedure allowing it to depart from that jurisdiction or be exported. The procedures of the Act to import the corporation and make it subject to the Act are then followed.

Section 188 of the Act deals with exports, which is the transfer of a corporation subject to the Act to another jurisdiction, so that the corporation becomes subject only to the laws of that other jurisdiction and no longer subject to the Act. The Director has the power to prevent an export if the proposed continuance would adversely affect creditors or shareholders.

At one time there was a question whether continuances gave rise to a fundamental constitutional problem. The issue was whether the federal government could delegate to a province (or any other jurisdiction) power over a corporation incorporated under federal law. The requirements of mutual reciprocity set out in the Act under which the exporting jurisdiction must discontinue, or give up its jurisdiction, and that the importing jurisdiction must have specific provisions in its corporate legislation accepting jurisdiction, seem to have resolved the issue.

The legal principle of a continuance is that a corporation can change the law by which it is governed, while retaining its existence and identity. That is, upon a continuance, there is not a reincorporation or creation of a new entity. Instead, the corporation, which was incorporated under the laws of its original jurisdiction, after continuation is in effect incorporated under, and governed by and subject to the rules in the Act, and not the rules of its original jurisdiction of formation.

Import

Any corporation (including one incorporated outside Canada) may apply for continuance under the Act under s. 187, provided that the corporation's own jurisdiction authorizes such continuance. Federal corporations not incorporated under the Act, but incorporated under the federal legislation or a special Act of Parliament, cannot be continued under s. 187, but instead use the provisions of s. 268 (which authorizes a proceeding under s. 187) and is discussed below in Chapter 17.

If a corporation desires to be continued under the Act, it must first follow the procedure to export itself from its former jurisdiction. For example, many of the provincial corporate statutes have an export procedure similar to that found in the Act. Once this is done, the corporation applies for articles of continuance in prescribed form (Form 11). The filing procedure is typical of such procedures under the Act. That is, duplicate articles of continuation duly executed by a director or officer are filed, together with the applicable fees, with notices of registered office and directors (Forms 3 and 6). Upon receipt of these documents, the Director follows the procedure set out in s. 262, discussed above under the heading "Procedure for amendments to articles". Upon receipt of the duly filed articles of continuance, the Director must issue articles of continuance. It appears that the Director has no discretion to refuse a corporation from continuing under the Act, provided that the corporation's own jurisdiction has duly consented to the continuance. Section 187(6) requires the Director to send a copy of the certificate of continuance of a corporation continued under the Act to the appropriate authorities of the jurisdiction from whence the corporation came.

The form of the articles of continuance is similar to that of articles of incorporation. The information required to be set forth in the articles of incorporation must be in the articles of continuance (see Chapter 2, "Formation of New Corporations"). Although a corporation may retain its former attributes upon continuance (subject to the amendments required to conform with the Act), it does not have to do so. Section 187(2) provides the articles of continuance may affect any amendment to the articles or other incorporating documents that could have been affected by articles of amendment under the Act.

Certain changes to the charter of a corporation must, however, be made upon continuance under the Act. For example, s. 24(1) of the Act prohibits par value shares. Section 24(2) provides rules that apply to a corporation which has par value shares before being continued under the Act. In such case, upon a continuation under the Act, the par value shares are deemed to be shares without par value. It is, understood that the Director has a policy that requires par value shares to be changed into no par value shares in the articles of continuance before the articles are accepted.

As well, the Act does not allow partly paid shares (s. 25(3)). Shares must be fully paid and non-assessable (s. 25(2)). It appears, however, that by virtue of s. 187(8) partly paid shares issued before continuance under the Act may still exist and shareholders may still be subject to a call thereon, after continuance. In addition, subss. 187(9) and (10) provide that share certificates in bearer form may be issued if such right of conversion existed prior to the continuation of the corporation and that share warrants as defined in the *Canada Corporations Act*, namely, warrants stating that the bearer is entitled to the share or shares therein specified and dividends being provided for by coupons or otherwise for the share or shares included in the warrant constitute a share for the purposes of subss. 187(8) and (9).

It is customary, and may well be necessary, to replace the by-laws for a corporation made subject to the Act by new by-laws conforming to the provisions of the Act.

Finally, it should be noted that a corporation is generally entitled to keep its former name after continuance, even if such name would otherwise contravene the provisions of s. 12. It is, however, noteworthy that the Director's policy on allowable corporate names is significantly stricter than the policy in most other jurisdictions, and so he may require a name change upon continuance if the existing name is confusingly similar to that of an existing corporation.

Export

Section 188 allows a corporation to be issued a certificate of discontinuance and to be continued under the laws of another jurisdiction. The formalities to be followed in making an application for discontinuance are relatively simple in form. However, since discontinuance involves a departure of a corporation from the Act and the loss by the shareholders of their rights given by the Act, there are three important procedural safeguards imposed on an exporting corporation. First, its shareholders must authorize the discontinuance by a special resolution. Second, shareholders may dissent. Third, in any event, the Director has the right to refuse to allow the export.

Before authorizing the discontinuance process, the directors of the corporation would ensure that the proposed new jurisdiction has suitable laws. In particular, s. 188(10) prohibits continuance to a new jurisdiction unless the laws of that jurisdiction provide that (a) the property of the corporation continues to be its property; (b) the obligations of the corporation continue; (c) any existing cause of action, claim or liability to prosecution is unaffected; (d) a civil, criminal or administrative claim or proceeding pending by or against the corporation may be continued by or against the corporation; (e) a conviction against, or ruling, order or judgment provided in favour of or against the corporation may be enforced by or against the corporation.

As well, there are certain regulatory restrictions on the discontinuance. For example, the Minister of Finance must consent to the continuance of any corporation to which the federal *Investment Companies Act* applies (s. 188(2)).

More generally, the Director has the power to refuse to allow the continuance unless it will not adversely affect creditors or shareholders. It appears that the Director has very broad powers in this regard: *Re Canada Business Corporations Act, supra.*

The Director has published a policy statement relating to the export of corporations. The Director will allow export to jurisdictions that have embodied in their legislation rights and obligations of shareholders and creditors similar to those in the Act. In particular, the Director will automatically allow export to eight of the Canadian common law jurisdictions that allow continuance. In the case of all other jurisdictions, the Director's guidelines include the requirement either that all the shareholders are in favour of the proposal or alternatively that at least 80 per cent of the votes cast are in favour (including 80 per cent of the minority, if any) and the laws of the accepting jurisdiction, or the articles of the corporation, contain an oppression remedy, a derivative action remedy, and dissent and appraisal rights, similar to those contained in the Act. It is understood that this policy statement is under review. The authority to prescribe a percentage of votes greater than that provided in the Act may be doubtful.

If the importing jurisdiction is suitable, under the criteria outlined above, the directors of the corporation would authorize the discontinuance procedure to commence. A notice of meeting, complying with the rules of s. 135 (See

Chapter 10 "Shareholders' Meetings") must be sent to all shareholders. As usual with proposed fundamental changes, the notice must specify that a dissenting shareholder is entitled to the fair value of his shares. However, failure to make that statement does not invalidate a discontinuance (s. 188(3)).

All shares, whether or not they are otherwise entitled to vote, are entitled to vote (s. 188(4)). Approval of a continuance must be by special resolution, but there is not a separate class vote. The resolution may authorize the directors of the corporation to abandon the application for continuance without further action of the shareholders (s. 188(6)). Presumably such a provision would be included if there was a concern that excessive dissents would impose an undue financial burden on the corporation.

Assuming that all of the foregoing are complied with, and upon payment of the required fees, the corporation would apply to the Director for a letter of satisfaction. Such a letter is then produced to the relevant authorities of the importing jurisdiction, together with any material required by such authorities. Upon receipt by the Director of a notice from the authorities of the new jurisdiction that the corporation has been continued under its laws, the Director will file (see s. 262) and issue a certificate of discontinuance. The certificate of discontinuance would normally be dated the day that the corporation was continued in its new jurisdiction.

Effect of continuance

It seems clear that, upon a continuance, the existence of the original corporation is not terminated and the corporation retains and maintains its identity. The only change is in the governing law. Although there are no cases directly on point, an examination of the Act makes that result obvious. Both ss. 187(7) and 188(10) repeat the operative word "continues". In *R. v. Black and Decker, supra*, the Supreme Court of Canada stated that, upon an amalgamation, no new corporation was created and made it clear that use of the word "continued" was important in the result. Accordingly, a continuance in another jurisdiction must inevitably result in the continued existence of the same corporation.

Borrowing powers

Section 189 is rather anomalous. Sections 189(1) and (2) deal with the borrowing powers of a corporation. Such powers have little connection with the balance of Part XV of the Act. On the other hand, subss. 189(3)-(9) deal with extraordinary sales, leases or exchanges of property for which the approval of shareholders by special resolution is required, since such transactions represent a fundamental change in the business of a corporation.

Section 189(1) provides that, unless the articles, by-laws or a unanimous shareholder agreement provide to the contrary, a corporation has broad powers to borrow or give security upon the corporation's property. It might be argued that s. 189(1) is unnecessary since, by virtue of s. 15(1) of the Act, a corporation has all the capacity, rights and powers of a natural person. In practice, however, financial institutions and their counsel will often require specific borrowing by-laws and other enabling proceedings to be taken to authorize a borrowing. Such actions are taken pursuant to the specific authority conferred by s. 189(1) of the Act. It is normal practice to include a specific borrowing power in the articles of incorporation.

More particularly, s. 189(1) provides that the directors may, without authorization of the shareholders, borrow money and issue, reissue, sell or pledge debt obligations of the corporation. As well, the corporation may, subject to the prohibitions of s. 44 (relating to financial assistance to shareholders, officers, directors or other employees, or to any person in connection with the purchase of shares of the corporation), guarantee the performance of an obligation of any person. In addition, the directors may mortgage or otherwise charge or give security generally over any property of the corporation (including subsequently acquired property) to secure any obligation of the corporation.

Sale of assets

Section 189(2) specifically authorizes the delegation of the borrowing powers to a single director or officer, or a committee of directors, provided that such delegation does not contravene the articles, by-laws or a unanimous shareholder agreement. This delegation may occur, notwithstanding the prohibitions on the delegation of powers set out in ss. 115(3) and 121(a) (see Chapter 8).

Section 189(3) describes certain transactions which should clearly be regarded as constituting fundamental changes to the business of a corporation, namely the sale, lease or exchange of all or substantially all of the property of a corporation, except in the ordinary course of business.

Such a transaction must be approved by shareholders. Section 189(4) describes the procedure for giving notice of a meeting to shareholders. Such notice must comply with s. 135 and must also contain a copy of or a summary of the proposed agreement of sale, lease exchange and the usual notice regarding the right to dissent (but failure to give this last notice will not invalidate the transaction). All shares, whether or not otherwise entitled to vote, are entitled to vote on the transaction (s. 189(6)), but there would not normally be a separate class (or series) vote unless a particular class or series was affected by the transactions in a manner different from other shares (s. 189(7)). At the shareholders' meeting, the shareholders may by special resolution approve the transactions or authorize the directors to fix the terms and conditions of the transactions (s. 189(5)). The shareholders may also authorize the directors to terminate the transactions before implementation (s. 189(9)).

The important question is, of course, what constitutes "all or substantially all" and there is some jurisprudence on the issue. The Canadian tax authorities apparently take the position that "all or substantially all" in the federal *Income Tax Act* means at least 90 per cent.

The issue does not, however, appear susceptible to such precise mathematical calculation: *Wood v. MNR* (1987), 87 D.T.C. 312 (T.C.C.). A better view would appear to be that both the quality as well as the quantity of the property in question must be examined: *Wardean Drilling Co. v. MNR* (1974), 74 D.T.C.

6164 (F.C.T.D.); affd 78 D.T.C. 6202 (F.C.A.). Since the purpose of the provision is to protect the shareholders from a destruction of the corporation's business, the transaction must be tantamount to the winding-up of the corporation's business in order to require a special resolution: *Good v. Lackawanna Leather Co.* (1967), 233 A. (2d) 201, quoted with approval in *85956 Holdings Ltd. v. Fayerman Brothers Ltd.*, [1986] 2 W.W.R. 754 (Sask. C.A.). It seems that the sale of as little as one third of the company's assets might trigger the operation of s. 189(3): *85956 Holdings, supra*; *Campbell v. Vose* (1975), 515 F. 2nd 256. Such extreme cases occur when the balance of the assets are monetary including cash, promissory notes or an investment portfolio. On the other hand, where a corporation carries on one or more businesses, the sale of one such business would not cause the provision to become operative, provided the corporation retains business assets: *Olympia and York Enterprises Ltd. v. Hiram Walker Resources Ltd.* (1986), 59 O.R. (2d) 254; *Martin v. F.B. Bourgault Industries Air Seeder Division Ltd.* (1987), 45 D.L.R. (4th) 296 (Sask.); *Re Vanalta Resources Limited* (unreported) (1976), (B.C. S.C.).

Interesting theoretical questions can arise where a corporation is engaged in a number of businesses and has a number of plants in each type of business. It would appear, although there is no authority in point, that such a corporation could sell off various divisions as a whole or plants of a particular division without being subject to the provision in question so long as a substantial business remains. At some point, however, it is apparent that the courts would intercede and thus if there was a series of debentures which became payable on the disposal of all or substantially all of the assets of the corporation, such debentures would be held to fall due somewhere in a process of disposal of the kind indicated. For example, if a corporation sells in ten separate transactions over a period of years an aggregate of 95 per cent of the original assets, the court might well say that the debentures had fallen due, but if there was still a substantial business in relation to the outstanding debentures, it probably would not.

Right to dissent

Section 190 of the Act gives to shareholders who disagree with a particular fundamental change the right to dissent from such change. The corporation must then purchase the shares of such dissenting shareholder and pay to such shareholder the fair value of such shares.

As noted throughout this chapter, fundamental changes generally give rise to the dissent right, except that the dissent right is not available to shareholders where a fundamental change occurs by virtue of a reorganization under s. 191. As to whether a shareholder can take advantage of both the dissent right and the oppression remedy under s. 241, see the discussion under Effect of Amalgamation, *supra*.

Subject to the foregoing, the dissent right is available to holders of shares of a particular class in each of the following circumstances: (i) a court permits such dissent in an application for approval of an arrangement (see discussion of s. 192 below under the heading "Arrangements"); (ii) the corporation resolves to amend its articles to add, change or remove any provisions restricting or constraining the issue, transfer or ownership of shares of that class; (iii) the corporation proposes to amend its articles to add, change or remove any restriction on the business that the corporation may carry on; (iv) an amalgamation is proposed (except a short-form amalgamation under s. 184); (v) it is proposed to continue the corporation out of the Act; (vi) a transaction described in s. 189(3) (extraordinary sale, lease or exchange) is approved (s. 190(1)).

In addition, the holder of shares of a class (or series) entitled to a separate class (or series) vote by virtue of s. 176 may dissent from an action described in that section (s. 190(2)).

It should be noted that s. 190(4) prevents any partial dissents. A dissenting shareholder may only dissent with respect to all the shares of a particular class held by him on behalf of any one beneficial owner.

Section 190(3) provides that a dissenting shareholder is entitled to be paid the fair value of the shares determined at the close of business on the day before the resolution in question was adopted. There are two important issues that arise in the interpretation of s. 190(3). The first question is whether the amount awarded to shareholders who exercise their dissent rights should include any benefit or value arising as a result of the fundamental change to which they are dissenting. The second issue is what is the intrinsic fair value of the shares, and how should such value be determined.

If there is an agreement between shareholders providing for the sale of shares in certain circumstances, the provisions of the agreement may override the dissent rights in the Act: *Mica Management Centre Inc. v. Lockett* (1986), 37 B.L.R. 209 (Ont. H.C.).

As to the first point, when there is a fundamental change in the direction of a corporation, the dissenters need not accept it and they are entitled to withdraw from the corporation after being paid a fair value for their interest. It is, however, now well settled that, in withdrawing from the corporation, dissenters are not entitled to receive any advantage from the fundamental change to which they have dissented. This principle is now clearly embedded in Canadian law, and the uncertainty on the point raised by earlier cases has been settled: *Brant Investments Ltd. v. KeepRite Inc.* (1991), 3 O.R. (3d) 289 (Ont. C.A.); *Smeenk v. Dexleigh Corp.* (1990), 74 O.R. (2d) 385; *LoCicero v. B.A.C.M. Industries* (1988), 49 D.L.R. (4th) 159 (S.C.C.); *Fraser Inc. v. Aitken* (1988), 41 B.L.R. 87 (Ont.). The principle holds true whether the transaction is an amalgamation or other combination to use tax losses, or a business combination designed to reduce costs by consolidating operations. For other cases on valuation see *Re VCS Holdings Ltd. and Helliwell*, [1978] 5 W.W.R. 559 (B.C.); *Robertson v. Canadian Canners Ltd.* (1978), 4 B.L.R. 290 (Ont.).

It is also clear that only a registered shareholder can exercise the dissent rights. A notice of dissent filed by a person other than a registered shareholder is a nullity: *Manitoba (Securities Commission) v. Versatile Cornat Corporation* (1979), 7 B.L.R. 38 (Man. Q.B.) (which deals with the *Manitoba Corporations Act* which has a dissent provision similar to that of s. 190 of the Act); *Westmin Resources Ltd. v. Hamilton*, [1991] 3 W.W.R. 716 (B.C. S.C.) deals with s. 190. Whilst having the advantage of certainty, this result seems inappropriate in the context of modern capital markets where significant numbers of shares are registered in the names of depository agencies, brokerage firms or other nominees.

Accordingly, in the case where a share depository, trust corporation, brokerage house or other registered holder of many shares belonging to a number of different beneficial shareholders, serious practical problems arise where some, but not all, such beneficial shareholders wish to exercise their dissent rights. For example, see *Bathurst Norsemines Ltd. (N.P.L.) v. Pitfield MacKay Ross Ltd.* (1984), 52 B.C.L.R. 115.

The somewhat lengthy and procedurally complicated dissent process is commenced when a dissenting shareholder sends a written notice to the corporation objecting to the proposed resolution. This notice may be delivered either at or before the meeting of shareholders at which the resolution in question is to be considered unless the corporation did not give notice to the shareholder of the purpose of the meeting and of his right to dissent (s. 190(5)). It would appear that the shareholder in such a case should give a dissent notice promptly on learning of the action. See *Denischuk v. Bonn Energy Corp.* (1983), 30 Sask. R. 37 (Sask. Q.B.) ; *Jepson v. Canadian Salt Co.*, [1979] 4 W.W.R. 35 (Alta.) (on the questions of time limits, this case may be subject to question); *Re Skye Resources Ltd. and Camskye Holdings Inc.* (1982), 38 O.R. (2d) 253; affd (1983), 40 O.R. (2d) 416 (C.A.); *Fitch v. Churchill Corp.* (1990), 66 D.L.R. (4th) 569 (Alta. C.A.).

Within ten days after the shareholders adopt the resolution, the corporation must send to each shareholder who has filed an objection a notice that the resolution was adopted (s. 190(6)). A particular shareholder who wishes to continue the dissent process must, within 20 days after receipt of such notice, send to the corporation a further written notice containing the name and address of the shareholder, the number and class of shares in respect of which the dissent right is to be exercised and a demand for payment of the fair value of such shares. It should be noted that the time frame of the dissent process is keyed to the receipt by the dissenting shareholder of notice from the corporation that the resolution has been adopted. A shareholder who does not receive notice of such adoption from the corporation may dissent within 20 days after learning that the resolution has been adopted. It is therefore incumbent on the corporation to ensure that the shareholder gets notice that the resolution has been adopted (s. 190(7)).

The process continues with the dissenting shareholder sending, within 30 days after sending a notice under s. 190(7), the certificates representing the shares in respect of which the dissent is made, to the corporation or its transfer agents (s. 190(8)). Failure to send the share certificates with the 30-day period invalidates any dissent rights (s. 190(9)).

Upon receipt of the share certificates, the corporation (or its transfer agent) must endorse thereon a notice that the shareholder is a dissenting shareholder, and forthwith return the share certificate to the dissenting shareholder (s. 190(10)).

When a notice demanding payment under s. 190(7) is sent, the dissenting shareholder sending such notice ceases to have any rights as a shareholder other than the right to be paid the fair value of the shares (s. 190(11)). There are three exceptions to this rule. First, a dissenting shareholder may withdraw the dissent notice at any time before the corporation sends a written offer to pay for the shares under s. 190(12), as described below. Second, if the corporation fails to make a written offer to pay for the shares the dissenting shareholder may withdraw. Finally, if the particular resolution contains a provision which allows the directors to revoke the resolution before it is implemented and such revocation rights are exercised, then the shareholder's dissent rights are nullified. In each such case, the shareholder's rights are reinstated *nunc pro tunc* as of the date when the notice of dissent was filed. Thus, it appears that there is a period during which a dissenting shareholder's rights *vis-à-vis* the corporation are suspended but nothing of practical importance appears to turn on this. It will be noted that the dissenting shareholder is entitled to be paid in cash and need not accept securities: *Canadian Gas & Energy Fund v. Sceptre Resources Ltd.* (1985), 29 B.L.R. 178 (Alta.).

As noted, the corporation must make a written offer to the shareholder to complete the dissent process. Such offer must be made within seven days after the later of the day on which the action approved by the resolution is effective, or the day the corporation received the demand for payment from the dissenting shareholder, as described in s. 190. The written payment offer must contain certain information as described in s. 190(12). The payment offer must contain a written offer to pay for the shares in an amount considered by the directors of the corporation to be the fair value thereof, accompanied by a statement showing how that fair value was determined (s. 190(12)(a)). If, however, the corporation is legally unable to pay for the shares because of the prohibition imposed by s. 190(26), see below, then it may so notify the dissenting shareholder (s. 190(12)(b)). In such case, the dissenter may, at his election, be reinstated as a shareholder of the corporation (s. 190(25)(a)).

All offers for shares of the same class or series must be on the same terms (s. 190(13)). Payment must be made by the corporation within ten days after the offer to pay has been accepted. If, however, the corporation does not receive such acceptance within 30 days the offer lapses (s. 190(14)).

Obviously there may be cases in which the corporation and a dissenting shareholder, or group of shareholders, disagree on the fair value of shares held by dissenters. Such disputes must ultimately be settled by a court. Subsections (15) to (23) of s. 190 of the Act provide a procedural code which must be followed by dissenting shareholders, the corporation and the court in resolving such disputes.

Section 190(15) provides that if a corporation decides not to make an offer to pay under s. 190(12), or alternatively, if such offer is made but the dissenting shareholders do not accept such offer, then the corporation may apply to a court to fix the fair value of the shares.

Section 190(17) specifies that the particular court will be a provincial court. The particular province will be where the corporation has its registered office, but may also be where a dissenting shareholder resides if the corporation carries on business in that province. It would normally be the case that where the corporation brings the court application it would choose the province of its registered office, whereas a dissenting shareholder might well choose the province where he resides. However, the Act does not require that this result occur.

The corporation's application to court must be made within 50 days after the shareholder resolution in question becomes effective, but the court may grant an extension of time (s. 190(5)). If the corporation fails to apply to court within the required time, a dissenting shareholder may make an application to court within a further period of 20 days after the corporation's time limit expires. The court may extend the time within which a dissenting shareholder must make an application (s. 190(16)).

The Act specifically provides that a dissenting shareholder is not required to give security for costs in a dissent application (s. 190(19)). This helps to ensure that a minority shareholder is not forced to accept an unfair price for his shares where he does not have the ability to enforce his rights.

Section 190(19) of the Act prevents a multiplicity of actions, and ensures that all dissenting shareholders receive the same price for their shares. Section 190(19)(a) provides that all dissenting shareholders whose shares have not been purchased by the corporation must be joined as parties to the action and are bound by the decision of the court. Section 190(19)(b) imposes an obligation on the corporation to notify each affected dissenter of the date and place of the court application, the consequences to a dissenting shareholder of the application, and that such shareholder has the right to appear and be heard, either in person or through counsel.

Section 190(20) gives the court broad powers to add any other person as a party to the action, and to fix the fair value of the shares for all shareholders. Note that the duty to fix the fair value rests in the court; neither party has an onus of proof: *Ultramar Canada Inc. v. Montreal Pipe Line Ltd.* (1990) 74 O.R. (2d) 136, additional reasons at (1990), 75 O.R. (2d) 498.

Section 190(21) gives the court discretion to appoint its own appraisers to assist in fixing fair value. A valuator may in some circumstances in Ontario be granted access to corporate records or the right to examine persons (see: *Xerox Canada Inc. v. Ontario Municipal Employees Retirement Board* (1991), 3 B.L.R. (2d) 68 (Ont. Gen. Div.)) however a valuator is not an arbitrator, referee, nor assessor, but a court expert. In Alberta, there is no procedural basis to permit a valuator to examine witnesses. (see: *Westfair Foods Ltd. v. Watt* (1992), 94 D.L.R. (4th) 733 (Alta. C.A.)).

Once the court has fixed the value, the court issues an order against the corporation in favour of the dissenters (s. 190(22)); *Bain Insulation and Supply Ltd. v. Ginther* (1988), 63 A.L.R. (2d) 403 (C.A.).

The court may award interest from the date the action approved by the offending resolution is effective to the date of the order. The court is not, apparently, bound by the rates of interest set out in its own rules of procedure or enabling legislation but may, by virtue of s. 190(23), award a reasonable rate of interest.

Of course, the vital question is what is the proper fair value of the shares and how should such fair value be calculated? It is now accepted in Canadian jurisprudence that there are four approved approaches to the valuation of shares: (a) the stock market value approach: the quoted stock market price of the shares; (b) the assets approach: the valuation of the net assets of the corporation at fair market value; (c) the earnings or investment value approach: the capitalization of maintainable earnings; and (d) some combination of these three approaches. Approval of these various approaches was given in, among other cases, *Brant Investments Ltd. v. Keeprite Inc., supra*; *Smeenk v. Dexleigh Corp., supra*; *LoCicero v. B.A.C.M. Industries, supra*; *Domglas Inc. v. Jarislowsky, Fraser & Co.* (1980), 13 B.L.R. 135 (Que. S.C.). See also *Kelvin Energy Ltd. v. Bahan* (1987), 52 Alta L.R. (2d) 71.

The courts have clearly established that no approach to determining fair value of shares is appropriate for all circumstances. Rather, they have indicated that the question is one of judgment, fairness and equity to be decided in every case on all circumstances of that case: *Cyprus Anvil Mining Corp. v. Dickson* (1986), 33 D.L.R. (4th) 641 (B.C. C.A.). See also *Smeenk v. Dexleigh, supra.*

It is clear that a court, asked to establish the fair value of particular shares, is free to look at any factor it considers relevant as part of the exercise of its judgment and its equitable jurisdiction. In the case of private corporations, the stock market value method is clearly not available and a court would look to one of the other methods, or more likely, a combination thereof: see *Diligenti v. RWMD Operations Kelowna Ltd. (No. 2)* (1977), 4 B.C.L.R. 134 (B.C. S.C.).

In the case of public corporations, it might be argued that the stock market value would, being an open market between willing buyers and sellers, automatically be the fair market value. This does not, however, reflect the fact that the shares of many public corporations are thinly traded, or that for many Canadian public corporations, a substantial block of shares is held by a small group of dominant shareholders. In such cases, the stock market does not work perfectly and the traded price of the shares may well be unrepresentative of the true fair value of a *pro rata* share of the corporation. Accordingly, the courts will not always be bound by stock market values in fixing fair value.

Thus, in *Neonex International v. Kolasa, supra*, the British Columbia Supreme Court rejected the stock market value approach because an individual controlled almost 50 per cent of the shares, and it was determined that this would have the effect of depressing stock market prices. Similarly, in *Re Whitehorse Copper Mines Ltd.* (1980), 10 B.L.R. 113 (B.C. S.C.) over two thirds of the shares were held by two groups of shareholders. This, coupled with the lack of trading of the remaining shares, led to the rejection of the stock market value by the court. There are several cases where the stock market value of shares which are thinly traded has been rejected as not representing fair value: *Domglas Inc. v. Jarislowsky, Fraser & Co.* (1980), 13 B.L.R. 135 (Que. S.C.); affd 22 B.L.R. 121 (Que. C.A.); *Brant Investments Ltd. v. Keeprite Inc., supra*; *Fraser Inc. v. Aitken, supra*. It is, therefore, not possible to assert, as a straightforward proposition, that the stock-market value of the shares of a public corporation will necessarily be considered to be the fair value for those shares.

On the other hand, not all cases involve shares that are thinly traded or have large shareholders. Therefore, it becomes important to attempt to establish tendencies in order to determine so far as is possible how likely a court is to use something other than stock market value as fair value for shares. *Re Montgomery and Shell Canada Ltd.* (1980), 111 D.L.R. (3d) 116 (Sask. Q.B.) is one of the relatively few fair value cases in which a large publicly held corporation was involved. Even there, two thirds of the class of shares involved were held by one shareholder as were all of the other two classes of shares. The remaining one-third of the class of shares in question was publicly held and there was active trading in a large number of shares over an extended period of time. In that case, it was found that the stock market value was, in fact, fair value.

Another case, *Canadian Gas and Energy Fund Ltd. v. Sceptre Resources Ltd.*, [1985] 5 W.W.R. 43 (Alta.) involved a public, widely held and actively traded corporation with no controlling shareholder. In that case, the stock market price was considered to "fairly [reflect] the public's perception of the market value of [the] shares". The stock market value was, therefore, considered to form the "main criterion to be utilized in establishing fair value". It was not, however, accepted as the only indicator of fair value and in this case the court checked the stock market value against the values arrived at by the other methods. See also *Lough v. Canadian Natural Resources Ltd.* (1983), 45 B.C.L.R. 335.

There is jurisprudence to the effect that, where there is a forceable taking or an expropriation of shares, the dissenting shareholder should be allowed a premium: *Domglas Inc. v. Jarislowsky, Fraser & Co.* (1980), 13 B.L.R. 135 (Que. S.C.); affd 22 B.L.R. 121 (Que. C.A.); *Investissements Mont-Soleil Inc. v. National Drug Ltd.* (1982), 22 B.L.R. 139 (Que. S.C.). See also *Jakobson v. Agassiz Enterprises Ltd.* (1987), 49 Man. R. (2d) 270. (Such cases involved an amalgamation squeeze-out, where minority shareholders were upon an amalgamation given redeemable shares which were redeemed immediately after the amalgamation.) It now, however, seems settled that the right to such a premium does not exist in Canadian law. See *LoCicero and B.A.C.M. Industries, supra*; also *Brant v. Keeprite Inc., supra*; *Fraser v. Aitken, supra, Westfair Foods Ltd. v. Watt* (1992), 94 D.L.R. (4th) 733 (Alta. C.A.) nor is there any right to a deduction for a minority interest. See: *Baniuk v. Carpenter* (1990), 281 A.P.R. 332 (N.B. Q.B.). As to costs see the discussion in Chapter 16.

It should be noted that a corporation is not obligated to pay dissenting shareholders in all circumstances. As already noted, it is possible (and is prudent practice) for the resolution authorizing the fundamental change to allow the directors not to implement such change where such action is in the best interests of the corporation. An example where such action may be necessary would be where there is a sufficient number of dissenting shareholders to impose a severe cash flow shortage on the corporation if the fundamental change was implemented.

Section 190(26) actually prevents the corporation making payments to dissenting shareholders where either of the two corporate solvency tests cannot be met. That is, if after making a payment to dissenting shareholders the corporation would be unable to pay its liabilities as they become due, or the realizable value of the corporation's assets would be less than the aggregate of its liabilities, the payment to dissenters cannot be made. If the corporation fails either of these solvency tests at the time when it would otherwise have to deliver an offer to pay dissenters under s. 190(12), it must instead notify the dissenters that it is not lawfully able to pay for their shares. For a discussion of the solvency test, see *Clarke v. Technical Marketing Associates Ltd. Estate* (1992), 8 O.R. (3d) 734 (Ont. Ct. Gen. Div.).

It is possible that a situation could arise where the corporation would not find out that it failed one of the solvency tests until after a court had determined the fair value of the shares of dissenters. Sections 190(24) and (25) deal with the problem. If the corporation is insolvent, it must, within ten days after the pronouncement of the order of the court fixing the fair value of the shares, notify such dissenting shareholders that it is unable lawfully to pay for their shares. Within 30 days of receipt of such notice, the dissenting shareholder must, by written notice to the corporation, choose between two courses of action. The dissenter may withdraw the notice of dissent — in which case the corporation is deemed to consent to the withdrawal, and the shareholder is reinstated in full as a shareholder of the corporation. In the alternative, the dissenter may retain the status of a claimant against the corporation to be paid as soon as the corporation is lawfully able to do so. If the corporation remains insolvent under the Act and is liquidated, such dissenting shareholder ranks subordinate to all other creditors of the corporation but in priority to other shareholders.

Reorganizations

Section 191 is basically a procedural provision. It enables certain fundamental and other changes to be made to a corporation where other federal statutes require such changes to be made, or where such changes are necessary to implement an order of a court made pursuant to the oppression remedy under s. 241 of the Act (see Chapter 16).

A reorganization, for purposes of s. 191, is defined in s. 191(1) to be a court order which is made pursuant either to the oppression remedy powers of s. 241, or an order under the *Bankruptcy and Insolvency Act* approving a proposal in bankruptcy, or any other federal act that affects the rights of a corporation, its shareholders and creditors. An example of such a federal statute would be the *Companies Creditors Arrangement Act*.

If a corporation is subject to a reorganization order described above, its articles may be amended by such order to make any change to the articles that could be made by filing articles of amendment pursuant to s. 173. In addition, the court may authorize the issue of debt obligations of the corporation, including debt convertible into any class of shares or debt having the right or option to acquire shares of any class.

Section 191(3)(b) authorizes the court to appoint additional directors of the corporation, or replace all or any of the existing board with new directors.

A reorganization order is implemented by filing duplicate articles of reorganization with the director in prescribed form (Form 14), together with the usual documents such as any notice of change of registered office, any applicable notice of change of directors and an appropriate name search if a new name is ordered. The Director then follows the usual s. 262 procedure and issues a certificate of amendment (s. 191(5)). This certificate is effective on the date shown thereon and amends the articles of the corporation as and from that date.

It should be noted that a shareholder cannot dissent from a reorganization order made pursuant to s. 191.

Arrangements

Arrangements have been part of the corporate law of Canada for the better part of a century. Arrangements under the Act are now dealt with in s. 192. Arrangements have currently two basic uses. First, and most common, an arrangement may be used in situations where it is not practical for a corporation to effect a fundamental change, or perhaps, a series of fundamental changes under the normal procedures. Second, arrangements are utilized as a method of reorganizing the affairs of a corporation in financial difficulty.

In the former Act, many fundamental changes to a corporation occurred using the procedure for arrangements and compromises. The term "arrangement" under the former Act included any change to the share capital, the capitalization, conversion or division of shares into different classes, the modification of the provisions of a particular class of shares, and also an amalgamation or reconstruction, that is, a business combination.

Section 192(1) of the Act defines "arrangements" to include: (a) an amendment to the articles; (b) an amalgamation of two corporations under the Act; (c) an amalgamation between a corporation subject to the Act, and a corporation subject to the laws of another jurisdiction, resulting in an amalgamated corporation subject to the Act; (d) a division of the business of a corporation; (e) the transfer of all or substantially all of the property of a corporation subject to the Act to any corporation (wherever incorporated) in exchange for property, money or securities of the transferee corporation; (f) the exchange of securities of any corporation, subject to the Act, for property, money or securities of the same corporation, a property, money or securities of a corporation not subject to the Act (provided that these exchanges do not constitute a take-over bid, as defined in s. 194 of the Act); (g) a liquidation or dissolution of the corporation; or (h) any combination of the foregoing.

From the foregoing list of enumerated transactions, and the use of the term "includes" it will be apparent that an arrangement is a broad term covering a wide range of corporate transactions. Many cases decided under the Act, the *English Companies Act* and under the acts of several provinces of Canada support this view. Moreover, the fact that the arrangement is similar in form or result to another form of fundamental change does not prevent use of the arrangement procedure: *Amoco Canada Petroleum Co. v. Dome Petroleum Ltd.* (unreported) (Alta. Q.B.); *Savage v. Amoco Acquisition Co.* (1988), 40 B.L.R. 188 (Alta. C.A.);

Re Hellenic & General Trust Ltd., [1975] 3 All E.R. 382; *In re Guardian Assurance Co.*, [1917] 1 Ch. 431 (C.A.); *Re West Humber Apartments Ltd.*, [1969] 1 O.R. 229 (Ont. H.C.); *Imperial Trust Co. v. Canbra Foods Ltd.* (1987), 50 Alta. L.R. (2d) 375; *Grouse Mountain Resorts v. Angeli* (1989), 42 B.L.R. 219 (B.C. C.A.).

The only constraints imposed by the cases are that a court cannot sanction an arrangement which is, by its terms, *ultra vires* the objects of the corporation or which would involve the corporation in the exercise of an *ultra vires* power; *In re Guardian Assurance, supra*; *In re Oceanic Steam Navigation Co.*, [1939] Ch. 41. Such constraints would not normally affect a corporation subject to the Act since, as discussed in Chapter 3, a corporation has the capacity of a natural person and would not normally have in its articles any restrictions on its objects or powers. Older authority to the effect that shares could not be converted into bonds is no longer applicable in view of the wording of the Act.

Section 192(3) sets out the conditions under which a corporation may apply to a court to affect a fundamental change in the nature of an arrangement. First, it must not be practicable for the corporation to make the proposed changes under any other provision of the Act. Second, the corporation must not be insolvent.

In practice, both these conditions impose only a minimal barrier to the bringing of an arrangement application. For example, the practicability test does not mean that the proposed arrangement must contemplate something that is impossible to achieve under the provisions of Part XV of the Act. The fact that the proposed transaction is difficult to put into practice using the normal provisions of Part XV will be sufficient to allow an arrangement application: *Imperial Trust Co. v. Canbra Foods Ltd., supra.*

Section 192(2) of the Act defines insolvency for the purposes of an arrangement, and contains the two solvency tests. That is, a corporation will be insolvent if it is unable to pay its liabilities as they become due, or if the net realizable value of its assets is less than the total of stated capital of all classes of shares. It appears that arrangements may not be applicable to an insolvency situation since s. 192(3) implies that only a corporation that is not insolvent can qualify for the arrangement procedure.

In the case of *Savage v. Amoco Acquisition Co., supra,* however, the court did not interpret s. 192(3) of the Act to limit applications for arrangements to situations where *none* of the corporations involved were insolvent. In that case, the principal corporation involved was clearly insolvent but the corporation making the application (a recently incorporated shell) was not itself insolvent. Since leave to appeal the *Savage* case was refused by the Supreme Court of Canada, the solvency requirement in s. 192(3) has essentially been rendered ineffective by the simple procedural device of having the application made by a solvent corporation specially formed for the transaction.

Where an arrangement or compromise is proposed to be made between a corporation and its creditors, whether secured or unsecured or any class of them, consideration should be given to the *Companies' Creditors Arrangement*

Act which is applicable to a debtor corporation having outstanding an issue of secured or unsecured bonds of that corporation or of a predecessor in title of that corporation issued under a trust deed or other instrument running in favour of a trustee and where the compromise or arrangement proposed includes a compromise or arrangement between the debtor corporation and the holders of such an issue (s. 3).

Where such a compromise or arrangement is proposed, the court may, on the application of the corporation of any creditor, the trustee in bankruptcy or liquidator of the corporation, order a meeting of the creditors or the particular class thereof and, if so determined by the court, of the shareholders of the corporation, to be summoned in such manner as the court may direct (ss. 4, 5). Where a majority in number representing three fourths in value of the creditors or class of creditors present and voting at such meetings agree to any compromise or arrangement, either as proposed or as altered or modified at such meeting, the compromise or arrangement may be sanctioned by the court and upon such sanctioning is binding on all the creditors or the class of creditors as the case may be and on any trustee for such class as well as the corporation; if an authorized assignment or receiving order has been made by or against the corporation it is also binding on such trustee and liquidator (s. 6).

Provision is made for the court to give directions with respect to an alteration or modification of any compromise or arrangement proposed after the court has directed a meeting or meetings to be summoned (s. 7).

The application is to be made to the court in the province where the head office or chief place of business of the corporation in Canada is situate or if there is no such place of business within Canada in any province where any assets of the corporation are situated (s. 9.1). The court is given power under s. 11 to restrain proceedings under the *Bankruptcy and Insolvency Act* or *Winding-up Act* and to determine the amount of any claim. Provision is made for appeals.

These provisions cannot be used where it is desired to deal with the position of shareholders and it will be noted that despite the wording of s. 192(3) of the Act, it is common practice to bring an application for an arrangement under s. 192 where the corporation is in financial difficulty (see *infra*).

Section 192(4) gives a court broad powers in respect of the procedure and practice in connection with the application for a proposed arrangement. In particular, the court may give (by way of interim or final order) any of the following: (a) an order determining that notice be given to any interested person, or that no person, other than the Director (who, by virtue of s. 192(5), must receive notice) shall receive notice; (b) an order appointing counsel to represent shareholders at the corporation's expense; (c) an order requiring the corporation to hold a meeting of security holders; (d) an order allowing shareholders to dissent; or (e) an order permitting the proposed arrangement, or any amendment or variation thereof.

It can be seen, therefore, that the court has broad jurisdiction to determine the conduct of shareholders' meetings in respect of an arrangement and who may appear before it on the application — subject, as noted, to the provisions for s. 192(5) which requires that the Director must be given notice and may appear before the court in person or by counsel.

There is a significant body of jurisprudence under the *English Companies Act*, former provincial statutes in Canada, and the former Act, dealing with the notice of shareholders' meetings, the form of notice, form of proxies, majority approval and the like. Such jurisprudence should be viewed with extreme caution in the context of the Act. Under those former statutes all fundamental changes were implemented by using an arrangement or compromise, and the related provisions dealing with amalgamations or reconstructions.

Under the Act, as it now reads, many of the procedures and practices set out in those older statutes have been replaced by the provisions of the Act. The arrangement provisions now contained in s. 192 are essentially a residual power to achieve fundamental changes that may be difficult, or impossible, under the more precise rules relating to specific fundamental changes. Accordingly the courts have correctly, it is submitted, not been overly concerned with procedural requirements in interpreting s. 192.

It will be observed that, in theory at least, a court would be free to make an order approving an arrangement without any meeting of shareholders being held but this would be most unusual. The course of conduct often followed is for the corporation to propose an arrangement and to hold a meeting of the holders of the relevant securities at which the arrangement is approved following which it is presented to the court for approval. It will be noted that the court may order the corporation to call, hold and conduct a meeting of the security holders in such manner as the court may direct (s. 192(4)(c)). It will also be observed that there is no stipulation of any percentage of the votes to be cast at any meeting of security holders in favour of the arrangement. While it might be argued that a simple majority was all that was necessary, it is suggested that the better view (and the rule that seems to be followed in practice) is that two thirds of the votes cast should be in favour of the arrangement. For a discussion of the procedures to be followed, see the decision of the Alberta Court of Appeal in *Savage v. Amoco Acquisition Co.*, (1988), 40 B.L.R. 188 (Alta. C.A.) (leave to appeal to S.C.C. refused (1988)).

One important point with respect to an arrangement is that unless the order or the court permits a shareholder to dissent under s. 190, there is no power for a shareholder to dissent under that provision. Presumably if the arrangement did not so provide, however, the Director might object.

In considering whether to approve an arrangement, there are two distinct lines of cases. The courts will scrutinize the arrangement to ensure that it is fair to the corporation, and that all classes of shareholders will benefit. Ordinarily, Canadian courts follow the long established principle that an arrangement cannot occur where the proposal in question calls for the diminution of rights of some shareholders without a compensatory payment or other accommodation by the corporation: *Re N.F.U. Development Trust*, [1973] 1 All E.R. 135 (Ch. D.); *Re Simco Ltée* (1977), 3 B.L.R. 318 (Que. S.C.); *Standard Manufacturing Co. v. Baird* (1984), 5 D.L.R. (4th) 697 (Nfld. T.D.); *Imperial Trust Co. v. Canbra Foods Ltd.*, *supra*. See also *Re Ripley International Ltd.* (1977), 1 B.L.R. 269 (Ont. H.C.).

There is, however, an exception to that rule found in the so-called "necessity" cases. Such cases involved situations where, without the actions proposed in the arrangement, there is a significant risk that the corporation might not survive, or that its financial stability will be seriously impaired. Examples of such cases would be where the corporation has an unworkable capital structure (see *Re The Hamilton Bridge Co.*, [1939] O.W.N. 327 (Ont. H.C.)) or is in serious financial difficulty (the *Dome* cases, *infra*) or requires a complete change of direction in its business to survive changing economic conditions.

Two recent cases have provided excellent examples of each of the foregoing principles. An example of the more traditional type of case is found in *Re Canadian Pacific Ltd.* (1990), 73 O.R. (2d) 212. By contrast, the various *Dome Petroleum* cases (*Amoco Canada Petroleum v. Dome Petroleum Ltd., supra*; *Savage v. Amoco Acquisition Co., supra*; *Bank of Montreal v. Dome Petroleum Limited*; *Premji v. Amoco Acquisition Co.* (1988), 61 Alta. L.R. (2d) 279 (C.A.) provide an example of an extreme necessity situation. The two lines of cases are discussed below.

In the normal situation, where there is no necessity that the arrangement occur, our courts state that they still apply the test laid down 100 years ago by the English Court of Appeal in *Re Alabama, New Orleans, Texas and Pacific Junction Railway Co.*, [1891] 1 Ch. 213 (C.A.).

In the case of *Re Canadian Pacific Ltd.* (1990), 73 O.R. (2d) 212, the Ontario High Court used *Re Alabama, New Orleans, Texas and Pacific Junction Railway Co.* as its starting point in determining whether or not to approve the arrangement. The tests are that the court will (i) ascertain that all the statutory requirements have been fulfilled; (ii) satisfy itself that the arrangement is put forward in good faith; (iii) consider whether the statutory majority who approved the scheme were acting *bona fide* or were seeking to promote interests adverse to those of the class who they preferred to represent; (iv) determine whether the arrangement is such as a man of business would reasonably approve; (v) determine whether the arrangement is fair and reasonable.

The first test, that all statutory requirements be met, is not really relevant in considering arrangements under the Act since s. 192(4) gives the court very broad powers. In this regard, the Act is therefore unlike some of the provincial statutes which have a specific scheme — usually involving a class vote — that must be adhered to when considering an arrangement.

The second test, good faith, would seem to be designed so that the court can quickly dismiss those cases that are, in effect, an expropriation by controlling shareholders of the shares of a minority on patently unreasonable terms: *Standard Manufacturing Co. v. Baird* (1984), 5 D.L.R. (4th) 697.

The third test, statutory majority, is also not really relevant to a determination under the Act since there is no statutory majority. As discussed below, however, the existence of a significant positive vote by shareholders would be a factor the court would consider.

The fourth test, "whether the arrangement is such that a man of business would reasonably approve", seems to imply that the court should impose an objective standard. So, too, does the fifth test, that the arrangement must be fair and reasonable. The result in the *Canadian Pacific* case does not appear entirely consistent with these views.

In that case it was proposed to spin off most of the shares of a major subsidiary of the applicant to its common shareholders. The evidence was that the parent corporation would lose some 14 to 16 per cent of its value. The parent corporation had assets with a value in the range of $17 billion; annual income, though variable, averaged over $400 million a year for the 5 years preceding the application. Over 90 per cent of the shareholders approved the transaction, but most of the preferred shareholders (primarily the members of one family) voted against the arrangement. The preferred shares in question carried a dividend of 4 per cent, representing a cash outlay of some $600,000 annually. On a purely objective basis, it would appear that any financial impact on the preferred shareholders was truly negligible.

It was found that the same transactions could have been accomplished by declaring a dividend on the shares of the subsidiary, in specie, to common shareholders. The preferred shareholders could not have prevented such a dividend. Such a dividend would, however, have resulted in a significant tax liability to the corporation and common shareholders. The same court had, in an earlier application (reported (1991), 72 O.R. (2d) 545) determined that the arrangement transaction was, in essence, a dividend.

Nevertheless, the court refused to sanction the arrangement. The court stated that because there was a difference in treatment of the two classes of shareholder, there was a heavy onus on the applicant: see *Palmer v. Carling O'Keefe Breweries of Canada Ltd.* (1989), 67 O.R. (2d) 161.

There does not appear to be any provision in s. 192(4) or elsewhere in the Act that would allow a court to change the normal rules of onus of proof in civil procedure. The better view, as stated by the court itself in *Canadian Pacific*, is that the applicant must establish, at least *prima facie*, that the proposed arrangement is fair and reasonable. If and when that has been accomplished, the burden then shifts to opposing parties to persuade the courts that they have rights or interests which have been significantly or appreciably affected: *Re National Bank Ltd.* (1966), 1 W.L.R. 819 (Ch. Div.) and *Re Universal Explorations Ltd. and Petrol Oil and Gas Co.* (1982), 16 B.L.R. 186.

From a close reading of *Canadian Pacific* it appears that the court felt that the case was very close to the line. Three factors — all of which would appear to be extraneous — appear to have influenced the result. The size of the transaction, the fact that the subsidiary held some of the original assets of the corporation and the complexity of the transaction were said to have affected the court's conclusion. Unfortunately the case was not appealed.

In any event, it appears in the normal situation the courts are very reluctant to sanction an arrangement without the approval of a significant majority of shareholders of all classes.

Where, however, the very survival of the corporation is at stake, the courts take a somewhat different view although the requirement of fairness and reasonableness is still present. In such cases, the rights of any special class of creditors or shareholders may be made subservient to the interests of the corporation and all creditors and shareholders thereof. For example, in the case of *Savage v. Amoco Acquisition Co*, *supra*, the preferred shareholders wanted a separate class vote and presumably, such vote would not have been positive. The court rejected the idea of separate votes and approved the arrangement, primarily on the basis that the proposal was an essential step in saving Dome Petroleum from bankruptcy and that it was fair and reasonable.

In summary, it appears that in all cases the courts will examine the merits and fairness of a particular proposal, as well as the degree of shareholder acceptance. Where the arrangement is not one of necessity, this latter factor will have great weight. However, where approval of the proposal is necessary to allow the corporation to continue, significantly less weight may be given to approval by a particular class of shareholder.

If a court has approved an arrangement and issued an order pursuant to s. 192(4)(e), articles of arrangement in the prescribed form (Form 14.1) are sent to the Director. The usual documents, for example, any applicable notice of change of registered office or notice of change of directors, must accompany the articles, together with a copy of the court order (s. 192(6)).

Upon receipt of the duly executed articles of arrangement and appropriate accorporationing documents, the Director must issue a certificate of amendment, in accordance with the usual procedures set out in s. 262 (s. 192(7)). The arrangement then becomes effective on the date shown in that certificate (s. 192(8)).

Chapter 13

PROSPECTUSES AND TAKE-OVER BIDS

Cross-references: Ontario Act, ss. 187-190;
Securities Act, R.S.O. 1990, c. S.5

General

One of the most important tasks which those engaged in the formation or management of a corporation have to perform is to make suitable arrangements to provide it with capital. Except where an existing business is being incorporated and no further capital is required, or the capital is privately arranged (as, for example, through a bank), an offer to the public of the shares or other securities of a new corporation will be necessary. Established corporations will also require additional capital from time to time and in order to obtain it may offer shares or other securities to the public or may arrange for private placements of securities with financial institutions. An offer to the public normally requires the issuance of a prospectus.

In what follows, no attempt is made to refer to any detailed provisions of the legislation of any jurisdiction; the broad principles applicable thereunder are indicated briefly. For a discussion of take-over bids, refer to the text under the heading "Take-over Bids" in this chapter; for a discussion of insider trading, see Chapter 9.

A corporation incorporated under the federal Act must comply with any provisions of provincial legislation applicable with regard to the offering of its shares or securities in any particular province; a copy of the prospectus or other offering document is to be filed with the Director (s. 193).

A corporation incorporated under the laws of a province or any other jurisdiction must comply with the applicable legislation with regard to offering its shares or other securities in which its shares or securities are offered.

Securities Acts

The Securities Acts provide for registration with provincial authorities of persons trading in securities, regulate trading by persons so registered and prohibit trading by persons not so registered. In addition, they provide for disclosure of prescribed details with respect to securities offered to the public. Generally speaking, the information required is full, true and plain disclosure of all material facts with respect to the securities offered and the corporation issuing the securities.

The persons who must register under such legislation include brokers, investment dealers and their salespeople. They also include corporations, usually described as "security issuers", which propose to offer their shares or securities to the public without the assistance of investment dealers or brokers.

The applicable statutes and regulations contain provisions of greater or less complexity with regard to applications for registration, the persons covered by the registration of a corporation or partnership, termination and renewal of registration, exemptions from registration and so on.

The terms "trade" or "trading in securities" are broadly defined, and the legislation in force in the different provinces regulates trading in varying degrees and gives the provincial authorities varying jurisdiction over traders and trading in securities. In all the provinces there is considerable control exercised over offers of securities to the public.

In what follows, reference is made to the *Securities Act* (Ontario).

This Act provides that no person or corporation is to trade in a security where such trade would constitute a distribution of such a security unless a preliminary prospectus and a prospectus have been filed with the Ontario Securities Commission and receipts obtained therefor. The prospectus is to provide full, true and plain disclosure of all material facts relating to the securities issued or that are proposed to be distributed (including information about the issuer) and is to comply with the requirements of the Act, the regulations and the policy statements issued by the Securities Commission. It will be noted that the regulations issued pursuant to the Act as well as the policy statements of the Securities Commission contain specific requirements as to the contents of prospectuses for various classes of issuer. The preliminary prospectus must comply substantially with the requirements of the Act and regulations with certain exceptions, namely that the report or reports of the auditors or accountants required by the regulations need not be included and information with respect to the price to the underwriter and the offering price of the securities and other matters dependent upon or relating to such pricing may be omitted. The final prospectus must contain such financial statements, reports or other documents as may be required. There is a waiting period of at least ten to fifteen days (depending on whether one or multi jurisdictions are involved) between the issuance of a receipt for a preliminary prospectus and the issuance of a receipt for the final prospectus. During this interval expressions of interest may be solicited from prospective purchasers if a copy of the preliminary prospectus is forwarded to them.

The final prospectus must be sent by mail or be delivered to every purchaser either before or not later than two business days after entering into an agreement of purchase and sale for any order or subscription. The purchaser may rescind the sale agreement if written or telegraphic notice to that effect is received by the dealer from whom the security was purchased not later than midnight on the second business day after receipt by the purchaser of the prospectus.

It will be noted that in order to avoid statutory civil liability the underwriter (and others involved in the distribution) must exercise due diligence with respect to a reasonable investigation of the securities offered and the issuer thereof of matters material to the issuer or the securities involved to ensure that there is no misrepresentation in the prospectus.

The Act contains a number of important definitions including those of "distribution", "security" and "reporting issuer". The term "security" is defined as including, among other things, any document, instrument or writing, commonly known as a security as well as a number of other documents or instruments constituting evidence of an interest in the capital, assets, property, profits, earnings or royalties of any person or corporation. The definition also extends to certain investment contracts other than an investment contract within the meaning of the *Investment Contracts Act*, R.S.O. 1990, c. I.14. There is a considerable body of jurisprudence in the United States and Canada concerning what constitutes an "investment contract". The most definitive analysis in Canada is found in *Pacific Coast Coin Exchange of Canada v. Ontario Securities Commission*, [1978] 2 S.C.R. 112, where it was held that agreements for the sale of bags of silver coins constituted investment contracts and fell within the definition of a "security". The Supreme Court's decision indicates that the definition of "security" should be read broadly to encompass new types of investment opportunities within the ambit of the *Securities Act*. See also *Superintendent of Brokers v. Lazerman Investment Metals International Inc.* (1985), 62 B.C.L.R. 376 (C.A.).

The Act provides for statutory civil liability for misrepresentation in a prospectus and gives the purchaser a right of action for damages against the issuer or selling security holder on whose behalf the distribution is made; each underwriter required to sign the full, true and plain disclosure certificate forming part of the prospectus; every director of the issuer at the time the prospectus was filed; and every person or corporation whose consent has been filed as required by the regulations, but only with respect to reports, opinions or statements that were made by them. (For example, the consent requirement includes auditors, consulting engineers, geologists and other experts.) In addition, every person or corporation is so liable who signed the prospectus other than the foregoing, for example, the chief executive officer, the chief financial officer of the issuer and any promoter. In the alternative, a right of rescission is given to the purchaser in certain cases. The Act provides that an action must be commenced in the case of an action for rescission no more than 180 days after the date of the transaction giving rise to the cause of action or in any other action no more than 180 days after the plaintiff first had knowledge of the facts giving rise to the cause of action or three years after the date of the transaction that gave rise to the cause of action, whichever is first. It will be noted that in addition to the statutory liability, there can also be liability at common law as to which, see the discussion under the heading "Liability at common law for misrepresentation in a prospectus", *infra*.

The Act also provides that reporting issuers are required to comply with the various continuous and timely disclosure requirements set out in the Act and the regulations. A "reporting issuer" is defined as including an issuer that has issued voting securities on or after May 1, 1967 for which a prospectus was filed, or in respect of whom or which a securities exchange take-over bid circular has been filed, or any of whose securities have been listed in a recognized stock exchange in Ontario since September 15, 1979. A reporting issuer is required to issue and file immediately a press release and to prepare and file a material change report within ten days with respect to any material change occurring in its affairs; provision is made for confidential disclosure where public disclosure would be unduly detrimental to the interest of the reporting issuer. A "material change" is defined as a change in the business, operations or capital of an issuer that would reasonably be expected to have a significant effect on the market price or value of the securities of an issuer and includes a decision to implement such a change made by the board of directors of the issuer or by senior management of the issuer who believe that confirmation of the decision by the board of directors is probable. National Policy Statement No. 40 issued by the Canadian Securities Administrators contains similar timely disclosure obligations but with respect to a broader category — material information. For a discussion of timely disclosure and whether information is material, see *Pezim v. British Columbia (Superintendent of Brokers)* (1992), 66 B.C.L.R. 257 (C.A.). It is understood that this case is under appeal to the Supreme Court of Canada.

The Act provides heavy penalties for persons in a special relationship with the reporting issuer who trade in securities of the reporting issuer with knowledge of a material fact or change which has not generally been disclosed or who inform or "tip" others about such fact or change, except in the necessary course of business. The term "persons in a special relationship with a reporting issuer" is defined as including any insider, affiliate or associate of the reporting issuer or a person proposing to make a take-over bid for the securities of the reporting issuer or proposing to become a party to a reorganization, amalgamation, merger, arrangement or similar business combination. The Act provides a penalty for the misuse of such information (resulting in a profit) of a fine of up to $1,000,000 (but not less than the amount of any profit) and an amount equal to triple the profit made by any person by reason of the contravention of the Act. In addition, there is civil liability to the seller or purchaser of the securities for damages. It will be observed that both the "tipper" and the "tippee" may be liable civilly with respect to such trades. The definition of a "person with a special relationship with a reporting issuer" also includes a person or company that is engaging or proposes to engage in any business or professional activity with or on behalf of the reporting issuer or the persons proposing to make a take-over bid or enter into a business combination with the reporting issuer. In addition, this group includes any director, officer or employee of the reporting issuer or of a person or corporation proposing to make a take-over bid or enter into a business combination with a reporting issuer, a person learning of the material fact or change while the person was one of the persons described above or a person learning of a material fact or change with respect to the issuer from any other person or corporation described in the definition including a person described in the clause and who knew or reasonably ought to have known that the person or corporation is a person or corporation in such a relationship.

Financial reporting is required of any reporting issuer, including unaudited quarterly statements as well as audited year-end financial statements. Corporations having a shareholder equity in excess of $10,000,000 or revenues in excess of $10,000,000 must in addition file an annual information form and prepare and send to shareholders a management's discussion and analysis of financial conditions and results of operations (which can be included in the annual report). See O.S.C. Policy 5.10, published in the O.S.C. Bulletin for January 1993 at p. 375 *et seq.*

In certain cases, reporting issuers having qualified as such for a period of 36 months and where the market value of their equity securities in the hands of the public is at least $75,000,000 may use an abbreviated form of prospectus incorporating by reference information from the public file of the issuer, known as the prompt offering prospectus qualification system (the POP system); where the public float is $300,000,000 or more, the 36 month period will not be required.

In addition, in 1991 the United States Securities and Exchange Commission and the various provincial jurisdictions in Canada entered into a reciprocal disclosure system for offering of securities. This is known as the multi-jurisdictional disclosure system and permits qualifying issuers in Canada or the United States to offer securities in the other jurisdiction using documentation based on the requirements of the jurisdiction where the securities are issued. The system is also applicable to a number of other securities transactions.

The Ontario Act also has detailed rules applicable to insider reporting, proxy solicitation and take-over bids, including compulsory acquisition and "going-probate" transactions. In a case where a provincial Securities Act or Acts are applicable to the corporation which is also subject to the *Canada Business Corporations Act*, the provincial Acts must also be complied with.

Provincial Legislation with Respect to Dealing in Securities

The general aim of security legislation is to regulate the manner in which the business of selling securities should be conducted and to ensure that persons who carry on such a business are honest and of good repute. See *Lymburn v. Mayland*, [1932] A.C. 318, 324; *Lumley v. Broadway Coffee Co.*, [1935] O.R. 278 at 282 (C.A.) and *Smith v. R.*, [1960] S.C.R. 776. See also *Multiple Access Ltd. v. McCutcheon*, [1982] 2 S.C.R. 161.

Such legislation is within the powers of provincial legislatures and extends to federal corporations and securities issued by such corporations: *Lymburn v. Mayland, supra.* In *R. v. Hazzard*, [1932] O.R. 139, Riddell J.A. affirmed the conviction under the then applicable *Security Frauds Prevention Act* of four officers of a federal corporation who were not registered as required by the Act, it being assumed that they were acting as officers of and for the corporation.

Liability at Common Law for Misrepresentation in a Prospectus

Criminal liability is dealt with in s. 122 of the *Securities Act* (Ontario) and civil liability is dealt with in s. 130 which relates to liability for misrepresentation in a prospectus. It will be noted in s. 130 where there is a misrepresentation in a prospectus, a purchaser who purchases a security offered thereby during the period of distribution is deemed to have relied on such misrepresentation and has a right of action for damages against the named individuals. At common law the action for misrepresentation was not actionable unless the person to whom it was made had in fact acted upon it and it may be difficult to prove such reliance. However, the general statement which follows of the liability at common law is still useful since there are limitation periods for civil liability under the *Securities Act* which are shorter than those at common law for misrepresentation and subs. (10) provides that the rights conferred by s. 130 are in addition to and without derogation from any other rights the purchaser may have at law. Accordingly, the provisions of the common law are still worthy of note. See *Jones v. F.H. Deacon Hodgson Inc.* (1986), 56 O.R. (2d) 540 (H.C.).

The duty of those who are responsible for the framing of a prospectus is stated by Lord Chelmsford in *Directors, Central Ry. Co. of Venezuela v. Kisch* (1867), L.R. 2 H.L. 99 at 113, as follows:

> But although, in its introduction to the public, some high colouring, and even exaggeration, in the description of the advantages which are likely to be enjoyed by the subscribers to an undertaking, may be expected, yet no misstatement or concealment of any material facts or circumstances ought to be permitted. In my opinion, the public, who are invited by a prospectus to join in any new adventure, ought to have the same opportunity of judging of everything which has a material bearing on its true character, as the promoters themselves possess. It cannot be too frequently or too strongly impressed upon those who, having projected any undertaking, are desirous of obtaining the co-operation of persons who have no other information on the subject than that which they choose to convey, that the utmost candour and honesty ought to characterize their published statements. As was said by Vice-Chancellor Kindersley in the case of the *New Brunswick and Canada Railway Co. v. Muggeridge* 1 Dr. & Sm. 381
>
>> those who issue a prospectus holding out to the public the great advantages which will accrue to persons who will take shares in a proposed undertaking, and inviting them to take shares on the faith of the representations therein contained, are bound to state everything with strict and scrupulous accuracy, and not only to abstain from stating as fact that which is not so, but to omit no one fact within their knowledge the existence of which might in any degree affect the nature, or extent, or quality of the privileges and advantages which the prospectus holds out as inducements to take shares.

The rights and remedies which may be open to a subscriber for or a purchaser of securities in respect of misrepresentation contained in a prospectus are:

1. Damages in the common law action for deceit.
2. Rescission of the contract.
3. Rectification of the register.
4. Defence of misrepresentation to an action for payment.
5. Compensation or damages under statutory provisions.
6. Criminal proceedings.

Before discussing these various remedies, the essential elements which are necessary to entitle a person to *any* relief in respect of misrepresentation and the persons entitled to relief will be considered.

Essential elements of misrepresentation

A misrepresentation is a representation which at the material time was false in substance and in fact. Before a subscriber for or a purchaser of securities can claim any relief for misrepresentation he must establish that the misrepresentation was one of fact, that it was material and that he acted upon it. A misrepresentation may be either innocent or fraudulent; an innocent misrepresentation is one made with an actual, honest belief in its truth while a fraudulent misrepresentation is one made either with knowledge that it was false, or recklessly, not caring whether it was true or false, or not believing it to be true. Fraud is an essential element only in the common law action for deceit and in criminal proceedings.

Misrepresentation must be of fact

The misstatement must be one of fact and not merely of law: *Beattie v. Lord Ebury* (1872), L.R. 7 Ch. App. 777. But a statement of fact which involves a statement of law is still a statement of fact: *Eaglesfield v. Marquis of Londonderry* (1876), 4 Ch. D. 693 at 702 (C.A.).

National Policy 48 now regulates future oriented financial material; but at common law mere expressions of hope and opinion were not representations of fact: *Bellairs v. Tucker* (1884), 13 Q.B.D. 562 at 573; *Re National Husker Co.* (1913), 4 O.W.N. 1077 (C.A.), affd (1913), 5 O.W.N. 875 (C.A.); *Dupaul v. Varyland Investment Co.* (1923), 35 Que. K.B. 328 (optimistic predictions); nor was anticipation of future results: *Bentley & Co. v. Black* (1893), 9 T.L.R. 580; but misrepresentation as to the state of a man's mind is a misstatement of fact, for example, a misstatement of the objects for which an issue of debentures was being made: *Edgington v. Fitzmaurice* (1885), 29 Ch. D. 459 at 483 (C.A.). A statement by an agent of the corporation that the shares would earn dividends of 30 per cent, which was unfounded and was not an honest expression of opinion, was held to be a false statement of fact, that is, a false statement of the agent's opinion: *Pioneer Tractor Co. v. Peebles* (1914), 18 D.L.R. 477 (Sask. C.A.), affd (1915), 8 W.W.R. 632 (S.C.C.).

Misrepresentation must be of an existing fact, not as to what may be reasonably expected to take place: *Modern Bedstead Co. v. Tobin* (1908), 12 O.W.R. 22 at 25 (Ch. Div.). While a representation of fact may be inherent in a statement of opinion and the existence of the opinion in the person stating it is a question of fact, a statement which is merely an opinion honestly held will not support a claim for rescission: *Bisset v. Wilkinson*, [1927] A.C. 177 (P.C.). This case must be considered in the light of the current requirements of due diligence.

A mere statement of intention on the part of the corporation to do something which in its then position it will be unable to carry out, viz., to use unissued common shares for the purpose of a bonus on the issuance of further preference shares confers no right of action: *Forget v. Cement Products Co. of Canada* (1916), 28 D.L.R. 717 (P.C.).

Mere non-disclosure of material facts will not be a ground for an action in the nature of an action for misrepresentation. For that purpose non-disclosure must have the effect of making that which is stated absolutely false: *Peek v. Gurney* (1873), L.R. 6 H.L. 377 at 403; *McKeown v. Boudard-Peveril Gear Co.*

(1896), 74 L.T. 712 (C.A.). The non-disclosure must be of something the disclosure of which would falsify some statements in the prospectus: *Re Christineville Rubber Estates Ltd.* (1911), 81 L.J. Ch. 63.

Misrepresentation must be material

The misstatement must be material. A misstatement is material when it is of such a nature that it induces, tends to induce or is part of the inducement to, a person to act on the faith of it: *Smith v. Chadwick* (1882), 20 Ch. D. 27 at 44 (C.A.)

The following Canadian cases may be referred to as illustrating statements held to be material: *Temperance Colonization Co. v. Fairfield* (1888), 16 O.R. 544, affd (1889), 17 O.A.R. 205 (representation that the corporation had the privilege of selecting a "compact choice tract of land" for the purpose of settlement free from the use of intoxicating liquors); *McCallam v. Sun Savings & Loan Co.* (1902), 1 O.W.R. 226 (representation that dividends were guaranteed by another corporation); *Ontario Ladies' College v. Kendry* (1905), 10 O.L.R. 324 (C.A.) (representation that named persons had subscribed for shares on condition that subscriptions for a specified amount were obtained by a certain date and that the representee's subscription was required to make up that amount); *Goold v. Gillies* (1908), 40 S.C.R. 437 (representation that the shares purchased were treasury stock); *Howard v. Canadian Automatic Transportation Co.* (1914), 6 O.W.N. 285, affd (1914), 6 O.W.N. 404 (C.A.) (misrepresentation as to the existence of a patent); *Young v. Smith* (1915), 21 D.L.R. 97 (Alta. C.A.) (a representation that other shareholders had paid cash for their shares); *Pioneer Tractor Co. v. Peebles* (1913), 15 D.L.R. 275 (Sask. T.D.), affd (1914), 18 D.L.R. 477 (Sask. C.A.), affd (1915), 8 W.W.R. 632 (S.C.C.) (a statement that thousands were interested in a corporation which guaranteed its success); *Allan v. McLennan* (1916), 10 W.W.R. 941, varied (1916), 31 D.L.R. 617 (B.C. C.A.) (representation that the shares purchased came direct from the corporation when part or all of them were issued shares belonging to another shareholder); *McCurdy v. Oak Tire & Rubber Co.* (1918), 44 O.L.R. 571 (representation, among others, that the factory superintendent had taken a specified amount of shares); *Aikens v. Waugh* (1919), 16 O.W.N. 390 (representation that the corporation was paying dividends); *Sissons v. Hassard*, [1923] 4 D.L.R. 186 (Alta. C.A.) (misrepresentation as to liabilities of the corporation); *Farmers Packing Co. v. Tully*, [1927] 2 D.L.R. 749 (Man. K.B.) (representation that corporation was a co-operative when it was in fact an ordinary corporation). See also *Dupuis v. Pan American Mines Ltd.* (1979), 7 B.L.R. 288 (Que. S.C.).

If the name of a person is improperly inserted as a director it will depend on the circumstances whether the misstatement is material: *Smith v. Chadwick* (1882), 20 Ch. D. 27 at 52, 69, 75 (C.A.).

As to statements which were not in the circumstances regarded as material, see *Kennedy v. Acadia Pulp & Paper Mills Co.* (1905), 38 N.S.R. 291 (C.A.) (representation that undrawn profits had been appropriated to a reserve fund); *Henry Hope & Sons of Canada Ltd. v. Sinclair* (1920), 17 O.W.N. 459 (statement amounted only to an expression of hope); *Butler v. Hamilton Lumber & Coal Co.* (1920), 18 O.W.N. 404 (alleged misrepresentation in prospectus not proved).

Misrepresentation must be acted upon

Misrepresentation is not actionable unless it is made with the intent that the person to whom it is made will act upon it and he does in fact so act.

The representation must have contributed to inducing the shareholder to purchase the shares, but it need not be the sole inducement: *Edgington v. Fitzmaurice* (1885), 29 Ch. D. 459 (C.A.); *Re London & Leeds Bank, Ex p. Carling* (1887), 56 L.T. 115; *Arnison v. Smith* (1889), 41 Ch. D. 348 at 359, 369 (C.A.).

Where an untrue representation has been made which is material, the onus of showing that it was not relied upon rests on the party who made it: *Baker v. Guaranty Savings & Loan Assn.*, [1931] S.C.R. 199; *Redgrave v. Hurd* (1881), 20 Ch. D. 1 at 21 (C.A.), per Jessel M.R. If it is shown that the party to whom the representation was made knew the true facts, his action will fail because he cannot successfully contend that he relied upon the representation: *Davison v. Priest* (1920), 51 D.L.R. 158 at 165 (N.S. C.A.).

The test is not whether the person complaining would have acted differently but whether he might have acted differently if the misrepresentation had not been made: *Young v. Smith* (1915), 21 D.L.R. 97 at 102 (Alta. C.A.).

In an action founded on deceit the misrepresentation must have been acted upon, i.e., the plaintiff must have been induced by the misstatement to take the shares: *Doyle v. Smith* (1907), 40 N.S.R. 157; but if it is proved that the defendant with a view to inducing the plaintiff to enter into the contract made a statement of a nature as would be likely to induce a person to enter into a contract and it is proved that the plaintiff entered into the contract it is a fair inference of fact that he was induced to do so by the statement: *Smith v. Chadwick* (1884), 9 App. Cas. 187 at 196; *Macleay v. Tait*, [1906] A.C. 24 at 31.

A misrepresentation made on a previous purchase of shares can be relied on where it remains uncorrected when the subscriber subsequently takes a further block of shares still relying on the truth of the original misrepresentation: *Fitzherbert v. Dominion Bed Manufacturing Co.* (1915), 23 D.L.R. 125 (B.C. C.A.).

Both materiality and whether the subscriber was induced to act on the misrepresentation are questions of fact: *Young v. Smith* (1915), 21 D.L.R. 97 (Alta. C.A.).

The person to whom the representation was made must have suffered damage; his loss must have been attributable to the misstatement: *Smith v. Chadwick* (1884), 9 App. Cas. 187, and see *Macleay v. Tait*, [1906] A.C. 24 at 26; *Johnson v. Johnson* (1913), 14 D.L.R. 756 (B.C. C.A.) (subscriber not misled to his prejudice).

Persons entitled to relief

It is ordinarily only the original subscriber who is entitled to rescission or damages for misrepresentation contained in a prospectus. Thus where applicants renounced the shares applied for in favour of the plaintiff, who was an undisclosed principal, the plaintiff, being in effect a transferee, could not obtain rescission for misrepresentation in the prospectus, it being impossible to treat the transaction between the corporation and the plaintiff as being based on the prospectus: *Collins v. Associated Greyhound Racecourses Ltd.*, [1930] 1 Ch. 1 (C.A.).

In order that a transferee may maintain an action for deceit in respect of loss occasioned by his belief in the prospectus and his consequent taking of shares, it would seem that he must show some connection between the persons responsible for the prospectus and himself in the communication of the prospectus and its influence upon his conduct in purchasing the shares: *Peek v. Gurney* (1873), L.R. 6 H.L. 377 at 400. In that case (which overruled many previous authorities) the House of Lords held that when the allotment is completed the office of the prospectus is exhausted and that a person who is not an allottee but a subsequent purchaser in the market is not so connected with the prospectus as to render those who issued it liable to him for his loss. However, in *Andrews v. Mockford*, [1896] 1 Q.B. 372 the Court of Appeal found that the object of the prospectus in question was not merely to induce application for an allotment of shares but also to induce persons to purchase shares in the market; consequently the function of the prospectus was not exhausted when the allotment was completed, and a person who bought shares on the market on the faith of the prospectus and thereby sustained loss was entitled to damages against those who were responsible for the issuing of the prospectus.

The plaintiff is not entitled to relief if he was a petitioner for incorporation and signed the memorandum of agreement which accompanies the petition. On the granting of the charter he becomes a shareholder and cannot repudiate his liability: *Bergeron v. Cie de meubles de Jonquière* (1913), 22 Que. K.B. 341. In *Buff Pressed Brick Co. v. Ford* (1915), 33 O.L.R. 264, the Ontario Court of Appeal in coming to the same conclusion held that any misrepresentation made to an incorporator is the act of a promoter, not the corporation; the corporation not being in existence, cannot make any misrepresentation. The shareholder's rights, if any, are against the promoters. An additional ground for refusing relief to an incorporator is that, by signing the memorandum of agreement, he becomes bound not only as between himself and the corporation but also as between himself and others who become shareholders. See *In re Metal Constituents Ltd.*, [1902] 1 Ch. 707.

A person who, relying on misrepresentations made to him, purchased shares as trustee for another, has the right himself to maintain an action for rescission; such right is not affected by the subsequent assignment of the beneficial interest of the *cestui que trust* to another: *Pigott v. Nesbitt, Thomson & Co.*, [1939] O.R. 66 (C.A.); affd (*sub nom. Nesbitt, Thomson & Co. v. Pigott*) [1941] S.C.R. 520.

An assignee of shares to which the circumstances attach as incidental and subsidiary a right of action to rescind is entitled to maintain the action for it does not savour of champerty or maintenance: *Nesbitt, Thomson & Co. v. Pigott*, *supra*. In this respect the right of action for rescission differs from a right of action for tort (i.e., action for deceit) which is not assignable: *Defries v. Milne*, [1913] 1 Ch. 98 (C.A.).

An underwriting subscriber is in a somewhat different position from an ordinary subscriber when he attempts to assert a claim in respect of a prospectus: *Baty v. Keswick* (1901), 85 L.T. 18 at 20; *Canada Food Co. v. Stanford* (1916), 28 D.L.R. 689 at 691 (N.S. C.A.).

Remedies and Defences Available at Common Law to a Subscriber for or Purchaser of Securities

Damages in common law action for deceit

Under the common law an action of deceit lies for misrepresentation in prospectuses, upon the faith of which persons are induced to take shares in a corporation to their loss. In addition to the essential elements of misrepresentation, which are discussed under the heading "Essential elements of misrepresentation" in this chapter, it is necessary in an action for deceit for a person to prove fraud and damages resulting therefrom.

An action for deceit brought by a purchaser of shares in a corporation and based on fraudulent misrepresentation must be brought against the particular individual responsible for the misrepresentation and not against the corporation: *Houldsworth v. City of Glasgow Bank* (1880), 5 App. Cas. 317 at 326; *Western Bank of Scotland v. Addie* (1867), L.R. 1 H.L. (Sc.) 145 at 157; *Milne v. Durham Hosiery Mills Ltd.* (1925), 57 O.L.R. 228 at 232 (C.A.). The House of Lords in the *Houldsworth* case laid down that the principle which entitles a person, who has been induced by fraud to purchase goods, to retain the goods and sue for damages does not apply to shares in a corporation. In that case a shareholder brought an action against the corporation for damages caused by the fraudulent misrepresentations of a director in inducing him to purchase shares and the House of Lords held that a person induced by the fraud of the agents of a corporation to become a partner (shareholder or member) in that corporation could not bring an action for damages for deceit against the corporation while he remained in it. His only remedy against the corporation is for rescission of the contract; and if that becomes impossible (by a winding-up of the corporation or by any other means) his action for damages against the corporation cannot be maintained. The *Houldsworth* case was followed and applied by the Ontario Court of Appeal in *Milne v. Durham Hosiery Mills Ltd.*, *supra*.

A claim for deceit against the directors as well as a claim for damages against them may be combined with a claim against the corporation for rescission in one action: *Frankenburg v. Great Horseless Carriage Co.*, [1900] 1 Q.B. 504. The distinction between an action for deceit and an action for the rescission of the contract to take shares is discussed in *Petrie v. Guelph Lumber Co.* (1886), 11 S.C.R. 450.

Fraud

Fraud is an essential element in an action for deceit and must be proved to enable the plaintiff to recover: *Derry v. Peek* (1889), 14 App. Cas. 337.

The clearest evidence of fraud is required: *Petrie v. Guelph Lumber Co.*, *supra*; *Beatty v. Neelon* (1885), 12 O.A.R. 50 (C.A.), affd (1887), 13 S.C.R. 1; *Clark v. Gray* (1902), 1 O.W.R. 370.

In order to prove fraud, it is necessary to establish that the statements were made fraudulently, that is, either with the knowledge that they were false, or recklessly, not caring whether they were true or false, or not believing them to be true.

If the statement complained of was believed in by the directors, the action fails. The statement must be shown to have been made dishonestly: *Angus v. Clifford*, [1891] 2 Ch. 449 (C.A.); but, if there is no reasonable foundation for an alleged belief in false statements, that may be sufficient to convince the court that there was no real belief in their truth: *Derry v. Peek* (1889), 14 App. Cas. 337 at 375; *Nesbitt, Thomson & Co. v. Pigott*, [1941] S.C.R. 520 at 530 where Taschereau J., delivering the judgment of the majority of the court, said that indifference as to whether the statements were false or true is sufficient to create civil liability; *Akerhielm v. De Mare*, [1959] A.C. 789 (P.C.) where Lord Jenkins stated at p. 805:

> The question is not whether the defendant in any given case honestly believed the representation to be true in the sense assigned to it by the court on an objective consideration of its truth or falsity, but whether he honestly believed the representation to be true in the sense in which he understood it albeit erroneously when it was made. This general proposition is no doubt subject to limitations. For instance, the meaning placed by the defendant on the representation made may be so far removed from the sense in which it would be understood by any reasonable person as to make it impossible to hold that the defendant honestly understood the representation to bear the meaning claimed by him and honestly believed it in that sense to be true.

Even although documents when read together gave a false impression there would be no fraudulent misrepresentation unless it was intended to give that false impression: *Gross v. Lewis Hillman Ltd.*, [1970] Ch. 445 (C.A.).

There must be a false statement of fact or at least such a partial statement that the omission to state that which is not disclosed renders that which is stated absolutely false: *Peek v. Gurney* (1873), L.R. 6 H.L. 377 at 403. And see *Aaron's Reefs Ltd. v. Twiss*, [1896] A.C. 273 at 287.

The court will look at the prospectus as a whole and read it in the sense in which the persons responsible for it must have known that the statements would be understood and may come to the conclusion that there was a false representation even though no individual statement is proved to be untrue. In *Aaron's Reefs Ltd. v. Twiss*, [1896] A.C. 273, Lord Halsbury L.C. said at p. 281: "If by a number of statements you intentionally give a false impression and induce a person to act upon it, it is not the less false although if one takes each statement by itself there may be a difficulty in showing that any specific statement is untrue".

Directors will be liable for misrepresentation by their agents: *Goold v. Gillies* (1908), 40 S.C.R. 437; but directors will not be liable for misrepresentation by an unauthorized agent or for statements in a prospectus not authorized to be issued by them: *Chapman v. Warren*, [1936] 2 D.L.R. 157 (Ont. H.C.).

Damage

Damage must be proved. Fraud without damages gives no cause of action: *Angers v. Mutual Reserve Fund Life Association* (1904), 35 S.C.R. 330 at 340.

The measure of damages is the difference between the actual value of the shares at the date of the allotment and the amount paid by the shareholder: *Peek v. Derry* (1888), 37 Ch. D. 541 at 594 (C.A.); or, at the time of the purchase, where issued shares have been wrongfully delivered: *Goold v. Gillies* (1908), 40 S.C.R. 437 at 452; but, in such a case, Macdonald C.J.A. in *Allan v. McLennan* (1916), 31 D.L.R. 617 at 619 (B.C. C.A.), was of the opinion that the measure of damages was the difference between the value of the shares at the time when the plaintiff discovered the fraud and what was paid for them with interest. *Prima facie* the value of the shares, if they had been as represented, is taken to be what was paid for them: *McConnel v. Wright*, [1903] 1 Ch. 546 (C.A.). If the defendant wants to show that the shares were worth so much more that, even on the true facts, they were worth what was paid he must produce evidence to that effect; and if the plaintiff wants to show that even if the shares had been as represented they were worth less than he paid for them he must produce evidence: *Sissons v. Hassard*, [1923] 4 D.L.R. 186 at 191 (Alta. C.A.). The time at which damages ought to be assessed is the date of allotment: *McConnel v. Wright, supra.*

While it is the plaintiff's duty to minimize damages he is under no obligation to spend money for that purpose; thus where the plaintiff, by reason of fraudulent misrepresentation inducing him to advance money on a debenture, had sustained damages amounting to the difference between the amount lent and the amount received in liquidation and subsequently purchased the assets of the corporation from the receiver and sold them at a profit he was not required to set off the profit against the loss: *Jewelowski v. Propp*, [1944] 1 K.B. 510.

Delay in proceedings

Where there has been concealment, the statute of limitations will be prevented from running. Thus, in *Gibbs v. Guild* (1882), 9 Q.B.D. 59 (C.A.) where the plaintiff did not discover and had no reasonable means of discovering the fraud until within six years before action and the existence of the fraud was fraudulently concealed by the defendant until within such six years the action was in time. But so long as there has been no laches on the part of the person defrauded it is immaterial whether or not there have been active measures taken by the wrongdoer to prevent detection: *Bulli Coal Mining Co. v. Osborne*, [1899] A.C. 351; *Twyford v. Bishopric* (1914), 20 D.L.R. 871 (Alta. C.A.); *Nesbitt, Thomson & Co. v. Pigott*, [1941] S.C.R. 520. In *Nesbitt* the plaintiff had made his first purchase of shares in 1927 and the writ was not issued until 1935. The plaintiff made no enquiries until 1932 and did not suspect fraud until an engineer employed by him made his report in 1934. It was held that the statute began to run then and that the plaintiff in commencing his definite enquiries in 1932 acted with reasonable promptness.

The only delay which will be a bar to relief is that fixed by the statute: *Peek v. Gurney* (1873), L.R. 6 H.L. 377 at 384. However, in *Dorsch v. Freeholders*

Oil Co., [1965] S.C.R. 670, the *Companies Act* of Saskatchewan required every person invited by a prospectus to purchase a security be furnished with a copy of the prospectus. It was held that non-compliance with the section could, at most, render the purchase of the shares voidable by the purchaser. Here the right to void the purchase had been lost by the shareholder who by his conduct in receiving the share certificate, voting at annual meetings and failing to take any steps repudiating until six years later had waived any right to rescind.

Whether the bankruptcy and subsequent discharge of a person against whom a claim for damages for misrepresentation on the sale of securities is made will operate as a release from liability in respect of such claim depends upon whether the liability was incurred by means of fraud. Under the *Bankruptcy Act* such a liability is not released by an order of discharge: *Boland v. Johnson*, [1934] O.R. 108 (C.A.).

Rescission of the contract

The remedy of rescission based on misrepresentation at common law is discussed here.

Under the general law of contract a contract induced by misrepresentation is voidable and may be set aside by the court. Thus, if a contract for the subscription for or purchase of shares is induced by misrepresentation, whether such misrepresentation is innocent or fraudulent, the court in an action by the subscriber or purchaser will rescind the contract and order restitution of the moneys paid under the contract with interest: *In re Metropolitan Coal Consumers' Association, Karberg's Case*, [1892] 3 Ch. 1 at 17 (C.A.). As to the rescission of executed contracts, see below.

Grounds for rescission

In an action for rescission, just as in an action for deceit, it is necessary to prove that the misrepresentation was one of fact, that it was material and that it was acted upon. For comment on these essential elements, see the discussion under the heading "Essential Elements of Misrepresentation" and following, in this chapter. On the other hand, in an action for rescission, unlike an action for deceit, it is not necessary to prove damages: *Gillett v. Peppercorne* (1840), 3 Beav. 78 at 84; *Hulton v. Hulton*, [1917] 1 K.B. 813 at 824 (C.A.), nor is it necessary, subject to the one possible exception discussed below, to prove that the misrepresentation was made fraudulently: *Redgrave v. Hurd* (1881), 20 Ch. D. 1 at 12 (C.A.); *Karberg's Case, supra*, at 13. It is immaterial that the directors may be ignorant of the untruth of the statement: *Reese River Silver Mining Co. v. Smith* (1869), L.R. 4 H.L. 64 at 79. The distinction between an action for rescission and one for deceit is discussed in *Petrie v. Guelph Lumber Co.* (1886), 11 S.C.R. 450.

The one possible exception to the rule that the court will grant rescission of a contract for shares without proof that the misrepresentation was fraudulent is in the case where the contract has been fully executed. Under the general law of contract, if a contract has been executed and property has passed the court will set it aside on the ground of misrepresentation only if fraud is shown:

Seddon v. North Eastern Salt Co., [1905] 1 Ch. 326 (sale of shares); *Angel v. Jay*, [1911] 1 K.B. 666 (C.A.). This principle was applied in *Abrey v. Victoria Printing Co.* (1912), 2 D.L.R. 208 (Ont. C.A.) where the subscriber had paid up his subscription in full and the court treated the contract as executed and refused to grant rescission on the ground of misrepresentation not amounting to fraud. In *First National Reinsurance Co. v. Greenfield*, [1921] 2 K.B. 260 at 272, where the authorities are considered, McCardie J. concluded that contracts for the taking of shares, even though followed by allotment and the placing of the name of the applicant on the register, did not fall within the principle of the *Seddon* case, *supra*; see also *Lecky v. Walter*, [1914] 1 I.R. 378, *infra*. However, in *Kingstone v. Dominion Alloy Steel Corp. Ltd.*, [1939] O.R. 286 at 293, Gillanders J.A. on the facts of the case (contract executed 15 years before action taken) followed *Abrey v. Victoria Printing Co., supra*. The principle established in the *Seddon* case, *supra*, has been criticized in a number of subsequent cases which are referred to in *Long v. Lloyd*, [1958] 2 All E.R. 402 at 404, 406 (C.A.), but the case has not been overruled.

There is no doubt that rescission of an executed contract to take shares will be granted if the action is based upon a fraudulent misrepresentation: *McGaffigan v. National Husker Co.* (1911), 2 O.W.N. 600; *Pigott Construction Co. v. Nesbitt, Thomson & Co.*, [1939] O.R. 66 (C.A.), affd [1941] S.C.R. 520. See also *Burns v. Ambler* (1963), 42 W.W.R. 254 (B.C. S.C.).

If there is a difference in substance between the thing bargained for and that obtained, there may be rescission for innocent misrepresentation after the contract has been executed, for example, a contract to buy mortgage debentures where the buyer takes delivery of what he believes to be such, but what he afterwards discovers to be ordinary shares: *Lecky v. Walter*, [1914] 1 I.R. 378 at 386, 387.

As to when parties will be deemed *ad idem*, see *Lindsey v. Heron & Co.* (1922), 50 O.L.R. 1 (C.A.), and *Baker v. Guaranty Savings & Loan Assn.*, [1931] S.C.R. 199.

Mere non-disclosure is insufficient as a ground for rescission. The facts not disclosed must be such that the omission to disclose them renders the statement actually made misleading: *McKeown v. Boudard-Peveril Gear Co.* (1896), 74 L.T. 712. Thus, in *Coles v. White City (Manchester) Greyhound Assn Ltd.* (1928), 45 T.L.R. 230, the plaintiff was entitled to rescission on the ground that a statement in the prospectus that the lands of the corporation were eminently suitable for the establishment of a track was clearly misleading where the prospectus did not disclose that the land purchased by the corporation for its operations was subject to a town planning scheme.

If a statement of fact in a prospectus was true at the date of the prospectus but becomes untrue before allotment, the allottee is entitled to rescind: *In re Scottish Petroleum Co., Anderson's Case* (1881), 17 Ch. D. 373 at 377; *In re Scottish Petroleum Co.* (1883), 23 Ch. D. 413 at 438 (C.A.); but see *Petrie v. Guelph Lumber Co.* (1886), 11 S.C.R. 450 at 482 where the allottee was not entitled to rescind by reason of the alleged concealment of a mortgage given after the prospectus was issued.

A fraudulent representation by the agent that the corporation would commence business within a certain time entitled the subscriber to rescind: *International Casualty Co. v. Thomson* (1913), 48 S.C.R. 167. So also a fraudulent representation that the business of the corporation was so great as to make it necessary to erect a second factory: *Howard v. Canadian Automatic Transportation Co.* (1914), 6 O.W.N. 285, affd (1914), 6 O.W.N. 404 (C.A.); and a false and misleading statement by an agent that an insurance corporation had made the required statutory deposit with the government: *Vancouver Life Insurance Co. v. Richards* (1919), 48 D.L.R. 707 (B.C. C.A.).

A representation by an agent which amounts to a *simplex commendatio*, unless made in bad faith, is not a ground for rescission: *North West Battery Co. v. Hargrave* (1913), 15 D.L.R. 193 (Man. K.B.).

It is sometimes stated in the contract of subscription that no representations of any kind shall be binding or affect its validity unless embodied therein. It has been held that such a provision in a contract is notice that the agent has no authority to bind his principals by any representations not embodied in the written contract: *Hughes v. Ojibway Realty Co.* (1922), 22 O.W.N. 574, affd (1924), 55 O.L.R. 611 (C.A.). This was not a case of a contract for the purchase of shares. A clause in a contract stating that no representations have been made by either party may be held to be a corroboration of the evidence of one party that no representations were made; although it was pointed out that such a clause might in some cases be part of a fraud and therefore of no avail: *Campbell v. Hamill*, [1925] 4 D.L.R. 958 (Sask. C.A.). In the case of such a contract, Kelly J. held that a special clause, designed to exonerate the vendor from responsibility for accuracy of statements made by its agent, was ineffective: *Mitchell v. Continental Bond Corp.* (1924), 27 O.W.N. 184 (C.A.).

Responsibility of corporation for misrepresentations

The action to rescind must be brought against the corporation, and accordingly the plaintiff must prove that the misstatement was made by someone having authority to bind the corporation, or that the prospectus in which the misstatement occurred was the act of the corporation. Thus in *Farrell v. Manchester* (1908), 40 S.C.R. 339, the misstatement in question had been made by a broker who had been employed to sell the shares and had prepared the prospectus. It was held that the prospectus having been proved to be the act of the corporation, the plaintiff was entitled to rescind and it was further held to be immaterial that the prospectus was marked "private". A corporation cannot escape liability on the ground that the misstatements were not authorized where the directors know that the person making the representations was acting for the corporation in raising money: *Hilo Manufacturing Co. v. Williamson* (1911), 28 T.L.R. 164; *Farah v. Capital Manufacturing Co.* (1913), 23 O.W.R. 918, affd 24 O.W.R. 808 (C.A.) (misrepresentation by managing director). For a discussion of the circumstances which will fix a corporation with responsibility for a document purporting to be the prospectus of the corporation, see *French Gas Saving Co. v. Desbarats Advertising Agency Ltd.* (1912), 1 D.L.R. 136 (Que. C.A.). Where the president of a bank, acting outside the scope of his authority, had sold issued shares to the plaintiff upon a representation that they were unissued shares, there being no contractual relationship between the plaintiff and the bank, the plaintiff failed as against the bank in respect of his claim for rescission: *Allan v. McLennan* (1916), 10 W.W.R. 941 at 943, varied (1916), 31 D.L.R. 617 at 625 (B.C. C.A.).

A prospectus for which the corporation is not in the first place responsible may become the act of the corporation if it is adopted by it. This may occur when the prospectus was issued prior to incorporation and the corporation has in effect adopted it by allotting the shares subscribed for: *Buff Pressed Brick Co. v. Ford* (1915), 33 O.L.R. 264 (C.A.); *In re Metropolitan Coal Consumers' Assn., Karberg's Case*, [1892] 3 Ch. 1 (C.A.). In such cases there may be a remedy against the corporation as well as against the promoters.

In *Karberg's Case, supra*, Lindley L.J. said at p. 13:

> Speaking generally, there is no doubt that a misrepresentation in order to vitiate a contract must be made by a party to it, or by his agent. But this rule is not without exception: *Stewart's Case* ((1866), L.R. 1 Ch. 574) and *Downes v. Ship* ((1868), L.R. 3 H.L. 343) warrant the proposition that an application to a company when formed for shares, based upon a prospectus issued by the promoters of the company before its formation, cannot be dissevered by the company from such prospectus.

It should be borne in mind that this case was one of rescission. For other cases where it was sought to hold a corporation responsible for statements in a prospectus, see *Henderson v. Lacon* (1867), L.R. 5 Eq. 249; *Peek v. Gurney* (1873), L.R. 6 H.L. 377; *Re Denham & Co.* (1884), 25 Ch. D. 752; *Tamplin's Case*, [1892] W.N. 94, 146. But if the misrepresentation is made by a promoter who is neither a director or general agent of the corporation nor a special agent to procure subscriptions nor authorized to make any representations on its behalf, and the application is not one made conditional upon, nor, to the knowledge of the directors based upon, any representations made by the promoter, the applicant is not entitled to rescission: *Lynde v. Anglo-Italian Hemp Spinning Co.*, [1896] 1 Ch. 178. The corporation will be bound by the acts of a director who has made representations in obtaining subscriptions for shares where the members of the board knew that the director was endeavouring to raise money on the corporation's behalf: *Hilo Manufacturing Co. v. Williamson* (1911), 28 T.L.R. 164.

As regards reports of experts, if the corporation assumes the authenticity of, and represents as facts, what is stated in the report, the corporation will be bound by the representation: *In re Reese River Mining Co., Smith's Case* (1867), L.R. 2 Ch. App. 604 at 611. And if the corporation puts out a prospectus embodying a report made by a director it is responsible at least for the absence of fraud in the misrepresentations contained in the report: *Mair v. Rio Grande Rubber Estates Ltd.*, [1913] A.C. 853. If a prospectus contains statements based upon a bona fide report of an expert any material inaccuracy in the corporation's statements, although based on the report, will be a ground for rescission, unless the prospectus clearly warns the public that the corporation does not vouch for the accuracy of the reports quoted or referred to therein: *In re Pacaya Rubber & Produce Co., Burns' Application*, [1914] 1 Ch. 542, and cases cited.

Where the plaintiff is an undisclosed principal he cannot rely upon a misrepresentation contained in the prospectus as a ground for rescission, without proving that the agent relied upon and was misled by the representation: *Collins v. Associated Greyhound Racecourses Ltd.*, [1930] 1 Ch. 1 (C.A.).

No order to return the moneys paid under the contract rescinded can be made against the directors separately or jointly: *Ross v. Estates Investment Co.* (1868), L.R. 3 Ch. App. 682, at 689-690; *Solloway v. Johnson*, [1934] A.C. 193 at 207.

A shareholder's remedy against the corporation is rescission and not an action for damages because, in view of the relationship between a shareholder and a corporation, he cannot retain his shares and seek damages against the corporation: *Houldsworth v. City of Glasgow Bank* (1880), 5 App. Cas. 317; *Milne v. Durham Hosiery Mills Ltd.* (1925), 57 O.L.R. 228 (C.A.).

Rescission relates back to the period when proceedings were taken to rescind notwithstanding that a winding-up order is subsequently made: *Reese River Silver Mining Co. v. Smith* (1869), L.R. 4 H.L. 64; *Dominion Bed Manufacturing Co. v. Fitzherbert* (1917), 36 D.L.R. 600 (B.C. C.A.).

Loss of right to rescind

A contract to take shares induced by misrepresentation contained in a prospectus is not void but voidable only; it is valid until repudiated and the subscriber may lose the right to repudiate in various ways. Thus, if after having obtained knowledge of the facts the subscriber does something indicating affirmation of the contract, for example, if he attends meetings, agrees to sell his shares, pays calls or otherwise shows that he regards himself as a shareholder, he loses the right to repudiate the contract: *Petrie v. Guelph Lumber Co.* (1886), 11 S.C.R. 450; *Pineau v. Neigette Co.* (1911), 22 R.L.N.S. 154; *Re National Husker Co., Worthington's Case* (1913), 14 D.L.R. 696 (Ont. C.A.); *Ward v. Siemon* (1918), 43 O.L.R. 113 at 118; *Re Burnsland Ltd., Barr's Case* (1920), 53 D.L.R. 439 (Alta. T.D.). Mere attendance at meetings without voting or taking part in the proceedings when the defendant was ignorant of the real character or nature of the corporation, believing it to be a co-operative association when it was in fact an ordinary corporation, may be insufficient to establish estoppel: *Farmers Packing Co. v. Tully*, [1927] 2 D.L.R. 749 (Man. K.B.).

The fact of a person seeing a prospectus wherein a corporation makes certain statements, which if true would affect such person's rights, and of not proceeding immediately to protest against such statements is no proof of acquiescence in such statements and of ratification of the acts or deeds therein described: *Consumers Cordage Co. v. Molson* (1912), 2 D.L.R. 451 (Que. C.A.).

Under the common law in regard to voidable contracts the rule is that the right to avoid must, if exercised at all, be exercised promptly on the discovery of the facts. Accordingly, the most common example of loss of the right to rescind is to be found in delay by the shareholder. He must proceed promptly after the misrepresentation is brought to his notice. In *In re Scottish Petroleum Co.* (1883), 23 Ch. D. 413 (C.A.) it was suggested that a delay of a fortnight might be too long. In *Central Venezuela Railway Co. v. Kisch* (1867), L.R. 2

H.L. 99, a delay of two months did not disentitle the shareholder to relief when time for investigation on his part had to be allowed for; and in *In re Pacaya Rubber & Produce Co., Burns' Application*, [1914] 1 Ch. 542 at 548, a delay of seven months did not disentitle the shareholder to relief as he had been ill. In the following cases the shareholder was held to be too late: *Morrisburgh & Ottawa Electric Ry. Co. v. O'Connor* (1915), 34 O.L.R. 161 (C.A.) (delay of two years); *Robert v. Montreal Trust Co.* (1918), 56 S.C.R. 342 at 354 (delay of two and a half years); *First National Reinsurance Co. v. Greenfield*, [1921] 2 K.B. 260 at 277 (delay of seven months); *Kingstone v. Dominion Alloy Steel Corp.*, [1939] O.R. 286 at 292 (no fraud alleged and action barred by Statute of Limitations).

In *Nelles v. Ontario Investment Association* (1889), 17 O.R. 129, a number of years intervened between the date of the subscription and the date of the action, but the plaintiff, not having become aware of the untruthfulness of the misstatements until shortly before the action, was entitled to recover. It was also held that the fact that the plaintiff had sold some of his shares did not prevent rescission as to the balance. And when no change occurs in the status of the corporation in the interval between subscription and the bringing of the action, delay by the shareholder in ascertaining his rights has been held not to be a bar: *Pioneer Tractor Co. v. Peebles* (1913), 15 D.L.R. 275 (Sask. T.D.), affd (1914), 18 D.L.R. 477 (Sask. C.A.), affd (1915), 8 W.W.R. 632 (S.C.C.).

The result of the authorities would appear to be that it is a question of fact in each case whether there has been undue delay, and the only safe course for the subscriber is to repudiate with the utmost promptness on discovery of the misrepresentation, otherwise his rights may be lost.

The same results do not follow from delay in bringing an action after repudiation has taken place. In *Farrell v. Manchester* (1908), 40 S.C.R. 339, it was held that, at any rate when the shares are fully paid up, a delay of almost a year between repudiation and the bringing of the action did not disentitle the shareholder to relief.

In an action for rescission on the ground of fraud the Statute of Limitations does not commence to run until the fraud is discovered; it is not necessary for the plaintiff to prove concealment and in the absence of laches he is entitled to succeed: *Pigott Construction Co. v. Nesbitt, Thomson & Co.*, [1937] O.R. 888 at 910, [1939] O.R. 66 at 82, affd (*sub nom. Nesbitt, Thomson & Co. v. Pigott*) [1941] S.C.R. 520.

The subscriber in order to make his repudiation effective should immediately bring an action against the corporation for rescission since the right to rescind is lost by the commencement of a winding-up before the action is brought: *In re Scottish Petroleum Co.* (1883), 23 Ch. D. 413 (C.A.); *Reese River Mining Co. v. Smith* (1869), L.R. 4 H.L. 64; *St. Roch Hotel Co. v. Barbeau* (1915), 48 Que. S.C. 94; but not by the corporation's having got into financial difficulties short of liquidation: *Fitzherbert v. Dominion Bed Manufacturing Co.* (1915), 23 D.L.R. 125 (B.C. C.A.). The reason why a winding-up destroys the right to rescind is because after a winding-up the shareholder's liability becomes a statutory liability to contribute the amount unpaid on his shares, and other rights, viz., those of creditors and contributories, intervene so that rescission is no longer possible: *Tennent v. City of Glasgow Bank* (1879), 4 App. Cas. 615. The same rule applies under the *Bankruptcy and Insolvency Act*: see *Trusts & Guarantee Co. v. Smith*, [1924] 2 D.L.R. 211 (Ont. C.A.).

In *Re Western Canada Fire Insurance Co.* (1915), 22 D.L.R. 19, the Court of Appeal in Alberta held that an unequivocal repudiation, where the subscriber was entitled to repudiate, was sufficient without the further step of bringing proceedings to set aside the subscription before a winding-up. The court further held that it was not bound by *In re Scottish Petroleum Co.* (1883), 23 Ch. D. 413 (C.A.). *Re Western Canada Fire Insurance Co., supra*, was followed in *Re Panama Pacific Grain Terminals Ltd.*, [1939] 4 D.L.R. 705 at 710 (Sask. K.B.). On the other hand, in Ontario *In re Scottish Petroleum Co.* has been followed: *Re National Stadium Ltd.* (1924), 55 O.L.R. 199 (C.A.); approved in *Milne v. Durham Hosiery Mills Ltd.* (1925), 57 O.L.R. 228 (C.A.).

Rectification of the register

The provision of the English *Companies Act*, empowering the court to rectify the register on the application of the person aggrieved will enable a person who has been induced by misrepresentation to take shares to obtain relief in such an application by having his name removed from the register: *In re London & Staffordshire Fire Insurance Co.* (1883), 24 Ch. D. 149; but he must not only repudiate but also take steps with reasonable promptness to have his name removed from the register: *Re Christineville Rubber Estates Ltd.* (1911), 81 L.J. Ch. 63; *First National Reinsurance Co. v. Greenfield*, [1921] 2 K.B. 260. And after discovering the misrepresentation he must not have done any act which recognizes the shares as his property: *Re Burnsland Ltd., Barr's Case* (1920), 53 D.L.R. 439 (Alta. T.D.) and cases cited.

Similar provisions appear in provincial Business Corporations Acts, for example, the Ontario Act, s. 250. It has been held that that section is not to be invoked except in a reasonably clear case: *Gramm Motor Truck Co. of Canada v. Bennett* (1914), 35 O.L.R. 224 (C.A.); *British American Timber Co. v. Jones*, [1941] 3 W.W.R. 296 (B.C. C.A.).

The provisions of s. 243 of the Federal Act for the rectification of the books of the corporation are similar and it would appear that they could be invoked for the purpose of having the name of a shareholder removed on the ground that his subscription was induced by misrepresentation.

See the comment in chapter 16 on this subject.

Defence of misrepresentation to an action for payment

Where an action is brought for calls, it has been held in England that the mere plea of fraud or material misrepresentation in the prospectus and repudiation is insufficient. The shareholder must allege and prove not only that he has repudiated but also that he has taken steps to rescind the contract and have his name removed from the register of shareholders. If the court to which the proceedings are taken is itself competent to rectify the register, it is sufficient to counterclaim for rectification: *First National Reinsurance Co. v. Greenfield*,

[1921] 2 K.B. 260 at 271; and see *Aaron's Reefs Ltd. v. Twiss*, [1896] A.C. 273 (counterclaim for rescission); *Hilo Manufacturing Co. v. Williamson* (1911), 28 T.L.R. 164 (counterclaim for rescission).

The rule enunciated in *First National Reinsurance Co., supra*, does not apply in the case of a shareholder in a federal corporation, and accordingly it is not necessary for him to take steps to have his name removed from the register before his defence of misrepresentation can be sustained: *Re Panama Pacific Grain Terminals Ltd.*, [1939] 4 D.L.R. 705 at 711 (Sask. K.B.). In *Farrell v. Manchester* (1908), 40 S.C.R. 339 at 353, it was held that the rule laid down in the English cases does not apply in the case of corporations incorporated under Acts which provide that the register of shareholders is only open to creditors and shareholders and not to everyone as is the case under the English *Companies Act.*

It has been held in the case of an Ontario corporation that misrepresentation may be set up as a defence to an action to enforce the contract of subscription. If the misrepresentations are fraudulent and the fraud induces the subscription, the shares are not to be forced on the subscriber: *Buff Pressed Brick Co. v. Ford* (1915), 33 O.L.R. 264 at 266 (C.A.). And in *Ontario Ladies' College v. Kendry* (1905), 10 O.L.R. 324 (C.A.) it was held that a material misrepresentation of an agent inducing the contract of subscription, whether made in good faith or not, was a good defence to an action by the corporation to enforce the contract.

In *Pioneer Tractor Co. v. Peebles* (1913), 15 D.L.R. 275 (Sask. T.D.), affd (1914), 18 D.L.R. 477 (Sask. C.A.), affd (1915), 8 W.W.R. 632 (S.C.C.) a defence of misrepresentation in an action upon the subscription was sustained, the English decisions referred to above being held to be inapplicable. This case was followed in *Re Panama Pacific Grain Terminals Ltd.*, [1939] 4 D.L.R. 705 at 711 (Sask. K.B.).

If a jury has found that the subscription was not induced by the alleged misrepresentation the subscription will not be set aside: *Gowganda Queen Mines Ltd. v. Boeckh* (1911), 24 O.L.R. 293, affd (1912), 46 S.C.R. 645; *Maritime United Farmers Co-operative Ltd. v. Dickie*, [1925] 1 D.L.R. 377 (N.B. C.A.). See also *Cie de Cerceuils en Verre v. Doyon* (1923), 29 Rev. Leg. 288 (representation true at time of subscription).

In *Skelton v. Frigon*, [1923] 4 D.L.R. 278, the Quebec Court of Appeal held that an untrue representation that all shareholders were on an equal footing was a good defence to an action on a note given for the amount of the subscription.

In *Britannia Collieries Ltd. v. Hauser*, [1922] 1 W.W.R. 811 (Alta. T.D.), Walsh J. said he was inclined to the view that the corporation could be held liable for the representation of a promoter made before it came into existence. In that case it was held that the misrepresentation complained of had not been established and the point was not dealt with in the judgment affirming the decision of the trial judge ([1922] 2 W.W.R. 885 (Alta. C.A.)).

Although the subscriber may have a good defence against the corporation, for example, that his subscription was induced by fraud and that he had never received any notice of allotment, by giving in payment of his shares a promissory note to the corporation which the latter has endorsed to a holder in due course, he may be liable to the holder on the note: *Standard Bank v. Stephens* (1908), 11 O.W.R. 582 (Div. Ct.). See also *Borden v. Stanford* (1915), 21 D.L.R. 209 (N.S. C.A.) where a subscriber was held liable to a holder in due course of a note given for shares agreed to be taken from brokers described as trustees.

Where the subscriber's shares have been forfeited for non-payment of calls, he ceases to be a shareholder and he can set up fraud as a defence to an action by the corporation for the call if he has done nothing to affirm the contract: *Aaron's Reefs Ltd. v. Twiss*, [1896] A.C. 273 (H.L.).

A trustee in bankruptcy is not entitled to enforce a subscription obtained through misrepresentation as to the corporation's solvency: *Re Macdonald Lumber Co.*, [1923] 4 D.L.R. 44 (Que. S.C.).

Compensation or damages under the statutory provisions

In *Derry v. Peek* (1889), 14 App. Cas. 337, it was held that in an action of deceit the plaintiff must prove actual fraud, and that a false statement made through carelessness and without reasonable grounds for believing it to be true may be evidence of fraud, but does not necessarily amount to fraud; and further, that such statement, if made in the honest belief that it is true, is not fraudulent and does not render the person making it liable to an action of deceit. The practical effect of this decision would have been to leave those deceived by untrue statements in prospectuses without a remedy, except where something practically amounting to pre-conceived and deliberate fraud in the publication of such statements could be shown. As to *Derry v. Peek* and the common law action for deceit see the discussion under the headings "Damages in the common law action for deceit" and "Fraud", in this chapter.

The securities legislation creates a liability which did not exist apart from statute, viz., to pay compensation to all persons who subscribe for securities of the corporation on the faith of a prospectus issued by or on behalf of the corporation which invites persons to subscribe for securities of the corporation, for the loss or damage they may have sustained by reason of any untrue statements of a material fact or an omission to state a material fact that is required to be stated or that is necessary to make a statement not misleading in the light of the circumstances in which it is made in the prospectus, or by reference incorporated in the prospectus or issued with the prospectus.

The securities legislation does not prejudice the remedy which subscribers have at common law in damages for deceit against the individual who makes any fraudulent misrepresentation nor the equitable remedy of rescission in an action against the corporation. A claim against directors under the section as well as a claim for deceit against the directors and a claim against the corporation for rescission may be combined in one action: *Frankenburg v. Great Horseless Carriage Co.*, [1900] 1 Q.B. 504 (C.A.). In *Kingstone v. Dominion Alloy Steel Corp. Ltd.*, [1939] O.R. 286 at 294, it was suggested that the plaintiff may have to elect between a claim for rescission and his remedy against the directors under the statute as a shareholder.

Some damage must be proved: *Stevens v. Hoare* (1904), 20 T.L.R. 407. Where the corporation failed about a year after it was formed and the plaintiff lost the money he paid for his shares, that was *prima facie* evidence of some damage and the plaintiff was entitled to an enquiry as to the amount of his damages: *Shepheard v. Broome*, [1904] A.C. 342 at 347, per Lord Lindley. The measure of damages is the same as in the common law action of deceit: *Clark v. Urquhart*, [1930] A.C. 28 (P.C.), namely, the difference between the purchase price and value of the shares at the time of allotment: *McConnel v. Wright*, [1903] 1 Ch. 546; *Kingstone v. Dominion Alloy Steel Corp. Ltd.*, [1939] O.R. 286 at 294 (plaintiff's claim failed because no evidence adduced to show the fair value of the shares); *Broome v. Speak*, [1903] 1 Ch. 586 (C.A.); affd (*sub nom. Shepheard v. Broome*) [1904] A.C. 342 (H.L.). See, however, *Clark v. Urquhart*, *supra*, at 68, where Lord Atkin expressly reserved the right to further consider whether or not the formula in *McConnel v. Wright*, *supra*, was correct or expressed in too rigid terms. If the purchaser does not retain his shares, but repudiates his subscription, the measure of damages is the amount paid for them: *Johnson v. Johnson* (1913), 14 D.L.R. 756 (B.C. C.A.). See further the notes under the heading "Damages in the common law action for deceit", *supra*.

An untrue statement is one untrue in point of fact: *Broome v. Speak*, [1903] 1 Ch. 586 at 602, and it is immaterial that it was made innocently: *Shepheard v. Broome*, [1904] A.C. 342; *Johnson v. Johnson*, *supra*, at 758. A misleading statement may be an "untrue statement": *Greenwood v. Leather Shod Wheel Co.*, [1900] 1 Ch. 421 at 434.

The liability under the statute being founded on tort the maxim *actio personalis moritur cum persona* applies, and where a director is a defendant in an action brought under the statute the action will not survive against the executor in the absence of proof that the director's estate benefited by the tort: *Geipel v. Peach*, [1917] 2 Ch. 108.

The cause of action accrues at the time when the shares are subscribed for and the period of limitation within which an action must be brought is six years: *Thomson v. Lord Clanmorris*, [1900] 1 Ch. 718 (C.A.); *Kingstone v. Dominion Alloy Steel Corp. Ltd.*, [1939] O.R. 286 at 293.

If a director, knowing that a prospectus is being issued, does not read it or make any enquiry as to its contents, and gives no notice as required by the statute, it is too late for him to repudiate the prospectus if he waits until an action is brought against him for damages for an untrue statement in the prospectus: *Drincqbier v. Wood*, [1899] 1 Ch. 393.

The onus is on the defendant to show reasonable grounds for believing in the accuracy of any untrue statement, and particulars of such grounds will be ordered where this defence is set up: *Alman v. Oppert*, [1901] 2 K.B. 576 (C.A.).

As to what is required to be proved to establish reasonable grounds of belief, see *Greenwood v. Leather Shod Wheel Co.*, [1900] 1 Ch. 421 (C.A.); *Stevens v. Hoare* (1904), 20 T.L.R. 407; *Shepheard v. Broome*, [1904] A.C. 342.

The uncorroborated statements of a vendor-promoter afford by themselves no reasonable ground for belief in their truth: *Adams v. Thrift*, [1915] 2 Ch. 21 (C.A.).

It is usually desirable to set out any report or valuation in full without comment. The dangers attendant on commenting on or drawing conclusions from reports of experts are illustrated in *Pigott v. Nesbitt, Thomson & Co.*, [1937] O.R. 888, affd [1939] O.R. 66 (C.A.), affd (*sub nom. Nesbitt, Thomson & Co. v. Pigott*) [1941] S.C.R. 520.

The right of contribution is available against any other person who, if sued separately would have been liable to make the same payment, unless the person asserting the right of contribution was guilty of fraudulent misrepresentation and the other was not. Where a director is suing under the subsection, it is not sufficient to claim merely contribution on account of the judgment obtained against him, and which he has paid. The statement of claim must allege the defendant's responsibility for the issue of the prospectus, that the subscriber applied for the shares on the faith of it, and that he suffered loss by reason of one or more untrue statements therein: *Johnson v. Johnson* (1913), 14 D.L.R. 756 at 761 (B.C. C.A.). The plaintiff must establish such a case as a subscriber himself would be required to make if he were suing: *Johnson v. Johnson, supra.* The co-director should be brought in by third party notice: *Gerson v. Simpson*, [1903] 2 K.B. 197 (C.A.).

Criminal liability for false statements in a prospectus

In addition to the offences provided for under the various Securities Acts, Directors, officers and promoters may be criminally liable under the *Criminal Code* for making, circulating or publishing a prospectus, statement or account, whether written or oral, which they know to be false in any material particular, with the intent specified in s. 400 of the *Criminal Code*, which reads as follows:

> 400. (1) Every one who makes, circulates or publishes a prospectus, statement or an account, whether written or oral, that he knows is false in a material particular, with intent
>
> (a) to induce persons, whether ascertained or not, to become shareholders or partners in a company,
> (b) to deceive or defraud the members, shareholders or creditors, whether ascertained or not, of a company,
> (c) to induce any person to entrust or advance anything to a company, or
> (d) to enter into any security for the benefit of a company,
> is guilty of an indictable offence and is liable to imprisonment for a term not exceeding ten years.
>
> (2) In this section, "company" means a syndicate, body corporate or company, whether existing or proposed to be created.

The falsity of the statement and knowledge of the falsity are essential as is also intention to induce or to defraud: *R. v. Harcourt* (1930), 64 O.L.R. 566 (C.A.); intention to defraud may be presumed when it is proved that the statements are false to the knowledge of the accused: *R. v. Birt* (1899), 63 J.P. 328 or if it was intended that the false statement should influence and be acted upon by those it was designed to reach: *R. v. Miller*, [1940] 3 D.L.R. 293 at 296 (B.C. C.A.); *R. v. McLeod*, [1941] 1 D.L.R. 578 at 580 (B.C. C.A.), revd [1941] S.C.R.

228. As to what is a material particular within the statute, see *R. v. Harcourt*, *supra*; and *R. v. Gillespie* (1898), 1 C.C.C. 551 (Que. Q.B.).

Where the prospectus stated that the corporation had been incorporated to own and operate a building free and clear of bonds and mortgages and showed an engraving of a large building with the words "no bonds", "no mortgages" prominently displayed, the judge is justified in telling the jury that they are justified in finding the meaning of these representations to be that the property the corporation was incorporated to own and operate was *at the time* free from bonds and mortgages, although close scrutiny by a person accustomed to examine such documents with care would have disclosed that the corporation was *ultimately* to acquire the property free of bonds or mortgages: *R. v. Johnston*, [1932] 1 D.L.R. 655 (Ont. C.A.).

It will be noted that s. 400 applies to oral statements.

The section in its earlier form related to the issuing of a written prospectus, statement or account and where in a prosecution brought at that time the evidence disclosed that the accused obtained stock subscriptions on the strength of false oral statements the conviction was quashed: *R. v. Anderson* (1924), 55 O.L.R. 586 (C.A.); *R. v. Morgan*, [1947] O.R. 805 (C.A.).

Section 380 of the *Criminal Code* makes it an indictable offence by deceit, falsehood or other fraudulent means to defraud the public or any person, whether ascertained or not, of any property, money or valuable security or to affect the public market price of stocks, shares, merchandise or anything that is offered for sale to the public, whether such deceit, falsehood or other fraudulent means would or would not amount to a false pretence.

See also *Cox and Patton v. R.*, [1963] S.C.R. 500 and *R. v. Olan*, [1978] 2 S.C.R. 1175; *R. v. Colucci*, [1965] 4 C.C.C. 56 (Ont. C.A.); *Davidson v. R.*, [1971] 4 W.W.R. 731 (B.C. C.A.); and *R. v. Scallen* (1974), 15 C.C.C. (2d) 441 (B.C. C.A.).

Under similar legislation the directors were convicted of publishing fraudulent statements in a statement in lieu of a prospectus. Where a director knew that the document would be filed in a public office, that was evidence of publication in the place where the office was situated: *R. v. Hooley Macdonald & Wallis* (1923), 92 L.J.K.B. 78.

Section 84 of the English *Larceny Act, 1861* makes it a misdemeanour for a director of a body corporate or public company to make, publish or circulate with the intent specified in the section, any written statement or account, which he knows to be false in any material particular. A written statement may be false within the meaning of the section not only because of what it states but because of what it implies, conceals or omits, and where every statement in the prospectus for the issue of debenture stock issued by a corporation of which the accused was chairman was true, but the prospectus omitted information about the corporation's affairs with the result that the prospectus conveyed a false impression, it was held that the accused was rightly convicted of an offence under the section: *R. v. Kylsant (Lord)*, [1932] 1 K.B. 442 (C.C.A.).

So where the prospectus purported to describe the nature of the corporation's business, its assets and liabilities, but omitted to state that another business proposed to be acquired had large forward commitments incurred in an attempt to corner the pepper market, the prospectus was held to be false in a material particular, the essence of the document being to mislead the public as to the nature of the risk: *R. v. Bishirgian*, [1936] 1 All E.R. 586.

A balance sheet is false in a material particular where it shows as a cash asset a substantial sum which is in fact a temporary loan: *R. v. McLeod*, [1941] 1 D.L.R. 578 at 580 (B.C. C.A.), revd [1941] S.C.R. 228.

Promoters

The position of promoters

Promoters are the persons who form a corporation and take the necessary steps to enable it to commence operations. The term "promoter" has no exact meaning in law and in the preparation of prospectuses, subject to any statutory definitions, it is prudent to construe the term broadly rather than narrowly. Promoters stand in a fiduciary relationship to the corporation because their position gives them an extensive power and influence in shaping and controlling the affairs of the corporation. One of the results of such relationship is that promoters are not entitled to make a profit at the expense of the corporation without fully and fairly disclosing it. It is not enough to disclose the profit to a board of directors who are mere nominees of the promoters. Disclosure must be made to an independent quorum of the board or to the shareholders at large. It is also usually necessary under the statutory prospectus requirements to disclose in a prospectus particulars of payment of any kind to promoters within a particular period prior to the issuance of the prospectus.

Promoters have important duties to perform. They will have to see that any property or business taken over by the corporation is acquired on justifiable terms and that the capitalization of the corporation and the different kinds of shares and securities to be issued are appropriate. Often the promoters will also settle the terms of the preliminary agreements for acquisition of assets; secure the executive officers and directors; see that the articles of incorporation, charter or memorandum of association and by-laws or articles are properly framed, and assist in the preparation of the prospectus and plan of financing. In the technical details in connection with the above matters the promoters will have the assistance and guidance of their legal advisers and of the investment dealers or other persons responsible for distributing the corporation's shares or securities to the public. For the risks they run and the services they render promoters may properly insist on being remunerated. As there is considerable danger of their incurring liability to the corporation and others if legal requirements as to disclosure of their interest in transactions with the corporation or otherwise are not complied with, promoters should always seek competent advice.

The word "promoter" has no very definite meaning: *Emma Silver Mining Co. v. Lewis* (1879), 4 C.P.D. 396 at 407.

The *Securities Act* (Ontario) in s. 1(1) provides that the term "promoter" means:

(a) a person or company who, acting alone or in conjunction with one or more other persons, companies or a combination thereof, directly or indirectly, takes the initiative in founding, organizing or substantially reorganizing the business of an issuer, or

(b) a person or company who, in connection with the founding, organizing or substantial reorganizing of the business of an issuer, directly or indirectly, receives in consideration of services or property, or both services and property, 10 per cent or more of any class of securities of the issuer or 10 per cent or more of the proceeds from the sale of any class of securities of a particular issue, but a person or company who receives such securities or proceeds either solely as underwriting commissions or solely in consideration of property shall not be deemed to be a promoter within the meaning of this definition if such person or company does not otherwise take part in founding, organizing or substantially reorganizing the business.

The promoters are required to sign any prospectus pursuant to the *Securities Act* (Ontario) and the liabilities attaching to those who sign a prospectus are of course applicable to promoters.

The federal Act contains no definition of the word "promoter" and the courts have refrained from limiting the scope of the term by defining it. As Bowen J. said in *Whaley Bridge Calico Printing Co. v. Green* (1880), 5 Q.B.D. 109 at 111, it is " . . . a term not of law, but of business, usefully summing up in a single word a number of business operations familiar to the commercial world by which a corporation is generally brought into existence"; and Lindley L.J. in *Lydney & Wigpool Iron Ore Co. v. Bird* (1886), 33 Ch. D. 85 at 93 (C.A.), observed "... the word "promoter" is ambiguous, and it is necessary to ascertain in each case what the so-called promoter really did before his legal liabilities can be accurately ascertained". The state of being a promoter is not a definite legal status, such as that of a shareholder or a director to which the law annexes certain rights and burdens. While then the word does not admit of exact definition there is no practical difficulty in identifying as a promoter the person who is responsible for "getting up" the corporation, who negotiates the preliminary agreements, and who instructs solicitors as to incorporation. See *Lydney & Wigpool Iron Ore Co. v. Bird, supra.* It is in every case, however, a question of fact whether a person by his acts has constituted himself a promoter, and if so to what extent: *Emma Silver Mining Co. v. Grant* (1879), 11 Ch. D. 918.

An individual may be a promoter without actually being the person who forms the corporation, and in *Emma Silver Mining Co. v. Lewis* (1879), 4 C.P.D. 396, it was held that there had been evidence to go to the jury, and the latter's finding that the defendants were promoters was left undisturbed, where it was shown that the defendants arranged with the owner to assist in selling a mine to a corporation to be formed by him, and while they helped him to sell the mine let him form the corporation, fix the price and arrange the details of sale; they also permitted themselves to be appointed metal brokers of the corporation at a remuneration, allowed themselves to be referred to in the prospectus for information concerning the mine and received some paid-up shares from the vendor. See also *Emma Silver Mining Co. v. Grant, supra,* and *Nesbitt, Thomson & Co. v. Pigott*, [1941] S.C.R. 520 for instances of acts which will constitute promotion.

The purchase of assets with a view to their resale to a corporation to be formed by the purchasers where the purchasers have not taken any steps to form a corporation does not constitute them promoters at the time of the purchase: *Ladywell Mining Co. v. Brookes* (1887), 35 Ch. D. 400 (C.A.).

An agreement to purchase assets for cash and shares in a corporation to be formed by the purchaser does not necessarily constitute the purchaser a promoter at the time of entering into the agreement: *Gover's Case* (1875), 1 Ch. D. 182 (C.A.).

A solicitor who acts for the corporation in its early stages even if he allows his name to be printed on the prospectus is not thereby a promoter: *Re Great Wheal Polgooth Co.* (1883), 53 L.J. Ch. 42. A provisional director is not necessarily a promoter: *Federated Press Ltd. v. Archambault* (1924), 30 Rev. Leg. 220.

It will not avail the real promoter to interpose a nominal promoter and so attempt to avoid responsibility and Phillimore J. held in *Re Oarby, Ex p. Brougham*, [1911] 1 K.B. 95, that where the nominal promoter was a corporation, which was a mere "alias" for two individuals, the latter were the real promoters and liable as such.

The liability of promoters, to the corporation or to other persons, is now considered under the following headings:

Fiduciary relationship of promoters to the corporation.
Secret profit.
Sale of property by the promoter to the corporation.
Preliminary expenses and services performed before incorporation.
Personal liability of promoters for pre-incorporation contracts.
Promoters as partners or agents for one another.

Fiduciary relationship of promoters to the corporation

Promoters of a corporation stand in a fiduciary relationship to the corporation which they bring into existence. Their position as promoters gives them an extensive power and influence in shaping and controlling the affairs of the corporation which is created, and it is because of their possession of such power and influence that a fiduciary relationship is deemed to be established. This is in accord with the well-settled principles of equity which impress such a character upon the relationship subsisting between two persons when one of them is in a position to exercise a controlling influence over the minds or actions of the other. The principle as applied to the promoters of a corporation was first clearly enunciated in the case of *Erlanger v. New Sombrero Phosphate Co.* (1878), 3 App. Cas. 1218 at 1269 (H.L.); see also *Gray v. Yellowknife Gold Mines Ltd. (No. 1)*, [1947] O.R. 928 at 947 (C.A.).

The fiduciary relationship exists as from the time when promotion commences. It is an inference from all the facts when the period begins at which the character of promoter is assumed: *In re Olympia Ltd.*, [1898] 2 Ch. 153 at 182 (C.A.). See also the same case affirmed (*sub nom. Gluckstein v. Barnes*) [1900] A.C. 240, where Lord Robertson at p. 256 observed that taking a decisive step in shaping and limiting the corporation was conclusive as an act of promotion. The fiduciary relationship may commence before the corporation comes into existence: *Emma Silver Mining Co. v. Lewis* (1879), 4 C.P.D. 396, at 407; *Lagunas Nitrate Co. v. Lagunas Syndicate*, [1899] 2 Ch. 392 at 428 (C.A.).

No fiduciary agent may intentionally place himself in a position where his interest may conflict with his duty: *Lagunas Nitrate Co. v. Lagunas Syndicate, supra*, at 442. The duties resulting from such fiduciary relationship include the obligation not to sell property to the corporation at an exorbitant price; not to conceal anything that it is proper for the directors to know in order to permit them to form a fair judgment as to the value of such property; not to make any misrepresentation of facts material to the purchase; and the positive obligation to see that the fiduciary's contracts with the corporation are made through the medium of an independent board of directors: *In re Hess Manufacturing Co.* (1894), 23 S.C.R. 644 at 667; *Stratford Fuel, Ice, Cartage & Construction Co. v. Mooney* (1909), 21 O.L.R. 426 at 444 (C.A.); *Proprietary Mines Ltd. v. MacKay*, [1939] O.R. 461 at 488 (C.A.); affd (*sub nom. MacKay v. Proprietary Mines Ltd.*) [1941] 1 D.L.R. 240 (S.C.C.). But there is no duty on the part of promoters to provide the corporation with an independent board if the real truth is disclosed to those who are induced by the promoters to join the corporation: *Lagunas Nitrate Co. v. Lagunas Syndicate*, [1899] 2 Ch. 392 at 426 (C.A.); *Larocque v. Beauchemin*, [1897] A.C. 358 at 364.

Promoters cannot receive any personal advantage without the fullest possible disclosure to and assent of all concerned: *Bennett v. Havelock Electric Light & Power Co.* (1910), 21 O.L.R. 120 at 131. Disclosure to a board of directors who are mere nominees of the promoters is of no avail: *Gluckstein v. Barnes*, [1900] A.C. 240; and where the public are to be invited to subscribe there should be disclosure to the intended shareholders: *Gluckstein v. Barnes, supra*, at 249; *Bennett v. Havelock, supra*, at 130. Where all the shareholders of the corporation know the facts and approve of the transaction and there is to be no public issue of shares, such a course need not be followed, for *volenti non fit injuria*: *Salomon v. Salomon & Co.*, [1897] A.C. 22. And in *A.G. Can. v. Standard Trust Co. of New York*, [1911] A.C. 498, where the incorporating Act of a railway company authorized the purchase of certain assets, and all the persons interested in the capital of the company concurred in the purchase with full knowledge of the facts, it was held that the promoters were entitled to retain a profit made by them on the sale of such assets to the company, though there had been no independent board provided. In such a case the corporation cannot affirm the contract made with it and recover the profits made by its vendors: *In re Ambrose Lake Tin & Copper Mining Co., Ex p. Taylor* (1880), 14 Ch. D. 390 (C.A.).

Secret profit

Once a person becomes a promoter of a corporation his right to profit from dealings with it is severely restricted. Any profit he does make must be made with its knowledge and consent if he is to retain it; and he is accountable to it for any secret profit.

As a consequence of the fiduciary relationship between the promoter and the corporation the former is not entitled to make a profit at the expense of the latter; or, if he does make a profit, in order to retain it, he must make full disclosure to the corporation: *Bennett v. Havelock Electric Light & Power Co.* (1910), 21 O.L.R. 120; *In re Hess Manufacturing Co.* (1894), 23 S.C.R. 644 at 659; *Stratford Fuel, Ice, Cartage & Construction Co. v. Mooney* (1909), 21 O.L.R. 426 (C.A.); *Patton v. Yukon Consolidated Gold Corp.*, [1934] O.W.N. 321 (C.A.); *Proprietary Mines Ltd. v. MacKay*, [1939] O.R. 461 at 488, affd (*sub nom. MacKay v. Proprietary Mines Ltd.*) [1941] 1 D.L.R. 240 (S.C.C.). Everything material in relation to the transaction must be disclosed: *Emma Silver Mining Co. v. Grant* (1879), 11 Ch. D. 918 at 937. The promoter must disclose the fact that he is the real vendor to the corporation if such is the case: *In re Leeds & Hanley Theatres of Varities Ltd.*, [1902] 2 Ch. 809 (C.A.); *Dominion Royalty Corp. v. Goffatt*, [1935] S.C.R. 565.

Under some circumstances it may be necessary to disclose the amount of the profit. See *Gluckstein v. Barnes*, [1900] A.C. 240 at 258 and 259. On the other hand, non-disclosure of the amount of the profit made on a resale to the corporation has been held not to be fatal to the validity of the sale: *Lagunas Nitrate Co. v. Lagunas Syndicate*, [1899] 2 Ch. 392 at 431 (C.A.). In *In re Lady Forrest (Murchison) Gold Mine Ltd.*, [1901] 1 Ch. 582, where it was disclosed that some profit was being made on a resale to the corporation, it was held that there was a breach of duty on the part of the promoter, who was also a director, in not disclosing the amount of profit but that although the corporation might have had a right to rescind the contract, the promoter could not be ordered to repay the profit.

Disclosure must be real disclosure, not merely to directors who are nominees of the promoter, and the duty to disclose may extend to future shareholders where persons are invited to take shares in the corporation: *Gluckstein v. Barnes*, [1900] A.C. 240; *In re Leeds & Hanley Theatres of Varieties Ltd.*, [1902] 2 Ch. 809 (C.A.); *Proprietary Mines Ltd. v. MacKay*, [1939] O.R. 461 (C.A.), affd (*sub nom. MacKay v. Proprietary Mines Ltd.*) [1941] 1 D.L.R. 240 (S.C.C.); *Crown Reserve Consolidated Mines Ltd. v. MacKay*, [1941] 3 D.L.R. 461 (Ont. C.A.).

It has been held, where fraud was shown, that an incorporated syndicate may be a mere alias for promoters who are its principal shareholders and that the latter are personally liable for undisclosed profits ostensibly made by the syndicate: *In re Darby, Ex p. Brougham*, [1911] 1 K.B. 95.

The promoter who is making a profit out of his dealings with the corporation should provide it with an independent body of shareholders or board of directors who will protect the corporation in its dealings with him: *Gluckstein v. Barnes*, [1900] A.C. 240; at any rate where the public is invited to subscribe; for disclosure to a board of directors who are the mere nominees of the promoter, the board room being occupied by the enemy, as was said in the last mentioned case, is obviously a farce: *Bennett v. Havelock Electric Light & Power Co.* (1910), 21 O.L.R. 120 at 130 and see *Stratford Fuel, Ice, Cartage & Construction Co. v. Mooney* (1909), 21 O.L.R. 426 at 443 and 445 (C.A.); *Proprietary Mines Ltd. v. MacKay*, [1939] O.R. 461 at 488 (C.A.). Where, however, there was no concealment and no secret profit and the corporation's articles of association expressly provided that it should acquire the asset at the price named, even though the promoters had not provided the corporation with an independent board, the corporation could not make the promoters account for their profit: *Omnium Electric Palaces Ltd. v. Baines,* [1914] 1 Ch. 332 (C.A.).

As noted above under the heading "Fiduciary relationship of promoters to the corporation", the obligation to provide the corporation with an independent board does not exist when all the shareholders of the corporation know the facts and approve the transaction.

If a promoter fraudulently obtains an illicit profit on a sale of property to the corporation without making full disclosure he will be compelled to relinquish it: *Gluckstein v. Barnes,* [1900] A.C. 240. So if a promoter has purchased property for the corporation from a vendor who is to be paid by the corporation when formed, and, by a secret arrangement with the vendor, a part of the purchase price when the agreement is carried out comes into the hands of the promoter, that is a secret profit which he cannot retain: *In re Hess Manufacturing Co.* (1894), 23 S.C.R. 644; *Crawford v. Bathurst Land & Development Co.* (1918), 42 O.L.R. 256 at 270, 271 (C.A.), revd (*sub nom. Fullerton v. Crawford*) (1919), 59 S.C.R. 314. Other cases illustrating the principle are *Alexandra Oil & Development Co. v. Cook* (1907), 10 O.W.R. 781 (Div. Ct.), affd (1908), 11 O.W.R. 1054 (C.A.) (misrepresentation by promoter of price paid for the property) and *Hammond v. Silver Black Foxes Ltd.* (1924), 27 O.W.N. 303 (insufficient disclosure). So also where a promoter has received a secret profit from the vendor who is also a promoter, he cannot retain it: *Graham Island Collieries v. Canadian Development Co.* (1913), 12 D.L.R. 316 (B.C. S.C.).

A promoter who makes a secret profit at the expense of the corporation he promotes, by purchasing for the intended corporation property which he sells to it at an enhanced price, is liable in damages for the resulting loss to the promoted corporation: *Vitomen Cereal Ltd. v. Manitoba Grain Co.,* [1928] 4 D.L.R. 440 (B.C. S.C.). The remedy in such a case being damages, it is available though rescission may have become impossible: *In re Leeds & Hanley Theatres of Varieties Ltd.,* [1902] 2 Ch. 809 (C.A.).

Where a promoter had received shares of a corporation by way of secret profit, he was held to be accountable to the liquidator for the profit made by reselling the shares, whether the shares were void and worthless or not, since he had dealt with them as validly issued. As to a portion of the proceeds of the resale of the shares received by him in shares of other corporations, he was not to be treated as having received that amount in cash, but was only liable for the actual value of the shares: *Jubilee Cotton Mills Ltd. (Official Receiver) v. Lewis,* [1924] A.C. 958 (H.L.). See also the judgment of Warrington L.J. in the same case reported [1923] 1 Ch. 1 (C.A.) as to the alternative remedies open to the corporation.

Where the profit takes the form of paid-up shares in the corporation, insofar as they have not passed into the hands of innocent purchasers for value without notice, the certificates may be ordered to be cancelled: *Fire Valley Orchards v. Sly* (1914), 17 D.L.R. 3 (B.C. S.C.); *Proprietary Mines Ltd. v. MacKay,* [1939] O.R. 461 at 480, 483, 490, 501, affd (*sub nom. MacKay v. Proprietary Mines Ltd.*) [1941] 1 D.L.R. 240 (S.C.C.).

Sale of property by the promoter to the corporation

Where the promoter has already acquired property before the fiduciary relationship between him and the corporation has arisen, it is clear he is not debarred from making a profit on a resale to the corporation merely because he happens to promote it. In *Highway Advertising Co. v. Ellis* (1904), 7 O.L.R. 504 (C.A.), the defendants acquired a patent before the incorporation of the corporation and before they became promoters of it. The patent was then sold to the corporation and Moss C.J.O., in holding that the defendants were entitled to retain the consideration they had received, said that it would have been immaterial if the defendants had acquired their interests without consideration so long as these had not been acquired for the corporation. For other cases where the property which was sold to the corporation had been acquired by the promoter before the fiduciary relationship between him and the corporation arose, see *In re Hess Manufacturing Co.* (1894), 21 O.A.R. 66 at 67, per Osler J.A.; *Ruethel Mining Co. v. Thorpe* (1907), 9 O.W.R. 942, affd (1907), 10 O.W.R. 222 (Div. Ct.) (a case of a director); *Clark v. Mooers* (1922), 69 D.L.R. 448 (Sask. C.A.).

The fact that when the vendor purchased the property, later resold to the corporation, he had in contemplation the formation of the corporation or even the sale of the property to the corporation does not make him a person standing in a fiduciary relationship to the corporation at that time; *Ladywell Mining Co. v. Brookes* (1887), 35 Ch. D. 400 at 409 (C.A.), and cases cited.

The corporation is not entitled to treat the vendor as a trustee for it and entitled only to what he paid for the property unless, when he acquired the property, he either did so for the corporation or was in such a fiduciary relationship to the corporation that the purchase must be considered as having been made by him as trustee for the corporation: *In re Ambrose Lake Tin & Copper Mining Co., Ex p. Taylor* (1880), 14 Ch. D. 390 at 398 (C.A.). In support of the proposition that promoters may acquire property as trustees for a corporation, see *In re Hess Manufacturing Co.* (1894), 23 S.C.R. 644 at 659; *Graham Island Collieries v. Canadian Development Co.* (1913), 12 D.L.R. 316 at 318; *Jacobus Marler Estates Ltd. v. Marler* (1916), 85 L.J.P.C. 167 and *Vitomen Cereal Ltd. v. Manitoba Grain Co.*, [1928] 4 D.L.R. 440 at 458 (B.C. S.C.).

Whether promoters do in fact acquire assets as trustees for a corporation is a question of fact: *Omnium Electric Palaces Ltd. v. Baines*, [1914] 1 Ch. 332 at 347 (C.A.); *Clark v. Mooers* (1922), 69 D.L.R. 448 at 455 (Sask. C.A.); *Rumford v. Hinton* (1922), 52 O.L.R. 47 at 51 (C.A.). As regards property acquired before the corporation is incorporated promoters can rarely be shown to be trustees for the intended corporation: *In re Leeds & Hanley Theatres of Varieties Ltd.*, [1902] 2 Ch. 809 at 822 (C.A.); *In re Hess Manufacturing Co., supra*; *Rumford v. Hinton, supra*; and see *Omnium Electric Palaces Ltd. v. Baines, supra*, at 347, approving *In re Leeds & Hanley Theatres of Varieties Ltd., supra*, and *Clark v. Mooers, supra*, where, however, the action against the vendor failed because the corporation had done an act amounting to a waiver of its remedy.

Promoters who purchase property, which it is proposed that a corporation to be formed shall acquire, are not agents for the corporation in making the purchase, because a corporation which has not come into existence cannot have an agent: *Rumford v. Hinton* (1922), 52 O.L.R. 47 (C.A.); *Natal Land & Colonization Co. v. Pauline Colliery & Development Syndicate Ltd.*, [1904] A.C. 120 (P.C.).

Where the promoter sells property to the corporation, without disclosing that he is the real owner, the corporation on discovery of the facts is entitled to rescission and the repayment of the purchase price if it is in a position to make *restitutio in integrum*, but not otherwise: *Dominion Royalty Corp. v. Goffatt*, [1935] S.C.R. 565.

Rescission of the contract, repayment of the price paid and a reconveyance were ordered where the promoter acting in collusion with the vendors had fraudulently concealed the total price: *Lindsay Petroleum Co. v. Hurd* (1874), L.R. 5 P.C. 221.

If a person acquires property with the intention of reselling it to a corporation promoted by him he should provide the corporation with an independent board, and if he fails to do so the contract may be rescinded provided the parties can be restored to their original positions: *In re Hess Manufacturing Co.* (1894), 23 S.C.R. 644 at 677. See, however, *Lagunas Nitrate Co. v. Lagunas Syndicate*, [1899] 2 Ch. 392 (C.A.) where Lindley M.R. at p. 425 stated that a corporation cannot set aside an agreement entered into by it for the purchase of property simply because the directors are not an independent board; there must be secrecy or concealment of the true position of the directors and untrue statements as to what they did for the corporation.

If rescission has become impossible, the corporation may be left without a remedy, unless fraud or misrepresentation or breach of duty to make full disclosure on the part of the promoter can be proved.

If the vendor-promoter has by fraud induced the corporation to buy, the corporation will be entitled to keep its bargain and to get damages for fraud, though rescission is not possible and is not desired: *Rumford v. Hinton* (1922), 52 O.L.R. 47 (C.A.) and cases cited. In that case, where promoters failed to disclose to subscribers to a syndicate that they intended to sell property at a profit to the corporation to be formed but induced the subscribers to believe that, in acquiring the property at a price (which was in excess of the actual price paid) they were buying direct from the owner at the lowest possible price and without any intermediate profit and the promoters took the intermediate profit, it was held that they were guilty of fraud, and the corporation was entitled to damages, though rescission was not desired. The promoter was liable for the whole of the depletion which the assets of the corporation had suffered, less such sums as he could show to have been expended by him in acquiring, maintaining, subdividing or selling the property (lands) in question. Minority shareholders cannot make the promoter account unless the acts complained of are fraudulent or beyond the powers of the corporation: *Clark v. Mooers* (1921), 60 D.L.R. 542, affd (1922), 69 D.L.R. 448 (Sask. C.A.). Individual shareholders are not entitled to bring an action against promoters for damages caused by misrepresentation by the promoters as to contracts alleged to be held by them in connection with a business agreed by them to be sold to a corporation to be formed; the injury is an injury to the corporation and not to the respective shareholders: *Beatty v. Neelon* (1885), 12 O.A.R. 50 (C.A.), affd (1887), 13 S.C.R. 1.

If there has been a breach on the part of the promoter of the duty of full disclosure, even though rescission may not be possible, the corporation on discovery of the facts has the alternative remedy of requiring the promoter to pay damages for breach of the duty to disclose. Thus, where the prospectus prepared with the privity of the vendor-promoters did not disclose the fact that they were the real vendors of property sold by them at a profit through the medium of a trustee, the promoters were held liable in damages to the corporation: *In re Leeds & Hanley Theatres of Varieties Ltd.*, [1902] 2 Ch. 809. The measure of damages is the difference between the true value of the property and the selling price to the corporation: *In re Leeds & Hanley Theatres of Varieties Ltd., supra*, Vaughan Williams L.J., at p. 826, considered that the promoters were entitled to have the promotion expenses deducted in their favour. So also where vendors made a secret agreement with a promoter whereby he received part of the purchase price and attended a meeting of the purchasing syndicate at which by their silence the members of the syndicate who were not participants in the fraud were misled as to the real purchase price, while rescission, under the circumstances, was not ordered, the defendants were ordered to repay such part of the sum so received by the promoter to the trustee (in whose name the property was purchased and held pending incorporation of the corporation) as would enable the trustee to repay to the innocent members of the syndicate the excess amounts contributed by them: *Northrup Mining Co. v. Dimock* (1894), 27 N.S.R. 112 (C.A.).

The breach of duty need not amount to positive fraud: *Proprietary Mines Ltd. v. MacKay*, [1939] O.R. 461 at 501 (C.A.), adopting as applicable to cases of promoters the principle laid down in *Nocton v. Lord Ashburton*, [1914] A.C. 932. In *Proprietary Mines Ltd. v. MacKay, supra*, it was further held that shares of the corporation, issued by a promoter to himself without allotment by the directors and without consideration, to the extent they remained in his hands should be delivered up and cancelled.

As to the liability of promoters of a corporation (who are also directors) to refund gifts made to them by a vendor out of his profits on the sale of assets to the corporation, see *Fullerton v. Crawford* (1919), 59 S.C.R. 314.

Preliminary expenses and services performed before incorporation

By preliminary expenses are meant those connected with the formation and organization of the corporation, such as the fee paid for the articles of incorporation and the costs in connection therewith and in the holding of organization meetings, the drawing of preliminary agreements, the preparation of the prospectus, the printing of share certificates, and the purchase and entering up of the books required to be kept by the corporation. Some of these items of expense will, and certain of them must, be incurred before the corporation which benefits thereby comes into existence.

The promoters or other persons who make disbursements or incur liabilities for a corporation *to be formed* are not entitled subject to what follows to be reimbursed or to have their liabilities assumed by the corporation when it comes into existence: *In re English & Colonial Produce Co.*, [1906] 2 Ch. 435 (C.A.); *In re Rotherham Alum & Chemical Co.* (1884), 25 Ch. D. 103 (C.A.). It is usual to insert among the corporation's powers a clause to the effect that it may pay preliminary expenses, and while there is nothing to prevent the corporation from doing so, the existence of such a power without more will not enable a promoter to claim repayment of his outlay: *In re Empress Engineering Co.* (1881), 16 Ch. D. 125 (C.A.). The promoter must prove a new, express contract by the corporation after formation to reimburse him: *In re English & Colonial Produce Co., supra*, or some facts must exist from which the court can infer such an agreement: *Van Hummell v. International Guarantee Co.* (1913), 10 D.L.R. 306 (Man. K.B.).

The dictum of the Court of Appeal in *In re Hereford & South Wales Waggon & Engineering Co.* (1876), 2 Ch. D. 621 at 624, that, if the corporation adopts and takes the benefit of pre-incorporation services in respect of which such expenses arose, the corporation is liable in equity to pay for the services, was dissented from in *In re English & Colonial Produce Co., supra.*

As to the right of a solicitor under the laws of the province of Quebec to recover for professional services rendered before incorporation, see *Holdstock v. Joint Committee of the Ladies Hairdressing Trade of Montreal* (1941), 79 Que. S.C. 272.

It is usual to have the contract which, as indicated above, is required to entitle the persons concerned to reimbursement embodied in the sale agreement, or an agreement to render future services, so that there will be consideration to support the contract.

The principle would apply to incorporation fees paid to the Director as well as to other expenses: see *In re National Motor Mail-Coach Co., Clinton's Claim*, [1908] 2 Ch. 515 (C.A.). Where a corporation is incorporated by private Act, it is not liable for the expenses of procuring incorporation in the absence of agreement or a provision in the Act that the corporation shall be liable: *Re Crown Mutual Hail Insurance Co.* (1908), 18 Man. R. 51. This case is also important as regards the position of solicitors, since it was held that they have no equitable claim against the corporation for the costs of procuring the passing of the Act. However, the corporation having already made a payment to its solicitors on account of costs they were permitted to appropriate such payment to pre-incorporation costs. Even if the Act should contain the usual provision for payment of preliminary expenses, solicitors retained by a promoter would have no direct claim against the corporation for such services; per Mathers J., *Re Crown Mutual Hail Insurance Co., supra*, at p. 53, citing *Wyatt v. Metropolitan Board of Works* (1861), 11 C.B.N.S. 744, and *Re Skegness & St. Leonard's Tramways Co., Ex p. Hanly* (1889), 41 Ch. D. 215 (C.A.).

Where a promoter has performed services before incorporation he is not entitled to be indemnified in the absence of a new agreement: *Van Hummell v. International Guarantee Co.* (1913), 10 D.L.R. 306 (Man. K.B.). A promoter cannot sue a co-promoter for remuneration for such services in the absence of express agreement: *Van Hummell v. International Guarantee Co., supra*; *Holmes v. Higgins* (1822), 1 B. & C. 74; *Patterson v. Brown* (1905), 6 O.W.R. 204 (C.A.).

Personal liability of promoters for pre-incorporation contracts

For a general discussion of pre-incorporation contracts see the heading "Pre-incorporation contracts" in Chapter 3, and s. 14 of the federal Act.

The former cases on this question must be regarded with caution and in many cases will be superseded by the provisions of the Act.

The substance of the statutory provisions is contained in s. 14, which provides that a person who enters into a written contract in the name of or on behalf of a corporation before it comes into existence is personally bound by the contract and is entitled to the benefits thereof but subject to the provisions of the section

> 14(2). A corporation may, within a reasonable time after it comes into existence, by any action or conduct signifying its intention to be bound thereby, adopt a written contract made before it came into existence in its name or on its behalf, and on such adoption
>
> (a) the corporation is bound by the contract and is entitled to the benefits thereof as if the corporation had been in existence at the date of the contract and had been a party thereto; and
> (b) a person who purported to act in the name of or on behalf of the corporation ceases . . . to be bound by or entitled to the benefits of the contract.

Section 14(3) provides that a party to such a contract "may apply to a court for an order fixing obligations under the contract as joint or joint and several or apportioning liability between or among the corporation and a person who purported to act in the name of or on behalf of the corporation and on such application the court may make any order it thinks fit". Section 14(4) provides that if it is so expressly provided in the written contract, "a person who purported to act in the name of or on behalf of the corporation before it came into existence is not in any event bound by the contract or entitled to the benefits thereof".

Persons who incur obligations on behalf of a proposed corporation do so at their own peril, for if the corporation, after incorporation, chooses to repudiate the obligation, they will be personally liable: *Irwin v. Lessard* (1889), 17 R.L. 589 (C.A.). And though the form of the transaction be the giving of security for an advance to a projected corporation the promoter is primarily liable, for the corporation not being in existence cannot be the principal debtor: *Clergue v. Humphrey* (1901), 31 S.C.R. 966.

The liability proceeds upon the ordinary principles of the law of contract. As a general rule the same principle applies to the right of the corporation to claim the benefit of the acts of promoters — unless both are bound neither is bound. But sometimes the express provisions of a statute may enable the corporation to assert rights over property acquired or to claim the benefits of contracts made prior to incorporation. Also the terms of the Act may be such that upon incorporation the legal title to property theretofore acquired for the proposed corporation is *ipso facto* transferred to it. But even in such cases it is wise to evidence the transfer by a conveyance.

Where individuals intend to form a corporation but owing to non-compliance with the statute no corporation is created, but business is carried on and liabilities are incurred, they may find that they are in a sense partners and personally responsible to the creditors. See *Seiffert v. Irving* (1888), 15 O.R. 173 (C.A.). The distinction between the liability of proposed corporators and that of ordinary partners where business is carried on prior to incorporation is thus stated by Boyd C. in *Sandusky Coal Co. v. Walker* (1896), 27 O.R. 677 at 681 (C.A.):

> The whole body of proposed corporators are not necessarily liable as partners in the case of the prosecution of business prior to incorporation, for the whole concern is not a partnership in that sense; but it is a *quasi* partnership in this sense, that all those who take a practical part in the prosecution of the business or who sanction or ratify the conduct of affairs become liable as partners. The extent or proportion of liability between themselves depends upon the extent of their interest as manifested in their subscription for shares; on this footing the profits and losses would be proportioned among them. The practical difference as to evidence is that in the case of partners all would be liable without notice of the obligation incurred; in the other case some evidence must be given to shew knowledge or notice and assent on the part of each person to be charged.

A mere agreement to take shares in an intended corporation which proves abortive will not constitute the subscriber a partner in the undertaking: *Sylvester v. McCuaig* (1878), 28 U.C.C.P. 443 (C.A.). It has been held in the province of Quebec that signing the petition for incorporation renders provisional directors liable jointly and severally for the fees of the solicitor employed by the promoter to procure the incorporation of the corporation and before the corporation has in fact been incorporated: *Auger v. Corneillier* (1892), 2 Que. Q.B. 293; *sed quaere.* See also on the liability of corporators of a nominal corporation which has no legal status, *Gildersleeve v. Balfour* (1893), 15 P.R. 293 (C.A.).

There is no personal liability when the contract is a provisional one only to take effect upon the incorporation of the corporation: *Thomas Navigation Co. v. Reid* (1886), 13 O.A.R. 303.

As to the liability of persons who contract, not personally but as trustees for a corporation to be incorporated, see *T. W. Hand Fireworks Co. v. Baikie* (1913), 43 Que. S.C. 325 (Ct. of Rev.); and *Bonhomme v. Bickerdike* (1899), 17 Que. S.C. 28, affd (April 24, 1900) (Que. C.A.) (unreported); in the latter case the corporation never was incorporated. But now see s. 14 of the Act.

Promoters as partners or agents for one another

As a general rule promoters are not partners, although they may become liable as partners for the acts of their co-promoters ratified by them: *Sandusky Coal Co. v. Walker* (1896), 27 O.R. 677 (C.A.). Nevertheless it may often happen that the arrangements between the promoters, and their sanctioning and taking the benefit of contracts made on their behalf by certain of their number, or by persons acting in their interests, will render them all liable upon such contracts.

Some of their number may be given or allowed to take upon themselves an authority to bind the others. And persons who are promoters may at the same time become so associated by agreement that they are actually partners, when they will be liable for each others' acts as such: *Howard Stove Manufacturing Co. v. Dingman* (1907), 10 O.W.R. 127 (C.A.); and if the partnership is entered into for a single adventure or undertaking it can only be dissolved in accordance with the law relating to partnership: *Matthews v. Maurice* (1923), 54 O.L.R. 64. It must be a question of fact in every case: *Garvin v. Edmondson* (1909), 14 O.W.R. 435, affd (1910), 15 O.W.R. 210 (C.A.) (no relationship of partners); *Ellis v. Drummond* (1893), 4 Que. S.C. 473. See, however, *Pepin v. Dufour* (1925), 31 R.L. 446.

Promoters are not, as such, agents for each other: *Wilson v. Hotchkiss* (1901), 2 O.L.R. 261 (C.A.); affd (*sub nom. Milburn v. Wilson*) (1901), 31 S.C.R. 481; and *Hung Man v. Ellis* (1895), 3 B.C.R. 486. But where promoters have been authorized to act as agents for their co-promoters, the latter will be liable for the acts of the former according to the ordinary principles of the law of agency: *Wilson v. Hotchkiss, supra*. The corporation itself is not responsible for acts of the agents of promoters before its incorporation in the absence of express adoption thereof: *Gourlie v. Chandler & Hart* (1907), 41 N.S.R. 341 (C.A.).

Take-Over Bids

Generally, a take-over bid is an offer made to shareholders of a corporation to purchase a number of voting shares of the corporation in excess of a stipulated minimum percentage and is defined to include an offer by an issuer to acquire its own shares. The federal Act and the securities legislation of the provinces contain provisions regulating take-over bids. Careful consideration must be given to the provisions of any provincial securities legislation. It will be noted that such securities legislation must be complied with in addition to any requirements of the federal Act. The provisions of more than one province may be applicable if the take-over bid is directed to residents of the province in question and if the corporation is subject to the provisions of the securities legislation.

It will be observed that where the offeree company has both Canadian and foreign shareholders, the take-over bid may be made to the Canadian shareholders only. See *Re Gulf Canada Corp.* (1986), 9 O.S.C.B. 1903; however, see *Royal Trustco Ltd. v. Campeau Corporation (No. 1)* (1980), 31 O.R. (2d) 131 (C.A.).

Where a provincial commission issued a temporary cease trading order and commenced administrative proceedings pursuant to the take-over provisions of the provincial Act and actions were brought in court alleging fraud and conspiracy, an application was made to the commission to stay the proceedings by the commission pending disposition of the court proceedings. As similar issues of fact would arise in both proceedings, the commission hearing was stayed pending final disposition of the proceedings in court: *Re Comaplex Resources International Ltd.* (1989), 12 O.S.C.B. 1475.

In *Re Asbestos Corp.* (1988), 11 O.S.C.B. 3419, affd (1991), 1 O.R. (3d) 723, 76 D.L.R. (4th) 467 (Div. Ct.), aff'd (1992), 97 D.L.R. (4th) 144 (Ont. C.A.), leave to appeal to S.C.C. refused May 27, 1993, the majority shareholders of a corporation operating in Quebec but listed on The Toronto Stock Exchange and, in consequence, subject to the rules of the Ontario Securities Commission, sold the direct control of the corporation in question at a premium which would have required an offer to be made at the same price to minority shareholders. It was alleged that the target corporation was not subject to the laws of Ontario since the transaction had occurred outside Ontario and that the offeror corporation was a Quebec crown corporation. The Commission ruled that it had jurisdiction to proceed with the hearing and the allegations were sufficient to call for a reply by the offeror corporation.

In *Re H.E.R.O. Industries Ltd.* (1990), 13 O.S.C.B. 3775 where the offer to purchase shares complied with the statutory exemption but undermined the spirit behind the procedure; the Commission intervened to protect the public interest and to deny the exemption. See also *Re Canadian Tire Corporation* (1987), 10 O.S.C.B. 858 and *Re Selkirk Communications and Southam Inc.* (1988), 11 O.S.C.B. 286, both of which were cases in which the commission considered its role in protecting the public interest in the context of a take-over bid which technically complied with the Act.

A take-over bid means an offer (other than an exempt offer) made at approximately the same time to shareholders to acquire shares which when combined with shares beneficially owned or controlled directly or indirectly by the offeror (or an affiliate or associate of the offeror) would exceed 10 per cent of any class of issued shares of the corporation and includes any offer (other than an exempt offer) by an issuer to repurchase its own shares (s. 194). An exempt offer is defined as (i) an offer to fewer than 15 shareholders to purchase shares by way of separate agreements, (ii) an offer to purchase shares through a stock exchange or in the over-the-counter market in such circumstances as may be prescribed by regulation, (iii) an offer to purchase shares of a corporation having fewer than 15 shareholders, two or more joint holders of shares being counted as one shareholder, (iv) an offer exempted pursuant to the order of a court having jurisdiction in the place where the offeree corporation has its registered office, or (v) an offer by a corporation to repurchase its own shares to be held pursuant to constrained share provisions as set out in s. 32 (s. 194).

It will be observed that under the Ontario *Securities Act* the exemptions are different. For example, if the consideration paid for any of the securities is in excess of 115% of the market price of the securities at the date of the bid as determined in accordance with the regulations passed under the Act, the take-over bid is not exempt. Sections 104 and 105 of that Act give power to the Commission and to the court respectively to make orders requiring compliance with the provisions of the Act and in the case of an application to court to rescind a transaction with any interested party, to require the disposition of any security or to require or prohibit the exercise of any or all of the voting rights attaching to any securities. See *Crowborough Investments Ltd. v. Alcan Aluminum Ltd.* (1987), 10 O.S.C.B. 4408; *Ontario Securities Commission v. McLaughlin* (1983), 40 O.R. (2d) 405 (C.A.); *Elsley's Frosted Foods Ltd. v. Mid White Oak Square Ltd.* (1976), 14 O.R. (2d) 479; and see *Re Enfield*

Corp. (1990), 13 O.S.C.B. 3364 for a discussion of calculation of the relevant market price where a put is concerned. In that case it was held that the relevant date for determining the market price was the day when the put was granted (and not the date of exercise) as that was the date when the offeror's investment decision was made.

Where a take-over bid is for all the shares of any class (i) shares deposited pursuant to the take-over bid, if not taken up by the offeror, may be withdrawn by or on behalf of an offeree at any time after 60 days following the date of the take-over bid, (ii) the offeror cannot take up shares deposited pursuant to the take-over bid until ten days after the date of such take-over bid, and (iii) if the offeror intends to take advantage of the provisions of s. 206 (compulsory acquisition) he must so state and must in addition state that the offeree is entitled to dissent and to demand the fair value of his shares (s. 195).

Where a take-over bid is for less than all of the shares of any class (i) no shares may be taken up thereunder until 21 days after the date of the take-over bid, (ii) the period of time within which the shares may be deposited pursuant to the take-over bid or any extension thereof is not to exceed 35 days from the date of the take-over bid, and (iii) if a greater number of shares is deposited pursuant to the take-over bid than the offeror is bound or willing to take up and pay for, the shares to be taken up are to be taken up rateably, disregarding fractions, according to the number of shares deposited by each offeree (s. 196(1)).

Where a take-over bid for all the shares of any class is converted by amendment or otherwise to a bid for less than all the shares of a class the take-over bid is deemed to be for less than all the shares of the class and then the provisions of s. 196(1) apply (s. 196(2)).

The Act contains rules applicable to take-over bids generally governing the period of time when deposited shares may be withdrawn, when shares deposited must be taken up and paid for and the period of time within which the shares may be deposited (s. 197(a)-(c)). If the terms of the take-over bid are amended by increasing the consideration offered for the shares, the offeror must pay such increased consideration to each offeree whose shares are taken up whether before or after the amendment to the take-over bid (s. 197(d)). If there is a purchase by the offeror of shares to which a take-over bid relates other than pursuant to the take-over bid during the time within which shares may be deposited pursuant to the take-over bid, certain rules are applicable: (i) a payment greater than the amount set out in the take-over bid is deemed to be an amendment to which s. 197(d) is applicable, (ii) the offeror is to immediately notify the offerees of the increased consideration, (iii) the shares so acquired are to be counted to determine whether a condition as to minimum acceptance has been fulfilled, and (iv) the shares so acquired are not to be counted among the shares to be taken up rateably pursuant to s. 196(1)(c) where the take-over bid is for less than all of the shares of any class (s. 197(f)). If the offeror intends to purchase shares to which the take-over bid relates in the market during the period of time in which shares may be deposited pursuant to the take-over bid the offeror must so state in the take-over bid circular (s. 197(e)).

In a case where a take-over bid was made for non-voting and voting shares, the bid contained a condition permitting the offeror to withdraw it if the offer had not been accepted by 90 per cent of each class of shares. Shortly after the termination date, the offeror purported to waive the 90 per cent condition with respect to the voting shares but not with respect to the non-voting shares, with the result that the voting shares would be taken up, but not the non-voting shares. The commission held that the offeror must make a fresh offer to purchase all non-voting shares tendered and trading in respect of the voting shares taken up by the offeror was prohibited until the fresh offer was made. The condition and the bid were not unlawful, but the offeror was not entitled to take up the voting shares unless the 90 per cent condition was waived for both classes of shares: see *Rolland Inc. v. Cascades Inc.* (1987), 10 O.S.C.B. 1630. See also *Calgary Power Ltd. v. Atco Ltd.* (1980), 12 B.L.R. 16 (Alta. Q.B.); *Re Royal Trustco Ltd. and Campeau Corporation (No. 2)* (1980), 11 B.L.R. 298 (O.S.C.); *Re ATCO Ltd. and 99139 Canada Inc. (No. 1)* (1980), 12 B.L.R. 1 (Alta Sec. Comm.); and *Re 99139 Canada Inc. and ATCO Ltd.* (1980), 12 B.L.R. 9 (O.S.C.); and *Re ATCO Ltd. and 99139 Canada Inc. (No. 2)* (1980), 12 B.L.R. 7 (Alta. Sec. Comm.); *First City Financial Corp. v. Genstar Corp.* (1981), 33 O.R. (2d) 631; and see *Re Genstar Corp.* (1982), 20 B.L.R. 72 (O.S.C.); *Re Selkirk Communications Ltd. and Slaight Communications Inc.* (1985), 51 O.R. (2d) 205. It will be noted that both the Toronto Stock Exchange and the Ontario Securities Commission have policies requiring "coat tail" provisions in the articles of an issuer with restricted shares.

A take-over bid (including a copy of the take-over bid circular in prescribed form and any amendment of the take-over bid) is required to be sent concurrently to each director of the offeree corporation, to each shareholder of the offeree corporation resident in Canada, and to the Director; a take-over bid is deemed to be dated as of the date on which it is sent, and a shareholder is deemed to be resident in Canada if his latest address as shown in the securities register of the offeree corporation is an address within Canada (s. 198).

If a take-over bid is made by or on behalf of a body corporate the directors thereof are required to approve the take-over bid and the take-over bid circular and such approval is to be evidenced on the circular by the signature of one or more directors (s. 203(1)).

Where a take-over bid states that shares deposited are to be paid for in money or partly in money the offeror must make adequate arrangements to make sure that funds are available to make the required money payment for such shares (s. 199). Where a take-over bid provides either in whole or in part for an exchange of securities a take-over bid circular is to be sent in prescribed form (s. 200).

The directors of an offeree corporation are to send a directors' circular in prescribed form to each director of the offeree corporation, to each shareholder of the offeree corporation resident in Canada, to the offeror and to the Director (s. 201(1)). Unless such circular is sent within ten days of the date of the take-over bid the directors are forthwith to give notice in prescribed form to the offerees and the Director that a directors' circular will be sent and may recommend that the offerees do not tender their shares pursuant to the take-over bid until they receive the directors' circular (s. 201(2), (3)). The directors' circular must be sent to each offeree and to the Director at least seven days before the termination of the take-over bid or before the sixtieth day of the take-over bid, whichever is earlier (s. 201(4)). Provision is made for a statement by a director of an offeree corporation if he is of the opinion that a take-over bid is not advantageous to the shareholders of the offeree corporation or where he disagrees with any statement in a directors' circular and such opinion or disagreement is to be indicated in the directors' circular and is to be accompanied by his reasons (s. 201(5)).

The directors of an offeree corporation are required to approve a directors' circular that contains the recommendations of a majority of the directors and such approval is to be evidenced by the signature of one or more directors (s. 203(2)).

The consent in writing is required of a person whose profession lends credibility to a statement made by him before such statement may be used in a take-over bid circular or a directors' circular; if requested by the Director such person is to send to the Director a copy of any such statement together with a copy of his consent (s. 202).

If full disclosure is not made with respect to a material fact, in the take-over bid or the directors' circular, the court can quash the take-over bid. See *Behar c. Golden Pond Resources Inc.* (1986), 36 B.L.R. 56 (Que. S.C.), *Nalcap Holdings Inc. v. Kelvin Energy Ltd.*, [1988] R.J.Q. 2768.

Penalties are provided for offences arising as a result of a failure to comply with the statutory provisions and provision is made for restraining orders and orders rescinding any transaction (s. 205). Provisions are made for compulsory acquisition of the shares held by dissenting offerees who have the right to require that the fair value of their shares be paid to them (s. 206).

Under s. 205(3) where there has been a failure to comply with the Act or the regulations in connection with a take-over bid the Director or any interested person may apply to a court and on such application the court may make any order it thinks fit including an order restraining the distribution of the take-over bid circular, a directors' circular or other document used in connection with the take-over bid, an order requiring correction of any document if the take-over bid is to continue, an order varying the dates and times referred to in the take-over bid sections, an order requiring compliance with the Act, an order compensating an aggrieved person, an order rescinding a transaction, an order requiring an offeror to dispose of shares acquired pursuant to the take-over bid and also prohibiting the offeror from voting shares acquired pursuant to a take-over bid. In the case of *Sparling v. Royal Trust Co.* (1984), 24 B.L.R. 145 (Ont. C.A.), affd [1986] 2 S.C.R. 537, the Director had commenced an action against the directors of a corporation and the corporation itself alleging that there had been a failure to disclose material facts in a circular sent by the directors to the shareholders during a take-over. The Director sought among other things an order declaring that any shareholder grieved by such omission was entitled to be compensated by the defendants for any loss suffered. At trial, the claim for compensation was struck from the pleadings, but on appeal it was restored and it was held that the institution of the proceedings by means of an action was in the best interests of all parties and that the procedure followed was correct. For circumstances where a compliance order was held to be inappropriate see *Re Ontario Securities Commission and Electra Investments (Canada) Ltd.* (1984), 45 O.R. (2d) 246. See also *Re Genstar Corp.* (1982), 20 B.L.R. 72 (O.S.C.); *Royal Trustco Ltd. v. Ontario Securities Commission* (1983), 42 O.R. (2d) 147 (Div. Ct.); *Re Trizec Equities Ltd.; Re Bramalea Ltd. (No.1)* (1984), 25 B.L.R. 290 (O.S.C.); see *Re Noverco Inc.* (1990), 13 O.S.C.B. 3377; *Re CDC Life Sciences Inc.* (1988), 11 O.S.C.B. 2541 and *Re H.E.R.O. Industries Ltd.* (1990), 13 O.S.C.B. 3775.

Where an inadvertent breach of the take-over bid rules occurred, see *Re Gordon Capital Corp.* (1990), 13 O.S.C.B. 2035, affd (1991), 14 O.S.C.B. 2713 (Div. Ct.), where penalties were imposed. In a case where the Director had indicated that a squeeze out not conforming with s. 206 would be contrary to the Act, and possibly might lead to a challenge in the court, a take-over bid was made which did not refer to the Director's position. It was held that until the view of the Director had been tested in the courts or endorsed in decision or policy statements by a securities commission, the commission did not feel it necessary to disclose such position in the take-over bid circular: see *Re Core-Mark International Inc.* (1989), 12 O.S.C.B. 3797.

Poison Pills

Shareholders' rights plans, commonly known as "Poison Pills", may be implemented by the directors of a corporation in order to repel, or at least delay, potential hostile take-over bids. Such plans can take many forms, however the common theme underlying the various plans is that the Poison Pill will make it expensive, often prohibitively so, for a hostile acquiror to gain control of a target corporation without the cooperation of the board of directors of the target corporation. An example of a form of Poison Pill is the "flip in" whereby shareholders are given a special dividend consisting of, for example, a right to purchase one voting share per common share then held, exercisable within a stipulated time after a person or group has acquired beneficial ownership of 20% or more of the target corporation's stock, or after a date designated by the board following the commencement of a take-over bid. This Poison Pill gives non-tendering shareholders, except the potential hostile acquiror, the right to buy the voting shares in the target corporation at a substantially reduced price from market at the time of exercise. The board of directors retains the power to redeem the rights, for a nominal sum, within a specified time period. The effect of putting such a Poison Pill in place would be to substantially dilute a successful offeror's equity interest and therefore make the cost of the target corporation so high that, without board approval of a tender offer, acquisition might become a financial impossibility. The board of directors can therefore effectively use a Poison Pill as a tool in order to: i) encourage a hostile acquiror to seek to negotiate with the board; ii) provide the additional time needed to encourage other bidders to come forward with competing offers; or iii) provide the time necessary to put together an alternative proposal by the target corporation.

In adopting a Poison Pill and in deciding whether or not to redeem the rights which have been issued, the board of directors must act in the best interests of the corporation. However, there is a lack of certainty in Canadian jurisprudence with respect to what constitutes the "best interests of the corporation". If after investigation, the board of directors determines that implementing a Poison Pill will advance "the best interests of the corporation" the directors may do so, but may later be required to meet what appears to be one of three different tests as to what constitutes "acting in the best interests of the corporation". One line of cases stresses that directors must act in good faith, and must provide reasonable grounds for such belief. (*Teck Corp. Ltd. v. Millar*, [1973] 2 W.W.R. 385 (B.C.S.C.); *Olympia & York Enterprises v. Hiram Walker Resources Ltd.* (1986), 59 O.R. (2d) 254 (Div. Ct.)). A somewhat stricter approach is put forward in a later case which provides that the considerations of the board of directors upon which the decision to act was based must be consistent only with the best interests of the corporation and inconsistent with any other interests (*Exco Corp. v. Nova Scotia Savings & Loan Co.* (1987), 35 B.L.R. 149 (N.S.S.C.)). A more recent authority provides for the most stringent test in that an onus is placed on the directors to show that their act of implementing a Poison Pill was reasonable in relation to the threat posed by a take-over bid and was directed to the benefit of the corporation and its shareholders as a whole, and not for an improper purpose such as the entrenchment of the board of directors (*347883 Alberta Ltd. v. Producers Pipeline Inc.* (1991), 80 D.L.R. (4th) 359 (Sask. C.A.)).

Although such plans may be implemented by boards of directors, generally the regulatory authorities require that shareholders approve the adoption of a Poison Pill within a reasonable period of time after implementation. National Policy No. 38, published by the Canadian securities administrators, makes the point that prior shareholder approval of defensive tactics implemented by the board of directors of a target corporation in response to an apprehended or actual take-over bid (such as the implementation of a Poison Pill) would, in appropriate cases, allay the concerns of such administrators over potential abuse of shareholders' rights in such situations.

As well, while no action has been taken with respect to the implementation of a Poison Pill by a board of directors of a potential target corporation, it is indicated in National Policy No. 38 that intervention and appropriate action will be taken in a situation where defensive tactics used by the board of directors of a target corporation are likely to deny or severely limit the ability of the target corporation's shareholders to respond to a take-over bid or a competing bid. In a recent case involving a contested take-over bid, the Ontario Securities Commission made an order cease-trading any rights that might have become issuable under a Poison Pill in respect of a particular bid because, in the opinion of the Commission, the Poison Pill had outlived its usefulness in that it had succeeded in inducing a competing bid to come forward and had failed in its attempt to get the initial bidder to sweeten its offer. (*In the Matter of Canadian Jorex Limited and Mannville Oil & Gas Ltd.* (1992), 15 O.C.S.B. 257).

Acquisition of Minority Shares

As indicated above, where one corporation (an "offeror corporation") offers to acquire shares of another corporation (a "target corporation"), such an offer being commonly termed a "take-over bid", and the offer is accepted by the holders of a large majority of the shares of the target corporation affected, the Acts of certain jurisdictions make provision for the compulsory acquisition by the offeror corporation of the balance of the shares affected.

Under the federal Act where a take-over bid is made for all the shares of a class of shares and within 120 days after the date of such take-over bid the bid is accepted by the holders of not less than 90 per cent of the shares of any class to which the take-over bid relates (other than shares held at the date of the take-over bid by or on behalf of the offeror or an affiliate or associate of the offeror) the offeror is entitled, upon complying with the requirements of the section, to acquire the shares held by a person who has not accepted the offer or a subsequent holder of such shares. The offeror is required to send by registered mail within 60 days after the date of termination of a take-over bid, and in any event within 180 days after such date, an offeror's notice to each dissenting shareholder and to the Director setting out that (i) the holders of more than 90 per cent of the shares in question have accepted the take-over bid, (ii) the offeror is bound to take up and pay for such shares or has so taken up and paid for them, (iii) the dissenting offeree is required to elect to transfer his shares to the offeror on the same terms as set out in the take-over bid, or to demand the payment of the fair value of his shares in accordance with the provisions of the section by notifying the offeror within 20 days after he receives such notice, (iv) a dissenting offeree who does not demand payment of the fair value is deemed to have elected to transfer his shares on the same terms as the take-over bid, and (v) a dissenting offeree must send his shares to which the take-over bid relates to the offeree corporation within 20 days after he receives the offeror's notice. The offeror is to send to the offeree corporation concurrently with sending the offeror's notice a notice of adverse claim in accordance with s. 78 with respect to each share held by the dissenting offeree. The dissenting offeree is required within 20 days after receiving the offeror's notice to send his share certificates of the class of shares to which the take-over bid relates to the offeree corporation; the offeror, within 20 days after sending the notice to the dissenting offeree, is to pay or transfer to the offeree corporation the amount of money or other consideration that the offeror would have paid if the dissenting offeree had accepted the take-over bid. Within 30 days after the offeror's notice is sent the offeree corporation is to issue to the offeror a certificate in respect of the shares that were held by dissenting offerees and give to each dissenting offeree who elects to accept the take-over bid terms and who forwards his share certificates to the offeree corporation the money or other consideration to which such dissenting offeree is entitled (fractional shares may be paid for in money). If the dissenting offeree has not sent his share certificates to the offeree corporation notice is to be given to him by the offeree corporation that his shares have been cancelled and that the money or other consideration to which he is entitled is being held in trust for him and that the same will be sent to him after receiving his shares subject to his right to demand payment of the fair value of his shares (s. 206(1)-(8)).

If a dissenting offeree has elected to demand the fair market value of his shares the offeror may, within 20 days after it has paid or transferred the money or consideration to the offeree corporation with respect to the dissenting offeree, apply to a court to fix the fair value of the shares of such dissenting offeree. Provision is made for an application to a court by a dissenting offeree if the offeror fails to apply to a court, such application to be made within a further period of 20 days. Where a dissenting offeree also fails to make an application to a court within the specified 20-day period, he is deemed to have elected to transfer his shares to the offeror on the same terms that the offeror acquired the shares from the offerees who accepted the take-over bid. The application is made to the court having jurisdiction in the place where the corporation has its registered office or in the province where the dissenting offeree resides if the corporation carries on business in that province. No security for costs need be given by the dissenting offeree, and upon such an application all dissenting offerees who have demanded payment of the fair value for their shares are to be joined as parties and are to be bound by the decision of the court. The offeror is to notify each affected dissenting offeree of the date, place and consequences of the application and of the right of the dissenting offeree to appear and be heard in person or by counsel. Upon an application the court is to determine whether any other person is a dissenting offeree who should be joined as a party and is to fix a fair value for the shares of all dissenting offerees. Provision is made for the appointment of one or more appraisers to assist the court in fixing a fair value. The order of the court is to be made against the offeror in favour of each dissenting offeree and for the amount for his shares as fixed by the court. The court may make any order it thinks fit in connection with the proceedings under the provision including the allowance of interest to a dissenting offeree from the date upon which his share certificates are sent or delivered until the date of payment. Provision is also made for payment to the Receiver General in case a shareholder cannot be found (s. 206(9)-(18)).

In order for the provisions of the Act to be applicable, the offeror may, if a corporation, be incorporated under any jurisdiction; but, the offeree corporation must be incorporated or continued under the federal Act.

In *Manning v. Harris Steel Group Inc.*, [1987] 1 W.W.R. 86 (B.C. S.C.), affd [1990] 1 W.W.R. 346 (B.C. C.A.) a minority shareholder refused the amount offered in a take-over bid and applied to the court to fix the fair value of his shares. The court indicated that the offer price of $5.75 per share was inadequate and used an investment value basis for fixing the fair value of the shares which amounted to $12.10 per share. It was pointed out that there were two components in establishing the investment value, the first being the earnings per share and the second being the rate of capitalization. The court held that lost tax deferments were not to be considered, nor was there any premium due to be given for forcible taking. See also *Cyprus Anvil Mining Corp. v. Dickson* (1986), 8 B.C.L.R. (2d) 145 (C.A.). As the leading authority for the proposition that minority shareholders are not entitled to any premium for forcible taking see *LoCicero v. B.A.C.M. Industries Ltd.*, [1988] 1 S.C.R. 399, reversing the Manitoba Court of Appeal judgment in [1986] 3 W.W.R. 152.

In a compulsory acquisition under the English Act, a fair offer was to be made for the shares of the corporation in question. It was held in *Re Grierson, Oldham & Adams, Ltd.*, [1967] 1 All E.R. 192 (Ch. D.) that the test of fairness was whether the offer was fair as to the body of the shareholders as a whole and not as to the individual applicants. In coming to this conclusion, it was pointed out that the English statute provided that the dissenting offering corporation was entitled to acquire the shares unless the court thought fit to order otherwise. It had been pointed out in other cases dealing with this question that *prima facie* where the offer is accepted by not less than nine tenths of the shareholders, the offer must be taken to be a proper one and the onus rests on those making the application to give a reason why their shares should not be acquired by the offering corporation. The court in the present case also indicated that it was not unfair to offer a minority shareholder the value of what he possessed. That is, no minority shareholding premium should be paid for under a compulsory acquisition.

It will be noted that the federal Act has been interpreted differently than the English statute and that the fair value may not be the same as the market value: *Re Whitehorse Copper Mines Ltd.; Hudson Bay Mining & Smelting Co. Ltd. v. Lueck* (1980), 10 B.L.R. 113 (B.C. S.C.). See in addition to the cases cited above: *Les Investissements Mont-Soleil Inc. v. National Drug Ltd.* (1982), 22 B.L.R. 139 (Que. S.C.). For a discussion of the determination of fair value, see Chapter 12, *supra*.

In *Mormac Investments Ltd. v. Andres Wines Ltd.* (1980), 13 B.L.R. 58 (N.S. C.A.) it was held that the provisions of the *Nova Scotia Companies Act* did not permit the compulsory acquisition of shares where the offer was not made for a sufficient length of time. In that case the offer had been made for one month and there were various extensions. See also *Re Huber and Pocklington Financial Corp.* (1982), 134 D.L.R. (3d) 532 (N.S. T.D.).

Chapter 14

LIQUIDATION AND DISSOLUTION

Cross-references: Ontario Act, ss. 191-244.

Supervision of Court

Under Part XVIII of the federal Act, liquidation proceedings may be supervised by the court. "Court" is defined in s. 207 as a court having jurisdiction in the place where the corporation has its registered office. As a corporation's corporate existence is dependent upon the jurisdiction which brought it into being, a corporation can be dissolved only by the jurisdiction which created it. See *Lazard Bros. & Co. v. Midland Bank*, [1933] A.C. 289 (H.L.); *Russian & English Bank v. Baring Bros. & Co.*, [1936] A.C. 405 (H.L.); *Shoolbred v. Clarke* (1890), 17 S.C.R. 265; *National Trust Co. v. Ebro Irrigation & Power Co.*, [1954] O.R. 463 at 477 (H.C.). However, where a corporation has been continued in another jurisdiction, the original jurisdiction of incorporation would no longer have authority to take any further action with respect to the corporation. One jurisdiction may deal with the assets of a corporation incorporated in another jurisdiction, as for example in a winding-up, but it cannot affect the corporation's existence.

Application of Part

Part XVIII does not apply where a corporation desires to terminate its business and proceeds under either the *Bankruptcy and Insolvency Act*, R.S.C. 1985, c. B-3 or the *Winding-up Act*, R.S.C. 1985, c. W-11. See s. 208(1). Any proceedings taken under the federal Act to dissolve or to liquidate and dissolve a corporation will be stayed if, in a proceeding under the *Bankruptcy and Insolvency Act*, the corporation is found to be insolvent within the meaning of that Act. See s. 208(2). Where voluntary winding-up had been commenced under the former Manitoba *Companies Act* and a subsequent petition in bankruptcy was made against the corporation, the sole right to oppose the petition belonged to the liquidator. See *Re Elar Construction Ltd.* (1961), 3 C.B.R. (N.S.) 249 (Man. Q.B.). Where a liquidator had been appointed pursuant to the Manitoba *Companies Act*, and the liquidator found the corporation to be insolvent, it was proper for him to seek a court order directing him to make an assignment under what is now the *Bankruptcy and Insolvency Act*. See *Re Brandon Packers Ltd.* (1962), 33 D.L.R. (2d) 503 (Man. C.A.), or to file an assignment in bankruptcy, or take some other measure to put the corporation in bankruptcy. See *Re Western Hemlock Products Ltd.* (1961), 35 W.W.R. 184 (B.C. S.C.) and *Re Brandon Packers Ltd.*, *supra*, but see *Re Jarvis Construction Co.*, [1972] 1 W.W.R. 308 (B.C. S.C.) in which it was held that the powers of the liquidator on a voluntary winding-up under the former British Columbia Act did not include the power to make an assignment in bankruptcy. Because the existence and powers of the corporation continued notwithstanding the winding-up, the court held that the proper persons to make the assignment would be the directors or the creditors of the corporation. It will be noted that such power appears to be now implicit in the federal Act which specifically provides that the powers of the directors and shareholders cease and vest in the liquidator except as authorized by the court even though the corporation still continues in existence during liquidation. See s. 219(1) of the federal Act. However, such a provision is not found in the voluntary winding-up provisions of the Ontario Act which merely provides that the corporation continues to exist.

The termination of the operations of a corporation may also, in some cases, be achieved under the federal *Winding-up Act*. Dissolution is not ordinarily the same as winding-up. Any provincial corporation or a foreign corporation with assets in Canada may be wound up on the ground of insolvency. Section 3(3) of the federal Act, however, specifically provides that the *Winding-up Act* has no application with respect to CBCA corporations. For a detailed explanation of the provisions of the *Winding-up Act*, see Part II.

In jurisdictions where corporations are incorporated by memorandum and articles, the legislation may contain provisions for striking the corporation off the register for failure to comply with the provisions of the relevant Companies Act. Whether the striking of a corporation off the register effects a dissolution or not depends upon the provisions of the statute. See *International Mining Syndicate v. Stewart* (1914), 48 N.S.R. 172 (C.A.); *Dadson v. Grest*, [1928] 1 D.L.R. 479 (Sask. C.A.) (R.S.S. 1909, c. 72); *Engineer Mining Co. v. Fraser*, [1923] A.C. 228 (P.C.) (R.S.B.C. 1897, c. 135, s. 9); *Morris v. Harris*, [1927] A.C. 252 (H.L.) (*English Companies Act*, 1908, s. 223); *Sutherland v. Strawberry Valley Stock & Farm Produce Co.* (1922), 69 D.L.R. 269 (Sask. Q.B.) (R.S.S. 1920, c. 76, s. 32); *Leask Cattle Co. v. Drabble*, [1923] 1 W.W.R. 126 (Sask. C.A.) (dissolution imposed by s. 31(3) of R.S.S. 1920, c. 76, only a qualified dissolution by reason of provisions of subs. (4), the corporation having been restored to the register).

Revival

Where a corporation has been dissolved, s. 209 permits an "interested person" to apply to the Director to have the corporation revived. Articles of revival must be sent in the prescribed form to the director who then is required to issue a certificate of revival. Upon the issue of the certificate, the corporation is revived under the Act on the date shown in the certificate. The corporation has, thereafter, subject to any reasonable terms which may be imposed by the Director and to rights acquired by any person after dissolution, all the rights and privileges and is liable for the obligations it would have had if it had not been dissolved. See s. 209(1)-(4) of the federal Act and s. 241(4)-(7) of the Ontario Act.

Revival may also in certain circumstances be achieved by special Act. For example, the Ontario Act specifically provides for revival only where a corporation is dissolved for failure to comply with the *Corporations Tax Act*, the *Securities Act* or the *Corporations Information Act*, if an application is made within five years of dissolution. Similarly, if an application for revival is brought after the five-year limitation, revival could not be achieved under the Ontario Act. However, it would be possible to obtain revival pursuant to a private member's bill. See *546672 Ontario Ltd. v. Perricciolo* (1991), 3 O.R. (3d) 774 (Gen. Div.).

Whether an order of revival has or does not have a retrospective effect depends on the actual wording of the statutory provisions. Where the statute deems the corporation to have continued in existence, it is more likely the revival order has a retrospective effect.

In *Tymans Ltd. v. Craven*, [1952] 2 Q.B. 100 (C.A.) the Court of Appeal in construing s. 353(6) of the English *Companies Act, 1948*, which provided that the court may order the name of the corporation restored to the register and " . . . the company shall be deemed to have continued in existence as if its name had not been struck off . . ." held that these words were clearly designed to produce an "as you were" position and that the re-animation of the corporation by a restoration order was retroactive to the date that the company was struck off the register.

In *In re C.W. Dixon Ltd.*, [1947] Ch. 251 it was held that restoration to the register meant that the property of the corporation never vested in the Crown as *bona vacantia* and that no order for revesting was necessary. As to *bona vacantia*, see *infra*.

In *Re Boxco Ltd.*, [1970] 2 All E.R. 183 (Ch. D.) the corporation was struck off the register for failing to file certain returns. Not knowing the corporation was no longer in existence, the directors purported to create a charge on property being purchased by the corporation. Registration of the charge was denied on the basis of the non-existence of the corporation. The corporation sought an order of restoration and an order that the purported charge had been validly delivered for registration. Relying on the *Tymans* case, *supra*, Pennycuick J. held that the restoration order should have retrospective effect and validated the charge.

The current federal Act has no retrospective effect. In *Computerized Meetings & Hotel Systems Ltd. v. Moore* (1982), 40 O.R. (2d) 88 (Div. Ct.), revg (1982), 36 O.R. (2d) 708 (Master) the corporation commenced an action after it had been dissolved. A certificate of revival was subsequently issued under the Act. The court held that the certificate did not have a retrospective effect so as to validate the commencement of the action. Under the federal Act, a corporation is revived on the date shown on the certificate and thereafter has rights and privileges. See also *Profit Sharing Investors of Canada Ltd. v. Coffee Vending Services (Ottawa) Ltd.* (1983), 41 O.R. (2d) 470 (H.C.) (revival after the expiration of a limitation period where the writ was issued after dissolution under the federal Act does not validate the writ) and *Wolf Offshore Transport Ltd. v. Sulzer Canada Inc.* (1992), 100 Nfld. & P.E.I.R. 178 (Nfld. T.D.), where Riche J. held that plaintiff was not entitled to continue proceeding upon revival where action commenced after dissolution.

Conversely, the wording of the Ontario Act has been more broadly interpreted to have a retrospective effect. In *Zangelo Investments Ltd. v. Glasford State Inc.* (1988), 63 O.R. (2d) 542 (C.A.), affg (1987), 59 O.R. (2d) 510 (H.C.) a corporation which had been previously dissolved entered into an agreement of purchase and sale with an option to purchase. The corporation applied for a determination of its right to exercise the option. The Ontario Court of Appeal affirmed that on revival under the Ontario Act, a corporation is revived as of the date of dissolution so as to update all action taken during the period of dissolution. The order declaring the corporation entitled to exercise the option was stayed until it could produce evidence of revival.

In British Columbia, the current *Company Act*, R.S.B.C. 1979, c. 59, deems the company to have continued in existence. In interpreting this provision, the British Columbia Supreme Court concluded in *Canadian Sports Specialists Inc.*

v. Philippon (1990), 66 D.L.R. (4th) 188 (B.C. S.C.) that the provision has a retrospective effect because of the deeming clause. However, not every order made under that Act necessarily has a retrospective effect. In *Natural Nectar Products Canada Ltd. v. Theodor,* [1990] 5 W.W.R. 590 (B.C. C.A.) it was held that the purpose of the deeming provision was to overcome the possibility that a revived corporation would be revived as a distinct legal entity from the dissolved one and pre-dissolution claims would not therefore be maintainable. The deeming clause itself, however, was not necessarily considered to be retrospective. By virtue of s. 287 of the Act, a court could order the corporation placed in the same position as if it had not been dissolved and the effect of that order would be retrospective. Such an order is within the judge's discretion in the appropriate circumstances. Because the order in *Natural Nectar* omitted the words "as if its name had never been struck off", the Court of Appeal was of the view that the order of restoration as entered had no retrospective effect.

Restoration of the company to the register under the *Companies Act,* R.S.B.C. 1911, c. 39 as amended in 1913 and 1914 did not have the effect of revesting a lease in the company where there had been a legal re-entry by the lessor prior to the date of dissolution. See *British Columbia Thoroughbred Association v. Brighouse,* [1922] 3 W.W.R. 665 (B.C. C.A.). In *obiter* Galliher J.A. suggested that even if re-entry had occurred during dissolution, the statute which deemed the company to have continued was not to be interpreted to mean restored without regard to intervening rights.

Similarly, restoration of a corporation to the register under ss. 209 and 210 of the British Columbia *Companies Act,* R.S.B.C. 1948, c. 58, 12 years after it had been struck off the register did not have the effect of revesting land in the corporation where the *Escheats Act* of the province provided in effect that land of a dissolved corporation escheated to the provincial Crown unless the corporation was revived within one year from its dissolution. See *R. v. Lincoln Mining Syndicate Ltd.*, [1959] S.C.R. 736.

In *R. v. Gill* (1989), 40 B.C.L.R. (2d) 360 (Co. Ct.) it was held that a corporation cannot be required to comply with a demand to file income tax returns while dissolved and before restoration where the demand is made before restoration. A non-existent person cannot be required to file. The fact of restoration subsequent to the demand is irrelevant.

In Alberta, both the former *Companies Act* and the current *Business Corporations Act* clearly have a retroactive effect. Under the current Act, once restored to the register, the legislation deems the corporation to have continued in existence as if it had not been struck off. With respect to the former Act, in *Pocock Floors Ltd. v. Holmes Construction Ltd.*, [1971] 1 W.W.R. 394 (Alta. Dist. Ct.) it was held that where an action had been commenced by a corporation subsequently struck off the register, the order of the court restoring the corporation to the register had the effect of erasing any intervening disabilities leaving the corporation as if it had never been struck off.

Where the Boy Scouts of Canada (Edmonton Region) Foundation was a residual beneficiary under a will but had been dissolved for failure to file annual returns and later restored to the register, it was nevertheless entitled to its share of the residue. The revival provision which deemed the corporation to have continued in existence had a retrospective effect: see *Montreal Trust Co. v. Boy Scouts of Canada (Edmonton Region) Foundation*, [1978] 5 W.W.R. 123 (B.C. S.C.).

In *Royal Bank v. Cressler Hotels Ltd.* (1980), 14 Alta. L.R. (2d) 279 (Q.B.) a corporation was struck off the register for failure to file annual returns and subsequently restored. The corporation filed a builder's lien claim while struck off. It was held that the restoration order restored the corporation to the same position as if never struck off. Section 180(2) of the *Companies Act*, R.S.A. 1970, c. 60 (now R.S.A. 1980, c. C-20, s. 197(2)), which provided that unregistered companies were incapable of acquiring an interest in land had no application to companies restored to the register.

Where the defendant moved before a restoration order was made to have the plaintiff corporation's action struck on the ground that the corporation, after commencing the action, had been struck from the register, the court held that the right to apply for restoration remained. The action did not die on dissolution but the corporation could not proceed with it before restoration. See *Berroy Holdings Ltd. v. Cowen* (1977), 5 Alta. L.R. (2d) 5, 80 D.L.R. (3d) 701 (Dist. Ct.).

With respect to the current Alberta Act, where a corporation is struck from the register, the action then commenced, and subsequently a restoration order is made, the court will refuse to strike the claim. See *Culchoe Nu Lodge (1980) Ltd. v. Cando Contracting Ltd.* (1986), 73 A.R. 342 (Alta. Master); *Home Mortgage Ltd. v. Robertson*, [1988] 4 W.W.R. 260 (Sask. Q.B.).

Where a corporation entered into an agreement for sale of land subsequent to being struck off the register but prior to restoration, it was held that the restoration order had the effect of validating the agreement which the purchaser had repudiated. The purchaser had not relied on the corporation's incapacity when repudiating the agreement. See *Berezuk v. Bebube* (1985), 60 A.R. 131 (Q.B.).

In Manitoba, the current revival provision is identical to that found in the federal Act. In interpreting the former Manitoba Act which was similarly worded, the court held in *Steven Kulba Enterprises Ltd. v. Viking Investments Ltd.*, [1978] 4 W.W.R. 610 (Man. Q.B.) that the corporation, having been dissolved and not revived, had no legal existence. In *obiter*, the court concluded the revival section had no retrospective effect. But in *Helcor Enterprises Ltd. v. Moore & James Food Services Ltd.*, [1990] 5 W.W.R. 596 (Man. Q.B.), the court disagreed with this interpretation stating that the object of the revival section is to minimize the harmful effects flowing from dissolution and the objective is best achieved by giving the section a liberal interpretation.

Under the former Manitoba *Companies Act*, R.S.M. 1913, c. 35, s. 130 as amended, the order of revival restored the corporation "to its legal position as at the time of such revocation, cancellation or surrender in the same manner and to the same extent as if there had been no such revocation, cancellation or surrender, and the same shall thereupon be revived and restored accordingly". It was held that revocation operated as a mere suspension of the powers of the corporation. Thus, acts instituted between revocation and the order of reinstatement could be validated. Temporary revocation of a corporation's charter, subsequently revived, did not affect the prosecution of an appeal by the corporation during the period of revocation. See *Kildonan Investments Ltd. v. Thompson* (1917), 55 S.C.R. 272.

In Newfoundland, revival provisions which deemed the corporation to have continued as if not struck off have been held to be retroactive. Thus, where the plaintiff corporation was struck off the register, issued a writ of summons and subsequently restored, the plaintiff's action was not struck out. See *M. Hodge & Sons Ltd. v. Monaghan (No. 2)* (1983), 127 A.P.R. 163 (Nfld. C.A.), revg (1982), 104 A.P.R. 492 (T.D.).

Similarly, a defendant corporation's application to set aside service of a writ and strike out an action against it on the ground that the defendant corporation was not in existence at the time of issue of the writ, its registration having been revoked, but subsequently restored, was dismissed. The order of restoration was held to have a retroactive effect to the date of dissolution. See *A.G. Nfld. v. Sterrett* (1983), 43 Nfld. & P.E.I.R. 197, 127 A.P.R. 197 (Nfld. T.D.).

A reinstatement order in Nova Scotia had the effect of cancelling escheat retroactively. The corporate owner of land was dissolved but subsequently reinstated. The property had been sold at a tax sale by the municipality. The court concluded the tax sale was retroactively validated by the order of reinstatement. The escheat provisions of the *Dissolved Corporations Property Act*, R.S.N.S. 1967, c. 77 were not intended to override the provisions of the *Companies Act*, R.S.N.S. 1967, c. 42. See *Stewarts of Dartmouth Ltd. v. Dartmouth* (1981), 128 D.L.R. (3d) 547 (N.S..T.D.).

Dissolution Before Commencing Business

The current federal Act provides a simple means for dissolution of a corporation before it has commenced business. Corporations which have not issued any shares may be dissolved at any time by resolution of all the directors, see s. 210(1). A corporation that has no property and no liabilities may be dissolved by special resolution of the shareholders or where there are more than one class of shares, by special resolution of the holders of each class (s. 210(2)). Corporations that have property or liabilities or both may be similarly dissolved if, by the special resolution, the shareholders authorize the directors to cause the corporation to distribute property and discharge liabilities and the corporation does so before articles of dissolution are sent to the Director (s. 210(3)). The Director is to issue a certificate of dissolution and the corporation ceases to exist on the date shown in the certificate.

Proposing Liquidation and Dissolution

The directors of a corporation or those shareholders entitled to vote at annual meetings may make a proposal for the voluntary liquidation and dissolution of a corporation, see s. 211(1). Such a proposal requires authorization by special resolution of the shareholders, or by special resolution of the holders of each class of shares (s. 211(3)). Once the shareholders have approved the liquidation and dissolution, a statement of intent to dissolve must be sent to the Director (s. 211(4)). Upon receipt of the statement of intent, the Director is required to issue a certificate of intent to dissolve. Once this certificate is issued, the corporation is required to cease carrying on business except to the extent necessary for liquidation, but its corporate existence continues until the certificate of dissolution is issued. After the certificate of intent to dissolve is issued, the corporation is required to do the following:

(a) immediately give notice to each known creditor of the corporation;
(b) publish notice of the intended dissolution once a week for four consecutive weeks in a newspaper published or distributed in the place where the corporation has its registered office and take reasonable steps to give notice in each province where the corporation was carrying on business at the time it sent the statement of intent to dissolve to the Director;
(c) proceed to collect its property, to dispose of properties that are not to be distributed in kind to its shareholders, to discharge its obligations and do all other acts required to liquidate; and
(d) after giving the required notice and providing for payment or discharge of all its obligations, distribute the remaining property among the shareholders according to their respective rights. See s. 211(7).

At any time during liquidation, the Director or any interested person may apply to the court for an order that liquidation be continued under the court's supervision. The Director is entitled to notice of such application and the Director is entitled to appear and to be heard in person or by counsel, see s. 211(8) and (9) of the Act. Such an application must state the reasons, verified by an affidavit of the applicant, why the court should supervise the liquidation and dissolution. If the court makes the order, then the liquidation and dissolution continue under court supervision (s. 215(1), (2)).

The Act provides for revocation of the certificate of intent to dissolve if a statement of revocation of intention is sent to the Director as approved by the shareholder's special resolution and such statement is received before the issue of a certificate of dissolution. The Director will issue a certificate of revocation of intent to dissolve and the revocation is effective as of the date shown in the certificate. On that date, the corporation may continue to carry on business (s. 211(10)-(12)).

Providing that the corporation does not revoke its intention to dissolve and it has complied with all the requirements of the section, articles of dissolution are prepared and sent to the Director. A certificate of dissolution is issued by the Director and the corporation ceases to exist on the date shown on the certificate (s. 211(13)-(16)).

Dissolution by Director

In those jurisdictions with legislation based on the former federal Act, a corporation's charter can be forfeited for non-use. Liability to forfeiture may arise if the corporation does not go into bona fide operation or does not use its corporate powers. Under previous federal legislation (R.S.C. 1906, c. 79, s. 27) where liability to forfeiture arose if there was no use of the charter, it was held that there was sufficient use of the charter if the corporation became organized and shares were allotted. In the case of an association incorporated for the purpose of construction and maintaining a racecourse, it was held that the racecourse need not be constructed in order to keep the charter alive as it was sufficient that the association was organized and stock was allotted: see *Hepburn v. Connaught Park Jockey Club of Ottawa* (1916), 10 O.W.N. 333 (H.C.). Bringing and maintaining an action and the activities of the trustee, while the corporation was in bankruptcy under an order later vacated, constituted a user of the charter. See *Confederation Land Corp. v. C.P.R.*, [1942] 2 D.L.R. 70 at 73 (Alta. C.A.). See *Cie Generale des Boissons Canadiennes v. Procureur General* (1906), 15 Que. K.B. 536 (C.A.) as to what transactions will be sufficient to enable the court to refrain from declaring forfeiture on the ground that the corporation has failed to go into actual operation.

In *Re Earnscliffe Trust Co.* (1991), 305 A.P.R. 72 (P.E.I.T.D.), the Director's notice of intention to dissolve for non-user under the *Companies Act* was reversed. The corporation had submitted returns pursuant to the *Licensing Act* and the *Companies Act* in which the corporation was described as inactive. However, the corporation had made the required annual reports, applied for and received its annual licence and held meetings of directors and shareholders. Because the Director had determined that the corporation was carrying on business for purposes of the *Licencing Act*, he was estopped from dissolving the charter on the ground that the corporation was not "carrying on business" for purposes of the *Companies Act*.

Under the former federal Act where the charter of a corporation could be forfeited on the happening of certain events such as non-user, it has been held that the charter is not automatically forfeited on the happening of the event but a substantive judicial proceeding is necessary to terminate the existence of the corporation. See *Roy v. Quebec* (1888), 14 Q.L.R. 255; *Hardy Lumber Co. v. Pickerel River Improvement Co.* (1898), 29 S.C.R. 211 at 214; *Moto-Sway Corp. of America v. Standard Steel Construction Co.*, [1939] O.W.N. 311 (H.C.); *Sovereign Crude Oil & Asphalt Co. v. Hébert* (1925), 63 Que. S.C. 286; *Re Cooks & Waiters Club*, [1938] 3 W.W.R. 305 (Alta. T.D.). *Scire facias* was considered to be the proper judicial proceeding to take to have the charter annulled: see *R. v. Bailiffs of Bewdley* (1712), 1 P. Wms. 207; *Mayor of Colchester v. Brooke* (1845), 7 Q.B. 339 at 385; *R. v. Arnaud* (1846), 9 Q.B. 806.

In *Dominion Distillery Products Co. v. The King*, [1937] Ex. C.R. 145 at 157, it was held that non-user had the effect of automatic forfeiture, but on appeal the Supreme Court of Canada ([1938] S.C.R. 458) expressed no opinion on the point. In *Confederation Land Corp. v. C.P.R.*, [1942] 2 D.L.R. 70, the Alberta Appellate Division doubted the correctness of the decision in the *Dominion Distillery* case that non-user effects an automatic forfeiture of the charter.

The non-user provisions of the former federal Act did not confer any power to cancel the charter by order-in-council. The cancellation of the charter by order-in-council, in the absence of a provision in the governing Act authorizing cancellation in such manner, is a nullity: *Re Stanley Mineral Springs Co.* (1916), 10 W.W.R. 1368 (Man. K.B.).

It was unnecessary under the non-user provisions of the former Ontario Act to resort to the courts as was required under the former federal Act. See *A.G. v. Toronto Junction Club* (1904), 8 O.L.R. 440 (H.C.) and *Border Cities Press Club v. A. G. Ontario*, [1955] O.R. 14 (C.A.). Under that Act, forfeiture was not automatic but occurred when some step was taken by the executive: *Moto-Sway Corp. of America v. Standard Steel Construction Co.*, [1939] O.W.N. 311 (H.C.).

Forfeiture of the corporate charter may be used as a ground of defence. It has been held in Quebec that when a corporation has forfeited its charter by breach of its Act of incorporation, a defendant may have an action against him by the corporation stayed until proceedings can be taken to have the charter annulled. See *Windsor Hotel v. Murphy* (1877), 1 L.N. 74; *Quebec & Richmond Ry. Co. v. Dawson* (1851), 1 L.C.R. 366. However, where a corporation obtained judgment and proceeded to execute on the judgment before the corporate charter was annulled for failure to commence business within three years of incorporation, it was held that it is no defence to say the corporation had no legal existence. A corporation remains legally in existence until a court passes judgment annulling the charter and the judgment takes effect only from that date. See *Sovereign Crude Oil & Asphalt Co. v. Hébert* (1925), 63 Que. S.C. 286. A judgment against a non-existent or dissolved corporation is void. See *Simmons v. Liberal Opinion Ltd.*, [1911] 1 K.B. 966 (C.A.); *Lazard Bros. & Co. v. Midland Bank*, [1933] A.C. 289. Nor are corporate debts extinguished through forfeiture of the charter. Where the guarantor of corporate debts alleged that dissolution of the corporation for failure to file the annual return determines the liability of the guarantor, it was held that because provisions for revival exist there is no termination of corporate debts on the forfeiture of the charter. See *Bank of Montreal v. Stephen* (1989), 45 B.L.R. 80 at 89 (N.B. Q.B.), vard (*sub nom. Bank of Montreal v. Dobbin* (1991), 117 N.B.R. (2d) 106 (C.A.), leave to appeal to S.C.C. refused (1991), 119 N.B.R. (2d) 90 (note) (S.C.C.).

Under s. 212(1) of the current Act, in cases where a corporation:

> (a) has not commenced business within three years after the date shown in its certificate of incorporation,
> (b) has not carried on its business for three consecutive years, or
> (c) is in default for a period of one year in sending to the Director any fee, notice or document required by this Act,
>
> the Director may dissolve the corporation by issuing a certificate of dissolution . . . or he may apply to a court for an order dissolving the corporation . . .

However, the Director cannot dissolve the corporation until he has given 120 days' notice of his decision to dissolve to the corporation and to each of its directors and published notice of this decision in the *Canada Gazette*, in a periodical available to the public respecting insider reports and exemptions and in a newspaper published or distributed in the place where the corporate registered office is situated. Unless cause to the contrary has been shown or an order is made by the court requiring the Director to change his mind, the Director may, after expiry of the notice period, issue the certificate of dissolution and the corporation ceases to exist on the date shown in the certificate. If the Director applies to a court for an order of dissolution, the court has the power to make a liquidation order and order of dissolution.

In addition to the grounds set out in s. 212, the Director or any interested person (after giving notice to the Director) may apply to a court for an order dissolving a corporation if the corporation has

(a) failed for two or more consecutive years to comply with the requirements of the Act respecting the holding of annual meetings of shareholders;
(b) contravened s. 16(2) of the Act by carrying on business or exercising powers restricted by its articles or exercising its powers contrary to its articles, contravened s. 21 by failing to grant access to corporate records, contravened s. 157 by failing to prepare or permit examination of certain financial statements, contravened s. 159 by failing to forward copies of financial statements to shareholders; or
(c) procured any certificate under the Act by misrepresentation. (s. 213).

The court may order the corporation be dissolved, liquidated and dissolved under court supervision, or any other order it thinks fit. Once the Director receives the court order, he must issue the proper certificate and publish notice of the certificate. The corporation then ceases to exist on the date shown in the certificate.

Further Grounds

A court may order the liquidation and dissolution of a corporation or any affiliated corporations on the application of a shareholder where there is evidence of oppression. Where the court is satisfied that:

(a) the act or omission of the corporation or any affiliate effects a result,
(b) the business or affairs of the corporation or affiliate are or have been carried on or conducted in a manner, or
(c) the powers of the directors of the corporation or affiliate are or have been exercised in a manner "that is oppressive or unfairly prejudicial to or that unfairly disregards the interests of any security holder, creditor, director or officer", the court may make an order for liquidation and dissolution. (s. 214).

The court may also order liquidation and dissolution if it is satisfied that a unanimous shareholder agreement entitles the complaining shareholder to demand dissolution after the triggering event has occurred or if the court is satisfied that it is just and equitable to make such an order. It will be noted that the oppression remedy is also available under s. 241 and the court is entitled to make the order under either section. See Chapter 16 for a full discussion of the shareholder oppression remedy under the heading "Statutory remedies".

An application for an order under s. 214 must state the reasons, as verified by the affidavit of the applicant, why the corporation should be liquidated and dissolved. The court may order the directors and officers of the corporation to provide the court with all material information known to or reasonably ascertainable by them. Such information may include financial statements of the corporation, names and addresses of each shareholder, names and addresses of creditors and the names and addresses of persons with whom the corporation has a contract. The court may further order the corporation or any person having an interest in the corporation or a claim against it to show cause, at a time designated within four weeks of making the order, why the corporation should not be liquidated and dissolved. If the court makes a show cause order, a copy of the order must be published at least once in each week before the time appointed for the hearing in a newspaper published or distributed in the place where the corporation has its registered office. A copy of the order must be served on the Director and each person named in the order. Publication and service of the show cause order is the responsibility of the corporation or such other person as ordered by the court (s. 216(1)-(5)). In connection with the liquidation and dissolution, where the court is satisfied the corporation is able to pay or adequately provide for the discharge of all its obligations, the court may make a wide variety of orders as set out in s. 217 of the Act.

Liquidation

As noted earlier, the provisions respecting liquidation are not applicable where the corporation is found to be insolvent in a proceeding under the *Bankruptcy and Insolvency Act*, or where proceedings have been taken by a federal or provincial corporation under the *Bankruptcy and Insolvency Act* or where a provincial corporation proceeds under the *Winding-up Act*.

Under the current federal Act, a liquidator may be appointed and his remuneration fixed by court order, see ss. 217(b) and 220(1); some provincial legislation, for example, the Ontario Act, provides for the voluntary winding-up of the corporation's affairs under a liquidator and such appointment does not require a court order but instead voluntary winding-up is commenced by special resolution of the shareholders. At such a meeting the shareholders appoint one or more persons as liquidator and fix his remuneration and the costs, charges and expenses of the winding-up. See s. 193(1), (2) of the Ontario Act.

With respect to the principles of fixing the remuneration of the liquidator, in *Re Three Stars Excavating & Grading Ltd.* (1977), 25 C.B.R. (N.S.) 255 (Ont. H.C.), Southey J. concluded that the court had authority under the former Ontario *Business Corporations Act* to award the liquidator proper disbursements in fixing his compensation. He further held that where remuneration is claimed based on an hourly rate for time spent it is the responsibility of the liquidator to keep a careful record of hours spent. The liquidator is entitled to charge for all necessary work done by his associates. Finally, the liquidator is entitled to charge for time spent on investigating submissions made by rival groups of shareholders and attempting to settle conflicting claims.

A court may specifically provide in its order for the liquidation of a corporation that shareholders be personally responsible to pay all or a portion of a liquidator's fees and disbursements should realization of the corporation's assets by the liquidator result in insufficient funds to meet the outstanding obligations of the corporation. If a liquidator is uncertain whether there exist sufficient assets to pay his fees and disbursements, he should refuse to act as liquidator unless he obtains suitable guarantees from the directors, officers or shareholders of the corporation. See *Bawden v. Jackson* (unreported) December 14, 1990 (Ont. C.A.).

A liquidator is not a trustee within the meaning of the former British Columbia *Trustee Act* and therefore the provisions of that Act which limit a trustee's remuneration to five per cent of the gross value of the assets do not apply. See *Re Intermountain Building & Loan Association of Canada*, [1942] 2 W.W.R. 571 (B.C. S.C.).

The liquidation commences when the court order is made (see s. 218 of the federal Act). If such an order is made, the corporation continues in existence but ceases to carry on business, except the business required for orderly liquidation. As noted earlier, under the federal Act, the powers of the directors and shareholders vest in the liquidator although the liquidator is entitled to delegate those powers to the directors or shareholders (s. 219(1), (2)), but a corresponding provision is not found in the Ontario Act.

The duties of the liquidator are set out in s. 221 of the federal Act. The liquidator is required to give notice to the Director and to known claimants and creditors. He is also required to publish notice and to take steps to give notice in each province where the corporation carries on business requiring persons indebted to the corporation to pay to the liquidator the amount owing, requiring persons possessing property of the corporation to deliver it to the liquidator and requiring those persons having claims against the corporation to present particulars to the liquidator within two months. The liquidator essentially carries on the business of the corporation. The liquidator takes the property of the corporation into his custody and control and keeps account of moneys received and paid out. He may apply to the court for directions if he determines that the corporation is unable to pay or adequately provide for the discharge of its obligations. He is required to deliver financial statements to the court and to the Director.

Within one year after his appointment, and after paying or providing for claims against the corporation, the liquidator is required to apply to court for approval of his final accounts and permission to distribute the remaining property amongst the shareholders or to apply for an extension of time. Where the assets of the corporation were realized and the proceeds held in interest-bearing accounts with the result that interest accrued on the proceeds in the hands of the liquidator, the Ontario Court of Appeal held that the interest was not payable on distribution to the fundholders. See *Re Fund of Funds Ltd.* (1986), 59 C.B.R. (N.S.) 310 (Ont. H.C.) where Houlden J.A. was of the opinion that interest was not payable at common law pursuant to the provisions of either the former or current Ontario *Business Corporations Act* or by virtue of s. 38 of the *Judicature Act*, R.S.O. 1970, c. 228. Where the liquidator, as an officer of the court, has a duty to distribute money in his hands, a debtor-creditor relationship is not created. Therefore, on distribution there is no debt owing by the liquidator to the shareholders and hence the *Judicature Act* had no application.

The law is unclear whether the declaration of dividends by the liquidator in the distribution of realized assets creates a debtor-creditor relationship. See *Re Fund of Funds Ltd., supra,* but compare: *Re Northern Ontario Power Co.,* [1954] O.W.N. 105 (Master).

The costs of the liquidation are paid out of the property of the corporation (s. 223(1) of the federal Act). If the liquidator fails to make this application, the Act allows a shareholder to bring an application to court for an order requiring the liquidator to show cause why the final accounting and distribution should not be made. The liquidator must publish notice of his intention to make this application in the place where the registered office is and give notice to the Director, to inspectors appointed, to each shareholder and to persons who provided security or fidelity bond for the liquidation. Once he obtains court approval, he may distribute the property to the shareholders. See ss. 221 and 223(1)-(4) of the federal Act.

On approval of the final accounts the court will order the Director to issue a certificate of dissolution, direct the custody or disposal of corporate records and documents and discharge the liquidator. The corporation will cease to exist on the date shown in the certificate of dissolution. The person granted custody of the records remains liable to produce them for six years after dissolution or shorter period if so ordered. Contravention of this provision can result in summary conviction and a fine or imprisonment of six months or both. See ss. 223(5)-(7) and 225(1)-(2) of the federal Act.

The liquidator, in the exercise of his duties, is entitled to retain professional advisers such as lawyers, accountants, engineers and appraisers and to rely on their opinions and representations and on the financial statements represented to him by corporate officers or auditors. He is able to bring and defend actions or proceedings in the name of the corporation or settle or compromise claims, sell corporate property, do all acts and execute documents in the name of the corporation and borrow money on the security of the property of the corporation (s. 222(1)-(2) of the federal Act).

If the liquidator believes persons have corporate property in their possession or control or have concealed, withheld or misappropriated corporate property, he is entitled to make application to court for an order requiring the person to appear in court. If the court determines the person has concealed, withheld or misappropriated corporate property, the court may order the person to restore it to the corporation or compensate the liquidator (s. 222(3), (4) of the federal Act). A similar provision is found in the former and current Ontario Acts. The current Act provides that the court can summon persons suspected to have any of the estate or effects of the corporation in their possession before the court *or* the liquidator. In *Re Sky Beach Investments Ltd.* (1977), 3 B.L.R. 26 (H.C.) an application was made to summon persons to appear before the liquidator. Weatherston J.A., in interpreting the provisions of the former Act, granted the application and observed that the examinations must be carried out under oath; that the person being examined should have the right to counsel; that the public generally has no right of access to the proceedings; and that while no provision respecting production of documents is specifically found in that section, the obligation to produce documents is implicit in the Act. See s. 230 of the Ontario Act.

If in the course of liquidation the liquidator proposes or the shareholders resolve to exchange corporate property for securities of another corporation for distribution amongst the shareholders or to distribute corporate property to the shareholders in kind, shareholders are entitled to apply to court for an order requiring the distribution of corporate property to be in money. The court may order conversion of the property into money or that shareholder claims be satisfied by a distribution in money. In the latter case, the court then fixes the fair value of the shares of the shareholder or may appoint appraisers to assist in fixing the fair value and the final order is rendered against the corporation for the amount fixed. See ss. 224(1), (2) and 190(20)-(22) of the federal Act.

The voluntary winding-up provisions under the Ontario Act are similar to those in the federal Act, except, as stated above, winding-up is commenced by resolution of the shareholders and does not require a court order. Within 10 days after the special resolution is passed by a two-thirds majority, notice of the resolution must be filed with the Director and published in the *Ontario Gazette* within 20 days. When the shareholders resolve to wind up the business of the corporation, they are required to appoint a liquidator or may delegate this responsibility to a committee known as inspectors composed of shareholders, contributories or creditors. See ss. 193(2) and 194 of the Ontario Act.

The winding-up usually commences at the time of passing of the resolution, although by resolution can commence at any later time. From the date of commencement of the winding-up, the corporation ceases to carry on its undertaking except as required to wind up its business. However, the corporation retains its corporate existence and powers which continue until its affairs are wound up. See ss. 197 and 198 of the Ontario Act.

In interpreting a predecessor section of the Ontario Act, which provided that the corporation was dissolved on the expiration of three months from the date of filing of the liquidator's return with the provincial secretary, the Supreme Court of Canada concluded that although the corporation "disappears" after the three-month period, the shareholders were entitled thereafter to bring an action claiming their entitlement to any assets still remaining. See *Christie v. Edwards*, [1940] S.C.R. 410.

The duties and powers of the liquidator, subject to the approval of shareholders or the inspectors in certain cases, are set out in the Act and include the power (a) to make a compromise or other arrangement with creditors and claimants; (b) to compromise all debts and liabilities capable of resulting in debts and claims between the corporation and contributories; and (c) to receive cash or shares in the purchasing body corporate where the business of the corporation to be wound up is transferred to another corporation. See ss. 202-204 of the Ontario Act.

The liquidator is required to settle the list of contributories and call on them to the extent of their liability to pay sums necessary to satisfy the liabilities of the corporation and the expenses of winding up. If the winding-up continues for more than one year, the liquidator must call a meeting of the shareholders. See ss. 200 and 201(2) of the Ontario Act.

When the winding-up is complete, the liquidator makes an account showing the manner in which the winding-up has been conducted and lays the account before the shareholders at a meeting. Within ten days of the meeting, a notice of the meeting must be filed with the Director and on the expiration of three months after the date of filing, the corporation is dissolved. This date may be deferred if the liquidator or other interested person applies to court for such an order. The court may also order the corporation dissolved on application of the liquidator or other interested persons. See s. 205 of the Ontario Act.

Whether winding-up is voluntary or by court order under the Ontario Act, once winding-up has commenced, the Act does not permit an action or other proceeding to be commenced against the corporation, nor does it permit attachment, sequestration, distress or execution against the estate or effects of the corporation except with leave of the court. See ss. 199 and 216 of the Ontario Act. No such provision is found in the federal Act.

Continuation of Actions

Notwithstanding the dissolution of corporations, the federal Act provides for the continuation of actions by or against the corporation. Where the applicable corporation legislation failed specifically to provide for the continuation of actions, it had previously been held that a corporation struck off the register under the British Columbia *Companies Act* and not restored was incapable of continuing an action commenced by it before it was struck off and that further proceedings should be stayed. See *Bute Logging Co. v. Sanders* (1952), 5 W.W.R. 142 (B.C. S.C.). Similarly, in *Floen Holdings Ltd. v. Ruff*, [1978] 3 W.W.R. 172 (B.C. S.C.) the plaintiff corporation commenced an action but was subsequently dissolved pursuant to the *Companies Act*, S.B.C. 1973, c. 18 as amended. It was held that the plaintiff corporation could continue the action only if reinstated in the corporations register. Where a corporation had been struck off the register for failure to comply with the provisions of the Alberta *Companies Act*, it was not capable of taking an appeal from its income tax assessment to the Tax Appeal Board. See *Spray Construction Co. v. M.N.R.* (1950), 50 D.T.C. 282.

Currently, civil, criminal or administrative actions or proceedings commenced by or against the corporation prior to dissolution may be continued under the federal Act as if the corporation had not been dissolved. Civil, criminal or administrative actions or proceedings may also be brought against the corporation for a period of two years after dissolution as if the corporation had not been dissolved. The Act does not, however, provide for the bringing of actions by a corporation subsequent to its dissolution. See s. 226(2)(a), (b) of the federal Act and s. 242(1)(a), (b) of the Ontario Act. However, the Act demands strict compliance. See for example *Wolf Offshore Transport Ltd. v. Sulzer Canada Inc.* (1992), 100 Nfld. & P.E.I.R. 178 (Nfld. T.D.), where Riche J. held that the plaintiff was not entitled to continue action upon revival where action commenced after dissolution.

For example, where a corporate charter was revoked for non-payment of fees and the *Companies Act* continued the corporation for three years for the purpose of defending or prosecuting actions, but the corporation took no steps to prosecute an action commenced prior to the revocation until four years after the revocation, the action was dismissed for laches. See *Edmunston Chain Saw Ltd. v. Levesque* (1972), 17 N.B.R. (2d) 449 (Co. Ct.).

Where proceedings were commenced by the corporation after having been struck from the register and no order of restoration was made, the statement of claim was struck as an abuse of process. The plaintiff did not exist in law. See *J.J. Catering Ltd. v. M.G.M. Developments Ltd.* (1986), 45 Alta. L.R. (2d) 318 (Master).

A dissolved Ontario corporation is not incapable of instructing a solicitor or of continuing an action, but in the absence of revival, may only do so if the action is commenced before the dissolution. See *Cini v. Micallef* (1987), 60 O.R. (2d) 584 at 594 (H.C.). No corporation which has been dissolved exists for the purpose of conducting litigation unless the proceedings fall strictly within the provisions of the Act. Therefore a corporation which has been dissolved cannot appeal a tax assessment after the dissolution. See *460354 Ontario Inc. v. M.N.R.* (1988), 88 D.T.C. 1679 (T.C.C.), but see *495187 Ontario Ltd. v. Canada (M.N.R.)* (1992), 92 D.T.C. 6311 (F.C. T.D.) where a notice of reassessment was issued and an appeal of that assessment sought after dissolution, the sole shareholder and Director of the corporation was permitted to appeal the notice without prior revival of the corporation.

However, in *Estabrooks Pontiac Buick Ltd. v. General Motors Acceptance Corp. of Canada Ltd.* (1987), 86 N.B.R. (2d) 104 (Q.B.), the plaintiff corporation had commenced an action subsequent to the forfeiture of its charter. The defendant moved to dismiss the action by raising the defence of legal incapacity. Unlike the current federal Act, the statute did not distinguish between claims made by and against the corporation and merely provided that the corporation was continued for three years for the purpose of prosecuting or defending suits by or against it. The court rejected the argument that the continuation of actions provision was limited to the prosecution of suits commenced before forfeiture. The court refused to read in the words "which were commenced before forfeiture".

The federal Act also provides that any property that would have been available to satisfy any judgment or order if the corporation had not been dissolved remains available for that purpose. See s. 226(2)(c) of the federal Act and s. 242(1)(c) of the Ontario Act.

After dissolution, service of documents on the dissolved corporation may be effected by serving the document on a director of the corporation (s. 226(3) of the federal Act). In Ontario, service may also be effected on an officer of the corporation (s. 242(2) of the Ontario Act). The Ontario Act also requires notice of actions brought against the corporation and the initiating process be served on the public trustee, s. 242(3) of the Ontario Act.

Notwithstanding the dissolution of a corporation, shareholders to whom any property has been distributed are liable to persons initiating claims against the corporation after dissolution to the extent of the amount received by the shareholder. Actions to enforce shareholder liability may be brought within two years after dissolution (s. 226(4) of the federal Act). In Ontario such claims may be brought within five years of dissolution (s. 243(1) of the Ontario Act). These provisions now make it clear that claimants may take action against the shareholders to enforce the judgment obtained. In a predecessor section of the Ontario Act, shareholders remained liable to "creditors" for two years following dissolution. In *G. T. Campbell & Associates Ltd. v. Hugh Carson Co.* (1979), 7 B.L.R. 84 (Ont. C.A.) the court was of the view that to give any effect to s. 252 which provided for actions brought after dissolution, the word "creditor" in s. 253 which created shareholder liability would have to be broadly interpreted to include claimants under s. 252. In both the federal and Ontario Acts, the definition of "shareholder" has been extended to expressly include the heirs and legal representatives of the shareholder. See s. 226(1) of the federal Act and s. 243(3) of the Ontario Act.

Unknown Claimants

When the corporation is dissolved and a creditor or shareholder cannot be found, that portion of the property distributable to him is converted into money and paid to the Receiver General. That payment is deemed by the Act to be in satisfaction of the debt or claim of that creditor or shareholder. However, the amount of the debt or claim can be recovered from the Receiver General out of the Consolidated Revenue Fund, if the creditor or shareholder can establish his entitlement to the moneys paid to the Receiver General. See s. 227(1)-(3) of the federal Act.

Bona Vacantia

The common law doctrine of *bona vacantia* is codified in s. 228(1) of the federal Act. The property of the corporation which has not been disposed of at the date of dissolution, except that property necessary to satisfy judgments or orders obtained after dissolution and that property converted into money and paid to the Receiver General for unknown claimants, vests in the Crown. The doctrine of *bona vacantia* cannot be defeated by resolution of the shareholders to donate surplus moneys to charity. See *Re Prairie Fibreboard Ltd.* (1962), 38 W.W.R. 412 (Sask. Q.B.).

At common law, the personal property vested in the corporation at the time of its dissolution devolved to the Crown. See *In re Higginson & Dean*, [1899] 1 Q.B. 325; *In re Thomas Spencer Wells; Swinburne-Hanham v. Howard*, [1933] 1 Ch. 29 (C.A.); and *Russian & English Bank v. Barins Bros. & Co.*, [1936] A.C. 405 at 422, 426, 434, and 439 (H.L.). It is unclear whether the corporation's real estate vested in the corporation at the time of dissolution escheats to the Crown or reverts to the original grantor. With respect to the latter, see *In re Woking Urban District Council (Basingstoke Canal) Act, 1911*, [1914] 1 Ch. 300 (C.A.); *Canadian Fertilizer Co. v. Canadian Industries Ltd.*, [1938] 3 D.L.R. 765 (Ont. S.C.) following *Lindsay Petroleum Co. v. Pardee* (1875), 22 Gr. 18 (C.A.); and *R. v. Smith* (1985), 39 Alta. L.R. (2d) 180 (Q.B.). On the other hand, in

Stowell MacGregor Corp. v. John MacGregor Corp., [1942] 4 D.L.R. 120 at 126 (N.B. K.B.), Baxter C.J.N.B. expressed disagreement with the doctrine of reversion to the original grantor. Similarly, in *Re Jolin and Lart Investments Ltd.* (1977), 18 O.R. (2d) 161 (Dist. Ct.), the court rejected the theory of reversion to the original grantor and held that real property was forfeited to the Crown. The court noted that subsequent to the corporation's dissolution, amendments to the Ontario *Companies Act* were made which specifically provided that real property vest in the Crown.

The current federal and Ontario Acts do not specifically refer to both personal and real property, instead they refer to "property". This term would almost certainly be interpreted to include both real and personal property.

Where a plaintiff corporation agreed to sell to a defendant certain land which had been purchased by the plaintiff's predecessor but the previous transfer was not registered before the predecessor's charter expired, the Ontario Court of Appeal held that the predecessor's equitable interest in the land at the time of the expiration of its charter had been forfeited to the Crown and accordingly the plaintiff corporation, not having good title, was not entitled to specific performance of the agreement. See *Marcobalt Mining Syndicate v. Gray*, [1955] O.R. 761 (C.A.).

Both the common law doctrine of *bona vacantia* and the statutory forfeiture provisions are subject to the provisions respecting revival. See *A.G. B.C. v. Royal Bank*, [1937] S.C.R. 459 respecting revival. In *Re Ownership of Lands Known as "Monarch", "extension", "Prince Albert", "Saskatchewan" and "Huron" Mineral Claims*, [1984] 5 W.W.R. 761 (Sask. Q.B.) the Crown claimed the surface rights in land owned by a dissolved gold mine corporation which was subsequently revived. It was held that at common law, the Crown's title though *bona vacantia* is defeasible and terminates on revival. Statutory forfeiture is also subject to revival which restores the corporation to its former position subject to terms imposed by the revival order.

As to conflicting claims of two provinces to the same asset as *bona vacantia*, see *Re Hole Estate*, [1948] 4 D.L.R. 419 (Man. K.B.).

The right of a corporation as a creditor to participate in the assets of a bankrupt, in respect of a debt proved in the bankruptcy, survives the dissolution of the corporation and continues to be existing personal property, which devolves on the Crown as *bona vacantia*. See *In re Higginson & Dean*, [1899] 1 Q.B. 325.

The doctrine of *bona vacantia* extends to leaseholds. See *In re Thomas Spencer Wells; Swinburne-Hanham v. Howard*, [1933] 1 Ch. 29 (C.A.). In that case it was held that an equity of redemption in property subleased to the corporation and assigned to a mortgagee passed to the Crown as *bona vacantia* on the dissolution of the mortgagor corporation. Lawrence L.J. and Romer L.J. so held on the assumption that the term granted by the sublease was not extinguished on the dissolution of the corporation. The head lessor was not before the court. Lord Hanworth M.R. was of the opinion that on the dissolution of the corporation the equity of redemption was not extinguished.

Where the parties had admitted that the assets of a defunct English corporation formerly carrying on business in British Columbia were *bona vacantia*, it was held that such assets vest in the province as royalties under ss. 102 and 109 of the *British North America Act, 1867*. See *R. v. British Columbia (Attorney General)*, [1924] A.C. 213 (P.C.).

As to provincial legislation declaring to be *bona vacantia* unclaimed moneys held in trust, see *Manitoba (Provincial Treasurer) v. Canada (Minister of Finance)*, [1934] S.C.R. 370; *A.G. Can. v. Atts. G. Que., Sask., Alta. & Man.*, [1947] A.C. 33 at 45 (P.C.). In the last mentioned case provincial legislation aimed primarily at certain deposits in banks in Quebec was held to be *ultra vires* as relating to banking.

The shareholders of an electrical utility which is being wound up have no legal right to unclaimed deposits made by former customers, and therefore cannot defeat the doctrine of *bona vacantia*. See *Re Northern Ontario Power Co.*, [1954] O.W.N. 105 (Master).

Where a foreign corporation had been dissolved under its own law of incorporation and years later, on the discovery of assets in England, a winding-up order was made under the *Companies Act, 1948* the court held that the right of the Crown to *bona vacantia* extended only to any surplus existing after the proper administration of the assets in the English winding-up. See *Re Banque Industrielle de Moscou*, [1952] 2 All E.R. 532 (Ch. Div.).

While the reasons for judgment in *A.G. B.C. v. Royal Bank*, [1937] S.C.R. 459 do not appear to throw any doubt on the applicability of the doctrine of *bona vacantia* where the corporation has been finally dissolved "without successor or representative", it was held that the doctrine did not apply to a bank deposit in the name of a British Columbia corporation which had been struck off the register under s. 167 of the *Companies Act*, R.S.B.C. 1924, c. 38. Pursuant to ss. 199 and 200 of the British Columbia *Companies Act*, 1929, c. 11, an order had been made restoring the corporation to the register with the consequence that the corporation was to be deemed to have continued in existence as if it had not been struck off. See also *Confederation Land Corp. v. C.P.R.*, [1942] 2 D.L.R. 70 at 73 (Alta. C.A.); *Re Albion Machine Co.*, [1929] 1 D.L.R. 274 (N.S. T.D.); *In re C.W. Dixon Ltd.*, [1947] Ch. 251 (effect of order under s. 294 of the *Companies Act, 1929*).

In *Embree v. Miller* (1917), 33 D.L.R. 331 the Appellate Division of the Alberta Supreme Court held that, on an Alberta corporation having been struck off the register with the result that it was dissolved, shareholders were entitled to bring a representative action to recover assets belonging to the corporation. The basis of the decision was that the Crown was only entitled to the residue of the corporation's assets after its obligations had been satisfied and that shareholders were creditors of the corporation on its dissolution after payment of all its other obligations. As to the right of a shareholder of a Saskatchewan corporation which has been struck off the register to make other shareholders account for his *pro rata* part of the assets of the corporation which such shareholders have distributed among themselves without formal liquidation proceedings, see *Dadson v. Grest*, [1928] 1 D.L.R. 479 (Sask. C.A.).

Where the assets of a dissolved Dakota corporation and the trustees in whom they were vested were in the province, Hodgins J.A. in *McCormack v. Carman* (1919), 17 O.W.N. 241 (C.A.) said it was open for any creditor or anyone who held the status of a shareholder to have the assets administered here. It is clear, however, that the corporation in that case had not been finally dissolved "without successor or representative".

The principle that unclaimed property of a dissolved corporation vests in the Crown as *bona vacantia* does not apply to property held by the corporation in trust and where a corporation has sold its assets and then been dissolved without first effecting a legal transfer of the property sold to the purchaser, orders have been made appointing a new trustee under legislation such as s. 5 of the *Trustee Act*, R.S.O. 1990, c. T.23 in place of the dissolved corporation and vesting the particular property in the purchaser. See *In re General Accident Assurance Corp.*, [1904] 1 Ch. 147 (vesting order); *In re No. 9, Bomore Road*, [1906] 1 Ch. 359; *In re Albert Road, Norwood*, [1916] 1 Ch. 289 (the corporation had been ordered to assign leasehold premises in pursuance of a foreclosure order but had failed to do so; a new trustee was appointed and a vesting order made); *Canadian Fertilizer Co. v. Canadian Industries Ltd.*, [1938] 3 D.L.R. 765 (Ont. S.C.) (vesting order made); *Re Gair Company of Canada* (unreported) (Supreme Court of Ontario, Plaxton J., June 26, 1941) (vesting order made where the original vendor corporation, the purchaser corporation and second purchaser corporation whose assets had been sold to the applicant had all surrendered their charters). Where the subject matter was a patent granted by the Crown, on the dissolution of the corporation the legal interest in the patent was considered to have vested in the Crown, if it vested anywhere, and the application was refused. See *In re Taylor's Agreement Trusts*, [1904] 2 Ch. 737.

Where a corporation is revived, any property other than money which was forfeited to the Crown that has not been disposed of must be returned to the corporation and the corporation is to be paid an amount equal to any money received by the Crown. Where the property has been disposed of, the corporation is to receive an amount equal to the lesser of the value of that property at the date of vesting and any amount realized by the Crown on disposition of the property (s. 228(2)).

Chapter 15

INVESTIGATIONS

Cross-references: Ontario Act, ss. 161-167.

Investigation

The federal Act and the Acts of all provinces except Prince Edward Island provide for the appointment of inspectors to investigate the affairs of a corporation either by a government official, by court order or alternatively, in those jurisdictions with legislation based on the former Canada *Companies Act*, by resolution of the shareholders. Under business corporations legislation investigations may be ordered by a court on application by a "security holder", which by definition would include shareholders, or by the Directors, but inspectors cannot be appointed by a corporation by shareholder resolution.

Both levels of government are constitutionally competent to enact legislation for the appointment of inspectors. The inspector does not occupy a judicial or quasi-judicial position and has no power to adjudicate. Therefore, the appointment of an inspector is *intra vires* a province as he does not exercise the jurisdiction of a judge pursuant to s. 96 of the *Constitution Act, 1867*: see *Re First Investors Corp.*, [1988] 4 W.W.R. 22, 58 Alta. L.R. (2d) 38 (Q.B.), affd (1988), 59 Alta.

L.R. (2d) 334 (C.A.). Nor does the federal appointment of inspectors trench on provincial jurisdiction over property and civil rights. Under a predecessor section of the federal Act, the Minister could apply to the Restrictive Trade Practices Commission and the Commission could order an investigation and appoint an inspector. A shareholder of a corporation under such investigation applied for an order of prohibition to stop the investigation on the ground that the provision was *ultra vires* the Parliament. The court held that neither Parliament nor the provincial legislatures have exclusive jurisdiction to legislate with respect to investigations. Authority is provincial where investigations concern provincial matters and is federal in all other cases. Moreover, Parliament has authority under the "peace, order and good government" clause to legislate with respect to the incorporation of corporations with non-provincial objects: see *Re Doyle and Restrictive Trade Practices Commission (No. 2)* (1983), 7 D.L.R. (4th) 524 (Fed. C.A.), leave to appeal to S.C.C. refused (1983), 51 N.R. 236. The fact that an investigation ordered may reveal evidence which could form the basis of a subsequent criminal charge does not vitiate the constitutionality of the inquiry. The Alberta Act has been held not to entrench on the federal power over criminal law in s. 91(27) of the *Constitution Act, 1867*: see *Re First Investors Corp., supra*, at 41-42 (W.W.R.). Further, the fact that evidence of criminal activity may emerge does not breach either s. 7 or s. 15 of the *Canadian Charter of Rights and Freedoms.* See *Re First Investors Corp., supra*, at 43-45 (W.W.R.).

In those jurisdictions with legislation based on the former Canada *Companies Act*, the power of the court to intervene in the affairs of a private corporation is exercised with caution. Before the court will appoint an inspector, it must be *prima facie* in the interests of the corporation or the security holders: see *Re Baker and Paddock Inn Peterborough Ltd.* (1977), 16 O.R. (2d) 38 (H.C.). To justify an order on application of the shareholders, "it should appear that there is reason on substantial grounds to believe that material information regarding the affairs or management of the company is being concealed or withheld from shareholders whose interests entitle them to the disclosure": *Re Town Topics Co.* (1911), 20 Man. R. 574 at 576, per Robson J. To show a difference of opinion respecting management decisions is not enough, although in cases of serious mismanagement or where there are indications of bad faith or an intention to injure or damage the corporation or its shareholders, a court might be persuaded to intervene: see *Re Baker and Paddock Inn Peterborough Ltd., supra*; *Re Sabex Internationale Ltée* (1979), 6 B.L.R. 65 (Que. S.C.).

Where corporate assets were used without the knowledge of one director who also held 40 per cent of the corporation's shares, an investigation was warranted: see *Baniuk v. Carpenter et al. (No. 1)* (1986), 85 N.B.R. (2d) 372 (Q.B.). Where the directors caused the corporation to deal with other corporations in which they had pecuniary interests without disclosure of this fact, the petitioner, a minority shareholder, had good reason for requiring the investigation: see

Hong v. Rice Bowl Ltd. (1985), 153 A.P.R. 329 (Nfld. T.D.). It has been held under the British Columbia *Companies Act* that where a corporation has already fully disclosed to its shareholders a breach of duty and misfeasance on the part of the directors, these are not matters to be inquired into under this section: see *Re Automatic Phone Recorder Co.* (1955), 15 W.W.R. 666 (B.C. S.C.). The fact that no dividends have been declared by a profit-making corporation has been held insufficient to warrant an order under the federal *Companies Act* as originally enacted: *Re Sarnia Ranching Co.* (1915), 8 W.W.R. 697 (Alta. T.D.). The court never interferes to prescribe to a corporation what it shall do as to its own purely internal affairs: *Lambert v. Neuchatel Ashphalte Co.* (1882), 30 W.R. 913.

Under the Quebec *Companies Act*, where the provincial secretary appointed an inspector upon the application of a shareholder without notice to the corporation, it was held that as the section provided no special procedure in connection with an appointment other than that which was in the opinion of the provincial secretary sufficient and as it must be presumed that the provincial secretary had acted in accordance with this section, no injunction would be granted to restrain the inspector from proceeding with his inspection: *Johnson Woollen Mills Ltd. v. Southern Canada Power Co.*, [1944] Que. P.R. 337, affd [1945] Que. K.B. 134. In England, it has been held that the rules of natural justice do not apply to the appointment of inspectors by the Secretary of State and therefore the corporation is not entitled to an opportunity to state its case before the decision to order an investigation is made. Such appointment could not be challenged so long as the Secretary of State acted *bona fide* and within his powers under the Act: see *Norwest Holst v. Secretary of State for Trade*, [1978] 3 All E.R. 280 (C.A.).

A corporation incorporated under legislation similar to the former federal Act may itself, by resolution of its shareholders at any annual or special general meeting called for the purpose, appoint inspectors to investigate its affairs. Where the Act requires a special resolution for the appointment of inspectors, an ordinary resolution will not suffice and will be inoperative as being an interference with the management of the business of the corporation by the directors: see *Scott v. Scott*, [1943] 1 All E.R. 582.

Where the governing Act authorizes the appointment of an inspector on the application of a specified proportion in value of the shareholders, it has been held that the owners of shares standing in the name of a bare trustee may be counted to make up the proportion: see *Re Kootenay Valley Fruit Lands Co.* (1911), 18 W.L.R. 145. It has been held under the British Columbia *Companies Act*, S.B.C. 1973, c. 18, s. 230(1), which makes provision for the appointment of an inspector on the "application of a member . . . holding not less than one-fifth of the issued shares of any class of the corporation", that the section only applies to an application by a single individual holding the proportion of shares and not to a group of shareholders collectively holding the required one-fifth shares: see *Re Peterson and Kanata Investments Ltd.* (1975), 60 D.L.R. (3d) 527 (B.C. S.C.). Note the *Interpretation Act*, S.B.C. 1974, c. 42, s. 24(3) stated that in a statute, "words in the singular include the plural and words in the plural include the singular". Query whether the basis for the decision in *Re Peterson and Kanata Investments Ltd., supra,* is correct in light of s. 24(3) of the *Interpretation Act.*

The inspector merely performs an investigatory role and therefore he is under no duty to comply with the rules of natural justice: see *Canadian Javelin Ltd. v. Sparling*, [1979] 1 F.C. 334, affd (1979), 106 D.L.R. (3d) 495 (Fed. C.A.), leave to appeal to S.C.C. refused (1980), 106 D.L.R. (3d) 495n. However, he is under a duty to act fairly: see *Grebely v. Seven Mile High Group Inc.* (1990), 46 B.C.L.R. (2d) 240 (S.C.); *Re Associated Investors of Canada Ltd.* (1988), 63 Alta. L.R. (2d) 69 (Q.B.); *Re Ferguson and Imax Systems Corp.* (1984), 47 O.R. (2d) 225 (Div. Ct.); and *Re Pergamon Press Ltd.*, [1971] 1 Ch. 388 (C.A.) and must not only be impartial but appear to be impartial: see *Re Ferguson amd Imax Systems Corp., supra.*

However, in British Columbia, while the Supreme Court has agreed that inspectors must be impartial, it has held that in order to successfully attack the inspector's conduct on the basis of bias, the applicant must establish strong evidence of actual operative bias and proof of a reasonable apprehension of bias will be insufficient. The concern that justice not only be done but also be seen to be done should not generally be applied to the functions of an investigator: see *Grebely v. Seven Mile High Group Inc.* (1990), 46 B.C.L.R. (2d) 240 at 258 (S.C.).

The scope of the duty of fairness depends upon the nature of the report, its circulation to the public, its degree of influence on the ultimate decision, the seriousness of the allegations, the possible penalties which might result, and the publicity surrounding the proceedings: see *Re Associated Investors of Canada Ltd.* (1988), 63 Alta. L.R. (2d) 69 (Q.B.). The nature of the investigation may give rise to the reasonable expectation that those persons adversely affected should have an opportunity to state their case especially where the outcome of the investigation is likely to be prejudicial: *Re Associated Investors of Canada Ltd., supra.* It is sufficient for inspectors holding inquiries to put to witnesses those statements made against them which appear to call for an explanation or answer but they need not put their tentative conclusions to the witnesses: see *Maxwell v. Department of Trade & Industry*, [1974] 2 All E.R. 122 (C.A.).

When the inspector has made his report his duties are at an end. The report merely sets out information. It binds no one and cannot be made the foundation of any subsequent proceeding, nor will the report be evidence of the existence of any fact therein stated, but, if duly authenticated, it will be admissible in any legal proceeding as evidence of the opinion of the inspector: see *Re Grosvenor and West End Railway Terminus Hotel Co.* (1897), 76 L.T. 337; *Re Town Topics Co.* (1911), 20 Man. R. 574 (K.B.); *Re Shell Castle Fire Place Ltd.* (1927), 33 O.W.N. 195; and *Grebely v. Seven Mile High Group Inc.* (1990), 46 B.C.L.R. (2d) 240 at 245. But see *Re Armvent*, [1975] 3 All E.R. 441 (Ch. D.) where it was held that the contents of the report may be *prima facie* admissible evidence on which to base a winding-up of the corporation even if the report is challenged, although the decision as to whether it is just and equitable to do so remains with the judge. In some jurisdictions the admissibility of the report as evidence of the opinion of the inspector has been statutorily enacted. In Alberta, the *Companies Act*, R.S.A. 1980, c. C-20, s. 77(10) specifically makes a copy of the inspector's report admissible as evidence of the facts stated therein. There is no such provision in the federal Act.

Business corporations legislation also provides for appointment of inspectors by court order. Under the federal Act, on the application of a security holder or the Director, the court having the jurisdiction in the place where the corporation has its registered office may order an investigation to be made of the corporation and any of its affiliated corporations: see s. 229(1)-(2) of the federal Act and s. 161(1)-(2) of the Ontario Act.

The Act now clarifies that subsidiary corporations may be investigated. The predecessor section of the Ontario Act allowed only the investigation of the "affairs and management of the corporation". In interpreting this section it was suggested in *obiter* that this would likely not include the investigation of a wholly owned subsidiary corporation: see *Re H. Flagal (Holdings) Ltd.*, [1966] 1 O.R. 33 (H.C.).

Such applications may be brought on an *ex parte* basis and heard *in camera*: see s. 229(5) of the federal Act and s. 161(5) of the Ontario Act.

The circumstances in which such an order may be made include the following: where the business of the corporation or an affiliate is or has been carried on with intent to defraud; where the business has been carried on or the powers of the directors have been exercised in a manner that is oppressive or unfairly prejudicial to a security holder; the corporation or affiliate was formed or is to be dissolved for fraudulent purposes; or where persons concerned with the corporation or affiliate have acted fraudulently or dishonestly.

The Ontario High Court in *obiter* has suggested that the legislation may only apply to the actions of directors *qua* directors and not to their activities as individuals or to the actions of officers who are not directors: see *Re Royal Trustco Ltd. (No. 3)* (1981), 14 B.L.R. 307 at 315 (Ont. H.C.).

With respect to the test to be applied in deciding whether the conduct complained of falls within this section, a court is entitled to make an order for an investigation "if it appears on the face of the materials submitted to the court that there is good reason to think that the conduct complained of may have taken place": *Re Royal Trustco Ltd. (No. 3), supra.* An applicant is not required to prove beyond a reasonable doubt or on the balance of probabilities those acts enumerated in s. 229(2) in order to obtain a court order. Such order may be made where there are "sufficient grounds" to warrant an investigation: see *Re First Investors Corp.*, [1988] 4 W.W.R. 22 at 32 (Alta. Q.B.), affd (1988), 59 Alta. L.R. (2d) 334 (C.A.). The predecessor section of the Ontario Act provided that the application was to be supported by such evidence as the court required. It was held that an order could not be made based on an affidavit containing serious allegations of bad faith and misconduct made on information and belief where the sources of information were available: see *Re H. Flagal (Holdings) Ltd., supra.*

An order under these sections should only be made where the application primarily focuses on facts and not on disputed or uncertain questions of law which are more properly resolved in a lawsuit. An investigation is only that, not a proceeding for a determination of rights: see *Re Royal Trustco Ltd. (No. 3), supra*, at 311. However, the Alberta Court of Appeal has stated that the inspector is not simply a data gatherer. He is entitled to analyze and characterize evidence and report to the court the legal framework which guided his investigation. The Alberta Act though does not confer on the inspector the power to determine civil or criminal responsibility, nor can he report his opinion with respect to whether an individual, corporation or government agency committed fraud or illegal acts or is liable for negligence or illegality: see *Re First Investors Corp., supra*, at 36-38 (W.W.R.).

Powers of Court

In connection with these investigations, a court may make any order it thinks fit, such as ordering the appointment of an inspector, authorizing the inspector to enter any premises and examine any documents and records; conduct hearings; order any person to produce documents or to attend the hearing and give evidence on oath. The court may order the inspector to make interim or final reports to the court. Under the federal Act, the inspector is required to send to the Director a copy of every report made (s. 230(1)-(2)). The Ontario Act also requires an inspector to send his report to the Director and to the Ontario Securities Commission if the corporation under investigation is an offering corporation (s. 162(1)-(2)).

Power of Inspector

The inspector's powers are set out in the court order appointing him. The inspector is entitled to seek production of documents from third parties so long as a sufficient nexus can be established between the contents of the documents which the inspector seeks production of and the subject matter under investigation: see *Re First Investors Corp. (No. 2)* (1988), 87 A.R. 279 at 283 (Q.B.). Whether or not the documents requested are properly producible is a question of relevance: *Re First Investors Corp. (No. 2), supra*, at 281.

In addition to the powers in the court order, an inspector is entitled to exchange information and co-operate with other public officials who exercise investigatory powers and who are investigating similar conduct in respect of the corporation. See s. 231(1)-(2) of the federal Act and s. 163(1)-(2) of the Ontario Act. This additional power is not found in the legislation of all provinces; however, a power to disclose information to certain third parties seems implicit in corporate law legislation. It has been held that even in the absence of an explicit power to exchange information, legislation which authorizes investigations is in part enacted in the public interest and therefore to carry out his statutory duties properly, the inspector must be able to exchange information on a confidential basis with other regulatory bodies even if the information is private and of a confidential nature. However, it cannot be interpreted as abrogating solicitor-client privilege: see *Canadian Javelin Ltd. v. Sparling* (1978), 91 D.L.R. (3d) 64 (Fed. C.A.), affg (1978) 4 B.L.R. 153 (Fed. T.D.).

Hearing *In Camera*

In certain provinces, the statute does not specify whether investigations are to be held *in camera*. However, in interpreting English legislation similar to the former federal Act, it was held that investigations are to be held in private: see *Hearts of Oak Assurance Co. v. A.G.*, [1932] A.C. 392 at 403 (H.L.). The inspector is entitled to have the assistance at the inquiry of any person whom he may reasonably require, for example, a shorthand writer: see *In re Gaumont-British Picture Corp.*, [1940] 1 Ch. 506.

Under the federal Act, hearings conducted by an inspector may be held *in camera* upon the application of an interested person to the court. Persons under investigation or who are being examined at a hearing have the right to be represented by counsel: see s. 232(2) of the federal Act and s. 164(2) of the Ontario Act.

Criminating Statements and Solicitor-Client Privilege

No one is excused from attending such hearing by reason that their evidence tends to incriminate them, but that evidence cannot be used against them in subsequent proceedings except for certain criminal prosecutions: see s. 233 of the federal Act. There is no corresponding provision in the Ontario Act but such provision is found in other jurisdictions. However, similar provisions are also found in s. 5(1)-(2) of the *Canada Evidence Act*, R.S.C. 1985, c. C-5 and s. 9(1)-(2) of the Ontario *Evidence Act*, R.S.O. 1990, c. E.23. These statutes apply to proceedings, actions and matters over which Parliament and the legislature, respectively, have jurisdiction. Such "matters" should include investigatory hearings and therefore the protections of the federal and provincial Evidence Acts would be available to witnesses.

In interpreting the provisions of the former Ontario *Business Corporations Act*, the court held that although the statute required production of accounts and records for examination by an inspector, documents may be subject to a claim of solicitor-client privilege. Such privilege applies even though no litigation is in progress or contemplated, but only to communications made between the corporation and the solicitor acting in that capacity. Where privilege is claimed and disputed, reference to the master is appropriate: see *Re Presswood and International Chemalloy Corp.* (1975), 11 O.R. (2d) 164 (H.C.). The federal Act specifically protects solicitor and client privilege and whether particular information is deserving of such protection remains a question for the courts: see s. 236 of the federal Act and s. 166 of the Ontario Act.

Absolute Privilege

Oral or written statements and the report made by the inspector or any other person connected with an investigation are protected by statutory privilege: see s. 234 of the federal Act and s. 165 of the Ontario Act. This affords those individuals with absolute privilege in respect of statements made in the course of an investigation in any subsequent action for defamation.

Information Respecting Ownership and Control and Inquiries

The Director is given certain powers under Part XIX of the federal Act. If he is satisfied that there is reason to inquire into the ownership or control of a security of a corporation or of its affiliates, he may require any person that he reasonably believes has or has had an interest in the security or who acts or has acted for such a person to provide information respecting present and past interests in the security and the names and addresses of such persons. Non-compliance with this section constitutes an offence and penalties are provided: see s. 235. There is no corresponding power in the Ontario Act, although such a power is found in other jurisdictions. The Director is also allowed to make inquiries of any person relating to compliance with the Act: see s. 237 of the federal Act and s. 167 of the Ontario Act.

Costs

In those provinces operating under legislation based on the former Canada *Companies Act*, the cost of the investigation is generally borne by the applicant unless the corporation is ordered to pay the expenses. In some of the jurisdictions the applicant may be required to give security for costs before the appointment of an inspector: see *Hong v. Rice Bowl Ltd.* (1985), 153 A.P.R. 239 (Nfld. T.D.).

As to the principles on which costs will be awarded as to an investigation under the former Ontario *Companies Act*, see *Re Shell Castle Fire Place Ltd.* (1927), 33 O.W.N. 195 (Master); *Re Clinton Knitting Co.*, [1942] O.W.N. 174 (C.A.).

The focus of the business corporations legislation is to shift the cost burden from the applicant to the corporation. In *Mexican Light & Power Co. v. Mexican Light & Power Co. (Shareholders of)* (1989), 46 B.L.R. 14 at 20 (H.C.) Potts J. stated that the corporation ought to pay the costs of the investigation otherwise "minority shareholders could never realistically take advantage of the provisions of Part XIII of the Ontario *Business Corporations Act, 1982*". A security holder applying to the court for an order directing an investigation is generally not required to give security for costs: see s. 229(4) of the federal Act and s. 161(4) of the Ontario Act. The court may make an order requiring the corporation to pay the costs of the investigation: see s. 230(1)(l) of the federal Act and s. 162(1)(l) of the Ontario Act.

The usual order respecting costs where an inspector has been appointed would require the corporation to pay the costs of the inspection and the costs of the application for the appointment. However, it appears that s. 230(1) of the federal Act gives the court discretion to make an award of costs against the complainant where the court determines that the application had no merit. Where the corporation was found on appeal to have had good reason to object to the appointment, the order respecting costs required the corporation to pay those costs, but was varied to reserve to the judge hearing the balance of the motion the power to direct the complainant to reimburse the corporation for all or part of the costs paid to the inspector: see *Re Ferguson and Imax Systems Corp.* (1984), 47 O.R. (2d) 225 at 239-240 (Div. Ct.).

The provisions of the business corporations legislation also permit wider orders. Where the preparation of the inspector's report was in the interests of the corporation and its creditors and the applicants had been reasonable in asking for the investigation, the court ordered that costs be paid by the corporation or its directors jointly and severally: see *Re Teperman & Sons Ltd.* (1984), 29 B.L.R. 1 (Ont. H.C.).

Chapter 16

REMEDIES, OFFENCES AND PUNISHMENT

Cross-references: Ontario Act, ss. 245-261.

Procedural matters

Institution of actions

An abbreviation of the name of the corporation, the word "company" being abbreviated to "co.", will be a sufficient legal description for the purpose of suit: *Continental Marble Co. v. Langs*, [1937] 4 D.L.R. 39 (B.C. C.A.). The principle of this case would also apply to the abbreviation of "corporation" to 'corp." or "co." Where a defendant corporation objected to the style of cause in an action on the ground that the word "Limited" had been omitted, the court held that the omission did not invalidate the description of the corporation: *Côté v. Lake St. John Distributing Co.*, [1956] Que. P.R. 314 (Sup. Ct.). The omission of the word "Limited" after the name of the corporation in the body of an affidavit where the name is correctly stated in the style of cause does not make the affidavit void: *Dalhousie Lumber Co. v. Walker* (1916), 30 D.L.R. 498 (N.B. C.A.).

As to the right of a corporation to bring an action in its original name where the name has been changed, see *Provincial Insurance Co. v. Cameron* (1881), 31 U.C.C.P. 523, affd (*sub nom. Provincial Insurance Co. v. Worts*) (1883), 9 O.A.R. 56.

Where an action had been commenced under the name of one of the amalgamating corporations, an application to substitute the correct corporate name was granted as the defendant was not misled or prejudiced by the use of the wrong name: *C & J Enterprises (1971) Ltd. v. Curtis* (1978), 25 N.B.R. (2d) 537 (Q.B.). Where a writ was issued after amalgamation in the name of one of the amalgamating corporations, the writ could be amended even though a limitation period had passed: *Witco Chemical Co. v. Oakville (Town)*, [1975] 1 S.C.R. 273. Where the plaintiff amalgamated with another corporation having a separate but similar cause of action against the defendant, but for which the limitation period had expired, the plaintiff's application to substitute the amalgamated corporation as plaintiff was denied. There was no real or substantial connection between the claims of the original plaintiff and of the corporation now amalgamated and no reasonable explanation for the failure to advance the corporation's claim within the limitation period. See *J.C. Kerkhoff & Sons Construction Ltd. v. British Columbia & Yukon Territories Building and Construction Trades Council* (1987), 24 C.P.C. (2d) 299 (B.C. S.C.).

An amendment will be allowed to correct the corporate name of the plaintiff in an action on terms as to costs: *Macklin School District No. 2420 v. Saskatchewan Guarantee & Fidelity Co.*, [1919] 2 W.W.R. 396 (Sask. K.B.) and cases cited. As to the procedure to be followed by a defendant where the plaintiff's name is incorrectly set out, see *Cornish Silver Mining Co. v. Bull* (1874), 21 Gr. 592 (demurrer); *Great North Western Telegraph Co. v. McLaren* (1884), 1 Man. R. 358 (application to complete plaintiff to amend). See, however, *D. Glanville & Co. v. Lyne*, [1942] W.N. 65 (leave refused to amend by substituting correct name of corporation so as to make it, instead of the solicitors, liable for costs). Where the defendant corporation named in a lawsuit was a corporation having the same mailing address and the same president as another corporation which was properly the defendant, an application to amend the statement of claim to change the name of the defendant after the expiration of the appropriate limitation period was allowed because the defendant had notice of the claim within the limitation period and there was no actual prejudice: see *Dyck v. Sweeprite Manufacturing Inc.* (1989), 33 C.P.C. (2d) 230 (Man. Q.B.). A conviction for a criminal or *quasi*-criminal offence will be set aside if the exact name of the corporation is not used: *R. v. Pelissiers Ltd.*, [1926] 1 D.L.R. 574 at 578 (Man. C.A.).

The failure of a plaintiff to plead and prove that it is a body corporate under the laws of certain jurisdictions may be fatal to the corporation's action and result in the claim being dismissed. See, for example, *International Harvester Credit Corp. v. Knight* (1975), 19 N.B.R. (2d) 620 (Co. Ct.), but see *Pen Air Federal Credit Union v. Vandermark* (1980), 91 A.P.R. 430 (Nfld. Dist. Ct.), in which leave to amend the pleadings was granted.

The directors, in pursuance of their general powers of management are the persons authorized to direct the bringing of an action in the name of the corporation. In general the only way in which the shareholders can control the bona fide exercise of the powers of the directors is by altering the by-laws or by refusing to re-elect directors whose policy they disapprove or by removing the directors if the articles or by-laws permit: *Automatic Self-Cleansing Filter Syndicate Co. v. Cuninghame*, [1906] 2 Ch. 34 (C.A.); *Gramophone & Typewriter Ltd. v. Stanley*, [1908] 2 K.B. 89 at 105, 106 (C.A.); and see *Quin & Axtens Ltd. v. Salmon*, [1909] A.C. 442 (H.L.). If an action has been authorized by the directors, the court will not give effect to a resolution of the shareholders directing the corporation's solicitors not to proceed further: *John Shaw & Sons (Salford) Ltd. v. Shaw*, [1935] 2 K.B. 113 at 134, 143 (C.A.); *Macson Development Co. v. Gordon* (1959), 19 D.L.R. (2d) 465 at 470 (N.S. T.D.). It has been held that a majority shareholder, in the absence of any contrary provisions in the articles, may overrule the decision of the directors against bringing an action in the name of the corporation: *Marshall's Valve Gear Co. v. Manning, Wardle & Co. Ltd.*, [1909] 1 Ch. 267 (criticized in *John Shaw & Sons (Salford) Ltd. v. Shaw, supra*, at 143). It has been held that where the scope of authority of the managing director comes from an agreement that he carry out the ordinary day-to-day business activities, such authority includes instructing solicitors to commence an action for the recovery of corporate property. See *Lake Aircraft Sales (Pty.) Ltd. v. Northwest Lake Sales & Service Ltd.* (1978), 6 B.C.L.R. 387 (S.C.).

Where an action had been brought in the name of the corporation at the instance of persons claiming to be legal directors, an order having been made setting aside the writ of summons with costs to be paid by the plaintiff's solicitors on the ground that it had been issued without authority of the defendants who claimed to be the legal directors of the corporation, successive appeals to the Appeal Division of the Supreme Court of New Brunswick and to the Supreme Court of Canada were dismissed: *St. John & Quebec Railway Co. v. Jones* (1921), 57 D.L.R. 477 (N.B. C.A.), affd (1921), 62 S.C.R. 92.

Where directors are improperly elected and act as such against the wishes of a majority of the shareholders, the majority are entitled to use the name of the corporation in an action to set aside the election: *Colonial Assurance Co. v. Smith* (1912), 4 D.L.R. 814 (Man. K.B.).

As to cases involving actions to set aside a contract between a director and the corporation or to make a director account for profits, see Chapter 8.

In a case of emergency a shareholder may use the corporation's name as plaintiff subject to his being able to show that he has proper authority but if it later appears that the corporation's name has been used improperly it will be struck out: *Harben v. Phillips* (1883), 23 Ch. D. 14 (C.A.); *Colonial Assurance Co. v. Smith* (1913), 12 D.L.R. 113 at 127 (Man. K.B.). The court may grant interlocutory relief in the meantime: *Pender v. Lushington* (1877), 6 Ch. D. 70.

An officer has no implied authority to bring an action in the name of the corporation: *Standard Construction Co. v. Crabb* (1914), 7 W.W.R. 719 (managing director). However, under special circumstances, where the corporation is named as defendant, individual officers may be entitled to enter a defence on the corporation's behalf: *Legge v. Legge*, [1939] 4 D.L.R. 740 (Man. K.B.). In that case, where there was a deadlock between the members of the board, two of the four directors of the corporation brought an action against one of the other two directors on behalf of all shareholders, joining the corporation as defendant. It was held that it was the duty of the other two directors, one of whom was a defendant and the owner of a majority of the shares, as officers not to allow the action against the corporation to go undefended. See also *Mayo Lumber Co. v. Kapoor Lumber Co.*, [1939] 4 D.L.R. 812 (B.C. S.C.), where a writ had been issued against the corporation on the instructions of one of the corporation's two directors and owing to his refusal to attend a directors' meeting no resolution could be passed authorizing the filing of a conditional appearance. On an *ex parte* application of the other director a solicitor was authorized to act for the corporation with authority to enter a conditional appearance without prejudice to the making of an application to set aside the writ.

Where on a petition to wind up the corporation one of the directors who controlled 50 per cent of the shares appointed a counsel to act for the corporation, and the other director who controlled the remaining 50 per cent of the shares objected to the appointment, there being no provision for a casting vote at directors' or shareholders' meetings, the court refused to recognize the appointment of the counsel as valid on the ground that it had not been made by the board of directors: *Re Rothlish Investments Ltd.* (1953), 61 Man. R. 195. The court distinguished the case of *Legge v. Legge, supra*, on the basis that one of the directors who made the appointment in that case was also the majority shareholder and so could be considered as having control of the corporation.

Where there are competing factions, each claiming the right to represent the corporation, and the corporation's name is used as plaintiff, the court will direct the proceedings to be stayed until the wishes of the majority can be ascertained: *MacDougall v. Gardiner* (1875), 1 Ch. D. 13 at 22 (C.A.); *Harben v. Phillips* (1883), 23 Ch. D. 14 (C.A.); *Leavens v. Great West Permanent Loan Co.*, [1927] 2 W.W.R. 401 (Man. K.B.), affd (1927), 36 Man. R. 606 (C.A.); *DuMart Packing Co. v. DuMart*, [1928] 1 D.L.R. 640 (Ont. H.C.).

If the name of the corporation has been used without the authority of the directors and on an application to strike out its name the court can see that there is no possibility of obtaining the sanction of the shareholders to its use, the name will be struck out; but if there is any reasonable doubt concerning the wishes of the shareholders the name will be allowed to remain until their wishes are ascertained: *Leavens v. Great West Permanent Loan Co.*, [1927] 2 W.W.R. 401, and cases cited at 403.

The directors, acting as a board, are entitled to determine whether an action brought against the corporation is to be defended: *Campbell v. Taxicabs Verrals Ltd.* (1912), 27 O.L.R. 141 at 144. But where the directors, being a majority of the shareholders, in collusion with the president, refused to defend an action brought by him against the corporation, it was held that a minority shareholder, on behalf of himself and others, was entitled to defend the action in the name of the corporation: *Dimock v. Central Rawdon Mining Co.* (1903), 36 N.S.R. 337 (C.A.).

Where it is claimed that the action has been brought without authority, the proper course is to apply at an early stage to have the action stayed, where questions of fact have to be considered on which it is necessary to decide the existence or non-existence of the authority: *Richmond v. Branson & Son*, [1914] 1 Ch. 968 at 974; *Russian Commercial & Industrial Bank v. Comptoir d'Escompte de Mulhouse*, [1923] 2 K.B. 630 at 672, [1925] A.C. 112 at 148 (H.C.); as explained in *John Shaw & Sons (Salford) Ltd. v. Shaw*, [1935] 2 K.B. 113 at 145 (C.A.). However, the court has inherent jurisdiction to order an action to be struck out if it is established that the action has been brought without authority: *Daimler Co. v. Continental Tyre & Rubber Co. (Great Britain) Ltd.*, [1916] 2 A.C. 307 (H.L.); *John Shaw & Sons (Salford) Ltd. v. Shaw, supra*, at 131, 145; *Lytton Gold Mines Ltd. v. Muno* (1933), 49 B.C.R. 18 at 21.

Where the action was brought without the authorization of the board of directors, but at the instance of a person for whom a large block of shares was held in trust, the action was struck as irregular. An action by a corporation should be commenced only on the authority of the board of directors; although when started without authority, the directors have the power to ratify within a reasonable time: see *Car-Rite (1964) Ltd. v. Ferguson* (1967), 59 W.W.R. 636 (Alta. Dist. Ct.).

Where an officer of a corporation, without authority, instructed a solicitor to issue a writ on behalf of the corporation, on an application to stay the proceedings the solicitor was ordered to pay the costs. The court will not order an officer of the corporation who gave the instructions to issue the writ acting in good faith on what he considered sufficient authority, to pay the costs of an action brought without authority. The remedy, if any, is against the solicitors who issued the writ: *Standard Construction Co. v. Crabb* (1914), 7 W.W.R. 719 (Sask. C.A.); *Pacific Coast Coal Mines Ltd. v. Arbuthnot*, [1926] 1 D.L.R. 670 (B.C. S.C.).

A solicitor who starts proceedings in the name of a corporation without verifying whether he has the proper authority to do so, or starts them under an erroneous assumption as to his authority, does so at his peril. If he has no sufficient authority, the action is not properly constituted, but it is open at any time for the corporation to ratify the solicitor's act, to adopt the proceedings and to continue them. Hence, where an action had been started in the name of a corporation without its authority, and later the corporation went into liquidation and the liquidator adopted the proceedings on behalf of the corporation, the defendant's objection that the action was improperly constituted failed: *Danish Mercantile Co. v. Beaumont*, [1951] 1 Ch. 680 (C.A.).

The Ontario Rules of Civil Procedure codify certain rules respecting authority to commence proceedings. Pursuant to Rule 15.02, a solicitor who is named in an originating process as the solicitor for the plaintiff or applicant shall if served with a demand in writing from any person who has been served with the process declare in writing whether he or she commenced or authorized the commencement of the proceeding or whether the corporation authorized the commencement of the proceedings. If the solicitor fails to comply with the demand, a court may order the solicitor to comply, the proceedings may be stayed, and the solicitor may be ordered to pay the costs of the proceedings. If the solicitor declares that he or she did not commence or authorize the commencement of the proceedings, the court may dismiss the proceedings. If the solicitor has commenced the proceedings without authority, the court may stay or dismiss the proceedings and the solicitor may be ordered to pay the costs of the proceedings. If proceedings have been stayed, no further steps may be taken without leave of the court. See also *Sternig v. Pallett* (1982), 29 C.P.C. 13 (Ont. Master) (action stayed); *Bomanak Delicatessan Ltd. v. Minakakis* (1974), 4 O.R. (2d) 9 (H.C.) (action dismissed where commenced in the name of the corporation without a meeting of the directors or shareholders); *Brismil Mines Ltd. v. Globe Exploration & Mining Co.*, [1970] 3 O.R. 622 (Master) (action stayed where commenced on behalf of a corporation without a resolution of the board of directors); but see *Melgold Construction Management Ltd. v. Banton Investments Ltd.* (1988), 32 C.P.C. (2d) 153 (Ont. Master) (lien action allowed to proceed where corporate plaintiff commenced the action in the ordinary course of business but without a resolution authorizing the litigation) and *Bank of Montreal v. Vola* (1980), 31 O.R. (2d) 60 (H.C.) (action arising out of transactions within the normal course of the bank's business commenced by bank's solicitor on the written instructions of accounts manager, but without a resolution of the board of directors, allowed to proceed).

The plaintiff's solicitors were not required to pay the costs of the defendants incurred where the corporate plaintiff had been added at trial but had been previously dissolved, where the fact of the dissolution was unknown to the solicitors and the defendant's solicitors had eight months' notice of the plaintiff's motion to add the corporate plaintiff: see *Cini v. Micallef* (1987), 60 O.R. (2d) 584 (H.C.). Similarly, in *Marley-King Line Construction Ltd. v. Marley*, [1962] O.W.N. 253 (Master) the solicitor was not ordered to pay costs personally where the court determined he had not been negligent and had acted bona fide.

As to an action brought in the name of the corporation after a liquidator has been appointed, see Chapter 14. As to the position of a corporation that has been dissolved during litigation, see *Kildonan Investments Ltd. v. Thompson* (1917), 55 S.C.R. 272; *Bute Logging Co. v. Sanders* (1952), 5 W.W.R. (N.S.) 142 (B.C. S.C.), and cases cited therein.

A corporation has the same right as an individual to withdraw its name from litigation to which it has been made a party plaintiff, but of which it does not approve: *International Wrecking Co. v. Murphy* (1888), 12 P.R. 423.

Defendants who are mere outsiders have no *locus standi* to object that the corporation's name is being improperly used as plaintiff on the ground that the action was authorized by a *de facto* board: *DuMart Packing Co. v. DuMart*, [1928] 1 D.L.R. 640 (Ont. H.C.).

Where an action has been brought in the corporation's name for breach of trust against directors and shareholders, the latter cannot vote at a meeting directed to be called to decide whether the corporation's name may be used as plaintiff: *Leavens v. Great West Permanent Loan Co. (No. 2)*, [1927] 3 W.W.R. 486 (Man. K.B.).

Where the corporation sues to set aside an *ultra vires* transaction the joinder of a shareholder as co-plaintiff is unnecessary and will be visited with costs: *Toronto Finance Corp. v. Banking Service Corp.* (1925), 57 O.L.R. 514, affd (1926), 59 O.L.R. 278 (C.A.), affd [1928] 2 W.W.R. 443 (P.C.).

A corporation can sue for libel reflecting on the management of its trade or business without alleging special damage: *South Hetton Coal Co. v. North-Eastern News Association*, [1894] 1 Q.B. 133 (C.A.); *Owen Sound Building & Savings Society v. Meir* (1893), 24 O.R. 109 (C.A.) (statement capable of the construction that the business of the corporation was being illegally transacted); *Journal Printing Co. of Ottawa v. MacLean* (1894), 25 O.R. 509 (charge of corruption in the conduct of the paper of a newspaper publishing corporation). Similarly, a corporation can sue for spoken words calculated to injure its reputation in relation to its trade or business without alleging special damage: *D. & L. Caterers Ltd. v. D'Ajou*, [1945] W.N. 88 (C.A.).

Originally, it had been held that a corporation appearing in legal proceedings must do so by counsel because, the corporation being an artificial entity, it could not appear in person: see *Frinton & Walton Urban District Council v. Walton & District Sand & Mineral Co.*, [1938] 1 All E.R. 649 (Ch. D.); *Tritonia Ltd. v. Equity & Law Life Assurance Society*, [1943] A.C. 584.

Initially, this was also the position in Canada. See, for example, *Western Producers Mutual Hail Insurance Co. v. Stewart*, [1928] 1 W.W.R. 320 (Sask. Dist. Ct.) and *Spurr v. Albert Mining Co.* (1874), 15 N.B.R. 260 (C.A.). However, the law has evolved over time so that in most jurisdictions a corporation is now allowed to appear before the courts through properly authorized officers. The various rules of civil procedure of the provinces now codify this development. For example, Ontario Rules provide that where a corporation is a party to a proceeding, it shall be represented by a solicitor, except by leave of the court. One of the factors to be taken into account in decisions whether to grant leave is the internal situation of the corporation and whether the person seeking to represent the corporation in court is a senior representative of the corporation who has been duly authorized by the board of directors, who themselves have been properly elected. Another factor is fairness to the opposing party, that is, whether the representative will be properly able to carry out the duties of a litigant under the rules. See *419212 Ontario Ltd. v. Astrochrome Crankshaft Toronto Ltd.* (1991), 3 O.R. (3d) 116 (Master). Conversely, the combined effect of the provisions of the Quebec Code of Civil Procedure and the *Act Respecting the Barreau du Quebec*, R.S.Q., c. B-1, mean that in Quebec, a corporation can only appear in court through counsel and representation of the corporation by any person other than by a member of the Bar is invalid: see *Banque National du Canada v. Atomic Slipper Co.* (1991), 2 B.L.R. (2d) 1 (S.C.C.). The Federal Court Rules also require representation by counsel, see *infra*.

In the following cases, such leave was granted to authorized officers to institute proceedings and appear in court on behalf of the corporation: *Northern Homes Ltd. v. Steel-Space Industries Ltd.*, [1975] 5 W.W.R. 115 (N.W.T. S.C.); *Bural v. Thomas Custom Brokers Ltd.* (1978), 20 O.R. (2d) 600 (H.C.) (corporation without a solicitor of record not subject to having statement of defence struck out or dismissed); *Valley Credit Ltd. v. Greentree* (1979), 15 B.C.L.R. 28 (Co. Ct.); *92417 Canada Ltd. v. Bank of Montreal* (1984), 45 C.P.C. 149 (Ont. Master) (officer permitted to represent corporation where the corporate plaintiff had insufficient funds to retain solicitor); *92417 Canada Ltd. v. Bomac Batten Ltd.* (1984), 45 O.R. (2d) 593 (Master) (officer of impecunious corporation granted leave although officer not entitled to appear for corporation throughout litigation and each instance to be dealt with on the merits).

In the following cases, officers were denied leave to act for the corporation in proceedings: *Youngson v. Chromex Nickel Mines Ltd.* (1977), 81 D.L.R. (3d) 158 (B.C. Co. Ct.) (president not allowed to appear); *BMI Canada Ltd. v. Kildonan Motor Hotel Ltd.* (1982), 67 C.P.R. (2d) 204 (Fed. T.D.) and *Baldasaro v. Canada* (1986), 4 F.T.R. 120 (Fed. T.D.) (Federal Rules require representation by counsel).

In the *Baldasaro* case, the action was stayed until the Federal Rules were complied with and a solicitor obtained. *Canren Systems Corp. v. Canada* (1986), 6 F.T.R. 75 (Fed. T.D.) (nor do the provisions of the British Columbia Act which empower a member to bring an action in the name of the corporation exempt a corporation from the requirement of the Federal Rules which require representation by a solicitor); *Father Don's Natural Products Ltd. v. McKenzie* (1984), 47 C.P.C. 156 (Fed. T.D.), affd (1986), 65 N.R. 62 (Fed. C.A.) (president denied leave where he had filed affidavit in support of the proceedings and it would be undesirable for him to appear both as witness and advocate on behalf of the corporation); *Shinkaruk Enterprises Ltd. v. Commonwealth Insurance Co.* (1986), 47 Sask. R. 308 (Q.B.) (the leave provisions of the Saskatchewan Act respecting derivative actions were not intended to allow the president of a corporation to prosecute an action where the corporation was unable to retain counsel to represent it); *Great West Life Assurance Co. v. Royal Anne Hotel Co.* (1986), 6 B.C.L.R. (2d) 175 (C.A.) (where president had a record of frivolous and vexatious litigation, he was denied leave to represent the corporation); *Guccio Gucci S.p.A. v. Cebuchier* (1988), 22 C.I.P.R. 254 (Fed. T.D.) (officer of the corporation who was also co-defendant denied leave to represent the corporation and court ordering corporation be represented by solicitor as there was no evidence that the corporation was impecunious or that the officer was authorized to represent the corporation); *Aylward's Ltd. v. St. Lawrence (Town)* (1988), 38 M.P.L.R. 26 (Nfld. C.A.) (president not entitled to represent corporation because he was not a member of the law society, his appearance thus constituting the unauthorized practice of law contrary to the *Law Society Act*), and *Professional Sign Crafters (1988) Ltd. v. Wedekind* (1993), 8 Alta. L.R. (3d) 11 (Master) — *Legal Professions Act* precludes non-lawyer from appearing on behalf of the corporation and the Alberta Rules of Court, being procedural only, could not grant new or substantive rights, but see *Vernrose Holdings Ltd. v. Pacific Press Ltd.* (1977), 4 B.C.L.R. 193, affd (1978), 7 B.C.L.R. 298 (C.A.) (there being no prohibition in the British Columbia Rules against a corporation appearing by other than a solicitor and the officer not appearing in the expectation of any reward, the officer was not unlawfully engaged in the practice of law); *54129 Manitoba Ltd. v. MacGillivray* (1989), 35 C.P.C. (2d) 146 (Man. Q.B.).

The court maintains ultimate control over the decision as to whom to grant an audience and can limit the right of a corporation to appear in person or through a solicitor. Interference with the corporate litigant's decision to be represented by a lawyer or through a duly authorized officer of the corporation is rare but will be justified in a case where the issues are extremely complex, the facts are in issue and matters of credibility may arise.

It would not appear that a court will exercise its discretion to allow an employee who is not an officer or director to act on behalf of the corporation. See, for example, *B.C. Telephone Co. v. Rueben*, [1982] 5 W.W.R. 428 (B.C. S.C.) (while the court has a discretionary power to allow persons other than solicitors to act on the corporation's behalf, that discretion should be exercised carefully and the fact that an employee is not an officer was a sufficient ground for the court to refuse to exercise such discretion); *MacLab Enterprises Inc.*

(Midwest Property Management) v. Rawdah (1983), 27 Alta. L.R. (2d) 164 (Q.B.) (an Alberta corporation has the right to appear in person in court but an employee was not permitted to present the case for the corporation since an employee unlike a director is not the brain of the corporation or a representative of the mind and will of the corporation.

The following additional decisions relating to proceedings by a corporation are noted.

Where, on an appeal, it appears that supplementary letters patent or by-laws, not produced at the trial, may be relevant, the court may require them to be produced: *Sinclair v. Blue Top Brewing Co.*, [1945] O.R. 359 (C.A.), affd [1947] 4 D.L.R. 561 at 567 (S.C.C.); *Smith v. Walkerville Malleable Iron Co.* (1896), 23 O.A.R. 95 at 105.

An incorporated corporation cannot itself give information which can be used to substantiate a deponent's statement of belief; it can do so only by one or more of its officers: *In re Mintz; Malauf v. Mintz*, [1930] 1 W.W.R. 198 (Sask. C.A.). Where an application for leave to serve a writ of summons *ex juris* was supported by an affidavit by the solicitor for the plaintiff, an incorporated corporation, in which the paragraphs purporting to show a good cause of action began with the words "I am advised by the plaintiff . . ." it was held that the paragraphs were worthless as they did not state a proper source from which the belief was derived: *K. J. Preiswerck Ltd. v. Los Angeles-Seattle Motor Express Inc.* (1957), 22 W.W.R. 93 (B.C. S.C.). It is not necessary for a president of a corporation when making an affidavit to recite that he is duly authorized to make such affidavit on behalf of the corporation; the authority is implied by his office: *Stolberg Mill Construction Ltd. v. Selkirk Spruce Mills Ltd.* (1957), 22 W.W.R. 605 (B.C. S.C.).

A corporate creditor of a deceased person may prove its claim against the deceased's estate by the evidence of one of its servants and corroboration as required by the *Evidence Act* is not necessary: *Re Bell, Ex p. Sabiston-Hughes Ltd.*, [1940] O.R. 88 (C.A.).

Service on the corporation

The rules of practice in the various provinces provide for the manner of service of process on corporations.

Where a person is served with a writ of summons as an officer of a corporate defendant, a motion to set aside the service on the ground that the person served is not an officer of the corporation should be made on behalf of the corporation when the proceedings come to its notice and not by the person served, unless service on him will not bring the writ to the notice of the corporation: *Dixon v. Gibson* (1931), 40 O.W.N. 60 (Master).

In Ontario, the Rules of Civil Procedure provide for service of originating process on corporations other than municipal corporations by leaving a copy of the document with an officer, director or agent of the corporation, or with a person at any place of business of the corporation who appears to be in control or management of the place of business. It has been held that a corporation is to be served at its statutory registered office, and it is not enough to serve the inhabitants of the office without addressing the notice to the company. To do so would be an intolerable burden where a number of corporations share the same registered office or where it is the premises of a law firm with numerous clients. See *841656 N.W.T. Ltd. v. Jodphur Holdings Ltd.* (1992), 7 C.P.C. (3d) 165 (N.W.T. C.A.). Where the corporation did not carry on any of its business in Ontario but merely maintained assets in Ontario and did not make any corporate decisions about the assets in Ontario, service on an officer, director or agent who is in Ontario for reasons which are not related to the corporation's business does not constitute proper service: *Santa Marina Shipping Co. S.A. v. Lunham & Moore Ltd.* (1978), 18 O.R. (2d) 315 (H.C.). Nor is service proper where a corporate officer is attending a trial in Ontario. Attendance at a trial is not the conduct of "any of the business of" the corporation: *Sarco Canada Ltd. v. Pyrotherm Equipment Ltd.*, [1969] 1 O.R. 426 (Master). In Saskatchewan, where a statement of claim was served on an independent contractor rather than a clerk, manager, agent, employee or other representative, the service was validated by the court as the defendant corporation had notice of the facts and of the nature of the claim: *Emigh v. Diamond Messenger Services (Saskatoon) Ltd.* (1987), 21 C.P.C. (2d) 238 (Sask. Q.B.). Service on the corporation's "public relations man" was not good service as he was not an officer, agent or employee of the corporation as required by the New Brunswick Rules of Court: *J.D. Irving Ltd. v. Omega Pipeline Ltd.* (1977), 16 N.B.R. (2d) 474 (Q.B.). Similarly, service on a receptionist employed by the corporation was not proper service as required by the British Columbia Rules because she was not a manager, cashier, superintendent, treasurer, secretary, clerk or agent of the corporation. The Rule assumes that such individuals have status and responsibility in the organization so as to be expected to react properly to the receipt of the writ of summons. See: *Molson v. Vitale* (1991), 47 C.P.C. (2d) 302 (B.C. Master). A comptroller did not come within the class of persons upon whom service was proper under the Federal Court Rules: *MCA Canada Ltd. v. Robert Simpson Productions*, [1971] F.C. 445 (T.D.).

The word "person" in the rule includes a corporation: therefore, a corporation which sold tickets for a foreign corporation was properly served as agent of the foreign corporation carrying on business in Ontario: *Doreske v. Champlain Coach Lines*, [1939] O.R. 560 (C.A.).

Where the plaintiff obtained judgment by default in an action against the defendant corporation of which he was president, and the writ in the action was served upon the plaintiff only and there was no other service upon, or notice of the pendency of the action given to, anyone connected with the corporation or concerned in its affairs, it was held that the mode of service was one that could not be adopted, and that the judge to whom the application was made had the right to set it aside as an abuse of the process of the court: *Holmes v. Stewiacke Railway Co.* (1899), 32 N.S.R. 395.

Service on the liquidator of a corporation is not good service on the corporation: *Re Flowers* (1896), 75 L.T. 306.

The rules also provide that where the head office, registered office or principal place of business of a corporation cannot be found at the last address recorded with the appropriate government ministry, service may be made on the corporation by mailing by prepaid first class mail or by registered or certified mail a copy of the document to the corporation at that address.

Discovery

The Ontario Rules provide that production of documents may be ordered where the documents are in the possession or control of a subsidiary or affiliated corporation or where a corporation is directly or indirectly controlled by one of the parties. See *Peters v. General Motors of Canada Ltd.* (1986), 14 C.P.C. (2d) 147 (Ont. Dist. Ct.).

The general rule as to the production of documents by a corporation in litigation with its shareholders is that it can claim privilege only if the document was obtained by the corporation for the purpose of defending itself against litigation. Thus, where a corporation has obtained advice in the common interest and paid for it out of the corporation's moneys the shareholder has a right to see it; but a shareholder is not entitled to see opinions of counsel, given after a claim has been made against him, in connection with litigation between the corporation and the shareholder: *Woodhouse & Co. v. Woodhouse* (1914), 30 T.L.R. 559.

Shareholders are entitled in an action against the corporation to production of communications between the corporation and its solicitors before the action is brought: *Gourand v. Edison Bell Telephone Co.* (1887), 57 L.J. Ch. 498. Where directors, in the performance of their duty in attempting to resolve the interpretation of one of the articles and not because of a possible action against them, instructed accountants to make a report, shareholders were entitled to see the report notwithstanding that before it was made they had commenced proceedings against the corporation: *Dennis & Sons Ltd. v. West Norfolk Farmers' Manure & Chemical Co-operative Co.*, [1943] Ch. 220.

Communications between lawyers of a corporation and the employees of a wholly-owned subsidiary of the same corporation were held to be privileged where there was a close relationship between the management of the two corporations: *Mutual Life Assurance Co. of Canada v. Canada (Deputy A.G.)* (1988), 28 C.P.C. (2d) 101 (Ont. H.C.).

Where the lawyer is an employee of the client, the communications will be privileged where they relate to the employee's function as lawyer but not in respect of business or other functions: *Mutual Life Assurance Co. of Canada v. Canada (Deputy A.G.), supra.* The Alberta Rules of Court provide for examination of "officers" of a corporation. Where the defendant sought to examine the plaintiff's agent who had been involved in contract negotiations and was also at the material time the plaintiff's solicitor, the defendant's motion to examine the agent as an "officer" pursuant to the Rules was granted. See *Simpson's Num Ti Jah Lodge Ltd. v. Lange* (1991), 2 C.P.C. (3d) 39 (Alta. Q.B.).

Where the minutes of board of director meetings recorded the legal advice of in-house counsel, discovery was denied as the report of counsel fell within solicitor-client privilege: *Nova Scotia Power Corp. v. Surveyer, Nenniger & Chevert Inc.* (1986), 180 A.P.R. 327 (N.S. T.D.), affd (1987), 193 A.P.R. 217 (N.S. C.A.).

Where the plaintiff desired production of all the defendant's financial records from the corporation's inception when it was formed through the amalgamation of several corporations, the request was denied on the basis that full production would be prejudicial to the defendant if the production disclosed unrelated financial dealings and would amount to an invasion of the defendant's privacy: *MacDonald Estate v. Martin* (1987), 51 Man. R. (2d) 53 (Q.B.).

Generally, the various rules of practice allow for the selection or designation of an officer, director or employee to be examined on behalf of the corporation. Ordinarily, the proper person to be examined is the officer who is best able to provide the information and who is qualified to speak on behalf of the corporation. In Ontario the party examining is entitled to select the officer whom he wishes to examine and may name an officer who is a member of the firm of solicitors acting for the corporation: *Trinity College v. Levinter* (1924), 54 O.L.R. 290 (C.A.); *Tyack v. Western Freight Lines Ltd.*, [1942] O.W.N. 143. But in Saskatchewan where an officer was to be examined for the purpose of using such examination against the corporation it was held that that officer should be designated who had the greatest personal knowledge of the facts and circumstances relevant to the issue: *Regina (City) v. Robinson's Clothes Ltd.*, [1922] 2 W.W.R. 807 (Sask. Q.B.). A court will generally uphold a party's choice so long as it does not constitute an abuse of process or the circumstances of the particular case do not make the choice seem unreasonable. Examining counsel's *prima facie* right to select which officer or servant of a corporate party is to be examined is not an absolute right but the right was not denied on the ground that the representative lacked personal knowledge, on the ground that another person having more knowledge of the circumstances would provide a better examination, or on the ground that the representative is a past officer or director of the corporation. See *Cineplex Odeon Corp. v. Toronto Star Newspapers Ltd.* (1986), 11 C.P.C. (2d) 291 (Ont. Master); *Eversonic Inc. v. MacGirr* (1986), 53 O.R. (2d) 179 (Master); *Ipapo Estate v. Citadel Life Insurance Co.* (1986), 14 C.P.C. (2d) 258 (Man. Q.B.); *Kent Drugs Ltd. v. Kronson* (1986), 12 C.P.C. (2d) 249 (Man. C.A.) and *MacMillan Bloedel Ltd. v. Binstead* (1981), 29 B.C.L.R. 9 (C.A.). Where the officer selected for examination was ill, it was held that an order of substitution would not be granted, but if it is proved that the health of the officer is so poor as to make it impossible for the individual to be examined, an order of substitution may be granted: *Bank of Montreal v. Stephen* (1986), 76 N.B.R. (2d) 427 (C.A.).

However, the right of choice is not absolute. Where a plaintiff made serious allegations of misrepresentation, recklessness and fraud, the corporation was entitled to substitute another employee shown to have the greatest knowledge of the relevant circumstances: *Rainbow Industrial Caterers Ltd. v. C.N.R.* (1986), 6 B.C.L.R. (2d) 268 (S.C.). Where the officer selected for examination was subsequently dismissed by the defendant and charged with fraud and there was a likelihood of prejudice and hostility to the defendant, the defendant corporation successfully applied for an order that another person be examined: *Landmark Properties Ltd. v. Crown Trust Co.* (1983), 49 B.C.L.R. 268 (C.A.). Where the defendant designated an officer to be examined and the plaintiff desired to substitute an officer who took the position subsequent to the event in issue, the court held the defendant's right was not unqualified and that the officer selected by the plaintiff had the best knowledge relevant to the issues and held a position of responsibility which qualified him to speak on behalf of the corporation: *Winnipeg (City) v. Lewko* (1987), 15 C.P.C. (2d) 88 (Man. Q.B.). Where the director of the plaintiff corporation selected for examination by the defendant allegedly participated in the impugned transaction, it was held that the director was in a position of conflict with the plaintiff and was therefore an inappropriate selection: *Exhibition Association of Saint John (City & County) v. Canadian Imperial Bank of Commerce* (1987), 21 C.P.C. (2d) 88 (N.B. Q.B.).

Whether a person other than a director is an officer or not for the purpose of examination for discovery depends on the circumstances of each particular case: *McDonald v. United Air Transport Ltd.*, [1939] 3 D.L.R. 27 (B.C. C.A.) and cases cited. As to the principles applicable see *Morrison v. Grand Trunk Railway Co.* (1903), 5 O.L.R. 38 (C.A.).

The following have been held subject to examination for discovery as officers: the local agent of an insurance corporation: *Goring v. London Mutual Fire Insurance Co.* (1885), 10 P.R. 642; an architect employed by a corporation: *Smith v. Clarke* (1887), 12 P.R. 217; the locomotive superintendent and the locomotive foreman of a railway corporation: *Canada Atlantic Railway Co. v. Moxley* (1887), 15 S.C.R. 145; the conductor of a railway train: *Leitch v. Grand Trunk Railway Co.* (1888), 13 P.R. 369 (Ont. C.A.); an attorney appointed by an extra-provincial corporation as its representative on whom service of process may be made: *McNeil v. Lewis Bros. Ltd.* (1908), 16 O.L.R. 652; a solicitor who devotes his whole time to the service of a corporation at a remuneration: *Duncan v. Vancouver (City)* (1917), 36 D.L.R. 218 (B.C. C.A.); a pilot in sole charge of an air transport corporation's aeroplane: *McDonald v. United Air Transport Ltd.*, [1939] 3 D.L.R. 27 (B.C. C.A.); the only official of the corporation residing in the province: *Canadian Doughnut Co. Ltd. v. Canada Egg Products Ltd. (No. 1)* (1952), 6 W.W.R. (N.S.) 684 (Sask. C.A.); a person in complete control of the operations of the corporation: *Cleveland Browns Inc. v. Kissell*, [1954] O.W.N. 24; the volunteer chairman of a charitable organization who supervised the construction of a centre which the plaintiff builder had agreed to build: *Cana Construction Co. v. Calgary Centre for Performing Arts*, [1986] 6 W.W.R. 74 (Alta. C.A.); the current president of the corporate defendant notwithstanding that he had not been with the defendant corporation at the time of the disputed transaction: *Belray Farms Ltd. v. Zenon Park Co-operative Dehydrators Ltd.* (1985), 43 Sask. R. 71 (Q.B.); a sales representative who acts as a manufacturer's agent: *Bassett Furniture Industries Inc. v. Sargent Color T.V. & Furniture Ltd.*, [1981] 6 W.W.R. 270 (Man. Co. Ct.); the solicitor acting for a corporate party: *Burlington Northern Inc. v. Ferguson*, [1973] 2 W.W.R. 473 (B.C. S.C.).

The following have been held not to be examinable as officers: an engine driver: *Morrison v. Grand Trunk Railway Co.* (1903), 5 O.L.R. 38 (C.A.); a member of a firm, a part only of the business of which was to effect sales of the wares of a corporation on commission: *Nichols & Shepard Co. v. Skedanuk* (1912), 6 D.L.R. 115 (Alta. C.A.); a salesman: *Clavelle v. Oliver Ltd.*, [1939] 3 D.L.R.

806 (Sask. K.B.); an architect who had been in charge of a building project where it was shown that the architect functioned as an independent contractor: *Joseph Silaschi General Contracting (Kitchener) Ltd. v. Kitchener (City)* (1986), 8 C.P.C. (2d) 199 (Ont. H.C.).

As to an officer of a subordinate branch of an organization being examinable, see *Readhead v. Canadian Order of Woodmen of the World* (1905), 9 O.L.R. 321 (Master); *National Trust Co. Ltd. v. Canadian Order of Foresters*, [1923] 1 W.W.R. 932 (Alta. C.A.).

Where a defendant sought to discover an employee of a co-defendant's American parent corporation, it was held that discovery was proper. While the employee was not an officer or employee of a party to the action, he was the one person connected with the corporation best informed of the matters at issue: *Syncrude Canada Ltd. v. Canadian Bechtel Ltd.* (1990), 77 Alta. L.R. (2d) 328 (Master).

Pursuant to the provisions of various provincial rules of court, it is sometimes possible to examine past officers and employees. See *Bank of British Columbia v. North Shore Motors Ltd.* (1979), 12 C.P.C. 292 (B.C. S.C.) (where the fact that a former employee was hostile to the defendant corporation was no bar to her discovery under the British Columbia Rules); *Wenzel Oil Tool Co. v. Alberta (Treasury Branches)* (1990), 74 Alta. L.R. (2d) 24 (Q.B.) (the Alberta Rules force pre-trial disclosure from someone who is best informed and connected to the corporate party and thus are broad enough to encompass past officers and employees); *Kent Drugs Ltd. v. Kronson* (1986), 12 C.P.C. (2d) 249 (Man. C.A.) and *Merchants Consolidated Ltd. v. Henderson-McIvor Foods Ltd.*, [1991] 5 W.W.R. 348 (Man. C.A.) (Manitoba Rules permitting examination of former officers); *Scott Transport Ltd. v. Bondy*, [1973] 2 O.R. 159 (H.C.); *Stepps Investments Ltd. v. Security Capital Corp. Ltd.* (1973), 2 O.R. (2d) 648 (H.C.) (in Ontario under the former Rules it was held that the officer or director to be examined should be an officer or servant at the time of examination); *Buckley v. Students Union of St. Thomas University Inc.*, (1991), 120 N.B.R. (2d) 91 (Q.B.) (the New Brunswick Rules require the person to be examined on behalf of a corporate party to have been an officer, director or manager at the time of the examination); *Butler v. Dimitrieff* (1988), 66 O.R. (2d) 707 (Master); *Hamilton Harbour Commissioners v. J.P. Porter Co.* (1978), 19 O.R. (2d) 66 (H.C.) (under the current Ontario rules it has been held that where an officer, director or employee resigns in good faith before the examination takes place the right to examine is lost but where the resignation is not *bona fide*, the former officer may be ordered to attend the examination); *Fraser v. E.S. Gallagher Sales Ltd.* (1987), 22 C.P.C. (2d) 238 (Ont. Master) (motion for leave to examine former general manager of defendant dismissed as plaintiff failed to show inability to obtain information from defendant's designated representative who had already been examined); *Famous Players Development Corp. v. Central Capital Corp.* (1991), 6 O.R. (3d) 765 (Div. Ct.) affg (1990), 46 C.P.C. (2d) 90 (Gen. Div.) revg unreported August 10, 1990, Ont. Master (motion to examine former employee dismissed as plaintiff failed to show inability to obtain information from other persons to be examined).

With respect to the right to examine non-resident officers, see *General Motors Acceptance Corp. of Canada v. Bank of Montreal*, [1986] 3 W.W.R. 562 (Man. Q.B.), revd on other grounds [1987] 1 W.W.R. 192 (Man. C.A.) The Manitoba Rules allow examination of non-resident former officer who is willing to attend for discovery, but not where the corporation agreed to produce a person resident in Manitoba and who was knowledgeable in the matters in issue: *Bank of Nova Scotia v. Wesplain Insurance Management Inc.*, [1984] 3 W.W.R. 519 (Man. C.A.); *Hill Estate v. Chevron Standard Ltd.*, [1987] 5 W.W.R. 467 (Man. C.A.), revg in part [1986] 6 W.W.R. 440 (Man. Q.B.); *George Vann Inc. v. N.L. Industries Inc.* (1984), 1 C.P.R. (3d) 277 (Fed. T.D.) (application to examine former officer now living in foreign country dismissed although domestic examinable party ordered to become fully informed by making inquiries of the former officer now living in the foreign country); and *Lido Industrial Products Ltd. v. Teledyne Industries Inc.*, [1979] 1 F.C. 310 (C.A.) (no power in federal court to order the examination of persons living outside Canada); but see *Rasins v. Foodcorp Ltd.*, [1980] 1 F.C. 729 (T.D.) (corporate defendant ordered to produce officer living abroad for examination in Canada on the grounds that the officer living abroad had recently moved to England, was a proper witness to the dispute in question and was still under the control of the corporate defendant as the chairman of the defendant's board of directors). The examination of a non-resident officer by way of oral examination is the proper method of examination and not by way of interrogatories in New Brunswick. See *Von Muenchhausen v. Sunshine Beach Ltd.* (1992), 8 C.P.C. (3d) 5 (N.B. C.A.).

The officer called to give evidence on examination for discovery must not only answer as to his individual knowledge, but must also enquire and obtain what information he can from: other officers and servants of the corporation who have personal knowledge of the facts: see *Nichols & Shepard Co. v. Skedanuk* (1912), 6 D.L.R. 115 (Alta. C.A.); *Giddings v. Canadian Northern Railway*, [1919] 1 W.W.R. 909 (Sask. K.B.); *Goodbun v. Mitchell (No. 4)*, [1928] 2 W.W.R. 594 (Man. C.A.); *Star Electric Fixtures Ltd. v. Sussex Fire Insurance Co.*, [1936] O.W.N. 654; *Abel v. Cooke*, [1937] 1 W.W.R. 705 (Alta. T.D.) (ex-employees); *Fisher v. Pain*, [1938] O.W.N. 74; *Kerr v. Toronto Transportation Commission*, [1944] O.W.N. 250; *Anderson v. County of York*, [1945] O.W.N. 772; *Meilleur v. U.N.I.-Crete Canada Ltd.* (1982), 30 C.P.C. 80 (Ont. H.C.); *Signcorp Investments Ltd. v. Cairns Homes Ltd.* (1988), 24 C.P.C. (2d) 1 (Sask. Q.B.); *Quintette Coal Ltd. v. Bow Valley Resource Services Ltd.* (1988), 29 B.C.L.R. (2d) 109 (S.C.); but see *Carling O'Keefe Breweries of Canada Ltd. v. Anheuser-Busch Inc.* (1981), 60 C.P.R. (2d) 200 (Fed. T.D.) (corporation having no duty to obtain information from persons beyond its control); from agents of the corporation; and from a parent corporation where there is an exchange of information between the subsidiary and its parent: see *Scheuermann v. Jablanczy* (1984), 44 C.P.C. 97 (Ont. H.C.); but see *W.H. Brady Co. v. Letraset Canada Ltd.* (1981), 58 C.P.R. (2d) 167 (Fed. T.D.), affd (1981), 60 C.P.R. (2d) 144 (Fed. C.A.) (officer of subsidiary had no duty to inform himself or produce documents in possession of foreign parent corporation). Where the officer is examined on behalf of the corporation, he is obliged to answer any proper question if the answer is within his personal knowledge, whether that knowledge was acquired in his capacity as an officer of the corporation or not. Thus, if the questions put are relevant to the issues raised in the pleadings, the officer must divulge information that was obtained prior to becoming an officer of the corporation: see *Willroy Mines Ltd. v. New Cinch Uranium Ltd.* (1983), 34 C.P.C. 13 (Ont. Master), affd (1983), 34 C.P.C. 13n (Ont. H.C.); *British Columbia Lightweight Aggregate Ltd. v. Canada Cement LeFarge Ltd. (No. 3)* (1978), 8 B.C.L.R. 321, 9 C.P.C. 152 (S.C.); *Mobil Oil Corp. v. Project 200 Investments Ltd.*, [1975] 4 W.W.R. 663 (B.C. S.C.). In the earlier cases of *Fisher v. Pain*, [1938] O.W.N. 74; *MacGregor v. Canadian Pacific Railway*, [1938] 3 D.L.R. 687 (Alta. C.A.); *Edmonton (City) v. W. W. Sales Ltd.*, [1941] 3 D.L.R. 737 (Alta. T.D.), it was held that an officer could not be examined concerning matters knowledge of which he acquired not as an officer of the corporation but in some other capacity.

Where the officer has made inquiries of such individuals he must disclose such information but is not required to adopt it or reject it on discovery. The corporation can assert whether or not the information is accurate or not: see *Nova, An Alberta Corp. v. Guelph Engineering Co.* (1986), 57 Alta. L.R. (2d) 15 (Q.B.) and *Claiborne Industries Ltd. v. National Bank of Canada* (1986), 55 O.R. (2d) 289, additional reasons at (1986), 60 O.R. (2d) 33 (H.C.), vard (1989), 69 O.R. (2d) 65 (C.A.). Where the officer of a corporation gave answers on discovery which were based on information received from individuals not employed by the corporation, the corporation was bound by the answers as the officer had not qualified reliance on that information: see *Claiborne Industries Ltd. v. National Bank of Canada, supra.* It has been held that the British Columbia Rules do not allow the examining party to insist that the corporate representative to be examined be authorized by the corporation to give answers which are binding on the corporation: see *Dillingham Construction Ltd. v. British Columbia Hydro & Power Authority* (1990), 40 C.P.C. (2d) 220 (B.C. S.C.).

As to the procedure where an officer of a corporation has declined to answer questions asserted to be proper, see *Shaw v. Union Trust Co.* (1915), 35 O.L.R. 146 at 150; *Black v. Mutual Benefit Health & Accident Association*, [1942] O.W.N. 563 (Master), quashed [1942] O.W.N. 637 (H.C.) and cases cited.

As to the right of a plaintiff to production of the corporation's books of account in a class action, see *Therrien v. Dominion Construction Corp.*, [1944] 4 D.L.R. 400 (Ont. H.C.), and cases cited.

And as to the examination of a corporation as a judgment debtor, see *Charlebois v. Great North-West Railway Co.* (1892), 15 P.R. 10.

Injunction

Where a corporation is restrained by injunction from doing some act, it commits a breach of the injunction and is liable for contempt if the act is in fact done even though it was done by an officer or servant through carelessness or dereliction of duty: *Stancomb v. Trowbridge Urban District Council*, [1910] 2 Ch. 190.

A judgment requiring a corporation to do or abstain from doing an act is an injunction which must be obeyed by all officers of the corporation and can be enforced against the officers by attachment or committal: *Bolton v. Wentworth (County of)* (1911), 23 O.L.R. 390. The court cannot order the issue of a writ of attachment against a corporation for contempt of court but can order the corporation to pay a fine: *Canadian General Electric Co. v. Toronto Electric Supply Co.*, [1935] Ex. C.R. 16. As to whether a judgment can be enforced against a corporation in Ontario by sequestration of its property, see *Copeland-Chatterson Co. v. Business Systems Co.* (1908), 16 O.L.R. 481 at 498 (C.A.); *Bolton v. Wentworth (County of), supra*, at 393.

Corporate crime

A corporation may be indicted or fined for breach of duty imposed by law: *R. v. Birmingham Railway Co.* (1842), 3 Q.B. 223; *R. v. Tyler & International Commercial Co.*, [1891] 2 Q.B. 588 (C.A.); *Union Colliery Co. v. R.* (1900), 31 S.C.R. 81 (criminal negligence in the discharge of a duty); *Mousell Bros. Ltd. v. London & North-Western Railway Co.*, [1917] 2 K.B. 836 (penalty for breach of statutory duty committed by servant within scope of employment); *R. v. Canadian Allis-Chalmers Ltd.* (1923), 54 O.L.R. 38 (C.A.) (criminal negligence in operating machine in factory); *R. v. Uscan Engineering Corp.*, [1949] 1 W.W.R. 780 (penalty for breach of a statutory requirement).

Various federal and provincial statutes provide that corporations may face criminal (or what might be considered as quasi-criminal) liability for breach of that statute. Some statutes provide that the commission of the unlawful act by the corporation itself constitutes the offence. Corporations may in addition face criminal liability for the unlawful acts of its servants and agents since a corporation, not being a natural person, must necessarily act through its servants and agents. The corporation's liability is, however, not vicarious liability as a result of the doctrine of *respondeat superior* but based on the "directing mind" concept discussed *infra*. Where a corporation is guilty of a criminal offence, generally, the directing mind is also guilty: see *Canadian Dredge and Dock Co. v. The Queen*, [1985] 1 S.C.R. 662. The fact that the acts of the directing mind were in law those of the corporation does not prevent the conviction of the individual either as a principal or as an aider and abettor where the corporation is also convicted: see *R. v. Fell* (1981), 64 C.C.C. (2d) 456 (Ont. C.A.). Convictions of both the individual and the corporation for the same offence are permissible even where the individual charged is the sole director, shareholder and officer and directing mind of the accused corporation. The convictions do not constitute the penalizing of the same person twice: see *R. v. Shamrock Chemicals Ltd.* (1989), 4 C.E.L.R. (N.S.) 215 (Ont. Dist. Ct.).

Where the corporation faces criminal liability for the unlawful acts of its agents and servants, the key question is the outer limit of corporate responsibility, that is, for whose actions is the corporation in law responsible? *Canadian Dredge and Dock Co. v. The Queen*, [1985] 1 S.C.R. 662 establishes several guiding principles. The corporation was charged with conspiracy to defraud pursuant to former ss. 338 and 423 of the *Criminal Code* as a result of the bid-rigging activities of the manager and president of the corporation. The Supreme Court of Canada concluded that for offences requiring proof of *mens rea*, a corporation may be affixed with liability for the actions of a servant or agent where the individual is a vital organ of the corporation and its "directing mind and will". Where the identity of the directing mind and the corporation coincide and the actions of the directing mind are performed within the sector of corporate operations assigned to him, criminal liability will attach. However, where the unlawful act of the individual is totally in fraud of the corporation and by design or otherwise results in a benefit exclusively to that individual, the acts of the individual will not be attributed to the corporation. The identification doctrine will therefore only operate so as to fix a corporation with criminal responsibility where the individual is considered a "directing mind", his unlawful actions were taken within the field of operation assigned to him, his actions were not a total fraud on the corporation, and by design or otherwise results in the benefit of the corporation.

See also *R. v. St. Lawrence Corp.*, [1969] 2 O.R. 305 (C.A.) (corporation guilty of conspiracy to lessen competition); *R. v. Waterloo Mercury Sales Ltd.* (1974), 18 C.C.C. (2d) 248 (Alta. Dist. Ct.) (where the defendant corporation's used car manager who was neither a director or officer had caused the odometers on certain cars to be turned back in defiance of orders from corporate officials that odometers were not to be tampered with, the corporation was found guilty of fraud); *R. v. Spot Supermarket Inc.* (1979), 50 C.C.C. (2d) 239 (Que. C.A.) (corporate accused guilty of theft of sales tax collected in its grocery stores where the supervisor employed by the accused was in complete control of accounting procedures); *R. v. P.G. Marketplace* (1979), 51 C.C.C. (2d) 185 (B.C. C.A.) (corporation convicted of fraud where salesman of corporation sold car for more than the consignment price agreed and the transactions of the salesman were subject only to pro forma approval of an official of the corporation); *Re Commodore Business Machines Ltd. and Ontario (Minister of Labour)* (1984), 49 O.R. (2d) 17 (Div. Ct.) (corporation personally in breach of *Human Rights Code* where foreman of corporation sexually harassed female employees); *R. v. Syncrude Canada Ltd.*, [1984] 1 W.W.R. 355 (Alta. Q.B.). But where the actions of employees constitute the carrying out of a policy already in place, the employees' position is not of such stature that their acts fix the corporation with liability. A corporation is not criminally liable for the acts or omissions of all its employees and servants: *R. v. Dawson City Hotels Ltd.* (1986), 1 Y.R. 3 (Y.T. C.A.); but where a corporate manager was found not guilty of fraud, the corporation's conviction was unreasonable as its liability could only be based on the liability of the manager: *R. v. Kimco Steel Sales Ltd.* (1988), 43 C.C.C. (3d) 104 (Ont. Dist. Ct.) (salesman of corporate defendant who forged certificates of quality not a directing mind and corporation acquitted of fraud). See also *R. v. Shell Canada Products Ltd.* (1990), 45 B.L.R. 231 (Man. C.A.). In this case a corporation was convicted of retail price maintenance contrary to the provisions of the *Competition Act* where the corporation's marketing representative attempted to influence upward the price at which a retailer sold gasoline. While the marketing representative may have been too low in the corporate hierarchy to be the directing mind there was some evidence that his conduct was influenced by his superior who was in charge of pricing in Manitoba.

A corporation may be guilty of criminal offences where *mens rea* is an essential element: *R. v. Fane Robinson Ltd.*, [1941] 3 D.L.R. 409 (Alta. C.A.) and cases cited; *R. v. National Cafe Ltd.*, [1943] 1 D.L.R. 153 (B.C. S.C.); *Director of Public Prosecutions v. Kent & Sussex Contractors Ltd.*, [1944] 1 K.B. 146 (corporation convicted of making use of a document with intent to deceive and of making a statement known to be false in a material particular); *R. v. I.C.R. Haulage Ltd.*, [1944] 1 K.B. 551 (an indictment for common law conspiracy to defraud will lie against a corporation); *R. v. McGavin Bakeries Ltd. (No. 6)* (1951), 101 C.C.C. 22 (Alta. T.D.) (conspiracy in restraint of trade); *R. v. Bruin Hotel Co.* (1954), 109 C.C.C. 174 (Alta. C.A.) (conviction under the Alberta *Liquor Control Act*); *Couture v. Commissairies d'Ecoles de Lauzon*, [1950] Que. S.C. 201, 97 C.C.C. 218; *R. v. Howard Smith Paper Mills Ltd.*, [1955] O.R. 713 (C.A.) (conspiracy in restraint of trade); *R. v. Northern Electric Co.*, [1955] O.R. 431 (conspiracy in restraint of trade); *R. v. Dominion Steel & Coal Corp.* (1956), 116 C.C.C. 117 (Ont. H.C.) (conspiracy in restraint of trade); *Barreau De Richelieu v. St. Jean Automobile Ltée*, [1957] Que. S.C. 310 (violation of the *Bar Act*); *Sommers v. R.* (1959), 124 C.C.C. 241 (S.C.C.) (corporations convicted of giving bribes to a government official).

Where a corporation is charged with a criminal offence involving *mens rea*, the criminal acts must be proved to be the acts of the corporation: *R. v. Ash-Temple Co.*, [1949] O.R. 315 (C.A.).

A finding of guilt may be made against a wholly-owned subsidiary, there being no basis for excusing it because it acts under the control of its parent corporation: *R. v. Dominion Steel & Coal Corp.*, *supra.*

An amalgamated corporation can be held liable for the criminal acts of one of its amalgamating corporations committed prior to the amalgamation. Pursuant to the provisions of the former *Canada Corporations Act* (as well as the present federal Act) no new corporation is created and no old corporation is extinguished but rather both corporations are continued as one: see *R. v. Black & Decker Manufacturing Co.*, [1975] 1 S.C.R. 411 (amalgamated corporation liable for a breach of the *Combines Investigation Act*); and *R. v. Mercantile Distributing Ltd.*, [1975] 6 W.W.R. 187 (B.C. S.C.) (amalgamated corporation liable for the payment of a fine imposed on one of the amalgamating corporations for an offence pursuant to the *Income Tax Act*).

Exceptions to the general rule that a corporation can be indicted for criminal acts arise from the limitations which must attach to an artificial entity: *R. v. I.C.R. Haulage Ltd.*, [1944] K.B. 551. At p. 554 Stable J. delivering the judgment of the Court of Appeal said:

> Included in these exceptions are the cases in which, from its very nature, the offence cannot be committed by a corporation, as, for example, perjury, an offence which cannot be vicariously committed, or bigamy, an offence which a limited company, not being a natural person, cannot commit vicariously or otherwise. A further exception, but for a different reason, comprises offences of which murder is an example, where the only punishment the court can impose is corporal . . .

In *R. v. Great West Laundry Co.* (1900), 3 C.C.C. 614 (Man. K.B.) it was held that an indictment will not lie against a corporation for manslaughter, since criminal liability of a corporation cannot extend to cases where personal intent or malice is involved. Even if the corporation could be convicted, punishment, being life imprisonment, could not be imposed.

A corporation may be liable to a penalty for breach of a municipal by-law: *R. v. Toronto Railway Co.* (1898), 30 O.R. 214 (C.A.). It may also be liable to a penalty for breach of a regulation made pursuant to a statute where *mens rea* is not an essential ingredient of the offence: *Griffiths v. Studebakers Ltd.*, [1924] 1 K.B. 102.

There are many federal and provincial regulatory statutes which do not require proof of *mens rea* for conviction. Such statutes are considered to constitute public welfare legislation which create offences of strict liability but which are not criminal in the true sense. Such statutes usually provide that the corporation may avail itself of a defence of due diligence, proof of which is on the corporation, to avoid conviction.

The defence of due diligence for public welfare offences was established in *R. v. Sault Ste. Marie*, [1978] 2 S.C.R. 1299. The Supreme Court of Canada held that a conviction may be obtained for breach of a public welfare statute which does not require proof of *mens rea* where the accused is unable to establish that all due care has been taken. The availability of the defence to a corporation depends on whether such due diligence was taken by those who are the directing mind and will of the corporation, whose acts are in law the acts of the corporation. See also *Tesco Supermarkets v. Nattras*, [1972] A.C. 153 (H.L.).

The reverse onus aspect of the due diligence defence in respect of regulatory offences does not offend s. 7 or s. 11(d) of the *Canadian Charter of Rights and Freedoms.* In *R. v. Wholesale Travel Group Inc.*, [1991] 3 S.C.R. 154, which involved the misleading advertising provisions of the *Competition Act*, the court held that at least in the context of regulatory offences, a strict liability offence for which a defence of due diligence is available is constitutional. The requirement that the corporate accused "establish" that it took reasonable precautions on a balance of probabilities and exercised due diligence did infringe the provisions of s. 11(d) of the Charter; however, this was justifiable pursuant to s. 1 of the Charter. Because of the nature of public welfare offences, it would place an impossible burden on the Crown to prove the offence without such a reverse onus provision.

The *Interpretation Act*, R.S.C. 1985, c. I-21 (a similar provision is found in the Interpretation Acts of the various provinces) provides that in every Act unless the context otherwise requires "person" includes "any body corporate or politic". These words merely embody the principle stated in *Pharmaceutical Society v. London & Provincial Supply Association* (1880), 5 App. Cas. 857 at 862 (per Avory J. in *Law Society v. United Service Bureau Ltd.*, [1934] 1 K.B. 343 at 348). In the latter case, on the construction of the particular statute under consideration it was held that the context otherwise required and the words "any person" did not include a body corporate.

Section 2 of the *Criminal Code*, R.S.C. 1985, c. C-46, which extends to Acts of the legislatures of the provinces, defines "every one", "person", "owner", and similar expressions as including "bodies corporate" and "corporations" in relation to the acts and things that they are capable of doing and owning respectively.

The word "individual" as used in a statute may include a corporation: *R. v. Sommers (No. 4)* (1958), 26 W.W.R. 246 (B.C. S.C.).

There is nothing in those sections (now ss. 620-623) of the *Criminal Code* which provide the machinery for enforcing the provisions of the Code against corporations that limits the operation of such sections to corporations within the province where the indictment is found: *R. v. Container Materials Ltd.*, [1939] 4 D.L.R. 387 at 390 (Ont. H.C.); *R. v. McGavin Bakeries Ltd. (No. 1)*, [1950] 2 W.W.R. 735 at 748 (Alta. T.D.).

The *Criminal Code* has swept away all difficulties which previously existed as to a corporation being summoned, indicted, committed, appearing, pleading or being tried: *R. v. McGavin Bakeries Ltd., supra*, and cases cited.

A summons served on the "registered owner" of a motor vehicle is not bad because it does not use the word "limited" after the word "company": *Springate v. Questier*, [1952] 2 All E.R. 21 (C.A.).

In criminal proceedings against a corporation, it is sufficient to establish a *prima facie* case of incorporation of the accused by *viva voce* evidence and it is unnecessary to produce the certificate of incorporation: *R. v. Bantalor Trading Co.* (1983), 45 N.B.R. (2d) 394 (C.A.).

A corporation may be ordered in the course of a criminal trial to produce minute books in the possession of its solicitor as such minute books constitute *prima facie* evidence and cannot be the claim of solicitor-client privilege: *Purzon du Canada Ltée v. Cour Municipale de Montréal*, [1976] Que. P.R. 152 (C.A.).

The Canadian Charter of Rights and Freedoms

The *Canadian Charter of Rights and Freedoms* constitutionally entrenches certain rights. Clearly, some of the provisions are applicable to corporations. Certain provisions, however, confer constitutional protections on a human level and therefore a corporation may not have standing to challenge the provisions of a particular law. For example, s. 7 provides that *everyone* has the right to life, liberty and security of the person. Section 11 is applicable only where a *person* is charged with an offence. Section 15 provides that *everyone* is equal before and under the law.

The question was first addressed by the Supreme Court of Canada in *R. v. Big M Drug Mart*, [1985] 1 S.C.R. 295. Big M had been charged under the *Lord's Day Act* and claimed the constitutional protection of s. 2(a) which guarantees freedom of religion. The court stated that any accused, whether a corporation or an individual, may defend a criminal charge by arguing that the law under which the charge had been brought is constitutionally invalid. In the court's view, it is the nature of the law and not the status of the accused that is the issue.

Later, in *A.G. Quebec v. Irwin Toy Ltd.*, [1989] 1 S.C.R. 927, the Supreme Court of Canada determined that Irwin Toy, in asserting that the sections of the *Consumer Protection Act* which purported to regulate advertising violated s. 7, could not claim the constitutional protection of that section. The *Consumer Protection Act* did provide for penalties, notably a fine or imprisonment, upon contravention of the Act. The court noted that only the corporation and not its officers had been named as parties to the proceedings. Dickson C.J.C. held that, at pp. 1002-3.

> In order to put forward a s. 7 argument in a case of this kind where the officers of the corporation are not named as parties to the proceedings, the corporation would have to urge that its own life, liberty and security of the person was being deprived in a manner not in accordance with the principles of fundamental justice. In our opinion, a corporation cannot avail itself of the protection offered by s. 7 of the *Charter.*

Dickson C.J.C. added that the section read as a whole appeared to confer protection on a human level but nevertheless suggested that the principle articulated in the *Big M Drug Mart* case remains applicable because in the instant case no penal proceedings were pending.

In *R. v. Amway Corp.*, [1989] 1 S.C.R. 21, Amway claimed the protection of s. 11(c) which provides that a person charged with an offence has the right not to be compelled to be a witness in proceedings against that person. Amway had been charged with making a false declaration with respect to goods imported into Canada. Before it was convicted, the Crown claimed a forfeiture of the goods and duty pursuant to the *Customs Act* and sought an order under the Federal Court Rules that an officer of the corporation be produced for examination. Sopinka J. held that in order to obtain the benefit of s. 11(c), the accused must establish that it is a person, it is charged with an offence, and that it will be a witness against that person. The case was decided on the last point. Sopinka J. was of the view that a corporation could not be a witness against itself. Thus it is permissible to compel an officer of a corporation to testify against the corporation.

It has been held that a corporation cannot claim the right to a trial by jury as guaranteed by s. 11(f) of the Charter as a corporation could not be subject to imprisonment. See *R. v. Bogardus, Wilson Ltd.* (1982), 2 C.R.R. 110 (B.C. Prov. Ct.) and *Re PPG Industries Canada Ltd. and Canada (Attorney General)* (1983), 42 B.C.L.R. 334 (C.A.).

In *Slaight Communications Inc. v. Davidson*, [1989] 1 S.C.R. 1038, Slaight was found to have unjustly dismissed the respondent, and an adjudicator ordered that Slaight provide the respondent with a letter of recommendation which contained certain facts. Slaight was prohibited from answering a request for information about the respondent except by sending the letter of recommendation. Slaight appealed the adjudicator's order on the basis that the prohibition infringed the corporation's freedom of expression contrary to s. 2(b) of the Charter. The Supreme Court of Canada held that the prohibition did infringe the guarantee of s. 2(b), but the prohibition was saved by s. 1 of the Charter as a reasonable limit justified by law in a free and democratic society. Thus, the term "everyone" in s. 2 of the Charter includes a corporation.

In *Thomson Newspapers v. Canada (Director of Investigations and Research, Combines Investigation Branch)*, [1990] 1 S.C.R. 425, the court dealt with the issue of whether the provisions of the *Combines Investigation Act* which permitted the examination of witnesses and the production of business records in the course of an investigation under the Act infringed either s. 7 or s. 8. A majority of the court held that the corporation could not claim the benefit of s. 7 on the basis of the decision in *Irwin Toy*. Four of the judges noted that the case, however, stood on a somewhat different footing because three of the appellants in the *Thomson* case were individuals while in *Irwin Toy* no individuals had been named as parties. Wilson J., for example, concluded that if the *Consumer Protection Act* violated the rights of these individuals and could not be justified under s. 1, then it would be equally of no force or effect in respect of corporations. The Act in that case did not provide for separate treatment of human beings and individuals.

In *R. v. Wholesale Travel Group Inc.*, [1991] 3 S.C.R. 154, a majority of the court clarified the application of ss. 7 and 11 to corporations. The court held that because the provisions of the *Competition Act* applied both to an individual and a corporate accused, the corporate accused had standing pursuant to ss. 7 and 11 of the Charter to challenge the provisions of the Act. If a provision infringes individual rights and is therefore unconstitutional, the provision is equally inapplicable to a corporate accused. However, Lamer C.J. suggested that if the provisions had applied solely to corporations, a corporation would have no standing to challenge the provision.

In *R. v. C.I.P. Inc.*, [1992] 1 S.C.R. 843, the Supreme Court of Canada held that corporations are entitled to invoke the protection guaranteed by s. 11(b) of the Charter which provides that "any person charged with an offence has the right to be tried within a reasonable time". A corporation has a legitimate interest in being tried within a reasonable time because corporations could be prejudiced by the passage of time in that the availability of witnesses and the reliability of their testimony could have a significant impact on its ability to put forward a defence.

It has been held that the provisions of s. 14 which guarantee the assistance of an interpreter do not apply to a corporation: *Restaurant Diana Inc. v. Quebec (Regie des Permis d'Alcool)* (1988), 13 A.C.W.S. (3d) 249 (Que. S.C.).

Whether or not the protections of s. 15 are available to corporations has not been clearly answered by the Supreme Court of Canada. In *Edmonton Journal v. Alberta (Attorney General)*, [1989] 2 S.C.R. 1326, three members of the court held that this section was not applicable to corporations. However, the weight of lower court decisions overwhelmingly supports the view that the word "individual" applies only to natural persons. See, for example, *R. v. Paul Magder Furs Ltd.* (1989), 49 C.C.C. (3d) 267 (Ont. C.A.); *Smith, Kline & French Laboratories Ltd. v. Canada (Attorney General)*, [1986] 1 F.C. 274, affd (1986) 34 D.L.R. (4th) 584 (C.A.); *Re PPG Industries Ltd. and Canada (Attorney General)* (1983), 42 B.C.L.R. 334 (C.A.); *General Bearing Service Inc. v. Canada* (1990), 34 F.T.R. 37 (T.D.).

Remedies

Introduction

Supremacy of the majority

The will of the majority of the shareholders of an corporation is the will of the corporation, and whatever the corporation has power to do, a majority of shareholders may cause to be done against the will of a minority: *Australian Auxiliary Steam Clipper Co. v. Mounsey* (1858), 4 K. & J. 733 at 740; *In re Horbury Bridge, Coal, Iron & Waggon Co.* (1879), 11 Ch. D. 109 (C.A.), unless, of course, there is some express provision to the contrary which is applicable to the particular corporation.

This principle of the supremacy of the majority is embodied in the *Interpretation Act*, which provides that in every federal Act, unless the contrary intention appears, words making any association or number of persons a corporation or body politic and corporate shall vest in a majority of the members of the corporation the power to bind the others by their acts. A similar provision appears in the Interpretation Acts of the provinces: see *Noble v. Cameron*, [1955] O.R. 608 (Ont. C.A.) for an examination of the Ontario provision.

Generally speaking, a person when he acquires shares in a corporation may be said to agree to submit himself to the decision of the majority at shareholders' meetings on all matters which are within the competence of such meetings. Thus, it has been held that at any meeting of shareholders the majority, in the absence of express provisions to the contrary, will bind the minority: *In re Horbury Bridge, Coal, Iron & Waggon Co., supra; Patrick v. Empire Coal & Tramway Co.* (1907), 3 N.B. Eq. 571 4 E.L.R. 98 (N.B. S.C.); *Noble v. Cameron, supra.*

Such majority must, however, be a bona fide majority: *Davidson v. Grange* (1854), 4 Gr. 377 (C.A.), and must proceed regularly and with *bona fides*; *Harben v. Phillips* (1883), 23 Ch. D. 14 (C.A.); *Henderson v. Bank of Australasia* (1890), 45 Ch. D. 330; and thus minorities are, as will appear below, entitled to protection against the wrongful acts of majorities.

The Rule in Foss v. Harbottle

The rule as to the supremacy of the majority has an important application as regards litigation in respect of wrongs alleged to be done the corporation. Prior to the enactment of statutory shareholder remedies, according to the rule in *Foss v. Harbottle* (1843), 2 Hare 461, the corporation was ordinarily the proper plaintiff in any action to redress a wrong done to the corporation or to recover its property, as the corporation was considered capable of determining as a matter of internal management whether or not litigation should be instituted on behalf of the corporation for either of such purposes. The decision of the corporation, as represented by the majority of the shareholders, on this question ordinarily bound all the shareholders. The corporation, as represented by the majority, may and presumably will sue if the majority considers that a wrong has been done to the corporation. If the corporation does not consider itself to have been wronged, it will not sue. The courts, therefore, did not ordinarily interfere or permit interference with such internal management by allowing individual shareholders to sue in the place of the corporation. The principle applied both where the majority of the shareholders lawfully approved and where it might lawfully approve the acts of which a minority complained.

The exceptions to the rule in *Foss and Harbottle* have been replaced by statutory remedies and there is no longer a common law representative action. See the authorities cited below under the heading "Statutory Remedies". However, the discussion which follows has been retained since it is applicable in provinces where the common law provisions have not been codified.

The rule in *Foss v. Harbottle* was summarized by Jenkins L.J. in *Edwards v. Halliwell*, [1950] 2 All E.R. 1064 at 1066-7 (C.A.), as follows:

> The rule in *Foss v. Harbottle*, as I understand it, comes to no more than this. First, the proper plaintiff in an action in respect of a wrong alleged to be done to a company or association of persons is *prima facie* the company or the association of persons itself. Secondly, where the alleged wrong is a transaction which might be made binding on the company or association and on all its members by a simple majority of the members, no individual member of the company is allowed to maintain an action in respect of that matter for the simple reason that, if a mere majority of the members of the company or association is in favour of what has been done, then *cadit quaestio*. No wrong had been done to the company or association and there is nothing in respect of which anyone can sue. If, on the other hand, a simple majority of members of the company or association is against what has been done, then there is no valid reason why the company or association itself should not sue. In my judgment, it is implicit in the rule that the matter relied on as constituting the cause of action should be a cause of action properly belonging to the general body of corporators or members of the company or association as opposed to a cause of action which some individual member can assert in his own right.

The rule in *Foss v. Harbottle* was concerned with wrongs alleged to have been done to the corporation or association. When the rights invaded were not the rights of the corporation or association but the rights of the individual members thereof, the rule had no application: *Edwards v. Halliwell*, [1950] 2 All E.R. 1064 (C.A.).

The rule in *Foss v. Harbottle* has been restated and followed in many cases, for example, *MacDougall v. Gardiner* (1875), 1 Ch. D. 13 (C.A.); *Burland v. Earle*, [1902] A.C. 83; *Rose v. British Columbia Refining Co.* (1911), 16 B.C.R. 215 at 227 (C.A.); *Johnston v. Thompson* (1914), 15 D.L.R. 546 (B.C. S.C.), afffd (*sub nom. Johnston v. Carlin)* (1914), 20 B.C.R. 520 (C.A.); *Wheeler v. Freame* (1914), 7 W.W.R. 191 (Alta. T.D.); *Brown v. Menzies Bay Timber Co.* (1917), 34 D.L.R. 452 (B.C. C.A.); *Watson v. Barrett* (1929), 41 B.C.R. 478; as well as *Edwards v. Halliwell, supra*; *Burrows v. Becker*, [1969] S.C.R. 162; *D'Amore v. McDonald*, [1973] 1 O.R. 845, (1973), affd 1 O.R. (2d) 370 (C.A.).

The rule meant that if the act done, though it be the act of the directors only, be one which could have been sanctioned by a majority of the shareholders, an action by some of the shareholders, on behalf of themselves and others, to impeach the act could not be sustained because the majority might immediately sanction the act complained of: *Bagshaw v. Eastern Union Railway Co.* (1849), 7 Hare 114; *Re Bolt & Iron Co., Livingstone's Case* (1887), 14 O.R. 211; affd

(1889), 16 O.A.R. 397 (C.A.); *Purdom v. Ontario Loan & Debenture Co.* (1892), 22 O.R. 597.

An act which is *intra vires* and consented to by every shareholder was not open to attack: *MacDonald Bros. v. Godson* (1916), 31 D.L.R. 363 at 365 (B.C. C.A.).

The rule applied where the act complained of was an irregularity and could be ratified by a properly constituted meeting: *Burland v. Earle*, [1902] A.C. 83 (P.C.); *Dominion Cotton Mills Co. v. Amyot*, [1912] A.C. 546 (P.C.); *In re Pacific Coast Coal Mines & Hodges*, [1926] 4 D.L.R. 759 (B.C. C.A.); *Slone v. Sidler (No. 2)* (1957), 12 D.L.R. (2d) 507 (N.S. C.A.).

Thus, irregularities or informalities, for example, in connection with the election of directors or in the notice of a shareholders' meeting, where no questions of fraud or *ultra vires* are involved, did not give a minority shareholder a cause of action to attack the validity of the proceedings: *Watt v. Commonwealth Petroleum Ltd.*, [1938] 4 D.L.R. 701 (Alta. C.A.) (election of directors); *Normandy v. Ind, Coope & Co.*, [1908] 1 Ch. 84 (defective notice); *Pelech v. Ukrainian Mutual Benefit Assn.*, [1940] 4 D.L.R. 342 (Man. K.B.) (defective notice).

The rule in *Foss v. Harbottle* was applicable to a registered trade union: *Cotter v. National Union of Seamen*, [1929] 2 Ch. 58 (C.A.). In that case the plaintiffs, members of a trade union, purported to sue on behalf of themselves and all the members of the union other than the named defendants claiming, *inter alia*, a declaration that a certain special general meeting was invalidly convened and that resolutions passed thereat were invalid. It was held that, as regards the alleged irregularities, the court must treat the union as a legal entity which held property and was governed by the code contained in its rules and that the rule laid down in *Foss v. Harbottle* and *MacDougall v. Gardiner* (1875), 1 Ch. D. 13 (C.A.), applied. Therefore, irregularities committed in the convening and conduct of the meeting, at which the resolutions complained of were passed, could be regularized by the passing of fresh resolutions. The court therefore refused to interfere by injunction at the instance of individual members of the union.

While a director is precluded from entering into engagements in which he has a personal interest conflicting with that of the corporation, a contract so entered into may be adopted by the corporation, provided that its adoption is not brought about by unfair or improper means, and is not illegal or fraudulent or oppressive towards those shareholders who oppose it: *North-West Transportation Co. v. Beatty* (1887), 12 App. Cas. 589 (P.C.). In such a case, a director has a perfect right to acquire further shares, and to exercise his voting power in such a manner as to secure the election of directors whose views upon policy agree with his own and to support his views at a shareholders' meeting: *North-West Transportation Co. v. Beatty*, *supra*, at p. 601; and see also *Christopher v. Noxon* (1884), 4 O.R. 672; *Goldex Mines Ltd. v. Revill* (1974), 7 O.R. (2d) 216 (C.A.); and *Wotherspoon Ltd. v. Canadian Pacific Ltd.*, [1987] 1 S.C.R. 952, 39 D.L.R. (4th) 169. In these cases it was held that a controlling shareholder may sell corporate property to itself or a subsidiary if a full disclosure is made and if the transaction is not oppressive or unfair to the minority shareholders. Thus in *Garvie v. Axsmith*, [1962] O.R. 65, where an agreement was approved at a shareholders' meeting purchasing the assets of another corporation, the resolution of the directors approving such an agreement being invalid since three of the five directors of the corporation were interested in the agreement and there was no independent quorum, it was held that the purchase could be validated by confirmation of a majority of the shareholders so long as the interest of the directors was declared in the notice calling the meeting. In order to set aside the resolution of the shareholders' meeting the plaintiff had to do more than show that the transactions were improvident. He had to show that they were a fraud upon the minority shareholders and that the wrongdoers were in control of the corporation. These facts could not be proven in the present case. There was not sufficient inside information given with the materials sent out with the notice as to the method of valuation of the two corporations and therefore there was no proper notice and the resolutions were set aside on this ground.

The majority may modify the nature of the business carried on as long as they do not engage in anything *ultra vires*: *A.G. v. Gould* (1860), 28 Beav. 485; *Grant v. United Kingdom Switchback Railway Co.* (1889), 40 Ch. D. 135 (C.A.); *Pardee v. Humberstone Summer Resort Co.*, [1933] 3 D.L.R. 277 (Ont. H.C.) (law substantially complied with and directors not acting illegally, fraudulently or oppressively).

As to the reluctance of the court to interfere in the internal management of corporations see *McDougald v. Wilson*, [1933] 3 D.L.R. 111 (Que. S.C.) (interlocutory injunction to restrain the calling of a special general meeting of the corporation's shareholders as an ancillary to an action for a declaration as to the ownership of certain shares of the corporation refused as there was no illegality or fraud on the part of the corporation in the calling of the meeting); *Western Ontario Natural Gas Co. v. Aikens*, [1946] O.R. 661 (action for damages for conspiracy dismissed as no fraud or lack of good faith on part of majority); *Majich v. Croatian Home of Noranda Inc. & Krancevic*, [1958] Que. S.C. 525 (court refused to interfere in the internal management of a corporation as the directors had not formally refused to carry out a legal duty, that is, to convene a meeting to elect new directors); *Pylypchuk v. Dell Hotel Ltd.* (1958), 15 D.L.R. (2d) 589 (B.C. S.C.) (interlocutory injunction enjoining directors from making changes in the operation of the corporation pending litigation set aside as fraud was not alleged and the operational changes were not *ultra vires* the directors).

In *Trade Auxiliary Co. v. Vickers* (1873), L.R. 16 Eq. 303 at 305, Malins V.C. expressed the opinion that if there is no properly constituted governing body of a corporation or there are such dissensions in the governing body that it is impossible to carry on the business, the court will interfere "but only for a limited time, and to as small an extent as possible", that is, until a governing body is appointed. In that case at the instance of a shareholder the court appointed a receiver for two months and later extended the appointment for another two months. This decision was approved in *Stanfield v. Gibbon*, [1925] W.N. 11, but in *Young v. Alberta Petroleum Consolidated*, [1930] 1 D.L.R. 903, the Alberta Court of Appeal set aside an order appointing a receiver on the ground that the court would not interfere with the internal affairs of the corporation.

There is a distinction between the powers of a majority of shareholders in a going concern and of a majority of contributories in a winding-up: *Ferguson v. Wallbridge*, [1935] 3 D.L.R. 66 at 80 (P.C.). Thus, as held in that case, once a liquidation has commenced, a majority of contributories cannot require a minority to approve a payment out of surplus assets distributable amongst the contributories.

Exceptions to the Rule in Foss v. Harbottle

The rule in *Foss v. Harbottle* (1843), 2 Hare 461, was subject to certain exceptions which are summarized in *Gray v. Yellowknife Gold Mines Ltd. (No. 1)*, [1947] O.R. 928 at 963 (C.A.). In *Edwards v. Halliwell*, [1950] 2 All E.R. 1064 (C.A.), Jenkins L.J. indicated at p. 1067 that the rule in *Foss v. Harbottle* was subject to the following exceptions:

1. The majority cannot confirm an act which is *ultra vires* or illegal.
2. The majority cannot confirm an act which constitutes a fraud against the minority where the wrongdoers are themselves in control of the company.
3. The majority cannot confirm an act which can only be validly done or sanctioned, not by a simple majority but by some special majority; otherwise a company could *de facto* do by simple majority something which required a special majority.

Ultra vires or illegal acts

A majority cannot validate an *ultra vires* contract: *Ernest v. Nichols* (1857), 6 H.L.C. 401; nor an *ultra vires* conveyance: *Stanishewski v. Tkachuk*, [1955] O.R. 667.

In *Caulfield v. Sunland Biscuit Co.*, [1941] 4 D.L.R. 714 (Alta. T.D.), an injunction was continued restraining the holding of a shareholders' meeting to approve increases of capital and allotments of shares which were attacked on the ground of illegality.

A by-law or resolution of the directors will be invalid and *ultra vires* of the corporation if it operates unequally towards the interests of any class of the shareholders: *North-West Electric Co. v. Walsh* (1898), 29 S.C.R. 33.

A majority cannot divert corporate funds to purposes other than those for which they were advanced: *Bagshaw v. Eastern Union Railway Co.* (1849), 7 Hare 114; *Brogdin v. Bank of Upper Canada* (1867), 13 Gr. 544; *Grier v. Plunket* (1868), 15 Gr. 152 (Ont. Ch.). See also the following cases respecting *ultra vires* and illegal acts: *Holmes v. Newcastle-upon-Tyne Freehold Abattoir Co.* (1875), 1 Ch. D. 682; *Hope v. International Financial Security* (1876), 4 Ch. D. 327; *Lindsay v. Imperial Steel & Wire Co.* (1910), 21 O.L.R. 375 (C.A.); *Carr v. British Columbia Nickel Mines Ltd. (No. 2)*, [1937] 3 W.W.R. 61 (B.C. S.C.) (voting power must be exercised *bona fide*); *Caulfield v. Sunland Biscuit Co., supra*; *Lauzon v. Charbonneau*, [1946] Que. S.C. 337; *Stanishewski v. Tkachuk*, [1955] O.R. 667.

Fraud or harsh treatment

If there be fraud or if in the absence of proof of actual fraud the facts make out a case of harsh treatment being practised by the majority of the shareholders against the minority, the court will interfere: *Waddell v. Ontario Canning Co.* (1889), 18 O.R. 41. So, if it is shown that the majority are banded together against the minority for the express purpose of taking advantage of their position to obtain a personal benefit to themselves at the expense of those who are in the minority, the court will interfere: *Waddell v. Ontario Canning Co., supra.*

A resolution passed by majority shareholders will constitute a fraud on the minority if it was not passed "*bona fide* for the benefit of the company as a whole" or if the effect of it was "to discriminate between the majority shareholders and the minority shareholders so as to give the former an advantage of which the latter were deprived": *Greenhalgh v. Arderne Cinemas Ltd.*, [1950] 2 All E.R. 1120 at 1126 (C.A.), per Evershed M.R.

A leading English case is that of *Menier v. Hooper's Telegraph Works* (1874), L.R. 9 Ch. App. 350. There the majority of the shares were owned by another corporation, and Mellish L.J. said that the majority could not be allowed to sell the assets of the corporation and keep the consideration, but must allow the minority to have their share of any consideration that might come to them. So also a corporation cannot use its preponderate vote in a controlled corporation to dispose of a product of the controlled corporation in order to satisfy an obligation of its own to the detriment of the minority shareholders of the controlled corporation: *General Asphalt Co. v. Anglo-Saxon Petroleum Co.* (1932), 48 T.L.R. 276 (H.L.). Nor may a corporation abuse its position of majority shareholder of a subsidiary and in breach of its duty imposed by such relationship acquire assets of the subsidiary: *Gray v. Yellowknife Gold Mines Ltd. (No. 1)*, [1947] O.R. 928 at 947 (C.A.). Where there are common directors of two corporations, it is a breach of good faith for such directors to promote the interests of one of the corporations (a majority shareholder in the other) against those of the other by imposing upon the other a one-sided option to take up a block of its shares, thus using their position as directors to the detriment of the controlled corporation and to the advantage of the controlling corporation: *Gray v. Yellowknife Gold Mines Ltd. (No. 2)*, [1947] O.R. 994 (C.A.).

Where a minority shareholder sought to bring an action against the corporation and its directors for damages for negligence, alleging gross negligence in effecting a sale of an asset of the corporation at a price greatly below its true market value, but not that the sale was beyond the powers of the corporation nor that the directors had acted fraudulently, the court held that the action could not be maintained: *Pavlides v. Jensen*, [1956] 1 Ch. 565.

In *Cameron v. Blair Holdings Corp.*, [1955] O.W.N. 61 (C.A.), escrowed shares representing control of Stanwell Oil & Gas Ltd. had been issued to Blair Holdings under an agreement between Stanwell and Blair Holdings which both corporations agreed should be rescinded and the persons who had acquired the escrowed shares did not deny the facts on the basis of which rescission was claimed. In a class action brought by the minority shareholders of Stanwell, the Ontario Court of Appeal granted an interlocutory injunction restraining the voting of the escrowed shares on the ground that it would be inequitable that persons who possess voting powers attached to shares issued under an agreement which both parties thereto said should be rescinded should continue to occupy and control the affairs and destiny of the corporation pending the final determination of the issues in the action.

The minority may invoke the aid of the court when they suffer a special detriment by the directors taking the profits or using the assets for their own ends: *Hodgkinson v. National Live Stock Insurance Co.* (1859), 4 DeG. & J. 422; *Hichens v. Congreve* (1828), 4 Russ. 562; *Nolan v. Parsons*, [1942] O.R. 358 (where the directors fraudulently voted to themselves the greater part of the profits of the corporation as directors' fees).

Where directors had made a misapplication of the funds to their own purposes, it was held that they could not subsequently validate it by a directors' by-law, ratified at a shareholders' meeting, at which they controlled the majority of votes: *Waddell v. Ontario Canning Co.* (1889) 18 O.R. 41. And in this case the circumstances were considered ample by Robertson J. to bring it within the rule as to harsh treatment. As to a shareholder using his voting power to commit a breach of trust see further the notes under the heading "Voting", in chapter 10.

Where a *prima facie* case of fraud, oppression or unfairness had been made out an injunction may be granted restraining a meeting: *Fuller v. Bruce*, [1935] 3 D.L.R. 256 (N.S. C.A.). The court will interfere to restrain directors from fixing a date for holding the annual meeting for the purpose of preventing shareholders from exercising their voting power: *Cannon v. Trask* (1875), L.R. 20 Eq. 669. And where it was alleged that certain resolutions, if passed, would constitute an illegal oppression of the minority, and it appeared that, if an injunction were refused, the plaintiff would have finally lost his remedy, an interim injunction was granted restraining the passing of the resolutions: *Carr v. British Columbia Nickel Mines Ltd.*, [1937] 2 W.W.R. 399 (B.C. S.C.).

The majority will be restrained from paying dividends on common shares in derogation of the rights of the holders of preferred shares: *Henry v. Great Northern Railway Co.* (1857), 4 K. & J. 1; *Bannatyne v. Direct Spanish Telegraph Co.* (1887), 34 Ch. D. 287 (C.A.); *Sturge v. Eastern Union Railway Co.* (1885), 7 DeG. M. & G. 158. And similarly when special rights are given to ordinary shareholders as to division or appropriation of profits: *Fawcett v. Laurie* (1860), 1 Dr. & Sm. 192; but see *Johnston v. Consumers' Gas Co.* (1895), 27 O.R. 9. The majority cannot agree to levy calls otherwise than on every shareholder alike: *Preston v. Grand Collier Dock Co.* (1840), 11 Sim. 327.

See also the following cases in respect of fraud or harsh conduct: *Fraser v. Whalley* (1864), 2 Hem. & M. 10; *In re London & Mercantile Discount Co.* (1865), L.R. 1 Eq. 277; *Atwool v. Merryweather* (1867), L.R. 5 Eq. 464n; *Waddell v. Ontario Canning Co.* (1889), 18 O.R. 41; *Bennett v. Havelock Electric Light & Power Co.* (1910), 21 O.L.R. 120, revd (1912), 25 O.L.R. 200 (C.A.); *Shaw v. Union Trust Co.* (1915), 35 O.L.R. 146; *Cook v. Deeks*, [1916] 1 A.C. 554 (P.C.) (a breach of trust by directors); *Stockford v. McPherson* (1916), 9 W.W.R.

1192 (Alta. T.D.); *Houston v. Victoria Machinery Depot Ltd.*, [1924] 2 D.L.R. 657 (B.C. S.C.); *Shiesel v. Kirsch*, [1931] O.R. 41 (C.A.); *Patterson & Hidson v. Livingstone*, [1931] 1 D.L.R. 386 (S.C.C.) (requirements as to statement of claim alleging fraud); *Sass v. St. Nicholas Mutual Benefit Association*, [1937] S.C.R. 415 at 420 (plaintiff's right to sue limited to cases of *ultra vires* act or attempt by majority to practise fraud or oppression on minority); *Zwicker v. Stanbury*, [1953] 2 S.C.R. 438 (breach of trust by directors); *Bakal v. Petursson*, [1953] 4 D.L.R. 449 (S.C.C.); *Slone v. Margolian* (1958), 12 D.L.R. (2d) 507 (N.S. C.A.) (nominal damages assessed against directors for violation of shareholders' agreement, which violation resulted in benefit to company); *Ellis v. McQueen*, [1967] 2 O.R. 399 (action alleging fraud dismissed where wrongdoers' shares had passed into the control of a third party and the pleadings did not demonstrate that the defendants were in control of the corporation); *Glass v. Atkin*, [1968] 1 O.R. 65 (plaintiff shareholders holding 50 per cent of the shares allowed to bring an action alleging fraud where they were powerless to compel an action by the corporation and their position in relation to such an action was tantamount to that of a minority); *D'Amore v. McDonald*, [1973] 1 O.R. 845, affd (1973), 1 O.R. (2d) 370 (C.A.) (fraud in the sense that those committing the alleged acts must be endeavouring to secure either a direct or indirect advantage over other shareholders).

Special majorities

The third exception to the rule in *Foss v. Harbottle* arises where the governing Act or the by-laws or the articles of a corporation require that certain acts are to be done or sanctioned by a special majority. A simple majority cannot confirm acts which can only be validly done or sanctioned by a special majority: *Baillie v. Oriental Telephone & Electric Co.*, [1915] 1 Ch. 503 (C.A.).

In *Edwards v. Halliwell*, [1950] 2 All E.R. 1064 (C.A.), where the contributions of members of a trade union to the union could under its rules be altered only if a ballot vote of the members had been taken and a two-thirds majority obtained, and a resolution increasing the contributions was passed at a delegate meeting without a ballot being taken, two members of the union were granted a declaration that the increase was invalid on the ground, among others, that the failure to obtain a two-thirds majority vote of the members in favour of the increase brought the case within the third exception stated above to the rule in *Foss v. Harbottle.*

Qualified minority rights

Under the governing Act or by-laws or articles minority shareholders holding a specified proportion of the shares may have the right to take certain action.

The main qualified minority right found in most governing Acts is the right to requisition shareholders' meetings. Thus, for example, under s. 143(1) of this Act and under s. 105(1) of the Ontario Act, shareholders holding not less than five per cent of the issued shares carrying voting rights may requisition a special general meeting. Where a statute gives this right, the directors may not limit it: *Austin Mining Co. v. Gemmel* (1886), 10 O.R. 696 (C.A.); *Re Cambrian Peat & Fuel Co.* (1875), 23 W.R. 405. See further the notes on "Special Meetings", in Chapter 10.

Individual shareholder's rights

Apart from his rights as one of the majority or minority, a shareholder has a number of rights in his individual capacity which he may enforce by action regardless of the wishes of the majority.

Perhaps the most important of the rights appertaining to his status as a shareholder is the right to insist that the corporation observe all the provisions governing it: *Salmon v. Quin & Axtens Ltd.*, [1909] 1 Ch. 311 (C.A.), affd [1909] A.C. 442 (H.L.); *Smith v. Humbervale Cemetery Co.* (1915), 33 O.L.R. 452 at 459 (C.A.), and cases cited. In the *Smith* case a single shareholder was granted an injunction restraining the corporation from doing an *ultra vires* act.

A shareholder of a corporation whose property interest or rights are injured by *ultra vires* acts committed through breach of the criminal law is entitled to relief, including an injunction, against the corporation: *Kozlowski v. Workers' Benevolent Society*, [1934] 1 D.L.R. 237 at 243, per Trueman J.A.

In *Theatre Amusement Co. v. Stone* (1914), 50 S.C.R. 32, it was held that a single shareholder was entitled to succeed in an action against the corporation and the directors for breach of the statutory articles (as to vacating the office of director). At pp. 36-37 Duff J. said:

> The articles of association are binding upon the comapny, the directors and the shareholders, until changed in accordance with the law. So long as they remain in force, any shareholder is entitled, unless he is estopped from taking that position by some conduct of his own, to insist upon the articles being observed by the company, and the directors of the company. This right he cannot be deprived of by the action of any majority. In truth, the articles of association constitute a contract between the company and the shareholders which every shareholder is entitled to insist upon being carried out.

Where the contributions of members of a trade union had been increased contrary to the rules of the trade union (which correspond to the articles of a corporation: *Cotter v. National Union of Seamen*, [1929] 2 Ch. 58), the Court of Appeal held that two members of the union were entitled to a declaration that the increase was invalid on the ground that the personal and individual rights of membership of each of them had been invaded by the invalid increases: *Edwards v. Halliwell*, [1950] 2 All E.R. 1064.

The Act confers a number of individual rights on shareholders and if these rights are breached, the shareholder may sue to restrain the violation of his rights or for other relief.

If a shareholder's share carries a vote but the corporation refuses to record his vote, an individual right is infringed: *Pender v. Lushington* (1877), 6 Ch. D. 70 where Jessel M.R. stated at p. 80:

> This is an action by Mr. *Pender* for himself. He is a member of the company, and whether he votes with the majority or the minority he is entitled to have his vote recorded — an individual right in respect of which he has a right to sue. That has nothing to do with the question like that raised in *Foss v. Harbottle* and that line of cases. He has a right to say, "Whether I vote in the majority or minority, you shall record my vote, as that is a right of property belonging to my interest in this company, and if you refuse to record my vote I will institute legal proceedings against you to compel you."

In the absence of a provision to the contrary, a shareholder has the right to demand a poll at a shareholders' meeting; see the notes under the heading "Poll", in Chapter 10.

A shareholder has the right to bring an action against the corporation for a dividend which has been declared and is payable: *In re Severn & Wye & Severn Bridge Railway Co.*, [1896] 1 Ch. 559.

The right to inspect certain books of the corporation is a right attaching to a shareholder in his individual capacity: *Cooper v. Premier Trust Co.*, [1945] O.R. 35 at 43 (C.A.).

Section 190 of the federal Act gives the holder of shares of any class of a corporation the right to dissent by following a prescribed procedure if certain matters of a fundamental nature are authorized such as an amendment to change or remove any provisions restricting or restraining the issue, transfer or ownership of shares of any class, an amendment to the articles to change, remove or add any restriction on the business or businesses that the corporation may carry on, an amalgamation, the continuance under the laws of another jurisdiction, or the sale, lease or exchange of all or substantially all of its property. In such event, an offer is to be made to the dissenting shareholder by the corporation for payment for his shares at the fair value thereof. An application may be made to the court either by the corporation or the shareholder to determine the fair value for the shares of any dissenting shareholder. Some question may arise under the provisions of the federal Act as to whether a shareholder is entitled to sue to restrain a course of action which would otherwise be regarded as improper if he is entitled to follow the process for dissent set out in s. 190.

While there is no case exactly on point it is suggested that two recent cases indicate that the remedy of an injunction against a proposed statutory amalgamation squeeze out is still available. In the case of *Re Brant Investments Ltd. v. KeepRite Inc.* (1991), 80 D.L.R. (4th) 161 (Ont. C.A.) it was held that a shareholder could apply both for an oppression remedy under what is now s. 241 as well as bringing an action for the fair value of his shares pursuant to what is now s. 190 as a dissenting shareholder. It was held that on the facts of the case there was no oppression and the fair value of the shares was fixed by the court. A court has power under s. 241(3) to restrain the conduct complained of, and in *Palmer v. Carling O'Keefe Breweries of Canada Ltd.* (1989), 41 B.L.R, 128 (Ont. Div. Ct.) the court suggested that an order to set aside the amalgamation was available but it was not prepared to make such an order as there were many changes in the 18 months which had elapsed since the amalgamation and there would be most unfortunate tax consequences. While in theory an amalgamation could be "undone" the issue of securities or debt or the acquistion of assets might well make this impossible from a practical point of view and there is some question whether an amalgamation once completed can be undone, cf. *Ruskin v. Canada All-News Radio Ltd.* (1979), 7 B.L.R. 142 (Ont. H.C.). However, if an application for injunction is brought immediately after the notice of the proposed meeting is received, it would appear that the court can grant an injunction against the proposed amalgamation and that the existence of the valuation remedy would not debar the applicant. It may be, however, that in a case where there were good business reasons for the statutory amalgamation squeeze out a court would be reluctant to interfere with the business judgment of the directors by prohibiting the proposed amalgamation, and might grant some other form of relief contemplated by s. 241(3): see *General Accident Assurance Co. of Canada v. Lornex Mining Corp.* (1988), 40 B.L.R. 299 (Ont. H.C.). On the other hand, it is doubtful in the ordinary case that there can be good business reasons which would justify confiscation of the interests of the minority shareholders. The mere saving of expense would not appear to be sufficient. See also the discussion in Chapter 12 under the heading "Amalgamations".

A shareholder has a right to share proportionately in a distribution of assets on a surrender of the charter of the corporation or as incidental to a liquidation.

Prima facie minority shareholders had the right to use the corporation's name in cases they alleged fell within one of the exceptions to the rule in *Foss & Harbottle Colonial Assurance Co. v. Smith* (1913), 12 D.L.R. 113 (Man. K.B.). However, as in such a case the issues may be clouded by the right of minority shareholders to use the corporation's name, it was preferable and the more common practice to bring an action in the form of a representative or class action: *Alexander v. Automatic Telephone Co.*, [1900] 2 Ch. 56 at 69 (C.A.). See further the notes under "Procedural matters", *supra*, in this chapter.

Where an action was taken by the shareholders of a corporation against a shareholder-director, it was held that such defendant should be excepted from the general body of shareholders referred to in the style of cause as plaintiffs: *Wheeler v. Freame* (1914), 7 W.W.R. 191 (Alta. T.D.).

The requirements at common law were similar to those now codified in the federal Act in respect of obtaining leave to being a derivative action. The current requirements will be discussed later. In order that an action by one shareholder might be maintained on behalf of the corporation, though he sued on behalf of himself as well as all shareholders other than the defendants, it was not sufficient to show that the corporation was under the absolute control of the defendants in the action, unless it was clearly indicated that the control was exercised at the time the action was commenced: *Weatherbe v. Whitney* (1897), 30 N.S.R. 49 (C.A.).

The plaintiff was required to account for the fact that the corporation had not seen fit to bring action on its own behalf. This was done by showing refusal or that by reason of wrongdoers being in control at the time of bringing the action it would be idle to apply. The facts on which the shareholder relied for his justification had to be pleaded: *Fisher v. Saint John Opera House Co.*, [1937]

4 D.L.R. 337 at 342 (N.B. C.A.). And see *Birch v. Sullivan*, [1958] 1 All E.R. 56 (Ch. Div.), and *Ellis v. McQueen*, [1967] 2 O.R. 399, where it was held that a statement of claim in a minority shareholder's action was defective as it did not allege that, because the alleged wrongdoer was in control of the corporation, the action could not be brought in the name of the corporation.

The minority shareholder was required to show that he had exhausted every effort to secure the joinder of the corporation as plaintiff and that he had failed: *Ferguson v. Wallbridge*, [1935] 3 D.L.R. 66 at 83 (P.C.); *Lloyd-Owen v. Bull*, [1936] 4 D.L.R. 273 at 275 (P.C.); *Lauzon v. Charbonneau*, [1946] Que. S.C. 337; *Burrows v. Becker*, [1969] S.C.R. 162; *Fisher v. Western Surety Co.* (1979), 19 A.R. 612 (Q.B.), see also *Plummer v. Terra Mining & Exploration Ltd.* (1974), 47 D.L.R. (3d) 268 (B.C. S.C.) wherein it was held that it must be clearly shown that an attempt was made to obtain proper authority from the corporate body in a public meeting or that such an attempt would be futile. As pointed out in *Lloyd-Owen v. Bull, supra*, if the corporation is in liquidation the necessity for any such expedient in procedure disappears and "the minority shareholders are no longer at the mercy of the majority, wrongly retaining the property of the corporation by the strength of their votes." *Quaere*, however, whether the liquidator could be compelled to bring the action. He could, of course, be removed by the court under s. 32 of the *Winding-up Act* and, doubtless, if the liquidator refused to apply to the court under s. 35 for leave to bring an action, the court might remove him.

The class action was not maintainable, if it was not shown that the corporation declined to bring the action: *Rose v. British Columbia Refining Co.* (1911), 16 B.C.R. 215 (C.A.); or, if it did not appear that the consent of the directors or shareholders could not have been obtained for the institution of proceedings in the name of the corporation: *McMurray v. Northern Railway Co.* (1875), 22 Gr. 476; (1876), 23 Gr. 134; or if the demand was insufficient: *Fremont Canning Co. v. Wall*, [1941] O.R. 379 (C.A.). In *Cockburn v. Newbridge Sanitary Steam Laundry Co.*, [1915] 1 I.R. 237, the plaintiff's solicitors by written notice called upon the corporation to bring the action and the plaintiff's action on behalf of himself and others was brought after failure of the corporation to comply with the notice.

However, the action was maintainable if it appeared that an application to the corporation to authorize the suit would be futile: *Russell v. Wakefield Waterworks Co.* (1875), L.R. 20 Eq. 474 at 482 (for a statement of the cases where this doctrine applies); *McMurray v. Northern Railway Co.* (1876), 23 Gr. 134 (form of pleadings); *Elliot v. Hatzic Prairie Ltd.* (1912), 6 D.L.R. 9 (B.C. S.C.); *Houston v. Victoria Machinery Depot Ltd.*, [1924] 2 D.L.R. 657 (B.C. S.C.); *Bryant v. Dingman*, [1929] 1 W.W.R. 507 (Alta. T.D.) (motion to strike out certain paragraphs of statement of claim dismissed where enough was alleged to warrant holding that it would be useless to require plaintiff to go through the form of requesting permission from the corporation to use its name); *Patton v. Yukon Consolidated Gold Corp.*, [1934] O.W.N. 321 (C.A.) (objection ineffective if it has been waived).

Where the defendant moved at the trial for the dismissal of the action, without notice of intention so to do, on the ground that an allegation in the statement of claim that an application to the corporation for permission to bring an action in its name was refused was insufficient, it was held that (assuming an amendment was necessary) the plaintiff ought to be given leave to amend his pleadings to allege that such application would have been futile: *Levi v. MacDougall*, [1941] 4 D.L.R. 340 (S.C.C.).

Where an objection was successfully taken at a late stage to the competency of the proceedings, it was held that a special order will be made as to the costs thrown away as a result of the delay; but if the plaintiff has refused to withdraw charges of conspiracy and fraud, not supported by the evidence, the court may deprive him of costs: *Ferguson v. Wallbridge*, [1935] 3 D.L.R. 66 (P.C.).

Where after a minority shareholder's action had been brought the corporation itself brought an action for substantially the same relief, the shareholder's action was on the application of the corporation dismissed: *Wheeler v. Annesley* (1958), 11 D.L.R. (2d) 573 (B.C. S.C.).

A shareholder could be personally disqualified from bringing an action against the will of the majority if he participated or acquiesced in the acts he impeached: *Henderson v. Strang* (1920), 60 S.C.R. 201; *Fullerton v. Crawford* (1919), 59 S.C.R. 314 and cases there cited: *Griffin v. Baker* (1923), 24 O.W.N. 367; *Shiesel v. Kirsch* (1930), 66 O.L.R. 174, [1931] O.R. 41 (C.A.); *Fisher v. Saint John Opera House Co.*, [1937] 4 D.L.R. 337 at 341 (N.B. C.A.). See also *Irvin v. Irvin Porcupine Gold Mines Ltd.*, [1940] O.W.N. 315 (shareholder complaining of lack of information in notice of meeting with respect to an agreement, where shareholder aware of terms of agreement).

It was also held that a shareholder should not be added as a co-plaintiff by the corporation where he had received and sought to retain a benefit received under an *ultra vires* transaction which was being attacked: *Toronto Finance Corp. v. Banking Service Corp. Ltd.* (1926), 59 O.L.R 278 (C.A.).

A shareholder suing on his own behalf and on behalf of all other shareholders of two corporations, making the directors and the corporations defendants, could not succeed where the plaintiff and the individual defendants were all parties to an illegal scheme: *Shiesel v. Kirsch*, [1931] O.R. 41 (C.A.). Mulock C.J.O., with whom Magee J.A. concurred, agreed with the trial judge basing his judgment on acquiescence on the part of the plaintiff.

But acquiescence by a shareholder who had received no benefit under an *ultra vires* act did not estop him from attacking it: *Pacific Coast Coal Mines Ltd. v. Arbuthnot*, [1917] A.C. 607 (P.C.); *McKenna v. Spooner Oils Ltd.*, [1934] 1 W.W.R. 255 (Alta. T.D.). See also *Sass v. St. Nicholas Mutual Benefit Assn.* [1936] 4 D.L.R. 474 (Man. C.A.), affd [1937] S.C.R. 415, and followed in *Sokil v. Zawidowski*, [1938] 2 D.L.R. 602 at 605 (Man. K.B.), as to the effect of acquiescence in disqualifying a plaintiff. In *Sass v. St. Nicholas Mutual Benefit Assn.*, *supra*, on appeal to the Supreme Court of Canada, the court having arrived at the conclusion that the plaintiff had no status to bring the action found it unnecessary to consider the objections to the plaintiff's status based on acquiescence.

In *Brown v. Can-Erin Mines Ltd.* (1960), 25 D.L.R. (2d) 250 (Ont. H.C.), it was held that the fact that there might be amongst the shareholders, other than the plaintiffs and the defendants, certain persons who had acquiesced in the transaction attacked did not bar the plaintiffs from bringing an action "on behalf of themselves and all other shareholders of the company" except the defendants.

In an action where the plaintiff assumed a representative capacity to attack proceedings "all personal objections against the individual plaintiff must be gone into and considered before relief can be granted", per Robson J.A. in *Kozlowski v. Workers' Benevolent Society*, [1934] 1 D.L.R. 237 at 245 (Man. C.A.), and cases cited; approved in *Sykes v. One Big Union*, [1936] 1 D.L.R. 662 at 665 (Man. C.A.). If a person was disentitled to sue on his own behalf, he could not do so on behalf of others interested: *Harris Maxwell Larder Lake Mining Co. v. Gold Fields Ltd.* (1911), 23 O.L.R. 625; *Sykes v. One Big Union, supra*. A shareholder had no greater rights by reason of the action being in form one by himself and all other shareholders; he must succeed by his own merits: *Towers v. African Tug Co.*, [1904] 1 Ch. 558 at 572 (C.A.). Where a shareholder had participated in an arrangement explained to the shareholders and unanimously approved he was estopped from impeaching it: *Waschysyn v. Kildonan Ice & Fuel Co.*, [1937] 2 D.L.R. 653 (Man. C.A.); *Gray v. Yellowknife Gold Mines Ltd. (No. 1)*, [1947] O.R. 928 at 949 and 962 (C.A.). And where a shareholder had sold all his shares he could not sue the corporation on behalf of himself and other shareholders: *Lund v. Walker* (1928), 34 O.W.N. 262 (Master); *International Mercantile Marine Co. v. Oceanic Steam Navigation Co.* (1934), 78 Sol. Jo. 350. And see *Birch v. Sullivan*, [1958] 1 All E.R. 56 (Ch. Div.), for the rights of a bankrupt shareholder to bring a minority shareholder's action.

A class action to make the defendants account as trustees for profits on dealings with the corporation could not be maintained if the corporation was in liquidation; nor could an amendment adding the corporation as plaintiff be made in the action if the corporation was in liquidation: *Ferguson v. Wallbridge*, [1935] 3 D.L.R. 66 (P.C.).

Where all the shareholders of a corporation had surrendered their shares and the corporation was practically defunct and there were no shareholders, a plaintiff suing former directors on behalf of himself and all other shareholders had no standing: *Clarkson v. Davies*, [1923] A.C. 100 (P.C.).

At common law, joinder of personal and representative claims was generally not permitted. It is unclear whether that rule has been continued under the current federal statutory scheme, as the cases are conflicting in their results. A discussion of the provisions of the current Act follows, *infra*. A claim put forward by a plaintiff in his own right was improperly joined in an action brought by him on behalf of himself and others against the corporation: *Thomas v. Hobler* (1861), 4 DeG. F. & J. 199; *Stroud v. Lawson*, [1898] 2 Q.B. 44 (C.A.); *Ruggles v. Ruse* (1929), 36 O.W.N. 17 at 19; *Gray v. Yellowknife Gold Mines Ltd. (No. 1)*, [1947] O.R. 928 at 949 (C.A.); and *Overholt v. Williams*, [1956] O.W.N. 891 (class action for an alleged breach of trust by directors could not be joined with a personal claim for alleged dismissal and failure to pay salary). In *Slone v. Margolian* (1957), 8 D.L.R. (2d) 115, affd (*sub nom. Slone v. Sidler (No. 2)*) (1957),

12 D.L.R. (2d) 507 (N.S. C.A.), the Nova Scotia Supreme Court allowed an individual claim for damages for breach of an agreement to be joined with the shareholder's class action although pointing out that it was not considered good practice to join such a personal claim with a representative action. Generally, the court would order the plaintiff either to abandon his personal claim or to elect to proceed first with his individual claim or with the claim on behalf of the class: *Ruggles v. Ruse, supra*; *Overholt v. Williams, supra*.

It was improper to join a claim that it was just and equitable that the defendant corporation be wound up in an action claiming other relief and such a claim was struck out: *McDougall v. Gamble*, [1942] 2 D.L.R. 604 (Ont. C.A.); but see *Atwool v. Merryweather* (1867), L.R. 5 Eq. 464n where an order was made declaring that the corporation ought to be wound up.

If the action was by a *cestui que trust* to restrain the voting of shares held in trust the corporation was considered a necessary party: *Petrie v. Brown*, [1934] 3 W.W.R. 380 (B.C. S.C.).

As to the right of minority shareholders to maintain a counterclaim against majority shareholders, who are suing the minority for contribution in respect of a guarantee, setting up that the majority had fraudulently converted assets of the corporation to the prejudice of the minority shareholders, see *Rickerd v. Weber*, [1934] 1 W.W.R. 116 (Alta. T.D.).

Costs incurred in defending a corporation against attacks in respect of valid corporate acts, and the directors in respect of resolutions regularly passed authorizing the same, were generally borne by the corporation: *Northern Life Assurance Co. of Canada v. McMaster, Montgomery, Fleury & Co.*, [1928] S.C.R. 512.

Where wrongs against the shareholder personally alleged

Under the rule in *Foss v. Harbottle*, the corporation was the proper plaintiff in proceedings to redress a wrong done the corporation and the individual shareholder could not bring an action to secure such redress except in respect of the recognized exceptions to the rule.

There were certain rights which belong to the shareholder in his individual capacity, however, and which the shareholder could enforce by action regardless of the wishes of the majority.

Statutory remedies

Reform of the common law rules has taken place in most Canadian jurisdictions through the enacting of statutory representative and personal actions. With respect to the representative action, s. 239 of the federal Act was intended to do away with some of the procedural problems facing litigants as a result of the rule in *Foss v. Harbottle* as discussed above. The Act requires "complainants" who wish to bring such an action to apply to court for leave to bring the action. Leave will be granted only where the court is satisfied that reasonable notice has been given to the directors, the complainant acts in good faith and it is in the interest of the corporation that the action be brought. See s. 239. The courts have not required applicants to meet an onerous standard, instead granting leave so long as it appears that the action is not frivolous or vexatious and could reasonably succeed. The current statutory scheme abolishes the common law rule that approval by the shareholders was a bar to the bringing of an action, although such approval is now relevant in the court's determination of whether it is in the interests of the corporation to grant leave. See s. 242.

The oppression remedy is a statutory creation which was previously unavailable at common law. Limited personal actions could be brought at common law as an exception to the rule in *Foss v. Harbottle*, as discussed above. Nevertheless, at common law, the fairness of the actions and policy decisions of corporate management could not be questioned. The Act was intended, in light of the existing common law, to widen the class of persons who could bring personal actions against the corporation or its directors and widen the scope of the conduct to be reviewed.

In addition to the remedies set out below see also to the remedies under the Securities Acts which are referred to in Chapter 13.

"Complainants"

The federal Act (ss. 239 and 241) allows "complainants" standing to bring derivative actions and to claim relief from acts which are "oppressive", "unfairly prejudicial" or which "unfairly disregard the interests of" a complainant. "Complainant" as defined in the federal Act, expressly includes current and former shareholders, current and former directors and officers of the corporation or any of its affiliates, the Director, or any other person who, in the discretion of the court, is a proper person to make an application for such remedy: see s. 238.

The Ontario Act in addition provides that in the case of offering corporations the Ontario Securities Commission may apply for relief. See the Ontario Act, s. 248(1) and *Ontario Securities Commission v. McLaughlin* (1987), 11 O.S.C.B. 442 (Ont. Div. Ct.), where the Commission was granted standing even though the corporation had ceased to be an offering corporation. It was held sufficient for the acts complained of to have taken place at the time the corporation was an offering corporation.

The court may make a variety of orders, as discussed below, if satisfied that in respect of a corporation or any of its affiliates any act or omission of the corporation or any of its affiliates effects a result, the business or affairs of the corporation or any of its affiliates are or have been carried on or conducted in a manner, or the powers of the directors of the corporation or any of its affiliates are or have been exercised in a manner that is oppressive or unfairly prejudicial to or that unfairly disregards the interest of any security holder, creditor, director or officer: s. 241.

A literal interpretation of s. 241 should allow anyone to bring an action on behalf of other security holders, creditors, directors or officers even though there has been no wrong done to the applicant himself, provided the applicant otherwise qualifies as a "complainant" as defined in s. 238. The following cases, however, do not adopt this approach.

In *Goldbelt Mines Inc. (N.P.L.) v. New Beginnings Resources Inc.* (1984), 28 B.L.R. 130 (B.C. C.A.), the court held that the applicant, a shareholder of the defendant corporation, was not entitled to invoke the prejudice to warrant holders who lacked status as shareholders of record for the purpose of voting at an extraordinary meeting and where the applicant shareholder had not been oppressed or unfairly prejudiced pursuant to the provisions of the British Columbia Act.

In *Re Abraham and Inter Wide Investments Ltd.* (1985), 51 O.R. (2d) 460 at 468 (H.C.), Griffiths J. commented in respect of the parallel provision in the Ontario Act that the right to relief is dependent on there being conduct which is oppressive, unfairly prejudicial or which unfairly disregards the interests of the *complainant.* The respondent directors of Inter Wide therefore did not have status in respect of their cross-application for an order directing Inter Wide to purchase Abraham's shares.

Bayda C.J.S., in a dissenting opinion in *347883 Alberta Ltd. v. Producers Pipelines Inc.*, [1991] 4 W.W.R. 151, revd [1991] 4 W.W.R. 577 (Sask. C.A.), was of the view that the conduct complained of must relate to the complainant. Bayda C.J.S. at p. 619 stated that while the word "any" in s. 234 of the Saskatchewan Act may suggest that it is sufficient to prove that other security holders have suffered prejudice, as a general rule only persons who have suffered wrongs are entitled to ask a court for a remedy to redress that wrong. While a legislature could, if it so chose, depart from that general rule, it would need to do so in unambiguous terms. The word "any" in Bayda C.J.S.'s opinion fell short of the clarity needed to abrogate the general rule.

It has been held that the right to bring a statutory claim for an oppression remedy is assignable. Where the plaintiff bank had purchased the assets of another bank and the asset purchase included an assignment of the right of action in respect of loans made by the assignor, the plaintiff bank was entitled to bring a claim for an oppression remedy against the shareholders of the debtor corporation pursuant to the provisions of the Ontario Act: see *Lloyds Bank Canda v. Canada Life Assurance Co.* (June 5, 1990), Doc. Toronto 18929/87, Van Camp J. (Ont. H.C.).

Security holders, Directors and officers

In addition to shareholders or former shareholders, holders or former holders of a debt obligation of a corporation may complain; a debt obligation is defined as a bond, debenture or other evidence of indebtedness or guarantee of a corporation. Directors, officers and former directors and officers are all included in the definition of the term "complainant" (s. 238(a) and (b)). See *Berdugo v. Lalique Glassworks Inc.*, unreported, Ont. Gen. Div., Dec. 18, 1992, Carruthers J. — while no corporate records showed complainants to be officers or directors, they had been so acknowledged and had standing under the Ontario Act. It will be noted that any of the above with respect to an affiliate of the corporation have standing.

Where the corporation has made an assignment in bankruptcy, by virtue of s. 71 of the *Bankruptcy and Insolvency Act* all property of the bankrupt vests in the trustee, including rights of action. Thus, bankruptcy prevents the shareholder from bringing a derivative action. See *Churchill Pulpmill Ltd. v. Government of Manitoba*, [1977] 6 W.W.R. 109 (Man. C.A.); *Gibson v. Manitoba Development Corp.*, [1982] 5 W.W.R. 168 (Man. C.A.); *Re Mattagami Pulp & Paper Co.* (1926), 8 C.B.R. 67 (Ont. S.C.) and *Rickerd v. Weber*, [1934] 1 W.W.R. 116 (Alta. T.D.). It remains open to the shareholder to apply pursuant to the provisions of the *Bankruptcy and Insolvency Act* for a reassignment of the cause of action and an order authorizing him to take the proceeding in his own name and at his own expense: *Ozesezginer v. Royal Bank* (1990), 102 A.R. 296 (Q.B.). Where the trustee in bankruptcy had declined to pursue legal proceedings on behalf of the corporation, it was held that there was still a legal argument to be made that the applicants were entitled to an order pursuant to the provisions of the British Columbia Act authorizing them to continue proceedings in the name of the corporation for wrongs done to the corporation: *Liu v. Sung* (1991), 57 B.C.L.R. (2d) 229 (C.A.), revg (1988), 39 B.L.R. 236 (B.C. S.C.).

The Act specifically provides that former shareholders have standing as "complainants". However, in *Michalak v. Biotech Electronics Ltd.* (1986), 35 B.L.R. 1 (Que. S.C.), affd unreported, April 19, 1989 (Que. C.A.), former shareholders lacked standing under the oppression provisions of the federal Act to bring an application for the appointment of an inspector. The court held that because the standing provisions of the Act specifically refer to former registered holders of securities, former shareholders have a *prima facie* right to relief. However, that right may be displaced where there is no current oppression at the time of the application. Because the complainants had previously sold their shares to the respondent, there was no oppression when the application was heard.

The case law is divided as to the question of whether persons claiming to be entitled to have shares issued pursuant to a pre-incorporation contract have standing to bring an oppression action. In *Csak v. Aumon* (1990), 69 D.L.R. (4th) 567 (Ont. H.C.), Lane J. held that the applicants were the beneficial owners of the shares in question. In his opinion, "beneficial owner" would include a situation where shares are registered in someone else's name and the applicant is the acknowledged owner and also a situation where the applicant claims to be the beneficial owner. To require the claimant to first prove his legal entitlement to the shares would defeat the broad remedial intent of the Act.

Conversely, in *Bernstein v. 335861 (Alberta) Ltd.* (1986), 73 A.R. 188 (Master) the plaintiff, a prospective shareholder, was denied standing pursuant to the Alberta Act to bring a motion for relief pursuant to the oppression provisions of the Alberta Act. The Master was unwilling to interpret the words "security holder" as including an "anticipated security holder".

The *Bernstein* case was followed in *Innocan Inc. v. Canadian Pacific Air Lines Ltd.*, [1987] R.J.Q. 2451 (C.S.), appeal dismissed [1991] R.J.Q. 2186 (C.A.). The shareholders of Nordair, which subsequently amalgamated with CPAL and continued under the name CPAL, obtained warrants to purchase the common shares of CPAL if CPAL made a public offering prior to December 31, 1988. The warrant holders alleged that the value of their warrants had been substantially reduced as a result of the proposed sale by CPAL of one of CPAL's divisions. The warrant holders, as former shareholders of Nordair, were denied standing to attack the proposed sale of the division because the warrants were neither shares nor debts of the corporation. The interest of the plaintiffs were only eventual and would disappear after December 31, 1988 if there was no public offering. Therefore, the court characterized the warrant holders' interest as, at most, that of an anticipated security holder.

The remedial provisions of the British Columbia Act grant a "member" standing. The definition of "member" in this statute is somewhat more limited in scope than the federal or Ontario counterparts but includes beneficial owners of shares and proper persons. In *Benarroch v. City Resources (Canada) Ltd.* (1991), 54 B.C.L.R. (2d) 373 (C.A.), a director who held an option to purchase shares sought relief pursuant to both the derivative action and oppression provisions of the Act in respect of alleged fraud, negligence and breach of duty of the other directors. The court denied the petitioner standing in respect of the oppression provisions on the basis that the director had no direct financial interest in how the corporation was managed and the option to purchase shares did not make him a member of the corporation in the ordinary sense. See also *Lee v. International Consort Industries Inc.* (1992), 63 B.C.L.R. (2d) 119 (C.A.) — "proper person" is one with a legitimate interest in the manner in which the affairs of the corporation are managed and a person in a position analagous to that of a minority shareholder. The petitioner, being a director but not a shareholder, had no standing to apply for relief.

Where the plaintiffs were minority shareholders of a New York corporation which was the parent of a wholly-owned Ontario subsidiary corporation, they were allowed to continue their action against the officers and directors of both corporations and majority shareholders of the parent corporation. White J. was of the opinion that the issue should be determined by a trial judge; nevertheless, he commented that while the issue was unclear, if the plaintiffs were denied standing then the Ontario Act would have no effect with respect to oppressive or unfair conduct committed in Ontario: *Moriarity v. Slater* (1989), 42 B.L.R. 52 (Ont. H.C.). In view of the definitions in the Act (ss. 245, 1(1) and 1(4)) it would not appear that there was any issue.

In *Ginther v. Rainbow Management Ltd.* (July 24, 1989), Doc. CA010720 (B.C. C.A.), the British Columbia Court of Appeal held that shareholders who are not direct shareholders in the corporation, but who hold shares in another corporation which is a minority shareholder of the corporation, are proper persons within the meaning of the Act.

While the section was obviously designed to protect the rights of minority shareholders, the weight of authority would suggest that the remedy may in some circumstances be available to shareholders holding a majority of the shares or where control of the corporation is equally divided.

In *Vedova v. Garden House Inn Ltd.* (1985), 29 B.L.R. 236 (Ont. H.C.), the applicant shareholders who held 50 per cent of the issued and outstanding common shares challenged financing arrangements, which required a restructuring of the capital stock of the corporation as proposed by the shareholders holding the remaining 50 per cent of the shares, as oppressive. Anderson J. held that the oppression provisions of the Ontario Act should be confined to the protection of minorities and the Act was not intended as a method of mediating disputes between opposing groups of shareholders acting from positions of equality.

However, in *Re Gandalman Investments Inc. and Fogle* (1985), 52 O.R. (2d) 614 (H.C.), the beneficiary of a 50 per cent shareholder's interest in the corporation moved to be elected to the board of directors of the corporation. Upon the defeat of the motion by the other shareholder an application was made pursuant to the oppression section of the Ontario Act. Callon J. held that the Act should not be interpreted narrowly. The Act did not, in his opinion, specifically restrict the availability of the remedy to minority shareholders. Callon J. concluded that the percentage of shares held should not determine the issue. Instead, the crucial question should be whether power and authority in the corporation are equally divided.

In *Credit Foncier Franco-Canadien v. C.S.W. Enterprises Ltd.* (1986), 54 Sask. R. 97 (Q.B.), a 50 per cent shareholder brought an application for an order appointing a receiver-manager where the managing shareholder was acting detrimentally in handling the financial matters of the corporation and prejudicially to the interests of the applicant. The order was not granted, however, as the court considered it appropriate to order the managing shareholder to purchase the shares of the applicant.

Gillespie v. Overs (August 14, 1987), Doc. RE 1088/87, RE 1115/87 (Ont. H.C.) purported to follow the *Gandalman* case, *supra*, in holding that a majority shareholder was a proper complainant. In Sutherland J.'s opinion, the provisions of the Ontario Act should receive a broad and purposeful interpretation and where a unanimous shareholders' agreement is used to oppress a majority shareholder, relief should be granted.

In *Cairney v. Golden Key Holdings Ltd. (No. 1)* (1987), 40 B.L.R. 263 (B.C. S.C.), the court refused to grant the respondent's cross motion to dismiss a 55 per cent shareholder's motion for the appointment of an inspector/receiver pursuant to the oppression provisions of the British Columbia Act. MacDonald L.J.S.C. noted that while the cases generally involve oppression of the minority, there was nothing in the British Columbia Act which suggested that the remedy need be reserved for minority shareholders. Further, it was possible to oppress the majority where the minority had control over the financial management of the corporation.

In *Liu v. Sung* (1988), 39 B.L.R. 236 (B.C. S.C.), revd (1991), 57 B.C.L.R. (2d) 299 (C.A.), the plaintiffs, holding 50 per cent of the shares, brought an action alleging conspiracy against the corporation, its directors and trustee in bankruptcy. The defendants applied to strike out the claim on the basis that it was a derivative claim which could only be brought by the corporation. The plaintiffs applied for leave to commence a derivative action pursuant to the provisions of the British Columbia Act. The Court of Appeal set aside the order of the chambers judge in which the action had been dismissed on the basis that the alleged wrongs were committed against the corporation and that the applicants could not bring the action as the cause of action had on bankruptcy vested in the trustee.

In *Chrysler Canada Ltd. v. Shury* (April 12, 1988), Doc. Vancouver C850504 (B.C. S.C.), affd (June 5, 1989), Doc. CA009426 (B.C. C.A.), Hinds J. noted that the provisions of the federal Act are broader than those of the British Columbia Act. In this case the plaintiff, while not a minority shareholder, qualified as a complainant. Shury held 99 per cent of the issued common and preference shares of a Chrysler dealership, but Chrysler Canada through a voting trust agreement and stock agreement had the legal right to control the affairs of the dealership. Hinds J. concluded that Shury was for practical purposes in the position of a minority shareholder.

Where the directors of a corporation holding 10 per cent of the shares passed a resolution to issue further shares to themselves, which would have the effect of reducing the majority interest to 5 per cent, the court granted the relief sought by the majority shareholder and set aside the share issue: see *Yok Wing Hui v. Yamato Japanese Steak House Inc.* (January 6, 1988), Doc. 1936/87, Gray J. (Ont. H.C.).

In *Jabaco Inc. v. Real Corporate Group Ltd.* (unreported) (January 20, 1989), Doc. Toronto RE 2680/88, Doherty J. (Ont. H.C.), Jabaco, which held 60 per cent of the equity and 50 per cent of the voting power in the corporation, brought an application pursuant to the federal Act. Doherty J. rejected the respondent's contention that oppression remedies should be reserved to complainants whose power and authority is less than that of those who engaged in the oppressive conduct. In Doherty J.'s opinion, such an interpretation would be to unduly restrict the language of the Act and he concluded that an applicant may qualify as a complainant regardless of the size of his share position, or the degree of authority which the constitution of the corporation permits him to exercise over the affairs of the corporation. Where a complainant has a position of superiority or equality within the corporation, his claim may be more tenuous or difficult to establish but he should not be prevented from bringing it.

Where it was alleged that an equal shareholder with control of the management of the corporation had mismanaged the affairs of the corporation, thus unfairly prejudicing the interests of the other shareholder, the court ordered the by-laws of the corporation varied to revest the management of the corporation in the applicant: *Trnkoczy and Multi-Scale Charge Ltd. v. Shooting Chrony Inc.* (1991), 1 B.L.R. (3d) 202 (Ont. Gen. Div.).

In *Tilley & Alex Tilley Holdings Inc. v. Hails et al* (1992), 7 O.R. (3d) 257 (Gen. Div.), varied (1992), 8 O.R. (3d) 169 (Div. Ct.), affd. (1992), 9 O.R. (2d) 255 (C.A.), the applicant, a 50% shareholder, was granted a remedy pursuant to the oppression provisions of the Ontario Act without comment on this point.

The Director

The Director appointed pursuant to s. 260 of the federal Act is specifically granted standing to bring an action pursuant to the remedial provisions of the Act. The regulations to the Ontario Act (Reg. 45) set out specific circumstances in which the Director under that Act may apply to the court for a remedy pursuant to the oppression provisions of the Ontario Act. These include cases where it appears that conduct referred to in s. 248(1) constitutes or threatens to constitute a breach of the Act or regulations; conduct requiring the Director to perform a duty under the Act or the regulations and where the performance of the duty would, in the opinion of the Director, effect a result that is oppressive or unfairly prejudicial to or that unfairly disregards the interests of the persons referred to in s. 248(2) of the Act, or, in the Director's opinion, a person with the status of complainant is unable to make an application and it is in the public interest that an application be made. For cases in which the Director has taken such action, see, for example, *Sparling v. Royal Trustco Ltd.* (1984), 6 D.L.R. (4th) 682 (Ont. C.A.), affd [1986] 2 S.C.R. 537 (S.C.C.), *Sparling v. Southam Inc.* (1988), 66 O.R. (2d) 225 (H.C.) and *Doyle v. Sparling,* [1992] R.J.Q. 11 (C.A.).

"Proper persons"

The last category of persons with status as "complainant" are "proper persons". There is no definition of "proper persons" in the Act. The broad definition of "complainant" in the Act supports the view that creditors have standing. The question is whether all creditors should be considered proper persons to invoke the remedial provisions of the Act or whether the Act contemplates that only a limited class of creditors have standing.

With respect to the question of whether creditors generally have any standing under the remedial provisions of the Act, see *Re Daon Development Corp.* (1984), 54 B.C.L.R. 235 (S.C.) (debenture holder seeking leave to bring a derivative action not qualified as complainant); *R. v. The Sands Motor Hotel Ltd.*, [1985] 1 W.W.R. 59 (Sask. Q.B.) (federal Crown as creditor qualified as complainant pursuant to the oppression provisions); *Bank of Montreal v. Dome Petroleum Ltd.* (1987), 67 C.B.R. (N.S.) 296 (Alta. Q.B.) (creditor qualified as complainant); *Tsuru v. Montpetit,* [1989] R.J.Q. 2452 (C.S.) (creditor qualified as complainant); *Canadian Opera Co. v. 670800 Ont. Inc.* (1990), 75 O.R. (2d) 720 (Div. Ct.) (creditor qualified as complainant); *First Edmonton Place v. 315888 Alta. Ltd.* (1988), 40 B.L.R. 28 (Alta. Q.B.), revd [1990] 2 W.W.R. 670 (Alta. C.A.) (creditor had status as a complainant but unable to bring oppression remedy because not a creditor at time of oppression); *Lloyds Bank Canada v. Canada Life Assurance Co.* (unreported) (June 5, 1990), Doc. Toronto 18929/87, Van Camp J. (Ont. H.C.) (assignee of creditor entitled to bring claim for oppression remedy in respect of assignor's loan to debtor corporation) and *Prime Computer of Canada Ltd. v. Jeffrey & Robinson & Jeffrey Ltd.* (1991), 6 O.R. (3d) 733 (Gen. Div.) (unpaid judgment creditor entitled to apply for order under oppression provisions.)

The term "creditor" is not defined in the Act. Creditors to whom a liquidated debt is owing have been granted standing pursuant to either the derivative action or the oppression provisions. For example, in *Tsuru v. Montpetit,* [1989] R.J.Q. 2452 (C.S.) a creditor who had made a loan to the debtor corporation was granted standing as a complainant pursuant to the provisions of the federal Act.

In *Prime Computer of Canada Ltd. v. Jeffrey & Robinson & Jeffrey Ltd. supra,* the vendor of computer equipment to which the defendant corporation owed payment for purchases was permitted to bring an action alleging that the stripping of corporate assets was oppressive or unfairly prejudicial to the interests of the judgment creditor.

It is unclear, however, whether the term "creditor" should be restricted to persons to whom a debt is owing, or whether it should have an extended meaning to include persons with unliquidated claims for damages. There is authority for the proposition that "creditor" should be interpreted in the latter sense.

In *G.T. Campbell & Associates Ltd. v. Hugh Carson Co.* (1979), 24 O.R. (2d) 758 (C.A.), the Court of Appeal considered the provisions of the 1970 Ontario Act which provided for the commencement of actions against the corporation and its shareholders within two years of dissolution. In interpreting the meaning of "creditor" in s. 253 a majority of the court was of the view that to ascribe the common law meaning to the word would lead to an unjust and unreasonable result, in that otherwise, persons with unliquidated claims against the corporation would be unable to satisfy their judgment as against the shareholders to whom the property of the corporation had been distributed. It would be practically impossible to obtain judgment against the corporation, commence an action against the shareholders and obtain judgment within the two-year period required by the Act. Therefore, for the purpose of those provisions, "creditor" included persons with unliquidated claims for damages.

The Ontario Divisional Court relied upon the *G. T. Campbell* case *supra*, in ascribing an extended meaning to the word "creditor" to s. 248 of the current Ontario Act. In *Canadian Opera Co. v. 670800 Ontario Inc., supra*, the Canadian Opera Corporation sought summary judgment pursuant to the oppression remedy when property for which the full purchase price had been paid was not delivered. At first instance, Hollingworth J. accepted the argument that a debtor-creditor relationship was established as soon as the purchase price had been paid. The defendant argued before the Divisional Court that the word "creditor" in s. 248 should be restricted to its common law meaning and therefore be limited to persons having claims for liquidated amounts. The Divisional Court rejected the argument, relying on the *G. T. Campbell* case.

In *First Edmonton Place Ltd. v. 315888 Alta Ltd., supra*, a creditor brought an application for leave to bring an action in the name of the respondent corporation pursuant to the oppression provisions or, alternatively, the derivative action provisions of the Alberta Act. McDonald J. allowed the latter claim but denied the former claim.

The corporate defendant, a shell corporation, entered into an oral agreement with the plaintiff to rent office space. As an inducement to enter into the lease, the plaintiff granted the defendant an 18-month rent-free period, a leasehold improvement allowance and a cash payment. The cash payment was distributed to the directors. No written lease was executed and after the expiration of the rent-free period, the defendant vacated the premises. The plaintiff took the position that the actions of the directors constituted breaches of their obligations to the corporation.

In determining whether the lessor was a "complainant" with standing to advance the claims against the defendant, McDonald J. concluded that "proper person" may include a creditor and furthermore, a person toward whom a contingent liability was owed. However, in order to bring an action for oppression, the creditor would also have to point to evidence of oppression or that the debtor disregarded the interests of a security holder, creditor, director or officer in addition to evidence that in the circumstances of the case, justice and equity require the claim to be tried. Such circumstances would be made out where the conduct of the directors constituted the use of the corporation to commit a fraud upon the applicant or where the conduct constituted a breach of an underlying and objectively reasonable expectation of the applicant arising from the circumstances in which the applicant's relationship with the corporation arose.

McDonald J. granted leave to bring a derivative action. However, he refused leave to bring the oppression action, noting that leave to commence an action could only be granted if the applicant had been a creditor at the time of the wrongful acts. McDonald J. characterized the applicant's claim as an unliquidated claim for damages and held that at the time of the acts complained of, there was not yet any rent due under the lease. He distinguished the *G.T. Campbell* case on the basis that the concerns for justice and reasonableness were not present in the case before him. Therefore, he concluded that the term "creditor" did not include a lessor in respect of rent not yet owing. (See also: *Trillium Computer Resources Inc. v. Taiwan* (1992), 10 O.R. (3d) 249 (Gen. Div.) — creditor denied standing because it was alleged that it became a creditor as a result of the respondent's actions. A complainant creditor must be a creditor at the time of the alleged oppressive conduct.)

The defendant appealed on the issue of the derivative action claim. Stevenson J.A. granted the appeal. He noted that in order to succeed in the derivative action, the landlord would have to establish the liability of the tenant. That determination would be made in the lawsuit against the numbered corporation which was already underway. Therefore, in his view the basis for the derivative action was speculative and it was premature to make the order granting leave to bring the derivative action. He did, however, leave open the question of whether leave would be available to a creditor to bring a derivative action in the proper circumstances.

It has been held that a debenture holder does not have standing as a proper person pursuant to the provisions of the British Columbia Act: see *Re Daon Development Corp.* (1984), 54 B.C.L.R. 235 (S.C.). The decision may not be applicable in other jurisdictions given the more restricted definition of "member" in the British Columbia statute.

The trustee in bankruptcy of a bankrupt corporation was denied standing as a "proper person" to seek an oppression remedy. In *Canada (Attorney General) v. Standard Trust Co.* (1991), 5 O.R. (3d) 660 (Gen. Div.), the trustee in bankruptcy contended that the loan by the bankrupt corporation to its subsidiary was oppressive of the interests of the creditors of the bankrupt corporation and claimed standing as the representative of the creditors. The court held that the trustee had no higher rights than the bankrupt corporation which could not have attacked the transaction as it had been unanimously approved by the board of directors.

Commencing a derivative action

The codification of the representative action embraces all causes of actions that a shareholder may sue for on behalf of a corporation and thus there no longer exists a common law representative action. The statute must be complied with, and leave must be obtained from the court. See *Farnham v. Fingold*, [1973] 2 O.R. 132 (C.A.), revg on other grounds [1972] 3 O.R. 688 (H.C.); *Goldex Mines v. Revill*, [1973] 3 O.R. 869 (Div. Ct.), revg [1973] 1 O.R. 659, affd (1974), 7 O.R. (2d) 216 (C.A.); and *Shield Development Co. v. Snyder*, [1976] 3 W.W.R. 44 (B.C. S.C.). Any interlocutory orders obtained without leave are therefore invalid: see *Goldex Mines v. Revill, supra.*

It has been held that if there was any doubt as to whether the provisions of the former Ontario Act permitted the granting of leave to bring a derivative action *nunc pro tunc* in the proper circumstances (see, for example, *Goldex Mines v. Revill, supra*, wherein Hughes J.A. noted that in appropriate cases leave might be granted *nunc pro tunc*; *Re Goldhar and Quebec Manitou Mines Ltd.* (1975), 9 O.R. (2d) 740 (Div. Ct.) and *Olympia & York Enterprises Ltd. v. Hiram Walker Resources Ltd.* (1986), 59 O.R. (2d) 254 (Div. Ct.), where leave had not been sought and notice had not been given to the directors, the application was considered a nullity), the change in the wording of the 1982 Act clearly now permits such an order to be made. See *Vadeko International Inc. v. Philosophe* (1990), 1 O.R. (3d) 87 (Gen. Div.); *McBride v. Airphoto Analysis Associates Consultants Ltd.* (unreported) (January 22, 1990), Doc. Toronto 4598/85, Montgomery J. (Ont. H.C.), vard (August 26, 1991) (Ont. C.A.), leave to appeal to S.C.C. refused (1992), 138 N.R. 414 (note) (S.C.C.), but see *Pappas v. Acan Windows Inc.* (1991), 90 Nfld. & P.E.I.R. 126 (Nfld. T.D.), where an order *nunc pro tunc* pursuant to the provisions of the Newfoundland Act was refused.

Clearly, the application for leave is not intended to be an exhaustive analysis of the merits of the claim, and courts have granted leave where convinced that the action is not frivolous or vexatious and has some chance of success: see *Marc-Jay Investments Ltd. v. Levy* (1974), 5 O.R. (2d) 235; *Armstrong v. Gardner* (1978), 20 O.R. (2d) 648; *Title Estate v. Harris* (1990), 72 O.R. (2d) 468 (H.C.); *Georbay Developments Inc. v. Smahel* (1990), 72 O.R. (2d) 200 (H.C.).

The application for leave is brought by way of motion or application. The moving party must establish three elements in order to obtain an order granting leave, namely, notice, good faith and that it is in the interests of the corporation.

First, the applicant must prove that reasonable notice has been given to the directors of the corporation and that it is unlikely that the directors will bring, prosecute, defend or discontinue an action. This section of the Act is not construed in a technical or restricted manner and thus "notice" has been held to include the request to bring the action together with details of the nature of the claim: see *Re Daon Development Corp.* (1984), 54 B.C.L.R. 235 (S.C.); *Re Bellman and Western Approaches Ltd.* (1981), 17 B.L.R. 117 (B.C. C.A.); and *Armstrong v. Gardner* (1978), 20 O.R. (2d) 648 (H.C.) (a letter to the board of directors constitutes notice); but see *Re Daon Development Corp., supra,* where a letter written to the board by the complainant's solicitor after the motion had been filed was not considered to constitute notice. It is not necessary to include a draft statement of claim: *Loeb v. Provigo Inc.* (1978), 88 D.L.R. (3d) 139 (Ont. H.C.). The notice must be directed to the directors and not simply to the corporation itself: *Johnson v. Meyer* (1987), 57 Sask. R. 161 (Q.B.). Sufficient notice is established even though each and every cause of action is not specified in the notice: *Re Bellman and Western Approaches Ltd., supra.* "Notice" is no more than the knowledge which would be disclosed in a generally endorsed writ of summons: *Re Northwest Forest Products Ltd.*, [1975] 4 W.W.R. 724 (B.C. S.C.). The technicalities as to notice may be satisfied by serving a notice of motion: *Baniuk v. Carpenter (No. 2)* (1987), 217 A.P.R. 394 (N.B. Q.B.).

With respect to the question of the likelihood that the corporation will not bring the action, it has been held that the applicant must make reasonable efforts to cause the corporation to bring the action: *Appotive v. Computrex Centres Ltd.* (1981), 16 B.L.R. 133 (B.C. S.C.). In *Re Daon Development Corp., supra,* reasonable efforts were interpreted to include reasonable notice to the director and details of the nature of the claim, where this can be done without undue expense or effort. In this case, the applicant was not relieved of the requirements of the Act simply because his solicitor presumed that the directors would decline to bring the action. But in *Gorner v. Martin* (1985), 4 C.P.C. (2d) 72 (Nlfd. T.D.) it was held that the plaintiff was not required to make a request of the shareholders or directors where the circumstances make it plain that such request would be futile.

The second requirement is that the applicant must be acting in good faith. Good faith is not defined in the Act and each case is decided on its own facts. It has been held that the requirement was satisfied even where someone allied in interest with the applicant was more knowledgeable about the facts of the case and would have been a better subject for cross-examination: *Solmon v. Elkind* (1976), 3 C.P.C. 31 (Ont. H.C.). Where the applicant sought leave to bring both a personal and a derivative action for substantially the same relief, it was argued that this demonstrated bad faith. The court, however, concluded that the relief sought was not the same: *Re Bellman and Western Approaches Ltd.* (1981), 17 B.L.R. 117 (B.C. C.A.). Where the applicant sought leave to bring an action against one of the directors for compensation because the director had been operating his own business on the corporation's premises rent-free for several years, the court concluded the applicant was not acting in good faith. The applicant had previously requested to be made a director and been refused, had been using the corporation's premises to run his own business and had waited 10 years to bring the action: *Ledrew v. Ledrew Lumber Co.* (1988), 223 A.P.R. 71 (Nfld. T.D.). Where the motive for bringing the application was to obtain a tactical advantage against the defendant shareholders, this was considered to be evidence of bad faith: *Vedova v. Garden House Inn Ltd.* (1985), 29 B.L.R. 236 (Ont. H.C.). Good faith was established notwithstanding that the applicant stood to personally benefit from any recovery of corporate assets appropriated by the defendants: *Title Estate v. Harris* (1990), 72 O.R. (2d) 468 (H.C.). Where the complainant sought to substitute himself as plaintiff and continue an action brought by another shareholder which had been settled, the *bona fides* of the complainant was in question. He had previously taken no interest in the proceedings: *Abraham v. Prosoccer Ltd.* (1980), 31 O.R. (2d) 475 (H.C.). Where the complainant failed to file an affidavit to establish his good faith, leave was not granted. See *8th Street Theatre Co. v. Besenski* (1981), 15 Sask. R. 182 (Q.B.); but see also *Appotive v. Computrex Centres Ltd.* (1981), 16 B.L.R. 133 (B.S. S.C.), where Rae J. commented that it was likely the applicant was acting in good faith based on information contained in the affidavit of his solicitor, notwithstanding there was no personal affidavit of the applicant.

Finally, the court must be satisfied that granting leave to bring the action is in the best interests of the corporation. It is sufficient that an arguable case be shown. Thus, where it appeared that the directors in deciding not to sue may have been prevented from exercising an unprejudiced judgment, an arguable case had been shown: *Re Bellman and Western Approaches Ltd., supra.* A *prima facie* case does not have to be proved and the applicant need only deduce sufficient evidence which on the face of it at first disclosure suggests that it is in the interests of the corporation to pursue the action: *Re Northwest Forest Products Ltd.*, [1975] 4 W.W.R. 724 (B.C. S.C.). Where the material failed to disclose the nature of the proposed action and the circumstances upon which a court could decide that it would be in the interests of the corporation that the action be brought, the court was unable to make a proper determination: *8th Street Theatre Co. v. Besenski, supra.*

Power of the court regarding derivative actions

The court may at any time make any order it sees fit, including: (1) an order authorizing the complainant or any other person to control the conduct of the action; (2) an order giving directions for the conduct of the action; (3) an order directing that any amount adjudged payable by the defendant be paid in whole or in part directly to former and present security holders; and (4) an order requiring the corporation to pay the complainant's legal fees incurred in connection with the action (s. 240).

With respect to the payment of fees, it has been held that the complainant's right to indemnification is a *prima facie* right. However, where the minority shareholder was likely to benefit financially, an order was made requiring the corporation to indemnify the shareholder to the extent of one-half of the fees and costs: *Turner v. Mailhot* (1985), 50 O.R. (2d) 561 (H.C.). An order for costs is appropriate only where the applicant can demonstrate a financial need to the court to ensure that the action proceeds: *Johnson v. Meyer* (1987), 62 Sask. R. 34 (Q.B.). Such right of indemnification would also appear to be available in respect of the common law action in those jurisdictions which have not enacted the statutory representative action: *Wallersteiner v. Moir (No. 2)*, [1975] 1 All E.R. 849 (C.A.). However, such application should not be made on an *ex parte* basis and the corporation is entitled to have access to all of the evidence unless protected by privilege: *Smith v. Croft*, [1986] 2 All E.R. 551 (Ch. Div.). Where the plaintiff seeks an interim order, the plaintiff must demonstrate that the order is genuinely needed because he has insufficient funds to finance the litigation: *Smith v. Croft, supra.*

Grounds establishing oppression

Section 241 sets out the grounds which constitute oppression. These include: (1) acts or omissions by a corporation or affiliate; (2) the carrying on of the business or affairs of a corporation or affiliate; or (3) the exercise of the powers of the directors of the corporation or affiliate that is oppressive or unfairly prejudicial to or that unfairly disregards the interests of a security holder, creditor, director or officer.

It is unclear whether the words "oppressive", "unfairly prejudicial", and "unfairly disregards" establish different standards in descending thresholds of proof or whether they overlap. In *Westfair Foods Ltd. v. Watt*, [1991] 4 W.W.R. 695 (Alta. C.A.), Kerans J.A. stated that the adjectives simply provide that the classes mentioned are to be treated "fairly" in the sense of "justly" by corporations. See also *Keho Holdings Ltd. v. Noble* (1987), 38 D.L.R. (4th) 368 (Alta. C.A.); but see *Dancey v. 229281 Alta. Ltd.* (1988), 40 B.L.R. 180 (Alta. Q.B.) (wherein it was held that the words "unfairly prejudicial" had an effect different from and going beyond that ascribed to "oppressive"); *Re Mason and Intercity Properties Ltd.* (1987), 59 O.R. (2d) 631 (C.A.) (wherein Blair J.A. commented that "oppressive" conduct is a more rigorous standard than that of "unfairly prejudicial conduct" or conduct which "unfairly disregards"); *Re Abraham and Inter Wide Investments Ltd.* (1985), 51 O.R. (2d) 460 (H.C.) (wherein Griffiths J. commented that conduct which is oppressive has an element of coercion, but that such element need not be proved to support a finding that the actions complained of are unfairly prejudicial or unfairly disregard the applicant's interests); and *Gillespie v. Overs* (August 14, 1987), Doc. RE 1088/87, RE 1115/87 (Ont. H.C.) (in which Sutherland J., noting the comments of Griffiths J., expressed the view that the threshold which is required to prove conduct which is "unfairly prejudicial" may involve a lesser test than that required to prove conduct which is "oppressive". In turn, conduct that "unfairly disregards" may require a lower threshold of proof than that required to prove conduct that is "unfairly prejudicial").

"Oppressive" has been interpreted as meaning burdensome, harsh or wrongful. See, for example, *Scottish Co-operative Wholesale Society Ltd. v. Meyer*, [1959] A.C. 324 (H.L.), and *Burnett v. Tsang* (1985), 29 B.L.R. 196 (Alta. Q.B.). "Unfairly prejudicial" has been interpreted to mean "acts that are unjustly or inequitably detrimental": *Diligenti v. RWMD Operations Kelowna* (1976), 1 B.C.L.R. 36 (S.C.). "Unfairly disregards" has been interpreted to mean "unjustly or without cause pay no attention to, ignore or treat as of no importance the interests of security holders, creditors, directors or officers": *Stech v. Davies* (1987), 53 Alta. L.R. (2d) 373 (Q.B.).

It is not a requirement of the Act that evidence of bad faith or a want of probity must be established by the complainant, although evidence of bad faith may be relevant in a determination of whether the quality or propriety of the conduct is oppressive or unfair: see *Brant Investments Ltd. v. Keeprite Inc.*

(1991), 3 O.R. (3d) 289 (C.A.), and *Palmer v. Carling O'Keefe Breweries of Canada Ltd.* (1989), 67 O.R. (2d) 161 (Div. Ct.). However, in a small, closely held corporation, conduct which is not bona fide may effect a result which is oppressive or unfairly prejudicial: *Ferguson v. Imax Systems Corp.* (1983), 43 O.R. (2d) 128 (C.A.).

It is unclear whether the applicant must have "clean hands". See, for example, *Journet v. Superchef Foods Industries Ltd.* (1984), 29 B.L.R. 206 (Que. S.C.) and *In re London School of Electronics Ltd.*, [1986] Ch. 211 (doctrine of "clean hands" not applicable); but see *Cairney v. Golden Key Holdings Ltd.* (1988), 40 B.L.R. 289 (B.C. S.C.) (the doctrine of "clean hands" may preclude relief where there is an immediate and necessary relation between the relief sought and the misbehaviour in question such that it would be unjust to grant the relief); *Gillespie v. Overs, supra* ("clean hands" doctrine may be applicable) and *Frey v. Scheper,* unreported Sept. 23, 1992, Ont. Gen. Div., Rosenberg J. (where plaintiff convicted of fraud and defendant attempted to coerce Frey into purchasing his shares for more than their real value, the defendant's conduct was oppressive but the defendant was denied the first ground of relief on the basis that he did not have clean hands. The corporation was, however, ordered wound up.)

It would appear that an applicant will be successful only if the oppression exists at the time of the application or is contemplated to be done at a meeting at which notice is given. Hence, the Act does not recognize "anticipatory oppression". See *Michalak v. Biotech Electronics Ltd.* (1986), 35 B.L.R. 1 (Que. S.C.); *Bank of Montreal v. Dome Petroleum Ltd.* (1987), 67 C.B.R. (N.S.) 296 (Alta. Q.B.). However, the remedying, before the hearing, of the acts or conduct complained of is relevant to the issue of whether orders need be made to protect a petitioner in the future and does not deprive a court of the powers conferred by the British Columbia Act: *Low v. Ascot Jockey Club Ltd.* (1986), 1 B.C.L.R. (2d) 123 (S.C.).

Several guiding principles have been articulated in the case law which assist courts in interpreting the oppression provisions. Clearly, the provisions are remedial and should be interpreted broadly to carry out the intended purpose: see *Ferguson v. Imax Systems Corp.* (1983), 43 O.R. (2d) 128 (C.A.), leave to appeal to S.C.C. refused (1983), 52 N.R. 317n (S.C.C.). In *Westfair Foods Ltd. v. Watt*, [1991] 4 W.W.R. 695 (Alta. C.A.), it was held that the test in determining whether or not an action is oppressive is fact specific and courts should be guided by the reasonable expectations of the parties. See pp. 702-3. On an application, the court must consider the nature of the acts complained of and the method by which they were carried out. Judges are, however, not entitled to substitute their own business judgment for that of managers or directors: see *Brant Investments Ltd. v. Keeprite Inc.* (1991), 3 O.R. (3d) 289 (C.A.).

In the following cases, the conduct complained of was considered to be oppressive or unfairly prejudicial or to constitute conduct which unfairly disregarded the interests of the applicant: *Re National Building Maintenance Ltd.*, [1971] 1 W.W.R. 8 (B.C. S.C.), affd (*sub nom. National Building Maintenance Ltd. v. Dove*), [1972] 5 W.W.R. 410 (B.C. C.A.) (majority shareholder secretly taking management fees without board approval and falsifying financial statements to induce minority shareholder to sell shares); *Re Peterson and Kanata Investments Ltd.* (1975), 60 D.L.R. (3d) 527 (B.C. S.C.) (granting of voting control through share issue and sale of only substantial asset of the corporation); *Diligenti v. RWMD Operations Kelowna Ltd.* (1976), 1 B.C.L.R. 36 (S.C.) (removal from management position and board and excessive management fees and compensation paid in a closely held corporation of which the petitioner was one of four equal founders); *Jackman v. Jackets Enterprises Ltd.* (1977), 2 B.L.R. 355 (B.C. S.C.) (advance of money without security to a corporation wholly owned by majority shareholder and mortgage given, funds of which used to benefit majority shareholder's corporation oppressive as diminishing plaintiff's equity without any offsetting benefit); *Rowe v. National Wholesalers Ltd.* (1978), 22 Nfld. & P.E.I.R. 26 (Nfld. T.D.) (directors paying themselves unusually large directors' fees and a portion of the fees lent back to the corporation at one and one-half per cent above prime rate with the result that the directors were unjustly enriched to the exclusion of the minority); *Alexander v. Westeel Rosco Ltd.* (1978), 4 B.L.R. 313 (Ont. H.C.) (a proposed amalgamation squeeze-out in which it was proposed that minority shareholders receive non-voting preference shares which were to be redeemed for cash while the majority shareholders received common shares in the new corporation); *Redekop v. Robco Construction Ltd.* (1978), 89 D.L.R. (3d) 507 (B.C. S.C.) (majority shareholder caused corporation to enter into a contract in which the majority had an interest); *Beauchamp v. Contenants Sanitaires C.S. Inc.* (1979), 7 B.L.R. 200 (Que. S.C.) (directors issued new shares with the aim of maintaing their control and which had the effect of reducing the value of the shares and without giving the applicant an invitation to participate in order to maintain his percentage shareholdings); *Burdon v. Zeller's Ltd.* (1981), 16 B.L.R. 59 (Que. S.C.) (proposed amalgamation squeeze-out); *Re Romana Inn Ltd.* (1982), 48 B.C.L.R. 65 (S.C.) (where business and assets of corporation sold and net proceeds distributed to other shareholders, and petitioner received no notice of any meetings or resolutions concerning the sale, petitioner had established oppression); *Ferguson v. Imax Systems Corp.* (1983), 43 O.R. (2d) 128 (C.A.) (failure to pay dividends and reorganization was intended to force applicant to sell shares); *Mason v. M.O.W. Holdings Ltd.* (1983), 23 B.L.R. 255 (Man. Q.B.) (special resolution passed respecting an application for articles of amendment which would allow respondent corporation to buy out minority shareholder for $25,000). A court will not allow one side to arbitrarily fix the share price: *Ferguson v. Imax Systems Corp.*, *supra* (failing to pay dividends and proposing a reorganization whereby the non-redeemable shares held by the applicant would be converted into redeemable shares and subsequently redeemed where motivated out of a desire to force a shareholder out of the corporation); *Re Little Billy's Restaurant (1977) Ltd.* (1983), 21 B.L.R. 246 (B.C. S.C.) (directors' resolution approved payment of franchise fee thus diverting anticipated funds of the corporation to another corporation owned and controlled by the directors); *Miller v. F. Mendel Holdings Ltd.*, [1984] 2 W.W.R. 683 (Sask. Q.B.) (majority shareholder removed plaintiffs as directors, terminated their privileges as shareholders, prevented them from transferring their shares, and caused the corporation to exercise an option to purchase lands and to transfer the lands to her solely-owned corporation at the same price, with the result that the holding corporation received no consideration for the option and retained a rental expense); *Journet v. Superchef Foods Industries Ltd.* (1984), 29 B.L.R. 206 (Que. S.C.) (shareholder/director failed to call general meeting to fill vacancy on board, failed to prepare financial statements in accordance with the Act, opened and operated bank account of the corporation without authorization, issued shares to himself in an attempt to obtain voting control, attempted to acquire or appropriate by dubious legal means the shares of the other shareholders, operated corporation in disregard of other shareholders' rights as if he were the only shareholder, the net result of all of the above being that the shareholder took control of the corporation for his own benefit and the other shareholders were rendered helpless); *Eiserman v. Ara Farms Ltd.*, [1988] 5 W.W.R. 97 (Sask. C.A.) (the majority shareholder in a closely-held family farm caused the minority shareholder to feel that management control of the farm had become intolerable and that his real control of the farm had essentially ceased); *Re Abraham and Inter Wide Investments Ltd.* (1985), 51 O.R. (2d) 460 (H.C.) (payment of unauthorized directors' fees and serious departures by the directors from legal and normal business practices); *Low v. Ascot Jockey Club Ltd.* (1986), 1 B.C.L.R. (2d) 123 (S.C.) (majority shareholder siphoning off profits of corporation by claiming bonuses and management fees and corporation making unsecured interest-free loans); *Heyl v. Lac Minerals Ltd.* (1985), 50 O.R. (2d) 535 (H.C.), affd (1985), 52 O.R. (2d) 224 (note) (Div. Ct.) (failure to register individuals as shareholders); *Mazzotta v. Twin Gold Mines* (1987), 37 B.L.R. 218 (Ont. H.C.) (directors made private placement of a large number of shares without informing the minority shareholders despite knowing that they were interested in acquiring the shares and as a result the minority's position was diluted); *Palmer v. Carling O'Keefe Breweries of Canada Ltd.* (1989), 67 O.R. (2d) 161 (Div. Ct.) (vertical amalgamation which involved incurring debt leaving the corporation highly leveraged as a result was oppressive of the preference shareholders even though the shareholders' dividend entitlement was supported by an agreement with the parent corporation guaranteeing payment of the dividends); *Keho Holdings Ltd. v. Noble* (1987), 52 Alta. L.R. (2d) 195 (C.A.) (granting of stock option to majority shareholder and borrowing of money advanced to majority shareholder's personal corporation without security oppressive but allegations of exercise of control over corporation and exclusion of minority shareholder from management not oppressive as applicant failed to prove underlying participation tantamount to partnership); but see *Re Bird Precision Bellows Ltd.*, [1984] 3 All E.R. 444 (Ch. D.) (where the corporation was a quasi-partnership from the date of incorporation and there was an understanding that the petitioners would participate in the management of the corporation the denial of the right of participation was oppressive); *Brown v. MacFarlane* (unreported), Ont. H.C., Doc. No. Re 760/87, Rosenberg J., July 8, 1988, revd (June 9, 1989), Doc. No. 738/88 (Ont. Div. Ct.) (majority shareholder issued to itself special shares which paid substantial dividends and refused to give information to minority shareholder); *Chicago Blower Corp v. 141209 Canada Ltd.* (1988), 40 B.L.R. 201

(Man. Q.B.) (transfer of assets to corporation owned and controlled by majority shareholders in exchange for unsecured promissory note); *Welichka v. Bittner Investments Ltd.* (1988), 90 A.R. 224 (Q.B.) (the making of business decisions which favoured a holding corporation at the expense of an associated corporation of which the plaintiff was a minority shareholder); *Naaykens v. Bayes Equipment (Neepawa) Ltd.* (1988), 56 Man. R. (2d) 272 (Q.B.) (upon the taking over of the assets of a corporation in which the applicant was an officer and shareholder, no independent valuation occurred); *Metropolitan Commercial Carpet Centre Ltd. v. Donovan* (1989), 42 B.L.R. 306 (N.S. T.D.) (shareholders paid to themselves a management fee and a bonus and applicant paid no fee and bonus held in trust upon applicant leaving corporation's employ and starting competitive corporation); *PCM Construction Control Consultants Ltd. v. Heeger* (1989), 67 Alta. L.R. (2d) 302 (Q.B.) (plaintiff forced out of employment, continued briefly as director but excluded from decisions and information and remaining shareholders stripping corporation of assets); *Explo Syndicate v. Explo Inc.* (unreported), (June 29, 1989) Gravely L.J.S.C., Doc. Niagara North 6007/87 (Ont. H.C.) shareholders' agreement for the purchase of shares provided the plaintiff syndicate, an investment vehicle for minority shareholders, with representation on the board of directors of the target corporation; changes were effected to the management of the target corporation which had the effect of shutting the minority shareholders out of the management of the corporation); *Goguen v. Metro Oil Co.* (1989), 42 B.L.R. 30 (N.B. C.A.) (majority shareholder selling shares and removing assets from the corporation; minority shareholder's employment terminated and corporation refusing to purchase the shares granted pursuant to the minority shareholder's employment contract); *Oliver v. Ruge* (1989), 46 B.L.R. 50 (Ont. H.C.) (although there existed no written shareholders' agreement indicating a restriction on transfer which required approval, sale of the shares owned by the two directors was oppressive as shareholders owed fiduciary duty to other shareholders to advise of a transfer which passes control); but see *Brant Investments Ltd. v. Keeprite Inc.* (1991), 3 O.R. (3d) 289 (C.A.) (wherein it was held that majority shareholders owe no fiduciary duty to minority shareholders); *347883 Alberta Ltd. v. Producers Pipelines Inc.*, [1991] 4 W.W.R. 577 (Sask. C.A.), revg. [1991] 4 W.W.R. 151 (Sask. Q.B.) (where the applicant made a takeover bid and the corporate directors used an issuer bid and a shareholder rights agreement as a poison pill, the application to set aside the rights agreement was granted as the shareholder agreement was an attempt to force the issuer bid on the shareholders); *Loveridge Holdings Ltd. v. King-Pin Ltd.* (1991), 5 B.L.R. (2d) 195 (Ont. Gen. Div.), (where the respondent corporation made interest free, unsecured loans to corporations owned or controlled by other shareholder, such use of the respondent corporation was considered as unfairly prejudicial, even though there had been no intent to prejudice the applicant's rights and nothing illegal or dishonest had been done); *820099 Ontario Inc. v. Harold E. Ballard Ltd.* (1991), 3 B.L.R. (2d) 113 (Ont. Div. Ct.), affg. (1991), 3 B.L.R. (2d) 123 (Ont. Gen. Div.) (where the capital structure of the corporation was altered for the benefit of the majority shareholder, and the corporation purchased several pieces of the shareholder's real estate and issued common shares in return, the Court concluded that the major transactions had been undertaken without proper valuations and did not benefit the corporation. The directors had acted in an oppressive manner that unfairly disregarded the interests of a minority shareholder); *Millar v. McNally et al.* (1991), 3 B.L.R. (2d) 102 (Ont. Gen. Div.) (a 1/3 shareholder was effectively shut out of the running of the business, was not provided with notices of director and shareholder meetings, was given no information about the corporation and the remaining shareholders refused to purchase his shares when he ceased employment); *Doyle et al. v. Doyle et al.* (1991) 292 A.P.R. 75 (Nfld. T.D.) (mismanagement of corporate resources, mixing of personal expenses and corporate expenses by one of the shareholder/directors, failure to call shareholder meetings and to provide audited financial statements); *Hamilton v. Sartorio*, [1991] 3 W.W.R. 670 (Alta. Q.B.) (applicant's employment had been terminated, he had been excluded from the usual remuneration package and his bonus not paid by way of set off); *Rivers v. Denton* (1992), 5 B.L.R. (2d) 212 (Ont. Gen. Div.) (financial information not provided to shareholder, he was effectively shut out of meaningful participation in the corporation, and the corporation had failed to remit withholding taxes without his knowledge or assent and for which the directors could be personally liable); *Tilley and Alex Tilley Holdings Inc. v. Hails et al.* (1992) 7 O.R. (3d) 257 (Gen. Div.), varied (1992), 8 O.R. (3d) 169 (Div. Ct.), affd. (1992), 9 O.R. (3d) 255 (C.A.) (severe animosity developed between the two 50% shareholders and the respondent shareholder had harrassed the applicant to the point where the operation of the corporation was in jeopardy and trust and confidence had disappeared).

In the following cases, the actions complained of were held not to be oppressive or unfairly prejudicial or to constitute conduct which unfairly disregarded the interests of the applicant: *Case v. Edmonton Country Club Ltd.*, [1974] 5 W.W.R. 157 (Alta. T.D.) (proposal to consider a special resolution at extraordinary general meeting to transfer all the assets of the defendant corporation to another corporation, thus leaving the defendant corporation a holding corporation of the shares of the purchasing corporation); *Turner v. North Shore Taxi* (1980), 26 B.C.L.R. 367 (S.C.) (voting procedure for election of directors in which ballots provided on the basis of units of shares owned not oppressive); *de la Giroday v. Giroday Sawmills Ltd.* (1983), 49 B.C.L.R. 378 (S.C.) (articles amended for selective redemption of preferred shares not oppressive in a closely-held family business where these shares received by the petitioner were gifts); *Burnett v. Tsang* (1985), 29 B.L.R. 196 (Alta. Q.B.) (petitioner had been dismissed from a management position); *O'Connor v. Winchester Oil & Gas Inc.* (1986), 69 B.C.L.R. 330 (S.C.) (actions of defendant directors in negotiating share exchange offer with another corporation in which United States resident shareholders were excluded not oppressive or unfairly prejudicial because the directors' actions were based on bona fide legal advice suggesting that American securities law prevented the inclusion of American shareholders and prejudice to the exchange offer and significantly increased legal costs were avoided by excluding the American shareholders); *Dicore Resources Ltd. v. Goldstream Resources Ltd.* (1986), 2 B.C.L.R. (2d) 244 (S.C.)

(private placement of shares by directors resulting in loss of majority shareholding of the petitioners not oppressive or unfairly prejudicial as the petitioners had no vested right to retain control of the corporation); *Wotherspoon v. Canadian Pacific Ltd.*, [1987] 1 S.C.R. 952 (sale of land to subsidiary of majority shareholder not oppressive); *Callander v. Eveline Holdings Ltd.* (1987), 48 Man. R. (2d) 308 (Q.B.) (dividends withheld for reinvestment purposes not constituting unequal treatment where shareholders treated alike according to shareholders' agreement and the corporate by-laws and where the treatment was consistent with the financial state and performance of the corporation); *Stone v. Stonehurst Enterprises Ltd.* (1987), 202 A.P.R. 290 (N.B. Q.B.) (majority shareholder accepting lesser of two offers for purchase of corporation's assets not oppressive or unfairly prejudicial or unfairly disregarding minority shareholders' interests where the decision was an honest one made in the best financial interests of the corporation); *Bernard v. Montgomery* (1987), 36 B.L.R. 257 (Sask. Q.B.) (applicant disputed valuation placed on his shares where there was no evidence of wrongful collusion between shareholders or the parties doing the valuation); *General Accident Assurance Co. of Canada v. Lornex Mining Corp.* (1988), 40 B.L.R. 299 (Ont. H.C.) (an amalgamation squeeze-out is *prima facie* oppressive, but oppression is rebutted where a price in excess of two independent valuations is obtained); *Dancey v. 229281 Alberta Ltd.* (1988), 40 B.L.R. 180 (Alta. Q.B.) (corporation continued by special resolution without notice to applicant, applicant denied right to be a director, further borrowing of money without means to repay, and procedural flaws in share transfer); *Re A Corporation*, [1988] 1 W.L.R. 1068 (Ch. D.) (reinvesting of profits instead of payment of dividends has equal effect on all shareholders so not oppressive but may defeat a legitimate expectation thus justifying a winding-up order on just and equitable grounds); *Lindzon v. International Sterling Holdings Inc.* (1989), 45 B.L.R. 57 (B.C. S.C.) (allegations that corporation gratuitously paying a debt due from a third person to one of the directors without benefit to the corporation, that the corporation was selling its real property without shareholder approval, that advances were made to an affiliate in which the directors had a personal interest and without adequate security); *Camroux v. Armstrong* (1990), 47 B.L.R. 302 (B.C. S.C.) (majority shareholder failing to buy petitioner's shares at fair market value as stipulated in the petitioner's employment contract is mere breach of contract and not oppression); *Westfair Foods Ltd. v. Watt*, [1991] 4 W.W.R. 695 (Alta. C.A.) (corporation implementing new dividend policy whereby entire net earnings were distributed as dividends which had the effect of capping the break-up value of the shares and favouring the holders of the common shares, however, the corporation's conduct in not advising the shareholders of a pending delisting by the Toronto Stock Exchange and in characterizing the corporation as a wholly-owned subsidiary was considered to unfairly disregard the interests of the Class A shareholders); *Brant Investments Ltd. v. Keeprite Inc.* (1991), 3 O.R. (3d) 289 (C.A.) (the purchase of the assets of a subsidiary corporation, the acquisition cost to be raised by an issue of rights to existing shareholders); *Culford v. Carey Elite Limousine Service Ltd.* (1991), 115 A.R. 275 (Q.B.) (plaintiff shareholder, who was also director and officer, relinquished control of corporation but continued to be employed as manager brought application in respect of the actions of directors in firing plaintiff and removing her as officer and director. Because a lack of probity or fair dealing could not be established, the application was dismissed.).

Powers of the court re oppression

The Act grants the court broad remedial powers, and permits the court to make both interim and final orders. Specific powers are enumerated in the Act including the power to make an order:

(1) to restrain the conduct complained of;
(2) to appoint a receiver or a receiver-manager;
(3) to regulate the corporation's affairs by amending the articles or by-laws or creating or amending a unanimous shareholders' agreement;
(4) to direct the issue or exchange of securities;
(5) to appoint directors in place of or in addition to all or any of the directors then in office;
(6) to direct the corporation or other person to purchase securities of a security holder;
(7) to direct the corporation or other person to pay to a security holder any part of the moneys paid by him for securities;
(8) to vary or set aside a transaction or contract to which a corporation is a party and compensating the corporation or any other party to the transaction or contract;
(9) to require the corporation to produce financial statements;
(10) to compensate an aggrieved person;
(11) to direct the rectification of the register or other corporate records;
(12) to liquidate and dissolve the corporation (such order is also available pursuant to s. 214 of the federal Act);
(13) to direct an investigation; and
(14) to require the trial of any issue.

See the federal Act, s. 241(3); Ontario Act, s. 248(3). Certain of these orders are obviously extreme measures which may interfere significantly with the exercising of corporate management powers while other of the remedies are less drastic.

It has been held that even if a Court has jurisdiction to grant relief under this section, a court may refuse to intervene where the association of the parties was governed by a shareholder's agreement because deadlock was anticipated, and the agreement provided remedies in the event of deadlock. Those remedies and not those of the Court were to be invoked. See: *Korogonas v. Andrew*, [1992] 4 W.W.R. 399 (Alta. Q.B.).

Order restraining the conduct complained of

In *Re Peterson and Kanata Investments Ltd.* (1975), 60 D.L.R. (3d) 527 (B.C. S.C.), the court found that the granting of voting control through a share issue and the sale of the only substantial asset of the corporation was oppressive and therefore enjoined the special meeting of the shareholders to approve the sale until a new date for such a meeting was set by a new board of directors to be elected at the next annual meeting.

In *Re Alexander and Westeel-Rosco Ltd.* (1978), 4 B.L.R. 313 (Ont. H.C.), where the court found that the proposed amalgamation squeeze-out was oppressive of the minority shareholders, it was ordered that the convening of any shareholder meeting in respect of the proposed amalgamation be restrained and that the corporation be restrained from taking any steps in furtherance of the amalgamation. See also *Carlton Realty Co. v. Maple Leaf Mills Ltd.* (1978), 4 B.L.R. 300 (Ont. H.C.) and *Burdon v. Zeller's Ltd.* (1981), 16 B.L.R. 59 (Que. S.C.).

In *Ruskin v. Canada All-News Radio Ltd.* (1979), 7 B.L.R. 142 (Ont. H.C.), a minority shareholder applied to enjoin a proposed amalgamation. The court found that while the reorganization might have positive advantages for some of the respondents, it would be oppressive of the applicant who would suffer irreparable harm if the injunction was not granted. The injunction was granted restraining the respondents from taking any steps to carry out the decisions made at a shareholders' meeting held earlier that day and from acting on the certificate of amalgamation which had been procured by the respondents on the day of the application.

In *Re Little Billy's Restaurant (1977) Ltd.* (1983), 21 B.L.R. 246 (B.C. S.C.), the corporation paid franchise fees to a corporation owned by the majority before the actual franchise agreement was executed. The court ordered that the majority be enjoined from entering into the agreement so long as the majority owned and controlled the other corporation.

In *Ferguson v. Imax Systems Corp.* (1983), 150 D.L.R. (3d) 718 (C.A.), leave to appeal to S.C.C. refused (1983), 52 N.R. 317n, the proposed reorganization whereby the non-redeemable shares held by the applicant would be converted into redeemable shares and subsequently redeemed, which was motivated by a desire to force the shareholder out of the corporation was enjoined by the court. The corporation was forever restrained from implementing the resolution.

In *Heslop v. Heslop* (unreported), (December 5, 1985), Rowles L.J.S.C., (B.C. S.C.), an interim order was granted enjoining the directors from disposing of assets or taking any action to reduce the value of the corporation where the directors had threatened to abandon the corporation if the applicant exercised her rights as a shareholder.

In *Keho Holdings Ltd. v. Noble* (1987), 52 Alta. L.R. (2d) 195 (C.A.), the majority shareholder and the corporation were enjoined from exercising a share option.

In *Homestead Development Ltd. v. Lehman Resources Ltd.* (1988), 40 B.L.R. 1 (B.C. S.C.), a shareholder's resolution in which the incumbent board was voted out and replaced with another board was set aside and the incumbent board restored where the complainant shareholder alleged that an agreement had been reached that management was to remain with the founding shareholders.

Appointment of a receiver or receiver-manager

In *Re Peterson and Kanata Investments Ltd.* (1975), 60 D.L.R. (3d) 527 (B.C. S.C.), the court also found that the controlling shareholder had abused his control in order to personally profit at the expense of the corporation. The court, therefore, ordered that the shareholder sell his shares to the corporation in order that a new board of directors could be elected free of the influence of the shareholder. To assist in effecting this purpose, the court appointed a receiver-manager to hold office until the next annual meeting of the corporation was concluded.

A receiver was also appointed in *Inversiones Montfore S.A. v. Javelin International Ltd.* (1982), 17 B.L.R. 230 (Que. S.C.), for the period of time required for an investigation by the Restrictive Trade Practices Commission.

Where the controlling shareholder operated the corporation as if he were the only shareholder in disregard of the rights of other shareholders and with the effect that he took control of the corporation for his own benefit, the court ordered that he be removed as a director and officer of the corporation and a receiver-manager be appointed for an initial term of six months with full power to carry on the business and affairs of the corporation until such time as discharged by court order or the term of the appointment expired and a new board was elected: *Journet v. Superchef Food Industries Ltd.* (1984), 29 B.L.R. 206 (Que. S.C.).

Where the minority shareholder exercised control over the financial management of the corporation and had not accounted for the moneys received by the corporation, the petitioner was entitled to an order appointing a receiver and an inspector: *Cairney v. Golden Key Holdings Ltd. (No. 1)* (1987), 40 B.L.R. 263 (B.C. S.C.).

The appointment of a receiver was initially ordered in *Chicago Blower Corp. v. 141209 Canada Ltd.* (1988), 40 B.L.R. 201 (Man. Q.B.) additional reasons (1989), 56 Man. R. (2d) 316 as in Dureault J.'s view what was needed was management independent of the three directors who had caused the transfer of assets of the corporation to another corporation owned and controlled by them. However, in subsequent reasons the court substituted a different order upon submissions by the parties that the previous order would materially and adversely affect the intervenor, the Bank of Montreal.

Such an order was considered inappropriate in *Credit Foncier Franco-Canadien v. C.S.W. Enterprises Ltd.* (1986), 54 Sask. R. 97 (Q.B.). The majority shareholders had paid rent to themselves, made unauthorized loans and wilfully placed a mortgage in arrears; however, the court stated that although the managing shareholder had acted improperly or unreasonably, the situation did not warrant the appointment of a receiver-manager where there were other appropriate remedies available.

Amendment of articles, by-laws, and shareholders' agreements

There are few reported cases respecting amendments of a shareholders' agreement. An amendment of an existing shareholders' agreement to include a buy-out provision was not ordered where the shareholders' agreement had been in force for 20 years, entered into with the benefit of independent legal advice and represented a workable arrangement: *Lecce v. Lecce* (1990), 72 O.R. (2d) 540 (H.C.). An amendment to a unanimous shareholders' agreement was ordered in *Gillespie v. Overs* (unreported) (August 17, 1987) Sutherland J., (Ont. H.C.). The court ordered that a provision of the agreement which provided that Gillespie was to be president of Pizza Pizza Ltd. be deleted from the agreement on the basis that Gillespie had acted as president in a manner which was unfairly prejudicial to Overs. An amendment to a shareholders' agreement was ordered in *Explo Syndicate v. Explo Inc.* (unreported), (June 29, 1989), Gravely L.J.S.C., (Ont. H.C.). The court ordered that the agreement for the purchase of shares which provided for representation on the board of directors by members of the minority investors' syndicate be amended to provide that the agreement could be amended only by unanimous resolution of all shareholders.

It is noteworthy that the provisions of the Alberta Act are somewhat narrower in this regard and provide only that the articles and by-laws may be amended and that the amendment operates notwithstanding any unanimous shareholders' agreement. The Institute of Law Research and Reform in commenting on this provision was of the view that the Alberta Act should not follow the federal model. See Institute of Law Research and Reform, *Proposed Alberta Business Corporations Act* (1980), pp. 311-312.

In *Yok Wing Hui v. Yamato Japanese Steak House Inc.* (unreported), Ont. H.C., Gray J., January 6, 1988, the issuance of additional shares for nominal consideration which had the effect of reducing the majority shareholder's status to that of a minority shareholder was oppressive or unfairly prejudicial conduct and the court ordered the articles of incorporation amended to provide that no further shares could be issued without the consent of all the shareholders.

In *Daniels v. Fielder* (1988), 65 O.R. (2d) 629 (H.C.), the court ordered that the provisions of the corporate by-laws which provided for the chairman of the meeting to have a casting vote be deleted. The existence of a casting vote provision was considered inimical to the partnership basis upon which the two-man corporation had been operated prior to the death of one of the shareholders. In view of the fact that the granting of this particular relief could give rise to a deadlock and future applications to the court, further relief which is discussed below was granted.

In *Trnkoczy and Multi-Scale Charge Ltd. v. Shooting Chrony Inc.* (1991), 1 B.L.R. (2d) 202 (Ont. Gen. Div.), the corporate by-laws were ordered amended to remove the defendant Volk as manager of the corporation and vest management of the corporation in the control of the applicant.

In *Doyle et al v. Doyle et al* (1991), 292 A.P.R. 75 (Nfld. T.D.), it was ordered that the by-laws be amended to provide for a minimum number of 3 directors and that the non-redeemable voting preferred shares be made redeemable and non-voting.

If an order to amend the articles or by-laws of the corporation is made pursuant to s. 241(3), the Act requires the directors to submit articles of reorganization and no other amendment of the articles or by-laws is permitted without the consent of the court until ordered otherwise. See the federal Act, s. 241(4) and Ontario Act, s. 248(4). If an amendment to the articles is ordered by the court, that order prevents the shareholder from exercising his right to dissent, as discussed in Chapter 12.

Directing the corporation to purchase shares

This remedy may be granted in lieu of a winding-up order where there has been a loss of confidence, but where a remedy short of winding-up is desirable. However, both remedies are considered to be drastic measures and courts will strive to do equity without resorting to a forced purchase when possible: see *Heslop v. Heslop* (unreported), (December 5, 1985) Rowles L.J.S.C. (B.C. S.C.) and *Baniuk v. Carpenter* (1988), 228 A.P.R. 1 (N.B. Q.B.), revd in part (1989), 261 A.P.R. 196 (N.B. C.A.).

Any order made pursuant to s. 241(3)(f) and (g) is subject to s. 241(6) of the federal Act which provides that no payment can be made to a shareholder where there are reasonable grounds to believe that the corporation is or would after the payment be unable to pay its liabilities as they become due or where the realizable value of the corporation's assets would thereby be less than the aggregate of its liabilities. For a discussion of the principles of valuation, see Chapter 12.

The remedy is particularly appropriate where the complainant has been excluded from meaningful participation in the corporation. For example, where the plaintiffs had been removed as directors and prevented from transferring their shares, and assets were transferred to a corporation owned by the majority shareholder, the corporation and the majority shareholder were ordered to purchase the shares of the minority shareholders: *Miller v. F. Mendel Holdings Ltd.*, [1984] 2 W.W.R. 683 (Sask. Q.B.). See also *Re Bird Precision Bellows Ltd.*, [1984] 3 All E.R. 444 (Ch. D.), affd [1986] 2 W.L.R. 158 (C.A.) (where minority were removed from the board and denied their equitable right to participate in management, the court ordered the majority shareholder to purchase the shares of the minority); *Re Mason and Intercity Properties Ltd.* (1987), 59 O.R. (2d) 631 (C.A.) (where minority shareholder and director excluded from participation by the corporation president, the corporation was ordered to purchase the shares of the minority); *Eiserman v. Ara Farms Ltd.*, [1988] 5 W.W.R. 97 (Sask. C.A.) (plaintiff minority shareholder and director in a closely-held family farm resigned as director and employee where the course of conduct of the defendants had made continued participation intolerable and where plaintiff ceased to have any real management control); *Daniels v. Fielder* (1988), 65 O.R. (2d) 629 (H.C.) (forced purchase of the shares of the beneficiary of one of the 50 per cent shareholders by the other shareholder ordered by the court where the evidence did not justify a winding-up order as there was no evidence of mismanagement or of questionable dealings and the widow had little interest and had taken no role in the business; such relief was consistent with the provisions of the shareholders' agreement which had not been invoked by the surviving shareholder, and which contemplated the purchase of shares of a deceased shareholder by the survivor). In *Lajoie v. Lajoie Brothers Contracting Ltd.* (1989), 45 B.L.R. 113 (Ont. H.C.), where two brothers incorporated a corporation previously operated as a partnership and the applicant's participation was effectively terminated, the court ordered the corporation and the other shareholders to purchase his shares.

Where the minority shareholder was negotiating the purchase of his shares and the majority shareholder paid himself management fees which reduced the value of the shareholder's equity in the corporation and presented false financial information in an attempt to induce the petitioner to believe his shares were of little value, the court ordered the majority shareholder to purchase the shares of the petitioner at the value they would have had but for the defendant's oppressive actions: *Re National Building Maintenance Ltd.*, [1971] 1 W.W.R. 8 (B.C. S.C.), affd (*sub nom. National Building Maintenance Ltd. v. Dove*), [1972] 5 W.W.R. 410 (B.C. C.A.).

Where the corporation failed to hold annual meetings and to provide the minority shareholder with financial statements, improperly elected a director and dismissed the minority shareholder from its employ, the court held that there were no grounds for a "just and equitable" winding-up but ordered the corporation or its shareholders to purchase the minority's shares: *Meltzer v. Western Paper Box Co.* (1977), 3 B.L.R. 113 (Man. Q.B.).

Where the majority shareholder was guilty of a conflict of interest in using corporate assets for his own benefit and taking a maturing business opportunity from the corporation, the court ordered that the corporation or the majority shareholder purchase the shares of the minority: *Redekop v. Robco Construction Ltd.* (1978), 7 B.C.L.R. 268 (S.C.).

Where a shareholder in the securities business was required by law to sell his shares to his former employer before he could purchase shares in his new employer, and the former employer corporation elected to postpone the repurchase, the court ordered the corporation to purchase the shares, as no motive for the conduct of the corporation was suggested except to embarrass or punish the applicant: *Re Bury and Bell Gouinlock Ltd.* (1984), 12 D.L.R. (4th) 451 (Ont. H.C.), affd (1985), 14 D.L.R. (4th) 448 (Ont. Div. Ct.).

Where the shareholder had obtained an order that his shares be purchased either by the corporation or its directors at their choice, the shareholder sought an amendment to the order which required the purchase of the shares by a person other than the corporation in order to improve his tax position. The court held that amendment was inappropriate after the judgment had been relied upon by the respondents. Any tax advantage derived by the corporation from the purchase would be taken into account in the valuation: *Abraham v. Inter Wide Investments Ltd.* (1988), 55 D.L.R. (4th) 377 (Ont. H.C.).

In *Credit Foncier Franco-Canadien v. C.S.W. Enterprises Ltd.* (1986), 54 Sask. R. 97 (Q.B.) (as discussed above in respect of appointment of receivers), although the court was of the view that the appointment of a receiver-manager was inappropriate, the court ordered the majority to purchase the shares of the minority.

Where the corporation was highly leveraged as a result of a vertical amalgamation and the amalgamation was for the benefit of the parent corporation and of no benefit to the preference shareholders, the court ordered that the corporation redeem the preference shares at their redemption price:

Palmer v. Carling O'Keefe Breweries of Canada Ltd. (1989), 67 O.R. (2d) 161 (Div. Ct.).

Where the majority shareholder had removed assets from the corporation which had the effect of decreasing the value of the minority shareholder's shares, the minority shareholder's employment was terminated and the corporation refused to purchase his five per cent share interest, the court was of the view that in the circumstances it was appropriate to order the majority shareholder to purchase the shares: *Goguen v. Metro Oil Co.* (1989), 42 B.L.R. 30 (N.B. C.A.).

Where the Class A shareholders of a corporation disputed a new dividend policy which had the effect of capping the break-up value of the shares and favoured the holders of common shares, the directors had failed to respond to a letter from the Toronto Stock Exchange regarding delisting and the directors characterized the corporation as a wholly-owned subsidiary, while the shareholders had no expectation beyond their preferential dividend to profits, the other actions of the directors unfairly disregarded the interests of the Class A shareholders and the court ordered the forced purchase of the Class A shares by the corporation: *Westfair Foods Ltd. v. Watt*, [1991] 4 W.W.R. 695 (Alta. C.A.).

Where the applicant had been excluded from meaningful participation in the corporation and the respondent shareholders failed to purchase his shares when he ceased employment, the Court ordered the respondent shareholders to purchase the 1/3 interest of the applicant: *Millar v. McNally et al* (1991), 3 B.L.R. (2d) 102 (Ont. Gen. Div.).

Where the applicant's employment was terminated, he was excluded from the usual remuneration package and his bonus not paid by way of set-off, the corporation or the majority shareholder was ordered to purchase his shares: *Hamilton v. Sartorio*, [1991] 3 W.W.R. 670 (Alta. Q.B.).

Where two 50% shareholders had developed great animosity to one another and a deadlock had developed, the Court concluded that the respondent had been the cause of the deadlock and the applicant was therefore entitled to purchase the respondent's shares at fair market value. See: *Tilley and Alex Tilley Holdings Inc. v. Hails et al.* (1992), 7 O.R. (3d) 257 (Gen. Div.), varied (1992), 8 O.R. (3d) 169 (Div. Ct.), affd. (1992), 9 O.R. (3d) 255 (C.A.).

Where the applicant, a 50% shareholder alleged that a deadlock had developed with the respondent and sought an order winding-up the corporation, the Court refused such order on the basis that the corporation was conducting a viable business. Instead, the Court ordered that the respondent purchase the applicant's shares even though such relief had not been requested. See: *S.G. & S. Investments (1972) Ltd. v. Golden Boy Foods Inc.* (1991), 81 D.L.R. (4th) 649 (B.C. C.A.).

The order for the purchase of shares was not granted in *Jackman v. Jackets Enterprises Ltd.* (1977), 4 B.C.L.R. 358 (S.C.) where the minority shareholder had received the shares as a gift from the majority shareholder and the minority shareholder had never expected to share in the management of the corporation. Nor was the order granted in *Brown v. MacFarlane* (unreported), (Ont. H.C.), Doc. No. RE 760/87, Rosenberg J. (July 8, 1988), revd (June 9, 1989), Doc.

No. 738/88 (Ont. Div. Ct.), but the court ordered compensation for the improper declaration of dividends and in addition, a penalty of 100 per cent of the amount which was defalcated. On appeal, the Divisional Court ordered a trial of the issue, being of the view that on the particular facts of the case, a disposition based on affadavit evidence was inappropriate.

The remedy was not granted in *Baniuk v. Carpenter* (1988), 228 A.P.R. 1 (N.B. Q.B.), revd in part (1989), 261 A.P.R. 196 (N.B. C.A.), wherein the Court of Appeal stated that an order of buy-out of shares is a drastic remedy to be used in only the most serious and compelling of cases. In this case, the applicant could not realistically claim to lack confidence in the respondent's management abilities. See also *Heslop v. Heslop*, (unreported) (Decemberr 5, 1985), Rowles L.J.S.C. (B.C. S.C.) — in respect of the denial of financial information and dividends, the failure to register the complainant as a shareholder and the threats to cease operating the corporation, the Court ordered the production of financial information, rectification of the register and enjoined the directors from disposing of assets or acting to reduce the value of the corporation. Nor was this remedy ordered in *Loveridge Holdings Ltd. v. King-Pin Ltd.* (1991), 5 B.L.R. (3d) 195 (Ont. Gen. Div.), where the corporation was insolvent, however, the majority shareholder could be so ordered.

Order to pay to the security holder the moneys paid for the securities.

The order to pay moneys to the security holder is subject to the solvency test set out in s. 241(6) of the federal Act described above.

Where the plaintiff had been induced to invest $25,000 in the corporation, the court ordered the defendant to pay the $25,000 back to the plaintiff: *Welichka v. Bittner Investments Ltd.* (1988), 90 A.R. 224 (Q.B.).

Order varying or setting aside a contract or transaction and compensating complainant

In several cases, an oppressive or unfairly prejudicial issuance of shares has been set aside. See, for example, *Yok Wing Hui v. Yamato Japanese Steak House Inc.* (unreported), Ont. H.C., Gray J., January 6, 1988 (issuance of shares which had the effect of reducing the majority shareholder's interest to that of a minority shareholder set aside) and *Mazzotta v. Twin Gold Mines* (1987), 37 B.L.R. 218 (Ont. H.C.), where the board of directors of the defendant corporation authorized the sale of shares by private placement and the issue of shares had the effect of increasing the control of the corporation by the majority shareholder and his relatives, but where the minority had not been canvassed as to their willingness to pay a higher price, the minority interests had been disregarded and the court ordered the issue of shares set aside and that any profit received from the shares be accounted for.

Where the directors had paid themselves unusually large director fees and a portion of the fees were loaned to the corporation, the moneys were ordered repaid to the corporation: *Rowe v. National Wholesalers Ltd.* (1978), 22 Nfld. & P.E.I.R. 26 (Nfld. T.D.).

Where the corporation had paid franchise fees to another corporation owned by the majority, the resolution which approved the franchise agreement and the agreement itself were set aside: *Re Little Billy's Restaurant (1977) Ltd.* (1983), 21 B.L.R. 246 (B.C. S.C.).

In *Palmer v. Carling O'Keefe Breweries of Canada Ltd.* (1989), 67 O.R. (2d) 161 (Div. Ct.), the vertical amalgamation could not be unwound because of the passage of time and the undesirable tax consequences which would result and accordingly a redemption of the preference shares was ordered. See also the comment under the heading, "Directing the corporation to purchase shares," above.

Order to produce financial statements

The federal Act provides that the court may order the corporation to produce to the court or to any interested person financial statements or an accounting in another form as determined by the court. There is no definition of "interested person" in the Act, but it would likely include all those individuals who would otherwise qualify as a complainant. Such an order may be helpful in providing information previously unavailable to potential complainants which would indicate that further remedies may be desirable.

In *Jackman v. Jackets Enterprises Ltd.* (1977), 2 B.L.R. 335 (B.C. S.C.), notwithstanding that the plaintiff's shares had been acquired by way of gift and she had no legal or equitable right to be consulted on management, the directors were ordered to observe strictly the requirements of the British Columbia Act respecting the providing of information.

In *Burnett v. Tsang* (1985), 29 B.L.R. 196 (Alta. Q.B.) the complainant contended that she had been improperly dismissed from a management position and denied the right as a shareholder to participate in the affairs of the corporation. She sought a winding-up or alternatively a forced purchase of her shares in conjunction with an order to produce certain financial statements. The application was successful in part as she obtained an order for disclosure of financial statements and an accounting of funds.

Where the petitioner who acquired shares pursuant to a separation agreement was not provided with financial information, the share register had not been amended to reflect her shareholdings, and the principals of the corporation threatened to abandon the corporation if the petitioner attempted to exercise her rights as a shareholder, the court refused to grant the remedies of winding-up or the purchase of the petitioner's shares, but ordered the corporation to provide financial information: *Heslop v. Heslop* (unreported) (December 5, 1985), Rowles L.J.S.C., (B.C. S.C.).

Rectification of records

Section 243 of the federal Act provides for the rectification of records. If the name of a person is alleged to be or to have been wrongly entered or retained in, or wrongly deleted or omitted from the registers or records of a corporation, the corporation, a security holder or any aggrieved person may apply for an order of rectification. Upon such application being made, notification must be given to the Director who is entitled to appear. Rectification may also be granted in the following circumstances: rectification of registers or records where oppression has been proved (s. 241(3)(k)); rectification of proxies where a form of proxy, management proxy circular or dissident's proxy circular contains an untrue statement or a material fact or omits to state a material fact (s. 154(1)(b)); and rectification of take-over bid circulars, director's circulars or other documents where in connection with a take-over bid there has been non-compliance with the Act or regulations (s. 205(3)(b)). For a discussion of the latter two remedies, see Chapters 10 and 13, respectively.

In connection with an application for rectification, the court may make any order it sees fit including: (1) an order requiring the registers or other records of the corporation to be rectified; (2) an order restraining the corporation from calling or holding a meeting of shareholders or paying a dividend before such rectification; (3) an order determining the right of a party to the proceedings to have his name entered or retained in, or deleted or omitted from the registers or records of the corporation; and (4) an order compensating a party who has incurred a loss (see the federal Act, s. 243(3) and the Ontario Act, s. 250(2)).

In *Re British Columbia Aircraft Propeller & Engine Co.* (1968), 66 D.L.R. (2d) 628 (B.C. S.C.), the petitioner had entered into an agreement which allowed him to purchase 25 per cent of the shares held by the respondent. A share certificate was drawn up, but destroyed by the respondent. The petitioner applied for rectification of the register and the claim was granted as the applicant was entitled under the agreement to a transfer of the shares.

Where a corporation was incorporated to be owned equally by three shareholders, and one shareholder, as president and manager of the corporation, directed the corporate solicitor to change the records in order that he obtain far in excess of his one-third shares, an order of rectification was granted and the records amended to reflect the proper one-third shareholdings of each shareholder: *Davis v. Davis* (1981), 9 Man. R. (2d) 236 (Q.B.).

In *Mitchell v. Miller* (1983), 21 Sask. R. 407 (C.A.) the only voting share of a holding corporation was bequeathed to the respondent by her father although no formal transfer occurred. She applied to be registered as a shareholder and the order was granted by the lower court. The applicant, another daughter, appealed this order requesting that the share be jointly held by both herself and the respondent. The appeal was dismissed as the deceased father clearly intended that the respondent control the holding corporation. An order was granted to register the respondent as holder of the voting share.

Where the petitioner acquired shareholdings under the terms of a separation agreement, but the corporation, of which the petitioner's husband was the principal, refused to amend the share register, the court ordered that the register be amended to reflect the petitioner's interest: *Heslop v. Heslop*, unreported (December 5, 1985), Rowles L.J.S.C. (B.C. S.C.).

In *Mathers v. Mathers* (1989), 230 A.P.R. 354 (N.S. C.A.), two brothers acted as directors of a corporation but the articles of association required there to be three directors. One brother transferred a share to his wife. The other brother objected and applied to strike out the wife's registration as invalid on the basis that there were only two directors. The court dismissed the application on the basis that there was no requirement in the articles of association that the directors approve a share transfer validly made.

Where the relief sought is the substitution of the applicant on the register as owner in the place of some other person, that other person is a necessary party: *Ontario Jockey Club Ltd. v. McBride*, [1927] A.C. 916 at 918. But in an action for damages for wrongful removal of the plaintiff's name from the register the person whose name has been substituted on the register need not and should not be joined as a defendant: *Lovibond v. G.T.R.*, [1936] 3 D.L.R. 449 at 460. Directors are not necessary or proper parties to a motion for rectification: *In re Keith Prowse & Co.*, [1918] 1 Ch. 487.

No doubt s. 243 is not to be invoked except in a reasonably clear case: *Gramm Motor Truck Co. v. Bennett* (1914), 35 O.L.R. 224 (C.A.). See also *Lorsch & Co. v. Shamrock Consolidated Mines Ltd.* (1917), 39 O.L.R. 315 (C.A.) (where an order was made under the corresponding section of the former Ontario Act directing registration); *Scott v. Frank F. Scott (London) Ltd.*, [1940] Ch. 794 (C.A.) (executrix entitled to rectification by substituting her name for that of the testator in whose name the shares stood); *Re Champion & White Ltd.*, [1943] 1 D.L.R. 283 (B.C. S.C.), revd on other grounds, [1943] 2 D.L.R. 145 (B.C. C.A.) (application under the former British Columbia *Companies Act* for an order that the register of members be rectified by entering the name of the petitioner, a purchaser of shares in a private corporation); *Warren v. Union Gas Co. of Canada*, [1943] 4 D.L.R. 668 (Ont. C.A.) (question of validity or interpretation of a provision of the Ontario *Succession Duty Act* not to be determined on a motion for rectification of books); *Re Imperial Hotel Ltd.* (1956), 19 W.W.R. 132 (B.C. S.C.) (an application under the British Columbia *Companies Act* for an order that the name of a shareholder be removed from the share register was dismissed); *Moodie v. Shepherd (Bookbinders) Ltd.*, [1949] 2 All E.R. 1044 (H.L.) (executors entitled to be registered where the directors had invalidly exercised the right to refuse which was given them under the articles).

The former Ontario Act did not enable the court to relieve a shareholder declared to be such in the charter: *Re J. A. French & Co.* (1910), 1 O.W.N. 864, vard (1910), 2 O.W.N. 498 (C.A.); but on the appeal rectification of the register was permitted by reducing the applicant's holding to one share.

The powers of the court under s. 243 are exercisable whether the corporation is in liquidation or not: *In re Sussex Brick Co.*, [1904] 1 Ch. 598 (C.A.).

On an application by a shareholder an order was made under the former Ontario Act for the rectification of the share register by restoring to it the names of a number of shareholders whose names had been deleted pursuant to a resolution of the board of directors. The shares in question had been issued in apparent conformity with the terms on which all the shares of the same class had been issued and it was held that the board of directors was not entitled summarily to determine that the holders were not and never had been properly on the register without giving them an opportunity to be heard, where it was known that such holders were asserting or attempting to assert their rights as such: *Guest v. Dominion Royalty Corp.*, [1933] O.W.N. 379. Garrow J. said at

p. 380 that no doubt in a plain case the directors would be justified in causing obvious errors to be rectified.

Directors who had refused to register a transfer of shares were held personally liable for the costs of the application brought to rectify the register, there being evidence of bad faith on their part in the refusal: *Re Shoal Harbour Marine Service Ltd.* (1956), 20 W.W.R. 312 (B.C. S.C.), vard (1956), 20 W.W.R. 448 (B.C. S.C.).

Notwithstanding long delay an order for rectification may be made: *Montgomery v. Beardmore* (1929), 36 O.W.N. 99; *Cooper v. Cayzor Athabaska Mines Ltd.* (1960), 24 D.L.R. (2d) 544 (Ont. C.A.). But laches and acquiescence may defeat a claim made for rectification of the register by adding the plaintiff's name as a shareholder: *Patterson v. Vulcan Iron Works Ltd.*, [1929] 4 D.L.R. 508 (B.C. S.C.), affd, [1930] 2 D.L.R. 961 at 973 (B.C. C.A.). Rectification may be ordered where an allottee proceeds promptly upon ascertaining that the shares were illegally issued: *Twigg v. Thunder Hill Mining Co.* (1893), 3 B.C.R. 101. Where, however, the shareholder's name had been taken off the register in consequence of an alleged release of the shareholders from liability involving a purchase by the corporation of its own shares, the court directed the plaintiff's name to be restored, after a lapse of years, the shares not having in the meantime been reissued or otherwise dealt with by the corporation: *Bellerby v. Rowland & Marwood's Steamship Co.*, [1902] 2 Ch. 14 (C.A.).

Liquidation and dissolution

An order of liquidation and dissolution is the most extreme remedy provided for in the Act. Winding-up of the corporation on grounds of oppression is also provided for in s. 214 of the federal Act. A winding-up remedy is also applicable to non-share capital corporations: *Sobrinho v. Oakville Portuguese Canadian Club* (1982), 37 O.R. (2d) 581 (H.C.).

Where there were irregularities in the keeping of corporation records, one of the applicants had been dismissed from his employment with one of the corporations and it was alleged that financial statements had not been provided, the applicants alleged that the conduct of the respondent was oppressive and unfairly prejudicial. The court found that the majority shareholder had turned the corporation into a successful business, was justified in terminating the employment of one of the minority shareholders, and had offered the minority shareholders a good price for their shares. The application for winding-up was dismissed and the court ordered the majority shareholder to purchase the shares of the applicants after an independent valuation: *Meltzer v. Western Paper Box Co.*, [1978] 1 W.W.R. 451 (Man. Q.B.).

Where the majority shareholders used a holding corporation to maintain the profitability of another corporation in which they had an interest, the scheme was oppressive to minority interests and a winding-up order was granted: *Fedoruk v. Fedoruk Holdings Ltd.*, [1978] 6 W.W.R. 40 (Man. Q.B.).

In *Burnett v. Tsang* (1985), 29 B.L.R. 196 (Alta. Q.B.), the petitioner, an employee, shareholder and director, was not successful in obtaining a winding-up order, but the court did order the corporation to produce certain financial statements and to account for the funds it had received and expended. The petitioner's employment as manager had been terminated and she was removed as a director of the corporation. She alleged that her wrongful dismissal justified a winding-up order, either on just and equitable grounds or because the dismissal was oppressive. The court held that the actions of the corporation were not oppressive or unfairly prejudicial to the petitioner, nor did they unfairly disregard her interests as director.

In *Stech v. Davies* (1987), 53 Alta. L.R. (2d) 373 (Q.B.), the winding-up order was refused. In this case, Stech and Davies were equal partners in two corporations. Because the relationship had deteriorated, each offered to buy the other's interest in one of the corporations but were unable to come to terms. Davies took certain financial steps which resulted in a large tax liability for Stech. He also refused to provide Stech with financial information concerning both of the corporations. The court held that an order of liquidation was not in the best interests of either party. While the actions of Davies were oppressive or unfairly prejudicial to or unfairly disregarded the interests of Stech, the court was of the view that the fairest and most equitable way to settle the dispute would be to make an order pursuant to s. 234 whereby Davies would end up owning the total number of shares in one of the corporations and Stech would own the total number of shares in the other corporation.

In *Keho Holdings Ltd. v. Noble* (1987), 52 Alta. L.R. (2d) 195 (C.A.), the court refused to invoke the drastic step of dissolution. In this case, a loan had been made to a corporation owned by the majority shareholder and a share option had been granted to the majority shareholder. The court was of the view that the share option was oppressive and unfairly prejudicial to the respondents and that there was a loss of confidence in management. In the circumstances, the court made an order pursuant to s. 234 of the Act that the share option be cancelled and the loan repaid or security given within 30 days.

Where the plaintiff was excluded from the operation of the business, there had been an improper share transfer and appointment of a director, and the defendant refused to exercise the right to buy out the plaintiff's interest, the conduct was oppressive but the remedy of winding-up was not granted. There was no evidence of financial mismanagement and what the plaintiff wanted was a forced purchase of shares: *Daniels v. Fielder* (1988), 65 O.R. (2d) 629 (H.C.).

In *Westfair Foods Ltd. v. Watt* (1991), 79 Alta. L.R. (2d) 363 (C.A.), affg (1990), 73 Alta. L.R. (2d) 326 (Q.B.), a winding-up order or alternatively the forced repurchase of the respondent's Class A shares by the appellant corporation was sought. The Class A shareholders had complained that a significant portion of the earnings of the corporation had been retained and the net annual earnings had been paid as dividends. The Class A shareholders were only entitled to a $2 preferential dividend. The court held that the Class A shareholders had no reasonable expectation beyond the preferential dividend. The failure of the directors to increase the amount of the Class A shareholders' fixed dividend was not oppressive, unfairly prejudicial, nor did it unfairly disregard the interests of the Class A shareholders. However, the failure to inform shareholders of a pending Toronto Stock Exchange delisting and a characterization of the corporation as a wholly-owned subsidiary justified an order that the corporation repurchase the Class A shares.

In *Doyle et al v. Doyle et al* (1991), 292 A.P.R. 75 (Nfld. T.D.), the Court held that if its other orders proved ineffective within 9 months, then a winding-up was ordered.

In *Rivers v. Denton* (1992), 5 B.L.R. (2d) 212 (Ont. Gen. Div.), the lack of financial information provided would not be a ground for dissolution, however it was part of a pattern of exclusion of the applicant from important decision making. Where decisions had been made that exposed the applicant to personal liability and destroyed the trust and confidence between the partners, a winding-up order was granted notwithstanding that the corporation had recently become marginally profitable.

In *Korogonas v. Andrew*, [1992] 4 W.W.R. 399 (Q.B.), additional reasons at (1992), 3 Alta. L.R. (3d) 8 (Q.B.), Veit J. refused to grant a winding-up order concluding that where a corporation is in a strong financial position, winding-up should not be considered. See also: *S.G. & G. Investments (1972) Ltd. v. Golden Boy Foods Inc.* (1991), 81 D.L.R. (4th) 649 (B.C. C.A.).

Section 214 of the federal Act provides that winding-up may be obtained on just and equitable grounds. Winding-up on just and equitable grounds is also provided for in the federal *Winding-up Act.* Such an order may be made in the following circumstances: (1) where a considerable proportion of the shareholders have justifiably lost confidence in the management of the corporation's affairs and the directors have a preponderance of voting power; (2) where the subject matter of the business for which the corporation was incorporated has disappeared (substratum lost); (3) where the affairs of a corporation are brought to a deadlock; (4) and where the corporation is analogous to a partnership and circumstances such as animosity would justify dissolution of a partnership.

Loss of confidence

With respect to lack of confidence in management, it has been held that a lack of confidence must not arise from dissatisfaction at being outvoted on the domestic policy of the corporation: *Re R.C. Young Insurance Ltd.*, [1955] O.R. 598 (C.A.). There must be some reason founded upon the wrongful actions of those in control: *Re Florentine Co.* (1926), 31 O.W.N. 70; *Re Sydney & Whitney Pier Bus Service Ltd.*, [1944] 3 D.L.R. 468 at 473 (N.S. S.C.); *Re James Lumbers Co.* (1925), 58 O.L.R. 100; *Re Toronto Finance Corp.* (1930), 65 O.L.R. 351; *Re Martello & Sons Ltd.*, [1945] O.R. 453 (C.A.); *Bannerman v. Concrete Column Clamps Ltd.*, [1953] Que. S.C. 107; *Re Columbia Gypsum Co.* (1958), 17 D.L.R. (2d) 280 (B.C. S.C.).

The following cases illustrate circumstances which were held to establish a justifiable lack of confidence; *In re Amalgamated Syndicate*, [1897] 2 Ch. 600 (directors were contemplating embarking on business that was *ultra vires* the corporation); *Thompson v. Drysdale*, [1925] S.C. 211 (majority shareholder was acting on the basis that the whole assets of the corporation belonged to him); *In re Davis & Collett Ltd.*, [1935] Ch. 693 (director of a private corporation was endeavouring by irregularities to acquire complete control and exclude other directors from management); *In re Companies Act; Delip Singh v. Moody Shingles Ltd.*, [1947] 1 W.W.R. 480 (B.C. C.A.) (no general meeting of the corporation had been held for 10 years, no proper books had been kept and assets of corporation were being sold to one of the directors).

Where the control of a public corporation was in the hands of a new interest group and in the first week of its administration the single valuable asset of the corporation was liquidated without explanation, an order of winding-up was granted. A duty of fair dealing devolves upon those who take control of a public corporation: *Re J.R. Jowsey Mining Co.*, [1969] 2 O.R. 549 (C.A.), affg [1969] 1 O.R. 437 (H.C.).

Where the petitioner complained that a majority shareholder had secretly and wrongfully paid to himself management fees, thus reducing the value of the shareholders' equity in the corporation and falsely prepared balance sheets, such conduct was oppressive to the petitioner in his capacity as a shareholder. This was a case where because of a complete lack of confidence engendered by such conduct, a winding-up order was justified. Such an order would, however, unfairly prejudice the petitioner since it would not give him the relief he sought in respect of his essential complaint, namely, the wrongful taking of the management fees. The petitioner was entitled to an order that the majority shareholder buy all of the petitioner's shares on the basis of a valuation of his shares as of the date of the petition: *Re National Building Maintenance Ltd.*, [1971] 1 W.W.R. 8 (B.C. S.C.); affd (*sub nom. National Building Maintenance Ltd. v. Dove*) [1972] 5 W.W.R. 410 (B.C. C.A.).

Where the applicant, an employee of the corporation and a 50 per cent shareholder, had been dismissed for alcohol-related problems, and the other shareholders transferred the corporation's inventory to another corporation owned by themselves, the application for winding-up was granted. There had been a freeze-out of the plaintiff and improper conduct leading to a lack of confidence in the management of the corporation: *Rafuse v. Bishop* (1979), 34 N.S.R. (2d) 70 (T.D.).

In *Dunwoody Ltd. v. 358074 Ontario Ltd.* (1984), 5 O.A.C. 288 (Div. Ct.), revg (1983), 45 C.B.R. (N.S.) 136 (Ont. S.C.), the order for winding-up was allowed where the following acts of a director were considered to give rise to a justifiable loss of confidence: payment to director of excessive salaries, dividends and unsecured personal loans; purchase of luxury items and transfer of those items into the director's name; causing the loss of real estate holdings; and causing the corporation to provide benefits to a corporation owned by the director.

Where one of two equal shareholders disposed of property owned by the corporation without the knowledge and consent of the beneficiary of the other shareholder's estate, there was a loss of trust and confidence sufficient to warrant an order of liquidation and dissolution: *Reznick v. Bilecki* (1986), 49 Sask. R. 232 (C.A.).

The refusal by the directors of a private corporation to register the executors of a deceased shareholder, in the absence of evidence of improper exercise of their discretion, is insufficient to justify a winding-up order on this ground: *Re Cuthbert Cooper & Sons Ltd.*, [1937] Ch. 392.

A dissatisfied minority shareholder is not entitled to a winding-up order on the ground that the corporation's undertaking is so speculative and hazardous that the corporation should not be permitted to continue: *Re Jury Gold Mine Development Co.* (1928), 63 O.L.R. 109 (C.A.) and *Re Hugh-Pam Porcupine Mines Ltd.*, [1942] O.W.N. 544 (situation falling short of deadlock).

Where the applicant had been a shareholder in the corporation for only two years and had paid only a small portion of the purchase price for his shares and was in default thereof, and the other shareholder had been a shareholder for 25 years and the evidence indicated that winding-up would cause much damage to the business and benefit competitors, the application was refused: *Higgins v. Brock & Higgins Insurance Agencies Ltd.* (1976), 22 C.B.R. (N.S.) 248 (Ont. S.C.).

The dismissal, by two of the three equal shareholders in a private corporation, of the third shareholder as managing director and his removal from the board because of an honest dissatisfaction with his services and his policies is not, by itself, a ground for ordering the corporation wound up under the just and equitable rule: *Scott v. Northland Beverages (1956) Ltd.* (1960), 31 W.W.R. 287 (B.C. C.A.).

But where the plaintiff was a director and one of three equal shareholders in a corporation, and the plaintiff had been dismissed from employment with the corporation, effectively removed from management and had received no information regarding the conduct of the affairs of the corporation, the order for winding-up was granted: *Strickland v. Tricom Associates (1979) Ltd.* (1982), 38 Nfld. & P.E.I.R. 451 (Nfld. T.D.).

Mere dissension within the corporation is not sufficient to justify a winding-up order on the ground of lack of confidence. In such cases the remedy of the shareholders is by action: *Re Harris-Maxwell Larder Lake Gold Mining Co.* (1910), 1 O.W.N. 984; *Re Jury Gold Mine Development Co.* (1928), 63 O.L.R. 109 (C.A.); *Re Sovereign Oil Co.*, [1934] 3 W.W.R. 317 (B.C. S.C.); *Re Winnipeg Saddlery Co.* (1935), 42 Man. R. 448. Where the dispute amounted to a domestic policy quarrel, the application was refused. The applicant lacked "clean hands" where he had over-reacted to trivial incidents: *Jordan v. McKenzie* (1980), 30 O.R. (2d) 705 (H.C.).

As to the unsatisfactory position of minority shareholders, see *Re Imperial Steel & Wire Co.* (1919), 17 O.W.N. 324. In *Noden Hallitt v. Johnson Ltd.* (1924), 26 O.W.N. 269 (H.C.), leave to appeal refused (1924), 26 O.W.N. 330 (C.A.), a minority shareholder's petition was dismissed where he could not show that the majority had acted fraudulently or dishonestly.

In the absence of fraud, loss of confidence by one of the three shareholders in the conduct and management of the corporation's affairs by the remaining shareholders is not in itself a ground to justify an order winding-up the corporation. Extricating a shareholder from a poor investment is not a proper ground for winding-up: *Re Chetal Enterprises Ltd.* (1973), 39 D.L.R. (3d) 116 (Sask. Q.B.).

An order was denied where the petitioning shareholders alleged mismanagement and that the corporate powers had been violated but could not establish fraud, bad faith, or a lack of probity on the part of the directors or management and where the evidence did not show a lack of confidence: *Shacket v. Universal Factors Corp.* (1966), 10 C.B.R. (N.S.) 166 (Que. S.C.); *B. Love Ltd. v. Bull Steel & Salvage Ltd.* (1982), 38 O.R. (2d) 691, additional reasons (1982), 40 O.R. (2d) 1 (H.C.).

Where one-eighth of the corporation's shares had been sold to an employee and the majority shareholders retained the right to repurchase the shares if the employee ceased his employment with the corporation, a winding-up order was not granted upon the termination of the shareholder's employment. There was no evidence that the majority shareholders had been guilty of any misconduct: *Re D & D Holdings Ltd.*, [1981] 4 W.W.R. 13 (Alta. Q.B.).

Where the minority shareholder was entitled to a 25 per cent interest in the corporation and the respondent destroyed the share certificate and procured the minority shareholder's dismissal as manager and his removal as director, the just and equitable ground could not be utilized merely because of changes in the board of directors or dismissal of employees: *Re B.C. Aircraft Propeller and Engine Co.* (1968), 63 W.W.R. 80 (B.C. S.C.).

Loss of substratum

Where the substratum of the corporation is gone, the court may order a winding-up: *In Re Haven Gold Mining Co.* (1882), 20 Ch. D. 151 (C.A.); *Re Hamilton Ideal Manufacturing Co.* (1915), 34 O.L.R. 66; *Dominion Trust Co. v. Boyce* (1917), 43 D.L.R. 538 (B.C. C.A.), affd (*sub nom. Macpherson v. Boyce*) (1919), 59 S.C.R. 691; *Re Blériot Manufacturing Aircraft Co.* (1916), 32 T.L.R. 253 (substratum gone: proven misconduct by director); *Marzitelli v. Verona Construction Ltd.* (1979), 33 C.B.R. (N.S.) 180 (Que. S.C.). In *Re Coolgardie Consolidated Gold Mines Ltd.* (1911), 13 T.L.R. 301, Lindley L.J. said that the court ought to look at whether the primary object had failed so that the substratum was gone not merely as lawyers but as businessmen, and in so doing, came to the conclusion that the framers of the memorandum of association had the working of a particular property in view.

In *Re British Empire Steel Corp.*, [1927] 2 D.L.R. 964 (N.S. T.D.), the court was asked to decide that it was just and equitable to wind up the corporation on the ground of loss of confidence, loss of substratum and impairment of capital. The corporation was a holding corporation. The petitioner was a minority shareholder and the majority of the shareholders opposed the application. The corporation controlled a number of corporations, one of which on the ground of jeopardy had been placed in the hands of a receiver. The court refused assent to the proposition that when such was the case the substratum of the holding corporation was necessarily gone. As to impairment of capital, it was held unless destruction of substratum was thereby caused, this was a matter to be left to the shareholders to deal with.

The mere fact that there has been depreciation in the value of the assets or that the assets have become frozen does not establish that the substratum has disappeared: *Re Toronto Finance Corp.* (1930), 65 O.L.R. 351. Nor was the substratum gone where the ability of corporation to achieve its objects was still a question of speculation: *Re Columbia Gypsum Co.* (1958), 17 D.L.R. (2d) 280 (B.C. S.C.).

Where a corporation had been incorporated with wide powers, but its principal business which had been dealing in second mortgages on real estate had become unprofitable and it was the professed intention of the directors, or some of them, to engage in other lines of business, it was held that it could not be said that the substratum was gone, on the ground that when a corporation is established for several purposes it may abandon one of them and carry on the others: *Re Toronto Finance Corp.* (1930), 65 O.L.R. 351 (following *Re Norwegian Titanic Iron Co.* (1865), 35 Beav. 223).

It was alleged in another case that an insurance corporation had lost the substance of its insurance business, that its assets were mainly frozen, that the corporation had changed its nature from that of an active insurance corporation to a holding corporation and that it had little prospect of regaining its insurance business or property. The corporation, however, had made a vigorous attempt to rebuild its insurance business, liquidate its frozen assets and regain its true ends. Some progress had been made although it could not be determined whether the attempt would be successful. The vast majority of shareholders opposed the petition. Under these circumstances it was held that a case had not been made out for a winding-up order on the just and equitable ground: *Re Canada National Fire Insurance Co.*, [1930] 3 W.W.R. 113 (Man. K.B.), leave to appeal refused [1930] 3 W.W.R. 209 (Man. C.A.).

In *Marzitelli v. Verona Construction Ltd.* (1979), 33 C.B.R. (N.S.) 180 (Que. S.C.), where the corporation had not pursued its principal object since 1975, the corporation had existed since that time for the primary benefit of its principal shareholder and its assets had diminished appreciably, a winding-up order was granted on the basis that the substratum of the corporation had disappeared. The court noted that generally an application to wind up on this basis should not be granted where the sole motive of the applicant is to recover their investment. In the present instance, the corporation was not operating and had suffered serious losses. Under these circumstances, minority shareholders wanted to assure themselves that they would recover as much of their investment as possible. There was no indication of bad faith on their part and it did not preclude an application for winding-up.

Where two of a corporation's operating subsidiaries were bankrupt, two were inactive and some of the corporation's real estate property had been sold, the substratum of the corporation was gone and an order for winding-up was justified. A solvent corporation may be wound up where its substratum has failed: *Dunwoody Ltd. v. 358074 Ont. Ltd.* (1984), 5 O.A.C. 288 (Div. Ct.).

If a material part of the substratum is gone, then the court will look at all the other circumstances in order to see whether it is just and equitable to wind up the corporation. That the corporation was fraudulent from its inception and that a winding-up order was the best means of enabling defrauded shareholders to recover their money was held material: In *Re Thomas Edward*

Brinsmead & Sons, [1897] 1 Ch. 45; affd [1897] 1 Ch. 406 (C.A.). But an order has been refused where a mining corporation still retained its property and there was still a means of working it under the charter: *Re Harris Maxwell Larder Lake Gold Mining Co.* (1910), 1 O.W.N. 984. See also the following cases where a material part of the substratum was gone and the court looked at other circumstances to ascertain whether it was just and equitable to wind up the corporation: *Re Suburban Hotel Co.* (1867), L.R. 2 Ch. App. 737; *Re Red Rock Gold Mining Co.* (1889), 61 L.T. 785; *Re Anglo-Mexican Mint Co.*, [1875] W.N. 168; *In re Crown Bank* (1890), 44 Ch. D. 634; *Re Florida Mining Co.* (1901), 9 B.C.R. 108 (C.A.).

Deadlock

The third basis for winding-up on just and equitable grounds is deadlock. See *Re Sailing Ship Kentmere*, [1897] W.N. 58; *Re Town Topics Co.* (1911), 20 Man. R. 574 at 578 (K.B.); *In re American Pioneer Leather Co.*, [1918] 1 Ch. 556; *Re Bondi Better Bananas Ltd.*, [1951] O.R. 845 (C.A.); *Prussin v. Park Distributors Inc.* (1963), 6 C.B.R. (N.S.) 31 (Que. S.C.); *Re Humberbank Investment Development Ltd.* (1972), 17 C.B.R. (N.S.) 220 (Ont. S.C.) (where two groups equally shared control and capital and there were serious and persistent disagreements with respect to questions relating to the management of the corporation and normal operations became impossible, there was deadlock); *Kelly v. Condon* (1986), 190 A.P.R. 196 (Nfld. T.D.) (where a 50 per cent shareholder was denied information about the corporation's assets and the corporation's failure to sell any of its 240 holdings, the differences between the two majority shareholders resulted in a complete deadlock as to the operation of the business and a winding-up order was granted); *Cablecasting (Manitoba) Ltd. v. Selkirk Communications Ltd.* (1987), 50 Man. R. (2d) 225 (C.A.), revg (1986), 50 Man. R. (2d) 227 (Q.B.) (where two corporations were 50 per cent shareholders, there was a conflict over the management of the corporation and the parties were deadlocked on how to resolve the issue of mismanagement, a winding-up order was granted).

In *Re Jury Gold Mine Development Co.* (1928), 63 O.L.R. 109 at 111 (C.A.), Middleton J.A., delivering the judgment of the court, quoted with approval the explanation of what is meant by deadlock given in *Symington v. Symington's Quarries Ltd.* (1906), 8 Sess. Cas. (5th series) 121 at 129:

> The situation referred to is one analogous to that existing in a partnership where there is a small number of persons equally or nearly equally divided, so that it is impossible that the business of the company can be carried on. "That is a rule that would very seldom be applicable to a company under the Companies Act — never certainly where the company appeals to the public for subscription to its shares — because if the directors are equally divided, or if there is such a division as makes it difficult to carry on the company's affairs, the remedy of the shareholders is to turn them out and to elect a harmonious board of directors."

Even a position short of a complete deadlock may suffice: *Re Yenidje Tobacco Co. Ltd.*, [1916] 2 Ch. 426 (C.A.) (corporation was carrying on business but the only two shareholders and directors became so hostile that neither would speak to the other); *Re Winding-up Ordinance and Timbers Ltd.* (1917), 35 D.L.R. 431 (Alta. C.A.) (the applicant holding 49 per cent of the shares was deprived of all voice in the management of the corporation's affairs); *St. Joseph Lithuanian Benefit Society v. Wasilianskas* (1924), 27 O.W.N. 318 (C.A.) (irreconcilable attitude of two factions); *Re White Castle Inn Ltd.*, [1946] O.W.N. 773 (order made on the ground of substantial deadlock where two shareholders owned the shares in practically equal proportions, although one had a casting vote as president).

The court has refused to make an order though apparently there was a deadlock: *Re Dewey & O'Heir Co.* (1909), 13 O.W.R. 32 at 38 (C.A.) (deadlock caused by domestic quarrel precipitated by applicant for the winding-up); *Re Shipway Iron Bell & Wire Manufacturing Co.* (1926), 58 O.L.R. 585 (deadlock caused by domestic quarrel and substantial majority opposed to the winding-up of the corporation); *Morton v. Aspe* (1989), 62 Man. R. (2d) 1 (Q.B.).

An alleged deadlock, caused by the petitioners, was held under the circumstances not to constitute a ground for a winding-up order: *Re James Lumbers Co.* (1925), 58 O.L.R. 101. Where the deadlock was only temporary, the court refused to make a winding-up order: *Re Toronto Finance Corp.* (1930), 65 O.L.R. 351. There must be an existing material deadlock and therefore where the deadlock has been resolved at the time of the application, there was no basis for a winding-up order: *Re Welport Investments Ltd.* (1985), 31 B.L.R. 232 (Ont. H.C.). And where on appeal the court reached the conclusion that, with the exercise of tolerance and good sense, there was no reason why the alleged deadlock should continue, a winding-up order was set aside: *Re Michael P. Georgas Co.*, [1948] O.R. 708 (C.A.).

Where two minority shareholders petitioned the court for an order to wind up the corporation on grounds that it was being mismanaged, and was violating its powers under the charter, the application was dismissed because no fraud, bad faith or lack of probity existed and the evidence did not demonstrate a loss of confidence: *Shacket v. Universal Factors Corp.* (1966), 10 C.B.R. (N.S.) 166 (Que. S.C.).

Where the respondent procured the petitioner's dismissal as manager and his removal as director, the winding-up order was denied. Although the petitioner lacked confidence in the respondent who had treated him unfairly, the respondent had not affected the petitioner's proprietary rights as a shareholder: *Re B.C. Aircraft Propeller and Engine Co.* (1968), 63 W.W.R. 80 (B.C. S.C.).

And where the deadlock in a corporation's affairs in no way involved improper conduct on the part of the directors but had been brought about wholly by the failure of one shareholder to complete his contract to purchase some of the corporation's stock, the court refused to make a winding-up order on the basis that if an agreement could be reached on the contract the corporation's operations could continue: *Re Balfour Fashions Ltd.*, [1957] O.W.N. 91.

In *Western Quebec Investments Ltd. v. J. G. Bisson Construction & Engineering Ltd.*, [1972] Que. S.C. 331, the shareholder's petition alleged that the corporation's board of directors was deadlocked, that there had never been an annual meeting of the shareholders nor a properly constituted meeting of its board of directors and that this constituted grounds for winding up. The petition was, however, dismissed and the court stated that a winding-up order could not be granted on the just and applicable principle where the petitioner had unclean hands, where there were other remedies available, where the consequences to other shareholders would be unduly harsh or where the petitioner was merely a dissatisfied shareholder analogous to an unhappy partner in a partnership.

For a situation in a corporation to be recognized as a deadlock equal holdings of stock by the contesting factions is not required: *Re Davis & Collett Ltd.*, [1935] 1 Ch. 693; *Re Purvis Fisheries Ltd.*, [1955] 1 D.L.R. 93 (Man. C.A.).

Partnership

Finally, in the case of a private corporation analogous to a partnership, the circumstances (for example, continued quarrelling, a state of animosity which precludes all reasonable hope of reconciliation and friendly co-operation, a deadlock) which justify the dissolution of a partnership are circumstances which induce the court to exercise its jurisdiction under the "just and equitable" clause and wind up such a corporation: *Re Yenidje Tobacco Co.*, [1916] 2 Ch. 426 (C.A.); *Re Davis & Collett Ltd.*, [1935] 1 Ch. 693; *Re Bondi Better Bananas Ltd.*, [1951] O.R. 845 (C.A.); *Bannerman v. Concrete Column Clamps Ltd.*, [1953] Que. S.C. 107; *Re National Drive-In Theatres Ltd.*, [1954] 2 D.L.R. 55 (B.C. S.C.); *Bonar v. Toth*, [1957] O.W.N. 268 (C.A.); *Ebrahimi v. Westbourne Galleries Ltd.*, [1972] 2 All E.R. 492 (H.L.); *Re Pre-Delco Machine & Tool Ltd.*, [1973] 3 O.R. 115 (H.C.); *Rogers v. Agincourt Holdings Ltd.* (1976), 12 O.R. (2d) 386 (Div. Ct.), affd (1976), 14 O.R. (2d) 489 (C.A.); *DiRisio v. DeLorenzo* (1981), 38 C.B.R. (N.S.) 154 (Ont. H.C.); *Dunham v. Appollo Tours Ltd. (No. 2)* (1978), 20 O.R. (2d) 9 (H.C.); *Kapeluck v. Professional Industries Ltd.* (1983), 25 Sask. R. 58 (Q.B.).

In *Ebrahimi v. Westbourne Galleries Ltd. supra*, the parties carried on business as a partnership which was later incorporated. Soon after the incorporation, the son of one of the parties was appointed a director and each of the parties transferred to him a certain number of shares. Differences about the running of the business arose. At a general meeting, an ordinary resolution was passed pursuant to which the appellant was removed as officer and director and was thereafter excluded from any share in the conduct of the business. The appellant applied for a winding-up order. The House of Lords held that the right course was to dissolve the association by a winding-up. Lord Wilberforce, at p. 500, articulated the following principles:

> It would be impossible, and wholly undesirable, to define the circumstances in which these considerations may arise. Certainly the fact that a company is a small one, or a private company, is not enough. There are very many of these where the association is a purely commercial one, of which it can safely be said that the basis of association is adequately and exhaustively laid down in the articles. The super-imposition of equitable consideration requires something more, which typically may include one, or probably more of the following elements: (i) an association formed or continued on the basis of a personal relationship, involving mutual confidence — this element will often be found where pre-existing partnership has

> been converted into a limited company; (ii) an agreement, or understanding, that all, or some (for there may be "sleeping" members) of the shareholders shall participate in the conduct of the business; (iii) restriction on the transfer of the members' interest in the company — so that if confidence is lost, or one member is removed from management, he cannot take out his stake and go elsewhere.

In *Re R.C. Young Insurance Ltd.*, [1955] O.R. 598 (C.A.), five principles are outlined with respect to the winding-up of private corporations which are essentially a partnership of two persons. These are:

1. It is right to consider what is the precise position of a private corporation such as this, and in what respect it may be fair to call a partnership in the guise of a private corporation.
2. The same principles ought to be applied where there is, in substance, a partnership in the form of guise of a private corporation. The circumstances which would justify the winding-up of a partnership are circumstances that should induce the court to exercise its jurisdiction under the "just and equitable" clause and to wind up the corporation.
3. As the foundation of applications for winding-up on the "just and equitable" rule there must be a justifiable lack of confidence in the conduct and management of the corporation's affairs.
4. That lack of confidence must be grounded on the conduct of the directors in regard to the corporation's business. It may rest on lack of probity, good faith or other improper conduct on the part of a majority of directors.
5. It must not spring from dissatisfaction at being out-voted in the business affairs or what is called the "domestic policy" of the corporation.

In *DiRisio v. DeLorenzo* (1981), 38 C.B.R. (N.S.) 154 (Ont. H.C.), the court noted that the principles stated in the *Ebrahimi* case represent a broadening of the principles adopted in the *R.C. Young Insurance* case. The court noted that cases in which winding-up is ordered on the basis of the just and equitable rule cannot be conclusively determined by reference to fixed principles and that it would be wrong to assume that all of the five circumstances set out in the *R.C. Young Insurance* case must be satisfied before a winding-up order can be made. The principles are meant only to act as guidelines to assist the court in determining whether or not it is just and equitable in a broad sense to wind up a corporation on particular facts. In this case, three equal shareholders had operated a restaurant business for nearly 20 years. When differences developed among them over the alleged misconduct and breach of trust on the part of one of the shareholders, the court granted a winding-up order.

It is not necessary for an applicant to provide any documentary evidence of partnership. The nature of the arrangement may be drawn from the events and circumstances surrounding the incorporation and the operation of the corporation: *Mammone v. Doralin Investments Ltd.* (1985), 54 C.B.R. (N.S.) 171 (Ont. S.C.).

In *Re Bondi Better Bananas*, [1951] O.R. 845 (C.A.), a private corporation had been formed to take over the assets and undertaking of a partnership, each of the two former partners having equal shareholdings and equal control in the management of the corporation. Dissension and mistrust developed between the two former partners and a deadlock in the affairs of the corporation arose. The Ontario Court of Appeal held that the deadlock was sufficient to warrant the winding-up of the corporation but in addition it held that as the corporation was analogous to a partnership and as circumstances existed which would justify the dissolution of a partnership, these facts were also a sufficient ground to order the corporation wound up.

For other cases where the court has ordered the corporation wound up on the basis of the partnership doctrine, see *Bannerman v. Concrete Column Clamps Ltd.*, [1953] Que. S.C. 107 (other grounds in this case included justifiable loss of confidence in the management of the corporation and a deadlock in the affairs of the corporation); *Re National Drive-in Theatres Ltd.*, [1954] 2 D.L.R. 55 (B.C. S.C.) (quarrelling and animosity between two family groups each owning one-half of the issued shares, but the casting vote at meetings gave one family sole control); *Bonar v. Toth*, [1957] O.W.N. 268 (C.A.) (a serious deadlock had existed for several years in the affairs of a corporation analogous to a partnership and there was not the slightest hope of a reconciliation being effected between the two opposing interests); *Re Pre-Delco Machine & Tool*, [1973] 3 O.R. 115 (exclusion of the partner-shareholder in the decision-making process); *Kapeluck v. Professional Industries Ltd.* (1983), 25 Sask. R. 58 (Q.B.) (respondents deliberately violating agreement intended to safeguard minority rights in changing capital structure and limiting number of directors where a relationship of trust and confidence between the shareholders was found to be akin to partnership).

Where two shareholders operated a corporation as a joint venture, both having the same number of shares but one having a casting vote, the serious differences between them which made the operation of the corporation impossible justified the making of a winding-up order. The fact that one shareholder had a casting vote did not prevent the court from exercising its power to order a winding-up: *Dunham v. Appollo Tours Ltd. (No. 2)* (1978), 20 O.R. (2d) 9 (H.C.).

In *Re Levine Developments (Israel) Ltd.* (1978), 5 D.L.R. 164 (Ont. H.C.), the petition for winding-up was dismissed. The applicants had alleged that the corporation was supposed to function as a corporate partnership in full good faith, trust and confidence and with active participation by the principals of the petitioner. However, the court found that no steps had been taken by contract to impose the elements of partnership. A draft shareholders' agreement which had not been signed was not considered as evidence of the spirit and intent of the parties. This was not a case where a partnership in a corporate form consisting of unsophisticated people had been incorporated to carry on the business formerly carried on as a partnership. In this case, the incorporation, financing and operation of the corporation had been the subject of careful consideration and professional advice.

The winding-up order was also refused in *Marmel v. Burshtein*, [1973] 4 W.W.R. 643 (Man. C.A.), revg (*sub nom. Re Broadway Enterprises Ltd.*) [1972] 6 W.W.R. 673 (Man. Q.B.). No fraud or dishonesty had been alleged and the petitioner had failed to demonstrate that the assets of the corporation would be sold at a price far below their true value.

However, where the corporation had more than ten shareholders it was held that the partnership doctrine may not necessarily be applicable. Further, even if a partnership operated under the guise of a corporation, there must be a justifiable lack of confidence in the conduct and management of the corporation's affairs: *Re Sharon Golf & Country Club* (1975), 20 C.B.R. (N.S.) 159 (Ont. H.C.).

In *B. Love Ltd. v. Bulk Steel & Salvage Ltd.* (1982), 38 O.R. (2d) 691, additional reasons (1982), 40 O.R. (2d) 1 (H.C.), an order for winding-up of the corporation was denied. The court noted that there is a heavy onus on the applicant to establish the grounds for the making of a winding-up order. The applicant in this case failed to show that the business relationship and the corporation was based on mutual trust and confidence and without this relationship the shareholders would never have agreed to carry on the business in common. Even where a partnership analogy can be proved, a winding-up order will not be granted unless the applicant can show a lack of probity or good faith on the part of the directors managing the corporation's business or a complete breakdown in mutual confidence.

Where two individuals operated two corporations in partnership and each held 50% of the shares, a winding-up order was denied. Although it was just and equitable to wind-up the corporations, it was clear that the corporations continued to operate and Dea J. was of the view that it would be better to see each of the parties purchase one of the corporations as a going concern. See: *Lamoureux v. Golden Flooring Accessories Ltd.* (1991), 79 Alta. L.R. (2d) 178 (Q.B.).

In *Gattuso Investments Inc. v. Gattuso Corp.* (1969), 14 C.B.R. (N.S.) 161 (Que. S.C.), a dispute arose between the former owner of the business who had become a minority shareholder and the present majority holder who it was alleged had unlawfully acquired the control by exerting pressure upon the former owners and by an illegal issue of treasury stock. The court refused the winding-up order on the partnership grounds. In this case, the petitioner had a preference over his adversaries in the return of capital on a liquidation. If the assets of the corporation were insufficient to reimburse all the shareholders on winding up, the petitioner would not be prejudiced. Accordingly, the court held that it would be manifestly unfair to apply the principles applicable to the dissolution of partnerships. The parties in this case were not on the same footing as partners. Additionally, the corporation, being a public corporation as opposed to a private corporation, could not be dissolved under the just and equitable rule on the ground of partnership unless fraud or dishonesty was alleged.

Shareholder ratification

Section 242 of the federal Act provides that shareholder ratification of the alleged breach of a right or duty no longer has the effect of precluding an action by the shareholder. Prior to the statutory reforms, shareholder ratification, unless the conduct fell within the narrow exceptions to the rule in *Foss v. Harbottle*

(1843), 2 Hare 461, absolutely barred any action by a shareholder. The Act does, however, provide that evidence of ratification may be taken into account by the court in making an order under Part XX or pursuant to s. 214 of the federal Act. The counterpart in the Ontario Act is s. 249(1).

Security for costs

A complainant is not required to give security for costs in any application made or action brought. See s. 242(3).

Costs

Section 242(4) provides that in an application brought under Part XX, the court may order the payment to the complainant of his interim costs including legal fees and disbursements. However, on final disposition of the matter, the complainant may be held accountable for such interim costs. In respect of an application pursuant to s. 242, as compared to a similar application in respect of s. 240, it has been held that different considerations apply. An order is appropriate where the applicant is in financial difficulty, the financial difficulty arises out of the alleged oppressive conduct of the corporation, and the applicant has made out a *prima facie* case. See *Wilson v. Conley* (1990), 1 B.L.R. (2d) 220 (Ont. Gen. Div.).

However, in *Alles v. Maurice* (1992), 5 B.L.R. (2d) 146 (Ont. Ct. Gen. Div.), Blair J. ordered the respondents to pay the complainant interim costs, holding that the complainant must "establish that there is a case of sufficient merit to warrant pursuit and that the applicant is genuinely in financial circumstances which but for an order under s. 284(4) [now s. 249(4)] would preclude the claim from being pursued". Blair J. accepted the first criterion from *Wilson v. Conley, supra*, but took issue with both the second and third criteria, stating that in his view, the inability to fund an otherwise meritorious law suit need not be directly caused by the alleged oppression and that it is unnecessary to apply language and concepts applicable to injunctive relief to the exercise and discretion pursuant to s. 249(4). See also *Organ et al v. Barnett et al* (1992), 11 O.R. (3d) 210 (Gen. Div.) - wherein MacDonald J. agreed with Blair J.

As to the disposition of final costs, the awarding and scale of costs are within the discretion of the court. A court will consider the complexity of the proceeding, the importance of the legal issues, and the respondent's conduct. A complete indemnification of costs might be awarded in what the court considers to be a proper case.

For example, in *Millar v. McNally et al* (1992), 3 B.L.R. (2d) 102n (Ont. Gen. Div.), additional reasons to (1992), 3 B.L.R. (2d) 102, a complete indemnification was not warranted. Two shareholders of G Ltd. had ignored the applicant shareholder's rights by failing to purchase his shares after he ceased employment, failed to give him notice of the director and shareholder meetings and refused his requests for information. The two shareholders also incorporated a new corporation, W Ltd., to operate G Ltd.'s business. The applicant was awarded party and party costs, 90% to be paid by G Ltd. and 10% to be paid by W Ltd. None of the costs were awarded against the respondent shareholders.

Practice and procedure

It is unclear whether a complainant can bring an action in the nature of a derivative claim pursuant to the oppression provisions. To allow such a claim to proceed under s. 234 would allow the complainant to circumvent the leave provisions of the Act.

In practice, these two sections overlap a great deal as the parties which are able to bring both a derivative action and an oppression action can be the same and both actions can be the result of the same fact situation. Courts throughout Canada have expressed varying views as to when leave must be sought for derivative actions which coincide with an oppression action.

Two cases which were decided prior to the enactment of today's oppression remedy sections have been relied upon by many courts as the basis for determining when leave for a derivative action must be sought. *Farnham v. Fingold*, [1973] 2 O.R. 132 (C.A.), discusses the difference between personal and derivative actions and states clearly that if an action is not personal but is brought for and on behalf of a corporation, leave must be sought. In this case, it was found that the action, argued to be a personal action, was in fact a derivative action and the claim was struck without prejudice to the right to commence a separate action for which leave must be sought.

In *Goldex Mines Ltd. v. Revill* (1974), 7 O.R. (2d) 216 the Court of Appeal stated that even if there is a personal action which accompanies a derivative action, leave must be obtained for the derivative portion of the claim. Once leave is obtained then both the derivative and personal actions may be heard together. The court found that both the derivative and personal claims were woven together and as such the court could not rule upon the personal claims. The court discussed whether the entire claim should be struck or whether the claim would be struck with leave to amend. The court struck the claim as no limitation period was involved and a new claim could be issued and because a separate claim could be issued for the derivative action. But see *Feld v. Glick* (1975), 8 O.R. (2d) 7 (H.C.), where all parties would be before the court, the claim was not struck out for failure to obtain leave. However, the court held that at the conclusion of the trial, if the claims were found to be derivative, the defendant could assert the failure to comply with the leave provisions as a defence.

In the following cases it has been held that actions of a derivative nature cannot be commenced under the oppression provisions: *Re Goldhar and Quebec Manitou Mines Ltd.* (1975), 9 O.R. (2d) 740 (Div. Ct.); *Shield Development Co. v. Snyder*, [1976] 3 W.W.R. 44 (B.C. S.C.); *Winchill v. Del Zotto* (1976), 1 C.P.C. 338 (Ont. H.C.); *Loeb v. Provigo Inc.* (1978), 4 B.L.R. 272 (Ont. H.C.); *Hoskin v. Price Waterhouse Ltd.* (1982), 37 O.R. (2d) 464 (Div. Ct.); *Beckwith v. Natural Nectar Products Canada Ltd.* (unreported) (June 14, 1985), B.C.S.C., Cowan L.J.S.C. (B.C. S.C.); *Re Goldstream Resources* (1986), 2 B.C.L.R. (2d) 244 (S.C.); *Pizzo v. Crory* (1986), 171 A.P.R. 419 (N.S. T.D.); *Stone v. Stonehurst Enterprises Ltd.* (1987), 202 A.P.R. 290 (N.B. Q.B.); *Cini v. Micallef* (1987), 60 O.R. (2d) 584 (H.C.); *Skorchid v. Edgewater Marine Ltd.* (1988), 9 A.C.W.S. (3d) 247 (Ont. H.C.); *Pappas v. Acan Window Inc.* (1991), 2 B.L.R. (2d) 180 (Nfld. T.D.).

Conversely, the following cases suggest that derivative actions can be commenced under the oppression provisions: *Re Peterson and Kanata Investments Ltd.* (1975), 60 D.L.R. (3d) 527 (B.C. S.C.); *Inversiones Montforte S.A. v. Javelin International Ltd.* (1982), 17 B.L.R. 230 (Que. S.C.); *Re Wismer and Javelin International Ltd.* (1982), 38 O.R. (2d) 26 (H.C.); *Ontario (Securities Commission) v. McLaughlin* (1987), 11 O.S.C.B. 442 (H.C.); *Sparling v. Javelin International Ltd.*, [1986] R.J.Q. 1073 (Que. S.C.), affd [1987] R.D.J. 307 (Que. C.A.). For a thorough review of the issue, see: MacIntosh, J., "The Oppression Remedy: Personal or Derivative?", (1981), 70 *Canadian Bar Review*, 29.

It has been held that in Quebec a complainant may not pursue a class action as provided in the *Code of Civil Procedure* in combination with an application for a statutory remedy pursuant to s. 234 of the federal Act: *Fradet c. Sociéte Asbestos Ltée*, [1990] R.D.J. 180 (C.A. Que.) leave to appeal to S.C.C. refused (1990), 116 N.R. 157n (S.C.C.).

Section 190 (11) of the federal Act provides that a dissenting shareholder upon submitting a notice for payment "ceases to have any rights as a shareholder other than the right to be paid the fair value of his shares". Thus, it has been argued that upon invoking the dissenting shareholder rights, the shareholder has no status to bring a parallel action pursuant to s. 241 of the federal Act. It has, however, been held that a complainant retains his right to pursue the remedies granted by s. 241. This approach is consistent with the definition of "complainant" in s. 238 which expressly includes former security holders. See *Brant Investments Ltd. v. Keeprite Inc.* (1987), 37 B.L.R. 65 (Ont. H.C.), affd (1991), 3 O.R. (3d) 289 (C.A.); *Chicago Blower Corp. v. 141209 Canada Ltd.* (1988), 40 B.L.R. 201 (Man. Q.B.); but see *McConnell v. Newco Financial Corp.* (1979), 8 B.L.R. 180 (B.C. S.C.) wherein Esson J. commented in *obiter* that he could see no need to restrict the meaning of the words "rights as a shareholder" to matters such as voting and receiving dividends.

It seems clear that under the federal Act, proceedings in respect of the oppression remedy may be brought either in the form of an action or by application. Section 248 specifically provides that the application may be made in a summary manner by petition, originating notice, or otherwise as the rules of court provide. In *Sparling v. Royal Trust Co.* (1983), 143 D.L.R. (3d) 112 (Ont. H.C.), revd on other grounds (1984), 45 O.R. (2d) 484 (Ont. C.A.), affd [1986] 2 S.C.R. 537, it was argued that as that section made reference to application and not action, relief could not be obtained pursuant to the oppression provisions by way of action. Trainor J. held that the provisions were merely directory and therefore relief could be obtained by way of action. The Court of Appeal agreed stating that the inclusion of the words "or otherwise" contemplated institution of proceedings by action. See also *Bank of Montreal v. Dome Petroleum Ltd.* (1987), 67 C.B.R. (N.S.) 296 (Alta. Q.B.) (pursuant to the federal Act and the Alberta Rules of Court, an application for relief pursuant to s. 234 may be brought in a summary manner by originating notice of motion).

It was, until recently, unclear whether the Ontario Act permits such relief to be obtained by action. In *Title Estate v. Harris* (1990), 72 O.R. (2d) 468 (H.C.), Granger J. noted that there is no equivalent to s. 248 of the federal Act in the

Ontario Act. In his opinion, such omission was indicative of the legislature's intent that such applications should come before the court in a timely fashion to be dealt with in a summary manner and by way of action.

Conversely, in *Muljadi v. O'Brien* (1990), 75 O.R. (2d) 270 (Gen. Div.) (leave to appeal to the Divisional Court denied) Gilbert J. declined to follow the *Title* case, preferring the approach in the *Sparling* case, and concluded that s. 247(1) [now s. 248(1)] of the Ontario Act which simply provides that a complainant may apply to court was permissive and allows the moving party to decide whether they will bring an action or make an application to court.

The Ontario Court of Appeal in *Chilean v. Augdome Corp.* (1991), 2 O.R. (3d) 696 (C.A.) agreed with the conclusions and approach of Gilbert J. in the *Muljadi* case.

The Director is entitled to bring a class action for compensation on behalf of all shareholders: see *Sparling v. Royal Trust Co.* (1984), 45 O.R. (2d) 484 (C.A.), affd [1986] 2 S.C.R. 537.

Other matters

Part XX of the Act contains a number of other general provisions which are discussed below.

It is provided that the Director may apply to a court for directions in respect of any matter concerning his duties under the Act and in such application the court may give such directions and may make such further orders that it thinks fit (s. 244). If the Director refuses to file any articles or other document required to be filed by him before the articles or other document becomes effective he is required within 20 days after receipt by him (or within 20 days after he receives any approval required under any other Act, whichever is the later) to give notice of his refusal to the person who has submitted the articles giving his reasons; failure to file or give written notice of the refusal is deemed to be a refusal itself (refusal to file the articles or document in question) (s. 245). An appeal is provided in s. 246 from the decision of the Director by a person who feels aggrieved by such decision. The appeal is by way of an application to a court for an order requiring the Director to change his decision and on such application the court may so order and make any further order it thinks fit (s. 246).

Section 247 provides that if a corporation or any director, officer, employee, agent, auditor, trustee, receiver, receiver-manager or liquidator does not comply with the Act, the regulations, articles, by-laws or any unanimous shareholders' agreement, a complainant or creditor of the corporation may, in addition to any other rights he may have, apply to a court for an order directing such person to comply with, or to restrain any such person from acting in breach of, any provisions thereof, and on such application the court may so order and it may make any further order it thinks fit.

An application to court under any provision of the Act may be made in a summary manner by petition, originating notice of motion or otherwise as the rules of the court may provide and subject to any order respecting notice to interested parties or costs, or any other order the court may think fit (s. 248).

An appeal lies to the court of appeal (that is, the court to which an appeal lies) from any order made by a court under the Act (s. 249). It does not matter whether the order appealed from is interlocutory or final. See: *McKechnie v. Equipement de pollution Hurum Ltee*, [1991] R.D.J. 6 (C.A. Que.) as approved in *Kelvin Energy Ltd. v. Lee et al.*, [1992] 3 S.C.R. 235. However, the appeal must be in respect of an order made pursuant to the provisions of the Act. In the *Kelvin Energy* case, in conjuction with a previous application under the oppression provisions of the federal Act, an order was obtained pursuant to the Quebec Code of Civil Procedure for authorization to summon two witnesses for an examination for discovery. An appeal of that decision was dismissed on the basis that the "order" was not one which could be appealed pursuant to s. 249 because it was made pursuant to the Code and not pursuant to the federal Act.

Offences

The federal Act contains many specific offence provisions in addition to a general offence provision. Generally, the contravention of specific offence provisions by the corporation and by individuals constitutes an offence punishable on summary conviction to a fine not exceeding $5,000. Individuals may also be imprisoned for a term not exceeding six months. Certain offence provisions may also apply to the actions of directors and officers of the corporation even if the corporation is not prosecuted or convicted. The general offence provision is found in s. 251 of the federal Act and provides that contravention of a provision of the Act or the regulations for which no punishment is prescribed is punishable on summary conviction. The prosecution of any offences pursuant to the Act must be undertaken within two years after the subject matter of the complaint arose (see the federal Act, s. 252(2)). Where such person is found guilty of the offence, a court may, in addition to the punishment imposed, order compliance with the provisions of the Act or regulations which have been contravened (see the federal Act, s. 252(1)).

The following are the specific offence provisions and penalties contained in the federal Act:

1. s. 20(6) — Failure to comply with the provisions respecting the preparation and maintenance of corporate and director's records constitutes an offence punishable on summary conviction to a fine not exceeding $5,000.

2. s. 21(10) — Contravention of the provisions respecting shareholder lists constitutes an offence punishable on summary conviction to a fine not exceeding $5,000 or to imprisonment for a term not exceeding six months or to both.

3. s. 22(3) — Contravention of the provisions which establish the form of the records required to be prepared and maintained and the precautions to be observed in respect of loss, destruction or falsification of and inaccuracies in the records constitutes an offence punishable on summary conviction to a fine not exceeding $5,000 or to imprisonment for a term not exceeding six months or to both.

4. s. 32(3) — Contravention of the provisions respecting prohibited transfers constitutes an offence punishable on summary conviction to a fine not exceeding $5,000.

5. s. 85(6) — Contravention of the provisions respecting the use of the list of security holders of debt obligations constitutes an offence punishable on summary conviction to a fine not exceeding $5,000 or to a term of imprisonment not exceeding six months or to both.

6. s. 127(9) — Contravention of the provisions respecting insider reports constitutes an offence punishable on summary conviction to a fine not exceeding $5,000 or to a term of imprisonment not exceeding six months or to both.

7. s. 127(10) — Where a body corporate contravenes the insider report provisions, any director or officer who knowingly authorized, permitted or acquiesced in the commission of the offence is also liable on summary conviction to a fine not exceeding $5,000 or to a term of imprisonment not exceeding six months or to both, whether or not the corporation has been prosecuted or convicted.

8. s. 130(4) — Contravention of the provisions prohibiting short sales, puts or calls constitutes an offence punishable on summary conviction to a fine not exceeding $5,000 or to a term of imprisonment not exceeding six months or to both.

9. s. 149(3) — Failure to send a form of proxy with a notice of meeting constitutes an offence punishable on summary conviction to a fine not exceeding $5,000.

10. s. 149(4) — Where a corporation commits the offence of failing to send a form of proxy, any director or officer who knowingly authorized, permitted or acquiesced in the commission of the offence commits an offence punishable on summary conviction to a fine not exceeding $5,000 or to a term of imprisonment not exceeding six months or to both, whether or not the corporation has been prosecuted or convicted.

11. s. 150(3) — Failure to observe the provisions respecting the solicitation of proxies constitutes an offence punishable on summary conviction to a fine not exceeding $5,000 or to a term of imprisonment not exceeding six months or to both, whether or not the corporation has been prosecuted or convicted.

12. s. 150(4) — Where a body corporate commits an offence respecting the solicitation of proxies, any officer or director who knowingly authorized, permitted or acquiesced in the commission of the offence commits an offence punishable on summary conviction to a fine not exceeding $5,000 or to a term of imprisonment not exceeding six months or to both, whether or not the corporation has been prosecuted or convicted.

13. s. 153(8) — Where a registrant of shares who does not beneficially own those shares fails to comply with the provisions respecting the voting of

those shares, he commits an offence punishable on summary conviction to a fine not exceeding $5,000 or to a term of imprisonment not exceeding six months or to both.

14. s. 153(9) — Where the registrant is a body corporate and contravenes the provisions respecting the voting of shares of which the body corporate is not the beneficial owner, any officer or director who knowingly authorized, permitted or acquiesced in the commission of the offence commits an offence punishable on summary conviction to a fine not exceeding $5,000 or to a term of imprisonment not exceeding six months or to both, whether or not the corporation has been prosecuted or convicted.

15. s. 159(2) — A corporation which fails to send a copy of the annual financial statements to each shareholder 21 days before the annual meeting or before a resolution is signed in lieu of such meeting commits an offence punishable on summary conviction to a fine not exceeding $5,000.

16. s. 160(6) — Offering corporations or those whose revenues exceed $10,000,000 or whose assets exceed $5,000,000 which fail to send annual financial statements to the Director commit an offence punishable on summary conviction to a fine not exceeding $5,000.

17. s. 168(4) — Failure by an auditor or former auditor of the corporation to attend a meeting of shareholders upon written notice by a shareholder or director constitutes an offence punishable on summary conviction to a fine not exceeding $5,000 or to a term of imprisonment not exceeding six months or to both.

18. s. 171(9) — Where a director or officer fails to notify the audit committee and auditor of errors in the financial statements that the auditor has reported on, or where they have been notified by the auditor of errors in the financial statements and failed to prepare and issue revised statements or informed the shareholders or, if required, to inform the Director of errors in the financial statements, an offence is committed punishable on summary conviction to a fine not exceeding $5,000 or to a term of imprisonment not exceeding six months or to both.

19. s. 205(1) — Offerors who fail to comply with the provisions respecting take-over bids commit an offence punishable on summary conviction to a fine not exceeding $5,000 or to a term of imprisonment not exceeding six months or to both.

20. s. 225(2) — Persons who have been granted custody of the records of a dissolved corporation who fail to produce such documents and records within the required time period following dissolution commit an offence punishable on summary conviction to a fine not exceeding $5,000 or to a term of imprisonment not exceeding six months or to both.

21. s. 235(4) — Persons who fail to comply with the request of the Director to report to him information concerning the ownership or control of a security

commits an offence punishable on summary conviction to a fine not exceeding $5,000 or to a term of imprisonment not exceeding six months or to both.

22. s. 235(5) — Where a body corporate fails to comply with the Director's request for information concerning the ownership or control of a security, any officer or director who knowingly authorized, permitted or acquiesced in the commission of the offence commits an offence punishable on summary conviction to a fine not exceeding $5,000 or to a term of imprisonment not exceeding six months or to both.

23. s. 250(1) — Persons who make or assist in making a report, return, notice or other document required by the Act or the regulations to be sent to the Director or other person which contain untrue statements of material facts or omit material facts which make the statement misleading in the circumstances commits an offence punishable on summary conviction to a fine not exceeding $5,000 or to a term of imprisonment not exceeding six months or to both.

24. s. 250(2) — Where a corporation makes untrue statements in a report, return, notice or other document, or omits material facts which make a statement misleading in the circumstances, any director who knowingly authorized, permitted or acquiesced in the commission of the offence commits an offence punishable on summary conviction to a fine not exceeding $5,000 or to a term of imprisonment not exceeding six months or to both, whether or not the corporation is prosecuted or convicted.

In addition to the general and specific offence provisions of the federal Act, there are numerous other federal and provincial statutes which contain offence provisions which apply to corporations and to directors and officers. These statutes regulate diverse matters ranging from agricultural products and environmental pollution to weights and measures.

Section 126(1) of the *Criminal Code* provides that every person who without lawful excuse contravenes a federal Act by wilfully doing anything forbidden by that Act or by wilfully omitting to do anything required to be done by such Act is, unless a punishment is expressly provided by law, guilty of an indictable offence and liable to imprisonment for a term not exceeding two years.

Chapter 17

NOTICES AND RETURNS

Cross-references: Ontario Act, ss. 262-278;
Corporations Information Act, s. 3.

Notices

Section 253(1) of the Act provides that a notice or document required by the Act, regulations, articles or by-laws to be sent to a shareholder or director of a corporation may be sent by prepaid mail addressed to, or may be delivered, personally, to the shareholder at his latest address as shown on the records of the corporation or its transfer agent and to a director at his latest address as shown on the records of the corporation or on the last notice filed with the Director pursuant to the Act. A notice or document sent in accordance with this provision is deemed to be received by a shareholder or director at the time it would be delivered in the ordinary course of mail, unless there are reasonable grounds for believing that the shareholder or director did not receive the notice or document at that time or at all (s. 253(3)). If a notice or document to a shareholder is returned on three consecutive occasions, the corporation is not required to send any further notices or documents to that shareholder until he informs the corporation in writing of his new address (s. 253(4)). It will be observed that a director named in a notice sent by a corporation to the Director pursuant to the Act and filed by the Director is presumed for the purposes of the Act to be a director of the corporation referred to in the notice (s. 253(2)). For discussion of this last provision see Chapter 8 under the heading "Resignation".

Section 254 provides that a notice or a document required to be sent to or served on a corporation may be sent by registered mail to the registered office of the corporation shown on the last notice filed with the Director and if so sent is deemed to be received or served at the time it would be delivered in the ordinary course of the mail, unless there are reasonable grounds for believing that the corporation did not receive the notice or document at that time or at all.

Section 255 provides that where a notice or document is required by the Act or regulations to be sent, the sending may be waived or the time for the notice or document may be waived or abridged at any time with the consent in writing of the person entitled thereto.

Certificates

Section 256 of the Act provides that where the Act requires or authorizes the Director to issue a certificate or certify any fact, the certificate shall be signed by the Director or Deputy Director authorized pursuant to s. 260 and is conclusive proof of the facts so certified without proof of the signature or official character of the person appearing to have signed the certificate, except in a proceeding under s. 213 to dissolve a corporation.

A certificate issued on behalf of a corporation stating any fact that is set out in the articles, by-laws, the unanimous shareholder agreement, minutes of the meetings of directors or shareholders or in a trust indenture or other contract to which the corporation is a party may be signed by a director, officer or a transfer agent of the corporation (s. 257(1)); when introduced as evidence in a criminal, civil or administrative action or proceeding, such certificate is, in the absence of evidence to the contrary, proof of the facts so certified without proof of the signature or official character of the person appearing to have signed the certificate (s. 257(2)); an entry in the securities register of or a security certificate issued by a corporation is, in the absence of evidence to the contrary, proof that the person in whose name the security is registered is owner of the security registered in the register or in the certificate (s. 257(3)).

Where a matter is declared to be *prima facie* evidence, the case thereby made out may be rebutted by other evidence: *Arnot's Case* (1887), 36 Ch. D. 702 (C.A.); *Re International Electric Co.* (1914), 31 O.L.R. 348 at 358; *Re Lake Ontario Navigation Co.* (1910), 20 O.L.R. 191 at 195 (C.A.).

Common law

At common law entries of a public nature in the public books of a corporation were *prima facie* evidence of the truth thereof, even against strangers, provided that the entries were made by the proper officer or his substitute: *R. v. Motherwell* (1718), 1 Stra. 93. A public book is one that the corporation was under a legal duty to keep for the benefit or information of some portion of the public: *Sturla v. Freccia* (1880), 5 App. Cas. 623. However, entries in the public books of a corporation as to private matters and entries in private books were only receivable as admissions against and not in favour of a corporation: *Hill v. Manchester Waterworks* (1833), 5 B. & Ad. 866; *Branksea Island Co.; Ex p. Bentinck (No. 2)* (1888), 1 Meg. C.R. 12 (C.A.); and against and not in favour of members of the corporation who acquiesced in the entries: *Waterford v. Price* (1847), 9 Ir. L.R. 310; *Hallmark's Case* (1878), 9 Ch. D. 329 (C.A.). In *Furlong v. Burns & Co.*, [1964] 2 O.R. 3, the court indicated that minutes of the meetings of the board of directors and shareholders were admissible in evidence in favour of a corporation as well as against it. The by-laws of a corporation have been held to be an entry of a public nature: *Holdsworth v. Dartmouth Corp.* (1838), 1 Ros. Civ. Ev. (19th ed.) 193; while particulars of irregularities in the execution of a bond have been held to be an entry of a private nature: *Hill v. Manchester Waterworks, supra.* By statute (for example, s. 257(2) of this Act) certain certificates of a corporation are often made *prima facie* or conclusive evidence, for specified purposes, of the matters set out therein.

At common law, entries in the public books of a corporation are provable either by the production of the original books or by examined copies: *Brocas v. Lord Mayor of London* (1766), 1 Stra. 307. Entries of a private nature must be proved by the production of the original, and copies, though long preserved among the corporate papers, are not admissible: *R. v. Gwyn* (1721), 1 Stra. 401. In Canada the provisions of the various Evidence Acts govern the proof of the above matters.

Books irregularly kept

A corporation's books have been received in evidence notwithstanding the omission of a shareholder's address or the amount paid up. See *Wolverhampton New Waterworks Co. v. Hawkesford* (1861), 11 C.B.N.S. 456. A paper containing the names of the shareholders was rejected in this case as not being a "register", and in *Re Printing, Telegraph & Construction Co. of Agence Havas; Ex p. Cammell*, [1894] 2 Ch. 392 (C.A.), similarly, a series of allotment sheets was held not intended as a register under the English *Companies Act.* Nor was a ledger page, which did not comply with the provisions of s. 28 of the Saskatchewan *Companies*

Act (R.S.S. 1909, c. 72), considered as a register of members: *Morse Co-operative Supply Co. v. Coates* (1918), 38 D.L.R. 92 (Sask. C.A.).

The court will, however, where the case demands it, take cognizance of entries in books irregularly or improperly kept: *Re Sprouted Food Co.; Hudson's Case* (1905), 6 O.W.R. 514; and for other illustrations see *Re Central Bank; Baines' Case* (1889), 16 O.A.R. 237; *Boultbee v. Gzowski* (1898), 29 S.C.R. 54; *Union Bank v. Morris & Code* (1900), 27 O.A.R. 396.

Provisions relating to the Director

Section 260 of the Act provides that the Minister may appoint a Director and one or more Deputy Directors to carry out the duties and exercise the powers of the Director under the Act.

The Director may require that a document or fact stated in a document required by the Act or the regulations be sent to him is to be verified by affidavit made under oath or by statutory declaration under the *Canada Evidence Act* before any commissioner for oaths or for taking affidavits: see s. 259.

Section 258 of the Act provides that where a notice or document is required to be sent to the Director under the Act, the Director may accept a photostatic or photographic copy thereof.

Regulations

Section 261 of the Act provides that the Governor in Council may make regulations describing any matter required or authorized by the Act to be prescribed; requiring the payment of a fee in respect of the filing, examination or copying of any document or in respect of any action that the Director is required or authorized to take under the Act and prescribing the amount thereof; prescribing the format and contents of annual returns, notices and other documents required to be sent to the Director or to be issued by him; prescribing rules with respect to exemptions permitted by the Act; and prescribing that the standards for the purposes of s. 155(1)(a) as they exist from time to time of an accounting body named in the regulations are to be followed. Such regulations are to be published at least 60 days in advance in the *Canada Gazette* and in the periodical published pursuant to s. 129 (the Canada Corporations Bulletin) and a reasonable opportunity is to be afforded to interested persons to make representations with respect thereto; such publication is not required if the proposed regulation grants an exemption or relieves a restriction, establishes or amends a fee, has been previously published whether or not amended, or makes no material substantive change in an existing regulation.

Regulations have been published pursuant to the Act. They deal with forms and the format of documents; what constitutes the class of resident Canadians; corporate names; insider trading; proxies and proxy solicitation; financial disclosure; exemption therefrom; constrained share corporations; take-over bids; rules of procedure for application for exemption; and set out, in addition, the prescribed fees. The forms set out in Schedule 1 to the regulations contain the prescribed forms to be sent to the Director or which are issued by him under the Act.

In *Re MacMillan Bloedel Industries Ltd. and Minister of Consumer & Corporate Affairs* (1974), 46 D.L.R. (3d) 464 (Fed. Ct.) it was argued that the fees payable under the regulations for an amalgamation were so excessive as to amount to a tax rather than a fee. It was held that the amount in question was a fee and was properly chargeable.

The regulations are discussed under the various headings of this work to which they apply.

Section 267 of the Act provides that the records required to be kept under the Act by the Director may be in bound or looseleaf form, photographic film form or may be entered or recorded by any system of mechanical or electronic data processing or any other information storage device that is capable of reproducing any required information in intelligible written form within a reasonable time; where such records are maintained by the Director in other than a written form, copy in an intelligible written form is to be provided by the Director and such report certified by the Director is admissible in evidence to the same extent as the original written records would have been; no production by the Director of any document other than a certificate and attached articles or statements filed under s. 262 need be made after six years from the date he receives it.

Section 266 provides that a person who has paid the prescribed fee is entitled during usual business hours to examine a document required by the Act or the regulations to be sent to the Director except a report sent to him under s. 230(2) by an inspector pursuant to Part XIX and to make copies of or extracts therefrom. A copy is to be furnished on request.

Filing of articles

Where articles or a statement of intent to dissolve or a statement of revocation of intent to dissolve (as referred to in s. 211) are to be sent to the Director pursuant to the Act, unless otherwise specifically provided, s. 262 provides that two copies of the document in question are to be signed by a Director or an officer of the corporation or, in the case of articles of incorporation by an incorporator; on receiving duplicate originals or such statement in prescribed form, any other required documents and the prescribed fee, the Director is to endorse on each of the duplicate originals the word "filed" and the date of filing, issue in duplicate the appropriate certificate and attach to each certificate one of the duplicate originals of the articles or statement, file the copy of the certificate on the attached articles or statement, send to the corporation or its representative the original certificate and attached articles or statement and publish in the *Canada Gazette* and in the Canada Corporations Bulletin the notice of the issue of the certificate. A certificate to be issued by the Director may be dated as of the day he receives the material in question or as of any later date specified by the court or the person who signed the articles or statement; the signature required on a certificate may be printed or otherwise mechanically reproduced and a certificate of discontinuance may be dated as of the day a corporation is continued under the laws of another jurisdiction.

The practice is to permit such request to be made by the solicitors submitting the material.

Section 264 provides that the Director may alter a notice or document, other than an affidavit or statutory declaration, if so authorized by the person who sent the document or by his representative. Where any certificate containing an error is issued to a corporation by the Director, the directors or shareholders of the corporation, at the request of the Director, are to pass the resolution and send in the documents required to comply with the Act and to take such other steps as the Director may reasonably require; the Director may demand the surrender of the certificate and issue a corrected certificate which is to bear the date of the certificate it replaces; if there is a material alteration of the terms of the original certificate notice of the corrections to be given in the *Canada Gazette* or in the Canada Corporations Bulletin (s. 265).

Annual return

Under s. 263(1) of the Act every corporation is on the prescribed date to send to the Director an annual return in prescribed form (Form 22). A fee is payable with respect to such annual return.

Where a corporation is in default for a period of one year in sending to the Director any fee, notice or document required by the Act, the Director may dissolve the corporation by issuing a certificate of dissolution under s. 212(1) or may apply to a court for an order dissolving the corporation under s. 217. The Director is not to dissolve a corporation unless he has given 120 days' notice of his decision to the corporation and to each director thereof and publishes notice of his decision in the *Canada Gazette*, in the Canada Corporations Bulletin and in a newspaper published or distributed in the place where the corporation has its registered office (s. 212(2)); following such publication, unless cause to the contrary has been shown or a court order made under s. 246, the Director may issue a certificate of dissolution in prescribed form (Form 18) (s. 212(3)) whereupon the corporation ceases to exist on the date shown in the certificate (s. 212(4)). As to the revival of a dissolved corporation, see Chapter 14 under the heading "Revival".

Upon the bankruptcy of a corporation the trustee in bankruptcy is not concerned in filing the returns. It is the duty of the directors and shareholders to do so if they desire to keep the corporation alive: *Re Canadian Cereal & Flour Mills Co.* (1921), 51 O.L.R. 316.

Certificates of compliance

Section 263(2) of the Act provides that the Director may furnish any person with a certificate that a corporation has sent to him a document required to be sent to the Director under the Act.

Continuance of federal corporations

Section 268 of the Act provides that corporations incorporated under an Act of the federal Parliament other than the *Canada Business Corporations Act* may by special resolution authorize the directors of the corporation to apply under s. 187 for a certificate of continuance under the Act and by the same resolution make any amendment to the charter that a corporation incorporated under the Act may make to its articles. No resolution may affect a class or series of shares unless it is authorized in accordance with s. 176 of the Act and is of the nature referred to in s. 176(1))(a), (b) or (c). A shareholder is not entitled to dissent pursuant to the provisions of s. 190 in respect of an amendment made pursuant to the foregoing provisions. Such continuance may also be authorized by the directors of such a corporation if the articles of continuance do not require any amendment other than an amendment required to conform to the *Canada Business Corporations Act.* Power is given to the Governor in Council (under s. 268(6)) to require certain corporations incorporated under an Act of Parliament to which Part I or Part II of the *Canada Corporations Act* does not apply, other than a bank or a corporation to which the *Insurance Companies Act* or the *Trust and Loan Companies Act* is applicable, to apply for a certificate of continuance under the Act.

It will be observed that no fee is payable in respect of a continuation authorized by s. 268. Failure to make the application ordered by the Governor in Council will result in the dissolution of the corporation on the expiration of the prescribed period.

The provisions are also applicable to a body corporate to which Part IV of the *Canada Corporations Act* applies other than corporation to which the *Insurance Companies Act* or the *Trust and Loan Companies Act* is applicable. A non-profit corporation is not entitled to apply for a certificate of continuance under s. 187.

Chapter 18

OTHER FEDERAL CORPORATE BODIES

General

The *Canada Business Corporations Act* was originally proclaimed in force effective December 15, 1975. It applied to business corporations except those specified in the Act: s. 3(2) (now repealed) provided that the federal Act did not apply to a body corporate that was a bank including a bank to which the *Quebec Savings Bank Act* applied, an insurance corporation within the meaning of the *Insurance Companies Act*, a trust corporation within the meaning of the *Trust Companies Act* or a loan corporation within the meaning of the *Loan Companies Act.*

Corporations incorporated under the federal jurisdiction include those incorporated under the *Insurance Companies Act* and the *Trust and Loan Companies Act* as well as the *Bank Act* and corporations that are incorporated by special Act of the Parliament of Canada. In addition, there are a number of Crown corporations so called which have been incorporated to carry on a particular function.

Non-profit corporations

Part II of the *Canada Corporations Act* (which is still in force) is applicable to non-share corporations incorporated for the purpose of carrying on without pecuniary gain to its members objects to which the legislative authority of the Parliament of Canada extends of a national, patriotic, religious, philanthropic, charitable, scientific, artistic, social, professional or sporting character or the like objects: see s. 154(1). The Act contains detailed provisions as to the application and by-laws and provides that existing corporations created by or under any Act of the Parliament of Canada for such purposes may be continued by letters patent under s. 156. Section 157 of the Act makes a number of the provisions of Part I applicable to corporations without share capital. Part III of the *Canada Corporations Act* (which is still in force) applies to non-share capital corporations incorporated for the purposes aforesaid by any special Act of the Parliament of Canada.

Separate legislation has been enacted by the Parliament of Canada with regard to railway, banking, insurance, loan and trust corporations. These and other corporations respecting which special legislation has been passed are governed primarily by their special Acts of incorporation and also by the appropriate general statute, for example, the *Bank Act*, to the extent this is not inconsistent with the terms of the particular special Act.

Except in the case of railway, banking and certain insurance corporations, and except where the particular special Act otherwise provides, Part IV of the Act applies to all corporations incorporated by special Act. In addition certain sections of Part I are by s. 161(1) made applicable to corporations to which Part IV applies, namely, ss. 68-84 (information as to mortgages and charges, prospectuses and offers to the public); ss. 98-99 (interest of directors, liability for wages); ss. 100-100.6 (annual meeting); ss. 114-133 (investigations, accounts and audit, annual returns); and ss. 135.1-135.93 (take-over bids).

In some instances, for example, s. 167 (qualification of directors) the requirements of Part IV are more severe than those of Part I of the Act. However, any of the provisions of Part IV may be excepted under the special Act (s. 162(2)), although such exclusion is in each case a matter to be determined by Parliament.

The transfer of shares of a corporation incorporated by special Act may be restricted by a provision in the Act or in the corporation's by-laws. (s. 176).

The liability of holders of shares which are not fully paid to creditors is set out in s. 188. Under s. 188 *scire facias* is a proper and appropriate proceeding against a shareholder by a creditor who holds an unsatisfied execution against the corporation: *Moore v. Kirkland* (1856), 5 U.C.C.P. 452; *Tyre v. Wilkes* (1856), 13 U.C.Q.B. 482; *Jenkins v. Wilcock* (1862), 11 U.C.C.P. 505; *Fraser v. Hickman* (1863), 12 U.C.C.P. 584; *Brice v. Munro* (1885), 12 O.A.R. 453 at 465.

A statutory provision similar to s. 209 (service of process on company) has been held valid: *Jordan v. McMillan; C.P.R. Garnishee* (1901), 8 B.C.R. 27; *Royal Bank v. Canadian National Fire Ins. Co.*, [1920] 3 W.W.R. 517 (B.C.); but see *Tytler v. C.P.R.* (1899), 26 O.A.R. 467.

The provisions of the *Winding-up Act* apply to corporations incorporated by special Act (s. 211).

So far as non-profit corporations are concerned, a new statute dealing with non-profit corporations has been suggested from time to time and the *Canada Non-Profit Corporations Act* received first reading in the Senate on November 15, 1977. However, the bill has not appeared on the order paper of either the Senate or the House of Commons for a number of years and accordingly the enactment of this bill must be taken as being subject to considerable delay.

Other corporations

Part IV of the *Canada Corporations Act* provides that a number of provisions of Part I are applicable to any corporation incorporated by special Act of the

Parliament of Canada. Section 162(1) of the Act provides that, except as provided in the part, it applies to every joint stock corporation incorporated subsequently to June 22, 1869, by any special Act of the Parliament of Canada for any of the purposes to which the legislative authority of the Parliament of Canada extends and so far as applicable to the undertaking not expressly varied or excepted by the special Act. Part IV is incorporated in the special Act and forms parts thereof and is to be construed therewith as forming one Act. A code of provisions is set out in the Act from ss. 160-214 inclusive. Part V of the *Canada Corporations Act* sets out certain incidental powers of corporate bodies created otherwise than by letters patent and Part VI contains certain provisions of general application.

As the by-laws of a corporation governed by Part II are either incorporated in the letters patent or are on file in the Department of the Secretary of State it is submitted that they are public documents and any person dealing with such corporations must satisfy himself in all cases that the provisions of the by-laws have been complied with; for the public will be deemed to have notice of the contents of such by-laws. See *Gold v. Maldaver* (1912), 4 O.W.N. 106.

The right of corporations without share capital to acquire and hold land will in all cases be subject to the provisions of provincial legislation (if any) respecting mortmain or other restrictions.

In *Kerr v. Dominion Millers Association* (1930), 38 O.W.N. 290, the defendant association was incorporated and was given the right to issue shares to participating members but no shares were ever issued. Ultimately a resolution was passed for the distribution of the property among its members. It was held that any member of a corporation without share capital, who, by reason of death or other cause, ceases to be such, loses his right to share upon any division of assets; when there is no share capital the member's right is to an aliquot share along with other actual members and such right arises only upon distribution.

The provisions of s. 5(4) of Part I as to the winding-up or the dissolution of a corporation in the circumstances set out in clauses (a), (b) and (c) thereof do not apply to corporations without share capital under Part II. Under the common law, however, such corporations may be wound up and dissolved in the circumstances set out in s. 5(4): *A.G. Can. v. Hellenic Colonization Association,* [1946] 3 D.L.R. 840.

PART II

THE WINDING-UP ACT

Chapter 19

INTRODUCTORY; GROUNDS FOR WINDING-UP ORDER

Section 1. Short Title
Section 2. Definitions
Section 3. When corporation deemed insolvent
Section 4. When corporation deemed unable to pay its debts
Section 5. Commencement of winding-up
Section 6. Application of Act
Section 7. Act does not apply to certain corporations
Section 8. Part I subject to Part II in the case of banks
Section 9. Part I subject to Part III in the case of insurance corporations
Section 10. Cases where a winding-up order may be made

Cross references: Section 11
Ontario Act, s. 207

Winding-up procedure

The winding-up or, as it is often called, the liquidation of a corporation is a statutory procedure for terminating the operations of the corporation, realizing its assets, distributing the proceeds of such realization among the creditors and shareholders in accordance with their respective entitlements, and dissolving the corporation.

The vast majority of realizations for the benefit of creditors in cases of insolvency are pursuant to the *Bankruptcy and Insolvency Act* (Canada). In addition, the court may make an order that a corporation be liquidated and dissolved pursuant to s. 214 of the *Canada Business Corporations Act* upon an application by the persons listed therein, including a security holder or former security holder, if the court is satisfied that such action is just and equitable. *The Companies' Creditors Arrangement Act*, R.S.C. 1985, c. C-36 is also frequently used where a compromise or arrangement is sought between a corporation and its creditors and it is desired to keep the operations of the corporation going. However, certain types of corporations such as banks, insurance corporations and trust and loan corporations, if insolvent, may be wound up only under the provisions of the *Winding-up Act*, and the provisions of the *Bankruptcy and Insolvency Act* are not applicable to them. It will be noted that s. 3(3) of the *Canada Business Corporations Act* provides that the *Winding-Up Act* is not applicable to corporations incorporated or continued under that Act.

The first federal *Winding-up Act* was passed in 1882 (45 Vict., c. 23). The present Act is chapter W-11 of the Revised Statutes of Canada, 1985. Any federal corporation (not incorporated under the *Canada Business Corporations Act*) or provincial corporation and, if it has assets in Canada, any foreign corporation may be wound up under this Act on the ground of insolvency. A corporation is deemed to be insolvent in the circumstances set out in s. 3 of the Act; these include the inability to pay debts as they become due and the permitting of an execution against it to remain unsatisfied. An eligible federal corporation may also be wound up under the Act on other specified grounds.

An application for a winding-up order based on insolvency may be made by the corporation, by a shareholder or, as is the usual case, by a creditor; in certain cases the Attorney General of Canada is empowered to make the application. The court has discretion as to whether the order will be granted or not, and an order will be refused or the application directed to stand over in special cases. If the application is granted, the court orders that the corporation be wound up under the Act, appoints a provisional liquidator and then a permanent liquidator and delegates to an officer of the court the powers of the court in relation to the winding-up.

The making of a winding-up order does not destroy the corporation's corporate state; but from the making of the order the corporation is to cease to carry on its business except so far as is necessary for the beneficial winding up of the corporation.

Upon the appointment of the liquidator, all the powers of the directors cease, except insofar as the court or the liquidator sanctions their continuance. No transfer of shares may be made except with the sanction of the liquidator under the authority of the court, and no suit, action or other proceeding may be proceeded with or commenced against the corporation except with leave of the court. Secured creditors, such as mortgagees and bondholders, must also obtain leave from the court before enforcing their rights.

Immediately upon his appointment, the liquidator takes into his custody or control all the property of the corporation and proceeds to collect moneys owing to the corporation. In this connection he prepares a list of contributories or shareholders; shareholders whose shares are not fully paid (now most rare) will be liable to contribute the amounts unpaid thereon, and those whose shares are fully paid will be entitled to share in any surplus. The creditors file their claims against the corporation with the liquidator, and any contested claims are disposed of by the court. Subject to the requirement of valuation, secured creditors, if they wish, may rely on their security instead of filing claims in the winding-up. With the court's approval, the liquidator may compromise debts due to the corporation and make compromises with the creditors.

After the creditors have been paid and the costs of the winding-up have been satisfied, the court will divide the balance, if any, among the shareholders according to their rights under the charter and by-laws or articles. An order will then be made discharging the liquidator.

The Act does not expressly provide for the dissolution of a corporation upon completion of the winding-up. In the case of a federal corporation, the appropriate Department on receiving evidence that the winding-up has been completed and the liquidator discharged, will treat the corporation as dissolved. In the case of a provincial corporation that has been wound up under this Act, the effect of the completion of the winding-up will be determined under the applicable provincial legislation; see for example, s. 218 of the Ontario Act, which provides for the dissolution of the corporation after certain formalities have been complied with.

The foregoing is a brief summary of the procedure for, and the effect of, winding up a corporation under this Act; the various points mentioned are dealt with below in more detail.

It will be noted that an assignment under the *Bankruptcy and Insolvency Act* will be set aside where there is a previous application for winding up: *Re C. Rossi Inc.* (1967), 12 C.B.R. (N.S.) 17 (Que. C.S.).

Under provincial legislation, which may be contained in the Companies

Act or in a separate Act, a provincially incorporated corporation may be wound up on various grounds but not on the ground of insolvency. Under the federal Act and some of the provincial Companies Acts, a corporation that has ceased carrying on business, and has no debts or liabilities or has obtained the consent of its creditors, on compliance with the requisite formalities may surrender its charter.

This Act is *intra vires* of Parliament, being in the nature of an insolvency law: *Clarke v. Union Fire Insurance Co.* (1890), 17 S.C.R. 265; and Parliament is alone competent to enact such legislation: *B.N.A. Act*, s. 91, head 21; *Canada (Attorney General) v. Ontario (Attorney General)*, [1898] A.C. 700 at 715 (P.C.).

A provincial Act passed to relieve a particular society that is shown on the face of the Act to be in a state of financial embarrassment, is, however, *intra vires* as coming within s. 92: *Union St. Jacques de Montréal v. Belisle* (1874), L.R. 6 P.C. 31.

It has been held that a provincial statute providing for the sale of a provincially subsidized railway when it is insolvent or has not complied with its charter or ceases to carry on its undertaking, applies to a corporation that is subject to the federal legislative jurisdiction: *Nantel v. Cie de Chemin de fer de la Baie des Chaleurs* (1896), 9 Que. S.C. 47; affd (1896), 5 Que. Q.B. 64 (C.A.).

Where the effect of a provincial Act was to confiscate a provincial railway corporation in accordance with the Act, but the Act did not in its terms purport to wind up the corporation on the ground of insolvency, the Act was held not to be *ultra vires* as trenching on the federal field in relation to bankruptcy and insolvency: *Saint John & Quebec Railway v. Jones* (1921), 57 D.L.R. 477 at 484 (N.B. C.A.) ; appeal dismissed (1921), 62 S.C.R. 92.

As to the winding up of provincial corporations under this Act on the ground of insolvency, see the notes under the heading "Insolvent provincial corporations" in this chapter. As to the provisions of the Ontario Act with regard to the winding up of Ontario corporations, see the notes under the heading "Winding-up under the Ontario Act" in this chapter.

Definitions of *Winding-up Act* (s. 2)

Some of the terms defined in s. 2 are dealt with below.

"Company"

The Act is valid as regards a federal corporation (not incorporated under the C.B.C.A.) carrying on business outside Canada: *Re I.O.S. Ltd. (No. 2)* (1973), 43 D.L.R. (3d) 759 (N.B. C.A.); an insolvent provincial corporation: *Clarke v. Union Fire Insurance Co.* (1890), 17 S.C.R. 265; and an insolvent foreign corporation: *Allen v. Hanson* (1890) 18 S.C.R. 667. See further the notes under the heading "Application of Act" in this chapter.

"Contributory"

While the definition in the Act is wide enough to include any person indebted to the corporation the term is limited in its application to the liability of shareholders as such: *Re Central Bank of Canada (sub nom. Yorke's Case)* (1888), 15 O.R. 625 (H.C.); *Re Monarch Bank* (1914), 42 O.L.R. 207 (C.A.). See also the notes to s. 53, which section elaborates on the meaning of "contributory": *Re National Savings Bank Assn. Ltd.* (1866), 1 Ch. App. 547 at 551.

A fully paid shareholder is a contributory within the meaning of the provision: *Re National Savings Bank Assn.* (1866), 1 Ch. App. 547; *Re Timbers Ltd.* (1917), 35 D.L.R. 431 (Alta. C.A.); *Re Pe Ben Pipelines Ltd. (sub nom. Charles T. Ivan Investments Ltd. v. Pe Ben Pipelines Ltd.)* (1978), 90 D.L.R. (3d) 262 (Alta. T.D.). A shareholder may be placed on the list of contributories even though he has paid his shares in full: *Re Anglesea Colliery Co.* (1866), 1 Ch. App. 555, followed in *Re Monarch Bank* (1914), 42 O.L.R. 207 (C.A.) (where a fully paid subscriber was placed on the list so that he would be able to claim in the distribution of the surplus remaining after the creditors of the bank had been paid); *Re Colonial Assurance Co.* (1916), 29 D.L.R. 488 (Man. K.B.); *Christie v. Edwards*, [1939] O.R. 48 at 53 (H.C.) and cases cited; revd [1940] O.R. 28 at 32 (C.A.); revd [1940] S.C.R. 410.

"Contributory" does not include a mere debtor who is a stranger to the corporation, but only a shareholder or member: *Re Central Bank of Canada (sub nom. Yorke's Case)* (1888), 15 O.R. 625 (H.C.).

Section 53 providing for the liability of contributories, is limited in its application to the liability of a member or shareholder in his character as such. Thus, a former holder of bonus shares, who has transferred them to a person who (a) has been accepted by the corporation as transferee and (b) who is entitled to hold those shares as fully paid, is not liable to be placed on the list of contributories so as to be liable to contribute *qua* shareholder: *Re Wiarton Beet Sugar Co.* (1906), 12 O.L.R. 149 (H.C.); *Re Winnipeg Hedge & Wire Fence Co.* (1912), 1 D.L.R. 316 (Man. K.B.). And a person who might have been liable as a contributory by reason of the fact that he acquired shares in consideration for assets without complying with the provision of s. 42 of the *Quebec Companies Act* (requiring that contracts providing for the issuance of shares for a consideration other than cash be filed with the Provincial Secretary) was not so liable when he had validly transferred his shares and ceased to be a registered shareholder prior to the bankruptcy of the corporation: *Tremblay v. Vermette*, [1959] S.C.R. 690. In *Wiarton, supra*, it was held, however, that if the transferor was a director he would be liable for breach of trust if he was a party to the allotment of the shares as fully paid, and also for transferring them as fully paid shares to the prejudice of the corporation, and was caught by what is now s. 124 (old s. 125). In *Re Winnipeg Hedge & Wire Fence Co., supra*, Robson J., at 323, expressed the view that s. 125 could not be invoked on an application to settle a list of contributories.

See also the following cases supporting the principle that the liability of contributories is limited in its application to the liability of a shareholder in his character as such: *Tilsonburg Agricultural & Manufacturing Co. v. Goodrich*

(1885), 8 O.R. 565 (C.A.); *Re Standard Fire Insurance Co.* (1885), 7 O.R. 488 (H.C.); affd (1885), 12 O.A.R. 486; affd (1886), 12 S.C.R. 644; *Cole v. Canada Fire & Marine Insurance Co.* (1885), 8 O.R. 92 (H.C.); *Re London Speaker Printing Co.* (1889), 16 O.A.R. 508.

"Court"

In Quebec "the Superior Court" means the court for the district where the head office of the corporation is situated: *Dupont v. Cie de moulin à bardeau Chanfréné* (1885), 11 L.N. 225.

The jurisdiction of the court is analogous to the jurisdiction in administration actions: *Re Mercantile Trading Co., Stringer's Case* (1869), 4 Ch. App. 475; *Re County Marine Insurance Co., Rance's Case* (1870), 6 Ch. App. 104.

A local judge of the Supreme Court in British Columbia has no jurisdiction to make a winding-up order under the Act: *Re Kootenay Brewing Co.* (1898), 7 B.C.R. 131; likewise, a prothonotary of the Quebec Superior Court has no jurisdiction to grant a petition for a winding-up order under the Act: *Re Lievre Lumber Cie v. Prevost*, [1954] Que. S.C. 249. In Ontario a petition may be presented to a judge in chambers: *Re Toronto Brass Co.* (1898), 18 P.R. 248 (H.C.); *Re J.F. Cunningham & Son Ltd.*, [1955] O.W.N. 668 (H.C.); and thus the Master has jurisdiction to deal with an application relating to the conduct of the matter. See also s. 110, which provides for the powers of the court to be exercised by a judge in chambers. The modern practice, however, is to apply to the court or a judge in chambers for a winding-up order, and for any matter relating to the conduct of the same.

In British Columbia an order under the Act must take the form of a court order although applied for by way of chamber summons or motion in chambers: *Re Bank of Vancouver*, [1920] 1 W.W.R. 816 (B.C. S.C.).

The decisions under the Act in one province are not binding on the courts of another province: *Re Central Bank* (1889), 30 C.L.T. 271 (Ont.); but as a general rule the court of one province should follow the decision of the highest court of another province upon a federal statute: *R. v. Glenfield*, [1935] 1 D.L.R. 37 (Alta. C.A.); *Hudson's Bay Co. v. Peters*, [1937] 2 D.L.R. 786 (Alta. C.A.).

"Trading corporation"

In ascertaining whether a corporation is a "trading corporation", apparently it is sufficient if any of the objects bring it within the subsection: *Re Lake Winnipeg Transportation, Lumber & Trading Co.* (1891), 7 Man. R. 255 at 259 (Q.B.); *Re Canadian General Service Corp. (No. 1)* (1914), 16 D.L.R. 15 (K.B.). Whether the corporation has actually exercised the powers that bring it within the definition is immaterial: *Re Anchor Investment Co.* (1912), 7 D.L.R. 915 (B.C. S.C.). These cases may be of less relevance now that most corporation statutes do not require a statement of objects, and it may now be necessary to look more at the actual activities of the corporation in question.

Under the term "trading corporation" will be included a gas manufacturing corporation: *De Lorimier v. Canadian Gas & Oil Co.* (1908), 34 Que. S.C. 381; but not a social club: *Montreal City Club v. Stevenson* (1895), 8 Que. S.C. 527;

Re St. James' Club (1852), 2 De G.M. & G. 383; nor a literary society: *Re Bristol Athenaeum* (1889), 43 Ch. D. 236.

Application of Act

Section 6 sets out the corporations to which the Act applies. It is subject to ss. 7-9; regarding these, see the subheadings below.

The federal Parliament appears to have the power to legislate for the winding up (a) of all corporations incorporated under federal legislation (whether or not business is carried on outside Canada): *Re I.O.S. Ltd. (No. 2)* (1973), 43 D.L.R. (3d) 759 (N.B. C.A.); (b) of all corporations incorporated under legislation of any of the provinces of Canada, provided the corporation is insolvent; and (c) of a foreign corporation, provided the corporation is insolvent and has assets in Canada.

The principal questions arising under s. 6 have related to the jurisdiction and constitutional powers of Parliament with respect to foreign and provincial corporations.

By virtue of s. 3(3) of the *Canada Business Corporations Act*, the *Winding-up Act* is not applicable to any corporation incorporated or continued under that Act.

Solvent provincial corporations being wound up provincially

The question has arisen whether paragraph (b) of s. 6 empowers the court to supersede a provincial or voluntary winding-up in the case of a solvent corporation incorporated under provincial charter.

In *Re Colonial Investment Co. of Winnipeg* (1913), 15 D.L.R. 634, the Manitoba Court of Appeal held that a provincial corporation if in the process of voluntary liquidation pursuant to a resolution of its shareholders, though not actually insolvent, may be brought within this provision of the *Winding-up Act* and ordered to be wound up on the petition of a shareholder (under s. 10(b)). The decision proceeds on the basis that federal Parliament, in the exercise of its exclusive regulative power respecting bankruptcy and insolvency under s. 91 (head 21) of the *Constitution Act, 1867* can declare that a voluntary liquidation constitutes a species of insolvency.

In *Re Cramp Steel Co.* (1908), 16 O.L.R. 230 at 231 (H.C.), Mabee, J., said "the only clauses of the . . . Act which can be made to apply to an Ontario corporation are those dealing with insolvency." The *Cramp* case was followed and the *Colonial Investment* case was not followed by Orde, J., in *Re Empire Timber, Lumber & Tie Co.* (1920), 48 O.L.R. 193 (S.C.). There it was pointed out that the Act does not declare that a voluntary liquidation is a "species of insolvency" but rather indicates that there may be cases of liquidation or winding-up that do not necessarily constitute insolvency. The *Empire Timber* case was followed in *Re North American Lumber Co.* (1921), 20 O.W.N. 232 (S.C.); *Dominion Savings & Investment Society v. Huron & Erie Mortgage Corp.* (1923), 25 O.W.N. 339 (H.C.); affd (1924), 25 O.W.N. 603 (C.A.).

The *Cramp* case, accordingly, must be regarded as being law in Ontario, and the Act does not there apply to a provincially incorporated corporation unless it is insolvent. The *Cramp* case has been followed in Quebec: *Druker v. Quebec (Securities Commission)*, [1960] Que. Q.B. 1082 (C.A.). See also the cases referred to under the next heading.

Section 6 applies also to corporations that are insolvent though not technically being wound up and against which proceedings are being taken to realize their assets and pay their debts: *Re Union Fire Insurance Co.* (1886), 13 O.A.R. 268.

Insolvent provincial corporations

A corporation, though incorporated by a provincial legislature, may be put into compulsory liquidation and wound up under this Act if it is insolvent. The *Winding-up Act* is in the nature of an insolvency law: *Clarke v. Union Fire Insurance Co.* (1887), 14 O.R. 618 (H.C.); affd (1890), 16 O.A.R. 161; affd (1890), 17 S.C.R. 265; *Re Eldorado Union Store Co.* (1886), 17 N.S.R. 514 (C.A.); *Re British Columbia Iron Works Co.* (1899), 6 B.C.R. 536 (C.A.); *Gouin v. Title Guarantee & Trust Corp.*, [1939] 2 D.L.R. 796 (Que. S.C.) (Quebec corporation having the powers of a trust corporation and also of a loan corporation with borrowing powers).

If a provincially incorporated corporation is not shown to be insolvent, the Act does not apply: *Re Cramp Steel Co.* (1908), 16 O.L.R. 230 (H.C.), and cases noted above; *Re Nelson Ford Lumber Co.* (1908), 1 Sask. L.R. 108 (T.D.); *Re Outlook Hotel Co.* (1909), 2 Sask. L.R. 435 at 439 (T.D.); *Mutual Enterprises Inc. v. Dettner*, [1938] 2 D.L.R. 778 (Que. S.C.).

A corporation incorporated under the Ontario Companies Act and carrying on business in Ontario is "doing business in Canada" within the meaning of this Act: *Re Ontario Forge & Bolt Co.* (1894) 25 O.R. 407 (H.C.).

The provincial Act dealing with winding-up did not apply to a corporation incorporated in that province where an application was made to wind up on the ground of insolvency, because provincial legislatures have no jurisdiction in matters of bankruptcy or insolvency: *Re Iron Clay Brick Manufacturing Co.* (1889), 19 O.R. 113 (H.C.); *Re Tober Enterprises Ltd.* (1980), 109 D.L.R. (3d) 184 (B.C. S.C.).

Foreign corporations

The federal Parliament can, in the exercise of its powers respecting insolvency and bankruptcy, legislate respecting insolvent corporations doing business in Canada and with reference to the property of such corporations within its jurisdiction: *Allen v. Hanson* (1890), 18 S.C.R. 667; *Re Breakwater Co.* (1914), 33 O.L.R. 65 (H.C.).

The business of a foreign corporation having assets in Canada may be wound up here although the corporation is in process of being wound up elsewhere: *Re Stewart River Gold Dredging Co.* (1912), 7 D.L.R. 736 (Y.T. Ct.); *Re Breakwater Co., supra.*

Canadian policyholders petitioned for distribution of the deposit made by a foreign corporation, with the Minister of Finance, under 31 Vict., c. 48 (Dom.) and 34 Vict., c. 9 (Dom.), the corporation being insolvent. It was held that they were entitled to the relief asked, notwithstanding that proceedings to wind up the corporation were pending before the English courts: *Re Briton Medical & General Life Assn.* (1886), 12 O.R. 441 (H.C.).

Where liquidation was sought in Canada with the concurrence of the foreign liquidator and as ancillary to the foreign winding up, the Supreme Court of Canada held that this Act warranted the making of the order and that the statute is not *ultra vires* of Parliament: *Allen v. Hanson* (1890) 18 S.C.R. 667, commenting on and partially overruling the following cases: *Re Steel Co. of Canada* (1884), 17 N.S.R. 49 (C.A.); revd *(sub nom. Merchants' Bank of Halifax v. Gillespie Moffat & Co.)* (1885) 10 S.C.R. 312; *Re Halifax Sugar Refinery Co.* (1889), 22 N.S.R. 71 (C.A.).

All the *Winding-up Act* seeks to do in the case of foreign corporations is protect and regulate the property in Canada and protect the rights of the creditors of such corporations relating to their property in Canada. Although not all the provisions of the Act are applicable to foreign corporations, those which are should be acted upon: *Allen v. Hanson, supra.*

However, in *Re Breakwater Co.* (1914) 33 O.L.R. 65 (H.C.), Middleton, J., held that once the winding-up order is made, the provisions of the Act apply and control the whole situation; and that the winding-up order under the Act is in no sense ancillary to the proceedings in the foreign court, but is an independent and self-contained proceeding. It was also held that it was the duty of the Canadian liquidator to distribute the Canadian funds among all the creditors whether residing in Canada or elsewhere, and that he could not discharge himself by remitting them to the foreign liquidator. In *Allen v. Hanson, supra*, Strong, J., at 674, appears to have taken a somewhat different view of the nature of the proceedings and of the duties of the Canadian liquidator, viz., that the effect of the winding-up order here was only to entitle the liquidator to realize the assets, and after paying all creditors (not merely those within the jurisdiction), to remit the balance (if any) of the assets to the foreign liquidator to be applied and distributed as might be directed by the proper person; and also that the Canadian winding-up was a subsidiary proceeding.

In *Re National Benefit Assurance Co.*, [1927] 3 D.L.R. 289 (Man. C.A.), the actual point decided was that a policyholder under a policy of insurance was not entitled to rank as a preferred creditor, in respect of a claim on his policy, on deposits made in connection with licences for kinds of insurance other than that covered by his policy. The liquidator had got in the deposits and had provided in full for all claims under licensed branches of insurance. Apart from claims in respect of unlicensed branches and the balance of the deposit, the corporation had no other liabilities or assets in Canada. Trueman, J.A., however, at 300-302, adopted the view that the corporation in question being an English corporation with substantial liabilities, of which but a fractional amount was owing in Canada, a double liquidation should be avoided by treating the duties of the Canadian liquidator as ancillary to the English winding-up proceedings. He also pointed out that if, in the Canadian liquidation, the Canadian assets were retained here it would only be for the purpose of paying the Canadian creditors *pari passu* with the English and other creditors. He therefore considered that, since there could be no apprehension that the Canadian creditors would not have equal treatment with all other creditors, there was no reason why the assets in the hands of the Canadian liquidator should not be remitted to the English liquidator. Some of the English decisions cited by Trueman, J.A., in support of the above view and other decisions may be briefly summarized as follows: the court sanctioned the acceptance of an undertaking by the solicitor for the English agent of the corporation that the English assets should remain in *statu quo* until further order: *Re Matheson Bros. Ltd.* (1884), 27 Ch. D. 225; the operations of the liquidator, without special direction of the court, should be limited to getting in the assets and making a list of the creditors in the jurisdiction: *Re Commercial Bank of South Australia* (1886), 33 Ch. D. 174 at 178; a compulsory winding-up order in Australia did not supersede but was ancillary to a voluntary winding-up in England of a corporation having its registered office in England but having a branch office in Australia; *North Australian Territory Co. v. Goldsbrough, Mort & Co.* (1889), 61 L.T. 716; the powers of the liquidator were limited to the collecting of the English assets and the settling of the list of English creditors and a limitation placed on the liquidator's remuneration: *Re Federal Bank of Australia Ltd.* (1893), 62 L.J. Ch. 561 (C.A.); any surplus should be administered under the principal liquidation proceedings: *Re Briton Medical & General Life Assn.* (1886), 12 O.R. 441 at 447 (H.C.).

If, however, a winding-up order has been made under the Act in the usual form, while it may be difficult to see how the operation of the liquidation can be limited (subject to the special provisions applicable to certain insurance corporations, contained in s. 165) as indicated in some of the above decisions. The modern practice is that Canadian creditors should not have their rights remitted in the foreign liquidation but are entitled to have them determined in the Canadian proceedings, if there should be any conflict between the Canadian and foreign law. See *Re Breakwater Co.* (1914), 33 O.L.R. 65 at 67 (H.C.).

In *Re Hibernian Merchants Ltd.*, [1958] 1 Ch. 76, Roxburgh, J., held that in view of the words " . . . all the provisions of this Act with respect to winding-up shall apply . . . [to a foreign corporation]" in s. 399 of the *English Companies Act*, 1948, the court had no power to limit the operation of an order made on the winding up of a foreign corporation to the English assets.

The liquidation of a corporation in a foreign country where it is domiciled will not release it from liability under a contract made and to be performed in England, and the other party to the contract can sue on it in England notwithstanding the foreign liquidation proceedings: *Gibbs & Sons v. Société Industrielle et Commerciale des Métaux* (1890), 25 Q.B.D. 399 (C.A.).

The English statutory provisions with regard to the winding-up of foreign corporations have never been similar to section 6 of the Canadian Act.

While in the following cases it has been held that foreign corporations doing business in England can be wound up there, the cases are based on the statutory provisions in force at the time. They are mentioned here only as illustrations of the circumstances that may constitute "doing business" for this purpose: *Re Commercial Bank of India* (1868), L.R. 6 Eq. 517; *Re Matheson Bros. Ltd.* (1884),

27 Ch. D. 225; *Re Commercial Bank of South Australia* (1886), 33 Ch. D. 174, (1887), 36 Ch. D. 522; *Re Mercantile Bank of Australia*, [1892] 2 Ch. 204; *Re Federal Bank of Australia Ltd.* (1893), 62 L.J. Ch. 561 (C.A.). In *Re Lloyd Generale Italiano* (1885), 29 Ch. D. 219, the court held that under the provisions then in force, it had no jurisdiction to wind up a foreign corporation that had no branch office of its own in England but merely carried on business through an agent in England.

Under s. 666 of the English *Companies Act*, 1985, a foreign corporation that has carried on business in England can be wound up by the court in a greater variety of circumstances than a foreign corporation under s. 6 of the Canadian Act. The circumstances in which a foreign corporation may be wound up under s. 666(5) are:

(a) if the company is dissolved, or has ceased to carry on business, or is carrying on business only for the purpose of winding-up its affairs;
(b) if the corporation is unable to pay its debts;
(c) if the court is of opinion that it is just and equitable that the company should be wound up.

Under s. 670 of the *English Companies Act*, 1985, a foreign corporation that was carrying on business in England, but has ceased to do so, may be wound up in England even if it has been dissolved according to its own law of incorporation: *Re Russian Bank for Foreign Trade*, [1933] Ch. 745; *Re Tea Trading Co., K. & C. Popoff Bros.*, [1933] Ch. 647; *Russian & English Bank v. Baring Bros. & Co.*, [1936] A.C. 405; *Banque des Marchands de Moscou (Koupetschesky) v. Kindersley*, [1951] Ch. 112 (C.A.); *Re Azoff-Don Commercial Bank*, [1954] Ch. 315.

In *Banque des Marchands de Moscou (Koupetschesky) v. Kindersley*, [1951] 1 Ch. 112 (C.A.), it was held that a foreign corporation could be wound up under the above provisions even though it did not have an established place of business in England, it being sufficient that there were assets and creditors in England, as these were sufficient indications of a business having been carried on by the corporation in England.

Where the court in England has made a winding-up order with respect to a foreign corporation, the winding-up is conducted in accordance with English, not foreign, law: *Re Suidair International Airways Ltd. (In Liquidation)*, [1951] 1 Ch. 165.

Foreign creditors are entitled to prove in the English winding-up in the same manner as English creditors: *Re Azoff-Don Commercial Bank*, [1954] Ch. 315. If by English law the debt which is sought to be proved in the English winding up is locally situated in a foreign country, and if by the law of that country the debt was discharged at the date of the winding-up in England, the debt cannot be proved: *Re Banque des Marchands de Moscou (Koupetschesky), Royal Exchange Assurance v. Liquidator; Re Banque des Marchands de Moscou (Koupetschesky), Wilenkin v. Liquidator*, [1952] 1 All E.R. 1269; *Re Banque des Marchands de Moscou (Koupetschesky)*, [1954] 2 All E.R. 746.

Where a foreign corporation had been dissolved under its own law of incorporation, and where years later, on the discovery of assets in England, a winding-up order was made under the *Companies Act*, 1948, the court held that the right of the Crown to *bona vacantia* extended only to any surplus existing after the proper administration of the assets in the English winding-up: *Re Banque Industrielle de Moscou*, [1952] 2 All E.R. 532; *Re Banque des Marchands de Moscou (Koupetschesky)*, [1958] Ch. 182.

Special classes of corporations

The following have been ordered to be wound up: corporations incorporated by a royal charter: *Re Bank of South Australia (No. 2)*, [1895] 1 Ch. at 587 (C.A.); corporations incorporated by special Act: *Re Portsmouth Borough (Kingston, Fratton & Southsea) Tramways Co.*, [1892] 2 Ch. 362.

A tram corporation incorporated by a special Act may be wound up, not being a railway corporation: *Re Brentford & Isleworth Tramways Co.* (1884), 26 Ch. D. 527; *Re Portsmouth Borough (Kingston, Fratton & Southsea) Tramways Co., supra.*

The court will be most cautious about winding up a corporation that is in the nature of a public undertaking, when the legislature has declared it to be of great public benefit: *Re Free Fishermen of Faversham (Co. or Fraternity of)* (1887), 36 Ch. D. 329 (C.A.); *Re Exmouth Docks Co.* (1873), L.R. 17 Eq. 181. See *contra: Re Barton-upon-Humber & District Water Co.* (1889), 42 Ch. D. 585; *Re Portsmouth Borough (Kingston, Fratton & Southsea) Tramways Co., supra.*

A social club is not an association or a trading corporation within the *Winding-up Act*: *Montreal City Club v. Stevenson* (1895), 8 Que. S.C. 537; *Re St. James' Club* (1852), De G. M. & G. 383; *Langevin v. Stadium Co.* (1917), 19 Que. P.R. 245; *Durocher v. Club champêtre Canada* (1917), 19 Que. P.R. 178. A club that has only subsidiary power to do certain acts of a commercial nature is not a commercial corporation: *Langevin v. Stadium Co., supra.* Nor is a literary society: *Re Bristol Athenaeum* (1889), 43 Ch. D. 236.

A corporation dissolved after a winding-up cannot again be ordered to be wound up: *Coxon v. Gorst*, [1891] 2 Ch. 73; unless the winding-up can be impeached for fraud: *Re London & Caledonian Marine Insurance Co.* (1879), 11 Ch. D. 140 (C.A.); *Re Pinto Silver Mining Co.* (1878), 8 Ch. D. 273 (C.A.). But see *Re Crookhaven Mining Co.* (1866), L.R. 3 Eq. 69, where it was held that the dissolution of a corporation under the English *Companies Act*, 1862, did not deprive the court of its jurisdiction over such corporation under the Act.

Where a corporation has been struck off the register pursuant to the provisions of the Nova Scotia Companies Act and in consequence is dissolved, no winding-up order should be made while the corporation remains off the register: *Re Albion Machine Co.*, [1929] 1 D.L.R. 274 (N.S. T.D.).

A corporation irregularly incorporated is non-existent and cannot be wound up: *Re National Debenture & Assets Corp.*, [1891] 2 Ch. 505 (C.A.); *Oakes v. Turquand & Harding; Peek v. Turquand & Harding; Re Overend, Gurney & Co.* (1867), L.R. 2 H.L. 325.

The same applies to an illegal corporation: *Re Padstow Total Loss & Collision*

Assurance Assn. (1882), 20 Ch. D. 137 (C.A.); *Re Ilfracombe Permanent Mutual Benefit Building Society*, [1901] 1 Ch. 102.

It is immaterial whether the corporation was carrying on business at the date of the winding-up: *Scott v. Hyde* (1908), 18 Que. K.B. 138 (C.A.). An incorporated bank that has never become entitled to commence business as a bank may be wound up: *Re Monarch Bank of Canada* (May 29, 1908) [unreported].

The fact that a corporation's sphere of action is outside of the country of incorporation is no bar to its being wound up in that country provided it is insolvent: *Re Madrid & Valencia Ry. Co.; Ex parte Turner; Ex parte James* (1849), 3 De G. & Sm. 127; *Re Factage Parisien Ltd.* (1865), 34 L.J. Ch. 142 (note). Nor is it a bar that all its members are foreigners: *Re General Co. for Promotion of Land Credit* (1870), 5 Ch. App. 363 (L.J.).

The court has jurisdiction to wind up a Manitoba corporation having its head office in the province if it has assets in Canada, although it never carried on any business in Manitoba: *Re Stewart & Matthews Ltd.* (1916), 26 Man. R. 277 (K.B.).

Excepted corporations (s. 7)

By s. 7, certain corporations (building societies not having a capital stock, and railway or telegraph corporations) are excepted from the application of the Act. See *Clarke v. Union Fire Insurance Co.* (1890), 17 S.C.R. 264 at 274.

Financial Institutions

It will be noted that in the case of banks and insurance corporations, the petition is usually made by the Attorney General of Canada on the request of the minutes.

Banks (s. 6)

By s. 8 the provisions of Part I of the Act are subject to the provisions of Part II (s. 151 ff.) in the case of banks other than saving banks.

The provisions in s. 151 ff. must be complied with before the winding-up can proceed. See *Mott v. Bank of Nova Scotia* (1887), 14 S.C.R. 650; *Re Central Bank of Canada* (1887), 15 O.R. 309 at 310 (H.C.).

Insurance corporations (s. 9)

By s. 9 the provisions of Part I of the Act are subject to the provisions of Part III (s. 159 ff.) in the case of insurance corporations. See *A.G. Canada v. Cardinal Insurance Co.* (1982), 39 O.R. (2d) 204 (H.C.) where a winding-up was granted when one insurance company was being administered by the Superintendent. See also *Re Advocate General Insurance Co. of Canada* (1989), 60 Man. R. (2d) 186 (Q.B.).

Loan, Trust and Insurance Corporations

Under s. 84(3) of the *Loan Companies Act*, R.S.C. 1985, c. L-12, the Minister may request the Attorney General of Canada to apply for an order to wind up the corporation under the *Winding Up Act* when the Superintendent has control of the corporation concerned pursuant to the provisions of the Act. A similar provision is contained in the *Trust Companies Act*, R.S.C. 1985, c. T-20, s. 95(3) and in the *Insurance Companies Act*, S.C. 1991, c. 47, s. 685, which is applicable to domestic and foreign insurance companies or societies. See *A.G. Canada v. Cardinal Insurance Co.* (1982), 39 O.R. (2d) 204 (H.C.). See also *Advocate General Insurance Co. of Canada, Re* (1989), 60 Man. R. (2d) 186 (Q.B.).

When corporation deemed insolvent (s. 3)

Section 3 sets out eight different situations in which a corporation will be deemed insolvent.

Unable to pay its debts (subs. (a))

A corporation is deemed insolvent if it is unable to pay its debts as they become due. Section 4 provides that a corporation is deemed to be unable to pay its debts as they become due if a demand has been served and default made as provided in that section.

In Manitoba it has been held by Taylor C.J., that s. 3(a) and s. 4 are to be read together, that s. 4 defines what "unable to pay its debts" means and that a petitioning creditor who seeks to show insolvency within s. 3(a) can only succeed by proceeding in the manner provided in s. 4: *Re Rapid City Farmers' Elevator Co.* (1894), 9 Man. R. 574 (Q.B.); see also *Re Qu'Appelle Valley Farming Co.* (1888), 5 Man. R. 160 (Q.B.); *Re Catholic Publishing & Bookselling Co.* (1864), 2 De G. J. & Sm. 116. There are cases in Ontario to the same effect: *Re Briton Medical & General Life Assn.* (1886), 11 O.R. 478 (Ch. D.); *Re Ewart Carriage Works Ltd.* (1904), 8 O.L.R. 527 (where the petitioner was given leave to amend, offer additional evidence and again present his petition within fourteen days); *Re Cobalt Development Co.* (1908), 12 O.W.R. 83 (T.D.). These cases have been followed in British Columbia: *Re Anchor Investment Co.* (1912), 7 D.L.R. 915 (B.C. S.C.); and in Saskatchewan: *Re Great West Brick & Coal Co.* (1916), 9 Sask. L.R. 240 (T.D.).

The above decisions may be regarded as doubtful in light of later decisions.

In *Re Home Bank of Canada*, [1923] 4 D.L.R. 891 (Ont. H.C.), Fisher, J., at p. 895 said:

> It seems to me if a creditor could shew by any other means than that pointed out by sec. 4 that a company is unable to pay its debts as they become due, the Court would be bound to regard that evidence. Section 4 only provides one of the modes by which a company may be deemed unable to pay its debts. I do not understand the decision of the *Briton Medical etc. Life Ass'n*, 11 O.R. 478, and the *Ewart Carriage Works, Ltd.*, 8 O.L.R. 527, to go so far as to decide that if there was sufficient proof apart from what sec. 4 provides that no order could be made. In those cases there were only bare allegations of the facts that the company was unable to pay and no evidence which would have been conclusive apart from sec. 4.

See also *Re G. Minerals Ltd.* (1967), 61 D.L.R. (2d) 186 (B.C. S.C.) to the same effect.

However, it should be observed that in *Re Home Bank of Canada* there was a written acknowledgment based on a resolution passed by the directors admitting insolvency, so that the order was actually made under s. 3(d).

In *Re Milo Wheat Co.*, [1925] 2 D.L.R. 1170 (Man. C.A.), Perdue C.J.M. and Dennistoun J.A., expressed the same view as Fisher J., in the *Home Bank* case, although the petition failed because the material was insufficient, the petitioner having failed to prove that the corporation was insolvent and that non-payment of his claim was due the corporation's inability to pay. See also *Cushing Sulphite Fibre Co. v. Cushing (sub nom. Re Cushing Sulphite Fibre Co.)* (1905), 37 N.B.R. 254 at 302 (C.A.).

In Quebec it has been held that when insolvency is alleged in the petition, the petitioning creditor is not compelled to prove that he demanded payment from the corporation conformably to s. 4: *McKay v. Assn. coloniale de construction & de placements* (1884) 13 R.L.O.S. 383 (Que. S.C.). But the petitioner must allege and prove the insolvency otherwise: *Eddy v. Henderson* (1890), M.L.R. 6 S.C. 137; *Moore Carpet Co. v. Mitchell* (1908), 5 E.L.R. 248 (Que. C.A.); *Re Dominion Antimony Co.* (1908), 6 E.L.R. 177; *Calumet Metals Co. v. Eldredge* (1914), 17 D.L.R. 276 (Que. C.A.); *H. Walters & Sons Ltd. v. Walters* (1921), 30 Que. K.B. 525 (C.A.).

Where extension of the time for paying accounts was the usual practice in a trade, the Quebec court held that it would be unreasonable and unjust, as well as contrary to the spirit of the Act, to hold that a corporation availing itself of a few extensions of this kind had ceased to pay its debts as they became due so as to justify a creditor commencing proceedings under the Act to wind up the corporation: *Allure Sportswear Inc. v. Beiner*, [1960] Que. S.C. 628.

In Manitoba, it was held that a corporation should be deemed to be insolvent under subs. (a) where it appeared that the petitioners had recovered judgment against the corporation on a debt and that the bailiff had made a seizure under an execution, under which certain moneys were realized which were being held for distribution among creditors: *Re Manitoba Commission Co.* (1913), 9 D.L.R. 436 (Man. K.B.); affd (1913), 4 W.W.R. 255 (Man. C.A.).

The English courts have held a corporation unable to pay its debts where the corporation's acceptances were dishonoured: *Re Globe New Patent Iron & Steel Co.* (1875), L.R. 20 Eq. 337; and where the creditor was told by the corporation's solicitor that there were no assets on which he could levy: *Re Flagstaff Silver Mining Co. of Utah* (1875), L.R. 20 Eq. 268; *Re Yate Collieries & Limeworks Co.*, [1883] W.N. 171.

In *Re Rapid City Farmers' Elevator Co.* (1894), 9 Man. R. 574 (Q.B.), Taylor, C.J., distinguished *Re Globe New Patent Iron & Steel Co.* and *Re Flagstaff Silver Mining Co. of Utah, supra*, on the ground that the *Winding-up Act* contains no clause corresponding to s. 80, subs. 4, of the English *Companies Act*, 1862; cf. *Re Ewart Carriage Works Ltd.* (1904), 8 O.L.R. 527 at 528.

"Unable to pay its debts" means inability to pay debts absolutely as they become due, that is, debts that the creditor may demand be paid instantly: *Re*

European Life Assurance Society (1869), L.R. 9 Eq. 122. This does not mean "demanded" but "demandable": *Re Bristol Joint Stock Bank* (1890), 44 Ch. D. 703.

A corporation is not unable to pay its debts because it is carrying on a losing business if its assets exceed its liabilities; *Re Joint Stock Coal Co.* (1869), L.R. 8 Eq. 146; *Re Spence's Patent Non-Conducting Composition & Cement Co.* (1869), L.R. 9 Eq. 9.

An allegation that a corporation is insolvent and unable to pay petitioners' debts is not a sufficient allegation within the meaning of subs. (a): *Re Rapid City Farmers' Elevator Co.* (1894), 9 Man. R. 574 (Q.B.).

The non-payment of a disputed debt is no proof of insolvency: *Re Wheal Lovell Mining Co.; Ex parte Wyld* (1849), 1 Mac. & G. 1 (L.C.); *Re Gold Hill Mines* (1883), 23 Ch. D. 210 (C.A.). Whether there is a debt must be settled by action before petition: *Re Great Britain Mutual Life Assurance Society* (1880), 16 Ch. D. 246 (C.A.); but the court will determine the existence of the debt, if possible on hearing the petition: *Re Imperial Silver Quarries Co.* (1868), 16 W.R. 1220; *Re Anglo-Bavarian Steel Ball Co.*, [1899] W.N. 80.

Calling meeting of creditors to compound with them (subs. (b))

A corporation will be deemed insolvent if it calls a meeting of its creditors for the purpose of compounding with them.

Where a letter sent by a corporation to a creditor merely stated "please have a representative meet the creditors" at a certain time and place, but did not state the purpose of the meeting, the court held that without any account of what took place at the meeting, it would be impossible to infer from the letter that it was a meeting of the corporation's creditors called for the purpose of compounding with them: *Re Manitoba Commission Co.* (1912), 2 D.L.R. 1 (Man. K.B.). However, where the corporation called a meeting of its creditors, and at the meeting the manager stated that the corporation was unable to pay its debts and offered to compound with the creditors, that was a sufficient acknowledgment of the purposes of the meeting for the purposes of subs. (b): *Re Manitoba Commission Co.* (1913), 9 D.L.R. 436 (Man. K.B.); affd (1913), 4 W.W.R. 255 (Man. C.A.).

Exhibiting statement showing inability to meet liabilities (subs. (c))

If a corporation exhibits a statement showing its inability to meet its liabilities, it will be deemed insolvent; see *Re G. Minerals Ltd.* (1967), 61 D.L.R. (2d) 186 (B.C.S.C.).

This subsection is *intra vires* of Parliament: *Re Lake Winnipeg Transportation, Lumber & Trading Co.* (1891), 7 Man. R. 255 at 262 (Q.B.).

The liabilities referred to in the subsection are those to creditors as distinguished from those to shareholders: *Re United Canneries of British Columbia Ltd.* (1903), 9 B.C.R. 528 (S.C.); *Re Great West Brick & Coal Co.* (1916), 9 Sask. L.R. 240 (T.D.). The statement exhibited must be the corporation's statement. Thus, where the corporation's president threw open the books of the corporation to an accountant employed by a creditor, and the accountant made a report to the creditors showing the corporation to be insolvent, these facts were held not to bring the corporation within the subsection, for the acts of the accountant were not those of the corporation: *Re Manitoba Commission Co.* (1912), 2 D.L.R. 1 (Man. K.B.).

Where a petition is filed under this subsection, the statement must be taken as correct and cannot be attacked by the petitioner: *Re United Canneries, supra.*

Otherwise acknowledging its insolvency (subs. (d))

A corporation may acknowledge its insolvency in some way other than those enumerated in clauses (a), (b) and (c), above, and if it does so, it is deemed insolvent.

As a matter of pleading, where it is intended to rely upon an acknowledgement of insolvency, such acknowledgement must be stated and set forth in the petition: *Re Briton Medical & General Life Assn.* (1886), 11 O.R. 478 (Ch. D.); see also *Re Ewart Carriage Works Ltd.* (1904), 8 O.L.R. 527, at 529.

A debtor is insolvent when his property, subject to execution, if sold under legal process at a sale fairly and reasonably conducted, would not be sufficient to pay his debts: *Dominion Bank v. Cowan* (1887), 14 O.L.R. 465 at 466 (H.C.).

The acknowledgement must be "some formal act of the directors or of the shareholders or of some officer expressly or impliedly authorized to make such an acknowledgement on the corporation's behalf": *Re Manitoba Commission Co.* (1912), 2 D.L.R. 1 (Man. K.B.) at 7 per Mathers C.J. It must be a corporate act: *Re Atlas Canning Co.* (1897), 5 B.C.R. 661 (C.A.). Thus, a resolution passed by the directors to the effect that the creditors be notified and requested to file claims with a trustee for *pro rata* payment, followed by notification to the creditors, is sufficient: *Re Anchor Investment Co.* (1912), 7 D.L.R. 915 (B.C. S.C.). Moreover, where the corporation called a meeting of creditors at which the manager stated that the corporation was unable to meet its debts and offered to compound with the creditors, it was held that this was a sufficient acknowledgement of the corporation's insolvency: *Re Manitoba Commission Co.* (1913), 9 D.L.R. 436 (Man. K.B.), affd (1913), 4 W.W.R. 255 (Man. C.A.).

The fact that the corporation has not paid the debt and has allowed itself to be sued, and judgment to be recovered and execution returned *nulla bona*, is not an acknowledgement of insolvency within the subsection: *Re Qu'Appelle Valley Farming Co.* (1888), 5 Man. R. 160 (Q.B.); nor are affidavits of the corporation's officers to the effect that the corporation is insolvent, when those do not give a statement of assets and liabilities, sufficient; see also *Re Great West Brick & Coal Co.* (1916), 9 Sask. L.R. 240 (T.D.). Nor is failure to appear and oppose the petition enough: *Re Lake Winnipeg Transportation, Lumber & Trading Co.* (1891), 7 Man. R. 255 (Q.B.); nor is admission by counsel, for the material filed must bring the case within the section: *Re Grundy Stove Co.* (1904), 7 O.L.R. 252 (H.C.).

The mere fact that according to its statement the corporation's assets are valued higher than is reasonable, and that there is a deficit rather than a surplus, is not sufficient material on which to base an order for winding up: *Re Canuck Automobiles Ltd.* (1919), 17 O.W.N. 328 (H.C.).

If a petition for the winding-up of a bank can bring the bank within subs. (d) a winding-up order may be made, notwithstanding the appointment of a curator under the *Bank Act: Re Home Bank of Canada*, [1923] 4 D.L.R. 891 at 894 (Ont. H.C.).

Assigning, removing its property to defeat creditors (subs. (e))

If a corporation assigns, removes or disposes of any of its property, or attempts or is about to do so, with intent to defraud, defeat or delay any of its creditors, it will be deemed insolvent.

A winding-up petition that alleges fraud, for example, by promoters and directors, must state the facts that constitute the fraud though not the evidence. If there is only a vague general allegation of fraud, evidence will not be admitted of particular acts of fraud: *Re Rica Gold Washing Co.* (1879), 11 Ch. D. 36 (C.A.). See also *Re Qu'Appelle Valley Farming Co.* (1888), 5 Man. R. 160 at 164; and *Re Ewart Carriage Works Ltd.* (1904), 8 O.L.R. 527.

Where a corporation that had ceased operations and was so heavily indebted it could have been put in liquidation, was proceeding to transfer its assets, against the will of dissentient shareholders and creditors, in consideration of the issue of paid-up shares of another corporation, it was held that the corporation was brought within subs. (e) as being about to assign some of its property with intent to defraud and delay creditors: *Calumet Metals Ltd. v. Eldredge* (1914), 17 D.L.R. 276 (Que. C.A.).

Procuring execution against its property (subs. (f))

If a corporation procures an execution against its money, goods, chattels, land or property with intent to defraud, defeat or delay any of its creditors, it will be deemed insolvent.

Making general assignment (subs. (g))

Under this clause, a corporation will be deemed insolvent if it has made a general conveyance or assignment of its property for the benefit of its creditors; or if, being unable to pay its creditors, without their consent or without satisfying their claims it sells or conveys the whole or the main part of its stock in trade or its assets.

A corporation unable to meet its liabilities in full conveyed the main part of its assets to another corporation without the consent of its creditors and without satisfying their claims. It was held that a winding-up order might issue: *Re Qu'Appelle Valley Farming Co.* (1888), 5 Man. R. 160 (Q.B.). See also *Calumet Metals Co. v. Eldredge, supra.*

The fact a corporation is in voluntary liquidation is *prima facie* evidence of insolvency: *Northampton Coal, Iron & Waggon Co. v. Midland Waggon Co.* (1878), 7 Ch. D. 500 (C.A.); *Pure Spirit Co. v. Fowler* (1890), 25 Q.B.D. 235 (D.C.). The court may, however, refuse an order in such a case: *Re Strathy Wire Fence Co.* (1904), 8 O.L.R. 186 (C.A.).

In Manitoba it has been decided that a corporation cannot be deemed insolvent within the meaning of the Act because an execution has been returned *nulla bona* by a county court bailiff: *Re Rapid City Farmers' Elevator Co.* (1894), 9 Man. R. 574 (Q.B.); following *Re Qu'Appelle Valley Farming Co., supra.*

Permitting execution to remain unsatisfied (subs. (h))

If a corporation permits an execution against it to remain unsatisfied until four days prior to the sheriff's sale of the property or until fifteen days after the property has been seized, it will be deemed insolvent under this clause.

In computing the time under this subsection, the day fixed for the sale is not included. Where the writ was in the sheriff's hands on December 30 and the sale was fixed for January 3, it was held that this proved insolvency within subs. (h): *Re Lake Winnipeg Transportation, Lumber & Trading Co.* (1891), 7 Man. R. 255 (Q.B.).

Evidence of actual seizure is necessary: *Rapid City Farmers' Elevator Co.* (1894), 9 Man. R. 574 (Q.B.); *Re Ewart Carriage Works Ltd.* (1904), 8 O.L.R. 527; *Re Great West Brick & Coal Co.* (1916), 9 Sask. L.R. 240 (T.D.).

This subsection is not affected by s. 4: *Re Installations, Ltd.* (1913) 14 D.L.R. 679.

Section 4

This section provides that a corporation is deemed to be unable to pay its debts as they become due if a demand has been served and the corporation neglects to pay the sum within the time specified in and as provided by the section.

When the debt was not due when demand was made, it was held that non-payment was not evidence of insolvency within the meaning of the section: *Re Briton Medical & General Life Assn.* (1886), 11 O.R. 478 (Ch. D.).

A delay by a creditor (for example, for eight months) in following up a statutory demand is not an implied withdrawal of his demand and does not disentitle him to found a winding-up petition on the corporation's non-compliance: *Re Imperial Hydropathic Hotel Co., Blackpool Ltd.* (1882), 23 Ch. D. 1 (C.A.).

The petitioner's delay may, however, affect the court's discretion to grant or refuse the order: *Re Strathy Wire Fence Co.* (1904), 8 O.L.R. 186 at 191 (C.A.).

Service of a specially endorsed writ is not equivalent to service of a demand under the Act: *Re Abbott-Mitchell Iron & Steel Co.* (1901) 2 O.L.R. 143. In Quebec it has been held that service of a winding-up petition is equivalent to service of a demand: *Alex Bremner v. Dominion Floor & Wall Tile Co.* (1915), 17 Que. P.R. 278.

What constitutes neglect to pay

An order for a winding-up is not rendered invalid by the fact that the petitioning creditor demanded payment of a larger sum than was really due, where the corporation did not offer to pay the sum due: *Cardiff Preserved Coal & Coke Co. v. Norton* (1867), L.R. 2 Ch. 405.

Where proof that the corporation is unable to pay its debts is rested on non-payment of the debt after notice, the whole period mentioned must have expired before the petition for winding-up is presented: *Re Catholic Publishing & Bookselling Co.* (1864), 2 De G. J. & Sm. 116.

The court is bound to treat "neglect" by the corporation to comply with the statutory demand as conclusive evidence of the corporation's insolvency: *Re Imperial Hydropathic Hotel Co., Blackpool Ltd.* (1882), 23 Ch. D. 1 (C.A.).

The mere failure, unless without reasonable cause, to comply with a statutory notice for payment of a debt is not "neglect" to pay within the meaning of the section: *Re London & Paris Banking Corp.* (1874), L.R. 19 Eq. 444. However, if no reason is given why the payment is not made, the corporation must be deemed insolvent: *Cushing Sulphite Fibre Co. v. Cushing (sub nom. Re Cushing Sulphite Fibre Co.* (1905), 37 N.B.R. 254 (C.A.).

In proceeding under this section, it is not sufficient to show that several demands of payment have been made by the creditors without success, unless a demand in writing has been served on the corporation in the manner in which process may legally be served on it: *Re Rapid City Farmers' Elevator Co.* (1894), 9 Man. R. 574 (Q.B.).

Where a petitioning creditor claimed as assignee of a judgment debt, and founded his application under this section, he was held liable to prove that not only the date of the judgment, but also its assignment to him, were prior to his statutory demand: *Re Rapid City Farmers' Elevator Co.* (1895) 10 Man. R. 681 (Q.B.).

A secured creditor may make the demand under the section: *Re Cushing Sulphite Fibre Co. v. Cushing, supra*. See also the notes to s. 3(a).

Commencement of winding-up (s. 5)

The winding-up of the business of the corporation commences from the time that the notice of presentation of the petition for winding-up is served under s. 5: *Fuches v. Hamilton Tribune Co.* (1884), 10 P.R. 409 (H.C.); *Re Fashion Shop Co.* (1915), 33 O.L.R. 253 at 254 (H.C.). The Act contains no provision as to when the winding-up commences where the application for winding-up is by the corporation for in that case, under s. 12(2), no notice of presentation of the petition is required. See also the notes to ss. 12 (in Chapter 20) and 19 (in Chapter 21); and *Bank of Hamilton v. Kramer-Irwin Co.* (1912), 1 D.L.R. 475 (Ont. Master). It is doubtful, as was observed in this case, whether a corporation could consent to judgment after the service of a petition.

A debenture holder who, after and with knowledge of the presentation of a petition, advanced money to the corporation, before the making of the winding-up order, to pay the wages of workmen, was held entitled to a declaration of the validity of the debenture given as security, notwithstanding that s. 105(2) of the *Companies (Consolidation) Act*, 1908, makes every disposition of the property of the corporation made after the commencement of the winding-up void unless the court otherwise orders: *Re Park Ward & Co.*, [1926] Ch. 828; applied in *Re Steane's (Bournemouth) Ltd.*, [1950] 1 All E.R. 21 (Ch. D.); *Re T.W. Construction Ltd.*, [1954] 1 All E.R. 744 (Ch. D.).

Service of petition

The requirements as to service are governed by the general rules of practice in the particular province unless special rules have been made, which will then apply, under s. 136. See the notes to ss. 11-12 under the heading "Notice of application" in Chapter 20.

Service of a winding-up petition must be a real, substantial service. Thus, where the corporation's office had been pulled down and the corporation had ceased to do business for more than eight years, service on a workman employed on the former site was held insufficient: *Re Manchester & London Life Assurance & Loan Assn.* (1870), L.R. 9 Eq. 643.

If the corporation's head office is closed, the petition may be left in the letter box, but in such a case it is desirable that the petition should be served on a member of or on one of the directors of the corporation or on the corporation's solicitor: *Re London & Westminster Wine Co.* (1863), 12 W.R. 6.

Where a corporation had transferred its business and closed its office, the court ordered service of a winding-up petition on any five of the directors: *Re Unity General Assurance Assn.* (1863), 11 W.R. 355.

Service of a winding-up petition on a person authorized by the directors to accept service, for example, on a solicitor appointed by the corporation, is sufficient, though such service be not at the registered office of the corporation: *Re Regent United Service Stores* (1878), 8 Ch. D. 75 (C.A.).

Where a corporation had no known place of business, the court directed service of the petition on the chairman and general manager: *Re National Credit & Exchange Co.* (1862), 11 W.R. 161.

Service on the vice-president is insufficient: *Kearns Ink Co.*, (1907) Anglin, J. [unreported]; so also is service on an assignee for the benefit of creditors: *Re Rodney Casket Co.* (1908) 12 O.L.R. 409 (H.C.).

As to service out of the jurisdiction, see s. 112.

Grounds for winding-up

Under section 10 of the Act, the court may make a winding-up order on five grounds, which are discussed below under these headings: Expiration or dissolution of corporation; Resolution of shareholders to wind up; Insolvency; Capital impaired; and Just and equitable.

Expiration or dissolution of corporation (para. (a))

If the time provided in the governing instruments for the duration of a corporation has expired, or if an event provided in the governing instruments for the dissolution of a corporation has occurred, the corporation may be wound up.

Resolution of shareholders to wind-up (para (b))

Shareholders at a special general meeting called for the purpose may pass a resolution requiring the corporation to be wound up.

As to whether this paragraph applies to a solvent corporation incorporated under a provincial Act, see *Re Cramp Steel Co.* (1908), 16 O.L.R. 230 (H.C.) and the discussion of this point under the heading "Solvent provincial corporations being wound up provincially" in this Chapter.

As to what notice of the shareholders' meeting is sufficient, see *Stimson v. North West Cattle Co.* (1902), 5 Que. P.R. 30 (S.C.). The intention to pass the resolution should be stated in the notice: *Re Lemay Ltd.* (1924), 26 O.W.N. 443 (H.C.).

As a result of a reorganization, preferred shares were reclassified as Class A and Class B preference shares. The Class B preference shares were not redeemable and participated equally with the common shares by way of a dividend. Almost all of the common shares were held by a holding corporation. A number of years after the reorganization, this corporation called a meeting for the purpose of passing a resolution to wind itself up. The resolution to authorize the winding up was approved by the holding corporation, which owned all but 30 of the shares represented at the meeting. At this meeting only the common shareholders voted, no notice of the meeting having been given to the A or B shareholders. Certain Class B preference shareholders objected on the grounds that the preference shareholders were entitled to notice and to vote, and that the court had an equitable jurisdiction which should be exercised against the granting of the winding-up order. It was held that the holders of preference shares were not entitled to notice of the meeting or to vote thereat because of the conditions attaching to the preference shares. The conditions attached to the Class B preference shares provided for their redemption on a voluntary winding up, and it was held that the common shareholder was entitled to act as it did: *Fallis v. United Fuel Investments Ltd.*, [1963] S.C.R. 397. Cf. *Mexican Light & Power Co. v. Shareholders of Mexican Light & Power Co.* (1989), 46 B.L.R. 14 (Ont. H.C.), a case under the Ontario Act.

Insolvency (Para (c))

An insolvent corporation may be wound up; as to what constitutes insolvency, see ss. 3 and 6 and the notes thereon above.

Capital impaired (para. (d))

The court may make a winding-up order if the capital stock of the corporation is impaired to the extent of 25 per cent thereof and if it is shown that the lost capital will not likely be restored within a year. As to whether a provincially incorporated corporation, not insolvent, may be wound up under this paragraph, see *Re Cramp Steel Co.*, *supra*, and the notes under the heading "Solvent provincial corporations being wound up provincially" in this chapter.

Where the state of affairs provided for in para. (d) exists, the petitioner is *prima facie* entitled to a winding-up order, which should be made unless it can be shown that the court should exercise its discretion (which is a narrow one) to refuse the order: *Re Base-O-Lite Products Ltd.*, [1933] O.R. 156 (H.C.). In the same case it was further held that the fact that after the petition was filed, a large majority of shareholders had voted that the corporation should continue in business, was not sufficient to justify the refusal of the order.

Where the order is asked for under para. (d), it is the duty of the court to determine first, the extent of the impairment of the capital stock and second, whether the lost capital will likely be restored within one year; and the petition must allege facts that, if proved, will satisfy the court on these points: *Re Eastern Fur Finance Corp.*, [1934] 1 D.L.R. 611 (N.B. C.A.). As pointed out in that case, it is not necessary for the court to find that the substratum of the corporation is gone. The court appears to have taken the view that its discretion in granting or refusing a winding-up order is not the narrow discretion suggested by Sedgewick, J., in *Re Base-O-Lite, supra.* While the petition was also based on para. (e), the order was made only because the court was satisfied that the reduction in the market value of the corporation's assets had impaired the corporation so that it could not profitably go on and that it was in the interest of all concerned that the corporation be wound up. See, however, *Re British Empire Steel Corp. Ltd.*, [1927] 2 D.L.R. 964 at 968, 969 (N.S. T.D.), where the court held that impairment of capital (unless it caused a destruction of the substratum) was not a ground for winding-up a corporation.

In determining the extent of the impairment of the capital stock, arrears of dividends accrued but undeclared on cumulative preferred shares are not liabilities of the corporation: *Re Farmers' Oil & Supply Co.*, [1944] 3 W.W.R. 110 (Sask. K.B.).

Just and equitable (para. (e))

If the court is of the opinion that for any reason, other than those set forth in paragraphs (a) to (d) above, it is just and equitable to wind up the corporation, it may make a winding-up order.

The principal grounds on which winding-up orders have been made under the just and equitable clause have been these: justifiable lack of confidence in the management of the corporation's affairs, loss of the substratum of the corporation, deadlock in the corporation's affairs and (in the case of a private corporation) the existence of facts that would justify the dissolution of a partnership. These grounds are discussed under the comment on ss. 214 and 241 of the *Canada Business Corporations Act* in Chapters 14 and 16 respectively.

Winding-up under the Ontario Act

Voluntary winding-up

Part XVI of the Ontario Act provides for the winding-up of corporations incorporated under that Act. Section 193 provides that a corporation may be wound up voluntarily when a special resolution for that purpose has been passed. Part XVI is made use of where the corporation is solvent as regards creditors and for some special reason it is undesirable or impossible to liquidate the corporation by way of distribution of assets (if any) and surrender of the charter. As to the procedure for distributing corporate assets and surrendering a corporate charter, see the notes to s. 214 of the *Canada Business Corporations Act.*

The resolution should follow the words of the Act: *Duncan & Gray Ltd. v. Silver Spring Brewery*, [1925] 4 D.L.R. 724 (B.C. S.C.) (resolution irregular;

liquidator not properly appointed and disentitled to sue). *Quaere* whether the court has power to interfere in the operation of a winding-up resolution passed by the shareholders on any ground short of the invalidity of the action taken by the shareholders: *Montreal Trust Co. v. Oxford Pipe Line Co.*, [1942] O.R. 490 at 493 (C.A.) per Robertson C.J.O.

The powers of a liquidator in a voluntary winding-up are set out in s. 223 of the Ontario Act. These include the power to carry on the business so far as may be required as beneficial for the winding up of the corporation. A liquidator in the exercise of such statutory power is justified in carrying on the business if he *bona fide* and reasonably forms the opinion that the carrying on of the business is necessary for the beneficial winding up of the corporation: *Re Great Eastern Electric Co.*, [1941] Ch. 241.

Section 204 provides, *inter alia*, that where a corporation is proposed to be or is in the course of being wound up voluntarily, and the whole or a portion of its business or property is proposed to be transferred or sold to another corporation, the liquidator of the first mentioned corporation, with the sanction in general meeting of the corporation by which he was appointed, conferring either a general authority or an authority in respect of any particular arrangement, may receive, in compensation or in part compensation for such sale or transfer, shares or other like interest in the other corporation for distribution among the shareholders of the first mentioned corporation.

On an application under the above section for an order approving an agreement for the amalgamation of the corporation with another corporation, objection was made on behalf of certain bondholders and holders of "talons" carrying the right to share in the profits of the corporation during the currency of the bonds, on the ground that the amalgamation would terminate such right. The application was granted, and the bondholders were left to assert their rights under the bond mortgage by other proceedings: *Re Spanish River Pulp & Paper Mills Ltd.* (1928) 34 O.W.N. 250 (H.C.).

The provisions of the *Bankruptcy Act* are not applicable to the proceedings in a voluntary winding-up under a provincial statute. If the corporation is insolvent, the liquidator's proper course is to file an assignment in bankruptcy or proceed under the bankruptcy legislation: *Re Western Hemlock Products Ltd.* (1961), 27 D.L.R. (2d) 457 (B.C. S.C.).

Winding-up under order of the court

Section 207 of the Ontario Act provides that a corporation may be wound up by order of the court in the specified circumstances.

Where an application is made for a winding-up order, an affidavit negativing insolvency is required: *Re Waltham Motors Corp.* (1922), 23 O.W.N. 123 (H.C.). If the corporation is insolvent, the petition will be dismissed: *Re Shipway Iron Bell & Wire Manufacturing Co.* (1926), 58 O.L.R. 585 (C.A.). The examinations in bankruptcy proceedings of a director and his fellow directors are not admissible on a petition of the bankruptcy trustee for the winding up of the corporation: *Re Fox Johnson & Co.*, [1942] 2 D.L.R. 784 (Ont. H.C.).

It was suggested in *Oxweld Acetylene Co. v. Oxyweld Co. of Canada* (1923)

53 O.L.R. 455 (C.A.) that the court might make a winding-up order under the present para. (b)(iv) on the ground that the affidavit in support of the application for incorporation contained misstatements of fact.

A liquidator appointed by the shareholders may be removed as provided in s. 196. Under s. 211 the court has the power to remove for cause a liquidator appointed by it.

Dissolution

Section 204 provides that where the affairs of the corporation have been fully wound up voluntarily, the liquidator is to (a) make up an account showing the manner in which the winding up has been conducted and the property of the corporation disposed of and (b) call a meeting of the shareholders or members to consider the account. Within ten days after the meeting, the liquidator is to make and file a return to the Director; in addition, a notice is to be published in the *Ontario Gazette*; and on the expiration of three months from the date of filing, the corporation is *ipso facto* to be dissolved.

Where the report has been filed and the statutory period has elapsed, the court has no power to go behind the dissolution except in the case of fraud: *Re Pinto Silver Mining Co.* (1878), 8 Ch. D. 273 (C.A.); *Re London & Caledonian Marine Insurance Co.* (1879), 11 Ch. D. 140 (C.A.); *Christie v. Edwards*, [1940] O.R. 28 at 31 (C.A.). This last case was reversed by the Supreme Court of Canada, in [1940] S.C.R. 410, which held that shareholders of a defunct corporation suing on behalf of themselves and others were entitled to an accounting of moneys alleged to be wrongfully withheld by the liquidator.

Section 205 provides that at any time during the three-month period, the court may, on the application of the liquidator or any other interested person, defer the date on which the dissolution of the corporation is to take place until a date fixed in its order. See section 218 for dissolution by court order on a winding-up ordered by the court.

Chapter 20

WINDING-UP ORDER

Cross references: Sections 3, 10, 110, 120, 130, 136, 137, 152 ff.; Ontario Act, ss. 208, 209

Practice

A creditor or shareholder who is the applicant for an order that a corporation be wound up, is to give four days' notice to the corporation of his application (s. 12(2)). At the expiration of that time he presents his petition, verified by affidavit, to the court. Notice of the time and place that the petition will be presented should be served on the corporation along with the petition and affidavit. In the case of banks, it is necessary to take the preliminary proceedings provided by s. 151 ff. It will be noted that in the case of banks and insurance corporations, the petition is usually made by the Attorney General of Canada on the request of the Minister.

Where a petitioner dies before the order is granted, an order of revivor will be granted to his executors: *Re Dynevor Duffryn Collieries Co.*, [1878] W.N. 199; *Re Commercial Bank of London*, [1888] W.N. 214.

Petitioning without reasonable and probable cause is a ground for action by the corporation: *Quartz Hill Consolidated Gold Mining Co. v. Eyre* (1883), 11 Q.B.D. 674 (C.A.). Where a creditor commenced proceedings under the Act in bad faith and failed to establish the truth of any of the allegations upon which the petition for the winding-up order was based, the court held that the unjustified institution of the proceedings and the libellous allegations contained in the petition were injurious to the corporation's reputation and business and that the corporation was entitled to damages: *Allure Sportswear Inc. v. Beiner*, [1960] Que. S.C. 628. *Suppressio veri* will defeat the petition: *Re Ipswich, Norwich & Yarmouth Railway Co.; Ex parte Barnett* (1849), 1 De G. & Sm. 744.

A petitioner may discontinue proceedings before the winding-up order is made; other creditors who are not themselves petitioners are not entitled to be substituted: *Doyle v. Atlas Canning Co.* (1897), 5 B.C.R. 279 (S.C.).

Where an order had been obtained in chambers by one creditor, the conduct of proceedings was in the special circumstances given to other creditors who had also applied for such order: *Re Joseph Hall Co.* (1884), 10 P.R. 485 (Ont. H.C.).

Creditors may show cause against or may appear and assist the petitioning creditor: *Re Lake Winnipeg Transportation, Lumber & Trading Co.* (1891), 7 Man. R. 255 (Q.B.).

The procedure, unless specific rules are in force under the Act, are governed by the general Rules of Practice in force in a particular province where the application is brought. See *Re Preformed Laminates Inc.*, [1961] Que. S.C. 439. Persons not parties to the winding-up are not entitled to cross-examine on affidavits filed in support of a motion for the appointment of a permanent liquidation: *A.G. Canada v. Pitts Insurance Co.* (1982), 42 C.B.R. (N.S.) 313 (Master).

The Petition (or application)

The petition itself must allege facts sufficient to justify a winding-up order. It is not enough that a proper case can be shown on the evidence: *Re Wear Engine Works Co.* (1875), 10 Ch. App. 188 at 191; *Re Companies' Winding-up Acts* (1898), 6 B.C.R. 112 (S.C.); *Re Outlook Hotel Co.* (1909), 2 Sask. L.R. 435 at 439 (T.D.); but in *Re Michael P. Georgas Co.*, [1948] O.R. 708 (C.A.), it was held to be sufficient that the grounds and facts relied upon should be set out in an affidavit annexed to the application.

It is prudent to draw a petition so as to bring the corporation within as many of the subsections of s. 3 as possible.

The petition should state the circumstances with sufficient detail that the court is able to see from the petition itself that a winding-up order ought to be made: *Re Wear Engine Works Co.* (1875), 10 Ch. App. 188 at 191; *Re Patent Cocoa Fibre Co.* (1876), 1 Ch. D. 617; *Re Langham Skating Rink Co.* (1877), 5 Ch. D. 669 (C.A.); *Re Rica Gold Washing Co.* (1879), 11 Ch. D. 36 (C.A.); *Re White Star Consolidated Gold Mining Co.* (1883), 48 L.T. 815; *Re Eldorado Union Store Co.* (1886), 17 N.S.R. 514 (C.A.); *Re Atlas Canning Co.* (1897), 5 B.C.R. 661 at 667 (C.A.).

If a creditor petitions for a compulsory order after the commencement of voluntary winding-up proceedings, he should recite the voluntary winding-up and allege that he will be prejudiced thereby: *Re Electrical Engineering Co.* (1891), 64 L.T. 658; *Re Russell, Cordner & Co.*, [1891] 3 Ch. 171; *Re Medical Battery Co.*, [1894] 1 Ch. 444.

One petition to wind up two corporations is wrong: *Re Shields Marine Insurance Co.*, [1867] W.N. 296.

It has been held under the provision of the Ontario Act corresponding to s. 12(2) that the style of cause in a winding-up proceeding should not include the names of shareholders as applicants or co-respondents: *Re J.F. Cunningham & Son Ltd.*, [1955] O.W.N. 668 (H.C.).

Amendment

A petition may be amended by leave of the court: *Re Queen's Benefit Building Society* (1871), 6 Ch. App. 815. And although a petition was opened and evidence was gone into, leave was given to amend: *Re White Star Consolidated Gold Mining Co.* (1883), 48 L.T. 815, followed in *Re Eastern Fur Finance Corp.*, [1934] 1 D.L.R. 611 at 612 (N.B. C.A.).

The court has the power to permit amendments under ss. 129 and 130 of the Act: *Re Canadian General Service Corp.* (No. 2) (1914), 16 D.L.R. 17 (Man. K.B.); *Re Steel Realty & Development Co.* (1923), 25 O.W.N. 285 (H.C.) (leave given to amend and submit proof that corporation came within s. 6); *Re Eastern Fur Finance Corp.*, [1934] 1 D.L.R. 611 (N.B. C.A.) (allegations insufficient; leave given after substantial amount of evidence taken). Where sufficient particulars were given in the petition to make it appear advisable that the corporation should be wound up, the court granted leave to amend, offer additional evidence and again present the petition: *Re Redpath Motor Vehicle Co.* (1904), 4 O.W.R. 515 (H.C.); *Re Ewart Carriage Works Ltd.* (1904), 8 O.L.R. 527; *Re Abbott-Mitchell Iron & Steel Co.* (1901), 2 O.L.R. 143.

Where the amendment would involve alleging facts of insolvency arising since the date that the petition was filed, leave to amend will be refused; for, by s. 5, the winding-up commences from the service of notice of presentation of the petition, and the rights of other persons may be affected by such amendment: *Re Companies' Winding-up Acts* (1898), 6 B.C.R. 112 (S.C.). On the other hand, amendments were permitted to verify an allegation of insolvency at the time of the filing of the petition to reflect the fact that the bank had, since the petition was filed, acknowledged insolvency; also so as to include s. 10(d) and (e) of the Act: *Re Home Bank of Canada* (1923), 54 O.L.R. 606 (H.C.).

In *Swift Canadian Co. v. Island Creamery Association* (1912), 10 D.L.R.

833 (B.C. S.C.), on an application by the petitioner after the order had been made incorrectly reciting the name of the corporation, the amendment of the petition and of the winding-up proceedings by correcting the name of the corporation was directed.

Notice of application

The four days' notice need not be clear days: *Re Arnold Chemical Co.* (1901), 2 O.L.R. 671 (H.C.). Thus, a notice given on the first day of the month for a hearing on the fifth is sufficient: *Re Maritime Wrapper Co.* (1902), 35 N.B.R. 682 (C.A.). Under the rules in force in Manitoba, apparently four clear days' notice is necessary except in cases of special hardship; and a Sunday will not be included: *J.H. Ashdown Hardware Co. v. Residential Building Co.* (1914), 7 W.W.R. 690 (Man. K.B.).

The provision for four days' notice of the application cannot be waived by the corporation, and in the absence of requisite notice the order cannot be made; and although the court has the power to grant an adjournment under s. 13, this will not be done if there are other applications pending: *Re Farmers Bank of Canada* (1910), 22 O.L.R. 556 (H.C.). In *Re Installations Ltd. (sub nom. Great West Supply Co. v. Installations Ltd.)* (1914), 15 D.L.R. 896 (Alta. T.D.), it was held that notice could be waived; this was followed in the same province in *Re Consumers' Coal Co.*, [1917] 2 W.W.R. 143 (Alta. T.D.), where it was held that service of notice could be dispensed with in proper circumstances, for example, where instructions to counsel to appear had been authorized at a meeting of the board, and counsel had in fact appeared.

Apparently notice is dispensed with where the corporation is a party to the application: *Pontbriand Co. v. Coskey* (1912), 14 Que. P.R. 19, and s. 12(2).

The notice referred to in the section applies to the hearing of the application and not to the presentation of the petition for winding-up provided for in s. 5: *Re Halifax Power Co.* (1917), 36 D.L.R. 393 (N.S. C.A.). See also *Re I.O.S. Ltd. (No. 2)* (1973), 43 D.L.R. (3d) 759 (N.B. C.A.) and *Re G. Minerals Ltd.* (1967), 61 D.L.R. (2d) 186 (B.C. S.C.). See *Re Preformed Laminates Inc.*, [1961] Que. S.C. 439, where insufficient notice was given.

The notice must be served on the corporation: *Re J.F. Cunningham & Son Ltd.*, [1955] O.W.N. 668 at 670 (H.C.). Service on an assignee for creditors is not a compliance with s. 12(2): *Re Rodney Casket Co.* (1908), 12 O.L.R. 409 (H.C.).

Service on the creditors, contributories or shareholders is not required, but notice of application to appoint a liquidator should be given to them: *Re Qu'Appelle Valley Farming Co.* (1888), 5 Man. R. 160 (Q.B.). Such persons may, however, appear *ex gratia*: *Re McLean, Stinson & Brodie, Ltd.* (1910), 2 O.W.N. 294 (H.C.). The curator of an insolvent bank is entitled to notice of the presentation of the petition: *Re Farmers Bank of Canada* (1910), 22 O.L.R. 556 (H.C.).

The requirements as to service are governed by the general rules of practice in force in the relative province, unless special rules have been made under s. 136, which will then apply. However, the Rules of Practice in Ontario are not made applicable by the *Winding-up Act*; this is so the court can shorten the period of notice of the application: *Re Farmers Bank, supra.*

Evidence in support of application

The petitioner must prove his case: *Re Grundy Stove Co.* (1904), 7 O.L.R. 252 (H.C.); *Re Manitoba Commission Co.* (1912), 2 D.L.R. 1 (Man. K.B.) and cases cited; and the allegations in the petition should be verified by affidavit, for there must be evidence for the court to act upon. While the Act does not require an affidavit, the rules in force in the various provinces generally do, because a petition is not evidence: *Re Atlas Canning Co.* (1897), 5 B.C.R. 661 (C.A.); and see *Re Michael P. Georgas Co.*, [1948] O.R. 708 (C.A.). In *Re Maritime Wrapper Co.* (1902) 35 N.B.R. 682 (C.A.) it was held that the allegations in the petition could be proved at the hearing and need not be verified by affidavit.

Where the rules require an affidavit to be filed before the presentation of the petition, this requirement must be observed: *Re Companies' Winding-up Acts* (1898), 6 B.C.R. 112 (S.C.); leave to file a supplementary affidavit will generally be refused.

When there are two competing petitions and the order is made on the later one, because of a failure to file the affidavit in support of the earlier one before service of the later one as required by the rules, this is not a proper case for appellate interference: *Re Belding Lumber Co.* (1911), 23 O.L.R. 255 (H.C.).

The affidavit should be made by the petitioner, but an affidavit made by the petitioner's agent or solicitor may be sufficient: *Re Qu'Appelle Valley Farming Co.* (1888), 5 Man. R. 160 at 166 (Q.B.); and see *Re African Farms Ltd.*, [1906] 1 Ch. 640.

It has been held in Manitoba that a petition for a winding-up order cannot be supported by statements verified by affidavit on information and belief: *Re Manitoba Commission Co.* (1912), 2 D.L.R. 1 (Man. K.B.); *Re Canada Provident Insurance & Investment Corp. (sub nom. Canada Provident & Investment Corp., Re)* (1913), 14 D.L.R. 782 at 785 (Man. K.B.). The English practice, and that in Ontario and British Columbia, is otherwise: *Re Colonial Investment Co. of Winnipeg* (1913), 14 D.L.R. 563 at 572 (Man. K.B.). An affidavit of a person who deposes on information and belief, and who on cross-examination appears to have no knowledge of the facts, is a nullity: *Re Atlas Canning Co.* (1897), 5 B.C.R. 661 (C.A.); see also *Re Outlook Hotel Co.* (1909), 2 Sask. L.R. 435 (T.D.). Where the rules, as in Manitoba, did not permit an affidavit on information and belief, a general verification by affidavit of various paragraphs of the petition is not to be encouraged, but constitutes evidence that may be given effect to in the absence of any conflicting material: *Re Colonial Investment Co. of Winnipeg, supra.*

It is the practice in Ontario to serve the affidavits with the application (or petition), but *quaere* whether this is necessary unless the rules locally applicable specifically require it. For the practice in Saskatchewan, see *Re Outlook Hotel Co., supra.*

Unless or until rules of procedure are made under s. 136 of the Act, the rules in force in the relative province are made applicable by s. 137: *Re Belding*

Lumber Co. (1911), 23 O.L.R. 255 (H.C.). So where the practice of the court is to support petitions by affidavits and *viva voce* evidence, shareholders petitioning for a winding-up are held entitled to examine the corporation's directors as witnesses in support of the petition: *Re Baynes Carriage Co.* (1912), 27 O.L.R. 144 (H.C.).

A petitioner is not normally entitled to discovery: *Re West Devon Great Consols Mine* (1884), 27 Ch. D. 106 (C.A.); but in *Canada Deposit Insurance Corp. v. Commonwealth Trust Co.* (1991), 2 C.B.R. (3d) 87 (B.C. S.C.) it was held that in an appropriate case the court might order examinations for discovery under the Act. In Ontario, the evidence of any witnesses including officers of the corporation, may be obtained for use in support of the petition: see Rule 39.03.

Sometimes the corporation itself or its officers admit the insolvency. In such cases the preferred practice is for the corporation to appoint counsel to appear on its behalf at the hearing and admit the insolvency, rather than to obtain an affidavit from one of the officers of the corporation, whose statement, having regard to the decisions below noted, may prove insufficient.

It is usually desirable to supplement the affidavit verifying the petition, by such additional evidence as is obtainable, and if any question is likely to arise regarding the existence or validity of the petitioner's claim, he can then set forth fully the facts proving it.

Where the evidence includes statements that have been produced by officers of the corporation, or written admissions or correspondence, these should be set forth as exhibits to the affidavit filed.

Where the rules prescribe a form of affidavit and provide that such affidavit is to be *prima facie* evidence of the statements in the petition, an affidavit in the prescribed form is sufficient: *Re Great West Permanent Loan Co.*, [1927] 2 W.W.R. 15 (Man. K.B.). In *Re S.A. Hawken Ltd.*, [1950] 2 All E.R. 408 at 413 (Ch. D.), Wynn-Parry, J., expressed the view that additional evidence, supplementing this form of affidavit, was necessary where the petition was based on allegations of fraud; and was desirable where the petition was based on allegations that the affairs of the corporation required investigation (even though no charge of fraud was made) and where a petitioner had to rely on certain documents if the petition was opposed.

The deponent in an affidavit filed in support of the petition may be cross-examined thereon: *Re Manitoba Commission Co.* (1912), 2 D.L.R. 1 at 4 (Man. K.B.); so also the affiant of an affidavit in opposition under the Manitoba Winding-up Act and rules: *Re Manitoba Commission Co.* (1911), 19 W.L.R. 893 (Man. K.B.); in Ontario see *Re Steel Realty Development Corp.; Re L.R. Steel Co.* (1924), 26 O.W.N. 329 where the cross-examination on the affidavit of a non-resident was ordered.

Under the rules applicable in Manitoba, where the petitioner has been examined by counsel for the corporation, an order for further examination by counsel for shareholders will be refused in the absence of a suggestion that the first examination was not proper: *Re Great West Permanent Loan Co.*, [1927] 2 W.W.R. 433 (Man. K.B.). Petitioners are not entitled to a preliminary order that certain of the corporation's officers should produce the books of the corporation and auditors' reports on their examination as compulsory witnesses in support of the petition: *Re Baynes Carriage Co.* (1912), 8 D.L.R. 309 (Ont. H.C.).

While, as a general rule, a disputed claim may not form the basis of a petition, this rule will not be applied when the petitioner would otherwise be without redress: *Re Russian & English Bank*, [1932] 1 Ch. 663 (corporation dissolved and Act permitting winding-up of such corporations).

If the dispute is *bona fide* and the corporation is solvent, the court has jurisdiction to restrain by injunction a person claiming to be a creditor from presenting a petition: *Cercle Restaurant Castiglione Co. v. Lavery* (1881), 18 Ch. D. 555; *Niger Merchants Co. v. Capper* (1877), 18 Ch. D. 557n.

Misconduct of directors has been held not to be a ground for a shareholder's petition unless producing insolvency: *Re Anglo-Greek Steam Co.* (1866), L.R. 2 Eq. 1. In that case, objection was made to the remuneration of and the payment of commissions to directors.

The affidavits in support of the petition must bring that petition strictly within the words of the section. An affidavit of "insolvency within the meaning of the section" without a statement of facts is insufficient: *Re Chapel House Colliery Co.* (1883), 24 Ch. D. 259 at 270 (C.A.); *Re Qu'Appelle Valley Farming Co.* (1888), 5 Man. R. 160 (Q.B.); *Re Lake Winnipeg Transportation, Lumber & Trading Co.* (1891), 7 Man. R. 255 (Q.B.); *Re Rapid City Farmers' Elevator Co.* (1894), 9 Man. R. 574 (Q.B.).

Where the petitioner was president of the corporation and also a large creditor, and made an affidavit that he knew the corporation was unable to pay in full, but gave no comparative statement of its assets and liabilities, it was held that this was not sufficient evidence of insolvency: *Re Lake Winnipeg Transportation, Lumber & Trading Co., supra.*

Where the court was satisfied on the evidence that the corporation was unable to pay its debts, a winding-up order was made, though a call had been made that the corporation alleged would meet its embarrassments: *Re International Contract Co.; Ex parte Spartali & Tabor* (1886), 14 L.T. 726.

Where a banking corporation had stopped payment, and the petitioning creditor proved his debt and refusal to pay, the court refused to assent to a suggestion that the corporation would resume business in a few days, and made the order as *ex debito justitiae*: *Re Consolidated Bank* (1886), 14 L.T. 656.

A shareholder's petition on the ground of impairment of capital must be accompanied by evidence thereof, apart from his affidavit: *Re "A" Co.* (1917), 34 D.L.R. 396 (Man. K.B.).

Adjournment

A petition is not allowed to stand over unless this is clearly necessary: *Re Metropolitan Railway Warehousing Co.* (1867), 15 W.R. 1121 (L.J.J.); *Re Edmonton Brewing & Malting Co.*, [1918] 2 W.W.R. 350 (Alta. T.D.) (hearing of petition enlarged because of unsettled conditions in the industry); not even where all parties desire this, unless the evidence shows that such course is desirable: *Re*

Federal Bank of Australia (1893), 62 L.J. Ch. 561 (C.A.); or where the debt is disputed, in view of the provisions of s. 5: *Re Meaford Manufacturing Co.* (1919), 46 O.L.R. 282 (H.C.).

In the following cases a petition by a creditor was ordered to stand over so that it could be seen if means could be found for paying dissentient creditors: *Re Western of Canada Oil, Land & Works Co.* (1873), L.R. 17 Eq. 1; *Re St. Thomas' Dock Co.* (1876), 2 Ch. D. 116; *Re Exmouth Docks Co.* (1873), L.R. 17 Eq. 181; *Re Brighton Hotel Co.* (1868), L.R. 6 Eq. 339.

The order as between the petitioning creditor and the corporation is *ex debito justitiae*, and the enlargement of the hearing is granted on the representations and wishes of creditors other than the petitioner, not on the application of the corporation or of contributories: *Re Consolidated Bank* (1886), 14 L.T. 656.

Where the petitioner was a debenture holder, the petition was ordered to stand over for inquiry as to whether the corporation had any assets other than those comprised in the debentures: *Re Olathe Silver Mining Co.* (1884), 27 Ch. D. 278.

Where the petition was opposed by a majority of the creditors, it was ordered to stand over for six months on terms, this being considered more beneficial to the other creditors than dismissing it: *Re Great Western (Forest of Dean) Coal Consumers' Co.* (1882), 21 Ch. D. 769.

Under s. 14 of the Act, the corporation may request that the petition be allowed to stand over; see the notes under the heading "Adjournment at request of corporation and resulting inquiry" in this chapter.

Application by creditor

A person may be a "creditor" within the meaning of s. 11 and s. 2 and therefore entitled to petition when a corporation has become insolvent, even though he is not a creditor to whom a debt is "then due" within the meaning of s. 4.

See the judgment in *Re Atlas Canning Co.* (1897), 5 B.C.R. 661 at 668 (C.A.), in which Drake J., said:

> ... creditor, in its primary meaning, imports one to whom a debt is due, in a secondary meaning, one to whom money is owing but the period of payment has not arrived, *debitum in praesenti solvendum in futuro*. Section 6 [now s. 4] of the Act refers to a creditor whose debt is "then due"; in section 8 [now s. 11] the term is "creditor" only. The distinction is not unmeaning. In the one case the debt must be due, in the other it need not be due. In the latter case, when a company has become insolvent such a creditor can be a petitioner.

A secured creditor may petition even though he has a lien for the full amount of his claim: *Re Strathy Wire Fence Co.* (1904), 8 O.L.R. 186 at 192 (C.A.); and *Re Great Western (Forest of Dean) Coal Consumers' Co.* (1882), 21 Ch. D. 769; but he need not state the value of his security: *Moor v. Anglo-Italian Bank* (1879), 10 Ch. D. 681; *Cushing Sulphite Fibre Co. v. Cushing (sub nom. Re Cushing Sulphite Fibre Co.)* (1905), 37 N.B.R. 254 (C.A.).

Whether a bondholder is entitled to petition depends on the terms of his security. If a direct debt from the corporation to the holder is created in the bonds, and if there is no covenant in the bond with the trustees of the covering trust deed, the bondholder may petition: *Re Olathe Silver Mining Co.* (1884), 27 Ch. D. 278; but he may not if the covenant is with the trustees only: *Re Uruguay Central & Hygueritas Railway Co. of Monte Video* (1879), 11 Ch. D. 372. In *Cushing Sulphite Fibre Co., supra*, two judges thought that the bonds in question fell under the *Uruguay Central* case, but the majority of the court held that the bondholder was entitled to petition. See also *Re Mid-West Glass Co.*, [1931] 3 W.W.R. 165 (Man. K.B.), where the bonds gave the holder thereof a first floating charge on the undertaking and assets of the corporation, present and future, and the court held that he was entitled to petition.

Holders of debenture stock—secured by a trust deed in which the covenant to pay principal and interest is between the corporation and the trustee, although the covenant is to pay the debenture stockholders—are not creditors entitled to present a winding-up petition. They are *cestuis que* trust only: *Re Dunderland Iron Ore Co.*, [1909] 1 Ch. 446.

In *Re Nelson Ford Lumber Co.* (1908), 1 Sask. L.R. 108 (T.D.), the court refused to recognize an unlicensed corporation as being a creditor entitled to petition, where the claim arose in respect of business carried on in contravention of provincial legislation.

The following have been held entitled to petition: an executor of a creditor: *Re Masonic & General Life Assurance Co.* (1885), 32 Ch. D. 373; an assignee legal or equitable or bona fide holder of a debt: *Re Ooregum Gold Mining Co.* (1885), 29 Sol. J. 204; the holder of a bearer debenture deposited with him as security for a debt of the original holder: *Re Olathe Silver Mining Co., supra*; *Re Montgomery Moore Ship Collision Doors Syndicate Ltd.* (1903), 72 L.J. Ch. 624; but the real and beneficial owners of the debt should join in the petition and proof: *Re People's Loan & Deposit Co.* (1906), 7 O.W.R. 253 (H.C.); an assignee of a definite part of a debt: *Re Steel Wing Co.; Petition of F. T. Lord*, [1921] 1 Ch. 349; a corporation: *Ex parte Mexican Santa Barbara Mining Co.* (1890), 34 Sol. J. 269; an assignee to whom the corporation has made an assignment for the benefit of its creditors: *Re National Automobile Woodworking Co.* (1914), 7 O.W.N. 22 (H.C.), in which it was directed that the order should go on the filing of a written consent by a creditor or shareholder to the amount required by s. 11; an execution creditor: *Re Lake Winnipeg Transportation, Lumber & Trading Co.* (1891), 7 Man. R. 255 (Q.B.).

The debt must be unquestioned and liquidated: *Schneider v. Laurentide* (1913), 15 Que. P.R. 271.

An equitable debt will support a petition: *Re London & Birmingham Flint & Alkali Glass Co.; Ex parte Wright* (1859), 1 De G. F. & J. 257 (L.C.).

A garnishee order against a corporation does not make the garnishor a creditor of the corporation: *Re Combined Weighing & Advertising Machine Co.* (1889), 43 Ch. D. 99 (C.A.).

An hypothecary creditor, who is not personally a creditor of the corporation, but can only take hypothecary action against it by reason of being in possession of immoveables, has no status to demand that the corporation be put in liquidation: *Leduc v. Kensington Land Co.* (1899), 16 Que. S.C. 213.

Persons who are parties to a deed of assignment made by the corporation for the benefit of its creditors and whereby an extension of time for payment of the corporation's debts is agreed to, are estopped from presenting a winding-up petition until the period of extension has expired: *Re Atlas Canning Co.* (1897), 5 B.C.R. 661 (C.A.).

Cases in which creditor's petition has been granted

In the following cases the order was made on the petition of a creditor, though opposed by the corporation: *Re General Rolling Stock Co.* (1865), 34 Beav. 314; *Re Isle of Wight Ferry Co.* (1865), 2 Hem. & M. 597; *Re Family Endowment Society* (1870), 5 Ch. App. 118; *Re National Provincial Life Assurance Society* (1870), L.R. 9 Eq. 306; *Re General Co. for Promotion of Land Credit* (1870), 5 Ch. App. 363 (L.J.); affd (*sub nom. Reuss (Princess) v. Bos* (1871), L.R. 5 H.L. 176; *Re King's Cross Industrial Dwellings Co.* (1870), L.R. 11 Eq. 149; *Re Home Assurance Assn. (No. 2)* (1871), L.R. 12 Eq. 112; *Re Flagstaff Silver Mining Co. of Utah* (1875), L.R. 20 Eq. 268; *Re Globe New Patent Iron & Steel Co.* (1875), L.R. 20 Eq. 337; *Re Commercial Bank of South Australia* (1886), 33 Ch. D. 174.

Cases in which creditor's petition has been dismissed

In the following cases a petition by a creditor was dismissed.

Association illegal: *Re Padstow Total Loss & Collision Assurance Assn.* (1882), 20 Ch. D. 137 (C.A.).

Petitioner a debenture holder: *Re Herne Bay Waterworks Co.* (1878) 10 Ch. D. 42; *Re Uruguay Central & Hygueritas Ry. Co. of Monte Video* (1879), 11 Ch. D. 372.

Petition opposed by the majority of creditors, and it did not appear that the petitioner would gain anything by an order: *Re Free Fishermen of Faversham (Co. or Fraternity of)* (1887), 36 Ch. D. 329 (C.A.); *Re Chapel House Colliery Co.* (1883) 24 Ch. D. 259 (C.A.); *Re Uruguay Central & Hygueritas Ry. Co. of Monte Video, supra.*

Petitioners' debt assigned since petition was presented: *Re Paris Skating Rink Co.* (1877), 5 Ch. D. 959 (C.A.).

Requisite period after demand had not expired when petition presented: *Re Catholic Publishing & Bookselling Co.* (1864), 2 De G. J. & Sm. 116.

Petitioner's debt small and attached by judgment creditor of his own: *Re European Banking Co.; Ex parte Baylis* (1866), L.R. 2 Eq. 521.

Petitioners' debt not disputed, but the majority of creditors preferred a voluntary winding-up: *Re Langley Mill Steel & Iron Works Co.* (1871), L.R. 12 Eq. 26; *Re Oro Fino Mines Ltd.* (1900), 7 B.C.R. 388 (C.A.).

Corporation had made a voluntary assignment for the benefit of creditors, and it was the desire of the great majority in number and value of the creditors that liquidation should proceed under the assignment: *Wakefield Rattan Co. v. Hamilton Whip Co.* (1893), 24 O.R. 107 (H.C.); *Re Maple Leaf Dairy Co.* (1901),

2 O.L.R. 590 (H.C.); *Re British American Feldspar Ltd.* (1920), 18 O.W.N. 313 (Master).

Creditor held to be a shareholder as a result of special resolution under trust deed and not entitled to bring petition as creditor: *Quebec Production Corp. v. Lavigne*, [1972] Que. C.A. 172.

No evidence of doing business in Canada, or that the corporation had an office or place of business in Canada, or that petitioners would benefit: *Re Steel Realty Development Co.* (1924), 27 O.W.N. 37 (C.A.).

It is well settled that a creditor's petition brought to enforce payment of a debt disputed in good faith will be dismissed with costs, as such a petition is an abuse of the process of the court: *Re Imperial Hydropathic Hotel Co., Blackpool Ltd.* (1882), 23 Ch. D. 1 (C.A.); *Re Meaford Manufacturing Co.* (1919), 46 O.L.R. 282 (H.C.); *Re Wells*, [1944] 3 D.L.R. 651 (Ont. S.C.) (under the then Bankruptcy Act). In the following cases not only was the debt disputed but the circumstances indicated also existed: *Re Pen-y-van Colliery Co.* (1877), 6 Ch. D. 477 (claim for unliquidated damages); *Re Gold Hill Mines* (1883), 23 Ch. D. 210 (C.A.) (debt small and no proof of insolvency); *Re Cobalt Development Co.* (1908), 12 O.W.R. 83 (T.D.) (no proof of insolvency); *Re Steel Realty Development Co.* (1923), 25 O.W.N. 468 (only asset in Canada was the right to receive dividends from another corporation in liquidation in the United States; corporation had not traded in Canada; no proof of insolvency). See also *Re Aril Canada Ltd.* (1976), 22 N.S.R. (2d) 515, where the application was refused when foreclosure proceedings were underway, and there was no evidence that the position of the unsecured creditors would be improved in a winding-up.

Application by shareholder

A shareholder may, under s. 11, petition for a winding-up order on the ground that the period fixed in the charter for the duration of the corporation has expired, or that a resolution requiring the corporation to be wound up has been passed at a special meeting of shareholders called for the purpose. If he holds shares in the capital stock to the amount of at least 500 dollars par value or holds 5 shares without nominal or par value, he may under the same section petition on the ground of insolvency or impairment of capital, or under the just and equitable rule, subject to the limitation that a shareholder in a bank or insurance corporation may not petition on the ground of insolvency. In *Re "A" Co.* (1917), 34 D.L.R. 396 (Man. K.B.), a shareholder of an insurance corporation was held to have no *locus standi*, in view of s. 11, to petition on the ground of insolvency.

A shareholder may petition notwithstanding that his shares are fully paid: *Re National Savings Bank Assn.* (1866), 1 Ch. App. 547; *Re Timbers Ltd.* (1917), 35 D.L.R. 431 (Alta. C.A.); or that he carries no voting rights: *Re Canada Provident Insurance & Investment Corp. (sub nom. Canada Provident & Investment Corp., Re)* (1913), 14 D.L.R. 782 (Man. K.B.).

However, if the petitioner's shares are fully paid, the court will not grant a winding-up order except under special circumstances: *Re Patent Artificial Stone Co.* (1864), 34 Beav. 185; this is on the basis that he has no interest in the winding-up unless he alleges that there is a surplus and supports this allegation by evidence: *Re Rica Gold Washing Co.* (1879), 11 Ch. D. 36 (C.A.); *Re Vron Colliery Co.* (1882), 20 Ch. D. 442 at 447 (C.A.); *Re Diamond Fuel Co.* (1879) 13 Ch. D. 400 at 411 (C.A.). The court refused the order where the shareholder's shares were valueless: *Re Shipway Iron Bell & Wire Manufacturing Co.* (1926), 58 O.L.R. 585 (C.A.); and where there was no reasonable probability of sufficient assets being left for the shareholders to give the petitioning shareholder a tangible interest in the corporation: *Re Tangier Amalgamated Mining Co.* (1906), 39 N.S.R. 373 (C.A.).

A shareholder must petition for the winding-up of the corporation for a *bona fide* purpose and not merely for the purpose of bringing pressure on the corporation: *Re "A" Co., supra*, and cases cited therein at 399. An action for damages will lie against the shareholder if he presents a petition falsely and maliciously even though no pecuniary loss or special damage to the corporation is proved, for the presentation of a petition is from its very nature calculated to injure the credit of the corporation: *Quartz Hill Consolidated Gold Mining Co. v. Eyre* (1883), 11 Q.B.D. 674 (C.A.); *Allure Sportswear Inc. v. Beiner*, [1960] Que S.C. 628.

Where a shareholder has established a case under s. 10(d) (impairment of capital), it has been held that he is *prima facie* entitled to the order even though the majority of the shareholders are against the application, and that the court should make the order unless it is shown that the court should exercise its discretion to refuse the order: *Re Base-O-Lite Products Ltd.*, [1933] O.R. 156 at 158 (H.C.). However, in *Re British Empire Steel Corp.*, [1927] 2 D.L.R. 964 at 968, 969 (N.S. T.D.), and *Re Eastern Fur Finance Corp.*, [1934] 1 D.L.R. 611 (N.B. C.A.), the court considered the wishes of the majority of shareholders.

The fact that the petitioning shareholder is in arrears as to calls is not a ground in itself for dismissing the petition; but the petition will not be allowed to proceed until the calls have been paid into court or an undertaking has been given to submit to such order as the court may make as to payment of the calls: *Re Diamond Fuel Co.* (1879), 13 Ch. D. 400 at 404 (C.A.); *Re Crystal Reef Gold Mining Co.*, [1892] 1 Ch. 408.

Where the petitioner had acquired his shares as collateral security and the shares had not been transferred on the books of the corporation, an objection that the petitioner had no status was sustained: *Blatt Ray Inc. v. Gavsie* (1939), 20 C.B.R. 447 (Que. S.C.).

Executors of a deceased shareholder are shareholders and entitled to petition even though they have not procured registration of the shares in their names: *Re Great West Permanent Loan Co.*, [1927] 2 W.W.R. 15 (Man. K.B.).

A trustee in bankruptcy of a shareholder who has not caused himself to be registered as the holder of the shares, is not entitled to petition: *Re Fox Johnson & Co. Ltd.*, [1942] 2 D.L.R. 784 (Ont. H.C.); *Re H.L. Bolton Engineering Co.*, [1956] 1 Ch. 577.

Power of court on application

Discretion of the court

It has been said that on insolvency being shown, a creditor is entitled to an order *ex debito justitiae*, but the words of the section imply a discretion in the court: *Re Strathy Wire Fence Co.* (1904), 8 O.L.R. 186 at 192 (C.A.), where Garrow, J.A., said, "Some discretion must, in my opinion, be exercised in every case. The court must before granting the order see that the petitioner has a lawful claim, that the company is insolvent, that there are assets to be administered, and that the proceedings proposed are necessary"; followed in *Re Olympia Co.* (1915), 25 D.L.R. 620 (Man. C.A.).

The most that can be said is that when a creditor has made out a case under the Act, he is generally or *prima facie* entitled to an order: *Bowes v. Hope Life & Insurance Guarantee Co. (Directors of)* (1865), 11 H.L. Cas. 389; *Re Isle of Wight Ferry Co.* (1865), 2 Hem. & M. 597; *Re Western of Canada Oil, Land and Works Co.* (1873), L.R. 17 Eq. 1; *Re West Hartlepool Ironworks Co.* (1875), 10 Ch. App. 618; *Re Uruguay Central & Hygueritas Ry. Co. of Monte Video* (1879), 11 Ch. D. 372; *Re Great Western (Forest of Dean) Coal Consumers' Co.* (1882), 21 Ch. D. 769; *Re Chapel House Colliery Co.* (1883), 24 Ch. D. 259 (C.A.).

This rule does not apply as between the petitioning creditor and other creditors, and if the majority oppose, the court ought to regard their wishes: *Re West Hartlepool Ironworks Co., supra*; *Re Western of Canada Oil, Land and Works Co., supra.*; *Re Chapel House Colliery Co., supra*; *Re E. Bishop & Sons Ltd.*, [1900] 2 Ch. 254; but the opposing creditors must prove their case: *Re Krasnapolsky Restaurant & Winter Garden Co.*, [1892] 3 Ch. 174.

A winding-up will only be ordered when it is in the best interests of all the creditors; in the case of a conflict between the creditors and shareholders, the rights of the former are regarded: *Fortin v. Dorchester Electric Co.* (1915), 48 Que. S.C. 258.

Where the petitioner is the only creditor desiring the order, and it is not shown that he has a substantial interest, the order will not be made: *Marsden v. Minnekahda Land Co.* (1918), 40 D.L.R. 76 (B.C. C.A.).

When the petition is opposed by the majority of the creditors, whose prospects of being paid would be diminished by a winding-up under the Act, the order will be refused: *Re Ocean Falls Co.* (1913), 13 D.L.R. 265 (B.C. S.C.); *Re Edmonton Brewing & Malting Co. (No. 2)* (1918), 43 D.L.R. 748 (Alta. K.B.). In such circumstances, if the petition was presented by a judgment creditor, he will not be ordered to pay costs: *Re R.W. Sharman, Ltd.*, [1957] 1 All E.R. 737 (Ch. D.). However, in a proper case the rights of minority creditors will be regarded: *Re Charles H. Davis & Co.* (1907), 9 O.W.R. 993.

Where a petition is not made for a *bona fide* purpose, but merely to serve some collateral object, for example, to put pressure on the corporation to repay money paid on account of a stock subscription, the petition will be dismissed: *Re "A" Co.* (1917), 34 D.L.R. 396.

When a winding-up petition is pending, it is a contempt of court for the corporation to issue a circular to shareholders containing misrepresentations, with intent to obtain a resolution for voluntary winding-up and thereby influence the court not to make a winding-up order: *Re Septimus Parsonage & Co.*, [1901] 2 Ch. 424.

The court will not interfere with a voluntary winding-up and order a compulsory winding-up unless it is shown that the rights of the petitioners will be prejudiced by the voluntary liquidation: *Re Oro Fino Mines Ltd.* (1900), 7 B.C.R. 388 (C.A.). In *Re National Distribution of Electricity Co.*, [1902] 2 Ch. 34 (C.A.), the court refused to upset a voluntary liquidation and make a compulsory order at the instance of a shareholder, the evidence being insufficient that any benefit would thereby result to the shareholders.

The rule in England is that where a corporation is in voluntary liquidation and a creditor presents a petition for its compulsory winding-up, the court is bound to have regard to the wishes not only of the petitioning creditor but of all the creditors. If the majority of the creditors wish to continue the voluntary liquidation, and if no valid reason is shown why effect should not be given to their wishes, the court will not make a winding-up order: *Re Home Remedies, Ltd.*, [1943] 1 Ch. 1 at 3, followed in *Re B. Karsberg Ltd.*, [1955] 3 All E.R. 854 at 860 (C.A.).

It does not necessarily follow, when a corporation is controlled by one shareholder and the liquidator in a voluntary liquidation may be regarded as a nominee of that shareholder, that a voluntary winding-up cannot be continued with due regard to the interests of the creditors: *Adebayo v. Nigeria (Official Receiver)*, [1954] 2 All E.R. 197 (P.C.).

In *Re Hough Lithographing Co.* (1915), 8 O.W.N. 377 (In Chambers), Sutherland, J., following *Re Crigglestone Coal Co. (No. 1)*, [1906] 2 Ch. 327 (C.A.), granted a winding-up order at the request of an unsecured creditor, notwithstanding that a liquidator appointed under the provisions of the Ontario *Companies Act* had disposed of the corporation's assets and had proceeded generally with the liquidation under that Act.

If it does not appear that the proceedings proposed are necessary, an order will not be made: *Re Strathy Wire Fence Co.* (1904), 8 O.L.R. 186 (C.A.); nor will it be made if the petitioner would gain nothing by the order: *Re East Kent Colliery Co.* (1914), 30 T.L.R. 659. But see *Cushing Sulphite Fibre Co. v. Cushing (sub nom. Re Cushing Sulphite Fibre Co.)* (1905), 37 N.B.R. 254 (C.A.).

A single creditor is not entitled to an order where his rights could be exercised as effectively by action and judgment: *Re International Electric Co. Ltd.* (1914), 31 O.L.R. 348 at 353 (H.C.).

An order will not be made where it is shown that there are no assets which the liquidator can receive: *Re Chapel House Colliery Co.* (1883), 24 Ch. D. 259 (C.A.); *Re Okell & Morris Fruit Preserving Co.* (1902), 9 B.C.R. 153 (C.A.); *Re Georgian Bay Ship & Power Aqueduct Canal Co.* (1898), 29 O.R. 358 (H.C.); *Re Ocean Falls Co.* (1913), 13 D.L.R. 265 (B.C. S.C.). But see *contra*, *Re Alexander Dunbar & Sons Co.* (1910), 9 E.L.R. 217 (N.B. K.B.) (no assets, order made). It is different if there are some assets: *Re Manitoba Commission Co.* (1913), 9 D.L.R. 436 (Man. K.B.); affd (1913), 4 W.W.R. 255 (Man. C.A.); *Re Lacey & Co.* (1877), 46 L.J. Ch. 660; or if it is not clear that there will be none, for example, where there are shares subscribed for but not fully paid up: *Re Georgian Bay Ship Canal & Power Aqueduct Co., supra*; or if there is a probability that the creditors will derive some benefit from the order: *Re South East Corp.* (1915), 23 D.L.R. 724 (Alta. C.A.). The onus is on those opposing the petition to show that the creditors will derive no benefit.

In special circumstances, for example, where a receiver for debenture holders has carried on the business of the corporation and has incurred further liabilities, an order may be made even though the assets are small and more than covered by the debentures, and even though the petitioners cannot show that there will be any surplus for them: *Re Chic Ltd.*, [1905] 2 Ch. 345. See also *Dominion Trust Co. v. Boyce* (1917), 43 D.L.R. 538 (B.C. C.A.); affd (*sub nom. Macpherson v. Boyce)* (1919), 59 S.C.R. 691 (petitioner for winding-up order had failed to exchange his shares in the old corporation for shares in a new corporation created to take over the business and assets of the old corporation; the court held that he was entitled to an order for the winding-up of the old corporation).

Where debenture holders were carrying on the business of the corporation although no receiver had been appointed, an order was made in favour of petitioning judgment creditors on the ground that it was just and equitable to wind up the corporation, even assuming that the assets were insufficient for the debenture holders: *Re Alfred Melson & Co.*, [1906] 1 Ch. 841; *Re Clandown Colliery Co.*, [1915] 1 Ch. 369. Under later English decisions, the order was not refused because the assets were insufficient or because there were no assets; and if the order would be useful, though not necessarily fruitful, there was jurisdiction to make it: *Re Crigglestone Coal Co. (No. 1)*, [1906] 2 Ch. 327 (C.A.).

For other instances in which creditors' petitions were and were not granted, see the notes to ss. 11-12 under the headings "Cases in which creditor's petition has been granted" and "Cases in which creditor's petition has been dismissed" in this chapter.

The objection that a second application for a winding-up order cannot be made after the first application has failed on the ground that the matter is *res judicata*, is not effective where on the second application the parties are not the same and where the material urged in favour of the application is different. This, even though the purpose of the later application is similar to that of the former: *Re Manitoba Commission Co.* (1913), 9 D.L.R. 436 (Man. K.B.); affd (1913), 4 W.W.R. 255 (Man. C.A.).

For cases in which the petition has been allowed to be amended, see the notes to ss. 11-12, under heading "Amendment" in this chapter.

For cases in which the petition has been adjourned, see the notes to ss. 11-12, under the heading "Adjournment" in this chapter, and to s. 14, *infra*. *Semble* the court has no power under s. 13, upon an adjournment of a hearing, to prevent the retroactive effect under s. 5 of a winding-up order: *Re Meaford Manufacturing Co.* (1919), 46 O.L.R. 282 at 284 (H.C.).

The court has no authority under section 13 to appoint a receiver and manager: *Anderson v. Newton*, [1934] 3 D.L.R. 224 at 228 (Man. C.A.).

Competing petitions

Where there are several competing petitions, the first applicant whose material is wholly regular will in general have the carriage of the order: *Re Commercial Discount Co.* (1863), 32 Beav. 198; *Re Farmers Bank of Canada* (1910), 22 O.L.R. 556 at 558 (H.C.); *Re Joseph Hall Co.* (1884), 10 P.R. 485 (Ont. H.C.); *Re Simpson & Hunter Ltd.* (1916), 10 W.W.R. 922 (Alta. T.D.). If the procedure of the applicant first in point of time is irregular, for example, if he has failed to file the affidavit in support of his petition as required by the rules, the order will be made upon the second petition: *Re Belding Lumber Co.* (1911), 23 O.L.R. 255 (H.C.). In *Re Estates Ltd.* (1904), 8 O.L.R. 564 (H.C.), there were two petitions, and the order was in the circumstances made on both petitions, but the conduct of the proceedings was given to the later petitioner, who was a creditor for money that was paid to the corporation under a contract, in preference to the prior petitioner, who was an employee in close touch with the officers and management. In *Re Constantinople & Alexandria Hotel Co.* (1865), 13 W. R. 851, where one petition was presented by a fully paid-up shareholder and another petition by a partly paid-up shareholder, the former was given the conduct of the proceedings. See *Re Auberge du port Inc.* (1963), 6 C.B.R. (N.S.) 144 (Que. S.C.).

Costs

In England the parties entitled to be heard on the petition are the corporation and its contributories and creditors; other people may be heard as *amici curiae* but no appeal is allowed them: *Re Bradford Navigation Co.* (1870), 5 Ch. App. 600 (L.J.). A shareholder may appear to support or object: *Re British Nation Life Assurance Assn.* (1872), L.R. 14 Eq. 492 at 501.

In Canada creditors may show cause against or may appear and assist the petitioning creditor, and are entitled to costs of so doing: *Re Commercial Bank of Manitoba* (1893), 9 Man. R. 342 (Q.B.); *Re Alpha Oil Co.* (1887), 12 P.R. 298 (Ont. H.C.).

A creditor presenting a winding-up petition with notice of an earlier one does so at his own risk as to costs and can recover costs subsequently incurred only if he can show that the first petition was presented *mala fide* or collusively: *Re Manitoba Milling & Brewing Co.* (1891), 8 Man. R. 426 (Q.B.); *Re General Financial Bank* (1882), 20 Ch. D. 276 (C.A.); *Re Building Societies' Trust Ltd.* (1890), 44 Ch. D. 140; *Re Scott & Jackson Ltd.*, [1893] W.N. 184. If, on the other hand, the second petition was made in good faith and without notice of the first, the second petitioner's costs should be allowed: *Re Algoma Commercial Co.* (1904), 3 O.W.R. 140 (H.C.). In *Re Manitoba Milling & Brewing Co., supra*, the order made was that the second petitioner should have his share of the costs of creditors supporting a winding-up order, as well as the costs of his own petition up to and including presentation, when he first had notice of the earlier application. Any attempt to forestall a *bona fide* application by a friendly and possibly collusive one will not be encouraged: *Re Enterprise Hosiery Co.* (1904), 4 O.W.R. 56 (H.C.).

If an offer were made to pay the petitioner's debt and costs, and he afterwards brought the petition to a hearing, costs incurred after the offer would not be allowed: *Re Times Life Assurance & Guarantee Co.* (1869), L.R. 9 Eq. 382.

If any director is attacked in the petition, he appears separately; and if the case against him fails, he is entitled to his costs: *Re Anglo-Greek Steam Co.* (1866), L.R. 2 Eq. 1.

With regard to costs of the petition, a general rule was laid down by Romilly, M.R., in *Re Humber Ironworks Co.* (1866), L.R. 2 Eq. 15, to the following effect:

1. Where the court refuses to make the order, shareholders or creditors or others supporting the petition will not have their costs; nor will parties opposing the petition. But any one of the directors or shareholders who is personally assailed by a charge that is disproved, and is free from blame, will receive his costs, these to be paid personally by the petitioners; and the corporation opposing the order will have its costs from the petitioner.
2. Where the court makes the order, no costs will be given to persons who appear to oppose the petition; and shareholders or creditors who together or separately appear to support the petition will get only one set of costs among them all. The costs incurred by the petitioner and the corporation will be given out of the estate.

This rule was reviewed in various subsequent cases. The practice in England now is to give costs to the petitioner if the petition succeeds, and to the corporation if it fails; and further, to give one set of costs to the contributories and one to the creditors who support the winning side. See also *Re Olympia Co.* (1915), 9 W.W.R. 405 (Man. K.B.); affd (1915), 25 D.L.R. 620 (Man. C.A.). If the petition succeeds, these costs are given out of the corporation's estate; if it fails, they are given against the petitioner: *Re European Banking Co.; Ex parte Baylis* (1866), L.R. 2 Eq. 521; *Re Peckham, etc., Tramways Co.* (1888), 57 L.J. Ch. 462; *Re Wiarton Beet Sugar Co.* (1904), 3 O.W.R. 393 (H.C.). However, where a petition for a winding-up order presented by a judgment creditor was dismissed because the majority of creditors opposed the petition, the court refused to order the petitioning judgment creditor to pay costs, because it was only by the opposition of the majority of the creditors that he was deprived of what would otherwise have been his right as a judgment creditor, that is, to have the corporation wound up: *Re R.W. Sharman, Ltd.*, [1957] 1 All E.R. 737 (Ch. D.).

Some sufficient grounds for appearing must be shown: *Re Hull & County Bank* (1878), 10 Ch. D. 130; *Re Winding-up Act* (1904), 10 B.C.R. 351 (S.C.).

Where the petition is withdrawn or is dismissed by consent, the petitioner will be ordered to pay one set of costs to the creditors supporting the petition and one set to those opposing it: *Re British Electric Street Tramways Co.*, [1903] 1 Ch. 725. However, it appears that this rule is not an inflexible one, and the court will consider in each case the circumstances giving rise to the withdrawal or the dismissal.

Where a creditor's petition was ordered to stand over to establish a debt, and the debt was established, it was held that the petitioner was entitled to costs of establishing the debt as well as of presenting the petition: *Re Railway Finance Co.* (1866), 14 W.R. 785.

The costs of a successful petitioner payable out of the corporation's assets are a first charge on the assets: *Re Baden Machinery Co.* (1906), 12 O.L.R. 634 (H.C.); *Re Audley Hall Cotton Spinning Co.* (1868), L.R. 6 Eq. 245. These costs may include the costs of establishing his claim: *Re Universal Non-Tariff Fire Assurance Co.*, [1875] W.N. 54. The petitioner is entitled to be paid in full and is not required to prove his claim: *Re Home Investment Society* (1880), 14 Ch. D. 167; *Madrid Bank v. Pelly* (1869), L.R. 7 Eq. 442; and is entitled to the costs free of set-off: *Re General Exchange Bank* (1867), L.R. 4 Eq. 138. Even if the assets are deficient, the petitioner's costs rank before costs incurred in the winding-up and before the liquidator's remuneration: *Re Massey Co.; Re Freehold Land & Brickmaking Co.* (1870), L.R. 9 Eq. 367; *Re Dominion of Canada Plumbago Co.* (1884), 27 Ch. D. 33 (C.A.).

However, if a corporation is in voluntary liquidation, the costs of the voluntary liquidator are paid in priority to those of the petitioner: *Re New York Exchange Co.*, [1893] 1 Ch. 371. As to costs of the voluntary liquidator at the hearing, see *Re A.W. Hall & Co.*, [1885] W.N. 190, and *Re Monte de Piété of England Ltd.*, [1892] W.N. 166.

This priority is only enjoyed by petitioners for the winding-up order, not for costs awarded on other proceedings in the winding-up: *Re Marlborough Club Co.* (1868), L.R. 6 Eq. 519.

Security for costs

Security for costs may be required where the petitioner lives out of the jurisdiction: *Re Home Assurance Assn. (No. 2)* (1871), L.R. 12 Eq. 112; also where the petitioner cannot be found at his business address and his solicitor does not know his private address: *Re Sturgis (British) Motor Power Syndicate Ltd.* (1885), 53 L.T. 715; but if a petitioner out of the jurisdiction has an unsatisfied judgment, no security need be given: *Re Contract & Agency Corp.* (1887), 57 L.J. Ch. 5.

Adjournment at request of corporation and resulting inquiry

If the corporation opposes the application for a winding-up order on any of the grounds set out in s. 14, the court may adjourn the proceedings and order an inquiry into the affairs of the corporation.

An accountant will only be appointed under s. 14 where there has been a *prima facie* case of insolvency made out such as would justify a winding-up order: *Re Manitoba Commission Co.* (1912), 2 D.L.R. 1 (Man. K.B.).

Where the corporation had committed an act of insolvency, but a writ of execution had been withdrawn and a majority of the shareholders favoured the corporation continuing in business, the petition was adjourned and an accountant was appointed to inquire and report: *Re Imperial Steel & Wire Co.* (1919), 17 O.W.N. 11 (H.C.).

The corporation and its officers are under a duty to exhibit to the person making the inquiry all books of account, etc., requested by him (s. 15).

Upon receiving the report of the person ordered to inquire into the corporation's affairs, and after hearing any of the shareholders or creditors that desire to be heard, the court may either refuse the application or make the winding-up order (s. 16).

Stay of proceedings against corporation

At any time after the petition for a winding-up order has been presented, before making the order, the court may stay further proceedings in any action or proceeding against the corporation (s. 17).

A restraining order to prevent the execution by judgment creditors of process against the corporation can only be applied for after the petition has been presented, and such petition can only be presented after four days' notice: *Re Eldorado Union Store Co.* (1886), 17 N.S.R. 514 (C.A.).

The enforcing of an execution is a "proceeding" under the section: *Re Artistic Colour Printing Co.* (1880), 14 Ch. D. 502; *Re Tobique Gypsum Co.* (1903), 6 O.L.R. 515 (C.A.).

A creditor within the jurisdiction will be restrained from proceeding with an action beyond the territorial jurisdiction of the court: *Re International Pulp & Paper Co.* (1876), 3 Ch. D. 594; *Re Tobique Gypsum Co., supra.*

The court in the winding-up proceedings has jurisdiction to restrain proceedings in another court against the corporation or its liquidator as such: *Re Central Bank Winding-up* (1890), 20 O.R. 214 (H.C.); but it cannot deal with an action in another court against the liquidator personally: *Re G.B. Wood Ltd.*, [1932] 3 W.W.R. 525 at 532 (Man. K.B.).

The application under this section for an injunction restraining any actions or proceedings against the corporation will be made to the judge before whom the winding-up petition is pending, wheresoever pending. Usually the application is made on notice to the plaintiff in the action sought to be stayed, but in a proper case the order may be made, on an *ex parte* application: *Re Tobique Gypsum Co., supra.* The application may be made in chambers.

The better practice is for the order to specify each action or proceeding in which the proceedings are to be restrained, but an order in general terms will not be invalid: *Re Tobique Gypsum Co., supra.*

Where the sheriff had, notwithstanding an order staying proceedings, proceeded with a sale under an execution against the lands of the corporation in the province of New Brunswick and had executed a deed to the purchaser, it was held that there was no jurisdiction in the court to make an order under the Act summarily declaring the sale void so far as the purchaser and a mortgagee of the purchaser were concerned. Moss, C.J.O., stated that it would be different as regards the execution creditor, and perhaps the sheriff: *Re Tobique Gypsum Co., supra.*

As to the stay of actions against the corporation after a winding-up order has been made, see the notes under the heading "Actions against corporation stayed when winding-up order made" in Chapter 21.

Chapter 21

EFFECT OF WINDING-UP ORDER

Section 18. The court may stay winding-up proceedings
Section 19. Company to cease business except as provided but corporate state and powers to continue
Section 20. Transfers of shares after the commencement of the winding-up are void
Section 21. Actions against the company are stayed after the winding-up has been made
Section 22. Executions, etc., after the making of the winding-up order are void

Cross references: Sections 17, 86, 135
Ontario Act, ss. 197-98, 216

Effect on assets and carrying on of business

On the making of a winding-up order, the liquidator appointed by the court takes control of all the assets that are in the possession of the corporation (s. 33), and the corporation is to cease to carry on its business except to the extent contemplated by s. 19, that is, "except in so far as is, in the opinion of the liquidator, required for the beneficial winding-up thereof." Under s. 35, the carrying on of the business is subject to the approval of the court. As to the getting in of the assets by the liquidator, see the notes under the heading "Taking possession of assets (s. 33)" in Chapter 22; as to the carrying on of the business by the liquidator, see the notes under the heading in Chapter 22.

On the appointment of the liquidator, the powers of the directors cease, except in so far as the court or the liquidator sanctions their continuance (s. 31).

The winding-up relates back to the date of service of the notice of presentation of the petition (s. 5): *Bank of Hamilton v. Kramer-Irwin Co.* (1912), 20 O.W.R. 999.

After the winding-up order has been made, new rights are given by the Act of Parliament — rights that did not exist before the winding-up and that can be enforced only under the winding-up: *Re National Funds Assurance Co.* (1878), 10 Ch. D. 118 at 125.

The Statute of Limitations does not run against a creditor after the order has been made: *Re General Rolling Stock Co.; Joint Stock Discount Co.'s Claim* (1872), 7 Ch. App. 646. Modern practice is to take out two orders, the first finding the corporation in question properly to be the subject matter of the Act and ordering that it be wound up, the second specifying in detail the manner of the liquidation and the terms of the stay as to proceedings.

Effect on corporate status and powers

The making of a winding-up order does not destroy the corporation's corporate status: s. 19; *Soucy v. Cie d'imprimerie industrielle* (1902), 5 Que. P.R. 195; *Jolicoeur v. Boivin & Cie*, [1951] Que. P.R. 369 at 372. Its corporate powers also continue, although some powers, for example, the power to sue, must be exercised by the liquidator under the authority of the court: *Kent v. La Communauté des Soeurs de Charité de la Providence*, [1903] A.C. 220; *Re Home Bank* (1930), 66 O.L.R. 264. For the power to give a proxy, see *Carle v. Rango*, [1961] Que. Q.B. 405 (C.A.).

As to the dissolution of the corporation upon completion of the winding-up, see the notes under the heading "Dissolution of corporation" in Chapter 22.

Effect on interest on debts

Unless there should turn out to be a surplus of assets available after payment of the principal of the debts, all interest ceases at the commencement of the winding-up: *Humber Ironworks & Shipbuilding Co., Re; Warrant Finance Co.'s Case* (1869), 4 Ch. App. 643; *Re International Contract Co.; Hughes' Claim* (1872),

L.R. 13 Eq. 623; *Re Collie; Ex parte Findlay* (1881), 17 Ch. D. 334 (C.A.); *Re London, Windsor & Greenwich Hotels Co.*, [1892] 1 Ch. 639. Interest must be calculated to the date on which the petition is presented: *Re Agricultural Wholesale Society*, [1929] 2 Ch. 261; *Re Parent Trust & Finance Co.*, [1936] 1 All E.R. 641. A creditor whose debt carries interest may enter a claim for interest, and if the corporation should have a surplus, he will be paid: *Dominion Gresham Guarantee & Casualty Co. v. Hermant* (1933), 35 Que. K.B. 564 (right reserved to claimant to be collocated for interest against surplus, if any).

To the extent of any surplus, judgment creditors who obtained judgments after the commencement of the winding-up as well as those who obtained judgments before the winding-up are alike entitled to interest: *Re Colonial Assurance Co.*, [1928] 3 W.W.R. 703 (Man. K.B.); *Re Fine Industrial Commodities Ltd.*, [1956] Ch. 256. In the latter case it was also held that simple contract creditors were not entitled to interest on their debts out of such surplus. *Roberlson v. Carlile Ltd.*, [1949] 2 D.L.R. 525 (Alta. C.A.), there existed a surplus of assets after the principal of all the approved claims against the corporation had been paid by the liquidator. The Court of Appeal (O'Connor J.A., dissenting in part) held that interest on interest-bearing notes, computed from the date of the commencement of the liquidation up to the date of payment, should be paid before any payment was made to shareholders.

As to the position of secured claimants, see the notes under the heading "Secured creditors" in Chapter 24.

Effect on existing contracts

Contracts are not terminated by the mere fact of liquidation. A contract made by the corporation before it goes into liquidation can be enforced by the liquidator, but the other party to the contract cannot enforce it without the leave of the court and on such terms as the court may direct. In the case of a contract entered into before liquidation for the purchase and delivery of goods by instalments, the liquidator cannot require the vendors to make further deliveries without paying for them in cash and also paying for the goods already delivered: *William Hamilton Manufacturing Co. v. Hamilton Steel & Iron Co.* (1910), 23 O.L.R. 270 (C.A.); *P. Lyall & Sons Construction Co. v. Baker*, [1933] O.R. 286 at 294 (C.A.).

In the case of a contract to supply services, where the creditor has reserved the right to discontinue the services in the event of default, the liquidator may be put to his election either to reject the contract or to accept and continue the contract, making good the default to secure such continuation: *Bell Telephone Co. v. Duclos*, [1942] 3 D.L.R. 738 at 743 (Que. C.A.).

Where a trust corporation under arrangement with a client is entitled to retain as its remuneration a percentage of the return on an investment made by it for the client, on the insolvency of the trust corporation the benefit of the arrangement passes to the liquidator who will not be compelled to surrender the security to the *cestui que trust*; nor will the court appoint a special trustee for carrying the arrangement into effect: *Dominion Trust Co. v. Harper* (1915), 24 D.L.R. 670 (B.C. C.A.). But the liquidator of a trust corporation cannot continue in the name of the trust corporation to function as administrator of the property of an intestate: *Re Hiebert*, [1934] 4 D.L.R. 799 (Sask. K.B.).

In respect of goods sold to a corporation under a conditional sale agreement, the liquidator stands in no higher position than the corporation and if he sells the goods, the unpaid vendor is entitled to recover out of the estate the full amount due under the agreement: *Re Canadian Camera & Optical Co.* (1901), 2 O.L.R. 677 (C.A.). If the agreement is unregistered and there is an execution creditor of the corporation, the contract is void against the liquidator to the extent only of the amount owing to such execution creditor: *Re Northern Creameries Co.*, [1921] 3 W.W.R. 355.

In Ontario a liquidator has the same power to disclaim a lease as a trustee in bankruptcy; the practice varies from province to province.

Where a lessee from the corporation had an option to purchase property, it was held that the winding up of that corporation did not cut down his rights; the corporation was held liable in damages to the lessee when the liquidator sold the property without giving the lessee an opportunity to exercise his option: *McCarter v. York County Loan Co.* (1907), 14 O.L.R. 420.

If the liquidator elects to perform a contract previously entered into by the corporation he can compel the other party likewise to carry it out: *Mersey Steel & Iron Co. v. Naylor Benzon & Co.* (1884), 9 App. Cas. 434.

Where a person did work for a corporation, and agreed to accept either shares or cash in payment, it was held that on a winding-up he could not be compelled by the liquidators to accept shares against his wish: *Re Alexandra Park Co.*, [1866] W.N. 231.

Discharge of employees of corporation

An order for the winding-up of the corporation is a notice of discharge to the employees of the corporation: *Re Imperial Wine Co.; Shirreff's Case* (1872), L.R. 14 Eq. 417; *Re General Rolling Stock Co.; Chapman's Case* (1866), L.R. 1 Eq. 346; *Re Oriental Bank Corp.; MacDowall's Case* (1886), 32 Ch. D. 366; *Rolfe v. Canadian Timber & Saw Mills Ltd.* (1906), 12 B.C.R. 363 (C.A.); *Re City Cold Storage Co.* (1916), 30 D.L.R. 574 (Sask. T.D.).

Where a director holds office upon the terms of the articles or by-laws, the effect of liquidation is to terminate his contract of service: *Re T.N. Farrer Ltd.*, [1937] Ch. 352.

When there is a written agreement appointing a managing director, and the corporation goes into voluntary liquidation with the assent or approval of that managing director, it does not follow that he should lose all right to recover damages for the breach of the agreement: *Fowler v. Commercial Timber Co.*, [1930] 2 K.B. 1 (C.A.).

The method of dealing with a claim for salary is to ascertain the present value of an annuity equal to the salary for the unexpired term, regard being had to the risk of health and life, and a deduction being made for the liberty to obtain new employment: *Hawkins v. Allied Truck Co.* (1919), 16 O.W.N. 381 at 382.

Where the business is continued after the winding-up and the former employees are actually employed, the old contract between the corporation and its employees continues in force. The notice of discharge must be given pursuant thereto: *Re English Joint Stock Bank; Ex parte Harding* (1867), L.R. 3 Eq. 341.

Where a secretary, who had been appointed without any fixed term of office, acted as the secretary of the corporation to the time of the passing of the resolution for the voluntary winding-up of the corporation, the court held that he was entitled to his salary to that date, as he held office during the pleasure of the board of directors, or until he resigned, or until some event (in this case the winding-up of the corporation) happened that involved a termination of his employment: *Re Jubilee Theatre Ltd.* (1956), 3 D.L.R. (2d) 624 (N.S. C.A.).

Effect on voluntary winding-up

A winding-up order under the Act will supersede a voluntary winding-up, but does not render a voluntary winding-up void *ab initio*; and a subsequent proceeding under the federal Act will not vitiate the proceedings under the statute governing the voluntary liquidation: *Imperial Canadian Trust Co. v. Potter* (1917), 34 D.L.R. 457 (Alta. C.A.).

Effect on liens

A winding-up order does not defeat a valid lien claimed by a solicitor on the documents of the corporation in his hands at the presentation of the petition: *Re Capital Fire Insurance Assn.* (1883), 24 Ch. D. 408 (C.A.).

The order does not interfere with the right of a mortgagee to appoint a receiver under a power in the mortgage deed: *Re Henry Pound, Son & Hutchins* (1889), 42 Ch. D. 402 (C.A.); but the receiver cannot take possession without the leave of the court. In effect, there is a stay until the provisions of the Act have been complied with. See further the notes on ss. 78-84 under the heading "Bondholders and mortgagees" in Chapter 24.

Contingent liabilities

The winding-up order will not prevent a contingent liability on the part of the corporation from ripening into a debt; therefore, the holder of a fire policy issued by a corporation may prove in the winding-up for the full amount of loss covered by the policy, though the fire occurred after the date of the winding-up order: *Re Northern Counties of England Fire Insurance Co.; Macfarlane's Claim* (1880), 17 Ch. D. 337.

Effect on shareholders

As to the effect of a winding-up order on a shareholder's right to rescind his contract for shares, see the notes under the heading "Loss of right to rescind" in chapter 13.

It has been held in England that a provision in the articles that a call should not be made without the consent of three fourths of the shareholders, does not apply to a call made in the winding-up: *Re Coed Madog Slate Co.*, [1877] W.N. 190. Nor does a provision apply as to the instalments by which calls are to be payable: *Re Cordova Union Gold Co.*, [1891] 2 Ch. 580. See s. 61 of this Act.

Provisions in the articles as to interest upon calls do not apply to calls made in the winding-up: *Re Welsh Flannel & Tweed Co.* (1875), L.R. 20 Eq. 360.

Effect on transfer of shares

Under s. 20, transfers of shares (except as sanctioned by the liquidator with the authority of the court) are forbidden after the commencement of the winding-up, that is, after the date of service of the notice of presentation of the petition (s. 5). The Act contains no provision as to when the winding-up commences where the application for winding-up is by the corporation, for in that case no notice is required (s. 12(2)).

After a winding-up, a transfer of shares may be made with the sanction of the liquidator acting under the authority of the court: *Redfern v. Polson* (1894), 25 O.R. 321 (C.A.); compare s. 35 (powers of liquidator); and see *Pacaud v. Tourigny* (1883), 10 Q.L.R. 54 (C.A.).

The leave of the court will only be granted upon special grounds: *Re Onward Building Society*, [1891] 2 Q.B. 463 (C.A.). The general scheme of the Act is that " 'as the tree falls so it must lie', unless the court chooses to alter the existing state of things", per Bowen, L.J., at 482.

For a case where the sanction by the liquidator of transfers was subject to special statutory provisions as to entitlement to hold shares, see *Re Saskatchewan Co-operative Elevator Co.*, [1927] 4 D.L.R. 804 (Sask. K.B.).

Where the shares are listed on a stock exchange, an order in general terms authorizing the liquidator to sanction transfers is sometimes made.

The liquidator alone is powerless to accept transfers void under s. 20; nor will the fact that he has inadvertently placed the names of the transferees on the list of contributories and obtained a judgment against the transferees release the transferors: *Re Ontario Bank* (1912), 27 O.L.R. 192 (C.A.).

The application of the section is limited to transfers of shares and alterations of the status of members: *Trusts & Guarantee Co. v. Munro* (1909), 19 O.L.R. 480 at 487 and 488 (C.A.).

Actions against corporation stayed when winding-up order made (s. 21)

Under s. 21, after the winding-up order is made, no suit, action or other proceeding is to be proceeded with or commenced against the corporation, except with the leave of the court and subject to such terms as the court imposes.

The object of s. 21 is "to prevent litigation being carried on by any one prejudicial to the estate, to prevent the assets being dissipated by lawsuits, and to have all matters decided promptly by a summary petition": Brodeur, J. in *Stewart v. Lepage* (1916), 53 S.C.R. 337 at 351. The court will not allow its administration of assets to be interfered with by other proceedings affecting the estate; and creditors of such estate must bring their rights into the Master's office, which the Act substitutes for proceedings at law: *Clarke v. Union Fire Insurance Co.; Caston's Case* (1884), 10 P.R. 339. See *Doxtator v. DeLeary* (1982),

44 C.B.R. (N.S.) 133 (Ont. C.A.) for a case where application for leave was granted in a claim against an insurer in a car accident.

The section must be read with s. 135 of the Act, which lays down the general rule that all remedies of the types therein set out may be obtained by an order of the court on summary petition. See the notes on s. 135 in Chapter 25.

It should be noted (as was observed in *Re J. McCarthy & Sons* (1916), 38 O.L.R. 3 at 10 (C.A.) and in *Stewart v. Lepage* (1916), 53 S.C.R. 337 at 348) that the English Act contains no provision corresponding to s. 135. This should be kept in mind when consideration is given to English cases dealing with the granting of leave to bring or continue actions.

There is authority for the view that where s. 135 applies, it provides the only remedy available, and that leave cannot in such cases be granted under s. 21. The better view appears to be that the sections must be read together, and that even if a case comes within s. 135, leave to bring or proceed with an action may be granted under s. 21 in exceptional cases. For a discussion of the two views referred to, see the notes to s. 135 under the heading "Whether the remedy under s. 135 is exclusive" in Chapter 25.

The leave to proceed with or commence an action provided for in s. 21 is obtainable only where there are such exceptional circumstances present as justify it being granted: *Re Raven Lake Portland Cement Co.* (1911), 24 O.L.R. 286 (C.A.). Where nothing more than the amount and ordinary questions of fact and law are involved, that is not enough: *Re J. McCarthy & Sons, supra.* For cases where the court has granted or refused leave, see the notes under the headings "Discretion to grant leave" and "Mortgagees and bondholders" in this chapter.

The section should further be compared with s. 86, which, as regards the proceedings to which it applies, viz., those of a judicial nature, has a retroactive effect. Section 21, on the other hand, while general in its application, only affects proceedings taken after the winding-up order has been made. Those taken before will not be affected unless they are caught by s. 86: *Re E. C. Colwell Candy Co.* (1902), 35 N.B.R. 613 (C.A.).

An action continued by leave of the court in the winding-up does not become a proceeding in the winding-up, but proceeds as a provincial action subject to the provincial law, which may impose a moratorium that may be limited to a special class of action or suitor or to one particular action or suitor: *Abitibi Power & Paper Co. v. Montreal Trust Co.*, [1943] A.C. 536 at 548.

As to distress, which is a proceeding within the meaning of s. 21, see the notes under the heading "Distress" in this chapter.

The section does not bind the Crown: *A.G. Canada v. Ettenberg* (1936), 18 C.B.R. 144 (Que. C.A.).

Where the governing legislation does not provide for an automatic stay, and the court is asked to stay an action, the only material question to be considered is this: are there any circumstances which render it necessary that the action be continued, or can the claim of the plaintiff be as easily dealt with in the winding-up as in any other way? If the claim sought to be enforced is capable of being satisfactorily dealt with in the winding-up, other proceedings to enforce it will be stayed: *Re Hermann Loog Ltd.* (1887), 36 Ch. D. 502; *Re International Pulp & Paper Co.* (1876), 3 Ch. D. 594; *Re Australian Direct Steam Navigation Co.* (1875), L.R. 20 Eq. 325; *Re Briton Medical & General Life Assurance Assn.* (1886), 32 Ch. D. 503.

Leave of court necessary for commencing or continuing proceedings

The court having charge of the winding-up has overriding jurisdiction, and the operation of s. 21 extends to any province in which proceedings are sought to be taken. Thus the original court will prevent an action being brought against the corporation or its liquidator in another province, without leave from the court that made the winding-up order and has charge and control of the winding-up proceedings: *Stewart v. Lepage* (1916), 53 S.C.R. 337; *Re Central Bank* (1890), 20 O.R. 214 (H.C.); *Robillard v. Blanchet* (1901), 19 Que. S.C. 383; *Re Tobique Gypsum Co.* (1903), 6 O.L.R. 515 at 518 (C.A.); *Blais v. Bankers' Trust Corp. Ltd.* (1913), 14 D.L.R. 277 (T.D.); *H.J. Carson & Co. v. Montreal Trust Co.* (1915), 49 N.S.R. 50 (C.A.); *Hobbs v. Kenabeek Consolidated Silver Mines Ltd.* (1918), 14 O.W.N. 358 (H.C.).

See also *A.G. Can. v. Astra Trust Co.* (1983), 47 C.B.R. (N.S.) 218 (Ont. S.C.), where leave to make the trust corporation being wound up a party was refused, since there would be little benefit to the creditors and there could be lengthy and expensive litigation involved.

Thus, in *Wood Gundy Inc. v. Northland Bank* (1989), 73 C.B.R. (N.S.) 297 (Man. Q.B.), the court dismissed an application on the basis that another provincial jurisdiction was the most convenient forum and that the courts had a duty to minimize litigation.

In Quebec, leave must be given by the Superior Court of the district where the liquidation proceedings are in progress or by a judge of such court: *Organ v. Gamache* (1913), 22 Que. K.B. 389 (C.A.); *Plante v. Cie de pulpe de Dalmas* (1914), 20 D.L.R. 983 (Que. C.A.); *Royer v. Dupuis Ltd.* (1940), 44 Que. P.R. 178.

Ignorance of the existence of the winding-up order made in another province will not help the plaintiff, except possibly as to costs: *Lavell v. Canadian Mineral Rubber Co.* (1913), 14 D.L.R. 521 at 523 (Alta.).

Where the judgment in an action against a corporation had been reserved, the court refused to render judgment upon a winding-up order being made: *Molleur v. St. Laurent Pulp & Paper Co.* (1887), M.L.R. 3 S.C. 273.

After a winding-up order is made in Manitoba, a second order by an Alberta court under the Alberta Insurance Act appointing a receiver to administer the securities deposited in Alberta for the benefit of creditors in that province, cannot be made without leave of the Manitoba court in the winding-up proceedings: *Re Continental Fire & Casualty Co. (In Liquidation)*, [1924] 1 W.W.R. 1080. See, in addition, as to insurance corporations, s. 165.

However, it has been held that the corresponding section of the English *Companies Act* has no application to proceedings in foreign courts: *Re Vocalion (Foreign) Ltd.*, [1932] 2 Ch. 196, (where the cases are collected). Parliament never legislates respecting strictly foreign courts: *Re Oriental Inland Steam Co.; Ex parte Scinde Ry. Co.* (1874), 9 Ch. App. 557, per Mellish, L.J., at 560.

On the other hand, the court can restrain a creditor within the jurisdiction from proceeding with an action in a foreign court: *Re Oriental Inland Steam Co.; Ex parte Scinde Ry. Co., supra* (English corporation ordered to withdraw attachment against property in India of corporation being wound up in England); *Re North Carolina Estate Co.* (1889), 5 T.L.R. 328 (injunction against British subject permanently residing in England from proceeding with an action in the United States); *Falck's Case*, [1894] 1 Ch. 369 (English creditor resident in England restrained from proceeding against property of corporation in Brazil under judgment obtained in Brazilian courts, the order preserving for him such security as he had by the effect of the judgment); *Re Belfast Ship Owners Co.*, [1894] 1 I.R. 321 (British subjects resident in England, who were petitioners for winding-up order, restrained from proceeding in the United States). The court can exercise such jurisdiction against a foreign corporation registered in England and properly served there: *Re Vocalion (Foreign) Ltd., supra*; but in the same case, Maugham, J., held that as against such foreign corporation, domiciled abroad, the court ought *prima facie* not to exercise such jurisdiction for the reason that in general it will be more conducive to substantial justice that the foreign proceedings be allowed to continue.

A mortgagee of immovable property in a foreign country will not be restrained from continuing proceedings instituted by him in that country to enforce his security, even though the mortgagor is a corporation in the course of winding up; at all events, when all the parties can appear in the foreign court and have their rights settled: *Moor v. Anglo-Italian Bank* (1879), 10 Ch. D. 681, followed in *Re Vocalion (Foreign) Ltd., supra.*

After a winding-up order had been made, P., a resident of Ontario, brought an action against the corporation in the State of Michigan, to attach certain property of the corporation there. The liquidator brought an action in Ontario for an injunction to restrain P. from proceeding with his action in Michigan. It was held that this case could not be distinguished in principle from *Re Taylor; Ex parte Williams; Re Ry. Steel & Plant Co.* (1878), 8 Ch. D. 183; and upon the facts disclosed, the injunction was refused and P. was allowed to continue his action in Michigan: *Re Lake Superior Native Copper Co.* (1885), 9 O.R. 277.

If the court is of the opinion that the action ought not to be stopped because it is instituted against directors and other individuals as well as against the corporation, the court will allow the proceedings to continue, but will require the plaintiff to undertake not to issue execution against the corporation without leave of the court: *McEwan v. London Bombay & Mediterranean Bank*, [1866] W.N. 407; *Hagell v. Currie; Breech-Loading Armoury Co., Re*, [1867] W.N. 75.

The section does not prevent a defendant from taking without leave the necessary steps to defend himself in an action brought against him by the liquidator or the corporation in liquidation, for example, an application to set aside a concurrent writ of summons for service out of the jurisdiction and service thereof: *Frid Lewis Co. v. Holmes* (1915), 8 Sask. L.R. 185. If the subject matter of a counterclaim is not outside of and independent of the subject matter of the claim made by the liquidator, it is in the nature of a defence and no leave is necessary: *Dominion Trust Co. v. Brydges* (1920), 28 B.C.R. 451 (S.C.).

It has been held that the section does not relate to obligations incurred by the liquidator in the course of the liquidation: *Scott v. Silver* (1915), 8 O.W.N. 552. In the last mentioned case, Middleton, J., dismissed a motion for an order prohibiting the enforcement of a judgment against a liquidator garnishee in respect of wages payable by the liquidator. He did not deal with the question whether leave should originally have been obtained to sue the liquidator independently of the section. But see *Re G.B. Wood Ltd.*, [1932] 3 W.W.R. 525 (Man. K.B.), where it was held that leave was required to sue in respect of negligent use of a chattel of the corporation after the making of the winding-up order. In that case Montague, J., said, at 530, that to reach the estate it is only necessary to sue the corporation and that he could not conceive of any circumstances where the liquidator must be sued as such; but he also observed that such actions have been often brought, citing *Robillard v. Blanchet* (1901), 19 Que. S.C. 383; *H.J. Carson & Co. v. Montreal Trust Co.* (1915), 49 N.S.R. 50 (C.A.) and *Stewart v. Lepage* (1916), 53 S.C.R. 337.

See also the notes under s. 22 as to the effect of attachments, distress, etc., after the making of the winding-up order.

Application for leave

The application must be made to the court in Canada that has the conduct of the winding up, even though the application is for leave to continue an action begun before the winding up in a province other than that in which the winding up is proceeding: *Brewster v. Can. Iron Corp.* (1914), 7 O.W.N. 128. In Quebec, leave can be granted only by the tribunal of the judicial district in which the winding-up proceedings are being carried on: *Plante v. Cie de pulpe de Dalmas* (1914), 20 D.L.R. 983 (C.A.).

Application for leave, after an order of reference has been made under s. 111, should except in exceptional cases be made to the Master or Referee: *Re J. McCarthy & Sons Co.* (1916), 38 O.L.R. 3 (C.A.), per Hodgins, J.A. Prior to that decision applications had frequently been made to a judge in chambers, not only in Ontario but in the other provinces. A county court judge has no jurisdiction under the section: *Goldrich v. Colonial Assurance Co.* (1916), 28 D.L.R. 542 (Man. C.A.).

A person who applied to the court under s. 21 for leave to sue the liquidator was not required to give notice to the liquidator of his intention so to apply: *Maranda-Desauliers v. Peckham et The Title Guarantee & Trust Corp. of Canada*, [1950] Que. K.B. 366 (C.A.).

Discretion to grant leave

As to the object of s. 21 and the principle that leave should be granted thereunder only in special circumstances, see the notes under the heading "Actions against corporation stayed when winding-up order made (s. 21)" in this chapter.

Where it applies (as to which see the notes to that section), s. 135 makes it necessary to show special grounds when justifying the granting of leave under s. 21: *Re Raven Lake Cement Co.* (1911), 24 O.L.R. 286 (C.A.); *Re J. McCarthy & Sons Co.* (1916), 38 O.L.R. 3 (C.A.).

Leave will be granted to bring action against the corporation for arrears of wages, so that after a return of *nulla bona* the plaintiff might sue the directors under the Manitoba *Companies Act*: *Re Lake Winnipeg Transportation, Lumber & Trading Co.*, (1891), 7 Man. R. 602 (Q.B.); and leave will be granted to continue an action to enable the plaintiff to enforce a statutory remedy against directors requiring a judgment and execution against the corporation with a return by the sheriff: *Risler v. Alberta Newspapers Ltd.* (1919), 46 D.L.R. 536 (Alta. C.A.). For the principles governing the granting of leave to secured creditors see the notes under the heading "Mortgagees and Bondholders" in this chapter.

When, before the winding up, a shareholder had been sued by the corporation for unpaid calls, and had delivered a defence, and had counterclaimed for the cancellation of his subscription on the ground of misrepresentations in the prospectus, the shareholder's application for leave to proceed in the action was refused, on the ground that he could have in the winding up all the relief claimed in the action: *Re Pakenham Pork Packing Co.* (1903), 6 O.L.R. 582 (H.C.). But when a shareholder had sued for cancellation of his subscription on the ground of fraud, and costs had been incurred and the action was on the list for trial, leave was granted in Quebec: *Johnston v. Ewart Co.* (1907), 31 Que. S.C. 336. When, although the amount to be claimed in the proposed action is considerable, nothing more than the amount and ordinary questions of fact and law are involved, leave is not to be granted: *Re J. McCarthy & Sons Co.* (1916), 38 O.L.R. 3 (C.A.). So also an application was refused for leave to bring an action to set aside stock subscriptions on failure of the applicant to show such special and unusual circumstances as to make it reasonably clear that the Master could not satisfactorily deal with the question: *Titterington v. Distributors Co.* (1906), 8 O.W.R. 328.

On the other hand, the applicability of the provisions of a provincial Insurance Act, under which securities of an insurance corporation deposited under such Act are to be administered for the benefit of and distributable among policyholders and creditors in that province, justifies the granting of leave to take proceedings in the provincial courts directed to secure the administration of the securities for the purposes indicated in the provincial Act: *Re Continental Fire & Casualty Co.*, [1924] 1 W.W.R. 132 (Man.).

When an action has already been dismissed, and has become barred by lapse of time when the winding-up order is made, a new action should not be authorized: *Goldrich v. Colonial Assurance Co.* (1916), 28 D.L.R. 542 (Man. C.A.).

When the rights of the parties have changed since an action brought without leave has been commenced, for example, by the running of the Statute of Limitations, an order should not be made *nunc pro tunc* that would maintain the action as having been brought in time: *Re G.B. Wood Ltd.*, [1932] 3 W.W.R. 525 (Man.K.B.).

Mortgagees and bondholders

Mortgagees or bondholders cannot proceed to enforce their remedies without leave: *Re Winnipeg & Western Development Co.* (1916), 33 W.L.R. 749. In *British Columbia Tie & Timber Co.* (1909), 14 B.C.R. 204, Clement, J., refused to interfere with a mortgagee's sale proceedings on the ground that such a sale did not fall within s. 21 (and so require the leave of the court); but this case seems to be opposed not only to the authorities elsewhere but also to *Re Lenora Mount Sicker Copper Mining Co.* (1902), 9 B.C.R. 471, which was decided in the same province.

In general, the secured creditor has a right to apply for and obtain leave to bring an action to enforce his security: *Re Lenora Mount Sicker Copper Mining Co., supra*; *Re Dominion Milling Co.* (1912), 3 D.L.R. 897; *Re Winnipeg & Western Development Co., supra.*

When, in addition to the claims of the applicant and of the liquidator, an interest in the assets in question was alleged by a mortgagee, who would not be bound by the determination of the issue as between the liquidator and the claimant by summary proceedings under what is now s. 135, Mulock, C.J., K.B., made an order that, if the mortgagee was unwilling to come in under the winding-up proceedings, leave should be granted to bring an action: *Kurtz v. McLean Ltd.* (1908), 11 O.W.R. 437.

When bondholders made no claim in the winding up, and their security was known to be insufficient to meet the mortgaged debt, and they were proceeding with an action to enforce their security, leave to proceed was *ex debito justitiae: Abitibi Power & Paper Co. v. Montreal Trust Co.*, [1943] A.C. 536 at 547.

In *Re Raven Lake Portland Cement Co.* (1911), 24 O.L.R. 286 (C.A.), trustees for bondholders obtained leave to bring an action against the liquidators of the mortgagor corporation in respect of assets alleged to be mortgaged under the trust deed, claiming the proceeds or damages for conversion.

Leave was granted to commence an action that a debenture constituted a first charge upon the property of the corporation: *Holdsworth v. Refrigerated Express Lines Ltd.* (1954), 13 W.W.R. 542 (B.C.), following *Michigan Trust Co. v. Canadian Puget Sound Lumber Co.*, [1918] 3 W.W.R. 273 (B.C. C.A.) (mortgage to secure a debenture issue).

When a bondholder's application for leave to commence an action was opposed by the majority of the bondholders, the court refused leave: *Re Excelsior Brick Co., Ltd.* (1916), an unreported decision of Middleton, J.

In granting leave to a secured creditor to commence or continue an action, the court may impose terms. For example, in *Re Dominion Milling Co.* (1912), 3 D.L.R. 897, the liquidator was given time to ascertain the value of the property and to pay the mortgagee, otherwise the mortgagee could proceed with a sale; in *Re Martin International Trap Rock Co.* (1915), 8 O.W.N. 599, an order was made granting the mortgagees for the bondholders leave to enforce their security after the expiration of three months, the liquidator having this time to effect a sale; and in *Re Winnipeg & Western Development Co.* (1916), 33 W.L.R. 749, successive adjournments were ordered conditionally on the corporation's making certain payments of arrears of interest and taxes with a view to protecting the corporation and permitting the assets to be sold. However a liquidator is not entitled to the conduct of a sale under foreclosure proceedings, and an order made by a judge at his instance that directed the winding-up proceedings postponing the sale, and that directed the referee to advertise, and that fixed a subsequent date for sale, was held to be bad: *Re Cushing Sulphite Fibre Co.* (1906), 38 N.B.R. 581 (C.A.).

The fact that before the winding-up order is made, judgments against the corporation have been registered, does not disentitle a mortgagee or bondholder from obtaining leave to proceed to enforce his security: *Re Giant Mining Co.* (1904), 10 B.C.R. 327 (C.A.).

A mortgagee will not generally be restrained from enforcing his rights against the mortgaged property: *David Lloyd & Co., Re.; Lloyd v. David Lloyd & Co.* (1877), 6 Ch. D. 339 (C.A.); *Re Longdendale Cotton Spinning Co.* (1878), 8 Ch. D. 150; *Re Cushing Sulphite Fibre Co.* (1906), 38 N.B.R. 581 (C.A.); *Abitibi Power & Paper Co. v. Montreal Trust Co.*, [1943] A.C. 536 at 547. It is otherwise when there is only an equitable charge and not a mortgage: *Andrew v. Swansea Cambrian Benefit Bldg. Soc.* (1880), 50 L.J. Q.B. 428. See also the notes under the subheading "Distress," in this chapter.

See further the notes to s. 135 of this Act in Chapter 25.

Appeal from order made under s. 21

An appeal lies from an order made under s. 21, giving leave to bring an action: *Re J. McCarthy & Sons Co.* (1916), 38 O.L.R. 3 (C.A.). When the court cannot say that the discretion of the judge or official to whom the application was made was exercised wrongly, his order granting or refusing leave will not be disturbed on appeal: *Re Raven Lake Portland Cement Co.* (1911), 24 O.L.R. 286 (C.A.); *Re Toronto Cream & Butter Co.* (1909), 14 O.W.R. 81 (C.A.).

When leave had been granted to the applicant to sue the corporation for specific performance of an agreement for exchange of lands, or in default for cancellation of the agreement and recovery of the applicant's lands, of which the corporation was in possession, the Master's discretion in granting leave was held on appeal to have been properly exercised: *Re Transcontinental Townsite Co.* (1915), 21 D.L.R. 291.

The discretion may be reviewed on appeal: *Re Cushing Sulphite Fibre Co.* (1906), 38 N.B.R. 581 (C.A.). Moreover, when the order appealed from was made on a wrong principle, it was set aside by the Ontario Court of Appeal: *Re J. McCarthy & Sons Co., supra.* The rule still stands, however, that an exercise of a discretion proceeding on proper principles is not generally to be interfered with, *ibid.*, per Meredith, C.J.C.P.

Effect of s. 21 on unauthorized proceedings

In *Blais v. Bankers' Trust Corp.* (1913), 14 D.L.R. 277 (T.D.), and *Lavell v. Canadian Mineral Rubber Co.* (1913), 14 D.L.R. 521 (Alta.), it was held that when an action commenced without leave is irregular, it only should be stayed until leave is granted; so also to the same effect: *Stewart v. Lepage* (1916), 53

S.C.R. 337; *H.J. Carson & Montreal Trust Co.* (1915), 49 N.S.R. 50 (C.A.); *Trusts & Guarantee Co. v. Brenner*, [1932] O.R. 245 at 251 (C.A.); *Re G.B. Wood Ltd.*, [1932] 2 W.W.R. 525 at 527 (Man. K.B.).

An action brought without leave will be dismissed in Quebec on exception to the form: *Marcotte v. Turcot* (1902), 4 Que. P.R. 342; *Soucy v. Cie d'imprimerie industrielle* (1902), 5 Que. P.R. 195. For Quebec cases where it was held that unauthorized proceedings were a nullity, see *Ruffer v. Rattray & Sons Ltd.* (1911), 39 Que. S.C. 245 (defence raised by another defendant party); *Cossette v. Cdn. Marine Engineering Co.* (1920), 22 Que. P.R. 368 (action dismissed).

An order made on an application in a provincial court pursuant to the provisions of a provincial statute, if it is without leave in the winding-up proceedings, is a nullity: *Re Continental Fire & Casualty Co. (In Liquidation)*, [1924] 1 W.W.R. 1080.

In Ontario a motion to dismiss an action brought without leave for want of prosecution was refused on the ground that the section imposed an absolute stay: *Duke v. Ulrey* (1909) 14 O.W.R. 932.

When proceedings had been continued without leave after a winding-up order had intervened, mortgagees were deprived of costs incurred after the winding-up order, and the costs of the motion for leave to proceed were awarded to the liquidator: *Re Winnipeg & Western Development Co.* (1916), 9 W.W.R. 1360 (Man. K.B.) (leave to continue proceedings granted on terms).

A judgment entered against the corporation after a winding-up order has been made is wholly void and nugatory: *Keating v. Graham* (1895), 26 O.R. 361 (C.A.); *Graham v. Casselman Lumber Co.* (1893), 4 Que. S.C. 91.

A garnishee summons depending on an unauthorized action is ineffective and will be set aside: *Lavell v. Canadian Mineral Rubber Co.* (1913), 14 D.L.R. 521 (Alta.).

Effect of s. 22

Section 22 provides that every attachment, sequestration, distress or execution put in force against the estate or effects of the corporation after the making of the winding-up order is void.

Sections 21 and 22 must be read together. An attachment, sequestration, distress or execution is not void under s. 22 unless "put in force" after the making of the winding-up order. It is not void even then if leave has been obtained under s. 21: *Risler v. Alberta Newspapers Ltd.* (1919), 46 D.L.R. 536 at 538 (Alta. C.A.).

However, it has been held that, owing to the provisions of s. 86 of the Act, Canadian courts have no discretion under s. 22 to allow attachments, distresses, etc.: *Shaver v. Cotton* (1896), 23 O.A.R. 426 at 435.

An execution is "put in force" when the sheriff by virtue of the writ enters into possession: *Re London & Devon Biscuit Co.* (1871), L.R. 12 Eq. 190 at 194; *Re Penny Lumber Co.*, [1921] 3 W.W.R. 352 (Alta.). A winding up supersedes the execution: *Re Ideal Foundry & Hardware Co.* (1918), 42 O.L.R. 411.

The section will apply in all provinces where the corporation's assets may be situate: *Re Producers Rock & Gravel Co., Ltd.* (1913), 14 D.L.R. 289. The operation of the section is limited to creditors of the corporation: *Good v. Nepisiguit Lumber Co.* (1912), 11 D.L.R. 850 (N.B. C.A.); *Re Regent United Service Stores* (1878), 8 Ch. D. 616 (C.A.).

The effect of this section with ss. 19 and 86 is to prevent a liquidator from allowing a preference or priority, unless this has been impressed upon assets before the same were taken possession of by him: *Re Faulkner Ltd.* (1915), 34 O.L.R. 536 at 538 (H.C.), followed in *Re Beaver Drugs* (1926), 7 C.B.R. 719 (Ont. S.C.).

In *Plummer v. Sullivan Machinery Co.* (1917), 24 B.C.R. 104, a vendor of machinery, under a conditional sale contract whereby the property remained in him until payment, seized and resold the machinery after the corporation had been wound up and without obtaining leave from the court. An action brought by the liquidator for wrongful seizure was dismissed on the ground that, at worst, the vendor's conduct was irregular; and that if necessary, leave to repossess would be granted *nunc pro tunc* — the vendor was simply enforcing a claim to its own property.

The section does not bind the Crown: *Canada (A.G.) v. Ettenberg* (1936), 18 C.B.R. 144 (Que. C.A.).

By virtue of s. 22, the making of a winding-up order is a complete defence to an action by a judgment creditor of the corporation after a winding-up order has been made against a shareholder who has not paid up his stock in full: *Shaver v. Cotton, supra.*

Sequestration

It appears that the term "sequestration" as used in s. 22 means sequestration to recover payment of a judgment already obtained: *Richelieu & Ontario Navigation Co. v. SS. "Imperial"* (1909), 12 Ex. C.R. 243; but see *Re Australian Direct Steam Navigation Co.* (1875), L.R. 20 Eq. 325.

Distress

A distress made before the making of a winding-up order is not avoided thereby: *Re E.C. Colwell Candy Co.* (1902), 35 N.B.R. 613 (C.A.); similarly, when the seizure under distress was constructive: *National Trust Co. v. Leeson Estate* (1916), 26 D.L.R. 422 (Alta. C.A.); and see the notes on s. 86 in Chapter 24. There is nothing in ss. 21, 22 and 86 to prevent a landlord from realizing, when the distress has been put into effect before the commencement of the winding up: *Re Shirleys Ltd.* (1916), 29 D.L.R. 273.

The right to restrain after the making of a winding-up order depends on whether the rent accrued due before or after the order was made.

If the rent accrued due before the commencement of the winding up, the landlord will not be allowed to distrain: *Re Traders North Staffordshire Carrying Co.; Re North Staffordshire Ry. Co.* (1874), L.R. 19 Eq. 60; *Thomas v. Patent Lionite Co.* (1881), 17 Ch. D. 250 (C.A.); *Re G.B. Cloak & Suit Co.* (1932), 36 Que. P.R. 57; even though the liquidator may have retained possession of and carried on the corporation's works upon the land: *Re North Yorkshire Iron Co.* (1878), 7 Ch. D. 661; *Re Brown, Bayley & Dixon; Ex parte Roberts & Wright*

(1881), 18 Ch. D. 649. The landlord must prove for his debt like any other creditor: *Re South Kensington Co-op. Stores* (1881), 17 Ch. D. 161; *Re Oak Pits Colliery Co.* (1882), 21 Ch. D. 322; *Fuches v. Hamilton Tribune Co.* (1884), 10 P.R. 409.

When the landlord has no right of proof against the corporation, the court will not restrain the landlord from levying a distress on the corporation's goods: *Re Lundy Granite Co.; Ex parte Heaven* (1871), 6 Ch. App. 462; *Re Carriage Co-op. Supply Assn.; Ex parte Clemence* (1883), 23 Ch. D. 154; *Re Exhall Coal Mining Co.* (1864), 4 De G. J. & Sm. 377, 46 E.R. 964; *Re Regent United Service Stores* (1878), 8 Ch. D. 616 (C.A.).

A provisional liquidator in possession undertook to pay a landlord's claim for overdue rent, this claim to be paid preferentially. After service of notice of an order for the winding up of the corporation, this undertaking was held, by virtue of sections corresponding to ss. 21 and 22 of this Act, void, unless the permission of the court was first obtained: *Fuches v. Hamilton Tribune Co., supra.*

If the rent accrued after the commencement of the winding up, the landlord will be allowed to distrain for it or receive payment in full, if the liquidator has retained possession of the property for the purposes of winding up, or for carrying on the corporation's business, or in order to sell it or to do the best he can with it; for in these circumstances the rent is considered as one of the expenses of the winding-up and should be paid in full like any other debt properly incurred by the liquidator: *Re Lundy Granite Co.; Ex parte Heaven* (1871), 6 Ch. App. 462; *Re North Yorkshire Iron Co.* (1878), 7 Ch. D. 661; *Re Silkstone & Dodworth Coal & Iron Co.* (1881), 17 Ch. D. 158; *Re South Kensington Co-op. Stores* (1881), 17 Ch. D. 161; *Re Brown, Bayley & Dixon; Ex parte Roberts & Wright* (1881), 18 Ch. D. 649; *Re Oak Pits Colliery Co.* (1882), 21 Ch. D. 322.

After a winding-up order has been granted, leave is necessary in order to distrain, for a distress is a "proceeding" within s. 21: *Re Ottawa Porcelain & Carbon Co.* (1900), 31 O.R. 679 at 689; *Re Jasper Liquor Co.* (1915), 25 D.L.R. 84 (Alta. C.A.).

If the corporation by its liquidator remains in possession for the purpose of realizing its property to better advantage, it can only do so on the terms of the lease. The lessor is entitled to receive out of the assets got in by the liquidator the sum required to put the premises in the repair required by the covenants and not merely to prove for his claim: *Re Levi & Co., Ltd.*, [1919] 1 Ch. 416.

If the rent has accrued due partly before and partly after the commencement of the winding up, and if the landlord establishes his right to distrain, or to be paid in full, for the latter portion of the rent, the rent will be apportioned, and the distress will be allowed for so much as accrued after the winding up commenced: *Re South Kensington Co-op. Stores, supra.*

As regards distress, the sections under consideration only apply to a landlord who seeks to distrain upon goods of a corporation that is his legal tenant. Therefore, in *Re New City Constitutional Club Co.; Ex parte Purssell* (1887), 34

Ch. D. 646 (C.A.), the court decided that it could not prevent a landlord from distraining upon goods that, although originally the property of the corporation, had ceased to be so by being charged for more than their full value in favour of debenture holders.

Execution

When an execution has been issued before the winding-up petition is presented, the legal position may first be considered independently of s. 86 of the Act. When a creditor has actually issued an execution against a corporation before a petition to wind it up has been presented, and the sheriff is in possession when it is presented, the court will not interfere and deprive the creditor of the fruits of his diligence: *Re Withernsea Brickworks* (1880), 16 Ch. D. 337 (C.A.); *Merchants Bank v. Roche Percee Coal Co.* (1897), 3 Terr. L.R. 463; unless under any special circumstances, for example, oppression or fraud: *Re Perkins Beach Lead Mining Co.* (1877), 7 Ch. D. 371. There may be a question, however, as to how far this principle would be applied in Ontario, having regard to the policy of equal distribution among creditors established by the *Creditors' Relief Act*: *Dawson v. Moffatt* (1886), 11 O.R. 484 (C.A.), and *contra, McLean v. Allen* (1890), 14 P.R. 84 (Ont. H.C.). It would not appear to be good law when there is an assignment under the *Bankruptcy and Insolvency Act.*

But as a rule, if the sheriff does not seize before the commencement of the winding up, the execution will be stayed: *Re Taylor; Re Williams; Ex parte Ry. Steel & Plant Co.* (1878), 8 Ch. D. 183. And receivers appointed in the same interval will be restrained from acting: *Campbell v. Compagnie Générale de Bellegarde; Re Compagnie Générale de Bellegarde* (1876), 2 Ch. D. 181; *Perry v. Oriental Hotels Co.* (1870), L.R. 5 Ch. App. 420.

When the execution preceded the petition to wind up, the court, while staying the execution, has directed the liquidator to sell for the benefit of the execution creditor — see *Re Taylor; Re Williams; Ex parte Ry. Steel & Plant Co.* (1878), 8 Ch. D. 183, thus substantially securing to him the fruits of his diligence. *A fortiori* the court will not interfere with an execution creditor who actually got his money before the winding-up order was made: *Re United English & Scottish Assurance Co.; Ex parte Hawkins* (1868), L.R. 3 Ch. App. 787.

Section 86 of this Act, however, provides in effect that an execution creates no lien if, before payment over to the plaintiff of the moneys actually levied, the winding up of the corporation's business has commenced, that is, the notice of presentation of the petition has been served (s. 5). See the notes on s. 86 in Chapter 24.

Executions issued after a petition for a winding-up order has been presented stand in a different position: *Re Taylor; Re Williams; Ex parte Ry. Steel & Plant Co., supra.* These are void, and the sheriff is not entitled to his fees in respect thereof, notwithstanding that they were levied in a province other than that in which the winding-up order was made and in ignorance of the existence of the order: *Re Producers Rock & Gravel Co.* (1913), 14 D.L.R. 289 (B.C.); *Pilote v. Leclerc* (1917), 52 Que. S.C. 127; *Richards v. Producers Rock & Gravel Co.* (1914), 17 D.L.R. 588. When an execution has been filed after a winding-up order has been made and is therefore void under s. 22, there is no lien whatsoever, even for costs, under s. 86: *Re Leitch Collieries Ltd.*, [1926] 1 D.L.R. 1183 (Alta.).

A person who executes a judgment in contravention of the section may be obliged to pay the liquidator's costs of opposing the execution: *Great Northwestern Telegraph Co. v. La Cie du Journal "Le Monde"* (1899), 5 Que. P.R. 379.

Under the English Act prior to 1947, the court granted leave to issue execution after the winding up when the creditor had been prevented from doing so before the winding up by trickery, or something equivalent to dishonesty, on the part of the corporation: *Armorduct Manufacturing Co. v. General Incandescent Co.*, [1911] 2 K.B. 143 (C.A.). By an amendment in 1947, the court was given the power to grant an execution creditor any relief it thought fit, if that creditor failed to complete execution by the commencement of the winding up of the corporation. Under this provision the court has jurisdiction to do what is right and fair according to the circumstances of each case; accordingly, its jurisdiction is much wider than it was prior to 1947, when the court's power to interfere was justified only if there was trickery or dishonesty on the part of the corporation: *Re Grosvenor Metal Co., Ltd.*, [1950] 1 Ch. 63 (corporation persuaded the creditor to delay execution, and court granted creditor leave to issue execution), and *Re Suidair International Airways Ltd. (In Liquidation)*, [1951] 1 Ch. 165 (corporation placed every possible obstacle in the way of the creditor and court granted leave to issue execution). See also *Engineering Industry Training Board v. Samuel Talbot (Engineers) Ltd.*, [1969] 2 Q.B. 270 (C.A.).

A return of *nulla bona* by the sheriff after the winding-up order to a writ of execution issued and received by him before the making of the order does not fall within the section and is not void: *Pukulski v. Jardine* (1912), 26 O.L.R. 323.

Once a winding-up order has been made, a payment for the purpose of avoiding an execution is illegal: *Richards v. Producers Rock & Gravel Co.* (1914), 17 D.L.R. 588.

Garnishee

In the case of an execution by a writ of *fi. fa.*, the important date is that on which the sheriff seizes; in the case of an attachment of a debt by means of a garnishee order, the date to be considered is the date on which the order *nisi* is served; in other respects the rule applicable to the stay of these two forms of proceedings is the same: *Re Stanhope Silkstone Collieries Co.* (1879), 11 Ch. D. 160 (C.A.).

But see s. 86, which negatives the lien unless the moneys have been paid over before the winding up has commenced: *Lavell v. Canadian Mineral Rubber Co.* (1913), 14 D.L.R. 521 (Alta. T.D.); *Re Wayne Coal Co.* (1920), 55 D.L.R. 327 (Alta. T.D.) (claim for money paid twice by mistake).

A garnishee summons issued after a winding-up order is ineffective for the purpose of attaching moneys owing to the corporation and will be set aside: *Lavell v. Canadian Mineral Rubber Co., supra.*

Stay of winding-up proceedings

A winding-up order, once pronounced, can be got rid of in three ways:

(a) Before the order is entered, the petition may be withdrawn and the order rescinded, assuming there is only one petitioner: *Re Crown Bank* (1890), 44 Ch. D. 634. Once the order is entered, the court has no jurisdiction to cancel it, except in special circumstances, for example, where it was obtained by fraud or concealment of material facts: *Re Equitable Savings Loan & Building Assn.* (1903), 6 O.L.R. 26 at 31 (C.A.), and compare *McNabb v. Oppenheimer* (1885), 11 P.R. 214.

(b) The order may be appealed; see the notes to ss. 103 and 106 in Chapter 25.

(c) An application may be made under s. 18 by any creditor or contributory (but not by the corporation: *Re Baxters, Ltd.*, [1898] W.N. 60) that all proceedings under the winding-up order be stayed. The court has a discretion as to whether the stay should be granted and whether it should be absolute or limited, and as to the terms and conditions thereof.

The principles on which the court will act in the exercise of its jurisdiction with reference to staying proceedings under a winding-up order are stated by Buckley, J., in *Re Telescriptor Syndicate Ltd.*, [1903] 2 Ch. 174 at 180, to be the same as when an application is made in bankruptcy to rescind a receiving order or annul an adjudication in bankruptcy, where

> . . . the Court refuses to act upon the mere assent of the creditors in the matter, and considers not only whether what is proposed is for the benefit of the creditors, but also whether it is conducive or detrimental to commercial morality and to the interests of the public at large. The mere consent of the creditors is but an element in the case.

In exercising its discretion, the court will have regard to such facts as these: there was an undisclosed agreement between promoter and vendor providing for participation by the former in the share consideration payable on the sale; there was a gift of paid-up shares to the directors; there were other matters connected with the promotion, formation or failure of the corporation, or the conduct of its business, that appear to call for investigation: *Re Telescriptor Syndicate Ltd. supra*, at 180.

A stay may properly be asked for when some scheme of reorganization is contemplated: *Re Marine Investment Co.; Ex parte Exors* (1873), L.R. 8 Ch. App. 702. When a large number of the creditors desired that the liquidation should proceed under some form of voluntary liquidation already entered upon as being more expeditious and inexpensive, a stay was granted under the section: *Re Belding Lumber Co.* (1911), 23 O.L.R. 255 (H.C.). In this case the stay was until the court should further order on application of any creditor upon notice.

When a shareholder obtained in Manitoba a winding-up order against a corporation that was incorporated in that province but had the major part of its assets in Saskatchewan and was carrying on business in the United States, and when an order of adjudication in bankruptcy had been made against it, the majority of the creditors and shareholders applied for a stay. All the unsecured creditors had proved their claims in the bankruptcy court. It was held that once everything necessary had been accomplished to make the assets of the corporation not vested in the trustee in bankruptcy available for the Canadian creditors *pari passu* with the creditors in the United States, nothing further should be done under the order until it became necessary to take some action in aid of the bankruptcy proceedings: *Re Stewart & Matthews Ltd.* (1916), 26 Man. R. 277 (K.B.).

A stay may be granted pending the preparation of a complete list of contributories: *Banque de St. Jean v. Bienvenu* (1908), 10 Que. P.R. 223.

In *Re Installations Ltd.* (1913), 14 D.L.R. 679 (Alta.), a stay was granted until the trial of an interpleader issue that had been pending.

See the following cases illustrating the conditions under which a stay will be granted: *Ex parte Barber* (1849), 1 Mac. & G. 176; *Re Worcester, Tenbury & Ludlow Ry. Co.* (1850), 3 De G. & Sm. 189; *Re South Barrule Slate Quarry Co.* (1869), L.R. 8 Eq. 688; *Carew's Case* (1854), 5 De G. M. & G. 94; *Re Eastern Counties Junction & Southend Ry. Co.; Underwood's Case* (1854), 6 De G.M. & G. 677; *Dover & Deal Ry., Clinique Ports, Thanet & Coast Junction Co., Re; Clifton's Case* (1854), 5 De G.M. & G. 743; *Re Continental Bank Corp.; Re London & Mediterranean Bank* (1867), 15 W.R. 548; *Re European Ass'n Co.*, [1872] W.N. 85. And as to costs, see *Clark's Case* (1854), 1 K. & J. 22; *Ex parte Woolmer* (1851), 5 De G. & Sm. 117.

Chapter 22

LIQUIDATORS

Cross references: Sections 19, 48, 49, 65, 66, 69, 70, 110, 123, 133, 141, 151
Ontario Act, ss. 210, 220-224, 227-229.

Appointment of liquidator (Ss. 23-25, 29)

Section 23 provides that the court, in making the winding-up order, may appoint a liquidator or more than one liquidator. It need not do so at that time; the practice now is, in many cases (and always in the case of a bank), to appoint a provisional liquidator as permitted by s. 28: *Re Army & Navy Clothing Co. of Toronto* (1901), 3 O.L.R. 37 (C.A.); *Great West Supply Co. v. Installations Ltd.* (1914), 15 D.L.R. 896. As to the powers of the provisional liquidator, see *Villeneuve Co. v. Price Bros. Ltd.* (1909), 36 Que. S.C. 395.

The winding-up order may delegate to the Master or an Official Referee the powers of the court, as under s. 119. See the notes to that section in Chapter 25. The more usual practice is to apply to the court itself. A permanent liquidator is then appointed after notice as prescribed by s. 26.

Notice previous to appointment of permanent liquidator (s. 26)

A notice is to be sent out for the appointment of a permanent liquidator. Previous notice of the appointment of the permanent liquidator must be given to the creditors, contributories and shareholders or members in compliance with s. 26; otherwise the appointment will be set aside: *Shoolbred v. Union Fire Insurance Co.* (1887), 14 S.C.R. 624; *Re Guelph Linseed Oil Co.* (1903), 2 O.W.R. 1151; *Great West Supply Co. v. Installations Ltd.* (1914), 15 D.L.R. 896; *Stimson v. North West Cattle Co.* (1902), 14 Que. K.B. 279 (C.A.). See however s. 125 and *I.O.S. Ltd. (No. 2), Re* (1973), 43 D.L.R. (3d) 759 (N.B. C.A.).

As to the nature of the notice, see *Villeneuve v. Price Bros. Ltd.* (1909), 36 Que. S.C. 395.

Who will be appointed

It will be noted that s. 23(2) provides that except in the case of certain special corporations which are listed, no liquidator is to be appointed who is not licensed as a trustee under the *Bankruptcy and Insolvency Act.*

The court abstains from laying down any such rule as that the nominee of the petitioning creditor should have a preference. The court will consider the condition of affairs to ascertain which parties are most interested in the due administration of the estate in liquidation and, other things being equal, will act upon their recommendation: *Re Alpha Oil Co.* (1887), 12 P.R. 298.

Other things being equal, the petitioner's nominee is preferred: *Re General Provident Assurance Co.* (1868), 17 W.R. 42; *Re Albert Average Assurance Assn.* (1870), 5 Ch. App. 597. No hard and fast rule to this effect exists. The wishes of those most interested are to be regarded: *Re Northern Assam Tea Co.* (1870), 5 Ch. App. 644; *Re Hoyland Silkstone Colliery Co.*, [1883], 53 L.J. Ch. 352; *Re Land Financiers, Assn.* (1878) 10 Ch. D. 269.

Where the creditors have the chief and immediate concern in realizing the assets, their nominees will be appointed as against the nominees of the shareholders: *Re Central Bank of Canada* (1887), 15 O.R. 309 (H.C.). It is not necessary for both creditors and shareholders to be represented: *Forsythe v. Bank of Nova Scotia; In Re The Bank of Liverpool* (1890), 18 S.C.R. 707. Where the nominee of the successful creditors is appointed, one set of costs will be allowed them: *Re Alpha Oil Co., supra; Re Northern Assam Tea Co., supra.*

The court has a discretion, and is not merely to register the result of the determination of the creditors and contributories, and it may refuse to accept their nominee: *Re International Contract Co.* (1866), 1 Ch. App. 523; *Re London, Bombay & Mediterranean Bank* (1866), 1 Ch. App. 525; *Re Northern Assam Tea Co., supra; Re Johannisberg and Gold Trust Co.*, [1892] 1 Ch. 583; *Re Land Development Assn.*, [1892] W.N. 23; *Re Commercial Bank of Manitoba* (1893), 9 Man. L.R. 342; *Re Radford & Bright Ltd.* [1901] 1 Ch. 272.

Liquidators should be disinterested persons, and neither creditors, debtors nor shareholders should be appointed: *Re Central Bank of Canada* (1887), 15 O.R. 309; *Re Commercial Bank of Manitoba, supra; Re Men's Wear, Ltd.* (1914), 22 D.L.R. 530. The appointment of a shareholder is not favoured: *Re Northumberland & Durham District Banking Co.* (1858), 2 De G. & J. 508; *Société des journalistes canadiens Inc. v. Photogravure nationale Ltée* (1936), 42 R. de Jur. 241. If, however, all the creditors desire the appointment of an individual who happens to be a shareholder, he may be appointed: *Re New Westminster Gas Co.* (1897), 5 B.C.R. 618. The fact that the liquidator in a voluntary liquidation is the nominee of the shareholder who controls the corporation is no reason why the voluntary winding-up cannot continue with due regard to the interests of the creditors: *Adebayo v. Nigeria (Official Receiver)*, [1954] 2 All E.R. 197

(P.C.). See also *Commonwealth Trust Co. v. Canada Deposit Insurance Corp.* (1990), 79 C.B.R. (N.S.) 196 (B.C. S.C.) where a choice among various proposed liquidators was made.

Where a voluntary winding-up is superseded by a compulsory order, the voluntary liquidator is usually continued: *Re London & Mediterranean Banking Ltd.* (1866), 15 W.R. 33.

It has been held in Quebec that a provisional liquidator who is not a creditor has no status to demand to be named as liquidator and to demand the nomination of inspectors designated by him: *Société des journalistes canadiens Inc. v. Photogravure nationale Ltée* (1936), 42 R. de Jur. 241.

It is not usual to appoint more than one liquidator: *Dignard v. Angers* (1910), 11 Que. P.R. 389. However, where it is necessary for the proper winding up of the affairs of a corporation, two liquidators may be appointed jointly: *Re Solloway Mills & Co.* (1933), 14 C.B.R. 208 (Que. S.C.).

An incorporated corporation may be appointed liquidator in which case the incorporated corporation may act through one or more of its principal officers designated by the court (s. 29).

Appeal

A right of appeal from an order appointing a liquidator may exist under provincial rules of practice: *Markle v. Ross* (1889), 13 P.R 135. However, the court of appeal will not interfere with the discretion of the judge in the appointment of a liquidator: *Re International Contract Co.* (1866), Ch. App. 523; *Re Railway Finance Co.* (1866), 14 W.R. 956; *Re Albert Averages Assurances Assn.* (1870), 5 Ch. App. 597, and see *Forsythe v. Bank of Nova Scotia* (1890), 18 S.C.R. 707, affg (1890), 22 N.S.R. 97.

Security (ss. 27, 30)

No special rules, instructions or forms regarding security have been adopted in Ontario.

The security most usually given is the bond of a guarantee corporation, but other security has frequently been accepted.

When the liquidation has been partially completed the security is sometimes reduced.

The security need not be fixed by the winding-up order; it may be left to the Master under s. 111; *Clarke v. Union Fire Insurance Co.* (1890), 17 S.C.R. 265.

As to a certificate of the liquidator's liability on default, see *Re Birmingham Brewery Malting & Distilling Co.* (1883), 52 L.J. Ch. 358. The sureties have a right to appeal against the Master's certificate where the bond provides that such certificate shall be sufficient evidence of the amount of the liquidator's liability: *Re Army & Navy Clothing Co. of Toronto* (1901), 3 O.L.R. 37 (C.A.).

In a suit on a bond guaranteeing the true accounting of a liquidator, it was held that the condition of the bond was limited to moneys that were moneys of the corporation or for which the corporation was accountable and that the guarantee corporation was not liable in respect of moneys received by the liquidator as the personal agent of a creditor: *McFarland v. London & Lancashire Guarantee & Accident Co.*, [1928] S.C.R. 57.

Section 29 provides that an incorporated corporation may be appointed liquidator; and s. 30 provides that, where under the laws of any province a trust corporation is accepted by the courts of such province and is permitted to act as administrator, assignee or curator without giving security, such trust corporation may be appointed as liquidator without giving security: *Forsythe v. Bank of Nova Scotia* (1890), 18 S.C.R. 707.

Effect of appointment on powers of directors (S. 31)

On the appointment of the liquidator, the powers of the directors cease, except as their continuance is sanctioned by the court or the liquidator.

Even without an express provision as contained in s. 31 the powers of the directors do in fact cease on the appointment of a liquidator in a compulsory liquidation: *Re Farrow's Bank Ltd.*, [1921] 2 Ch. 164 at 173 (C.A.); but it would seem that they still continue to be directors of the corporation: *Davey v. Gibson* (1929), 64 O.L.R. 627 at 630, affd (1930), 65 O.L.R. 379 (C.A.).

When powers of the directors are not continued as provided by s. 31, their fiduciary relation to the corporation or its shareholders is at an end, and a sale to them by the liquidator of the corporation is valid: *Re Mabou Coal & Gypsum Co.* (1894), 27 N.S.R. 305 (C.A.); *Chatham National Bank v. McKeen* (1895), 24 S.C.R. 348.

The corporation as a defendant, before a liquidator was appointed, was summoned to answer interrogatories upon articulated facts, but a liquidator was appointed before the day fixed for answering. The rule was continued by consent to a subsequent day, and on that day, no one appearing to answer, default was entered. It was held that inasmuch as by s. 34 (now s. 31) of the *Winding-up Act*, upon the appointment of a liquidator, all the powers of the directors cease, except insofar as the court or the liquidator sanction their continuance, the directors after the appointment of a liquidator could not authorize any person to answer for them unless their powers had been specially continued to that effect. The corporation was, therefore, relieved from the default and the liquidator allowed to answer: *Graham v. Casselman Lumber Co.* (1893), 4 Que. S.C. 91.

Where, on a reference, a resolution passed by the shareholders was tendered in evidence, the resolution having been passed at a meeting held after the winding-up order, and having been objected to on the ground that the corporation was in liquidation and the directors and shareholders could not exercise the powers they professed to exercise in passing the resolution, the referee was directed to receive the evidence in question. No opinion was expressed whether the resolution was effective: *Re Galt Reporter Ltd.* (1923), 25 O.W.N. 89 (H.C.). See also the notes to s. 19 in Chapter 21.

Resignation and removal of liquidator (S. 32)

Section 32 provides that a liquidator may resign or may be removed by the court on due cause shown; and s. 142 provides, *inter alia*, that a liquidator failing to comply with the requirements and directions of any order made by the court under the Act may in the discretion of the court be removed. Insufficiency of assets alone is not a ground to permit a liquidator to resign: *Re Blanche Industries Ltd.*, [1966] Que. S.C. 474 (assets not sufficient to pay liquidator's out of pocket expenses).

Intention to leave the country is a due cause for resignation: *Re Woodburn Sons Co. (Liquidators of) v. Duggan* (1910), 11 Que. P.R. 393.

Where there is want of harmony between the liquidators, the court will remove one of them on the advice of the creditors: *Cloyes v. Darling* (1884), 16 R.L. 649; *Exchange Bank v. Campbell* (1885), 15 R.L. 373.

In an application to remove a liquidator, the interests of the liquidation are the main consideration, and it is not necessary to show personal unfitness: *Re Adam Eyton, Ltd.; Ex parte Charlesworth* (1887), 36 Ch. D. 299 (C.A.). However, personal unfitness is a ground for removal: *Re Sir John Moore Gold Mining Co.* (1879), 12 Ch. D. 325 (C.A.) (favouritism to persons whose interests were opposed to those of the creditors); *Re Mansel; Ex parte Newitt* (1884), 14 Q.B.D. 177 (C.A.) (vexatious obstruction in the realization of the estate in the interest of a debtor).

Removal has been directed by the court in the following cases: *Re Flour Co.* (1868), 16 W.R. 553 (liquidator guilty of misconduct in petitioning for the winding-up); *City & County Investment Co.* (1877), 25 W.R. 342 (one person acting as liquidator of two corporations, the interests of which conflicted); *Re Devonshire Silkstone Coal Co.*, [1878] W.N. 71 (duty conflicted with interest, the liquidators of the corporation selling the corporation's assets to a new corporation in which they took shares); *Re Assiniboine Valley Stock & Dairy Farming Co.* (1889), 6 Man. L.R. 184 (the majority of the creditors requested the change; the proposed liquidators would act without remuneration and one of them had a business connection that would be of value to the corporation); *Re Rubber & Produce Investment Trust*, [1915] 1 Ch. 382 (liquidator and committee of inspection proposed to spend assets in misfeasance proceedings against the wishes of the creditors); *Re Hatzic Prairie Co.* (1914), 15 D.L.R. 772 (B.C. C.A.) (the liquidators wrongfully delegated their power to sell the assets); *Commonwealth Trust Co. v. Canada Deposit Insurance Corp.* (1990), 79 C.B.R. (N.S.) 183 (B.C. S.C.) (it was proposed to sue the liquidator for misadministration and the liquidator was permitted to resign as there would be a conflict of interest and it was not able to make an independent assessment of the merits of the case). For a case where it was proposed to sue the liquidator and his removal was not ordered, see *Re United Fuel Investments Ltd. (No. 1)*, [1964] 2 O.R. 411, affd [1966] 1 O.R. 165 (C.A.).

A liquidator has a right of appeal against his removal: *Re Adam Eyton, Ltd.; Ex parte Charlesworth* (1887), 36 Ch. D. 299 (C.A.).

The majority shareholder of a trust company brought an application to discharge the current liquidator in a case where the winding-up had been ongoing for 20 years. The Court dismissed the application holding that in the hostile climate between the parties, the continued presence of the liquidator was essential to assist the Court: *Canada Deposit Insurance Corp. v. Commonwealth Trust Co.* (1991), 4 C.B.R. (3d) 16 (B.C. S.C.).

In the following cases the court refused to direct the removal of the liquidator: *Re Marseilles Extension Ry. & Land Co.* (1867), L.R. 4 Eq. 692 and *Re British Nation Life Assurance Assn.* (1872), L.R. 14 Eq. 492 (in both cases, some creditors opposed the liquidators' continuance in office but failed to satisfy the court that removal would be in the best interests of the estate); *Re Plymouth Patent Sugar Co.*, [1870] W.N. 84 (refusal to employ as solicitor the nominee of the creditors); *Rigaud Granite Co. v. Wylie* (1916), 18 Que. P.R. 266 (liquidator was an employee of one of the inspectors). See also *United Fuel Investments Ltd. and Deacon v. Union Gas Co. of Canada Ltd.*, [1966] 1 O.R. 165 (C.A.).

In an application for compulsory winding up and removal of the liquidator appointed in the voluntry liquidation, the order was refused, since, although the liquidator had been dilatory and had failed to meet certain statutory requirements, the administration was almost complete and the burden of showing that the liquidation could not be continued with due regard to the interests of the creditors was not satisfied. The petition was dismissed: *Re J. Russell Electronics Ltd.*, [1968] 1 W.L.R. 1252.

The application to remove should be made by motion to the officer of the court to whom the reference to wind up has been directed, and supported by affidavits establishing the grounds relied on.

Under the British Columbia *Companies Act*, a corporation that resolves to wind up voluntarily is to appoint a liquidator in general meeting. Where, at such a shareholders' meeting, only one shareholder was present at the time a resolution appointing a liquidator was put, the meeting was not properly constituted and the liquidator was not properly appointed and was accordingly removed by the court: *Re Primary Distributors Ltd.*, [1954] 2 D.L.R. 438.

If any vacancy in the office of liquidator occurs all the property of the corporation is deemed to be in the custody of the court (s. 48).

Position and duties of liquidator

The liquidator is an officer of the court, appointed by the court to perform the functions prescribed by the Act and exercising his powers and performing his duties under the court's supervision. The corporate state and all the powers of the corporation continue after a winding-up order is made; but from the time of such order the corporation is to cease to carry on business, except in so far as the liquidator considers it necessary for its beneficial winding up (s. 19). Even then, the liquidator must have the court's approval to do so under s. 35. As to the liquidator carrying on the business, see below under the heading "Powers of liquidator".

As stated by Lord Davey in *Kent v. La Communauté des Soeurs de Charité de la Providence*, [1903] A.C. 220 at 226:

> The office of the liquidator has in fact a double aspect. On the one hand he wields the powers of the company, and on the other hand he is the representative for some purposes of the creditors and contributories.

Following are some of the judicial expressions of opinion in the English and Canadian courts regarding the position of the liquidator and the extent to which they represent creditors as well as the corporation:

> "In a winding-up the liquidator acts not only for creditors, but for contributories, and for the company also . . . . The liquidator does not act more for the creditors than he does for the company": per Page-Wood, V.-C., in *Re Marine Mansions Co.* (1867), L.R. 4 Eq. 601 at 610.
>
> "Generally speaking, he is said to represent the company, the creditors, and the general body of contributories": per Cairns, L.J., in *Re Joint Stock Discount Co.; Sichell's Case* (1867), 3 Ch. App. 119 at 122.
>
> ". . . the liquidator represents the creditors . . . but only because he represents the company, and through the company the rights of the creditors are to be enforced": per Cairns, L.J., in *Re Duckworth* (1867), 2 Ch. App. 578 at 580, and adopted by Lord Westbury in *Waterhouse v. Jamieson* (1870), L.R. 2 Sc. & Div. 29 at 38.
>
> "The liquidator seems to be somewhat in the position of a receiver or agent appointed by the Court to represent the company for the purposes of the Act; not as an assignee, but as the statutory representative of the company for the purposes of winding-up": per Mabee, I., in *McCarter v. York County Loan Co.* (1907), 14 O.L.R. 420 at 422.

A liquidator is subject only to the control of the court and there is no limitation upon the discretionary power of the court in the exercise of this control: *Maranda-Desaulniers v. Peckham*, [1953] Que. Q.B. 163 (C.A.) at 172.

He is an officer of the court and, like other officers, may be ordered to refund money paid to him under mistake of law: *Re Opera Ltd.*, [1891] 3 Ch. 260; or where it would be dishonest for him to retain it: *Re Regent Finance & Guarantee Corp. Ltd.*, [1930] W.N. 84. He is expressly made subject to the jurisdiction that the court may exercise under s. 124 in respect of misfeasance in office. The court can compel performance of the liquidator's duties by s. 135.

The High Court of Justice in Ontario, in which proceedings were pending under this Act for the winding-up of the Central Bank, granted an injunction to restrain a claimant from proceeding in the courts of Quebec against the liquidators for things done in their official capacity: *Re Central Bank Winding-Up* (1890), 20 O.R. 214 (H.C.).

To a limited extent, the liquidator seems to be in the position of a trustee. In a voluntary winding-up he stands in a fiduciary position to the shareholders and is required to make disclosure: *Christie v. Edwards*, [1939] O.R. 48 at 57 (C.A.) and cases cited. In the same case on appeal to the Supreme Court of Canada ([1940] 3 D.L.R. 65), it was held that the liquidator was liable to an accounting in an action. But his true position is that of agent for the corporation. Where a liquidator takes out insurance in his capacity as liquidator, then the insured is the corporation in liquidation: *Montreal Trust Co. v. Caledonian Insurance Co.*, [1932] 1 D.L.R. 116 (Alta. C.A.). He is not, strictly speaking, a trustee for either the creditors or contributories; therefore, in the absence of fraud, *mala fides* or personal misconduct, an action for damages will not lie against him at the suit either of a creditor or contributory for delay in paying the creditor's claims, or in handing over to the contributory his proportion of the surplus assets: *Knowles v. Scott*, [1891] 1 Ch. 717.

Where the sale of an undertaking of a corporation by its liquidator to himself had been set aside on the ground of fraud, the liquidator was ordered to repay the rents and profits that had accrued, but not the interest on the same: *Silkstone & Haigh Moor Coal Co. v. Edey*, [1900] 1 Ch. 167.

It is the duty of the liquidator to identify the creditors from the records of the corporation and to communicate with any creditor who fails to file a claim: *Pulsford v. Devenish*, [1903] 2 Ch. 625; *James Smith & Sons (Norwood) Ltd. v. Goodman*, [1936] Ch. 216 (C.A.).

It is clear that against a lessee from the corporation, the liquidator stands in no higher position than the corporation itself: *McCarter v. York County Loan Co.* (1907), 14 O.L.R. 420; and against a person who has duly registered a mechanics' lien for material supplied and work performed before the commencement of the winding-up the liquidator represents no higher claim than the corporation, so that the lienholder will be entitled to his statutory priority: *Re Clinton Thresher Co.* (1910), 20 O.L.R. 555 (H.C.). And the liquidator stands in no higher position than the corporation to dispute the authority of an officer to sign a promissory note, at any rate where all the shareholders have ratified or are estopped: *Re Almur Fur Trading Co.*, [1932] S.C.R. 150.

As to whether the liquidator has, on behalf of creditors, the right to object to formal defects or want of registration of a security given by the corporation, for example, a chattel mortgage and the following cases: *Re Andrews* (1877), 2 O.A.R. 24; *Re Rainy Lake Lumber Co.* (1888), 15 O.A.R. 749; *Parkes v. St. George* (1882), 2 O.R. 342 at 347 (H.C.); *Kitching v. Hicks* (1883), 6 O.R. 739 at 745 (C.A.); *Harrison v. Nepisiguit Lumber Co.* (1911), 11 E.L.R. 314 (C.A.); *Re William Hamilton Mfg. Co.* (1909), 1 O.W.N. 61 (H.C.); *Security Trust Co. v. Stewart* (1918), 39 D.L.R. 518 (C.A.); *Dominion Trust Co. v. Royal Bank* (1929), 59 D.L.R. 224 (S.C.).

The rights and powers possessed by the liquidator sometimes exceed those which the corporation itself could have asserted: *Waterhouse v. Jamieson* (1870), L.R. 2 Sc. & Div. 29 at 32; *Re Exchange Banking Co.; Flitcroft's Case* (1882), 21 Ch. D. 519 at 527 (C.A.); *Re Florence Land & Public Works Co.; Nicol's Case; Tufnell & Ponsonby's Case* (1885), 29 Ch. D. 421 at 429 (C.A.); *Re London Celluloid Co.* (1888), 39 Ch. D. 190 at 204 (C.A.); *Re Ebsworth & Tidy's Contract* (1889), 42 Ch. D. 23 at 43 (C.A.); *Re Sharpe; Bennett Masonic & General Life Assurance Co. v. Sharpe*, [1892] 1 Ch. 154 at 167 (C.A.).

Where liquidators purchase the interest of a dissentient shareholder they have no power to release him from his liability to the creditors of the corporation: *Re Imperial Land Co. of Marseilles, Vining's Case* (1870), 6 Ch. App. 96.

Taking possession of assets (s. 33)

The liquidator's first duty as regards the estate is to take charge of all of the corporation's assets. He will then proceed to convert them into money, collect outstanding accounts and generally administer the affairs of the corporation with a view to realization and applying the proceeds in payment of the corporation's creditors. As to the carrying on of the corporation's business by the liquidator, see under the heading "Powers of liquidator" below.

After a winding-up order, the power of collecting the assets of the corporation is vested solely in the liquidator: *Shaver v. Cotton* (1896), 23 A.R. 426 at 429 and 434; *Bank of Hochelaga v. Garth* (1886), M.L.R. 2 S.C. 201; *Richards v. Producers Rock & Gravel Co.* (1914), 17 D.L.R. 588; *Victoria & Montreal Fire Insurance Co. v. Derome* (1902), 21 Que. S.C. 319.

Where an asset of the insolvent corporation has been illegally applied by one of its officers and there is sufficient identification of the fund that it can be followed, the liquidator can follow it into the hands of a third party: *Chandler & Massey Ltd. v. Irish* (1913), 29 O.L.R. 112 (C.A.).

A liquidator may recover dividends improperly declared, at any rate where the shareholder cannot plead good faith: *Hyde v. Scott* (1918), 47 D.L.R. 260 at 267 (C.A.).

Where a trust corporation had possession, as bailee or trustee for the plaintiffs, of certain share certificates in which the trust corporation asserted that another corporation (of which the trust corporation was the liquidator) claimed an interest, the trust corporation was held liable, on its refusal to deliver up the certificates to the liquidator of the plaintiffs, to pay damages based on an estimate of what had been lost by the detention: *Elgin Loan & Savings Co. v. National Trust Co.* (1905), 10 O.L.R. 41 (C.A.).

A winding-up order supersedes an execution, and the liquidator will be entitled to possession of the goods pending inquiry as to validity of the claims asserted in respect of them: *Re Ideal Foundry & Hardware Co.* (1918), 42 O.L.R. 411. See further as to executions, the notes to s. 22 in Chapter 21.

Where the liquidator has been in possession as assignee for the creditors, on his appointment as liquidator the estate is in his hands as liquidator: *Re Army & Navy Clothing Co. of Toronto* (1901), 3 O.L.R. 37 (C.A.).

Though the title to the corporation's estate is not by the Act vested in the liquidator, it is his duty to protect any property in his custody for the benefit of the creditors. This duty extends to any property of which he takes over possession from an assignee for creditors of the corporation: *National Trust Co. v. Trusts & Guarantee Co.* (1912), 26 O.L.R. 279 at 289 (H.C.).

As to the claim of a liquidator to proceeds of book debts assigned by a corporation and collected by it where the corporation is subsequently wound up, see *Re Cope Fruit Co.*, (1917) 32 D.L.R. 346 (Alta. C.A.); also *Re Kootenay Valley Fruit Lands Co.* (1912), 3 D.L.R. 428 (K.B.).

The court will not divest the liquidator of an insolvent trust corporation of a trust that is coupled with an interest held by the corporation and that is an asset in the winding-up: *Dominion Trust Co. v. Harper* (1915), 24 D.L.R. 670 (B.C. C.A.).

In *Re Colonial Investment Co. of Winnipeg* (1914), 15 D.L.R. 650 (Man.), an application by the liquidator for delivery to him of the assets in the hands of the voluntary liquidator was ordered to stand over, pending a reference to the Master to pass the accounts of the voluntary liquidator.

A liquidator in England for the voluntary winding up there of a corporation incorporated in England cannot intervene in Quebec to prevent Canadian creditors realizing there on assets in the province. *Quaere* if such liquidator has any standing before the Canadian court: *Powis v. Quebec Bank* (1893), 2 Que.

O.B. 566 (C.A). See, however, *Grant v. British Canadian Lumber Co.* (1891), 18 S.C.R. 708.

Accounts and returns

The statute does not prescribe the records to be kept by the liquidator, except the bank passbook referred to in ss. 69 and 70; however, apart from specific enactment, the liquidator is bound to keep true and complete accounts.

As to the documents required to be forwarded by the liquidator to the Chief Statistician of Canada see s. 40.

Canada's *Income Tax Act* requires that a return of income be filed for each taxation year in prescribed form and containing prescribed information, by or on behalf of the corporation. The Act also provides that every liquidator, or other person administering, managing, winding up, controlling or otherwise dealing with the property, business, estate or income of a person who has not filed a return for a taxation year, must file a return in prescribed form for that person for the year or years in question. Such person (other than a trustee in bankruptcy) is not to make any distribution of any property over which he has control in his capacity as a responsible representative, without first obtaining a certificate from the Minister of National Revenue certifying that all taxes for which any taxpayer is liable, or for which the responsible representative is or can reasonably be expected to become liable in his capacity as the responsible representative, have been paid or that security has been accepted by the Minister. Failure to obtain such a certificate will result in the responsible representative being personally liable for the payment of any tax to the extent of the value of the property distributed by him.

Powers of liquidator (S. 35)

Under s. 35, the liquidator is given broad powers, which are, however, exercisable only with the approval of the court. See *Traders Leasing Ltd. v. Marcotte* (1963), 6 C.B.R. (N.S.) 153 (Que. S.C.) for a review of a liquidator's conduct.

The principles by which the court will be guided in giving or withholding its approval are these: (1) it will check anything that might prejudice the estate; (2) it will not sanction anything that is improper or contrary to the ordinary course of trade; (3) it will exercise its discretion for the benefit of the general body of creditors: *Re Commercial Bank Corp. of India & The East; Smith, Fleming & Co.'s Case; Gledstanes & Co.'s Case* (1866), 1 Ch. App. 538. As to the effect of absence of previous notice to creditors, see *Re Arnold* (1916), 31 D.L.R. 786 (H.C.); *Brigman v. McKenzie* (1897), 6 B.C.R. 56 (C.A.).

As a general rule, the principle of estoppel is not applicable to anything said or done by the liquidator without the authority of the court: *Re People's Trust Co.* (1918), 25 B.C.R. 138; *Re Ontario Bank* (1912), 27 O.L.R. 192 (C.A.).

Under s. 39, the court may provide, by any order subsequent to the winding-up order, that the liquidator may exercise any of the powers conferred upon him by the Act, without the sanction or intervention of the court. For an example of the application of s. 39, see *Re Victoria-Montreal Fire Insurance Co. v. Hyde*

(1902), 4 Que. P.R. 315, where an order was made covering all cases in which the amount involved was under $100. The court may under this section give the liquidator general authority to bring actions without applications to the court: *Kendall v. Webster* (1910), 15 B.C.R. 268 (C.A.).

Conduct of litigation (subs. (a))

A corporation, notwithstanding that it is in liquidation, retains the power to sue, but this power must be exercised by the liquidator with the authority of the court: *Kent v. Communauté des Soeurs de Charité de la Providence*, [1903] A.C. 220. As to the obtaining of such authority, see the notes under the heading "Approval of court to legal proceedings" in this chapter. Once leave has been given, the court will not interfere with the liquidator's conduct of the litigation; *quaere* whether it can do so: *Dominion Trust Co. v. New York Life Insurance Co.*, [1918] 1 W.W.R. 614 (B.C.S.C.).

A liquidator may appeal from any order without the leave of the court, but in such case he does so at his own risk as to costs. See *Re Silver Valley Mines* (1882), 21 Ch. D. 381 (C.A.), where the practice as to appeals by liquidators is stated very fully. He may appeal against an order refusing him his costs out of the estate, or against an order for his removal: *Re Adam Eyton, Ex parte Charlesworth* (1887), 36 Ch. D. 299 (C.A.).

As to reversal on appeal of a direction to bring an action, see *Re Auto Top & Body Co.* (1916), 10 O.W.N. 76.

Actions begun before the liquidation should be continued in the name of the corporation, and a fresh action should not be begun: *Ross v. Perras* (1894), 5 Que. S.C. 470.

Permission may be given to continue in the name of the corporation an action brought by it to recover calls commenced before the liquidation: *Victoria & Montreal Fire Insurance Co. v. Derome* (1902), 21 Que. S.C. 319 (shareholder permitted to plead that obligation to contribute could only be made through a fresh call made by the liquidator based on the amount required to discharge the debts of the corporation).

Under s. 35(1)(a) any suit may be brought or defended by the liquidator (with the approval of the court) either in his own name as liquidator or in the name and on behalf of the corporation. See the notes under the next heading "Whether liquidator should sue in own name or name of corporation", below.

When a liquidator applies for an interim injunction he may be required to give a personal undertaking as to damages: *Westminster Assn. Ltd. v. Upward* (1880), 24 Sol. Jo. 690; but there is no established practice to this effect: *Rosling & Flynn Ltd. v. Law Guarantee & Trust Co.* (1903), 47 Sol. Jo. 255. See also *Brenner (Trustee of) v. Brenner*, [1923] 3 D.L.R. 1097 at 1099 (S.C.) where Orde, J., concluded that in cases where there was any doubt as to the sufficiency of the estate, the liquidator's personal undertaking as to damages should be a condition to the granting of the interim injunction.

A creditor of the corporation may intervene in an action begun by the liquidator: *Communauté des Soeurs de Charité de la Providence v. Bastien* (1900),

11 Que. K.B. 64. As to the extent of this right of intervention, see *Kent v. Communauté des Soeurs de Charité de la Providence* (1901), 19 Que. S.C. 556.

A creditor may also apply for leave to bring an action in the name of the liquidator: *Re Bailey Cobalt Mine Ltd.* (1915), 8 O.W.N. 433.

The liquidator is not a necessary or proper party to an action against the corporation brought before the winding-up to set aside as fraudulent a chattel mortgage made to the corporation and continued against the corporation in liquidation: *Cole v. British Cdn. Fur & Trading Co.* (1918), 42 O.L.R. 587.

Proceedings to enforce the liability of contributories are properly brought by the liquidator and not by the petitioner: *Re Sarnia Oil Co.* (1891), 14 P.R. 335 (Ont. C.A.).

Section 35(1)(a) read with s. 19 is wide enough to justify a summary application to the court to place a contributory on the list instead of applying for leave to bring an action for specific performance of a contract to take shares, where the corporation before insolvency is entitled to apply for rectification of the register: *Monarch Oil Co. (Liquidator of) v. Chapin* (1917), 37 D.L.R. 772 (T.D.).

Where a liquidator desires to reimburse himself out of the assets in respect of litigation in Ontario, but the winding-up and the assets are in the control of the court in Quebec where the order was made, the Quebec court that has control of the assets alone can make the order: *Boyd v. Dominion Cold Storage Co.* (1897), 17 P.R. 545.

When the liquidator seeks to enforce completion by a vendor of a contract to deliver goods to the corporation, and the vendor at the same time has a claim against the corporation for goods already supplied, the liquidator can only recover nominal damages for the vendor's breach of contract: *William Hamilton Mfg. Co. v. Hamilton Steel & Iron Co.* (1910), 23 O.L.R. 270 at 284 (C.A.).

If a liquidator desires to recover a payment made by the corporation to one of its creditors and alleged to constitute an illegal preference, the proper procedure is to commence an action by writ of summons and not to apply to the court by way of summary petition: *Ross Bros. & Co. v. Vermette*, [1952] Que. Q.B. 178 (C.A.), following *Re Tobique Gypsum Co.* (1903), 6 O.L.R. 515 (C.A.).

Whether liquidator should sue in own name or in name of corporation.

Under s. 35(1)(a), as already indicated, the liquidator may, with the approval of the court, bring any suit in his own name as liquidator or in the name of and on behalf of the corporation.

On the authorities, the question whether he should sue in his own name or in that of the corporation depends on the nature of the cause of action and whether he therein represents the corporation or the creditors and contributories. See *Kent v. Communauté des Soeurs de Charité de la Providence*, [1903] A.C. 220, per Lord Davey, at 226:

> There are . . . many cases in which he may sue in his own name, as e.g., to impeach some act or deed of the company before winding-up which is made voidable in the interests of creditors and contributories. But their Lordships think that wherever

the object of the action is to recover a debt, or to recover or protect property the title to which is in the company, the action should be brought in the name of the company.

The liquidator must sue in his own name when he acts as the representative of creditors and contributories, but in that of the corporation when he is recovering its debts or its property: *William Hamilton Mfg. Co. v. Hamilton Steel & Iron Co.* (1910), 23 O.L.R. 270 at 282 (C.A.); *Re Home Bank* (1930), 66 O.L.R. 264 (H.C.). It is proper for the liquidator to sue in his own name alone where the action is founded on alleged wrongful interference with his possession: *Crain v. Wade* (1917), 55 S.C.R. 208 at 214, 215 (action by liquidator in own name in detinue for seizure by defendant of certain brick). If there is any doubt, it is prudent for the corporation and the liquidator to join as co-plaintiffs.

If the liquidator has incorrectly brought the action in his own name, but the defendant has not objected to the form of the action but has admitted the debt and pleaded a set-off, leave should be given to amend: ibid.

Illustrations of the distinction are to be found in *Hyde v. Thibaudeau* (1910), 20 Que. K.B. 200 (C.A.); *Lapierre v. Banque de St.-Jean* (1910), 17 R.L.N.S. 428 (Que. C.A.); *Royal Paper Box Co. v. Canada Cement Construction Co.* (1915), 48 Que. S.C. 287; *Roberge v. Grimard* (1938), 41 Que. P.R. 342.

The liquidator of an insolvent corporation represents the creditors of that corporation for actions that belong to the creditors themselves. Therefore, an action to nullify a payment made by the corporation to a creditor who knew about the insolvent state of that corporation, being in the nature of an action "*paulienne*," may be begun by the liquidator: *Kent v. Blandy* (1896), 10 Que. S.C. 255.

Approval of court to legal proceedings

The liquidator of a corporation in liquidation cannot begin proceedings against the debtors of that corporation without the previous consent of the court on notice to creditors, contributories, shareholders or members as the court prescribes, and it is not sufficient to seek that consent in the case of proceedings already begun against the debtors of the corporation: *Ross v. Perras* (1894), 5 Que. S.C. 470.

The liquidator of a corporation must be specially authorized to institute an action for the recovery of an amount due the corporation, and a general authorization to recover all the corporation's assets is not sufficient: *Freygang v. Daveluy* (1892), 2 Que. S.C. 505. This case does not reflect modern practice.

In British Columbia, the leave of the court to continue a proceeding begun by the corporation may be granted to the liquidator on an *ex parte* application: *Goldstein v. Vancouver Timber & Trading Co.* (1912), 4 D.L.R. 172 (B.C. C.A.).

In *Sarnia Agricultural Implement Mfg. Co. v. Hutchinson* (1889), 17 O.R. 676 (H.C.), it was objected that the liquidator had not obtained the authorization of the court. Proudfoot, J., held that the objection was made too late, when it came at the trial after evidence had been given. *Semble*, that the proper course is to move in chambers to dismiss the action for want of authority: *ibid.*

In *William Hamilton Manufacturing Co. v. Hamilton Steel & Iron Co.* (1910), 23 O.L.R. 270 at 281 (C.A.), the judgment of Britton, J., at the trial indicates that an application to stay is the proper procedure, and that none having been made, the objection of want of approval was not to be given effect to. In *Re G. B. Wood Ltd.*, [1932] 3 W.W.R. 525 (K.B.), an application was made in the winding-up proceedings for an order dismissing or staying actions brought without leave, and an order was made staying the actions permanently.

See also the following decisions with regard to the approval of the court to legal proceedings: *Common v. McCaskill* (1897), 13 Que. S.C. 282 (the approval obtained by the liquidator covered a smaller sum than that for which he sued and his action was dismissed on that ground); *Cie d'opéra comique de Montréal v. Desaulniers* (1904), 7 Que. P.R. 83 (the failure of the liquidator to serve notice of his application for approval on a debtor was held not a ground for dismissing the action against the debtor); *Fecteau v. Ideal Confectionery Co.* (1911), 12 Que. P.R. 360 (the liquidator was not compelled to continue an action against the corporation pending at the time of the winding-up order); *Ruffer v. Rattray & Sons Ltd.* (1911), 39 Que. S.C. 245 (the liquidator must obtain approval to defend an action, even though his defence is that such action was improperly commenced without leave); *Bank of Hamilton v. Kramer-Irwin Co.* (1912), 20 O.W.R. 999 (the proper procedure for a liquidator to take to set aside a consent judgment is by way of action, not by a motion).

Costs

The general rule is that the liquidator is entitled to the costs of all proceedings properly taken: *Re Silver Valley Mines Co.* (1882), 21 Ch. D. 381 (C.A.); unless he has done something to make himself personally liable: *Re R. Bolton & Co. Salisbury-Jones & Dale's Case*, [1895] 1 Ch. 333 (C.A.). See also *Re London Metallurgical Co.*, [1895] 1 Ch. 758, where the authorities on this point are fully discussed. See also *Re Wilson, Lovatt & Sons Ltd.*, [1977] 1 All E.R. 274. In certain cases retrospective sanction may be given or the liquidator authorized to incur legal expenses as part of the expenses of winding up where the retainer of the solicitors had not been previously authorized: *Re Associated Travel Leisure & Services Ltd. (In Liquidation)*, [1978] 1 W.L.R. 547.

If an action is proceeding to which the corporation is a party and the corporation by its liquidator determines to prosecute or defend the action on behalf of the estate, the estate must be regarded as the party litigant, and in the event of failure the costs will be payable in full out of the estate: *Re Wenborn & Co.*, [1905] 1 Ch. 413 at 416; *Re Transcontinental Townsite Co.* (1915), 25 D.L.R. 597 (K.B.) (unconditional judgment for costs against defendant corporation in liquidation); but must be paid out of the corporation's own assets and cannot be paid out of assets in its hands as a trustee or in a fiduciary capacity: *Canadian Guaranty Trust Co. v. Young*, [1933] 3 D.L.R. 558 (Man. C.A.).

When an action is brought or defended by the liquidator in the name of the corporation in liquidation and he is not otherwise a party to it, he cannot be ordered personally to pay the costs of it: *Ontario Forge & Bolt Co. v. Comet Cycle Co.* (1896), 17 P.R. 156 (C.A.). See *Fraser v. Brescia Steam Tramways*

Co. (1887), 56 L.T. 771; *Re Cosmopolitan Life Assn.* (1893), 15 P.R. 185 (C.A.), a case under the Ontario *Winding-up Act*; *Re Transcontinental Townsite Co., supra*, at 599; *Re Primary Distributors Ltd.* (1956), 19 W.W.R. 181 (B.C.), a case under the British Columbia *Companies Act*.

The court will not attach the liquidator's bank account in garnishee proceedings for payment of costs when an action brought by a corporation in liquidation is dismissed with costs: *Lancaster Motor Co. (London) v. Bremith Ltd.*, [1941] 1 K.B. 675 (C.A.).

Where proceedings are taken in the name of the liquidator and the liquidator is unsuccessful, the usual order is that the liquidator is to pay the costs out of the assets in his hands: *Re Transcontinental Townsite Co., supra*, at 600, and cases cited. As pointed out in *Re Dominion of Canada Plumbago Co.* (1884), 27 Ch. D. 33 at 41 (C.A.), the order for payment of costs by the liquidator may be drawn in various forms. Where the order was that the liquidator should pay to successful appellants costs out of the assets of the corporation, it was held that such costs were payable in priority to those incurred by the liquidator, though subject to (a) certain costs payable by the liquidator to petitioning creditors, and (b) certain costs of realization and reasonable compensation in connection with such realization payable out of the assets so realized.

Where the liquidator at his request was added as a party, defendant judgment for costs was given against the liquidator personally as well as against the corporation: *Boyd v. Dominion Cold Storage Co.* (1897), 17 P.R. 545; similarly where the liquidator sued in his own name: *Jackson v. Cannon* (1903), 10 B.C.R. 73 (C.A.).

Where there are encumbrances and the mortgaged property is realized by the liquidator in the winding up, the liquidator's costs of realization are a first charge, the encumbrances rank next, and the general costs of the winding up are payable out of the surplus: *Re Oriental Hotels Co.; Perry v. Oriental Hotels Co.* (1871), L.R. 12 Eq. 126; *Batten v. Wedgwood Coal & Iron Co.* (1884), 28 Ch. D. 317.

The solicitor of the liquidator has no claim for costs against the liquidator personally: *Re Trueman's Estate; Hooke v. Piper* (1872), L.R. 14 Eq. 278; *Re Anglo-Moravian Hungarian Junction Ry. Co.; Ex parte Watkin* (1875), 1 Ch. D. 130 (C.A.). Nor has he any lien on the file of proceedings for his costs: *Union Cement & Brick Co., Re; Ex parte Pulbrook* (1869), 4 Ch. App. 627.

A claimant filed a claim for travelling expenses with the liquidator of a corporation being wound up. The expenses were in connection with enquiries as to the status of shares in the estate. The claim was disallowed as no authorization had been given by the liquidator and the information could have been obtained as easily by correspondence: *Re vonKlitzing* (1984), 57 N.B.R. (2d) 32 (Q.B.).

The costs of an action for calls that had been discontinued by the liquidator on voluntary liquidation were directed to be set off against any sum recovered by the liquidator under originating summons: *Re United Service Assn.* (1901), 1 Ch. 97.

Upon an application for leave to continue or to commence an action against the corporation the court may make it a term of the leave granted that the plaintiff, if successful, is to add his costs to the amount recovered, that is, that the costs should not be paid in full but should be provable in the usual way: *Re Wenborn & Co.*, [1905] 1 Ch. 413 at 417; *Re Transcontinental Townsite Co.* (1915), 25 D.L.R. 597 at 598 (K.B.).

Where the liquidator has been made a party at his own request and has no assets in the province in which the litigation is proceeding, he may be ordered to give security for costs: *Boyd v. Dominion Cold Storage Co., supra.* Where the liquidator is bringing action to set aside a sale of the corporation's assets on the ground of fraud, and the action does not appear to be frivolous or vexatious, it is not a proper case to order security: *Montreal Trust Co. v. McDougall*, [1930] 3 D.L.R. 159.

Discovery by liquidator

As the liquidator represents the corporation in litigation, he may be compelled to make discovery: *Re Barned's Banking Co., Ex parte Contract Corp.* (1867), 3 Ch. App. 105; *Re Contract Corp., Gooch's Case* (1872), 7 Ch. App. 207; *Re Traders Trust Co.* (1915), 8 W.W.R. 1080 (B.C. S.C.).

A liquidator, however, being an officer of the court, is not in the position of an ordinary litigant and will not, in the absence of special circumstances, be required to make an affidavit as to documents in his possession, though he is bound to show to the adverse litigant all the documents he requires to see: *Re Mutual Society* (1883), 22 Ch. D. 714 at 718 (C.A.); *Dominion Trust Co. v. Royal Bank* (1919), 27 B.C.R. 166 (S.C.) (order refused compelling liquidator to make an affidavit of documents when he was willing to make disclosure).

See also *Surrey Credit Union Ltd. v. Northland Bank* (1989), 62 Man. R. (2d) 285 (C.A.), where an order requiring the liquidator to provide access to documents and information in the hands of the liquidator was refused, as it would not be for the benefit of the winding up nor in the interests of the bank or creditors generally. See also *Canada Deposit Insurance Corp. v. Commonwealth Trust Co.* (1990), 2 C.B.R. (3d) 87 (B.C. S.C.).

Liquidator carrying on business of corporation (subs. (b))

Unless the liquidators are authorized to carry on the business of the corporation, their duty is only to wind it up, and they are bound to distribute the assets according to the liabilities as they exist at the date of the stoppage; they have no power to alter those liabilities by making a fresh contract: *Re East of England Banking Co.* (1868), 4 Ch. App. 14; *Re Steel Co. of Canada* (1884), 17 N.S.R. 17.

The power of the liquidator, with the approval of the court, is to carry on the business of the corporation so far as is necessary for the beneficial winding up of the same. The necessity must be determined by the court, and the business must be carried on with a view to winding up the corporation and not with a view to its continuance: *Re Wreck Recovery & Salvage Co.* (1880), 15 Ch. D. 353, 360 at 361 (C.A.). It is sufficient to forward an application to the court for approval if the liquidator *bona fide* and reasonably forms the opinion that the carrying on of the business is necessary for the beneficial winding up of the corporation; and his reasonable opinion, in the event that it is falsified by subsequent events, is not to be judged by those events: *Re Great Eastern Electric Co.*, [1941] Ch. 241 at 245, 246.

If an advance is made after the presentation of the petition, the person making the advance is entitled to the benefit of security taken if the advance was made under s. 19 with the sanction of the liquidator and for the beneficial winding up of the corporation: *Clarkson v. Dominion Bank* (1919), 58 S.C.R. 448.

If the liquidator in the proper exercise of his powers incurs obligations, those to whom he incurs them are entitled to rank on the assets of the corporation ahead of the pre-liquidation creditors: *Re Great Eastern Electric Co., supra.*

A liquidator, unlike a receiver and manager appointed by the court, is the agent of the corporation: *Re Anglo-Moravian Hungarian Junction Ry. Co., Ex p. Watkin* (1875), 1 Ch. D. 130 (C.A.). Where a liquidator wrote to the vendors of goods under an existing contract asking that payments should be made after delivery instead of before delivery, as provided in the contract, to which the vendors acceded and a delivery of goods was subsequently not accepted by the corporation or the liquidator, it was held (a) that even if the letter and its acceptance constituted a new contract, it was one that purported to be by the liquidator as agent for the corporation, and (b) that he did not purport to contract nor did the vendors give him credit on his own behalf, and accordingly, he was not personally liable: *Stead, Hazel & Co. v. Cooper*, [1933] 1 K.B. 840.

Authority to carry on the corporation's business does not authorize the liquidator of a trust corporation to part with the corporation's right of retainer, as this would involve a reduction of the assets, and as such would require a substantive approval of the court under s. 37: *Re Arnold* (1916), 31 D.L.R. 786 (H.C.).

The offices of liquidator and of administrator of an estate are incompatible; a trust corporation in liquidation cannot continue to exercise the duties of trustee unless so directed by a court having jurisdiction over the trust: *Re Hiebert Estate*, [1934] 4 D.L.R. 799 (Sask. K.B.) (liquidator removed as administrator).

As to the effect of adopting an outstanding contract, see *Re Bishop Construction Co.* (1914), 15 D.L.R. 911 (Que. C.A.).

If the liquidator supplies goods in pursuance of a contract made before the winding up commenced, the purchaser cannot set off a debt incurred to himself by the corporation prior to the winding up: *Re Ince Hall Rolling Mills Co. v. Douglas Forge Co.* (1882), 8 Q.B.D. 179; *Mersey Steel & Iron Co. v. Naylor, Benzon & Co.* (1882), 9 Q.B.D. 648 (C.A.). See also the following cases where the question of the set-off of a debt incurred prior to the winding up was considered: *Re English Joint Stock Bank, Ex p. Harding* (1867), L.R. 3 Eq. 341; *Re Oriental Hotels Co., Perry v. Oriental Hotels Co.*; (1871), L.R. 12 Eq. 126; *Wiltshire Iron Co. v. Great Western Ry. Co.* (1871), L.R. 6 Q.B. 101 and 776; *Re Regent's Canal Ironworks Co.; Grissell, Ex parte* (1875), 3 Ch. D. 411 (C.A.); *Re Asphaltic Wood Pavement Co., Lee & Chapman's Case* (1885), 30 Ch. D. 216 (C.A.); *Re Llangennech Coal Co.* (1887), 56 L.T. 475.

Sale of property (subs. (c))

The power to sell is conferred on the liquidator; it is not exercisable by the court, but by the liquidator after first having obtained the court's approval.

Until forms, rules and regulations are made under s. 136 the ordinary Court practice in sales will apply. For the practice and what must be shown where a private sale is desired, see *Re Bolt & Iron Co.* (1884), 10 P.R. 434 (Ont. Master) P.R. 434. See also *Re Atlantic Felt Inc.*, [1962] Que. S.C. 195.

In the case of *Northland Bank (Liquidator of) v. Kuperman*, [1989] 4 W.W.R. 701 (Man. C.A.), the liquidator had agreed to sell property subject to obtaining court approval. A subsequent and higher offer was obtained before the court's approval was obtained, and the court suggested that there be a further tender by the two bidders. The original offeror appealed the decision. It was held that the appeal should be allowed and the earlier sale approved. The discretion approving or disapproving the sale by the liquidator was to be exercised fairly and was not to be used as a means of getting a higher price due to changed circumstances. Once the court was satisfied with the process of sale, it should have exercised its discretion in favour of the sale, assuming that the price was not improvident at the material time, which in these circumstances it was not.

In *Re Atlantic Felt Inc.* (1962), 3 C.B.R. (N.S.) 318, it was held that the court has a duty to protect the interests of creditors against erroneous decisions of the liquidator, and that any person who considers that the purposes of the Act are being jeopardized has a right to come before the court to ask it to exercise its right and duty of control over acts of the liquidator. In the aforementioned case, the liquidator advertised for tenders, and the applicant's bid was considerably higher than the next highest bid. The inspectors instructed the liquidator to refuse all bids but to invite new tenders. It was shown that most of the inspectors were interested in the lower bid and that they had refused the tender so that they themselves could purchase the assets. The court held that the liquidator should be directed to accept the applicant's tender; it was pointed out that the decision of the inspectors was contrary to the best interests of the creditors at large, and that the call for tenders was defective in that no advertising was to be made. In view of the conflict of interest and the absence of any guarantee that any higher bid would be received, the original first higher bid was to be accepted.

In Quebec, on an application of the liquidator for an order authorizing him to call for tenders, the order should be granted and the judge is not entitled to direct that the assets be sold by the sheriff: *Mount Royal Park Incline Railway v. Robson* (1919), 26 Rev. Leg. N.S. 198.

For the purpose of registering in Ontario a conveyance of lands by the liquidator, the registrar requires (a) a certified copy of the court order appointing the liquidator and authorizing the sale of the real property, (b) an affidavit of the solicitor for the liquidator stating that the court order is in full force and effect and that the order affects the lands referred to in the application, and (c) that the actual transfer contain the certificate of the liquidator (or an officer) to the same effect.

Where the powers of the court have been delegated to the Official Referee, and the latter has approved of a sale, there is no need to have the sale confirmed by a judge in chambers: *Re McCann Knox Milling Co.* (1910), 1 O.W.N. 579.

Where a creditor was dissatisfied with an offer that the Master had directed the liquidator to accept, the creditor was given a limited time to produce a better offer: *Re Oakoal Co.* (1921), 21 O.W.N. 53.

There must be a valid contract in existence between the liquidator and the purchaser before the liquidator can be compelled to carry out a proposed sale: *Re Canada Woollen Mills Ltd.* (1905), 9 O.L.R. 367 (C.A.).

An agreement to purchase the assets of an insolvent corporation at a certain rate on the dollar of unascertained claims of the creditors is of doubtful validity when there is no affidavit of estimated value: *Re Bolt & Iron Co.* (1884), 10 P.R. 434 (Ont. Master).

As to the meaning of the phrase "free from encumbrances" in a sale by a liquidator, see *Dominion Linen Mfg. Co. v. Langley* (1911), 19 O.W.R. 648, affd (1912), 46 S.C.R. 633.

The liquidator is bound by the corporation's covenant in a lease not to assign the demised premises without the consent of the lessor: *Re Farrow's Bank Ltd.*, [1921] 2 Ch. 164 (C.A.).

Where a liquidator has sold the assets, expressly including an asset the title to which has not passed and in respect of which there is a liability of the corporation to pay deferred instalments of the purchase price, he must be taken to have intended to give the purchaser a good title and therefore to have adopted the contract of purchase. Accordingly, the vendor is entitled to be paid the balance of the purchase price out of the assets of the corporation in liquidation: *In re Anchor Line (Henderson Brothers) Ltd.*, [1937] Ch. 483 (C.A.).

The Act does not contain any provisions permitting a sale of an immovable with the effect of a judicial decree: *Re Limoges & Co. & Russell* (1932), 36 Que. P.R. 144.

Under the provisions of subss. (c) (before the amendment of 1924 by expressly providing that a sale might be made for such consideration as approved by the court) and (h), the court had power to sanction the acceptance by the liquidator of an offer to purchase the corporation's assets for a consideration other than money, for example, shares of a new corporation; and when a very large majority of the shareholders desired that the offer be accepted, it was held that the court should give effect to their wishes: *Re Bailey Cobalt Mines Ltd.* (1920), 47 O.L.R. 13 (C.A.), following *Re Cambrian Mining Co.* (1882), 48 L.T.R. 114.

It should be noted in the *Bailey Cobalt* case that the sale involved payment of the creditors of the old corporation by the new corporation, and that a majority of the creditors had approved. It was further held, the corporation being an Ontario corporation, that s. 23(m) (now see s. 184(3)) of the Ontario Act applied.

If a sale has the effect of allowing an insolvent corporation, or its shareholders, to participate in the proceeds of the sale, notwithstanding that the creditors are not paid in full, then it is an arrangement: *Re Thompson Cadillac Mining Corp.*, [1943] 2 D.L.R. 255 (S.C.C.). That case was decided under a provision (corresponding to the present s. 30(l)(a) of the *Bankruptcy and*

Insolvency Act) authorizing the trustee, with the permission of the inspectors, to sell or dispose of the property of the bankrupt. It was held that the sale was not within the powers exercisable under the paragraph, and no doubt the same rule would apply to a sale by a liquidator that is in fact an arrangement.

As to whether the purchaser from a liquidator of assets and claims is entitled to continue the liquidation for the purpose of realizing the claims, or whether he must enforce them by action, see *Re Port Arthur Waggon Co.* (1919), 45 O.L.R. 260 at 266, 271, affd (1920), 47 O.L.R. 565 (C.A.); *Re Port Arthur Waggon Co.*; *Smyth's Case* (1918), 57 S.C.R. 388. In *Re Canadian Cordage & Mfg. Co.* (1923), 54 O.L.R. 486 (H.C.), it was held that the purchaser from the liquidator of claims against contributories was not entitled to use the machinery of the winding up to enforce them. The same objection, however, was held to be of no avail in *Re Port Arthur Waggon Co., supra*; and see *Re Port Arthur Waggon Co., supra*, at 570. In *Re Canadian Cordage & Mfg. Co., supra*, it is pointed out that the liability of a contributory is a relative one; that on payment of a call there is a corresponding right to contribution from the other contributories and a right to a refund of a proportionate share of any surplus; and that where the creditors as a result of the liquidation had received a fraction over 9 cents on the dollar, *quaere* whether any contributory, when called upon by the assignee of the claims to pay, was not entitled to insist that any surplus realized over and above the amount realized on the sale of the claims should go to the creditors, and whether, if the creditors were satisfied with the amount of their dividend, the contributories should be called on for more.

Special provision is made in the Acts of certain of the provinces of Canada for the sale of the business of a corporation by its liquidator, in pursuance of a resolution of the shareholders, to a new corporation in consideration for shares of the new corporation. These are distributed among the shareholders of the corporation that is being wound up. Any shareholder of the transferor corporation who did not vote in favour of the resolution and who expresses his dissent in the manner prescribed may require the liquidator either (a) to abstain from carrying the resolution into effect or (b) to purchase his interest, at a price to be determined by agreement or by arbitration in the manner provided by the Act.

In jurisdictions where a statutory provision such as the above is in force and applies, when the corporation is "proposed to be or is in the course of being wound up", the corporation cannot make a sale of shares to another corporation without complying with the section: *Bisgood v. Henderson's Transvaal Estates, Ltd.*, [1908] 1 Ch. 743 (C.A.). A sale cannot be made to a foreign corporation under the English Act, owing to the definition clauses of the Act: *Thomas v. United Butter Cos. of France Ltd.*, [1909] 2 Ch. 484; although this may be effected as an arrangement: *Re Anglo-Continental Supply Co.*, [1922] 2 Ch. 723. The requirements of the section are not complied with by passing an ordinary resolution sanctioning a sale for shares and special resolutions providing for winding up and distribution: *Etheridge v. Central Uruguay Northern Extension Ry. Co.*, [1913] 1 Ch. 425.

A corporation can, however, sell its assets and undertaking for shares of another corporation in pursuance of a charter power, provided that the resolution passed by the shareholders merely authorizes the sale and no distribution is involved: *Hemstreet v. North West Biscuit Co.*, [1926] 2 D.L.R. 829 (Alta. C.A.).

Raising funds (subs. (g))

The liquidator should apply to the court for leave to borrow before obtaining a loan. Where the order authorizing a loan provided that the same should be a first mortgage on all the assets of the corporation subject only to existing liens, charges and encumbrances, it was held that the lender's lien took priority over the costs and charges of the winding-up proceedings, including the fees of the liquidator and solicitor: *Keyes v. Hannington* (1913), 13 D.L.R. 139 (N.B. C.A.). See also *Re British Columbia Timbers Ltd.* (1921), 1 C.B.R. 392 (authorization to borrow from a specified bank not in excess of a stated amount).

Section 94 of the Act only gives priority to the winding-up costs over claims against the corporation that were in existence at the time of going into liquidation: *Keyes v. Hannington, supra.*

General powers (subs. (h))

In *Re Bailey Cobalt Mines Ltd.* (1920), 47 O.L.R. 13, the Court of Appeal expressed the view that the generality of this clause should not be limited; and held that it gave the liquidator, with the sanction of the court, power to do anything that might be thought expedient with reference to the assets of the corporation, in that case to accept an offer to purchase the assets of the corporation for a consideration other than a money payment.

Wynn-Parry, J., regarded the corresponding clause of the English Act (s. 245(2)(h)) as "a mopping-up provision at the end of a list of functions which the liquidator was enabled to perform in connection with the administration of the particular company's affairs and no more." He pointed out that the clause was in very general terms and that it did not indicate among whom the assets were to be distributed, nor how this was to be ascertained. These facts must be determined by reference to s. 265 (corresponding to s. 95 of the federal Act), which was the only operative section as regards the actual distribution; and that accordingly, in a compulsory winding up, an order of the court was always necessary before the liquidator was entitled to distribute the assets; and that this was so whether or not an adjustment of the rights of the contributories among themselves was required: *Re Phoenix Oil & Transport Co. (No. 2)*, [1958] Ch. 565.

When solicitor may be appointed (S. 36)

Under s. 36, the liquidator may with the approval of the court appoint a solicitor to assist him in the performance of his duties.

Who may be appointed

It is preferable to have the proceedings under an order for winding up a corporation conducted by solicitors who are totally unconnected with the corporation to be wound up: *Re Joseph Hall Mfg. Co.* (1884), 10 P.R. 485 (Ont. H.C.).

A solicitor who is acting also for claimants whose claims must be contested by the liquidator should not act for the liquidator: *Re Trueman's Estate; Hooke v. Piper* (1872), L.R. 14 Eq. 278; *Re Anglo-Moravian Hungarian Junction Ry. Co., Ex parte Watkin* (1875), 1 Ch. D. 130 (C.A.).

In a proceeding for the winding up of a corporation, a solicitor who is acting for claimants whose claims must be contested by the liquidator cannot obtain the sanction of the court to his acting also as solicitor for the liquidator. Nor will the court sanction the appointment of a special solicitor to act for the liquidator in the matter of the contested claims. The winding up must be prosecuted by one disinterested solicitor whose services will not be divided by the assertion of antagonistic claims: *Re Charles Stark Co. (No. 2)* (1893), 15 P.R. 471 (Ont. H.C.).

A liquidator may not appoint his partner: *Re Universal Private Telegraph Co.* (1870), 23 L.T. 884.

Change of solicitor

Where the liquidator desires to change solicitors, he need only allege that the change is in the best interests of the winding up: *Re Bank of Vancouver* (1919), 27 B.C.R. 457 (fact that solicitor has been acting for claimants not sufficient ground for withholding of approval; but solicitor, before such approval, must cease to act for such claimants); *Re Continental Fire & Casualty Co.*, [1924] 3 D.L.R. 9. See also the discussion in *Canada Deposit Insurance Corp. v. Commonwealth Trust Co.* (1991), 4 C.B.R. (3d) 16 at 29ff (B.C. S.C.), which involved an application to remove lawyers for the liquidator on the grounds of conflict.

Costs of liquidator's solicitor

The costs of the solicitor employed come out of the assets next after the liquidator's necessary disbursements and before his remuneration.

The solicitor of the liquidator has no claim for costs against the liquidator personally and must look to the assets: *Re Trueman's Estate; Hooke v. Piper* (1872), L.R. 14 Eq. 278; *Re Anglo-Moravian Junction Ry. Co., Ex parte Watkin* (1875), 1 Ch. D. 130 (C.A.); *MacInnes v. Daly*, [1921] 2 W.W.R. 869 (B.C. C.A.) (liquidator entitled, as against garnishing creditor of solicitor, to set off against costs owing to solicitor a debt owing by solicitor to the corporation). The liquidator's solicitor has no claim on the creditors for his fees: *Beaubien v. Corticelli Silla Co.* (1912), 14 Que. P.R. 194.

Where a creditor of a contributory applied for a charging order, it was held that the solicitor for the liquidator was entitled to his properly taxable costs as a first charge on the fund — that is, any dividend which might be paid — and that the creditor must look to the balance for his claim and for any costs that might be awarded to him: *Re Saskatchewan Co-operative Elevator Co.*, [1928] 2 W.W.R. 256 (Sask. K.B.).

Costs that the liquidator is ordered to pay to an adverse litigant must be paid in priority to costs due to the solicitor of the liquidator: *Re Dominion of Canada Plumbago Co.* (1884), 27 Ch. D. 33 (C.A.). A liquidator should not pay a large bill of a solicitor without taxation or court approval: *Re Prudential Life Insurance Co.*, [1920] 2 W.W.R. 628 (K.B.).

Upon the reference for the winding up of a corporation, the referee appointed a firm of solicitors to represent the general body of creditors, and ordered that representatives of this firm be notified to attend whenever he so directed, and that their costs as between solicitor and client be paid out of the assets. It was held that this class of order and liability was not favoured by the courts and should be invoked and that their attendance thereunder had, only when there was any special question on which the appearance of someone to represent the creditors was desirable. Also, that attendances and services should not be paid for out of the assets except where contemporaneously approved of by the referee; and that it was not proper practice for the referee to extend this approval at the close of the proceedings in the form of a certificate stating that, had he been applied to from time to time, he might have provided for other attendances and services: *Re Drury Nickel Co.* (1895), 16 P.R. 525 (Ont. H.C.).

Compromises and arrangements (Ss. 37, 38)

With the approval of the court, a liquidator may compromise or arrange any debts due to the corporation (s. 37) or any debts due by the corporation (s. 38).

In sanctioning such a compromise or arrangement, the court is exercising a judicial discretion, and therefore will not give its sanction without having the means to form an opinion of the propriety of the compromise or arrangement proposed: *Re Northumberland & Durham District Banking Co., Ex parte Totty* (1860), 1 Dr. & Sm. 273 (compromise with contributories); *Morin v. Bilodeau* (1898), 8 Que. Q.B. 330 (C.A.) (compromise of pending litigation).

The court may rescind a compromise made with its sanction, if it was obtained by misrepresentation: *Re Leeds Banking Co.; Ex parte Clarke* (1866), 14 W.R. 856; and see *Re Home Counties Life Assurance Co.; Ex parte Garstin* (1862), 10 W.R. 457; *Re Central Darjeeling Tea Co.*, [1866] W.N. 361.

The section corresponding to s. 37 was construed very widely in the earlier English cases. See *Re Commercial Bank Corp. of India & The East* (1869), L.R. 8 Eq. 241.

The court has no jurisdiction to compel the liquidator to compromise with a contributory: *East of England Banking Co.; Pearson's Case* (1872), 7 Ch. App. 309.

Without the consent of the court, the liquidator cannot accept less than payment in full of a debt due to the corporation: *Re Ontario Bank* (1912), 27 O.L.R. 192 at 202 (C.A.); *Re Arnold* (1916), 31 D.L.R. 786 (H.C.); *Laurie Engine Co. v. Mackie* (1906), 7 Que. P.R. 431. The modern practice is to provide a general approval rather than individual applications.

Since the liquidator has no power to release anyone without the court's approval, laches on his part will not release contributories: *Re Ontario Bank, Massey & Lee's Case, supra.*

The power of the court to authorize the liquidator to act in the name of the corporation to settle pending litigation by or against the corporation is a discretionary power; and the liquidator is not obliged to consult the creditors of the corporation before applying to the court for authority to effect a settlement: *Morin v. Bilodeau* (1898), 8 Que. Q.B. 330 (C.A.).

Contingent claims (for example, a claim of guarantors of the corporation's indebtedness to the bank), as well as direct claims, may be compromised under s. 38: *Re Stratford Fuel Ice & Construction Co.* (1912), 28 O.L.R. 481 at 487.

A compromise to entitle a debtor to regain its assets must include a settlement not only of the unsecured debts but of the secured debts: *Re Stinson Reeb Builders Supply Co.* (1935), 16 C.B.R. 308 (Que. S.C.).

If the creditors have consented to a compromise of their claims, the court will not be astute to find technical defects in the proceedings: *Re Dynevor, Dyffryn & Neath Abbey Collieries Co.* (1879), 11 Ch. D. 605.

Where the liquidator sought approval of an agreement for the sale of the corporation's assets, at a price equal to 25 cents on the dollar of the claims of the creditors of the corporation "as may be admitted or adjudicated", the court refused to sanction the agreement. *Quaere*, whether an agreement to purchase the assets of a corporation at a certain rate on the dollar of the unascertained claims of the creditors of such corporation would be valid: *Re Bolt & Iron Co.* (1884), 10 P.R. 434 (Ont. Master).

If a liquidator, without obtaining the sanction of the court, settles and pays an invalid claim, he will be liable for the amount so misapplied: *Re Windsor Steam Coal Co. (1901)*, [1929] 1 Ch. 151 (C.A.).

Under s. 66 of the Act, the court has power to compel a minority of creditors to accept a compromise; and such a compromise is likewise binding on the liquidator and contributories.

Deposit of corporation's money (Ss. 44-47)

The liquidator is required to deposit all money that he has in his hands belonging to the corporation in a bank designated by the court (s. 44). These moneys are to be kept in a separate account in the name of the liquidator as such (s. 45). Within three days after the final winding up of the corporation's business, the liquidator must deposit any money not required for any other purpose authorized by the Act (s. 46), and he is liable for failure to do so (s. 47). See also the notes under ss. 138-139 on "Unclaimed deposits" in Chapter 25. For a decision of alleged improprieties in handling deposit accounts see *Canada Deposit Insurance Corp. v. Commonwealth Trust Co.* (1991), 6 C.B.R. (3d) 293 (B.C. S.C.).

The court will normally permit investments of a specified type by the liquidator and permit deposits in banks generally rather than a specific bank.

Court discharging functions of liquidator

Under section 48, if at any time there is no liquidator, all the property of the corporation is deemed to be in the custody of the court (s. 48).

The word "liquidator" in s. 48 includes a provisional liquidator: *System Theatre Operating Co. v. Pulos*, [1955] S.C.R. 448 at 453.

If the realization and the distribution of the assets have proceeded to such a stage that the court considers it expedient that final realization and distribution be under the direction of the court, it may so order (s. 49). In such a case, the liquidator is discharged and the assets are turned over to an officer of the court.

An order for the sale of an asset by the court after the liquidator's discharge, and an order vesting such asset in the purchaser, have been granted under ss. 48 and 49.

Inspectors (S. 41)

The duty of the inspectors is to assist and advise the liquidator in the liquidation. They have no control over the liquidator, who is subject only to the control of the court: *Maranda-Desaulniers v. Peckham*, [1953] Que. Q.B. 163 at 172 (C.A.). See also *Commonwealth Trust Co.*, [1971] 20 D.L.R. (3d) 170 (B.C.). Their remuneration is provided for by s. 43.

So long as he holds that office, an inspector is disqualified from becoming a purchaser of the corporation's assets, unless he has the consent of his *cestuis que trust* — that is, the contributories and creditors — or at least an order of the court after notice to all concerned; for he is in the position of a trustee for sale of the assets of the insolvent corporation: *Re Canada Woollen Mills Ltd.* (1905), 9 O.L.R. 367 (C.A.), per Moss, C.J.O., at 368. Where the sale to an inspector had been made pursuant to an order of the court, it was held that, in the absence of fraud or preference, the sale could not be set aside: *Montreal Exhibition Co. c. Ducles* (1937), 18 C.B.R. 248 (C.S. Qué.). In *Morrison v. Watts* (1892), 19 O.A.R. 622 (C.A.), a sale to an inspector was set aside, there being evidence of fraud. See also *Goldsmith & Co. v. Druker*, [1962] Que. S.C. 195, where the conduct of the inspectors was criticized.

In the event of an inspector becoming a purchaser while the fiduciary relationship continues, the purchase may be set aside on the motion of the liquidator or a creditor: *Re Canada Woollen Mills Ltd., supra*, and (1904), 8 O.L.R. 581; *Gastonguay v. Savoie* (1899), 29 S.C.R. 613. Where the transaction is completed, the creditors may be entitled to a reference to ascertain what profit, if any, the inspector has derived therefrom: *Segsworth v. Anderson* (1894), 24 S.C.R. 699.

However, where an inspector has purchased shares that formed part of the assets without knowing that they formed part of the estate, while the court will order him to return the shares retained subject to his lien for the price paid, it will not order him to replace the shares sold but will only require him to account for the proceeds thereof: *Re Bulmer; Ex parte Greaves*, [1937] Ch. 499 (C.A.).

An inspector, after his discharge from that office, may tender for and buy the corporation's assets: *Christin v. Hudon* (1919), 58 Que. S.C. 397.

Remuneration of liquidators and inspectors (Ss. 42, 43)

The word "liquidator" in s. 42 includes a provisional liquidator: *System Theatre Operating Co. v. Pulos*, [1955] S.C.R. 448 at 453; thus, where a winding-up order has been set aside, the court has power under this section to determine the amount of fees and disbursements to be allowed the provisional liquidator: *ibid.*

The cases noted below reflect the traditional approach for the method of settling the liquidator's compensation and many of the principles therein set forth will still be applicable. However, in modern practice the usual course is to set an hourly rate for the liquidator and his employees and associates.

The liquidator's compensation for his services was usually a percentage based on the time occupied, work done and responsibility imposed; and when fixed goes to the liquidator, or, if more than one, is distributed amongst them: *The Central Bank of Canada* (1887), 15 O.R. 309 (H.C.); *Re Waldron Drouin Co.* (1916), 17 Que. P.R. 358.

The remuneration of the liquidators should be spread over the whole period of liquidation so as to insure vigilance at all stages: *Re Central Bank* (1892), 22 O.R. 247 (*sub nom. Lye's Claim*); and ought not to be fixed at the time of their appointment; but the court adopted the suggestions of the shareholders and creditors as to the proportions in which the several liquidators should share in the amount to be allowed: *Re Commercial Bank of Man.* (1893), 9 Man. R. 342.

The liquidator should furnish proof of the services rendered, work done, etc.: *Exchange Bank v. Campbell* (1885), 15 R.L. 373; *Re Assiniboine Valley Stock & Dairy Farming Co.* (1889), 6 Man. R. 184. On an application for interim remuneration, the liquidator may be examined on his affidavit and as to moneys recovered subsequent to the date to which remuneration is being claimed; and if the application is dismissed, the liquidator may be ordered to pay costs personally: *Re Prudential Life Insurance Co.* [1920] 2 W.W.R. 628 (K.B.).

No fixed scale of remuneration has been adopted in Ontario. An hourly rate in addition to the normal percentage fee was held to be justified where special duties had to be performed: *Re J. West & Co.* (1966), 9 C.B.R. (N.S.) 32 (Ont. S.C.).

In Manitoba the scale of remuneration fixed in England has been followed, not as absolutely binding, but as a guide: *Re Saskatchewan Coal Mining Co.* (1890), 6 Man. R. 593 (Q.B.); but in *Re Prudential Life Insurance Co.*, [1920] 2 W.W.R. 628, at 630 (K.B.), Galt, J., said "Five per cent. consisting of two and a half per cent. on collections and the same for distributions, seems to be recognized both in Ontario and Manitoba as a reasonable remuneration for a complete winding-up, but there is no hard and fast rule."

In *Eastern Trust Co. v. Nova Scotia Steel & Coal Co.* (1938), 13 M.P.R. 237 (N.S. C.A.), where the liquidators were respectively one of the receivers and the paid technical advisor of the receivers, and it was difficult to differentiate between the services rendered in one capacity and those rendered in the other, their remuneration was fixed at 1 per cent of the money passing through their hands.

A liquidator was held not entitled to claim fees based on the tariff of the association of chartered accountants of which he was a member: *Re Waldron Drouin Co.* (1916), 17 Que. P.R. 358.

A liquidator in a winding-up subject to the supervision of the court is not a trustee within the provisions of the *Trustee Act*, of British Columbia so as to make applicable the restriction on remuneration in s. 80 of that Act: *Re Intermountain Building & Loan Assn.* [1942] 3 D.L.R. 779 (B.C.S.C.).

Decisions on the remuneration of executors, trustees and receivers may be helpful as indicating the principles on which the remuneration of liquidators may be determined. *Re Toronto General Trusts Corp. v. Central Ontario Ry.* (1905), 6 O.W.R. 350 at 354 (H.C.), Teetzel, J., said that it was proper to take the following circumstances into account when fixing the amount of remuneration of an executor: the magnitude of the trust; the care and responsibility springing therefrom; the time occupied in performing the duties; the skill and ability displayed; and the success attending the administration. These elements suggested by Teetzel, J., are still considered the governing factors in determining the remuneration of executors, and have been approved in a number of decisions; see *Re MacDonald Estate*, [1933] 1 W.W.R. 421 at 426 (Sask. C.A.); *Re Mortimer*, [1936] O.R. 438 at 441 (C.A.); *London & Western Trusts Co. v. Dougall Building Co.*, [1947] O.W.N. 386 at 387; *Hinkson v. Canada Permanent Trust Co.*, [1948] 2 W.W.R. 515 at 527 (Sask. C.A.).

While compensation is generally estimated by the application of percentages, it was pointed out in *Re Atkinson*, [1952] 3 D.L.R. 609 at 612 (Ont. C.A.) that percentages "should be employed only as a rough guide to assist in the computation of what may be considered a fair and reasonable allowance . . . ." At 615-616 of the report, the percentages used in arriving at an executor's compensation in a large estate are set out.

The amount that may be considered "a fair and reasonable allowance" will vary greatly, and each case necessarily will depend on its own merits. However, the following cases on the remuneration of executors, trustee or receivers, may be of assistance: *Re Stobie Forlong & Co.* (1933), 14 C.B.R. 237 (Ont. S.C.) (method of calculating trustee's remuneration); *Re Jenny Lind Candy Shops Ltd.* (1939), 21 C.B.R. 182 (Ont. S.C.) (remuneration of trustee calculated at 192); *Re George Coles Ltd.* [1940] 2 D.L.R. 786 (an interim receiver was allowed 4 per cent on part of the gross receipts, but only 2.5 per cent on the balance, which came from a government contract, and a lump sum for special services); *London & Western Trusts Co. v. Dougall Building Co., supra*, (3 per cent allowed for realization and distribution of capital where no extraordinary degree of skill required); *Re McQuay*, [1948] O.W.N. 304 (4 per cent on capital receipts; and management fee increased from the usual 0.2 of 1 per cent to 0.4 of 1 per cent); *Hinkson v. Canada Permanent Trust Co., supra* (discussion of allowance to executor in connection with the management of a business); *Re Heap Estate* (1951), 4 W.W.R. (N.S.) 206 (B.C.N.S.) (allowance of 2 per cent of aggregate value of estate to executor-solicitor); *Re Cauchon* [1952] O.W.N. 335 (C.A.) (compensation payable to executor-solicitor set out at 337-8).

No charge can be made by a liquidator for time spent in procuring his own appointment or opposing his discharge: *Re Assiniboine Valley Stock & Dairy Farming Co.* (1889), 6 Man. R. 184 (scale of remuneration and business for which it is allowed discussed); his compensation will be reduced if the liquidation is unduly prolonged: *Re A.E. Mundle & Co.* (1975), 21 C.B.R. (N.S.) 242 (N.B. Q.B.).

The fiduciary relationship that exists between a liquidator and the shareholders or creditors prevents a liquidator who is a solicitor from receiving profit costs of non-contentious legal business done by him as solicitor: *Re Gertzenstein Ltd.*, [1937] Ch. 115.

A corporation acting as liquidator cannot charge fees for legal documents drawn by its clerk; nor, as a disbursement, commissions on collections made by its own branch office in another province; nor, as a disbursement, a commission paid to a solicitor in addition to his full ordinary costs. Also, the liquidator should not pay a solicitor's bill in a large amount without taxation or without the sanction of the court; and it is doubtful whether a corporation acting as liquidator should charge as a disbursement rent for space in a building owned by it and occupied for the purposes of the liquidation unless under the sanction of the court: *Re Prudential Life Insurance Co.*, [1920] 2 W.W.R. 628 (K.B.).

Creditors can have the liquidator's remuneration fixed by a taxing officer: *Re Laurie Engine Co.* (1906), 8 Que. P.R. 59.

As to the priority of the liquidator's remuneration and disbursements when there is a deficiency of assets, see the following cases: *Re London Metallurgical Co.*, [1895] 1 Ch. 758; *Re Massey; Re Freehold Land & Brickmaking Co.* (1870), L.R. 9 Eq. 367; *Re Dronfield Silkstone Coal Co. (No. 2)* (1883), 23 Ch. D. 511; *Re Dominion of Canada Plumbago Co.* (1884), 27 Ch. D. 33 (C.A.); *Batten v. Wedgwood Coal & Iron Co.* (1886), 31 Ch. D. 346; *Re Sanitary Burial Assn.* [1900] 2 Ch. 289; *Re Baden Machinery Co.* (1906), 12 O.L.R. 634.

Under s. 94, the winding-up expenses, including the remuneration of the liquidator, are payable out of the assets of the corporation in priority to all other claims. The liquidator is only entitled to remuneration out of the assets of the corporation available for that purpose: *Re Dronfield Silkstone Coal Co. (No. 2)* (1883), 23 Ch. D. 511. As in a normal case, the whole of the expenses that the liquidator incurs in the winding-up should be provided for by him before he is entitled to any remuneration. If his position is that there will be no balance available for his remuneration, he should arrange with the creditors or other persons interested to indemnify him or put up a fund for his benefit: *Re Beni-Felkai Mining Co.* [1934] Ch. 406 at 422.

The remuneration of the liquidator ranks after the rights of mortgagees and debenture-holders, but in priority to unsecured creditors: *Re Regent's Canal Iron works Co.; Ex parte Grissell* (1875), 3 Ch. D. 411 (C.A.); *Re Ormerod, Grierson & Co.*, [1890] W.N. 217.

The liquidator has no lien for his fees: *Ross v. Walker* (1899), 10 Que. P.R. 428 (C.A.).

Under s. 43, the court also determines the remuneration of the inspectors, if such have been appointed. Their remuneration will be based upon the services performed by them.

Discharge of liquidator

The Act contains no provision enabling the liquidator to apply for his discharge after completing the winding-up. No difficulty, however, arises in practice. The liquidator, having completed the winding up of the corporation's affairs, passes his accounts before the Master or Official Referee upon notice to all parties. The costs of the solicitors for the liquidator and for the creditors are taxed. After the accounts have been passed, and the sums remaining in the liquidator's hands for distribution have been paid out to the parties entitled, and proof of such payment has been furnished to the Master or Official Referee, the liquidator applies for and obtains an order directing his discharge and the cancellation of the liquidator's bond.

When the liquidator of an insurance corporation petitioned for his discharge, and it appeared that he had appropriated to himself from the funds received an amount exceeding the remuneration fixed by the court, and the evidence did not disclose the exact amount in which he was indebted to the estate, the court refused to grant his discharge without fixing the amount to be paid by him as a condition of obtaining his discharge: *Plender v. Fitzgerald* (1888), M.L.R. 5 Q.B. 446 (C.A.).

No action will lie against a liquidator as such after he has been discharged: *Toronto (City) v. Wade*, [1932] O.R. 500 (C.A.).

Dissolution of corporation

The Act contains no express provisions for the dissolution of the corporation upon completion of the winding up. It has been suggested that s. 19 of this Act (which provides that the corporation's corporate state shall continue until its affairs are wound up), by implication, operates to terminate the corporation's existence when the winding up has been completed; but it seems doubtful that the section has such effect. It is understood, however, that in the case of a federal corporation, when evidence is furnished to the Corporations Branch that the winding up has been completed and that the liquidator has been discharged, and when the letters patent are returned, the Corporations Branch will treat the corporation as dissolved.

Solicitors for a corporation that had been wound up entered an appearance on instructions from the former president, who had funds for distribution; the corporate defendant deemed to continue as party to the action because of the special circumstances: *C.R.F. Holdings Ltd. v. Fundy Chemical Int. Ltd.* (1980), 21 B.C.L.R. 345; vard on other grounds, [1982] 2 W.W.R. 385 (B.C. C.A.); leave to appeal to S.C.C. refused (1982), 42 N.R. 358 (*sub nom. Smerchanski v. C.R.F. Holdings Ltd.*).

Section 217 of the Ontario Act, which is applicable to Ontario corporations wound up under that Act, provides for the making of an order by the court after the business and affairs of the corporation have been fully wound up, on application by the liquidator or any other person interested, and the corporation is dissolved on the date fixed in the order. The effect of the predecessor section (which requires a general meeting of shareholders and a return to be filed with the Provincial Secretary) was held to be that the cannot go behind it unless it was established that the dissolution was obtained by fraud: *Christie v. Edwards*, [1939] O.R. 48 (C.A.), affd on this point by the Supreme Court of Canada, [1940] 3 D.L.R. 56 at 70.

Chapter 23

CONTRIBUTORIES

Section 50. List of contributories to be settled
Section 51. Classes of contributories distinguished
Section 52. Adding heirs of deceased contributory to list
Section 53. Liability of shareholders to contribute amount unpaid on shares
Section 54. Liability after transfer of shares
Section 55. Liability of contributory creates a debt
Section 56. Liability is provable against estate of a bankrupt or insolvent contributory
Section 57. Contributory may in certain events be ordered to hand over money and books
Section 58. Court may order payment by contributory of amounts due apart from calls under the Act
Section 59. When calls may be made on contributories
Section 60. Consideration by court of possible failure by some contributories to pay calls
Section 61. Court order for payment by contributory into bank
Section 62. The court is to adjust the rights of contributories among themselves

Cross references: Section 2
Ontario Act, ss. 191, 200, 203, 215(2), 225, 226.

Definition of contributory

The term "contributory" is defined in s. 2 of the Act as a person liable to contribute to the assets of a corporation under the Act. See the notes to that section in Chapter 19.

The cases that follow deal almost without exception with situations where a shareholder is alleged to owe money on the shares held by him. Most of the Business Corporations Acts in Canada (including the Federal Act) do not provide for the issue of partially paid shares (although a corporation can be continued under the Federal Act with partially paid shares), and accordingly, many of the cases will, strictly speaking, not be applicable. However, partially paid shares can exist under a number of federal statutes—for example, banks and insurance corporations, and certain corporations incorporated by private act or pursuant to provincial legislation. Accordingly, these cases are retained in this volume, although their usefulness is much diminished.

Cases dealing with procedural matters are still applicable even where the contributory is not a shareholder. Note that under the definition, a "contributory" is a person liable to contribute to the assets, and this could include a director who has acquiesced in an improper dividend or in other like cases (see the notes under the heading "Director's liability" in the comment, *supra*, at Chapter 8).

The Federal Act by s. 25(3) provides that a share is not to be issued until the consideration for the share is fully paid in (a) money or (b) property or past service that is not less in value than the money that the corporation would have received if the share had been issued the money. *Quaere* whether, if the share had been issued for property that violates the requirements of the section, some liability might attach to the holder of the share or shares, at least if he were the original shareholder and took the shares with the knowledge of the violation. The Act is silent on the point; but, for example, under s. 38(4) of the Federal Act by s. 25(3), a creditor is entitled to apply to a court for an order compelling a shareholder to repay amounts improperly distributed pursuant to a reduction of capital. Note that under s. 118(1) of the Act, a director will be liable for an improper issue of shares, but any action in such regard must be brought within two years of the date of the resolution authorizing the issue (s. 118(7)).

Settling list of contributories

The liquidator is required to make out a list of the contributories of the corporation from the corporate records received by him. The list is to contain the name, address and description of each of the contributories, and (if a shareholder) the number of shares in respect of which each contributory appears to be liable. After making this list, he should obtain an order from the court (a) appointing a date and time for settling the list of contributories and (b) directing service of a copy of the order, a copy of the winding-up order, and of the order of reference and the list of contributories prepared in accordance with s. 50 on all the persons whose names appear on it. The order usually provides for service by registered mail. The order further provides that any person who objects to being fixed on the list as a contributory is to file and serve on the liquidator, by a certain date, his defence or contestation setting out the grounds of his defence; and that in default of defence the persons appearing on the list will be settled on it without further notice.

Upon the return of the appointment before the Master or Referee the liquidator should attend with an affidavit of service, in accordance with the orders above mentioned and with the requisite documents to prove the liability of the contributories where necessary. If any person objects to being fixed on the list, it is usual to fix a special day for hearing the case. At the hearing, the evidence to fix the alleged contributory on the list is first produced by the liquidator, and then the alleged contributory produces his evidence in opposition. It is not the practice in Ontario, as it has been in England, for the liquidator himself to sit judicially to determine whether the alleged contributory ought or ought not to be settled upon the list, but the liquidator brings into the office of the Master to whom the reference in the winding-up has been assigned a list of such contributories as from the books he alleges ought to be settled upon such list; and these persons are thereupon, after the notice above mentioned, heard before the Master and their rights determined. From the decision of the Master so given, an appeal lies to the court, as in ordinary cases. Upon hearing the case, the Master may issue an order or report embodying his decision with respect to the question and awarding costs to either party. As to the practice in Quebec, see *Citizens Insurance Co. v. Montreal Trust & Deposit Co.* (1904), 6 Que. P.R. 275; *Banque de St. Jean v. Bienvenue* (1908), 10 Que. P.R. 223; *Frank v. Boston Shoe Co.* (1915), 24 Que. K.B. 267 (C.A.); *Compagnie d'Immeubles v. St.-Amour* (1920), 59 Que. S.C. 391.

As to the principles to be followed in settling contributories on the list, see *Re Atlas Loan Co.* (1903), 3 O.W.R. 604. For the effect of laches by the liquidator, see *Re Ontario Bank* (1912), 27 O.L.R. 192 at 202 (C.A.) (delay by liquidator in adding name to the list did not create estoppel); *Deslongchamps v. Lord* (1922), 34 Que. K.B. 134 (C.A.) (liquidator neglected to ask the court to settle the list, and court did so at the request of a creditor and one of the inspectors).

The provisional liquidator has no power to prepare the list of contributories: *Villeneuve Co. v. Price Bros. Ltd.* (1909), 36 Que. S.C. 395. It has been held in Quebec that each contributory has a right to a complete list: *Banque de St. Jean v. Bienvenue, supra.* The several members of a partnership firm are contributories in respect of a balance due on shares held by the firm: *Re Distributors Co.* (1909), 13 O.W.R. 735.

The mere fact that a corporation has commenced business before it was legally entitled to do so does not entitle shareholders to be struck off the list of contributories: *Re Western Canadian Fire Insurance Co.; Craig's Case* (1914), 19 D.L.R. 170; so also as regards shareholders of a bank that never became entitled to begin business: *Re Monarch Bank of Canada* (1914), 32 O.L.R 207 (C.A.).

Shareholders who have not subscribed for their shares, but have obtained them as fully paid by transfer from the original allottee, cannot be placed on the list of contributories in an action by the liquidator for calls: *National Trust Co. v. Frank*, [1917] 3 W.W.R. 43, and cases cited.

The liquidator and the court must proceed in the manner provided by the Act. Thus it has been held that the liquidator cannot by petition pray to have the persons therein named declared contributories, and cannot have them summoned to hear themselves so declared contributories: *Frank v. Boston Shoe Co.* (1915), 24 Que. K.B. 267 (C.A.).

If at the time of settling the list, a contributory is dead, the list should be amended by the substitution of the personal representatives of the contributory upon due notice to them of an application for that purpose. If this is not done, the executors or administrators have a valid defence on that ground: *Re Canadian Cordage & Mfg. Co.* (1923), 54 O.L.R. 486. For further proceedings to enforce liability, see the notes to s. 55 under the heading "Nature of liability of contributory" in this chapter.

A holder of fully paid shares may be placed on the list of contributories on the application of the liquidator or on his own application: *Re Monarch Bank of Canada* (1914), 32 O.L.R. 207, per Maclaren, J.A., at 213; *Re Colonial Assurance Co.* (1916), 29 D.L.R. 488; *Christie v. Edwards*, [1939] O.R. 48 at 52, and cases cited; [1940] O.R. 28 at 32 (C.A.) and [1940] S.C.R. 410; *Re Aidall Ltd.*, [1933] Ch. 323 at 333, (where it is possible that surplus assets will be distributable to the shareholders); *Pe Ben Pipelines Ltd.* (1978), 90 D.L.R. (3d) 262 (Alta. T.D.). If, however, the corporation is insolvent and there is nothing distributable to the shareholders, a fully paid shareholder is entitled to object to being put on the list of contributories for the purpose of giving the court jurisdiction over him as a debtor of the corporation: *Re Marlborough Club Co.* (1868), L.R. 5 Eq. 365.

When an alleged contributory claims that some other person is liable in his stead, he should bring such other person before the court: *Re European Arbitration; Thomas Brown's Case* (1872), 17 Sol. Jo. 289.

But if he is entitled to have his name removed, the mere fact that there is no person who can be substituted, will not prevent him from enforcing his right; as, for instance, in *Re Joint Stock Discount Co.; Fyfe's Case* (1869), 4 Ch. App. 768, where the transferee was dead and had no legal representative; or as in *Re European Assn. Soc.; Bentinck's Case* (1873), 18 Sol. Jo. 224, where shares had been transferred to an infant and the transferor could not be found, and the infant's name was struck off. And see *Re Imperial Mercantile Credit Assn.; Curtis's Case* (1868), L.R. 6 Eq. 455; *Re Commercial Bank Corp. of India; Wilson's Case* (1873), L.R. 8 Eq. 455; *Re Central Bank & Hogg* (1890), 19 O.R. 77, all cases where infants were successful in having their names removed from the list.

As to the limitation on the power of the liquidator under the English Act to vary the list of contributories after it has been finally settled, see *Re Westways Garage, Ltd.*, [1942] Ch. 356.

Jurisdiction of master or referee

Under the usual order of delegation under s. 111, the Master or Referee may settle the list of contributories: *Clarke v. Union Fire Insurance Co.* (1889), 16 O.A.R. 161 at 167; *Shoolbred v. Clarke; Re Union Fire Insurance Co.* (1890), 17 S.C.R. 265 at 280; *Re Farmers Bank of Canada; Lindsay's Case* (1916), 35 O.L.R. 470 at 473.

Where the court's powers have been delegated to a local Master, such officer has jurisdiction in settling the list of contributories, to inquire whether shares, in respect of which certificates are held purporting to be fully paid up, have in fact had anything paid thereon: *Re Cornwall Furniture Co.* (1909), 18 O.L.R. 101 (C.A.). In the absence of fraud, however, neither the court nor the delegated officer will inquire into the adequacy of any consideration taken by the corporation in lieu of money payment for the shares: *Re Hess Mfg. Co.* (1894), 23 S.C.R. 644 at 653, as explained in *Re Cornwall Furniture Co., supra; Hood v. Eden* (1905), 36 S.C.R. 476.

Costs of contributories

If a contributory successfully resists the application to put him on the list, he will be entitled to costs out of the estate: *Re Joint Stock Discount Co.; Nation's Case* (1866), L.R. 3 Eq. 77; *Ship's Case* (1865), 13 W.R. 450; *Re London Hamburg & Continental Exchange Bank; Emmerson's Case* (1866), 1 Ch. App. 433; *Re Limehouse Works Co.; Coate's Case* (1873), L.R. 17 Eq. 169; *Re Hercules Ins. Co.; Lowe's Case* (1870), L.R. 9 Eq. 589. Even when the contributory is unsuccessful, in some cases costs have been allowed. See *Re Metropolitan Public Carriage & Repository Co.; Cleland's Case* (1872), L.R. 14 Eq. 387, where the decision turned on the construction of a new statute; *Re Bank of London Assurance Assn.; Part's Case* (1870), L.R. 10 Eq. 622, which was a test case; *Walker's Case* (1866), L.R. 2 Eq. 554; *Re Imperial Land Co. of Marseilles; Jeaffreson, Ex parte* (1871), L.R. 11 Eq. 109; *Re Mutual Society; Grimwade v. Mutual Soc.* (1881), 18 Ch. D. 530. But except in special circumstances, when a contributory contests his liability and fails he must pay the costs: *Re London & Provincial Starch Co.; Gower's Case* (1868), L.R. 6 Eq. 77; *Re Birbeck Life Assurance Co.* (1865), 2 Dr. & Sm. 321; *Re Overend, Gurney & Co.; Musgrave & Hart's Case* (1867), L.R. 5 Eq. 193; *Re Barned's Banking Co.; Andrew's Case* (1867), 3 Ch. App. 161; *Oakes & Peek, Ex parte* (1867), L.R. 3 Eq. 576 at 633.

As to the costs of the liquidator, see the notes to ss. 33-40 in Chapter 22.

A person whose name has been wrongly placed on the list of contributories does not, by delaying in making application to have it removed, thereby raise an equity against his right to have his name removed but in such circumstances he is not entitled to costs: *Re Mexican & South American Co.; Shewell's Case* (1867), 2 Ch. App. 387; *Re Joint Stock Co.; Fyfe's Case* (1869), 4 Ch. App. 768; *Re Alexandra Park Co.; Hart's Case* (1868), L.R. 6 Eq. 512; *Re United Ports & General Ins. Co.; Nelson's Case*, [1874] W.N. 196.

In the case of a bank, those who have held shares that have not been fully paid before the suspension would be liable as contributories: *Re Central Bank of Canada; Baines' Case* (1889), 16 A.R. 237; *Re Ontario Bank* (1912), 27 O.L.R. 192. And a person to whom such shares are transferred is also liable: *Re Central Bank* (1889), 17 O.R. 110. In the case of a building society that had made advances to members on the security of real estate, it was held that the mortgagee members were not liable to be placed on the list of contributories: *Re Saint John Building Society* (1889), 28 N.B.R. 597 (C.A.).

Under former Bank Acts, shareholders of a bank were under double liability, that is, each shareholder was liable for the bank's deficiency to an amount equal to the par value of the shares held by him, in addition to any amount not paid up on such shares.

For an instance of double liability under the terms of a particular statute, see *Re Provincial Building Society* (1891), 30 N.B.R. 628 (C.A.).

A director of a corporation owning partly paid-up shares therein transferred some of such shares to another director, the sums paid up on all the shares being attributed to the retained shares by informal agreement between these two directors and another. A new certificate was issued with respect to the retained shares, bearing an endorsement as to the agreed amount paid up thereon. It was held that the liquidator of the corporation was right in placing the original owner of shares upon the list of contributories, and in treating the retained shares as if only the original payments had been made thereon: *Re Federal Mortgage Corp. & Stewart*, [1917] 2 W.W.R. 52.

Nature of liability of contributory (s. 55)

After a winding-up order, the liability to contribute no longer depends on the original contract alone but is a statutory liability resulting from s. 55.

It had been held under the Bankruptcy Acts of England that the liability to pay calls that had not been made at the date of the adjudication was not a debt payable presently or at a future time; and that accordingly, such calls could not be proved against the bankrupt's estate: *South Staffordshire Ry. v. Burnside* (1851), 5 Exch. 129; *General Discount Co. v. Stokes* (1864), 17 C.B.N.S. 765. And the same principle applied whether the call was made by a continuing corporation or under the Winding-up Acts: ibid.

The section of the English Act corresponding to s. 55 was intended to meet these decisions, and also to remove the difficulties arising from the conflict of the decisions: see *Re Warwick & Worcester Ry; Parburv's Case* (1861), 3 De G.F. & J. 80; *Chapple's Case* (1852), 5 De G. & Sm. 400; *Re Liverpool Marine Assurance Co.; Greenshield's Case* (1852), 5 De G. & Sm. 599.

It has also been held under the section that the liability of a contributory to calls commenced when he became a member: *Re Vaughan; Canwell, Ex parte* (1864), De G.J. & Sm. 539; but the question is not free from doubt, cf. *Maritime Bank v. Troop* (1888), 16 S.C.R. 456 at 471.

No action lies in respect of a claim for an unpaid balance owing on shares where the contributory has already been settled on the list and the liquidator is in a position to enforce payment by execution against the executors of the contributory: *Re Dominion Permanent Loan Co.* (1926), 7 C.B.R. 420 (Ont. S.C.).

Bankruptcy or insolvency of contributory (s. 56)

Section 56 provides that in the case of the bankruptcy or insolvency of any contributory, the estimated value of his liability to future calls, as well as calls already made, may be proved against his estate.

Under a corresponding statutory provision of an earlier English Act, it has been held that if the winding-up preceded the shareholder's bankruptcy, all future calls might be proved against his estate; but that when he was adjudicated bankrupt before the winding-up, calls made in the winding-up could not be proved at all: *Financial Corp. Ltd. v. Lawrence* (1869), L.R. 4 C.P. 731; *Pickering, Ex parte* (1868), 4 Ch. App. 58; *Re Bank of Hindustan, China & Japan; Mitchell's Case* (1870), 5 Ch. App. 400; *Re Land Credit Co. of Ireland, McEwen's Case* (1871), 6 Ch. App. 582; *Marshall, Ex Parte* (1872), 7 Ch. App. 324.

Contributory may in certain events be ordered to hand over money and books (s. 57)

After a winding-up order has been made, the court may require any contributory settled on the list "as" trustee, receiver, banker, agent or officer of the corporation, to hand over any money and books that are in his hands and to which the corporation is *prima facie* entitled (s. 57).

The word "as" before the words "trustee, receiver, banker, agent or officer" in s. 57 may be a misprint for the word "or" as ordinarily the type of person described would not be on the list of contributories. Cf. the comparable provision in the English Act (s. 258) which read "and any".

These summary powers cannot be exercised against a person who is not a contributory, trustee, receiver, banker, agent or officer of the corporation: *Re United English & Scottish Assurance Co.; Hawkins, Ex parte* (1868), L.R. 3 Ch. App. 787; *Hollingsworth's Case* (1849), 3 De G. & Sm. 102; *Cox's Case* (1850), 3 De G. & Sm. 180; *Re Imperial Land Co. of Marseilles; Re National Bank* (1870), L.R. 10 Eq. 298; *Re Northfield Iron & Steel Co.*, [1866] W.N. 253; *Grant v. British Canadian Lumber Co.* (1891), 18 S.C.R. 708 (order made against agent of corporation).

The following cases show that the court will exercise these summary powers whenever it can do so without injustice: *Re Caerphilly Colliery Co; Pearson's Case* (1877), 5 Ch. D. 336 (C.A.); *Re Morvah Consols. Tin Mining Co.; McKay's Case* (1875), 2 Ch. D. 1 (C.A.); *Re Mercantile Trading Co.; Stringer's Case* (1869), 4 Ch. App. 475; *Re County Marine Ins. Co.; Rance's Case* (1871), 6 Ch. App. 104; *Cardiff Preserved Coal & Coke Co. v. Norton* (1867), 2 Ch. App. 405. In the earlier cases it was held that these powers ought to be exercised with the greatest hesitancy; but in the later cases the power was exercised more freely.

In *Re British Imperial Corp.* (1877), 5 Ch. D. 749, leave was given to serve a summons out of the jurisdiction. This section has been held not to apply to persons residing out of the jurisdiction: *British Canadian Lumbering v. Grant* (1887), 12 P.R. 301. See, however, s. 112 of this Act providing for service out of the jurisdiction.

Court may order payment of amounts due by contributories (s. 58)

Under s. 58, the court may order the payment of amounts due by contributories to the corporation, apart from amounts due under calls made in the winding-up.

The procedure authorized by s. 58 is a summary statutory proceeding in lieu of an action commenced by writ: *Ex parte Whinney* (1884), 13 Q.B.D. 476 at 478. The section excludes calls made in the winding-up, which are governed by s. 59, but would include a call made before the winding-up: *Re Whitehouse & Co.* (1878), 9 Ch. D. 595 at 601. The nature of the remedy under the section is discussed by Lindley, L.J., in *Westmoreland Green & Blue Slate Co. v. Feilden*, [1891] 3 Ch. 15 at 25 (C.A.). The summary procedure authorized by the section is optional and not obligatory: *Masecar v. McKenzie & Son*, [1924] 2 D.L.R. 1242 (Sask. C.A.), and cases cited. The court has power under this section and s. 124 to order a contributory or a director to repay a dividend declared and paid under a delusive and fraudulent balance sheet: *Re Mercantile Trading Co.; Stringer's Case* (1869), 4 Ch. App. 475.

The jurisdiction to make a summary order under the section does not arise until a list of contributories has been settled, and the order can only be made against a person whose name is placed on the list: *Masecar v. McKenzie & Son, supra*.

If the corporation is insolvent and there is nothing distributable to the shareholders, a fully paid shareholder is entitled to object to being put on the list of contributories for the purpose of giving the court jurisdiction under s. 58 as a debtor of the corporation: *Re Marlborough Club Co.* (1868), L.R. 5 Eq. 365. A fully paid shareholder may, however, be put on the list of contributories: *Re Monarch Bank of Canada* (1914), 32 O.L.R. 207 at 217 (C.A.); *Re Colonial Assurance Co.* (1916), 29 D.L.R. 488; and where it is possible that surplus assets will be distributable to the shareholders, fully paid shareholders ought to be placed on the list of contributories: *Re Aidall Ltd.*, [1933] Ch. 323 at 333 (C.A.). In that case it was held that the jurisdiction under the provision rests on the fact of the person being settled on the list; and that a fully paid shareholder settled on the list, having received too large a sum on a distribution knowing that provision had not been made for a debt of the corporation, may be ordered to pay the amount of the debt to the liquidator.

Calls in winding-up

After the list of contributories has been settled, calls may be levied upon contributories whose names appear on the list, pursuant to the provisions of s. 59; and for that purpose the liquidator should bring before the Master an affidavit setting forth the facts on which to found an order for the call. If the call is not paid, the court gives judgment directing payment, and on further default execution may be issued.

The settling of the list of contributories is a condition precedent to the making of a call: *Re English Bank of the River Plate*, [1892] 1 Ch. 391.

As to the meaning of "debts and liabilities" as used in s. 59, see *Re Contract Corp.* (1866), 2 Ch. App. 95 and *Re Barned's Banking Co.; Contract Corp., Ex parte* (1867), 3 Ch. App. 105.

The discretion of the Master as to the quantum of a call will not be interfered with on appeal without strong grounds being shown for so doing: *Re Barned's Banking Co., supra.* The court will not on appeal from the Master enter upon an enquiry as to whether or not the whole of the amount due should be paid: *Re Home Bank of Canada* (1926), 59 O.L.R. 654 (C.A.). An order making a call, after payment of which there would still remain an unpaid liability on shares, should not refer to the call as a "final call", even though no further calls are anticipated: *Re City of London Insurance Co.*, [1932] 1 Ch. 226.

The liability of the contributory under the Act commences on the date of the call, until which time the Statute of Limitations does not commence to run: *Re Johnston Bros. Ltd.* (1920), 29 B.C.R. 183.

Under the English Act, which contains no provision similar to that in s. 60(2) to the effect that no call shall compel payment of a debt before the maturity thereof, a contract for payment for shares by instalments is determined by the winding-up, and the liquidator is entitled to make an immediate call: *Re Cordova Union Gold Co.*, [1891] 2 Ch. 580. Under the Act, contracts for payment for shares in a special manner, for example, otherwise than in cash, are terminated by the winding-up: *Re Wiarton Beet Sugar Co.* (1905), 5 O.W.R. 542. And it may be that the same reasoning applies to a contract for payment by instalments: *Re Imperial Canadian Trust Co. & McKeague*, [1929] 4 D.L.R. 381 (Man. C.A.); *Re National Stadium Ltd.* (1924), 55 O.L.R. 199 at 204. However, in *Re Victoria & Montreal Fire Insurance Co.* (1904), 26 Que. S.C. 282, decided under the former s. 49 (corresponding to ss. 59 and 60 of the present Act), it was held that the liquidator could not with or without the authorization of the court make calls of such a nature as to make the obligations of the contributories more onerous than provided in the charter; and in *Re Alliance Investment Co.*, [1919] 1 W.W.R. 17, decided under the present section, it was held that leave will not be granted to call up the whole balance unpaid on shares where the time fixed for payment under the application has not arrived. This latter decision was overruled by the Supreme Court of Canada in *Burton v. Contributories of Home Assurance Co. of Canada*, [1950] S.C.R. 591. In that case the liquidator applied to the court for an order making a call on each of the shareholders for 100 per cent of the amounts for which they were respectively settled upon the list of contributories; and it was contended that the "maturity of the debt" referred to in s. 60(2) was determined by certain provisions of the Alberta Insurance Act and that calls must be made in the amounts and at the intervals specified in that Act. The majority of the court took the view that the "maturity of the debt" was the time set by the court in making the calls and not the time as determined by the Alberta Insurance Act, and consequently, that calls could be made on the contributories for the full balance still owing on each share.

In the case of a corporation governed by the provisions of the *Alberta Companies Act*, R.S.A. 1922, c. 156, s. 47 of which provided that in the event of a corporation being wound up, every present and past member was to be liable to contribute to the assets of the corporation to an amount (not exceeding the amount unpaid on his shares) sufficient for payment of the debts and liabilities — the effect of the section was held to be that upon a winding-up, any provisions (whether appearing in the articles or by express agreement) postponing payment for the shares beyond the commencement of the winding-up proceedings were abrogated; and that the shareholder was bound to pay in accordance with the provisions of the statute governing the winding-up. So a contributory of an insolvent Alberta corporation being wound up under the *Bankruptcy Act* was bound to pay immediately the balance owing upon his shares, although instalments under the subscription contract were not due: *Re Irma Co-operative Co.*, [1925] 1 D.L.R. 27.

In New Brunswick it has been held that an attachment of the person for non-payment of money ordered by a judge to be paid under s. 61 should be granted by the judge who made the order: *St. John Building Society, Ex parte; Haggart's Case* (1890), 30 N.B.R. 251 (C.A.).

As to suing for judgment on a call made in a winding-up, see *Maritime Trust Co. v. Alcock* (1916), 22 B.C.R. 399.

As to suing for the balance due on shares a person who is not entered on the register, see *Masecar v. McKenzie & Son*, [1924] 2 D.L.R. 1242 (Sask. C.A.).

As to set-off, see the notes to s. 73 under the heading "Shareholders" in Chapter 24.

Under s. 77(2) of the *Bankruptcy and Insolvency Act*, the amount that the contributory is liable to contribute is a debt payable to the trustee forthwith upon the bankruptcy of the corporation.

Adjustment of rights of contributories among themselves (s. 62)

The need to adjust the rights of contributories among themselves may arise from the fact that some shareholders have paid more than others on their shares. See *Re Monarch Bank of Canada* (1914), 32 O.L.R. 207 (C.A.). In that winding-up, it was found that some subscribers had paid in full, and others varying proportions on their shares, and that the whole nominal share capital subscribed was not required for meeting creditors' claims. The liquidator accordingly made a call for the purpose of equalization on all subscribers who had paid less than one half on their subscriptions.

As well, the above section is frequently applied when holders of preferred shares have a prior right to a return of capital in a winding-up, and a surplus of assets is realized, as to which see s. 95 of this Act and the notes under the heading "Preference as to return of capital and rights on distribution of surplus assets" in Chapter 5. As indicated in the last-mentioned notes, where there are several classes of shares, their respective rights will depend on the articles, letters patent and by-laws or memorandum and articles. If these contain provisions as to the rights of any class on a winding-up, such provisions will be exhaustive: *Scottish Insurance Corp. v. Wilsons & Clyde Coal Co.*, [1949] A.C. 462; *Prudential Assurance Co. v. Chatterley-Whitfield Collieries Co.*, [1949] A.C. 512; *Re Isle of Thanet Electric Supply Co.*, [1950] Ch. 161.

In the absence of a contrary provision regulating the distribution of surplus assets, where there are fully paid and partly paid shares, so much of the uncalled capital must be called up or treated as called up as is necessary to equalize the capital account and the balance distributed among the shareholders in proportion to the number of shares held by them respectively: *Re Hodge's Distillery Co., Maude, Ex parte* (1870), 6 Ch. App. 51; *Birch v. Cropper; Re Bridgewater Navigation Co.* (1889), 14 App. Cas. 525; *Re Anglo-Continental Corp of Western Australia*, [1898] 1 Ch. 327. The rule may be excluded by apt words in the provisions: *Re Kinatan (Borneo) Rubber Ltd.*, [1923] 1 Ch. 124. In adjusting the rights of contributories *inter se*, holders of shares issued at a discount (unauthorized by law) are treated as holders of partly paid shares and are liable for the amount unpaid: *Re Weymouth & Channel Islands Steam Packet Co.*, [1891] 1 Ch. 66; *Welton v. Saffery*, [1897] A.C. 299.

Where some shareholders have made payment on their shares in advance of calls, such shareholders are entitled, on a return of capital, to repayment of the amount so paid plus interest before other holders of shares of equal rank receive anything: *Re Exchange Drapery Co.* (1888), 38 Ch. D. 171; *Re Wakefield Rolling Stock Co.*, [1892] 3 Ch. 165 at 174.

In the following cases, calls were made on holders of partly paid shares for the purpose of adjusting rights between them and the holders of fully paid shares: *Re Holyford Mining Co.* (1867), 3 I.R. Eq. 208; *Re Anglesea Colliery Co.* (1867), L.R. 2 Eq. 379; *Re Scinde, Punjaub & Delhi Corp.* (1871), 6 Ch. App. 53n; *Re Provision Merchants' Co.* (1872), 26 L.T. 862; *Re Coed Madog Slate Co.*, [1877] W.N. 190.

The jurisdiction of the court under a section such as s. 62 is to adjust the right of contributories *qua* contributories only: *Re Alexandra Palace Co.* (1883), 23 Ch. D. 297.

As to distribution of profits earned before and after liquidation, see *Bishop v. Smyrna & Cassaba Ry. Co.*, [1895] 2 Ch. 265; and *Re Bridgewater Navigation Co.*, [1891] 2 Ch. 317, which decision was said not to be in conflict with *Birch v. Cropper, supra*, in *Re Canada Trust Co. & Guelph Trust Co.*, [1950] O.R. 245, at 251.

Liability of shareholders to contribute

The application of s. 53 is limited to shareholders or members: *Tremblay v. Vermette*, [1959] S.C.R. 690; *Re Winnipeg Hedge & Wire Fence Co.* (1912), 1 D.L.R. 316. See also *Re Wiarton Beet Sugar Co.* (1906), 12 O.L.R. 149 at 152; *Re Monarch Bank of Canada* (1914), 32 O.L.R. 207; *Re Central Bank of Canada* (1888), 15 O.R. 625. Where shares are held by A in trust for B the latter is not a contributory: *Re Great Wheal Busy Mining Co.; King's Case* (1871), 6 Ch. App. 196; *Re Winnipeg Hedge & Wire Fence Co., supra*. An equitable mortgagee of shares is not a contributory: *Re Joint Stock Discount Co.; Sichell's Case* (1867), 3 Ch. App. 119.

As to liability of members of an incorporated club who seek to resign while dues are unpaid, see *Re Cedar Brook Golf & Country Club Ltd.* (1936), 18 C.B.R. 34 (decision of Registrar).

It should be noted, however, that some of the defences open to a person where the corporation seeks to enforce his liability to it as a shareholder, are not available in proceedings by a liquidator after a winding-up has occurred and the rights of creditors and other contributories have intervened. For example, a shareholder cannot, after a winding-up order, escape liability on the ground that his subscription was induced by fraud: *Oakes v. Turquand & Harding* (1867), L.R. 2 H.L. 325; *Kent v. Freehold Land Co. & Brick-Making Co.* (1868), 3 Ch. App. 493; *Re Central Bank of Canada* (1889), 17 O.R. 110 at 117; *Stephens v. Riddell* (1910), 21 O.L.R. 484; or by setting up that the winding-up order has been made under a mistake of law: *Re Arthur Average Assn.* (1876), 3 Ch. D. 522. On the other hand, the rule in *Oakes v. Turquand & Harding, supra*, has no application where there has never been a concluded agreement to take shares, or where the agreement, though concluded in fact, is in point of law a nullity: *Re Northwestern Trust Co.*, [1926] S.C.R. 412 at 419. Thus, where the name of a person has been recorded on the books of the corporation as a shareholder in pursuance of an agreement that is wholly void, that person will not be liable as a contributory in the absence of acts constituting an independent contract under which he might be made liable: *Re London & Northern Ins. Corp.; Stace & Worth's Case* (1869), 4 Ch. App. 682; *Re Oriental Commercial Bank, Alabaster's Case* (1868), L.R. 7 Eq. 273 at 284; *Re Lake Ontario Navigation Co.* (1910), 20 O.L.R. 191 at 195 (C.A.) (sufficient if shareholder promptly repudiates so that he does not become liable by estoppel). In *Re Home Assurance Co. of Canada; Patterson v. Burton*, [1950] S.C.R. 578, the conduct of the holders of shares was such that they were held liable as contributories even though the original contracts of sale of the shares to them were void.

Once a winding-up order is made, the liability of a shareholder in no way depends upon the terms of the contract under which he took his shares; the sole question then is whether he is in fact a shareholder owing a balance on his shares, and the Statute of Limitations is no answer to the statutory liability of the shareholder under the section: *Imperial Canadian Trust Co. v. McKeague*, [1929] 4 D.L.R. 381 (Man. C.A.).

With regard to liability to the extent of the amount unpaid in respect of the contributory's shares, the same questions arise as are discussed in the notes to s. 25 of the *Canada Business Corporations Act* in Chapter 5.

For the liability of executors and administrators of a deceased shareholder, and of beneficiaries holding under an unregistered transfer, see *Clarkson v. McLean* (1918), 42 O.L.R. 1.

Liability after transfer (s. 54)

The general rule is that where a person has transferred his shares, and the transferee has been registered as the holder thereof, the transferor is no longer to be regarded as a shareholder and cannot be made a contributory: *Re Winnipeg Hedge & Wire Fence Co.* (1912), 1 D.L.R. 316, approved and followed in *Tremblay v. Vermette*, [1959] S.C.R. 690 at 699.

Unless a past shareholder is subjected to liability by the Act under the authority of which the corporation is created, or by some Act relating to it, he cannot be placed on the list of contributories: *Re Wiarton Beet Sugar Co.* (1906), 12 O.L.R. 149, approved and followed in *Tremblay v. Vermette, supra.*

Section 54 provides that a shareholder who has transferred his shares will still be liable as a contributory if the transfer did not by law free him from liability (see below), or if he is by law liable to the corporation or its creditors for an amount over and above the amount unpaid on his shares.

Thus, there will still be liability on past members who have transferred their shares in circumstances that do not by law free them from liability in respect thereof — for example, when the transfer has been fraudulent or collusive to avoid liability. In *Tremblay v. Vermette*, [1959] S.C.R. 690, Locke, J., said at 701 that the reference in s. 54 to transfers made in circumstances that do not by law free the shareholder from liability in respect of the shares presumably relates to transfers that may be impeached for, *inter alia*, fraud or other irregularity. It also provides that if any shareholder "is by law liable to the company or its members or creditors beyond the amount unpaid on his shares he shall be deemed a member." This provision will cover such cases as were dealt with in *Re Maria Anna & Steinbank Coal & Coke Co.; Hill's Case* (1875), L.R. 20 Eq. 585; *Peninsular Co. v. Fleming* (1872), 27 L.T. 93; *Re Maria Anna & Steinbank Coal & Coke Co.; McKewan's Case* (1877), 6 Ch. D. 447 (C.A.).

Chapter 24

CREDITORS

Section 96. Contracts made without consideration during three months preceding liquidation are presumed to be with intent to defraud creditors
Section 97. Contracts injuring or obstructing creditors are presumed in certain events to be with intent to defraud creditors
Section 98. Contracts injuring or obstructing creditors made within 30 days preceding liquidation are voidable
Section 99. Contracts made with intent to defraud or delay creditors in certain events are void
Section 100. Sales or transfers involving unjust preference to creditor are void
Section 101. Certain payments made by the corporation within thirty days next before the commencement of the winding-up are void
Section 102. Debts of the corporation transferred to contributories or persons indebted to the corporation are not to be set-off

Cross references: Sections 2, 11, 19, 21, 22, 38, 59, 121, 133, 135
Ontario Act, s. 220.

Meetings of creditors, contributories and shareholders

Under s. 63, the court may direct meetings of the creditors, contributories, shareholders or members to be held for the purpose of ascertaining their wishes. Sections 63-69 contain certain provisions with regard to procedure and voting at such meetings. Under s. 152(2) meetings of creditors and shareholders must be held for this purpose prior to making a winding-up order with respect to a bank.

As to the action of the court when there is a conflict as to the appointment of a liquidator, see *Re Central Bank* (1887), 15 O.R. 309 (H.C.); *Re Alpha Oil Co.* (1887), 12 P.R. 298; *Forsythe v. Bank of Nova Scotia* (1889), 22 N.S.R. 97 (C.A.); *Re Commercial Bank of Manitoba* (1893), 9 Man. R. 342 (Q.B.); *Cloyes v. Darling* (1884), 16 R.L. 649.

If creditors pass resolutions that are not *bona fide* in the interests of the winding-up but are for some ulterior object, the liquidator may get the leave of the court to disregard the resolutions: *Ex parte Cocks; Re Poole* (1882), 21 Ch. D. 397 (C.A.). Compare *Ex parte Strawbridge*; *Re Hickman* (1883), 25 Ch. D. 266 (C.A.).

A proxy must stand or fall as at the date of the meeting: *Re Andrew Motherwell Ltd.* (1923), 4 C.B.R. 265 (Ont. S.C.) (evidence of subsequent confirmation excluded).

Creditors who do not attend after notice are presumed to be willing to be bound by the action of those who do attend: *Exchange Bank v. Campbell* (1885), 15 R.L. 373.

Compromises or arrangements

Prior to the passing of ss. 65 and 66, the only power to compromise claims against the corporation was that given by s. 38. The present ss. 65 and 66 provide that the court may, on application of the liquidator or any creditor of the corporation, order that a meeting of creditors (or of a class or classes of creditors) be called to consider a proposed compromise or arrangement of the type specified; and that, if a majority in number representing three quarters in value of such creditors represented in person or by proxy at such meeting agree to any such arrangement or compromise, such arrangement or compromise is, if sanctioned by an order of the court, binding on the creditors, the liquidator and the contributories.

Sections 65 and 66 are in supplement of s. 38, and do not modify it: *Ward v. Mullin* (1904), 14 Que. K.B. 49 (C.A.).

Compromises or arrangements between a corporation and its creditors may now be effected in certain events under the *Companies' Creditors Arrangement Act*, s. 6 of which provides that, when a corporation is in course of being wound up under the *Winding-up Act*, a compromise or arrangement sanctioned in the manner provided by that section is to be binding upon the liquidator and contributories. Section 19 of the *Companies' Creditors Arrangement Act* provides that ss. 65 and 66 of the *Winding-up Act* are not to apply to any compromise or arrangement to which the *Companies' Creditors Arrangement Act* applies.

Production of pass books

At every meeting of the contributories, creditors, shareholders or members, the liquidator is required to produce a bank pass book containing certain particulars (s. 69); and he is also required to produce the bank pass book whenever ordered to do so by the court (s. 70).

Creditors' claims

Right of creditors to rank

Under s. 71, all claims, present or future, certain or contingent, and for liquidated or unliquidated damages, may be proven against the corporation.

The definition of "creditor" contained in s. 2(e) is consistent with the provisions of s. 71 with regard to the proof of claims. It is the policy of the Act that all claims against the corporation are to be dealt with and disposed of in the winding-up proceedings. See s. 21 and the notes thereon in Chapter 21.

As to the right of creditors to interest, see the notes on the effect of a winding-up order on interest under the heading "Effect on interest on debts" in Chapter 21.

A secured creditor who realizes his security is entitled to apply the proceeds in or toward payment of principal, interest and costs: *Re London, Windsor & Greenwich Hotels Co.; Quartermaine's Case*, [1892] 1 Ch. 639. See the notes under the heading "Secured creditors" in this chapter.

For the distribution of bank assets where there is a surplus, see *Re Commercial Bank of Manitoba* (1894), 10 Man. R. 61 (Q.B.).

Where the relationship between a depositor and the corporation is that of creditor and debtor, the mere use of the term "in trust" in the agreement between the parties cannot change the character of the transaction, and the depositor is only entitled to rank as an ordinary creditor: *Re Bergethaler Waisenamt*, [1947] 2 D.L.R. 234 (Man. K.B.). Depositor creditors, if their claims do not arise out of *ultra vires* transactions, are entitled to rank along with other creditors: *Re Bergethaler Waisenamt*, [1949] 1 D.L.R. 769 (Man. C.A.). For a discussion of whether an emergency financial assistance arrangement constituted a loan or a capital investment, see *Canada Deposit Insurance Corp. v. Canadian Commercial Bank*, [1992] 3 S.C.R. 558.

A depositor whose deposit had been partially withdrawn is bound to rank: *Re Commercial Bank of Manitoba, supra.* Where a trust corporation had lost the power to receive money on deposit, depositors claiming for moneys on deposit prior to its losing such power were held to be entitled to payment in full before depositors claiming for deposits made after its losing such power: *Re Nippon Kinu Sha Ltd.* (1923), 3 C.B.R. 673 (B.C. S.C.). But where the relationship between the creditor and the insolvent corporation is not that of customer and banker, but principal and agent, moneys collected by the agent for the principal will be impressed with a trust, if traceable, in favour of the principal: *Re International Mercantile Agency Ltd.* (1906), 7 O.W.R. 795 (H.C.). For the right to rank as a claimant against a guaranteed fund which constituted a trust fund under the trust company legislation where the monies sent for this purpose were used for another purpose without authorization, see *Liquidator of Principal Savings and Trust Co. v. Smallwood* (1992), 6 Alta. L.R. (3d) 394 (Q.B.).

When a depositor had left a cheque with the president of a bank with instructions to draw the money out and invest it in a mortgage as soon as a suitable security could be found, and the president the day before the suspension drew the money out and put it in an envelope addressed to the depositor, it was held that the depositor must rank only as an ordinary creditor: *Re Commercial Bank of Manitoba* (1894), 10 Man. R. 61 (Q.B.).

Shareholders who had made a voluntary payment to the corporation's reserve fund were held not to be entitled to rank as creditors therefor: *Re Atlas Loan Co.* (1904), 7 O.L.R. 706 (H.C.); affd (1905), 9 O.L.R. 468 (C.A.). Shareholders who had surrendered their shares in the corporation in exchange for promissory notes of the corporation were held not to be entitled to rank as creditors in respect of such promissory notes: *Re Stodacona-Rouyn Mines Ltd.*, [1942] Que. S.C. 275.

When a judgment was recovered for damages against a corporation that went into liquidation, and the insurance corporation with which the corporation in liquidation was insured paid the amount of the damages to the liquidator, it was held that the money formed part of the assets of the corporation, and that the person who had recovered the judgment had no right to require the liquidator to hand the money over to him: *Re Harrington Motor Co.; Ex parte Chaplin*, [1928] Ch. 105 (C.A.). See also *Treverton v. Superintendant of Insurance* (1987), 62 O.R. (2d) 556 (H.C.).

Where parties in the position of trustees for a corporation have purchased claims against the corporation at a discount, they may rank for the face value of the claims but are entitled to receive dividends only to the extent of their actual payments made to acquire the claims: *Re Catholic Register; Ex parte Foy & Coffee* (February 10, 1900), (Ont. Master-in-Ordinary) (unreported); *Re Humber Ironworks Co.* (1869), L.R. 8 Eq. 122; *Ex parte Larking; Re Imperial Land Co. of Marseilles* (1877), 4 Ch. D. 566 (C.A.).

A liquidator may validly reject a claim founded upon an *ultra vires* contract, even though the claim has merged into a judgment against the corporation: *Re Jon Beauforte (London) Ltd.*, [1953] 1 Ch. 131.

Claims that are statute barred at the date of the winding-up order may not be paid by the liquidator: *Re Fleetwood & District Electric Light & Power Syndicate*, [1915] 1 Ch. 486; but the Statute of Limitations ceases to run against a creditor from the date of the winding-up order, and claims not then barred can be proved: *Re General Rolling Stock Co.; Joint Stock Discount Co.'s Claim* (1872), 7 Ch. App. 646 (a compulsory winding-up order had been made). It was held in the following cases that the same rule applies with equal force to a voluntary winding-up: *Re Fleetwood & District Electric Light & Power Syndicate, supra*; *Re Art Reproduction Co.*, [1952] Ch. 89; *Re Northern Ontario Power Co.*, [1954] O.W.N. 105 (Master); *Re Canada Tea Co.*, [1959] O.W.N. 378 (H.C.).

Where the claim of a foreign creditor for a debt due in foreign currency is converted into Canadian currency, the rate of exchange at which the conversion is to be made is the rate ruling on the date of the breach of contract that gave rise to the debt: *Re British American Continental Bank Ltd.; Goldzieher & Penso's Claim*, [1922] 2 Ch. 575 (C.A.); and where there is an account current, and the account is closed before the winding-up order, the date when the account is closed is the date of conversion: *Re British American Continental Bank; Credit General Liègeois' Claim*, [1922] 2 Ch. 589.

Nothing in this section alters or interferes with the *lex loci contractus*: *Re Harte v. Ontario Express & Transportation Co.* (1893), 22 O.R. 510 (Master).

Because the Act is silent as to the relevant ranking to be given to privileged creditors, result must be had, under s. 110 (now s. 109) of the Act, to the law of the jurisdiction in question. Thus, liquidation costs, including the liquidator's fee and costs of seizure incurred by a lessor should take precedence. Then follow provincial sales tax, provincial income tax and corporation tax, which are ranked equally; then a claim for municipal taxes; and then a claim for rent. Finally are payable federal claims for income tax and unemployment insurance contributions: *Re Kiddy's City Inc.* (1967), 12 C.B.R. (N.S.) 22 (Que. S.C.).

Present, future, certain or contingent claims

As already indicated, the claims that may be proven include present or future and certain or contingent claims (s. 71). Under s. 71(2), the court is to determine the amount for which contingent claims are to rank.

When the corporation has undertaken to indemnify a person against certain contingent liabilities, such person can prove in respect of the liability, though he has paid nothing: *Re Panther Lead Co.*, [1896] 1 Ch. 978; *Hardy v. Fothergill* (1888), 13 App. Cas. 351 (H.L.); *Re British Provident Life & Fire Assurance Co.; Anglo-Australian Co.'s Case* (1864), 10 L.T. 326; *Re National Financial Co.; Ex parte Oriental Commercial Bank* (1868), 3 Ch. App. 791.

So in the case of a surety: *Ex parte Delmar; Re Herepath and Delmar* (1890), 38 W.R. 752.

And a guarantor who has not paid anything under his guarantee has a right to prove in respect of his contingent liability: In *Re Blackpool Motor Car Co.; Hamilton v. Blackpool Motor Car Co.*, [1901] 1 Ch. 77. In *Re Stratford Fuel,*

Ice & Construction Co. (1913), 28 O.L.R. 481 (C.A.), affd (*sub nom. Brown v. Coughlin)* (1914), 50 S.C.R. 100, the position of guarantors on a bond limited in amount for the ultimate balance due to a bank by the corporation, which later became insolvent, was considered. The bond was in the common form permitting compounding with the corporation, the primary debtor, and taking and giving up securities without releasing the guarantors. In pursuance of the terms of settlement of litigation between the bank and the liquidator in respect of this and other securities held by the bank, it was agreed *inter alia* that the bank was not to rank upon the estate; that the bond in question should be declared valid; that the bank reserved all its rights against all securities in its hands and against the guarantors. The claimants, the guarantors, sought to rank against the estate of the corporation in respect of the payments that they had made to the bank under the guarantee. The guarantors were held entitled to rank, for they had a right to prove that had not been taken away by the dealings between the bank and the primary debtor. It was further held that it is not double proof, but double ranking so as to compel the payment of two dividends for the same debt, that is objectionable; that even if there could be no double proof, the estate was not wound up; and that as the creditor had been paid in full, the sureties could prove for the amount of the debt paid by them. See also, as to double ranking, *Ontario Bank v. Chaplin* (1891), 20 S.C.R. 152.

In Northland Bank (in Liquidation) v. Kocken et al. (B.C.C.A.), an unreported judgment handed down on April 2, 1993 (Vancouver Registry 13560), there was a dispute by a debtor to the bank alleging a counterclaim with a right of set off against the claim by the bank. After discussing the matter the Court held that despite the factual difficulties with their position, the debtors were entitled to their day in court and the counter-claim by the debtors was directed to be set down for trial.

The winding-up order will not prevent a contingent liability of the corporation from ripening into a debt: *Re Northern Counties of England Fire Insurance Co.; Macfarlane's Claim* (1880), 17 Ch. D. 337. In this case the holder of a fire policy issued by the corporation was held entitled to prove for the full amount of a loss accruing after the winding-up. For the treatment of potential insurance claims of which policyholder is not yet aware, see *A.G. Canada v. Northumberland General Insurance Co.* (1986), 56 O.R. (2d) 609 (H.C.).

The holder of a contingent claim is entitled to have provision made therefor under s. 71 and s. 95 (distribution): *Re Armstrong Whitworth Securities Co.*, [1947] Ch. 673.

A surety who has paid a creditor's claim that has priority of payment over other debts of the corporation, is entitled, under the *Mercantile Law Amendment Act, 1856*, to stand in the place of the original creditor: *Re Lamplugh Iron Ore Co.*, [1927] 1 Ch. 308.

As to the position where a corporation in liquidation is itself a contributory of another corporation, see the notes to ss. 55 and 56 in Chapter 23.

Claims for damages

As already indicated, claims for liquidated or unliquidated damages may be proven (s. 71).

A claim for damages for repudiation of an obligation is provable: *Northern Ontario Power Co. v. LaRoche Mines Ltd.*, [1937] O.R. 824 (C.A.), revd on other grounds, [1938] 3 D.L.R. 657 (P.C.); *Re Apex Supply Co.*, [1941] W.N. 254 (stipulated sum payable under hire-purchase agreement by way of compensation for depreciation of goods, provable).

Rent

The landlord can, of course, prove for past rent, but will invariably desire to take advantage of the special rights and remedies reserved by law or by the terms of the lease. The right of distress is discussed in the notes to ss. 21, 22 (Chapter 21) and 86 (below); the right to preferential payment in a winding-up is discussed under ss. 86 and 22.

As to a landlord proving for the future rent, if the landlord accepts a surrender of the lease, he may prove for the loss occasioned by such surrender: *Hardy v. Fothergill* (1888), 13 App. Cas. 351 (H.L.); *Re Panther Lead Co.*, [1896] 1 Ch. 978; *Re Midland Coal, Coke & Iron Co.*; *Craig's Claim*, [1895] 1 Ch. 267; but this can only be done when the landlord accepts a surrender: *Re New Oriental Bank Corp. (No. 2)*, [1895] 1 Ch. 753. As to proving for future rent when there is an acceleration clause in the lease, see *Shackell & Co. v. Chorlton & Sons*, [1895] 1 Ch. 378. Before the case of *Hardy v. Fothergill, supra*, it had been held in *Re London & Colonial Co.; Horsey's Claim* (1868), L.R. 5 Eq. 561, and *Re Haytor Granite Co.* (1865), 1 Ch. App. 77, that a landlord could not prove in respect of damage sustained for loss of future rent; but in *Re Midland Coal, supra*, and *Re Panther Lead Co., supra*, it was said that *Hardy v. Fothergill* introduced a new rule in respect of this class of claims.

Under a somewhat similar provision, a claim by a landlord for future rent against a tenant under a lease that has been assigned, is a liability for which proof can be made: *James Smith & Sons (Norwood) Ltd. v. Goodman*, [1936] 1 Ch. 216 (C.A.), followed in *Re House Property & Investment Co.*, [1954] 1 Ch. 576.

If the liquidator disclaims the lease, as he has a right to do under s. 39 of the *Landlord and Tenant Act*, R.S.O. 1990, c. L.7, (and in some other provinces), the landlord cannot rank as a creditor for damages in respect of breach of contract: see *Re Mussens Ltd.*, [1933] O.W.N. 459 (S.C.).

A subtenant of the lessee, against whom a receiving order or winding-up order has been made, where the under-lease has been consented to in writing by the head lessor, if the trustee or liquidator disclaims, has the rights reserved under subsection (2) of section 39 of the *Landlord and Tenant Act*. Where the consent of the head lessor has not been obtained (the sub-lease being expressed to be subject to the rights of the owner and to the head lease), the sub-lessee is entitled to rank against the estate of the sub-lessor as an ordinary creditor for damages recovered against the sub-lessor for failure to put the sub-lessee in possession of the premises: *Re Schulte-United Ltd.*, [1934] O.R. 453 (C.A.) (basis of determining damages discussed).

Taxes

As to the statutory lien or priority of certain taxes, see the notes to s. 86, below.

The right to prove for a claim for municipal taxes imposed before the winding-up depends on the right to maintain an action therefor, which only exists when the taxes cannot be recovered in any special manner provided for by the *Assessment Act*, for example, distress or sale: *Re Ottawa Porcelain & Carbon Co.* (1900), 31 O.R. 679 (Master). The principle is there stated by Street, J., at 690, as follows:

> The principle is that where there is no right of action, and therefore no privity between the person entitled to distrain and the company in liquidation, the person entitled to distrain may pursue his only remedy, viz., that of distress, and reap the fruits of it as if there had been no liquidation. But where there is a right of action, even though there be also a right of distress, then the creditor is within the Winding-up Act, and must prove as an ordinary creditor.

So it was held that there was a right of proof for a water rate, where a corporate liability was imposed: ibid.

Municipal taxes imposed before the winding-up can only rank as ordinary debts in the absence of a statutory lien or charge or other statutory priority; but taxes imposed after the commencement of the winding-up must be paid in full as part of the expenses of liquidation, if the liquidator has remained in possession and such possession has been a "beneficial occupation": *Re Ideal House Furnishers Ltd.* (1909), 18 Man. R. 650 (K.B.). As to what constitutes such occupation by the liquidator as will create a liability to pay municipal taxes, see *Re National Arms & Ammunition Co.* (1885), 28 Ch. D. 474 (C.A.), and the cases there cited; see also the notes to s. 22 in Chapter 21. Where the corporation is assessed for municipal taxes subsequent to the winding-up order, that is not intended as an assessment of the liquidator either personally or in his capacity as such, even though the name of the corporation is followed by the words "A. B. liquidator," and no statutory liability is imposed on the liquidator personally: *Toronto (City) v. Wade*, [1932] O.R. 500 (C.A.). *Semble,* if electric current were supplied to a liquidator at his request, he would be under contractual liability to pay the rates; and if he were to allow the liquidation to be completed without indemnifying himself out of the assets, he would be bound to pay: ibid.

Apart from legislation creating a lien, charge or priority, the claim for municipal taxes must be treated as an ordinary and not a preferential claim where the municipality being entitled to distrain before the winding-up order, has not done so: *Re Faulkner Ltd.* (1915), 34 O.L.R. 536 (H.C.). See also *Re Beaver Drugs* (1926), 7 C.B.R. 719 (Ont. S.C.), and cases cited.

As to the right of a municipality to rank in respect of business tax, see *Re Ideal House Furnishers Ltd., supra.* In Ontario, a corporation that has been duly assessed for business tax in a year in which it was carrying on business, remains liable to pay the tax levied in the following year based upon such assessment, even though it goes into liquidation in the course of the year for which the assessment was made and carries on no business during the year in which the tax is levied: *Re Lyman Brothers*, [1933] O.R. 159 (C.A.).

A corporation in liquidation, if it has income, is liable for income tax thereon; and interest on deferred payments on account of the sale price of the corporation's assets is income and subject to taxation: *North Pacific Lumber Co. v. Minister of National Revenue*, [1928] Ex. C.R. 68; *Re Saskatchewan Co-operative Elevator Co.*, [1933] 3 W.W.R. 669 (Sask.). Income tax assessed against a corporation in liquidation, in respect of the profits of its business carried on by the liquidator, is part of the expenses of the liquidation: *Re Beni-Felkai Mining Co.*, [1934] 1 Ch. 406.

Under s. 159(2) and (3) of the *Income Tax Act (Canada)*, a liquidator is required to obtain a certificate from the Minister of National Revenue certifying that all amounts owing under the *Income Tax Act* by the taxpayer have been paid, prior to final distribution, failing which the liquidator will be personally liable for the same up to the amount of the distribution.

Priority of wage earners

The claims for arrears of salary and wages of the persons specified in s. 72 enjoy a special privilege over other creditors, but as the Crown is not mentioned therein, the claim of the Crown to priority is not affected. See s. 17 of the *Interpretation Act*, R.S.C. 1985, c. I-21.

Where the claim comes into conflict with other privileged claims, for example, that of a lessor, the local law governs: *Re White Star Hotel Co.* (1916), 17 Que. P.R. 299.

As to the position where a claim under the section comes into competition with security held by a bank under the *Bank Act*, see *Re Alberta Ornamental Iron Co. & Imperial Bank* (1917), 35 W.L.R. 126.

As to the priority of wage earners and materialmen, see *Re Canadian Mineral Rubber Co.* (1916), 10 O.W.N. 456 (H.C.), affd (1916), 11 O.W.N. 135 (Div. Ct.), and as to the effect of taking a promissory note for the amount of wages, see *Armstrong v. Watson* (1919), 45 D.L.R. 501 (Alta. T.D.); and of taking a judgment, *Ball v. Thorne* (1919), 46 O.L.R. 261 (C.A.).

Any claim by a wage earner for damages for failure to give reasonable notice of termination would be provable in the same manner as a claim by an ordinary creditor.

Clerks or other persons

As to the meaning of "clerk", see *Re Morlock & Cline Ltd.* (1911), 23 O.L.R. 165 at 166 (H.C.). A managing director is not a clerk: *Re Newspaper Proprietary Syndicate*, [1900] 2 Ch. 349; nor is a manager: *Re White Star Hotel Co.* (1916), 17 Que. P.R. 299. See also the notes to s. 122 of the Canadian Business Corporations Act.

There are numerous cases in which the courts have had to decide who will be included under the term "other persons." It has been held that it is better to give such words a restricted interpretation, and that the *ejusdem generis* rule applies: *Re Ritchie-Hearn Co.* (1905), 6 O.W.R. 474 (H.C.); *Moore Carpet Co. v. Howard* (1909), 15 R. de J. 191; *Miquelon v. Vilandre Co.* (1913), 16 D.L.R. 316 (Que. S.C.); *Re Shirleys Ltd.* (1916), 29 D.L.R. 273 (Sask. T.D.).

The person seeking the special privilege must not be in an independent position — for example, an auditor or a solicitor who might do work for many corporations: *Re Ontario Forge & Bolt Co.* (1896), 27 O.R. 230 (H.C.). A managing director has been held disentitled to any special privilege. "Other persons" must be "of the servant and not of the executive or master class": *Re Ritchie-Hearn Co.* (1905), 6 O.W.R. 474. A director is not a servant but a manager: *Re Newspaper Proprietary Syndicate Ltd.*; *Hopkinson v. Newspaper Proprietary Syndicate Ltd.*, [1900] 2 Ch. 349. The element of control by the corporation is important: *Re Western Coal Co.* (1913), 12 D.L.R. 401 (Alta. T.D.); *Re Parkin Elevator Co.* (1916), 37 O.L.R. 277 (C.A.).

Where, however, a director is employed as a commercial traveller and takes no active part in the management of the corporation, he has been held entitled to priority: *Re Morlock & Cline Ltd.* (1911), 23 O.L.R. 165 (H.C.); and see *Fayne v. Langley* (1899), 31 O.R. 254 (H.C.), where an officer related to a corporation in two capacities (i.e., as president or vice-president, and as officer in receipt of salary) was held entitled to priority.

Persons are in the employment of the corporation "in or about its business or trade" when, for example, they are employed in connection with the construction of a mill and such construction comes directly within the purposes and objects of the corporation: *Re Lake Sulphite Pulp Co.*; *Crawley & McCracken Co.'s Claim* (December 10, 1938), (Ont. S.C.) (unreported).

Salary or wages

The words "salary or wages" import a contract for service as distinguished from a contract for services, and an independent contractor is not covered by the section: *Re Parkin Elevator Co., supra,* per Masten, J.; and see *Re Dominion Shipbuilding & Repair Co.* (1921), 51 O.L.R. 144 (C.A.); *Saunders v. Toronto (City)* (1899), 26 O.A.R. 265.

An assignee of the privileged creditor may make the claim: *Lee v. Friedman* (1909), 20 O.L.R. 49 (C.A.); *Re Morlock & Cline Ltd., supra.*

Where a servant is remunerated by a fixed sum and expenses, the latter are to be treated as part of the wages for which a privilege may be claimed: *Re Morlock & Cline Ltd., supra.* A bonus payable in addition to salary may come within the privilege: *Abeles v. Turgeon* (1914), 13 D.L.R. 210 (Que. C.A.). Where a person came within the class, his claim was not disallowed because his remuneration was payable by way of commission: *Re Hartwick Fur Co.* (1914), 17 D.L.R. 853 (Ont. H.C.). These cases have been criticized in the Ontario Court of Appeal in *Re Parkin Elevator Co.* (1916), 37 O.L.R. 277 (C.A.), where Meredith, C.J.C.P., observed at 283 that they reach if they do not overstep the limits of the law. In the last mentioned case, Meredith, C.J.C.P., held that it was contrary to any reasonable meaning that could be attributed to the words "salary or wages," to include the proportion of the price of the goods that the claimant was to have for the sales made by him. The judgment of Masten, J., went on the ground that the claimant was not one of the classes of persons entitled to priority, holding that receipt of a commission in lieu of wages looks in the direction of an independent contractor but is not conclusive. Riddell and Lennox, JJ., concurred in the result but gave no reasons.

Decisions as to entitlement to priority under s. 72

The following have been held entitled to priority:

A commercial traveller: *Re Morlock & Cline Ltd.* (1911), 23 O.L.R. 165 (H.C.); *Re Hartwick Fur Co.* (1914), 17 D.L.R. 853 (Ont. H.C.); *Abeles v. Turgeon* (1914), 13 D.L.R. 210 (Que. C.A.).

A salesman on salary, notwithstanding that he also acted as secretary; *semble*, as secretary he would have been preferred: *Re S.E. Walker Co.* (1913), 12 D.L.R. 769 (Alta. T.D.) (decided under a similar section of the N.W.T. *Companies Winding-up Ordinance*, 1911).

A teamster using his own wagon and team, who is not an independent contractor but is subject to the direction and control of his employer: *Re Western Coal Co.* (1913), 12 D.L.R. 401 (Alta. T.D.) (also decided under the N.W.T. *Companies Winding-up Ordinance*, 1911).

An editor under separate contract, although also a director: *Re Beeton & Co.*, [1913] 2 Ch. 279.

The following have been held not entitled to priority:

An accountant temporarily employed by the corporation to audit its books and who is not subject to any direction or control in so doing: *Miquelon v. Vilandre Co.* (1913), 16 D.L.R. 316 (Que. S.C.).

An auditor, who is remunerated by "audit fee": *Re Ontario Forge & Bolt Co.* (1896), 27 O.R. 230 (H.C.).

A manager: *Moore Carpet Co. v. Howard* (1909), 15 R. de J. 191; *Re Shirleys Ltd.* (1916), 29 D.L.R. 273; *Girard v. Garégpy* (1916), 49 Que. S.C. 284 (C.A.); *Re White Star Hotel Co.* (1916), 17 Que. P.R. 299.

A managing director: *Re Ritchie-Hearn Co.* (1905), 6 O.W.R. 474 (H.C.); also a managing director who also served as a salesman, when it was impossible to apportion his salary between his two functions: *Re S.E. Walker Co., supra.*

A secretary-treasurer: *Moore Carpet Co. v. Howard, supra.*

A mechanical expert and inspector: *Re American Tire Co.* (1903), 2 O.W.R. 29 (C.A.).

See also the notes under the heading "Priority of wage earners".

Decisions as to entitlement to priority under provisions of the Bankruptcy and Insolvency Act corresponding to s. 72

The following cases, which have been decided under what is currently s. 136(1)(d) of the *Bankruptcy and Insolvency Act* may be referred to. That section gives priority to all wages, salaries, commissions or compensation of any clerk, servant, travelling salesman, labourer or workman in respect of services rendered to the bankrupt or assignor during six months before the date of the receiving order or assignment to the extent of $2000 and proper disbursements by a travelling salesman up to an additional $1000.

The following have been held entitled to priority:

Travelling salesman (salary and expenses): *Re Stockton* (1921), 2 C.B.R. 204 (N.B. K.B.); *Re Corson Shoe Co.*, [1924] 1 D.L.R. 555 (Ont. S.C.).

Travelling salesmen whose services were not exclusive, whose territory was limited and whose orders were subject to acceptance: *Re Hercules Rubber Co.* (1922), 22 O.W.N. 610 (S.C.).

President and managing director, where there was a contract of employment: *Re Eastern Ontario Milk Products Co.* (1922), 52 O.L.R. 67 (S.C.).

Secretary-treasurer performing duties of a bookkeeper, even though he was also a director: *Re Eastern Ontario Milk Products Co., supra.*

Manager and secretary, where there was a letter setting out salary and terms of employment: *Re N.A. Macdonald & Co.*, [1923] 1 D.L.R. 620 (Que. S.C.) (but see *Parisian Cleaners & Laundry Ltd. v. Blondin, infra*).

Accountant not exclusively employed: *Re Gordean Furniture Co.*, [1923] 4 D.L.R. 1198 (Alta. T.D.); *Re Kellerman* (1933), 15 C.B.R. 197 (Ont. S.C.).

Truck driver's salary as such, where there was a contract: *Re Sexton* (1930), 66 O.L.R. 313 (C.A.).

The following have been held not entitled to priority:

Travelling salesman selling on commission: *Re Specialty Bags Co.* (1923), 53 O.L.R. 35 (C.A.) (position that of buyer and seller).

Director and manager, where no services performed: *Re Continental Publishing Co.* (1924), 25 O.W.N. 610 (S.C.).

Manager's commission, where there was a contract of employment: *Parisian Cleaners & Laundry Ltd. v. Blondin*, [1939] 4 D.L.R. 791 (Que. C.A.), disapproving *Re N.A. Macdonald & Co., supra.*

Truck driver's claim for gasoline for truck supplied by him under a contract: *Re Sexton, supra.*

Section 140 of the *Bankruptcy and Insolvency Act* provides that no officer or director of a bankrupt corporation is entitled to have his claim preferred as provided by s. 136 in respect of wages, salary, commission or compensation for work done or services rendered to the corporation in any capacity.

Set-off

Under s. 73, the law of set-off is to apply to all claims against the corporation and to proceedings for the recovery of debts of the corporation as though the corporation were not being wound up.

The law of set-off applicable in each case will be the law in force in the province where the proceedings are taken.

As to the nature of set-off, see *Thompson v. Big Cities Realty & Agency Co.* (1910), 21 O.L.R. 394 at 402 (C.A.); *Grills v. Farah* (1910), 21 O.L.R. 457 (H.C.); and for the distinction between counterclaim and set-off, see *Gates v. Seagram* (1909), 19 O.L.R. 216. See also *Standard Trust Co. v. Turner Crossing Inc.* (1992), 15 C.B.R. (3d) 75 (Sask. Q.B.); Cf. *Canada Deposit Insurance Corp. v. Canadian Commercial Bank* (1989), 76 C.B.R. (N.S.) 116 (Alta. Q.B.). The distinction is important under this section; see the subheading "Mutual debts", below.

In Quebec, legal compensation does not take place except as regards debts exigible before the corporation goes into liquidation: *Chagnon v. Hutchison* (1921), 31 Que. K.B. 545.

Where a subscriber had recovered judgment against a corporation in liquidation for moneys paid on his application, on the ground that issued shares had been delivered, it was held that there could be no set-off of moneys paid by the corporation by way of dividends on the shares subscribed for: *Brydges v. Dominion Trust Co.*, [1919] 3 W.W.R. 345 (B.C. S.C.).

As to the position where there has not been in fact any attempt to set off advances and payments made to the corporation against payments made by the corporation, see *Re B.P. Fowler Ltd.*, [1938] Ch. 113.

Under s. 102 persons indebted to the corporation may not set off against their liability to the corporation debts of the corporation transferred to them in the circumstances specified in the section. See further the notes under the heading "Transfer of debts" in this chapter.

Mutual debts

It is only "mutual debts" which are properly the subject of set-off, as distinguished from counterclaims which fall within s. 71: *Crain v. Wade* (1917), 55 S.C.R. 208 at 218.

It is a fundamental principle of the law of set-off that the right shall be mutual. A corporation is not entitled to set off damages against a claim based on a lease, there being lack of mutuality: *Re Montreal Cold Storage & Freezing Co.* (1902), 4 Que. P.R. 340. If, however, a claim originally for damages has by judgment become a debt, it can be set off: *Moody v. Canadian Bank of Commerce* (1891), 14 P.R. 258. For want of mutuality, a misfeasant cannot set off money due to him from the corporation against sums due for his misfeasance: *Re Anglo-French Co-operative Society; Ex parte Pelly* (1882), 21 Ch. D. 492 (C.A.); *Re Bolt & Iron Co.* (1887), 14 O.R. 211 (H.C.), affd (1889), 16 O.A.R. 397; *Re Disappearing Propellor Boat Co.* (1925), 5 C.B.R. 679 (Ont. Ref.). Similarly, for want of mutuality, a claim in detinue and damages cannot be the subject of set-off: *Eberle's Hotels & Restaurant Co. v. Jonas* (1887), 18 Q.B.D. 459 (C.A.); *Crain v. Wade* (1916), 35 O.L.R. 402 at 411 (C.A.). A debt of the corporation as a going concern cannot be set off against a debt that becomes due or accruing due after the making of the winding-up order, set-off failing for lack of mutuality: *P. Lyall & Sons Construction Co. v. Baker*, [1933] O.R. 286 (C.A.), and cases there cited; and see the cases under "Liquidator carrying on business of corporation," under Chapter 22.

The operation of what is now the *Courts of Justice Act*, R.S.O. 1990, c. C.43, with respect to set-off, is not limited to cases of debts arising out of or connected with the same transaction: *Kallio v. Russell Timber Co.*, [1942] S.C.R. 346, and cases cited (judgments against plaintiff in another court assigned to defendant could be set off).

Partners had applied to a bank for credit to their firm, agreeing to give joint and several notes in their individual names and to become jointly and severally liable for the transactions of the firm, so that the firm was the principal debtor and the partners were sureties and liable for its debts to the extent of their joint and several notes. Each partner, as well as the firm, had a deposit to his and its credit in the bank that became insolvent. The debts of the partners to the bank and the bank's debt to the partners were due before the winding-up order. The debts were held to be mutual debts at the date of the failure. It was further held that the defendants, being obliged to pay the firm's shortage, had the right to have their individual deposits applied upon that shortage; and that the defendants, being proceeded against jointly and severally, could not be prevented from setting up any right possessed by or accruing to them in either capacity: *Clarkson v. Robinet*, [1925] 4 D.L.R. 778 (Ont. C.A.).

There is no right of set-off of a joint indebtedness of a firm against the separate indebtedness of a corporation to one of the partners: *Re Pennington & Owen Ltd.*, [1925] Ch. 825 (C.A.). But where a bank took security on the separate account of one partner of a firm, customers of the bank, for the indebtedness of the firm to the bank, an equity arose which prevented the bank from asserting the joint liability of the firm without first giving credit for the amount standing to the credit of the partner: *Clarkson v. Smith (Sub nom. Clarkson v. Smith & Goldberg)* (1926), 58 O.L.R. 241 (C.A.).

A debt owing to the corporation by a debtor who has a claim against a fund that came into the hands of the liquidator impressed with certain trusts, should be set off against an amount payable to the debtor out of the general assets of the corporation, and not set off against the sum payable out of the trust fund: *Re Canadian Home Investment Co.*, [1917] 3 W.W.R. 629 (B.C. C.A.).

A claim on a policy that has matured before the winding-up can be set off: *Sovereign Life Assurance Co. v. Dodd*, [1892] 2 Q.B. 573 (C.A.).

Where by set-off the debt on one side is satisfied, the security for that debt is freed: *Re Barnett* (1874), L.R. 9 Ch. App. 293. And see *Clarke v. Union Fire Insurance Co.* (1884), 4 C.L.T. 249; *Re Kindsgrove Steel Co.*, [1894] W.N. 25; *Re Washington Diamond Mining Co.*, [1893] 3 Ch. 95 (C.A.).

As to set-off against an assignee of a director against whom the liquidator has, subsequent to the assignment, recovered damages for misfeasance, see *Re Milan Tramways Co.; Ex parte Theys* (1882), 22 Ch. D. 122 at 125, 126 (C.A.); *Re Bailey Cobalt Mines Ltd.* (1919), 44 O.L.R. 1 (C.A.) where the cases are collected.

Debts due or accruing due

As to the significance of the words "debts due or accruing due to the corporation at the commencement of the winding-up", see *Crain v. Wade* (1917), 55 S.C.R. 208.

There is no debt due or accruing due within the meaning of s. 73 where there is merely an executory agreement that may ripen into a debt in the event of certain contingencies: *P. Lyall & Sons Construction Co. v. Baker*, [1933] O.R. 286 (C.A.), where the cases are collected.

Duty to make good amount owing

Even where there is no set-off, the rule that where an estate is being administered by the court, or where a fund is being distributed, a party cannot take anything out of the fund until he has made good what he owes to the fund, will prevent a director against whom the liquidator has recovered damages for misfeasance from obtaining payment of his claim against the corporation without paying in what he has been found liable to contribute: *Re Rhodesia Goldfields Ltd.; Partridge v. Rhodesia Goldfields Ltd.*, [1910] 1 Ch. 239; *Re Bailey Cobalt Mines Ltd., supra.*

The rule does not apply so as to permit a liquidator to set off a joint debt owing to the corporation by two shareholders against a debt owing by the corporation to one of them or his assign: *Re Pennington & Owen Ltd.*, [1925] Ch. 825 (C.A.).

Shareholders

A shareholder who is also a creditor has no right to set off a debt due to him by the corporation prior to the winding-up against his liability as a contributory: *Re Wiarton Beet Sugar Manufacturing Co.* (1905), 10 O.L.R. 219 (H.C.); *Re Overend, Gurney & Co.; Grissell's Case* (1866), 1 Ch. App. 528; *Re White Star Life Ltd.*, [1938] Ch. 458 at 479 (C.A.); or against the double liability formerly imposed on shareholders under the *Bank Act*: *Maritime Bank v. Troop* (1888), 16 S.C.R. 456; or against calls made by a bankruptcy trustee, when there has been no call before bankruptcy: *Re Comptoir agricole Ltée* (1924), 4 C.B.R. 649 (Que. S.C.). The reason in both cases is the absence of mutuality between the claims of the liquidator against the contributory and the claim of the latter as creditor of the corporation as a going concern. Moreover, as observed by Teetzel, J., in *Re Wiarton Beet Sugar Manufacturing Co., supra*, at 223: "To allow a set-off by a shareholder who is also a creditor would violate the spirit and intention of the Winding-up Act, the ruling object of which is the distribution of the assets of an insolvent company amongst its creditors *pari passu*"; and Panneton, J., in *Re Comptoir agricole Ltée, supra*, observed that to allow a set-off under these circumstances would involve payment of the shareholder in full to the detriment of other creditors.

The rule applies even though the right to set off may have been expressly stipulated in an agreement or contract between the corporation and the shareholder: *Re Paraguassu Steam Tramroad Co.*; *Black & Co.'s Case* (1872), 8 Ch. App. 254; *Re Law Car & General Insurance Corp.*, [1912] 1 Ch. 405.

The rule applies to a claim for goods supplied to the corporation under agreement: *Re Jones & Moore Electric Co.* (1909), 18 Man. R. 549 (C.A.); *Re Mimico Sewer Pipe & Brick Manufacturing Co.* (1895), 26 O.R. 289 (H.C.) is not a useful decision on the question of set-off: *Re Wiarton Beet Sugar Manufacturing Co., supra*, at 224.

In some jurisdictions, set-off in the case of contributories is excluded by the governing Companies Act: *Re Irma Co-operative Co.*, [1925] 1 D.L.R. 27 (Alta. T.D.); or may be permitted: *Re Globe Fire Assurance Co.; Robertson's Case* (1909), 11 W.L.R. 45, 293.

A creditor who is also a shareholder may set off his debt against calls made on his shares before the winding-up: *Re Ontario Fire Insurance Co.* (1915),

10 W.W.R. 911 (Alta. T.D.). Such is not the case in England (see *Re Overend, Gurney & Co.*; *Grissell's Case* (1866), 1 Ch. App. 528; *Re Breech-Loading Armoury Co.*; *Calisher's Case* (1868), L.R. 5 Eq. 214; *Re Stranton Iron & Steel Co.*; *Barnett's Case* (1875), L.R. 19 Eq. 449), but the provisions of the English Act regarding set-off differ from s. 73.

If the debt is incurred by the liquidator in the winding-up, it may be set off: *Re London & Colonial Co.*; *Ex parte Clark* (1869), L.R. 7 Eq. 550; and see *Re Pyle Works* (1890), 44 Ch. D. 534 (C.A.), where the shareholder creditors had a charge on the calls.

The question as to whether, in the case of a provincially incorporated corporation being wound up under the Federal Act, the provincial legislature may confer a right of set-off on a shareholder that cannot be curtailed by federal legislation, was raised but not decided in *Re Wiarton Beet Sugar Manufacturing Co., supra.*

See also *Re Consolidated Investments Ltd.*, [1918] 2 W.W.R. 581 (Alta. T.D.) (no call, arrangement for set-off made with directors, but set-off not allowed); *Re Consolidated Investments Ltd.*, [1919] 3 W.W.R. 105 (Alta. Master) (set-off refused).

Time for sending in claims (s. 74)

Under s. 74, the court may fix a time at or within which creditors may send in their claims, and may direct notice thereof to be given by the liquidator.

If a claimant seeks to come in after the time allowed for filing claims, he should show on affidavit the merit of his application and explain the cause of his delay: *Re Merchants Life Assn.* (1901), 22 C.L.T. 21 (Ont. H.C.); cf. also s. 77.

Where the Official Referee made an order in the liquidation of a bank barring all claims that were not put in and proved in response to advertisements, this did not affect the claim of the Crown or the Minister of Finance in respect of unclaimed depositors' balances and outstanding circulation; and the Minister had no *locus standi* to appeal from the order: *Re Ontario Bank* (1916), 38 O.L.R. 242 (H.C.).

As to corroboration of disputed claims, see *Josephs v. Morton* (1916), 26 D.L.R. 433 (N.S. C.A.).

Proof of claims (s. 75)

If the liquidator considers that a creditor's claim should not be allowed without proof, he may send the creditor notice to attend before the court and prove his claim (s. 75(l)).

The court cannot make an order staying proceedings under the section pending the disposition of certain selected claims: *Re Dominion Trust Co.* (1916), 27 D.L.R. 580 (B.C. C.A.).

As to delay by a creditor in demanding particulars of contestation by the liquidator, see *Re Montreal Cold Storage & Freezing Co.* (1902), 4 Que. P.R. 340. See also *Re Stratford Fuel, Ice & Construction Co.* (1913), 28 O.L.R. 481 (C.A.), affd (*sub nom. Brown v. Coughlin*) (1914), 50 S.C.R. 100.

As to the duty of a liquidator when examining a claim, see *Re Home & Colonial Insurance Co.*, [1930] 1 Ch. 102, at131.

The service of notice under this section does not prevent the liquidator, before the claimant has taken the necessary steps, from contesting the claim under s. 87 of this Act: *Re Stadacona-Rouyn Mines Ltd.*, [1942] Que. S.C. 275.

As to the duty of the liquidator to ascertain the corporation's liabilities accrued or contingent as shown by the corporation's records, see *Re Armstrong Whitworth Securities Co.*, [1947] Ch. 673.

Distribution of assets (ss. 76, 77)

After the time for sending in claims has expired, and after all claims of which proof was required have been settled, the liquidator may distribute the assets of the corporation (s. 76(1)).

Under the English Act, if the liquidator in a voluntary winding-up distributes the assets of the corporation without making provision for its debts, he may be liable in damages to a creditor of whose claim he was aware: *Pulsford v. Devenish*, [1903] 2 Ch. 625; *James Smith & Sons (Norwood) Ltd. v. Goodman*, [1936] Ch. 216 (C.A.).

Section 76 is for the protection of the liquidator. The actual distribution of the assets is governed by ss. 93-95.

In the circumstances provided for in s. 77, a creditor will be allowed to rank, notwithstanding that his claim was presented and proved after the time fixed for proving claims; but will only be entitled to participate *pari passu* in the undistributed assets, and will not be allowed, out of such undistributed assets, the dividend already paid to other creditors: *Re Peoples Loan & Deposit Co.*, [1917] 3 W.W.R. 981 (B.C. S.C.). See also *Re Armstrong Whitworth Securities Co.*, [1947] Ch. 673, where creditors' claims were admitted although they were put in after a partial distribution among the shareholders had been made.

Secured creditors

A creditor is a secured creditor if he has any security for his claim upon the property of the corporation: *Re Printing & Numerical Registering Co.* (1878), 8 Ch. D. 535. See also *Canada Deposit Insurance Corp. v. Canadian Commercial Bank* (1992), unreported, Doc. No. 8503-23319, November 18, 1992 (Alta. Q.B.).

A landlord who has exercised his right of distress before the winding-up is a secured creditor: *Thomas v. Patent Lionite Co.* (1881), 17 Ch. D. 250 (C.A.); as to the rights of a landlord, see further the notes to s. 86, below. A person who has obtained the appointment of a receiver before the winding-up is a secured creditor: *Anglo-Italian Bank v. Davies* (1878), 9 Ch. D. 275 (C.A.).

A construction or mechanics' lien is a secured claim under the *Winding-up Act: Re Empire Brewing & Malting Co. (sub nom. Re Rourke & Cass' Claims)* (1891), 8 Man. R. 424 (Q.B.).

Where a security is transferred outright to the creditor, he is not a secured creditor within the section: *Bourbeau Co. v. Stewart Macdonald Export Co.* (1917), 26 Que. K.B. 315.

The holder of a personal guarantee of directors of the corporation is outside s. 78, and the position is not altered by the fact that the directors hold a mortgage on the property of the corporation by way of indemnity: *Re Hardstone Brick Co.*, [1917] 1 W.W.R. 541 (Alta. T.D.). A principal creditor is not entitled to the benefit of collateral security given by the principal debtor to the surety: *Re Walker, Sheffield Banking Co. v. Clayton*, [1892] 1 Ch. 621.

Thus, when equipment was purchased pursuant to a contract whereby title was not to pass until the purchase price was completely paid, and when the equipment was, prior to payment, attached to a truck belonging to a corporation that was subsequently ordered to be wound up, the supplier of the equipment claimed to rank as a secured creditor and was held entitled to do so because of the contract: *Re Conserverie St-Denis Ltée*, [1967] Que. S.C. 292.

Rights of secured creditors

Secured creditors may (1) stand outside the liquidation proceedings and realize upon their securities in any manner the general law authorizes; or (2) release their security and prove for the amount of their claim as unsecured creditors; or (3) come into the liquidation proceedings and value their security and prove for the balance: *Deacon v. Driffil* (1879), 4 O.A.R. 335 at 338 (C.A.); *McFarland v. London & Lancashire Guarantee & Accident Co.*, [1926] 3 D.L.R. 974 at 979 (B.C. C.A.); affd [1927] 3 D.L.R. 67 (S.C.C.).

Right to remain outside liquidation

Secured creditors cannot be compelled to file their claims and prove under the Act, if they prefer to rely on their security and not to share in the distribution of the assets: *Re Brampton Gas Co.* (1902), 4 O.L.R. 509 (C.A.); *Capital Trust Corp. v. Yellowhead Pass Coal & Coke Co.* (1916), 27 D.L.R. 25 (Alta. C.A.). See also *Re Rant & Ker Ltd.*, [1930] 2 W.W.R. 274 (B.C. S.C.) (disputes between liquidator and bank as to ownership of certain bonds directed to be determined by action). But see *Re Lenora Mount Sicker Copper Mining Co.* (1902), 9 B.C.R. 471 (S.C.); *Montreal Trust Co. v. Abitibi Power & Paper Co.*, [1943] A.C. 536 at 547 (P.C.) .

A secured creditor who realizes his security is entitled to apply the proceeds in or toward payment of his principal, interest and costs: *Re London, Windsor & Greenwich Hotels Co.; Quartermaine's Case*, [1892] 1 Ch. 639.

If the secured creditor elects to rely on his security, he cannot rank against the estate for any deficiency. Consequently, if the secured creditor retains his securities, staying outside the liquidation, and gives the liquidator authority to realize them for him, the liquidator does so as agent and not as liquidator. The secured creditor cannot recover against the surety for the liquidator for the misappropriation by the liquidator of the proceeds of the securities: *McFarland v. London & Lancashire Guarantee & Accident Co.*, *supra*. As to the limitation on the expenses that a liquidator is entitled to claim in priority to a mortgagee who has assented to a sale of the mortgaged assets by the liquidator, see *Scott v. Siemen* (1911), 2 O.W.N. 697 (H.C.), and cases cited.

As to the right of the secured creditor to bring an action for the enforcement of his security, see the notes under the heading "Right of secured creditor to sue" in this chapter.

Right to value security and prove in liquidation for balance of claim

For cases where the secured creditor determines to come into the liquidation proceedings, value his security and prove for the balance of his claim, the procedure is set out in ss. 78-84. As there indicated, the liquidator, with the court's approval, is then to consent to the retention of the security by the creditor, or to require the creditor to turn it over to the estate at the specified value.

When a creditor had inadvertently proved without valuing his security, he was allowed to amend his proof: *Re Lake Winnipeg Transportation, Lumber & Trading Co.* (1892), 8 Man. R. 463 (Q.B.); *Re Henry Lister & Co.; Ex parte Huddersfield Banking Co.*, [1892] 2 Ch. 417; and see *Re Frith; Ex parte Schofield* (1879), 12 Ch. D. 337; *Re Arden; Ex parte Arden* (1884), 14 Q.B.D. 121 (D.C.); *Re Barned's Banking Co.; Ex parte Bank of England* (1870), 18 W.R. 944.

A creditor cannot withdraw his valuation and enforce his security: *Re British Columbia Pottery Co.* (1895), 4 B.C.R. 525 (S.C.); but where secured creditors, without any intention to submit to the adjudication of their claims in the winding-up, have filed affidavits in proof thereof, leave has been granted for the withdrawal of the claims: *Re Brampton Gas Co.* (1902), 4 O.L.R. 509 (C.A.).

A security need be given up by a secured creditor only if it will augment the estate of the corporation: *Re Toronto Dairies Ltd.*, [1952] O.W.N. 84 (S.C.). In that case the dairy had deposited a guarantee bond and certain Dominion of Canada bonds with the Milk Control Board to protect the milk producers in the event that the dairy defaulted in paying their accounts.The Senior Master held that the proceeds of the guarantee bond, if given up, would not have augmented the estate of the corporation, as the bond had never been the property of the corporation; but that the proceeds of the Dominion of Canada bonds, which bonds were originally an asset of the corporation, if given up, would augment the corporation's estate and be available for distribution among all the dairy's creditors. Consequently, the milk producers were entitled to prove the balance of their claims after deducting only the proceeds of the Dominion of Canada bonds; the proceeds of the guarantee bond, it being an outside security, did not need to be deducted, provided that the producers were not to receive more than one hundred cents on the dollar.

Where a creditor in a voluntary winding-up under the British Columbia *Companies Act* valued its security at a certain sum for which it accepted certain book debts, the price thereof being deducted from its claim, it was held that the debt was extinguished to the extent of the valuation, and a surety was discharged *pro tanto: Canadian Bank of Commerce v. Martin* (1918), 40 D.L.R. 155 (B.C. C.A.).

As to the right of revaluing securities, see *Box v. Bird's Hill Sand Co.* (1912), 8 D.L.R. 768 (Man. K.B.); affd (1913), 12 D.L.R. 556 (Man. C.A.); *Canada Furniture Co. v. Banning* (1918), 39 D.L.R. 313 at 319 (Man.K.B.); as to release of sureties, see *Canadian Bank of Commerce v. Martin, supra.*

Where a secured creditor has consented to the sale of an asset of the estate free from encumbrances, he will be deemed to have assented to the conversion of the asset free from his security and will not be entitled, on filing his claim and valuing his security after the sale, to any special charge on the proceeds of the sale: *Traders Bank v. Lockwood* (1913), 48 S.C.R. 593.

When a mortgage is made by a corporation to a trustee to secure several creditors of the corporation, any one creditor has the right to value his interest in such security and maintain his claim on the estate except as reduced by such valuation. The liquidator cannot insist on either getting an assignment of the whole security or relegating the creditor to his rights under the security and refusing to let him rank, but can only force him to assign his interest therein. The principle of the Act in reference to secured creditors is one of election and not forfeiture: *Re Thunder Hill Mining Co.* (1896), 5 B.C.R. 21 (C.A.), and see *Moor v. Anglo-Italian Bank* (1879), 10 Ch. D. 681 at 689; *Ex parte Schofield* (1879), 40 L.T. N.S. 464, 823; *Re Henry Lister & Co.; Ex parte Huddersfield Banking Co.*, [1892] 2 Ch. 417.

As to the right of a creditor to rank on estates of joint debtors and also prove under the above section, see *Ontario Bank v. Chaplin* (1891), 20 S.C.R. 152.

A secured creditor who has exhausted his security without satisfying his debt is not entitled to apply the proceeds of the security in payment, first of interest subsequent to the winding-up and then in reduction of principal, and to prove in the winding-up for the balance of the principal. His proof must be limited to what was due for principal and interest at the commencement of the winding-up after deducting therefrom proceeds of sale or realization received in respect of the security: *Re London, Windsor & Greenwich Hotels Co.; Quartermaine's Case*, [1892] 1 Ch. 639, following *Ex parte Penfold* (1871), 4 De G. & Sm. 282. It should be noted that these cases were decided under the English Bankruptcy rules entitling a secured creditor who realizes his security to prove for the balance after deducting the net amount realized. However, in *Re St. Lawrence Investment & Trust Co.* (1936), 74 Que. S.C. 496, where a secured creditor had sold the security without having been required to value his securities, he was held entitled to rank as an ordinary creditor for the balance of his claim.

Right of secured creditor to sue

A secured creditor has a right to apply for and obtain leave to bring or proceed with an action for enforcing his securities: *Re David Lloyd & Co.; Lloyd v. David Lloyd & Co.* (1877), 6 Ch. D. 339 (C.A.); *Re Longdendale Cotton Spinning Co.* (1878), 8 Ch. D. 150; *Re Joshua Stubbs Ltd.; Barney v. Joshua Stubbs Ltd.*, [1891] 1 Ch. 475 (C.A.); *Re London, Windsor & Greenwich Hotels Co.; Quartermaine's Case, supra.* See also *The "Zafiro"; John Carlbom & Co. v. S.S. Zafiro (owners)*, [1959] 3 W.L.R. 123.

Bondholders and mortgagees

The mere fact that a winding-up order has been made does not prevent a debenture holder or mortgagee of the corporation from bringing an action to realize his security: *Re Longdendale Cotton Spinning Co., supra*; and in *Re*

David Lloyd & Co.; Lloyd v. David Lloyd & Co., supra, it was held that when an order has been made to wind up a corporation, a mortgagee who has commenced an action against the corporation to realize his security ought to have leave under the section of the English *Companies Act* (1862), corresponding to s. 21 of this Act, to proceed with his action, except under special circumstances or unless he can obtain the same relief in the winding-up. And see *Re Joshua Stubbs Ltd.; Barney v. Joshua Stubbs Ltd., supra; Re Canadian Western Steel Corp.* (1922), 51 O.L.R. 615 (C.A.). See the notes to ss. 21 (Chapter 21) and 135 (Chapter 25) of this Act.

So also a trustee for bondholders may cause himself to be put into possession of the assets without prejudice to the rights of privileged creditors: *Canadian Brass Bedsteads Ltd. v. Duclos* (1916), 18 Que. P.R. 206.

In Alberta it has been held that leave cannot be refused on an application under the Alberta Winding-up Rules unless the court is prepared to say that the mortgagee's claim will be at once recognized and allowed in the liquidation proceedings: *Capital Trust v. Yellowhead Pass Coal & Coke Co.* (1916), 27 D.L.R. 25 (Alta. C.A.).

On a petition by a mortgagee in the winding-up proceedings under the Act, asking for the conveyance to him by the liquidator of the corporation's equity of redemption, the court has jurisdiction to make the usual order for foreclosure or sale. It is a matter of discretion with the court whether an action will be directed or summary proceedings sanctioned: *Re Essex Land & Timber Co.* (1891), 21 O.R. 367 (H.C.).

The court ought not to confirm a sale by a mortgagee until the security has been valued, and offered to the liquidator at that value: *Re Thunder Hill Mining Co.* (1894), 3 B.C.R. 351 (S.C.).

A subsequent encumbrancer is not bound to prove as a secured creditor where the property has already been surrendered under the Act to a prior mortgagee and cannot, therefore, be given up to the claimant as required by s. 79: *Re Ottawa Porcelain & Carbon Co.* (1900), 31 O.R. 679, 692 (Master).

As to the compromise of secured claims and double ranking, see *Re Stratford Fuel, Ice & Construction Co.* (1913), 28 O.L.R. 481 (C.A.); affd (*sub nom. Brown v. Coughlin*) (1914), 50 S.C.R. 100.

The Crown has no right to displace creditors holding a security upon specific assets: *Re Imperial Paper Mills* (1915), 7 O.W.N. 630 (H.C.).

Priority of the Crown

The Crown is entitled to a priority in a winding-up over other creditors of equal degree, whether the claim is asserted in right of the Dominion or of one of the provinces: *R. v. Bank of Nova Scotia* (1885), 11 S.C.R. 1; *Maritime Bank of Canada (Liquidators) v. New Brunswick (Receiver-General)*, [1892] A.C. 437 (P.C); *New South Wales Taxation Commissioners v. Palmer*, [1907] A.C. 179 (P.C.); *Re Sid. B. Smith Lumber Co.*, [1917] 3 W.W.R. 844 (B.C. S.C.); *Re Simpson & Hunter Ltd.*, [1917] 1 W.W.R. 402 (Alta. T.D.); *R. v. Lithwick* (1921), 57 D.L.R. 1 (Ex. Ct.); *Toronto (City) v. Wade*, [1931] O.R. 470 (S.C.) (taxes and power rates not constituting a lien or charge); *North Pacific Lumber Co. v. Minister of National Revenue*, [1928] Ex. C.R. 68; *MacLaren v. Minister of National Revenue*, [1934] Ex. C.R. 13; *Re General Fireproofing Co. of Canada*, [1937] S.C.R. 150; *Barclay Furniture Manufacturing Co. v. Grobstein* (1939), 21 C.B.R. 123 (Que. S.C.); but not where the priority is contrary to any local law: *Exchange Bank of Canada v. R.* (1886), 11 App. Cas. 157 (P.C.).

The priority of the Crown as between creditors of equal degree extends to a claim for unliquidated damages for breach of contract: *Toronto (City) v. Wade, supra*, and ibid., [1932] O.R. 500 (C.A.) (appeal dismissed on grounds which made it unnecessary to consider the Crown's priority).

In England the priority of the Crown in a winding-up was abrogated by the *Companies (Consolidation) Act, 1908*: see *Re H.J. Webb & Co.*, [1922] 2 Ch. 369, where the prerogative right of the Crown is fully discussed.

In the case of an assignment for the benefit of creditors under the Ontario Act, it was held that different principles are applicable, *sed quaere: Clarkson v. Canada (Attorney General)* (1888), 15 O.R. 632 (H.C.); affd (1889), 16 O.A.R. 202; but see *New South Wales Taxation Commissioners v. Palmer*, [1907] A.C. 179 at 185 (P.C.).

In *Re Sid B. Smith Lumber Co.*, [1917] 3 W.W.R. 844 (B.C. S.C.), following *New South Wales Taxation Commissioners v. Palmer, supra*, the claim of the Crown in the right of the Province of British Columbia was held entitled to priority as regards moneys due to the Accident Fund of the British Columbia Workmen's Compensation Board, which is "simply an adjunct or administrative body exercising its powers and acting for the Provincial Government on behalf of the province." See also *Re White Star Hotel Co.* (1916), 17 Que. P.R. 299. Where the board is really a separate body and the corporation is not in truth a debtor of the government, there is no priority: *Fox v. Newfoundland Government*, [1898] A.C. 667 (P.C.).

The Crown's priority will not affect creditors holding a specific security: *Re Imperial Paper Mills* (1915), 7 O.W.N. 630 (H.C.).

Effect of s. 86

Section 86 provides that no lien or privilege shall be created by execution, etc., after the commencement of the winding-up.

The effect of this and other sections is to show that "the power of dealing with and collecting the assets after the making of the winding-up order is vested in the liquidator alone": *Shaver v. Cotton* (1896), 23 O.A.R. 426, per Osler, J.A., at 434. The section goes "only on the extent of prohibiting the *creation* of any lien or privilege by the issue or delivery to the sheriff of any execution, or by the filing or registering of any memorial of judgment, or by the issue or making of any attachment or garnishee order or other process or proceeding", per Barry, J., in *Good v. Nepisiguit Lumber Co.* (1912), 41 N.B.R. 57 at 75 (C.A.). It applies only to judicial proceedings: *Re E.C. Colwell Candy Co.* (1902), 35 N.B.R. 613 (C.A.); *Re Shirleys Ltd.* (1916), 29 D.L.R. 273 (Sask. T.D.); and to proceedings commenced before the winding-up: ibid.

Under s. 22, every attachment, sequestration, distress or execution put in force against the estate or effects of the corporation after the making of the winding-up order is void.

Lien or privilege

"The expression lien is generally used to designate a right which a party has to retain that which is in his possession or power until certain demands are satisfied, and a particular lien may arise by mere operation of law": *Re Heyden* (1869), 29 U.C.Q.B. 262 at 264 (Ont. C.A.). "The word privilege is frequently used in the Lower Canada laws as referring to certain preferential or secured rights or claims, and in all probability that word was used in reference to that province, and the word lien as applicable to Upper Canada": ibid.

For the distinction between a privileged claim and a lien see *Grobstein v. Quebec (Workmen's Compensation Commission)*, [1940] 4 D.L.R. 811 (assessment owing to Quebec Workmen's Compensation Commission a privileged claim but not a lien).

Judgments

No lien is created on the property of the corporation by the filing of a judgment if, before payment thereof, winding-up proceedings have commenced: *Re A.S. McDonald Co.* (1919), 50 D.L.R. 417 (N.S. C.A.). The lien constituted by a provincial statute is taken away by this section: ibid.; *sed quaere*: cf. s. 82 and the dissenting judgment of Mellish, J. In this case the court made the order on the application of the liquidator, following *Re Toronto Wood & Shingle Co.* (1894), 30 C.L.T. 353 (Ont.).

Executions

The result of the section is that a writ of execution cannot become a lien on the property of the corporation after the service of notice of presentation of the winding-up petition, which is the date of the commencement of the winding-up: *Re Ideal Furnishing Co.* (1908), 17 Man. R. 576 (K.B.). In that case Mathers, J., was uncertain what the result would be under what is now s. 86 where the sheriff had sold the goods of the corporation and had the proceeds of sale in his hands when notice of the petition was served; under the present provision, the money would presumably become payable to the liquidator.

As there is no lien, the liquidator is entitled to register a transfer of the corporation's lands free of the execution: *Re Leitch Collieries Ltd.*, [1926] 1 D.L.R. 1183 (Alta. T.D.); *Re A.S. McDonald Co.* (1919), 50 D.L.R. 417 (N.S. C.A.).

Lien for costs

A judgment creditor who has an execution in the sheriff's hands at the commencement of the winding-up is protected to the extent of his costs: *Re Heyden* (1869), 29 U.C.Q.B. 262 (Ont. C.A.); *Re Fair Buist* (1866), 2 C.L.J. 216. The fees of the sheriff will also be allowed up to a certain date, for example, where a sheriff was entitled to hold goods seized before the winding-up until an order was made for their delivery up to the liquidator, his fees and possession money were allowed until the date of such order: *Re Oshawa Heat, Light & Power Co.* (1906), 8 O.W.R. 415 (Master). A sheriff is not entitled to poundage or possession money under an execution levied subsequent to a winding-up order, the seizure being illegal under s. 22; and a payment out of the corporation's funds to avoid or in consequence of such a seizure is illegal and can be demanded back by the liquidator: *Richards v. Producers Rock & Gravel Co.* (1914), 17 D.L.R. 588 (B.C.). Assuming a legal seizure, the onus is on the sheriff claiming poundage to satisfy the court that a compromise payment is the direct consequence of the seizure and not an agreement entered into previously between the parties: ibid.

If the *fi. fa.* is not in the sheriff's hands to be executed, but he has instructions not to seize, there is no lien for costs: *Re Saw Bill Lake Gold Mining Co.* (1903), 2 O.W.R. 1143 (H.C.).

Construction or Mechanics' liens

The section does not destroy mechanics' liens, so a lien duly registered for materials supplied and work done prior to the service of the winding-up petition will have priority over ordinary creditors: *Re Clinton Thresher Co.* (1910), 20 O.L.R. 555 (H.C.); *Re Empire Brewing & Malting Co. (sub nom. Re Rourke & Cass' Claim)* (1891), 8 Man. R. 424 (Q.B.); and see *Re Ibex Mining & Development Co.* (1903), 9 B.C.R. 557 (C.A.). The lien arises by virtue of doing the work and registering the lien and subsequently the certificate of action as statement of claim: *Re Empire Brewing & Malting Co., supra.*

If the statement of claim or certificate of action required by the provincial construction or mechanics' lien statutes has not been filed before the winding-up, leave should be obtained under s. 21.

Woodmen's liens

Similarly as regards liens under the *Woodmen's Lien Act*, C.S.N.B., 1903, c. 148, the lien arises when the work is done: *Good v. Nepisiguit Lumber Co.* (1912), 41 N.B.R. 57 (C.A.). In such cases the plaintiffs will be entitled to an order allowing them to proceed and enforce their liens.

Section 22 prevents lien holders from pursuing their remedies without leave, which is obtainable by an order of the court on summary petition under s. 135. However, s. 22 does not apply to the mere filing of a claim of lien; such may be filed after the winding up has commenced without obtaining permission: *Good v. Nepisiguit, supra*, at 74.

Section 86 applies to the creation and not to the enforcement of a lien; and both ss. 22 and 86 apply to creditors only and not to outsiders: *Good v. Nepisiguit, supra.* In the last-mentioned case, the plaintiffs were woodsmen employed by contractors who were engaged in cutting timber for a corporation subsequently ordered to be wound up. Since they were not creditors of the corporation, it was held that s. 86 did not stand in their way so as to prevent them from enforcing their lien.

Maritime liens

For a case where maritime liens for seamen's wages were considered, see *Traders Bank v. Lockwood* (1913), 48 S.C.R. 593 (not affected by loss of ship after sale by liquidator and entitled to recover their claims out of the fund realized).

Lien on documents

With respect to a solicitor's lien, the share register and minute books are not subject to such lien which the directors have no power to create; as to other documents that come into the solicitor's hands pending the winding-up, the solicitor cannot assert any lien that would interfere with the conduct of the winding-up; but as to documents regarding which there is no special provision in the *Companies Act* or the governing documents of the corporation, for example, letters of application and other papers relating to the allotment of shares, the winding-up order will not defeat any existing valid lien: *Re Capital Fire Insurance Assn.* (1883), 24 Ch. D. 408 (C.A.); *Re Boston Wood Rim Co.* (1904), 5 O.W.R. 149 (Master); *Re Land Traction Co.* (September 20, 1915), (Alta.), Stuart J. (unreported); followed in *Re Pioneer Tractor Co.*, [1918] 1 W.W.R. 329; *Re Residential Building Co.* (1916), 26 Man. R. 638 (Q.B.), distinguishing *Re Alpha Mortgage & Investment Co.* (1916), 22 B.C.R. 513 (S.C.). Production of such documents could, however, be compelled under s. 120.

Where documents come into the hands of solicitors in the general course of their business for the corporation, they have only a "passive" or "retaining" lien thereon. Production of such documents "without prejudice" to such lien will not confer priority on their claim over the claims of other creditors: *Executors & Administrators Trust Co. v. Seaborn, Taylor, Pope & Quirk* (1916), 27 D.L.R. 427 (Sask. C.A.). See also s. 121.

Trust creditors

If a trustee intermingles trust property with its own property, the whole will be treated as trust property except insofar as the trustee may be able to distinguish what is its own: *Re Saskatchewan General Trusts Corp.*, [1938] 3 D.L.R. 544 (Sask. C.A.), and cases cited. In that case a trust corporation took moneys from trust funds for the purpose of advancing moneys to estates under its administration. All the trust funds were kept in one general trust account, and there was no indication from which estate the money was taken. The trust creditors were willing to be treated as a class and to rank *pari passu*, and it was held that those creditors who should have funds in the trust account should have a first lien and charge on the fund described as "advances to estates, trusts and agencies," and that until such trust accounts were paid in full such moneys should be distributed ratably among such trust creditors in proportion to their claims, with interest at 5 per cent per annum.

As to the rights of holders of participation certificates in a mortgage to be paid out of the proceeds of such mortgage *pro rata*, see *Re Title Guarantee & Trust Corp. of Canada* (1939), 20 C.B.R. 290.

Preferential claim of landlord

In Ontario, under the *Landlord and Tenant Act*, R.S.O. 1990, c. L.7, s. 37, the landlord has a preferential lien for arrears of rent due during the period of three months next preceding and for three months following the commencement of the liquidation. This means that the landlord has a statutory lien upon goods available for distress, independent of actual distress or possession, for the amount of the rent as limited by the section: *Re Fashion Shop Co.* (1915), 33 O.L.R. 253 at 254 (H.C.). Such preferential lien is not a mere preferential lien in liquidation but is a statutory lien as a substitute for distress: *Re General Fireproofing Co. of Canada*, [1937] S.C.R. 150 at 165.

Where a landlord has already distrained before the winding-up order was made, the distress will not be invalidated by the order, for s. 21 only applies to proceedings taken after the order is made: *Re E.C. Colwell Candy Co.* (1902), 35 N.B.R. 613 (C.A.); *National Trust v. Leeson Estate* (1916), 26 D.L.R. 422 (Alta. C.A.) (constructive distress).

So also, a constructive seizure under verbal arrangement between agents of the lessor and lessee prior to the winding-up order will entitle the landlord to hold the goods distrained as against the liquidator: *Re Shirleys Ltd.* (1916), 29 D.L.R. 273 (Sask. T.D.). The majority of the court in *Re E.C. Colwell Candy Co., supra*, held that a distress is not a "proceeding" within the meaning of s. 86. Boyd, C., in *Fuches v. Hamilton Tribune Co.* (1884), 10 P.R. 409 (H.C.), took a different view, stating that s. 86 was fatal to a claim for a preference if, before the payment over of the moneys under the distress, the winding-up of the corporation had commenced. It should be observed, however, that in that case no steps had been taken by the lessors to assert their claim until after the winding-up had begun. The view of Boyd, C., was disapproved and *Re E.C. Colwell Candy Co.* followed in *Re Shirleys Ltd.* (1916), 29 D.L.R. 273 (Sask. T.D.), where the court held that a distress levied before the winding-up, not being a judicial proceeding, was not affected by the section. So where the corporation had taken possession under a lease in pursuance of an invalid resolution, it was held that the corporation accepted the tenancy on the terms set forth in the resolution and that the landlord was entitled to his preferential lien where he had distrained before the winding-up: *Re D. & S. Drug Co.* (1917), 31 D.L.R. 643 (Alta. C.A.). See also *Re Nutri-Bioy Canada Ltd.* (1964), 49 W.W.R. 678 (B.C. S.C.).

In Quebec a lessor has a privileged claim for rent due and to become due, in accordance with the rights conferred by the *Civil Code*. See *Harte of Quebec v. Ontario Express & Transportation Co.* (1893), 22 O.R. 510 (Master); *Brodeur Co. v. Merrill* (1917), 26 Que. K.B. 461.

Statutory lien or priority of certain taxes

As to the lien or priority of certain taxes, see *Re General Fireproofing Co. of Canada*, [1936] O.R. 510 (C.A.); varied [1937] S.C.R. 150; *Barclay Furniture Mfg. Co. v. Grobstein* (1939), 21 C.B.R. 123 (Que. S.C.).

In Quebec certain costs of the liquidation have priority over municipal water rates and business tax: *Welland Hotel Co. v. Montreal (City)* (1919), 56 D.L.R. 411 (Que. S.C.).

Certain federal or provincial statutes may also give, or purport to give, priority for amounts owing thereunder; careful consideration must be given to such provisions.

If prior to the passing of the by-law to levy taxes, the trustee has disposed of all distrainable assets, the municipality will not be a preferred creditor under the foregoing provision: *Re D.W. McIntosh Ltd.* (1940), 21 C.B.R. 245 (Ont. C.A.).

Under s. 136(1)(e) and (f) of the *Bankruptcy and Insolvency Act*, municipal taxes assessed or levied against the bankrupt within two years preceding his bankruptcy rank ahead of a landlord's claim for arrears of rent. See *Re General Fireproofing Co. of Canada*, [1937] S.C.R. 150.

The result may be different under the *Winding-up Act*, which contains no provision corresponding to s. 136 of the *Bankruptcy and Insolvency Act*. Tax liens of the Province, as decided in the above case under the *Bankruptcy and Insolvency Act*, would also have priority over the landlord under the *Winding-up Act*.

Contesting claims

Under s. 87, any liquidator, creditor or contributory, or shareholder or member may object to any claim filed with the liquidator, or to any dividend declared. This section applies only to those claims that are made in the winding-up proceedings; and, since a secured creditor is not bound to enter such a claim for the purpose of enforcing his security, a general creditor has no standing to attack such security the enforcement of which is sought by an independent foreclosure action: *Capital Trust Corp. v. Yellowhead Pass Coal & Coke Co.* (1916), 27 D.L.R. 25 (Alta. C.A.); *Ward v. Montreal Cold Storage & Freezing Co.* (1904), 26 Que. S.C. 310 (C.A.); *Re Standard Cobalt Mines Ltd.* (1911), 18 O.W.R. 555 (H.C.).

The liquidator may not, by counterclaiming for damages against a director by way of contestation of the latter's claim against the corporation as a creditor, in effect take misfeasance proceedings against him: *Re Boston Shoe Co.* (1914), 16 D.L.R. 856 (Que. S.C.). See *Union Brewery Co. v. Hyde* (1904), 6 Que. P.R. 395; *Re Laurie Engine Co.* (1906), 8 Que. P.R. 59. Where a liquidator desires to take misfeasance proceedings, he must do so by an independent and principal proceeding under the Act: *Re Boston Shoe Co., supra*.

As to a claimant obtaining security for costs from a contesting creditor, see *Re Montreal Cold Storage & Freezing Co.* (1902), 4 Que. P.R. 294.

The liquidator is not precluded from contesting a claim under s. 87 by reason of his having served a notice of contestation under s. 75: *Re Stadacona-Rouyn Mines Ltd.*, [1942] Que. S.C. 275.

Distribution of assets of corporation

Section 93 provides that the property of the corporation is to be applied in satisfaction of its debts and liabilities and of the charges, costs and expenses incurred in the winding-up.

In *Re Toronto Dairies Ltd.*, [1952] O.W.N. 84 (S.C.), it was held that the proceeds of a guarantee bond and of certain securities deposited by the dairy with the Milk Control Board, and held by it as trustee for the milk producers in the event of default by the dairy in paying their accounts, were not property of the corporation within the corresponding section of the Ontario Act.

Section 94 provides that costs, charges and expenses properly incurred in the winding-up, including the remuneration of the liquidator, are payable out of the assets of the corporation in priority to any other claims.

The effect of s. 94 is to confer priority only over claims against the corporation in existence at the time when it went into liquidation. Thus, where an order authorizing a loan to a liquidator provided that the loan should be a first charge on the assets subject only to existing liens, charges or encumbrances, the lender was held entitled to priority over the costs and charges of the winding-up proceedings, including the liquidator's costs and the solicitor's fees: *Keyes v. Hannington* (1913), 13 D.L.R. 139 (N.B. C.A.).

As to the costs and charges of proceedings taken during the winding-up, see the notes under the heading "Costs" in Chapter 22.

If the assets of the corporation are subject to mortgage, the equity of redemption only will be available for payment of costs, subject to any costs of preservation and realization to which the liquidator may be entitled: *Re Touquoy Gold Mining Co.* (1906), 2 E.L.R. 39 (N.S. T.D.).

When the liquidator carries on the business of the corporation at a profit, income tax assessed against the corporation is part of the expenses of the liquidation: *Re Beni-Felkai Mining Co.*, [1934] Ch. 406.

As to the priority of the costs of liquidation over water rates and business tax, see *Welland Hotel Co. v. Montreal (City)* (1919), 56 D.L.R. 411 (Que. S.C.), and cases cited.

Where a corporation in liquidation is a party to an action and costs are given against it, these take priority over the cost of the winding-up: *Re Home Investment Society* (1880), 14 Ch. D. 167; *Re Pacific Coast Syndicate Ltd.*, [1913] 2 Ch. 26. In such a case the party awarded costs is entitled to immediate payment: *Re Dominion of Canada Plumbago Co.* (1884), 27 Ch. D. 33 (C.A.). This priority in favour of the successful litigant does not extend to assets realized by litigation undertaken by the liquidator, the costs of which have not been paid, on the basis that a claimant cannot insist on payment out of assets that he admits have been properly realized and yet seek to have the costs of the realization disallowed: *Re Baden Machinery Co.* (1906), 12 O.L.R. 634 at 636 (H.C.). In the same case it was held that the liquidator should also have priority for a reasonable sum as compensation for his care and trouble in such realization.

See also *Re Peoples Trust Co.*, [1918] 1 W.W.R. 342 (B.C. S.C.); *Scott v. Siemen* (1911), 18 O.W.R. 538 (H.C.); *Dominion Trust Co. v. von Alvensleben*, [1919] 3 W.W.R. 209 (B.C. S.C.).

Basis of distribution of surplus

After the corporation's creditors have been paid and the costs of the winding-up have been satisfied, it is the duty of the liquidator to divide the balance (if any) of the assets among the shareholders or members of the corporation. The provisions of the Act do not require distribution in specie among the shareholders of the assets remaining after the sale of sufficient assets to satisfy the liabilities of a corporation. The ordinary rule is that the assets be sold and that the shareholders then receive a *pro rata* share of the net proceeds of the winding up: *Re United Fuel Investments Ltd. (No. 2)*, [1966] 1 O.R. 165 (C.A.).

The distribution must be preceded by an inquiry by the liquidator as to the persons entitled, and by an order of the court: *Re Phoenix Oil & Transport Co.*, [1958] Ch. 560 at 570; and see the notes to ss. 33-40, in Chapter 22.

Distribution among the shareholders will be made according to their rights under the provisions of the articles, the letters patent and by-laws or memorandum and articles of association. See *Birch v. Cropper; Re Bridgewater Navigation Co.* (1889), 14 App. Cas. 525 (H.L.). In such provisions, the term "surplus assets" may mean either the surplus remaining after payment only of outside liabilities, or the surplus remaining after payment of such outside liabilities and the return to the shareholders of the capital contributed by them. Where the surplus assets are to be distributed between the holders of different classes of shares according to the amount paid up thereon, the term has the former meaning: *Re Crichton's Oil Co.*, [1902] 2 Ch. 86 (C.A.). Where the surplus assets are to be divided between different classes of shares without reference to the par value or the amounts paid on the shares, the term *prima facie* has the latter meaning: *Re Ramel Syndicate Ltd.*, [1911] 1 Ch. 749, and cases cited. It may be doubted, however, whether the reasoning adopted in determining the construction of the provisions arrived at in the last mentioned case would be applicable when one or both classes of shares was without par value.

Before making distribution, the liquidator must comply with the *Income Tax Act*.

Return of capital

Preferred shares commonly carry a preferential right to the return of capital on a winding-up, in which case the amounts paid in by the preferred shareholders must be repaid to them before the common shareholders get anything.

Further participation after return of capital

Whether the holders of preferred shares will be entitled to participate in the surplus assets after the capital has been returned on all the shares depends on the construction of the documents whereby the rights of such holders are defined.

Payment in advance of calls

Where payments have been made by shareholders in advance of calls, such shareholders are entitled to the return of such sums, with interest, before other shareholders of equal rank receive anything: *Re Wakefield Rolling Stock Co.*, [1892] 3 Ch. 165 at 174.

Fraudulent preferences

When contracts presumed to be made with intent to defraud

Two classes of contracts are, under ss. 96 and 97, presumed to be made with intent to defraud creditors: (1) Contracts made without consideration, or with a merely nominal consideration, within three months before, or at any time after, the commencement of the winding-up (s. 96); and (2) Contracts in which there may be consideration, but which are made with a person who knows, or has probable cause for believing, that the corporation is unable to meet its engagements or after such inability is public and notorious and in respect of which corporation a winding-up order under the Act is afterwards made, if such contracts injure, obstruct or delay creditors (s. 97): *Skinner v. McLeod* (1874), 15 N.B.R. 131 (C.A.). See also *Angers v. American Motors (Can.) Ltd.*, [1968] Que. S.C. 460, where the liquidator could not succeed when the action was brought after the provincial limitation period.

While there is authority for the proposition that pressure by a creditor will rebut the presumption of intent to defraud arising under these sections; this may now be regarded as doubtful.

The presumption of intent to defraud creditors arising under s. 96 from the transaction taking place within three months of the winding-up was held to be rebuttable: *Hammond v. Bank of Ottawa* (1910), 22 O.L.R. 73 (C.A.). In this case, pressure by the creditor was shown. See also *Campbell v. Barrie* (1871), 31 U.C.Q.B. 279 at 298, 290 (Ont. C.A.); *Dominion Trust Co. v. Royal Bank* (1921), 59 D.L.R. 224 (B.C. S.C.).

An overdue debt is consideration that takes the case out of s. 96: *Adams v. Bank of Montreal* (1901), 32 S.C.R. 719. A mortgage is included in the term "contract": *Canadian Bank of Commerce v. Smith* (1911), 17 W.L.R. 135 (Alta. T.D.); *Hammond v. Bank of Ottawa, supra.*

The expression "unable to meet its engagements" in s. 97 points to an insufficiency of assets if realized under fair conditions: *Canadian Bank of Commerce v. Smith, supra*, at 143; *Dominion Bank v. Cowan* (1887), 14 O.R. 465 (H.C.).

The phrase "with a person who knows such inability or has probable cause for believing such inability to exist" in s. 97 does not import actual knowledge on the part of the creditor; nor does it seem necessary that he should have any actual belief on the subject; and belief will not protect a party if there is probable cause for believing otherwise: *McInnes v. Davidson* (1877), 24 Gr. 414.

The presumption mentioned in s. 97 was held to be rebuttable on proof of pressure by the creditor: *Adams v. Bank of Montreal* (1901), 32 S.C.R. 719; affg (1899), 8 B.C.R. 314 (C.A.).

As to the position where a contract is made with intent to defraud creditors, see the notes on s. 99 under the heading "Transactions made with intent to defraud," below.

The following are cases in which the transaction was set aside under the combined effect of the sections of the *Insolvency Act* corresponding to these sections and s. 99: *Payne v. Hendry* (1873), 20 Gr. 142; *Coates v. Joselin* (1867), 12 Gr. 524; *Brooks v. Taylor* (1876), 26 C.P. 443; *McFarlane v. McDonald* (1874), 21 Gr. 319; *Squire v. Watt* (1869), 29 U.C.R. 328; *Newton v. Ontario Bank* (1869), 15 Gr. 283; on appeal from (1867), 13 Gr. 652.

Contracts injuring or obstructing creditors voidable in certain events (s. 98)

Under section 98, contracts or conveyances injuring or obstructing creditors made within 30 days next before the commencement of the winding-up with a person who is ignorant of the corporation's inability to meet its engagements may be set aside by the court, which may impose terms protecting such person from loss or liability under the contract.

In the following cases the transaction was set aside as a fraud on creditors: *Black v. Fountain* (1876), 23 Gr. 174; *Masson v. McGowan* (1866), 2 L.C.L.J. 37.

The section does not mean that all contracts and conveyances made within the 30-day period are voidable, but only those by which creditors are injured or obstructed; thus, the section does not apply where the purchaser receives full value for the goods he buys: *Bank of Montreal v. McWhirter* (1867), 17 C.P. 506.

Where the transferee knows that the debtor is unable to meet his obligations, the provision as to protection does not apply: *Kalus v. Hergert* (1875), 1 O.A.R. 75. See also *Mathers v. Lynch* (1867), 27 U.C.Q.B. 244; *Skinner v. McLeod* (1874), 15 N.B.R. 131 (C.A.); *Walter v. Leduc Lumber Co.* (1915), 8 W.W.R. 360 (Alta. T.D.); *Re Allenby Garment Co.* (1964), 6 C.B.R. (N.S.) 109 (Ont. Master); and see also *Re United Fuel Investments Ltd.* (1962), 33 D.L.R. (2d) 336 (S.C.C.); affd [1962] S.C.R. 771.

This section cannot be construed as making null and void any dealings by a bank with its customers in the ordinary course of its banking business within 30 days next before the commencement of the winding-up of its customer; thus, discounts by a bank of a customer's trade paper in the ordinary course of business are not conveyances in contemplation of the section: *Canadian Bank of Commerce v. Burnett*, [1923] 2 D.L.R. 166 (Que. C.A.). A bank is entitled to rely on a statement of the customer's assets and liabilities showing a surplus as showing that it had no knowledge of the debtor's insolvency: *Re Archambault Ltd.*, [1923] 4 D.L.R. 362 (Que. S.C.). It was also held in the same case that delay in serving notice of an assignment of book debts was not a ground for setting aside the transfer; and that the bank could apply advances thereunder to payment of prior debts owing to itself.

Transactions made with intent to defraud (s. 99)

Under s. 99, contracts or conveyances made and acts done by the corporation with intent to defraud or delay creditors, and so made, done and intended with the knowledge of the person contracting or acting with the corporation, and that have the effect of obstructing or delaying creditors, are void.

The usual interpretation placed upon the word "void" in acts of this kind is "voidable": *Meriden Britannia Co. v. Braden* (1894), 21 O.A.R. 352. And this would seem to indicate that a good title can be conferred by a person who holds what is under the Act a void title: *Re Vansittart; Ex parte Brown*, [1893] 2 Q.B. 377; *Re Brall; Ex parte Norton*, [1893] 2 Q.B. 381; *Re Carter & Kenderdine's Contract*, [1897] 1 Ch. 776 (C.A.).

A banking firm, having become embarrassed, applied to the plaintiffs, to whom they owed $50,000, to advance $15,000 more. The debtors agreed to secure both debts by a mortgage on the real estate of one of the partners. The plaintiffs made the advance and obtained the mortgage. In less than three months thereafter, the debtors became insolvent. Though they were indebted beyond their means of paying at the time of executing the mortgage, they did not consider themselves so, nor were the mortgagees aware of it. The mortgage was not given from a desire to prefer the mortgagees over the other creditors, but solely as a means of obtaining the advance that they thought would enable them to go on with their business and pay their creditors. As respecting the antecedent debt, it was held that the mortgage was valid as against the assignee: *Royal Canadian Bank v. Kerr* (1870), 17 Gr. 47.

See also the following cases adopting the same principle: *Allan v. Clarkson* (1870), 17 Gr. 570; *Risk v. Sleeman* (1874), 21 Gr. 250; *Jackson v. Bowman* (1867), 14 Gr. 156; *Hyman v. Cuthbertson* (1886), 10 O.R. 443 (H.C.); *Ross v. Dunn* (1889), 16 O.A.R. 552. See, however, *Re Allenby Garment Co.* (1964), 6 C.B.R. (N.S.) 109 (Ont. S.C.) where an assignment of the proceeds of a fire insurance claim was set aside as the creditor knew at the time of the assignment that the debtor was unable to carry on business and to pay its accounts.

Actual knowledge on the part of the creditor, not mere constructive notice, is necessary under this section. A note given in violation of the law laid down in this section has been held to be an absolute nullity and to be void, *ab initio*, even in the hands of a third party who was an innocent holder for value before maturity: *Davis v. Muir* (1869), 13 L.C.J. 184.

Sale or transfer in contemplation of insolvency (s. 100)

Under s. 100(1), certain sales, deposits, pledges and transfers, and certain payments, are null and void if they result in one creditor obtaining an unjust preference over other creditors. The sales, deposits, pledges and transfers affected by the section are those made by a corporation in contemplation of insolvency by way of security for payment to any creditor; under s. 100(2), where such sale, deposit, pledge or transfer is made within 30 days before or at any time after the commencement of the winding-up, it is presumed to have been made in contemplation of insolvency.

The doctrine of pressure referred to in the notes on ss. 96 and 97 has no application under s. 100: *Davidson v. Ross* (1876), 24 Gr. 22. The cases decided under the English *Bankruptcy Acts* were distinguished on the ground that there the intention is made an ingredient, while under this section it is simply a question of what effect the transaction will have, coupled with the contemplation of insolvency. "If it has the effect of preventing the ratable distribution of an insolvent estate by transferring assets in security for, or satisfaction of a claim, which would not be entitled to priority over the claims of general creditors upon insolvency supervening," it is an unjust preference, per Moss, J., at 80. The court in this case was divided as to whether the presumption referred to in the latter half of the section was rebuttable. It has since been held to be rebuttable: *Kirby v. Rathbun Co.* (1900), 32 O.R. 9 (H.C.); *Dominion Trust Co. v. Royal Bank* (1921), 59 D.L.R. 224 at 236 (B.C. S.C.). And see *Webster v. Crickmore* (1898), 25 O.A.R. 97, which was decided under the Ontario Act respecting assignments and preferences, and *Lawson v. McGeoch* (1892), 22 O.R. 474 (H.C.), affd (1893), 20 O.A.R. 464.

It remains to be considered whether the decision in *Davidson v. Ross, supra*, has been overruled by decisions on similar enactments such as the Ontario *Assignments and Preferences Act*. In this connection, it should be observed that the wording of the section under which *Davidson v. Ross* was decided was, so far as material, identical with the wording of s. 100, and one ought to be careful in coming to the conclusion that it is overruled by cases decided under sections differently worded. It should also be noted that *The Bank of Australasia v. Harris* (1861), 15 Moo. P.C.C. 97, and *Harris v. The Bank of Australasia*, ibid., at 116, were cited in *Davidson v. Ross*. The wording of the section under consideration in *The Bank of Australasia v. Harris*, and that of the sections under consideration in such cases as *Molsons Bank v. Halter* (1890), 18 S.C.R. 88, and *Stephens v. McArthur* (1891), 19 S.C.R. 446, might appear to be practically identical with this section; but the court in *Davidson v. Ross, supra*, held that there was a distinction between a "preference," which under the English decisions had been held to mean a fraudulent preference and to be rebuttable by pressure, and an "unjust preference," which the court in *Davidson v. Ross* held not to mean a fraudulent preference and not to be rebuttable by pressure. See the judgment of Moss, J., at 81-83.

On the above grounds, it is submitted that the decisions on the Ontario *Assignments and Preferences Act* and similar enactments as to pressure do not apply to this section; that *Davidson v. Ross* is still good law; and that therefore, under the above enactment, pressure will not validate a transaction "whereby such creditor obtains or will obtain an unjust preference." And see *Kirby v. Rathbun Co., supra; Adams v. McCall* (1865), 25 U.C.R. 219.

See further on the question of pressure: *Ivey & Co. v. Knox, Morgan & Co.* (1885), 8 O.R. 635; *Brayley v. Ellis* (1884), 9 O.A.R. 565; *Long v. Hancock* (1884), 12 O.A.R. 137; *Johnson v. Hope* (1890), 17 O.A.R. 10; *Davies v. Gillard* (1891), 21 O.R. 431; *Beattie v. Wenger* (1897), 24 O.A.R. 72 (C.A.); *Gaslight Improvement Co. v. Terrell* (1870), L.R. 10 Eq. 168; *Re W. Blackburn & Co.*; *Buckley's Case*, [1899] 2 Ch. 725.

It is not an unjust preference when the transfer is made in pursuance of a bona fide agreement to give a security in return for an advance made, if the agreement is made more than 30 days before the commencement of the winding-up: *Suter v. Merchants Bank* (1876), 24 Gr. 365; *Re Central Bank* (1891), 21 O.R. 515 (H.C.); *Newton v. Ontario Bank* (1867), 13 Gr. 652; *Allan v. Clarkson* (1870), 17 Gr. 570; *Smith v. McLean* (1878), 25 Gr. 567, but see *Kalus v. Hergert* (1875), 1 O.A.R. 75. But where the taking of the security is deliberately postponed till the debtors are insolvent, it cannot be sustained: *Webster v. Crickmore* (1898), 25 O.A.R. 97; *Breese v. Knox* (1896), 24 O.A.R. 203; *Jones v. Kinney* (1885), 11 S.C.R. 708.

In *Marsh v. Sweeny* (1875), 15 N.B.R. 454 (C.A.), decided under the corresponding section in the *Insolvency Act* of 1869, which section did not contain the words "under this Act," it was held that the words "in contemplation of insolvency" did not mean in contemplation of insolvency under the Act.

The meaning of this phrase was explained by Patterson, J., in *Davidson v. Ross* (1877), 24 Gr. 22, at 69, as follows:

> I take the object of the law to be to make it the duty of a trader who, from the knowledge which he has of his own affairs or of the intentions of his creditors, has reason to apprehend either that proceedings under the Insolvent Act will be taken against him, or that he may have to resort to the Act for relief, to do nothing which will prejudice the ratable distribution of his assets, by giving one creditor an unjust preference over the others, and, I apprehend, that if under such circumstances he gives a preference, he does so in contemplation of insolvency, whether he does it from a desire to favour the preferred creditor, or only because that creditor has succeeded by urgency in overcoming his reluctance to give the preference.

Moss, J., in the same case, at 87, citing *Gibson v. Muskett* (1842), 4 Man. & G. 160, says that money was paid in contemplation of bankruptcy "if it was paid under such circumstances that any prudent man taking a reasonable view of his situation and the surrounding circumstances at the time might fairly expect bankruptcy would follow."

As to the meaning of the words "in contemplation of insolvency" see *Morgan v. Brundrett* (1833), 5 B. & Ad. 296, which supports the view that actual insolvency must be expected by the debtor at the time of the transaction. See also *Atkinson v. Brindall* (1835), 2 Bing N.C. 225, and *Gibson v. Brand* (1842), 4 Man. & G. 179; *Re Hunt; Ex parte Simpson* (1844), De G. 9 (Ct. of R.). If circumstances exist from which an ordinary man would conclude that a debtor was unable to meet his liabilities, knowledge of insolvency may be presumed: *National Bank of Australasia v. Morris*, [1892] A.C. 287 (P.C.). Securities are not to be deemed to have been given in contemplation of insolvency merely because the manager of the corporation knew of its insolvent condition, if the person receiving them had no such knowledge: *Dominion Trust Co. v. Royal Bank* (1921), 59 D.L.R. 224 at 236 (B.C.S.C.).

It should be observed that the presumption referred to in subs. (2) of the section is a presumption that the sale, deposit, pledge or transfer was made in contemplation of insolvency. This presumption is not displaced by merely showing that the sale or transfer was bona fide or that the creditor did not know or had no probable cause for believing the insolvent was unable to meet his engagements: *Evans v. Ross* (1880), 30 C.P. 121.

While, as indicated above, s. 100(1) also deals with payments, the presumption referred to in subs. (2) does not apply in the case of a payment, which is provided for in s. 101: *Canadian Bank of Commerce v. Burnett*, [1923] 2 D.L.R. 166 at 168 (Que. C.A.).

As to the meaning of pledge, see *Canadian Bank of Commerce v. Smith* (1911), 17 W.L.R. 135 (Alta. T.D.).

Under the English Companies Acts, an issue of debentures or debenture stock may be invalidated as a fraudulent preference: *Gaslight Improvement Co. v. Terrell* (1870), L.R. 10 Eq. 168; but debentures issued *bona fide* to prevent winding-up were held not to be avoided: *Re Inns of Court Hotel Co.* (1868), L.R. 6 Eq. 82.

It has also been held by the English courts that debenture holders are not as such entitled to attack a fraudulent preference in a winding-up on the ground that the provisions of the *Companies Act* are intended for the benefit of the general creditors: *Willmott v. London Celluloid Co.* (1886), 34 Ch. D. 147 (C.A.).

The Master, or other officer of the court to whom the Master's powers are delegated, is not a court of competent jurisdiction within this section of the Act for the purpose of trying the question as to the propriety and value of any transfer of property: *Harte v. Ontario Express & Transportation Co.* (1894), 25 O.R. 247 (H.C.). In such a case the liquidator should proceed under s. 35 of the *Winding-up Act*: *Re Sun Lithographing Co.* (1892), 22 O.R. 57 (C.A.).

See further as to unjust preference: *Smyth v. Morton* (1880), 30 C.P. 566; *City Bank v. Smith* (1869), 20 C.P. 93; *McWhirter v. Thorne* (1869), 19 C.P. 302; *Newton v. Ontario Bank* (1867), 13 Gr. 652; *Campbell v. Barrie* (1871), 31 U.C.Q.B. 279 at 291 (Ont. C.A.); *Larue v. Dohan* (1915), 48 Que. S.C. 374.

The failure by a liquidation to commence action within the limitation period prescribed by the laws of the province will bar any action for the alleged preferential transfer of assets: *Angers v. Amer. Motors (Canada) Ltd.*, [1968] Que. S.C. 460; *Gingras v. Bédard*, [1973] Que. S.C. 33.

Payments by corporation (s. 101)

Under s. 101, payments made within 30 days before the commencement of the winding-up by a corporation unable to meet its engagements in full, to a person knowing such inability or having probable cause for believing it to exist, are void.

The payment must be by the debtor himself: *McWhirter v. Thorne* (1869), 19 C.P. 302. See *Exchange Bank v. Counsell* (1885), 8 O.R. 673 (H.C.), where on the facts it was held that there was no payment.

Under s. 101, the payment is void when made to a person who knows that the corporation is unable to meet its engagements in full or has probable cause for believing that such inability exists. The view of the debtor in making the payment is not an element to be inquired into in the application of the section: *Trusts & Guarantee Co. v. Munro* (1909), 19 O.L.R. 480 at 487 (C.A.).

Where a bank in the ordinary course of business discounts commercial paper for a customer and makes advances, s. 101 and not s. 96 is applicable; and the liquidator, in order to recover, must show that the bank knew of the corporation's inability to meet its engagements in full, or had probable cause for believing such inability to exist: *Canadian Bank of Commerce v. Burnett*, [1923] 2 D.L.R. 166 (Que. C.A.).

When a bank sold a stock of goods held by it and agreed to accept in payment cheques of a third party drawn on his deposit account and subsequently accepted, and for which cheques the purchaser gave his acceptance to the third party, it was held that an action would not lie by the liquidators of the bank against the third party to recover back the amount paid on his cheques, as he had received no valuable consideration from the bank that he should be ordered to repay: *Exchange Bank v. Stinson* (1885), 8 O.R. 667 (H.C.).

Where an officer of the corporation has transferred to the latter, in breach of trust, trust moneys that being subsequently used in the corporation's business are no longer capable of being ear-marked and followed by the *cestuis que trust*, so that the corporation becomes merely a debtor to the trust estate for the moneys, the withdrawal and payment of the moneys to the trustee for the protection of the *cestuis que trust* on the eve of the winding-up is a payment to creditors and void under s. 101: *Trusts & Guarantee Co. v. Munro, supra.*

The repayment by a corporation on the eve of insolvency of advances made and that have benefited its creditors is not a preferential payment: *Larue v. Dohan* (1915), 48 Que. S.C. 374.

A payment by an insolvent after attachment against him on account of a draft that was discounted by the defendants for him and then dishonoured by non-acceptance was recoverable back by the official assignee, though the defendants were ignorant of the insolvency when they received the note from him: *Roe v. Royal Canadian Bank* (1868), 19 C.P. 347; followed in *Roe v. Bank of British North America* (1870), 20 C.P. 351.

Moneys recovered by the liquidator from a creditor on the ground that the payment was a fraudulent preference do not become part of the general assets of the corporation, so as to be covered by a floating charge that crystallized before the moneys were recovered, but are received by the liquidator impressed with a trust for those creditors among whom the assets of the corporation are distributable: *Re Yagerphone Ltd.*, [1935] Ch. 392.

"Valuable security" as used in s. 101(2) means some property of the debtor that has been given up to him or of which he has had the benefit; or some security upon which the creditor, if still the holder of it, would be bound to place a value: *Beattie v. Wenger* (1897), 24 O.A.R. 72 (C.A.). See also *R. v. Brady* (1866), 26 U.C.Q.B. 13 (C.A.). See also as to what will constitute a valuable security given up in consideration of the payment: *Churcher v. Johnston* (1874), 34 U.C.Q.B. 528; and *Re Wallis* (1874), 29 U.C.Q.B. 313; *Re Lamb* (1866), 4 P.R. 16.

Transfer of debts (s. 102)

Section 102 has the effect of preventing contributories or other persons indebted to the corporation from setting off against their liability to the corporation the debts of the corporation transferred to them in the circumstances specified in the section.

Before the amending Act, 52 Vict. (Dom.) c. 32, s. 16, was passed, it was held that the prohibition in s. 73 of the former Act against acquiring debts for the purpose of set-off was limited to the case of contributories; and that even in the case of a contributory who was also a debtor, he might acquire a debt owing to the corporation and set it off against the debt due by him, for he was not a contributory *quoad* the debt: *Re Central Bank of Canada (sub nom. Yorke's Case)* (1888), 15 O.R. 625 (H.C.), following *Ings v. Bank of Prince Edward Island* (1885), 11 S.C.R. 265. The provisions of the section are now applicable to all persons indebted or liable in any way to the corporation.

Formerly, claims acquired after a bank suspended payment but before the presentation of the petition could be set off: *Maritime Bank v. Robinson* (1887), 26 N.B.R. 297 (C.A.), but not claims acquired after the presentation of the winding-up petition: ibid. Now, after a bank has suspended payment and its insolvency is notorious, compensation of a debt due to the bank cannot be effected by a transfer to the debtor of debts due by the bank to third parties, where such transfer has been made after the suspension and within 30 days prior to the winding-up proceedings: *Communauté des Soeurs de Charité de la Providence v. Kent* (1904), 13 Que. S.C. 483 C.A.).

Chapter 25

PROCEDURE

Section 133. The court may appoint solicitors and counsel to represent classes of creditors
Section 134. The liquidator is subject to the summary jurisdiction of the court
Section 135. All remedies for enforcing any claim to any property in the hands of the liquidator may be obtained by an order of the court on summary petition
Section 136. Judges may make and settle rules, regulations and forms to be used in proceedings
Section 137. Pending action under section 137, the ordinary procedures of court to apply
Section 138. Unclaimed dividends to remain in bank for three years and then to be paid over to the Minister of Consumer and Corporate Affairs
Section 139. Money deposited by the liquidator but not paid out to claimants for three years to be paid over to the Minister of Consumer and Corporate Affairs
Section 140. The court may direct criminal proceedings against certain persons with respect to the company
Section 141. The destruction of books or the making of false entries there is an indictable offence, if intent to defraud or deceive
Section 142. Failure to comply with an order of the court is a contempt of court
Section 143. Refusal by officers, directors or employees of a company to give all the information possessed by them to a person appointed by the court to enquire into the company's affairs is a contempt of court
Section 144. If the liquidator fails to deposit in a bank the money of the estate he is liable to a penalty
Section 145. Refusal of a witness appearing before the court for examinaiton to answer any question put to him is contempt of court
Section 146. All books of the company as between contributories are *prima facie* evidence of the truth of contents
Section 147. Persons before whom affidavits or declarations are to be sworn
Section 148. Judicial notice to be taken of certain seals, stamps, or signatures.
Section 149. Office copy of an order may by a court of one province is evidence of the order
Section 150. How the failure to produce the liquidator's bank pass-book is proved

Cross references: Sections 21, 35(l)(a)
Ontario Corporations Act, ss. 227-236.

Right of Appeal

Under s. 103, leave may be granted in certain events to appeal from orders of the court or a single judge in winding-up proceedings; as to when leave may be granted, see the notes below on paragraphs (a), (b) and (c) of s. 103. The appeal is to the provincial or territorial courts of appeal (s. 104); as to appeals to the Supreme Court of Canada from such courts, see the notes on s. 107 below.

The right of appeal exists only in cases falling within s. 103: *Re Solloway Mills & Co. Ltd., In Liquidation, Ex p. I. W. C. Solloway*, [1935] O.R. 37 (C.A.) 47; see also *Traders Leasing Ltd. v. Marcotte* (1963), 6 C.B.R. (N.S.) 153 (Que. S.C.); and no appeal lies from an order refusing to set aside an appointment for the examination of an officer of the petitioner: *Re McLean, Stinson & Brodie, Ltd.* (1910), 18 O.W.R. 163; see also *Canada Deposit Insurance Corp. v. Commonwealth Trust Co.* (1992), unreported November 13, 1992 (B.C. C.A.).

The appeals provided for by s. 103 relate not to the direct appeal from the Master or Referee before whom the reference is proceeding, but to the appeal subsequently to be taken to the court of appeal. The first appeal from the Master or Referee who is conducting the reference exists as of right in Ontario, on the general principle that when the court has delegated to a subordinate tribunal any of its powers, a right of appeal always exists from such tribunal to the court itself: *Markle v. Ross* (1889), 13 P.R. 135. The appeal from a Master is to a single judge of the Supreme Court of Ontario.

As to appeals in the province of Quebec, see Re *Compagnie des Théatres & Turgeon & Courval* (1909), 10 Que. P.R. 215; *In re Banque de St. Jean* (1911), 12 Que. P.R. 353; *Banque de St. Jean v. Bienvenu* (1916), 17 Que. P.R. 443; *Brodeur Company Ltd. v. Merrill et al.* (1918), 57 Que. S.C. 137.

The jurisdiction of the court to rescind orders that have been issued inadvertently and in error is not fettered by s. 103: *In re The Central Bank of Canada, Hogaboom v. The Receiver General of Canada* (1897), 28 S.C.R. 192 at 205.

It was stated by Boyd, C., in *Re Belding Lumber Co. Ltd.* (1911), 23 O.L.R. 255 at 258, that:

> The matters in regard to which an appeal is contemplated are as to substantial matters of property or rights arising in the winding-up proceedings—an order having been granted, and something having arisen in the prosecution of the order affecting the assets and the creditors' rights therein.

No leave is necessary where the proceeding is not under the Act but is an ordinary civil action, even though the liquidator has sued in his capacity as liquidator: *Auger v. Ross* (1929), 47 Que. K.B. 444 (C.A.).

A shareholder and a creditor may appeal against a judgment against the corporation given in proceedings to which they were not original parties; they are persons dissatisfied within the meaning of s. 103 and have an interest in the final judgment; they may take advantage of extensions of time for appeal granted to the liquidator: *Re Stadacona Rouyn Mines Ltd.*, [1945] 1 D.L.R. 420 (Que. C.A.).

The proper procedure in seeking a revision of a judgment made under the *Winding-up Act* authorizing the sale of immovable property is an appeal under s. 103 rather than the issuance of a writ of summons: *Maranda-Desaulniers v. Peckham et al.*, [1953] Que. Q.B. 163 (C.A.).

When winding-up proceedings had commenced in Manitoba and a related issue was directed to be determined by the Supreme Court of Ontario, it was held that the proper forum for appeal from the decision with respect to the related issue was the Ontario Court of Appeal and not the Manitoba Court of Appeal: *Genovese v. York Lambton Corpn.* (1969), 67 W.W.R. 355, 4 D.L.R. (3d) 58, affd [1969] S.C.R. vi.

Questions as to future rights (s. 103(a))

Paragraph (a) of s. 103 provides for an appeal by leave if the question to be raised on appeal involves future rights.

The words "future rights" should be given a wide interpretation: *Re J. McCarthy & Sons Co.* (1916), 38 O.L.R. 3 (C.A.), where Meredith, C.J.C.P., in the appellate division, dealing with an appeal involving leave to bring an action, stated the following to be "future rights" sufficient under this section:

"the right of trial by ordinary methods involving future possible trial by jury and future unrestricted rights to appeal to this Court and to the Supreme Court of Canada, and other such like rights of the ordinary litigant."

See also, on the meaning of "future rights", *Re Union Fire Insurance Co.* (1886) 13 O.A.R. 268 at 295 (an order for the winding-up of a corporation involves future rights); *Re Canada National Fire Insurance Co.*, [1931] 1 D.L.R. 751 (Man. C.A.) (an order dismissing a petition by a shareholder for the winding-up of the corporation is within the section, as it involves the future rights of the shareholder); *Re Kern Agencies Ltd.*, [1931] 2 D.L.R. 614 (Sask. C.A.) ("future rights" is wide enough to include an appeal from a refusal to approve a proposed composition); *Re Ditchburn Boats & Aircraft (1936) Ltd.*, [1938] 3 D.L.R. 751 (Ont. C.A.) (future rights means legal rights only and does not include commercial advantages that may accrue to creditors from the superior administrative qualities of one trustee over another); *Bell Telephone Co. v. Duclos*, [1942] 3 D.L.R. 738 (Que. C.A.) (appeal by a creditor from an order requiring it to continue its services without interruption involves future rights).

An order granting leave to serve a misfeasance summons *ex juris* is not a matter affecting future rights, but is a mere matter of procedure: *Brown v. Cadwell*, [1918] 2 W.W.R. 229 (B.C. C.A.).

Where a shareholder, who was not satisfied with the dividend sheet of the liquidator, had petitioned unsuccessfully for an order requiring the liquidator to render a detailed account of his administration and appointing auditors to report on such account, a petition for leave to appeal was dismissed on the ground that the judgment in question involved no future rights of the parties: *Re Stadacona Rouyn Mines Ltd.; Silverstone v. Duclos*, [1945] 1 Que. K.B. 351.

Appeal from winding-up order

The original winding-up order is an order from which an appeal will lie under this section: *Re Shoolbred Union Fire Insurance Co.* (1886), 13 O.A.R. 268. Such an appeal involves future rights: ibid., at 295; *Marsden v. Minnekahda Land Co.* (1918), 40 D.L.R. 76; though it cannot be said that any sum of money is involved: *Cushing Sulphite Fibre Co. v. Cushing* (1906), 37 S.C.R. 427. See also *Re McGill Chair Co., Munro's Case* (1912), 26 O.L.R. 254; *Re Winding-up Act; Re Canada National Fire Insurance Company*, [1930] 4 D.L.R. 572 (appeal from order dismissing petition).

After a winding-up order has been made and become effective, the proper way to attack it is by appeal, not by application to rescind it directed to the judge who made the order: *Re Equitable Savings Long & Building Assn* (1903), 6 O.L.R. 26 at 31; nor by motion to set aside the order: *Re New York Dress & Cloaks Ltd.* (1926), 8 C.B.R. 372. A judge has no power to rescind his winding-up order, at all events where he has no additional material before him and it is not apparent that he was previously misled or that any fact was suppressed: ibid. See also *Re Auberge du Port Inc.* (1963), 6 C.B.R. (N.S.) 144 (Que.). But see *Siche Light Co. v. Fortin* (1911), 13 Que. P.R. 235 (S.C.); also *Pontbriand Co. v. Coskey* (1912), 14 Que. P.R. 19. An order directing the winding up of a foreign corporation doing business in Ontario made by one judge will not be set aside by another: *Re Lake Superior Native Copper Co.* (1885), 9 O.R. 277. Nor has a judge, on appeal from the findings of the Official Referee, jurisdiction to review the winding-up order: *Re Farmers Bank* (1916), 35 O.L.R. 470.

An appeal may be taken from an order refusing to grant a winding-up order: *Marsden v. Minnekahda Land Co.* (1918), 40 D.L.R. 76; and see *Re Martello & Sons, Ltd.*, [1945] O.R. 453 (C.A.) at 465. Where the order appealed from was considered right apart from the point of law involved, leave was refused: *Re Dominion Savings & Investment Society* (1923), 25 O.W.N. 475.

An appeal lies from an order by a judge revoking his order for dissolution: *Re Equitable Savings Loan & Building Assn* (1903), 6 O.L.R. 26.

Where an order had been made on the petition of the corporation launched in pursuance of a resolution of the shareholders, and proceedings were pending to annul the resolution as being fraudulent and illegal, the order was quashed and the petition directed to be held in suspense pending the conclusion of the litigation: *Bélanger v. Union Abitibi Mining Co.* (1916), 32 D.L.R. 700.

If a winding-up order has not been appealed against, a contributory or other person who is not a stranger to the winding-up proceedings cannot call into question its validity on any of the proceedings in the winding-up: *Re London Marine Assn* (1869) L.R. 8 Eq. 176; *Re Arthur Average Association* (1875), 3 Ch. D. 522, (1875), L.R. 10 Ch. App. 542; *Re Haycock's Policy*, [1876] 1 Ch. 611 at 616, 617; *Re Padstow Total Loss & Collision Assurance Assn* (1882), 20 Ch. D. 137 (C.A.), at 145; *Strick v. Swansea Tin-Plate Co.* (1887), 36 Ch. D. 558; *Re Sunderland 32nd Building Society* (1888) 21 Q.B.D. 349. But a stranger to the winding-up may dispute the validity of the order: *Re Bowling & Welby's Contract*, [1895] 1 Ch. 663 (C.A.).

Decisions affecting other similar cases (s. 103(b))

Paragraph (b) of s. 103 provides for an appeal by leave if the order or decision is likely to affect other cases of a similar nature in the winding-up proceedings.

Test cases brought by one or more contributories to obtain a decision on some question affecting a group or class furnish an example of the application of this subsection: *Re Monarch Bank* (1914), 42 O.L.R. 207; so also an appeal involving the question of liability on bonus stock, all the corporation's stock having been so issued: *Re McGill Chair Co., Munro's Case* (1912), 26 O.L.R. 254. See also *Re Bailey Cobalt Mines Ltd.* (1920), 47 O.L.R. 13, where leave was granted, apparently in part on the ground that the decision would affect similar cases likely to arise under the *Winding-up Act.*

Amount involved exceeding $500 (s. 103(c))

Paragraph (c) of s. 103 provides for an appeal by leave if the amount involved in the appeal exceeds $500.

Where the order appealed from is one setting aside a previous order confirming the disallowance of a claim to be a creditor in an amount in excess of $500, the case falls within para. (c): *Re Winding up Act & Gibson Mining Co. Ltd.*, [1923] 3 D.L.R. 1052 (B.C. C.A.).

Proof of the amount involved can be made by affidavit, and it is the duty of the court hearing the application to determine the amount from the affidavits filed: *Re Prudential Life Insurance Co.*, [1918] 3 W.W.R. 508 (Man. C.A.).

In ascertaining the amount involved, interest and costs are not to be included: *Dufresne v. Guevremont* (1896), 26 S.C.R. 216; *Re Wiarton Beet Root Sugar Co., Kydd's Case* (1905), 6 O.W.R. 590. Where the amount in question, while nominally just beyond $500, was very uncertain, as the parties on whom the liability was imposed were said to be financially worthless — except in the case of one, whose position was problematical — leave was refused: *Re McGill Chair Co., Munro's Case* (1912), 26 O.L.R. 254. See, however, *Re J. McCarthy & Sons Co.* (1916), 38 O.L.R. 3 at 6; and *Brown v. Cadwell*, [1918] 2 W.W.R. 229 (B.C. C.A.), where the amount in question was more than $500 and the right to appeal was upheld.

Where the question raised concerns the right of a creditor for more than $500 to rank as a preferred or ordinary creditor, there is an amount involved in the appeal exceeding $500, and an appeal would be under the similar provision of the *Bankruptcy and Insolvency Act* (which has been increased from $500 to $10,000): *Apex Lumber Co. v. Johnstone*, [1925] 3 D.L.R. 1050.

In the case of a judgment declaring a shareholder a contributory, the amount to which the liability of the contributory extends is the amount involved in the appeal: *Re Joyce Dress Corp., Horowitz v. Greenberg*, [1934] S.C.R. 212.

See further on the question as to the amount involved in an appeal the notes to s. 107, under the heading "Appeal to Supreme Court of Canada" in this chapter.

Cases in which no appeal lies

Appeals from interlocutory orders do not come within s. 103: *Re Solloway Mills Co. Ltd. & I. W. C. Solloway*, [1936] O.R. 416 (C.A.).

A contest between solicitors of creditors competing for the carriage of the order is not a proper case for appellate interference: *Re Belding Lumber Co. Ltd.* (1911), 23 O.L.R. 255, per Boyd, C.

There is no appeal from an order giving leave to appeal in cases in which there is power to give leave, but where there is no such power, the order granting leave is ineffectual and the appellate court will, of its own motion, refuse to enter on the appeal: *Re J. McCarthy & Sons Co.* (1916), 38 O.L.R. 3 (C.A.); *Cushing Sulphite Fibre Co. v. Cushing* (1906), 37 S.C.R. 427 (appeal quashed). In the *McCarthy* case, the appeal was subsequently heard on the merits.

Where leave has been refused, there is no appeal from such refusal, and successive applications to other judges or to the court to which the appeal lies will not be entertained: *Re Sarnia Oil Co.* (1893), 15 P.R. 347; *Re Solloway Mills & Co., In Liquidation, Ex parte Solloway*, [1935] O.R. 37 at 47 (C.A.).

Discretion to grant leave

Leave must be granted in the exercise of judicial discretion and may be refused where there is no prospect of any advantage to the insolvent estate: *Re Ontario Sugar Co., McKinnon's Case* (1911), 44 S.C.R. 659, at 661, 662.

Leave, generally speaking, ought to be refused unless there appears to be some reason for doubting the validity of the judgment in review: *Re Ontario Bank* (1917), 12 O.W.N. 245; *Re Durnford Elk Shoes Ltd.* (1916), 11 O.W.N. 105; *Re Winding-up Act, In re Canada National Fire Insurance Co.*, [1930] 4 D.L.R. 572; *Re Noden Hallitt v. Johnson Ltd.* (1924), 26 O.W.N. 330.

Where the decision affected other cases in the particular winding-up, and the point involved was of importance, and the amount involved was considerable, leave was granted; but where no other cases were involved in the liquidation, and no future rights were involved, and the amount in question, while nominally just beyond $500, was uncertain, leave was refused: *Re McGill Chair Co.* (1912), 5 D.L.R. 393. See also *Re Carpenter Ltd.* (1916), 10 O.W.N. 122; *Re Canadian Shipbuilding Co.* (1912), 4 O.W.N. 157 (leave refused); *Re Sovereign Bank of Canada, Clark's Case* (1916), 35 O.L.R. 448 at 454 (C.A.) (leave granted where the appeal appeared to be clearly arguable, and the case was one of great hardship, and a prolongation of the litigation could not be regarded as vexatious); *Re Port Arthur Wagon Co., Smyth's Case* (1916), 11 O.W.N. 162 (points of considerable importance raised, which should be authoritatively settled).

Practice on appeals

Section 105 requires that all appeals shall be regulated by the practice governing appeals in the province in which the appeal is taken.

Where notice of appeal to the court of appeal has been given without leave, it is not necessary to have the notice set aside: *Re Sarnia Oil Co.* (1893), 15 P.R. 182 (C.A.); and where the appellant has sought to proceed without leave the case has been struck off the list: *Re Canadian Shipbuilding Co.* (1912), 4 O.W.N. 157.

The time may be extended even where the application for extension is made after the 14 days specified in s. 105 have elapsed: *Re Monarch Bank of Canada* (1911), 18 O.W.R. 743; *Calumet Metals v. Eldredge* (1913), 15 D.L.R. 461, where the authorities are collected; *Canadian Bank of Commerce v. Burnett* (1921), 61 D.L.R. 604; *Re Winding-up Act & Gibson Mining Co. Ltd.*, [1923] 3 D.L.R. 1052 (B.C. C.A.). See also *Re Flash Stone Mfg. Co.* (1963), 6 C.B.R. (N.S.) 172 (Que.).

A respondent, by demanding, or applying to increase the amount of, security for costs, thereby waives his right to object that security was not originally furnished in time: *Re Florida Mining Co.* (1901), 8 B.C.R. 388 (C.A.); *Re Oro Fino Mines Ltd.* (1900), 7 B.C.R. 388 (C.A.).

The section is also referred to in *Re Belding Lumber Co. Ltd.* (1911), 23 O.L.R. 255.

Appeal to Supreme Court of Canada (s. 107)

Under s. 107 of this Act there is an appeal to the Supreme Court of Canada, by leave, if the amount involved exceeds $2,000. In other words, the appeal lies only where monetary questions are under consideration, for example, the liability of a contributory. Leave to appeal to the Supreme Court of Canada cannot, therefore, be granted from a judgment refusing to set aside a winding-up order: *Cushing Sulphite Fibre Co. v. Cushing* (1906), 37 S.C.R. 427. However, see *Re United Fuel Investments Ltd.* (1962), 33 D.L.R. (2d) 336 (S.C.C.), where leave to appeal a winding-up order was granted, and also the dismissal of a motion to quash such appeal reported at [1962] S.C.R. 771. The court held that there was an amount involved in excess of the figure stipulated since a shareholder would have lost over this amount in a winding-up. Where the appeal involves the liability of several contributories, the fact that the aggregate amount for which these are sought to be made liable exceeds $2,000 will not give the Supreme Court jurisdiction. The appeal must be treated as if proceedings had been separately taken against each: *Stephens v. Gerth, Re Ontario Express Co.* (1895), 24 S.C.R. 716.

The jurisdiction depends on the amount involved in the judgment appealed from and not on the amount demanded in the proceedings in which the judgment was rendered: *Re Great Northern Construction Co.* (1916), 53 S.C.R. 128, per Brodeur, J. Thus, where a contributory by the judgment appealed from had been fixed on the list for an amount sufficient to give jurisdiction, but it was shown that a call of 50 per cent only had been made on contributories and that no further calls were proposed to be made, so that less than $2,000 would be demanded from the contributory, Brodeur, J., held that the court had jurisdiction: *Re Monarch Bank of Canada; Murphy's Case* (June 17, 1919). (unreported).

Leave to appeal

In order to obtain leave to appeal under s. 107, it is not enough to show merely that the necessary amount is in controversy. If no important principle of law, nor the construction of a public Act, nor any question of public interest is involved, leave to appeal to the Supreme Court of Canada will not be granted: *Re Ontario Sugar Co., McKinnon's Case* (1911), 44 S.C.R. 659; *Riley v. Curtis & Harvey* (1919), 59 S.C.R. 206; *Re Joyce Dress Corp.; Re Horowitz v. Greenberg*, [1934] S.C.R. 212.

By the *Supreme Court Act*, the appeal may ordinarily only be brought if the Court is of the opinion that any question involved is sufficiently important, by reason of its public importance, or by reason of the importance of any issue of law (or of mixed law and fact) being raised, that it should be decided by the Supreme Court; or is, for any other reason, of such a nature or significance that it warrants a decision by the Court. Certain time limits are provided within which the application for leave to appeal must be brought, namely, 60 days after the date of the judgment appealed from, excluding the months of July and August; this time may be extended in special circumstances.

An action by a beneficiary against a trust corporation executor of a testator and the trust corporation's liquidator under a winding-up order to recover the proceeds of life insurance policies that were collected by the executor and which had been bequeathed to the plaintiff, is not subject to the provisions of what is now s. 107 and no leave to appeal is necessary: *Arnold v. Dominion Trust Co.* (1918), 56 S.C.R. 433, Idington and Brodeur, JJ., dissenting.

Description of liquidator in proceedings (s. 108)

Under s. 108 the liquidator is to be described in all proceedings as the liquidator of the corporation and not by his individual name only.

In *Bank of Hochelaga v. Masson* (1884), M.L.R. 1 S.C. 62, it was held that the purpose of this section was to simplify procedure so as to render substitution unnecessary where one liquidator was replaced by another; but that the section did not invalidate proceedings where the personal name of the liquidator was used.

Procedure to be similar to that in ordinary action (s. 109)

The effect of s. 109 is, generally speaking, to adopt for the purposes of the winding-up the procedure of the courts of the province in which the winding-up is being conducted. See *Re Toronto Rowing Club* (1916), 37 O.L.R. 23.

In certain provinces, special rules have been passed applicable to winding-up proceedings. No special rules have been passed in the province of Ontario, where the procedure of the Supreme Court of Ontario as established by the *Courts of Justice Act* and the Consolidated Rules applies save insofar as varied by the provisions of the *Winding-up Act*, which govern in case of variance: *Re Solloway Mills & Co., In Liquidation; Ex parte Solloway*, [1935] O.R. 37 at 47 (C.A.).

Section 109 indicates that the ordinary civil proceedings in the courts apply to contestants who litigate their rights and claims in a winding-up; consequently, such a litigant may not also be entitled to the special powers given by s. 118: *Re Sovereign Bank of Canada; Newman's Case* (1915), 34 O.L.R. 577 at 579.

Where an affidavit has been filed in opposition to a petition, the deponent may be cross-examined thereon: *Re Manitoba Commission Co.* (1912), 2 D.L.R. 1. For a discussion of holding an examination for discovery to resolve an issue under the Act, see *Canada Deposit Insurance Corp. v. Commonwealth Trust Co.* (1990), 2 C.B.R. (3d) 87 (B.C. S.C.).

The rule that the courts should not be called upon to decide merely theoretical propositions applies to an application to the court by a liquidator for the approval by the court of his action in adopting a certain procedure: *Re Great West Permanent Loan Co.*, [1928] 3 W.W.R. 628.

Since the Act is silent as to the relevant ranking to be given to privileged creditors, result must be had, under s. 109 of the Act, to the law of the jurisdiction in question. Thus, costs of liquidation, including liquidator's fees and costs of seizure incurred by a lessor, should take precedence; then follow provincial sales tax, provincial income tax and corporation tax, these ranked equally; after this, a claim for municipal taxes; and then a claim for rent; and finally are payable federal claims for income tax and unemployment insurance contributions: *Re Kiddy's City Inc.* (1967), 12 C.B.R. (N.S.) 22 (Que.).

Single judge may exercise powers of court (s. 110)

Under s. 110, the powers of the court under the Act may be exercised by a single judge in chambers. However, it has been held that the court has no power on a chambers application to determine the validity of instruments held by strangers to the corporation: *Re Maritime Trust Co.; Burns & Co.* (1916), 26 D.L.R. 92.

Order of reference (s. 111)

Under s. 111, the court may delegate any of its powers under the Act to any officer of the court. In the past, the winding-up order usually delegated the powers of the court to the Master or an Official Referee; see the notes to s. 23 in Chapter 22 but the modern practice is generally for the court to supervise the subsequent proceedings.

Section 111 is *intra vires* of the federal Parliament: *Re Farmers Bank* (1916), 35 O.L.R. 470; *Re Solloway Mills & Co.* [1937] 4 D.L.R. 26.

For the form of order of reference, see *Re Army & Navy Clothing Co. of Toronto* (1901), 3 O.L.R. 37 at 38 (C.A.).

Where the reference has been carried into the Master's office, the Master is, under the terms of the order of reference, vested with all the powers to apply the Act that are conferred upon the court and is enabled to exercise all those powers that a judge of the court could exercise if the matter were being dealt with directly by him.

The proceedings before the Master are substantially analogous to the proceedings in an administration action, subject only to such variation and modification as the general requirements of the case may demand.

In the Master's office, formal pleadings are not commonly delivered; but where it appears that advantage would be gained by defining the issue beforehand, the Master may direct pleadings to be delivered as in an ordinary action. He may also direct discovery, and may order the parties to deliver affidavits upon production as in an ordinary action, and may direct the examination of parties preliminary to the formal hearing of the matter. In this, as in all other respects, the procedure is entirely flexible and within the control of the Master before whom the proceeding is conducted; and he may, to the extent that the particular circumstances of the case render it desirable, adopt any or all of the proceedings in an action as may appear conducive to the best results in the particular matter to be determined. He should generally cause the proceedings so to be carried on in a manner that lessens expense and expedites the winding-up.

The officer to whom matters are referred has all the powers ordinarily possessed by a Master or Referee to whom a matter is referred; and it is, in general, his duty to determine the matters referred without interlocutory proceedings and in the most expeditious way possible: *Re Solloway Mills & Co. Ltd.*, [1935] O.R. 275.

While interlocutory decisions are subject to review by a judge, thereafter the provisions of s. 110 apply, and further appeals are limited to those permitted by ss. 103-107: *Re Solloway Mills Co. & I. W. C. Solloway*, [1936] O.R. 416.

The Master or other subordinate judicial officer has no jurisdiction unless by delegation to make an order in a winding-up proceeding: *Re Sarnia Oil Co.* (1893) 15 P.R. 182 (C.A.); *Re G. B. Wood Ltd.*, [1932] 3 W.W.R. 525.

"The powers to be delegated are confined to those conferred by the Act. The officer is not made the recipient of any of the original jurisdiction possessed by the court": *Re Cornwall Furniture Co.* (1909), 18 O.L.R. 101 (C.A.), per Moss, C.J.O., at 103.

The power to fix the security to be given by the liquidator may be delegated under the section: *Shoolbred v. Clarke* (1890), 17 S.C.R. 265 at 272, 279; so also the power to settle the list of contributories: *Re Farmers Bank* (1916), 35 O.L.R. 470; *Re Winding-up Act; Re Alberta Loan & Investment Co.* (1917), 32 D.L.R. 795. The delegated official has authority, when settling the list, to enquire whether shares in respect of which certificates for paid-up stock have been issued have in fact had anything paid thereon: *Re Cornwall Furniture Co., supra.* But in the absence of fraud, the court will not enquire into the value of the consideration taken for the issue of paid-up shares, and the Master accordingly is not competent to make such enquiry: *Re Hess Mfg. Co.* (1894), 23 S.C.R. 644, as explained in *Re Cornwall Furniture Co.* by Moss, C.J.O., at 105, who threw doubt on *Re Harris* (1905), 5 O.W.R. 649.

The Master, or other officer of the court to whom its powers are delegated, is not a court of competent jurisdiction within s. 100 for the purpose of trying the question of the propriety and value of a transfer of property alleged to be an unjust preference: *Harte v. Ontario Express & Transportation Co.* (1894), 25 O.R. 247 (H.C.); *Re Raven Lake Portland Cement Co.* (1911), 24 O.L.R. 286 (C.A.) at 292. The Master has no power to set aside conveyances as against strangers to the winding-up. See s. 135 in this chapter.

The Referee to whom the winding-up is referred is *functus officio* as to all matters dealt with by his report, and cannot directly or indirectly interfere with any appeal therefrom, for example, by directing the amendment of a notice of appeal from the report: *Re Anglo-American Fire Insurance Co.* (1919), 16 O.W.N. 149.

Where a proposed appeal is from a report of the Master, an application for security for costs should be made to that Master: *Bailey Cobalt Mines v. Benson* (1918), 43 O.L.R. 321 (C.A.).

Attachment of debts (s. 115)

Under s. 115 provision is made for attaching and garnishing debts due to any person against whom an order for the payment of money and costs or expenses has been made under the Act.

A garnishee order *nisi* issued by the Supreme Court of Ontario at the instance of the liquidator of an insolvent corporation is no answer to a workman's claim for judgment under the *Master and Servant Act*, R.S.S. 1909, c. 149, for wages earned in Saskatchewan: *Henderson v. Canadian Pacific Railway* (1916), 30 D.L.R. 62 (Sask. C.A.).

Attendance of witnesses (s. 116)

Section 116 provides that in any action, suit, proceeding or contestation under the Act, the court may order the issue of a writ of *subpoena ad testificandum* or of *subpoena duces tecum* commanding the attendance, as a witness, of any person within Canada.

Power of arrest (s. 117)

Under s. 117, orders for the arrest of contributories and officers of the corporation may be made in certain events.

As to the requirements and form of the affidavit necessary to found an order for arrest under this section, see *Central Bank v. Earle* (1889), 28 N.B.R. 173 (C.A.), in which it was held that it must appear by the affidavit that the order is sought at the direction of the liquidator. And see *Re Imperial Mercantile Credit Co.* (1867), L.R. 5 Eq. 264 (order of arrest refused when the only evidence was a hearsay statement that the contributory intended to leave the country); *Re Cotton Plantation Co. of Natal*, [1868] W.N. 79 (order for arrest made).

Examination under s. 118

After a winding-up order has been made, the court may summon the persons described in s. 118 to give information concerning the trade, dealings, estate or effects of the corporation.

The section "confers a special power, of an inquisitorial character, intended to be used by the liquidator for his own guidance in the conduct of the liquidation": *Re Sovereign Bank of Canada; Newman's Case* (1915), 34 O.L.R. 577, per Boyd, C., at 579. It is a proceeding not for the purpose of taking evidence, but for obtaining information. On this ground, creditors were refused, under the corresponding provisions of the English *Companies Act, 1862*, leave to attend at the examination to obtain information for the purpose of establishing a claim against the corporation: *Re Norwich Equitable Fire Insurance Society* (1884), 27 Ch. D. 515 (C.A.).

The application, when made by the liquidator, is *ex parte* without affidavit; but where a contributory desires to put the section in force, he must give notice to the liquidator; and *semble*, the person summoned to be examined has no *locus standi* to appeal against the order directing his examination: *Re Gold Co.* (1879), 12 Ch. D. 77 at 82, 83.

The issuing of a summons is a matter wholly in the discretion of the court: *Re Imperial Continental Water Corp.* (1886), 33 Ch. D. 314 at 319 (C.A.).

Where the order to examine is made at the instance of a contributory, the latter may not take advantage of the section for the purpose of enforcing his own rights against the person examined, and thereby obtain a means of discovery greater than the law affords: *Re Imperial Continental Water Corp. supra*. In certain circumstances, however, there may be a defined right of discovery open to a contributory; and in *Re Sovereign Bank of Canada, supra*, the court, on the liquidator's refusal of the liquidator to enter on the examination proposed by the contesting contributories, and the Official Referee's refusal to allow the contributories to examine certain persons, directed that the Official Referee should consider the appellant's application to examine a former general manager of the insolvent bank, on the basis that the contributories might have a claim to invoke the aid of this section.

Under the section, a bank manager may be summoned to give information regarding transactions between his bank and the company: *Re McMillan Grain Co.*, [1927] 3 D.L.R. 229.

A corporation is a "person": the *Interpretation Act*, R.S.C. 1985, c. I-21, s. 28; and in *Re Toronto Rowing Club* (1916), 37 O.L.R. 23, an order was made for the production and inspection of all books and documents in the possession or control of a corporation to which the lands of the insolvent corporation had been transferred.

Production of documents (s. 120)

A person summoned under s. 120 may be required to produce certain material relating to the corporation.

Where the object of the liquidator is to challenge the validity of debentures issued by the corporation, an order requiring a director of another corporation to which the debentures had been issued, to attend and produce, should not be made: *Re Maville Hose Ltd.*, [1939] Ch. 32. Also raised, but not decided, was the question as to whether a director could properly be said to have in his custody or power documents in the possession of the corporation.

Production of documents "without prejudice" to the lien does not, where the same is a "passive" lien, in any wise affect it so as to entitle the claimant to priority over the claims of other creditors: *Executors & Administrators Trust Co. v. Seaborn, Taylor, Pope & Quirk* (1916), 27 D.L.R. 427. See also *Re Toronto Rowing Club, supra.*

Inspection of documents (s. 123)

Under s. 123 the court may permit inspection of the books and papers of the corporation by creditors and shareholders.

Special circumstances must generally be shown in order to obtain an order for inspection: *Re Buchanan's Case* (1866), 15 W.R. 99; *Re Imperial Land Co. of Marseilles*, [1882] W.N. 173; *Colonial Engineering Co. v. Dominion Light, Heat & Power Co.* (1912), 13 Que. P.R. 436. Where inspection is sought for some purpose other than that of the winding-up, the order will be refused: *Re North Brazilian Sugar Factories, Ltd.* (1888), 37 Ch. D. 83. And see *Ex parte Walker* (1851), 15 Jur. 853; *Lancashire Cotton Spinning Co. v. Greatorex* (1866), 14 L.T. 290; *Re Emma Silver Mining Co.* (1875), L.R. 10 Ch. App. 194; *Re Lisbon Steam Tramways Co.*, [1875] W.N. 54; *Re National Financial Co., Ex parte Oriental Commercial Bank* (1868), L.R. 3 Ch. App. 791.

The court may dispense with notice (s. 125)

Notice may be dispensed with expressly or tacitly: see *Christin v. Hudon*

(1919), 58 Que. S.C. 397 and *Re I.O.S. Ltd. (No. 2)* (1973), 43 D.L.R. (3d) 759 (N.B. C.A.).

Auxiliary nature of provincial courts (s. 126)

Under s. 126 the courts of the various provinces are made auxiliary to one another for the purposes of the Act, and provision is made for the transfer from one court to another of the winding-up or any matter or proceeding relating thereto.

The court that has made the winding-up order is a federal court *ad hoc* and can restrain by injunction proceedings against the liquidator in the courts of other provinces: *Re Central Bank Winding-up* (1890), 20 O.R. 214. Generally speaking, a provincial court should not act except at the request of the federal court, but if requested should in every way assist such court: *Mowat v. Dominion Trust Co.* (1915), 8 Sask. L.R. 404 (C.A.). As to transfer of a proceeding from one court to another, see *Stewart v. Lepage* (1916), 53 S.C.R. 337 at 349.

The section does not authorize the courts of one province to entertain an application for leave to proceed with an action there commenced after a winding-up order has been made in another province. The application should be made in the winding-up proceedings to the court that made the order: *Brewster v. Canada Iron Corp.* (1914), 7 O.W.N. 128. See also *Re Dominion Cold Storage Co.* (1898), 18 P.R. 68.

On an application in Saskatchewan for leave to proceed there against the defendant corporation and its liquidators for an order requiring the latter to account for property in their hands locally situate in Saskatchewan, the court in British Columbia having made the winding-up order, it was held that the provincial court should not intervene except on the ground of emergency which was not made out on the application: *Mowat v. Dominion Trust Co., supra.*

Before an action against the corporation was commenced in Alberta, a winding-up order had been made by the Supreme Court of British Columbia, where the corporation was domiciled. It was held in view of s. 21, that the courts of other provinces could not exercise the jurisdiction which they would otherwise possess without leave of the court administering the provisions of the Act; but that the proceedings taken were only irregular, and not void; and that the Alberta court would act as ancillary to the British Columbia court should the latter desire the action to proceed. The action was stayed in the meantime: *Blais v. Bankers' Trust Corp.* (1913), 14 D.L.R. 277. For discussions to the same effect, see *Re Dome Lode Development Co. Ltd.* (1911), 17 W.L.R. 610; *Stewart v. LePage* (1916), 53 S.C.R. 337; *Re Fairweathers Ltd.* (1921), 51 O.L.R. 235; *Re Continental Fire & Casualty Co.*, [1924] 1 W.W.R. 132.

As to the extra-territorial jurisdiction of the court of a province under the *Winding-up Act*, see *Henderson v. Canadian Pacific Railway* (1916), 30 D.L.R. 62.

See also the notes to s. 21 in Chapter 21.

Enforcement of order in courts of another province

Where it is desired to enforce an order of a court of one province in a court of another province, a certified copy of the order, under the seal of the court that made the order, must be produced (s. 127); and upon such production the court in which it is sought to enforce the order must take the same enforcement proceedings as if the order was one made by it (s. 128).

The practice in Ontario is that on production of an office copy of the order certified as required by s. 127, execution may be issued on the order of the court of another province without making such order a rule of court or obtaining the direction of a judge: *Re Dominion Cold Storage Co.* (1898), 18 P.R. 68.

In New Brunswick the practice is, on production of the order to the registrar, to enter the order as a judgment of the court without any formal motion to that effect: *Re Sovereign Bank* (1915), 43 N.B.R. 519.

In British Columbia a motion is not necessary for the issue of execution on an order against contributories in the Supreme Court of Ontario. The registrar should, without direction, enter such orders as orders of the Supreme Court of British Columbia and proceed upon the same as ordinary records of that court: *Re Home Bank of Canada*, [1925] 1 D.L.R. 734.

As to the practice in Quebec, see *Clarkson v. Marcoux (de Succession)* (1913), 14 Que. P.R. 309.

Amendment of proceedings (s. 129)

Under s. 129, the rules of procedure as to amendments of pleadings and proceedings in the court apply to all pleadings and proceedings under the Act.

As to amending the winding-up petition, see the notes to s. 11 in Chapter 20. Where the liquidator incorrectly has brought an action in his own name, instead of in that of the corporation, leave may be given to amend. See *Kent v. Communauté des Soeurs de Charité*, [1903] A.C. 220.

As to amending the winding-up order where the name of the corporation has been incorrectly stated, see *Swift Canadian Co. v. Island Creamery Assn* (1912), 10 D.L.R. 833.

Solicitor and counsel to represent classes of creditors (s. 133)

Under s. 133, the court may appoint solicitors and counsel to represent classes of creditors, claimants or shareholders, the procedure for and effect of such appointment being set out in the section.

No meeting is required under s. 133: *Re London Fence Ltd.; Brown's Case* (1911), 21 Man. R. 91.

The services of a solicitor and counsel appointed under the section are confined to the proceedings in the winding-up and the court has no power to award to the solicitors for the shareholders, costs incurred prior to the presenting of the petition: *Re Prudential Life Insurance Co.* (1919), 47 D.L.R. 706.

Under a provision of a former *Companies Act* of Ontario authorizing an application to the court for advice in matters arising in a voluntary winding-up, it was held that by analogy to the Rules of Practice of the Supreme Court of Ontario regarding unrepresented persons and class actions, the Master has power to appoint some person to represent the interest of any person or class otherwise unrepresented: *Re Northern Ontario Power Co. Ltd.*, [1954] O.W.N.

105, following the procedure in *Re Artisans' Land & Mortgage Corp.*, [1904] 1 Ch. 796.

Liquidator as officer of court (s. 134)

Under s. 134 the liquidator is subject to the summary jurisdiction of the court in the same manner as the ordinary officers of the court, and the court may compel him to perform his duties.

The word "liquidator" in this section includes a provisional liquidator: *System Theatre Operating Co. v. Pulos*, [1955] S.C.R. 448 at 453.

As by s. 134 a liquidator is an officer of the court, leave must be obtained from the court before he can be sued: *Re G. B. Wood Ltd.*, [1932] 3 W.W.R. 525, at 531.

Misfeasance summons (s. 124)

Under s. 124 any liquidator, creditor or contributory of the corporation may apply to the court to examine the conduct of past or present officers of the corporation or certain other designated persons if it appears that they have misapplied or retained or become liable or accountable for any moneys of the corporation or been guilty of misfeasance or breach of trust in relation to the corporation. See *Friefeld v. Maxwell* (1966), 9 C.B.R. (N.S.) 214 (Que.). See also *Commonwealth Trust Co. v. Canada Deposit Insurance Corp.* (1990), 79 C.B.R. (N.S.) 183 (B.C.), at 196. There was a surplus of assets after liquidation, and a shareholder applied for leave to bring an action for damages in the name of the corporation against the liquidator and other parties outside the liquidation. The liquidator sought leave to withdraw on the grounds of conflict of interest. It was held that a new liquidator would be appointed to make the assessment. In the subsequent case it was decided that a large accounting firm was an appropriate liquidator, in that the corporation in question was involved in complex litigation. It was noted that the new liquidator was acceptable to both parties. See also *Re United Fuel Investments (No. 1)*, [1966] 1 O.R. 165 (C.A.).

Section 124 is *intra vires: Re Solloway Mills & Co.*, [1937] 4 D.L.R. 26.

The corresponding English provision, is somewhat wider in its terms, including "any person who has taken part in the formation or promotion of the company." The English cases must accordingly be applied with caution as regards the classes of persons liable under s. 124.

Claims to be disposed of in winding-up

The principle of the *Winding-up Act* is that all claims which are capable of being satisfactorily dealt with in the winding-up should be so disposed of, and a shareholder will not be permitted to bring an action against the directors and officers for misfeasance: *Re Farmers' Loan & Savings Co.* (1898), 8 O.W.R. 12. If, however, the cause of action against a director is a personal wrong, the right of the shareholder to sue the director persists, and no leave is necessary under s. 21, for the assets of the corporation would not be benefited or affected by the result of the litigation: ibid.

A misfeasance summons will not be set aside simply because it was obtained on an *ex parte* application: *Re Solloway Mills & Co. Ltd. (In Liquidation) Ex parte I.W.C. Solloway*, [1935] O.R. 37 (C.A.) 40.

Effect of section

Section 124 creates no new right, its effect being merely to provide a summary procedure for enforcing against an officer of the corporation liability for breach of trust or other misconduct, which prior to the Act might have been enforced by action: *Re Irish Provident Assurance Co.* [1913] 1 Ir. 352; *Re City Equitable Fire Insurance Co.*, [1925] Ch. 407 (C.A.).

"The misfeasance section . . . is one which does not create liability but relates to procedure alone . . . the liability must be found outside the section": *Re Owen Sound Lumber Co.* (1915), 34 O.L.R. 528, per Middleton, J. The summary procedure is in addition to other rights of action, and if the liquidator prefers to obtain leave and bring an action he may do so: *Northern Trust Co. v. Butchart* (1917), 35 D.L.R. 169.

It is not part of the duty of the court to direct the discontinuance of proceedings by summons, when such proceedings are adequate, so that other proceedings by way of writ may be taken; in proceedings by summons, third-party procedure is not applicable: *Re A. Singer & Co. (Hat Mfg.) Ltd.*, [1943] Ch. 121 (C.A.).

Master's jurisdiction

The Master has jurisdiction under the order of delegation to deal with questions of misfeasance: *Re Bolt & Iron Co.*, (1887), 14 O.R. 211, affd (1889), 16 O.A.R. 397; *Re Owen Sound Lumber Co.* (1917), 38 O.L.R. 414 at 420 (C.A).

The inquiry is intended to be conducted in a summary way, and while the Master has power to direct that particulars be given, such particulars cannot be regarded as formal pleadings: *Re Solloway Mills & Co. Ltd.*, [1935] O.R. 275 (order of Master directing statement of claim to be delivered vacated).

Procedure

The application, which may be made by any liquidator, creditor or contributory, is *ex parte* when made by the liquidator, and on notice to the liquidator if made by a creditor or contributory. *Semble*, if the application is by a contributory, he must have a direct pecuniary interest in the success of the application: *Cavendish Bentinck v. Fenn* (1887), 12 App. Cas. 652. The procedure authorized by the section is an independent and principal one and cannot be taken in an incidental proceeding by the liquidator, as, for example, by counterclaiming for damages against a director in contesting the latter's claim against the corporation as a creditor: *Re Boston Shoe Co.* (1914), 16 D.L.R. 856 (Que. S.C.). See also *Friefeld v. Maxwell* (1966), 9 C.B.R. (N.S.) 214 (Que. S.C.).

Directors are entitled to the same rights of discovery against the liquidator as in an action: *Re Traders Trust Co.* (1915), 8 W.W.R. 1080.

Costs

If the liquidator is unsuccessful, the costs are usually given out of the estate, but the liquidator may be compelled by the order to pay the costs out of his own pocket: *Re W. Powell & Sons*, [1896] 1 Ch. 681. Costs may be imposed against the defendants even though they succeed in showing that their misconduct has caused the corporation no pecuniary loss so that the liquidator's claim fails: *Re David Ireland & Co.*, [1905] 1 Ir. 133. However, in *Re City Equitable Fire Insurance Co. Ltd.*, *supra*, costs were allowed to auditors and directors who escaped liability by reason of an article exonerating them except in cases of wilful default, as otherwise they would have been deprived to a material extent of the protection that the article afforded.

Misfeasance or breach of trust

Misfeasance has been defined so as to include a breach of duty by an officer of a corporation, the direct consequence of which has been a misapplication of the corporation's assets resulting in pecuniary loss to the corporation for which that officer could be made responsible by an action at law or in equity: *Re Kingston Cotton Mill Co. (No. 2)*, [1896] 2 Ch. 279 (C.A.) at 283. Misconduct involving misapplication of funds or property of the corporation is generally termed "breach of trust". And see *Coventry & Dixon's Case* (1880), 14 Ch. D. 660 (C.A.); *Cavendish Bentinck v. Fenn* (1887), 12 App. Cas. 652; *Re B. Johnson & Co. (Builders) Ltd.*, [1955] 1 Ch. 634. A delay of 43 years did not prevent the granting of equitable relief: *Canada Trust Co. v. Lloyd*, [1968] S.C.R. 300.

Under the section, three questions are involved: (1) Has the person sought to be charged been guilty in relation to the corporation of one or more of the acts specified in the section? (2) If so, has loss resulted to the corporation or its assets for which compensation ought to be directed to be made? and (3) What is the extent of the compensation that ought to be directed?: *Re Manes Tailoring Co.; Crawford's Case* (1908), 18 O.L.R. 572 (C.A.) per Moss, C.J.O., at 580.

The section is not applicable to all cases in which the corporation has a right of action against one of its officers, but is limited to cases where there has been something in the nature of a breach of duty by an officer as such which has caused pecuniary loss to the corporation. Consequently, where the claim was for repayment by the secretary of expenses advanced with the consent of the managing director, and the secretary claimed a right of set-off, it was held that the claim should be raised in an action and the summons was dismissed: *Re Etic Ltd.*, [1928] Ch. 861; *Re Winding-up Act & Panama Pacific Grain Terminals*, [1940] 4 D.L.R. 194 (corporation suffered no loss).

The courts will not attempt a precise definition of what conduct is and what is not within the section. At one end of the scale, it is *prima facie* clear that a wrongful act involving misapplication of property in the hands of the person charged would be covered. At the other end of the scale, a claim based exclusively on common law negligence, or an ordinary claim for damages for negligence, would not be covered; nor is such a claim brought within the section by the mere expedient of adding epithets to the negligence charged, (e.g., "gross" or "deliberate"). In between these extremes there is a large range of conduct that may or may not be within the section: *Re B. Johnson & Co. (Builders), supra.*

Pecuniary loss to the corporation

In order to bring a case within the section, it must be shown that pecuniary loss to the corporation resulted from the act or default complained of: *Cavendish Bentinck v. Fenn* (1887), 12 App. Cas. 652 at 661-2; *Re Mashonaland Exploration Co.*, [1892] 3 Ch. 577; *Re Irish Provident Assurance Co.*, [1913] 1 Ir. 352. Loss to the corporation is an essential ingredient of the offence: *Re Dominion Trust Co.; Dominion Trust Co. v. McKay* (1917), 32 D.L.R. 63; *Re Stewart, Howe & Meek Ltd.* (1913), 25 O.W.R. 211 (C.A.); and see *Re Norwalk Mining Co.* (1915), 9 O.W.N. 41 (corporation suffered no loss); *McFarland v. London & Lancashire Guarantee & Accident Co.*, [1928] S.C.R. 57 (claim in respect of moneys not belonging to, or accountable for, by the corporation); *Re Winding-up Act & Panama Pacific Grain Terminals Ltd., supra*, (corporation suffered no loss).

Directors

The powers and duties of directors have been considered under Chapter 8. Reference should also be made to the notes under the headings "Right to remuneration" and "Personal liability of directors" in that chapter. See also the discussion in *Re Northland Bank* (1991), 3 C.B.R. (3d) 14 (Man. Q.B.).

A director may be liable even though he may only have been guilty of a mistake of law and not of any moral wrongdoing: *Re Manes Tailoring Co.; Crawford's Case* (1909), 18 O.L.R. 572. It has been held, however, that a bona fide transaction with the corporation that is impeachable only on the ground of *ultra vires* will be set aside subject only to the terms that both parties are restored to their original rights: *Re Irish Provident Assurance Co.*, [1913] 1 Ir. 352. If the act of misfeasance is neither *ultra vires* nor fraudulent nor dishonest, it must be shown that the directors did not really exercise their discretion or judgment as such: *Re Mashonaland Exploration Co.*, [1892] 3 Ch. 577. Directors who have taken no active part in the management of the corporation's business, who have attended no meetings, and who are not cognizant of any of the acts or omissions of the board are not liable: *Re Dominion Trust Co. (Directors' Case)* (1917), 32 D.L.R. 63. This case would not be decided the same way at the present time, as the total failure to perform his duties as a director would itself be regarded as actionable if other directors had acted improperly.

Directors who knowingly or without the exercise of ordinary prudence, sanction the payment of an improper dividend, are jointly and severally liable: *Northern Trust Co. v. Butchart* (1917), 35 D.L.R. 169; but negligence must be so gross as to amount to a breach of trust: ibid., at 183. Where, however, directors in declaring dividends in diminution of capital have acted honestly and have not been guilty of wilful blindness or carelessness, they have been excused: *Re Owen Sound Lumber Co.* (1917), 38 O.L.R. 414 (C.A.). *Quaere* whether this case is still good law on this point.

Where directors have no power to authorize payment of commissions out of the corporation's funds to persons who have procured subscriptions for the corporation's shares, they are liable on a misfeasance summons to repay to the liquidator the sums so improperly expended under their authority: *Re Monarch Bank of Canada* (1910), 22 O.L.R. 516; so also where the directors knowingly or without the exercise of ordinary prudence, sanction an illegal remuneration of directors or any *ultra vires* or illegal payments: *Northern Trust Co. v. Butchart, supra.* Likewise, a commission on shares subscribed for in the memorandum of association by the director in question is recoverable under a misfeasance summons where the commission was not authorized by the articles or referred to in the prospectus and was therefore illegal under the governing *Companies Act*: *Re Canadian Diamond Co.* (1913), 11 D.L.R. 251. And where a director received a commission, not authorized by the charter, on the sale of shares, he was liable to repay it: *Re Disappearing Propeller Boat Co.* (1925), 5 C.B.R. 679 (Ont. Ref.).

Moneys taken by directors in payment of services, where such payment is not authorized are taken in breach of trust and are recoverable: *Re Bolt & Iron Co.* (1887), 14 O.R. 211, affd (1889), 16 O.A.R. 397. In *Re Owen Sound Lumber Co., supra*, a director was held liable to refund moneys paid to him for guaranteeing the corporation's indebtedness in pursuance of a resolution of the directors that was invalid for lack of confirmation by the shareholders.

Directors of a corporation obtained money on the representation that the funds would be invested on mortgage. In fact, they used these moneys to discharge pressing claims of the corporation's creditors. All the directors who stood by in circumstances that should have aroused their suspicions were held personally liable on a misfeasance summons for the amount so misapplied, the sum being directed to be paid to the liquidator for repayment to the person defrauded: *In re Traders Trust Co. & Kory* (1916), 26 D.L.R. 41.

A director joined in sanctioning the issue to himself of shares as paid up that were, in fact, not fully paid; and then transferred his shares, receiving $125 more than he had paid. When the shares having were subsequently forfeited for non-payment of calls, he was held liable for breach of trust in assuming to accept the shares as paid up; but the measure of damages was held to be the market value of the shares at the date of allotment; and since at that date the shares had no market value, his profit, the sum of $125, was the extent of his liability: *Re Manes Tailoring Co., Crawford's Case* (1908), 18 O.L.R. 572 (C.A.). Where a promoter had distributed shares not fully paid up to directors, they were liable as contributories in respect of any shares still in their hands but were not liable for misfeasance under the Act, as the corporation had suffered no loss, the shares having no value at the date of allotment; further, one director was not liable under the Act because he had sold his shares prior to the winding-up in circumstances not involving a violation of duty: *Re Owen Sound Lumber Co.* (1917) 38 O.L.R. 414 (C.A). If a director sells his partly paid up shares in breach of his duty to take care and caution in procuring a responsible transferee, he is liable under the Act: *Re Peterborough Cold Storage Co.* (1907), 14 O.L.R. 475. See, however, *McGuire & Forester Ltd. v. Cadzow*, [1933] 1 D.L.R. 192 (Alta. C.A.), where it was pointed out that the only method available for enforcing payment of shares issued other than as fully paid was by way of call, which could only be made against a member of the corporation, and that the director, having sold his shares, had ceased to be a member and was not liable.

Where directors adopt a system of doing business that disregards a provision of the governing statute — for example, a requirement that corporate and trust moneys are to be kept separate — that is *prima facie* a defective and negligent system; and if loss can be shown to have resulted therefrom, they will be guilty of misfeasance: *Re Dominion Trust Co. (Directors' Case)* (1917) 32 D.L.R. 63 at 65.

As to awarding interest, in *Re National Bank of Wales Ltd.*, [1899] 2 Ch. 629 (C.A.) the rate allowed was 5 per cent, though the director eventually escaped liability in the House of Lords. In Canada the ordinary rules of the particular provinces to interest before and after judgment would be applicable.

It is not necessary that a director to be liable under the section, be validly appointed; *de facto* directors will be liable: *Coventry & Dixon's Case* (1880), 14 Ch. D. 660; *Re Owen Sound Lumber Co., supra; Northern Trust Co. v. Butchart* (1917), 35 D.L.R. 169 at 180. Provisional directors are covered by the section: *Re Monarch Bank of Canada* (1910) 22 O.L.R. 516.

Officers

An auditor is an officer under the section: *Re Kingston Cotton Mill Co. (No. 1)*, [1896] 1 Ch. 6; but not an accountant called in by the directors to do a specific piece of work: *Re Western Counties Steam Bakeries & Milling Co.*, [1897] 1 Ch. 617; nor is a banker: *Re Imperial Land Co. of Marseilles; Re National Bank* (1870) L.R. 10 Eq. 298; nor is a solicitor of the corporation: *Re Great Western Forest of Dean Coal Consumers Co.; Carter's Case* (1886), 31 Ch. D. 496, unless employed at a fixed salary: *Re Liberator Permanent Benefit Building Society* (1894), 71 L.T. 406; nor is a trustee for bondholders: *Astley v. New Tivoli Ltd.*, [1899] 1 Ch. 151 at 154 (per North, J.).

Where promoters by reason of being officers of the corporation are within the section, their liability for undisclosed profits may be enforced by misfeasance summons: cf. *Re Leeds & Hanley Theatres of Varieties Ltd.*, [1902] 2 Ch. 809 (C.A.).

Liquidator

A liquidator in a voluntary winding-up is not, apart from negligence, liable for wrongly admitting an invalid claim. However, a high standard of care is required; and where a liquidator paid a large claim that was in fact invalid without legal advice and without the approval of the court, it was held that he had not discharged his duty and was liable for misfeasance. In fixing the amount that a person liable for misfeasance should be ordered to pay the court has a discretion, and in the aforementioned circumstances the liquidator was ordered to pay such sum as would enable all creditors to be paid in full with interest at 5 per cent: *Re Home & Colonial Insurance Co. Ltd.*, [1930] 1 Ch. 102. In the same case it was held that a liquidator does not come within the words "other officers of the company" in an article exonerating directors and officers from liability.

Where a liquidator, without obtaining the opinion or sanction of the court, settled and paid a claim for damages that was later held to be invalid, he was held liable on a misfeasance summons for the whole amount so applied; and it was further held that he was not entitled to indemnity or relief under the *Trustee Act*: *Re Windsor Steam Coal Co.*, [1929] 1 Ch. 151 (C.A.).

Acts not constituting misfeasance

Neglect or omission to attend meetings is not the same as neglect or omission of a duty that ought to be performed thereat: *Marquis of Bute's Case*, [1892] 2 Ch. 100. This case might not be decided in the same manner today. Merely voting in favour of a resolution authorizing payment to a co-director, when that resolution fails to have any binding effect because it was not confirmed by the shareholders, is not misfeasance: *Re Owen Sound Lumber Co.* (1917) 38 O.L.R. 414 (C.A.). Where an illegal payment of money has been authorized by an *ultra vires* resolution, mere concurrence in the resolution is not sufficient to impose liability where the director has not taken part in the payment: *Cullerne v. London & Suburban General Permanent Building Society* (1890), 25 Q.B.D. 485; *Young v. Naval, Military & Civil Service Co-operative Society of South Africa*, [1905] 1 K.B. 687, and see *Re Monarch Bank of Canada*, (1910) 22 O.L.R. 516.

Acceptance of paid-up shares of a corporation for pre-incorporation services, where the memorandum of association authorized the issue (though the prospectus in effect stated that the power to make such issue would not be exercised), and when, there was no claim of fraud as to the rendering or value of the services, and no allegation of loss to the corporation, was held not to be misfeasance: *Re Canadian Diamond Co.* (1913), 11 D.L.R. 251.

Acting as a director without qualification is not misfeasance, no loss being shown: *Coventry & Dixon's Case* (1880), 14 Ch. D. 660.

Set-off

There is no right of set-off against a claim made by the liquidator for misfeasance: *Re Anglo-French Co-operative Society; Ex parte Pelly* (1882), 21 Ch. D. 492 (C.A.); *Re Bolt & Iron Co.* (1887), 14 O.R. 211, affd (1889), 16 O.A.R. 397; *Re Disappearing Propeller Boat Co.* (1925), 5 C.B.R. 679 (Ont. Ref.).

Statute of limitations

As to the operation of the Statute of Limitations, see *Flitcroft's Case* (1882), 21 Ch. D. 519 (C.A.); *Masonic & General Life Assurance Co. v. Sharpe*, [1892] 1 Ch. 154: *Re National Distribution of Electricity Co. Ltd.*, [1902] 2 Ch. 34 (C.A.); *North American Land & Timber Co. v. Watkins*, [1904] 1 Ch. 242, affd [1904] 2 Ch. 233; *Re Norwalk Mining Co.*, (1915), 9 O.W.N. 41.

Limitation of liability

Articles exonerating directors and officers, including auditors, except in case of dishonesty or wilful neglect or default, are a protection where a claim is made under the section for negligence or acts or omissions not constituting wilful neglect or default: *Re Brazilian Rubber Plantations & Estates, Ltd.*, [1911] 1 Ch. 425; *Re City Equitable Fire Insurance Co.*, [1925] Ch. 407 (C.A.). Negligence is not "wilful" unless the officer "knows that he is committing and intends to commit a breach of his duty, or is recklessly careless in the sense of not caring whether his act or omission is or is not a breach of duty": ibid., at 453, 498.

A liquidator is not protected by such an article: *Re Home & Colonial Insurance Co.*, [1930] 1 Ch. 102.

Effect of s. 135

The section lays down the general rule that the liquidator and the estate are to be protected from vexatious litigation and that claims against the estate must in general be disposed of in the winding-up and not otherwise. See *Re J. McCarthy & Sons Co.* (1916), 38 O.L.R. 3 (C.A.); *Re Ontario Bank* (1916), 38 O.L.R. 242; *Comptoir Mobilier-Canadien v. Jules Gallet de La Menardière et Paul L. Turgeon* (1933), 36 Que. P.R. 146. See also *Canada Deposit Insurance Corp. v. Canadian Commercial Bank* (1990), 108 A.R. 267.

As to the relation between this section and s. 21, see the notes under the heading "Whether the remedy under s. 135 is exclusive", in this chapter. As has been observed in the notes on s. 21, the English Act contains no provision corresponding to s. 135.

A suit cannot be entered against the liquidator without leave of the court: *Robillard v. Blanchet* (1901), 19 Que. S.C. 383. Where a trust corporation is in process of liquidation under order of the court in one province, this section and s. 21 will prevent a suit being brought in another province to have the liquidator declared a trustee of moneys deposited with the corporation for investment, and for his removal and the substitution of a new trustee and the vesting in the latter of the securities representing the moneys deposited: *Stewart v. Lepage* (1916), 53 S.C.R. 337. The proper procedure in such a case is an application by summary petition: ibid., per Idington and Anglin, JJ. So also, where the plaintiff claimed the right to sue the liquidator for the price of goods alleged to have been taken and sold by the latter, whereby the plaintiff was deprived of his right of stoppage *in transitu*, it was held that an action, having been begun without leave, was barred by what is now s. 135: *H. J. Carson & Co. v. Montreal Trust Co.* (1915), 23 D.L.R. 690.

Where, however, the plaintiffs, who were trustees for bondholders, had obtained leave to bring an action against the defendants, who were liquidators of the mortgagor corporation, in respect of assets alleged to be mortgaged under the trust deed, claiming (1) the proceeds or (2) damages for conversion, it was held on appeal from the order granting leave that the language of s. 136 (now s. 135) was not applicable to the first claim, and that its applicability to the second was doubtful, but that in any event leave to bring an action was properly granted: *Re Raven Lake Portland Cement Co.* (1911), 24 O.L.R. 286 (C.A.). As regards land mortgages, it has been held that the section is applicable to the case of a single mortgage only, and not where there are subsequent mortgages: *Re Canada Cabinet Co.* (1907), 9 O.W.R. 818.

Special circumstances and very substantial reasons are required to justify the granting of leave under s. 21; and if such leave has been granted on a wrong principle, the plaintiff may be remitted by the appellate court to his rights under this section: *Re J. McCarthy & Sons Co.* (1916), 38 O.L.R. 3 (C.A.). See further the notes under the heading "Application for leave" in Chapter 21.

Where a tort is alleged to have been committed after the making of the winding-up order, through the negligent handling of one of the assets of the corporation, claims for damages by the injured parties do not come within the language of the section: *Re G. B. Wood Ltd.*, [1932] 3 W.W.R. 525 at 528.

Who are affected

The words "all remedies sought," apply to creditors who have proved or can prove: *Archibald v. Haldan* (1870) 30 U.C.Q.B. 30 at 36. The claimant need not be a creditor in the strict sense; proceedings by *cestuis que trust* are covered by the section: *Stewart v. Lepage* (1916), 53 S.C.R. 337, Davies, J., dissenting; but the section does not apply to a creditor who is not seeking to enforce his claim, for example, a mortgagee who prefers to stand outside the liquidation: *Kurtz v. McLean Ltd.* (1908), 11 O.W.R. 437 at 439. It was, held, however, under s. 50 of the *Insolvent Act, 1869*, that where a mortgagee desired to obtain possession of assets in the hands of the liquidator, he must proceed by summary application: *Crombie v. Jackson* (1874), 34 U.C.Q.B. 575. A lienholder may obtain leave to pursue his remedies by application under this section: *Good v. Nepisiguit Lumber Co.* (1912), 11 N.B.R. 57 (C.A.); *Re Clinton Thresher Co.* (1910), 20 O.L.R. 555; *Re Fashion Shop Co.* (1915), 33 O.L.R. 253 (H.C.) (landlord). See also the notes under the following heading and on s. 21 in Chapter 21.

Whether the remedy under s. 135 is exclusive

It has been held by the Ontario Court of Appeal that the remedy by way of summary petition given by s. 135 is not exclusive; that the provision must be read with s. 21, with the former section laying down the general rule, the latter (providing for leave to bring actions) providing the exception; and that s. 21 is to be followed only where there are exceptional circumstances: *Re Raven Lake Portland Cement Co.* (1911), at 24 O.L.R. 286 (C.A.) at 292. It was pointed out in that case that some matters are beyond the jurisdiction of the Master or Referee in a winding-up proceeding. It was also held that even if the Referee had jurisdiction to adjudicate on the claims made in that case, he had a discretion under s. 21 to give leave to bring an action, and that it could not be said that the discretion had been improperly exercised. And where in another case the Referee refused leave to bring an action on the application of bondholders, his discretion was held to have been wrongly exercised, and the order was reversed on appeal: *Re Canadian Western Steel Corp. Ltd.* (1922), 51 O.L.R. 615 (C.A.); but see the observations of Ferguson, J.A., at 619. See also *Montreal Ltd. v. Laurentian Development Corp.*, [1964] Que. S.C. 111.

In *Kurtz & McLean Ltd.* (1908), 11 O.W.R. 437, in addition to the claims of the applicant (an unpaid vendor) and the liquidator, a mortgagee claimed an interest in the assets in question. Mulock, C.J. Ex., ordered that if the mortgagee was willing to attorn to the jurisdiction (which he could not be compelled to do), then the rights of the three parties should be disposed of under the Act, but that otherwise the applicant should be entitled to bring an action.

On the other hand, in Nova Scotia, in a case heard before the full court, it was said that, apart from the prohibition of s. 136 (now s. 135) against proceeding by action, where the section applies the remedy is exclusive, the general rule being that where a new statutory remedy is provided, it is the exclusive remedy: *H. J. Carson & Co. v. Montreal Trust Co.* (1915), 23 D.L.R. 690. In *Stewart v. Lepage* (1916), 53 S.C.R. 337, an action had been commenced without leave being obtained under s. 21; Anglin, J., at 348, regarded the petition under what is now s. 135 as the exclusive means of obtaining relief so far as the claimants sought a declaration of trust and allocation to the trust of assets in the hands of the liquidator. Idington, J., stated at 345 that if the claim was not of a clear and undoubted character, the court might permit some more suitable remedy. Brodeur, J., was apparently of the opinion that if leave had been obtained, the action might properly have been brought. Duff, J., gave no reasons. Davies, J., dissented. Both of the last mentioned cases were instances of actions brought without leave; but in *H. J. Carson & Co. v. Montreal Trust Co., supra*, the court held in effect that s. 135, which prohibited actions against the liquidator, and not s. 21, which prohibited actions against the corporation, governed. The judgment of Anglin, J., in *Stewart v. Lepage, supra*, looks in the same direction.

The question whether the remedy under s. 135 is exclusive was considered by the Court of Appeal in British Columbia in *Michigan Trust Co. v. Canadian Puget Sound Lumber Co.*, [1918] 3 W.W.R. 273 (C.A.). The plaintiff trustee for bondholders under a mortgage trust deed was held entitled to a final order of foreclosure, leave to bring the action having been given. Macdonald, C.J.A., held that the contention that the remedy under the section was exclusive could only prevail, if at all, when the case fell strictly within the class of cases mentioned therein; and that the case did not fall within the section because the mortgaged premises were never "in the hands, possession or control of the liquidator." McPhillips, J.A., stated that *Stewart v. Lepage* was not conclusive on this point and held that where leave was obtained, such an action was maintainable. Galliher, J.A., concurred in upholding the right of action.

In *Holdsworth v. Refrigerated Express Lines Ltd.* (1954), 13 W.W.R. (N.S.) 542, an application was made for leave to commence an action to establish that a certain debenture constituted a first charge upon the property of the corporation that was in liquidation under the Act. In granting leave and commenting upon the objection that what is now s. 135 of the Act prohibited such an action, Macfarlane J. said, at 543:

> It seems to me impossible to say that in proceedings of the kind proposed here, there will not arise issues which could not much better be tried by action. Just what can be dealt with by summary proceedings it is difficult to say and judges have refused to answer that question categorically. My own opinion is that the section was intended to deal with 'claims' in respect of the liens or mortgages referred to rather than with proceedings to realize the security which is held by the person desiring to realize. The object of the section, I think clearly is to save expensive litigation and multiplication of suits but that, if it is to be construed as depriving persons of their rights in any way, it must be construed I think most strictly.

For cases where the court has granted or refused leave to bring or proceed with an action see the notes under the subheadings "Discretion to grant leave" and "Mortgagees and bondholders" in Chapter 21.

Rules, regulations and forms

Under s. 136, a majority of the judges of the court may make and settle rules, regulations and forms to be observed in proceedings under the Act. Until rules are made under s. 136, the procedure of the court is to be the same, as nearly as may be, as that of the court in other cases (s. 137).

Until rules are made under s. 136, the general rules of practice in force in the court administering the Act are incorporated by reference in s. 137: *Re Belding Lumber Co.* (1911), 23 O.L.R. 255; *System Theatre Operating Co. v. Pulos*, [1955] S.C.R. 448.

Section 137 read with s. 2 and s. 136 renders applicable in Ontario the procedure, including therein the rules and methods of practice current in the Supreme Court of Ontario, which are to be adapted, as nearly as may be, to the uses of the profession under the *Winding-up Act: Re Baynes Carriage Co.* (1912), 27 O.L.R. 144. So, where the practice of the court is to support petitions by affidavits and *viva voce* evidence, shareholders petitioning for a winding-up were held entitled to examine the corporation's directors as witnesses in support of the petition: ibid.

Where rules have been made in pursuance of s. 136 they will govern: *Re Federal Mortgage Corp. & Stewart; Re Dominion Winding-up Act*, [1917] 2 W.W.R. 52. Rules have been promulgated under s. 136 or its predecessor in the following provinces: Alberta, British Columbia, Manitoba, Nova Scotia and Saskatchewan. Such rules may be *ultra vires* if not authorized by the statute, thus fixing a rate of interest was held to be a substantive right not authorized by the statute: *Canada Deposit Insurance Corp. v. Commonwealth Trust Co.* (1992), 16 C.B.R. (3d) 66 (B.C. S.C.).

As to the application in Manitoba of the rules made by the Judges of the Court of Queen's Bench as authorized by statute, see *Re Canada National Fire Insurance Co.*, [1931] 2 D.L.R. 875 (C.A.); *Re Purvis Fisheries Ltd.*, [1955] 1 D.L.R. 93 (Man. C.A.).

As regards sales, the ordinary practice of the court will apply until rules are made under s. 136: *Re Bolt & Iron Co.*, (1884,) 10 P.R. 434.

Unclaimed deposits

Under s. 138 all unclaimed dividends are to remain in a bank for three years and are then to be paid over by the bank, with interest accrued thereon, to the Minister of Consumer and Corporate Affairs. Section 139 provides that the money deposited in a bank by the liquidator after the final winding-up of the business of the corporation is to be left for three years, and that any unclaimed balance is then to be paid over, with the interest accrued thereon, to the Minister of Consumer and Corporate Affairs.

Where the liquidators had passed their final accounts and paid into court the balance in their hands, and that balance had by inadvertence been paid out of court to parties not entitled to it, it was held that the Receiver-General had such an interest in the fund that, even before three years from the time of payment in had expired, he might apply to the court for an order for repayment into court of the fund: *Hogaboom v. The Receiver-General of Canada, In re The Central Bank of Canada* (1897) 24 O.A.R. 470, (1898) 28 S.C.R. 192. Where certain securities were held by a trust corporation as trustee for unpaid depositors of a loan corporation, the moneys, representing the proceeds of realization of the securities coming into the hands of the liquidator of the trust corporation, were held to be subject to the same trusts and, accordingly, the sections did not apply: *Manitoba (Provincial Treasurer) v. Canada (Minister of Finance); Manitoba (Attorney General) v. Canada (Minister of Finance) and Canada (Attorney General)*, [1943] S.C.R. 370, where two actions had been brought by the Crown in the right of Manitoba claiming the moneys. In the first action, the moneys were claimed as *bona vacantia*, and the province failed on the ground that the evidence did not support a finding of abandonment. In the second action, the claim was under the *Vacant Property Act, 1940* (Man.), c. 57, which vested in the province all personal property (including money) held in trust by any person in the province that remained unclaimed for a specified period. The specified period having elapsed, the moneys being held in trust, and the liquidator being in Manitoba, the province was held entitled to succeed. See also *A.G. (Can.) v. A.G. (Que.)*, [1947] A.C. 33 at 45.

Offences and penalties

If it appears in the course of the winding-up of a corporation that any past or present director, manager, officer or member of the corporation is guilty of an offence in relation to the corporation for which he is criminally liable, the court may direct criminal proceedings against such person (s. 140).

Under s. 141, the destruction of books or documents belonging to the corporation, or any false entry therein with intent to defraud or deceive any person, is an indictable offence; in this connection, see also s. 397 of the Criminal Code, which provides that a person who with intent to defraud falsifies books or documents is guilty of an indictable offence and liable to five years' imprisonment.

The Act provides that certain courses of conduct amount to contempt of court; these courses are the failure of specified persons to comply with an order of the court (s. 142), the refusal by officers, directors or employees of the corporation to give all the information possessed by them to persons authorized by the court to inquire into the affairs of the corporation (s. 143) and the refusal of a witness appearing before the court for examination to answer any question put to him (s. 145).

If a liquidator fails to comply with the provisions of s. 144 as to the depositing of the corporation's money in a bank, he is liable to the penalty therein provided.

Evidence

Under s. 146, all the books of the corporation and of the liquidators are, as between contributories, *prima facie* evidence of the truth of all matters recorded therein. Thus, an entry in an allotment book (though there was no record of a meeting on the date of the entry), coupled with the admission of the contributory that he had applied for shares, was *prima facie* evidence of allotment and threw on the contributory the burden of proving the allotment invalid: *Re Great Northern Salt & Chemical Works, Ex parte Kennedy* (1890), 44 Ch. D. 472.

The entries in the books being *prima facie* evidence only the facts therein stated may be rebutted: *Page v. Austin* (1885), 10 S.C.R. 132. See also *Re International Electric Co.* (1914), 31 O.L.R. 348.

In proceedings in a court of a province other than that where the winding-up order was made to set aside an attachment made after the winding-up order, an affidavit by one of the liquidators setting out the fact of the making of the order was held to be sufficient proof thereof: *Salter v. St. Lawrence Lumber Co.* (1896), 28 N.S.R. 335.

Chapter 26

BANKS

The application of the Act to incorporated banks and savings banks is provided for by s. 6. Part II (ss. 151-158) of the Act, which applies to banks other than savings banks, contains specific provisions regarding the application for a winding-up order (s. 152(1)), the conduct of meetings of shareholders and creditors (ss. 153(2)-154), the appointment of a liquidator (ss. 155-156), the reservation of dividends in respect of outstanding bank notes (s. 157) and the manner of giving notice to the holders of bank notes (s. 158). It will be noted that the provisions with respect to bank notes are no longer applicable as all such notes have been assumed by the Bank of Canada. The practice is to appoint a provisional liquidator in the first instance.

It will be noted that the *Bank Act* provides for the liquidation and dissolution of a bank in sections 339 to 369. Section 340 of that Act provides that sections 341 to 368 do not apply to a bank which is insolvent within the meaning of the *Winding-up Act*; any such proceedings are to be stayed if the bank is found to be so insolvent. Section 543 of the *Bank Act* provides that the Attorney General of Canada on request of the minister may make an application to the court for winding-up.

Section 369 of the *Bank Act* sets out a list of priorities for payment. The first charge is for any amount due to the Federal Crown whether in trust or otherwise except for subordinate indebtedness; the second charge is for similar amounts due to the Crown in right of a province. The third charge is for deposit liabilities and non-subordinated indebtedness. Then follows subordinate indebtedness and all liabilities ranking equally with or subsequent to subordinate indebtedness, and lastly any fines and penalties for which the bank is liable. The priorities within each of the above rankings is to be determined in accordance with the laws governing priorities and where applicable by the terms of the particular indebtedness or liability.

It is provided in the section that the listed priorities are not to prejudice or affect the priority of the holder of any security interest in any bank property permitted to be created under s. 419(1) of the *Bank Act* (which permits the creation of a security interest in property of the bank where the obligation is to the Bank of Canada or the Canada Deposit Insurance Corporation or where the Superintendent of Financial Institutions has approved of the creation of the security interest in writing). The restriction does not apply to a security interest created on such classes of personal property as the Superintendent of Financial Institutions may by order designate or having a aggregate value less than that specified by order of the Superintendent.

In *Re Home Bank of Canada* (1923), 54 O.L.R. 606 (H.C.), the court directed the interim liquidator to call the meetings of shareholders and creditors referred to in s. 152.

In general, it may be stated that the court will appoint the nominee of that class which is most interested in the liquidation.

When the double liability of the shareholders of a bank was likely to be called up, the nominee of the creditors was preferred to the nominee of the shareholders: *Re Central Bank of Canada* (1887), 15 O.R. 309 (Ch. D.); *Re Bank of Liverpool* (1889), 22 N.S.R. 97 (C.A.), affd (1890), 18 S.C.R. 707 (*sub nom. Forsythe v. Bank of Nova Scotia*). Under the current *Bank Act*, double liability no longer exists.

There is nothing in the provisions of the *Winding-up Act* which requires that both creditors and shareholders should be represented on the board of liquidators: *Forsythe v. Bank of Nova Scotia* (1890), 18 S.C.R. 707.

In *Re Commercial Bank of Manitoba* (1893), 9 Man. R. 342 (Q.B.), it was said that the court is confined to a selection between the persons nominated at the meeting provided for in these sections, but may exercise its discretion; and is not bound to accept the choice of the majority. Where the corporation is solvent, the nominees of the shareholders will be preferred, but if it be insolvent or its solvency questionable, the wishes of the creditors should be preferred. It was further considered undesirable to appoint a debtor of a corporation, even if the corporation held securities, if the security was at all doubtful.

For the distribution of bank assets where there is a a surplus, see *Re Commercial Bank of Manitoba; Rev. Dr. Robertson's Claim* (1896), 10 Man. R. 61 (Q.B.).

For a discussion of whether emergency financial assistance constituted a loan or a capital investment, see the judgment of the Supreme Court of Canada in *Canada Deposit Insurance Corp. v. Canadian Commercial Bank*, [1992] 3 S.C.R. 558.

Chapter 27

INSURANCE CORPORATIONS

The application of the Act to insurance corporations is provided for by s. 6 and Part III (ss. 159-172) of the Act. Section 159 contains certain definitions which are applicable to expressions in Part III and s. 159.1 provides that Part III is applicable only to insurance corporations. Section 160 deals with special cases where an insurance corporation is deemed to be insolvent and provides that the Attorney General of Canada on request of the Minister may make an application to the Court for winding-up; s. 161 provides for priority of certain claims including claims by or relating to policy holders; special provisions are applicable to a foreign insurer; s. 162 empowers the liquidator to arrange for re-insurance; s. 163 provides for the computation of the value of insurance policies where no re-insurance has been effected and no claim has arisen thereunder; s. 164 provides for the transfer of funds and securities on deposit for the benefit of the corporation or for the protection of the policy holder to be transferred to the liquidator on Court order and for the failure to do so in the case of a deposit with a state or country outside Canada; s. 165 provides in the case of a foreign insurer for the transfer of the Canadian assets to the foreign liquidator on authorization of the Treasury Board if it deems such transfer advisable and in the interest of the Canadian policy holders. Section 166 provides for the preparation of a statement of creditors and claimants under every policy, such statement may be rectified by the liquidator or the Court with respect to any omissions or errors therein discovered by the liquidator or of which notice is given to him; s. 168(1) provides for a copy of this statement to be filed within a stipulated period of time with the office of the Superintendent of Financial Institutions after the liquidator has given notice of his intention so to do in the Canada Gazette, the provincial gazette and two newspapers published at or nearest the place where the head office or chief agency of the corporation in Canada is situate; s. 169 provides that notice of such filing is to be sent by mail by the liquidator to each creditor or claimant; s. 170 provides that the liquidator is to report every six months or more often if required to the Superintendent of Financial Institutions; s. 168(2) provides that any claim arising under the terms of a policy of which notice is received by the liquidator after the filing above referred to is to rank only for the value entered in the statement unless the amounts under administration are sufficient to pay claimants in full in which case the policy holder will rank as a creditor for the balance of his claim; s. 172 provides that nothing in Part III is to affect the priority of any mortgage, lien or charge on the property of the insurance corporation. By virtue of s. 167 if the assets under administration are not sufficient to cover all claims referred to in the above statement the policy holders are not barred from any recourse in law or equity against the issuing corporation or against any shareholder or director thereof except in respect of any amount received in the distribution of the assets in question.

Where an insurance corporation incorporated under the laws of Quebec was being wound up under the *Winding-up Act*, it was held that the deposit with the Provincial Treasurer to meet the claims of Quebec insurers should be made available to those insurers and administered for their benefit: *Re Strathcona Fire Insurance Co.; Lemire v. Nichol*, [1924] S.C.R. 402.

Where an insurance corporation in liquidation in one province under the *Winding-up Act* has deposited securities with the government of another province under the local Insurance Act for the benefit of creditors or policyholders in that province, leave may be given in the winding-up proceedings to take the requisite steps to have the securities administered in that province for the benefit of such policyholders or creditors: *Re Continental Fire & Casualty Co. (In Liquidation)*, [1924] 1 W.W.R. 132 (K.B.), and *Re Continental Fire and Insurance Co. (In Liquidation)*, [1924] 1 W.W.R. 1080. Where there is a different priority for deposited securities under the provincial Insurance Act and the *Winding-up Act*, the priorities in the latter Act apply: *A.G. Ontario v. Wentworth Insurance Co.*, [1969] S.C.R. 779.

Where an insurance corporation goes into liquidation under the Act, and as a result the policyholder cancels his policy, the agent must account for the part of the commission that corresponds to the unearned premiums on the cancelled policy: *Dominion Gresham Guarantee & Casualty Co. v. Crooks*, [1934] 1 D.L.R. 405 (Que. C.A.). For a discussion of the priority between unearned premiums and losses under policies of insurance, see *A.G. Canada v. Northumberland General Insurance Co.* (1988), 63 O.R. (2d) 706 (H.C.).

For a discussion of circumstances in which an insurance corporation that had been wound up was added as a party defendant as well as the liquidators, see *Re Pitts Insurance Co.; Doxtator v. De'Leary* (1982), 44 C.B.R. (N.S.) 133 (Ont.).

Where the Superintendent had seized the assets of an insurance corporation and withdrawn its certificate of registry, his refusal to pay claims rendered the corporation insolvent under the Act, and a winding-up order would be granted: *A.G. Can. v. Cardinal Insurance Co.* (1982), 39 O.R. (2d) 204, 20 B.L.R. 9 (H.C.).

Section 161 of the Act provides for a system of priorities in the winding-up of an insurance corporation as follows: (i) costs of liquidation; (ii) claims of preferred creditors under s. 72 of the Act; (iii) policy holder claims; and (iv) policyholder values and adjustments. It will be noted that different priorities may arise depending on whether re-insurance is effected or not as set out in s. 162; ordinary creditors will rank after all of the foregoing including the cost of the premium payable to any re-insurer. The case of *Trustee of Cooperants Mutual Insurance Society*, an unreported decision of the Quebec Superior Court delivered on December 4, 1992, dealt with the question of whether deposit administration contracts relating to pension plans constituted policies (which expression is defined in the Act as including annuities). After an extensive analysis of the applicable law the Court held that the deposit administration contracts did not constitute policies entitled to priority under the Act. The result was that the amounts under the deposit administration contracts ranked with the ordinary creditors and there was a substantial deficiency. It is interesting to note that apparently it was not argued that a trust was applicable to the assets in question so that they never formed part of the assets available for distribution. It is understood that an appeal has been brought from this decision.

Appendix 1

CANADA BUSINESS CORPORATIONS ACT

R.S.C. 1985, c. C-44, amended by R.S.C. 1985 (1st Supp.), c. 27, Sch. V, item 3; R.S.C. 1985 (2nd Supp.), c. 27, S.C. 1988, c. 2, S.C. 1990, c. 17, s. 6, S.C. 1991, c. 45, ss. 551-556; S.C. 1991, c. 46, 595-597; S.C. 1991, c. 47, 719-724; S.C. 1992, c. 1, 53-57; S.C. 1992, c. 27, s. 90(1)(h).*

An Act respecting Canadian business corporations.

SHORT TITLE

1. Short title. — This Act may be cited as the *Canada Business Corporations Act.*

PART I
INTERPRETATION AND APPLICATION

INTERPRETATION

2. (1) Definitions. — In this Act,

"affairs". — "affairs" means the relationships among a corporation, its affiliates and the shareholders, directors and officers of such bodies corporate but does not include the business carried on by such bodies corporate;

"affiliate". — "affiliate" means an affiliated body corporate within the meaning of subsection (2);

"articles". — "articles" means the original or restated articles of incorporation, articles of amendment, articles of amalgamation, articles of continuance, articles of reorganization, articles of arrangement, articles of dissolution, articles of revival and includes any amendments thereto;

"associate". — "associate" when used to indicate a relationship with any person means

(a) a body corporate of which that person beneficially owns or controls, directly or indirectly, shares or securities currently convertible into shares carrying more than ten per cent of the voting rights under all circumstances or by reason of the occurrence of an event that has

* S.C. 1985, 1986 and 1988 to be included in 1st, 2nd and 4th Supps, respectively, to the revision.

occurred and is continuing, or a currently exercisable option or right to purchase such shares or such convertible securities,
(b) a partner of that person acting on behalf of the partnership of which they are partners,
(c) a trust or estate in which that person has a substantial beneficial interest or in respect of which he serves as a trustee or in a similar capacity,
(d) a spouse or child of that person, and
(e) a relative of that person or of his spouse if that relative has the same residence as that person;

"auditor". — "auditor" includes a partnership of auditors;

"beneficial interest". — "beneficial interest" means an interest arising out of the beneficial ownership of securities;

"beneficial ownership." — "beneficial ownership" includes ownership through any trustee, legal representative, agent or other intermediary;

"body corporate". — "body corporate" includes a company or other body corporate wherever or however incorporated;

"call". — "call" means an option transferable by delivery to demand delivery of a specified number or amount of securities at a fixed price within a specified time but does not include an option or right to acquire securities of the corporation that granted the option or right to acquire;

"corporation." — "corporation" means a body corporate incorporated or continued under this Act and not discontinued under this Act;

"court". — "court" means
(a) in the Provinces of Newfoundland, Nova Scotia, Prince Edward Island and Ontario, the trial division or branch of the Supreme Court of the Province,
(b) in the Province of British Columbia, the Supreme Court of the Province,
(c) in the Provinces of Manitoba, Saskatchewan, Alberta and New Brunswick, the Court of Queen's Bench for the Province,
(d) in the Province of Quebec, the Superior Court of the Province, and
(e) in the Yukon Territory and the Northwest Territories, the Supreme Court thereof;

[Paras. (a) and (b) repealed and substituted by R.S.C. 1985 (2nd Supp.), c. 27, Sch., item 5; para. (a) repealed and substituted by paras. (a) and (a.1) by S.C. 1990, c. 17, s. 6.]

"court of appeal". — "court of appeal" means the court to which an appeal lies from an order of a court;

"debt obligation". — "debt obligation" means a bond, debenture, note or other evidence of indebtedness or guarantee of a corporation, whether secured or unsecured;

"Director". — "Director" means the Director appointed under section 260;

"director", "directors" and "board of directors". — "director" means a person occupying the position of director by whatever name called and "directors" and "board of directors" includes a single director;

"incorporator". — "incorporator" means a person who signs articles of incorporation;

"individual." — "individual" means a natural person;

"liability". — "liability" includes a debt of a corporation arising under section 40, subsection 190(25) and paragraphs 241(3)(f) and (g);

"Minister." — "Minister" means such member of the Queen's Privy Council for Canada as is designated by the Governor in Council as the Minister for the purposes of this Act;

"ordinary resolution". — "ordinary resolution" means a resolution passed by a majority of the votes cast by the shareholders who voted in respect of that resolution;

"person". — "person" includes an individual, partnership, association, body corporate, trustee, executor, administrator or legal representative;

"prescribed". — "prescribed" means prescribed by the regulations;

"put". — "put" means an option transferable by delivery to deliver a specified number or amount of securities at a fixed price within a specified time;

"redeemable share". — "redeemable share" means a share issued by a corporation

(a) that the corporation may purchase or redeem on the demand of the corporation, or

(b) that the corporation is required by its articles to purchase or redeem at a specified time or on the demand of a shareholder;

"resident Canadian". — "resident Canadian" means an individual who is

(a) a Canadian citizen ordinarily resident in Canada,

(b) a Canadian citizen not ordinarily resident in Canada who is a member of a prescribed class of persons, or

(c) a permanent resident within the meaning of the *Immigration Act* and ordinarily resident in Canada, except a permanent resident who has been ordinarily resident in Canada for more than one year after the time at which he first became eligible to apply for Canadian citizenship;

"security". — "security" means a share of any class or series of shares or a debt obligation of a corporation and includes a certificate evidencing such a share or debt obligation;

"security interest". — "security interest" means an interest in or charge on property of a corporation to secure payment of a debt or performance of any other obligation of the corporation;

"send". — "send" includes deliver;

"series". — "series", in relation to shares, means a division of a class of shares;

"special resolution". — "special resolution" means a resolution passed by a majority of not less than two-thirds of the votes cast by the shareholders who voted in respect of that resolution or signed by all the shareholders entitled to vote on that resolution;

"unanimous shareholder agreement". — "unanimous shareholder agreement" means an agreement described in subsection 146(2) or a declaration of a shareholder described in subsection 146(3);

(2) Affiliated bodies corporate. — For the purposes of this Act,

(a) one body corporate is affiliated with another body corporate if one of them is the subsidiary of the other or both are subsidiaries of the same body corporate or each of them is controlled by the same person; and

(b) if two bodies corporate are affiliated with the same body corporate at the same time, they are deemed to be affiliated with each other.

(3) Control. — For the purposes of this Act, a body corporate is controlled by a person if

(a) securities of the body corporate to which are attached more than fifty per cent of the votes that may be cast to elect directors of the body corporate are held, other than by way of security only, by or for the benefit of that person; and

(b) the votes attached to those securities are sufficient, if exercised, to elect a majority of the directors of the body corporate.

(4) Holding body corporate. — A body corporate is the holding body corporate of another if that other body corporate is its subsidiary.

(5) Subsidiary body corporate. — A body corporate is a subsidiary of another body corporate if it is controlled by that other body corporate.

(6) Deemed distribution to the public. — For the purposes of this Act, securities of a corporation

(a) issued on a conversion of other securities, or

(b) issued in exchange for other securities

are deemed to be securities that are part of a distribution to the public if those other securities were part of a distribution to the public.

(7) Distribution to the public. — Subject to subsection (8), for the purposes of this Act a security of a body corporate

(a) is part of a distribution to the public where, in respect of the security, there has been a filing of a prospectus, statement of material facts, registration statement, securities exchange take-over bid circular or similar document under the laws of Canada, a province or a jurisdiction outside Canada; or

(b) is deemed to be part of a distribution to the public, where the security has been issued and a filing referred to in paragraph (a) would be required if the security were being issued currently.

(8) Exemption. — On the application of a corporation, the Director may determine that a security of the corporation is not or was not part of a distribution to the public if he is satisfied that such determination would not prejudice any security holder of the corporation.

APPLICATION

3. (1) Application of Act. — This Act applies to every corporation incorporated and every body corporate continued as a corporation under this Act that has not been discontinued under this Act.

(2) [Repealed by S.C. 1991 c. 45, s. 551(1); repealed by S.C. 1991, c. 46, s. 595(1); repealed by S.C. 1991, c. 47, s. 719(1).]

(3) Certain Acts do not apply. — No provision of the *Canada Corporations Act*, chapter C-32 of the Revised Statutes of Canada, 1970, or the *Winding-up Act* applies to a corporation.

(4) Limitations on business that may be carried on. — No corporation shall carry on the business of

(a) a bank;

[Para. (a) repealed and substituted by S.C. 1991, c. 46, s. 595(2); S.C. 1992, c. 1, Sch. V, Item 11(2).]

(b) a company to which the *Insurance Companies Act* applies; or

[Para. (b) repealed and substituted by S.C. 1991, c. 47, s. 719(2).]

(c) a company to which the *Trust and Loan Companies Act* applies.

[Subsec. 4 repealed and substituted by S.C. 1991, c. 45, s. 551(2); repealed and substituted by S.C. 1991, c. 46, s. 595(3); repealed and substituted by S.C. 1991, c. 47, s. 719(3).]

PURPOSES OF ACT

4. Purposes. — The purposes of this Act are to revise and reform the law applicable to business corporations incorporated to carry on business throughout Canada, to advance the cause of uniformity of business corporation law in Canada and to provide a means of allowing an orderly transference of certain federal companies incorporated under various Acts of Parliament to this Act.

PART II
INCORPORATION

5. (1) Incorporators. — One or more individuals not one of whom

(a) is less than eighteen years of age,

(b) is of unsound mind and has been so found by a court in Canada or elsewhere, or

(c) has the status of bankrupt,

may incorporate a corporation by signing articles of incorporation and complying with section 7.

(2) Bodies corporate. — One or more bodies corporate may incorporate a corporation by signing articles of incorporation and complying with section 7.

6. (1) Articles of incorporation. — Articles of incorporation shall follow the prescribed form and shall set out, in respect of the proposed corporation,

(a) the name of the corporation;

(b) the place within Canada where the registered office is to be situated;

(c) the classes and any maximum number of shares that the corporation is authorized to issue, and

(i) if there will be two or more classes of shares, the rights, privileges, restrictions and conditions attaching to each class of shares, and

(ii) if a class of shares may be issued in series, the authority given to the directors to fix the number of shares in, and to determine the designation of, and the rights, privileges, restrictions and conditions attaching to, the shares of each series;

(d) if the issue, transfer or ownership of shares of the corporation is to be restricted, a statement to that effect and a statement as to the nature of such restrictions;

(e) the number of directors or, subject to paragraph 107(a), the minimum and maximum number of directors of the corporation; and

(f) any restrictions on the businesses that the corporation may carry on.

(2) Additional provisions in articles. — The articles may set out any provisions permitted by this Act or by law to be set out in the by-laws of the corporation.

(3) Special majorities. — Subject to subsection (4), if the articles or a unanimous shareholder agreement require a greater number of votes of directors or shareholders than that required by this Act to effect any action, the provisions of the articles or of the unanimous shareholder agreement prevail.

(4) Idem. — The articles may not require a greater number of votes of shareholders to remove a director than the number required by section 109.

7. Delivery of articles of incorporation. — An incorporator shall send to the Director articles of incorporation and the documents required by sections 19 and 106.

8. Certificate of incorporation. — On receipt of articles of incorporation, the Director shall issue a certificate of incorporation in accordance with section 262.

9. Effect of certificate. — A corporation comes into existence on the date shown in the certificate of incorporation.

10. (1) Name of corporation. — The word or expression "Limited", "Limitée", "Incorporated", "Incorporée", "Corporation", "Société par actions de régime fédéral" or "Société commerciale canadienne" or the abbreviation "Ltd.", "Ltée", "Inc.", "Corp.", "S.A.R.F." or "S.C.C." shall be part, other than only in a figurative or descriptive sense, of the name of every corporation, but a corporation may use and be legally designated by either the full or the abbreviated form.

[Subsec. (1) repealed and substituted by S.C. 1992, c. 1, s. 53(1) and shall be deemed to have come into force on December 12, 1988 by S.C. 1992, c. 1, s. 53(2).]

(2) Exemption. — The Director may exempt a body corporate continued as a corporation under this Act from the provisions of subsection (1).

(3) Alternate name. — Subject to subsection 12(1), a corporation may set out its name in its articles in an English form, a French form, an English form and a French form or in a combined English and French form and it may use and may be legally designated by any such form.

(4) Alternative name outside Canada. — Subject to subsection 12(1), a corporation may, for use outside Canada, set out its name in its articles in any language form and it may use and may be legally designated by any such form outside Canada.

(5) Publication of name. — A corporation shall set out its name in legible characters in all contracts, invoices, negotiable instruments and orders for goods or services issued or made by or on behalf of the corporation.

(6) Other name. — Subject to subsections (5) and 12(1), a corporation may carry on business under or identify itself by a name other than its corporate name.

11. (1) Reserving name. — The Director may, on request, reserve for ninety days a name for an intended corporation or for a corporation about to change its name.

(2) Designating number. — If requested to do so by the incorporators or

a corporation, the Director shall assign to the corporation as its name a designating number determined by him.

12. (1) Prohibited names. — A corporation shall not be incorporated with, have, carry on business under or identify itself by a name

(a) that is, as prescribed, prohibited or deceptively misdescriptive; or

(b) that is reserved for another corporation or intended corporation under section 11.

(2) Directing change of name. — If, through inadvertence or otherwise, a corporation

(a) comes into existence or is continued with a name, or

(b) on an application to change its name, is granted a name

that contravenes this section, the Director may direct the corporation to change its name in accordance with section 173.

(3) Name of continued corporation. — Notwithstanding subsections (1) and (2), a corporation that is continued under this Act is entitled to be continued with the name it had before such continuance unless that name is identical with or confusingly similar to the name of an existing body corporate.

(4) Idem. — If a corporation has a designating number as its name, the Director may direct the corporation to change its name to a name other than a designating number in accordance with section 173.

(5) Revoking name. — When a corporation has been directed under subsection (2) or (4) to change its name and has not within sixty days from the service of the directive to that effect changed its name to a name that complies with this Act, the Director may revoke the name of the corporation and assign to it a name and, until changed in accordance with section 173, the name of the corporation is thereafter the name so assigned.

13. (1) Certificate of amendment. — When a corporation has had its name revoked and a name assigned to it under subsection 12(5), the Director shall issue a certificate of amendment showing the new name of the corporation and shall forthwith give notice of the change of name in the *Canada Gazette* or in the periodical referred to in section 123.

(2) Effect of certificate. — The articles of the corporation are amended accordingly on the date shown in the certificate of amendment.

14. (1) Personal liability. — Subject to this section, a person who enters into a written contract in the name of or on behalf of a corporation before it comes into existence is personally bound by the contract and is entitled to the benefits thereof.

(2) Pre-incorporation and pre-amalgamation contracts. — A corporation may, within a reasonable time after it comes into existence, by any action or

conduct signifying its intention to be bound thereby, adopt a written contract made before it came into existence in its name or on its behalf, and on such adoption

(a) the corporation is bound by the contract and is entitled to the benefits thereof as if the corporation had been in existence at the date of the contract and had been a party thereto; and

(b) a person who purported to act in the name of or on behalf of the corporation ceases, except as provided in subsection (3), to be bound by or entitled to the benefits of the contract.

(3) Application to court. — Subject to subsection (4), whether or not a written contract made before the coming into existence of a corporation is adopted by the corporation, a party to the contract may apply to a court for an order fixing obligations under the contract as joint or joint and several or apportioning liability between or among the corporation and a person who purported to act in the name of or on behalf of the corporation and on such application the court may make any order it thinks fit.

(4) Exemption from personal liability. — If expressly so provided in the written contract, a person who purported to act in the name of or on behalf of the corporation before it came into existence is not in any event bound by the contract or entitled to the benefits thereof.

PART III
CAPACITY AND POWERS

15. (1) Capacity of a corporation. — A corporation has the capacity and, subject to this Act, the rights, powers and privileges of a natural person.

(2) Idem. — A corporation may carry on business throughout Canada.

(3) Extra-territorial capacity. — A corporation has the capacity to carry on its business, conduct its affairs and exercise its powers in any jurisdiction outside Canada to the extent that the laws of such jurisdiction permit.

16. (1) Powers of a corporation. — It is not necessary for a by-law to be passed in order to confer any particular power on the corporation or its directors.

(2) Restricted business or powers. — A corporation shall not carry on any business or exercise any power that it is restricted by its articles from carrying on or exercising, nor shall the corporation exercise any of its powers in a manner contrary to its articles.

(3) Rights preserved. — No act of a corporation, including any transfer of property to or by a corporation, is invalid by reason only that the act or transfer is contrary to its articles or this Act.

17. No constructive notice. — No person is affected by or is deemed to have notice or knowledge of the contents of a document concerning a corporation

by reason only that the document has been filed by the Director or is available for inspection at an office of the corporation.

18. Authority of directors, officers and agents. — A corporation or a guarantor of an obligation of the corporation may not assert against a person dealing with the corporation or with any person who has acquired rights from the corporation that

(a) the articles, by-laws and any unanimous shareholder agreement have not been complied with,

(b) the persons named in the most recent notice sent to the Director under section 106 or 113 are not the directors of the corporation,

(c) the place named in the most recent notice sent to the Director under section 19 is not the registered office of the corporation,

(d) a person held out by a corporation as a director, an officer or an agent of the corporation has not been duly appointed or has no authority to exercise the powers and perform the duties that are customary in the business of the corporation or usual for such director, officer or agent,

(e) a document issued by any director, officer or agent of a corporation with actual or usual authority to issue the document is not valid or not genuine, or

(f) financial assistance referred to in section 44 or a sale, lease or exchange of property referred to in subsection 189(3) was not authorized,

except where the person has or ought to have by virtue of his position with or relationship to the corporation knowledge to the contrary.

PART IV
REGISTERED OFFICE AND RECORDS

19. (1) Registered office. — A corporation shall at all times have a registered office in the place within Canada specified in its articles.

(2) Notice of registered office. — A notice of registered office in prescribed form shall be sent to the Director together with any articles that designate or change the place of the registered office of the corporation.

(3) Change of address. — The directors of a corporation may change the address of the registered office within the place specified in the articles.

(4) Notice of change of address. — A corporation shall send to the Director, within fifteen days of any change of address of its registered office, a notice in prescribed form and the Director shall file it.

20. (1) Corporate records. — A corporation shall prepare and maintain, at its registered office or at any other place in Canada designated by the directors, records containing

(a) the articles and the by-laws, and all amendments thereto, and a copy of any unanimous shareholder agreement;

(b) minutes of meetings and resolutions of shareholders;

(c) copies of all notices required by section 106 or 113; and

(d) a securities register that complies with section 50.

(2) Directors records. — In addition to the records described in subsection (1), a corporation shall prepare and maintain adequate accounting records and records containing minutes of meetings and resolutions of the directors and any committee thereof.

(3) Records of continued corporations. — For the purposes of paragraph (1)(b) and subsection (2), where a body corporate is continued under this Act, "records" includes similar records required by law to be maintained by the body corporate before it was so continued.

(4) Place of directors records. — The records described in subsection (2) shall be kept at the registered office of the corporation or at such other place as the directors think fit and shall at all reasonable times be open to inspection by the directors.

(5) Records in Canada. — Where accounting records of a corporation are kept at a place outside Canada, there shall be kept at the registered office or other office in Canada accounting records adequate to enable the directors to ascertain the financial position of the corporation with reasonable accuracy on a quarterly basis.

(6) Offence. — A corporation that, without reasonable cause, fails to comply with this section is guilty of an offence and liable on summary conviction to a fine not exceeding five thousand dollars.

21. (1) Access to corporate records. — Shareholders and creditors of a corporation, their agents and legal representatives and the Director may examine the records referred to in subsection 20(1) during the usual business hours of the corporation, and may take extracts therefrom, free of charge, and, where the corporation is a distributing corporation as defined in subsection 126(1), any other person may do so on payment of a reasonable fee.

(2) Copies of corporate records. — A shareholder of a corporation is entitled on request and without charge to one copy of the articles and by-laws and of any unanimous shareholder agreement.

(3) Shareholder lists. — Shareholders and creditors of a corporation, their agents and legal representatives, the Director and, where the corporation is a distributing corporation as defined in subsection 126(1), any other person, on payment of a reasonable fee and on sending to a corporation or its agent the affidavit referred to in subsection (7), may on application require the corporation or its agent to furnish within ten days from the receipt of the affidavit a list (in this section referred to as the "basic list") made up to a date not more than

ten days before the date of receipt of the affidavit setting out the names of the shareholders of the corporation, the number of shares owned by each shareholder and the address of each shareholder as shown on the records of the corporation.

(4) Supplemental lists. — A person requiring a corporation to supply a basic list may, if he states in the affidavit referred to in subsection (3) that he requires supplemental lists, require the corporation or its agent on payment of a reasonable fee to furnish supplemental lists setting out any changes from the basic list in the names or addresses of the shareholders and the number of shares owned by each shareholder for each business day following the date the basic list is made up to.

(5) When supplemental lists to be furnished. — The corporation or its agent shall furnish a supplemental list required under subsection (4)

(a) on the date the basic list is furnished, where the information relates to changes that took place prior to that date; and

(b) on the business day following the day to which the supplemental list relates, where the information relates to changes that take place on or after the date the basic list is furnished.

(6) Holders of options. — A person requiring a corporation to furnish a basic list or a supplemental list may also require the corporation to include in that list the name and address of any known holder of an option or right to acquire shares of the corporation.

(7) Contents of affidavit. — The affidavit required under subsection (3) shall state

(a) the name and address of the applicant;

(b) the name and address for service of the body corporate if the applicant is a body corporate; and

(c) that the basic list and any supplemental lists obtained pursuant to subsection (4) will not be used except as permitted under subsection (9).

(8) Idem. — If the applicant is a body corporate, the affidavit shall be made by a director or officer of the body corporate.

(9) Use of shareholder list. — A list of shareholders obtained under this section shall not be used by any person except in connection with

(a) an effort to influence the voting of shareholders of the corporation;

(b) an offer to acquire shares of the corporation; or

(c) any other matter relating to the affairs of the corporation.

(10) Offence. — A person who, without reasonable cause, contravenes this section is guilty of an offence and liable on summary conviction to a fine not

exceeding five thousand dollars or to imprisonment for a term not exceeding six months or to both.

22. (1) Form of records. — All registers and other records required by this Act to be prepared and maintained may be in a bound or loose-leaf form or in a photographic film form, or may be entered or recorded by any system of mechanical or electronic data processing or any other information storage device that is capable of reproducing any required information in intelligible written form within a reasonable time.

(2) Precautions. — A corporation and its agents shall take reasonable precautions to

(a) prevent loss or destruction of,

(b) prevent falsification of entries in, and

(c) facilitate detection and correction of inaccuracies in

the registers and other records required by this Act to be prepared and maintained.

(3) Offence. — A person who, without reasonable cause, contravenes this section is guilty of an offence and liable on summary conviction to a fine not exceeding five thousand dollars or to imprisonment for a term not exceeding six months or to both.

23. Corporate seal. — An instrument or agreement executed on behalf of a corporation by a director, an officer or an agent of the corporation is not invalid merely because a corporate seal is not affixed thereto.

PART V
CORPORATE FINANCE

24. (1) Shares. — Shares of a corporation shall be in registered form and shall be without nominal or par value.

(2) Transitional. — When a body corporate is continued under this Act, a share with nominal or par value issued by the body corporate before it was so continued is, for the purpose of subsection (1), deemed to be a share without nominal or par value.

(3) Rights attached to shares. — Where a corporation has only one class of shares, the rights of the holders thereof are equal in all respects and include the rights

(a) to vote at any meeting of shareholders of the corporation;

(b) to receive any dividend declared by the corporation; and

(c) to receive the remaining property of the corporation on dissolution.

(4) Rights to classes of shares. — The articles may provide for more than one class of shares and, if they so provide,

(a) the rights, privileges, restrictions and conditions attaching to the shares of each class shall be set out therein; and

(b) the rights set out in subsection (3) shall be attached to at least one class of shares but all such rights are not required to be attached to one class.

25. (1) Issue of shares. — Subject to the articles, the by-laws and any unanimous shareholder agreement and to section 28, shares may be issued at such times and to such persons and for such consideration as the directors may determine.

(2) Shares non-assessable. — Shares issued by a corporation are non-assessable and the holders are not liable to the corporation or to its creditors in respect thereof.

(3) Consideration. — A share shall not be issued until the consideration for the share is fully paid in money or in property or past services that are not less in value than the fair equivalent of the money that the corporation would have received if the share had been issued for money.

(4) Consideration other than money. — In determining whether property or past services are the fair equivalent of a money consideration, the directors may take into account reasonable charges and expenses of organization and reorganization and payments for property and past services reasonably expected to benefit the corporation.

(5) Definition of "property". — For the purposes of this section, "property" does not include a promissory note or a promise to pay.

26. (1) Stated capital account. — A corporation shall maintain a separate stated capital account for each class and series of shares it issues.

(2) Entries in stated capital account. — A corporation shall add to the appropriate stated capital account the full amount of any consideration it receives for any shares it issues.

(3) Exception for non-arm's length transactions. — Notwithstanding subsection 25(3) and subsection (2), where a corporation issues shares

(a) in exchange for

(i) property of a person who immediately before the exchange did not deal with the corporation at arm's length within the meaning of that term in the *Income Tax Act*, or

(ii) shares of a body corporate that immediately before the exchange or that, because of the exchange, did not deal with the corporation at arm's length within the meaning of that term in the *Income Tax Act*, or

(b) pursuant to an agreement referred to in subsection 182(1) or an arrangement referred to in paragraph 192(1)(b) or (c) to shareholders of an amalgamating body corporate who receive the shares in addition to or instead of securities of the amalgamated body corporate,

the corporation may, subject to subsection (4), add to the stated capital accounts maintained for the shares of the classes or series issued the whole or any part of the amount of the consideration it received in the exchange.

(4) Limit on addition to a stated capital account. — On the issue of a share a corporation shall not add to a stated capital account in respect of the share it issues an amount greater than the amount of the consideration it received for the share.

(5) Constraint on addition to a stated capital account. — Where a corporation proposes to add any amount to a stated capital account it maintains in respect of a class or series of shares, if

(a) the amount to be added was not received by the corporation as consideration for the issue of shares, and

(b) the corporation has issued any outstanding shares of more than one class or series,

the addition to the stated capital account must be approved by special resolution unless all the issued and outstanding shares are shares of not more than two classes of convertible shares referred to in subsection 39(5).

(6) Other additions to stated capital. — When a body corporate is continued under this Act, it may add to a stated capital account any consideration received by it for a share it issued and a corporation at any time may, subject to subsection (5), add to a stated capital account any amount it credited to a retained earnings or other surplus account.

(7) Transitional. — When a body corporate is continued under this Act, subsection (2) does not apply to the consideration received by it before it was so continued unless the share in respect of which the consideration is received is issued after the corporation is so continued.

(8) Idem. — When a body corporate is continued under this Act, any amount unpaid in respect of a share issued by the body corporate before it was so continued and paid after it was so continued shall be added to the stated capital account maintained for the shares of that class or series.

(9) Idem. — For the purposes of subsection 34(2), sections 38 and 42, subsection 44(1) and paragraph 185(2)(a), when a body corporate is continued under this Act its stated capital is deemed to include the amount that would have been included in stated capital if the body corporate had been incorporated under this Act.

(10) Restriction. — A corporation shall not reduce its stated capital or any stated capital account except in the manner provided in this Act.

(11) Exception for an open-end mutual fund. — Subsections (1) to (10)

and any other provisions of this Act relating to stated capital do not apply to an open-end mutual fund.

(12) Definition of "open-end mutual fund". — For the purposes of this section, "open-end mutual fund" means a corporation that makes a distribution to the public of its shares and that carries on only the business of investing the consideration it receives for the shares it issues, and all or substantially all of those shares are redeemable on the demand of a shareholder.

27. (1) Shares in series. — The articles may authorize the issue of any class of shares in one or more series and may authorize the directors to fix the number of shares in and to determine the designation, rights, privileges, restrictions and conditions attaching to, the shares of each series, subject to the limitations set out in the articles.

(2) Series participation. — If any cumulative dividends or amounts payable on return of capital in respect of a series of shares are not paid in full, the shares of all series of the same class participate rateably in respect of accumulated dividends and return of capital.

(3) Restrictions on series. — No rights, privileges, restrictions or conditions attached to a series of shares authorized under this section shall confer on a series a priority in respect of dividends or return of capital over any other series of shares of the same class that are then outstanding.

(4) Amendment of articles. — Before the issue of shares of a series authorized under this section, the directors shall send to the Director articles of amendment in prescribed form to designate a series of shares.

(5) Certificate of amendment. — On receipt of articles of amendment designating a series of shares, the Director shall issue a certificate of amendment in accordance with section 262.

(6) Effect of certificate. — The articles of the corporation are amended accordingly on the date shown in the certificate of amendment.

28. (1) Pre-emptive right. — If the articles so provide, no shares of a class shall be issued unless the shares have first been offered to the shareholders holding shares of that class, and those shareholders have a pre-emptive right to acquire the offered shares in proportion to their holdings of the shares of that class, at such price and on such terms as those shares are to be offered to others.

(2) Exception. — Notwithstanding that the articles provide the pre-emptive right referred to in subsection (1), shareholders have no pre-emptive right in respect of shares to be issued

(a) for a consideration other than money;

(b) as a share dividend; or

(c) pursuant to the exercise of conversion privileges, options or rights previously granted by the corporation.

29. (1) Options and rights. — A corporation may issue certificates, warrants or other evidences of conversion privileges, options or rights to acquire securities of the corporation, and shall set out the conditions thereof

(a) in the certificates, warrants or other evidences; or

(b) in certificates evidencing the securities to which the conversion privileges, options or rights are attached.

(2) Transferable rights. — Conversion privileges, options and rights to acquire securities of a corporation may be made transferable or non-transferable, and options and rights to acquire may be made separable or inseparable from any securities to which they are attached.

(3) Reserved shares. — Where a corporation has granted privileges to convert any securities issued by the corporation into shares, or into shares of another class or series, or has issued or granted options or rights to acquire shares, if the articles limit the number of authorized shares, the corporation shall reserve and continue to reserve sufficient authorized shares to meet the exercise of such conversion privileges, options and rights.

30. (1) Corporation holding its own shares. — Subject to subsection (2) and sections 31 to 36, a corporation

(a) shall not hold shares in itself or in its holding body corporate; and

(b) shall not permit any of its subsidiary bodies corporate to acquire shares of the corporation.

(2) Subsidiary holding shares of a corporation. — A corporation shall cause a subsidiary body corporate of the corporation that holds shares of the corporation to sell or otherwise dispose of those shares within five years from the date

(a) the body corporate became a subsidiary of the corporation; or

(b) the corporation was continued under this Act.

31. (1) Exception. — A corporation may in the capacity of a legal representative hold shares in itself or in its holding body corporate unless it or the holding body corporate or a subsidiary of either of them has a beneficial interest in the shares.

(2) Idem. — A corporation may hold shares in itself or in its holding body corporate by way of security for the purposes of a transaction entered into by it in the ordinary course of a business that includes the lending of money.

32. (1) Exception relating to Canadian ownership. — Subject to subsection 39(8), a corporation may, for the purpose of assisting the corporation or any of its affiliates or associates to qualify under any prescribed law of Canada or a province to receive licences, permits, grants, payments or other benefits by reason of attaining or maintaining a specified level of Canadian ownership or control, hold shares in itself that

(a) are not constrained for the purpose of assisting the corporation or any of its affiliates or associates to so qualify; or

(b) are shares into which shares held under paragraph (a) were converted by the corporation that are constrained for the purpose of assisting the corporation to so qualify and that were not previously held by the corporation.

(2) Prohibited transfers. — A corporation shall not transfer shares held under subsection (1) to any person unless the corporation is satisfied, on reasonable grounds, that the ownership of the shares as a result of the transfer would assist the corporation or any of its affiliates or associates to achieve the purpose set out in subsection (1).

(3) Offence. — A corporation that, without reasonable cause, fails to comply with subsection (2) is guilty of an offence and liable on summary conviction to a fine not exceeding five thousand dollars.

(4) Directors of corporation. — Where a corporation commits an offence under subsection (3), any director of the corporation who knowingly authorized, permitted or acquiesced in the commission of the offence is a party to and guilty of the offence and is liable on summary conviction to a fine not exceeding five thousand dollars or to imprisonment for a term not exceeding six months or to both, whether or not the corporation has been prosecuted or convicted.

(5) Where shares are transferred. — Where shares held under subsection (1) are transferred by a corporation, subsections 25(1), (3), (4) and (5), paragraph 115(3)(c) and subsection 118(1) apply, with such modifications as the circumstances require, in respect of the transfer as if the transfer were an issue.

(6) Transfer not void. — No transfer of shares by a corporation shall be void or voidable solely because the transfer is in contravention of subsection (2).

33. Voting shares. — A corporation holding shares in itself or in its holding body corporate shall not vote or permit those shares to be voted unless the corporation

(a) holds the shares in the capacity of a legal representative; and

(b) has complied with section 153.

34. (1) Acquisition of corporation's own shares. — Subject to subsection (2) and to its articles, a corporation may purchase or otherwise acquire shares issued by it.

(2) Limitation. — A corporation shall not make any payment to purchase or otherwise acquire shares issued by it if there are reasonable grounds for believing that

(a) the corporation is, or would after the payment be, unable to pay its liabilities as they become due; or

(b) the realizable value of the corporation's assets would after the payment be less than the aggregate of its liabilities and stated capital of all classes.

35. (1) Alternative acquisition of corporation's own shares. — Notwithstanding subsection 34(2), but subject to subsection (3) and to its articles, a corporation may purchase or otherwise acquire shares issued by it to

(a) settle or compromise a debt or claim asserted by or against the corporation;

(b) eliminate fractional shares; or

(c) fulfil the terms of a non-assignable agreement under which the corporation has an option or is obliged to purchase shares owned by a director, an officer or an employee of the corporation.

(2) Idem. — Notwithstanding subsection 34(2), a corporation may purchase or otherwise acquire shares issued by it to

(a) satisfy the claim of a shareholder who dissents under section 190; or

(b) comply with an order under section 241.

(3) Limitation. — A corporation shall not make any payment to purchase or acquire under subsection (1) shares issued by it if there are reasonable grounds for believing that

(a) the corporation is, or would after the payment be, unable to pay its liabilities as they become due; or

(b) the realizable value of the corporation's assets would after the payment be less than the aggregate of

(i) its liabilities, and

(ii) the amount required for payment on a redemption or in a liquidation of all shares the holders of which have the right to be paid prior to the holders of the shares to be purchased or acquired.

36. (1) Redemption of shares. — Notwithstanding subsection 34(2) or 35(3), but subject to subsection (2) and to its articles, a corporation may purchase or redeem any redeemable shares issued by it at prices not exceeding the redemption price thereof stated in the articles or calculated according to a formula stated in the articles.

(2) Limitation. — A corporation shall not make any payment to purchase or redeem any redeemable shares issued by it if there are reasonable grounds for believing that

(a) the corporation is, or would after the payment be, unable to pay its liabilities as they become due; or

(b) the realizable value of the corporation's assets would after the payment be less than the aggregate of

(i) its liabilities, and

(ii) the amount that would be required to pay the holders of shares that have a right to be paid, on a redemption or in a liquidation, rateably with or prior to the holders of the shares to be purchased or redeemed.

37. Donated shares. — A corporation may accept from any shareholder a share of the corporation surrendered to it as a gift, but may not extinguish or reduce a liability in respect of an amount unpaid on any such share except in accordance with section 38.

38. (1) Other reduction of stated capital. — Subject to subsection (3), a corporation may by special resolution reduce its stated capital for any purpose including, without limiting the generality of the foregoing, for the purpose of

(a) extinguishing or reducing a liability in respect of an amount unpaid on any share;

(b) distributing to the holder of an issued share of any class or series of shares an amount not exceeding the stated capital of the class or series; and

(c) declaring its stated capital to be reduced by an amount that is not represented by realizable assets.

(2) Contents of special resolution. — A special resolution under this section shall specify the stated capital account or accounts from which the reduction of stated capital effected by the special resolution will be deducted.

(3) Limitation. — A corporation shall not reduce its stated capital for any purpose other than the purpose mentioned in paragraph (1)(c) if there are reasonable grounds for believing that

(a) the corporation is, or would after the reduction be, unable to pay its liabilities as they become due; or

(b) the realizable value of the corporation's assets would thereby be less than the aggregate of its liabilities.

(4) Recovery. — A creditor of a corporation is entitled to apply to a court for an order compelling a shareholder or other recipient

(a) to pay to the corporation an amount equal to any liability of the shareholder that was extinguished or reduced contrary to this section; or

(b) to pay or deliver to the corporation any money or property that was paid or distributed to the shareholder or other recipient as a consequence of a reduction of capital made contrary to this section.

(5) Limitation. — An action to enforce a liability imposed by this section

may not be commenced after two years from the date of the act complained of.

(6) Remedy preserved. — This section does not affect any liability that arises under section 118.

39. (1) Adjustment of stated capital account. — On a purchase, redemption or other acquisition by a corporation under section 34, 35, 36, 45 or 190 or paragraph 241(3)(f), of shares or fractions thereof issued by it, the corporation shall deduct from the stated capital account maintained for the class or series of shares of which the shares purchased, redeemed or otherwise acquired form a part an amount equal to the result obtained by multiplying the stated capital of the shares of that class or series by the number of shares of that class or series or fractions thereof purchased, redeemed or otherwise acquired, divided by the number of issued shares of that class or series immediately before the purchase, redemption or other acquisition.

(2) Idem. — A corporation shall deduct the amount of a payment made by the corporation to a shareholder under paragraph 241(3)(g) from the stated capital account maintained for the class or series of shares in respect of which the payment was made.

(3) Idem. — A corporation shall adjust its stated capital account or accounts in accordance with any special resolution referred to in subsection 38(2).

(4) Idem. — On a conversion of issued shares of a corporation into shares of another class or series or a change under section 173, 191 or 241 of issued shares of a corporation into shares of another class or series, the corporation shall

(a) deduct from the stated capital account maintained for the class or series of shares converted or changed an amount equal to the result obtained by multiplying the stated capital of the shares of that class or series by the number of shares of that class or series converted or changed, divided by the number of issued shares of that class or series immediately before the conversion or change; and

(b) add the result obtained under paragraph (a) and any additional consideration received pursuant to the conversion or change to the stated capital account maintained or to be maintained for the class or series of shares into which the shares have been converted or changed.

(5) Stated capital of interconvertible shares. — For the purposes of subsection (4) and subject to its articles, where a corporation issues two classes of shares and there is attached to each such class a right to convert a share of the one class into a share of the other class, if a share of one class is converted into a share of the other class, the amount of stated capital attributable to a share in either class is the aggregate of the stated capital of both classes divided by the number of issued shares of both classes immediately before the conversion.

(6) Cancellation or restoration of shares. — Shares or fractions thereof of

any class or series of shares issued by a corporation and purchased, redeemed or otherwise acquired by it shall be cancelled or, if the articles limit the number of authorized shares, may be restored to the status of authorized but unissued shares of the class.

(7) Exception. — For the purposes of this section, a corporation holding shares in itself as permitted by subsections 31(1) and (2) is deemed not to have purchased, redeemed or otherwise acquired such shares.

(8) Idem. — For the purposes of this section, a corporation holding shares in itself by paragraph 32(1)(a) is deemed not to have purchased, redeemed or otherwise acquired the shares at the time they were acquired, but

(a) any of those shares that are held by the corporation at the expiration of two years, and

(b) any shares into which any of those shares were converted by the corporation and held under paragraph 32(1)(b) that are held by the corporation at the expiration of two years after the shares from which they were converted were acquired

are deemed to have been acquired at the expiration of the two years.

(9) Conversion or change of shares. — Shares issued by a corporation and converted into shares of another class or series or changed under section 173, 191 or 241 into shares of another class or series shall become issued shares of the class or series of shares into which the shares have been converted or changed.

(10) Effect of change of shares on number of unissued shares. — Where the articles limit the number of authorized shares of a class of shares of a corporation and issued shares of that class or of a series of shares of that class have become, pursuant to subsection (9), issued shares of another class or series, the number of unissued shares of the first-mentioned class shall, unless the articles otherwise provide, be increased by the number of shares that, pursuant to subsection (9), became shares of another class or series.

(11) Repayment. — Debt obligations issued, pledged, hypothecated or deposited by a corporation are not redeemed by reason only that the indebtedness evidenced by the debt obligations or in respect of which the debt obligations are issued, pledged, hypothecated or deposited is repaid.

(12) Acquisition and reissue of debt obligations. — Debt obligations issued by a corporation and purchased, redeemed or otherwise acquired by it may be cancelled or, subject to any applicable trust indenture or other agreement, may be reissued, pledged or hypothecated to secure any obligation of the corporation then existing or thereafter incurred, and any such acquisition and reissue, pledge or hypothecation is not a cancellation of the debt obligations.

40. (1) Enforceability of contract. — A contract with a corporation providing for the purchase of shares of the corporation is specifically enforceable against

the corporation except to the extent that the corporation cannot perform the contract without thereby being in breach of section 34 or 35.

(2) Burden of proof. — In any action brought on a contract referred to in subsection (1), the corporation has the burden of proving that performance thereof is prevented by section 34 or 35.

(3) Status of contracting party. — Until the corporation has fully performed a contract referred to in subsection (1), the other party retains the status of a claimant entitled to be paid as soon as the corporation is lawfully able to do so or, in a liquidation, to be ranked subordinate to the rights of creditors but in priority to the shareholders.

41. Commission for sale of shares. — The directors may authorize the corporation to pay a reasonable commission to any person in consideration of his purchasing or agreeing to purchase shares of the corporation from the corporation or from any other person, or procuring or agreeing to procure purchasers for any such shares.

42. Dividends. — A corporation shall not declare or pay a dividend if there are reasonable grounds for believing that

(a) the corporation is, or would after the payment be, unable to pay its liabilities as they become due; or

(b) the realizable value of the corporation's assets would thereby be less than the aggregate of its liabilities and stated capital of all classes.

43. (1) Form of dividend. — A corporation may pay a dividend by issuing fully paid shares of the corporation and, subject to section 42, a corporation may pay a dividend in money or property.

(2) Adjustment of stated capital account. — If shares of a corporation are issued in payment of a dividend, the declared amount of the dividend stated as an amount of money shall be added to the stated capital account maintained or to be maintained for the shares of the class or series issued in payment of the dividend.

44. (1) Prohibited loans and guarantees. — Subject to subsection (2), a corporation or any corporation with which it is affiliated shall not, directly or indirectly, give financial assistance by means of a loan, guarantee or otherwise

(a) to any shareholder, director, officer or employee of the corporation or of an affiliated corporation or to an associate of any such person for any purpose, or

(b) to any person for the purpose of or in connection with a purchase of a share issued or to be issued by the corporation or affiliated corporation,

where there are reasonable grounds for believing that

(c) the corporation is or, after giving the financial assistance, would be unable to pay its liabilities as they become due, or

(d) the realizable value of the corporation's assets, excluding the amount of any financial assistance in the form of a loan and in the form of assets pledged or encumbered to secure a guarantee, after giving the financial assistance, would be less than the aggregate of the corporation's liabilities and stated capital of all classes.

(2) Permitted loans and guarantees. — A corporation may give financial assistance by means of a loan, guarantee or otherwise

(a) to any person in the ordinary course of business if the lending of money is part of the ordinary business of the corporation;

(b) to any person on account of expenditures incurred or to be incurred on behalf of the corporation;

(c) to a holding body corporate if the corporation is a wholly-owned subsidiary of the holding body corporate;

(d) to a subsidiary body corporate of the corporation; and

(e) to employees of the corporation or any of its affiliates

(i) to enable or assist them to purchase or erect living accommodation for their own occupation, or

(ii) in accordance with a plan for the purchase of shares of the corporation or any of its affiliates to be held by a trustee.

(3) Enforceability. — A contract made by a corporation in contravention of this section may be enforced by the corporation or by a lender for value in good faith without notice of the contravention.

45. (1) Shareholder immunity. — The shareholders of a corporation are not, as shareholders, liable for any liability, act or default of the corporation except under subsection 38(4), 146(5) or 226(5).

(2) Lien on shares. — Subject to subsection 49(8), the articles may provide that the corporation has a lien on a share registered in the name of a shareholder or his legal representative for a debt of that shareholder to the corporation, including an amount unpaid in respect of a share issued by a body corporate on the date it was continued under this Act.

(3) Enforcement of lien. — A corporation may enforce a lien referred to in subsection (2) in accordance with its by-laws.

PART VI
SALE OF CONSTRAINED SHARES

46. (1) Sale of constrained shares by corporation. — A corporation that has constraints on the issue, transfer or ownership of its shares of any class or series may,

(a) in order to assist the corporation or any of its affiliates or associates to qualify under any prescribed law of Canada or a province to receive licences, permits, grants, payments or other benefits by reason of attaining or maintaining a specified level of Canadian ownership or control, or

(b) in order to assist the corporation to comply with

(i) section 379 of the *Trust and Loan Companies Act*, or

(ii) section 411 of the *Insurance Companies Act*,

sell, for that purpose or for the purpose of attaining or maintaining a level of Canadian ownership or control specified in its articles, under such conditions and after giving such notice as may be prescribed, as if it were the owner thereof, any of those constrained shares that are owned, or that the directors determine in such manner as may be prescribed may be owned, contrary to the constraints.

[Subsec. (1) repealed and substituted by S.C. 1991, c. 45, s. 552, S.C. 1991, c. 47, s. 720(1); para. (b) repealed and substituted by S.C. 1991, c. 47, s. 720(2).]

(2) Obligations of directors in sale. — Where shares are to be sold by a corporation under subsection (1), the directors of the corporation shall select the shares for sale in good faith and in a manner that is not unfairly prejudicial to, and does not unfairly disregard the interests of, the holders of the shares in the constrained class or series taken as a whole.

(3) Effect of sale. — Where shares are sold by a corporation under subsection (1), the owner of the shares immediately prior to the sale shall by that sale be divested of his interest in the shares, and the person who, but for the sale, would be the registered owner of the shares or a person who satisfies the corporation that, but for the sale, he could properly be treated as the registered owner or registered holder of the shares under section 51 shall, from the time of the sale, be entitled to receive only the net proceeds of the sale, together with any income earned thereon from the beginning of the month next following the date of the receipt by the corporation of the proceeds of the sale, less any taxes thereon and any costs of administration of a trust fund constituted under subsection 47(1) in relation thereto.

(4) Subsections 51(4) to (6) apply. — Subsections 51(4) to (6) apply in respect of the person who is entitled under subsection (3) to receive the proceeds of a sale of shares under subsection (1) as if the proceeds were a security and the person were a registered holder or owner of the security.

47. (1) Proceeds of sale to be trust fund. — The proceeds of a sale by a corporation under subsection 46(1) constitute a trust fund in the hands of the corporation for the benefit of the person entitled under subsection 46(3) to receive the proceeds of the sale, and any such trust fund may be commingled by the corporation with other such trust funds and shall be invested in such manner as may be prescribed.

(2) Costs of administration. — Reasonable costs of administration of a trust

fund referred to in subsection (1) may be deducted from the trust fund and any income earned thereon.

(3) Appointment of trust company. — Subject to this section, a corporation may transfer any trust fund referred to in subsection (1), and the administration thereof, to a trust company in Canada registered as such under the laws of Canada or a province, and the corporation is thereupon discharged of all further liability in respect of the trust fund.

(4) Discharge of corporation and trust company. — A receipt signed by a person entitled under subsection 46(3) to receive the proceeds of a sale that constitute a trust fund under subsection (1) shall be a complete discharge of the corporation and of any trust company to which a trust fund is transferred under subsection (3), in respect of the trust fund and income earned thereon paid to such person.

(5) Vesting in Crown. — A trust fund described in subsection (1), together with any income earned thereon, less any taxes thereon and costs of administration, that has not been claimed by a person entitled under subsection 46(3) to receive the proceeds of a sale that constitute the trust fund for a period of ten years after the date of the sale vests in Her Majesty in right of Canada.

(6) *Escheats Act applies.* — Sections 3 to 5 of the Escheats Act apply in respect of a trust fund that vests in Her Majesty in right of Canada under subsection (5).

PART VII
SECURITY CERTIFICATES, REGISTERS AND TRANSFERS

INTERPRETATION AND GENERAL

48. (1) Application of Part. — The transfer or transmission of a security shall be governed by this Part.

(2) Definitions. — In this Part,

"adverse claim". — "adverse claim" includes a claim that a transfer was or would be wrongful or that a particular adverse person is the owner of or has an interest in the security;

"bearer". — "bearer" means the person in possession of a security payable to bearer or endorsed in blank;

"*bona fide* purchaser". — "bona fide purchaser" means a purchaser for value in good faith and without notice of any adverse claim who takes delivery of a security in bearer form or order form or of a security in registered form issued to him or endorsed to him or endorsed in blank;

"broker". — "broker" means a person who is engaged for all or part of his time in the business of buying and selling securities and who, in the transaction concerned, acts for, or buys a security from, or sells a security to a customer;

"delivery". — "delivery" means voluntary transfer of possession;

"fiduciary". — "fiduciary" means a trustee, guardian, committee, curator, tutor, executor, administrator or representative of a deceased person, or any other person acting in a fiduciary capacity;

"fungible". — "'fungible", in relation to securities, means securities of which any unit is, by nature or usage of trade, the equivalent of any other like unit;

"genuine". — "genuine" means free of forgery or counterfeiting;

"good faith." — "good faith" means honesty in fact in the conduct of the transaction concerned;

"holder". — "holder" means a person in possession of a security issued or endorsed to him or to bearer or in blank;

"issuer". — "issuer" includes a corporation

(a) that is required by this Act to maintain a securities register, or
(b) that directly or indirectly creates fractional interests in its rights or property and that issues securities as evidence of such fractional interests;

"overissue". — "overissue" means the issue of securities in excess of any maximum number of securities that the issuer is authorized by its articles or a trust indenture to issue;

"purchaser". — "purchaser" means a person who takes an interest in a security by sale, mortgage, hypothec, pledge, issue, reissue, gift or any other voluntary transaction;

"security" or "security certificate". — "security" or "security certificate" means an instrument issued by a corporation that is

(a) in bearer, order or registered form,
(b) of a type commonly dealt in on securities exchanges or markets or commonly recognized in any area in which it is issued or dealt in as a medium for investment,
(c) one of a class or series or by its terms divisible into a class or series of instruments, and
(d) evidence of a share, participation or other interest in or obligation of a corporation;

"transfer". — "transfer" includes transmission by operation of law;

"trust indenture". — "trust indenture" means a trust indenture as defined in section 82;

"unauthorized". — "unauthorized", in relation to a signature or an endorsement, means one made without actual, implied or apparent authority and includes a forgery;

"valid". — "valid" means issued in accordance with the applicable law and the articles of the issuer or validated under section 52.

(3) Negotiable instruments. — Except where its transfer is restricted and noted on a security in accordance with subsection 49(8), a security is a negotiable instrument.

(4) Registered form. — A security is in registered form if

(a) it specifies a person entitled to the security or to the rights it evidences, and its transfer is capable of being recorded in a securities register; or

(b) it bears a statement that it is in registered form.

(5) Order form. — A debt obligation is in order form where, by its terms, it is payable to the order or assigns of any person therein specified with reasonable certainty or to him or his order.

(6) Bearer form. — A security is in bearer form if it is payable to bearer according to its terms and not by reason of any endorsement.

(7) Guarantor for issuer. — A guarantor for an issuer is deemed to be an issuer to the extent of his guarantee whether or not his obligation is noted on the security.

49. (1) Rights of holder. — Every security holder is entitled at his option to a security certificate that complies with this Act or a non-transferable written acknowledgement of his right to obtain such a security certificate from a corporation in respect of the securities of that corporation held by him.

(2) Fee for certificate. — A corporation may charge a fee of not more than three dollars for a security certificate issued in respect of a transfer.

(3) Joint holders. — A corporation is not required to issue more than one security certificate in respect of securities held jointly by several persons, and delivery of a certificate to one of several joint holders is sufficient delivery to all.

(4) Signatures. — A security certificate shall be signed manually by at least one director or officer of the corporation or by or on behalf of a registrar, transfer agent or branch transfer agent of the corporation, or by a trustee who certifies it in accordance with a trust indenture, and any additional signatures required on a security certificate may be printed or otherwise mechanically reproduced thereon.

(5) No manual signature required. — Notwithstanding subsection (4), a manual signature is not required on

(a) a security certificate representing

(i) a promissory note that is not issued under a trust indenture,

(ii) a fractional share, or

(iii) an option or a right to acquire a security; or

(b) a scrip certificate.

(6) Continuation of signature. — If a security certificate contains a printed or mechanically reproduced signature of a person, the corporation may issue the security certificate, notwithstanding that the person has ceased to be a director or an officer of the corporation, and the security certificate is as valid as if he were a director or an officer at the date of its issue.

(7) Contents of share certificate. — There shall be stated on the face of each share certificate issued by a corporation

(a) the name of the corporation;

(b) the words "Incorporated under the *Canada Business Corporations Act*";

(c) the name of the person to whom it was issued; and

(d) the number and class of shares and the designation of any series that the certificate represents.

(8) Restrictions. — If a security certificate issued by a corporation or by a body corporate before the body corporate was continued under this Act is or becomes subject to

(a) a restriction on its transfer other than a constraint under section 174,

(b) a lien in favour of the corporation,

(c) a unanimous shareholder agreement, or

(d) an endorsement under subsection 190(10),

such restriction, lien, agreement or endorsement is ineffective against a transferee of the security who has no actual knowledge of it, unless it or a reference to it is noted conspicuously on the security certificate.

(9) Limit on restriction. — A corporation any of the issued shares of which are or were part of a distribution to the public and remain outstanding and are held by more than one person shall not have a restriction on the issue, transfer or ownership of its shares of any class or series except by way of a constraint permitted under section 174.

(10) Notation of constraint. — Where the articles of a corporation constrain the issue, transfer or ownership of shares of any class or series in order to assist

(a) the corporation or any of its affiliates or associates to qualify under any prescribed law of Canada or a province to receive licences, permits, grants, payments or other benefits by reason of attaining or maintaining a specified level of Canadian ownership or control, or

(b) the corporation to comply with

(i) section 379 of the *Trust and Loan Companies Act*, or

(ii) section 411 of the *Insurance Companies Act*,

the constraint or a reference to it shall be noted conspicuously on every security certificate of the corporation evidencing a share that is subject to such constraint where the security certificate is issued after the day on which the share becomes subject to the constraint under this Act.

[Subsec. (10) repealed and substituted by S.C. 1991, c. 45, s. 553; repealed and substituted by S.C. 1991, c. 47, s. 721(1); para. (b) repealed and substituted by S.C. 1991, c. 47, s. 721(2).]

(11) Failure to note. — The failure to note a constraint or a reference to it pursuant to subsection (10) shall not invalidate any share or security certificate and shall not render a constraint ineffective against an owner, holder or transferee of the share or security certificate.

(12) Transitional. — If a body corporate continued under this Act has outstanding security certificates, and if the words "private company" appear on the certificates, those words are deemed to be a notice of a restriction, lien, agreement or endorsement for the purpose of subsection (8).

(13) Particulars of class. — There shall be stated legibly on a share certificate issued by a corporation that is authorized to issue shares of more than one class or series.

(a) the rights, privileges, restrictions and conditions attached to the shares of each class and series that exists when the share certificate is issued; or

(b) that the class or series of shares that it represents has rights, privileges, restrictions or conditions attached thereto and that the corporation will furnish a shareholder, on demand and without charge, with a full copy of the text of

(i) the rights, privileges, restrictions and conditions attached to each class authorized to be issued and to each series in so far as the same have been fixed by the directors, and

(ii) the authority of the directors to fix the rights, privileges, restrictions and conditions of subsequent series.

(14) Duty. — Where a share certificate issued by a corporation contains the statement mentioned in paragraph (13)(b), the corporation shall furnish a shareholder, on demand and without charge, with a full copy of the text of

(a) the rights, privileges, restrictions and conditions attached to each class authorized to be issued and to each series in so far as the same have been fixed by the directors; and

(b) the authority of the directors to fix the rights, privileges, restrictions and conditions of subsequent series.

(15) Fractional share. — A corporation may issue a certificate for a fractional

share or may issue in place thereof scrip certificates in bearer form that entitle the holder to receive a certificate for a full share by exchanging scrip certificates aggregating a full share.

(16) Scrip certificates. — The directors may attach conditions to any scrip certificates issued by a corporation, including conditions that

(a) the scrip certificates become void if not exchanged for a share certificate representing a full share before a specified date; and

(b) any shares for which such scrip certificates are exchangeable may, notwithstanding any pre-emptive right, be issued by the corporation to any person and the proceeds thereof distributed rateably to the holders of the scrip certificates.

(17) Holder of fractional share. — A holder of a fractional share issued by a corporation is not entitled to exercise voting rights or to receive a dividend in respect of the fractional share, unless

(a) the fractional share results from a consolidation of shares; or

(b) the articles of the corporation otherwise provide.

(18) Holder of scrip certificate. — A holder of a scrip certificate is not entitled to exercise voting rights or to receive a dividend in respect of the scrip certificate.

50. (1) Securities records. — A corporation shall maintain a securities register in which it records the securities issued by it in registered form, showing with respect to each class or series of securities

(a) the names, alphabetically arranged, and the latest known address of each person who is or has been a security holder;

(b) the number of securities held by each security holder; and

(c) the date and particulars of the issue and transfer of each security.

(2) Central and branch registers. — A corporation may appoint an agent to maintain a central securities register and branch securities registers.

(3) Place of register. — A central securities register shall be maintained by a corporation at its registered office or at any other place in Canada designated by the directors, and any branch securities registers may be kept at any place in or out of Canada designated by the directors.

(4) Effect of registration. — Registration of the issue or transfer of a security in the central securities register or in a branch securities register is complete and valid registration for all purposes.

(5) Branch register. — A branch securities register shall only contain particulars of securities issued or transferred at that branch.

(6) Central register. — Particulars of each issue or transfer of a security

registered in a branch securities register shall also be kept in the corresponding central securities register.

(7) Destruction of certificates. — A corporation, its agent or a trustee defined in subsection 82(1) is not required to produce

(a) a cancelled security certificate in registered form, an instrument referred to in subsection 29(1) that is cancelled or a like cancelled instrument in registered form six years after the date of its cancellation;

(b) a cancelled security certificate in bearer form or an instrument referred to in subsecton 29(1) that is cancelled or a like cancelled instrument in bearer form after the date of its cancellation; or

(c) an instrument referred to in subsection 29(1) or a like instrument, irrespective of its form, after the date of its expiration.

51. (1) Dealings with registered holder. — A corporation or a trustee defined in subsection 82(1) may, subject to sections 134, 135 and 138, treat the registered owner of a security as the person exclusively entitled to vote, to receive notices, to receive any interest, dividend or other payments in respect of the security, and otherwise to exercise all the rights and powers of an owner of the security.

(2) Constructive registered holder. — Notwithstanding subsection (1), a corporation whose articles restrict the right to transfer its securities shall, and any other corporation may, treat a person as a registered security holder entitled to exercise all the rights of the security holder he represents, if that person furnishes the corporation with evidence as described in subsection 77(4) that he is

(a) the executor, administrator, heir or legal representative of the heirs, of the estate of a deceased security holder;

(b) a guardian, committee, trustee, curator or tutor representing a registered security holder who is an infant, an incompetent person or a missing person; or

(c) a liquidator of, or a trustee in bankruptcy for, a registered security holder.

(3) Permissible registered holder. — If a person on whom the ownership of a security devolves by operation of law, other than a person described in subsection (2), furnishes proof of his authority to exercise rights or privileges in respect of a security of the corporation that is not registered in his name, the corporation shall treat such person as entitled to exercise those rights or privileges.

(4) Immunity of corporation. — A corporation is not required to inquire into the existence of, or see to the performance or observance of, any duty owed to a third person by a registered holder of any of its securities or by anyone whom it treats, as permitted or required by this section, as the owner or registered holder thereof.

(5) Infants. — If an infant exercises any rights of ownership in the securities of a corporation, no subsequent repudiation or avoidance is effective against the corporation.

(6) Joint holders. — A corporation may treat as owner of a security the survivors of persons to whom the security was issued as joint holders, if it receives proof satisfactory to it of the death of any such joint holder.

(7) Transmission of securities. — Subject to any applicable law relating to the collection of taxes, a person referred to in paragraph (2)(a) is entitled to become a registered holder or to designate a registered holder, if he deposits with the corporation or its transfer agent

(a) the original grant of probate or of letters of administration, or a copy thereof certified to be a true copy by

(i) the court that granted the probate or letters of administration,

(ii) a trust company incorporated under the laws of Canada or a province, or

(iii) a lawyer or notary acting on behalf of the person referred to in paragraph (2)(a), or

(b) in the case of transmission by notarial will in the Province of Quebec, a copy thereof authenticated pursuant to the laws of that Province,

together with

(c) an affidavit or declaration of transmission made by a person referred to in paragraph (2)(a), stating the particulars of the transmission, and

(d) the security certificate that was owned by the deceased holder

(i) in case of a transfer to a person referred to in paragraph (2)(a), with or without the endorsement of that person, and

(ii) in case of a transfer to any other person, endorsed in accordance with section 65,

and accompanied by any assurance the corporation may require under section 77.

(8) Excepted transmissions. — Notwithstanding subsection (7), if the laws of the jurisdiction governing the transmission of a security of a deceased holder do not require a grant of probate or of letters of administration in respect of the transmission, a legal representative of the deceased holder is entitled, subject to any applicable law relating to the collection of taxes, to become a registered holder or to designate a registered holder, if he deposits with the corporation or its transfer agent

(a) the security certificate that was owned by the deceased holder; and

(b) reasonable proof of the governing laws, of the deceased holder's interest in the security and of the right of the legal representative or the person he designates to become the registered holder.

(9) Right of corporation. — Deposit of the documents required by subsection (7) or (8) empowers a corporation or its transfer agent to record in a securities register the transmission of a security from the deceased holder to a person referred to in paragraph (2)(a) or to such person as the person referred to in that paragraph may designate and, thereafter, to treat the person who thus becomes a registered holder as the owner of those securities.

52. (1) Overissue. — The provisions of this Part that validate a security or compel its issue or reissue do not apply to the extent that validation, issue or reissue would result in overissue, but

(a) if a valid security, similar in all respects to the security involved in the overissue, is reasonably available for purchase, the person entitled to the validation or issue may compel the issuer to purchase and deliver such a security to him against surrender of the security that he holds; or

(b) if a valid security, similar in all respects to the security involved in the overissue, is not reasonably available for purchase, the person entitled to the validation or issue may recover from the issuer an amount equal to the price the last purchaser for value paid for the invalid security.

(2) Retroactive validation. — When an issuer amends its articles or a trust indenture to which it is a party to increase its authorized securities to a number equal to or in excess of the number of securities previously authorized plus the amount of the securities overissued, the securities so overissued are valid from the date of their issue.

(3) Payment not a purchase or redemption. — A purchase or payment by an issuer under subsection (1) is not a purchase or payment to which section 34, 35, 36 or 39 applies.

53. Burden of proof. — In an action on a security,

(a) unless specifically denied in the pleadings, each signature on the security or in a necessary endorsement is admitted;

(b) a signature on the security is presumed to be genuine and authorized but, if the effectiveness of the signature is put in issue, the burden of establishing that it is genuine and authorized is on the party claiming under the signature;

(c) if a signature is admitted or established, production of the instrument entitles a holder to recover on it unless the defendant establishes a defence or a defect going to the validity of the security; and;

(d) if the defendant establishes that a defence or defect exists, the plaintiff has the burden of establishing that the defence or defect is ineffective against him or some person under whom he claims.

54. Securities fungible. — Unless otherwise agreed, and subject to any applicable law, regulation or stock exchange rule, a person required to deliver securities may deliver any security of the specified issue in bearer form or registered in the name of the transferee or endorsed to him or in blank.

ISSUE — ISSUER

55. (1) Notice of defect. — Even against a purchaser for value without notice of a defect going to the validity of a security, the terms of the security include those stated on the security and those incorporated therein by reference to another instrument, statute, rule, regulation or order to the extent that the terms so incorporated do not conflict with the stated terms, but such a reference is not of itself notice to a purchaser for value of a defect going to the validity of the security, notwithstanding that the security expressly states that a person accepting it admits such notice.

(2) Purchaser for value. — A security is valid in the hands of a purchaser for value without notice of any defect going to its validity.

(3) Lack of genuineness. — Subject to section 57, the fact that a security is not genuine is a complete defence even against a purchaser for value without notice.

(4) Ineffective defences. — All other defences of an issuer, including non-delivery and conditional delivery of a security, are ineffective against a purchaser for value without notice of the particular defence.

56. Staleness as notice of defect. — After an event that creates a right to immediate performance of the principal obligation evidenced by a security, or that sets a date on or after which a security is to be presented or surrendered for redemption or exchange, a purchaser is deemed to have notice of any defect in its issue or of any defence of the issuer,

(a) if the event requires the payment of money or the delivery of securities, or both, on presentation or surrender of the security, and such money or securities are available on the date set for payment or exchange, and he takes the security more than one year after that date; or

(b) if he takes the security more than two years after the date set for presentation or surrender or the date on which such performance became due.

57. Unauthorized signature. — An unauthorized signature on a security before or in the course of its issue is ineffective, except that the signature is effective in favour of a purchaser for value and without notice of the lack of authority, if the signing has been done by

(a) an authenticating trustee, registrar, transfer agent or other person entrusted by the issuer with the signing of the security, or of similar securities, or their immediate preparation for signing; or

(b) an employee of the issuer or of a person referred to in paragraph (a) who in the ordinary course of his duties handles the security.

58. (1) Completion or alteration. — Where a security contains the signatures necessary for its issue or transfer but is incomplete in any other respect,

(a) any person may complete it by filling in the blanks in accordance with his authority; and

(b) notwithstanding that the blanks are incorrectly filled in, the security as completed is enforceable by a purchaser who took it for value and without notice of such incorrectness.

(2) Enforceability. — A completed security that has been improperly altered, even if fraudulently altered, remains enforceable but only according to its original terms.

59. (1) Warranties of agents. — A person signing a security as authenticating trustee, registrar, transfer agent or other person entrusted by the issuer with the signing of the security warrants to a purchaser for value without notice that

(a) the security is genuine;

(b) his acts in connection with the issue of the security are within his authority; and

(c) he has reasonable grounds for believing that the security is in the form and within the amount the issuer is authorized to issue.

(2) Limitation of liability. — Unless otherwise agreed, a person referred to in subsection (1) does not assume any further liability for the validity of a security.

PURCHASE

60. (1) Title of purchaser. — On delivery of a security the purchaser acquires the rights in the security that his transferor had or had authority to convey, except that a purchaser who has been a party to any fraud or illegality affecting the security or who as a prior holder had notice of an adverse claim does not improve his position by taking from a later *bona fide* purchaser.

(2) Title of *bona fide* purchaser. — A bona fide purchaser, in addition to acquiring the rights of a purchaser, also acquires the security free from any adverse claim.

(3) Limited interest. — A purchaser of a limited interest acquires rights only to the extent of the interest purchased.

61. (1) Deemed notice of adverse claim. — A purchaser of a security, or any broker for a seller or purchaser, is deemed to have notice of an adverse claim if

(a) the security, whether in bearer or registered form, has been endorsed "for collection" or "for surrender" or for some other purpose not involving transfer; or

(b) the security is in bearer form and has on it a statement that it is the property of a person other than the transferor, except that the mere writing of a name on a security is not such a statement.

(2) Notice of fiduciary duty. — Notwithstanding that a purchaser, or any broker for a seller or purchaser, has notice that a security is held by a third person or is registered in the name of or endorsed by a fiduciary, he has no duty to inquire into the rightfulness of the transfer and has no notice of an adverse claim, except that where a purchaser knows that the consideration is to be used for, or that the transaction is for, the personal benefit of the fiduciary or is otherwise in breach of the fiduciary's duty, the purchaser is deemed to have notice of an adverse claim.

62. Staleness as notice of adverse claim. — An event that creates a right to immediate performance of the principal obligation evidenced by a security or that sets a date on or after which the security is to be presented or surrendered for redemption or exchange is not of itself notice of an adverse claim, except in the case of a purchase

(a) after one year from any date set for such presentation or surrender for redemption or exchange; or

(b) after six months from any date set for payment of money against presentation or surrender of the security if funds are available for payment on that date.

63. (1) Warranties to issuer. — A person who presents a security for registration of transfer or for payment or exchange warrants to the issuer that he is entitled to the registration, payment or exchange, except that a purchaser for value without notice of an adverse claim who receives a new, reissued or re-registered security on registration of transfer warrants only that he has no knowledge of any unauthorized signature in a necessary endorsement.

(2) Warranties to purchaser. — A person by transferring a security to a purchaser for value warrants only that

(a) the transfer is effective and rightful;

(b) the security is genuine and has not been materially altered; and

(c) he knows of nothing that might impair the validity of the security.

(3) Warranties of intermediary. — Where a security is delivered by an intermediary known by the purchaser to be entrusted with delivery of the security on behalf of another or with collection of a draft or other claim to be collected against such delivery, the intermediary by such delivery warrants only his own good faith and authority even if he has purchased or made advances against the draft or other claim to be collected against the delivery.

(4) Warranties of pledgee. — A pledgee or other holder for purposes of security who redelivers a security received, or after payment and on order of the debtor delivers that security to a third person, gives only the warranties of an intermediary under subsection (3).

(5) Warranties of broker. — A broker gives to his customer, to the issuer and to a purchaser, as the case may be, the warranties provided in this section and has the rights and privileges of a purchaser under this section, and those warranties of and in favour of the broker acting as an agent are in addition to warranties given by his customer and warranties given in favour of his customer.

64. Right to compel endorsement. — When a security in registered form is delivered to a purchaser without a necessary endorsement, he may become a *bona fide* purchaser only as of the time the endorsement is supplied, but against the transferor the transfer is complete on delivery and the purchaser has a specifically enforceable right to have any necessary endorsement supplied.

65. (1) Definition of "appropriate person". — In this section, "appropriate person" means

(a) the person specified by the security or by special endorsement to be entitled to the security;

(b) if a person described in paragraph (a) is described as a fiduciary but is no longer serving in the described capacity, either that person or his successor;

(c) if the security or endorsement mentioned in paragraph (a) specifies more than one person as fiduciaries and one or more are no longer serving in the described capacity, the remaining fiduciary or fiduciaries, whether or not a successor has been appointed or qualified;

(d) if a person described in paragraph (a) is an individual and is without capacity to act by reason of death, incompetence, infancy, minority or otherwise, his fiduciary;

(e) if the security or endorsement mentioned in paragraph (a) specifies more than one person with right of survivorship and by reason of death all cannot sign, the survivor or survivors;

(f) a person having power to sign under applicable law or a power of attorney; or

(g) to the extent that a person described in paragraphs (a) to (f) may act through an agent, his authorized agent.

(2) Determining "appropriate person". — Whether the person signing is an appropriate person is determined as of the time of signing and an endorsement by such a person does not become unauthorized for the purposes of this Part by reason of any subsequent change of circumstances.

(3) Endorsement. — An endorsement of a security in registered form is made when an appropriate person signs, either on the security or on a separate document, an assignment or transfer of the security or a power to assign or transfer it, or when the signature of an appropriate person is written without more on the back of the security.

(4) Special or blank. — An endorsement may be special or in blank.

(5) Blank endorsement. — An endorsement in blank includes an endorsement to bearer.

(6) Special endorsement. — A special endorsement specifies the person to whom the security is to be transferred, or who has power to transfer it.

(7) Right of holder. — A holder may convert an endorsement in blank into a special endorsement.

(8) Immunity of endorser. — Unless otherwise agreed, the endorser by his endorsement assumes no obligation that the security will be honoured by the issuer.

(9) Partial endorsement. — An endorsement purporting to be only of part of a security representing units intended by the issuer to be separately transferable is effective to the extent of the endorsement.

(10) Failure of fiduciary to comply. — Failure of a fiduciary to comply with a controlling instrument or with the law of the jurisdiction governing the fiduciary relationship, including any law requiring the fiduciary to obtain court approval of a transfer, does not render his endorsement unauthorized for the purposes of this Part.

66. Effect of endorsement without delivery. — An endorsement of a security whether special or in blank does not constitute a transfer until delivery of the security on which it appears or, if the endorsement is on a separate document, until delivery of both the security and that document.

67. Endorsement in bearer form. — An endorsement of a security in bearer form may give notice of an adverse claim under section 61 but does not otherwise affect any right to registration that the holder has.

68. (1) Effect of unauthorized endorsement. — The owner of a security may assert the ineffectiveness of an endorsement against the issuer or any purchaser, other than a purchaser for value without notice of an adverse claim who has in good faith received a new, reissued or re-registered security on registration of transfer, unless the owner

(a) has ratified an unauthorized endorsement of the security; or

(b) is otherwise precluded from impugning the effectiveness of an unauthorized endorsement.

(2) Liability of issuer. — An issuer who registers the transfer of a security on an unauthorized endorsement is liable for improper registration.

69. (1) Warranties of guarantor of signature. — A person who guarantees a signature of an endorser of a security warrants that at the time of signing

(a) the signature was genuine;

(b) the signer was an appropriate person as defined in section 65 to endorse; and

(c) the signer had legal capacity to sign.

(2) Limitation of liability. — A person who guarantees a signature of an endorser does not otherwise warrant the rightfulness of the particular transfer.

(3) Warranties of guarantor of endorsement. — A person who guarantees an endorsement of a security warrants both the signature and the rightfulness of the transfer in all respects, but an issuer may not require a guarantee of endorsement as a condition to registration of transfer.

(4) Extent of liability. — The warranties referred to in this section are made to any person taking or dealing with the security relying on the guarantee and the guarantor is liable to such person for any loss resulting from breach of warranty.

70. (1) Constructive delivery of a security. — Delivery to a purchaser occurs when

(a) the purchaser or a person designated by him acquires possession of a security;

(b) the broker of the purchaser acquires possession of a security specially endorsed to or issued in the name of the purchaser;

(c) the broker of the purchaser sends him confirmation of the purchase and the broker in his records identifies a specific security as belonging to the purchaser; or

(d) with respect to an identified security to be delivered while still in the possession of a third person, that person acknowledges that he holds it for the purchaser.

(2) Constructive ownership. — A purchaser is the owner of a security held for him by his broker, but a purchaser is not a holder except in the cases referred to in paragraphs (1)(b) and (c).

(3) Ownership of part of fungible bulk. — If a security is part of a fungible bulk, a purchaser of the security is the owner of a proportionate interest in the fungible bulk.

(4) Notice to broker. — Notice of an adverse claim received by a broker or by a purchaser after the broker takes delivery as a holder for value is not effective against the broker or the purchaser, except that, as between the broker and the purchaser, the purchaser may demand delivery of an equivalent security as to which no notice of an adverse claim has been received.

71. (1) Delivery of security. — Unless otherwise agreed, if a sale of a security is made on an exchange or otherwise through brokers,

(a) the selling customer fulfils his duty to deliver when he delivers the security to the selling broker or to a person designated by the selling broker or causes an acknowledgement to be made to the selling broker that it is held for him; and

(b) the selling broker, including a correspondent broker, acting for a selling customer fulfils his duty to deliver by delivering the security or a like security to the buying broker or to a person designated by the buying broker or by effecting clearance of the sale in accordance with the rules of the exchange on which the transaction took place.

(2) Duty to deliver. — Subject to this section and unless otherwise agreed, a transferor's duty to deliver a security under a contract of purchase is not fulfilled until he delivers the security in negotiable form to the purchaser or to a person designated by the purchaser, or causes an acknowledgement to be made to the purchaser that the security is held for him.

(3) Delivery to broker. — A sale to a broker purchasing for his own account is subject to subsection (2) and not subsection (1), unless the sale is made on a stock exchange.

72. (1) Right to reclaim possession. — A person against whom the transfer of a security is wrongful for any reason, including his incapacity, may against anyone except a *bona fide* purchaser reclaim possession of the security or obtain possession of any new security evidencing all or part of the same rights or claim damages.

(2) Recovery if unauthorized endorsement. — If the transfer of a security is wrongful by reason of an unauthorized endorsement, the owner may reclaim possession of the security or a new security even from a *bona fide* purchaser if the ineffectiveness of the purported endorsement may be asserted against such purchaser under section 68.

(3) Remedies. — The right to reclaim possession of a security may be specifically enforced, its transfer may be restrained and the security may be impounded pending litigation.

73. (1) Right to requisites for registration. — Unless otherwise agreed, a transferor shall on demand supply a purchaser with proof of his authority to transfer or with any other requisite that is necessary to obtain registration of the transfer of a security, but if the transfer is not for value a transferor need not do so unless the purchaser pays the reasonable and necessary costs of the proof and transfer.

(2) Rescission of transfer. — If the transferor fails to comply with a demand under subsection (1) within a reasonable time, the purchaser may reject or rescind the transfer.

74. Seizure of security. — No seizure of a security or other interest evidenced thereby is effective until the person making the seizure obtains possession of the security.

75. No conversion if good faith delivery by agent. — An agent or bailee who in good faith, including observance of reasonable commercial standards if he is in the business of buying, selling or otherwise dealing with securities of a corporation, has received securities and sold, pledged or delivered them according to the instructions of his principal is not liable for conversion or for participation in breach of fiduciary duty although the principal has no right to dispose of them.

REGISTRATION

76. (1) Duty to register transfer. — Where a security in registered form is presented for transfer, the issuer shall register the transfer if

(a) the security is endorsed by an appropriate person as defined in section 65;

(b) reasonable assurance is given that that endorsement is genuine and effective;

(c) the issuer has no duty to inquire into adverse claims or has discharged any such duty;

(d) any applicable law relating to the collection of taxes has been complied with;

(e) the transfer is rightful or is to a *bona fide* purchaser; and

(f) any fee referred to in subsection 49(2) has been paid.

(2) Liability for delay. — Where an issuer has a duty to register a transfer of a security, the issuer is liable to the person presenting it for registration for loss resulting from any unreasonable delay in registration or from failure or refusal to register the transfer.

77. (1) Assurance that endorsement effective. — An issuer may require an assurance that each necessary endorsement on a security is genuine and effective by requiring a guarantee of the signature of the person endorsing, and by requiring

(a) if the endorsement is by an agent, reasonable assurance of authority to sign;

(b) if the endorsement is by a fiduciary, evidence of appointment or incumbency;

(c) if there is more than one fiduciary, reasonable assurance that all who are required to sign have done so; and

(d) in any other case, assurance that corresponds as closely as practicable to the foregoing.

(2) Definition of "guarantee of the signature". — For the purposes of subsection (1), a "guarantee of the signature" means a guarantee signed by or on behalf of a person reasonably believed by the issuer to be responsible.

(3) Standards. — An issuer may adopt reasonable standards to determine responsible persons for the purpose of subsection (2).

(4) Definition of "evidence of appointment or incumbency". — In paragraph (1)(b) "evidence of appointment or incumbency" means

(a) in the case of a fiduciary appointed by a court, a copy of the order certified in accordance with subsection 51(7), and dated not earlier than sixty days before the date a security is presented for transfer; or

(b) in any other case, a copy of a document showing the appointment or other evidence believed by the issuer to be appropriate.

(5) Standards. — An issuer may adopt reasonable standards with respect to evidence for the purposes of paragraph (4)(b).

(6) No notice to issuer. — An issuer is deemed not to have notice of the contents of any document referred to in subsection (4) except to the extent that the contents relate directly to appointment or incumbency.

(7) Notice from excess documentation. — If an issuer demands assurance additional to that specified in this section for a purpose other than that specified in subsection (4) and obtains a copy of a will, trust or partnership agreement, by-law or similar document, the issuer is deemed to have notice of all matters contained therein affecting the transfer.

78. (1) Limited duty of inquiry. — An issuer to whom a security is presented for registration has a duty to inquire into adverse claims if

(a) written notice of an adverse claim has been received at a time and in a manner that affords the issuer a reasonable opportunity to act on it before the issue of a new, reissued or re-registered security and the notice discloses the name and address of the claimant, the registered owner and the issue of which the security is a part; or

(b) the issuer is deemed to have notice of an adverse claim from a document that is obtained under subsection 77(7).

(2) Discharge of duty. — An issuer may discharge a duty of inquiry by any reasonable means, including notifying an adverse claimant by registered mail sent to the address furnished by him or, if no such address has been furnished, to his residence or regular place of business, that a security has been presented for registration of transfer by a named person, and that the transfer will be registered unless within thirty days from the date of mailing the notice either

(a) the issuer is served with a restraining order or other order of a court; or

(b) the issuer is provided with an indemnity bond sufficient in the issuer's judgment to protect the issuer and any registrar, transfer agent or other agent of the issuer from any loss that may be incurred by any of them as a result of complying with the adverse claim.

(3) Inquiry into adverse claims. — Unless an issuer is deemed to have notice of an adverse claim from a document that is obtained under subsection 77(7) or has received notice of an adverse claim under subsection (1), if a security presented for registration is endorsed by the appropriate person as defined in section 65, the issuer has no duty to inquire into adverse claims, and in particular,

(a) an issuer registering a security in the name of a person who is a fiduciary or who is described as a fiduciary is not bound to inquire into the existence, extent or correct description of the fiduciary relationship and thereafter the issuer may assume without inquiry that the newly registered owner continues to be the fiduciary until the issuer receives written notice that the fiduciary is no longer acting as such with respect to the particular security;

(b) an issuer registering transfer on an endorsement by a fiduciary has no duty to inquire whether the transfer is made in compliance with the document or with the law of the jurisdiction governing the fiduciary relationship; and

(c) an issuer is deemed not to have notice of the contents of any court record or any registered document even if the record or document is in the issuer's possession and even if the transfer is made on the endorsement of a fiduciary to the fiduciary himself or to his nominee.

(4) Duration of notice. — A written notice of adverse claim received by an issuer is effective for twelve months from the date when it was received unless the notice is renewed in writing.

79. (1) Limitation of issuer's liability. — Subject to any applicable law relating to the collection of taxes, the issuer is not liable to the owner or any other person who incurs a loss as a result of the registration of a transfer of a security if

(a) the necessary endorsements were on or with the security; and

(b) the issuer had no duty to inquire into adverse claims or had discharged any such duty.

(2) Duty of issuer in default. — If an issuer has registered a transfer of a security to a person not entitled to it, the issuer shall on demand deliver a like security to the owner unless

(a) subsection (1) applies;

(b) the owner is precluded by subsection 80(1) from asserting any claim; or

(c) the delivery would result in overissue, in which case the issuer's liability is governed by section 52.

80. (1) Notice of lost or stolen security. — Where a security has been lost, apparently destroyed or wrongfully taken, and the owner fails to notify the issuer of that fact by giving the issuer written notice of his adverse claim within a reasonable time after he knows of the loss, destruction or taking and if the issuer has registered a transfer of the security before receiving such notice, the owner is precluded from asserting against the issuer any claim to a new security.

(2) Duty of issuer to issue a new security. — Where the owner of a security claims that the security has been lost, destroyed or wrongfully taken, the issuer shall issue a new security in place of the original security if the owner

(a) so requests before the issuer has notice that the security has been acquired by a *bona fide* purchaser;

(b) furnishes the issuer with a sufficient indemnity bond; and

(c) satisfies any other reasonable requirements imposed by the issuer.

(3) Duty to register transfer. — If, after the issue of a new security under subsection (2), a *bona fide* purchaser of the original security presents the original security for registration of transfer, the issuer shall register the transfer unless registration would result in overissue, in which case the issuer's liability is governed by section 52.

(4) Right of issuer to recover. — In addition to any rights on an indemnity bond, the issuer may recover a new security issued under subsection (2) from the person to whom it was issued or any person taking under him other than a *bona fide* purchaser.

81. (1) Agent's duties, rights, etc. — An authenticating trustee, registrar, transfer agent or other agent of an issuer has, in respect of the issue, registration of transfer and cancellation of a security of the issuer,

(a) a duty to the issuer to exercise good faith and reasonable diligence; and

(b) the same obligations to the holder or owner of a security and the same rights, privileges and immunities as the issuer.

(2) Notice to agent. — Notice to an authenticating trustee, registrar, transfer agent or other agent of an issuer is notice to the issuer with respect to the functions performed by the agent.

PART VIII

TRUST INDENTURES

82. (1) Definitions. — In this Part,

"event of default". — "event of default" means an event specified in a trust indenture on the occurrence of which

(a) a security interest constituted by the trust indenture becomes enforceable, or

(b) the principal, interest and other moneys payable thereunder become or may be declared to be payable before maturity,

but the event is not an event of default until all conditions prescribed by the trust indenture in connection with such event for the giving of notice or the lapse of time or otherwise have been satisfied;

"trustee". — "trustee" means any person appointed as trustee under the terms of a trust indenture to which a corporation is a party and includes any successor trustee;

"trust indenture". — "trust indenture" means any deed, indenture or other instrument, including any supplement or amendment thereto, made by a corporation after its incorporation or continuance under this Act, under which the corporation issues debt obligations and in which a person is appointed as trustee for the holders of the debt obligations issued thereunder.

(2) Application. — This Part applies to a trust indenture if the debt obligations issued or to be issued under the trust indenture are part of a distribution to the public.

(3) Exemption. — The Director may exempt a trust indenture from this Part if the trust indenture, the debt obligations issued thereunder and the security interest effected thereby are subject to a law of a province or a country other than Canada that is substantially equivalent to this Part.

83. (1) Conflict of interest. — No person shall be appointed as trustee if there is a material conflict of interest between his role as trustee and his role in any other capacity.

(2) Eliminating conflict of interest. — A trustee shall, within ninety days after he becomes aware that a material conflict of interest exists

(a) eliminate such conflict of interest; or

(b) resign from office.

(3) Validity. — A trust indenture, any debt obligations issued thereunder and a security interest effected thereby are valid notwithstanding a material conflict of interest of the trustee.

(4) Removal of trustee. — If a trustee contravenes subsection (1) or (2), any interested person may apply to a court for an order that the trustee be replaced, and the court may make an order on such terms as it thinks fit.

84. Qualification of trustee. — A trustee, or at least one of the trustees if more than one is appointed, shall be a body corporate incorporated under the laws of Canada or a province and authorized to carry on the business of a trust company.

85. (1) List of security holders. — A holder of debt obligations issued under a trust indenture may, on payment to the trustee of a reasonable fee, require the trustee to furnish, within fifteen days after delivering to the trustee the statutory declaration referred to in subsection (4), a list setting out

(a) the names and addresses of the registered holders of the outstanding debt obligations,

(b) the principal amount of outstanding debt obligations owned by each such holder, and

(c) the aggregate principal amount of debt obligations outstanding

as shown on the records maintained by the trustee on the day that the statutory declaration is delivered to that trustee.

(2) Duty of issuer. — On the demand of a trustee, the issuer of debt obligations shall furnish the trustee with the information required to enable the trustee to comply with subsection (1).

(3) Corporate applicant. — If the person requiring the trustee to furnish a list under subsection (1) is a body corporate, the statutory declaration required under that subsection shall be made by a director or officer of the body corporate.

(4) Contents of statutory declaration. — The statutory declaration required under subsection (1) shall state

(a) the name and address of the person requiring the trustee to furnish the list and, if the person is a body corporate, the address for service thereof; and

(b) that the list will not be used except as permitted under subsection (5).

(5) Use of list. — A list obtained under this section shall not be used by any person except in connection with

(a) an effort to influence the voting of the holders of debt obligations;

(b) an offer to acquire debt obligations; or

(c) any other matter relating to the debt obligations or the affairs of the issuer or guarantor thereof.

(6) Offence. — A person who, without reasonable cause, contravenes subsection (5) is guilty of an offence and liable on summary convicton to a fine not exceeding five thousand dollars or to imprisonment for a term not exceeding six months or to both.

86. (1) Evidence of compliance. — An issuer or a guarantor of debt obligations issued or to be issued under a trust indenture shall, before doing any act under paragraph (a), (b) or (c), furnish the trustee with evidence of compliance with the conditions in the trust indenture relating to

(a) the issue, certification and delivery of debt obligations under the trust indenture;

(b) the release or release and substitution of property subject to a security interest constituted by the trust indenture; or

(c) the satisfaction and discharge of the trust indenture.

(2) Duty of issuer or guarantor. — On the demand of a trustee, the issuer or guarantor of debt obligations issued or to be issued under a trust indenture shall furnish the trustee with evidence of compliance with the trust indenture by the issuer or guarantor in respect of any act to be done by the trustee at the request of the issuer or guarantor.

87. Contents of declaration, etc. — Evidence of compliance as required by section 86 shall consist of

(a) a statutory declaration or certificate made by a director or an officer of the issuer or guarantor stating that the conditions referred to in that section have been complied with; and

(b) where the trust indenture requires compliance with conditions that are subject to review

(i) by legal counsel, an opinion of legal counsel that such conditions have been complied with, and

(ii) by an auditor or accountant, an opinion or report of the auditor of the issuer or guarantor, or such other accountant as the trustee may select, that such conditions have been complied with.

88. Further evidence of compliance. — The evidence of compliance referred to in section 87 shall include a statement by the person giving the evidence

(a) declaring that he has read and understands the conditions of the trust indenture described in section 86;

(b) describing the nature and scope of the examination or investigation on which he based the certificate, statement or opinion; and

(c) declaring that he has made such examination or investigation as he believes necessary to enable him to make the statements or give the opinions contained or expressed therein.

89. (1) Trustee may require evidence of compliance. — On the demand of a trustee, the issuer or guarantor of debt obligations issued under a trust indenture shall furnish the trustee with evidence in such form as the trustee may require as to compliance with any condition thereto relating to any action required or permitted to be taken by the issuer or guarantor under the trust indenture.

(2) Certificate of compliance. — At least once in each twelve month period beginning on the date of the trust indenture and at any other time on the demand

of a trustee, the issuer or guarantor of debt obligations issued under a trust indenture shall furnish the trustee with a certificate that the issuer or guarantor has complied with all requirements contained in the trust indenture that, if not complied with, would, with the giving of notice, lapse of time or otherwise, constitute an event of default, or, if there has been failure to so comply, giving particulars thereof.

90. Notice of default. — The trustee shall give to the holders of debt obligations issued under a trust indenture, within thirty days after the trustee becomes aware of the occurrence thereof, notice of every event of default arising under the trust indenture and continuing at the time the notice is given, unless the trustee reasonably believes that it is in the best interests of the holders of the debt obligations to withhold such notice and so informs the issuer or guarantor in writing.

91. Duty of care. — A trustee in exercising his powers and discharging his duties shall

(a) act honestly and in good faith with a view to the best interests of the holders of the debt obligations issued under the trust indenture; and

(b) exercise the care, diligence and skill of a reasonably prudent trustee.

92. Reliance on statements. — Notwithstanding section 91, a trustee is not liable if he relies in good faith on statements contained in a statutory declaration, certificate, opinion or report that complies with this Act or the trust indenture.

93. No exculpation. — No term of a trust indenture or of any agreement between a trustee and the holders of debt obligations issued thereunder or between the trustee and the issuer or guarantor shall operate so as to relieve a trustee from the duties imposed on him by section 91.

PART IX

RECEIVERS AND RECEIVER-MANAGERS

94. Functions of receiver. — A receiver of any property of a corporation may, subject to the rights of secured creditors, receive the income from the property and pay the liabilities connected with the property and realize the security interest of those on behalf of whom he is appointed, but, except to the extent permitted by a court, he may not carry on the business of the corporation.

95. Functions of receiver-manager. — A receiver of a corporation may, if he is also appointed receiver-manager of the corporation, carry on any business of the corporation to protect the security interest of those on behalf of whom he is appointed.

96. Directors' powers cease. — If a receiver-manager is appointed by a court or under an instrument, the powers of the directors of the corporation that the receiver-manager is authorized to exercise may not be exercised by the directors until the receiver-manager is discharged.

97. Duty to act. — A receiver or receiver-manager appointed by a court shall act in accordance with the directions of the court.

98. Duty under instrument. — A receiver or receiver-manager appointed under an instrument shall act in accordance with that instrument and any direction of a court made under section 100.

99. Duty of care. — A receiver or receiver-manager of a corporation appointed under an instrument shall

(a) act honestly and in good faith; and

(b) deal with any property of the corporation in his possession or control in a commercially reasonable manner.

100. Directions given by court. — On an application by a receiver or receiver-manager, whether appointed by a court or under an instrument, or on an application by any interested person, a court may make any order it thinks fit including, without limiting the generality of the foregoing,

(a) an order appointing, replacing or discharging a receiver or receiver-manager and approving his accounts;

(b) an order determining the notice to be given to any person or dispensing with notice to any person;

(c) an order fixing the remuneration of the receiver or receiver-manager;

(d) an order requiring the receiver or receiver-manager, or a person by or on behalf of whom he is appointed, to make good any default in connection with the receiver's or receiver-manager's custody or management of the property and business of the corporation, or to relieve any such person from any default on such terms as the court thinks fit, and to confirm any act of the receiver or receiver-manager; and

(e) an order giving directions on any matter relating to the duties of the receiver or receiver-manager.

101. Duties of receiver and receiver-manager. — A receiver or receiver-manager shall

(a) immediately notify the Director of his appointment and discharge;

(b) take into his custody and control the property of the corporation in accordance with the court order or instrument under which he is appointed;

(c) open and maintain a bank account in his name as receiver or receiver-manager of the corporation for the moneys of the corporation coming under his control;

(d) keep detailed accounts of all transactions carried out by him as receiver or receiver-manager;

(e) keep accounts of his administration that shall be available during usual business hours for inspection by the directors of the corporation;

(f) prepare at least once in every six month period after the date of his appointment financial statements of his administration as far as practicable in the form required by section 155; and

(g) on completion of his duties, render a final account of his administration in the form adopted for interim accounts under paragraph (f).

PART X
DIRECTORS AND OFFICERS

102. (1) Power to manage. — Subject to any unanimous shareholder agreement, the directors shall manage the business and affairs of a corporation.

(2) Number of directors. — A corporation shall have one or more directors but a corporation, any of the issued securities of which are or were part of a distribution to the public and remain outstanding and are held by more than one person, shall have not fewer than three directors, at least two of whom are not officers or employees of the corporation or its affiliates.

103. (1) By-laws. — Unless the articles, by-laws or a unanimous shareholder agreement otherwise provide, the directors may, by resolution, make, amend, or repeal any by-laws that regulate the business or affairs of the corporation.

(2) Shareholder approval. — The directors shall submit a by-law, or an amendment or a repeal of a by-law, made under subsection (1) to the shareholders at the next meeting of shareholders, and the shareholders may, by ordinary resolution, confirm, reject or amend the by-law, amendment or repeal.

(3) Effective date. — A by-law, or an amendment or a repeal of a by-law, is effective from the date of the resolution of the directors under subsection (1) until it is confirmed, confirmed as amended or rejected by the shareholders under subsecton (2) or until it ceases to be effective under subsection (4) and, where the by-law is confirmed or confirmed as amended, it continues in effect in the form in which it was so confirmed.

(4) Idem. — If a by-law, an amendment or a repeal is rejected by the shareholders, or if the directors do not submit a by-law, an amendment or a repeal to the shareholders as required under subsection (2), the by-law, amendment or repeal ceases to be effective and no subsequent resolution of the directors to make, amend or repeal a by-law having substantially the same purpose or effect is effective until it is confirmed or confirmed as amended by the shareholders.

(5) Shareholder proposal. — A shareholder entitled to vote at an annual meeting of shareholders may, in accordance with section 137, make a proposal to make, amend or repeal a by-law.

104. (1) Organization meeting. — After issue of the certificate of incor-

poration, a meeting of the directors of the corporation shall be held at which the directors may

(a) make by-laws;

(b) adopt forms of security certificates and corporate records;

(c) authorize the issue of securities;

(d) appoint officers;

(e) appoint an auditor to hold office until the first annual meeting of shareholders;

(f) make banking arrangements; and

(g) transact any other business.

(2) Exception. — Subsection (1) does not apply to a body corporate to which a certificate of amalgamation has been issued under subsection 185(4) or to which a certificate of continuance has been issued under subsection 187(4).

(3) Calling meeting. — An incorporator or a director may call the meeting of directors referred to in subsection (1) by giving not less than five days notice thereof by mail to each director, stating the time and place of the meeting.

105. (1) Qualifications of directors. — The following persons are disqualified from being a director of a corporation:

(a) anyone who is less than eighteen years of age;

(b) anyone who is of unsound mind and has been so found by a court in Canada or elsewhere;

(c) a person who is not an individual; or

(d) a person who has the status of bankrupt.

(2) Further qualifications. — Unless the articles otherwise provide, a director of a corporation is not required to hold shares issued by the corporation.

(3) Residency. — A majority of the directors of a corporation must be resident Canadians.

(4) Exception for holding corporation. — Notwithstanding subsection (3), not more than one-third of the directors of a holding corporation need be resident Canadians if the holding corporation earns in Canada directly or through its subsidiaries less than five per cent of the gross revenues of the holding corporation and all of its subsidiary bodies corporate together as shown in

(a) the most recent consolidated financial statements of the holding corporation referred to in section 157; or

(b) the most recent financial statements of the holding corporation and its subsidiary bodies corporate as at the end of the last completed financial year of the holding corporation.

106. (1) Notice of directors. — At the time of sending articles of incorporation, the incorporators shall send to the Director a notice of directors in prescribed form and the Director shall file the notice.

(2) Term of office. — Each director named in the notice referred to in subsection (1) holds office from the issue of the certificate of incorporation until the first meeting of shareholders.

(3) Election of directors. — Subject to paragraph 107(b), shareholders of a corporation shall, by ordinary resolution at the first meeting of shareholders and at each succeeding annual meeting at which an election of directors is required, elect directors to hold office for a term expiring not later than the close of the third annual meeting of shareholders following the election.

(4) Staggered terms. — It is not necessary that all directors elected at a meeting of shareholders hold office for the same term.

(5) No stated terms. — A director not elected for an expressly stated term ceases to hold office at the close of the first annual meeting of shareholders following his election.

(6) Incumbent directors. — Notwithstanding subsections (2), (3) and (5), if directors are not elected at a meeting of shareholders the incumbent directors continue in office until their successors are elected.

(7) Vacancy among candidates. — If a meeting of shareholders fails to elect the number or the minimum number of directors required by the articles by reason of the disqualification, incapacity or death of any candidates, the directors elected at that meeting may exercise all the powers of the directors if the number of directors so elected constitutes a quorum.

107. Cumulative voting. — Where the articles provide for cumulative voting,

(a) the articles shall require a fixed number and not a minimum and maximum number of directors;

(b) each shareholder entitled to vote at an election of directors has the right to cast a number of votes equal to the number of votes attached to the shares held by him multiplied by the number of directors to be elected, and he may cast all such votes in favour of one candidate or distribute them among the candidates in any manner;

(c) a separate vote of shareholders shall be taken with respect to each candidate nominated for director unless a resolution is passed unanimously permitting two or more persons to be elected by a single resolution;

(d) if a shareholder has voted for more than one candidate without specifying the distribution of his votes among the candidates, he is deemed to have distributed his votes equally among the candidates for whom he voted;

(e) if the number of candidates nominated for director exceeds the number of positions to be filled, the candidates who receive the least number of votes shall be eliminated until the number of candidates remaining equals the number of positions to be filled;

(f) each director ceases to hold office at the close of the first annual meeting of shareholders following his election;

(g) a director may not be removed from office if the votes cast against his removal would be sufficient to elect him and such votes could be voted cumulatively at an election at which the same total number of votes were cast and the number of directors required by the articles were then being elected; and

(h) the number of directors required by the articles may not be decreased if the votes cast against the motion to decrease would be sufficient to elect a director and such votes could be voted cumulatively at an election at which the same total number of votes were cast and the number of directors required by the articles were then being elected.

108. (1) Ceasing to hold office. — A director of a corporation ceases to hold office when

(a) he dies or resigns;

(b) he is removed in accordance with section 109; or

(c) he becomes disqualified under subsection 105(1).

(2) Effective date of resignation. — A resignation of a director becomes effective at the time a written resignation is sent to the corporation, or at the time specified in the resignation, whichever is later.

109. (1) Removal of directors. — Subject to paragraph 107(g), the shareholders of a corporation may by ordinary resolution at a special meeting remove any director or directors from office.

(2) Exception. — Where the holders of any class or series of shares of a corporation have an exclusive right to elect one or more directors, a director so elected may only be removed by an ordinary resolution at a meeting of the shareholders of that class or series.

(3) Vacancy. — Subject to paragraphs 107(b) to (e), a vacancy created by the removal of a director may be filled at the meeting of the shareholders at which the director is removed or, if not so filled, may be filled under section 111.

110. (1) Attendance at meeting. — A director of a corporation is entitled to receive notice of and to attend and be heard at every meeting of shareholders.

(2) Statement of director. — A director who

(a) resigns,

(b) receives a notice or otherwise learns of a meeting of shareholders called for the purpose of removing him from office, or

(c) receives a notice or otherwise learns of a meeting of directors or shareholders at which another person is to be appointed or elected to fill the office of director, whether because of his resignation or removal or because his term of office has expired or is about to expire,

is entitled to submit to the corporation a written statement giving the reasons for his resignation or the reasons why he opposes any proposed action or resolution.

(3) Circulating statement. — A corporation shall forthwith send a copy of the statement referred to in subsection (2) to every shareholder entitled to receive notice of any meeting referred to in subsection (1) and to the Director unless the statement is included in or attached to a management proxy circular required by section 150.

(4) Immunity. — No corporation or person acting on its behalf incurs any liability by reason only of circulating a director's statement in compliance with subsection (3).

111. (1) Filling vacancy. — Notwithstanding subsection 114(3), but subject to subsections (3) and (4), a quorum of directors may fill a vacancy among the directors, except a vacancy resulting from an increase in the number or minimum number of directors or from a failure to elect the number or minimum number of directors required by the articles.

(2) Calling meeting. — If there is not a quorum of directors or if there has been a failure to elect the number or minimum number of directors required by the articles, the directors then in office shall forthwith call a special meeting of shareholders to fill the vacancy and, if they fail to call a meeting or if there are no directors then in office, the meeting may be called by any shareholder.

(3) Class director. — Where the holders of any class or series of shares of a corporation have an exclusive right to elect one or more directors and a vacancy occurs among those directors,

(a) subject to subsection (4), the remaining directors elected by that class or series may fill the vacancy except a vacancy resulting from an increase in the number or minimum number of directors for that class or series or from a failure to elect the number or minimum number of directors for that class or series; or

(b) if there are no such remaining directors any holder of shares of that class or series may call a meeting of the holders thereof for the purpose of filling the vacancy.

(4) Shareholders filling vacancy. — The articles may provide that a vacancy among the directors shall only be filled by a vote of the shareholders, or by a vote of the holders of any class or series of shares having an exclusive right

to elect one or more directors if the vaçancy occurs among the directors elected by that class or series.

(5) Unexpired term. — A director appointed or elected to fill a vacancy holds office for the unexpired term of his predecessor.

112. (1) Number of directors. — The shareholders of a corporation may amend the articles to increase or, subject to paragraph 107(h), to decrease the number of directors, or the minimum or maximum number of directors, but no decrease shall shorten the term of an incumbent director.

(2) Electing additional number of directors where articles amended. — Where the shareholders adopt an amendment to the articles of a corporation to increase the number or minimum number of directors, the shareholders may, at the meeting at which they adopt the amendment, elect the additional number of directors authorized by the amendment, and for that purpose, notwithstanding subsections 179(1) and 262(3), on the issue of a certificate of amendment the articles are deemed to be amended as of the date the shareholders adopt the amendment to the articles.

113. (1) Notice of change of directors. — Within fifteen days after a change is made among its directors, a corporation shall send to the Director a notice in prescribed form setting out the change and the Director shall file the notice.

(2) Application to court. — Any interested person, or the Director, may apply to a court for an order to require a corporation to comply with subsection (1), and the court may so order and make any further order it thinks fit.

114. (1) Meeting of directors. — Unless the articles or by-laws otherwise provide, the directors may meet at any place, and on such notice as the by-laws require.

(2) Quorum. — Subject to the articles or by-laws, a majority of the number of directors or minimum number of directors required by the articles constitutes a quorum at any meeting of directors, and, notwithstanding any vacancy among the directors, a quorum of directors may exercise all the powers of the directors.

(3) Canadian majority. — Directors, other than directors of a corporation referred to in subsection 105(4), shall not transact business at a meeting of directors unless a majority of directors present are resident Canadians.

(4) Exception. — Notwithstanding subsection (3), directors may transact business at a meeting of directors where a majority of resident Canadian directors is not present if

(a) a resident Canadian director who is unable to be present approves in writing or by telephone or other communications facilities the business transacted at the meeting; and

(b) a majority of resident Canadian directors would have been present had that director been present at the meeting.

(5) Notice of meeting. — A notice of a meeting of directors shall specify any matter referred to in subsection 115(3) that is to be dealt with at the meeting but, unless the by-laws otherwise provide, need not specify the purpose of or the business to be transacted at the meeting.

(6) Waiver of notice. — A director may in any manner waive a notice of a meeting of directors; and attendance of a director at a meeting of directors is a waiver of notice of the meeting, except where a director attends a meeting for the express purpose of objecting to the transaction of any business on the grounds that the meeting is not lawfully called.

(7) Adjournment. — Notice of an adjourned meeting of directors is not required to be given if the time and place of the adjourned meeting is announced at the original meeting.

(8) One director meeting. — Where a corporation has only one director, that director may constitute a meeting.

(9) Participation by telephone. — Subject to the by-laws, a director may, if all the directors of the corporation consent, participate in a meeting of directors or of a committee of directors by means of such telephone or other communications facilities as permit all persons participating in the meeting to hear each other, and a director participating in such a meeting by such means is deemed for the purposes of this Act to be present at that meeting.

115. (1) Delegation. — Directors of a corporation may appoint from their number a managing director who is a resident Canadian or a committee of directors and delegate to such managing director or committee any of the powers of the directors.

(2) Canadian majority. — If the directors of a corporation, other than a corporation referred to in subsection 105(4), appoint a committee of directors, a majority of the members of the committee must be resident Canadians.

(3) Limits on authority. — Notwithstanding subsection (1), no managing director and no committee of directors has authority to

(a) submit to the shareholders any question or matter requiring the approval of the shareholders;

(b) fill a vacancy among the directors or in the office of auditor;

(c) issue securities except in the manner and on the terms authorized by the directors;

(d) declare dividends;

(e) purchase, redeem or otherwise acquire shares issued by the corporation;

(f) pay a commission referred to in section 41;

(g) approve a management proxy circular referred to in Part XIII;

(h) approve a take-over bid circular or directors' circular referred to in Part XVII;

(i) approve any financial statements referred to in section 155; or

(j) adopt, amend or repeal by-laws.

116. Validity of acts of directors and officers. — An act of a director or officer is valid notwithstanding an irregularity in his election or appointment or a defect in his qualification.

117. (1) Resolution in lieu of meeting. — A resolution in writing, signed by all the directors entitled to vote on that resolution at a meeting of directors or committee of directors, is as valid as if it had been passed at a meeting of directors or committee of directors.

(2) Filing resolution. — A copy of every resolution referred to in subsection (1) shall be kept with the minutes of the proceedings of the directors or committee of directors.

118. (1) Directors' liability. — Directors of a corporation who vote for or consent to a resolution authorizing the issue of a share under section 25 for a consideration other than money are jointly and severally liable to the corporation to make good any amount by which the consideration received is less than the fair equivalent of the money that the corporation would have received if the share had been issued for money on the date of the resolution.

(2) Further directors' liabilities. — Directors of a corporation who vote for or consent to a resolution authorizing

(a) a purchase, redemption or other acquisition of shares contrary to section 34, 35 or 36,

(b) a commission contrary to section 41,

(c) a payment of a dividend contrary to section 42,

(d) financial assistance contrary to section 44,

(e) a payment of an indemnity contrary to section 124, or

(f) a payment to a shareholder contrary to section 190 or 241,

are jointly and severally liable to restore to the corporation any amounts so distributed or paid and not otherwise recovered by the corporation.

(3) Contribution. — A director who has satisfied a judgment rendered under this section is entitled to contribution from the other directors who voted for or consented to the unlawful act on which the judgment was founded.

(4) Recovery. — A director liable under subsection (2) is entitled to apply to a court for an order compelling a shareholder or other recipient to pay or deliver to the director any money or property that was paid or distributed to

the shareholder or other recipient contrary to section 34, 35, 36, 41, 42, 44, 124, 190 or 241.

(5) Order of court. — In connection with an application under subsection (4) a court may, if it is satisfied that it is equitable to do so,

(a) order a shareholder or other recipient to pay or deliver to a director any money or property that was paid or distributed to the shareholder or other recipient contrary to section 34, 35, 36, 41, 42, 44, 124, 190 or 241;

(b) order a corporation to return or issue shares to a person from whom the corporation has purchased, redeemed or otherwise acquired shares; or

(c) make any further order it thinks fit.

(6) No liability. — A director is not liable under subsection (1) if he proves that he did not know and could not reasonably have known that the share was issued for a consideration less than the fair equivalent of the money that the corporation would have received if the share had been issued for money.

(7) Limitation. — An action to enforce a liability imposed by this section may not be commenced after two years from the date of the resolution authorizing the action complained of.

119. (1) Liability of directors for wages. — Directors of a corporation are jointly and severally liable to employees of the corporation for all debts not exceeding six months wages payable to each such employee for services performed for the corporation while they are such directors respectively.

(2) Conditions precedent to liability. — A director is not liable under subsection (1) unless

(a) the corporation has been sued for the debt within six months after it has become due and execution has been returned unsatisfied in whole or in part;

(b) the corporation has commenced liquidation and dissolution proceedings or has been dissolved and a claim for the debt has been proved within six months after the earlier of the date of commencement of the liquidation and dissolution proceedings and the date of dissolution; or

(c) the corporation has made an assignment or a receiving order has been made against it under the *Bankruptcy and Insolvency Act* and a claim for the debt has been proved within six months after the date of the assignment or receiving order.

(3) Limitation. — A director is not liable under this section unless he is sued for a debt referred to in subsection (1) while he is a director or within two years after he has ceased to be a director.

(4) Amount due after execution. — Where execution referred to in paragraph

(2)(a) has issued, the amount recoverable from a director is the amount remaining unsatisfied after execution.

(5) Subrogation of director. — Where a director pays a debt referred to in subsection (1) that is proved in liquidation and dissolution or bankrupcty proceedings, he is entitled to any preference that the employee would have been entitled to, and where a judgment has been obtained he is entitled to an assignment of the judgment.

(6) Contribution. — A director who has satisfied a claim under this section is entitled to contribution from the other directors who were liable for the claim.

[S. 119 amended by substituting "*Bankruptcy and Insolvency Act*" wherever the expression "*Bankruptcy Act*" occurs by S.C. 1992, c. 27, s. 90(1)*(h)*]

120. (1) Disclosure of interested director contract. — A director or officer of a corporation who

(a) is a party to a material contract or proposed material contract with the corporation, or

(b) is a director or an officer of or has a material interest in any person who is a party to a material contract or proposed material contract with the corporation,

shall disclose in writing to the corporation or request to have entered in the minutes of meetings of directors the nature and extent of his interest.

(2) Time of disclosure for director. — The disclosure required by subsection (1) shall be made, in the case of a director,

(a) at a meeting at which a proposed contract is first considered;

(b) if the director was not then interested in a proposed contract, at the first meeting after he becomes so interested;

(c) if the director becomes interested after a contract is made, at the first meeting after he becomes so interested; or

(d) if a person who is interested in a contract later becomes a director, at the first meeting after he becomes a director.

(3) Time of disclosure for officer. — The disclosure required by subsection (1) shall be made, in the case of an officer who is not a director,

(a) forthwith after he becomes aware that the contract or proposed contract is to be considered or has been considered at a meeting of directors;

(b) if the officer becomes interested after a contract is made, forthwith after he becomes so interested; or

(c) if a person who is interested in a contract later becomes an officer, forthwith after he becomes an officer.

(4) Time of disclosure for director or officer. — If a material contract or

proposed material contract is one that, in the ordinary course of the corporation's business, would not require approval by the directors or shareholders, a director or officer shall disclose in writing to the corporation or request to have entered in the minutes of meetings of directors the nature and extent of his interest forthwith after the director or officer becomes aware of the contract or proposed contract.

(5) Voting. — A director referred to in subsection (1) shall not vote on any resolution to approve the contract unless the contract is

(a) an arrangement by way of security for money lent to or obligations undertaken by him for the benefit of the corporation or an affiliate;

(b) one relating primarily to his remuneration as a director, officer, employee or agent of the corporation or an affiliate;

(c) one for indemnity or insurance under section 124; or

(d) one with an affiliate.

(6) Continuing disclosure. — For the purposes of this section, a general notice to the directors by a director or officer, declaring that he is a director or officer of or has a material interest in a person and is to be regarded as interested in any contract made with that person, is a sufficient declaration of interest in relation to any contract so made.

(7) Avoidance standards. — A material contract between a corporation and one or more of its directors or officers, or between a corporation and another person of which a director or officer of the corporation is a director or officer or in which he has a material interest, is neither void nor voidable by reason only of that relationship or by reason only that a director with an interest in the contract is present at or is counted to determine the presence of a quorum at a meeting of directors or committee of directors that authorized the contract, if the director or officer disclosed his interest in accordance with subsection (2), (3), (4) or (6), as the case may be, and the contract was approved by the directors or the shareholders and it was reasonable and fair to the corporation at the time it was approved.

(8) Application to court. — Where a director or officer of a corporation fails to disclose his interest in a material contract in accordance with this section, a court may, on the application of the corporation or a shareholder of the corporation, set aside the contract on such terms as it thinks fit.

121. Officers. — Subject to the articles, the by-laws or any unanimous shareholder agreement,

(a) the directors may designate the offices of the corporation, appoint as officers persons of full capacity, specify their duties and delegate to them powers to manage the business and affairs of the corporation, except powers to do anything referred to in subsection 115(3);

(b) a director may be appointed to any office of the corporation; and

(c) two or more offices of the corporation may be held by the same person.

122. (1) Duty of care of directors and officers. — Every director and officer of a corporation in exercising his powers and discharging his duties shall

(a) act honestly and in good faith with a view to the best interests of the corporation; and

(b) exercise the care, diligence and skill that a reasonably prudent person would exercise in comparable circumstances.

(2) Duty to comply. — Every director and officer of a corporation shall comply with this Act, the regulations, articles, by-laws and any unanimous shareholder agreement.

(3) No exculpation. — Subject to subsection 146(5), no provision in a contract, the articles, the by-laws or a resolution relieves a director or officer from the duty to act in accordance with this Act or the regulations or relieves him from liability for a breach thereof.

123. (1) Dissent. — A director who is present at a meeting of directors or committee of directors is deemed to have consented to any resolution passed or action taken thereat unless

(a) he requests that his dissent be or his dissent is entered in the minutes of the meeting;

(b) he sends his written dissent to the secretary of the meeting before the meeting is adjourned; or

(c) he sends his dissent by registered mail or delivers it to the registered office of the corporation immediately after the meeting is adjourned.

(2) Loss of right to dissent. — A director who votes for or consents to a resolution is not entitled to dissent under subsection (1).

(3) Dissent of absent director. — A director who was not present at a meeting at which a resolution was passed or action taken is deemed to have consented thereto unless within seven days after he becomes aware of the resolution he

(a) causes his dissent to be placed with the minutes of the meeting; or

(b) sends his dissent by registered mail or delivers it to the registered office of the corporation.

(4) Reliance on statements. — A director is not liable under section 118, 119 or 122 if he relies in good faith on

(a) financial statements of the corporation represented to him by an officer of the corporation or in a written report of the auditor of the corporation fairly to reflect the financial condition of the corporation; or

(b) a report of a lawyer, accountant, engineer, appraiser or other person whose profession lends credibility to a statement made by him.

124. (1) Indemnification. — Except in respect of an action by or on behalf of the corporation or body corporate to procure a judgment in its favour, a corporation may indemnify a director or officer of the corporation, a former director or officer of the corporation or a person who acts or acted at the corporation's request as a director or officer of a body corporate of which the corporation is or was a shareholder or creditor, and his heirs and legal representatives, against all costs, charges and expenses, including an amount paid to settle an action or satisfy a judgment, reasonably incurred by him in respect of any civil, criminal or administrative action or proceeding to which he is made a party by reason of being or having been a director or officer of such corporation or body corporate, if

(a) he acted honestly and in good faith with a view to the best interests of the corporation; and

(b) in the case of a criminal or administrative action or proceeding that is enforced by a monetary penalty, he had reasonable grounds for believing that his conduct was lawful.

(2) Indemnification in derivative actions. — A corporation may with the approval of a court indemnify a person referred to in subsection (1) in respect of an action by or on behalf of the corporation or body corporate to procure a judgment in its favour, to which he is made a party by reason of being or having been a director or an officer of the corporation or body corporate, against all costs, charges and expenses reasonably incurred by him in connection with such action if he fulfils the conditions set out in paragraphs (1)(a) and (b).

(3) Indemnity as of right. — Notwithstanding anything in this section, a person referred to in subsection (1) is entitled to indemnity from the corporation in respect of all costs, charges and expenses reasonably incurred by him in connection with the defence of any civil, criminal or administrative action or proceeding to which he is made a party by reason of being or having been a director or officer of the corporation or body corporate, if the person seeking indemnity

(a) was substantially successful on the merits in his defence of the action or proceeding, and

(b) fulfils the conditions set out in paragraphs (1)(a) and (b).

(4) Directors' and officers' insurance. — A corporation may purchase and maintain insurance for the benefit of any person referred to in subsection (1) against any liability incurred by him

(a) in his capacity as a director or officer of the corporation, except where the liability relates to his failure to act honestly and in good faith with a view to the best interests of the corporation; or

(b) in his capacity as a director or officer of another body corporate where he acts or acted in that capacity at the corporation's request, except where the liability relates to his failure to act honestly and in good faith with a view to the best interests of the body corporate.

(5) Application to court. — A corporation or a person referred to in subsection (1) may apply to a court for an order approving an indemnity under this section and the court may so order and make any further order it thinks fit.

(6) Notice to Director. — An applicant under subsection (5) shall give the Director notice of the application and the Director is entitled to appear and be heard in person or by counsel.

(7) Other notice. — On an application under subsection (5), the court may order notice to be given to any interested person and such person is entitled to appear and be heard in person or by counsel.

125. Remuneration. — Subject to the articles, the by-laws or any unanimous shareholder agreement, the directors of a corporation may fix the remuneration of the directors, officers and employees of the corporation.

PART XI
INSIDER TRADING

126. (1) Definitions. — In this Part,

"distributing corporation". — "distributing corporation" means a corporation, any of the issued securities of which are or were part of a distribution to the public and remain outstanding and are held by more than one person;

"insider". — "insider" means, except in section 131,

(a) a director or officer of a distributing corporation,

(b) a distributing corporation that purchases or otherwise acquires, except by means of a redemption under section 36, shares issued by it,

(c) a distributing corporation that purchases or otherwise acquires or sells shares issued by any of its affiliates, or

(d) a person who beneficially owns more than ten per cent of the shares of a distributing corporation or who exercises control or direction over more than ten per cent of the votes attached to shares of a distributing corporation, excluding shares owned by an underwriter under an underwriting agreement while those shares are in the course of a distribution to the public;

"officer". — "officer" means

(a) the chairman, president, vice-president, secretary, treasurer, comptroller, general counsel, general manager, managing director or any other individual who performs functions for a corporation similar to those normally performed by an individual occupying any such office, and

(b) each of the five highest paid employees of a corporation including any individual mentioned in paragraph (a);

"share". — "share" means a share carrying voting rights under all circumstances or by reason of the occurrence of an event that has occurred and that is continuing, and includes

(a) a security currently convertible into such a share, and

(b) currently exercisable options and rights to acquire such a share or such a convertible security.

(2) Further interpretation. — For the purposes of this Part,

(a) a director or an officer of a body corporate that is an insider of a distributing corporation is deemed to be an insider of the distributing corporation;

(b) a director or an officer of a body corporate that is a subsidiary is deemed to be an insider of its holding distributing corporation;

(c) a person is deemed to own beneficially shares beneficially owned by a body corporate controlled by him directly or indirectly;

(d) a body corporate is deemed to own beneficially shares beneficially owned by its affiliates; and

(e) the acquisition or disposition by an insider of an option or right to acquire a share is deemed to be a change in the beneficial ownership of the share to which the option or right to acquire relates.

(3) Deemed insiders. — For the purposes of this Part,

(a) if a body corporate becomes an insider of a distributing corporation, or enters into a business combination with a distributing corporation, a director or an officer of the body corporate or a shareholder of the body corporate who is a person referred to in paragraph (d) of the definition "insider" is deemed to have been an insider of the distributing corporation for the previous six months or for such shorter period as he was a director, an officer or such a shareholder of the body corporate; and

(b) if a distributing corporation becomes an insider of a body corporate or enters into a business combination with a body corporate, a director or an officer of the body corporate or a shareholder of the body corporate who is a person referred to in paragraph (d) of the definition "insider" is deemed to have been an insider of the distributing corporation for the previous six months or for such shorter period as he was a director, an officer or such a shareholder of the body corporate.

(4) Definition of "business combination". — In subsection (3), "business combination" means an acquisition of all or substantially all the property of

one body corporate by another or an amalgamation of two or more bodies corporate.

127. (1) First insider reports. — Unless he has filed or has been exempted from filing an insider report under the *Canada Corporations Act*, chapter C-32 of the Revised Statutes of Canada, 1970, or has been exempted from filing an insider report by the regulations, a person who is an insider of a body corporate on the day on which it is continued as a corporation under this Act shall, if the corporation is a distributing corporation, send to the Director an insider report in prescribed form within ten days after the end of the month in which such day occurs.

(2) Idem. — A person who becomes an insider shall, within ten days after the end of the month in which he becomes an insider, send to the Director an insider report in the prescribed form.

(3) Constructive insider report. — A person who is deemed to have been an insider under subsection 126(3) shall, within ten days after the end of the month in which he is deemed to have become an insider, send to the Director the insider reports for the period in respect of which he is deemed to have been an insider that he would have been required to send under this section had he been otherwise an insider for such period.

(4) Subsequent insider reports. — An insider whose interest in securities of a distributing corporation changes from that shown or required to be shown in the last insider report sent or required to be sent by him shall, within ten days after the end of the month in which such change takes place, send to the Director an insider report in the prescribed form.

(5) One insider report. — An insider report of a person that includes securities deemed to be beneficially owned by that person is deemed to be an insider report of a body corporate referred to in paragraph 126(2)(c) and the body corporate is not required to send a separate insider report.

(6) Idem. — An insider report of a body corporate that includes securities deemed to be beneficially owned by the body corporate is deemed to be an insider report of an affiliate referred to in paragraph 126(2)(d) and the affiliate is not required to send a separate insider report.

(7) Contents. — An insider report of a person that includes securities deemed beneficially owned by that person shall disclose separately

(a) the number or amount of the securities owned by a body corporate; and

(b) the name of the body corporate.

(8) Exemption order. — On an application by or on behalf of an insider, the Director may make an order on such terms as he thinks fit exempting the insider from any of the requirements of this section, which order may have retrospective effect.

(9) Offence. — A person who, without reasonable cause, fails to comply with this section is guilty of an offence and liable on summary conviction to a fine not exceeding five thousand dollars or to imprisonment for a term not exceeding six months or to both.

(10) Officers, etc., of bodies corporate. — Where a body corporate commits an offence under subsection (9), any director or officer of the body corporate who knowingly authorized, permitted or acquiesced in the commission of the offence is a party to and guilty of the offence and is liable on summary conviction to a fine not exceeding five thousand dollars or to imprisonment for a term not exceeding six months or to both, whether or not the body corporate has been prosecuted or convicted.

128. Notice of purchase of own shares. — A corporation that proposes to purchase or otherwise acquire its own shares otherwise than by means of a purchase or redemption under section 36 shall, in the prescribed circumstances, give notice to the Director of the proposed purchase or other acquisition in the manner prescribed.

129. Publication. — The Director shall summarize in a periodical available to the public the information contained in insider reports sent to him under sections 127 and 128 and the particulars of exemptions granted under subsection 127(8) together with the reasons therefor.

130. (1) Prohibition of short sale. — An insider shall not knowingly sell, directly or indirectly, a share of the distributing corporation or any of its affiliates if the insider selling the share does not own or has not fully paid for the share to be sold.

(2) Calls and puts. — An insider shall not, directly or indirectly, buy or sell a call or put in respect of a share of the corporation or any of its affiliates.

(3) Exception. — Notwithstanding subsection (1), an insider may sell a share he does not own if he owns another share convertible into the share sold or an option or right to acquire the share sold and, within ten days after the sale, he

(a) exercises the conversion privilege, option or right and delivers the share so acquired to the purchaser; or

(b) transfers the convertible share, option or right to the purchaser.

(4) Offence. — An insider who contravenes subsection (1) or (2) is guilty of an offence and liable on summary conviction to a fine not exceeding five thousand dollars or to imprisonment for a term not exceeding six months or to both.

131. (1) Definition of "insider". — In this section "insider" means, with respect to a corporation,

(a) the corporation;

(b) an affiliate of the corporation;

(c) a director or an officer of the corporation;

(d) a person who beneficially owns more than ten per cent of the shares of the corporation or who exercises control or direction over more than ten per cent of the votes attached to the shares of the corporation;

(e) a person employed or retained by the corporation; and

(f) a person who receives specific confidential information from a person described in this subsection or in subsection (2), including a person described in this paragraph, and who has knowledge that the person giving the information is a person described in this subsection or in subsection (2), including a person described in this paragraph.

(2) Deemed insiders. — For the purposes of this section,

(a) if a body corporate becomes an insider of a corporation, or enters into a business combination with a corporation, a director or officer of the body corporate is deemed to have been an insider of the corporation for the previous six months or for such shorter period as he was a director or an officer of the body corporate; and

(b) if a corporation becomes an insider of a body corporate, or enters into a business combination with a body corporate, a director or an officer of the body corporate is deemed to have been an insider of the corporation for the previous six months or for such shorter period as he was a director or officer of the body corporate.

(3) Definition of "business combination". — In subsection (2), "business combination" means an acquisition of all or substantially all the property of one body corporate by another or an amalgamation of two or more bodies corporate.

(4) Civil liability. — An insider who, in connection with a transaction in a security of the corporation or any of its affiliates, makes use of any specific confidential information for his own benefit or advantage that, if generally known, might reasonably be expected to affect materially the value of the security

(a) is liable to compensate any person for any direct loss suffered by that person as a result of the transaction, unless the information was known or in the exercise of reasonable diligence should have been known to that person; and

(b) is accountable to the corporation for any direct benefit or advantage received or receivable by the insider as a result of the transaction.

(5) Limitation. — An action to enforce a right created by subsection (4) may be commenced

(a) only within two years after discovery of the facts that gave rise to the cause of action; or

(b) if the transaction was required to be reported under section 127, only within two years from the time of reporting under that section.

PART XII
SHAREHOLDERS

132. (1) Place of meetings. — Meetings of shareholders of a corporation shall be held at the place within Canada provided in the by-laws or, in the absence of such provision, at the place within Canada that the directors determine.

(2) Meeting outside Canada. — Notwithstanding subsection (1), a meeting of shareholders of a corporation may be held outside Canada if all the shareholders entitled to vote at that meeting so agree, and a shareholder who attends a meeting of shareholders held outside Canada is deemed to have so agreed except when he attends the meeting for the express purpose of objecting to the transaction of any business on the grounds that the meeting is not lawfully held.

133. Calling meetings. — The directors of a corporation

(a) shall call an annual meeting of shareholders not later than eighteen months after the corporation comes into existence and subsequently not later than fifteen months after holding the last preceding annual meeting; and

(b) may at any time call a special meeting of shareholders.

134. (1) Fixing record date. — For the purpose of determining shareholders

(a) entitled to receive payment of a dividend,

(b) entitled to participate in a liquidation distribution, or

(c) for any other purpose except the right to receive notice of or to vote at a meeting,

the directors may fix in advance a date as the record date for such determination of shareholders, but such record date shall not precede by more than fifty days the particular action to be taken.

(2) Notice of meeting. — For the purpose of determining shareholders entitled to receive notice of a meeting of shareholders, the directors may fix in advance a date as the record date for such determination of shareholders, but such record date shall not precede by more than fifty days or by less than twenty-one days the date on which the meeting is to be held.

(3) No record date fixed. — If no record date is fixed,

(a) the record date for the determination of shareholders entitled to receive notice of a meeting of shareholders shall be

(i) at the close of business on the day immediately preceding the day on which the notice is given, or,

(ii) if no notice is given, the day on which the meeting is held; and

(b) the record date for the determination of shareholders for any purpose other than to establish a shareholder's right to receive notice of a meeting or to vote shall be at the close of business on the day on which the directors pass the resolution relating thereto.

(4) When record date fixed. — If a record date is fixed, unless notice of the record date is waived in writing by every holder of a share of the class or series affected whose name is set out in the securities register at the close of business on the day the directors fix the record date, notice thereof shall, not less than seven days before the date so fixed, be given

(a) by advertisement in a newspaper published or distributed in the place where the corporation has its registered office and in each place in Canada where it has a transfer agent or where a transfer of its shares may be recorded; and

(b) by written notice to each stock exchange in Canada on which the shares of the corporation are listed for trading.

135. (1) Notice of meeting. — Notice of the time and place of a meeting of shareholders shall be sent not less than twenty-one days nor more than fifty days before the meeting,

(a) to each shareholder entitled to vote at the meeting;

(b) to each director; and

(c) to the auditor of the corporation.

(2) Exception. — A notice of a meeting is not required to be sent to shareholders who were not registered on the records of the corporation or its transfer agent on the record date determined under subsection 134(2) or (3), but failure to receive a notice does not deprive a shareholder of the right to vote at the meeting.

(3) Adjournment. — If a meeting of shareholders is adjourned for less than thirty days it is not necessary, unless the by-laws otherwise provide, to give notice of the adjourned meeting, other than by announcement at the earliest meeting that is adjourned.

(4) Notice of adjourned meeting. — If a meeting of shareholders is adjourned by one or more adjournments for an aggregate of thirty days or more, notice of the adjourned meeting shall be given as for an original meeting but, unless the meeting is adjourned by one or more adjournments for an aggregate of more than ninety days, subsection 149(1) does not apply.

(5) Business. — All business transacted at a special meeting of shareholders and all business transacted at an annual meeting of shareholders, except consideration of the financial statements, auditor's report, election of directors and reappointment of the incumbent auditor, is deemed to be special business.

(6) Notice of business. — Notice of a meeting of shareholders at which special business is to be transacted shall state

(a) the nature of that business in sufficient detail to permit the shareholder to form a reasoned judgment thereon; and

(b) the text of any special resolution to be submitted to the meeting.

136. Waiver of notice. — A shareholder and any other person entitled to attend a meeting of shareholders may in any manner waive notice of a meeting of shareholders, and attendance of any such person at a meeting of shareholders is a waiver of notice of the meeting, except where he attends a meeting for the express purpose of objecting to the transaction of any business on the grounds that the meeting is not lawfully called.

137. (1) Shareholder proposal. — A shareholder entitled to vote at an annual meeting of shareholders may

(a) submit to the corporation notice of any matter that he proposes to raise at the meeting, hereinafter referred to as a "proposal"; and

(b) discuss at the meeting any matter in respect of which he would have been entitled to submit a proposal.

(2) Information circular. — A corporation that solicits proxies shall set out the proposal in the management proxy circular required by section 150 or attach the proposal thereto.

(3) Supporting statement. — If so requested by the shareholder, the corporation shall include in the management proxy circular or attach thereto a statement by the shareholder of not more than two hundred words in support of the proposal, and the name and address of the shareholder.

(4) Nomination for director. — A proposal may include nominations for the election of directors if the proposal is signed by one or more holders of shares representing in the aggregate not less than five per cent of the shares or five per cent of the shares of a class of shares of the corporation entitled to vote at the meeting to which the proposal is to be presented, but this subsection does not preclude nominations made at a meeting of shareholders.

(5) Exemptions. — A corporation is not required to comply with subsections (2) and (3) if

(a) the proposal is not submitted to the corporation at least ninety days before the anniversary date of the previous annual meeting of shareholders;

(b) it clearly appears that the proposal is submitted by the shareholder primarily for the purpose of enforcing a personal claim or redressing a personal grievance against the corporation or its directors, officers or security holders, or primarily for the purpose of promoting general economic, political, racial, religious, social or similar causes;

(c) the corporation, at the shareholder's request, included a proposal in a management proxy circular relating to a meeting of shareholders held within two years preceding the receipt of such request, and the shareholder failed to present the proposal, in person or by proxy, at the meeting;

(d) substantially the same proposal was submitted to shareholders in a management proxy circular or a dissident's proxy circular relating to a meeting of shareholders held within two years preceding the receipt of the shareholder's request and the proposal was defeated; or

(e) the rights conferred by this section are being abused to secure publicity.

(6) Immunity. — No corporation or person acting on its behalf incurs any liability by reason only of circulating a proposal or statement in compliance with this section.

(7) Notice of refusal. — If a corporation refuses to include a proposal in a management proxy circular, the corporation shall, within ten days after receiving the proposal, notify the shareholder submitting the proposal of its intention to omit the proposal from the management proxy circular and send to him a statement of the reasons for the refusal.

(8) Shareholder application to court. — On the application of a shareholder claiming to be aggrieved by a corporation's refusal under subsection (7), a court may restrain the holding of the meeting to which the proposal is sought to be presented and make any further order it thinks fit.

(9) Corporation's application to court. — The corporation or any person claiming to be aggrieved by a proposal may apply to a court for an order permitting the corporation to omit the proposal from the management proxy circular, and the court, if it is satisfied that subsection (5) applies, may make such order as it thinks fit.

(10) Director entitled to notice. — An applicant under subsection (8) or (9) shall give the Director notice of the application and the Director is entitled to appear and be heard in person or by counsel.

138. (1) Shareholder list. — A corporation shall prepare a list of shareholders entitled to receive notice of a meeting, arranged in alphabetical order and showing the number of shares held by each shareholder,

(a) if a record date is fixed under subsection 134(2), not later than ten days after that date; or

(b) if no record date is fixed

(i) at the close of business on the day immediately preceding the day on which the notice is given, or

(ii) where no notice is given, on the day on which the meeting is held.

(2) Effect of list. — Where a corporation fixes a record date under subsection

134(2), a person named in the list prepared under paragraph (1)(a) is entitled to vote the shares shown opposite his name at the meeting to which the list relates, except to the extent that

(a) the person has transferred the ownership of any of his shares after the record date, and

(b) the transferee of those shares

(i) produces properly endorsed share certificates, or

(ii) otherwise establishes that he owns the shares

and demands, not later than ten days before the meeting or such shorter period before the meeting as the by-laws of the corporation may provide, that his name be included in the list before the meeting

in which case the transferee is entitled to vote his shares at the meeting.

(3) Effect of list. — Where a corporation does not fix a record date under subsection 134(2), a person named in a list prepared under paragraph (1)(b) is entitled to vote the shares shown opposite his name at the meeting to which the list relates except to the extent that

(a) the person has transferred the ownership of any of his shares after the date on which a list referred to in subparagraph (1)(b)(i) is prepared, and

(b) the transferee of those shares

(i) produces properly endorsed share certificates or otherwise establishes that he owns the shares, and

(ii) demands not later than ten days before the meeting or such shorter period before the meeting as the by-laws of the corporation may provide, that his name be included in the list before the meeting

in which case the transferee is entitled to vote his shares at the meeting.

(4) Examination of list. — A shareholder may examine the list of shareholders

(a) during usual business hours at the registered office of the corporation or at the place where its central securities register is maintained; and

(b) at the meeting of shareholders for which the list was prepared.

139. (1) Quorum. — Unless the by-laws otherwise provide, a quorum of shareholders is present at a meeting of shareholders, irrespective of the number of persons actually present at the meeting, if the holders of a majority of the shares entitled to vote at the meeting are present in person or represented by proxy.

(2) Opening quorum sufficient. — If a quorum is present at the opening of a meeting of shareholders, the shareholders present may, unless the by-laws

otherwise provide, proceed with the business of the meeting, notwithstanding that a quorum is not present throughout the meeting.

(3) Adjournment. — If a quorum is not present at the opening of a meeting of shareholders, the shareholders present may adjourn the meeting to a fixed time and place but may not transact any other business.

(4) One shareholder meeting. — If a corporation has only one shareholder, or only one holder of any class or series of shares, the shareholder present in person or by proxy constitutes a meeting.

140. (1) Right to vote. — Unless the articles otherwise provide, each share of a corporation entitles the holder thereof to one vote at a meeting of shareholders.

(2) Representative. — If a body corporate or association is a shareholder of a corporation, the corporation shall recognize any individual authorized by a resolution of the directors or governing body of the body corporate or association to represent it at meetings of shareholders of the corporation.

(3) Powers of representative. — An individual authorized under subsection (2) may exercise on behalf of the body corporate or association he represents all the powers it could exercise if it were an individual shareholder.

(4) Joint shareholders. — Unless the by-laws otherwise provide, if two or more persons hold shares jointly, one of those holders present at a meeting of shareholders may in the absence of the others vote the shares, but if two or more of those persons who are present, in person or by proxy, vote, they shall vote as one on the shares jointly held by them.

141. (1) Voting. — Unless the by-laws otherwise provide, voting at a meeting of shareholders shall be by show of hands except where a ballot is demanded by a shareholder or proxyholder entitled to vote at the meeting.

(2) Ballot. — A shareholder or proxyholder may demand a ballot either before or after any vote by show of hands.

142. (1) Resolution in lieu of meeting. — Except where a written statement is submitted by a director under subsection 110(2) or by an auditor under subsection 168(5),

(a) a resolution in writing signed by all the shareholders entitled to vote on that resolution at a meeting of shareholders is as valid as if it had been passed at a meeting of the shareholders; and

(b) a resolution in writing dealing with all matters required by this Act to be dealt with at a meeting of shareholders, and signed by all the shareholders entitled to vote at that meeting, satisfies all the requirements of this Act relating to meetings of shareholders.

(2) Filing resolution. — A copy of every resolution referred to in subsection (1) shall be kept with the minutes of the meetings of shareholders.

143. (1) Requisition of meeting. — The holders of not less than five per cent of the issued shares of a corporation that carry the right to vote at the meeting sought to be held may requisition the directors to call a meeting of shareholders for the purposes stated in the requisition.

(2) Form. — The requisition referred to in subsection (1), which may consist of several documents of like form each signed by one or more shareholders, shall state the business to be transacted at the meeting and shall be sent to each director and to the registered office of the corporation.

(3) Directors calling meeting. — On receiving the requisition referred to in subsection (1), the directors shall call a meeting of shareholders to transact the business stated in the requisition, unless

(a) a record date has been fixed under subsection 134(2) and notice thereof has been given under subsection 134(4);

(b) the directors have called a meeting of shareholders and have given notice thereof under section 135; or

(c) the business of the meeting as stated in the requisition includes matters described in paragraphs 137(5)(b) to (e).

(4) Shareholder calling meeting. — If the directors do not within twenty-one days after receiving the requisition referred to in subsection (1) call a meeting, any shareholder who signed the requisition may call the meeting.

(5) Procedure. — A meeting called under this section shall be called as nearly as possible in the manner in which meetings are to be called pursuant to the by-laws, this Part and Part XIII.

(6) Reimbursement. — Unless the shareholders otherwise resolve at a meeting called under subsection (4), the corporation shall reimburse the shareholders the expenses reasonably incurred by them in requisitioning, calling and holding the meeting.

144. (1) Meeting called by court. — If for any reason it is impracticable to call a meeting of shareholders of a corporation in the manner in which meetings of those shareholders may be called, or to conduct the meeting in the manner prescribed by the by-laws and this Act, or if for any other reason a court thinks fit, the court, on the application of a director, a shareholder entitled to vote at the meeting or the Director, may order a meeting to be called, held and conducted in such manner as the court directs.

(2) Varying quorum. — Without restricting the generality of subsection (1), the court may order that the quorum required by the by-laws or this Act be varied or dispensed with at a meeting called, held and conducted pursuant to this section.

(3) Valid meeting. — A meeting called, held and conducted pursuant to this section is for all purposes a meeting of shareholders of the corporation duly called, held and conducted.

145. (1) Court review of election. — A corporation or a shareholder or director may apply to a court to determine any controversy with respect to an election or appointment of a director or auditor of the corporation.

(2) Powers of court. — On an application under this section, the court may make any order it thinks fit including, without limiting the generality of the foregoing:

(a) an order restraining a director or auditor whose election or appointment is challenged from acting pending determination of the dispute;

(b) an order declaring the result of the disputed election or appointment;

(c) an order requiring a new election or appointment, and including in the order directions for the management of the business and affairs of the corporation until a new election is held or appointment made; and

(d) an order determining the voting rights of shareholders and of persons claiming to own shares.

146. (1) Pooling agreement. — A written agreement between two or more shareholders may provide that in exercising voting rights the shares held by them shall be voted as therein provided.

(2) Unanimous shareholder agreement. — An otherwise lawful written agreement among all the shareholders of a corporation, or among all the shareholders and a person who is not a shareholder, that restricts, in whole or in part, the powers of the directors to manage the business and affairs of the corporation is valid.

(3) Declaration by single shareholder. — Where a person who is the beneficial owner of all the issued shares of a corporation makes a written declaration that restricts in whole or in part the powers of the directors to manage the business and affairs of a corporation, the declaration is deemed to be a unanimous shareholder agreement.

(4) Constructive party. — Subject to subsection 49(8), a transferee of shares subject to a unanimous shareholder agreement is deemed to be a party to the agreement.

(5) Rights of shareholder. — A shareholder who is a party to a unanimous shareholder agreement has all the rights, powers and duties of a director of the corporation to which the agreement relates to the extent that the agreement restricts the powers of the directors to manage the business and affairs of the corporation, and the directors are thereby relieved of their duties and liabilities, including any liabilities under section 119, to the same extent.

PART XIII
PROXIES

147. Definitions. — In this Part,

"form of proxy". — "form of proxy" means a written or printed form that, on completion and execution by or on behalf of a shareholder, becomes a proxy;

"proxy". — "proxy" means a completed and executed form of proxy by means of which a shareholder appoints a proxyholder to attend and act on his behalf at a meeting of shareholders;

"registrant". — "registrant" means a securities broker or dealer required to be registered to trade or deal in securities under the laws of any jurisdiction;

"solicit" or "solicitation". — "solicit" or "solicitation" includes

(a) a request for a proxy whether or not accompanied by or included in a form of proxy,

(b) a request to execute or not to execute a form of proxy or to revoke a proxy,

(c) the sending of a form of proxy or other communication to a shareholder under circumstances reasonably calculated to result in the procurement, withholding or revocation of a proxy, and

(d) the sending of a form of proxy to a shareholder under section 149, but does not include

(e) the sending of a form of proxy in response to an unsolicited request made by or on behalf of a shareholder,

(f) the performance of administrative acts or professional services on behalf of a person soliciting a proxy,

(g) the sending by a registrant of the documents referred to in section 153, or

(h) a solicitation by a person in respect of shares of which he is the beneficial owner;

"solicitation by or on behalf of the management of a corporation". — "solicitation by or on behalf of the management of a corporation" means a solicitation by any person pursuant to a resolution or instructions of, or with the acquiescence of, the directors or a committee of the directors.

148. (1) Appointing proxyholder. — A shareholder entitled to vote at a meeting of shareholders may by means of a proxy appoint a proxyholder or one or more alternate proxyholders, who are not required to be shareholders, to attend and act at the meeting in the manner and to the extent authorized by the proxy and with the authority conferred by the proxy.

(2) Execution of proxy. — A proxy shall be executed by the shareholder or by his attorney authorized in writing.

(3) Validity of proxy. — A proxy is valid only at the meeting in respect of which it is given or any adjournment thereof.

(4) Revocation of proxy. — A shareholder may revoke a proxy

(a) by depositing an instrument in writing executed by him or by his attorney authorized in writing

(i) at the registered office of the corporation at any time up to and including the last business day preceding the day of the meeting, or an adjournment thereof, at which the proxy is to be used, or

(ii) with the chairman of the meeting on the day of the meeting or an adjournment thereof; or

(b) in any other manner permitted by law.

(5) Deposit of proxies. — The directors may specify in a notice calling a meeting of shareholders a time not exceeding forty-eight hours, excluding Saturdays and holidays, preceding the meeting or an adjournment thereof before which time proxies to be used at the meeting must be deposited with the corporation or its agent.

149. (1) Mandatory solicitation. — Subject to subsection (2), the management of a corporation shall, concurrently with giving notice of a meeting of shareholders, send a form of proxy in prescribed form to each shareholder who is entitled to receive notice of the meeting.

(2) Exception. — Where a corporation has fewer than fifteen shareholders, two or more joint holders being counted as one shareholder, the management of the corporation is not required to send a form of proxy under subsection (1).

(3) Offence. — If the management of a corporation fails to comply, without reasonable cause, with subsection (1), the corporation is guilty of an offence and liable on summary conviction to a fine not exceeding five thousand dollars.

(4) Officers, etc., of corporations. — Where a corporation commits an offence under subsection (3), any director or officer of the corporation who knowingly authorized, permitted or acquiesced in the commission of the offence is a party to and guilty of the offence and is liable on summary conviction to a fine not exceeding five thousand dollars or to imprisonment for a term not exceeding six months or to both, whether or not the corporation has been prosecuted or convicted.

150. (1) Soliciting proxies. — A person shall not solicit proxies unless

(a) in the case of solicitation by or on behalf of the management of a corporation, a management proxy circular in prescribed form, either as an appendix to or as a separate document accompanying the notice of the meeting, or

(b) in the case of any other solicitation, a dissident's proxy circular in prescribed form stating the purposes of the solicitation is sent to the auditor of the corporation, to each shareholder whose proxy is solicited, to each director and, if paragraph (b) applies, to the corporation.

(2) Copy to Director. — A person required to send a management proxy circular or dissident's proxy circular shall send concurrently a copy thereof to the Director together with a statement in prescribed form, a copy of the notice of meeting, the form of proxy and any other documents for use in connection with the meeting.

[Subsecs. (1) and (2) repealed and substituted by S. C. 1992, c. 1, s. 54.]

(3) Offence. — A person who fails to comply with subsections (1) and (2) is guilty of an offence and liable on summary conviction to a fine not exceeding five thousand dollars or to imprisonment for a term not exceeding six months or to both, whether or not the body corporate has been prosecuted or convicted.

(4) Officers, etc., of body corporate. — Where a body corporate commits an offence under subsection (3), any director or officer of the body corporate who knowingly authorized, permitted or acquiesced in the commission of the offence is a party to and guilty of the offence and is liable on summary conviction to a fine not exceeding five thousand dollars or to imprisonment for a term not exceeding six months or to both, whether or not the body corporate has been prosecuted or convicted.

151. (1) Exemption order. — On the application of an interested person, the Director may make an order on such terms as he thinks fit exempting such person from any of the requirements of section 149 or subsection 150(1), which order may have retrospective effect.

(2) Publication. — The Director shall set out in the periodical referred to in section 129 the particulars of exemptions granted under this section together with the reasons therefor.

152. (1) Attendance at meeting. — A person who solicits a proxy and is appointed proxyholder shall attend in person or cause an alternate proxyholder to attend the meeting in respect of which the proxy is given and comply with the directions of the shareholder who appointed him.

(2) Right of a proxyholder. — A proxyholder or an alternate proxyholder has the same rights as the shareholder who appointed him to speak at a meeting of shareholders in respect of any matter, to vote by way of ballot at the meeting and, except where a proxyholder or an alternate proxyholder has conflicting instructions from more than one shareholder, to vote at such a meeting in respect of any matter by way of any show of hands.

(3) Idem. — Notwithstanding subsections (1) and (2), where the chairman of a meeting of shareholders declares to the meeting that, if a ballot is conducted, the total number of votes attached to shares represented at the meeting by proxy required to be voted against what to his knowledge will be the decision of the meeting in relation to any matter or group of matters is less than five per cent

of all the votes that might be cast at the meeting on such ballot, unless a shareholder or proxyholder demands a ballot,

(a) the chairman may conduct the vote in respect of that matter or group of matters by a show of hands; and

(b) a proxyholder or alternate proxyholder may vote in respect of that matter or group of matters by a show of hands.

(4) Offence. — A proxyholder or alternate proxyholder who without reasonable cause fails to comply with the directions of a shareholder under this section is guilty of an offence and liable on summary conviction to a fine not exceeding five thousand dollars or to imprisonment for a term not exceeding six months or to both.

153. (1) Duty of registrant. — Shares of a corporation that are registered in the name of a registrant or his nominee and not beneficially owned by the registrant shall not be voted unless the registrant, forthwith after receipt of the notice of the meeting, financial statements, management proxy circular, dissident's proxy circular and any other documents other than the form of proxy sent to shareholders by or on behalf of any person for use in connection with the meeting, sends a copy thereof to the beneficial owner and, except where the registrant has received written voting instructions from the beneficial owner, a written request for such instructions.

(2) Beneficial owner unknown. — A registrant shall not vote or appoint a proxyholder to vote shares registered in his name or in the name of his nominee that he does not beneficially own unless he receives voting instructions from the beneficial owner.

(3) Copies. — A person by or on behalf of whom a solicitation is made shall, at the request of a registrant, forthwith furnish the registrant at that person's expense with the necessary number of copies of the documents referred to in subsection (1) other than copies of the document requesting voting instructions.

(4) Instructions to registrant. — A registrant shall vote or appoint a proxyholder to vote any shares referred to in subsection (1) in accordance with any written voting instructions received from the beneficial owner.

(5) Beneficial owner as proxyholder. — If requested by a beneficial owner, a registrant shall appoint the beneficial owner or a nominee of the beneficial owner as proxyholder.

(6) Validity. — The failure of a registrant to comply with this section does not render void any meeting of shareholders or any action taken thereat.

(7) Limitation. — Nothing in this section gives a registrant the right to vote shares that he is otherwise prohibited from voting.

(8) Offence. — A registrant who knowingly fails to comply with this section is guilty of an offence and liable on summary conviction to a fine not exceeding

five thousand dollars or to imprisonment for a term not exceeding six months or to both.

(9) Officers, etc., of bodies corporate. — Where a registrant who is a body corporate commits an offence under subsection (8), any director or officer of the body corporate who knowingly authorized, permitted or acquiesced in the commission of the offence is a party to and guilty of the offence and is liable on summary conviction to a fine not exceeding five thousand dollars or to imprisonment for a term not exceeding six months or to both, whether or not the body corporate has been prosecuted or convicted.

154. (1) Restraining order. — If a form of proxy, management proxy circular or dissident's proxy circular contains an untrue statement of a material fact or omits to state a material fact required therein or necessary to make a statement contained therein not misleading in the light of the circumstances in which it was made, an interested person or the Director may apply to a court and the court may make any order it thinks fit including, without limiting the generality of the foregoing,

(a) an order restraining the solicitation, the holding of the meeting, or any person from implementing or acting on any resolution passed at the meeting to which the form of proxy, management proxy circular or dissident's proxy circular relates;

(b) an order requiring correction of any form of proxy or proxy circular and a further solicitation; and

(c) an order adjourning the meeting.

(2) Notice to Director. — An applicant under this section shall give to the Director notice of the application and the Director is entitled to appear and to be heard in person or by counsel.

PART XIV
FINANCIAL DISCLOSURE

155. (1) Annual financial statements. — Subject to section 156, the directors of a corporation shall place before the shareholders at every annual meeting

(a) comparative financial statements as prescribed relating separately to

(i) the period that began on the date the corporation came into existence and ended not more than six months before the annual meeting or, if the corporation has completed a financial year, the period that began immediately after the end of the last completed financial year and ended not more than six months before the annual meeting, and

(ii) the immediately preceding financial year;

(b) the report of the auditor, if any; and

(c) any further information respecting the financial position of the corporation and the results of its operations required by the articles, the by-laws or any unanimous shareholder agreement.

(2) Exception. — Notwithstanding paragraph (1)(a), the financial statements referred to in subparagraph (1)(a)(ii) may be omitted if the reason for the omission is set out in the financial statements, or in a note thereto, to be placed before the shareholders at an annual meeting.

156. Exemption. — A corporation may apply to the Director for an order authorizing the corporation to omit from its financial statements any item prescribed, or to dispense with the publication of any particular financial statement prescribed, and the Director may, if he reasonably believes that disclosure of the information therein contained would be detrimental to the corporation, permit such omission on such reasonable conditions as he thinks fit.

157. (1) Consolidated statements. — A corporation shall keep at its registered office a copy of the financial statements of each of its subsidiary bodies corporate and of each body corporate the accounts of which are consolidated in the financial statements of the corporation.

(2) Examination. — Shareholders of a corporation and their agents and legal representatives may on request therefor examine the statements referred to in subsection (1) during the usual business hours of the corporation and may make extracts therefrom free of charge.

(3) Barring examination. — A corporation may, within fifteen days of a request to examine under subsection (2), apply to a court for an order barring the right of any person to so examine, and the court may, if it is satisfied that such examination would be detrimental to the corporation or a subsidiary body corporate, bar such right and make any further order it thinks fit.

(4) Notice to Director. — A corporation shall give the Director and the person asking to examine under subsection (2) notice of an application under subsection (3), and the Director and such person may appear and be heard in person or by counsel.

158. (1) Approval of financial statements. — The directors of a corporation shall approve the financial statements referred to in section 155 and the approval shall be evidenced by the signature of one or more directors.

(2) Condition precedent. — A corporation shall not issue, publish or circulate copies of the financial statements referred to in section 155 unless the financial statements are

(a) approved and signed in accordance with subsection (1); and

(b) accompanied by the report of the auditor of the corporation, if any.

159. (1) Copies to shareholders. — A corporation shall, not less than twenty-one days before each annual meeting of shareholders or before the signing of a resolution under paragraph 142(1)(b) in lieu of the annual meeting, send a

copy of the documents referred to in section 155 to each shareholder, except to a shareholder who has informed the corporation in writing that he does not want a copy of those documents.

(2) Offence. — A corporation that, without reasonable cause, fails to comply with subsection (1) is guilty of an offence and liable on summary conviction to a fine not exceeding five thousand dollars.

160. (1) Copies to Director. — A corporation

(a) any of the securities of which are or were part of a distribution to the public, remain outstanding and are held by more than one person, or

(b) the gross revenues of which, as shown in the most recent financial statements referred to in section 155, exceed ten million dollars or the assets of which as shown in those financial statements exceed five million dollars

shall, not less than twenty-one days before each annual meeting of shareholders or forthwith after the signing of a resolution under paragraph 142(1)(b) in lieu of the annual meeting, and in any event not later than fifteen months after the last date when the last preceding annual meeting should have been held or a resolution in lieu of the meeting should have been signed, send a copy of the documents referred to in section 155 to the Director.

(2) Affiliates. — For the purposes of paragraph (1)(b), the gross revenues and assets of the corporation include the gross revenues and assets of its affiliates.

(3) Exemption. — On the application of a corporation, the Director may make an order on such reasonable conditions as the Director thinks fit exempting the corporation from the application of subsection (2) in such circumstances as may be prescribed.

[Subsec. (3) repealed and substituted by S.C. 1992, c. 1, s. 55.]

(4) Further disclosure. — If a corporation referred to in subsection (1)

(a) sends to its shareholders, or

(b) is required to file with or send to a public authority or a stock exchange

interim financial statements or related documents, the corporation shall forthwith send copies thereof to the Director.

(5) Subsidiary corporation exemption. — A subsidiary corporation is not required to comply with this section if

(a) the financial statements of its holding corporation are in consolidated or combined form and include the accounts of the subsidiary; and

(b) the consolidated or combined financial statements of the holding corporation are included in the documents sent to the Director by the holding corporation in compliance with this section.

(6) Offence. — A corporation that fails to comply with this section is guilty of an offence and liable on summary conviction to a fine not exceeding five thousand dollars.

161. (1) Qualification of auditor. — Subject to subsection (5), a person is disqualified from being an auditor of a corporation if he is not independent of the corporation, any of its affiliates, or the directors or officers of any such corporation or its affiliates.

(2) Independence. — For the purposes of this section,

(a) independence is a question of fact; and

(b) a person is deemed not to be independent if he or his business partner

(i) is a business partner, a director, an officer or an employee of the corporation or any of its affiliates, or a business partner of any director, officer or employee of any such corporation or any of its affiliates,

(ii) beneficially owns or controls, directly or indirectly, a material interest in the securities of the corporation or any of its affiliates, or

(iii) has been a receiver, receiver-manager, liquidator or trustee in bankruptcy of the corporation or any of its affiliates within two years of his proposed appointment as auditor of the corporation.

(3) Duty to resign. — An auditor who becomes disqualified under this section shall, subject to subsection (5), resign forthwith after becoming aware of his disqualification.

(4) Disqualification order. — An interested person may apply to a court for an order declaring an auditor to be disqualified under this section and the office of auditor to be vacant.

(5) Exemption order. — An interested person may apply to a court for an order exempting an auditor from disqualification under this section and the court may, if it is satisfied that an exemption would not unfairly prejudice the shareholders, make an exemption order on such terms as it thinks fit, which order may have retrospective effect.

162. (1) Appointment of auditor. — Subject to section 163, shareholders of a corporation shall, by ordinary resolution, at the first annual meeting of shareholders and at each succeeding annual meeting, appoint an auditor to hold office until the close of the next annual meeting.

(2) Eligibility. — An auditor appointed under section 104 is eligible for appointment under subsection (1).

(3) Incumbent auditor. — Notwithstanding subsection (1), if an auditor is not appointed at a meeting of shareholders, the incumbent auditor continues in office until a successor is appointed.

(4) Remuneration. — The remuneration of an auditor may be fixed by ordinary resolution of the shareholders or, if not so fixed, may be fixed by the directors.

163. (1) Dispensing with auditor. — The shareholders of a corporation that is not required to comply with section 160 may resolve not to appoint an auditor.

(2) Limitation. — A resolution under subsection (1) is valid only until the next succeeding annual meeting of shareholders.

(3) Unanimous consent. — A resolution under subsection (1) is not valid unless it is consented to by all the shareholders, including shareholders not otherwise entitled to vote.

(4) Exemption from appointing auditor. — On the application of a corporation that is a wholly-owned subsidiary of a holding body corporate, the Director may make an order on such reasonable conditions as the Director thinks fit exempting the corporation from appointing an auditor in such circumstances as may be prescribed.

[Subsec. (4) repealed and substituted by S.C. 1991, c. 1, s. 56.]

164. (1) Ceasing to hold office. — An auditor of a corporation ceases to hold office when

(a) he dies or resigns; or

(b) he is removed pursuant to section 165.

(2) Effective date of resignation. — A resignation of an auditor becomes effective at the time a written resignation is sent to the corporation, or at the time specified in the resignation, whichever is later.

165. (1) Removal of auditor. — The shareholders of a corporation may by ordinary resolution at a special meeting remove from office the auditor other than an auditor appointed by a court under section 167.

(2) Vacancy. — A vacancy created by the removal of an auditor may be filled at the meeting at which the auditor is removed or, if not so filled, may be filled under section 166.

166. (1) Filling vacancy. — Subject to subsection (3), the directors shall forthwith fill a vacancy in the office of auditor.

(2) Calling meeting. — If there is not a quorum of directors, the directors then in office shall, within twenty-one days after a vacancy in the office of auditor occurs, call a special meeting of shareholders to fill the vacancy and, if they fail to call a meeting or if there are no directors, the meeting may be called by any shareholder.

(3) Shareholders filling vacancy. — The articles of a corporation may provide that a vacancy in the office of auditor shall only be filled by vote of the shareholders.

(4) Unexpired term. — An auditor appointed to fill a vacancy holds office for the unexpired term of his predecessor.

167. (1) Court appointed auditor. — If a corporation does not have an auditor, the court may, on the application of a shareholder or the Director, appoint and fix the remuneration of an auditor who holds office until an auditor is appointed by the shareholders.

(2) Exception. — Subsection (1) does not apply if the shareholders have resolved under section 163 not to appoint an auditor.

168. (1) Right to attend meeting. — The auditor of a corporation is entitled to receive notice of every meeting of shareholders and, at the expense of the corporation, to attend and be heard thereat on matters relating to his duties as auditor.

(2) Duty to attend. — If a director or shareholder of a corporation, whether or not the shareholder is entitled to vote at the meeting, gives written notice not less than ten days before a meeting of shareholders to the auditor or a former auditor of the corporation, the auditor or former auditor shall attend the meeting at the expense of the corporation and answer questions relating to his duties as auditor.

(3) Notice to corporation. — A director or shareholder who sends a notice referred to in subsection (2) shall send concurrently a copy of the notice to the corporation.

(4) Offence. — An auditor or former auditor of a corporation who fails without reasonable cause to comply with subsection (2) is guilty of an offence and liable on summary conviction to a fine not exceeding five thousand dollars or to imprisonment for a term not exceeding six months or to both.

(5) Statement of auditor. — An auditor who

(a) resigns,

(b) receives a notice or otherwise learns of a meeting of shareholders called for the purpose of removing him from office,

(c) receives a notice or otherwise learns of a meeting of directors or shareholders at which another person is to be appointed to fill the office of auditor, whether because of the resignation or removal of the incumbent auditor or because his term of office has expired or is about to expire, or

(d) receives a notice or otherwise learns of a meeting of shareholders at which a resolution referred to in section 163 is to be proposed,

is entitled to submit to the corporation a written statement giving the reasons for his resignation or the reasons why he opposes any proposed action or resolution.

(6) Circulating statement. — The corporation shall forthwith send a copy

of the statement referred to in subsection (5) to every shareholder entitled to receive notice of any meeting referred to in subsection (1) and to the Director unless the statement is included in or attached to a management proxy circular required by section 150.

(7) Replacing auditor. — No person shall accept appointment or consent to be appointed as auditor of a corporation if he is replacing an auditor who has resigned, been removed or whose term of office has expired or is about to expire until he has requested and received from that auditor a written statement of the circumstances and the reasons why, in that auditor's opinion, he is to be replaced.

(8) Exception. — Notwithstanding subsection (7), a person otherwise qualified may accept appointment or consent to be appointed as auditor of a corporation if, within fifteen days after making the request referred to in that subsection, he does not receive a reply.

(9) Effect of non-compliance. — Unless subsection (8) applies, an appointment as auditor of a corporation of a person who has not complied with subsection (7) is void.

169. (1) Examination. — An auditor of a corporation shall make the examination that is in his opinion necessary to enable him to report in the prescribed manner on the financial statements required by this Act to be placed before the shareholders, except such financial statements or part thereof that relate to the period referred to in subparagraph 155(1)(a)(ii).

(2) Reliance on other auditor. — Notwithstanding section 170, an auditor of a corporation may reasonably rely on the report of an auditor of a body corporate or an unincorporated business the accounts of which are included in whole or in part in the financial statements of the corporation.

(3) Reasonableness. — For the purpose of subsection (2), reasonableness is a question of fact.

(4) Application. — Subsection (2) applies whether or not the financial statements of the holding corporation reported on by the auditor are in consolidated form.

170. (1) Right to information. — On the demand of an auditor of a corporation, the present or former directors, officers, employees or agents of the corporation shall furnish such

(a) information and explanations, and

(b) access to records, documents, books, accounts and vouchers of the corporation or any of its subsidiaries

as are, in the opinion of the auditor, necessary to enable him to make the examination and report required under section 169 and that the directors, officers, employees or agents are reasonably able to furnish.

(2) Idem. — On the demand of the auditor of a corporation, the directors of the corporation shall

(a) obtain from the present or former directors, officers, employees and agents of any subsidiary of the corporation the information and explanations that the present or former directors, officers, employees and agents are reasonably able to furnish and that are, in the opinion of the auditor, necessary to enable him to make the examination and report required under section 169; and

(b) furnish the auditor with the information and explanations so obtained.

171. (1) Audit committee. — Subject to subsection (2), a corporation described in subsection 102(2) shall, and any other other corporation may, have an audit committee composed of not less than three directors of the corporation, a majority of whom are not officers or employees of the corporation or any of its affiliates.

(2) Exemption. — A corporation may apply to the Director for an order authorizing the corporation to dispense with an audit committee, and the Director may, if he is satisfied that the shareholders will not be prejudiced by such an order, permit the corporation to dispense with an audit committee on such reasonable conditions as he thinks fit.

(3) Duty of committee. — An audit committee shall review the financial statements of the corporation before such financial statements are approved under section 158.

(4) Auditor's attendance. — The auditor of a corporation is entitled to receive notice of every meeting of the audit committee and, at the expense of the corporation, to attend and be heard thereat; and, if so requested by a member of the audit committee, shall attend every meeting of the committee held during the term of office of the auditor.

(5) Calling meeting. — The auditor of a corporation or a member of the audit committee may call a meeting of the committee.

(6) Notice of errors. — A director or an officer of a corporation shall forthwith notify the audit committee and the auditor of any error or mis-statement of which he becomes aware in a finanical statement that the auditor or a former auditor has reported upon.

(7) Error in financial statements. — If the auditor or former auditor of a corporation is notified or becomes aware of an error or mis-statement in a financial statement on which he has reported, and if in his opinion the error or mis-statement is material, he shall inform each director accordingly.

(8) Duty of directors. — When under subsection (7) the auditor or former

auditor informs the directors of an error or mis-statement in a financial statement, the directors shall

(a) prepare and issue revised financial statements; or

(b) otherwise inform the shareholders and, if the corporation is one that is required to comply with section 160, it shall inform the Director of the error or mis-statement in the same manner as it informs the shareholders.

(9) Offence. — Every director or officer of a corporation who knowingly fails to comply with subsection (6) or (8) is guilty of an offence and liable on summary conviction to a fine not exceeding five thousand dollars or to imprisonment for a term not exceeding six months or to both.

172. Qualified privilege (defamation). — Any oral or written statement or report made under this Act by the auditor or former auditor of a corporation has qualified privilege.

PART XV
FUNDAMENTAL CHANGES

173. (1) Amendment of articles. — Subject to sections 176 and 177, the articles of a corporation may by special resolution be amended to

(a) change its name;

(b) change the place in which its registered office is situated;

(c) add, change or remove any restriction on the business or businesses that the corporation may carry on;

(d) change any maximum number of shares that the corporation is authorized to issue;

(e) create new classes of shares;

(f) reduce or increase its stated capital which, for the purposes of the amendment, is deemed to be set out in the articles;

(g) change the designation of all or any of its shares, and add, change or remove any rights, privileges, restrictions and conditions, including rights to accrued dividends, in respect of all or any of its shares, whether issued or unissued;

(h) change the shares of any class or series, whether issued or unissued, into a different number of shares of the same class or series or into the same or a different number of shares of other classes or series;

(i) divide a class of shares, whether issued or unissued, into series and fix the number of shares in each series and the rights, privileges, restrictions and conditions thereof;

(j) authorize the directors to divide any class of unissued shares into series and fix the number of shares in each series and the rights, privileges, restrictions and conditions thereof;

(k) authorize the directors to change the rights, privileges, restrictions and conditions attached to unissued shares of any series;

(l) revoke, diminish or enlarge any authority conferred under paragraphs (j) and (k);

(m) increase or decrease the number of directors or the minimum or maximum number of directors, subject to sections 107 and 112;

(n) add, change or remove restrictions on the issue, transfer or ownership of shares; or

(o) add, change or remove any other provision that is permitted by this Act to be set out in the articles.

(2) Termination. — The directors of a corporation may, if authorized by the shareholders in the special resolution effecting an amendment under this section, revoke the resolution before it is acted on without further approval of the shareholders.

(3) Amendment of number name. — Notwithstanding subsection (1), where a corporation has a designating number as a name, the directors may amend its articles to change that name to a verbal name.

174. (1) Constraints on shares. — Subject to sections 176 and 177, a corporation any of the issued shares of which are or were part of a distribution to the public and remain outstanding and are held by more than one person may by special resolution amend its articles in accordance with the regulations to constrain

(a) the issue or transfer of shares of any class or series to persons who are not resident Canadians;

(b) the issue or transfer of shares of any class or series to enable the corporation or any of its affiliates or associates to qualify under any prescribed law of Canada or a province

(i) to obtain a licence to carry on any business,

(ii) to become a publisher of a Canadian newspaper or periodical, or

(iii) to acquire shares of a financial intermediary as defined in the regulations;

(c) the issue, transfer or ownership of shares of any class or series in order to assist the corporation or any of its affiliates or associates to qualify under any prescribed law of Canada or a province to receive licences, permits, grants, payments or other benefits by reason of attaining or maintaining a specified level of Canadian ownership or control; or

(d) the issue, transfer or ownership of shares of any class or series in order to assist the corporation to comply with

(i) section 379 of the *Trust and Loan Companies Act*, or

(ii) section 411 of the *Insurance Companies Act.*

[Subsec. (1) amended by striking out the word "or" at the end of para. (b), by adding the word "or" at the end of para. (c) and by adding para. (d) by S.C. 1991, c. 45, s. 554 and S.C. 1991, c. 47, s. 722(1); para. (d) substituted and replaced by S.C. 1991, c. 47, s. 722(2).]

(2) Exception in respect of paragraph (1)(c). — Paragraph (1)(c) does not permit a constraint on the issue, transfer or ownership of shares of any class or series of which any shares are outstanding unless

(a) in the case of a constraint in respect of a class, the shares of the class, or

(b) in the case of a constraint in respect of a series, the shares of the series

are already subject to a constraint permitted under that paragraph.

(3) Limitation on ownership of shares. — A corporation may, pursuant to paragraph (1)(c), limit the number of shares of that corporation that may be owned, or prohibit the ownership of shares, by any person whose ownership would adversely affect the ability of the corporation or any of its affiliates or associates to attain or maintain a level of Canadian ownership or control specified in its articles that equals or exceeds a specified level referred to in paragraph (1)(c).

(4) Change or removal of constraint. — A corporation referred to in subsection (1) may by special resolution amend its articles to change or remove any constraint on the issue, transfer or ownership of its shares.

(5) Termination. — The directors of a corporation may, if authorized by the shareholders in the special resolution effecting an amendment under subsection (1) or (4), revoke the resolution before it is acted on without further approval of the shareholders.

(6) Regulations. — Subject to subsections 261(2) and (3), the Governor in Council may make regulations with respect to a corporation that constrains the issue, transfer or ownership of its shares prescribing

(a) the disclosure required of the constraints in documents issued or published by the corporation;

(b) the duties and powers of the directors to refuse to issue or register transfers of shares in accordance with the articles of the corporation;

(c) the limitations on voting rights of any shares held contrary to the articles of the corporation;

(d) the powers of the directors to require disclosure of beneficial ownership of shares of the corporation and the right of the corporation and its directors, employees and agents to rely on such disclosure and the effects of such reliance; and

(e) the rights of any person owning shares of the corporation at the time of an amendment to its articles constraining share issues or transfers.

(7) Validity of acts. — An issue or a transfer of a share or an act of a corporation is valid notwithstanding any failure to comply with this section or the regulations.

175. (1) Proposal to amend. — Subject to subsection (2), a director or a shareholder who is entitled to vote at an annual meeting of shareholders may, in accordance with section 137, make a proposal to amend the articles.

(2) Notice of amendment. — Notice of a meeting of shareholders at which a proposal to amend the articles is to be considered shall set out the proposed amendment and, where applicable, shall state that a dissenting shareholder is entitled to be paid the fair value of his shares in accordance with section 190, but failure to make that statement does not invalidate an amendment.

176. (1) Class vote. — The holder of shares of a class or, subject to subsection (4), of a series are, unless the articles otherwise provide in the case of an amendment referred to in paragraphs (a), (b) and (e), entitled to vote separately as a class or series on a proposal to amend the articles to

(a) increase or decrease any maximum number of authorized shares of such class, or increase any maximum number of authorized shares of a class having rights or privileges equal or superior to the shares of such class;

(b) effect an exchange, reclassification or cancellation of all or part of the shares of such class;

(c) add, change or remove the rights, privileges, restrictions or conditions attached to the shares of such class and, without limiting the generality of the foregoing,

(i) remove or change prejudicially rights to accrued dividends or rights to cumulative dividends,

(ii) add, remove or change prejudicially redemption rights,

(iii) reduce or remove a dividend preference or a liquidation preference, or

(iv) add, remove or change prejudicially conversion privileges, options, voting, transfer or pre-emptive rights, or rights to acquire securities of a corporation, or sinking fund provisions;

(d) increase the rights or privileges of any class of shares having rights or privileges equal or superior to the shares of such class;

(e) create a new class of shares equal or superior to the shares of such class;

(f) make any class of shares having rights or privileges inferior to the shares of such class equal or superior to the shares of such class;

(g) effect an exchange or create a right of exchange of all or part of the shares of another class into the shares of such class; or

(h) constrain the issue, transfer or ownership of the shares of such class or change or remove such constraint.

(2) Exception. — Subsection (1) does not apply in respect of a proposal to amend the articles to add a right or privilege for a holder to convert shares of a class or series into shares of another class or series that is subject to a constraint permitted under paragraph 174(1)(c) but is otherwise equal to the class or series first mentioned.

(3) Deeming provision. — For the purpose of paragraph (1)(e), a new class of shares, the issue, transfer or ownership of which is to be constrained by an amendment to the articles pursuant to paragraph 174(1)(c), that is otherwise equal to an existing class of shares shall be deemed not to be equal or superior to the existing class of shares.

(4) Limitation. — The holders of a series of shares of a class are entitled to vote separately as a series under subsection (1) only if such series is affected by an amendment in a manner different from other shares of the same class.

(5) Right to vote. — Subsection (1) applies whether or not shares of a class or series otherwise carry the right to vote.

(6) Separate resolutions. — A proposed amendment to the articles referred to in subsection (1) is adopted when the holders of the shares of each class or series entitled to vote separately thereon as a class or series have approved such amendment by a special resolution.

177. (1) Delivery of articles. — Subject to any revocation under subsection 173(2) or 174(5), after an amendment has been adopted under section 173, 174 or 176 articles of amendment in prescribed form shall be sent to the Director.

(2) Reduction of stated capital. — If an amendment effects or requires a reduction of stated capital, subsections 38(3) and (4) apply.

178. Certificate of amendment. — On receipt of articles of amendment, the Director shall issue a certificate of amendment in accordance with section 262.

179. (1) Effect of certificate. — An amendment becomes effective on the date shown in the certificate of amendment and the articles are amended accordingly.

(2) Rights preserved. — No amendment to the articles affects an existing cause of action or claim or liability to prosecution in favour of or against the

corporation or its directors or officers, or any civil, criminal or administrative action or proceeding to which a corporation or its directors or officers is a party.

180. (1) Restated articles. — The directors may at any time, and shall when reasonably so directed by the Director, restate the articles of incorporation as amended.

(2) Delivery of articles. — Restated articles of incorporation in prescribed form shall be sent to the Director.

(3) Restated certificate. — On receipt of restated articles of incorporation, the Director shall issue a restated certificate of incorporation in accordance with section 262.

(4) Effect of certificate. — Restated articles of incorporation are effective on the date shown in the restated certificate of incorporation and supersede the original articles of incorporation and all amendments thereto.

181. Amalgamation. — Two or more corporations, including holding and subsidiary corporations, may amalgamate and continue as one corporation.

182. (1) Amalgamation agreement. — Each corporation proposing to amalgamate shall enter into an agreement setting out the terms and means of effecting the amalgamation and, in particular, setting out

(a) the provisions that are required to be included in articles of incorporation under section 6;

(b) the name and address of each proposed director of the amalgamated corporation;

(c) the manner in which the shares of each amalgamating corporation are to be converted into shares or other securities of the amalgamated corporation;

(d) if any shares of an amalgamating corporation are not to be converted into securities of the amalgamated corporation, the amount of money or securities of any body corporate that the holders of such shares are to receive in addition to or instead of securities of the amalgamated corporation;

(e) the manner of payment of money instead of the issue of fractional shares of the amalgamated corporation or of any other body corporate the securities of which are to be received in the amalgamation;

(f) whether the by-laws of the amalgamated corporation are to be those of one of the amalgamating corporations and, if not, a copy of the proposed by-laws; and

(g) details of any arrangements necessary to perfect the amalgamation and to provide for the subsequent management and operation of the amalgamated corporation.

(2) Cancellation. — If shares of one of the amalgamating corporations are held by or on behalf of another of the amalgamating corporations, the amalgamation agreement shall provide for the cancellation of such shares when the amalgamation becomes effective without any repayment of capital in respect thereof, and no provision shall be made in the agreement for the conversion of such shares into shares of the amalgamated corporation.

183. (1) Shareholder approval. — The directors of each amalgamating corporation shall submit the amalgamation agreement for approval to a meeting of the holders of shares of the amalgamating corporation of which they are directors and, subject to subsection (4), to the holders of each class or series of such shares.

(2) Notice of meeting. — A notice of a meeting of shareholders complying with section 135 shall be sent in accordance with that section to each shareholder of each amalgamating corporation, and shall

(a) include or be accompanied by a copy or summary of the amalgamation agreement; and

(b) state that a dissenting shareholder is entitled to be paid the fair value of his shares in accordance with section 190, but failure to make that statement does not invalidate an amalgamation.

(3) Right to vote. — Each share of an amalgamating corporation carries the right to vote in respect of an amalgamation whether or not it otherwise carries the right to vote.

(4) Class vote. — The holders of shares of a class or series of shares of an amalgamating corporation are entitled to vote separately as a class or series in respect of an amalgamation if the amalgamation agreement contains a provision that, if contained in a proposed amendment to the articles, would entitle such holders to vote as a class or series under section 176.

(5) Shareholder approval. — Subject to subsection (4), an amalgamation agreement is adopted when the shareholders of each amalgamating corporation have approved of the amalgamation by special resolutions.

(6) Termination. — An amalgamation agreement may provide that at any time before the issue of a certificate of amalgamation the agreement may be terminated by the directors of an amalgamating corporation, notwithstanding approval of the agreement by the shareholders of all or any of the amalgamating corporations.

184. (1) Vertical short-form amalgamation. — A holding corporation and one or more of its wholly-owned subsidiary corporations may amalgamate and continue as one corporation without complying with sections 182 and 183 if

(a) the amalgamation is approved by a resolution of the directors of each amalgamating corporation; and

(b) the resolutions provide that

(i) the shares of each amalgamating subsidiary corporation shall be cancelled without any repayment of capital in respect thereof,

(ii) except as may be prescribed, the articles of amalgamation shall be the same as the articles of incorporation of the amalgamated holding corporation, and

(iii) no securities shall be issued by the amalgamated corporation in connection with the amalgamation.

(2) Horizontal short-form amalgamation. — Two or more wholly-owned subsidiary corporations of the same holding body corporate may amalgamate and continue as one corporation without complying with sections 182 and 183 if

(a) the amalgamation is approved by a resolution of the directors of each amalgamating corporation; and

(b) the resolutions provide that

(i) the shares of all but one of the amalgamating subsidiary corporations shall be cancelled without any repayment of capital in respect thereof,

(ii) except as may be prescribed, the articles of amalgamation shall be the same as the articles of incorporation of the amalgamating subsidiary corporation whose shares are not cancelled, and

(iii) the stated capital of the amalgamating subsidiary corporations whose shares are cancelled shall be added to the stated capital of the amalgamating subsidiary corporation whose shares are not cancelled.

185. (1) Sending of articles. — Subject to subsection 183(6), after an amalgamation has been adopted under section 183 or approved under section 184, articles of amalgamation in prescribed form shall be sent to the Director together with the documents required by sections 19 and 106.

(2) Attached declarations. — The articles of amalgamation shall have attached thereto a statutory declaration of a director or an officer of each amalgamating corporation that establishes to the satisfaction of the Director that

(a) there are reasonable grounds for believing that

(i) each amalgamating corporation is and the amalgamated corporation will be able to pay its liabilities as they become due, and

(ii) the realizable value of the amalgamated corporation's assets will not be less than the aggregate of its liabilities and stated capital of all classes; and

(b) there are reasonable grounds for believing that

(i) no creditor will be prejudiced by the amalgamation, or

(ii) adequate notice has been given to all known creditors of the amalgamating corporations and no creditor objects to the amalgamation otherwise than on grounds that are frivolous or vexatious.

(3) Adequate notice. — For the purposes of subsection (2), adequate notice is given if

(a) a notice in writing is sent to each known creditor having a claim against the corporation that exceeds one thousand dollars;

(b) a notice is published once in a newspaper published or distributed in the place where the corporation has its registered office and reasonable notice thereof is given in each province where the corporation carries on business; and

(c) each notice states that the corporation intends to amalgamate with one or more specified corporations in accordance with this Act and that a creditor of the corporation may object to the amalgamation within thirty days from the date of the notice.

(4) Certificate of amalgamation. — On receipt of articles of amalgamation, the Director shall issue a certificate of amalgamation in accordance with section 262.

186. Effect of certificate. — On the date shown in a certificate of amalgamation

(a) the amalgamation of the amalgamating corporations and their continuance as one corporation become effective;

(b) the property of each amalgamating corporation continues to be the property of the amalgamated corporation;

(c) the amalgamated corporation continues to be liable for the obligations of each amalgamating corporation;

(d) an existing cause of action, claim or liability to prosecution is unaffected;

(e) a civil, criminal or administrative action or proceeding pending by or against an amalgamating corporation may be continued to be prosecuted by or against the amalgamated corporation;

(f) a conviction against, or ruling, order or judgment in favour of or against, an amalgamating corporation may be enforced by or against the amalgamated corporation;

(g) the articles of amalgamation are deemed to be the articles of incorporation of the amalgamated corporation and the certificate of amalgamation is deemed to be the certificate of incorporation of the amalgamated corporation.

187. (1) Continuance (import). — A body corporate incorporated otherwise

than by or under an Act of Parliament may, if so authorized by the laws of the jurisdiction where it is incorporated, apply to the Director for a certificate of continuance.

(2) Amendments in articles of continuance. — A body corporate that applies for continuance under subsection (1) may, without so stating in its articles of continuance, effect by those articles any amendment to its Act of incorporation, articles, letters patent or memorandum or articles of association if the amendment is an amendment a corporation incorporated under this Act may make to its articles.

(3) Articles of continuance. — Articles of continuance in prescribed form shall be sent to the Director together with the documents required by sections 19 and 106.

(4) Certificate of continuance. — On receipt of articles of continuance, the Director shall issue a certificate of continuance in accordance with section 262.

(5) Effect of certificate. — On the date shown in the certificate of continuance

(a) the body corporate becomes a corporation to which this Act applies as if it had been incorporated under this Act;

(b) the articles of continuance are deemed to be the articles of incorporation of the continued corporation; and

(c) the certificate of continuance is deemed to be the certificate of incorporation of the continued corporation.

(6) Copy of certificate. — The Director shall forthwith send a copy of the certificate of continuance to the appropriate official or public body in the jurisdiction in which continuance under this Act was authorized.

(7) Rights preserved. — When a body corporate is continued as a corporation under this Act,

(a) the property of the body corporate continues to be the property of the corporation;

(b) the corporation continues to be liable for the obligations of the body corporate;

(c) an existing cause of action, claim or liability to prosecution is unaffected;

(d) a civil, criminal or administrative action or proceeding pending by or against the body corporate may be continued to be prosecuted by or against the corporation; and

(e) a conviction against, or ruling, order or judgment in favour of or against, the body corporate may be enforced by or against the corporation.

(8) Issued shares. — Subject to subsection 49(8), a share of a body corporate

issued before the body corporate was continued under this Act is deemed to have been issued in compliance with this Act and with the provisions of the articles of continuance irrespective of whether the share is fully paid and irrespective of any designation, rights, privileges, restrictions or conditions set out on or referred to in the certificate representing the share; and continuance under this section does not deprive a holder of any right or privilege that he claims under, or relieve him of any liability in respect of, an issued share.

(9) Exception in case of convertible shares. — Where a corporation continued under this Act had, before it was so continued, issued a share certificate in registered form that is convertible to bearer form, the corporation may, if a holder of such a share certificate exercises the conversion privilege attached thereto, issue a share certificate in bearer form for the same number of shares to the holder.

(10) Definition of "share". — For the purposes of subsections (8), and (9), "share" includes an instrument referred to in subsection 29(1), a share warrant as defined in the *Canada Corporations Act*, chapter C-32 of the Revised Statutes of Canada, 1970, or a like instrument.

(11) Where continued reference to par value shares permissible. — Where the Director determines, on the application of a body corporate, that it is not practicable to change a reference to the nominal or par value of shares of a class or series that the body corporate was authorized to issue before it was continued under this Act, the Director may, notwithstanding subsection 24(1), permit the body corporate to continue to refer in its articles to those shares, whether issued or unissued, as shares having a nominal or par value.

(12) Limitation. — A corporation shall set out in its articles the maximum number of shares of a class or series referred to in subsection (11) and may not amend its articles to increase that maximum number of shares or to change the nominal or par value of those shares.

188. (1) Continuance (export). — Subject to subsections (2) and (10), a corporation may, if it is authorized by the shareholders in accordance with this section, and if it establishes to the satisfaction of the Director that its proposed continuance in another jurisdiction or under the *Bank Act*, the *Trust and Loan Companies Act* or the *Insurance Companies Act* will not adversely affect creditors or shareholders of the corporation, apply to the appropriate official or public body of the other jurisdiction, or to the Minister of Finance, as the case may be, requesting that the corporation be continued as if it had been incorporated under the laws of that other jurisdiction or under the *Bank Act*, the *Trust and Loan Companies Act* or the *Insurance Companies Act*.

[Subsec. (1) repealed and substituted by S.C. 1991, c. 45, s. 555(1); repealed and substituted by S.C. 1991, c. 46, s. 596(1) and (2); repealed and substituted by S.C. 1991, c. 47, s. 723(1) and (2).]

(2) Continuance (export) of investment company. — A corporation to which

the *Investment Companies Act* applies shall not apply for continuance in another jurisdiction without the prior consent of the Minister of Finance.

(3) Notice of meeting. — A notice of a meeting of shareholders complying with section 135 shall be sent in accordance with that section to each shareholder and shall state that a dissenting shareholder is entitled to be paid the fair value of his shares in accordance with section 190, but failure to make that statement does not invalidate a discontinuance under this Act.

(4) Right to vote. — Each share of the corporation carries the right to vote in respect of a continuance whether or not it otherwise carries the right to vote.

(5) Shareholder approval. — An application for continuance becomes authorized when the shareholders voting thereon have approved of the continuance by a special resolution.

(6) Termination. — The directors of a corporation may, if authorized by the shareholders at the time of approving an application for continuance under this section, abandon the application without further approval of the shareholders.

(7) Discontinuance. — On receipt of notice satisfactory to the Director that the corporation has been continued under the laws of another jurisdiction or under the *Bank Act*, the *Trust and Loan Companies Act* or the *Insurance Companies Act*, the Director shall file the notice and issue a certificate of discontinuance in accordance with section 262.

[Subsec. (7) repealed and substituted by S.C. 1991, c. 45, s. 555(2); repealed and substituted by S.C. 1991, c. 46, s. 596(3) and (4); repealed and substituted by S.C. 1991, c. 47, s. 723(3) and (4).]

(8) Notice deemed to be articles. — For the purposes of section 262, a notice referred to in subsection (7) is deemed to be articles that are in the prescribed form.

(9) Rights preserved. — This Act ceases to apply to the corporation on the date shown in the certificate of discontinuance.

(10) Prohibition. — A corporation shall not be continued as a body corporate under the laws of another jurisdiction unless those laws provide in effect that

(a) the property of the corporation continues to be the property of the body corporate;

(b) the body corporate continues to be liable for the obligations of the corporation;

(c) an existing cause of action, claim or liability to prosecution is unaffected;

(d) a civil, criminal or administrative action or proceeding pending by or against the corporation may be continued to be prosecuted by or against the body corporate; and

(e) a conviction against, or ruling, order or judgment in favour of or against, the corporation may be enforced by or against the body corporate.

189. (1) Borrowing powers. — Unless the articles or by-laws of or a unanimous shareholder agreement relating to a corporation otherwise provide, the articles of a corporation are deemed to state that the directors of a corporation may, without authorization of the shareholders,

(a) borrow money on the credit of the corporation;

(b) issue, reissue, sell or pledge debt obligations of the corporation;

(c) subject to section 44, give a guarantee on behalf of the corporation to secure performance of an obligation of any person; and

(d) mortgage, hypothecate, pledge or otherwise create a security interest in all or any property of the corporation, owned or subsequently acquired, to secure any obligation of the corporation.

(2) Delegation of borrowing powers. — Notwithstanding subsection 115(3) and paragraph 121(a), unless the articles or by-laws of or a unanimous shareholder agreement relating to a corporation otherwise provide, the directors may, by resolution, delegate the powers referred to in subsection (1) to a director, a committee of directors or an officer.

(3) Extraordinary sale, lease or exchange. — A sale, lease or exchange of all or substantially all the property of a corporation other than in the ordinary course of business of the corporation requires the approval of the shareholders in accordance with subsections (4) to (8).

(4) Notice of meeting. — A notice of a meeting of shareholders complying with section 135 shall be sent in accordance with that section to each shareholder and shall

(a) include or be accompanied by a copy or summary of the agreement of sale, lease or exchange; and

(b) state that a dissenting shareholder is entitled to be paid the fair value of his shares in accordance with section 190, but failure to make that statement does not invalidate a sale, lease or exchange referred to in subsection (3).

(5) Shareholder approval. — At the meeting referred to in subsection (4) the shareholders may authorize the sale, lease or exchange and may fix or authorize the directors to fix any of the terms and conditions thereof.

(6) Right to vote. — Each share of the corporation carries the right to vote in respect of a sale, lease or exchange referred to in subsection (3) whether or not it otherwise carries the right to vote.

(7) Class vote. — The holders of shares of a class or series of shares of the corporation are entitled to vote separately as a class or series in respect of a sale, lease or exchange referred to in subsection (3) only if such class or

series is affected by the sale, lease or exchange in a manner different from the shares of another class or series.

(8) Shareholder approval. — A sale, lease or exchange referred to in subsection (3) is adopted when the holders of each class or series entitled to vote thereon have approved of the sale, lease or exchange by a special resolution.

(9) Termination. — The directors of a corporation may, if authorized by the shareholders approving a proposed sale, lease or exchange, and subject to the rights of third parties, abandon the sale, lease or exchange without further approval of the shareholders.

190. (1) Right to dissent. — Subject to sections 191 and 241, a holder of shares of any class of a corporation may dissent if the corporation is subject to an order under paragraph 192(4)(d) that affects the holder or if the corporation resolves to

(a) amend its articles under section 173 or 174 to add, change or remove any provisions restricting or constraining the issue, transfer or ownership of shares of that class;

(b) amend its articles under section 173 to add, change or remove any restriction on the business or businesses that the corporation may carry on;

(c) amalgamate with another corporation, otherwise than under section 184;

(d) be continued under the laws of another jurisdiction under section 188; or

(e) sell, lease or exchange all or substantially all its property under subsection 189(3).

(2) Further right. — A holder of shares of any class or series of shares entitled to vote under section 176 may dissent if the corporation resolves to amend its articles in a manner described in that section.

(3) Payment for shares. — In addition to any other right he may have, but subject to subsection (26), a shareholder who complies with this section is entitled, when the action approved by the resolution from which he dissents or an order made under subsection 192(4) becomes effective, to be paid by the corporation the fair value of the shares held by him in respect of which he dissents, determined as of the close of business on the day before the resolution was adopted or the order was made.

(4) No partial dissent. — A dissenting shareholder may only claim under this section with respect to all the shares of a class held by him on behalf of any one beneficial owner and registered in the name of the dissenting shareholder.

(5) Objection. — A dissenting shareholder shall send to the corporation, at or before any meeting of shareholders at which a resolution referred to in subsection (1) or (2) is to be voted on, a written objection to the resolution,

unless the corporation did not give notice to the shareholder of the purpose of the meeting and of his right to dissent.

(6) Notice of resolution. — The corporation shall, within ten days after the shareholders adopt the resolution, send to each shareholder who has filed the objection referred to in subsection (5) notice that the resolution has been adopted, but such notice is not required to be sent to any shareholder who voted for the resolution or who has withdrawn his objection.

(7) Demand for payment. — A dissenting shareholder shall, within twenty days after he receives a notice under subsection (6) or, if he does not receive such notice, within twenty days after he learns that the resolution has been adopted, send to the corporation a written notice containing

(a) his name and address;

(b) the number and class of shares in respect of which he dissents; and

(c) a demand for payment of the fair value of such shares.

(8) Share certificate. — A dissenting shareholder shall, within thirty days after sending a notice under subsection (7), send the certificates representing the shares in respect of which he dissents to the corporation or its transfer agent.

(9) Forfeiture. — A dissenting shareholder who fails to comply with subsection (8) has no right to make a claim under this section.

(10) Endorsing certificate. — A corporation or its transfer agent shall endorse on any share certificate received under subsection (8) a notice that the holder is a dissenting shareholder under this section and shall forthwith return the share certificates to the dissenting shareholder.

(11) Suspension of rights. — On sending a notice under subsection (7), a dissenting shareholder ceases to have any rights as a shareholder other than the right to be paid the fair value of his shares as determined under this section except where

(a) the dissenting shareholder withdraws his notice before the corporation makes an offer under subsection (12),

(b) the corporation fails to make an offer in accordance with subsection (12) and the dissenting shareholder withdraws his notice, or

(c) the directors revoke a resolution to amend the articles under subsection 173(2) or 174(5), terminate an amalgamation agreement under subsection 183(6) or an application for continuance under subsection 188(6), or abandon a sale, lease or exchange under subsection 189(9),

in which case his rights as a shareholder are reinstated as of the date he sent the notice referred to in subsection (7).

(12) Offer to pay. — A corporation shall, not later than seven days after the later of the day on which the action approved by the resolution is effective

or the day the corporation received the notice referred to in subsection (7), send to each dissenting shareholder who has sent such notice

(a) a written offer to pay for his shares in an amount considered by the directors of the corporation to be the fair value thereof, accompanied by a statement showing how the fair value was determined; or

(b) if subsection (26) applies, a notification that it is unable lawfully to pay dissenting shareholders for their shares.

(13) Same terms. — Every offer made under subsection (12) for shares of the same class or series shall be on the same terms.

(14) Payment. — Subject to subsection (26), a corporation shall pay for the shares of a dissenting shareholder within ten days after an offer made under subsection (12) has been accepted, but any such offer lapses if the corporation does not receive an acceptance thereof within thirty days after the offer has been made.

(15) Corporation may apply to court. — Where a corporation fails to make an offer under subsection (12), or if a dissenting shareholder fails to accept an offer, the corporation may, within fifty days after the action approved by the resolution is effective or within such further period as a court may allow, apply to a court to fix a fair value for the shares of any dissenting shareholder.

(16) Shareholder application to court. — If a corporation fails to apply to a court under subsection (15), a dissenting shareholder may apply to a court for the same purpose within a further period of twenty days or within such further period as a court may allow.

(17) Venue. — An application under subsection (15) or (16) shall be made to a court having jurisdiction in the place where the corporation has its registered office or in the province where the dissenting shareholder resides if the corporation carries on business in that province.

(18) No security for costs. — A dissenting shareholder is not required to give security for costs in an application made under subsection (15) or (16).

(19) Parties. — On an application to a court under subsection (15) or (16),

(a) all dissenting shareholders whose shares have not been purchased by the corporation shall be joined as parties and are bound by the decision of the court; and

(b) the corporation shall notify each affected dissenting shareholder of the date, place and consequences of the application and of his right to appear and be heard in person or by counsel.

(20) Powers of court. — On an application to a court under subsection (15) or (16), the court may determine whether any other person is a dissenting shareholder who should be joined as a party, and the court shall then fix a fair value for the shares of all dissenting shareholders.

(21) Appraisers. — A court may in its discretion appoint one or more appraisers to assist the court to fix a fair value for the shares of the dissenting shareholders.

(22) Final order. — The final order of a court shall be rendered against the corporation in favour of each dissenting shareholder and for the amount of his shares as fixed by the court.

(23) Interest. — A court may in its discretion allow a reasonable rate of interest on the amount payable to each dissenting shareholder from the date the action approved by the resolution is effective until the date of payment.

(24) Notice that subsection (26) applies. — If subsection (26) applies, the corporation shall, within ten days after the pronouncement of an order under subsection (22), notify each dissenting shareholder that it is unable lawfully to pay dissenting shareholders for their shares.

(25) Effect where subsection (26) applies. — If subsection (26) applies, a dissenting shareholder, by written notice delivered to the corporation within thirty days after receiving a notice under subsection (24), may

(a) withdraw his notice of dissent, in which case the corporation is deemed to consent to the withdrawal and the shareholder is reinstated to his full rights as a shareholder; or

(b) retain a status as a claimant against the corporation, to be paid as soon as the corporation is lawfully able to do so or, in a liquidation, to be ranked subordinate to the rights of creditors of the corporation but in priority to its shareholders.

(26) Limitation. — A corporation shall not make a payment to a dissenting shareholder under this section if there are reasonable grounds for believing that

(a) the corporation is or would after the payment be unable to pay its liabilities as they become due; or

(b) the realizable value of the corporation's assets would thereby be less than the aggregate of its liabilities.

191. (1) Definition of "reorganization". — In this section, "reorganization" means a court order made under

(a) section 241;

(b) the *Bankruptcy and Insolvency Act* approving a proposal; or

(c) any other Act of Parliament that affects the rights among the corporation, its shareholders and creditors.

(2) Powers of court. — If a corporation is subject to an order referred to in subsection (1), its articles may be amended by such order to effect any change that might lawfully be made by an amendment under section 173.

(3) Further powers. — If a court makes an order referred to in subsection (1), the court may also

(a) authorize the issue of debt obligations of the corporation, whether or not convertible into shares of any class or having attached any rights or options to acquire shares of any class, and fix the terms thereof; and

(b) appoint directors in place of or in addition to all or any of the directors then in office.

(4) Articles of reorganization. — After an order referred to in subsection (1) has been made, articles of reorganization in prescribed form shall be sent to the Director together with the documents required by sections 19 and 113, if applicable.

(5) Certificate of reorganization. — On receipt of articles of reorganization, the Director shall issue a certificate of amendment in accordance with section 262.

(6) Effect of certificate. — A reorganization becomes effective on the date shown in the certificate of amendment and the articles of incorporation are amended accordingly.

(7) No dissent. — A shareholder is not entitled to dissent under section 190 if an amendment to the articles of incorporation is effected under this section.

[S. 191 amended by substituting "*Bankruptcy and Insolvency Act*" wherever the expression "*Bankruptcy Act*" occurs by S.C. 1992, c. 27, s. 90(1)(h).]

192. (1) Definition of "arrangement". — In this section, "arrangement" includes

(a) an amendment to the articles of a corporation;

(b) an amalgamation of two or more corporations;

(c) an amalgamation of a body corporate with a corporation that results in an amalgamated corporation subject to this Act;

(d) a division of the business carried on by a corporation;

(e) a transfer of all or substantially all the property of a corporation to another body corporate in exchange for property, money or securities of the body corporate;

(f) an exchange of securities of a corporation held by security holders for property, money or other securities of the corporation or property, money or securities of another body corporate that is not a take-over bid as defined in section 194;

(g) a liquidation and dissolution of a corporation; and

(h) any combination of the foregoing.

(2) Where corporation insolvent. — For the purposes of this section, a corporation is insolvent

(a) where it is unable to pay its liabilities as they become due; or

(b) where the realizable value of the assets of the corporation are less than the aggregate of its liabilities and stated capital of all classes.

(3) Application to court for approval of arrangement. — Where it is not practicable for a corporation that is not insolvent to effect a fundamental change in the nature of an arrangement under any other provision of this Act, the corporation may apply to a court for an order approving an arrangement proposed by the corporation.

(4) Powers of court. — In connection with an application under this section, the court may make any interim or final order it thinks fit including, without limiting the generality of the foregoing,

(a) an order determining the notice to be given to any interested person or dispensing with notice to any person other than the Director;

(b) an order appointing counsel, at the expense of the corporation, to represent the interests of the shareholders;

(c) an order requiring a corporation to call, hold and conduct a meeting of holders of securities or options or rights to acquire securities in such manner as the court directs;

(d) an order permitting a shareholder to dissent under section 190; and

(e) an order approving an arrangement as proposed by the corporation or as amended in any manner the court may direct.

(5) Notice to Director. — An applicant under this section shall give the Director notice of the application and the Director is entitled to appear and be heard in person or by counsel.

(6) Articles of arrangement. — After an order referred to in paragraph (4)(e) has been made, articles of arrangement in prescribed form shall be sent to the Director together with the documents required by sections 19 and 113, if applicable.

(7) Certificate of amendment. — On receipt of articles of arrangement, the Director shall issue a certificate of amendment in accordance with section 262.

(8) Effect of certificate. — An arrangement becomes effective on the date shown in the certificate of amendment.

PART XVI
PROSPECTUS QUALIFICATION

193. Distribution document. — A corporation that files or distributes in any jurisdiction a prospectus, statement of material facts, registration statement,

securities exchange take-over bid circular or similar document relating to the distribution to the public of the securities of the corporation shall forthwith send to the Director a copy of any such document.

PART XVII
TAKE-OVER BIDS

194. Definitions. — In this Part,

"exempt offer". — "exempt offer" means an offer

(a) to fewer than fifteen shareholders to purchase shares by way of separate agreements,

(b) to purchase shares through a stock exchange or in the over-the-counter market in such circumstances as may be prescribed,

(c) to purchase shares of a corporation that has fewer than fifteen shareholders, two or more joint holders being counted as one shareholder,

(d) exempted under section 204, or

(e) by a corporation to repurchase its own shares to be held under section 32;

"offer". — "offer" includes an invitation to make an offer;

"offeree". — "offeree" means a person to whom a take-over bid is made;

"offeree corporation". — "offeree corporation" means a corporation whose shares are the object of a take-over bid;

"offeror". — "offeror" means a person, other than an agent, who makes a take-over bid, and includes two or more persons who, directly or indirectly,

(a) make take-over bids jointly or in concert, or

(b) intend to exercise jointly or in concert voting rights attached to shares for which a take-over bid is made;

"share". — "share" means a share carrying voting rights under all circumstances or by reason of the occurrence of an event that has occurred and is continuing, and includes

(a) a security currently convertible into such a share, and

(b) currently exercisable options and rights to acquire such a share or such a convertible security;

"take-over bid". — "take-over bid" means an offer, other than an exempt offer, made by an offeror to shareholders at approximately the same time to acquire shares that, if combined with shares already beneficially owned or controlled, directly or indirectly, by the offeror or an affiliate or associate of the offeror on the date of the take-over bid, would exceed ten per cent of any class of issued shares of an offeree corporation and includes every offer, other than an exempt offer, by an issuer to repurchase its own shares.

195. Bid for all shares. — Where a take-over bid is for all the shares of any class,

(a) shares deposited pursuant to the take-over bid, if not taken up by the offeror, may be withdrawn by or on behalf of an offeree at any time after sixty days following the date of the take-over bid;

(b) the offeror shall not take up shares deposited pursuant thereto until ten days after the date of the take-over bid; and

(c) the offeror, if he so intends, shall state in the take-over bid circular that he intends to invoke the right under section 206 to acquire the shares of offerees who do not accept the take-over bid and that the offeree is entitled to dissent and to demand the fair value of his shares.

196. (1) Bid for less than all shares. — Where a take-over bid is for less than all the shares of any class,

(a) the offeror shall not take up shares deposited pursuant thereto until twenty-one days after the date of the take-over bid;

(b) the period of time within which shares may be deposited pursuant to the take-over bid or any extension thereof shall not exceed thirty-five days from the date of the take-over bid; and

(c) if a greater number of shares is deposited pursuant to the take-over bid than the offeror is bound or willing to take up and pay for, the shares taken up by the offeror shall be taken up rateably, disregarding fractions, according to the number of shares deposited by each offeree.

(2) Amendment by bid. — Where a take-over bid for all the shares of any class is converted by amendment or otherwise to a bid for less than all the shares of a class, the take-over bid is deemed to be a take-over bid to which subsection (1) applies.

197. Every bid for shares. — Whether a take-over bid is for all or less than all the shares of any class,

(a) shares deposited pursuant to the take-over bid may be withdrawn by or on behalf of an offeree at any time within ten days after the date of the take-over bid;

(b) shares deposited pursuant to the take-over bid shall, if the terms stipulated by the offeror and not subsequently waived by him have been complied with, be taken up and paid for within fourteen days after the last day within which shares may be deposited pursuant to the take-over bid;

(c) the period of time within which shares may be deposited pursuant to a take-over bid shall not be less than twenty-one days after the date of the take-over bid;

(d) if the terms of the take-over bid are amended by increasing the consideration offered for the shares, the offeror shall pay the increased consideration to each offeree whose shares are taken up pursuant to the take-over bid whether or not such shares have been taken up by the offeror before the amendment of the take-over bid;

(e) if the offeror intends to purchase shares to which the take-over bid relates in the market during the period of time within which shares may be deposited pursuant to the take-over bid, the offeror shall so state in the take-over bid circular; and

(f) if the offeror purchases shares to which a take-over bid relates other than pursuant to the take-over bid during the period of time within which shares may be deposited pursuant to the take-over bid,

(i) the payment other than pursuant to the take-over bid of an amount for a share that is greater than the amount offered in the take-over bid is deemed to be an amendment of the take-over bid to which paragraph (d) applies,

(ii) the offeror shall immediately notify the offerees of the increased consideration being offered for the shares,

(iii) the shares acquired other than pursuant to the take-over bid shall be counted to determine whether a condition as to minimum acceptance has been fulfilled, and

(iv) the shares acquired other than pursuant to the take-over bid shall not be counted among the shares taken up rateably under paragraph 196(1)(c).

198. (1) Sending bid. — A take-over bid, including a copy of the take-over bid circular in prescribed form and any amendment of the take-over bid, shall be sent concurrently to each director of the offeree corporation, to each shareholder of the offeree corporation resident in Canada and to the Director.

(2) Date of bid. — A take-over bid is deemed to be dated as of the date on which it is sent.

(3) Shareholders in Canada. — For the purposes of this section and section 201, a shareholder of an offeree corporation is deemed to be resident in Canada if his latest address as shown in the securities register of the offeree corporation is an address within Canada.

199. Arrangements for funds. — Where a take-over bid states that the consideration for the shares deposited pursuant thereto is to be paid in money or partly in money, the offeror shall make adequate arrangements to ensure that funds are available to make the required money payment for such shares.

200. Share-for-share bids. — Where a take-over bid states that the consideration for the shares of the offeree corporation is to be, in whole or in part, securities of the offeror or any other body corporate, the take-over bid circular shall be in prescribed form.

201. (1) Directors' circular. — The directors of an offeree corporation shall send a directors' circular in prescribed form to each director of the offeree corporation, to each shareholder of the offeree corporation resident in Canada, to the offeror and to the Director.

(2) Notice. — Unless the directors of an offeree corporation send a directors' circular under subsection (1) within ten days of the date of the take-over bid, the directors shall forthwith notify the offerees and the Director that a directors' circular will be sent and may recommend that the offerees do not tender their shares pursuant to the take-over bid until they receive the directors' circular.

(3) Contents of notice. — The notice required by subsection (2) shall be in prescribed form.

(4) Time of notice. — The directors shall send the directors' circular required by subsection (1) to each offeree and to the Director at least seven days before the date the take-over bid terminates or before the sixtieth day of the take-over bid, whichever is earlier.

(5) Dissent of director. — Where a director of an offeree corporation is of the opinion that a take-over bid is not advantageous to the shareholders of the offeree corporation or where a director disagrees with any statement in a directors' circular, he is entitled to indicate his opinion or disagreement in the directors' circular required by subsection (1) and, if he indicates his opinion or disagreement, he shall include in that circular a statement setting out the reasons for his opinion or disagreement.

202. (1) Expert's consent. — A report, opinion or statement of a solicitor, auditor, accountant, engineer, appraiser or other person whose profession lends credibility to a statement made by him shall not be included in a take-over bid circular or a directors' circular unless that person has consented in writing to the use of the report, opinion or statement.

(2) Copy to Director. — On the demand of the Director, a person referred to in subsection (1) shall forthwith send to the Director a copy of any report, opinion or statement referred to in that subsection that is made by that person together with a copy of his consent.

203. (1) Approval of take-over bid. — When a take-over bid is made by or on behalf of a body corporate, the directors of the body corporate shall approve the take-over bid and the take-over bid circular, and the approval shall be evidenced on the circular by the signature of one or more directors.

(2) Approval of directors' circular. — The directors of an offeree corporation shall approve a directors' circular that contains the recommendations of a

majority of the directors, and the approval shall be evidenced by the signature of one or more directors.

204. (1) Exemption order. — Any interested person may apply to a court having jurisdiction in the place where the offeree corporation has its registered office for an order exempting a take-over bid from any of the provisions of this Part, and the court may, if it is satisfied that an exemption would not unfairly prejudice a shareholder of the offeree corporation, make an exemption order on such terms as it thinks fit, which order may have retrospective effect.

(2) Notice to Director. — An applicant under subsection (1) shall give the Director notice of the hearing of an application under that subsection, and the Director is entitled to appear and be heard in person or by counsel.

(3) Publication. — The Director shall set out in the periodical referred to in section 129 the particulars of exemptions granted under this section.

205. (1) Offence. — An offeror who, without reasonable cause, fails to comply with this Part or the regulations is guilty of an offence and liable on summary conviction to a fine not exceeding five thousand dollars or to imprisonment for a term not exceeding six months or to both.

(2) Officers, etc., of bodies corporate. — Where a offeror who is a body corporate commits an offence under subsection (1), any director or officer of the body corporate who knowingly authorized, permitted or acquiesced in the commission of the offence is a party to and guilty of the offence and is liable on summary conviction to a fine not exceeding five thousand dollars or to imprisonment for a term not exceeding six months or to both, whether or not the body corporate has been prosecuted or convicted.

(3) Order of the court. — Where in connection with a take-over bid a person does not comply with this Act or the regulations, the Director or any interested person may apply to a court and on such application the court may make any order it thinks fit including, without limiting the generality of the foregoing,

(a) an order restraining the distribution of a take-over bid circular, a directors' circular, or other document used in connection with the take-over bid;

(b) an order, if the take-over bid is to continue, requiring correction of the take-over bid circular, directors' circular or other document and distribution of the corrected document to each offeree;

(c) an order varying the dates and times referred to in sections 195 to 197;

(d) an order requiring any person to comply with this Act or the regulations;

(e) an order compensating an aggrieved person;

(f) an order rescinding a transaction;

(g) an order requiring an offeror to dispose of shares acquired pursuant to the take-over bid; and

(h) an order prohibiting an offeror from voting shares acquired pursuant to a take-over bid.

(4) Definition of "interested person". — For the purposes of subsection (3), "interested person" includes

(d) exempted under section 204, or

(e) by a corporation to repurchase its own shares to be held under section 32;

"offer". — "offer" includes an invitation to make an offer;

"offeree". — "offeree" means a person to whom a take-over bid is made;

"offeree corporation". — "offeree corporation" means a corporation whose shares are the object of a take-over bid;

"offeror". — "offeror" means a person, other than an agent, who makes a take-over bid, and includes two or more persons who, directly or indirectly,

(a) make take-over bids jointly or in concert, or

(b) intend to exercise jointly or in concert voting rights attached to shares for which a take-over bid is made;

"share". — "share" means a share carrying voting rights under all circumstances or by reason of the occurrence of an event that has occurred and is continuing, and includes

(a) a security currently convertible into such a share, and

(b) currently exercisable options and rights to acquire such a share or such a convertible security;

"take-over bid". — "take-over bid" means an offer, other than an exempt offer, made by an offeror to shareholders at approximately the same time to acquire shares that, if combined with shares already beneficially owned or controlled, directly or indirectly, by the offeror or an affiliate or associate of the offeror on the date of the take-over bid, would exceed ten per cent of any class of issued shares of an offeree corporation and includes every offer, other than an exempt offer, by an issuer to repurchase its own shares.

195. Bid for all shares. — Where a take-over bid is for all the shares of any class,

(a) shares deposited pursuant to the take-over bid, if not taken up by the offeror, may be withdrawn by or on behalf of an offeree at any time after sixty days following the date of the take-over bid;

(b) the offeror shall not take up shares deposited pursuant thereto until ten days after the date of the take-over bid; and

(c) the offeror, if he so intends, shall state in the take-over bid circular that he intends to invoke the right under section 206 to acquire the shares of offerees who do not accept the take-over bid and that the offeree is entitled to dissent and to demand the fair value of his shares.

196. (1) Bid for less than all shares. — Where a take-over bid is for less than all the shares of any class,

(a) the offeror shall not take up shares deposited pursuant thereto until twenty-one days after the date of the take-over bid;

(b) the period of time within which shares may be deposited pursuant to the take-over bid or any extension thereof shall not exceed thirty-five days from the date of the take-over bid; and

(c) if a greater number of shares is deposited pursuant to the take-over bid than the offeror is bound or willing to take up and pay for, the shares taken up by the offeror shall be taken up rateably, disregarding fractions, according to the number of shares deposited by each offeree.

(2) Amendment by bid. — Where a take-over bid for all the shares of any class is converted by amendment or otherwise to a bid for less than all the shares of a class, the take-over bid is deemed to be a take-over bid to which subsection (1) applies.

197. Every bid for shares. — Whether a take-over bid is for all or less than all the shares of any class,

(a) shares deposited pursuant to the take-over bid may be withdrawn by or on behalf of an offeree at any time within ten days after the date of the take-over bid;

(b) shares deposited pursuant to the take-over bid shall, if the terms stipulated by the offeror and not subsequently waived by him have been complied with, be taken up and paid for within fourteen days after the last day within which shares may be deposited pursuant to the take-over bid;

(c) the period of time within which shares may be deposited pursuant to a take-over bid shall not be less than twenty-one days after the date of the take-over bid;

(d) if the terms of the take-over bid are amended by increasing the consideration offered for the shares, the offeror shall pay the increased consideration to each offeree whose shares are taken up pursuant to the take-over bid whether or not such shares have been taken up by the offeror before the amendment of the take-over bid;

(e) if the offeror intends to purchase shares to which the take-over bid relates in the market during the period of time within which shares may be deposited pursuant to the take-over bid, the offeror shall so state in the take-over bid circular; and

(f) if the offeror purchases shares to which a take-over bid relates other than pursuant to the take-over bid during the period of time within which shares may be deposited pursuant to the take-over bid,

(i) the payment other than pursuant to the take-over bid of an amount for a share that is greater than the amount offered in the take-over bid is deemed to be an amendment of the take-over bid to which paragraph (d) applies,

(ii) the offeror shall immediately notify the offerees of the increased consideration being offered for the shares,

(iii) the shares acquired other than pursuant to the take-over bid shall be counted to determine whether a condition as to minimum acceptance has been fulfilled, and

(iv) the shares acquired other than pursuant to the take-over bid shall not be counted among the shares taken up rateably under paragraph 196(1)(c).

198. (1) Sending bid. — A take-over bid, including a copy of the take-over bid circular in prescribed form and any amendment of the take-over bid, shall be sent concurrently to each director of the offeree corporation, to each shareholder of the offeree corporation resident in Canada and to the Director.

(2) Date of bid. — A take-over bid is deemed to be dated as of the date on which it is sent.

(3) Shareholders in Canada. — For the purposes of this section and section 201, a shareholder of an offeree corporation is deemed to be resident in Canada if his latest address as shown in the securities register of the offeree corporation is an address within Canada.

199. Arrangements for funds. — Where a take-over bid states that the consideration for the shares deposited pursuant thereto is to be paid in money or partly in money, the offeror shall make adequate arrangements to ensure that funds are available to make the required money payment for such shares.

200. Share-for-share bids. — Where a take-over bid states that the consideration for the shares of the offeree corporation is to be, in whole or in part, securities of the offeror or any other body corporate, the take-over bid circular shall be in prescribed form.

201. (1) Directors' circular. — The directors of an offeree corporation shall send a directors' circular in prescribed form to each director of the offeree corporation, to each shareholder of the offeree corporation resident in Canada, to the offeror and to the Director.

(2) Notice. — Unless the directors of an offeree corporation send a directors' circular under subsection (1) within ten days of the date of the take-over bid, the directors shall forthwith notify the offerees and the Director that a directors' circular will be sent and may recommend that the offerees do not tender their shares pursuant to the take-over bid until they receive the directors' circular.

(3) Contents of notice. — The notice required by subsection (2) shall be in prescribed form.

(4) Time of notice. — The directors shall send the directors' circular required by subsection (1) to each offeree and to the Director at least seven days before the date the take-over bid terminates or before the sixtieth day of the take-over bid, whichever is earlier.

(5) Dissent of director. — Where a director of an offeree corporation is of the opinion that a take-over bid is not advantageous to the shareholders of the offeree corporation or where a director disagrees with any statement in a directors' circular, he is entitled to indicate his opinion or disagreement in the directors' circular required by subsection (1) and, if he indicates his opinion or disagreement, he shall include in that circular a statement setting out the reasons for his opinion or disagreement.

202. (1) Expert's consent. — A report, opinion or statement of a solicitor, auditor, accountant, engineer, appraiser or other person whose profession lends credibility to a statement made by him shall not be included in a take-over bid circular or a directors' circular unless that person has consented in writing to the use of the report, opinion or statement.

(2) Copy to Director. — On the demand of the Director, a person referred to in subsection (1) shall forthwith send to the Director a copy of any report, opinion or statement referred to in that subsection that is made by that person together with a copy of his consent.

203. (1) Approval of take-over bid. — When a take-over bid is made by or on behalf of a body corporate, the directors of the body corporate shall approve the take-over bid and the take-over bid circular, and the approval shall be evidenced on the circular by the signature of one or more directors.

(2) Approval of directors' circular. — The directors of an offeree corporation shall approve a directors' circular that contains the recommendations of a majority of the directors, and the approval shall be evidenced by the signature of one or more directors.

204. (1) Exemption order. — Any interested person may apply to a court having jurisdiction in the place where the offeree corporation has its registered office for an order exempting a take-over bid from any of the provisions of this Part, and the court may, if it is satisfied that an exemption would not unfairly prejudice a shareholder of the offeree corporation, make an exemption order on such terms as it thinks fit, which order may have retrospective effect.

(2) Notice to Director. — An applicant under subsection (1) shall give the Director notice of the hearing of an application under that subsection, and the Director is entitled to appear and be heard in person or by counsel.

(3) Publication. — The Director shall set out in the periodical referred to in section 129 the particulars of exemptions granted under this section.

205. (1) Offence. — An offeror who, without reasonable cause, fails to comply with this Part or the regulations is guilty of an offence and liable on summary conviction to a fine not exceeding five thousand dollars or to imprisonment for a term not exceeding six months or to both.

(2) Officers, etc., of bodies corporate. — Where a offeror who is a body corporate commits an offence under subsection (1), any director or officer of the body corporate who knowingly authorized, permitted or acquiesced in the commission of the offence is a party to and guilty of the offence and is liable on summary conviction to a fine not exceeding five thousand dollars or to imprisonment for a term not exceeding six months or to both, whether or not the body corporate has been prosecuted or convicted.

(3) Order of the court. — Where in connection with a take-over bid a person does not comply with this Act or the regulations, the Director or any interested person may apply to a court and on such application the court may make any order it thinks fit including, without limiting the generality of the foregoing,

(a) an order restraining the distribution of a take-over bid circular, a directors' circular, or other document used in connection with the take-over bid;

(b) an order, if the take-over bid is to continue, requiring correction of the take-over bid circular, directors' circular or other document and distribution of the corrected document to each offeree;

(c) an order varying the dates and times referred to in sections 195 to 197;

(d) an order requiring any person to comply with this Act or the regulations;

(e) an order compensating an aggrieved person;

(f) an order rescinding a transaction;

(g) an order requiring an offeror to dispose of shares acquired pursuant to the take-over bid; and

(h) an order prohibiting an offeror from voting shares acquired pursuant to a take-over bid.

(4) Definition of "interested person". — For the purposes of subsection (3), "interested person" includes

(a) an offeree whether or not he deposits shares pursuant to a take-over bid;

(b) an offeree corporation;

(c) an offeror; and

(d) a rival offeror.

206. (1) Definitions. — In this section,

"dissenting offeree". — "dissenting offeree" means, where a take-over bid is made for all the shares of a class of shares, a holder of a share of that class who does not accept the take-over bid and includes a subsequent holder of that share who acquires it from the first mentioned holder;

"take-over bid". — "take-over bid" includes

(a) an offer to purchase shares of a class of shares to which no voting rights are attached if the offer complies with sections 195 to 203; and

(b) an offer to purchase shares, including shares to which no voting rights are attached, of a corporation having fewer than fifteen shareholders if the offer is made to all shareholders in the prescribed form and manner.

(2) Right to acquire. — If within one hundred and twenty days after the date of a take-over bid the bid is accepted by the holders of not less than ninety per cent of the shares of any class of shares to which the take-over bid relates, other than shares held at the date of the take-over bid by or on behalf of the offeror or an affiliate or associate of the offeror, the offeror is entitled, on complying with this section, to acquire the shares held by the dissenting offerees.

(3) Notice. — An offeror may acquire shares held by a dissenting offeree by sending by registered mail within sixty days after the date of termination of the take-over bid and in any event within one hundred and eighty days after the date of the take-over bid, an offeror's notice to each dissenting offeree and to the Director stating that

(a) the offerees holding more than ninety per cent of the shares to which the bid relates accepted the take-over bid;

(b) the offeror is bound to take up and pay for or has taken up and paid for the shares of the offerees who accepted the take-over bid;

(c) a dissenting offeree is required to elect

(i) to transfer his shares to the offeror on the terms on which the offeror acquired the shares of the offerees who accepted the take-over bid, or

(ii) to demand payment of the fair value of his shares in accordance with subsections (9) to (18) by notifying the offeror within twenty days after he receives the offeror's notice;

(d) a dissenting offeree who does not notify the offeror in accordance with subparagraph (c)(ii) is deemed to have elected to transfer his shares to the offeror on the same terms that the offeror acquired the shares from the offerees who accepted the take-over bid; and

(e) a dissenting offeree must send his shares to which the take-over bid relates to the offeree corporation within twenty days after he receives the offeror's notice.

(4) Notice of adverse claim. — Concurrently with sending the offeror's notice

under subsection (3), the offeror shall send to the offeree corporation a notice of adverse claim in accordance with section 78 with respect to each share held by a dissenting offeree.

(5) Share certificate. — A dissenting offeree to whom an offeror's notice is sent under subsection (3) shall, within twenty days after he receives that notice, send his share certificates of the class of shares to which the take-over bid relates to the offeree corporation.

(6) Payment. — Within twenty days after the offeror sends an offeror's notice under subsection (3), the offeror shall pay or transfer to the offeree corporation the amount of money or other consideration that the offeror would have had to pay or transfer to a dissenting offeree if the dissenting offeree had elected to accept the take-over bid under subparagraph (3)(c)(i).

(7) Consideration. — The offeree corporation is deemed to hold in trust for the dissenting shareholders the money or other consideration it receives under subsection (6), and the offeree corporation shall deposit the money in a separate account in a bank or other body corporate any of whose deposits are insured by the Canada Deposit Insurance Corporation or guaranteed by the Quebec Deposit Insurance Board, and shall place the other consideration in the custody of a bank or such other body corporate.

(8) Duty of offeree corporation. — Within thirty days after the offeror sends an offeror's notice under subsection (3), the offeree corporation shall

(a) issue to the offeror a share certificate in respect of the shares that were held by dissenting offerees;

(b) give to each dissenting offeree who elects to accept the take-over bid terms under subparagraph (3)(c)(i) and who sends his share certificates as required under subsection (5), the money or other consideration to which he is entitled, disregarding fractional shares, which may be paid for in money; and

(c) send to each dissenting shareholder who has not sent his share certificates as required under subsection (5) a notice stating that

(i) his shares have been cancelled,

(ii) the offeree corporation or some designated person holds in trust for him the money or other consideration to which he is entitled as payment for or in exchange for his shares, and

(iii) the offeree corporation will, subject to subsections (9) to (18), send that money or other consideration to him forthwith after receiving his shares.

(9) Application to court. — If a dissenting offeree has elected to demand payment of the fair value of his shares under subparagraph (3)(c)(ii), the offeror may, within twenty days after it has paid the money or transferred the other

consideration under subsection (6), apply to a court to fix the fair value of the shares of that dissenting offeree.

(10) Idem. — If an offeror fails to apply to a court under subsection (9), a dissenting offeree may apply to a court for the same purpose within a further period of twenty days.

(11) Status of dissenter if no court application. — Where no application is made to a court under subsection (10) within the period set out in that subsection, a dissenting offeree is deemed to have elected to transfer his shares to the offeror on the same terms that the offeror acquired the shares from the offerees who accepted the take-over bid.

(12) Venue. — An application under subsection (9) or (10) shall be made to a court having jurisdiction in the place where the corporation has its registered office or in the province where the dissenting offeree resides if the corporation carries on business in that province.

(13) No security for costs. — A dissenting offeree is not required to give security for costs in an application made under subsection (9) or (10).

(14) Parties. — On an application under subsection (9) or (10)

(a) all dissenting offerees referred to in subparagraph (3)(c)(ii) whose shares have not been acquired by the offeror shall be joined as parties and are bound by the decision of the court; and

(b) the offeror shall notify each affected dissenting offeree of the date, place and consequences of the application and of his right to appear and be heard in person or by counsel.

(15) Powers of court. — On an application to a court under subsection (9) or (10) the court may determine whether any other person is a dissenting offeree who should be joined as a party, and the court shall then fix a fair value for the shares of all dissenting offerees.

(16) Appraisers. — A court may in its discretion appoint one or more appraisers to assist the court to fix a fair value for the shares of a dissenting offeree.

(17) Final order. — The final order of the court shall be made against the offeror in favour of each dissenting offeree and for the amount for his shares as fixed by the court.

(18) Additional powers. — In connection with proceedings under this section, a court may make any order it thinks fit and, without limiting the generality of the foregoing, it may

(a) fix the amount of money or other consideration that is required to be held in trust under subsection (7);

(b) order that that money or other consideration be held in trust by a person other than the offeree corporation;

(c) allow a reasonable rate of interest on the amount payable to each dissenting offeree from the date he sends or delivers his share certificates under subsection (5) until the date of payment; and

(d) order that any money payable to a shareholder who cannot be found be paid to the Receiver General and subsection 227(3) applies in respect thereof.

PART XVIII
LIQUIDATION AND DISSOLUTION

207. Definition of "court". — In this Part, "court" means a court having jurisdiction in the place where the corporation has its registered office.

208. (1) Application of Part. — This Part does not apply to a corporation that is insolvent within the meaning of the *Bankruptcy and Insolvency Act* or that is a bankrupt within the meaning of that Act.

(2) Staying proceedings. — Any proceedings taken under this Part to dissolve or to liquidate and dissolve a corporation shall be stayed if the corporation is at any time found, in a proceeding under the *Bankruptcy and Insolvency Act*, to be insolvent within the meaning of that Act.

[S. 208 amended by substituting "*Bankruptcy and Insolvency Act*" wherever the expression "*Bankruptcy Act*" occurs by S.C. 1992, c. 27, s. 90(1)(h).]

209. (1) Revival. — Where a body corporate is dissolved under this Part or section 268 of this Act or section 261 of chapter 33 of the Statutes of Canada, 1974-75-76, any interested person may apply to the Director to have the body corporate revived as a corporation under this Act.

(2) Articles of revival. — Articles of revival in prescribed form shall be sent to the Director.

(3) Certificate of revival. — On receipt of articles of revival, the Director shall issue a certificate of revival in accordance with section 262.

(4) Rights preserved. — A body corporate is revived as a corporation under this Act on the date shown on the certificate of revival, and thereafter the corporation, subject to such reasonable terms as may be imposed by the Director and to the rights acquired by any person after its dissolution, has all the rights and privileges and is liable for the obligations that it would have had if it had not been dissolved.

210. (1) Dissolution before commencing business. — A corporation that has not issued any shares may be dissolved at any time by resolution of all the directors.

(2) Dissolution if no property. — A corporation that has no property and no liabilities may be dissolved by special resolution of the shareholders or, where it has issued more than one class of shares, by special resolutions of the holders of each class whether or not they are otherwise entitled to vote.

(3) Dissolution where property disposed of. — A corporation that has property or liabilities or both may be dissolved by special resolution of the shareholders or, where it has issued more than one class of shares, by special resolutions of the holders of each class whether or not they are otherwise entitled to vote, if

(a) by the special resolution or resolutions the shareholders authorize the directors to cause the corporation to distribute any property and discharge any liabilities; and

(b) the corporation has distributed any property and discharged any liabilities before it sends articles of dissolution to the Director pursuant to subsection (4).

(4) Articles of dissolution. — Articles of dissolution in prescribed form shall be sent to the Director.

(5) Certificate of dissolution. — On receipt of articles of dissolution, the Director shall issue a certificate of dissolution in accordance with section 262.

(6) Effect of certificate. — The corporation ceases to exist on the date shown in the certificate of dissolution.

211. (1) Proposing liquidation and dissolution. — The directors may propose, or a shareholder who is entitled to vote at an annual meeting of shareholders may, in accordance with section 137, make a proposal for, the voluntary liquidation and dissolution of a corporation.

(2) Notice of meeting. — Notice of any meeting of shareholders at which voluntary liquidation and dissolution is to be proposed shall set out the terms thereof.

(3) Shareholders resolution. — A corporation may liquidate and dissolve by special resolution of the shareholders or, where the corporation has issued more than one class of shares, by special resolution of the holders of each class whether or not they are otherwise entitled to vote.

(4) Statement of intent to dissolve. — A statement of intent to dissolve in prescribed form shall be sent to the Director.

(5) Certificate of intent to dissolve. — On receipt of a statement of intent to dissolve, the Director shall issue a certificate of intent to dissolve in accordance with section 262.

(6) Effect of certificate. — On issue of a certificate of intent to dissolve, the corporation shall cease to carry on business except to the extent necessary for the liquidation, but its corporate existence continues until the Director issues a certificate of dissolution.

(7) Liquidation. — After issue of a certificate of intent to dissolve, the corporation shall

(a) immediately cause notice thereof to be sent to each known creditor of the corporation;

(b) forthwith publish notice thereof once a week for four consecutive weeks in a newspaper published or distributed in the place where the corporation has its registered office and take reasonable steps to give notice thereof in each province in Canada where the corporation was carrying on business at the time it sent the statement of intent to dissolve to the Director;

(c) proceed to collect its property, to dispose of properties that are not to be distributed in kind to its shareholders, to discharge all its obligations and to do all other acts required to liquidate its business; and

(d) after giving the notice required under paragraphs (a) and (b) and adequately providing for the payment or discharge of all its obligations, distribute its remaining property, either in money or in kind, among its shareholders according to their respective rights.

(8) Supervision by court. — The Director or any interested person may, at any time during the liquidation of a corporation, apply to a court for an order that the liquidation be continued under the supervision of the court as provided in this Part, and on such application the court may so order and make any further order it thinks fit.

(9) Notice to Director. — An applicant under this section shall give the Director notice of the application, and the Director is entitled to appear and be heard in person or by counsel.

(10) Revocation. — At any time after issue of a certificate of intent to dissolve and before issue of a certificate of dissolution, a certificate of intent to dissolve may be revoked by sending to the Director a statement of revocation of intent to dissolve in prescribed form, if such revocation is approved in the same manner as the resolution under subsection (3).

(11) Certificate of revocation of intent to dissolve. — On receipt of a statement of revocation of intent to dissolve, the Director shall issue a certificate of revocation of intent to dissolve in accordance with section 262.

(12) Effect of certificate. — On the date shown in the certificate of revocation of intent to dissolve, the revocation is effective and the corporation may continue to carry on its business or businesses.

(13) Right to dissolve. — If a certificate of intent to dissolve has not been revoked and the corporation has complied with subsection (7), the corporation shall prepare articles of dissolution.

(14) Articles of dissolution. — Articles of dissolution in prescribed form shall be sent to the Director.

(15) Certificate of dissolution. — On receipt of articles of dissolution, the Director shall issue a certificate of dissolution in accordance with section 262.

(16) Effect of certificate. — The corporation ceases to exist on the date shown in the certificate of dissolution.

212. (1) Dissolution by Director. — Subject to subsections (2) and (3), where a corporation

(a) has not commenced business within three years after the date shown in its certificate of incorporation,

(b) has not carried on its business for three consecutive years, or

(c) is in default for a period of one year in sending to the Director any fee, notice or document required by this Act,

the Director may dissolve the corporation by issuing a certificate of dissolution under this section or he may apply to a court for an order dissolving the corporation, in which case section 217 applies.

(2) Publication. — The Director shall not dissolve a corporation under this section until he has

(a) given one hundred and twenty days notice of his decision to dissolve the corporation to the corporation and to each director thereof; and

(b) published notice of his decision to dissolve the corporation in the *Canada Gazette*, in the periodical referred to in section 129 and in a newspaper published or distributed in the place where the corporation has its registered office.

(3) Certificate of dissolution. — Unless cause to the contrary has been shown or an order has been made by a court under section 246, the Director may, after the expiration of the period referred to in subsection (2), issue a certificate of dissolution in prescribed form.

(4) Effect of certificate. — The corporation ceases to exist on the date shown in the certificate of dissolution.

213. (1) Grounds for dissolution. — The Director or any interested person may apply to a court for an order dissolving a corporation if the corporation has

(a) failed for two or more consecutive years to comply with the requirements of this Act with respect to the holding of annual meetings of shareholders;

(b) contravened subsection 16(2) or section 21, 157 or 159; or

(c) procured any certificate under this Act by misrepresentation.

(2) Notice to Director. — An applicant under this section shall give the Director notice of the application, and the Director is entitled to appear and be heard in person or by counsel.

(3) Dissolution order. — On an application under this section or section

212, the court may order that the corporation be dissolved or that the corporation be liquidated and dissolved under the supervision of the court, and the court may make any other order it thinks fit.

(4) Certificate. — On receipt of an order under this section, section 212 or 214, the Director shall

(a) if the order is to dissolve the corporation, issue a certificate of dissolution in prescribed form; or

(b) if the order is to liquidate and dissolve the corporation under the supervision of the court, issue a certificate of intent to dissolve in prescribed form and publish notice of such order in the *Canada Gazette* and in the periodical referred to in section 129.

(5) Effect of certificate. — The corporation ceases to exist on the date shown in the certificate of dissolution.

214. (1) Further grounds. — A court may order the liquidation and dissolution of a corporation or any of its affiliated corporations on the application of a shareholder,

(a) if the court is satisfied that in respect of a corporation or any of its affiliates

(i) any act or omission of the corporation or any of its affiliates effects a result,

(ii) the business or affairs of the corporation or any of its affiliates are or have been carried on or conducted in a manner, or

(iii) the powers of the directors of the corporation or any of its affiliates are or have been exercised in a manner

that is oppressive or unfairly prejudicial to or that unfairly disregards the interests of any security holder, creditor, director or officer; or

(b) if the court is satisfied that

(i) a unanimous shareholder agreement entitles a complaining shareholder to demand dissolution of the corporation after the occurrence of a specified event and that event has occurred, or

(ii) it is just and equitable that the corporation should be liquidated and dissolved.

(2) Alternative order. — On an application under this section, a court may make such order under this section or section 241 as it thinks fit.

(3) Application of s. 242. — Section 242 applies to an application under this section.

215. (1) Application for supervision. — An application to a court to supervise a voluntary liquidation and dissolution under subsection 211(8) shall state the

reasons, verified by an affidavit of the applicant, why the court should supervise the liquidation and dissolution.

(2) Court supervision. — If a court makes an order applied for under subsection 211(8), the liquidation and dissolution of the corporation shall continue under the supervision of the court in accordance with this Act.

216. (1) Application to court. — An application to a court under subsection 214(1) shall state the reasons, verified by an affidavit of the applicant, why the corporation should be liquidated and dissolved.

(2) Show cause order. — On an application under subsection 214(1), the court may make an order requiring the corporation and any person having an interest in the corporation or claim against it to show cause, at a time and place therein specified, not less than four weeks after the date of the order, why the corporation should not be liquidated and dissolved.

(3) Powers of court. — On an application under subsection 214(1) the court may order the directors and officers of the corporation to furnish the court with all material information known to or reasonably ascertainable by them, including

(a) financial statements of the corporation;

(b) the name and address of each shareholder of the corporation; and

(c) the name and address of each creditor or claimant, including any creditor or claimant with unliquidated, future or contingent claims, and any person with whom the corporation has a contract.

(4) Publication. — A copy of an order made under subsection (2) shall be

(a) published as directed in the order, at least once in each week before the time appointed for the hearing, in a newspaper published or distributed in the place where the corporation has its registered office; and

(b) served on the Director and each person named in the order.

(5) Person responsible. — Publication and service of an order under this section shall be effected by the corporation or by such other person and in such manner as the court may order.

217. Powers of court. — In connection with the dissolution or the liquidation and dissolution of a corporation, the court may, if it is satisfied that the corporation is able to pay or adequately provide for the discharge of all its obligations, make any order it thinks fit including, without limiting the generality of the foregoing,

(a) an order to liquidate;

(b) an order appointing a liquidator, with or without security, fixing his remuneration and replacing a liquidator;

(c) an order appointing inspectors or referees, specifying their powers, fixing their remuneration and replacing inspectors or referees;

(d) an order determining the notice to be given to any interested person, or dispensing with notice to any person;

(e) an order determining the validity of any claims made against the corporation;

(f) an order at any stage of the proceedings, restraining the directors and officers from

(i) exercising any of their powers, or

(ii) collecting or receiving any debt or other property of the corporation, and from paying out or transferring any property of the corporation, except as permitted by the court;

(g) an order determining and enforcing the duty or liability of any director, officer or shareholder

(i) to the corporation, or

(ii) for an obligation of the corporation;

(h) an order approving the payment, satisfaction or compromise of claims against the corporation and the retention of assets for such purpose, and determining the adequancy of provisions for the payment or discharge of obligations of the corporation, whether liquidated, unliquidated, future or contingent;

(i) an order disposing of or destroying the documents and records of the corporation;

(j) on the application of a creditor, the inspectors or the liquidator, an order giving directions on any matter arising in the liquidation;

(k) after notice has been given to all interested parties, an order relieving a liquidator from any omission or default on such terms as the court thinks fit and confirming any act of the liquidator;

(l) subject to section 223, an order approving any proposed interim or final distribution to shareholders in money or in property;

(m) an order disposing of any property belonging to creditors or shareholders who cannot be found;

(n) on the application of any director, officer, security holder, creditor or the liquidator,

(i) an order staying the liquidation on such terms and conditions as the court thinks fit,

(ii) an order continuing or discontinuing the liquidation proceedings, or

(iii) an order to the liquidator to restore to the corporation all its remaining property;

(o) after the liquidator has rendered his final account to the court, an order dissolving the corporation.

218. Effect of order. — The liquidation of a corporation commences when a court makes an order therefor.

219. (1) Cessation of business and powers. — If a court makes an order for liquidation of a corporation,

(a) the corporation continues in existence but shall cease to carry on business, except the business that is, in the opinion of the liquidator, required for an orderly liquidation; and

(b) the powers of the directors and shareholders cease and vest in the liquidator, except as specifically authorized by the court.

(2) Delegation by liquidator. — The liquidator may delegate any of the powers vested in him by paragraph (1)(b) to the directors or shareholders.

220. (1) Appointment of liquidator. — When making an order for the liquidation of a corporation or at any time thereafter, the court may appoint any person, including a director, an officer or a shareholder of the corporation or any other body corporate, as liquidator of the corporation.

(2) Vacancy. — Where an order for the liquidation of a corporation has been made and the office of liquidator is or becomes vacant, the property of the corporation is under the control of the court until the office of liquidator is filled.

221. Duties of liquidator. — A liquidator shall

(a) forthwith after his appointment give notice thereof to the Director and to each claimant and creditor known to the liquidator;

(b) forthwith publish notice in the *Canada Gazette* and in the periodical referred to in section 129 and by insertion once a week for two consecutive weeks in a newspaper published or distributed in the place where the corporation has its registered office and take reasonable steps to give notice thereof in each province where the corporation carries on business, requiring any person

(i) indebted to the corporation, to render an account and pay to the liquidator at the time and place specified any amount owing,

(ii) possessing property of the corporation, to deliver it to the liquidator at the time and place specified, and

(iii) having a claim against the corporation, whether liquidated, unliquidated, future or contingent, to present particulars thereof in writing to the liquidator not later than two months after the first publication of the notice;

(c) take into his custody and control the property of the corporation;

(d) open and maintain a trust account for the moneys of the corporation;

(e) keep accounts of the moneys of the corporation received and paid out by him;

(f) maintain separate lists of the shareholders, creditors and other persons having claims against the corporation;

(g) if at any time the liquidator determines that the corporation is unable to pay or adequately provide for the discharge of its obligations, apply to the court for directions;

(h) deliver to the court and to the Director, at least once in every twelve-month period after his appointment or more often as the court may require, financial statements of the corporation in the form required by section 155 or in such other form as the liquidator may think proper or as the court may require; and

(i) after his final accounts are approved by the court, distribute any remaining property of the corporation among the shareholders according to their respective rights.

222. (1) Powers of liquidator. — A liquidator may

(a) retain lawyers, accountants, engineers, appraisers and other professional advisers;

(b) bring, defend or take part in any civil, criminal or administrative action or proceeding in the name and on behalf of the corporation;

(c) carry on the business of the corporation as required for an orderly liquidation;

(d) sell by public auction or private sale any property of the corporation;

(e) do all acts and execute any documents in the name and on behalf of the corporation;

(f) borrow money on the security of the property of the corporation;

(g) settle or compromise any claims by or against the corporation; and

(h) do all other things necessary for the liquidation of the corporation and distribution of its property.

(2) Reliance on statements. — A liquidator is not liable if he relies in good faith on

(a) financial statements of the corporation represented to him by an officer of the corporation or in a written report of the auditor of the corporation to reflect fairly the financial condition of the corporation; or

(b) an opinion, a report or a statement of a lawyer, an accountant, an engineer, an appraiser or other professional adviser retained by the liquidator.

(3) Application for examination. — If a liquidator has reason to believe that any person has in his possession or under his control, or has concealed, withheld or misappropriated any property of the corporation, he may apply to the court for an order requiring that person to appear before the court at the time and place designated in the order and to be examined.

(4) Power of court. — If the examination referred to in subsection (3) discloses that a person has concealed, withheld or misappropriated property of the corporation, the court may order that person to restore it or pay compensation to the liquidator.

223. (1) Costs of liquidation. — A liquidator shall pay the costs of liquidation out of the property of the corporation and shall pay or make adequate provision for all claims against the corporation.

(2) Final account. — Within one year after his appointment, and after paying or making adequate provision for all claims against the corporation, the liquidator shall apply to the court

(a) for approval of his final accounts and for an order permitting him to distribute in money or in kind the remaining property of the corporation to its shareholders according to their respective rights; or

(b) for an extension of time, setting out the reasons therefor.

(3) Shareholder application. — If a liquidator fails to make the application required by subsection (2), a shareholder of the corporation may apply to the court for an order for the liquidator to show cause why a final accounting and distribution should not be made.

(4) Publication. — A liquidator shall give notice of his intention to make an application under subsection (2) to the Director, each inspector appointed under section 217, each shareholder and any person who provided a security or fidelity bond for the liquidation, and he shall publish the notice in a newspaper published or distributed in the place where the corporation has its registered office or as otherwise directed by the court.

(5) Final order. — If the court approves the final accounts rendered by a liquidator, the court shall make an order

(a) directing the Director to issue a certificate of dissolution;

(b) directing the custody or disposal of the documents and records of the corporation; and

(c) subject to subsection (6), discharging the liquidator.

(6) Delivery of order. — The liquidator shall forthwith send a certified copy of the order referred to in subsection (5) to the Director.

(7) Certificate of dissolution. — On receipt of the order referred to in subsection (5), the Director shall issue a certificate of dissolution in accordance with section 262.

(8) Effect of certificate. — The corporation ceases to exist on the date shown in the certificate of dissolution.

224. (1) Right to distribution in money. — If in the course of liquidation of a corporation the shareholders resolve or the liquidator proposes to

(a) exchange all or substantially all the property of the corporation for securities of another body corporate that are to be distributed to the shareholders, or

(b) distribute all or part of the property of the corporation to the shareholders in kind,

a shareholder may apply to the court for an order requiring the distribution of the property of the corporation to be in money.

(2) Powers of court. — On an application under subsection (1), the court may order

(a) all the property of the corporation to be converted into and distributed in money; or

(b) the claims of any shareholder applying under this section to be satisfied by a distribution in money, in which case subsections 190(20) to (22) apply.

225. (1) Custody of records. — A person who has been granted custody of the documents and records of a dissolved corporation remains liable to produce such documents and records for six years following the date of its dissolution or until the expiration of such other shorter period as may be ordered under subsection 223(5).

(2) Offence. — A person who, without reasonable cause, contravenes subsection (1) is guilty of an offence and liable on summary conviction to a fine not exceeding five thousand dollars or to imprisonment for a term not exceeding six months or to both.

226. (1) Definition of "shareholder". — In this section, "shareholder" includes the heirs and legal representatives of a shareholder.

(2) Continuation of actions. — Notwithstanding the dissolution of a body corporate under this Act,

(a) a civil, criminal or administrative action or proceeding commenced by or against the body corporate before its dissolution may be continued as if the body corporate had not been dissolved;

(b) a civil, criminal or administrative action or proceeding may be brought against the body corporate within two years after its dissolution as if the body corporate had not been dissolved; and

(c) any property that would have been available to satisfy any judgment or order if the body corporate had not been dissolved remains available for such purpose.

(3) Service. — Service of a document on a corporation after its dissolution may be effected by serving the document on a person shown in the last notice filed under section 106 or 113.

(3.1) Idem. — Service of a document on a company to which the *Canada Corporations Act*, chapter C-32 of the Revised Statutes of Canada, 1970, applied that has been dissolved by subsection 261(8) of the *Canada Business Corporations Act*, chapter 33 of the Statutes of Canada, 1974-75-76 and chapter 9 of the Statutes of Canada, 1978-79, may be effected by serving the document on a person shown as a director in the last annual summary filed by the company pursuant to the *Canada Corporations Act*.

[Subsec. (3.1) added by S.C. 1991, c. 1, s. 57.]

(4) Reimbursement. — Notwithstanding the dissolution of a body corporate under this Act, a shareholder to whom any of its property has been distributed is liable to any person claiming under subsection (2) to the extent of the amount received by that shareholder on such distribution, and an action to enforce such liability may be brought within two years after the date of the dissolution of the body corporate.

(5) Representative action. — A court may order an action referred to in subsection (4) to be brought against the persons who were shareholders as a class, subject to such conditions as the court thinks fit and, if the plaintiff establishes his claim, the court may refer the proceedings to a referee or other officer of the court who may

(a) add as a party to the proceedings before him each person who was a shareholder found by the plaintiff;

(b) determine, subject to subsection (4), the amount that each person who was a shareholder shall contribute towards satisfaction of the plaintiff's claim; and

(c) direct payment of the amounts so determined.

227. (1) Unknown claimants. — On the dissolution of a body corporate under this Act, the portion of the property distributable to a creditor or shareholder who cannot be found shall be converted into money and paid to the Receiver General.

(2) Constructive satisfaction. — A payment under subsection (1) is deemed to be in satisfaction of a debt or claim of such creditor or shareholder.

(3) Recovery. — If at any time a person establishes that he is entitled to any moneys paid to the Receiver General under this Act, the Receiver General shall pay an equivalent amount to him out of the Consolidated Revenue Fund.

228. (1) Vesting in Crown. — Subject to subsection 226(2) and section 227, property of a body corporate that has not been disposed of at the date of its dissolution under this Act vests in Her Majesty in right of Canada.

(2) Return of property on revival. — If a body corporate is revived as a corporation under section 209, any property, other than money, that vested in Her Majesty pursuant to subsection (1), that has not been disposed of shall be returned to the corporation and there shall be paid to the corporation out of the Consolidated Revenue Fund

(a) an amount equal to any money received by Her Majesty pursuant to subsection (1); and

(b) where property other than money vested in Her Majesty pursuant to subsection (1) and that property has been disposed of, an amount equal to the lesser of

(i) the value of any such property at the date it vested in Her Majesty, and

(ii) the amount realized by Her Majesty from the disposition of that property.

PART XIX
INVESTIGATION

229. (1) Investigation. — A security holder or the Director may apply, *ex parte* or on such notice as the court may require, to a court having jurisdiction in the place where the corporation has its registered office for an order directing an investigation to be made of the corporation and any of its affiliated corporations.

(2) Grounds. — If, on an application under subsection (1), it appears to the court that

(a) the business of the corporation or any of its affiliates is or has been carried on with intent to defraud any person,

(b) the business or affairs of the corporation or any of its affiliates are or have been carried on or conducted, or the powers of the directors are or have been exercised in a manner that is oppressive or unfairly prejudicial to or that unfairly disregards the interests of a security holder,

(c) the corporation or any of its affiliates was formed for a fraudulent or unlawful purpose or is to be dissolved for a fraudulent or unlawful purpose, or

(d) persons concerned with the formation, business or affairs of the corporation or any of its affiliates have in connection therewith acted fraudulently or dishonestly,

the court may order an investigation to be made of the corporation and any of its affiliated corporations.

(3) Notice to Director. — If a security holder makes an application under subsection (1) he shall give the Director reasonable notice thereof and the Director is entitled to appear and be heard in person or by counsel.

(4) No security for costs. — An applicant under this section is not required to give security for costs.

(5) Hearings *in camera.* — An *ex parte* application under this section shall be heard *in camera.*

(6) Consent to publish proceedings required. — No person may publish anything relating to *ex parte* proceedings under this section except with the authorization of the court or the written consent of the corporation being investigated.

230. (1) Powers of court. — In connection with an investigation under this Part, the court may make any order it thinks fit including, without limiting the generality of the foregoing,

(a) an order to investigate;

(b) an order appointing an inspector, who may be the Director, fixing the remuneration of an inspector, and replacing an inspector;

(c) an order determining the notice to be given to any interested person, or dispensing with notice to any person;

(d) an order authorizing an inspector to enter any premises in which the court is satisfied there might be relevant information, and to examine any thing and make copies of any document or record found on the premises;

(e) an order requiring any person to produce documents or records to the inspector;

(f) an order authorizing an inspector to conduct a hearing, administer oaths and examine any person on oath, and prescribing rules for the conduct of the hearing;

(g) an order requiring any person to attend a hearing conducted by an inspector and to give evidence on oath;

(h) an order giving directions to an inspector or any interested person on any matter arising in the investigation;

(i) an order requiring an inspector to make an interim or final report to the court;

(j) an order determining whether a report of an inspector should be published and, if so, ordering the Director to publish the report in whole or in part or to send copies to any person the court designates;

(k) an order requiring an inspector to discontinue an investigation;

(l) an order requiring the corporation to pay the costs of the investigation.

(2) Copy of report. — An inspector shall send to the Director a copy of every report made by the inspector under this Part.

231. (1) Power of inspector. — An inspector under this Part has the powers set out in the order appointing him.

(2) Exchange of information. — In addition to the powers set out in the order appointing him, an inspector appointed to investigate a corporation may furnish to, or exchange information and otherwise cooperate with, any public official in Canada or elsewhere who is authorized to exercise investigatory powers and who is investigating, in respect of the corporation, any allegation of improper conduct that is the same as or similar to the conduct described in subsection 229(2).

(3) Court order. — An inspector shall on request produce to an interested person a copy of any order made under subsection 230(1).

232. (1) Hearing *in camera*. — Any interested person may apply to the court for an order that a hearing conducted by an inspector under this Part be heard *in camera* and for directions on any matter arising in the investigation.

(2) Right to counsel. — A person whose conduct is being investigated or who is being examined at a hearing conducted by an inspector under this Part has a right to be represented by counsel.

233. Criminating statements. — No person is excused from attending and giving evidence and producing documents and records to an inspector under this Part by reason only that the evidence tends to criminate that person or subject that person to any proceeding or penalty, but no such evidence shall be used or is receivable against that person in any proceeding thereafter instituted against that person under an Act of Parliament, other than a prosecution under section 132 of the *Criminal Code* for perjury in giving the evidence or a prosecution under section 136 of the *Criminal Code* in respect of the evidence.

[Sec. 233 repealed and substituted by R.S.C. 1985 (1st Supp.), c. 27, Sch. v, Item3.]

234. Absolute privilege (defamation). — Any oral or written statement or report made by an inspector or any other person in an investigation under this Part has absolute privilege.

235. (1) Information respecting ownership and control. — If the Director is satisfied that, for the purposes of Part XI, XIII or XVII, or for the purposes of enforcing any regulation made under section 174, there is reason to inquire

into the ownership or control of a security of a corporation or any of its affiliates, the Director may require any person that he reasonably believes has or has had an interest in the security or acts or has acted on behalf of a person with such an interest to report to him or to any person he designates,

(a) information that such person has or can reasonably be expected to obtain as to present and past interests in the security; and

(b) the names and addresses of the persons so interested and of any person who acts or has acted in relation to the security on behalf of the persons so interested.

(2) Constructive interest in securities. — For the purposes of subsection (1), a person is deemed to have an interest in a security if

(a) he has a right to vote or to acquire or dispose of the security or any interest therein;

(b) his consent is necessary for the exercise of the rights or privileges of any other person interested in the security; or

(c) any other person interested in the security can be required or is accustomed to exercise rights or privileges attached to the security in accordance with his instructions.

(3) Publication. — The Director shall publish in the periodical referred to in section 129 the particulars of information obtained by him under this section, if the particulars

(a) are required to be disclosed by this Act or the regulations; and

(b) have not previously been so disclosed.

(4) Offence. — A person who fails to comply with this section is guilty of an offence and liable on summary conviction to a fine not exceeding five thousand dollars or to imprisonment for a term not exceeding six months or to both.

(5) Officers, etc., of bodies corporate. — Where a body corporate commits an offence under subsection (4), any director or officer of the body corporate who knowingly authorized, permitted or acquiesced in the commission of the offence is a party to and guilty of the offence and is liable on summary conviction to a fine not exceeding five thousand dollars or to imprisonment for a term not exceeding six months or to both, whether or not the body corporate has been prosecuted or convicted.

236. Solicitor-client privilege. — Nothing in this Part shall be construed as affecting the privilege that exists in respect of a solicitor and his client.

237. Inquiries. — The Director may make inquiries of any person relating to compliance with this Act.

PART XX
REMEDIES, OFFENCES AND PUNISHMENT

238. Definitions. — In this Part,

"action". — "action" means an action under this Act;

"complainant". — "complainant" means

(a) a registered holder or beneficial owner, and a former registered holder or beneficial owner, of a security of a corporation or any of its affiliates,

(b) a director or an officer or a former director or officer of a corporation or any of its affiliates,

(c) the Director, or

(d) any other person who, in the discretion of a court, is a proper person to make an application under this Part.

239. (1) Commencing derivative action. — Subject to subsection (2), a complainant may apply to a court for leave to bring an action in the name and on behalf of a corporation or any of its subsidiaries, or intervene in an action to which any such body corporate is a party, for the purpose of prosecuting, defending or discontinuing the action on behalf of the body corporate.

(2) Conditions precedent. — No action may be brought and no intervention in an action may be made under subsection (1) unless the court is satisfied that

(a) the complainant has given reasonable notice to the directors of the corporation or its subsidiary of his intention to apply to the court under subsection (1) if the directors of the corporation or its subsidiary do not bring, diligently prosecute or defend or discontinue the action;

(b) the complainant is acting in good faith; and

(c) it appears to be in the interests of the corporation or its subsidiary that the action be brought, prosecuted, defended or discontinued.

240. Powers of court. — In connection with an action brought or intervened in under section 239, the court may at any time make any order it thinks fit including, without limiting the generality of the foregoing,

(a) an order authorizing the complainant or any other person to control the conduct of the action;

(b) an order giving directions for the conduct of the action;

(c) an order directing that any amount adjudged payable by a defendant in the action shall be paid, in whole or in part, directly to former and present security holders of the corporation or its subsidiary instead of to the corporation or its subsidiary;

(d) an order requiring the corporation or its subsidiary to pay reasonable legal fees incurred by the complainant in connection with the action.

241. (1) Application to court re oppression. — A complainant may apply to a court for an order under this section.

(2) Grounds. — If, on an application under subsection (1), the court is satisfied that in respect of a corporation or any of its affiliates

(a) any act or omission of the corporation or any of its affiliates effects a result,

(b) the business or affairs of the corporation or any of its affiliates are or have been carried on or conducted in a manner, or

(c) the powers of the directors of the corporation or any of its affiliates are or have been exercised in a manner

that is oppressive or unfairly prejudicial to or that unfairly disregards the interests of any security holder, creditor, director or officer, the court may make an order to rectify the matters complained of.

(3) Powers of court. — In connection with an application under this section, the court may make any interim or final order it thinks fit including, without limiting the generality of the foregoing,

(a) an order restraining the conduct complained of;

(b) an order appointing a receiver or receiver-manager;

(c) an order to regulate a corporation's affairs by amending the articles or by-laws or creating or amending a unanimous shareholder agreement;

(d) an order directing an issue or exchange of securities;

(e) an order appointing directors in place of or in addition to all or any of the directors then in office;

(f) an order directing a corporation, subject to subsection (6), or any other person, to purchase securities of a security holder;

(g) an order directing a corporation, subject to subsection (6), or any other person, to pay to a security holder any part of the moneys paid by him for securities;

(h) an order varying or setting aside a transaction or contract to which a corporation is a party and compensating the corporation or any other party to the transaction or contract;

(i) an order requiring a corporation, within a time specified by the court, to produce to the court or an interested person financial statements in the form required by section 155 or an accounting in such other form as the court may determine;

(j) an order compensating an aggrieved person;

(k) an order directing rectification of the registers or other records of a corporation under section 243;

(l) an order liquidating and dissolving the corporation;

(m) an order directing an investigation under Part XIX to be made;

(n) an order requiring the trial of any issue.

(4) Duty of directors. — If an order made under this section directs amendment of the articles or by-laws of a corporation,

(a) the directors shall forthwith comply with subsection 191(4); and

(b) no other amendment to the articles or by-laws shall be made without the consent of the court, until a court otherwise orders.

(5) Exclusion. — A shareholder is not entitled to dissent under section 190 if an amendment to the articles is effected under this section.

(6) Limitation. — A corporation shall not make a payment to a shareholder under paragraph (3)(f) or (g) if there are reasonable grounds for believing that

(a) the corporation is or would after that payment be unable to pay its liabilities as they become due; or

(b) the realizable value of the corporation's assets would thereby be less than the aggregate of its liabilities.

(7) Alternative order. — An applicant under this section may apply in the alternative for an order under section 214.

242. (1) Evidence of shareholder approval not decisive. — An application made or an action brought or intervened in under this Part shall not be stayed or dismissed by reason only that it is shown that an alleged breach of a right or duty owed to the corporation or its subsidiary has been or may be approved by the shareholders of such body corporate, but evidence of approval by the shareholders may be taken into account by the court in making an order under section 214, 240 or 241.

(2) Court approval to discontinue. — An application made or an action brought or intervened in under this Part shall not be stayed, discontinued, settled or dismissed for want of prosecution without the approval of the court given on such terms as the court thinks fit and, if the court determines that the interests of any complainant may be substantially affected by such stay, discontinuance, settlement or dismissal, the court may order any party to the application or action to give notice to the complainant.

(3) No security for costs. — A complainant is not required to give security for costs in any application made or action brought or intervened in under this Part.

(4) Interim costs. — In an application made or an action brought or intervened in under this Part, the court may at any time order the corporation

or its subsidiary to pay to the complainant interim costs, including legal fees and disbursements, but the complainant may be held accountable for such interim costs on final disposition of the application or action.

243. (1) Application to court to rectify records. — If the name of a person is alleged to be or to have been wrongly entered or retained in, or wrongly deleted or omitted from, the registers or other records of a corporation, the corporation, a security holder of the corporation or any aggrieved person may apply to a court for an order that the registers or records be rectified.

(2) Notice to Director. — An applicant under this section shall give the Director notice of the application and the Director is entitled to appear and be heard in person or by counsel.

(3) Powers of court. — In connection with an application under this section, the court may make any order it thinks fit including, without limiting the generality of the foregoing,

(a) an order requiring the registers or other records of the corporation to be rectified;

(b) an order restraining the corporation from calling or holding a meeting of shareholders or paying a dividend before such rectification;

(c) an order determining the right of a party to the proceedings to have his name entered or retained in, or deleted or omitted from, the registers or records of the corporation, whether the issue arises between two or more security holders or alleged security holders, or between the corporation and any security holders or alleged security holders;

(d) an order compensating a party who has incurred a loss.

244. Application for directions. — The Director may apply to a court for directions in respect of any matter concerning his duties under this Act, and on such application the court may give such directions and make such further order as it thinks fit.

245. (1) Notice of refusal by Director. — If the Director refuses to file any articles or other document required by this Act to be filed by him before the articles or other document become effective, he shall, within twenty days after receipt thereof by him or twenty days after he receives any approval that may be required under any other Act, whichever is the later, give written notice of his refusal to the person who sent the articles or document, giving reasons therefor.

(2) Deemed refusal. — If the Director does not file or give written notice of his refusal to file any articles or document within the time limited therefor in subsection (1), he is deemed for the purposes of section 246 to have refused to file the articles or document.

246. Appeal from Director's decision. — A person who feels aggrieved by a decision of the Director

(a) to refuse to file in the form submitted to him any articles or other document required by this Act to be filed by him,

(b) to give a name, to change or revoke a name, or to refuse to reserve, accept, change or revoke a name under section 12,

(c) to refuse to grant an exemption under subsection 2(8), 10(2), 82(3), 127(8), 151(1), section 156, subsection 163(4) or 171(2) or subsection 160(3) and any regulations under that subsection,

(d) to refuse under subsection 187(11) to permit a continued reference to shares having a nominal or par value,

(e) to refuse to issue a certificate of discontinuance under section 188,

(f) to refuse to revive a corporation under section 209, or

(g) to dissolve a corporation under section 212,

may apply to a court for an order requiring the Director to change his decision, and on such application the court may so order and make any further order it thinks fit.

247. Restraining or compliance order. — If a corporation or any director, officer, employee, agent, auditor, trustee, receiver, receiver-manager or liquidator of a corporation does not comply with this Act, the regulations, articles, by-laws, or a unanimous shareholder agreement, a complainant or a creditor of the corporation may, in addition to any other right he has, apply to a court for an order directing any such person to comply with, or restraining any such person from acting in breach of, any provisions thereof, and on such application the court may so order and make any further order it thinks fit.

248. Summary application to court. — Where this Act states that a person may apply to a court, the application may be made in a summary manner by petition, originating notice of motion, or otherwise as the rules of the court provide, and subject to any order respecting notice to interested parties or costs, or any other order the court thinks fit.

249. Appeal. — An appeal lies to the court of appeal from any order made by a court under this Act.

250. (1) Offences with respect to reports. — A person who makes or assists in making a report, return, notice or other document required by this Act or the regulations to be sent to the Director or to any other person that

(a) contains an untrue statement of a material fact, or

(b) omits to state a material fact required therein or necessary to make a statement contained therein not misleading in the light of the circumstances in which it was made

is guilty of an offence and liable on summary conviction to a fine not exceeding five thousand dollars or to imprisonment for a term not exceeding six months or to both.

(2) Officers, etc., of bodies corporate. — Where a body corporate commits an offence under subsection (1), any director or officer of the body corporate who knowingly authorized, permitted or acquiesced in the commission of the offence is a party to and guilty of the offence and is liable on summary conviction to a fine not exceeding five thousand dollars or to imprisonment for a term not exceeding six months or to both, whether or not the body corporate has been prosecuted or convicted.

(3) Immunity. — No person is guilty of an offence under subsection (1) or (2) if the untrue statement or omission was unknown to him and in the exercise of reasonable diligence could not have been known to him.

251. Offence. — Every person who, without reasonable cause, contravenes a provision of this Act or the regulations for which no punishment is provided is guilty of an offence punishable on summary conviction.

252. (1) Order to comply. — Where a person is guilty of an offence under this Act or the regulations, any court in which proceedings in respect of the offence are taken may, in addition to any punishment it may impose, order that person to comply with the provisions of the Act or the regulations for the contravention of which he has been convicted.

(2) Limitation period. — A prosecution for an offence under this Act may be instituted at any time within but not later than two years after the time when the subject-matter of the complaint arose.

(3) Civil remedy not affected. — No civil remedy for an act or omission is suspended or affected by reason that the act or omission is an offence under this Act.

PART XXI
GENERAL

253. (1) Notice to directors and shareholders. — A notice or document required by this Act, the regulations, the articles or the by-laws to be sent to a shareholder or director of a corporation may be sent by prepaid mail addressed to, or may be delivered personally to,

(a) the shareholder at his latest address as shown in the records of the corporation or its transfer agent; and

(b) the director at his latest address as shown in the records of the corporation or in the last notice filed under section 106 or 113.

(2) Effect of notice. — A director named in a notice sent by a corporation to the Director under section 106 or 113 and filed by the Director is presumed for the purposes of this Act to be a director of the corporation referred to in the notice.

(3) Deemed receipt. — A notice or document sent in accordance with subsection (1) to a shareholder or director of a corporation is deemed to be received by him at the time it would be delivered in the ordinary course of mail unless there are reasonable grounds for believing that the shareholder or director did not receive the notice or document at that time or at all.

(4) Undelivered notices. — If a corporation sends a notice or document to a shareholder in accordance with subsection (1) and the notice or document is returned on three consecutive occasions because the shareholder cannot be found, the corporation is not required to send any further notices or documents to the shareholder until he informs the corporation in writing of his new address.

254. Notice to and service on a corporation. — A notice or document required to be sent to or served on a corporation may be sent by registered mail to the registered office of the corporation shown in the last notice filed under section 19 and, if so sent, is deemed to be received or served at the time it would be delivered in the ordinary course of mail unless there are reasonable grounds for believing that the corporation did not receive the notice or document at that time or at all.

255. Waiver of notice. — Where a notice or document is required by this Act or the regulations to be sent, the sending of the notice or document may be waived or the time for the notice or document may be waived or abridged at any time with the consent in writing of the person entitled thereto.

256. (1) Certificate of Director. — Where this Act requires or authorizes the Director to issue a certificate or to certify any fact, the certificate shall be signed by the Director or by a Deputy Director authorized under section 260.

(2) Evidence. — Except in a proceeding under section 213 to dissolve a corporation, a certificate referred to in subsection (1) or a certified copy thereof, when introduced as evidence in any civil, criminal or administrative action or proceeding, is conclusive proof of the facts so certified without proof of the signature or official character of the person appearing to have signed the certificate.

257. (1) Certificate of corporation. — A certificate issued on behalf of a corporation stating any fact that is set out in the articles, the by-laws, a unanimous shareholder agreement, the minutes of the meetings of the directors, a committee of directors or the shareholders, or in a trust indenture or other contract to which the corporation is a party, may be signed by a director, an officer or a transfer agent of the corporation.

(2) Proof. — When introduced as evidence in any civil, criminal or administrative action or proceeding,

(a) a fact stated in a certificate referred to in subsection (1),

(b) a certified extract from a securities register of a corporation, or

(c) a certified copy of minutes or extract from minutes of a meeting of shareholders, directors or a committee of directors of a corporation,

is, in the absence of evidence to the contrary, proof of the facts so certified without proof of the signature or official character of the person appearing to have signed the certificate.

(3) Security certificate. — An entry in a securities register of, or a security certificate issued by, a corporation is, in the absence of evidence to the contrary, proof that the person in whose name the security is registered is owner of the securities described in the register or in the certificate.

258. Copies. — Where a notice or document is required to be sent to the Director under this Act, the Director may accept a photostatic or photographic copy thereof.

259. (1) Proof required by Director. — The Director may require that a document or a fact stated in a document required by this Act or the regulations to be sent to him shall be verified in accordance with subsection (2).

(2) Form of proof. — A document or fact required by this Act or by the Director to be verified may be verified by affidavit made under oath or by statutory declaration under the *Canada Evidence Act* before any commissioner for oaths or for taking affidavits.

260. Appointment of Director. — The Minister may appoint a Director and one or more Deputy Directors to carry out the duties and exercise the powers of the Director under this Act.

261. (1) Regulations. — Subject to subsections (2) and (3), the Governor in Council may make regulations

(a) prescribing any matter required or authorized by this Act to be prescribed;

(b) requiring the payment of a fee in respect of the filing, examination or copying of any document, or in respect of any action that the Director is required or authorized to take under this Act, and prescribing the amount thereof;

(c) prescribing the format and contents of annual returns, notices and other documents required to be sent to the Director or to be issued by him;

(d) prescribing rules with respect to exemptions permitted by this Act; and

(e) prescribing that, for the purpose of paragraph 155(1)(a), the standards as they exist from time to time, of an accounting body named in the regulations shall be followed.

(2) Publication of proposed regulation. — Subject to subsection (3), the Minister shall publish in the *Canada Gazette* and in the periodical referred to in section 129 at least sixty days before the proposed effective date thereof a copy of every regulation that the Governor in Council proposes to make under

this Act and a reasonable opportunity shall be afforded to interested persons to make representations with respect thereto.

(3) Exceptions. — The Minister is not required to publish a proposed regulation if the proposed regulation

(a) grants an exemption or relieves a restriction;

(b) establishes or amends a fee;

(c) has been published pursuant to subsection (2) whether or not it has been amended as a result of representations made by interested persons as provided in that subsection; or

(d) makes no material substantive change in an existing regulation.

262. (1) Definition of "statement". — In this section, "statement" means a statement of intent to dissolve and a statement of revocation of intent to dissolve referred to in section 211.

(2) Execution and filing. — Where this Act requires that articles or a statement relating to a corporation shall be sent to the Director, unless otherwise specifically provided

(a) two copies (in this section called "duplicate originals") of the articles or the statement shall be signed by a director or an officer of the corporation or, in the case of articles of incorporation, by an incorporator; and

(b) on receiving duplicate originals of any articles or statement that are in the prescribed form, any other required documents and the prescribed fees, the Director shall

(i) endorse on each of the duplicate originals the word "Filed" and the date of the filing,

(ii) issue in duplicate the appropriate certificate and attach to each certificate one of the duplicate originals of the articles or statement,

(iii) file a copy of the certificate and attached articles or statement,

(iv) send to the corporation or its representative the original certificate and attached articles or statement, and

(v) publish in the *Canada Gazette* or in the periodical referred to in section 129 notice of the issue of the certificate.

(3) Date of certificate. — A certificate referred to in subsection (2) issued by the Director may be dated as of the day he receives the articles, statement or court order pursuant to which the certificate is issued or as of any later day specified by the court or person who signed the articles or statement.

(4) Signature. — A signature required on a certificate referred to in

subsection (2) or 263(2) may be printed or otherwise mechanically reproduced thereon.

(5) Date of certificate. — Notwithstanding subsection (3), a certificate of discontinuance may be dated as of the day a corporation is continued under the laws of another jurisdiction.

263. (1) Annual return. — Every corporation shall, on the prescribed date, send to the Director an annual return in prescribed form and the Director shall file it.

(2) Certificate of compliance. — The Director may furnish any person with a certificate that a corporation has sent to the Director a document required to be sent to him under this Act.

264. Alteration. — The Director may alter a notice or document, other than an affidavit or statutory declaration, if so authorized by the person who sent the document or by his representative.

265. (1) Corrections. — If a certificate containing an error is issued to a corporation by the Director, the directors or shareholders of the corporation shall, on the request of the Director, pass the resolutions and send to him the documents required to comply with this Act, and take such other steps as the Director may reasonably require, and the Director may demand the surrender of the certificate and issue a corrected certificate.

(2) Date of corrected certificate. — A certificate corrected under subsection (1) shall bear the date of the certificate it replaces.

(3) Notice. — If a corrected certificate issued under subsection (1) materially amends the terms of the original certificate, the Director shall forthwith give notice of the correction in the *Canada Gazette* or in the periodical referred to in section 129.

266. (1) Inspection. — A person who has paid the prescribed fee is entitled during usual business hours to examine a document required by this Act or the regulations to be sent to the Director, except a report sent to him under subsection 230(2), and to make copies of or extracts therefrom.

(2) Copies. — The Director shall furnish any person with a copy or a certified copy of a document required by this Act or the regulations to be sent to the Director, except a report sent to him under subsection 230(2).

267. (1) Records of Director. — Records required by this Act to be prepared and maintained by the Director may be in bound or loose-leaf form or in photographic film form, or may be entered or recorded by any system of mechanical or electronic data processing or by any other information storage device that is capable of reproducing any required information in intelligible written form within a reasonable time.

(2) Obligation to furnish. — Where records maintained by the Director are prepared and maintained other than in written form,

(a) the Director shall furnish any copy required to be furnished under subsection 266(2) in intelligible written form; and

(b) a report reproduced from those records, if it is certified by the Director, is admissible in evidence to the same extent as the original written records would have been.

(3) Retention of records. — The Director is not required to produce any document, other than a certificate and attached articles or statement filed under section 262, after six years from the date he receives it.

268. (1) Definition of "charter". — In this section, "charter" includes

(a) an act of incorporation and any amendments thereto; and

(b) letters patent of incorporation and any letters patent supplementary thereto.

(2) Amendment of charter. — In connection with a continuance under this Act, the shareholders of a body corporate incorporated or continued by or under an Act of Parliament other than this Act who are entitled to vote at annual meetings of shareholders may, notwithstanding any provision in any other Act of Parliament or any provision in the charter of the body corporate,

(a) by special resolution, authorize the directors of the body corporate to apply under section 187 for a certificate of continuance; and

(b) by the same resolution, make any amendment to the charter of the body corporate that a corporation incorporated under this Act may make to its articles.

(3) Change of class rights. — Notwithstanding subsection (2), the shareholders of a body corporate may not, by a special resolution under that subsection, make any change of the nature referred to in subsection 176(1) that affects a class or series of shares, unless

(a) the charter of the body corporate otherwise provides in respect of an amendment of the nature referred to in paragraph 176(1)(a), (b) or (e); or

(b) the holders of the class or series of shares approve the change in accordance with section 176.

(4) Authorizing continuance. — Subject to subsections (6) and (7), the directors of a body corporate incorporated or continued by or under an Act of Parliament other than this Act may, notwithstanding any provision in any other Act of Parliament or any provision in the charter of the body corporate, apply under section 187 for a certificate of continuance where the articles of continuance do not make any amendment to the charter of the body corporate other than an amendment required to conform to this Act.

(5) No dissent. — A shareholder is not entitled to dissent under section 190 in respect of an amendment made under subsection (2), (3) or (4).

(6) Discretionary continuance. — The Governor in Council may, by order, require that a body corporate incorporated by or under an Act of Parliament to which Part I or Part II of the *Canada Corporations Act*, does not apply, other than

(a) a bank,

[Para. (a) repealed and substituted by S.C. 1991, c. 46, s. 597; S.C. 1992, c. 1, Sch. V, Item 12.]

(b) a company or society to which the *Insurance Companies Act* applies;

[Para. (b) repealed and substituted by S.C. 1991, c. 47, s. 724.]

(c) a company to which the *Trust and Loan Companies Act* applies

shall apply for a certificate of continuance under section 187 within such period as may be prescribed.

[Subsec. (6) repealed and substituted by S.C. 1991, c. 45, s. 556.]

(7) Idem. — A body corporate to which Part IV of the *Canada Corporations Act* applies, other than a body corporate that carries on a business referred to in paragraph (6)(b), (c) or (d), may apply for a certificate of continuance under section 187.

(8) Fees. — A body corporate that obtains a certificate of continuance under this section is not required to pay any fees otherwise payable under this Act in respect of such continuance.

(9) Idem. — A body corporate referred to in subsection (6) that does not make an application to obtain a certificate of continuance within the period prescribed is dissolved on the expiration of that period.

(10) Continuance prohibited. — A body corporate to which Part II or Part III of the *Canada Corporations Act*, chapter C-32 of the Revised Statutes of Canada, 1970, applies or any similar body corporate incorporated otherwise than by or under an Act of Parliament may not apply for a certificate of continuance under section 187.

[Sections 263 and 264 of S.C. 1974-75-76, c. 33, were neither consolidated nor repealed by R.S.C. 1985. They were subsequently repealed by S.C. 1988, c. 2, s. 19.]

Appendix 2

WINDING-UP ACT

R.S.C. 1985, c. W-11, as amended by S.C. 1987, c. 23; c. 26; R.S.C. 1985 (and Supp.), c. 27, Sch., item 20; S.C. 1990, c. 17, ss. 43 and 44; S.C. 1991, c. 47, 747-752; S.C. 1992, c. 27, s. 90(1)(o).

An Act respecting the winding-up of insolvent companies.

SHORT TITLE

1. Short title. — This Act may be cited as the *Winding-up Act.* R.S., c. W-10, s. 1.

INTERPRETATION

2. Definitions. — In this Act

“capital stock”. — ”capital stock” includes a capital stock *de jure* or *de facto*;

“company”. — ”company” includes any corporation subject to this Act;

“contributory”. — ”contributory” means a person liable to contribute to the assets of a company under this Act; and, in all proceedings for determining the persons who are to be deemed contributories and in all proceedings prior to the final determination of such persons, it includes any person alleged to be a contributory;

“court”. — ”court” means,

(a) in Nova Scotia, British Columbia and Newfoundland, the Supreme Court,

(a.1) in Ontario, the Ontario Court (General Division),

- [Para. (a) repealed and substituted by paras. (a) and (a.1) by S.C. 1990, c. 17, s. 43.]

(b) in Quebec, the Superior Court,

(c) in New Brunswick, Manitoba, Saskatchewan and Alberta, the Court of Queen’s Bench, and

(c.1) in the Province of Prince Edward Island, the Trial Division of the Supreme Court,

- [Para. (c.1) added by R.S.C. 1985, c. 27, Sch., item 20.]

(d) in the Yukon Territory and Northwest Territories, the Supreme Court;

"creditor". — "creditor" includes all persons having any claim against the company present or future, certain, ascertained, or contingent, for liquidated or unliquidated damages; and in all proceedings for determining the persons who are to be deemed creditors it includes any person making any such claim;

"insurance company". — "insurance company" means a company transacting the business of insurance and includes any unincorporated association or reciprocal exchange transacting such business;

"Minister". — "Minister" means

(a) in Part I, the Minister of Consumer and Corporate Affairs, and
(b) in Parts II and III, the Minister of Finance;

"official gazette". — "official gazette" means the *Canada Gazette* and the gazette published under the authority of the government of the province where the proceedings for the winding-up of the business of the company are carried on, or used as the official means of communication between the lieutenant governor of that province and the people, and if no such gazette is published in the province, any newspaper published in the province and designated by a court for publishing the notices required by this Act;

"trading company". — "trading company" means any company, except a railway or telegraph company, carrying on business similar to that carried on by apothecaries, auctioneers, bankers, brokers, brickmakers, builders, carpenters, carriers, cattle or sheep salesmen, coach proprietors, dyers, fullers, keepers of inns, taverns, hotels, saloons or coffee houses, lime burners, livery stable keepers, market gardeners, millers, miners, packers, printers, quarrymen, sharebrokers, ship-owners, shipwrights, stockbrokers, stock-jobbers, victuallers, warehousemen, wharfingers, persons using the trade of merchandise by way of bargaining, exchange, bartering, commission, consignment or otherwise, in gross or by retail, or by persons who, either for themselves, or as agents or factors for others, seek their living by buying and selling or buying and letting for hire goods or commodities, or by the manufacture, workmanship or the conversion of goods or commodities or trees;

"winding-up order". — "winding-up order" means an order granted by a court under this Act to wind up the business of the company, and includes any order granted by the court to bring under this Act any company in liquidation or in process of being wound up.

3. When company deemed insolvent. — A company is deemed insolvent

(a) if it is unable to pay its debts as they become due;
(b) if it calls a meeting of its creditors for the purpose of compounding with them;
(c) if it exhibits a statement showing its inability to meet its liabilities;
(d) if it has otherwise acknowledged its insolvency;

(e) if it assigns, removes or disposes of, or attempts or is about to assign, remove or dispose of, any of its property, with intent to defraud, defeat or delay its creditors, or any of them;

(f) if, with the intent referred to in paragraph (e), it has procured its money, goods, chattels, land or property to be seized, levied on or taken, under or by any process of execution;

(g) if it has made any general conveyance or assignment of its property for the benefit of its creditors or if, being unable to meet its liabilities in full, it makes any sale or conveyance of the whole or the main part of its stock in trade or assets, without the consent of its creditors or without satisfying their claims; or

(h) if it permits any execution issued against it, under which any of its goods, chattels, land or property are seized, levied on or taken in execution, to remain unsatisfied till within four days of the time fixed by the sheriff or other officer for the sale thereof, or for fifteen days after the seizure.

4. Company deemed unable to pay its debts. — A company is deemed to be unable to pay its debts as they become due whenever a creditor, to whom the company is indebted in a sum exceeding two hundred dollars then due, has served on the company, in the manner in which process may legally be served on it in the place where service is made, a demand in writing, requiring the company to pay the sum so due, and the company has for ninety days, in the case of a bank, and for sixty days in all other cases, next succeeding the service of the demand, neglected to pay the sum or to secure or compound for the sum to the satisfaction of the creditor.

5. Commencement of winding-up. — The winding-up of the business of a company shall be deemed to commence at the time of the service of the notice of presentation of the petition for winding-up.

APPLICATION

6. Application. — This Act applies to all corporations incorporated by or under the authority of an Act of Parliament of the former Province of Canada, or of the Province of Nova Scotia, New Brunswick, British Columbia, Prince Edward Island or Newfoundland, and whose incorporation and the affairs whereof are subject to the legislative authority of Parliament; and to incorporated banks, savings banks, incorporated insurance companies, loan companies having borrowing powers, building societies having a capital stock, and incorporated trading companies doing business in Canada wherever incorporated and

(a) that are insolvent; or

(b) that are in liquidation or in process of being wound up, and, on petition by any of their shareholders or creditors, assignees or liquidators ask to be brought under this Act.

7. Certain corporations excepted. — This Act does not apply to building societies that do not have a capital stock or to railway or telegraph companies.

PART I
GENERAL

Limitation of Part

8. Subject to Part II. — In the case of a bank other than a savings bank the provisions of this Part are subject to the provisions of Part II.

9. Subject to Part III. — In the case of insurance companies the provisions of this Part are subject to the provisions of Part III.

Winding-up Order

10. Cases where winding-up order may be made. — A court may make a winding-up order in respect of a company

(a) where the period, if any, fixed for the duration of the company by the Act, charter or instrument of incorporation of the company has expired; or where an event, if any, has occurred, on the occurrence of which it is provided by the Act, charter or instrument of incorporation that the company is to be dissolved;
(b) where the company at a special meeting of shareholders called for the purpose has passed a resolution requiring the company to be wound up;
(c) when the company is insolvent;
(d) when the capital stock of the company is impaired to the extent of twenty-five per cent thereof, and when it is shown to the satisfaction of the court that the lost capital will not likely be restored within one year; or
(e) when the court is of opinion that for any other reason it is just and equitable that the company should be wound up.

Application for Order

11. Application for winding-up order. — An application for a winding-up order may

(a) in the cases mentioned in paragraphs 10(a) and (b), be made by the company or by a shareholder of the company;
(b) in the case mentioned in paragraph 10(c), be made by the company or by a creditor of the company for the sum of at least two hundred dollars, or, except in the case of banks and insurance corporations, by a shareholder holding shares in the capital stock of the company to the amount of at least five hundred dollars par value, or holding five shares without nominal or par value in the capital stock of the company, and
(c) in the cases mentioned in paragraphs 10(d) and (e), be made by a shareholder holding shares in the capital stock of the company to the amount of at least five hundred dollars par value, or holding five shares without nominal or par value in the capital stock of the company.

12. (1) How and where made. — An application for a winding-up order may be made by petition to the court in the province where the head office of the company is situated or, if there is no head office in Canada, then in the province where its chief place or one of its chief places of business is situated.

(2) Notice of application. — Except in cases where an application for a winding-up order is made by a company, four days notice of the application shall be given to the company before the making of the application.

13. Power of court. — A court may, on application for a winding-up order, make the order applied for, dismiss the application with or without costs, adjourn the hearing conditionally or unconditionally or make any interim or other order that it deems just.

14. Proceedings may be adjourned. — If a company opposes an application for a winding-up order on the ground that it has not become insolvent, that its suspension or default was only temporary and was not caused by a deficiency in its assets, that its capital stock is not impaired to the extent described in paragraph 10(d), that the impairment does not endanger the capacity of the company to pay its debts in full or that there is a probability that its lost capital will be restored within a year or within a reasonable time thereafter, and shows reasonable cause for believing that its opposition is well founded, the court, in its discretion, may, from time to time, adjourn proceedings on the application, for a time not exceeding six months after the date of the application, and may order an accountant or other person to inquire into the affairs of the company and to report thereon within a period not exceeding thirty days after the date of that order.

15. Duty of company. — On the service on the company of an order made under section 14 for an inquiry into the affairs of the company, the president, directors, officers and employees of the company and every other person shall respectively

(a) exhibit to the accountant or other person named for the purpose of making the inquiry the books of account of the company and all inventories, papers and vouchers referring to the business of the company or of any person therewith that are in their possession, custody or control; and
(b) give all such information as is required by the accountant or other person named for the purpose of the inquiry in order to form a just estimate of the affairs of the company.

16. Power of the court. — On receiving the report of the accountant or person ordered to inquire into the affairs of the company under section 14, and after hearing such shareholders or creditors of the company as desire to be heard thereon, the court may either refuse the application or make the winding-up order.

Staying Proceedings

17. Actions against company may be stayed. — A court may, on the application of a company, or of any creditor or contributory, at any time after the presentation of a petition for a winding-up order and before making the order, restrain further proceedings in any action, suit or proceeding against the company on such terms as the court thinks fit.

18. Court may stay winding-up proceedings. — A court may, on the application of any creditor or contributory, at any time after a winding-up order is made, and on proof, to the satisfaction of the court, that all proceedings in relation to the winding-up ought to be stayed, make an order staying those proceedings, either altogether or for a limited time, on such terms and subject to such conditions as the court thinks fit.

Effect of Winding-up Order

19. Company to cease business. — A company, from the time of the making of the winding-up order, shall cease to carry on its business, except in so far as is, in the opinion of the liquidator, required for the beneficial winding-up thereof, but the corporate state and all the corporate powers of the company, notwithstanding that it is otherwise provided by the Act, charter or instrument of incorporation of the company, continue until the affairs of the company are wound up.

20. Transfer of shares void. — All transfers of shares of a company referred to in section 19, except transfers made to or with the sanction of the liquidator, under the authority of the court, and every alteration in the status of the members of the company, after the commencement of the winding-up, are void.

21. Effect of winding-up order. — After a winding-up order is made in respect of a company, no suit, action or other proceeding shall be proceeded with or commenced against the company, except with the leave of the court and subject to such terms as the court imposes.

22. Execution, etc. — Every attachment, sequestration, distress or execution put in force against the estate or effects of a company after the making of a winding-up order is void.

Appointment of Liquidators

23. (1) Liquidator. — A court in making a winding-up order in respect of a company, may appoint a liquidator or more than one liquidator of the estate and effects of the company.

(2) Trustee under *Bankruptcy and Insolvency Act.* — In the case of any company except incorporated building societies, banks, savings banks, insurance companies, trust companies, loan companies and railway companies, a court shall not appoint as liquidator any person who is not licensed as a trustee under the *Bankruptcy and Insolvency Act.*

[S. 23 amended by substituting "*Bankruptcy and Insolvency Act*" in place of "*Bankruptcy Act*" by S.C. 1992, c. 27, s. 90(1)(o).]

24. If more than one liquidator. — If more than one liquidator is appointed under subsection 23(1), a court may declare whether any act to be done by a liquidator is to be done by all or any one or more of the liquidators.

25. Additional liquidators. — A court may, if it thinks fit, after the appointment of one or more liquidators, appoint an additional liquidator or liquidators.

26. Notice. — No liquidator shall be appointed under subsection 23(1) unless a previous notice is given to the creditors, contributories and shareholders or members of the company, and the court shall by order direct the manner and form in which the notice shall be given and the length of the notice.

27. Security. — The court shall determine what security shall be given by a liquidator on his appointment.

28. Provisional liquidator. — A court may, on the presentation of a petition for a winding-up order or at any time thereafter and before the first appointment of a liquidator, appoint provisionally a liquidator of the estate and effects of the company and may limit and restrict his powers by the order appointing him.

29. Incorporated company. — An incorporated company may be appointed liquidator to the goods and effects of a company under this Act, and if an incorporated company is so appointed, it may act through one or more of its principal offices designated by the court.

30. Trust company. — Where under the laws of any province a trust company is accepted by the courts of that province, and is permitted to act as administrator, assignee or curator without giving security, the trust company may be appointed liquidator of a company under this Act, without giving security.

31. Powers of directors. — On the appointment of a liquidator, all the powers of the directors of the company cease, except in so far as the court or the liquidator sanctions the continuance of those powers.

32. Resignation and removal. — A liquidator may resign or may be removed by the court on due cause shown, and every vacancy in the office of liquidator shall be filled by the court.

Powers and Duties of Liquidators

33. Duties after appointment. — A liquidator, on his appointment, shall take into his custody or under his control all the property, effects and choses in action to which the company is or appears to be entitled, and shall perform such duties in reference to winding up the business of the company as are imposed by the court or by this Act.

34. Liquidator to prepare statement. — A liquidator shall, within sixty days

after his appointment, prepare a statement of the assets, debts and liabilities of the company and of the value of those assets as shown by his books and records.

35. (1) Powers. — A liquidator may, with the approval of the court, and on such previous notice to the creditors, contributories, shareholders or members of the company as the court orders,

(a) bring or defend any action, suit or prosecution or other legal proceeding, civil or criminal, in his own name as liquidator or in the name or on behalf of the company, as the case may be;
(b) carry on the business of the company so far as is necessary to the beneficial winding-up of the company;
(c) sell the real and personal property, effects and choses in action of the company, by public auction or private contract, and transfer the whole thereof to any person or company, or sell them in parcels for such consideration as may be approved by the court;
(d) do all acts, and execute, in the name and on behalf of the company, all deeds, receipts and other documents, and for that purpose use, when necessary, the seal of the company;
(e) prove, rank, claim and draw dividends in the matter of the bankruptcy, insolvency or sequestration of any contributory, for any sum due the company from the contributory, and take and receive dividends in respect of the sum in the matter of the bankruptcy, insolvency or sequestration, as a separate debt due from that contributory and rateably with the other separate creditors;
(f) draw, accept, make and endorse any bill of exchange or promissory note in the name and on behalf of the company;
(g) raise on the security of the assets of the company any requisite sum or sums of money; and
(h) do and execute all such other things as are necessary for winding up the affairs of the company and distributing its assets.

(2) Company liable. — The drawing, accepting, making or endorsing of every bill of exchange or promissory note mentioned in subsection (1), on behalf of the company, has the same effect, with respect to the liability of the company, as if the bill or note had been drawn, accepted, made or endorsed by or on behalf of the company in the course of the carrying on of its business.

(3) No delivery of assets needed. — No delivery of the whole or of any part of the assets of the company is necessary to give a lien to any person taking security on the assets of the company.

36. Appointment of solicitor. — A liquidator may, with the approval of the court, appoint a solicitor or law agent to assist him in the performance of his duties.

37. (1) Debts due to the company. — A liquidator may, with the approval of the court, compromise all calls and liabilities to calls, debts and liabilities

capable of resulting in debts, and all claims, demands and matters in dispute in any way relating to or affecting the assets of the company or the winding-up of the company, on the receipt of such sums, payable at such times, and generally on such terms, as are agreed on.

(2) Security may be taken. — A liquidator may take any security for the discharge of the calls, debts, liabilities, claims, demands, or disputed matters referred to in subsection (1), and give a complete discharge in respect of all or any of those calls, debts, liabilities, claims, demands or matters.

38. Creditors may be compromised. — A liquidator may, with the approval of the court, make such compromise or other arrangements with creditors or persons claiming to be creditors of the company as he deems expedient.

39. Court may provide as to powers. — A court may provide, by any order subsequent to a winding-up order, that a liquidator may exercise any of the powers conferred on him by this Act, without the sanction or intervention of the court.

40. Documents to Chief Statistician of Canada. — A liquidator shall promptly after their receipt or preparation, mail to the Chief Statistician of Canada a true copy of

(a) the winding-up order referred to in section 10;
(b) the petition referred to in section 12;
(c) the statement of the debts, liabilities and assets of the company and statements of the value of the assets referred to in section 34; and
(d) the dividend sheets referred to in section 85.

Appointment of Inspectors

41. Inspectors. — A court may appoint, at any time when found advisable, one or more inspectors, whose duty it is to assist and advise a liquidator in the liquidation of a company.

Remuneration of Liquidators and Inspectors

42. (1) Remuneration. — A liquidator shall be paid such salary or remuneration, by way of percentage or otherwise, as the court directs, on such notice to the creditors, contributors, shareholders or members as the court orders.

(2) Distribution. — If there is more than one liquidator appointed for the liquidation of a company, the remuneration shall be distributed among them in such proportions as the court directs.

43. Remuneration of inspectors. — The court shall determine the remuneration, if any is deemed just, of inspectors.

Depositing in Bank

44. Moneys to be deposited in bank. — A liquidator shall deposit at interest in a bank or Government savings bank designated by the court all sums of

money that he has in his hands belonging to the company, whenever and as often as the sums amount to one hundred dollars.

45. Separate account. — Deposits under section 44 shall not be made in the name of the liquidator individually, on pain of dismissal, but a separate account shall be kept for the company of the moneys belonging to the company in the name of the liquidator as liquidator.

46. Balance on hand by liquidator. — A liquidator shall, within three days after the date of the final winding-up of the business of a company, deposit at interest in the bank, appointed or designated under Section 44, any money belonging to the estate then in his hands and not required for any other purpose authorized by this Act, with a sworn statement and account of that money, and that that money is all that he has in his hands.

47. Penalty for neglect. — In case any liquidator does not, within three days after the date of the final winding-up of the business of a company, deposit in the bank, appointed or designated under Section 44, any money belonging to the estate of which he is the liquidator, then in his hands, he shall be deemed a debtor to Her Majesty for that money, and may be compelled as such to account for and pay over that money.

Court Discharging Functions of Liquidator

48. If no liquidator. — If at any time no liquidator has been appointed to wind up the business of a company all the property of the company shall be deemed to be in the custody of the court.

49. (1) Provision for discharge of liquidator. — Whenever a company is being wound up and the realization and distribution of its assets has proceeded so far that in the opinion of the court it becomes expedient that the liquidator should be discharged, and that the balance remaining in his hands of the moneys and assets of the company can be better realized and distributed by the court, the court may make an order discharging the liquidator and for payment, delivery and transfer into court, or to such officer or person as the court may direct, of those moneys and assets, and the money and assets shall be realized and distributed, by or under the direction of the court, among the persons entitled thereto, in the same way, as nearly as may be, as if the distribution were being made by the liquidator.

(2) Disposal of books and documents. — In the case described in subsection (1), the court may make an order directing how the books, accounts and documents of the company and of the liquidator may be disposed of, and may order that they be deposited in court or otherwise dealt with as may be thought fit.

Contributories

50. List of contributories. — As soon as possible after the commencement of the winding-up of a company, the court shall settle a list of contributories.

51. Classes distinguished. — In the list of contributories referred to in section 50, persons who are contributories in their own right shall be distinguished from persons who are contributories as representatives of or liable for the debts of others.

52. Adding heirs to list. — It is not necessary, where the personal representative of any deceased contributory is placed on the list, to add the heirs or devisees of the contributory, but the heirs or devisees may be added as and when the court thinks fit.

53. (1) Liability of shareholders. — Every shareholder or member of a company or his representative is liable to contribute the amount unpaid on his shares of the capital, or on his liability to the company, or to its members or creditors, as the case may be, under the Act, charter or instrument of incorporation of the company, or otherwise.

(2) Liability an asset. — The amount that a shareholder is liable to contribute under subsection (1) shall be deemed an asset of the company, and a debt due to the company, payable as directed or appointed under this Act.

54. (1) Liability after transfer of shares. — Where a shareholder has transferred his shares under circumstances that do not, by law, free him from liability in respect thereof, or where he is by law liable to the company or its members or creditors , as the case may be, to an amount beyond the amount unpaid on his shares, he shall be deemed a member of the company for the purposes of this Act and is liable to contribute, under subsection 53(1), to the extent of his liabilities to the company or its members or creditors, independently of this Act.

(2) An asset. — The amount that a shareholder is liable to contribute under subsection (1) shall be deemed an asset and a debt described in subsection 53(2).

55. Liability of contributory a debt. — The liability of any person to contribute to the assets of a company under this Act, in the event of the business of the company being wound up, creates a debt accruing due from that person at the time when his liability commenced, but payable at the time or respective times when calls are made, under this Act, for enforcing that liability.

56. Provable against his estate. — In the case of the bankruptcy or insolvency of any contributory, the estimated value of his liability to future calls, as well as calls already made, may be proved against his estate.

57. Handing over money and books. — A court may, at any time after making a winding-up order, require any contributory for the time being settled on the list of contributories as trustee, receiver, banker, agent or officer of the company, to pay, deliver, convey, surrender or transfer forthwith, or within such time as the court directs, to or into the hands of the liquidator, any sum or balance, books, papers, estate or effects that are in his hands for the time being, and to which the company appears to be entitled.

58. Payment by contributory. — A court may, at any time after making

a winding-up order, make an order on any contributory for the time being settled on the list of contributories, directing payment to be made, in the manner mentioned in the order, of any moneys due from him or from the estate of the person whom he represents to the company, exclusive of any moneys that he or the estate of the person whom he represents is liable to contribute by virtue of any call made in pursuance of this Act.

59. Calls on contributories. — A court may, at any time after making a winding-up order, and either before or after it has ascertained the sufficiency of the assets of the company, make calls on and order payment thereof by all or any of the contributories for the time being settled on the list of contributories, to the extent of their liability, for payment of all or any sums it deems necessary to satisfy the debts and liabilities of the company, the costs, charges and expenses of winding up and for the adjustment of the rights of the contributories among themselves.

60. (1) Consideration of possible failure to pay. — A court may, in making a call, take into consideration the probability that some of the contributories on whom the call is made may partly or wholly fail to pay their respective portions of the call.

(2) Maturity of debt. — No call compels payment of a debt before the maturity thereof and the extent of the liability of any contributory is not increased by anything in this section.

61. (1) Order for payment. — A court may order any contributory, purchaser or other person from whom money is due to the company to pay the money into a bank or Government savings bank, to the account of the court instead of the liquidator.

(2) Enforcement. — An order made under subsection (1) may be enforced in the same manner as if it had directed payment to the liquidator.

62. Rights of contributories. — The court shall adjust the rights of the contributories among themselves.

Meetings of Creditors

63. Meetings. — A court may, if it thinks expedient, direct meetings of the creditors, contributories, shareholders or members of a company to be summoned, held and conducted in such manner as the court directs, for the purpose of ascertaining their wishes, and may appoint a person to act as chairman of any of those meetings, and to report the result of those meetings to the court.

64. (1) Votes according to amount of claim. — In the case described in Section 63, regard shall, with respect to creditors, be had as to the amount of the debt due to each creditor and with respect to shareholders or members, as to the number of votes conferred on each shareholder or member by law or by the regulations of the company.

(2) Preliminary proof. — The court may prescribe the mode of preliminary

proof of creditors' claims for the purpose of any meeting directed to be held under section 63.

65. Court may summon creditors to consider any proposed compromise. — Where any compromise or arrangement is proposed between a company in course of being wound up under this Act and the creditors of the company, or by and between any of those creditors or any class or classes of those creditors and the company, the court, in addition to any other of its powers, may, on the application, in a summary way, of any creditor or of the liquidator, order that a meeting of those creditors or class or classes of creditors shall be summoned in such manner as the court shall direct.

66. Sanction of compromise. — If a majority in number, representing three-fourths in value, of the creditors or class or classes of creditors referred to in section 65, present either in person or by proxy at the meeting summoned under that section, agree to any arrangement or compromise, the arrangement or compromise may be sanctioned by an order of the court, and in such case is binding on all the creditors, or on the class or classes of creditors, as the case may be, and also on the liquidator and contributories of the company.

67. Chairman of meeting. — In directing meetings of creditors, contributories, shareholders or members of a company to be held as provided in this Act, the court may either appoint a person to act as chairman of the meeting or direct that a chairman be appointed by the persons entitled to be present at the meeting, and, in the event the appointed chairman fails to attend the meeting, the persons present at the meeting may elect a qualified person as chairman who shall perform the duties prescribed by this Act.

68. Voting to be in person or by proxy. — No creditor, contributory, shareholder, or member of a company shall vote at any meeting unless present personally or represented by a person acting under a written authority, filed with the chairman or liquidator, to act as the representative at the meeting, or generally.

Production of Pass-books

69. Bank book of liquidator. — At every meeting of creditors, contributories, shareholders or members of a company, the liquidator shall produce a bank pass-book, showing the amount of the deposits made for the company, the dates at which the deposits were made, the amount withdrawn and dates of the withdrawal.

70. Other times. — The liquidator shall produce the pass-book referred to in section 69 whenever ordered to do so by the court.

Creditors' Claims

71. (1) What debts may be proved. — When the business of a company is being wound up under this Act, all debts payable on a contingency, and all

claims against the company, present or future, certain or contingent, and for liquidated or unliquidated damages, are admissible to proof against the company.

(2) Uncertain claims valued. — In case of any claim subject to any contingency or for unliquidated damages or which for any other reason does not bear a certain value, the court shall determine the value of the claim and the amount for which it shall rank.

72. Claims of clerks and employees privileged. — Clerks or other persons in, or having been in the employment of, a company, in or about its business or trade, shall be collocated in the dividend sheet by special privilege over other creditors, for any arrears of salary or wages due and unpaid to them at the time of the making of the winding-up order, not exceeding the arrears that have accrued to them during the three months immediately preceding the date of that order.

73. Law of set-off to apply. — The law of set-off, as administered by the courts, whether of law or equity, applies to all claims on the estate of a company, and to all proceedings for the recovery of debts due or accruing due to a company at the commencement of the winding-up of the company, in the same manner and to the same extent as if the business of the company was not being wound up under this Act.

74. Time for sending in claims. — A court may, with respect to the winding-up of a company, fix a certain day or certain days on or within which creditors of the company may send in their claims, and may direct notice thereof to be given by the liquidator, and may determine the manner in which notice of the day or days so fixed shall be given by the liquidator to the creditors.

75. (1) Creditors required to prove claims. — The liquidator may give notice in writing to creditors who have sent in their claims to him or of whose claims he has notice, and to creditors whose claims he considers should not be allowed without proof, requiring them to attend before the court on a day to be named in the notice and prove their claims to the satisfaction of the court.

(2) Disallowance on default. — Where a creditor does not attend in pursuance of the notice given under subsection (1), his claim shall be disallowed, unless the court sees fit to grant further time for the proof thereof.

(3) Disallowance on hearing. — Where a creditor attends in pursuance of the notice given under subsection (1), the court may on hearing the matter allow or disallow the claim of that creditor in whole or in part.

76. (1) Distribution of assets. — After the notices required by sections 74 and 75 have been given, and the respective times therein specified have expired and all claims of which proof has been required by due notice in writing by the liquidator in that behalf have been allowed or disallowed by the court in whole or in part, the liquidator may distribute the assets of the company or any part thereof among the persons entitled thereto and without reference to any claim against the company that has not then been sent to the liquidator.

(2) Claims not sent in. — The liquidator is not liable to any person whose claim has not been sent in at the time of distributing the assets or part thereof under subsection (1) for the assets or part thereof so distributed.

77. Rank of claims sent in after distribution started. — Where any claim or claims are sent in to the liquidator after any partial distribution of the assets of a company, the claim or claims, subject to proof and allowance as required by this Act, shall rank with other claims of creditors in any future distribution of assets of the company.

Secured Claims

78. Duty of creditor holding security. — If a creditor holds security on the estate of the company, he shall specify the nature and amount of such security in his claim, and shall therein, on his oath, put a specified value thereon.

79. Option of liquidator. — The liquidator, under the authority of the court, may either consent to the retention by the creditor of the property and effects constituting the security referred to in section 78 or on which it attaches, at the value specified thereon, or he may require from the creditor an assignment and delivery of the security, property and effects, at the specified value, to be paid by him out of the estate so soon as he has realized the security, together with interest on the value from the date of filing the claim until payment.

80. Ranking of secured creditor. — In the event of the retention referred to in section 79, the difference between the value at which the security is retained and the amount of the claim of the creditor shall be the amount for which he may rank in any future distribution of assets.

81. (1) Security by negotiable instrument. — If a creditor holds a claim based on negotiable instruments on which the company is only directly or secondarily liable and that is not mature or exigible, the creditor shall be considered to hold security within the meaning of sections 78, 79 and 80, and shall put a value on the liability of the person primarily liable thereon as being his security for the payment thereof.

(2) Revaluation. — After the maturity of the liability referred to in subsection (1) and its non-payment, the creditor is entitled to amend and revalue his claim.

82. Security by mortgage or charge. — Where the security of a creditor consists of a mortgage on ships or shipping or on real property, or of a registered judgment or an execution binding real property that is not by some other provision of this Act invalid for any purpose of creating a lien, claim or privilege on the real or personal property of the company, the property mortgaged or bound by the security shall only be assigned and delivered to the creditors

(a) subject to all previous mortgages, judgments, executions, hypothecs and liens thereon, holding rank and priority before his claim;
(b) on his assuming and binding himself to pay all such previous mortgages, judgments, executions, hypothecs and liens; and
(c) on his securing the estate of the company to the satisfaction of the

liquidator against any claim by reason of such previous mortgages, judgments, executions, hypothecs and liens.

83. In case of subsequent claims. — Where there are mortgages, judgments, executions, hypothecs or liens on ships or shipping or real property subsequent to those of a creditor referred to in section 82, he shall only obtain the property

(a) by consent of the subsequently secured creditors;
(b) on the subsequently secured creditors filing their claims specifying their security thereon as of no value;
(c) on his paying the subsequently secured creditors the value by them placed thereon; or
(d) on his securing the estate of the company to the satisfaction of the liquidator against any claim by reason of the subsequent mortgages, judgments, executions, hypothecs and liens.

84. Authority to retain. — On a secured claim being filed, with a valuation of the security, the liquidator shall procure the authority of the court to consent to the retention of the security by the creditor or shall require from him an assignment and delivery thereof.

Dividend Sheet

85. Preparing dividend sheet. — In the preparation of a dividend sheet, due regard shall be had to the rank and privilege of every creditor, but no dividend shall be allotted or paid to any creditor holding security on the estate of the company for his claim until the amount for which he may rank as a creditor on the estate, as to dividends therefrom, is established as herein provided.

Liens

86. (1) No lien by execution, etc., after commencement of winding-up. — No lien or privilege shall be created

(a) on the real or personal property of the company for the amount of any judgment debt, or of the interest thereon, by the issue or delivery to the sheriff of any writ of execution or by levying on or seizing under that writ the effects or estate of the company, or
(b) on the real or personal property of the company, or on any debts due or accruing or becoming due to the company, by the filing or registering of any memorial or minute of judgment or by the issue or taking out of any attachment or garnishee order or other process or proceeding,

if, before the payment over to the plaintiff of the moneys actually levied, paid or received under the writ, memorial, minute, attachment, garnishee order or other process or proceeding, the winding-up of the business of the company has commenced.

(2) Lien for costs expected. — This section does not affect any lien or privilege for costs that the plaintiff possesses under the law of the province in

which the writ, attachment, garnishee order or other process or proceeding was issued or taken out.

Contestation of Claims

87. Claims or dividend may be objected to. — Any liquidator, creditor, contributory, shareholder or member may object to any claim filed with the liquidator or to any dividend declared.

88. (1) Objections in writing. — Where a claim or dividend is objected to under section 87, the objections shall be filed in writing with the liquidator, together with the evidence of the previous service of a copy thereof on the claimant.

(2) Answers and replies. — The claimant shall have six days to answer the objections, or such further time as the court allows, and the contestant shall have three days to reply, or such further time as the court allows.

89. Day to be fixed for hearing. — On the completion of the issues on the objections filed under section 88, the liquidator shall transmit to the court all necessary papers relating to the contestation, and the court shall, on the application of either party, fix a day for taking evidence on the contestation and hearing and determining the contestation.

90. Costs. — The court may make such order as seems proper in respect of the payment of the costs of the contestation referred to in section 89 by either party or out of the estate of the company.

91. Default in answer by claimant. — Where, after a claim or dividend has been duly objected to, the claimant does not answer the objections, the court may, on the application of the contestant, make an order barring the claim or correcting the dividend, or may make such other order in reference thereto as appears right.

92. Security for costs. — The court may order the person objecting to a claim or dividend to give security for the costs of the contestation within a limited time, and may, in default, dismiss the contestation or stay proceedings thereon on such terms as the court thinks just.

Distribution of Assets

93. Distribution of property. — The property of the company shall be applied in satisfaction of its debts and liabilities, and the charges, costs and expenses incurred in winding up its affairs.

94. Winding-up expenses. — All costs, charges and expenses properly incurred in the winding-up of a company, including the remuneration of the liquidator, are payable out of the assets of the company, in priority to all other claims.

95. Distribution of surplus. — The court shall distribute among the persons entitled thereto any surplus that remains after satisfaction of the debts and

liabilities of the company, and the winding-up charges, costs and expenses, and unless otherwise provided by law or by the Act, charter or instrument of incorporation of the company, any property or assets remaining after the satisfaction shall be distributed among the members or shareholders according to their rights and interests in the company.

Fraudulent Preferences

96. Gratuitous contracts. — All gratuitous contracts, or conveyances or contracts without consideration, or with a merely nominal consideration, respecting either real or personal property, made by a company in respect to which a winding-up order under this Act is afterwards made, with or to any person whatsoever, whether a creditor of the company or not, within three months immediately preceding the commencement of the winding-up, or at any time afterwards, shall be presumed to have been made with intent to defraud the creditors of the company.

97. Contacts injuring or obstructing creditors. — All contracts by which creditors are injured, obstructed or delayed, made by a company unable to meet its engagements, and in respect of which a winding-up order under this Act is afterwards made, with a person whether a creditor of the company or not, who knows of that inability or has probable cause for believing that such inability exists, or after that inability has become public and notorious, shall be presumed to be made with intent to defraud the creditors of the company.

98. When contracts with consideration voidable. — A contract or conveyance for consideration, respecting either real or personal property, by which creditors are injured or obstructed, made by a company unable to meet its engagements with a person ignorant of that inability, whether a creditor of the company or not, and before that inability has become public and notorious, but within thirty days next before the commencement of the winding-up of the business of the company under this Act, or at any time afterwards, is voidable, and may be set aside by any court of competent jurisdiction, on such terms with respect to the protection of that person from actual loss or liability by reason of that contract as the court orders.

99. Contracts made with intent to defraud or delay creditors. — All contracts or conveyances made and acts done by a company respecting either real or personal property, with intent fraudulently to impede, obstruct or delay the creditors of the company in their remedies against the company, or with intent to defraud the creditors of the company or any of them, and so made, done and intended with the knowledge of the person contracting or acting with the company, whether a creditor of the company or not, and that have the effect of impeding, obstructing or delaying the creditors in their remedies, or of injuring them, or any of them, are void.

100. (1) Sale or transfer in contemplation of insolvency. — Where any sale, deposit, pledge or transfer is made of any property, real or personal, by a company in contemplation of insolvency under this Act, by way of security for payment

to any creditor, or where any property, real or personal, goods, effects or valuable security are given by way of payment by the company to any creditor, whereby that creditor obtains or will obtain an unjust preference over the other creditors, the sale, deposit, pledge, transfer or payment is void, and the subject thereof may be recovered back by the liquidator by suit or action in any court of competent jurisdiction.

(2) Presumption if within thirty days. — Where the sale, deposit, pledge or transfer under subsection (1) is made within thirty days next before the commencement of the winding-up under this Act, or at any time afterwards, it shall be presumed to have been so made in contemplation of insolvency.

101. (1) Payments by company within thirty days. -- Every payment made within thirty days next before the commencement of the winding-up under this Act by a company unable to meet its engagements in full, to a person who knows of that inability or has probable cause for believing that inability exists, is void, and the amount paid may be recovered back by the liquidator by suit or action in any court of competent jurisdiction.

(2) Restoration of security. — Where any valuable security is given up in consideration of a payment described in subsection (1), the security or the value thereof shall be restored to the creditor on the return of the payment.

102. Debts of company transferred to contributories. — When a debt due or owing by the company has been transferred within the time and under the circumstances mentioned in section 101, or at any time afterwards, to a contributory, or to any person indebted or liable in any way to the company, who knows or has probable cause for believing the company is unable to meet its engagements, or in contemplation of its insolvency under this Act, for the purpose of enabling that contributory or person to set up, by way of compensation or set-off, the debt so transferred, the debt shall not be set up by way of compensation or set-off against the claim on that contributory or person.

Appeals

103. Appeals. — Any person dissatisfied with an order or decision of the court or a single judge in any proceeding under this Act may,

(a) if the question to be raised on the appeal involves future rights,
(b) if the order or decision is likely to affect other cases of a similar nature in the winding-up proceedings, or
(c) if the amount involved in the appeal exceeds five hundred dollars,

by leave of a judge of the court, or by leave of the court or a judge of the court to which the appeal lies, appeal therefrom.

104. Court of Appeal. — An appeal under section 103 lies to the highest court of final resort in or for the province or territory in which the proceeding originated.

105. Practice. — All appeals shall be regulated, as far as possible, according

to the practice in other cases of the court appealed to, but no appeal hereinbefore authorized shall be entertained unless the appellant has, within fourteen days from the rendering of the order or decision appealed from, or within such further time as the court or judge appealed from allows, taken proceedings therein to perfect his appeal, or unless, within that time, he has made a deposit or given sufficient security according to the practice of the court appealed to that he will duly prosecute the appeal and pay such damages and costs as may be awarded to the respondent.

106. Dismissing appeal. — Where an appellant does not proceed with his appeal according to this Act and the rules of practice applicable, the court appealed to, on the application of the respondent, may dismiss the appeal with or without costs.

107. Appeal to Supreme Court of Canada. — An appeal, if the amount involved therein exceeds two thousand dollars, lies by leave of the Supreme Court of Canada to that Court from the highest court of final resort in or for the province or territory in which the proceedings originated.

Procedure

108. Describing liquidator. — In all proceedings connected with a company, a liquidator shall be described as the "liquidator of the (*name of company*)", and not by his individual name only.

109. Similar to ordinary suit. — The proceedings under a winding-up order shall be carried on as nearly as may be in the same manner as an ordinary suit, action or proceeding within the jurisdiction of the court.

110. Powers exercised by a single judge. — The powers conferred by this Act on a court may, subject to the appeal provided for in this Act, be exercised by a single judge thereof, and the judge may exercise those powers in chambers, either during term or in vacation.

111. Court may refer matters. — After a winding-up order is made, the court may, subject to an appeal according to the practice of the court in like cases, as to the court may seem meet, by order of reference, refer and delegate, according to the practice and procedure of the court, to any officer of the court any of the powers conferred on the court by this Act.

112. Service of process out of jurisdiction. — A court has the power and jurisdiction to cause or allow the service of process or proceedings under this Act to be made on persons out of the jurisdiction of the court, in the same manner, and with the like effect, as in ordinary actions or suits within the ordinary jurisdiction of the court.

113. Order of court deemed judgment. — Every order of a court or judge for the payment of money or costs, charges or expenses made under this Act shall be deemed a judgment of the court, and may be enforced against the person or goods and chattels, lands and tenements of the person ordered to pay in the manner in which judgments or decrees of any superior court obtained in

any suit may bind lands or be enforced in the province where the court making the order is situated.

114. Ordinary practice in case of discovery. — The practice with respect to the discovery of assets of judgment debtors, in force in the superior courts or in any superior court in the province where an order is made under section 113, is applicable to and may be availed of in like manner for the discovery of the assets of any person who by that order is ordered to pay any money or costs, charges or expenses.

115. Attachment and garnishment. — Debts due to any person against whom an order for the payment of money, costs or expenses has been obtained may, in any province where the attachment and garnishment of debts is allowed by law, be attached and garnished in the same manner as debts in that province due to a judgment debtor may be attached and garnished by a judgment creditor.

116. Witnesses attendance. — In any action, suit, proceeding or contestation under this Act, the court may order the issue of a writ of *subpoena ad testificandum* or of *subpoena duces tecum*, commanding the attendance, as a witness, of any person who is within Canada.

117. Arrest of absconding contributory, etc. — A court may, at any time before or after it has made a winding-up order, on proof being given that there are reasonable grounds to believe that any contributory or any past or present director, manager, officer or employee of the company is about to quit Canada or otherwise abscond, or to remove or conceal any of his goods or chattels, for the purpose of evading payment of calls, or for avoiding examination in respect of the affairs of the company, cause that person to be arrested, and his books, papers, moneys, securities for money, goods and chattels to be seized, and that person and property to be safely kept until such time as the court orders.

118. Examination. — A court may, after it has made a winding-up order, summon before it or before any person named by it any officer of the company or person known or suspected to have in his possession any of the estate or effects of the company or supposed to be indebted to the company, or any person whom the court deems capable of giving information concerning the trade, dealings, estate or effects of the company.

119. Person summoned refusing to attend. — If any person summoned under section 118, after being tendered a reasonable sum for his expenses, refuses, without a lawful excuse, to attend at the time appointed, the court may cause that person to be apprehended and brought up for examination.

120. Production of papers. — The court may require any officer or person described in section 118 to produce before the court any book, paper, deed, writing or other document in his custody or power relating to the company.

121. Lien on documents. — If any person claims any lien on papers, deeds, writings or documents produced by him, that production is without prejudice

to the lien, and the court has jurisdiction in the winding-up to determine all questions relating to the lien.

122. Examination on oath. — The court or person named by it may examine, on oath, either by oral or written interrogatories, any person appearing or brought up in the manner described in section 119, concerning the affairs, dealings, estate or effects of the company, and may reduce to writing the answers of the person and require him to subscribe the answers.

123. (1) Inspection of books and papers. — After a winding-up order has been made, the court may make such order for the inspection, by the creditors, contributories, shareholders or members of the company, of its books and papers, as the court thinks just.

(2) Limitation of inspection. — Any books and papers in the possession of the company may be inspected in conformity with the order of the court, but not further or otherwise.

124. Officer of company misapplying money. — When in the course of the winding-up of the business of a company under this Act it appears that any past or present director, manager, liquidator, receiver, employee or officer of the company has misapplied or retained in his own hands, or become liable or accountable for any moneys of the company, or been guilty of any misfeasance or breach of trust in relation to the company, the court may, on the application of any liquidator or of any creditor or contributory of the company, notwithstanding that the offence is one for which the offender is criminally liable, examine into the conduct of the director, manager, liquidator, receiver, employee or officer, and, after that examination, may make an order requiring him to repay any moneys so misapplied or retained, or for which he has become liable or accountable, together with interest at such rate as the court thinks just, or to contribute such sums of money to the assets of the company, by way of compensation in respect of the misapplication, retention, misfeasance or breach of trust, as the court thinks fit.

125. Dispensing with notice. — The court may, by any order made after a winding-up order and the appointment of a liquidator, dispense with notice to creditors, contributories, shareholders or members of the company required by this Act, where in its discretion such notice may properly be dispensed with.

126. Courts and judges auxiliary. — The courts of the various provinces, and the judges of those courts respectively, are auxiliary to one another for the purposes of this Act, and the winding-up of the business of a company or any matter or proceeding relating thereto may be transferred from one court to another with the concurrence, or by the order or orders, of the two courts or by an order of the Supreme Court of Canada.

127. Order of one court enforceable by another. — When any order made by one court is required to be enforced by another court, an office copy of the order so made, certified by the clerk or other proper officer of the court that

made the order, under the seal of that court, shall be produced to the proper officer of the court required to enforce the order.

128. Proceeding on order of another court. — The court required to enforce the order mentioned in section 127 shall, on the production of the certified copy of the order, take the same proceedings thereon for enforcing the order as if it were the order of that court.

129. (1) Rules with respect to amendments. — The rules of procedure, for the time being, with respect to amendments of pleadings and proceedings in the court, apply, as far as practicable, to all pleadings and proceedings under this Act.

(2) Authority to apply. — Any court before which proceedings under this Act are being carried on has full power and authority to apply to those proceedings the appropriate rules of that court with respect to amendments.

130. Irregularity or default. — No pleading or proceeding is void by reason of any irregularity or default that may be amended or disregarded, but the pleading or proceeding may be dealt with according to the rules and practice of the court in cases of irregularity or default.

131. Powers conferred are supplementary. — Any powers conferred by this Act on a court are in addition to, and not in restriction of, any other powers at law or in equity of instituting proceedings against any contributory or the estate of any contributory, or against any debtor of the company or the estate of any debtor of the company, for the recovery of any call or other sum due from the contributory, debtor or estate; and those proceedings may be instituted accordingly.

132. Wishes of creditors. — A court may, with respect to all matters relating to the winding-up of the business of a company, have regard, so far as it deems just, to the wishes of the creditors, contributories, shareholders or members of the company, as proved to it by any sufficient evidence.

133. (1) Solicitors and counsel representing classes of creditors. — A court, if satisfied that, with respect to the whole or any portion of the proceedings before it, the interests of creditors, claimants or shareholders can be classified, may, after notice by advertisement or otherwise, nominate and appoint a solicitor and counsel to represent each or any class for the purpose of the proceedings, and all the persons composing any such class are bound by the acts of the solicitor and counsel so appointed.

(2) Service on the solicitor appointed to represent a class of notices, orders or other proceedings of which service is required shall for all purposes be, and be deemed to be, good and sufficient service thereof on all the persons composing the class represented by him.

(3) Costs. — The court may, by the order appointing a solicitor and counsel for any class, or by subsequent order, provide for the payment of the costs of the solicitor and counsel by the liquidator of the company out of the assets

of the company, or out of such portion thereof as to the court seems just and proper.

134. Liquidator subject to summary jurisdiction of court. — A liquidator is subject to the summary jurisdiction of the court in the same manner and to the same extent as the ordinary officers of the court are subject to its jurisdiction, and the liquidator may be compelled to perform his duties by order of the court.

135. Remedies obtained by summary order. — All remedies sought or demanded for enforcing any claim for a debt, privilege, mortgage, lien or right of property on, in or to any effects or property in the hands, possession or custody of a liquidator may be obtained by an order of the court on summary petition, and not by any action, suit, attachment, seizure or other proceeding of any kind whatever.

Rules, Regulations and Forms

136. (1) Judges may make. — A majority of the judges of a court, of which the chief justice shall be one, may, from time to time,

(a) settle the forms and make the rules and regulations to be followed and observed in proceedings under this Act; and
(b) make rules respecting the costs, fees and charges that shall or may be had, taken or paid in those proceedings by or to attorneys, solicitors or counsel, officers of courts, whether for the officers or for the Crown, and sheriffs, or other persons, or for any service performed or work done under this Act.

(2) Ontario and Quebec. — In Ontario the judges of the Ontario Court (General Division), and in Quebec the judges of the Superior Court, or a majority of those judges, of which the chief justice shall be one, shall settle the forms and make the rules and regulations referred to in subsection (1).

[Subsec. (2) repealed and substituted by S.C. 1990, c. 17, s. 44.]

137. Until rules are made, procedure of court to apply. — Until the forms, rules and regulations referred to in section 136 are settled or made, the various forms and procedures, including the tariff of costs, fees and charges in cases under this Act shall, unless otherwise specially provided, be the same as nearly as possible as those of the court in other cases.

Unclaimed Deposits

138. (1) Unclaimed dividends. — All dividends deposited in a bank and remaining unclaimed at the time of the final winding-up of the business of a company shall be left for three years in the bank where they are deposited, subject to the claim of the persons entitled thereto.

(2) After three years. — If the dividends deposited under subsection (1)

are unclaimed at the expiration of three years, they shall be paid over by the bank, with interest accrued thereon, to the Minister.

(3) If afterwards claimed. — If the dividends deposited under subsection (1) are afterwards duly claimed, they shall be paid over by the bank, with interest accrued thereon, to the persons entitled thereto.

139. (1) Money deposited not paid after three years. — The money deposited in a bank by the liquidator after the final winding-up of the business of a company shall be left for three years in the bank, subject to be claimed by the persons entitled thereto.

(2) Unclaimed money. — Money not paid out pursuant to subsection (1) shall be paid over, with the interest accrued thereon, to the Minister, and if afterwards claimed shall be paid, with that interest, to the persons entitled thereto.

Offences and Punishment

140. Court may direct criminal proceedings. — When a winding-up order is made in respect of a company, if it appears in the course of the winding-up that any past or present director, manager, officer or member of the company is guilty of an offence in relation to the company for which he is criminally liable, the court may, on the application of any person interested in the winding-up, or of its own motion, direct the liquidator to institute and conduct a prosecution or prosecutions for the offence and may order the costs and expenses to be paid out of the assets of the company.

141. Destruction of books or false entry therein. — Every person who, with intent to defraud or deceive any person, destroys, mutilates, alters or falsifies any book, paper, writing or security, or makes or is privy to the making of any false or fraudulent entry in any register, book of account or other document belonging to a company, the business of which is being wound up under this Act, is guilty of an indictable offence and liable to imprisonment in the penitentiary for any term not less than two years or to imprisonment in any jail or in any place of confinement other than a penitentiary for any term less than two years, with or without hard labour.

142. (1) Failure to comply with order of court. — Any liquidator, director, manager, receiver, officer or employee of a company who fails to comply with the requirements or directions of any order made by a court under this Act is guilty of contempt of court and is subject to all processes and punishments of the court for contempt.

(2) Removal of liquidator. — Any liquidator who fails to comply as described in subsection (1) may, in the discretion of the court, be removed from office as liquidator.

143. Refusal by officers of company to give information. — Any refusal on the part of the president, directors, officers or employees of a company to give all information possessed by them respectively as to the affairs of the company required by the accountant or other person ordered by a court under

this Part to inquire into the affairs of the company and to report thereon is a contempt of court, and the president, directors, officers or employees are subject to all processes and punishments of the court for contempt.

144. Failure to deposit in bank money of estate. — Every liquidator who does not, within three days after the date of the final winding-up of the business of a company, deposit in the bank, designated under section 44, any money belonging to the estate of which he is the liquidator, then in his hands and not required for any other purpose authorized by this Act, together with an account of the money and a sworn statement that the money is all that he has in his hands, shall incur a penalty not exceeding ten dollars and not less than ten per cent per annum interest on the money in his hands for every day after the expiration of the said three days on which he neglects or delays the payment.

145. Refusal of witness to answer or subscribe. — Every person who is brought up for examination before a court after the court has made a winding-up order, or appearing before the court for the examination, and who refuses without lawful excuse to answer any question put to him or to subscribe any answer made by him on the examination is guilty of contempt of court and is subject to all processes and punishments of the court for contempt.

Evidence

146. Books to be proof of contents. — Where the business of a company is being wound up under this Act, all books of the company and of the liquidators are, as between the contributories of the company, in the absence of evidence to the contrary, proof of the truth of all matters purporting to be therein recorded.

147. Affidavits. — Every affidavit, solemn affirmation or declaration required to be sworn or made under or for the purposes of this Act, or to be used in a court in any proceeding under this Act, may be sworn or made

(a) in Canada before a liquidator, judge, notary public, commissioner for taking affidavits or justice of the peace; and
(b) outside Canada, before any judge of a court of record, any commissioner for taking affidavits to be used in any court in Canada, any notary public, the chief municipal officer of any town or city, any British consul or vice-consul or any person authorized by or under any statute of Canada, or of any province, to take affidavits.

148. Judicial notice of seals, stamp or signature. — All courts, judges, justices, commissioners and persons acting judicially shall take judicial notice of the seal, stamp or signature, as the case may be, of any court, liquidator, judge, notary public, commissioner, justice, chief municipal officer, consul, vice-consul, or other person referred to in section 147, attached, appended or subscribed to any solemn affidavit, affirmation or declaration referred to in that section or to any other document to be used for the purposes of this Act.

149. Copy of order. — When any order made by one court is required to be enforced by another court, the production of an office copy of the order

so made certified by the clerk or other proper officer of the court that made the order, under the seal of the court, is sufficient evidence of the order having been made.

150. Failure to produce pass-book. — The absence of mention in the minutes of any meeting of contributories, creditors, shareholders or members under this Act of the production of the liquidator's bank pass-book, is, in the absence of evidence to the contrary, proof that the pass-book was not produced at the meeting.

PART II
BANKS

151. Application of Part. — This Part applies to banks other than savings banks.

152. (1) Creditor to apply. — The application for a winding-up order shall be made by a creditor for a sum of not less than one thousand dollars.

(2) Direction of court. — A court shall, before making a winding-up order, direct a meeting of the shareholders of the bank and a meeting of the creditors of the bank to be summoned, held and conducted as the court directs, for the purpose of ascertaining their respective wishes respecting the appointment of liquidators.

153. (1) Chairman at meetings of shareholders. — The court may appoint a person to act as chairman of the meeting of shareholders, and in default of such appointment, the president of the bank, or other person who usually presides at a meeting of shareholders, shall be chairman.

(2) Chairman of meeting of creditors. — The court may appoint a person to act as chairman of the meeting of creditors, and in default of such appointment, the creditors at the meeting shall appoint a chairman.

154. (1) Voting at shareholders' meeting. — In taking a vote at the meeting of shareholders, regard shall be had to the number of votes conferred by law, or by the regulations of the bank, on each shareholder present or represented at the meeting.

(2) Voting at creditors' meeting. — In taking a vote at the meeting of creditors, regard shall be had to the amount of the debt due to each creditor.

155. Report to court and appointment of liquidators. — The chairman of each meeting of shareholders or creditors shall report the proceedings of the meeting to the court, and, if a winding-up order is made, the court shall appoint one or more liquidators not exceeding three to be selected, in its discretion, after such hearing of the parties as it deems expedient, from among the persons nominated by the majorities and minorities of the shareholders and creditors at their respective meetings.

156. Appointed by court. — If no one has been nominated under section 155, the liquidator or liquidators shall be chosen by the court.

157. (1) Reservation of dividends. — The liquidators shall ascertain as nearly as possible the amount of notes of the bank intended for circulation and actually outstanding, and shall reserve dividends on any part of that amount in respect of which claims are not filed, until the expiration of at least two years after the date of the winding-up order or until the last dividend, if the last dividend is not made until the expiration of that time.

(2) Applied to subsequently filed claims. — If claims are not filed and dividends applied for in respect of any part of the amount referred to in subsection (1) before the period limited by this section, the dividends reserved under that subsection shall form the last or part of the last dividend.

158. Publication of notices. — Publication in the *Canada Gazette* and in the official gazette of each province and in two newspapers issued at or nearest the place where the head office of a bank is situated, of notice of any proceeding of which, under this Act, creditors should be notified, is sufficient notice to holders of bank notes in circulation.

PART III
INSURANCE COMPANIES

159. Definitions. — In this Part,

"assets" means in respect of a foreign insurance company that is authorized under Part XIII of the *Insurance Companies Act* to insure

(a) risks in Canada falling within the class of life insurance, and

(b) risks in Canada falling within some other class of insurance, other than accident and sickness insurance, accident insurance, personal accident insurance and sickness insurance,

as the circumstances require, either the funds maintained in respect of the insurance by the foreign insurance company of risks falling within the classes of life insurance and accident and sickness insurance, accident insurance, personal accident insurance and sickness insurance or the funds maintained in respect of the insurance by the foreign insurance company of risks falling within some other class of insurance;

"company" means an insurance company;

"policy" includes, without limiting the generality of its meaning, "policy" as defined in the *Insurance Companies Act*;

"Superintendent" means the Superintendent of Financial Institutions appointed pursuant to subsection 5(1) of the *Office of the Superintendent of Financial Institutions Act.*

159.1 Application of Part. — This Part applies only to insurance companies.

[S. 159 repealed and substituted by ss. 159 and 159.1 by S.C. 1991, c. 47, s. 747.]

160. (1) When company deemed insolvent. — A company shall be deemed to be insolvent if,

(a) being a company to which this Part applies, it has failed to pay any undisputed claim arising under any policy of the company, or a disputed claim after final judgment in the regular course of law, for a period of ninety days after tender of a legally valid discharge and after notice of failure to pay has been given to the Minister;
(b) being a company, society or provincial company the commencement and carrying on of business by which has been approved by order of the Superintendent under the *Insurance Companies Act*, or a foreign company the insurance risks in Canada by which has been approved by order of the Superintendent under Part XIII of that Act, the Superintendent has made a report to the Minister that the Superintendent is of the opinion that the circumstances described in any of the subparagraphs 680(1)(b)(iii) to (ix) of that Act exist; or
(c) being a foreign company the insurance of risks in Canada by which has been approved by order of the Superintendent under Part XIII of the *Insurance Companies Act*, the order has been rescinded under section 655 of that Act and has not been remade within thirty days thereafter.

[Paras. (b) and (c) repealed and substituted by S.C. 1991, c. 47, s. 748.]

(2) Application for a winding-up order. — When any company is deemed to be insolvent under this Act or any other Act of Parliament, the Attorney General of Canada, on the request of the Minister, may apply to the court for an order that the company be wound up.

161. (1) Order of priority for payment of claims. — Subject to this Act, claims shall be paid in the following order of priority:

(a) costs of liquidation and the mortgage insurance and special insurance portions of the expenses described in paragraph 686(1)(a) of the *Insurance Companies Act* that were incurred by the Superintendent in respect of the company after March 31, 1986;
[Para. (a) repealed and substituted by S.C. 1991, c. 47, s. 749(1).]
(b) claims of preferred creditors, specified in section 72;
(c) claims of policyholders of the company ranking as follows:
  (i) if reinsurance is not effected as hereinafter provided,
    (A) firstly, any of the following claims:
      (I) in the case of policies of life insurance and policies of accident and sickness insurance, claims that have arisen under those policies of the company, in accordance with the terms thereof, prior to the date of the filing of the statement of the liquidator in the Office of the Superintendent of Financial Institutions as hereinafter provided, less any amount previously advanced by the company on the security of those policies, and claims of holders of policies of life insurance and policies of accident and

sickness insurance to the value of those policies computed as hereinafter provided,

(II) in the case of policies of insurance other than policies of life insurance and policies of accident and sickness insurance, claims that have arisen under those policies of the company by reason of the occurrence of the event insured against, in accordance with the terms thereof, prior to the date of filing of the statement of the liquidator in the Office of the Superintendent of Financial Institutions as hereinafter provided, less any amount previously advanced by the company on the security of those policies, and

(B) secondly, in the case of policies of insurance other than policies of life insurance and policies of accident and sickness insurance, the claims of such policy holders to the value of those policies computed as hereinafter provided or, as the case may be, claims that have arisen under those policies, in accordance with the terms thereof, prior to the date of the filing of the statement of the liquidator in the Office of the Superintendent of Financial Institutions as hereinafter provided, less any amount previously advanced by the company on the security of the policies, or

[Subpara. (i) repealed and replaced by S.C. 1987, c. 26, s. 52(1).]

(ii) if reinsurance is effected, firstly, claims that have arisen under the policies of the company, in accordance with the terms thereof, of which notice is received by the company prior to the date the reinsurance is effected, less any amount previously advanced by the company on the security of the policies, and secondly, the consideration payable for the reinsurance of policies under which no claims have arisen; and

(d) expenses described in paragraph 686(1)(a) of the *Insurance Companies Act* that were incurred by the Superintendent in respect of the company after March 31, 1986 and assessed against and paid by other companies pursuant to that Act, the *Canadian and British Insurance Companies Act* or the *Foreign Insurance Companies Act*, and interest in respect thereof at such rate as is specified by the Superintendent.

[Subsec. (1) amended by striking out the word "and" at the end of paragraph (b), by adding the word "and" at the end of paragraph (c) and by adding para. (d) by S.C. 1991, c. 47, s. 749(2).]

(2) Other creditors. — Other creditors and policyholders of the company, including policyholders claiming any minimum amount that a life company has agreed to pay under a policy or in respect of an amount in respect of which a segregated fund is maintained pursuant to section 451, 542 or 593 of the *Insurance Companies Act* for a deficiency if the assets of the fund are insufficient to satisfy such a claim, are entitled to receive a dividend on their claims only if the assets are more than sufficient to pay the claims specified in subsection (1).

(2.1) Claim of Superintendent. — Expenses described in paragraph 686(1)(a) of the *Insurance Companies Act* that were incurred by the Superintendent in respect of the company before April 1, 1986 and assessed against and paid by other companies pursuant to that Act, the *Canadian and British Insurance Companies Act* or the *Foreign Insurance Companies Act*, and interest in respect thereof at such rate as is specified by the Superintendent constitute a claim of Her Majesty against the assets of the company prior to any claim in respect of the shares, if any, of the company or any similar claim against those assets.

(3) Priority of claims of policyholders in foreign companies. — Notwithstanding anything in this Part, if a company is a foreign company the insurance of risks in Canada by which has been approved by order of the Superintendent under Part XIII of the *Insurance Companies Act*, no claim, after the payment of costs of liquidation and the mortgage insurance and special insurance portions of the expenses described in paragraph 686(1)(a) of the *Insurance Companies Act* that were incurred by the Superintendent in respect of the foreign company after March 31, 1986, other than claims of

(a) the preferred creditors referred to in paragraph (1)(b),
(b) holders of policies of a class of insurance specified in the order, and
(c) reinsurers of those policies, if any,

ranks against the assets in Canada maintained by the foreign company under that Act, if those assets are maintained solely for the protection of policyholders in Canada, and the balance, if any, of the assets remaining after the claims are paid shall be applied by the liquidator in satisfaction of the claims of any other creditors of the foreign company in Canada, but not including policyholders of the foreign company in respect of a class of insurance not specified in that order.

[Subsecs. (2) and (3) repealed and substituted by S.C. 1991, c. 47, s. 749(3).]

(4) Release of balance of assets to company. — The liquidator may, with the approval of the court and the Treasury Board, release to the company any balance of the assets in Canada remaining after payment of claims in the order of priority prescribed by subsection (3).

162. (1) Reinsurance of contracts by liquidator. — The liquidator may, without the consent of the policyholders, arrange for the reinsurance of

(a) the policies of the company, in the case of a company other than a foreign company, or
(b) the policies in Canada of a foreign company,

in a company, society, foreign company or provincial company within the meaning of the *Insurance Companies Act*, in which case the reinsurance shall be in lieu of the claim for the value of those policies computed as provided in section 163.

[Subsec. (1) repealed and substituted by S.C. 1991, c. 47, s. 750.]

(2) Reinsurance may be for a percentage of sum assured. — Where the assets of the company are insufficient to provide for the preferred claims specified in section 72, for claims under the policies of the company of which notice has been received by the company prior to the date of reinsurance and for the reinsurance in full of the policies of the company, the reinsurance may be effected for such a percentage of the full amount of the policies as the assets will secure.

(3) Approval of contracts of reinsurance. — No contract of reinsurance made in pursuance of this section becomes effective until approved by the court and by the Treasury Board.

163. (1) Holders of unmatured policies to claim for value computed. — Where the reinsurance is not effected, holders of policies of all classes of insurance on which no claims have arisen in accordance with the terms of the policies prior to the date of the winding-up order are entitled to claim against the assets of the company for the value of their respective policies computed as of the date of the winding-up order in accordance with such bases, methods and rules of computation as the Treasury Board may deem just and equitable, less any amount previously advanced by the company on the security of the policies.

(2) Bases and methods of valuation. — In prescribing bases, methods and rules of computation, the Treasury Board shall take into consideration the prospective indemnities, benefits and equities guaranteed under the terms of the policies of the several classes thereof, including any bonus or other additional indemnity or benefit granted after the date of issue of the policy and subsisting at the date of the winding-up order and profits apportioned to policies but not distributed, the prospective premium payments, if any, the contingencies on which the payment of indemnities, benefits and premiums may depend, and such rate or rates of interest as may be deemed appropriate, but in no case shall the value for which a policyholder may claim be less than the value for which he might have claimed under the terms of his policy on cancellation thereof as of the date of the winding-up order.

(3) Amendment thereof. — The bases, methods and rules of computation so prescribed by the Treasury Board are binding on all concerned, subject only to revocation or amendment by the Treasury Board.

(4) Computation by Superintendent. — The liquidator may require the Superintendent to compute the values of policies in respect of which claims are made and the expense of that valuation at the rate of three cents for each policy valued shall be paid by the liquidator to the Minister and applied toward payment of the expenses of the Office of the Superintendent of Financial Institutions.

[Subsec. (4) repealed and replaced by S.C. 1987, c. 23, s. 53.]

164. (1) Transfer of funds and securities to the liquidator. — The funds and securities of the company in Canada that may be on deposit with any government in Canada or with trustees or otherwise held for the company or

for the protection of the policyholders of the company of the class or classes that are affected by the winding-up order shall, on order of the court having jurisdiction, be transferred to the liquidator.(2) Assets on deposit outside Canada. — Where the company is a Canadian company that has deposited with the government of any state or country outside Canada, or with any trustee or other person in that state or country, any of its funds or securities for the protection of the company's policyholders in that state or country, the liquidator may request that government, trustee or other person to transfer those funds and securities to him and on such transfer being made, those funds and securities shall be used for the benefit of all the company's policyholders in the same manner as any other assets of the company.

(3) Consequence of non-transfer of assets. — Where a government, trustee or other person referred to in subsection (2) does not transfer the funds and securities deposited with it within such period commencing with the date of the liquidator's request therefor as the Court may fix, the policyholders of the company, for whose protection the deposit was made, shall be deemed to have refused the reinsurance, if any, arranged by the liquidator, and, whether reinsurance has been arranged or not, to have forfeited all right and claim to any share of the assets of the company other than the funds or securities so deposited for their protection outside Canada.

165. Transfer to foreign liquidator. — Where a foreign company the insurance of risks in Canada by which has been approved by order of the Superintendent under Part XIII of the *Insurance Companies Act* is in liquidation in the country in which its head office is situated, the Treasury Board may, if it deems it advisable and in the interests of the policyholders in Canada, authorize the liquidator, subject to the approval of the court, to transfer the assets in Canada of the foreign company to the liquidator in that country.

[S. 165 repealed and substituted by S.C. 1991, c. 47, s. 751.]

166. (1) Liquidator to prepare statement of claimants and creditors. — The liquidator shall, without the filing of any claim, notice or evidence or the taking of any action by any person, prepare a statement of all the persons appearing by the books and records of the company to be creditors of the company or to be claimants under any policy including any matured, valued, or cancelled policy, taking cognizance in that connection of all claims that have arisen in accordance with the terms of the policies of which he has notice.

(2) Collocation. — The statement described in subsection (1) shall show the amount, determined as provided in section 161 in respect of policyholders, for which each person is to rank as a claimant or a creditor and every such person shall be collocated and ranked as, and is entitled to the right of, a claimant or a creditor for the amount so ascertained by the liquidator, without filing any claim, notice or evidence, or taking any action.

(3) Objections. — Any collocation made pursuant to subsection (2) may be contested by any person interested, and any person who is not collocated,

or who is dissatisfied with the amount for which he is collocated, may file his own claim.

(4) Amendment of statement. — The liquidator or the court may rectify any statement prepared under subsection (1) on account of omissions or errors therein notified to the liquidator or discovered by him at any time before the completion of the liquidation, and only the claims appearing in the statement or amended statement shall be regarded in the distribution of the assets.

167. Right of action not debarred. — Where the assets are not sufficient to cover in full all claims appearing in the statement or amended statement described in section 166, the policyholders are not barred from any recourse they have, either in law or equity, against the company issuing the policy or against any shareholder or director thereof, except in respect of the share, if any, received in the distribution of those assets.

168. (1) Copy of statement filed in Office of the Superintendent of Financial Institutions. — A copy of the statement mentioned in section 167, certified by the liquidator, shall be filed in the Office of the Superintendent of Financial Institutions, after not less than thirty days notice of his intention to do so has been given by the liquidator by notice in the *Canada Gazette* and in the official gazette of each province and in two newspapers issued at or nearest the place where the head office of the company or the chief agency of the company in Canada, as the case may be, is situated.

[Subsec. (1) repealed and replaced by S.C. 1987, c. 23, s. 54.]

(2) When policyholder to rank as creditor. — Any claim that has arisen under the terms of a policy of which notice is received by the liquidator after the date of the filing of a statement mentioned in section 167 shall rank on the assets only for the value entered in the statement, unless the assets are sufficient to pay all claimants in full, and in that case, the policyholder shall rank as a creditor for the balance of his claim.

169. Notice of filing. — The liquidator shall forthwith send by prepaid mail a notice of the filing of the statement under subsection (1) to each claimant or creditor named in the statement, addressed to the latest address on record with the company, stating therein the amount for which the creditor or claimant is entitled to rank against the assets of the company.

170. Report to the Superintendent. — Where the company is a company, society, foreign company or provincial company within the meaning of the *Insurance Companies Act*, the liquidator shall report to the Superintendent once in every six months, or more often, as the Superintendent may require, on the condition of the affairs of the company, with such particulars as the Superintendent may require.

[S. 170 repealed and substituted by S.C. 1991, c. 47, s. 752.]

171. Publication of notice of proceedings. — Publication in the *Canada Gazette*, in the official gazette of each province and in two newspapers published

at or nearest to the place where the head office of the company or chief agency of the company in Canada, as the case may be, is situated, of notice of any proceedings of which, under this Act, creditors should be notified, is sufficient notice to holders of policies in respect of which no notice of claim has been received.

172. Priority of certain claims. — Nothing in this Part prejudices or affects the priority of any mortgage, lien or charge on the property of the company.

INDEX